Prepare a Path

An Account of My Life

Daniel Yordy

In the Presence of Whom
We Must Give an Account

Published by

Christ Revealed Bible Institute

Daniel Yordy
791 Cherry Creek Drive
Shepherd, Texas 77371

⟐ Introduction ⟐

In these pages you will find an unusual life story, even astonishing at times. You will find a devotion to God that will not turn aside, a love of the Bible that must see all word fulfilled, and a pursuit of Christ Community filled with a people who know the Father.

As you read these pages you will see a man stumbling through every step of the calling of God upon his life, yet carrying a vision of a Church without blemish, a Jerusalem that is a praise in all the earth. You will see a heart stretched wide by joy and by grief. You will walk with a man who needs his Savior to be REAL, the Lord Jesus Christ.

You will notice that this man is no different from any other, no different from you. Through the decades, he knows only haphazard confusion, stumbling from one mistake to the next, imagining a God far-away, a God of love, yet, somehow, hostile to him.

Yet at the end of this journey, he knows the Father inside his earthen vessel, sharing every part of his humanity with him – LIFE. That path from ignorance into knowing the Father every moment is the Path prepared for you, the Lord Jesus Christ.

As I finished the last portion of this account, I finally knew, in quiet certainty and unspeakable joy, what God's calling of me is and has always been, the Hand of God upon the unfolding of all my days.

My first task is to unveil the Word, an Apocalypse, one might say, of God's gospel of Life and the removal of all death placed upon the Word of God by those who have heeded the first deceit of the serpent.

My second task is to carry this precious Word through a gauntlet of death, through the refusal of all contempt against others, into setting forth my soul for the sake of my brothers and sisters, placing myself with Father beneath of each that each might be lifted up into life.

And my third task is to open the door of authority to God, that He might rush into His Church, that His knowledge might prevail in all the earth, that Rivers of Life might flow out to all, and to direct His mighty angels that all the kingdoms of darkness might crash into ruin.

Read these pages in the dawning realization that everything that is true of Jesus is true also of you, for He is your only life. My own life in God is a path prepared for you and Jesus, always together.

⟐ I Have a Dream ⟐

I have a dream.

I dream of the Church of Jesus Christ now upon this earth. I see her clothed with the Lord Jesus Christ; I see her bringing forth the knowledge of God into creation.

I see the Church, that she comes out from Jesus' side upon the cross. I see the Blood and the Water flowing out together, mixing into the dirt of the earth, the very Bride of Christ. I see the Lord

Jesus coming into His Church by the Spirit of Truth on the day of Pentecost. I see that Jesus is all inside of all who belong to Him.

I see the Church, a hundred million and more believers in Jesus all across this planet, walking together as the revelation of Jesus Christ in all of His glory revealed, right here on this earth, right now in this age.

You see, I care about God, that He would gain the desire of His Heart, to be seen and known by all creation through His only body, Christians loving one another with pure hearts fervently.

I dream of a firstfruits of Christ, giving their all for the sake of the Church, ready to sacrifice everything that they might be a point of gathering together. I see Christians everywhere gathering together around God's firstfruits into Christ Communities, more than a million Christian Communities across every land and among every people on earth.

I see the New Jerusalem coming out from God upon the earth inside of heaven.

I see Christians loving one another, with every thought that Father might be glorified through their gathering together, placing God Himself as all their connections together, a people filled with all the fulness of God.

I see Christians who place the Sacrifice of Jesus, one unlimited sacrifice for sins, as their only core, their only foundation, their absolute protection, their all.

I see Christians loving one another out from God, out from their personal union with the Lord Jesus Christ connecting them always with God and with one another.

I see great movements of the Devoted Spirit flowing inside of each community of Christ, among the Churches together, and out from them into all human society. I see the Word of the gospel being spoken everywhere.

I hear the ruling verses of the Bible on the lips of a hundred million or more Christians, spoken as their own self story, spoken together as the testimony and witness of Christ.

I hear the people of this world in awe, saying, "Now we know that God is true, for we can see Him. We can see Christians loving one another with all commitment and in all liberty. We know we are seeing God. We know that God sent Jesus into our lives."

I see Christians loving one another, committing their lives to each other and to the gathering together. I see sacrifice, I see steadfastness, I see faithfulness, I see giving, all in full reciprocity, back and forth, as the very revelation of God. I see Christians treating each other with utter respect and in the highest regard.

I see every Word spoken by Jesus and His apostles fulfilled in all completion right here on this earth, right now in this age, inside a hundred million or more believers in Jesus - the absolute proof that God is telling us the truth.

This is my story; this is my dream. This is the commitment of my heart and life. I know the cost; I know the tears. I know the joy unspeakable and filled with glory.

For Father's sake - a people for Father's sake. That God might be known by all.

I will know God in full, in all that God intends, and I will walk with a people who know God in the same way, right here on this earth, right now in this age.

I will walk in committed Christian Community with all who love Jesus made visible.

∼ Table of Contents ∼

∼ **Table of Contents** ∼

1. My Origins

Through December 1965

This Account

As I begin this account, I have just turned sixty years old. That seems strange to me since I was a young man only a short time ago. At the same time, I am nearly halfway through completing what will be the synthesis and culmination of all that God has taught me over many years, the five texts titled *Symmorphy*.

[I wrote this first chapter at that time; subsequent chapters began around three years later.]

As a writer, as a believer in Jesus, and as a lifelong student of the Bible, I have the silly idea that my texts on *Symmorphy* should and will replace Augustine and the Nicene Council in the thinking of Christians over the next thousand years. I know how ridiculous that claim sounds, thus I call it a "silly idea."

I have a reason for even imagining such a thing to be God's intention in the unfolding of history, and that is because I know, at least intellectually, that I am giving you the truth of God as it has never before been released to His church. And I am giving you that truth entirely out from the New Testament and entirely out from the Spirit of God.

So, if you are willing to entertain my foolishness for just a bit, we together must ask the obvious question – Why in God's good name would He, in fact, pick such a bumbling failure of a man as this unknown "Daniel Yordy" to speak the revelation of Christ as He is to His church?

I write this account for two reasons. First, I intend to prove to you that God has no good reason whatever to speak to His church through me – and many, many good reasons why He would not. And second, I am responsible to lay before you how God has taken me by the hand, step by faltering step, and led me into His own heart, that here, hiding entirely inside the heart of my Father, I might show that heart to you.

God, the God of the Bible, is entirely different from what they say.

If it is true, however, that I am, in fact, showing the Heart of Father to the church, a God never before seen or known as He really is, even in Christianity, then those now and in the future who may consider God through what I share have every right to know the path from which all this has come, all the experiences, all the issues, all the joys and sorrows.

Since my purpose in this account is somewhat academic, I will not attempt to turn these pages towards popular literature, a talent I don't necessarily have. At the same time, I hope to be complete in my account, that is, I hope to cover those many remembrances that are of meaning and value to me. Most parts of my history I will explore in depth, including the names of the many dear believers in Jesus with whom I have walked and my interactions with them.

I have two perspectives as I look back now over my sixty years of life. First, I see only the Lord Jesus Christ in every moment from my conception until now. Even before I asked Jesus into my heart at the age of seven, He carried me in all ways, and every part of me was found only inside of Him. Whatever actions of sin I may have committed, Jesus had already become upon the cross and taken them into an empty grave. And even though Jesus did not intend those actions of sin in my life, yet He did intend me through whatever those circumstances might have been. Yet it is not sin that I see, but Jesus. Thus, I now see Him revealing Himself in and as every part of me through every moment of my life.

And because I see my life as one seamless history of Christ, the Lord Jesus carrying me entirely inside Himself through all of it, I also look quite differently at all the people and all the circumstances through those years. For I see the same Jesus who carries me, also carrying them. As He reveals Himself through every moment of my own life, so He reveals Himself through theirs.

Sustaining all things by the Word of His power (Hebrews 1:3). Either Christ Jesus is all or He is nothing.

I find at the present moment no offense remaining inside of me. Every word or deed of any other person that I found to be offensive at that time, I no longer see as offense. And it is with joy alone that I place every person and every circumstance into the Mercy Seat of my heart, into the love of my Father for them flowing out of me.

Though I have forgiven all, there is no longer any need to forgive.

At the same time, I am compelled to honesty. For that reason, I must present many of those actions of others that, at that time, I imagined to be hurtful to me. My intention in honesty is in no way to point the finger, but rather to lead you and them by the hand, if it be possible, into knowing the same Mercy Seat of love in which I live, into the same seeing of Christ Jesus in every moment of your life.

On the other hand, I have also most certainly offended many, treated people badly, and acted in inconsiderate ways. I don't think my intention was ever to be destructive, yet my actions and words many times may well have been just that. For that reason, if any whom I have known might read this, I ask you to forgive me of any sins I may have committed against you. I was completely wrong.

In the joy of your forgiveness graciously extended to me, I begin my account.

One final note first: it is said that no autobiography can be truly accurate since its author is biased to the point of wearing blindfolds regarding many of life's circumstances. That is as it must be. It is certainly true that any individual who has interacted with me throughout my life will have their own different and personalized view of the circumstances I share, a view that will undoubtedly differ in some respects from mine. Yet I am convinced that they must agree that the general outline of all those events as I give them is accurate. I present things only as I, myself, know them; I can make no other claims.

Yet I also know this. Many who thought they knew me, knew me only by outward appearance. Many knew little of the real person inside of my shell, the one carried by the Lord Jesus through all things.

My Heritage

I was born on October 29, 1956 in a hospital in the small town of Mio, Michigan. My father was Emerson Edwin Yordy and my mother was Rhoda Marie (Handrich) Yordy. My father's parents were David Yordy and Sarah (Stauffer) Yordy. My mother's parents were William Handrich and Marie (Troyer) Handrich. We were Mennonites.

Tracing the line of my grandfather, David Yordy, takes us only to his father, John Yordy, born in Bavaria, Germany in 1838, of his mother, Mary Berkey. John was the child of a rape, assumed to be by a soldier. The genealogy of Mary and the Berkey family is well-developed on the Internet.

John immigrated to America at age ten with his mother. In the Mennonite community in Illinois where they settled, Mary met and married Peter Yordy, also newly come from Germany. There is no record of John's adoption by Peter; nevertheless, we bear his name, Yordy. John, apparently, was not accepted by the much younger children of that marriage, and went his separate way in life. Two things can be said about my great-grandfather, John's, life, he never stayed in the same situation long, he never felt that he fit. And he loved the Lord Jesus, whose grace was apparent on his life.

My grandfather, John's son, David Yordy, born in 1875, grew up in the corn country of Nebraska, but moved to Michigan at some point and purchased a farm in the Ashley area, north of Lansing where he became a dairy farmer. My cousin, Wallace Yordy, still runs that farm, though he no longer has a dairy. We visited there last in 2012.

My own father, Emerson Edwin, was the fifth of six children, born in Nebraska before the move to Michigan. Although I grew up in Oregon, I met all of his brothers and sisters in trips back to Michigan during my childhood. Dad grew up on the farm in Michigan. During WWII, dad worked for the government as a conscientious objector, building dams in Oregon, and then testing dairy cattle in Michigan. While conducting that job in Fairview, Michigan, dad attended the local Mennonite church. There he met Rhoda Handrich. He told me that from the first that he saw my mother, he never considered any other woman. They married there in Fairview, Michigan, in 1944; Dad was 27 and Mom was 22. Dad was 6'2" tall and Mom was 5'1".

My father's mother, Sarah Stauffer, was descended from a long line of Stauffer's, whose genealogy is found on the Internet all the way back to the Anabaptists of Switzerland in the 1500's. Stauffer is taken from Stauffen Mountain in the Bernese Alps. In the last part of the 1500's, many of the Anabaptists were driven out of Switzerland and found refuge and tolerance in the German states to the north, Alsace and Baden. Some were subsequently influenced by Jacob Amman in Alsace (the Amish) and others were influenced by Menno Simons of Holland (Mennonites). Three of my grandparents trace their ancestry to these same Anabaptists driven out of their homeland because of their faith in Jesus.

I know less about my mother's parents, even though I spent a few days with them several different times growing up. I liked playing shuffle board with my grandpa. I saw my grandfather, William, last in 1983, just after my grandmother had died. He was 91 and almost as spry as ever.

I did trace William Handrich's ancestry back once on the Internet. That search led me to the Kreighbol line, through one of the mothers. There I discovered that my mom's dad, William Handrich, was descended from a Kreighbol who had lived in a Christian community in Switzerland in the mid-1500's, along with a Stauffer in that same community, from whom came my dad's mother, Sarah.

I know little about the history of my grandmother, Marie Troyer, though I remember well her cheery smile. My grandmother, Sarah, had held me as a baby; I still have a Christmas card from her to me. She died before I was one.

My Family

Let me give, now, a quick history of my own family, up until the time we moved to Oregon in 1960, when I was three years old. My parents first lived in a little house on my grandfather's dairy farm, across the way from the big house, with Dad's mother, Sarah. Dad's older brother, John, had inherited part of the farm with the main house from their dad, David Yordy, who had been killed by one of his bulls in 1935. My mother was very different from my grandmother, and they did not have an easy time of it in that little house.

David was their first child, born in 1945, then Franz in 1947, Frieda in 1949, and Thomas in 1952. My parents then moved with their four children back up to the Fairview, Michigan area, to a house on the property belonging to my mother's sister and her husband, Floyd and Donna Esch. Dad bulldozed the road a mile through my uncle's property

back to the house, thus today that road is named Yordy Road. Dad worked for a while as a bulldozer operator. My sister, Cheryl, was born in 1954.

Then, in the fall of 1955, Dad was driving home with David and Thomas in the front seat and Franz and Frieda in the back seat. Not far from my Aunt and Uncle's farm, there was a slight hill in the gravel road. A car came flying over that hill and hit our car head on. Of course, in those days, there were neither seat belts nor car seats. Tommy and David were killed and Dad, Franz, and Frieda were badly injured. Little baby Cheryl had been home with Mom.

Dad had wanted to be a pastor in the church, a minister of the Lord Jesus, as I always have. Yet, though he prepared himself to that end, he was never really accepted by the Mennonite Church there in Fairview in a ministry role. After the terrible accident and the loss of two of their sons, it was indicated to my parents that this was the "judgment of God" upon them. Why God would exact such judgment upon my kind and generous parents who loved Jesus has never been clear to me.

I was conceived and born during the sorrow of those times, October 29, 1956, Daniel David Yordy, the David in memory of my brother who was lost. In May of 1958, my family moved up to a farm house near Gulliver, Michigan, in the upper peninsula. Dad had grown up as a farmer and wanted to try his hand at farming again. He was not able to make a living by it, though he always held farming close to his heart.

Dad had a number of cousins who had found a home in Oregon. In April of 1960, we moved to Tangent, Oregon and lived first in a little house that had belonged to my Great-Aunt Bella Schrock, who had passed on. That little house was next to the larger farmhouse where my Dad's cousin was a grass-seed farmer. The only thing I remember there was the big pear tree in the front yard.

In September, 1960, we moved to a larger house several miles north of Lebanon, Oregon. I do have memories from that time, playing with my sister, Cheryl, and sitting on the edge of the cucumber fields as Mom added a bit of income by picking cucumbers, a most nasty job in my childhood mind. Dad had been hired by Wah Chang, a rare metals factory in nearby Albany, Oregon, owned by the Telluride Corporation. He worked at that factory for the remainder of his working years, becoming a zirconium furnace operator. He was paid a decent wage, allowing my very thrifty and hands-on parents to provide a middle-class environment for us.

My family probably attended church at the stricter branch of Mennonites in the area, but Dad would never have taken to legalism. We attended the regular Mennonite church in Lebanon for a few months, but somehow Dad was not satisfied. Finally, we visited a non-Mennonite church called Calvary Community Church, just east of Albany. Dad must have liked it because we attended there for a couple of years.

I want to share one anecdote from this time that illustrates the type of person I would become. The Calvary Community Church had a picnic together near a rocky outcrop, probably Knox Butte. The rocky slope, not quite straight up, but with lots of ledges, was maybe 50 feet high. Sure enough, it wasn't long before I was found half-way up, determined to reach the top, but unable to go up or down. I might have been five. I was soon spotted, and a young man climbed up to where I was and carried me back to my anxious parents. This need to explore has been a major factor in my life.

Moving to Lacomb

Sometime in the summer of 1961, Dad was able to purchase a property of 29 acres up against the foothills of the Cascade Mountains, two miles east and north of the little village of Lacomb, Oregon. The property had just been logged and Dad bought it at a discount – $2500 at $25 a month.

Not long after, we moved to another house just south of Lebanon. Through my growing up years, I always shared a bedroom with my brother, Franz, who was nine years older than I. That was not easy for either one of us. I do remember that our little bedroom in this farmhouse was in an attic, which in my child's mind was pretty cool.

In August of 1962, Dad found a large white house for rent in Lacomb, right across from the little grocery store and right next to the little post office. Dad continued to work at Wah Chang, but now it was easier for him to go to our new property on his off times and work with my brother Franz, preparing the site for our new home. That September, I began attending first grade at Lacomb Elementary School, just down the street from us. I was five years old.

I did not know it, of course, but far to the southeast of us, just a few days before I turned six, a lit-

tle girl was born in a hospital in Albuquerque, New Mexico. Her name was Maureen Mack. Her parents were Claude and Roberta Mack; her father was in the U.S. Navy. Almost twenty-eight years later she would become the most important part of my life.

My "little" sister, Jenelle, was born in February, 1963. Dad and Franz began the construction of our new home in earnest that spring. They finished the first part of our new home for us to move in by March of 1965. Thus we were in the Lacomb house for about 2 ½ years.

Just down the street from us lived a boy my age, Randy Thorpe; we became friends. He attended the local Baptist church, just north of Lacomb. My parents, though Mennonite, were not sectarian. Anyone who loved Jesus was always enough for them. Thus I began attending side functions at the Lacomb Baptist Church, such things as Vacation Bible School and the weekly boys club, something I continued doing until my teen years.

Soon after our move to Lacomb, we as a family began to attend another local church in the Lacomb area, Providence Community Church, a historical landmark with a fascinating graveyard behind it.

Thus, in June of 1964 I attended the Vacation Bible School at the Baptist Church. For some reason, it is burned in my mind that my parents also took me to the VBS that summer at the Albany Mennonite Church, across the freeway from Wah Chang. Regardless, I remember distinctly the flannel board, and the teacher placing a black heart on that board, and then a red heart upon the black, and then a white heart upon the red. My own heart was deeply moved.

A few days later I was sitting on the back steps of our home, there in Lacomb, remembering that teaching.

"Jesus, would you come into my heart?" I asked.

As my heart was warmed in that moment, I knew that is exactly what He had done. I was seven years old.

We began attending Albany Mennonite Church in January of 1965, just before moving into our new home on our own property at 34769 East Lacomb Road. At this point in time, my childhood memory had become complete. Thus my childhood from age eight to age fifteen was set, now, in church attendance at Albany Mennonite Church, in growing up on our property next to the mountains and just above Crabtree Creek, and in attendance at Lacomb Elementary through eighth grade, going on, then, to Lebanon Union High School for ninth grade.

Let's back up a few months, however, to the fall of my third-grade year. Two things happened that fall. My first national memory came when the principal gathered the entire school onto the bleachers of the gym to inform us that our President, John F. Kennedy, had been shot and killed. That was a momentous moment in our hearts. It was also the event that would turn the generation of the sixties into the path of war and rebellion against mindless murder.

The second thing was that they lined us all up at school and shot a smallpox vaccination into our arms. By the time I turned nine, a light had gone out inside of me; of that I will talk later. A little boy who was the star of his school play in second grade, outgoing and friendly became confused and withdrawn, hiding from an internal pain he did not understand.

The final note of my family was the birth of my brother, Glenn Thomas, on Christmas Day, 1965. "Thomas" was in memory of our brother.

God with Me

I wrote the first part of this chapter six years ago, at the same time I was writing *Symmorphy III: King-*

dom. I did not know then what would happen to me as I wrote this account. Yet as I am finishing my life story, I am sitting here filled with overflowing joy.

But I will not tell you how or why, for this is a path, and you must follow it as I have, a path of entering into the knowledge of God as God speaks it in His Word.

At every step along the way, both in the months and years through which I lived and in the writing of this account, i imagined only that I stumbled from one failure to the next, from one painful experience to the next.

I did not know myself because I did not know my God.

At the beginning of this chapter I raised this question. – Why in God's good name would He, in fact, pick such a bumbling failure of a man as this unknown "Daniel Yordy" to speak the revelation of Christ as He is to His church?

As I complete this account, I still have no idea "why," yet I know, with all quiet certainty that He has.

My life is a path prepared for you, for your sake, dear reader, that you also might enter into the Joy in whom we live every day.

Our home on East Lacomb Rd. These are the picture windows of the living room facing east to Snow Peak.

My Family - I am ten years old.

From top left - Franz, Frieda, and Cheryl. From center left - me, dad and mom.
Bottom from left - Jenelle and Glenn.

2. My Childhood

March 1965 - July 1972

My Formative Years

So much of life is packed into the years from age eight to age fifteen. Seven years seems short, but to a child, those years define his or her life. My formative childhood years, then, were from March of 1965 when we moved into our home against the foothills of the Cascades, until July of 1972 when I turned my back on the knowledge of God to spend three-and-one-half years inside an awful darkness.

Now, there is no value for the testimony of Jesus Christ for me to share all I can remember from these years. Rather, I will first give an overview, then I will attempt to include a perspective of those things that are pertinent for my walk with God since those years.

As you will see, there is nothing in this history that is remarkable, let alone interesting. What I hope to do, however, is to give a sense of the milieu in which I grew up, the person I was inside that environment, and the more influential factors affecting me through those years.

I had wonderful parents; that is, I can assure you of that now. To a naïve boy growing up in the 1960's, I had no idea of that. My dad worked a rotating shift, which meant he often slept during the daytime. But though my dad was always kind to me – I think he whupped me only twice (well-deserved, though I did not think so then) – yet as I have grown older, I know my dad from the inside and understand the difficulties that bound his heart.

My dad never shared of himself with me. Yes, I worked with him many long hours clearing our property, building sheds and barns, and taking care of the farm animals he bought. But he never once shared of himself with me except that little bit he told me about seeing Mom for the first time – that came years later, when they visited me at the Albuquerque community. I knew that Dad worked at Wah Chang, but I did not even know what he did.

I now know how difficult it was inside for my Dad to share of himself. I came through the same difficulty with far more help than he ever knew.

My mother grew up in a very strict home and did not know herself how to speak words of encouragement. Yet both my mom and my dad loved us children with their lives, even though they did not really know how to communicate.

In actuality, my parents had no thought of "parenting." (I think that parenting is a modern invention.) Basically, I grew up like Topsy, mostly on my own. I did not know anything else. My mom worked hard at home, growing a large garden, preserving our food, stretching every penny dad brought home as far as it would go. Even in the late 70's, she was shocked when the pastor of the Assembly of God church they were attending held an elder and wives' meeting at a restaurant. Such a shocking waste of money, when Dad was required to buy a meal for the two of them at a restaurant!

I grew up in paradise. Let me describe the setting.

Growing up in Oregon

Our property just northeast of Lacomb was situated right on the western edge of the Cascade Mountains, where jumbles of ridges and hills punctuated the flat and richly soiled Willamette Valley. From the north windows of our house, the ground sloped down to the little valley of Crabtree Creek against the backdrop of Buzzard's Butte a thousand feet high. Through our eastern living room wall of large picture windows, Snow Peak, 4000 feet up, was framed in clear view, five miles away.

Following is a map of my dad's property of 29 acres and adjoining points. Writing of these things draws up just how real and deep the love of this area, this climate and vegetation, goes inside of me. In fact, if you type 34769 E. Lacomb Road, Lebanon, Oregon into Google maps set to "terrain," you can get an idea of the slope of East Lacomb Road towards Crabtree Creek below or up towards the crest above. [Google has removed the street view.] That slope in both directions features greatly in my

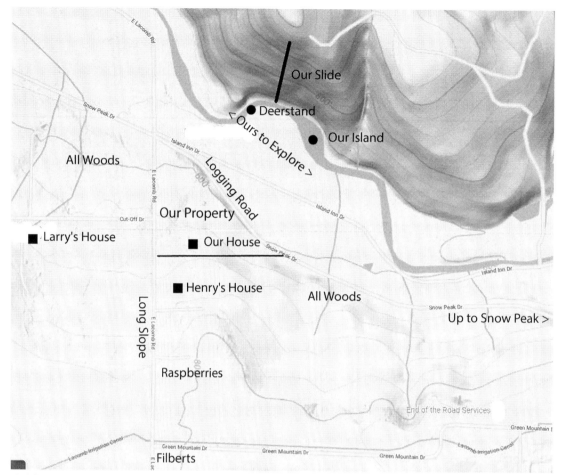

childhood memories. We made full use of it with bicycles, motorbikes, go-carts, wheelies, and whatever else would carry us fast. Of course, the property is no longer ours, but that part of the story will come much later.

The climate of the western slopes of the Pacific Northwest is West Coast Marine, similar to the British Isles and Northwest Europe, mild and wet. Our location was more like Ireland in that the upslope of the Cascades meant that much of the rain dropped right on us.

Rain is part of life to me, except our rain was rarely heavy, typically a light drizzle. Only in the summer months did it slack off. In the springtime it came in great waves from the coast range and in November it never stopped. Years later, I saw a twelve-year-old boy standing by the side of the road in the rain, waiting for the bus. He was hunched up, with water dripping steadily down his face. I was looking at me. No self-respecting boy in rural Oregon would be caught dead in the rain with any raincoat or hat or umbrella or any such nonsense. Rain was our life.

And because of the rain – green. Green of every shade and hue. Growing things, abundance of growing things. The logging road out of the mountains ran along the bottom edge of our property. I often watched log trucks driving by. When I was younger, a truck with one log on it, just the first part of one tree, was fairly common. Rarely did we see more than three or four logs on a truck. Trees grew big and full and green. And flowing streams were regular features. You could not walk half a mile without crossing flowing water. The ditch along our property ran year long. I loved to build dams and waterways, shaping the flow of the water to my pleasure. I loved finding a little stream and hiking down its course, finding every turn and spill and variation in its flow over rocks and around trees.

And berries. Let me give you the panorama of fruit from the earth in the life of an adolescent boy. The fruit season began in May, with cherries. I would climb up into the cherry tree at the edge of our yard and put away cherries like nobody's business. The goal was to keep a steady stream down one's gullet. My stomach was rock iron; I never got sick from unripe or too much fruit.

Then strawberries came in June. I did not like strawberries. We got in a bus that took us to the strawberry fields each morning. Strawberries hug the ground. There is no shade and you have to bend over on your knees to pick them. I would fill one carrier of berries, that is, six little boxes, worth thirty cents in wages. Then I would eat about the same amount; then I would sit in my row in the heat while my sister, Cheryl, picked my share on ahead, waiting through the long morning hours until the bus would take us home. I did not like strawberries.

Raspberries came in July, as well as plums, and huckleberries in the Coast Range and blueberries in the fields along the Roaring River. I liked raspberries, both their flavor and the fact that you could pick them standing up. The raspberry field was just at the top of the hill above our property. We picked through the morning, earning up to five bucks, then we sailed down the hill on our bicycles all the way to Crabtree Creek where we swam and explored and ran on the rocks all afternoon. I was very skilled at running fast across fields of boulders tipped helter skelter, without ever stumbling. We would climb way up Buzzard's Butte, not quite straight up from Crabtree Creek, about 500 feet above. There we turned around, sat down on the ground and slid the 500 feet back down as on a slide. It was just steep enough to go really fast, but not quite too steep. There was almost a trail seemingly made just for us, so that there were no trees or bushes in our path. We tried sliding on burlap, but that did not work. Penny's jeans would last one trip down, but Levis would go three times before they were shredded. It was such fun.

August was blackberries, my favorite. There were vast blackberry wildernesses covering acres on our property and everywhere else. But no one grew them for money, so we bussed to the bean fields, to pick pole beans for money. A kid could earn the most picking pole beans, but I preferred raspberries. Also in August were the thimbleberries, elderberries, and salmon berries. In September came the apples, apples of every kind, although I always started eating apples when they were not ripe. But for money, I picked up filberts in the hazelnut orchards just up the road. I enjoyed the shade under the trees, even though you had to work on your knees.

Finally, in October came the grapes. I can eat grapes. I squeeze the grape so that the flesh pops out of the skin, then I swallow it whole so that I don't bite on the bitter seeds. I put away a lot of grapes, fast. We had three kinds of grapes, pink, white, and blue. Lot's of blue grapes, at the neighbors and at home. Grapes are the one fruit I love tending the most. I have maintained a Concord grape arbor here in Houston, even though the climate is too hot. I wanted my children to know the pleasure of picking grapes off the vine and eating them fresh.

I went camping outside in the woods just off the driveway, first at the age of nine. Going camping along Crabtree Creek became a regular feature of my life. I ventured down to Crabtree Creek by myself at age nine as well, and there I taught myself how to swim. I was always safe because I was never foolish of danger. Even when caught in very difficult water when I was older, I would pause, calm myself, and proceed sensibly. Half of my summers was in the berry and bean fields and the other half was along or in Crabtree Creek (although I did work with my dad on our property quite a bit as well). The creek would become a raging torrent during the rainy months, but in the summer it was a just right, a good size for a "creek," but with many deep holes in which we could swim and with many channels in the solid rock through which we could slide.

I never knew of camping or having a picnic either with family or friends, that was not next to running water. The sound of water running over rocks is the sweetest music I know.

My Animals

I must include mention of some of the animals I raised and took care of growing up. My first dog was a little female mutt that I named "Mickey." I was working in the garden one day when the little thing came bounding towards me in front of my grinning mother. Mickey had a litter of puppies, but I did not have them long. Other than giving some of the puppies away, I don't remember what happened to them. My next dog was Topper, another mutt. He was my companion through most of these years until a neighbor's dog tricked him into going after a porcupine. Neither Henry nor I could get any of the quills out of his mouth, so I had to ask another neighbor to dispose of him.

My favorite dog came later, however, a full-grown Chesapeake Bay Retriever who came wandering in one day half-starved. He was the best of dogs; I named him "Gollum." All of my forays into mountains and woods and creeks were always with my dog. I had Gollum when I could drive up into the mountains. Exploring the mountains, just Gollum and me, was one of the most satisfying chapters of my life.

My first farm animal was a female goat, named Phoebe, who then had two little ones. I milked her until I got tired of goats and we sold them. Then I had a pig; I called her "Mama Pig." I would sit on her back until she woofed and ran off and I went flying. Dad liked to buy and raise calves, so I would take care of them. One year he brought home a milk cow, which I milked daily for a year. Then she broke into the feed bin and ate herself to death. Twice I raised ducks from little ones. Both times the foxes and weasels got them, one at a time.

Working with My Parents

We moved into our home at the beginning of this time period when it was finished enough to be occupied. For that reason, I grew up in the context of a house being built around me bit by bit. Dad more than doubled the size of the original three-bedroom house of around 1500 square feet, adding large extensions on each side. Towards the mountains, he built a large living/dining room with large picture window on three sides. Towards the road, he built a two story with a large basement/garage below and a second floor above containing two more bedrooms and a large "playroom." This made the house a split level, as the front of the "basement" was level with the drive.

I did not help much during my younger years, but as time went on, I did contribute a bit to the house construction. It was only natural that, when my friends were all building crude tree houses, I wanted to best them by building a real "house" on the ground in the woods just behind our house next to Henry Miller's property line. My little house was 8 feet by 10 feet with a loft; I was fifteen, but already taking full charge of my life. My bed was in the loft. I put in two windows and a wood stove. That was my bedroom, then, for several months.

Dad wanted to farm on the side. We worked together to clear about ten acres on the slope down from our house. I have done a lot of brush clearing. Dad had originally dynamited the huge stumps left on the property by the loggers. Some were several

feet across. The ground was filled with rocks. I have done a lot of rock hauling. We loaded them into a little trailer behind the tractor and then took them down to a drop at the bottom of our property. We would clean an area entirely of rocks, many trailer loads, and in a few weeks, the pigs would pull up as many rocks again. This growing of rocks out of cleared ground never really ended.

I also worked with Dad building sheds for the animals and putting a barbed wire fence all around the property. Dad always included space for my animals as well. In fact, our first little "barn" was for my goats.

Through these years I worked in my mom's garden. I also tended a good-sized garden of my own. One year I grew Indian corn, but the caterpillars ate the corn before it ever matured. I waged war against caterpillars for a while after that. One year I raised pumpkins that grew so big. I carved out one of the smaller ones and wore it on my head to school for Halloween dress-up, along with a white sheet. I thought it looked pretty cool, but I did not win the prize. Getting much of our food from our own garden was a large part of our lives.

I will talk more about my relationship with my parents in the next chapter.

My Friends

I was friends with a number of boys in my class at school. I would bike quite often up to Lacomb, to the school grounds two miles away. Or they would bike down to join us at Crabtree Creek. Rodney Gable and his younger brother Wade lived right next to the school property. Some of the most enjoyable times of my life was in their hay barn. Their dad had allowed them to create a system of tunnels deep under as they stacked the hay bales to the roof. We would snake through those tunnels or swing from a long rope into a deep mound of loose hay. One time, the chubby boy in our class was coming my way at the lowest point furthest back. He went over me, and got stuck. Yeah – "two boys suffocate to death under a pile of hay bales!" We kept wiggling, though, and eventually came free to continue on our way.

My best friend in my grade school years, however, was our next door neighbor, Henry Miller. And this was very odd, for Henry was the same age as my mom, that is, forty-two, when I first befriended him at age eight. Henry was a peculiar part of my life and a big part of my growing up. Henry was not retarded, but simple-minded. I understood that in his younger years he had rolled a bulldozer and knocked his head. Henry abhorred work, except when I made him help me. He lived, first with his mother, and then alone after she passed on. They were hill-billies, supported by meager government handouts. Yet Henry's mother owned their property, and it passed to his brother, Roy, when she died.

Henry was my friend. For that reason, I include a picture of him as well as a fuller description, a paper I wrote in college composition class, a character sketch.

☙

Henry Miller is probably the strangest and most astonishing person I have known. To must, he would be repulsive, but to me, as a child, he was my friend and companion. Henry lived next door to the place to which my family moved when I was eight; he had lived there with his mother in a ramshackle little house for most of his life. At that time, he was forty two years old.

Henry was a simple-minded man with a bushy read beard and long, stringy hair. He usually wore a cap to protect his partly-bald head from the sun. He dressed simply in work pants and shirt; often he would wear a plain suit-coat. The most noticeable thing about Henry, through, was that he was dirty. His cap was dirty, his face was dirty, his hands were dirty, his pants and shirt and suitcoat were dirty; though, occasionally, his pants and shirt would be washed. In all the years I knew him, he never washed his frying pan or the blankets on his bed. To sweep his house every few months was quite an endeavor for him, usually, that task was left to me. To take a shower once a month or two or three was an accomplishment to him, something to boast about. He did wash his plate ever couple of weeks or so, but carrying out the trash was nearly impossible. I once carted a year's worth of trash out of his kitchen for him. The trash filled my dad's pickup to the top of the stock racks. It was a formidable job.

Henry was simple, and he was lazy. I would try on occasion to get him to help me with my work at home. He would do well the first day; the second day – not so

well; on the third day, he would not show up. Because I knew him well, though, I could talk him into doing most anything for a little while. However, his favorite occupation remained watching television.

Henry was strange and obnoxious to most people, but my boyish eyes saw none of that, because Henry was my friend. From the time I was eight to the time I was nineteen, I spent many long hours with Henry. We hiked through the woods and went on picnics together. We built go-carts and worked on bicycles together. It would take a book to record the number of projects and contraptions we came up with to work on. I remember the time we attempted a bicycle built for two. This was one of many unsuccessful undertakings. It worked fine part way down the hill, but when we tried to turn a corner, it sort of folded up on us. Undiscouraged, we soon went on to our next brainstorm.

Well do I remember our wagon converted to a coaster-cart. Picture, if you will, stopping at a stop sign and looking up the hill to your left. The oddest sight meets your eyes. A twelve-year-old boy and a forty-six-year old man are perched precariously on a careening contraption made of a child's wagon with wooden sides. Behind them on the road are the strips of rubber that were the wagon tires before it started down the hill. As they go sailing by you on rubber-less tires, the old man's hat comes flying off his head and lands in the road directly in front of you. His long red hair blows freely in the wind as the two of them clatter past on down the road, unable to stop. The young boy leans eagerly

forward, his hands gripping the steering rope. Such was my relationship with Henry.

I learned much good from Henry, but much that was not good as well. Henry had a weakness; he loved to drink. Drink turned him into a fool and made him totally obnoxious. Though I loved Henry sober, over the years, I learned to dislike Henry drunk. Henry sober was my friend, but Henry drunk I did not like at all. I could maneuver Henry drunk, but, at least in my earlier years, that was not often.

⸎

Sometime in these years, I led a sober Henry to ask Jesus into his heart – which he did. Then, my mother told me that the next morning she heard him singing, "Jesus loves me," as he was tending his chickens. That was the extent of his "Christian" experience, but I have the right inside of God to call those who belong to me into salvation.

My best friend during my adolescence was Larry Jensen, from southern California. He came with his family to a property about a third of a mile away, up Cut-off Drive, in the summer before I entered ninth grade. We were the same age, but he was a year below me in school, since his birthday was in November instead of October. I was mucking about in the ditch half way to his house when he came walking by. He joined me mucking about, and, until we went separate ways years later, we did most everything together, especially camping and hiking, biking and motorbiking, exploring and arguing as boys do. Once he got his license, I rode with him to school every day. We even worked for the same employers. Yet we were never in classes at school together.

One time, Larry and I biked down to the very small town of Crabtree to visit his cousins. We hiked over to Crabtree Creek just north of the little town. Here, in the wide valley, it was a slow river with mud banks, not at all the way we knew it. There was a raft there, which we climbed onto fully clothed; we did not intend to swim. But we were boys, and so, pretty soon, we were rocking the raft back and forth until Larry's cousin, Bob, fell off. Only then did we remember that he could not swim. Bob lost his mind in full blown panic, screaming and flailing. Larry had no interest in expending himself to help someone in need, ever. So, what could I do? I jumped in, fully clothed, to "save" him. Only – once his hand touched me, he went straight up onto my shoulders and I went straight down under the water. I still had my boots on, so I could hardly tread water. I saw my whole life, in a flash, as they say, and I saw the headlines, "Two Boys Drown in Creek." But before it was too late, I found the bottom slope of mud under my feet and could then push up out of the water. Later, in high school swim class, we learned how to rescue correctly. I did not know that Bob was fine, so long as he was making noise.

Then, in my second year at high school, I became friends with Andy Wyatt, who lived on the south side of Lebanon. Andy would play a large role in my life, both through the "time of darkness" coming up and later, when he gave his heart back to the Lord at the same time as I, and we went to Church doings together. During my high school years, I disconnected from many of the fellows my age from Lacomb, spending time with Larry and Andy instead. Lebanon Union High School was large enough (1600 students) that we sifted out according to interest, and I sifted into the literary and intellectual group.

School and Church

Schol and church worked the same woe in my life. The greatest influence in the life of any child growing up in the modern world is the kids their same age with whom they are stuck inside the walled boxes of school or Sunday school and with whom they learn to function in every wrongful way. No kid has ever learned "social skills" from kids their own age. Instead they learn to bully and to be bullied, to shame and to be ashamed. Playing and learning with kids your own age is an important part of growing up healthy in the Lord, but only when such is balanced by about an equal time of interaction with adults in work and in fellowship. We learn the meaning of life from adults, and from the whole range of interaction with others, with other men besides our father and other women besides our mother, with old folks and little ones in daily life together. Only here is wholeness found, that is, belonging and purpose, giving and receiving.

My parents had no knowledge, in the sixties, of evil in this world. And when I turned towards darkness, it caught them completely unaware. Yet from my own trajectory, inside the arena of kids my own age in school and church, it was the only possible outcome.

Nonetheless, as I look back now, I call all of it by

Christ, and I see Him alone utterly together with me through every moment. And I see, now, His purposes in shaping me through every difficulty and every dark pressure. You see, Jesus lived in my heart. And through every part of my life, my Father was shaping my heart to fit His, though I knew it not.

I attended school for eight years at Lacomb Elementary School. School was always easy for me, so I never thought much about it. I never really "learned" to read. They gave me a book in first grade when I was five and told me what reading was. I read every type of book from then on. I saw a map when I was five as well and knowing the geography and the workings of the world became my all-consuming passion from then until now. When I was around twelve, I had the idea to write to every state capitol and ask for information and maps of their state. For weeks, our mailbox was filled with packages to my great delight. Texas sent me the most, and only Massachusetts sent me nothing. My parents had a set of geography books, and I absorbed them.

I need touch only a few highlights from my elementary school days. I started playing the trumpet in band in fifth grade and continued through my senior year in high school. I did not like to practice at home, however, so I was never really good. I just liked being part of the band. My most memorable learning experience was in fifth grade when Mrs. Sisson, "the tyrant teacher," read an entire book out loud to us, *Seven Alone*. In my teaching career, I have always read a book out loud to my English classes, one day a week. I know from the feedback that listening to the teacher read a story with full expression means a lot to them. I joined sports because I like being with the action, but I was never good enough to be sent out on the field or court, except when the score was 80 to 20 in our favor. Basically, my first two years at Lebanon Union High School ran in the same vein, except for no more failed sports.

Through these years we attended church at the Albany Mennonite Church, right across the freeway from my dad's place of work, Wah Chang. Church potlucks and having individual church families over for dinner after church was a big part of my childhood. I was taught good Bible things, but the people at Albany Mennonite were hardly born again, let alone knowing anything of the Spirit or of a relationship with a personal God. We were Mennonites, and so most of the young men served in the

Mennonite Voluntary service, including my brother, Franz. I remember one "rebellious" young man who joined the army, went to Vietnam, and came back a hardened drug addict.

The Bible was important to us, and we were taught Bible things. I believed that it was God's word to us, but I did not know it that well. When I was eleven or twelve, I had the bright idea of memorizing the three chapters of the Sermon on the Mount, just for fun. I would rattle through it to anyone who cared to listen. One time dad told me to chop down some brush trees, but I chopped down the wrong one. It affected me deeply that I had sorrowed him, so I sought the Lord earnestly, believing Him to raise the tree back to life again. To my great disappointment, it was still there, chopped down, when I went out to the bus in the morning.

But the general church environment is not what influences a child, and neither is it the general school environment. You can "fix" anything in school or Sunday school, and so long as it is a bunch of kids together, they WILL work their woe on one another, regardless. It was not the kids at our large public high school that pressed me towards drugs and rock music, but the kids at church, none of whom I really liked anyhow. I think that only one other kid in my age group, a girl, was born again. And the teacher simply followed whatever the "popular" boys demanded.

Throught these years I attended many week or week-end-long summer camps. Most of the time it was at the Mennonite campground in the Coast Range above Siletz, Oregon, called Drift Creek Camp. Two summers I went to a second, music camp there as well. I also attended nearby non-Mennonite camps on occasion. On the one hand, these were hyper out-of-control times for kids at that age. Mennonites were naïve and would bend over backward to satisfy kids. But on the other hand, those were deeply shaping experiences of togetherness in many activities, indoors and out. Mountains, woods, flowing streams, exploring, these things are written so deeply all through me. I have no idea how it is that I am living in Texas. I have never been able, in my estimation, to give my sons something similar.

When I Was Twelve

I am coming back now and filling in this little bit after I have completed this account and understand much better what was consequential to the unfolding of my life story.

In the summer and fall when I was twelve, which would be between seventh and eighth grades, I had three marked experiences that I now know were part of the whispering of God calling to me and to the song He had written in my heart.

The first experience was at Drift Creek Camp in June. We had all climbed into mini-busses and gone to the coast for an outing. On the way back I was sitting next to a black boy about my age, unusual in Oregon when I was young, This boy began having cramps and was doubled up in pain. He found some relief by pinching my leg just above the knee. In myself, I felt a sense of inclusion, that I was gathering him into myself that he might find some help. I would now call what I felt a Spirit of intercession.

After we had arrived back at Drift Creek and the boy was feeling better, the counselor who was with us remarked to me of the compassion and kindness that he saw in my expression. Yet outwardly, and for the most part, I was just a boy having fun.

The second experience took place in July in the raspberry field. I was picking raspberries in a row next to a girl about my age whom I did not know. She was that type of girl that likes to talk to boys and doesn't need a lot of responses back. In her stream of yakking, she asked me what I wanted to be when I grew up. I always take a question like that seriously and to the deepest levels. I had only one response, "I want to be married."

Yes, this was a desire for a wife and a family, something nearly impossible for me, yet I think it was also coming out from something far deeper, something I could not yet know.

The third experience came in August or September, with my brother, Franz's return from his Mennonite service in lieu of the military and Vietnam. I found on his little bookshelf a set of books titled *The Hobbit* and *The Lord of the Rings* by J.R.R. Tolkien. I was always a voracious reader and read widely even by that age. Yet there was something unique in this great story that touched the depths inside of me, and I could not stop reading it all the way through four times a year for the next few years until my dad, in concern, took the books from me.

He and I both thought that it was "fantasy" that intruged me, and that was true outwardly. I loved

to escape into wondrous dream worlds. I know now, however, that it was much deeper than that. The primary point of Tolkien's story is that victory comes through weakness, through stumbling and failing every step of the way. I know now that this was God calling to me.

And so my God marked me, even at the age of twelve, despite all my continued outward foolishness, with a heart of intercession for the sake of others, with a longing for the deepest levels of fellowship and community, and for the set of a journey stumbling through weakness, a path prepared, that others might be free, that I would come to know my God through weakness.

Trips and Other Events

I also want to include several road trips that we made as a family together through these years. Many events from these trips are marked vividly in my memories.

When I was younger, dad drove us down into southern Oregon on a weekend trip. We visited primarily the sand dunes on the southern Oregon coast, the Oregon caves, and Crater Lake National Park. I picture these things so clearly. We went often to the Oregon coast, but I never liked the ocean view, I always preferred mountains and deep valleys hidden away.

In the summer of 1968, also when I was twelve, we went to Michigan to visit mom and dad's brothers and sisters and all my cousins. We went again in the summer of 1972. Dad must have been like me, because he took a different route across the states coming and going each time. I really enjoyed playing shuffleboard with my grandpa, William, and I loved Grandma Marie's sweet smile. I enjoyed cousin Wally the most because he was always welcoming to me. I drove Uncle Orville's riding lawn mower all around and secretly "fell in love" with his cute daughters. I remember Yordy Drive and the grave stones where my two brothers were buried.

The trips were very long and tedious. I was confined to the back seat in-between Frieda and Cheryl. There was no air conditioning, and I had to be still or they would pinch me. The view out the windows was first mostly sage brush and second mostly corn fields. On one of our returns, I fell asleep in the front seat next to Mom as we drove down from Portland towards home. As the car went over the little hill on Meridian drive, I woke up. As my eyes opened, I saw the line of trees that was our property. Even though it was dark, the knowing that we were HOME went all through me instantly. I knew home; I knew what it looks like.

Then, in October of 1972, we drove a second time to Nebraska for Franz and Audrey's wedding in her home church and with her family, the Kennels. On this trip, I rode with Tim and Frieda who had been married a few years earlier. I think we went in Tim's 1965 Buick, which I would buy from him a few years later. I did not like the flat corn fields of Nebraska, but I remember Mr. Kennel saying to me, "This is how I make my bread and butter." He could not understand how anyone could stomach living in the mountains!

My Quirkiness

I did not know that I was Asperger's until I was 53 years old. I just thought I was peculiar. I was not outgoing, rather I was quite introverted, and I almost never talked to girls. Yet I loved being with other people and with my friends; I loved doing things with others. Although I didn't like working for my dad, I worked my tail off for Larry's dad, John Jensen, or with Henry, doing all the things I persuaded Henry to help me do.

So what did it mean, that I was what is called "high-performing" autism. First, from an early age, the most terrifying words I heard were, "Look me in the eye." It is something I never did.

Then, an Asperger's boy feels too much. For this reason, in order to cope, he must shut off and re-direct the overwhelming feelings and all the "noise" of external things. One way is to "feel" something else. And so I might smile or laugh when i hear or speak of terrible things; it's just how I place things away from myself. Another way to cope is by putting on "blinders" and focusing on pursuits that are fascinating to the boy. Those fascinating things for an Asperger's boy are typically related to patterns of some sort.

From the time I was twelve and first grabbed *The Hobbit* and *The Lord of the Rings* off my brother's bookshelf, or even earlier, my pattern was fantasy, creating complex fantastical worlds in my imagination. Now, a big part of this quality has given much benefit to my present readers, in that I am able to see and envision the things of God and of His kingdom. Nonetheless, in the years of my youth, a qual-

ity that God intended to use for good was turned into not-good directions. Nonetheless, I often draw from things during this time in order to share the good things of Christ with you.

Outwardly, I went from one nervous tick to another. For awhile I flapped my hands hard. Then for a while I made loud noises by squirting bubbles behind my lips. Then, I took to spitting all the time. This became embarrassing because it did not slow down well into my adult years. I drove my older sisters bananas. I really have no idea what my parents thought of me.

I drew endless maps in my bedroom. I conquered the world, one country at a time, many, many times. I built great cities and kingdoms and empires in my strictly ordered imagination, step by step.

I am a strange fish to bullies. They are drawn to suspect me as being an easy target, and, beginning with my grade school years, bullies have done much emotional and psychological harm against me. Yet they always found that I never come under control. I never play their games. I am never subject to any "dare." I could care less. I am astonished though, how many years of my life have been with bullies of all sorts, young and old, as my common companions. Yet greater than that, I have known many wonderful and kind friends whose friendships far exceed the norm.

Reading through this account, one must conclude that I grew up in tremendous abundance and blessing, and I did. I truly did.

Where Is Christ?

After I had completed the rough draft of what you have read thus far, I felt uneasy as to why I was providing this account to my readers. I looked through and thought, "There is no life in this." I felt as if I was "puffing myself up."

I did not want to abandon this project as one more "egg-on-the-face" experience, so I justified this to myself by the thought that, if I am to give God's people hope, as He instructed me to do, then they must know that there is NO "mark of God" or "signs of great calling," or anything like that by which "great men of God" show themselves to be superior to "lesser Christians."

I was just an ordinary boy growing up through the sixties right along with millions of similarly ordinary boys all across the country and the world. Regardless of the environment in which any child grows up, providing there is some degree of safety and stability, boys are interested in very similar things all across the board. If I dare to know my Father, then anyone can do the same.

But then I realized what was really going on inside of me.

The Lord has taken me over the years into specific and painful things inside this time period and showed me that it was not my fault, and that He was with me through each difficulty. But I had never gone with the Lord to look at the whole picture.

Writing this account takes me back into a bubble of feeling that is overwhelming to me. On the one hand, I loved that area around our house so much, but on the other hand, the feelings of a possessiveness it held over me had become stultifying. I do not come under the control of anything; for that reason, I have mostly stayed away from bringing these memories back.

The problem is that I have called large chunks of my life by "not-Christ." Through every moment of my childhood, I was coming out of my Father through the good speaking of Jesus. I walked as His revelation, that is, as the image and likeness of God. The problem is that we knew none of that. Rather, Christians have preferred to call themselves by "sin in the flesh" rather than by Christ.

It has been an exercise, now, of bringing the Lord Jesus into the strong emotions of these times and bringing that entire package of strong emotions and memories into the Lord Jesus Christ, as Paul commanded us to do – **Put on the Lord Jesus Christ.** I am no longer seeing a vain little boy, in spite of all my lack. Rather, I am seeing Jesus living as me through every moment. As I do that, all separation, as well as the twisted union of self-exaltation and self-condemnation, vanishes away into the peace and goodness of Christ.

Christ was in me, and inside of Christ was my Father, reconciling me and all my way unto Himself.

I have never been alone.

3. A Time of Darkness

July 1972 - December 1975

My Father

I now know what my Father is about in this experience of discovering memories I had not placed into the Lord Jesus. As I worked through the spiritual warfare required to place the Lord Jesus Christ upon my childhood, I came to understand what was missing.

The truth is, I had a heart to know the Lord, even as I was turning away. And so I know personally that the single most important NEED in human society is that the hearts of the fathers be turned towards their children. My own father's heart was most certainly turned towards me. The problem was simple; I did not know it.

It was as I became a father myself that I came to understand the agony of my own dad's heart, in that he could not share himself with his children. Yet I have done the same as he; I have covenanted with God that He would keep that which I cannot.

As a boy, I was enthusiastic, adventurous, always heading out in one direction or another, and utterly alone in an unsafe world. There was no one protecting me.

Because I have had so much help since, I was able to extend a measure of protection over my children. Protection does not mean "control," in fact, control is abuse, not protection. It means first, making sure that each one knows that I regard them as a person of respect and integrity. It means second, that I prevent any words of shame from entering into their self-story. It means third that, as they pass through normal human difficulties, I show them the same things in me, that I also went through these difficulties and that it is normal to being human and carried entirely inside of Jesus. And it means fourth, that I ensure that they are not placed into environments that would be destructive to them. That fourth is the hardest, and I was not always successful. Nonetheless, here is the difference. When my son ran from religious abuse, he ran to me, his father, where he found full safety inside of Christ.

I share this, because it is only by this contrast that I am able to place my childhood into Christ and to understand what went wrong and why.

I remain ashamed of one thing in my life. I am ashamed of my attitude towards my father, an animosity that began somewhere in the transfer from grade school at Lacomb to high school in Lebanon. By placing me out into the arena of the public school and the Sunday school classroom, my parents had placed me into great danger and into continual spiritual assault.

Because I had no protection from that assault, I blamed the one person who "ought to" have been my protection, my father. This connection was not conscious, that is, I had no idea of anything, just confusion and pain and an empty place where terrible things came against me and no one helped me at all.

The moment when I forgave my dad will come in a much later chapter of this story. I now know that my dad would have done anything to have protected me, if he had understood and been able to do so.

Yet I also realize that it was this lack in my life that was the surface reason why darkness prevailed through these years. The real reason, however, is that my Father required me to KNOW the critical importance of turning the hearts of the fathers towards their children, what that means and how it must be.

Experiences with God

Although twenty years ago I created a time-line of events in my life, there are still many things the timing of which I am not certain. Sometime around ninth grade, I began to smoke pot. I also began to smoke cigarettes, though not steadily. I had my first taste of alcohol sometime in here as well. This was the negative part of Henry Miller's involvement in my life. It's not that he influenced me in this direction, but rather, that I influenced him, that is, he was available to get what I requested from the store.

Then, I attended a revival service with my parents. When the preacher gave the call to come forward, something in the Spirit grabbed me by the shirt collar and sent me down to the front immediately. It was a good experience with God, but it could not last. That evening, in repentance, I gave my dad the pack of cigarettes I had. When I found it still in the pile of stuff on top of his dresser several weeks later, I interpreted that as meaning that he did not care. This interpretation was one hundred percent false, but it was all I knew.

I stopped going to church in August of 1972, so my other strange experience must have happened several months before. Our youth group had a get-together over the weekend at the Albany Mennonite Church, from Friday evening to Sunday morning. We slept in the classrooms and ate in the dining room below the auditorium. It was an incongruous experience because we listened to the Rolling Stones in the church and several of us smoked pot in a hiding place outside. Nonetheless, as I went home from this experience, something inside of me sang, over and over, "This is right, this living together inside the house of God is what it's all about."

In June of 1972, my brother and his wife, Franz and Audrey, were fellowshipping together with Del and Virginia Buerge whom we knew from the Albany church. Del's older brother, Jim Buerge and his wife had received the Baptism in the Holy Spirit a few years earlier and were attending a Spirit-filled church. As Franz and Audrey, Del and Virginia were seeking God together, the Holy Spirit came upon them. As they joyfully shared their new knowledge of God with my parents, both mom and dad received the infilling of the Holy Spirit along with my older sister, Frieda, and her husband, Tim Louden.

In July, then, as all this excitement was bubbling all around me, though I was pretty oblivious to it, I got into an argument with my friends, Larry Jensen and John McKinney. You see, it was normal for Larry and I to side together against John, who was younger and smaller than we were, but who was also a bit "stuck up." This time, Larry sided with John against me.

I went home in a huff, feeling cut off and lonely – a very good place to be.

For some strange reason, I grabbed a book my mother had bought recently, took it up to my bedroom and read it through in one sitting. The book

was *Prison to Praise* by Merlin Carothers. By the time I finished it, I was filled with such JOY beyond measure. I did not know it then, but my Savior had planted His most important seed into my heart, a seed that would grow of itself without any further input from any direction, a seed that would turn my heart into His pathway time and time again from then until now.

That seed is – give thanks. **In all things give thanks.**

This was an infilling of the Spirit, though I did not speak with tongues. Yet in the joy of the Lord, I cast off all the things of darkness and enjoined my parents to take me to every fellowship meeting there was. I even had the sensation of actually loving my little sister, Jenelle, something quite uncommon to a fifteen-year-old boy.

Turning Away

Sadly, there was so little understanding of the ways of God and so little teaching available. This experience with God lasted about three weeks.

Then, sometime in August, I went on our scheduled camping trip with Larry, this time up Crabtree Creek near where the logging bridge goes across. While I was with Larry, whom I now know was a bit less than just unregenerate, the "feelings" lifted. I wanted to smoke, but I had no cigarettes. I searched along the rocks where people came to swim, and after awhile I found a cigarette butt with enough remaining for me to light up and get a few whiffs of smoke.

When I did that, by my own decision, a light turned off inside of me. I entered a time of darkness that would last for three-and-one-half years. From that time on, I disconnected fully from my parents in going to church. I simply hid out in the woods until they were gone.

I went back to smoking, a habit that would soon grow to a pack a day. I smoked pot and drank beer with my friends from high school every chance I could. Besides Andy Wyatt and Larry, there were two other friends from my classes at school, Tim Steele and Tim Greiner. Actually, we were a foursome, Andy and I and the two Tim's. Larry was along with us, yes, but he returned to California for his senior year, so there was a period of time without him.

Andy was a bit older than us, so he was a driver

first. The three of them would come out from Lebanon to Henry's house. Then we would drive Henry up to the store in Lacomb where he would buy beer for us. We would return to his house, then, to drink and smoke.

Drugs were plentiful at school in the 1970's. In fact, Tim Greiner, who was the president of the honor society, was also the guy with the pot for sale which he carried in his hollowed-out textbook. We lived in a world that could end any moment by nuclear destruction. We lived under the horrors of a war that took the young men a few years older than us and turned them into hard and hate-filled men. Young people protesting this war at Kent State were shot dead by the government. Yet we were free as kids today are not. We would never have tolerated a policeman inside our school. Yet our freedom was now going in all the wrong directions.

Ignorant of Asperger's

I want to place a brief look at my final two years of high school inside this title, "Ignorant of Asperger's." There are many things inside this entire time period that are of no relevance. The time when the Lord took all this into Himself is pertinent here, however. As I was sitting waiting for my turn to experience prayer for deliverance, some fourteen years later at the Blueberry Christian Community, I was very apprehensive. My mind went back over this time of darkness. I heard the Lord speak, "Son, even in the darkness, you were still My son." I knew in that moment that He had taken all my iniquity upon Himself. I had imagined myself to be "unregenerate" during this time. I had not known that I have always belonged to Jesus.

I must warn you, however; I am opening a can of worms. Some might say, "Now that you know Jesus, don't open such a can of worms." But the worms are there, eating away, whether we open the can or not. Jesus said, "**You are clean.**" God told Peter, "**Do not call what I have made clean to be unclean.**" Being made clean, however, has never done anyone a bit of good unless we KNOW that we are every whit clean. We have not known such cleanness, not in those parts of our lives we have kept unopened because of the worms.

High School was easy for me. Whatever mental abilities I might have had, however, were devoted to gaming the system, to doing the least amount of work in order to maintain a B average. I always did my English class work, however, because I enjoyed it. I never did any Geometry homework, which meant straight F's on the daily grade. But we had a quiz every Friday, so I read the chapter on Thursday and got an A on Friday, which meant a C for the course. Matched with my A's in English and Band, that resulted in a B average – and so it went. So much of school was uninteresting; I never really connected with uninteresting even though I take great interest in many things.

I devoured books. In tenth grade we were required to read *A Tale of Two Cities* by Charles Dickens. At the end of the first week, I had finished it, but the other students were still crying over having to read chapter 2. I talked my dad into subscribing to a complete works of Charles Dickens in leather. By the end of high school I had read all his books, many of them twice. I became a student of WWII. I devoured history books, but I detested history class.

I have always loved being with other people, even though I've never been good at conversation except with Andy and Larry. And that was problematic. I did not understand until years later that both of them lied to me on a regular basis, Andy to get a rise out of me, and Larry, because he lived only in lies. It was years later that I realized that little that Larry claimed about himself was actually true. Yet I believed him at the time, with no reason to doubt. These relationships became very confusing to me.

A great darkness opened itself inside of me. I would sneak over to Henry's every night to watch TV (we did not have TV at home). I would sit there feeling deeply black about everything. I realize now the event that triggered this deep depression when I wasn't with my friends. Early in my eleventh grade year (if it was in October, I would still have been fifteen), I had occasion to purchase a tiny piece of paper that had been soaked in LSD from a girl at school. She told me that it was a "four-way" hit, but I had no idea what that meant. My parents were away at a church event that evening; only my foster brother, Ricky Bozek, was at home.

I swallowed the entire "four-way hit" around 11 PM. Within twenty minutes I was feeling wonderful. Then I was feeling TOO wonderful. Then it was way, way too much. I wandered around the house hollering for help. Ricky was in his room, but he never said a peep about it. I do not come under the control of anything, however. So when it became overwhelming to me, I took myself firmly in hand, went into my room, laid down on my bed, held the covers over me tightly, and refused to move or to do anything in response. For eight hours, I lay there in absolute FEAR to the sound of motorbikes gunning down the road and to the continuous swirl of fantastic images.

The fear was thick and palpable. On LSD, one finds oneself in the dimensions of the heavens with dark things all around. Through these hours I saw the gates of the heavenly city, and they were closed shut against me. In that moment, I believed that I was utterly and forever lost. When it faded at the end of the night and I arose to go about my day, I pretended that nothing had happened, though that was hard. My parents never knew. But from then on I believed that I was lost. This was the cause of my despair. For the next fifteen years, that darkness wrenched my gut in pain much of the time. None of my experiences with God removed it. But it became the whips that drove my darkness through the next three years.

It is so wonderful to me now as I place this experience into its context in my life. You see, no human lives by the truth, even though Jesus sustains each one every moment by His good speaking. All live by what they BELIEVE to be "the truth." I BELIEVED that I was lost, even though there was no truth in that belief. The Lord Jesus had shared with me every moment of that night. He did not intend my distress, but He did intend me, and He carried me through it far more safely than what I understood. But of course, I did not know Him then.

Yet it was this false belief that I was lost that drove me into seeking anything that could make me feel "not lost." My fantasy world, the structured and vastly complex daydreams I conjured up in my fierce mental drive became extensive. I figured out, not only how to conquer the entire world, but then also, the entire universe. I dreamed up how I, by science, could become "god" in my knowledge and power. To be honest with you, I came up with scenarios, in the early seventies, that would not become known as possibilities until the age of the Internet thirty years later.

Here is one of many places where Asperger's comes in. Although Asperger's often imagine the worst when it comes to how people think about them (mostly because they don't understand who or what these other "people" are), Asperger's are rarely dishonest with themselves. I have never con-fused my extensive fantasizing abilities with practical reality. What I did not know for many years is that this quality is not at all common. Most humans do mix fantasy with reality and never think twice about their confusion and dishonesty. It was this quality in my friends that so often threw me into further confusion; I did not know that they did not know the difference between make-believe and reality.

Seeking refuge in fantasy did not cease for me until I knew my precious union with the Lord Jesus Christ. Since the Lord sealed me into Himself in the summer of 2013, I can no longer find those fantasy realms that once were so important to me. I no longer have any need of them. And when I look back now, all I see is that I had done nothing more than turn the way God designed me into the wrong directions. I am the same person now, filled with Christ. I have always belonged to Jesus; I just did not know it.

A Bleak and Lonely Year

I want to give an overview of the year or so following my graduation from high school. It was a bleak and lonely year. I had designed my senior year to require doing no homework at all the entire year except one large project for English which I wanted to work on anyhow. And I had filled that year with involvement in activities with those classmates in my same literary bracket. My senior year was no work, all fun, and lots of doing things together including many quite imaginative pranks (or so I thought because most of them were my invention, including driving a Volkswagen Beetle into the school where it was pushed down the hall to the principal's office and successfully getting away with it, etc. etc.).

Graduation was another big activity together, also filled with, if not pranks, at least the dreaming of and laughing about the pranks we could pull. This was the age of "streaking," but only the president of the student body ever dared to do it. And so the morning after graduation came to me as a total shock, one for which I was completely unprepared. All that activity which had filled my life ceased, and it could not be regained. Larry was living in Southern California at the time, and my friends from school lived many miles away. I was alone. I did not like being alone. I don't quite understand myself. I love solitude, and I never get bored. But I also love doing things with others. I need both in equal measure.

I was not working, so I slept twelve hours a day and read books or drew maps and fantasized the other twelve hours. I almost became bored. The only way I could visit with my friends was if I borrowed money and the pickup from my dad, or if they got together and drove out to Henry's (whether he was in jail or not). I had little relationship then with the kids of the Lacomb area.

I had worked at the Stayton Cannery the fall of my senior year because Larry had gotten a job there. I disliked that kind of repetitive work, but it was money in one's pocket. The cannery opened up again in August, which brought the almost boring summer to an end. I worked the swing shift, from 3-11 PM, then I had the money to drive to my friends, wherever they were living, where we smoked pot, etc., until I came home around 3 AM. I will talk about that drive home night after night a little later.

Tim Steele, Tim Greiner, and Andy Wyatt had signed up to attend Linn Benton Community College. I had zero interest in any more school, for which I am grateful. College was not a worthwhile experience for anyone with whom I related. They did poorly because they took useless classes and partied most of the time. But Tim, Tim, and Andy had rented apartments right next to the college, and so that's where I went after work through the fall of 1974.

During this time we tried speed, that is, amphetamines. I always reacted to drugs a bit differently than most. Speed made me talk – non-stop, even while everyone else was talking non-stop. I shared everything about myself, things that should never be said. When the "high" left, then, I was utterly ashamed of the things I had blurted out. This became a dark pattern in my life that would last many years, that I would talk too much and then become deeply ashamed afterwards. It is still a foolish characteristic, but now I put it all into Jesus when I awake in the middle of the night; I no longer know shame. Needless to say, it was not long before I became utterly sick of amphetamines and stopped using them.

Sometime in December or January, Tim, Tim, and Andy found a large old house for rent with many bedrooms. A number of people who had lived at the apartment complex next to LBCC joined with them and they all rented it together. I was there many evenings, but I had no interest in staying overnight. We called it "Mad Hal," taken from the initials of those who lived there. It was a form of "community," but it did not end well. It was a very bleak winter.

By the time I started working in construction with Jimmy Barkley in May of 1975, Mad Hal had long since disbanded. But at that point I was working days, at a job that fitted me and that paid good money. Working with Jimmy became the first stability in my life since high school.

Through the summer of 1975 we drove up to Portland often to attend rock concerts, etc. I was usually the driver with quite a few piled into my car. I had bought an old 55' Chevy from my brother-in-law, Tim Louden, and had put a new engine into it, etc. My dad did not let me make it into a hot rod, however, so it remained a clunker. I wanted so much to buy a 1968 Triumph Spitfire after my income became regular, but dad refused to co-sign. He was willing to co-sign on a brand-new 1975 Honda Civic hatchback, however, so that became my car after I sold the 55' Chevy. My dad was right, because the two-seater Triumph would never have served my needs. I still dream of it to this day, however, when I'm out with my children, looking at cars for them to buy.

I remained at home in Lacomb. My friends lived in Albany and Corvallis and later Salem, so I drove long distances there and back most every day. I had dreamed of leaving home until I could. Then I realized that I had everything I needed at home at no cost and with no requirements. I had little relationship with my brothers and sisters; I was so far apart in age from my brothers; Franz was nine years older and Glenn nine years younger. I had little to do with my sisters. My parents placed no obligation on me. Dad always made sure I knew that I was free of him, that he would not control my life. My parents also received my friends as their own children, regardless. Andy even found refuge living with them for a few weeks after I went north to Canada. We were safe at home. Yet I was seldom there.

Following the Map

I want to bring in two more things before going on to that momentous fall of 1975 when I began to perceive the hound of heaven chasing me through all the dark ways of my life. First is the role of the map and the mountains in my life, and second is my places of work.

All through my childhood I had looked up at the mountains, and especially up the logging road with deep longing to see what was up there. But my dad never drove me up that road; I don't know why. I once went up the logging road all the way to Crabtree Lake with John McKinney's dad. I was utterly enthralled. Then, in May of 1972, I sold my awesome Schwinn bike in order to buy an un-awesome Honda 90 from Larry's dad. Larry already had a Bultaco, and so the logging roads that cover the Oregon Cascades were now ours.

The Honda just was not up to mountain inclines, so by August I sold it and purchased a second Bultaco from Larry's dad. We now had two equally matched bikes and oh, how we explored. I was in heaven. Give me a mountain road with a cliff on both sides, and a five speed manual tranny under my hand, and I am soaring.

I have over a hundred thousand miles of exploring the gravel logging roads of the mountains to the east of our home, primarily Snow Peak and Crabtree Mountain, fifty thousand miles in my Dad's pickups and fifty thousand in my Honda Car, plus several thousand miles on our Bultacos. I soon found maps of the logging roads. I love maps. I trace out a road on the map, and I must follow that road, regardless. I have been stuck many, many times, in mud and snow and water. I know how to get out of being stuck. But if that map says that this road goes over that hill, then by gum, I must follow that road over that hill regardless of what might be in the way. Larry and I started a number of the bike trails that became popular to many others later on until the logging company had to close them down because the bikers were gouging out the hillsides.

The mountains remained a huge part of my life until I moved away from Oregon to Christian Community in other places. Even when I returned to Oregon for two years with Maureen and our two little ones, I still took them often up into the mountains to drive and to hike and to explore. We even had a service together at a favorite spot.

I loved going up in the mountains with Gollum, my Chesapeake Bay Retriever. We climbed and explored so many places, just him and me.

Mad Hal was such a ridiculous caricature of "community"; nonetheless, it spoke to something deep inside of me, the same calling to community that I had experienced earlier. I would find this place or that in the mountains and sit there and dream up a community, many living together, and where our homes and gardens would be.

My Places of Work

Working at Stayton Cannery was not what I was designed to do, tedious work, doing the exact same thing over and over. I divided the clock into 15 minute periods and looked forward only to break, to lunch, to break and then to the quitting bell. Only in the most mundane of tasks could I find relief because then I could disconnect my mind from the useless task and into fantasy. One time I sang *Jesus Christ Superstar*, every song and every word. Weird, eh?

But I had one experience at the Stayton Cannery in my second season there that fits into the topic of the incredible protection in which I walked. My job for two weeks was "spotting" corn trucks as they came in from the local farms to dump their ears of corn. I would direct the truck to where it would drop its load, and then wait with two baskets to be filled with corn for a testing sample. One time a rickety old farm truck backed up, and it's tired mechanisms creaked as it slowly lifted up. My eyes were down on the baskets so that I could snatch them back after the first ears of corn came out. In that position, I heard a slight crack. Something registered in my brain that this "crack" was not right. I did not think. Instead, one second later I was turning around twenty feet away from that truck, which by this time was lying still on its side, having crushed the baskets where I was. That was the same careful instinct that kept me safe many times before and after, yes, but now I suspect that there was some angelic help involved.

Then, in May of 1975, Larry had returned from his final year of high school in Simi Valley, California. He was staying with his sister and brother-in-law, Jimmy and Sharon (Jensen) Barkley, who lived just a few miles from our house, on Ede Road – in the old Ede house. Jimmy was a carpenter, working as a sub-contractor framing houses for Republic Construction, a builder in Lebanon and Albany. Larry thought that we could get work with him. I went to his job site and, for some reason, Jimmy decided that I was worth hiring, since I was familiar with construction, having grown up inside of it. Larry came along as part of that package, but he lasted only a month before Jimmy decided that Larry was not a builder.

I took to construction; it fitted me as a creative and worthwhile occupation. Jimmy soon made me a junior partner with him and I worked with Jimmy through the next few years, even in-between my times at Graham River and Bowen's Mill. But when I walked onto the job site, my eyes saw the blueprints. I immediately asked to take them home for study. I had discovered one of the great loves God created me for – designing and building homes. In ninth grade I had taken an introductory occupational course that included nine weeks each of electricity, drafting, wood shop, and metal shop. The drafting was mostly mechanical drafting, but the work had sung all through me. I did not like "occupational" schooling however. I prefer to learn by doing it first.

Jimmy was about my older sister, Frieda's age; he was the first steady and good influence in my life. Jimmy always treated me as an equal, taught me all that he knew, and put up with all my nonsense. I have not seen Jimmy since the summer of 1979, though I have searched for him on the Internet without success. I miss him and would love to connect with him again.

The Hound of Heaven

By August of 1975, Andy and Tim Steele had found an apartment in Salem, Oregon. I drove up to Salem after work much of the time and then back home to Lacomb in the wee hours of the night drunk or stoned. But in August of 1975, I became aware of a shift in the heavens around me. There is no better metaphor to describe what I sensed than "the hound of heaven" baying down the paths of my life, haunting me with the calling of God.

I panicked, spending the next five months running from that insistent 'hound' on my tail. No matter what I did or where I went, I could not escape it. By this time I had become sick of chemical drugs and no longer used them. I became tired of alcohol and stopped drinking it. But I never tired of marijuana. I smoked a lot of pot, but although it could dull the baying of that hound, it could never silence it.

I want to talk about the wall of protection which I could often sense in the heavens around me and in physical circumstances. I want to relate a number of instances, though not necessarily in chronological order.

First, still during my high school years, I had watched a TV program about "mind over matter," using psychic power to heal. I became intrigued with the idea and thought all day at school about researching the topic more. When I got off the bus at home that day, my mom came right up to me. She said, "Daniel, I had a dream last night and the Lord warned me that you were touching something dangerous that will destroy you." My parents never tried to control me, so this statement from my mom meant something to me. I dropped the idea like a hot potato. Later, when my humanities seminar class were gathered at one of our homes for a class project, the rest of them decided to try to lift a table by levitation. I said, "No, I'm not interested," and sat and read a book while they failed at their attempt. My refusal did not bother them or me. I never did anything I did not want to do, and they accepted that as a given. By that one word from God through my mother, I have never touched spiritual evil.

One time, when we were up at Portland standing in line for a Pink Floyd concert, I was, of course, stoned on pot. Nonetheless, as we stood there in that line, a group of Hare Krishna dudes in orange robes went by us, chanting. As I stood there watching them pass, I knew that a wall of angels stood between me and all evil. I knew that I was safe, even though I imagined that I was lost. I had a number of opportunities to commit fornication, but every time my mind went blank and I could not see or hear until the opportunity had passed. God kept me, even against my will, from all those things that actually destroy.

I went three times down to Simi Valley, next to Los Angeles, to visit Larry. The first time was in October of 1974. I spent the night of my eighteenth birthday sitting all night in the Greyhound bus station on my way back home – not a very comfortable experience. Then, I went down with Larry for several days in July of 1975 after Jimmy had fired him. The last time was in November of 1975 when I spent another week in Los Angeles with Larry. During that visit, Larry and I went to a city park with a whole bunch of kids he knew. We were smoking pot and talking loudly. It was after dark. We were in a city neighborhood, but we did not care. Then, all of a sudden, I knew it was time to go. Larry easily agreed, and we left the others still making a lot of noise. We walked to the far corner of the park, went around a yard fence and down a quiet street to Larry's car, got in and drove to his home. We found out later that, at the very moment when Larry and I turned the corner, the cops came out of the woods behind the group and arrested everyone remaining. They all spent the night in jail. The truth is, I should have had a police record many times, but I never did. I could never have gone to Canada if I had.

One time I was driving up the logging road in my dad's pickup. It was crowded in the cab, so I suspect that it was Larry with Andy Wyatt and Tim Steele. We had just crossed the logging bridge and were on the narrow stretch between a deep and wide ditch filled with water on our right and a steep slope down to Crabtree Creek on our left. A logging truck came around the corner ahead at full speed. This was his road, and he was not about to move over in that too-narrow spot. If his wheel had gone off the pavement, it would likely have hurled him over the edge into the Creek. There was not enough room for us on the right. In that moment I knew that there was only one option. I gunned it as hard as I could. Just before we would have hit the logging truck, I swung the wheel hard to the right and then hard back again. Whoosh, we were back on the logging road on the other side of the truck. I cannot imagine it if I did not know it was true, but our right-side tires must have been above the water of the ditch as we went around the logging truck. Whether there were angels there holding us up, I don't know, but we were kept.

I imagined that I was "very good" at driving long miles home successfully in the early morning hours drunk and stoned. After the Lord received me back into Himself, I learned something different from my mom. Time and again, the Lord would wake her up in the middle of the night with me on her heart, she would drop to her knees and pray until she heard me driving in. I was not kept because of any virtue of my own; I was kept because my parents covenanted with God to keep me. I realize now that "knowing" just what to do, many times, must have come from the Spirit and through my parent's prayers.

I learned later that, sometime possibly in August, my dad stood out on the front steps of our home with his hands raised and tears streaming down his face and did what I have done for my own children. He placed me utterly upon a God who keeps covenant with us. The Lord spoke to him in that moment, "Daniel will return to Me before Christmas."

And so through these months I would swing back and forth between weeping on my way home in order to somehow find the Lord, to running towards evil as fast as I could. Yet no matter what I tried, evil things vanished from my reach and I could not touch them. Yet I could not find faith either. I stopped going to my high school friends as much. Rather, I spent many evenings smoking pot with Dural Sylvester, with whom I had been together in school since first grade. He was the only kid with whom I had tussled. He was taunting me once, so I threw my bicycle at him, after which he promptly knocked me and the bike into the ditch. That was the extent of any "fighting" I ever did, except that I hit my sister Cheryl in the back once, when she made me mad. Please, forgive me, Cheryl.

Dural, however, was the only one from my elementary school years at Lacomb with whom I maintained a relationship even after I was living in Christian community.

A Faithful Savior

On Saturday, December 20, I spent a quiet evening with Dural smoking a lot of marijuana. I drove home before midnight, and when I laid myself down upon my bed, I saw a vision. I saw two huge steel doors, like great bank vault doors, swinging shut with a clang that rang with all finality. I knew, without any question, that my life of running from God was finished and that I would never return to such a thing.

I got up the next day inside that certain knowledge. Yet I could not find faith; I did not know how to connect with God or what might be the path forward. That Sunday, I took all my drug paraphernalia and wrongful books, put it all in a large gunny sack and drove up into the mountains, this time to the west slope of Green Mountain, to an area I never went. I threw my gunny sack behind some bushes and sat there waiting, hoping God might show Himself by fire or something. Nothing happened, so I drove home in utter disconsolation.

The next day, Monday, I drove again up into the mountains, this time to one of my favorite areas, the west slopes of Crabtree Mountain. I had my Bible with me and, for some really strange reason, read the book of Job. Reading Job did nothing for me, and I finally went home in deeper despair. I could not go back, I could not go forward, and I did not know what to do.

Several months earlier, I had visited with my parents at Jim Buerge's home. Jim and Del both had purchased properties on the north slope of Thomas Creek several miles north of us. Thomas Creek drains the entire north slopes of Rogers Mountain, Snow Peak, and Crabtree Mountain. Jim Buerge was the only Christian figure in my childhood whom I respected.

That Tuesday morning, as I drove out from home, I decided that I needed help and that the only person to whom I could look for help was Jim Buerge. I drove up to his house and knocked on the door. A strange woman opened the door. When I asked about the Buerge's, she told me that they had moved to Canada a few months earlier.

I was alone. But I was also near the northern access to Snow Peak. This was a winter of little snow in the Western Cascades, which was unusual. Typically, "Snow" Peak is covered with snow during the winter months. You see, that morning, before I went to see Jim Buerge, I had attempted to drive again up the Snow Peak logging road which ran below our house. This time, however, when I had tried to cross the logging bridge, I found that the gate was closed and locked. Their would be no passage up that morning.

So as I left Jim's former home, I took the northern route up to the western shoulder of Snow Peak, looking out over the Willamette Valley. I stopped there at the highest point and sat in my car, unable to connect with the Lord. In my despair, I opened my Bible and read these words.

For it is impossible for those who were once enlightened, and have tasted of the heavenly gift, and were made partakers of the Holy Ghost, and have tasted the good word of God, and the powers of the world to come, if they shall fall away, to renew them again unto repentance; seeing they crucify to themselves the Son of God afresh, and put him to an open shame (Hebrews 6:4-6 – KJV).

I had tasted the good word of God and partaken of the Holy Ghost. These words, then, were the final axe. I was eliminated from God.

"Lord Jesus," I said, "Would You do the impossible for me? Would You be willing to be crucified and to be put to open shame again for me?"

I heard the words, "My son." Instantly I sat up, threw my pack of cigarettes out the window, and grabbed my Bible tightly to my heart. In that moment, I saw the closed logging gate. I knew that if I found that gate open when I came down the southwest slope of Snow Peak, I could be saved. Jesus would receive me.

I drove down the long and windy gravel logging road in trepidation. As I came down to the main Snow Peak line, I saw the camp watchman's pickup driving by just ahead. I knew I could be saved. Sure enough as I drove through, the gate was opened, and I could proceed the remaining three miles home.

You see, the problem was never on the side of my Savior, who had always been carrying me utterly inside of Himself. The problem was in my own mind, that I could not believe. The Lord gave me that picture of the open gate so that I could believe.

It was December 23, 1975, two days before Christmas. God is a Keeper of covenant.

⤸

Well, I did it. I opened that can of worms. And what did I find? I found no worms at all. Jesus has already taken to Himself all my loss and filled every moment of my life with all His gain. Yet seeing Jesus there with me through those eight hours of horror and fear when I overdosed on LSD brings an even further healing than I have yet known.

My Family - I am twenty-two years old.

From top left - Franz, Cheryl, Glenn, and me. From Bottom left - Jenelle, dad, mom, and Frieda.

4. A Season of Preparation

January 1976 - February 1977

Reflections

This has been quite an experience for me to open up again my childhood and youth. As I write these things, it's as if I am back there again with all the primary feelings of those times. Yet as I place every one of these moments into Jesus and He into them, Jesus Himself calms the raging storms and brings everything to a wondrous peace. After that, I can see everything with a new understanding, and I realize that at no point was I ever outside of the Way of Life, a Way that is not dependent on us, but is, in fact, Jesus Himself.

Those parts of this time that I once thought were major, I now see as relatively minor. And other parts that I thought were small and incidental, I now see as the true ruling points of these years. Dural Sylvester seemed to be minor, yet of all the non-Christians I knew through these years, I continue to hold him before the Lord as belonging to Salvation. The real major points, of course, were every instance of God with me. And the truly minor points were every instance of my own folly.

You see, for years after, I held a secret fear that, because my fantasizing was so great and because I had invented myself as a "god" by scientific knowledge and power, that the day might come that I would turn my back on God and become "the Antichrist." At times of great self-pity, this was a voiceless terror. Now, I can see that none of that ever had any meaning. God made us the way we are, and He brings all that we are into His goodness. Certainly we went in wrong directions, but what little one growing up has not? My grandson wanted to help his mother, so he put all his clean diapers into the dirty diaper pail. – Good things turned momentarily in the wrong directions.

Having opened these times back up in my consciousness, I have been zealous with the Lord that His peace would come into every turbulent moment. And so He is and does. The turbulence is there, buried deep inside, even if we stay unaware of it in the present moment. But when Jesus re-deemed us, He purchased from us all that we are and every moment of our lives. It all belongs to Him, even those most desperate times. What needs to be in His empty grave we count as being only there. But everything that was actually me becomes one seamless story of Christ.

A Slow Beginning

I was fully returned to the Lord Jesus, but Asperger's meant that I could not tell my parents so. It only took them a couple of weeks of evidence, however, before they knew. I was sneaking every Christian book into my room and going off to a church somewhere on Sunday mornings. I'm sure there was also a peace upon my face.

From the moment I threw that pack of cigarettes out my window, I never had any addictive need to smoke again. I still had two cigarettes in my glove box, however, and did not know how to get rid of them. Asperger's is very restrictive in things like this. So, I solved the problem by smoking them. Doing that, however, did not recreate any need to smoke. I had gone without cigarettes for a few days several months earlier and it was unbearable. This healing was a gift from God.

There were other things that I now know as Asperger's, but then I thought were just weird me. I could not turn my headlights on in the evening if there was another car coming my way, for they would see my "presumption." And I never got a hair cut for five years, not until just before I went north to visit Graham River for the first time. At first it was because I was by nature a long-haired hippy, but more than that, for others to see that I had altered my appearance would have been overwhelming to me. It would have been "presumptuous."

People often interpret Asperger's as being arrogant and haughty. We come across as harsh and rough at times, but our reasoning is NOT what people think. If you judge an Asperger's by outward appearance you will get it wrong. But – that's true regarding everyone. The little boy who said that the emperor "has no clothes," was likely Asperger's. You can see that blurting out honesty in the wrong places does not go over very well at all.

Probably by the second week of January I went to see Andy Wyatt again. He was living back home with his mom on the south side of Lebanon. Andy had his own room above the garage separate from the house. When I arrived, I was welcomed with a huge surprise.

Andy also had an experience with the Lord when he was younger, as had I. When he heard from Tim Steele that I had become a "Christian," that bit of news threw him into the proverbial "between the hammer and the anvil." As a result, he also had surrendered his heart back to the Lord. Andy became another awesome gift of God to me, that we had each other to begin our walk in this new life to which we had each committed ourselves.

After further reflection, another perspective that has come through this exercise of laying out the patterns of my life is that I can now see the very short time period between, let's say, September of 1975, when I first began to run from God's pursuit into every awful hiding place – until, say, September of 1977 when I sat in the glory of an open heavens with a Feast of Trumpets word entering into me by an anointing upon God's ministry beyond anything I have known. That's just two years, from age 18 to age 20.

Now I can see that what I imagined to be aimless wandering was never anything of the sort. Rather, I can see God's building blocks, step by step in my life, taking me always upon His path and making me that pathfinder He created me to be. And so I have titled this period of my life as "A Season of Preparation." I am looking for how my Father took me from one place to the other in such a short time.

However – I want to insert a brief caution. I just went looking for information from these times on an Internet search and found an obituary for Andy Wyatt, who passed on March 23, 2019. This picture is of him, probably still in his twenties. There is, of course, no mention of our time together, but it does describe him as he was – the laugh of the party.

Never imagine me as being some sort of "man of God." As I

ponder these things, I see just how much of a failure I am and have been in so many things including friendship. I am able to give hope to God's people ONLY because if Jesus takes all my misery into Himself, then it is a simple thing for Him to receive you as well.

I sought the Lord for one reason, and that is because I so desperately needed a Savior. Yet the difference with me was that whatever it was that satisfied others never, never satisfied me. I must go a different way; I must have God's real and final answer for everything in my life.

A Pentecostal Experience

Once Andy and I were connected together in this new life, we decided to attend Lebanon's primary Pentecostal Church, the Assembly of God Church at the north end of town at the corner of Highway 20 and Highway 34. When I look on Google maps, the satellite view shows the old building, but the street view shows a large empty lot; this landmark of Lebanon's history is gone.

The pastor of the church was H. D. Robeson, with C. O. Branson as his assistant pastor. This was a large and vibrant congregation. Pastor Robeson was of the old Pentecostal persuasion, and both he and Pastor Branson could preach up a storm. This church tended in the direction of the "holy roller" style. Now, as I place my time in this congregation, I am changing how I see. I have judged this church as "shallow," and certainly there was a level of "hype," of pretend performance. Nonetheless, as I look at all things, I am seeing Christ rather than outward appearance.

The Lord had put us in the right place. Lebanon's First Assembly church under Pastor Robeson was just what Andy and I needed at that time. And through our time there, the Lord did good things in our lives. Every season in our lives is a bridge connecting the prior season with the upcoming season. In each season, weeds are pulled out that would hinder a word yet to come. And important things are planted in our hearts out from which the season to come must grow.

Andy signed up for the pastor's ministry study program soon after we started there. Pastor Robeson was a wiry little man, filled with fire and passion. He was a strong Calvinist, of course, and the books he fed Andy, and through Andy to me, were Calvinist, which most Christians are, in spite of what they might imagine.

Right off the bat, Andy and I were prime candidates for receiving the Baptism in the Holy Spirit as the Pentecostals conceived that experience, that is, an experience to be sought with much tarrying and much laying on of hands and loud and fervent assistance. Andy and I, though good friends, were very different. I was an introvert; Andy was an extrovert. As an Asperger's, making myself subject to such a thing was not possible, but Andy was their perfect candidate. He gave them what they wanted and was filled with the Holy Spirit gloriously.

I had begun to read Watchman Nee right away. My mother had many of his books. During this time I read his book on *The Release of the Spirit*. Watchman Nee presented a different approach to the fullness of the Spirit, not as a "receiving," but as a "release." Since the Holy Spirit is one spirit with us the moment we are born again, Watchman Nee was seeing it correctly, that this experience is a release of the Holy Spirit into our souls, something for which God requires our permission first. In that book, Watchman Nee taught me that we ask God to fulfill His Word in our lives, and then we believe that we have received, waiting in full expectation of faith that what we have asked has already become ours. You can see that this mighty SEED planted in me by the Lord in the early months of 1976 has grown to a full-fruited tree that places that same seed of life all through everything I share with you.

So – when they asked me if I had received the Baptism of the Holy Spirit, I was caught between two things. On the one hand was a wrestling match with a chair if I said, "No, not yet," and the other was this word from Watchman Nee, to believe and to confess that I have received, since I had asked. My answer was a quiet and strained, "Yes," but it seemed to satisfy.

Now, God requires moments of surrender from each one of us. He does so because He never forces Himself on anyone, but rather He enters into our knowledge only through our express and willing permission. That permission, however, from our point of view, coming out of our unthankfulness as humans, seems to us to be a "terrible" surrender of ourselves to an "indomitable will." That moment of surrender does not come easily for most.

My own real surrender to God did not happen when I asked Jesus into my heart at age seven. It did not happen when I asked for forgiveness of my sins, for Jesus to take me back to Himself at age nineteen. It happened, in actuality, a few months later, I am guessing in April of 1976.

I was driving to work, framing houses with Jimmy, minding my own business, when another PERSON intruded Himself into my awareness. That Person stuck His bony finger into my forehead, so to speak, and spoke these words in question form, but it did not feel like a question. It felt much more like a fierce demand. – "Will you surrender all that you are to Me?"

That was a bit much. I did not like the sound of that at all. I managed to put the Fellow off through the hours of work, though my heart was much battered by that very insistent "question." On my way home, I continued to wrestle against such a thing, but, as I turned into the driveway, my stubbornness gave way. Before I came to a stop, I said, "Yes, Lord." I did not know then that I really said, **"Let it be to me according to Your word."**

As soon as I came to a stop, I HAD TO run up to my room as fast as I could, but before I could drop to my knees beside my bed, rivers of living water were already flowing up from my heart in a heavenly language separate from the control of my mind. I had known a measure of the release of the Spirit at age fifteen, after learning to give thanks for all things. This full release came as God's seal upon that Seed in me of asking and then believing we have already received.

I have not seen this before, how God set the demonstration of His Spirit upon the planting of His Word as mighty Seeds inside my heart, to confirm and to establish that Word in me, seeds that are now found all through all that I share with you.

There were strains taking place inside the ministry and congregation of Lebanon's First Assembly through those months, but Andy and I saw none of that. This was a good place for us and a good time of being grounded in the Word and in the Spirit.

The Bible and I
I was a reader of books; the Bible was a book, and so it seemed to me that one would read the Bible from beginning to end. Right from the start,

I determined that I would read the New Testament through a second time before beginning again at Genesis 1. And so, over the years, I have read the Bible through 24 times, but the New Testament, 47 times. When I am finished with the Jesus Secret version, I plan to read it as the second reading to bring my count to completion, although 25 and 50 sounds like a better set of numbers.

Prior to my conversion in December of 75, I had read Tolkien's *The Hobbit* and *The Lord of the Rings* through 18 times in six years. I put those books completely aside after my conversion. Reading the Bible through more often became a goal. I'm sure my first time was through the King James Version, but during our time at the Lebanon Assembly of God, I began to use the New American Standard, and thus it would have been my second time through, starting that probably by April.

In my childhood in the Mennonite and Baptist churches, the Bible was just there. It was God's word to us. Though I was taught it and though I memorized some verses, I had little more thought than that. But when the Lord turned my heart back to Himself, I turned to the Bible as my life.

I can be a very intense person in directions that are of supreme importance to me. I have never been more intense towards anything else than I have been towards the Bible from that time on. The Bible has always been God sharing Himself with me. I am simply uninterested in anything presented as "truth" that the Bible does not actually say.

Knowing God is and has always been the center of my life, and the Bible has always been the source of how I must know God. I have been taught by many Christian teachers and have read many outstanding Christian books, but the Bible, for me, is the only authority of truth.

I began reading the Bible from the first page to the last. In the first months after my return to the Lord, I spent little of my spare time doing anything else. I remember reading the Psalms in one sitting and the joy I knew afterwards. When I arrived at John 16 for the first time through the Bible, something wonderful happened. As I read **"and the Spirit of Truth will guide you into all truth,"** those words leaped off the page and entered into my heart by the Spirit as a personal word from God to me. You see, if the Word is not personally ours, it's not anything. I have never doubted that word,

a word that the same Spirit, who first spoke those words through John, made personal to me over 40 years ago. God has given us the Bible and the Spirit that we might know Him.

The idea that there are things in the Bible that are hidden from us or that we cannot know now, the idea that we cannot really know all "truth," not while we live on this earth, this idea is illogical and contrary to everything God says. It is an idea that I rejected from the start.

Even more than that, I did not read the Bible in order to know the Bible. Right from the start, I also conceived of God as a Person directly involved in my life. Even though at that time, I saw only dimly, still, my purpose in reading my Bible was always to know this Personal God and what He meant by being involved with me. I read the Bible because I had to know what this God actually says to me.

I also frequented the Christian book store and brought home many large tomes for Bible study, some of which I still have. One of those was *The Life and Times of Jesus the Messiah*, by Alfred Edersheim, of which I read nearly half (it was very dense). I also collected the same books Andy was studying in his course with Pastor Robeson, one of which was a large book on Romans and another was *The Total Depravity of Man* by Arthur W. Pink. This was a fascinating book to me, but before I could get half way through, it vanished. I bought it again a few years later, but before I could even begin reading, it vanished again. This was a way of thinking, placing utter depravity upon the Christian, that is, presenting a salvation of very little meaning, that God did not want planted in me alongside of the seeds of Christ.

My mother had all the popular charismatic paperback books, so I read those as well. Of these, Watchman Nee's books continued to be the most important. I do not remember when I first read *The Normal Christian Life*, through these months, but it had a major impact on my thinking from then until now. Whenever you read of me setting forth Blood – Cross – and Resurrection, you are reading of the Seed planted in me through Watchman Nee.

But more importantly at that time, I read from Watchman Nee that Christ was IN us. When I shared that with Andy, he rejected it instantly. You see, although we had little connection with the young people at the Pentecostal church, what little we had showed us levels of hypocrisy that did not fit with our zeal to know the Lord. Andy rejected the idea that Christ might be in them; it certainly seemed improbable to me. Then, later on, I think when Andy and I were sharing a house together, I read something more in Watchman Nee, that we are IN Christ. Again, Andy dismissed this idea as nonsense; it certainly was not part of Pentecostal Calvinism. But I pondered these things deeply not knowing at all what they meant.

Broader Charismatic Experiences

We became involved with other charismatic people and gatherings beyond the Pentecostal church. Through friends we knew at the Lebanon Assembly, we met other families in the area who gathered for fellowship in their homes. I connected with some of these more than Andy did, and continued fellowshipping with them even in-between my forays into faraway places. I connected with one family in particular, the Travers.

Mrs. Traver introduced me to Madame Guyon. I read her autobiography as well as her book, *Experiencing the Depths of Jesus Christ*. Here is something of great importance to know. Jesus said that we find what we seek. Those who seek to know Him find Him everywhere they look; those who seek other things, whatever those things might be, find Him not at all. I was looking for a direct and personal connection with God; Madame Guyon showed me that such a thing was real.

An anointed and godly young man we knew moved up to Portland, Oregon, so we went up a number of times to visit him and to spend time in the Lord with those whom he knew there. We also went up to Portland more than once to attend Full Gospel Business Men's conferences and Christian concerts. One well-known ministry I remember was Jack Hayford, a leading charismatic pastor from southern California.

We went up to Seattle one time to attend a Billy Graham crusade in the King Stadium, the largest stadium at that time, but a building that did not last long. We went in my car. I had a map. My map said that CANADA was only a couple hours up the road. During an off time I drove up by myself and crossed the border into British Columbia, went inside a short ways, turned around, and came back to Seattle. I did not know then that I would be a resident of British Columbia for twelve years and that I would make that drive dozens of times.

Through all these things a great tension was opening up inside of me, a travail for something I did not know. I will share more of that in the next chapter. Here I want to mention three things that created a deep cry for REAL inside of me.

First, although I was blessed by all the teaching I was receiving in the Pentecostal and charismatic circles, I went away from every such time with a sense of incompleteness. I could not put it into words, but there seemed to me to be such a shallowness, such a desire not to offend people, such a lack of authority in the speaking of the word. This sense was subconscious, but it increased a growing agony inside of me.

Once when we visited our Christian friends in Portland, we went with them one evening to a public park where some were "preaching the gospel." A young man got up on a little pedestal and began haranguing the people passing by, "You are sinners, you need to repent and turn to God." A young woman sauntered up to him and said, "I love sin."

I was seated with some others just behind this young "evangelist." As he began speaking, everything went haywire inside of me. I KNEW that his words were NOT Christ, though I did not know what Christ might be. His false face towards these non-Christians caused such distress in me that the brother sitting next to me had to calm me down.

This was one experience, but it was part of God's laying the groundwork in me for that great distress that would become the definition of my life.

Another time I went with a young man from the Pentecostal church to visit with Dural Sylvester. This young man was from our same class in school and Dural had known him well during his wild years separate from the Lord. Dural did not have a good memory of him, but he received us with an open face because of my friendship with him. At first we just visited, but before long this young man stood forth in all religious fervency and declared to Dural that if he did not repent, he would go to hell.

I cringed all through myself, most certainly, but what was even worse was watching Dural's face. The soft light towards us vanished and a dark hardness took its place. Dural soon sent us on our way, and he was right to do so. I knew that this young man had abused Dural just as he had done when they were younger, and I was ashamed that I had been part of such wickedness.

I knew that such was not the gospel of Christ, but I did not know what was.

Working with Jimmy

I continued working with Jimmy every week-day framing houses. Jimmy took my "conversion" in good stride, although, I can assure you, he also bore with a bit more nonsense from me. Jimmy's heart was towards the Lord, and he willingly confessed a simple belief in Jesus. Others were with us on the framing crew including Jimmy's dad for awhile, Jim Barkley. Then, in the late summer of 1976, we hired Andy as well to be part of our framing crew. Andy did all right on ground work, but he left running around on the tops of the walls and trusses for us.

It was an important foundation for me to begin with framing. By doing the same parts of a house frame over and over until they were utterly familiar gave me the basis out from which I could add every other part of construction in later years. Because I came to know every board in many different house designs by heart, I gained a fundamental part of designing homes. At the same time, I was busy creating a whole series of "house plans" for myself in my spare time.

From the time I was 18, I longed to build a house of my own design. I had no idea, however, that I ever would have such an opportunity. That type of thing is not typical in the commercial construction world. The desire only grew year by year, however. It would not be until I was 26 that I had the wondrous opportunity to do just that.

Framing houses is hard work. We were paid by the square foot, not by the hour, so in order to do well, we had to go at just short of a run day after day. We worked in all weather. In Oregon, if you don't work in the rain, you don't work; the rain was rarely heavy, however. As an Oregon boy I never considered either rain coat or rain hat. We just dripped.

I had a bad back, however, from my childhood. This problem was increased by one aspect of how we did the job. I wore a single pouch that hung heavy on my left side. I used my right hand all the time, so that side of me became very strong. My left hand, however, was the one that received all the missed blows and cuts and whacks. Anyhow, we would frame and side the walls as they were laid down on the deck. We had wall jacks, but often, we would all run over, grab a wall, and thrust it up. Sometimes it took all our strength and more.

This put great strain on the lower vertebrae of my back. One time we did not have enough strength (although Jimmy was incredibly strong), and a large wall came down right on top of me.

My back went out bad and often. There were times when I just lay in bed for a couple of days unable to move. This problem continued for years.

There was a young man whom we knew at the Lebanon Assembly who moved in great faith. Once, when my back was way out and very painful, he asked to pray for me. He had me sit and stretch out my legs. He picked my feet up in his hands and showed me how one leg was far shorter than the other. He asked God to heal, and immediately, by sight, the short leg "grew out" to match the long one, but in reality, all the disjointed vertebrate in my back went right into place. I could work and run without hindrance.

A number of times on the job site, when my back went out, I asked Jimmy to pray for me in that way. My back always went into place, and I could return to work without hindrance. One time, however, I thought to impress a non-believer that God works in power, so I said, "Come and watch." Of course, that time, nothing happened at all.

Then once, after I had returned from Nebraska, having witnessed the confidence of faith in the power of God in which my brother, Franz, moved, I was on the backside of a house we were framing. This time Andy was above me on top of a high wall. He fell off and landed hard on the ground just in front of me. He was unconscious, twisted in pain, and his face was pale, almost grey. I did not know what to do, so, in desperation, I went up to him, placed my hands on him, and said, "Be healed in the name of Jesus."

Instantly, Andy came wide awake, his face suddenly alight, and he stood up with no pain nor any effects from the fall. This was certainly not "of me," but God, who was always with us, whether we knew it or not.

Gone to Nebraska

My brother Franz had met Audrey, his wife, when she came to Oregon to attend college. After they were married, they lived in Oregon for a short time. Audrey, however, was from the corn region around Shickley, Nebraska, not far from where my dad was born. Her father owned a large corn farm, but they fed their corn to pigs and made their money by selling the pigs. Through Audrey's father, Franz was able to buy a small farmstead that included an old farm house and a number of large barns and outbuildings. They had moved there with their first two children, Jason and Rachelle, a couple of years prior. During that time, Franz had completely remodelled the old farmhouse, and had done a lot of work setting up an efficient pig-farm operation. He needed to do some more work inside his barns, so he invited me to come to Nebraska to work for him a couple of months.

Jimmy was always agreeable to whatever I wanted to do, so in August, I hopped in my car and away I went, by myself, across the country. Now, you must understand me. If I have a destination 2000 miles away, then the only option for me is to drive all over the place, adding hundreds of miles to the distance. If my map says something is sort of along the way, then I want to see it. I had been the long distances to Michigan and back with my parents when I was younger, along with the trip to Nebraska for my brother's wedding. Dad was actually a little bit like me, and thus took a different route each time. But the direct road from Oregon to Nebraska is almost the bleakest route in North America.

So, I headed up through the Idaho mountains towards Montana. I stayed in a motel in Salmon, Idaho, and then drove into Montana. I spent a bit of time at the Big Hole National Battlefield and became awed by the story of Chief Joseph and the Nez Perce. Standing on top of the hill where Custer's arrogance gave the Sioux a total victory was also a necessity. About half way across Montana, I picked up an Indian boy, about my age. He was on his way to Oklahoma. He was a good companion. When we got into the Black Hills, we found that all motels were filled. I tried to sleep alongside the road, but could not. We kept driving, all through the night and half the next day. I went 1500 miles in thirty hours. I left him along the road partway through Nebraska where he could catch a ride south.

I spent about two months working in Franz's pig barns, building doors, etc. I really loved their house, how they had transformed it. And I gained a fair bit of knowledge about raising pigs.

My brother was connected at that time with the teachings of Oral Roberts, and he moved in great confidence in God. God did some mighty things with them in Nebraska. I want to share a couple of instances that I experienced. Franz had some cattle as well as the pigs. One time, he needed to separate a particular heifer in order to treat some problem. He and I ran around and around, but we could not get the heifer away from the others. Then Franz stopped, pointed at the heifer and then at the open pen where we wanted her and commanded, "In the name of Jesus, you will go in there." The heifer stopped and looked. Franz repeated, "In the name of Jesus, go in there." Immediately, the heifer left the herd, went across the open space, and into the pen.

One time when I was at one end of a very heavy gate, carrying it with Franz, my back went out really bad. I could not stop, however, so, inspired by Franz' example, I said, inside myself, "In the name of Jesus, be healed." Instantly my back went entirely into place and was perfectly fine. The point is not that I experienced "miracles," but that I was learning to live in the full awareness and reality of God with us.

On my way home, then, my map said that the Colorado Rockies and San Francisco were sort of between me and home, so that's the way I went. The heights of Rocky Mountain National Park were beyond amazing. This was my first time to drive through San Francisco. I learned right away to keep the windows closed, eyes straight ahead, and to stop for nothing. I had visited the Redwoods once with my parents, but this time I walked awhile in their presence and was in awe of entities far, far larger than I. When I returned home, I went right back to work with Jimmy.

A Disaster between Two Dreams

From the time I was a boy, the dream of my life was to be married. From the time I gave my heart back to the Lord, I wanted to be married most every day. You see, my mom and dad were an incredible testimony to me of marriage. They loved one another. Never, in all my years, did I ever hear either of them speak a cross word to the other. Sadly, I have not measured to my father. My problem was simple, however. Hardly being able to talk with girls was normal, but the moment I thought I liked a girl, I could not get one word out from my mouth, no matter how hard I tried inside.

I saw girls in the Christian circles in which I moved who were attractive to me. They were entirely beyond my reach. At the same time, I struggled with Paul's ridiculous statements in 1 Corinthians about marriage. I feared that it might be "God's will" for me never to be married. I cannot express the despair such an idea brought me. One time, I was lying on my bed during the day. I thought this was September, but it had to be either before or after I went to Nebraska. I lifted up my heart in a deep cry of desire to God. I heard him speak to me. "Son, what does My word say." The only thing that came to mind was "**Delight thyself in the Lord, and He will give thee the desire of thy heart.**" Then the Lord said, "Is not My word My will?"

It would be fourteen long years before God fulfilled His promise to me, as Maureen came down the aisle to stand by my side, but in this moment He planted that Seed inside of me that God does what He says He will do.

After about six or so months at the First Assembly of God in Lebanon, Andy and I switched over to Skyline Assembly of God just south of Scio, Oregon, where my parents attended. My dad was an elder in this church. This had also been the church where Jim Buerge and his family attended before they went to Canada.

Skyline, pastored by Bob Adams, was a peaceful place, in contrast to the somewhat hyper Lebanon Church. But before we were there two weeks, some friends from the Lebanon Church broke some incredible news to us. All the pastors had resigned, and the church split apart with half of the congregation now going elsewhere. Andy and I had seen absolutely none of this. All we knew was the Lord meeting us in that season. The Lord had moved us on just before, since all that had nothing to do with what He was doing in our lives.

After I returned from Nebraska, Andy and I decided to rent the old Ede house where Jimmy and his family had lived. I had gone there with my dad when the Ede's still lived there, to pick apples and to get bales of twine from them. The house was little and old, but the property was amazing. Mr. Ede had started to plant an apple orchard in a large field, but had gotten only the outer row in, all the way around. That was still a lot of apples.

We moved in the first of November, my second foray away from home. I lasted three months.

I took the downstairs bedroom, and Andy took the upstairs room in the attic. There was a very old fashioned kitchen and a small living room. The house also had a large front porch. Now, Andy and I were living in the same house, working on the

same job, and going to the same church doings. Needless to say, we did not know how to communicate in practical everyday life. I later described it as taking two Tom cats, tying their tails together, and slinging them over a clothesline, although it was never so extreme as that. We just never talked things through, and so disagreements and frustrations only grew. There were things I blamed him for, but I am certain it went the other way as well.

But through that summer of 1976 and especially while I was sharing a house with Andy, another dream was growing inside of me. There was a large older two-story house for sale in Lebanon for $40,000, not far from the high school. My dream, which I shared with anyone who would hear, was for the Lord to give us that house so that we could establish a community house, a place of refuge for those needing such a place. I dreamed about such a community, but I did not even know how to get along with Andy.

At the end of January I moved back home; Andy did not stay much longer before returning to Lebanon. We did not speak to one another at all for another year. Yet after I had spent time in the move of God Christian communities, I think that Andy saw me as infected with the virus of heresy and seemed to want little more to do with me.

HOWEVER – here is one tiny, but wondrous part of the glory of our Salvation. When I found Andy's obituary and included his picture in this letter, I still felt remorse over the shadow that seemed to be there through all these years. For that reason, I engaged with the Lord Jesus in faith, bringing Him into my relationship with Andy. The second morning after, I opened this letter to continue working on it. I looked at Andy's picture and saw no shadow at all, only a dear and good friend.

That is the power of an endless life. Nothing is ever lost. All that is ours will return in its season. I will walk with Andy again through the beauty of Oregon's country paths, and we will know such joy.

In early February, Pastor Bob Adams of Skyline Assembly read a letter from Jim Buerge that had been addressed to the church. Most everyone there knew him and his family well. Hearing this letter being read awakened a great agony inside of me, a NEED to know a God I did not know, for I could not be found not knowing Him.

Hearing this letter changed my life forever.

5. Into the North

February 1977 - June 1977

Unexpected Patterns

Setting forth an account of my life has become something I did not expect. I did expect healing, and I did intend to call every moment by Christ, regardless. What I did not expect was to see the array of patterns opening up that demonstrate God's intentions towards me all the way through.

I hope, now, to show you those remarkable patterns of God in my life and what they meant. But I do not want you to think of me as anything other than a normal man somehow caught in the grip of Someone way bigger than me. I set this account of my life before you as an example that you also come out from your Father through the good speaking of Jesus and that, as you call every moment of your life by Christ as well, so you will see that God was always involved in your life just as much. "Superior saintliness" is not the mark of the Father; the mark of the Father is being carried through every stumbling step.

Always before I have looked at my failures as the defining points of my life. Now, it dawns on me that my many failures were just the background hum, the backdrop, so to speak. The defining points of my life were those specific moments either when God contended with me Forehead to forehead or when He planted a particular Word as a Seed in my heart, seeds that would lie hidden in my ground for years until they seemed to spring forth in full fruit as if they were the only things real.

This time period, from February of 1977 until May of 1979, is the foundation of my present knowledge of God. I have referred to it many times as a time of entering into a covenant with my Father. That final moment of that experience, in May of 1979, I have called "Cutting the Covenant." Indeed, Genesis 15 is apt, the "deep sleep," the cutting apart, the blood on the hillside, a God of fire passing through my split-open soul.

Yet I was just a boy of twenty to twenty-two experiencing life's joys and sorrows, fun times, good things, new experiences, and endless foolish mistakes and embarrassments.

The dissolving of my friendship with Andy opened a deep emptiness in me. But to understand my agony through February and March of 1977, I must share something about myself that I have only recently realized.

I experience, on a regular basis from my childhood until now, great depths of emotion that I have called an "angst," a wordless cry, a reaching towards something I cannot see, but that I know MUST BE. I'm not speaking of something small or occasional, but of a huge internal agony that is often. Until recently, I had thought of this as nothing more than "weird me." Or, at least for the last several years, as part of being Asperger's.

I now understand this quality as the pressures of "travail," the inexpressible groanings of the travailing Holy Spirit inside of whom we live. I used to call it awfulness or angst or "what is wrong with me?" Now, as I call my whole life to be one seamless story of Christ, regardless, I realize that from childhood, I have been seized in God's grip through every circumstance. When I look back now, calling everything in my life by Jesus, I see two things concerning this agony of travail that marked my person since I was nine. First, it was a quality of spirit, a reaching forward into something I knew must be there, but did not know at all. And second, it was a deep anguish to see and to know something real, life as it was meant to be.

Now, I am presenting myself as nothing more than a normal part of God's creation. Here is the reality of all. – **The entire creation groans together and travails together until now. Not only that, but even we ourselves, possessing the firstfruit of the Spirit, we also groan inside ourselves, eagerly expecting...** (Romans 8:22-23). Your entire life has been the same travail. See it as so, call it to be so, every moment. Call every moment of your life by the hand of God and not by any purposeless confusion.

February and March of 1977 were filled with this agony, far more than "normal," but in confusion and with no real understanding of God.

An Experience inside the Agony

In early February, Pastor Bob Adams read a letter to the Skyline Assembly, written by Jim Buerge and addressed to the congregation, who had known him well through his time as an elder in that church. In this letter, Jim shared about the work in which he and his family were involved, ministering to the First Nations people in the mountains above Ingenika at the north end of Lake Williston in northern British Columbia. They were living at a trapline in a place called "Eagle Rock." Everything he shared intrigued me – ministering to the "Indians," and living with others in the remote mountains of the North.

British Columbia – the North – had always intrigued me similar to looking up the logging road had intrigued me when I was a boy. Every mention of northern "wilderness" excited me.

Sometime in 1976, we had heard a terrible report of great loss. In order to get from Ingenika up to Eagle Rock, the Buerge's had to cross a mountain river on a raft. This was normal and reasonably safe. But that summer, as Jim and his wife, Jean, and their five children, accompanied by another brother by the name of John Clarke, going with them to minister to those at Eagle Rock, were making this normal crossing. The water was a bit high and rough and, for some reason, the raft was caught in the flood, and they were all tipped into the torrent. Jim's wife and their two youngest children did not make it to the shore, but were drowned.

Since all of us at Skyline knew of this tragedy, we gave ear to the things Jim shared.

Not long after the reading of this letter was Skyline Assembly's yearly "winter camp." Everyone in the church who wanted to participate went up to a lodge just off of Highway 20 in the high Cascades. I had been to many camps as a boy, but this time was different, this time it was the whole church, men, women, and children, with me as part of that church.

The lodge was large. The men slept in bunkrooms on one side and the women slept in bunkrooms on the other. The large room between was commodious, with around 50 people there. The snow outside was deep and the slopes were perfect for every kind of sledding and tubing. We were

there Friday evening through Sunday. We ate our meals together, we played together in the snow and sliding down the long hillsides. I had the chance to ride a snowmobile. I remember a prolonged game of chess with a brother from the church. We worshipped and shared communion together.

I drove home by myself that Sunday afternoon, weeping the entire way. "That was so right; that was so right," I told myself over and over, "that's what church is meant to be." I had never heard of Christian community, and I had no idea how this longing for life as it is meant to be could ever be fulfilled. Nonetheless, on that trip down the mountains out of the snow and into the wet valley below, I conceived the idea that maybe, just maybe, I could go up north to where Jim Buerge and his family lived at Eagle Rock. Maybe sharing time with them would begin to answer that deep longing for REAL.

You see, Jim had also shared in the letter that he and his remaining children were coming down to Oregon at the end of March and would visit Skyline Assembly.

One more thing that added to these two months of agony was the fact that I had recently read *Rees Howells: Intercessor* by Norman Grubb. The primary things I gained from reading this account of Rees Howells' life was first that a man could know and walk with God in close fellowship and second, that God is well able to do what He says in our lives. I see now that this was an increase of that which I had gained from reading Madame Guyon.

So here I was, caught through these two months, between emptiness and loss of friendship, confusion and disconnect on the one hand and a deep cry inside calling me towards something I did NOT know anything about. I was split apart, and I could find no answers.

Visitors at Skyline

The Buerge's came in late March, Jim, with his daughter, Pamela, and his two sons, Tony and Tim; Jim shared a greeting and testimony with the Skyline Assembly church. That Sunday afternoon, I went to visit with Jim at his mother's house in north Albany. I shared with him my desire to spend time with them in northern British Columbia.

"It may not be possible for you to come right out where we are," he said. "But my brother Del and my sister Rhonda and their families are living in a community called Graham River Farm. That is where we lived before we moved out to Eagle Rock (the trap line in the Rockies). I would suggest you spend some time there and get to know what we are about before you consider coming out to Eagle Rock. Graham River Farm covers us, and they have a say as well in who comes out to be with us."

Jim was a bit hesitant in sharing this. You see, standing before him was a 20-year-old boy with long stringy hair down to his belly and with a scrubby goatee on his face. Outwardly, I did not look like a "candidate" for the fellowship and way of life he knew was the experience of community at Graham River Farm.

As he suggested that I go to Graham River first, however, I felt a peace flow into my heart that it was the Lord. "Yes, I would like to go there," I said. He suggested also that I might want to cut my hair and shave first. For the first time, I was willing to do that – and did. That fact alone probably assured him that I was at least serious.

Jim and his children had driven down in his little Scout. He was in Oregon to close out some business endeavors he had been involved in and to buy a plane to take back north. He asked if I would drive the Scout back up to Graham River Farm while he and his children flew in the plane. I was quite willing. Thus, in early April of 1977, I headed north into what was for me the uncharted wilderness of northern British Columbia. I was twenty years old; and I love adventure.

Graham River had such an impact on me that I am taking more pages to cover these next two years than I have thus far.

The Trip Up

Jim Buerge asked me to take a cage full of pigeons up to his brother, Del. Jim had called the border and had fulfilled all the requirements they told him in order to take the pigeons across. However, when I arrived at the crossing at Sumas, Washington on a Friday evening in early April 1977, I learned that a Canadian vet would have to inspect the pigeons before they would be allowed to cross. The Canadian vet would not be available until Monday morning. So I turned around to go back, only now the American customs baulked at my bringing the pigeons into the States. So there I was caught in the no-man's land between two countries. The Americans soon believed my story and allowed me to proceed. I spent the weekend in a motel in Sumas.

On Monday morning, Jim flew up with his children, Pamela, Tony, and Tim. He took charge of the pigeons, so I did not have to worry about that part. However, when I went to the counter to ask for a visa, I made a mistake. I asked a question. I have never asked a question when crossing a border since. I asked, "What do I need to do to obtain a work permit in Canada?"

"Work?" the lady asked. "Work? You will not work in Canada!" At that point she was unwilling to let me through. Jim came in and talked with her; finally she was persuaded to give me a three-week visa on strict conditions. I had to post a $100 bond and lose the money if I was not out of Canada in three weeks. I had hoped to spend three months, so this was a disappointment to me at the time. She also said, "You can make your bed, but you cannot help wash the dishes or anything else. You may not work in Canada." I since learned that the border officials take a narrower view of things than do the immigration officers who supervise visitors in the interior. I was free to proceed north.

I drove up through the Fraser River canyon and across the Cariboo country to Prince George. This was the first time across a road I would travel dozens of times in the future. We spent the night at some friends of the Buerge's in Prince George, and the next day, Jim had Tony ride with me the rest of the way. We crossed the Pine pass and descended into the Peace River country. I was amazed to see solid grain farming country with tall silos this far to the north. It was the end of winter. There was still snow on the ground, though it was disappearing, and there were not yet leaves on the trees. It was the season of mud.

We drove north on the Alaska Highway from Fort St. John. Soon most signs of civilization disappeared. The pavement ended at Mile 93. At Mile 95 we turned west from the highway onto a primitive gravel road. We wound up and down for forty miles into the foothills of the Rockies. There was a bridge across the Halfway River, but none across the Graham. We came to a stop on the banks of the Graham River. I caught glimpses of log cabins on the other side. There were a number of vehicles parked on this side and a dirt road running down to the water. The ice was mostly gone, but the river was not yet high from the spring melt in the mountains. We honked the horn and waited; it was late afternoon. The spruce trees were green and dark, the poplar trees still leafless. The Graham River was a fairly large river, strong and full. This was an utterly new experience for me. Adventure beckoned, calling to the cry of my heart.

Adventure

After a short wait, we heard a tractor coming through the trees on the other side of the river. It soon appeared and plunged right into the water, pulling a long wooden hay wagon behind it. The water came up only to the tractor axles. The gravel bottom of the river had been smoothed to make a good ford. We put our things on the hay wagon and stood up, holding onto the rail in the front. There were no sidewalls to the trailer. We bounced across the river, wound through some trees on the other side, and then up a short embankment. Graham River Farm opened before us.

The community was like nothing I had ever seen before. All of the buildings were made of logs, roughly hewn together. On our left was a mechanics shop, to our right was a long, low building I would soon learn was called the Tabernacle. Just beyond it was a newly completed two-and-a-half-story building, the schoolhouse. On the nearer side of the Tabernacle was a row of small log cabins stringing out into the distance. This row was on the edge of an embankment overlooking muddy and partly snow-covered fields that would become the gardens during the summer months. Beyond the Tabernacle were three more rows of cabins, and beyond them, in the distance, I could see some large barns. The cabins themselves were unique. They were small, most about 20' x 20 or 25', all only one story with a low lean-to roof. They looked like rows of chicken coops, around twenty-five in all.

We stepped through a rough-hewn door into the Tabernacle. I looked out across a dining room

The Graham River Community

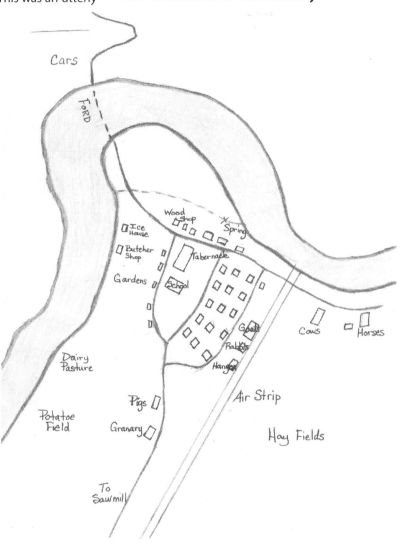

with a low wood ceiling and log walls. The room was probably about 30' wide by 70' long. There was a large wood stove not far from this entrance, and the room was filled with rough wood tables with backless benches on each side. On the right was the counter dividing the kitchen. I had never seen anything like it before.

Someone took me to a cabin whose occupants were away. I would be staying here for a few days. The cabin was low and dark. After a bit I heard a bell ringing; it was time for supper. This time the Tabernacle was filled with people! One hundred and fifty people sat down around those rough tables to share their supper meal together. What a sight! There were large numbers of children, adults of all ages, families and singles. They talked and laughed happily, joy and peace shining on all the faces. I was enthralled. We shared a simple meal together. I don't remember what it was, but I'm sure it was potatoes. I have eaten a lot of potatoes. I was greeted pleasantly, but no one made a big deal out of my being there.

There was no electricity except a generator in the welding shop. The Tabernacle had propane lights, and many of the cabins had one propane light in them. Otherwise kerosene lamps were used. I slept that night in a cabin by myself. The next morning after a hearty bowl of cracked grain for breakfast at the Tabernacle, I went to the work circle where the men received their assignments for the day. I don't remember what my first detail was, probably firewood, but I went to work. I began to meet the people. I had known Del Buerge and his family in Oregon, and had greeted them the evening before, but I did not know them well. All the rest of the people were complete strangers to me. It would take a long time to put together names, faces, and cabins.

For the next few days I went to the meals, worked with other men on whatever assignment I was given, and slept by myself in my cabin. No one invited me over to visit; no one talked with me about what this place was all about. I felt a bit lonely. Finally, after several days, I was moved to a cabin belonging to Bill and Dot Ritchie and their son Rohn. They were away from the farm, but a single young man named Harleigh Knapp was also staying there. He had a bed in the entry and I took Rohn's bed. I now had someone to talk with, although Harleigh was not the most talkative person and neither was I.

One job I did was to work with Tabor Mercier, a husky big-hearted man, on the firewood sawing detail. He had a large saw blade mounted on the front of a tractor. The blade had a platform in front of it. Tabor hoisted short lengths of log up onto the platform and swung it into the blade to make stove-sized pieces of wood. The members of his crew, including myself, handed the lengths of wood up to him, helping him get them on the platform, and then caught and stacked the firewood as it was cut. Another job I did was to go with Doug Witmer and Mallory Smith, young men my age, down to the grain bin. There we hooked a belt up between a tractor and a hammer mill, a device for grinding grain. The size of the screen would determine whether we produced flour for bread or cracked

grain for breakfast cereal. My job was to fill and lug buckets of grain from the grain bins to the hammer mill and to help tie the sacks and stack them when they were full. All of it was good, hard, basic-to-life sort of work.

Contending with the Word

The community had two services a week, besides the morning devotions. There was a sharing service on Wednesday night during which any member of the community could go up and share. The main service was on Saturday night during which only the elders preached. The praise services were long, strong, and anointed. I could sense the presence of God like I had never known. I did not understand most of what I heard. And the few things I did hear, I thought were really weird. One girl stood up and shared that she was learning that her life was really in her brothers and sisters. I thought "No way, my life is in Christ." I had forgotten that Christ was also in the people around me. Another brother shared that we needed to walk out the righteousness of Christ. I thought, "Baloney, Jesus is my righteousness, not what I do."

Harleigh suggested I attend a Bible study one evening at Ian and Isabelle Still's cabin. Ian and Isabelle were from Scotland and had immigrated to Canada specifically to live at Graham River Farm. I soon learned that most of the other people at Graham River were from the states: from Ohio, Pennsylvania, and New England, and had also immigrated to Canada to live at Graham River. Ian and Isabelle were a lively, good-hearted couple who spoke with a strong Scottish accent and laughed a lot. They were also very serious about the word and the truth God was speaking. They were unusual in the community in that they had only one child, a son, Gavin. Most of the families had five, six, seven children each. We were studying the book of Revelation. Isabelle said "Wasn't it so silly when we used to think that heaven had literal streets of gold?" I thought, "What are you talking about, of course heaven has streets paved with gold." She went on to say that the golden streets in John's vision meant that when we come to the fullness of all God has for us, we will be walking in the very nature of God, of which gold is a symbol. I had never heard of such a thing.

Somebody gave me some tapes by a man named Sam Fife. I had never heard of Sam Fife, but I took the tapes to the cabin and began to listen. It was only a few minutes before I slammed the tape recorder off and said loudly, "Baloney, this stuff is nonsense." Harleigh looked at me quietly, and said, "We can only walk in the light God gives us." I did not know what he was talking about. There was a problem for me, though. Sam Fife was the first preacher I had ever heard who spoke with the authority of the Holy Spirit. Something inside me was drawn to the anointing in which he was speaking. I spent a number of evenings alternately listening, and then slamming the tape recorder off and fuming.

From the very first moment that I slammed the "off" button on the tape recorder the very first time I heard Sam Fife speaking on a tape, I became deeply, deeply distressed about the Word God speaks. – What does God actually say in the Bible? This was an autistic agony of immeasurable proportions. Up until that moment, I had studied the Bible because I wanted to learn of God and of the power and meaning of the Christian life.

From that moment on, I KNEW that someone was misrepresenting what God says in the Bible. Of course, I knew that "someone" had to be Sam Fife. And so I opened my Bible to prove him wrong. I was 20 years old when this deep distress, this overwhelming desperation to know what God actually says in His word to me, began.

Finally, I worked one day with a crew of men cleaning the manure out of the pig barn. One of the men was Dan Kurtz, one of the elders. During a break, aside from the others, he asked me, "Daniel, where is Christ?" I hesitated and did not answer. He reached out a rough, tender finger and pointed it at me. "He is in you!" he said quietly. I knew from what the Lord had shown me the year before that it was true. Christ lived in me! That was the first word of this new strange-sounding teaching I was able to receive.

I was at Graham River for about two and a half weeks. I had to return to the states by Greyhound bus. I was glad at that point that I was allowed to stay in Canada for only three weeks. I was overwhelmed with the strangeness of it all, and I had much to think about and hash through in my own heart. I did not understand most of what I had heard and did not think it was true. I did not know why God had brought me there. I had the naive idea that maybe these people were in bondage and God wanted me to help them understand the "truth," as if I knew what the "truth" was.

Before I had left Oregon to go to Graham River, Pastor Bob Adams of Skyline Assembly had taken me aside to share his "concerns" about this group I was going to visit. He had been there for a short visit. "They believe there are three groups or levels in the church, and they are the top one of the three," he said. "Be very careful." I had no idea what he was talking about, but I had heard something about this concept at Graham River. It was now one of the many questions I had.

Yet prior to Jim's visit to Skyline, in response to things Pastor Bob knew were taught in the move fellowship, he had asked the congregation, "How many of you believe that a Christian can walk without sin," he asked. I was sitting in the back of the church that Sunday. I must always answer honestly, as far as I am able. I thought to myself, out from my reading of Rees Howells, **"With God all things are possible."** I raised my hand. All but one other did not.

This great contention now had me in its grip.

Dead-Ends

Upon returning to Oregon, I did not return to working with Jimmy and Andy. I did not want to go back to whatever hassles were inside of broken friendships. I tried two other jobs, but both ended quickly. I quit one, picking up branches in the National Forest for the forest service, because it was meaningless to me. I was fired from the other, a different construction crew, because I wore myself out and then called in sick. It seemed every direction was a dead-end.

Meanwhile, I searched my Bible. I had heard a number of things that had shaken my "Christian" beliefs to the core. I had to know what the Bible really said. Every spare moment I was not working, I was in the Word, searching and seeking to understand or to refute. I noticed something unusual. From the beginning of the Bible to the end, there were three divisions or levels of things: three feasts held by the nation of Israel, three parts of the tabernacle, three levels of fruitfulness - 30 fold, 60 fold, and 100 fold, and so on. I began to realize that three levels of knowing God was a Biblical concept. God was speaking something important.

I had no problem with the teaching I had heard about overcoming sin. I believed what Jesus said, **"With man it is impossible, but not with God; with God all things are possible."** Certainly, God can do whatever He wants to do in our lives.

I now know that it is only too normal for Christians, receiving a deeper understanding of God, to see themselves as "superior" and to become sectarian. But this is a problem for all Christians. The word which the brethren at Graham River had received was breaking free from some of the serpent's definitions common to all Nicene Christianity, some but not all.

Yet I have never seen a people who were so dedicated to a vision, or so willing to sacrifice everything valuable in this life to be a part of the kingdom of God, or so anointed in the power of the Holy Spirit. Whatever mistakes may have been made at Graham River or any other community I have been privileged to be a part of since, those mistakes were made out of misguided sincerity or personal weakness, never out of a lack of commitment to the Lord Jesus Christ.

There I was again in a dead-end place back in Oregon. I could see the Bible more clearly than I had before. I knew something was there beyond my acquired definitions of Christianity. I was simply waiting on God for the next step.

Then, one day in early June, I walked into a store in Albany, and whom should I meet but Jim Buerge! He had flown down again by himself to wrap up some business he had been unable to complete earlier. "Hey," I thought, "maybe I can go back to Graham River!" And so I did.

The Return Trip

Jim Buerge knew a family from Salem who were moving to a small community near Edmonton, Alberta that was associated with Graham River Farm. He suggested that I ask about traveling up with them. Once in Edmonton, I might be able to get a ride up to Fort St. John. This family, the Widmer's, agreed that I could ride with them.

We crossed the border at the crossing in northern Idaho. There my experience was opposite the first time. A kindly gentleman gave me a three-month visa to Canada with no problems. I would be able to get an extension through the immigration official in Dawson Creek, the town at the beginning of the Alaska Highway. We drove on to the town of St. Albert just north of Edmonton. Just beyond the outskirts of the city there was a small farm purchased by Christians who had established a small community there. Besides the main house there was a bunkhouse where I stayed with two other fellows, Patrick Downs and Rustin Myers. Patrick had just emigrated up from Houston, Texas and was working in Edmonton for a season before going on to a newly started community called Hilltop, also north of Fort St. John. I enjoyed a couple of days with them.

Then a couple of gentlemen came down from another Christian community called Shiloh that was not far from Graham River by a straight line, although by road it would be 80 miles. Their names were Don Deardorff and Fred Vanderhoof. They had come down to Edmonton in a truck to pick up a load of windows. They agreed to take me with them on their return trip. I found them to be hilarious. Don was short and skinny and Fred was tall and skinny. They told jokes and laughed all the way back to Fort St. John. Don Deardorff's laugh is quite infectious. Years later, at the Blueberry community, his table often erupted into gales of laughter during the meal, enough to cause heads to turn to see what was so funny. His children laugh the same way.

It was a pleasant trip for me from Edmonton to Fort St. John. It was June and full summer now. The whole Peace River country was considerably different than when I had seen it two months earlier. The north has four seasons, white, mud, green, and mud, and then white again. The white lasts the longest, six months, the green lasts only three months. The mud season is between them on both ends. Now it was green and breathtakingly beautiful.

Upon our arrival in Fort St. John, Don and Fred dropped me off at the home of a family, the Burnham's, who were associated with the communities and who made their house available to anyone coming into town from the farms needing a place to stay. I did not realize it at the time, but as I entered Fort St. John, that June of 1977, the Lord was turning my life into a different phase of experience with Him. It was a time of judgment. I was a mess inside and completely closed up, though I did not know it. Somehow God had to pry my shell apart so that He could eventually heal and restore. I was entering a furnace, a glorious furnace of affliction.

I spent two days at the Burnham's until the town trip from Graham River came to town. It was a van full of folks come to do their shopping. Many often came into town only once a month, though there was a town trip once a week. I had to wait all day until they were ready to return. It was late by the time we left Fort St. John, with a two-hour trip ahead of us. We were just a few miles from the turnoff to the Graham River when our tire blew. The driver, Todd Booth, did not have all that he needed to fix it, so he had to walk the few miles to get help. It was around three in the morning before we finally made it across the river and onto Graham River Farm. The delay must have been the Lord because right around the time we would have arrived, a bear was prowling around right at the Tabernacle. He tried to get into the cheese house, leaving marks on the window with his face. Then he meandered over to the butcher shop nearby, trying to get in there. He succeeded at that, only not the way he intended. One of the brothers shot him next day; they turned him into food for the table.

Origins of the Communities

There were several community farms in the Peace River region. Graham River, Shiloh, and Headwaters were all to the west of the Alaska Highway and north of Fort St. John, in the foothills of the Rockies. Blueberry, Evergreen, and Hilltop were to the east of the Alaska Highway and a little closer to Fort St. John. Finally, Peace River Farm was only a few miles west of Fort St. John in the canyon of the Peace river, and Hidden Valley was southwest of Dawson Creek, the furthest from the others. Peace River farm had just been bought out by the government in preparation for a dam that was never built. Some of the people from that community went on to other communities and some called it quits.

Most of the people in the communities had emigrated from the states specifically to establish these communities on the edge of the wilderness, a number also coming from eastern Canada. Graham River was the first to begin, in the early summer of 1972, with Headwaters and Shiloh starting later that summer. Hidden Valley had also begun in southern BC in early 1972, but had moved a couple of years later up into the Peace River Region. The others were established from 1973 to 1975, Hilltop being the "new" farm in the area. When I came to live at Graham River, Graham was five years old. I also began to learn of similar community farms in Alaska, across the States, in Latin America, and around the world.

Why community? For three basic reasons. The vision for the communities, and particularly the communities in the wilderness areas came from Brother Sam Fife, a former Baptist preacher from southern

Florida. His vision was to see God's people living together and sharing life together. There is clearly the pattern for such community in the New Testament, a pattern that has been practiced by many moves of the Spirit down through the centuries.

Establishing communities in wilderness places was unique to Brother Sam. Sam Fife believed in the early seventies that there were only a few more years left before a one-world government would be established and liberty would be no more.There were certainly many signs that seemed to agree with that. Brother Sam taught that God's people needed to establish community farms on the edge of the wilderness where they could support themselves and survive during a time when many Christians would perish.

The third thing that he taught was that during this time of difficulty that was coming, many Christians would be fleeing, looking for a place of refuge. It was Brother Sam's belief that God would use these communities in the wilderness to prepare a place of refuge for His people. That vision, "**to nourish her there**," gripped my heart from the beginning and remains to this day.

The urgency of Sam Fife's message persuaded around a thousand people to move into community in the Peace River area, as well as a similar number in the States, including Alaska, and a similar number in several Latin American countries, mostly Columbia. In 1972, Brother Sam predicted that we had only about five years left. It was at the end of those five years that I came to Graham River. With hindsight, many years later, we can look back and say, "Boy, he sure got the timing wrong." Yet, I believe that a large part of the urgency was from the Lord, regardless of the timetables of history.

At the same time, looking at the world today, there is more reason to be pessimistic now about how many years of liberty we have left than it was even then. Yes, many people moved to the communities in the wilderness out of a "herd" instinct, compelled by an external concern. At the same time, many sold all that they had, gave it away, and came to the communities out of obedience to a direct word from God to them personally. And God is always working together with those who love Him to turn all things towards goodness.

For me, for my life, God's timing was right on time.

6. Graham River Farm

June 1977 - March 1978

Living with the Davison's

I had returned to Graham River. I do not remember where I slept that first night, but for the first couple of weeks I stayed in a cabin by myself. I grew pretty lonely; I was not a socializer. I did not easily start relationships with people, and I was left alone by the people there as far as visiting was concerned. This was not an intentional oversight of the community; it's just the way it was. The communities have improved much in this regard. Of course I was with people all the time at meals, in services, and on the work details.

Graham River was beautiful any time of year. The fields stretching back from the cabins were sprouting green with new grain. The trees were in full leaf. The gardens were beginning to grow. I fitted into the work schedule in the same way I had done before, though there were different sets of tasks. The firewood season was over for a few months. The children were out of school, so they and their teachers were also on the work schedule now. There was a lot of activity on such a large community farm. One of my tasks was to work on the sawmill crew. The sawmill was a little distance from the rest of the community, at the far end of their small-plane landing strip. Warren Bowles, a young man my same age, was the saw operator. I helped roll the logs onto the carriage and helped take the fresh new lumber off on the other side. I loved watching the new boards being shaped by the saw.

After about two weeks, one of the women elders of the community, Ethelwyn Davison, approached me to say she would like to see me at her cabin that afternoon. Delighted at the chance to visit with someone, I went with anticipation.

"Daniel," she said as we sat in her small living room overlooking the gardens, "my husband, Dural, and I have been praying about having you come live with us. We asked for visions, before we said anything to you. They were positive, so we want to know if you would like to live with us."

"Yes, I would!" I answered.

"Good, bring your things over tomorrow."

So I was introduced to the practice in the communities of seeking for visions to confirm what someone feels God is speaking to them. I have obtained many sets of visions for directions I had from the Lord during my years in that fellowship. Almost every time, they were clearly for my situation and provided much comfort and assurance that the Lord was indeed working in my life.

Just then a young lady came into the Davison cabin wanting to talk to Sister Ethelwyn. She asked me if I wouldn't mind leaving so they could talk privately. Unbeknownst to Sister Ethelwyn, this was a crushing blow to me. I was so lonely and had so wanted to visit. I went back to my cabin and wept. But the next day I moved in with the Davison's.

The Davison's had doubled the size of their cabin with an addition, making it around 25 feet by 35 feet. I had my own room in the middle of the back wall. On one side of my room was a room shared by Mallory and David Smith, Ethelwyn's two sons. Between their room and the living room was a room occupied by Meri Smith, Ethelwyn's daughter. Mallory was just a year or so younger than me, Meri, a couple of years younger than him, and David was probably around 10 or 11. Dural and Ethelwyn shared a room on the opposite corner of the cabin. The living room and their bedroom were in the new addition. Dural was away for a couple of months on a ministry trip. He was a traveling ministry, going from group to group and community to community around North America, ministering to the various fellowships.

Dural and Ethelwyn were as opposite as could be and yet they shared the same heart. Brother D (as he was called) was slow and methodical. Though he had good things to say, I fell asleep under his preaching many times. His gift was in prayer, and he had one of the closest faith-filled relationships with the Lord of anyone I have ever known. Sister

Ethelwyn, on the other hand, was dynamic and creative. She was a trained musician and a music and drama teacher, and to her final day young people were out of breath to keep up with her creativity. I would live in their home for the first six months of my community experience.

Many Wonderful Experiences

I loved Christian community. Soon after my return one of the ladies, Janet Booth, told me with a smile, "I knew you would be back." I loved the shared meals in the Tabernacle with all the hubbub of people visiting with one another. I loved the services, upon which was an anointing of the Holy Spirit I had not known before, or since I have left community. There was an earnestness and devotion in worship and in the word that these people had that most once-a-week Christians never know. At the age of twenty, I loved the "primitive" conditions. It was like camping out all the time. Our water came fresh from the spring in buckets. We had

outhouses, each shared by two or three cabins. This was not new for me, since Henry Miller used only an outhouse. All the daily activities were involved with obtaining the basic necessities of life – food, warmth and shelter. Everything was real; there were none of the "cover-ups" produced by civilization to hide people from reality. I loved the simple hearty meals cooked on wood cook stoves. I loved working with the men on all the types of tasks I had read about in *Farmer Boy* by Laura Ingles Wilder when I was younger. And I loved seeing others whom I knew and cared for benefit personally from the work of my hands. I valued that reward far greater than any pay check.

July was hay month. The men who took care of the horses hooked them onto the hay wagons, and we rode out to the fields. These horses were large, powerful Belgians, hooked two to a wagon. The hay was laid out in neat rows across the fields. It had been cut and winnowed by horse-drawn machinery. A contraption pulled along behind the wagon picked up the hay and brought it up over the end

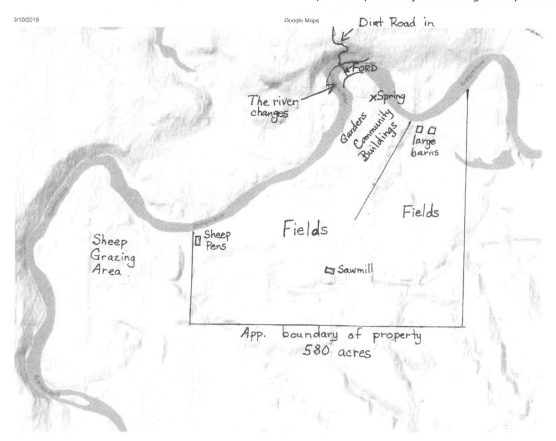

The Graham River Property and Surroundings
This place is written forever in my memories.

wall of the wagon. My job was to pitchfork the hay forward to the front of the wagon as it came up. The field was filled with crews of men and horses working together. When the wagon was piled high we rode back to the barns, lying on our backs on top of the pile seeing only the sky, rocking to the slow plod of the horses. It was a wonderful break before the hard work in the haymows.

There were two big barns, the cow barn and the horse barn. They had large high haymows above them. The wagon pulled up in front of the barn, and we climbed up to the haymow. Beyond the wagon was an ox tied to a rope. Rohn Ritchie, around 15 at the time, was the ox man. A large tong was suspended from a pulley riding on a track running the length of the haymow ceiling and attached to the rope on the other end from the ox. The great tong dug into the pile of hay on the wagon, and then Rohn urged the ox in the opposite direction, swinging the tong filled with hay up and back into the interior of the mow. At a certain point it released and dropped its load onto the growing pile of hay. There, a crew of men, myself included, forked the hay back up into the corners, keeping the pile growing. We went back and forth from fields to barns until both mows were brim full of fresh, sweet hay.

I had milked a cow when I was younger, so I joined the milking crew. We arose before breakfast, got the milking equipment and went out to the barn. Each of us took a cow, sat on a low wooden stool, buried our foreheads in the cow's flank, and milked a pail full of warm milk. The milking crew included Mallory, his friend, Doug Witmer, two younger fellows, Danny Reeser and Bobby Cole, a young elder named Paul Petrocinni, and myself. We each milked one cow except Doug and Mallory who were faster and milked two. We carried the milk up to the Tabernacle in a cart, usually Doug and myself, and ran it through a hand-cranked cream separator. The other fellows cleaned the barn and drove the cows to pasture for the day. While we were separating the cream from the milk, the girls from the goat barn came in with several buckets of goat milk, which we ran through the separator as well. The goat milk was separate from the cow milk, but the cream was mixed together. We finished just in time to clean up for breakfast. I was ready to eat!

The food was simple but good. There were many great cooks at Graham River, and indeed in every community where I have lived. Our diet consisted mostly of root vegetables and grain. We ate lots of potatoes as well as carrots and beets. We had potatoes fixed in every possible way. Each morning for breakfast, we ate cracked grain, and we had good homemade bread at every meal. Dinner, the big meal of the day, was our noon-meal, and supper was usually soup – leftovers plus water. We had a small amount of meat, four times a week. It takes a lot of meat to supply 150 people each with a portion. Most of our meat was moose and bear gotten in fall by hunting. Graham River did not raise beef cattle at that time. We also had pork, the occasional sheep, and rabbit once a month. Occasionally, we would even have horse, which is decent meat in spite of the thought, similar to moose. There was homemade cheese as well and peas, cabbage, and broccoli from the gardens. The greenhouses turned out tomatoes during the summer.

Sometimes I rode with Rohn Ritchie out to the sawmill to get a load of lumber for a building project. Those were always great days. It took half a day for the ox to lumber slowly out to the sawmill, for us to load up the wagon with rough-cut boards, and then for the ox to plod slowly back to the community. Only on the last stretch of the day, when it sensed that it was headed for the barn, did the ox pick up any speed, and even that was just a mild walk for us. We made two trips on such days, one in the morning and one in the afternoon.

It was soon discovered that I was a builder. Builders are in high demand on community farms. I worked with Steve Herman, a woodworker from Pennsylvania. He was preparing to build a carpenter shop right next to the welding and mechanics shop, on the corner where the road came up from the river. He enlisted my help. I enjoyed working with Steve; we had good conversation together. I had only framed before, but now I began a journey of learning by doing into every aspect of the construction trade. We built the carpenter shop through the summer. It was 40 foot square. The farm had some tools to put in it, a radial arm saw and a table saw as well as Steve's Shopsmith. The stove was right in the center. It became a great place in which to work as well as a gathering place for the men around the stove.

One morning as I was laying out the rafters on top of the wall, Ray Clark, the elder in charge of the work schedule came up to us. "We need all the men in the potato field to pull the weeds," he said. Steve was a bit perturbed at losing my help at this point of the construction. "You don't understand," he said, "we've got a carpenter here who can really help us with the building."

"Nope," said Brother Ray, "The potatoes are our food. We need every man weeding."

So that day I went to the potato field to pull out the lambsquarters from between the fast-growing rows of potatoes. It was actually an enjoyable experience. There were 30 to 40 men and boys on their hands and knees moving through the rows of potatoes, pulling out the thickly growing lambsquarters. Of course, the lambsquarters contain more nutrition than any plant in the garden, but they aren't the best tasting, so away they go. The sun was warm; the day was pleasant. The men laughed and talked together through the day. We weeded ten acres of potatoes in short order.

Contending with the Word

I ate my meals in the common dining room and worked with the men during the day, but in the evenings and on Sundays, I spent my time in my own room, steadfast at the most important task before me in those months. I spent hours searching the word, asking the Lord to show me if the strange things I was hearing were really true. My first question was concerning righteousness. Does God really expect us to walk in righteousness ourselves? I went through the New Testament from beginning to end and wrote out every verse on walking in the truth. I became astounded as I filled out page after page, copying nearly a third of the entire New Testament. By the time I was finished, I could only affirm that the New Testament did agree with the Apostle John, "**Do not be deceived, my little children. He that doeth righteousness is righteous, even as He is righteous.**"

The community gathered in the Tabernacle once a week to listen to a message on tape. One such evening, we listened to a tape by Sam Fife on what he called "the mystery of a man and a maid." I did not understand it much, but I thought it was the biggest bunch of baloney I had ever heard. This concept had two parts, one that the process of human reproduction was a picture created by God to show His plan for bringing forth His life in us. The other part of the concept is that Jesus plants His seed in the womb of His bride through the preaching of the ministry to the church.

I was so flabbergasted by this teaching that I spent the next two weeks pouring over the word trying to refute it. Then, one day, my eyes opened wide, and I saw that the process of human reproduction is indeed used in the Bible as a picture of God birthing His life in us. Suddenly, I saw this truth from Genesis to Revelation; it was as if the whole Bible were built upon it. And indeed it is. I am convinced that without understanding the pattern of the reproduction of life, it is impossible to understand the Bible, since the whole purpose of God is built on that pattern and so many references are made to it that have no meaning without understanding the pattern. And the seed that is Christ does often come through the ministry of the word.

Later in the summer, Dural Davison returned from his ministry trip. The farm had a long airstrip with one end between the community buildings and the barns. Brother D flew a small plane and used it to travel from place to place. One day he invited me to go with him to another community in the area, Headwaters, where he was going to minister. I eagerly went along. We climbed into his four-seater plane and headed down the airstrip. The moment the plane lifted off the ground, I was in love with flying. By plane it was only a few minutes to Headwaters. The airstrip there was several miles from the farm; we had to buzz the farm so they would come pick us up.

Although Headwaters was a community farm like Graham, it was different in many ways. It had just gone through a major split during which a number of families had moved away, but it still had more people than Graham River. Headwaters did not have a river to keep the vehicles out, so they were everywhere in the camp, turning everything into mud. I instantly appreciated the Graham River with no bridge. At least Graham was not muddy. Graham was also the only farm in the area that had a sandy soil. Everywhere else was clay, which meant that you could sink several inches into the mud with each step you took going back and forth to the Tabernacle for meals. At Graham, the cabins were all in neat rows, close to one another. At Headwaters, the closest cabin to the Tabernacle was as far as the furthest from it at Graham. There was a mile between the furthest cabin on one side and the furthest on the other side. In fact, the cow barn was closer to the Tabernacle than any but the one cabin. That cabin belonged to Danny Robertson and his family, and it was there we spent the night.

I shared a room with the Robertson's boy. Head-waters had a number of young people who did not like the farm and who were not seeking the Lord. The Robertson boy gave me an earful of complaint and intrigue, though it meant little to me. I was interested only in what the Lord was doing in my life.

A Time of Pruning

Upon my arrival at Fort St. John in June of 1977, I entered a time of judgment during which God began to dissolve the hard shell that encased me. I went through difficult situation after difficult situation. It seemed that I hardly got over one before I was hit with another. Very little of this was caused by other people's actions, most of it was caused by my own sensitivity or stupidity, whichever was convenient for God to use at the time. At least, that is what I thought. I had no idea then, nor did anyone else, that I was mildly autistic and lacked social abilities that most everyone else simply takes for granted.

Two incidents happened early on in my time at Graham that seemed "insulting" to me. A brother whom I became good friends with later, Bill Williams, came up to me one day in the Tabernacle with a vision God had given him for me. In the vision, he saw a chicken foot that gradually, over time, became the foot of an eagle. It seems silly now, but at the time, I took that as a personal insult from God. Me, a chicken foot? I was much more mature than that! The other incident was similar. I was reading Watchman Nee's *The Spiritual Man*. As I read the chapter on the experience of a soulish believer, I was reading a description of myself. I was stunned. I had considered myself to be a mature believer, not a "fleshy" one. That blow burdened me for nearly two weeks.

As I said, it seemed that I hardly got over one such blow, before the Lord through circumstances hit me with another. The worst single incident happened in the fall of the year. I went with Brother Eli Miller and Bobby Cole to a neighboring rancher, several miles from Graham. We spent the day putting up a corral fence for him in return for access to firewood from property he was clearing. As a young man in the north country, I had an unceasing hunger, and the food was really good. I ate a lot. We went in for dinner, the men of the family joined us, and the wife and daughter served us. I had seconds and thirds. I cleaned out the last of the stew. It was so good.

On our return to work, Brother Eli said, "Hey, fellows, take it easy on the food." Why, I know not, I answered, "Brother Eli, swallow your pride and join in." "Don't you realize, the wife and daughter had not eaten?" he answered, "You finished off their dinner."

Had Brother Eli swung a 2x4, it would not have hit me as hard. I was embarrassed, humiliated, mortified. I was so ashamed, I could hardly look at Brother Eli the rest of the afternoon or for several days after. I hardly wanted to leave my room; I was sure the whole community now viewed me as a pariah.

This incident was the most devastating of the several in which I felt like such a fool, but it certainly was not the only one. I was sensitive and withdrawn, on the one hand, but ready for adventure and new things on the other.

Let me say a word in my defence. I was helplessly naive, quite ignorant of other people as well as myself. My personality ranges between a designer and an achiever. Asperger's means I always feel threatened by others, and it includes a fear that makes confronting people or dealing with difficult relationships with people to be impossible. I had no one to help guide me through the emotional turmoil of adolescence. I had gone through some pretty black times emotionally. I was often ridiculed by others, especially Tim, Tim, and Andy, for saying something stupid. I had no idea why, so I closed my mouth and withdrew. I still liked to be around people, I just learned not to say anything.

Living with the Buerge's

With these problems, I entered community. I liked being around people; I loved the meals together. I just did not know how to relate to people. Though I usually kept to my room studying the word, the Davison house was a gathering place for the young people of the community. They would sit in the living room and chat; I could hear the hubbub of their voices through the thin walls of the cabin. One day, after quite a number of them had visited for over an hour, I joined them. I got a chair and quietly sat on the outside of the circle. I said nothing, but just enjoyed the conversation. A minute or so later, Mallory announced that he had to do something, got up and left the room. In less than five minutes I was the only person left in the room, sitting numbly in my chair. This same scenario happened a second and a third time as well. I did not blame them, but I did not understand why.

After I had lived with the Davison's for two months, Brother D and Sister Ethelwyn made plans to go on an extended ministry trip. In order not to leave us young people by ourselves in the cabin, they asked Del and Virginia Buerge to move into the cabin with their three children. Del and Virginia took D and Ethelwyn's room and their three small children had a small room on the backside of the porch. Solomon said, "**As iron sharpens iron, so a man sharpens the countenance of his friend**." Del was that to me. Del had a very different personality and view of life than mine. I enjoyed working, but it was not my life. To Del, work was everything. Someone taking a few minutes extra before going to the work schedule was inexcusable. Del was very exacting, and the slightest variation from his exact standards drew his wrath. Incident after incident built bitterness in my heart toward him.

One time when I went to town, Del asked me to pick up some coffee, the cheapest I could find. I spent several minutes laboring over the decision. Finally I picked what I thought was the cheapest coffee on the shelf. Upon arriving home, however, I was strongly informed that I had wasted his money irresponsibly. I had bought instant coffee, not regular. I had no idea at the time that without any means of making regular coffee, he would not want instant. Everyone else at the farm used instant. Another time he sat me down and took me to task for using too much jam on my crackers.

Del was the oversight of the goat program. In the fall, we began a remodel of the interior of the goat barn as well as adding a large haymow on top. So there I was, working all day with Del, eating with him and his family at the same table in the Tabernacle, and then going home to the same house. I became bitter, and the bitterness blocked my relationship with the Lord. I finally had to choose, would I be bitter, or would I humble myself and ask forgiveness. When I lived with Andy, I had faced the same thing, but there I just moved back home. I could not do that this time. Finally, I went to Del and asked his forgiveness for the way I was feeling towards him. The difficulties did not end, but the bitterness was broken. I still had ill feelings at times, but for the first time, with the Lord's help, I had overcome the emotional turmoil within.

This is one of the great advantages of Christian community. We can be so deceived about our own "spiritual maturity." We can think we are making great strides in our relationship with the Lord. We go to church on Sunday and are greeted with warm smiles and friendly handshakes. But when thrust into the closeness of community with these same beautiful people, we discover that they are not quite as beautiful as we had imagined them to be. Then comes the proving. I don't know how many people I watched over the years who imagined themselves to be spiritually mature, but who, in the crux of simply walking together with other like-minded believers, found that the press of bitterness and unforgiveness, not loving their brother as Christ loves the church, was more important to them than their relationship with the Lord, and away they went, bitter.

I must add this note, however. Although I did not see Del often in later years, yet I counted him as a friend, and Maureen and I spent a happy couple of days on our honeymoon enjoying Del and Virginia's hospitality at their home in the Yukon. Del also came down to be part of the first Graham River Tabernacle raising in 1992. But those stories come later.

Heart-Wrenching Desire

All of this, though, was only the smaller part of the circumstance the Lord was using to work on my hard shell. The larger part was my desire to be married. I had my eyes on a particular girl, about three years younger than me. Somehow, in my thinking, I came to believe that she was God's choice for me. God never actually spoke that, but I interpreted circumstance after circumstance to indicate that it was God's "will." As an Asperger's young man, once I thought I liked her, I could not possibly speak to her. Needless to say, I experienced innumerable disappointments. Another boy was also attracted to her. I did not know this, but I picked up on it after a while. I considered him to be less interested in the Lord than any other of the young people.

My personality, my desire for a wife, and my inhibitions all conspired to create many deeply disappointing moments through my time at Graham River.

Through all of these emotionally devastating blows, the Lord was working to open me up, a process that would take many years. Another vision received for me during this time showed me as a large rock with gold deep on the inside. It took great hammering and much work, but slowly cracks appeared in this rock that was so effectively hiding the gold.

Sometime in the late summer I traveled to Dawson Creek at the start of the Alaska Highway to see Mr. Wenham, the immigration officer. My three months were up, so I needed to ask for an extension. I was apprehensive when I presented my request to Mr. Wenham; I did not need to be. In all the years I went to see Mr. Wenham, he never cracked a smile, but he always gave me an extension. Mr. Wenham was a tremendous help to the people in the communities over the years. When his office was finally closed and he retired years later, we invited him to the Blueberry community for a special evening to honor him.

More Contending with the Word

In September 1977, I went to my first convention at Hidden Valley, south of Dawson Creek. A majority of the people from Graham River as well as from all the communities in the area – several hundred people, attended the convention. Hidden Valley had its own unique flavor. Most of the cabins had basements with the stove in the basement. This is a wise practice in the north country, but most of the communities did not follow it. I took a sleeping bag and slept on the floor of one of the cabins. That was the last time I failed to take a foamy with me to convention. Sleeping on a hard plywood floor with no cushion was not fun.

Many ministries from the local area, from Alaska, and across the states came to the convention. The move conventions were quite different from the charismatic conferences I had been to before. There was no program for the meetings. No one knew who would lead praise or who would preach in a given service. That is the way it is in all services throughout that fellowship. The Spirit of the Lord directs who will lead the praise and who will minister. Time and again I was awed at the clear thread that God wove through the songs chosen, the words that had been prepared, and the prophecies that were given. When the Lord is given room to direct the flow of the service, He does a much better job than we do. It was evident throughout that the anointing of the Lord was the focus and carrier of the meetings.

It was at this convention that I first saw Brother Sam Fife. He preached a word on endurance called "The Long Run." By this time he had realized that this thing would not be over in five years and that it could well last much longer than that. His word was that those who endure to the end will be saved. I have never heard anyone preach the way Brother Sam preached. I have never known anyone before or since who was more committed to the Lord, to His voice, and to the vision the Lord has for His church. Brother Sam was small and wiry with gray hair. He was around fifty years old at the time. For the first time, I heard someone preach with authority. I did not understand all that he said, but I did witness to the presence of the Holy Spirit that attended his words. This little man, with his iron devotion to the revelation of Jesus Christ, would impact my life more than any other. I had lived in community for three months, but for the first time I began to believe that this was, indeed, the move of the Spirit of God.

The word flowed endlessly. At this time in the move conventions, a short word was an hour-and-a-half long. Usually two or three preachers ministered in each service. The convention started on Wednesday evening and went until Sunday afternoon with two services a day. I counted a total of forty-three hours of praise and word. I was drawn in my spirit to the word and the anointing, but my human person was torn at the same time. It was an excruciating time for me, glorious and terrible.

I was not a blind believer, through all this my cry to the Lord was, "Lord Jesus, show me if this is of You or not." I wanted to know the Lord Jesus Christ above anything in this world. I know there were many others throughout the world with the same cry whom the Lord led in different ways, but this is the way He led me. Even now, I have to say, "Lord, I trust You." By this time, everything I had believed was Christianity had been ripped to shreds. Bit by bit my understanding of God and His word was being rebuilt.

Seeds Planted

Part of my purpose in this history is to recount the planting in me by God of the word that I share at the present time. Contending with what God says in the Bible had now become the overwhelming passion of my life. From 1977 until 2013, I have wrestled with God and with the Bible, that I might know the Salvation of God. If I heard anyone say something about the Bible or about "what God says," or about Christian "belief," that I did not know,

I was in BIG trouble inside. I could not rest. I have a Bible; I MUST KNOW what God says.

The first time I heard Sam Fife preaching on a tape, my confidence that Christians know what the Bible teaches was shattered. I do not trust what anyone says about anything; I have to know, myself, from evidence. The only solid evidence we have concerning God's intentions and workings is the Bible. My practice of writing out endless Bible verses began after my return to Graham River. All I had was a *Strong's Concordance* and a King James Bible, but that was enough.

Please understand, however, that my purpose was never to become a "Bible scholar." Such an idea would have been ludicrous to me. Two things were working inside of me. The first and most apparent was a desperate need to know what God actually says. I have always carried an unquenchable cry for SALVATION. The second deeper thing working in me was an intense calling of the deep inside of me to the deep inside of God. I did not want to know the Bible; I wanted to know God.

In the upcoming chapter, "Cutting the Covenant," I specify the points that I now understand to be God entering into a covenant with me, to fulfill His word in my life. Here is where the deepest part of that covenant was found. I am referring to the months of the fall and early winter of 1977.

⁓

Let me take you to a dark room in the back of a rough log cabin in the middle of the Canadian wilderness, to a 20-to-21-year-old boy on his knees beside his simple cot, in pain and agony of soul, in confusion, in shame, tears streaming down his face, in the loneliness of the night watches far from home, desiring to know the living God with all his heart. Allow me to draw back the veil, if you would, and show you a most holy thing.

There, inside this autistic, naïve, overly-sensitive boy, to whom most everything in life hurts, bringing confusion and endless misunderstanding, lives a daring, audacious, presumptuous HOPE. He cannot put it into words; he cannot explain it if you asked. But he knows it.

He bears inside his heart the incredible presumption that all this pain, all this confusion, all these tears possess a PURPOSE. That through them, Christ Jesus is reconciling the world to Himself. He bears in his heart the audacious belief that some-

day, somewhere, somehow, someone will break out of darkness and into light, someone will be spared the pain, someone will escape the confusion BE-CAUSE OF his tears and BECAUSE OF his hurt.

No, he does not see it, or how it could even be so. Yet he hopes, and HOPE is that which is not seen.

What he wants to know is that the Lord Jesus is IN his hurt and IN his affliction, that it is indeed holy and filled with great purpose. He wants it to be confirmed to him that Christ is indeed living as him in this world. He must know that the whisper inside, "You're difficulties are Me and I am in you, redeeming others to Myself," is truly founded in the gospel.

When he knows with all certainty the extent to which Christ Jesus reveals Himself in, as, and through his affliction, then, and only then, will healing be acceptable to him.

⁓

This was indeed the requirement I placed upon God (and Godly covenants are entirely one-sided – that which we require of a God who energeoes all inside of all), that my agony would result in blessing to others, that Father and I together would turn all my tears and confusion into hope arising inside of you that your Salvation is true and now and complete, that many would enter into the knowledge of God without hindrance as a result of my expectation of God in the midst of all my wrenching agony.

I will not explain here anything preached in the move fellowship that I now see as contrary to our knowledge of God and of Salvation. That contention must come later. You see, Jesus said that everyone finds exactly what they seek. Ideas that people have in their heads have no meaning. What counts is the desire of the heart. I sought God; therefore I found Him everywhere I looked and in every moment of my life.

I read an account in recent years written by a woman who says that she lived for a brief time in these same communities in the Peace River country of British Columbia, during this same time. She recounts that she saw no love of God anywhere she looked. That accusation completely astounded me, for I found the love of God outpoured towards me through wonderful Christian people everywhere I looked. Jesus was right; we find what we seek.

People are people, no matter where you find them. But the people I knew through all my years in Christian community, were the kindest, most loving, most devoted to God, most anointed, and most giving, of all I have known in my life. I am most willing to acknowledge any hurt anyone experienced by wrongful things and to show them Christ through all of it. But when false accusation comes against these precious people whom I knew and loved, then, well – let us say no more. Even now, when I think about those who were the most difficult for me personally, I remember well the goodness and love of God upon them and their desire to know Him as much as any.

Three seeds of God came into my life through Sam Fife during this season, and two seeds from the ongoing sharing of word in the community and conventions. The first and primary seed of life was, as I shared, the understanding that the pattern of the reproduction of life, whether plant life or human life, is the largest and most important metaphor God uses. The entire Bible is written out from that pattern and none who read the Bible can understand God's meaning apart from that pattern. I have taught you to practice that reality of God by responding to every word God speaks with "Let it be to me," that whatever God means by any word He speaks might enter into your heart to be written there as Christ Jesus Himself.

The second thing I received from Sam Fife was the shattering of "going to" heaven as the goal of the believer. Any thought of a someday Salvation and a someday Christ will block in the believer any need to know Christ as all that God speaks here and now.

The third thing I received through Sam Fife was the understanding of the world as I share it. Sam Fife preached regarding a world "conspiracy" intent upon forming a one-world government over the earth. This understanding was taught by many in that fellowship during the years I was part of it, but by September of 2001, that understanding had vanished and belief in "America" had replaced it. I do not teach what I teach about this world because I heard it preached, however. I don't teach anything because I heard it preached. I don't "believe" anything about this world. I require evidence gathered over years for anything I might consider to be true. Yet when I know the evidence, then I am unmoved by the fact that most humans and most Christians willfully prefer to believe things that cannot be true.

You cannot love this world and know the love of the Father.

I read two books that many had in the communities through this time. The first was *None Dare Call It Conspiracy* by Gary Allen. I still have copies of this book and at the present time, my knowledge of the facts of history remains in full agreement with what Gary Allen wrote. The second book was *Pawns in the Game* by William Carr.

From the time that I was five and understood a map of the world, my need to understand this world, what it is and how it works, has been great. Measured against other people's passions, this need in me to know would probably be counted greater. But it did not measure against my need to know what God says in the Bible. And, indeed, these two arenas of understanding do intermingle. This world is the setting of the proving of Christ through us.

Then, from the broader teachings of that fellowship, I gained first an understanding of the task set before the sons of God to set all creation free. This idea was new and strange, yes, but not difficult, especially since God says it so clearly in the most important chapter of the Bible. Nonetheless, inside of that word of setting creation free, there was another word, a word that became personal to me. While I sat in the powerfully anointed services in both the community and the conventions a desire grew in me to be part of that provision for God's church in her hour of deepest need. I longed to be a Joseph, one who stored up the word as grain during times of plenty so that God's people would have the nourishment they would need to take them through the darkness and into the revelation of Jesus Christ. I was just a boy, and I had no idea how I could be part of such a thing. But I wanted to be, somehow, with all my heart.

More Wondrous Adventure

I continued to have a range of tremendous experiences at Graham River. Sometime in late summer a couple of the men, Harold Witmer and Ralph Vega, took the young people on a several-day camping trip. We climbed the hill to the south of the farm and descended to Kobe's Creek. We crossed the creek and climbed to the top of Butler Ridge. From there we could see the peaks of the Rockies receding into the distance. To the south we could see the blue western arm of Williston Lake, though the huge Bennett Dam was hidden from view. The northern wilderness is beautiful and its wildness and remoteness exhilarating. Some of the young men talked about going on a different kind of wilderness trek the next summer. On this trip we carried our own food, but they were planning to go for several days without taking food, learning to live off what could be gathered from the land. I so wanted to participate in such an endeavor, though I never got the chance.

In the fall, also, I started working at two tasks quite new for me. The first was the butcher shop. I joined Harold Witmer and his sons, Steve and Doug, along with Mallory, and a brother named Al Rotundi. The butcher shop was a warm and inviting place to be. The men were kind and friendly. The work was different and interesting. Steve was in charge of the rabbit program that produced enough rabbits to feed the family a meal once a month. Butchering rabbits was kind of fun. The other young fellows could do one rabbit a minute. I never got that fast, but I did pretty well. We butchered bear, moose, pig, sheep, and even a horse. We ground meat, rendered fat into lard, and made cracklings. It is a fond memory.

The other task was herding sheep. I did that with two other younger fellows, Blake Cole and Paul van Dyke. The sheep were kept just beyond the farm property in a sheepfold up the river. We had license to graze them on crown land. We saddled up the horses in the morning and rode out to the sheepfold. We let the sheep out and then followed them with the horses as they grazed in the meadows along the river. It was fun just riding a horse all day through the fall of the year, watching the leaves turn yellow and gold. At first, I thought it was up to me to keep the sheep together. When they scattered through the trees, I panicked, trying to get them all back together again. I soon learned, however, that sheep with a shepherd stay together anyhow, and that the horse will always follow the sheep. So I lay back on the horse with my legs crossed on its neck and looked up at the sky and the leaves of the trees as the horse followed the sheep and the sheep stayed together. It was a great time. I learned a lot about sheep as well. The first thing I learned is that they are generally stupid. You can work and work to get them into an area of fresh grass that they have not trodden down, and they will run right through it, not taking a bite, heading back to familiar trodden pastures just as quickly as they can. They are also blind followers. If one leading ewe breaks through the fence into the grain

fields, all the rest will certainly follow – where they would all die from eating too much if you didn't chase them out.

Then winter came. Winter is the main season in the north. For six months the temperature stays below freezing, and snow covers the ground. The first morning that the temperature hit 55 degrees F below zero was quite memorable. We hugged close to the cows as we milked them, not daring to touch the metal buckets. Lucky for us that the cow's teats were warm, because you could not milk with mitts on. Once the temperature drops to minus 30, all outside work stops. Lungs can freeze at this temperature and machinery can crack. More than one person has tried to go jogging in this "free" time and was laid up for days as a result. On the other hand, the average temperature is around twenty below. In the north country, once it drops below zero, there is very little wind. Twenty below with the sun shining is actually comfortable. You dress for the weather, of course, but since the air is dry, if you dress properly and keep moving, you stay warm.

I had many memorable experiences during the winter months. One day I was assigned to go with Al Rotundi and Warren Bowles on a daylong trip to get some firewood logs from a site on the other side of the river. The men had made an ice-bridge across the Graham River during the winter months. They laid slabs and pumped water onto the ice until there was a slab thick enough to carry big trucks across the still fast-moving water. We went on a sleigh pulled by two horses. They did not travel fast. It took us most of the morning to get there, going through the sunny, still woods, listening to the clip-clop of the horses and the soft slush of the sleighs sliding over the snow, and talking quietly together. When we arrived at the log site, we spent maybe an hour of hard work loading them onto the sleigh. Then we built a fire, warmed our frozen sandwiches, boiled some tea, and ate lunch. It took the rest of the afternoon to ride back to the farm. It was one of those rare memorable experiences one has in life.

Another time, all the men went to the river to get ice for the ice house. This was straight out of *Farmer Boy*, a book I had read as a child many times, but never dreamed I would get to experience. The only difference was we used chain saws to cut the ice instead of crosscut saws. We sawed the ice into large square blocks and used metal tongs to hoist them out of the river. We loaded them onto a wagon pulled by horses and took them to the ice house where we packed them in sawdust. These blocks of ice would last through most of the summer, giving us ice for drinks and ice cream, and to cool an ice refrigerator.

Living with the Kurtz's

In the late fall, Dan Kurtz, one of the elders, came to me and asked me if I would remodel his cabin's enclosed porch. He wanted me to install a ceiling and a closet so that someone could use it for a bedroom. Dan Kurtz had a poor reputation among the young people, so, having absorbed some of their thinking, I resented doing the job. I ran into some problems that made it difficult work, so I did not relish the task. One day, I had time to work on Brother Dan's porch, but I did not want to. I chose to clean the cow barn out instead. As I walked past the Kurtz' cabin towards the barn, I heard the Lord speak to me, "Jonah." It was clear what He was insinuating. I was trying to find some other good deed to do to avoid the thing God had put before me. Reluctantly, I turned and went back to the porch job.

A few days after I completed that job, Brother Dan came to me and said "Daniel, we would like you to come live with us." If God was finished with my time with the Buerge's, so was I. I readily agreed. Here all those weeks I had been working on my own bedroom! I spent three months with the Kurtz's. It was the best three months I had in eighteen years of living in Christian community. Within the first week I was there, Brother Dan said to me, "Daniel, I see that you help yourself to the things in the kitchen cupboard. I'm glad you feel at home with us; you're welcome to whatever we have." What a difference between that and my previous experience. I have never felt more welcome or part of those I lived with than the time I spent with the Kurtz's. This is what I have always believed community should be; this is what my experience in community has not usually been for one reason or another. To be part of a community that has as its focus the intent of making any who comes feel utterly welcome is the desire of my heart and the reason why I am writing this story.

Dan and Joann had seven children, four girls and three boys. I do not remember all their names. The oldest, a girl, was maybe fifteen. They ranged from there down to a recently born little boy. There was also a single girl living with the Kurtz's, Kitty

Kiezebrink, who was walking out a year (that is, pre-engagement) with Harleigh Knapp. We all lived in a cabin 20' by 25'. I had my own room, the porch, Kitty had her own room, Dan and Joann had their room, the four girls were in another room in two sets of bunks, and the three boys were in the last room. There was also a living area with a kitchen counter in one corner and a small bathroom. There was no shower; we took basin baths. The cramped quarters were not a problem. We had the Spirit of Christ and a Christian love for one another.

In February we all loaded into vehicles to ride to Headwaters Farm for another convention. This time, many of the men got into the back of our wood truck, a large yellow Ryder truck. This was the only way for us to get to convention, so we did it. We did not see a thing, of course. What had taken twenty minutes by plane the summer before, now took two hours. By the time we arrived at Headwaters I was feeling pretty poorly. Headwaters, 1978, was my second convention. I was once again overwhelmed with the intensity of the anointing of the Spirit of Christ, and the flow and depth of the word.

In this February convention, I also heard a word, that I received as a missionary call to me, concerning the vision of being a provision for God's people all over the earth in their hour of greatest need, a vision of being a Joseph, gathering up word as food for God's Church during a time of great famine. I "raised my hand" inside me to God. I had no idea how I could possibly be part of such a thing, but I wanted to be, with all my heart, I wanted to be such a thing for God's entire church during her great travail.

When we returned to Graham, I began to think that my time there was nearing an end. Mr. Wenham had given me a six-months extension, due to run out in March. At the same time, I owed taxes to the US government for my work the year before. I needed to earn the money to pay those taxes before April 15. So in early March I boarded a Greyhound bus in Fort St. John and headed south, back home to Oregon. As I left Fort St. John, I felt an overwhelming peace flow over me. Then, it seemed as if the heavens opened and the Lord revealed to me that I was His son. The trip back to Oregon was filled with a precious fellowship with the Lord. It seemed that the spirit of judgment through embarrassment that had covered my life for the last nine months was for that time only. On a regular basis, at Graham River, I had done or said the most stupid and embarrassing things. That particular type of embarrassment did not happen to me again.

The picture on the right is Dural and Ethelwyn Davision several years after the time I lived in their home.

The Original Bowens Mill Buildings
at which I arrived the second week of June, 1978. I was 21 years old.

7. Into the South

March 1978 - October 1978

Returning to Oregon

Although my trip back to Oregon was filled with joy, something happened along the way that marked that fellowship. As I was riding the Greyhound bus south through Pine Pass, I was filled with such joy. Inside that joy, the Lord spoke to me, "You are My son."

After arriving at the Prince George bus station, however, I was standing in the large central waiting room with my stuff. There were a number of people in the room, although it was not packed. Suddenly, without warning, the fear of the Lord came upon me with intensity. I was trembling from head to foot, terrified of the Holy. I did not want anyone to see me in that state so I ran to the only private place I knew, a closed toilet stall. I sat down on the closed toilet seat to face whatever was coming.

It was the same as the morning of the day I received the full release of the Spirit with speaking in tongues two years earlier. It was as if a sharp bony finger was pointed straight at my forehead, and I heard the words, spoken with great intensity, "Will you surrender all that you are to Me right now?"

Who can give answer to the Almighty? There are times when one does not even say, "Yea" or "Nay," We close our mouth and are silent before Him. I managed to get out a terse, "Yes, Lord." The fear lifted, and I continued on my way. The sweet peace and fellowship continued, but with a deep soberness underneath of it.

I want to position this experience first, and then I want to give you a way to understand this seeming dichotomy between the truth of Christ our only life, even when we did not know such a thing, and the dealings of God in which He requires our willingness and the giving of thanks through great trials even for years. First, I don't care about "theology," but only about knowing this mighty Person who tells me to call Him, "Father," in spite of the fact that He is far bigger than me and to be feared. We know His love only inside of our regard for His fear.

Yet the fear of God leads only into living inside of absolute Love.

God establishes everything through two or three witnesses. The first time I experienced the demonstration of the Spirit with power was as God planted His Seed of giving thanks inside of me at age 15. The second time I experienced the demonstration of the Spirit with power was as God planted His Seed of asking and believing that we have received the fulfillment of His Word inside of me at age 19. Yet that second time was also attended with the fear of God and the bony finger and the demand that I surrender all to Him.

In my reading of the Annie visions, which I will introduce later in this chapter, I received this understanding of the Lord's ways. God does not control anyone, nor does He force Himself or compel anyone to love or serve Him. Yet God does have this right, that at a certain moment in a person's life, He is free to take a meaningful acceptance or rejection of Him and to seal a person for this present season into that decision. With Pharaoh, it was to hardness of heart, but with those whom He has chosen, it is that one, "Yes, Lord," that resonates at the depths God requires.

It seems to me now that when I said, "Yes, Lord," the first time, God placed me on probation. But when I said, "Yes, Lord," that second time at age 21 in the Prince George bus station, God sealed me into that decision. That is why, from then on, no matter how much I cried, "No, no, no," no matter how much I fought with God and tried my best to be rid of Him and to go my own way, it never worked. He never paid attention to any of that, but continued right on as if I was actually in full agreement with Him.

You see, I was about to enter twenty years of immense pressure and difficulty, contention, confusion, glory and grief, without the knowledge of Christ my life that is so precious to me now. I see now just how important these foundations of God would be in my life, both the planting of His Seed with power deep into my heart and His contention with me Forehead to forehead.

If God had not done so, you would never have heard of me for I would have nothing to share with you otherwise.

In the diagram below, I give another picture of how I now understand this great dichotomy between Christ living as me through every moment and these years of what can only be called the "deep dealings of God" in my heart and life.

Christ our life is the only thing that has ever been true. It was He all the way through, and as I call every moment of my life into His Story of me, I see NOW just how true it has been. The problem was I did not know any of that then. And God cannot just tell us, for we are given to pretending and to using anything at hand, including God, to abuse other people and to exalt ourselves. Our human psychosis is too great for God to spring His knowledge on us in the way that He really IS.

God has to draw us out of our self-thinking step by slow step until we can know His Christ-thinking which has been the only thing true. Except – that's how we see it, but that's not really what is happening. Consider this diagram of two paths.

The bottom path is the only true story of my life; the other path is the steps of my blind stumbling into the knowledge of what is already true. Where they come together is the beginning of my knowledge of Christ my life, and now I am always with Father through Jesus, regardless. As I walked through this seemingly split-path of my perceptions, I knew everything as the dealings of God with me. And that knowing is very important, for Jesus must win my heart.

BUT – here is what I discover after a season of walking with Father as one together. I discover that "God dealing with me," though important, was only how I perceived things. In reality the only thing real that was ever happening in my life was the shaping of my human heart to contain and to reveal the Heart of God All-Carrying.

And in the shaping of the human heart to contain Father's Heart, it is the Father who takes the mightiest blows. You see, that finished Hheart, my heart and Father's Heart together as one, is the Mercy Seat formed by the beating and beating of hammers. Father's Heart is always beaten in order to fit the shape of my own human heart far more than I, being pressed beyond measure, was being shaped to fit His Heart.

This joining of Heart with heart is the only thing meaningful taking place in the present age.

Now, I am sharing all this because I am about to open up an eight-year period of my life that I have rarely shared from in these letters. And as I open up these experiences of great difficulty, I want to know them in one way only, as the shaping of Father's Heart to fit mine and the shaping of my heart to fit His. There is no other treasure I would have.

A Time of Discontent

There is a whole lot of stuff packed into this short three-month space back in Oregon before my next grand adventure. I went right back to work with Jimmy. Andy was no longer around, and I saw him seldom after that.

One of the first things I did was go down to the Lebanon Airport and sign up for private pilot lessons. The very moment the plane flown by Brother D had lifted up off the runway at Graham River with me in the back seat, I was in love with flying small planes. I started with the instructor right away. I took naturally to the task and after seven hours with the instructor, he thought I was ready to solo. That first solo was quite an experience, one which I did successfully live through, but I was not willing to go up again by myself until after three more hours with the instructor. Then, my second solo flight was much smoother. I flew as far as the Pacific in one direction and up to The Dalles on the Columbia in the

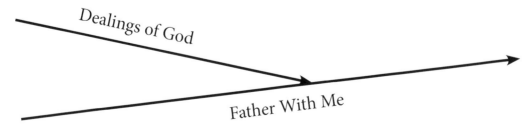

other direction. I did not start ground school, then, until I had already begun to solo. I was well on my way to a private pilot's license except my discontent sent me down the road before I finished it, and there was never again the opportunity to do so.

I also connected with a family in Albany who had known Jim Buerge, Don and Collette Manes and their two sons, Donny and Jerry. During my times in Oregon through the late seventies, I spent many evenings in their home in Bible study and fellowship. Mark Troyer also came to their fellowship times. His brother, John Troyer lived in the communities in BC with his family. My times of fellowship with the Manes's were rich. I also soon went up to Portland most Sundays for the services of the group there that were part of the same "move" fellowship as the communities in the north. I would visit after the services with David and Kim Johnson in their home. David was the primary elder in the Portland group. Portland was about seventy-five miles from my parents' home. I did not go up on I-5, however, but up the east side of the Willamette Valley, through Stayton, Silverton, and Oregon City. I became very familiar with that route over the years, including the long drive home after dark, which will factor greatly in the next chapter.

In May I rode down to the California convention in Van Nuys, California, with a sister from the Portland group, Kay Wallace, and her two young sons, Howard and Michael. Howard would spend five years in my English classroom at Blueberry, but I did not know that then.

Brother Dural and Sister Ethelwyn were at the California convention, so I visited briefly with them. Brother D shared with me that the move fellowships of the eastern United States under Brother Sam Fife's ministry had taken on the large task of building a community and convention center at a place called Bowens Mill, Georgia. Since Bowens Mill plays a large part in this history, let me recount the circumstances of its formation.

The same conventions that I went to at Hidden Valley and Headwaters were also held regularly by that fellowship throughout the world. The many traveling ministries went from convention to convention in a regular circuit that brought them to the same place at the same time each year. In the east, there had been an April convention in Canton, Ohio, then July in Miami, Florida, and October in Montreal, Quebec. As these conventions grew in

size, the costs for a meeting hall, food, and lodging had also gone up. Brother Sam set many important things in place in the practice of that fellowship. One was a corporate ministry. We rarely had services in which fewer than three people ministered the word, including in the conventions. And the pulpit was always open, even to those who may not have been part of the fellowship. At the same time, there were no costs for attending a convention, except for getting there. All the costs of food and lodging came out of the offerings during the convention services. If you had, you gave; if you did not have, you could still attend freely.

At the same time, the largest community in the move at that time, a Christian community at a place called Sapa, Mississippi, was forced, by circumstances, to leave Mississippi. A large property had become available at Bowens Mill, Georgia. For that reason, in February of 1978 more than a hundred people from Sapa and elsewhere in the South had moved into a trailer-house community at Bowens Mill and were in the process of building a convention center where the April, July, and October conventions could be held at a much lower cost.

Without explaining any of that, Brother D suggested to me that they sure could use builders to help get the convention site finished by the upcoming July convention.

Meanwhile, back in Oregon, I was caught between two things. On the one hand was a word of the revelation of Jesus Christ inside of me and on the other hand was a complete discontent with framing houses for people I did not know and a spiritual life that seemed to be going nowhere. I went with my parents a few times to charismatic services. At one such occasion, in Portland, I sat listening to a robed choir singing praises to God with great joy and in a lovely anointing. As I sat there, I could hear Sam Fife's voice as a loud crow cawing in my ear. Yet I knew that the word I had received from God through Sam Fife's ministry was the word to which I had begun to commit my life. I closed my ears to the siren's call of an easy Christianity and held to that Word I had received.

During this time, I read the two most important books in my life besides the Bible, both of which my mother possessed. The first was *I Looked and I Saw Visions of God*, edited by Ed Miller. The visions in this little book, seen by a young girl named Annie under Ed Miller's ministry in Argentina, caught my heart in their power. Every word I had heard in the move fellowship was confirmed to me mightily by these visions, particularly those visions that showed God planting of Himself into the lives and hearts of His chosen ones. To be one of those was more important to me than my breath, yet I had no idea how it could be so. The other book was *Hind's Feet on High Places* by Hannah Hurnard. The journey of Much Afraid step by stumbling step has always given me hope that my Savior would also carry me through all my inability into knowing Him.

In early June as I was nailing the plywood onto a roof, my discontent became too great. I threw my hammer down, said "Goodbye" to Jimmy and headed home. I'm not one to dilly-dally, so in a day or so I said "Goodbye" to my parents and headed down the road again. This time, it was into the South.

A Long Trip to a Strange Country

I had bought a big old white Buick for $200 from my brother in law, Tim Louden, during this time. It had a strong engine and ran well. I headed up Highway 20 over Santiam Pass into eastern Oregon. Except – something happened I was not expecting. For the first time in my life I felt and heard something inside, an incessant voice that would become as familiar to me as anything. I heard – "NO!"

Now, I have said that I have never won against the "No's" of God coming against me, restraining my way, bringing me to humbling myself and admitting my mistakes. That is true except twice. This was the first of those two times. As the "No" became unbearable, driving up over the Cascades, I would pull over for a bit, then keep going. The wrestling inside was fierce. Move community was life and adventure and the immediate knowledge of God and of the anointing and back home in Oregon was dullness and fleshiness and going nowhere at all. I did not know God well, and I was determined to know Him better, and I knew that I would never know Him at all if I just sat in Oregon in nothing. I could not turn around. Yet the "No's" continued through the stretch south to Nevada. In the end, my obstinacy did prevail and the "No's" slowly died away. I kept going, into what fire and affliction I did not know.

A straight line from Oregon to Georgia, would be a shorter route, but it would not include the Alamo. To drive within 500 miles of the Alamo and not visit it was inconceivable to me. So – my route had to include San Antonio, Texas. At the same time, I

left with only a hundred dollars. Even in 1978, that was not enough money. So, my first destination was Phoenix, Arizona where my sister, Frieda, and her family, Tim, April, and Ryan, were living at that time. After a detour through Death Valley, I arrived in Phoenix, which was at 112 degrees F. The summers of 1978-80 were much hotter than anything today. It was the first week of June.

I spent a couple of days with Tim and Frieda. I mentioned that I had no more money to continue my trip, so Tim gave me $150. Later, I got in trouble with my dad, who had just sent them that extra money for their own needs. Ignorant of that fact, I headed east. I did spend an afternoon at the Alamo. I had read the story many times, but I was disappointed because the charge of the Mexican army was now a wide boulevard filled with cars. It was hard to re-picture the story. But I did check out the places where Jim Bowie and Davy Crocket had died.

Crossing the border into Louisiana was a very strange experience. Going to British Columbia in Canada was the same country to me. There was little difference between BC and Oregon. But the South was a strange and foreign country. I had no air conditioning, so my windows were down. As I drove across the vast humid swamps of Louisiana, I thought my engine was going to pieces, but when I pulled over, the loud grinding noise of the Cicadas kept right on. Everything of the South was DIFFERENT to this Oregon boy. It was a strange land.

I had the address of Buddy and Dorothy Cobb who lived a couple of miles before the Bowens Mill community. In the late afternoon, I stopped at their house. Dorothy was the only one there, but she directed me down to the service taking place that evening. She called ahead, and so as I arrived at the Bowens Mill community, Brother Pat Stafford came out to greet me. A new adventure had begun.

My First Season at Bowens Mill

It is normal and expected in the move fellowship to go through a lengthy process of communication and confirmation of witness before showing up at one of the communities. I often paid no attention to that process, including this time. Yes, it raised some eyebrows, I'm sure, but my gentle spirit, my willingness to accept and to tackle anything, and the fact that I was a skilled builder opened the door to me every time. I have always plunged into any kind of adventure.

Bowens Mill was different than anything I had ever known. The people were different, the climate and vegetation were different, the food was different, the talk was different, the ways of doing things were different, the buildings were different, and the approach to construction was different. Yet I found the same Spirit and the same word that I had found at Graham River, the same open arms, warm smiles, and willing acceptance. I was back in community.

I placed a picture of the original Bowens Mill buildings on page 54. They are quite old. Originally this was a gas station on the left, a motel on the right and a community hall in the center. When I first arrived the community hall was the Tabernacle and meeting room and the motel was filled with families. Behind the motel and to the right of it was an open field filled with trailers of every sort.

Although there were people who had moved there straight from New Orleans, Miami, and elsewhere, most of the people at Bowens Mill were from the Sapa, Mississippi farm, a community that had a distinctly different view and practice. Sapa was a "deliverance" farm, a place to which troubled people could come to find help.

Brother Pat Stafford met me as I came up to the porch. The service was soon finished and I was directed to an empty bed in the men's dorm, one of the many trailers behind the motel. Several of the brothers in the men's dorm I would come to know later. Don Pettis was the "example," the term given at Sapa to a non-elder in charge of others. Two that I spent some of my off-time with were Lebron Tucker, a tall, strong, epileptic man with a willing heart and smile, and David Knowles who was venturing into the plumbing trade.

This was my home for the next three weeks and through the first convention at Bowens Mill. We had all our meals in the central building in the picture. I remember finding breakfast cereal on my plate for lunch. They did not have sugar with it, so I compensated by putting jelly on it. I had no idea why people ate unsweetened cereal. Only later did I learn that grits are different. I remember Bambi Hinson encouraging me to eat more, even after I was stuffed, to "keep up my strength." John and Bambi Hinson were the primary ministries of the Sapa group.

Sapa had been big on lots of meetings of every kind, so most evenings I was either in a service or a Bible study. On some evenings there was a choice as to which Bible study to attend. I gravitated towards one given by a gentle and anointed woman elder from the Mississippi farm by the name of Roberta Mack. I enjoyed her teaching.

A Fifteen-Year-Old Girl

One time, as several of us were sitting on the benches on the front porch of the community hall, a fifteen-year-old girl came up the steps of the porch carrying a big pot of soup that had been prepared elsewhere. I stepped up to her and offered to take the heavy pot. She did not smile or say anything, but she let me take it on into the serving counter.

I learned later that her name was Maureen, the youngest daughter of Claude and Roberta Mack. She was elegant, gentle and kind. Twelve years later she would walk down the aisle to become the most important part of my life.

Working on the Convention Site

The work on the convention site was managed by a brother named Don Billingsley who led a crew of many men, young and old, skilled and unskilled. By the time I arrived, the main Tabernacle frame and roof had been completed, although the screen all the way around, the doors, and the sawdust floor were not yet in place. The Tabernacle was 100 feet wide by 150 feet long. It could hold up to 1500 people. A large platform for the ministry was being built in the middle of one of the long walls.

My first task was to build the doors and to install them and the screen all the way around. I worked with an older brother named Tony Materick. He was a kindly gentleman from Ontario, Canada.

The slabs for the kitchen and the men's and women's bathrooms were being poured. It was above 110 degrees F through these weeks. I remember Lebron mixing concrete, stopping every little while to take his t-shirt off and wringing cups of sweat out of it. There was no air-conditioning, only fans in the trailers. That's why the Tabernacle was open all the way around with board-and-batten siding on the bottom half of the wall and screen on the top half.

A group of African-American men showed up to lay the cement blocks for the kitchen and bathrooms. They were led by an older gentleman, a true man of God, who was called Noah Nothing. I will refer to him as Brother Noah. His son, Daniel Bryant was also there. I was about to learn that Brother Daniel was one of the mightiest preachers I have ever been privileged to hear. Brother Noah had a church in Douglas, Georgia. Brother Sam loved to preach in his church, and they loved to hear him.

When we were finished with the screen, I was moved over to the task of framing the roofs for the bathrooms and kitchens. By this time it was seen that I was an experienced builder as well as a construction leader, so I was mostly in charge of this part. At the same time that we were framing these roofs, other men were bringing in truckloads of sawdust and spreading it out for the Tabernacle floor. The kitchen roof was the last roof we did. As we were framing it, storm clouds moved in. Everyone ran for cover. I stood on top of the wall laughing at them. "In Oregon, if we don't work in the rain," I said, "we don't work." No one paid attention. The first drops hit, way larger than any rain I had known. It's twenty-plus feet from the corner of the kitchen to the Tabernacle doors. When the first drop hit me I leaped to the ground. By the time I made it under the Tabernacle roof, the water was flowing two inches deep on the ground. It was a bit more than normal, but I was introduced to a different kind of rain.

On July 4, I was finishing the tin on the kitchen roof. (In the move we paid zero attention to any "holidays" except to place the conventions when people were getting off work.) It was 115 degrees F. The tin had to be on the roof. A thousand people would be showing up the next day for the convention, and they needed a place to eat. No one else was willing to brave the heat coming off the bright tin. I have always felt a sense of responsibility, however, which is why I was given charge of work crews early on. So I would get on the roof, throw a piece of tin into place, hammer the nails into it, and jump down back into the slightly cooler shade. I did that over and over. The roof would leak a bit, but it was finished by the end of the day. Other men brought in the kitchen stoves and counters the next day even as people were arriving for convention.

Move of God Conventions

July 5-9, Wednesday evening to Sunday afternoon, I experienced my first convention in the South. These conventions became a huge part of my life and of the shaping of the word inside of me. I would guesstimate that I spent around 1600 to 1800 hours of my life in the praise and preaching of these conventions. When Sam Fife was still alive, the conventions were around 45 hours of praise and preaching over several days. They shortened in length over the years, but they still remained times of penetration and shaping out from the power of a third feast word, that is, a Feast of Trumpets word, calling God's people towards the soon-coming fulfillment of Tabernacles in the life of the Church.

All the conventions have pretty much merged together for me, so I don't typically remember what I heard when. I just know that it was always mighty in God and that the word always went all through my soul. Nothing in any other realm of Christianity I have known has come anywhere close, not even a little bit. I sat in my chair, hour after hour, caught intently inside a vision of God among His people.

I would come to know personally most of the men and women who preached in these conventions. Many would play a large part in my life; all were examples to me of integrity and devotion to God. All gave of themselves utterly for the sake of the kingdom, that God's people might be established in the truth. I may understand some things differently now, but I was not connecting to ideas or theology, but to God. These ministries were different than any I have known before or since. There was no such thing as any "one-man-ministry." There was no "I-am-the-pastor" identity. The leading ministries in the move lived in the communities, in the cabin next door, one of the brothers and sisters right along with everyone else. I have stayed in their homes; I have eaten many meals with them. Nothing was hidden; no one was "superior."

Not all of those who preached in the northern conventions came to Bowens Mill, but most of those who did preach at Hidden Valley and Headwaters were also there. At the same time, there were a number of new faces at Bowens Mill. I want to recount some of their names.

Brother Dural and Sister Ethelwyn, with whom I had lived at Graham River, both preached in the conventions along with Eli Miller, also from Graham River. Sam Fife preached, of course, as well as Buddy

Cobb, originally from Hollywood, Florida, but who lived in another new community two miles down the road from Bowens Mill. There were Herb and Janet Myers – Herb was killed in a plane crash that summer of 1978, but I had heard him preach twice up north. There were Milton and Bonnie Vereide, who both preached in the conventions; they eventually lived at the Smithers, BC, community. John Clark, then from Hidden Valley, Joe McCord who has lived at the Lubbock, Texas community from then until now, and Tom Rowe from Atlanta were also primary ministries in the move. Many of these brethren were hilarious, and we laughed a lot. Brother Noah and Daniel Bryant both preached. John Hinson always preached in the Bowens Mill conventions, but he rarely went north. Don Stockbridge and Gary Shamblin were younger but deeply anointed ministries with fascinating messages as well as John Jeffries from the Haines, Alaska community. There were ministries from England, New England, and throughout the south, speaking in strange accents.

It was hot in the July conventions, of course, although the temperature dropped ten degrees the afternoon the convention started. Most everyone spent the services waving a fan to blow air across their faces. I determined that the effort required would produce as much heat as was being dissipated. I learned simply to ignore the heat.

When the convention was over, as people were still mingling after the last service, Brother John Hinson came up to me. "Brother Sam asked me if any good builders might be willing to come to the Citra Farm in Florida to help with the construction there," he said. "I mentioned you, and so Brother Sam said to ask." And so I got ready to drive to Citra.

The Citra Community

I arrived at the Citra community in the second week of July, 1978. Citra is a small southern town, just outside of Gainesville, Florida. At that time it was orange grove country, but frosts since then have moved the oranges south. I lived in the Citra community for four months. The fairly large property had been owned by Brother Noah Nothing; in fact, it was where he grew up. He had given it to Sam Fife for a community. Citra would be Sam Fife's community, although he did not get to spend much time there before he died. His wife, Lee Fife, lived there for many years. John and Bambi Hinson also had a small dwelling there and spent time back

and forth between Citra and Bowens Mill.

In the main house, a small southern house that had belonged to Noah Nothing's family, there lived an older couple who were called "Ma-mo" and "Pa-po." Ma-mo was an elder, but Pa-po was something else, a bit cantankerous, but good-hearted. Another elder was Howard Snodgrass who lived in a house next door with his family. Besides these married couples were a number of single young people, men and women, who had gathered there to help prepare a place for many more who were hoping to move to Citra. Art Jehle, a ministry in the move, and his wife, showed up a few weeks later. They came with a small travel trailer.

John and Bambi Hinson had differing ideas of how community should work than most others in the move. Their communities were much stricter than any others, and life was much more regulated. This was fine with me, although some of the particulars could be difficult. The move communities were never legalistic, however, as so many introverted groups become. One of the practices, coming out from Sam Fife, however, was that women wear dresses and men wear short hair and no beards. On the other hand, Sam Fife promoted women in ministry, along with many other non-legalistic things. The issue for Brother Sam was "the flesh." He had no tolerance for "fleshy things" like swimming pools and air conditioning, etc. He also held a strong line against the rebellious practices of that time and the demonic forces behind them. I just read an article from Vigilant Citizen this morning that confirmed that he was not wrong. Far worse things are now common in our world today.

Two young men showed up one day wanting to join the community. Both had long hair. Brother Sam sat them down at a picnic table and spoke with them. When he was done, Kurt went to town and got his hair cut, a precious brother in the Lord whom I knew for several years. The other young man I never saw again. Yes, I do believe that God places moments like this in our lives. The tree of life is a thorn tree and only those who desire to know the Father above all will dare press themselves up through the thorns to get the life of that tree.

There were three places for the several of us young men to sleep, on mattresses in the front porch, on bunks in the second bedroom of the house (Ma-mo and Pa-po had the other bedroom) and a small travel trailer in the back. Brother John

Hinson wanted to keep the young men at the Citra Farm from sinking into "self-identity." So he instituted a rotation. We spent a week in the front porch, a week in the bedroom, and a week in the travel trailer, rotating around each time.

I am now an opponent of such thinking; you will find the opposite concept in *Symmorphy V: Life*. But let me ask this question. How could I learn what was the Lord and what was not except I experience many things? I can say that never once in my years in community did I see any morally wrong practice, only sometimes quite misguided ones. This was a misguided practice; it prevented us from ever feeling at home.

Some of the brothers with whom I lived and worked were Lloyd Smith, an African American brother who gave me wise counsel concerning relating with blacks that I had never learned in Oregon. Another brother was Scott Risley. I don't remember most of the others.

Through most of this time I led the construction of an addition to the main house, about doubling it in size. This large room would become the meeting and dining room of the community as well as an extension of the kitchen. Later some brethren came down from Arkansas, Oklahoma, and Dallas to help build some larger family buildings in a back area of the property for families wanting to move to Citra. I worked with them some in pouring concrete. I became good friends with Al Danduran, his wife and, and his son-in-law, Billy Sims.

Citra was a good place for me overall. I was learning much, both in the Lord and in construction. It was in my spare time at Citra that I began the practice of writing out whole books of the Bible. Actually, someone had a typewriter, so I typed all the verses I wrote out. Typing is even better than writing for seeing the word entering into your understanding. At the same time, it continued to be a time of learning what was not appropriate in relating with other people. I could be a bit dense and even offensive at times. Ma-mo was a wonderful teacher in this regard; she was always trying to teach Pa-po to be kind, but she never succeeded.

Knowing how to walk together in harmony is not something anyone is born with. All of us must learn it, and the learning is very often painful. "Christ as me" never gives us the excuse to be rude and crude or to treat people badly. Treating people badly is something we have to learn not to do. For instance, Lloyd had to take me aside and let me know that "negro" was a word that was very hurtful to him. I appreciated that counsel, but it was not always easy to discover that I was being a pain in the rear.

While I was at Citra, a number of the young people there had the privilege of attending a rural, southern, Holy Ghost-filled black church associated with Brother Noah. The congregation welcomed us with open arms, escorted us down to the front rows, and we participated in one of the greatest experiences of my life, a worship unlike anything I had known.

Sam Fife

Sam and Lee Fife came to Citra in early September. Brother Sam was there as part of the community for about two weeks. There was a small building behind the main house that was just a bedroom. This was where John and Bambi  stayed when they were there. Since they were back at Bowens Mill, it's were Sam and Lee stayed.

Sam Fife never allowed anything to be written down regarding his life and ministry. He was so adamant about it that his wife, Lee Fife, continued to refuse permission to anyone to write a history of Sam Fife. We accept Christ living as our brother, yes, but this was an unfortunate fetish. At the present time if you go looking for information on Sam Fife online, you find only terrible reports, none of which are true. I reject any testimony about any Christian ministry that does not come from someone who walked closely with them over years. All the evil reports about Billy Graham and Joel Osteen, or about this Christian group or that, are just that, evil and false.

But no one ever told me not to write about Sam Fife, so I will. Here is an account I wrote for a college paper while I was at Blueberry. This gives an important, but idealistic view of Brother Sam. In the next chapter, I will give a differing view.

A Character Sketch of Sam Fife

He was a short, wiry, funny-looking little man, about five feet two or three inches tall. He had wavy white and gray hair and a rough, drawn face, very Scottish. He was usually dressed in casual unpretentious clothes – corduroy pants and a plain work shirt. Upon first meeting him he did not seem like much, sort of a vacant look on his face, a preoccupation with something obviously other than the person to whom he was speaking. He was not the kind of man to whom one would give much notice, sort of an absent-minded eccentric, a man who did not have his feet fully planted on this earth. His wife constantly followed him about, seeing that he did not forget to tie his shoes or to take his toothbrush along with him or to comb his hair.

Yet upon closer observance, one was struck with the depth of strength and even fire that was in this man. Disdaining trivialities and "how are you doing today," he had within him a bulldog determination that awed everyone who met him. One knew unequivocally that this man knew who he was, where he was going, and how to get there.

He was a man who loved judgment, who embraced judgment, who went out of his way to bring judgment into his life. He tried never to travel alone, even when accompanied by his wife. Always he would ask someone else to go with him so that his life was open and visible. Always he stayed on his knees before God. He would travel day and night, ministering the word, counseling, praying through the night, rarely stopping to sleep, never stopping to find his own pleasure. He would go a thousand miles out of his way to minister to a handful of saints. He had one view in life, the revelation of Jesus Christ.

It was when he stood up to speak that the quality that made him different became readily apparent. He spoke with authority. He knew the vision God had given him, he believed it with all of his heart, he had committed his life totally and irrevocably to its fulfillment, and that was all there was to it. His utter faith in the word that he preached could not but strike the very center of his listeners. His words demanded a decisive reaction; no one could hear him passively. Some that heard him speak found their lives totally re-oriented. They found themselves selling their belongings, forsaking their homelands, the only way of life thy had ever known, moving to far distant places, and adopting a far different lifestyle. Others who heard him speak rejected his words utterly, yet that word still left a mark upon them.

He opened the Bible like no one before him. He spoke of marriage union with God, of sitting in the throne of God, of being made just like God. He spoke of overcoming sin and putting death under our feet, of driving all the demons out of this earth and setting all creation free. His words were stirring and penetrating, permeated with the anointing of God. Though he himself has since gone to be with the Lord, his words continue today, alive in the hearts of those who heard and believe. He spoke also of a people who would love one another in this age, and there is no greater proof of the authenticity of his life and message than to see today, over eight years after his death, the firstfruits of that love in the lives of many who had loved to call him, "Brother Sam."

⸺

You can see from this description the source and the determination of so much that I teach. I truly want to give as full an account of this man, who influenced me more than any other, as I am able. It was his intensity that showed me face to face what I had seen from Madame Guyon and Rees Howells from a distance, that a man could know God and walk together with Him. The truth is, the things Sam Fife taught that I do not bring into the present word I share, are of less significance in my present understanding. Yes, a lot of people ran into great difficulties unprepared because Sam Fife did not know our present union with Christ, preached a false version of the cross and was not always gentle. That was wrong. But as I have said, the thing important to me was a man connecting with God, and that is what I remember.

Sam and Lee arrived at the start of the real garden season in the south. Planting a full garden in September was something new to me. But Brother Sam was a worker, and he had us all out there planting our food for the coming months. Seeing the "leader" of a movement numbering upwards of ten thousand people hard at work in the garden, or walking in his pajamas from the bathroom in the house to his bedroom out back was unusual in the realms of "leadership."

We were putting siding on the addition to the main house. Sam Fife wanted used painted-tin on it because we already had it from tearing down some buildings. Neither I nor the elders were in agreement. We wanted to match the siding that was on the rest of the house. They knew Sam Fife too well to raise the issue, so I was elected. When I made our argument, Sam Fife paused, then turned and walked away without saying anything. That evening, as he got up to preach, he spoke respectfully of our request. But then he presented a vision of giving all to the kingdom that was so clear and so inspiring that all I could think was, "Thank God for used painted-tin."

One time Brother Sam stepped into the young men's bedroom to talk with some of the brothers. The topic was the move communities in Columbia, South America. His eyes and his face glowed with the passion of absolute devotion to the Church of Jesus Christ and to her gathering together in community that I was simply enthralled. If you have heard me sing, "If I forget thee, Oh Jerusalem," you must realize how I have asked God to grant me such a heart for His people.

Most of the brothers and sisters went with Sam Fife to a meeting in the fellowship in Daytona Beach where he was ministering. There were quite a few groups throughout Florida, indeed all across North and South America, in England, Africa, Australia and Taiwan. For the drive home I was available, so Brother Sam had me ride back with Sister Lee and himself. There was not much conversation, but he always made sure his life was an open book.

Many of us from Citra then went up to the second convention at Bowens Mill, October 4-8, 1978. It's too hot in July, but October is the best time of year in the South. This was one of the most anointed times I have ever been privileged to attend. I have never known the Fire, the Purity and Power, the immanent Presence of a Holy God cut all through my heart and soul than listening to Sam Fife preach, prophecy, and pray during this convention. At this convention, I spent most of my time on the front row.

At the same time, a black brother from Jamaica was also there, by the name of Lester Higgins. Lest-er Higgins preached a word of union with Christ now. The power and anointing that was upon him and that word were as great as any in the move conventions. His words went across the congregation like lightning. I watched Sam Fife's face filled with joy and expectation at the hearing of such a word. I was deeply moved.

Returning to Oregon

I returned to Citra after the October convention in the front seat with Pa-po. Riding that distance with Pa-po was an experience like no other. I feared for my life every mile. You know we made it safely because I am writing this now, but it was only just. After a week or so, I realized that I did not feel at home at Citra. At the same time, my longing to return to Graham River Farm only grew. When I shared that with John Hinson, he said little more than, "Well, thanks for giving us your time here." He did ask me, however, if I could do one more task on my way. I was more than happy to comply.

That task was to stop at the former Sapa community in Mississippi, which had not yet been sold, in order to tear down a building and load the materials on a truck to be sent back to Citra for the building needs there. I readily agreed. Scott Risley, a young man around my age, cheerful and easy to get along with, went with me; he would drive the loaded truck back. We left probably by the end of the second week of October.

I spent about a week at the former Sapa community. Most of the core buildings were still there. Most of the people had lived in trailer houses which were gone to Bowens Mill, but there were two large dorms, the Tabernacle and school, as well as a smaller "dorm" that was more like a lodge. Jim and Joyce Fant had remained at Sapa with their daughter, Mary Ruth, to caretake the place until it could be sold. This was the first time that I met them. We had a wonderful time with them. Jim and Joyce would play a very large and positive role in my life.

After Scott and I had torn down one of the large dorms and loaded the material onto a truck, we said our goodbyes. I drove my Buick the long road home to Oregon, stopping at my brother's place in Nebraska for a few days along the way.

8. Cutting the Covenant

November 1978 - July 1979

Reassessing Everything

After completing the account of my time at the Citra community in Florida, I felt troubled, as if something was yet incomplete inside. I have never considered my time at Citra in this close way. Only as I wrote the last chapter did I realize that not feeling at home was indeed the primary reason why I did not stay.

My other question then was – have I presented an "idolized" view of Sam Fife?

In this chapter, I want to give a more complete picture including the great issues of God set before the move of God fellowship after Sam Fife's death. The truth is, In the present time I teach as much against things Sam Fife taught as I teach the same as what he taught.

The real issue for me was this trajectory from Madame Guyon to Rees Howells to Sam Fife – that I could know God and walk with Him in intimacy and in power. Nonetheless, I will tell you honestly that the desire to possess the same anointing God had placed upon Brother Sam is a meaningful temptation to me now, a temptation I am free to ignore because I know how God has dealt with me over many years, starting with this season of covenant.

God anoints me as He made me and for His expression through me, and not as or by the anointing or person of any other.

And I include a continual analysis because reading my story cannot benefit anyone unless, in some way, the Jesus who fills you with His glory can, by my stumbling steps and inadequate explanations, cause you to know Him inside of you and all through your own life story.

My life has no meaning except that, by it, I know the Father and Jesus Sent into me.

Through these years I was a mess inside. For you to know Christ also living as you, I must show you the difficulty of my own limitations through which Jesus carried me. Asperger's was not my primary problem, although it made my problem worse by blocking any understanding of these "people" all around me and by preventing meaningful communication.

My problem was that I was utterly ashamed of myself, that is, I lived for many years in the self-exaltation of extreme self-pity. Yet I can also honestly say that, underneath of that, my heart was true and that, in the core of my person, I remain the same from then until now.

If someone says, "Daniel, you are so different now than what you were back then," they are completely wrong. I am the same person inside I have always been. Yet they are also completely correct, for I am no longer ashamed of Christ Jesus living as me.

My conclusion is that through the many years from then until now, God masterfully used all the ongoing circumstances of my life, month after month, year after year, to bring me out of my ignorance into the wondrous knowledge of all Salvation in which I live now. Not one circumstance was ever out of place or unnecessary. The course of my life was perfect.

All of His ways concerning me are perfect. God has never led me wrong; God has never not led me. My testimony is honest and true.

I must also say that, regardless of whether anyone else reads this account of my life or obtains any benefit from it, my going through every specific time, person, and circumstance and seeing it filled with Jesus in truth, is accomplishing such incredible wonders for me in the filling up of every tiny hole or crack with the outpoured goodness of God.

Heading North Again

Returning to Oregon meant returning to my parent's home outside of Lacomb. This time I did not connect with Jimmy to work with him; I do not remember why. Rather, I found a job with a sub-contractor in Salem, Oregon, doing small construction jobs including sidewalks on city streets. I do not remember his name, but he was decent to work for. He was a Vietnam vet filled with the horror of the atrocities he had seen being committed by fellow soldiers against innocent people, and he was filled with a profound hatred of the American government. I worked with him almost a month.

In the first part of December, 1978, I headed north again to Graham River Farm, this time driving my large Buick. I had filled the trunk with oak boards when I left Citra. It was winter.

These years, 1977-80, were hotter summers and colder winters than normal, and I spent two of these winters in the far north and two of the summers in the deep South. I was just 22, so my brain was not completely in place yet; one does not drive into a brutal Canadian winter in an old car by one's self, unless you're young, adventurous, and foolhardy.

It was probably somewhere close to minus 30 degrees F as I approached Fort St. John. (Celsius and Fahrenheit are the same number at minus 40.) I was having trouble with overheating. The light would come on and I would stop. The temperature would cool rapidly and I could continue. Passing Fort St. John, I thought to myself that it had become cold enough that I didn't need a radiator. I stopped at the truck stop in Charlie Lake, however, and discovered that, indeed, I had no water at all. The cold outside was enough to cool the engine as I had stopped every little while. They had radiator hoses that fit, so I put new ones on. The problem was solved.

It was afternoon, Graham was only two hours away down long and winding, narrow and snow-banked roads of which I was mostly unfamiliar and for which I had no map. What could go wrong? This was December, when the days are barely eight hours long and the nights a full sixteen hours. I've always had a canny sense of navigation, either that, or the Lord has always helped me, because I reached the banks of the Graham River just before dark. The ice bridge was in place, so I could drive across.

As I arrived, however, I passed a trailer going back across the river filled with Steve Herman, most of his family, and all their belongings. This was my first taste of ones whom I knew and loved "leaving the farm," and "leaving the move." The Herman's two older boys had remained, primarily because they

were interested in the two young women at the farm whom they would eventually marry. At least I had a chance to say goodbye.

A Trying Winter

No one at Graham River knew I was coming. The only communication that could reach them was public service radio, which someone always listened to in order to hear any messages for Graham. I had not made use of that service, of course. Dan and Joann Kurtz and their family, with whom I had stayed the winter before, were gone from the farm on a trip down to the states visiting family. Since I had hoped to stay with them again, I went to their cabin, fired up the stove, and stayed there in my bed on the porch for a few nights.

I loved Graham River; I loved the people; I loved most every aspect of wilderness Christian community, but these next four months I spent at Graham River Farm were not as "romantic" as my memory of my earlier time there.

I fitted into the work schedule as before, but this was winter, and the work was mostly firewood. The Graham River community burned inordinate amounts of firewood. The two big stoves in the school sucked up over a cord of wood a day, and the perimeter of the rooms inside was still covered with frost. Poorly insulated buildings took far more wood and work to keep them heated than it would have taken to build a double wall and double roof, even with moss and dirt between. It was not until I designed the buildings years later that we built double-walled buildings. The Tabernacle I designed for the later Graham River community had only one small wood stove in the basement that heated a larger area than the earlier school building. A cord of wood would have lasted a month, not one day.

Not long after I arrived, some men elders met with me, including John Troyer, who had recently moved to Graham River with his family. John had the responsibility for a newly created "men's dorm." They asked me to move into that dorm instead of heating an empty cabin full time. The two Herman boys, Mike and Danny, were staying in the men's dorm cabin, along with another young man my age, Dan Dickout. Dan was pursing a relationship with Anne Kensley, who had lived with John and Bambi Hinson at Sapa before coming to Graham River. There were five of us in the dorm; I believe the fifth was Paul van Dyke. Since I was last in, I got the top bunk in the center, right on the other side of a thin wall from the wood stove.

I was outnumbered four to one. I went back to milking, so I went to bed early and got up early. They all went to bed late. Dan and Danny liked to sit up talking for hours after I needed to sleep. I liked to sleep in cooler temperatures; they liked to sleep in warmer temperatures. Their interests and conversational topics were not mine, and mine were not theirs. Night after night I lay in sweltering heat, unable to sleep, listening to the dull sounds of conversations that held no interest for me. More than that, Mike was the one who had "stolen" the admiration of the girl I had been imagining was the one the Lord had for me.

Now, I am speaking out from the point of view of a 22-year-old living with other young men my age. None of us knew how to get along, and there was no one older to temper our youthful inadequacies. Maureen and I spent many wonderful times with Dan and Ann Dickout in later years and count them as dear friends. Mike and Pamela are still married, with grandchildren, and I know they were meant for each other. But at that time, I did not care much for these fellows, and I know the feeling was mutual.

But this was all a good thing, you see. In my earlier months at Graham River I had spent most of my spare time in my bedroom, studying the Bible. After leaving there, I had regretted the fact that I had not known closely many of the people. Now, avoiding my "bedroom" was the thing I wanted to do, and the only way to do that was to invite myself over to visit with many other families in the community. It was a difficult reason, but an important result.

I visited with Al and Janet Rotundi, and their children, Rick and Monica. I visited with Bill Williams and his family. Bill had also been in Vietnam. He had volunteered as an act of committing suicide. After surviving untouched, he gave his heart to the Lord. I visited with Warren and Pamela Bowles, who were around my age. I made the rounds of a number of other families, including John and Betsy Troyer, trying not to visit any one place "too often." But often I would talk too much, and often I would return to my bed in deep self-pity that I had exposed my shame for others to see.

I still talk too much at times, but now I put it all into Father, and He carries me.

Sometime during this winter, the elders came up with the idea that, rather than assigning any specific work schedule for the men, everyone should simply be led by the Spirit. I was "led by the Spirit" to work in the warm carpenter shop making things for people. A lot of the men, however, were "led by the Spirit" to stay out of the bitter cold and in their warm cabins day after day.

I took on the project of building more comfortable benches for the services, which were now held in the school building. Before that, the only benches were flat, narrow, hard, and backless. I designed a simple frame that could be duplicated and that gave a curved seat and a curved back that fitted most people well. My benches were well appreciated and soon copied by others. But I was working by myself, so one day I gave an impassioned plea for some to be "led by the Spirit" to come help me. I remember that Warren Bowles showed up, cheerful and willing, and maybe one or two others.

It was not long before the elders reassessed this approach and returned to a form of planning and scheduling. [It actually takes years of trial and error to learn what works and what does not work in community. The suggestions in my book, Symmorphy V: Life, come out of years of such travail inside of basic and practical experience.]

Meanwhile, I was anxiously awaiting the return of Dan and Joanne Kurtz. I heard rumors that they were on their way, so I fired up their wood stove so that they would have a warm cabin upon arrival. Days went by and I eventually got into trouble for wasting firewood, so I stopped. They did return, probably in early February, just in time for the Headwaters convention, but, alas, I was not able to return to living with them. Unbeknownst to me, they were preparing to leave the community.

Except for the Headwaters convention, that is most of what I remember from my final time at the early Graham River community.

A Unique Convention

Later conventions were so common and similar; I will give specifics of only the few that were turning points for me. This Headwaters convention in February of 1979 was so unique and memorable that I will give a more detailed account. We went, as usual, in the back of the large wood truck, but I have only a vague memory of the cabin in which I stayed during the convention.

There were five hundred people from all the communities in the area packed into a space that would legally have held no more than two hundred. We sat on the narrow backless benches with our knees almost touching the backs of the people in front of us. It was a memorable and deeply anointed convention with long services and wonderful praise.

Sam Fife preached one sermon lasting five hours, a condensed version of what he would teach in April to the Hollywood, Florida, group, which became known as "The Hollywood Teachings." You have to understand the power of the word we were hearing because at no point did anyone "tire" of sitting there; we drew into ourselves with great eagerness every word God would have for us. Others wanted to preach, however, and so Brother Sam made room for them. That one service lasted nine hours.

Then, while Brother Joe McCord was preaching, I was wondering to the Lord about what I was hearing. I asked, "Lord, is this really Your move, is this really Your word?" I felt a deep assurance sweep over me, "You can trust this ministry; I have sent them."

One unique experience was when Edie Dwyer stood up to minister the word. I was watching 500 European Protestants, including major ministries, listening with full honor and respect to an African American woman preaching the word for an hour and a half. Such a thing was not known in Christian circles at that time; it was perfectly normal in the move fellowship.

The intensity, however, was upon Brother Sam. He ministered a second time, again a condensed form of what he had taught the month before in the Alaska communities, called "The Sapa Teaching." (One of the Alaska communities had called itself after Sapa, Mississippi, since many had come up from there.) One of the words Sam Fife preached was "God is a Farmer." You will find my version of that truth towards the end of *Symmorphy III: Kingdom*.

There was a heavy shadow resting upon Brother Sam throughout the whole convention, however. At one point during his teaching, he turned towards the ministries seated behind him and said, "One of you is resisting in the Spirit what I am teaching." No one responded, but Dan Kurtz would tell me later that it was him. I will share why in the next section. Brother Sam spoke of everyone trying to make him "king," trying to get him to make their decisions for them, something he always refused to do. He spoke of abandoning these people because of their lack of dedication and of his desire to draw out from them a few who would dedicate themselves utterly to the revelation of Jesus Christ, whatever it might cost.

At one time, in the sobriety of that Spirit, he looked my way and spent a long moment gazing into my eyes. He, of course, remembered me from September at Citra, six months earlier. I possessed, at that time, a nice suit. Unfortunately, I happened to be wearing it that day. I was ashamed that my "fleshiness" did not measure up to the standard he had raised.

After the convention, back at Graham River, I realized that I needed to work a few weeks in order to pay my taxes by April 15. So in March, I returned to Oregon. My Buick had driven its last mile, so I left it in the boneyard at Graham. This time I flew commercially from Fort St. John to Prince George. At Prince George I spent a couple of days with Bill Williams and his family who had also recently left the farm. I returned home, then, on the Greyhound bus.

A Covenant with God

One of the most important events in my life happened during these three months back home in Oregon. Before sharing that occasion, however, I want to give a fuller account of this time.

I went straight back to work with Jimmy. At this point it was just the two of us. Jimmy and I were very comfortable working together framing houses. Jimmy was the lead, of course, but we both knew what to do each step, and we simply did it together without saying anything. This kind of harmony in work together is a rare and priceless treasure. We framed one house for a private owner in the Hamilton Creek area just east of Lebanon. This house was custom-designed by an architect; from these untried blueprints I learned why architects need to frame houses before they begin to design them.

I continued fellowshipping often with Don and Colette Manes as well as driving up to Portland for Sunday services each weekend. In Portland, I continued fellowshipping with David and Kim Johnson after the services. In one such service I heard the shocking news that Dan and Joanne Kurtz had "left the move." In fact, they were coming down to Oregon to stay for a time with relatives who lived not far from Oregon City. This bit of news was overwhelming to me.

Let me explain. God created us to be filled with Himself, another Person, and to reveal the tender kindness of Father Himself through us to all creation. For that reason, we humans are designed to draw our identity out from our union with Christ Jesus and out from Father sharing all things with us. Because we do not know what we are, we desperately seek for an identity in every other direction. Animals and angels have no need to find an identity outside of themselves; humans do, for that is how we are created.

Identifying myself with "the move" was NO small thing, and it was an identity that had grown slowly over two years and through many wondrous and many difficult experiences. It was an identity that had come through a series of deeply personal decisions. When someone you knew and loved then chose to "leave the move," one's carefully (and wrongfully) cultivated identity is challenged. There was a deep sense of "betrayal."

This was one area where the people and ministry in the move of God fellowship failed badly. The attitude towards those who "left" was atrocious. Some of the things said to them were downright brutal. This propensity, however, is common to all and found in every type of Christian experience. Because we have not known that we are coming out of Father every moment through the good speaking of Jesus, we have been very religious in our bad treatment of others who "fail" our "lofty standards." And I put all this in quotation marks because this attitude and practice is abhorrent to me and became one of the primary reasons why I also left that fellowship. Nonetheless, I will wait to share more about this problem for after our move to Fort St. John in 1998.

In April and May of 1979, I had no idea of any of these things. Rather, God was challenging my false identity to its core. Then, on Sunday, April 29, I drove up to Portland again for the morning service. Right away, David Johnson said to me, "Brother Sam has been killed."

Brother Sam had been ministering in the move community in the mountains of Guatemala. As he flew his small plane to leave the valley that Friday, it was not climbing as it should. It was not able to clear the ridge and crashed. All on board were killed, including Sam Fife, Gary Shamblin, and another couple in the fellowship.

You see, Brother Sam had been preaching victory over death for years. A year or so earlier, he shared in a convention that he had been preaching for so long that we do not have to die that he was beginning to believe it. For that reason he said, "I am not going to die." He spoke this proclamation of faith a number of times in move conventions, a declaration of faith which we received as part of the mighty things God was doing in our midst.

Now he was dead.

My first thought, of course, was, "Wow, he had it wrong." That thought vanished, however, as the deeper assertion arose in me that it is better to die in faith, not having received the promises, than to live in any measure of unbelief. My third immediate thought, was that we would not turn back, regardless. We would go on to know the Lord.

Brother Joe McCord was coming to Portland in early May to minister to the group there. I had been in contact with Dan Kurtz on the phone. He asked me to pick him up on my way to Portland. He wanted to visit privately with Joe McCord, one of the primary ministries in that fellowship. It was dark as we drove back home.

As we drove that evening, Dan Kurtz shared with me some of the reasons why they had left the move. Now, I'm not good at remembering specific things said; more than that, I want to address the larger issue here. For that reason I will step aside from that particular conversation and share out from other things Dan has shared with me over the years as well as my present assessment of some of the problems in that fellowship. Part of my purpose is to "de-idolize" Brother Sam, a man of great devotion who was wrong on many important things.

Devotion that is true is a shining example to many, but devotion that is wrong hurts more people in more awful ways than one might realize.

Dan had a very good reason to sit there behind Brother Sam at the Headwaters convention resisting in his spirit what was being preached.

Brother Sam was reckless with his own safety and with the safety of others. And he was even more reckless in leading thousands of people into wilderness communities utterly unprepared. Then, in the midst of the great struggles they must face, he had nothing to help them know what to do. All he had was ever further "revelation," that, while containing truth from God, held nothing practical that was desperately needed by all of those five hundred people sitting there listening to him.

Sam Fife had one answer only – "Die to your flesh." If you have read what I write, then you know that I count this statement as contrary to God, and its outcome as only fruitless horror and mindless confusion.

The first couple of years Dan and Joanne had been at Graham River had been a wonderful time. It was new and exciting. Everyone was committed and worked hard to get along. God was among them and with Him came great blessing. They enjoyed wondrous times together in the Spirit. But time went on, and difficulties arose. The eldership at Graham River, about an equal number of men and women, including many married couples, were more than twenty very strong individuals. And each one had their own strong ideas about how any particular problem should be solved.

When your life and your family's well-being rests entirely on the decisions of the eldership, you can be sure that the stakes are high and that submitting to decisions with which you strongly disagree is next to impossible for most.

When strong Christians get a revelation of being "manifest sons of God" and of "ruling and reigning with Christ," religious arrogance is common. Some felt themselves "above" the laws of Canada, a conceit that the Canadian officials were well able to bring to a quick end. At the same time, in the conflict between "Christ is in you" versus, "Die to your flesh, brother," the flesh ALWAYS wins, and so disdain for people's "fleshy" concerns was often behind the decisions. There were even decisions made, at times, with resulting circumstances that, if you were outside looking in, and not in the press of the moment, you would call as bordering on immoral, at least from Dan Kurtz's view and memory.

Dan and Joanne, however, were the most kind to me of any I knew in that entire fellowship. That same kindness from them was normal towards all others. And so, as the years went by, deeply troubled individuals would come to them, pouring their hearts out, in all the confusion and despair that "preaching against the flesh" must ALWAYS bring. Dan and Joanne had no answers.

Dan is one who always carries others in his heart. And so he went to that Headwaters convention needing Brother Sam to guide these, nearly a thousand people in total, in real answers for real problems. Instead, all that he heard was extravagant and fairly useless "new revelation," along with this claim that all these people, who had sacrificed everything to follow the vision Sam Fife had set before them, were not "measuring up."

Yea. – I now understand Dan and Joanne's difficult decision completely.

Let's now return, however, to that twenty-two-year old boy back in Oregon, having just dropped Dan Kurtz off and who was now faced with an hour's drive home in the dark over a very familiar road.

I was shattered.

Every word I had received, every revelation from God, everything I then believed, every commitment I had made was ripped right out of me.

I wept most of the way home, bereft of any idea of what was true or right or of God. Every experience I had known through the prior two years I now weighed against the things Dan had shared and found them all wanting and empty. All of my carefully re-crafted identity was stripped away.

❧

So God said to Abram, "Bring Me a three-year-old heifer, a three-year-old female goat, a three-year-old ram, a turtledove, and a young pigeon." Then he brought all these to Him and cut them in two, down the middle, and placed each piece opposite the other; but he did not cut the birds in two. And when the vultures came down on the carcasses, Abram drove them away. Now when the sun was going down, a deep sleep fell upon Abram; and behold, horror and great darkness fell upon him…

And it came to pass, when the sun went down and it was dark, that behold, there appeared a smoking oven and a burning torch that passed between those pieces. On the same day the Lord made a covenant with Abram… (Genesis 15:9-18 – reduced).

❧

No, these words did not come to my mind on that drive home, but all the way home I CONTENDED with the Almighty. And in my cut-open soul, in my darkness, I made a covenant with God.

"God," I shouted at the top of my lungs, "I don't know what You are or what Your truth is, but I WILL know You in my life in this age, and I WILL walk with a people who know You."

God is a Keeper of Covenant.

Heading South Again

Dan Kurtz's experience had not been mine, nor was God's path for me the same as His path for Dan or any other. I went with my parents to a Full Gospel Business Men's meeting and the word preached was so shallow and so un-Biblical. Whatever faults might have been in the move fellowship, the things God actually says in the New Testament were more to be found in that fellowship than any other I knew. More than that, I loved community, and I did not know of any other people walking closely with God in the way I desired.

I talked Jimmy Barkley into going with me down to the California Convention in late May. Understand that when I am the driver, the route from one place to another must angle all over the place. I have no idea of our route then, just that I have been through every little part of California. Conventions were always a great contrasting press for me. Sitting under the word as it was being preached was glorious. Intermingling with crowds of people was always the loneliest thing I have known. I remember distinctly the agony of those times between services, particularly at this convention.

Two things of note happened here, however. First, a lady in a wheelchair whom I had not noticed before had someone push her forward on the stage to preach the word. I would remember her name only later, Charity Titus. I was struck by the anointing, power, and practicality of her word. Sister Charity would become one of the most important people in my life.

Brother Dural and Sister Ethelwyn were there as well. Brother Sam had not been at the California convention the year before and, of course, he was not there now. California was a small convention, however, and since the ministry had not yet gathered together after his death, little was said here. But again it was Brother D who shared with me about a little community starting in the high plains above Albuquerque, New Mexico, and about a small group of sisters who were struggling to build a little adobe house for the community. As I heard this story, a witness arose inside my heart that here was the next place God had for me.

After returning to Oregon, I again succeeded in convincing Jimmy to go with me to the convention that July in Bowens Mill, Georgia. We headed south at the end of June.

Jimmy and I visited the north rim of the Grand Canyon and drove into Canyon de Chelly National Monument on our way to the Albuquerque farm. I will share more of that community in the next chapter, but at that time, I shared with the elders there my leading to come and be a part of their community. We continued on towards Bowens Mill. We stopped at the move community in the Ozarks of Arkansas, only to discover that my calculations of when the convention was starting were wrong. We had to hurry on the next day.

Now, I was young and inconsiderate, immature and religious. Driving these long distances with Jimmy meant many arguments and my saying of wrongful and foolish things. Jimmy was always able to bear with my nonsense, but this long trip was wearing on him, I'm sure.

We arrived at Bowens Mill just as the first convention meeting was starting. We rushed in and found seats near the back. At the time, I would have defined myself in that moment as being "out of the Spirit." For the first couple of services, I sensed no connection to any anointing even though Sister Ethelwyn led the praise, and I could not connect with the word being preached.

Meanwhile Jimmy happened to overhear some things said in the men's bathroom that did not sit right with him. I don't know what he heard, or whether he simply misunderstood. The next morning he said goodbye to me and headed back to Oregon. I have not seen him since, though I miss his good friendship.

Issues Set by God before All

Slowly I came back "into the Spirit," that is, I could, again, hear the Lord speaking to me through the worship and the preaching of the word. There had been a memorial service for Brother Sam at Bowens Mill the first part of June, I believe, but this July was the first full convention after his death. Everyone had many questions, I'm sure.

Buddy Cobb had been right alongside of Brother Sam in anointing, in the preaching of the word, in faithfulness in ministry, and in wise counsel. For that reason everyone was positioned to yield to his leadership inside of a solidly corporate ministry.

At the beginning of a service midway through this convention, Don Stockbridge was leading the worship. By this time I was fully in tune, once again, with the Spirit of God. Brother Don was leading us in a fairly new worship song written by Brother Sam, one with which we were all well-familiar. We were singing it with great joy and confidence. Dancing in the Spirit had already begun in these conventions; we were enthusiastic in worship.

Here are the only words of the song that I can remember now: "Tell to creation – We're not going to die."

Halfway through the singing of this song, Brother Buddy Cobb stepped forward to pause the singing. He said to all (my paraphrase), "You cannot consider not dying until you have first stopped sinning."

Then he suggested that we sing the song in this way: "We're not going to die cause we're not going to sin." We sang it that way, but somehow a spark had vanished from our joy.

What was that? What had just happened?

I cannot give you an account of my life without also giving you an account of the move of God, for the two are intrinsically tied together as my life from age 20 to age 41. My wife grew up in the move fellowship from age 3 on. We were married in community, and our children were born in community.

My purpose in this account is to see the Lord Jesus in every moment of my life, to fill up any remaining holes with the goodness of God, and to draw from this account the determined purpose of God in setting before His Church a testimony regarding what He actually says in the New Testament.

This action of Buddy Cobb became a weight that slowly crushed me over the next nineteen years until that moment in the early months of 1998 when I KNEW that I would never be pleasing God or doing His will. Such a performance was entirely outside of my sphere. When I came to that utter knowing, I thought it was a time of great darkness. I did not know then that the light of Christ was now shining so brightly I could hardly see.

Lester Higgins had preached a word of "Christ our life," a word that was witnessed to by almost all including Sam Fife. There was much agreement between that word and many things Sam Fife taught.

Buddy Cobb preached a word of "Stop sinning first." It certainly sounded "right" to everyone. There was much agreement between that word and many things Sam Fife taught. But there was no agreement between Lester Higgin's word of "Christ our life" and Buddy Cobb's word of "Stop sinning first." The two words were as if from two different planets. In fact, they were the two trees standing before every person and every church, a tree of life, that is, Jesus living inside of us, versus a tree of "know what is right and do it and know what is wrong and stop doing it."

In this several-month period God set before the move fellowship the same choice He set before Adam in the garden and all through the Bible and before every Christian, the same choice He sets before you every moment, dear reader.

And then, in the semi-crisis created by Brother Sam's passing, the move fellowship chose the one and turned away from the other. The move fellowship, without even realizing it, turned away from the revelation of Jesus Christ through us, His body, and back to Calvinism, to full Nicene, that is Roman Catholic Christianity, back to the same belief system held by all Christians in this world. – *Look upon your sin; do not look upon Christ Jesus as your present Salvation in whom alone you live, but only as a "superior" One just beyond your reach.*

I want to give you a simple layout that will help you to understand this choice between two as it happened in the move fellowship.

I have not known any other fellowship that even comes close to the praise and worship we knew in the move. Yet, as I look at the lines we sang, I am astonished at the opposition found in the very words coming out of our mouth. We sang words of great faith; we sang words of longing to draw near without ever doing so, but mostly we sang words of outright unbelief.

Here is a song Brother Sam led us in, with deep connection to a glory just at the door. Consider the deep longing to know God along with the complete refusal that is found in it.

What more can I say, Lord,
What more can I say?
To unveil Your face, Lord,
Bring forth the new day?
That last final word, Lord,
That comes forth from You

Shall open the veil, Lord,
And we shall go through.

We sang the truth, yet we did not believe a word that we sang. Why? Because we did not care for God-Is, but we always wanted God to be something He is not. God says, "I am what I am." We answer, "God, I wish You were something else, something better."

Finally, in closing out this two-year time period that included direct involvement with Sam Fife, I want to show you how I now place the things that he taught. Again, this is vital to any account of my life because you will find things I learned through Sam Fife all through everything I teach now. Yet you will find many things Sam Fife taught that are repudiated with strength all the way through as well.

I understood the difference several years ago when I pulled out one of my favorite Sam Fife messages, "I Will Not Let You Go," and listened to it again. Every "what" Sam Fife presented was the same as what I teach now, and every "how" Sam Fife gave, as to how the "what" of God would be fulfilled in our lives, was the opposite of what I now know is Paul's gospel.

More than that, every wrenching difficulty that persuaded Dan and Joanne Kurtz that it was time to leave can be found inside of Sam Fife's "how." Yet the word that originally drew most into that fellowship was Sam Fife's "what."

As I realize now, the essential "why," out from which everything else must flow, was absent from Sam Fife's teaching. Buddy Cobb supplied a "why" for that fellowship, however, the horrific "why" of John Calvin. Since Buddy Cobb did not restore the typical Christian "what" of "go to heaven or go to hell," there was no "what" at all in his teaching. Nonetheless, the vision of the "what," that is, what God is doing, what the goal of the Christian life is really all about, that we had received from Sam Fife, remained for years in the hearts of many.

When I heard Lester Higgins preach Christ our life, I knew it was a true word. I cannot say, however, that it was a word God was planting in me then. Certainly Jesus lived in my heart, but the wondrous vision of present union with Christ was entirely beyond my reach.

I can tell you exactly what God's purpose for me through the next nineteen years would be. As I sought to know just what God says in His word to me, hiding His word in my heart with all fervency over years, so, under the crushing weight of the serpent's gospel, I would come to the depths of despair expressed by Paul in Romans 7.

Only the lost know salvation. Only those who KNOW they cannot, turn with joy to another Self, the Lord Jesus, now the only Life they are.

This path God set for me was perfect, for me and for you.

Nonetheless, the covenant I made with my God, that He would do what I require, stands. I WILL KNOW my Father in this present age, and I WILL walk with a people who KNOW the Father just as much.

The "How" of Sam Fife and Buddy Cobb	The "Why" of Buddy Cobb, that is, of John Calvin	The "What" of Sam Fife, all of which I also teach
• Die to your self. • Subdue your flesh. • Hear and obey. • Stay under the covering. • Submit to the ministry. • Stop "sinning." • Secure a Christ always just beyond your reach. • Prove that you love.	• God is a moral God, a God knowing good and evil and possessing an inflexible will. • God expects all to obey Him immediately and without question. • God sets the circumstances surrounding each solitary person, to determine if that person will walk in perfect obedience or not. • God loves you – BUT! • God hates what you are.	• The revelation of Jesus Christ through us, His body. • Christ as the Church, Christ community. • Defeating death; setting creation free. • Union with God. • Loving one another. • Christ our life, now. • Eliminate the false goal of "go to heaven or go to hell."

An Important Bit of History

If you were to search out information about Sam Fife, you would find more dark accusation against him than just about anyone.

One thing some like to discover happened in 1965-66, soon after the deliverance of Jane Miller. Sam Fife was deceived by a spirit of self-exaltation. Because he was very bold and because the whole pursuit of his soul was to know God, Sam Fife went fiercely in a wrong direction.

Except that did not last long. God very quickly dropped Sam Fife on his face before Him where he spent an entire year seeking God for His perspective, without preaching anything. After a year, God gave Brother Sam the same understanding of life and the knowledge of God that I also received from God through his preaching.

But God did not release Sam Fife to preach that word without a devastating warning, the same voice I have heard, speaking to him a similar warning that I also have heard. (I paraphrase, though I remember fairly clearly what Brother Sam shared.)

"If you ever turn away from Me again, I will take your life, rather than lose you to darkness. Do not turn away from Me again, My son."

As a result, Sam Fife always gathered a corporate ministry around himself, always kept himself covered, always kept his life as an open book for all to see. He shared these things openly, and I saw first hand the fear of God in which he kept himself.

Those who like to accuse will accuse even without knowing the truth.

Sadly, as I will share later, the hierarchy of ministry that Sam Fife presented to us as our covering became itself twisted because of the missing ingredient, our precious union with Jesus.

I never received anything from Sam Fife as an individual, but rather, all things I embraced came to me out from Scripture and out from the Spirit of God speaking personally to me. These are the things I have kept and now also teach. But God speaks through humans who are in-part. Thus, everything else never was part of me and is not part of what I teach.

You will find me sifting between what was of God and what was not all through my life story.

The picture is from *The Odyssey* played by Armand Assante. Odysseus is shooting an arrow straight through the axe hoops.

[Illustration is referenced on pages 79-80.]

9. Heart with Heart

Remembering the Most Important

As I am writing this unexpected chapter in my life story, I have just returned from a trip to the Nashville, Tennessee area where I taught this word of Christ our life to a small group of people and enjoyed rich fellowship with them.

Nonetheless, my Father and I shared some difficult experiences together in travail for His people. As I continued to ponder the meaning of these things the day after I returned home, the Lord enabled me to see a huge reality of my life through all the years I lived in move community; understanding the truth was like a sharp sword piercing through my soul.

Then I realized I had left out the most important thing God spoke to me as I was enjoying all those experiences at Graham River Farm through the summer and fall of 1977.

I cannot share the story of my life without sharing my experiences with other people and the sometimes wrenchingly difficult things I passed through. And I cannot share my interaction with others in such a way that leaves any shadow of blame upon them.

I now see such a mighty purpose of God for the next nineteen years of my life, greater than anything I could have imagined. I must frame these years, from July of 1979 with my arrival at the little community above Albuquerque, New Mexico to August of 1998 when my family and I left the Blair Valley community and the move, I must frame them a bit differently.

I intend to set forth my soul for the sake of each one with whom I interacted through these years. I intend to win the hearts of many, including those from whom I received the most hurt, confusion, and unending pain. In this chapter, I must set before you exactly what I mean, for you and I are about to walk together through the Holy, and it's best that no accusation of fault be found in your responses as a reader.

Yet, at the same time, there is no profit to any reader unless you can know and understand the reality and meaning of the utter hopelessness into which my soul was cast through those dark and lonely months of January and February, 1998, and the context out from which came the tears of agony through the winter of 2001-02 as the healing of God came to me through John Eldredge's wise counsel, step by terrible step.

The sword that thrust through my soul yesterday was of the same kind as the sword of desperate healing through my years of reading John Eldredge.

During the late summer and early fall of 1977, during my wonderfully romantic experience at Graham River Farm, I heard a word spoken in my spirit and in the heavens around me as I did the various tasks of my days.

I heard, "That the thoughts of many hearts may be revealed." I heard it over and over through many days, "**That the thoughts of many hearts may be revealed. – That the thoughts of many hearts may be revealed.**"

Finally, my curiosity became too great; I needed to know from whence this line came. I searched my Bible until one day I found it – Luke 2:35: "**Yea, a sword shall pierce through thine own soul also, that the thoughts of many hearts may be revealed.**"

This was not God speaking to Mary; this was God speaking to me. I was twenty years old when I heard this word, and it was as painful to me then as it would ever become. Now, forty-two years later, I want to show you exactly what God means.

The Press of God's People

I love community. I love gathering together with God's people. In the midst of the gathering and the back and forth, it would appear to you that I do well. What you would not see is the wrenching difficulty into which all that press of God's people places me.

Part of Father's purpose in this trip to Tennessee was to show me the boundaries of my ministry and calling in practical interaction with others.

God anoints me to write in the early morning hours as I hear Jesus singing in my heart. God anoints me to share that same word with you in every way that I can. God anoints me to fellowship together with those who have embraced the full reality of Christ our only life. And God anoints me to teach inside of a classroom to those who are eager to learn.

What God did not create me for is to share this word face to face with those who have forged a Christian identity that is not Christ our only life.

It is an exercise of love poured-out by which we see Christ Jesus living as each one and by which we impute no consciousness of sins. But it is not an act of blind foolishness. God's people identify themselves by many powerful things that are not real or true.

There is the "I am the pastor" identity that can be unwilling to accept that the gospel of the serpent has been their bottom line in spite of all the "love" that they teach. There is an "I am of the Spirit" identity that has no need for any "Bible word," but that calls its own thoughts as "God speaking" and imposes those thoughts on others as "the word of the Lord." There is the "America is God's country" identity that imagines that the U.S. government has always told the truth or that "God" and "America" are some sort of allies instead of the mortal enemies that they are.

The problem with all human identity derived from "not-Christ" is that the person who identifies him or herself with position or title, membership or country, flag or cause will oppose the Lord Jesus when push comes to shove. They will speak words concerning themselves that are not Christ our life. And the problem with that is a prolonged season of not knowing Father.

Here is the only entrance into Christ. – **That every mouth might be closed, and the entire cosmos brought under judgment before God** (Romans 3:19). As the entrance into Christ, the words "guilty before God" are fully appropriate.

Identifying with anything of our lives in this world WILL block our knowing that we come out from the Pro-Knowing of our Father through the good speaking of Jesus.

When we call our entire life in this world "GUILTY" and close our mouths about ourselves, AND, as we discover the wondrous glory of speaking Christ our only life, then we find that every real part of our entire life story has always been the story of Christ. We have not lost ourselves, but have gained ourselves back in full, true and good.

Justifying one's wrongful actions, on the other hand, works the same as accusing one's self for those actions, that is, it requires the spinning of a false identity.

Those who hold tightly to any former self-identity are still carried by the Lord Jesus all the way through death and into life, they just can't know that yet. Some may not know it for another thousand years. Holding a self-identity separate from "Jesus lives in my heart as every word God speaks through 'Let it be to me,'" is nothing more than the spinning of mental nonsense. It contains nothing real or true or good.

Now, this is not a teaching on "identity," but an attempt to position God's purpose for me and for my entire life story. It is such a relief to me, such joy and peace, to know that God did not design me to interact as a ministry with those who spin untrue "Christian" identities. They belong to Jesus, and He knows exactly what He is doing in their lives. They are not my focus or concern.

Coming to know such a thing, however, is not easy. Yet God did not just turn my heart away from a direction not for me, but, in the same set of circumstances, He turned it towards exactly those relationships He did design me for and for which He anoints me.

Let me explain. I put most of the cost of the trip to Tennessee on my wife's credit card. That means my "ministry" became her debt. Most of the money to cover that cost did not come into our possession until the day after I returned home. Yet it all came in. – But from whom? It came from three individuals who have embraced this word I share and who, far more than that, have walked with me heart with heart for some years.

And in that moment, the Lord made it clear to me, "This is how My Church is built, two walking together as equals, heart with heart."

Fixing People's Problems

I want to talk about the single most harmful thing done to me through all the years I lived in move of God Christian community. My purpose in this letter is to position these most difficult experiences in relating with others, especially with those who were "over me in the Lord." It is my intention to set forth my soul together with Father for the sake of each one of these through my writing of the next nineteen years.

Inside of the Christian experience there are many who see themselves as spiritually mature, or gifted, or called, or anointed, and thus see themselves as sent by God to help those who are less mature or gifted or anointed. They see themselves "above," and their brothers and sisters as specimens or guinea pigs upon which they are to work their superior insight into *What you ought to look like if you were to be like me (I mean like Christ).*

This conceit, coming out of the serpent's self-arrogance and Adam's contempt for others, is fairly common to us all. The only way I have ever known freedom from its entanglement is by the embracing of Christ my only life and by seeing my brother as Jesus living as him.

Yet as an Asperger's man, I have lived a life under the practice of those who are determined to "fix" my problem. Their words ALWAYS increased my difficulty because, even though their words had no connection with anything real inside of me, I did imagine that God was speaking to me through them.

This is the horror of imposing "Christ" on one another instead of seeing Christ with joy as our brother and sister. It creates hell for our victims.

I must share with you my interaction with three individuals on this trip to Tennessee because it was my consideration of what really happened that prepared me for the sword of God piercing my soul in hurt and healing at the same time, the day after I returned.

And out from my sword-pierced soul, I intend to open to you the thoughts of the hearts of many. Actually, I can do that now with one word. What are the heart thoughts of many about to be shown for all to see? I can sum up those thoughts with one word. – "Father."

I hope first to tell you and then to show you exactly what I mean.

I taught my "lessons" four times while in Tennessee, twice on Friday and twice on Saturday. Then, on Sunday morning, we continued sharing around the table in a true Christ-fellowship. It soon became clear that this was God's intention for us that morning. In fact, I was able to share in the flow of Christ with Christ the important things from the lessons for that day. This final gathering was of true hearts desiring to know Christ alone.

There was a couple, man and wife, in attendance in the first session on Friday morning. The brother in whose home the meetings were held opened our time together in the Spirit of Christ. Then the sister began to speak in prophetic utterance, directing the service as she wished, in exuberance, in dance, in outflowing abundance. She quoted from the "gospel of Thomas."

I receive all things as from my Father, so this did not bother me at all. Once I started sharing, several times I connected what I was sharing with what she had shared. I did this to honor Christ as her. After the session she visited with me regarding Asperger's, something shared by a member of her family.

This couple was not at the afternoon session, which is when I shared the true image of God, a Man on His face in the dirt under a cross He could not carry, carrying us inside Himself, carried by Father. The couple did attend the Saturday morning session.

For some reason, I don't really know why, I was not sleeping well. When I stood in front on Saturday morning, it was after two nights of only four-hours sleep, plus all the exercise of non-stop fellowship and interaction. I was doing well inside, but outwardly I was not overly expressive, shall we say. We had a time of praise during which I was definitely not exhibiting outwardly "full freedom in Spirit expression." Yet in all things, I see Father sharing any and all difficulty with me for the sake of His people. This is the deepest faith in God I have ever known, the greatest surrender, and the MOST WONDROUS blessing and goodness.

Sharing heart with Father is my treasure.

After the teaching, as we began to fellowship, the husband said to me that he had seen me in a dream from God the night before. He saw me inside a large wooden crate with thick boards nailed tightly. Then he saw a crowbar tearing off the first of the boards with great difficulty, but it was coming off. He also had the "interpretation," (something one should never do – "Let one speak and another interpret.") His interpretation was that I was penned in a cage and God was about to set me free.

I suffered no temptation whatever to imagine his dream or his interpretation as being "God speaking to me." I had no need to cast those words down, for they simply drifted off into their own nothingness with no help from me.

You can see the vital importance of our speaking BIBLE words as Christ our life. When we hear words that are not Christ, they have no meaning to us. How many times does God say that a believer in Jesus lives inside a cage? And how many times does God say that a believer in Jesus lives only inside of Christ? Never for the first; many, many times for the second.

Yet God does speak of a piece of wood causing problems. Had I been allowed to interpret the dream, I would have done so by God's words. "The wood is only in your eye, my dear brother. The crowbar is removing your wrong seeing so that you may see Christ as He already is."

Then, after we had eaten lunch, I was sitting at the table when the sister began to prophecy over me that I would rise up out of whatever it was she imagined to be "not-Christ" and be "free in the Spirit."

This has happened to me so many times in so many different ways. When I'm in the middle of it, I have no idea what is really going on and so I simply move in graciousness and wisdom of entreaty, which is God's intention anyway. Only later do I begin to understand what was really happening.

And so I was delighting in this sister, in her heart and in her expression. But her words were joining her husband's words in the nothingness that they were.

But in my care for her, I did not want her to continue to speak empty "spiritual" things. I wanted to win her heart. So I stopped her, and in gentleness and with great care, I explained to her Christ living as us. She began to listen. I shared with her that God had forged a treasure inside of me that, if she would know me, would be of inestimable value to her. (I do not remember my exact words.)

She sat down beside me with what looked to me like interest on her face. I refuse to imagine that I can know what is going on inside of any other person – unless they tell me, but I did have the hope that I had placed into her thinking something wonderful she may never have known before, that Christ can be as her AND as me and be very different in expression, yet fully the same Christ, that we can treasure our differences rather than impose ourselves on one another.

These two did not return for any more gatherings.

If I had imagined for one moment that it was "God speaking to me" through that couple, I would have had two options. Option 1 is to pretend with all my might to be what I am not and do what I cannot. Option 2, then, is to imagine that I have fallen short of God when I inevitably fail at being fake. Living inside such thinking is what "hades" means.

I must also mention another man who did not attend the sessions or participate in any fellowship, but with whom I visited briefly early one morning. This brother believes that Christ does live as him and that every thought that flits through his mind is God speaking through him. Jesus does carry this man all the way through, but his thoughts are not God's thoughts.

In the same way, there are many in "spiritual" Christianity who also imagine that, since God has "anointed" them, then the thoughts coming into their minds are God's "prophetic utterance" for this or that person. I realized later that the sister and this other man were identical in practice, though opposite in expression. Yet keep this concept in mind, for this is how the sword of God pierced through my soul after my return.

Now, I want to step aside from these individuals in order to talk about this universal practice in Christian circles, that of imposing our own religious expression on others as if they can be like Christ only if they pretend to be like our "anointed" and "superior" selves.

This was an almost universal practice throughout the move of God fellowship; it is the only possible expression of ministry that can come out from a false hierarchy. Indeed these things are universal to Christianity in this world and are the cause of the name of Jesus being held in contempt by most non-Christians today.

There is another word we use that IS this practice, including what the sister was speaking at me. It's called bullying, and it comes out from complete disrespect.

God's answer is simple. "Receive one another in the same way Jesus receives you."

The next day after I arrived back home, as I was sharing all these things with my wife, she said something I had not known before.

I cannot share my life without sharing my interaction with those who impacted my life for good or for ill. And thus I must bring in now by name an individual who factored in my life in a number of closely personal ways during the last several years I was in that fellowship, Barbara James. Sister Barbara was a traveling ministry who moved in a strong and effective deliverance ministry. She was anointed of the Lord with much wisdom and many good words. Although Sister Barbara is a specific individual, yet, of truth, she stands in for many throughout my years in that fellowship who thought and moved in the same way.

The only thing I ever received from Sister Barbara's input into me was increased confusion with a corresponding decrease in answers. Every word she spoke into me had no meaning to me; her words had no connection with anything real in my heart and life and experience. She always had it wrong.

Yet I believed that her ministry to me, along with all others to whom I had submitted my life, was God to me. And so God became more and more CONFUSION to me.

Maureen told me that Sister Barbara had shared with her that she had been taught and believed that, because she was an anointed ministry in the move of God, then the thoughts coming into her mind were God's thoughts towards this other person and that she should be confident in her "discernment" of them.

If we do not speak Bible words, that is, what God actually says in the gospel, written in our hearts as Christ made personal, our very and only life, then the words and ideas flowing through our minds are NOT God's words at all, no matter how anointed we imagine ourselves to be. The serpent's words RULE in the human and the Christian domain until we learn to speak only what God speaks as Christ Personal as us.

When I compared Sister Barbara's practice with that of the sister in Tennessee, I saw that they were identical. That realization was like a sword splitting my soul apart, that so much that people whom I held in high regard imposed on me as "God," so many things that were just made-up inside their own limited self-knowledge. It was a piercing of great pain that resulted first in great healing and second in determined purpose.

Winning Heart with Heart

I do not want to use this chapter to bring in things that must unfold through the circumstances of the next nineteen years ahead. I want only to position what is real and true along with my determined purpose in every upcoming chapter.

God walks with me through great difficulty, and in it shows me great contrast, so that I might understand, so that I might be able to share with you that which is real and precious. I no longer resist the difficulty, but I am glad that my Father and I together, through our shared difficulty, are enabling His people to know Him.

The Church of God is built in only one way, and that is two together, side by side as on a garden bench, sharing heart with heart. Speaking so-called "prophetic word" or so-called "discernment" at people is building a kingdom, yes; it's just not God's.

More than that, God has NEVER once told anyone what He is doing in the heart and life of another. And He never will. God never tells anyone that "so and so is sinning." If God remembers sin no more, how can He tell you what He does not know?

I do not know what is going on inside of you, what you are, how Jesus is showing Himself to you in your inward person – UNLESS you tell me. And such intimate conversation happens only as we are together, heart with heart, honoring one another with utmost respect.

There is no other Church.

And so, as I write forward from here, I am going to DARE something terrible out from my split-open soul.

I dare to seize every individual person with whom I interacted as mine, to seize them into the knowledge of Father, to seize them into the overflowing abundance of the joy of their Salvation, to seize them into honor and glory and respect forever.

I dare to win their heart.

And I will do so by setting forth my own soul for their sakes, that they and Father might meet together, here, above the Blood, and utterly free of me.

On page 74 is a picture that describes for me what I intend to do. This is a picture of the great test that Penelope set before the false suitors after Odysseus' return home, a test that only the true Odysseus could accomplish, that of stringing the bow of Odysseus and shooting an arrow through a line of axe hoops all the way to the target.

The first diagram below left represents the heart of each person, relating at me from a distance. Notice the wall between the two hearts maintained by the gospel of the serpent – *"Your heart, Christian, is evil. You ought to be like Christ, but you know full well that you are NOT."* Words can be thrown over the wall at one another, but never heart with heart.

The next diagram shows my intention through this recounting of all the interactions of my life. I intend to place my heart out over the heart of each person just enough that the sword of God might pass as that arrow through that place where our true hearts are joined.

Yea, a sword shall pierce through thine own soul also, that the thoughts of many hearts might be revealed.

Notice it says the thoughts of the hearts, not the thoughts of the mind.

And what is the thought of the heart of every believer in Jesus? "Father. – Father with me."

They made the mistake of involving themselves in my life; therefore I have the right to win their hearts for Father alone.

Yet I also realize that this will come in only one way, me and each one, sitting together, sharing heart with heart, in the full respect and honor of true friendship.

Consider the diagram again, not as "romance," but as a shared Hheart with Father, our one point of togetherness, the only Church of Christ.

Few episodes of my life are better at showing the thick wall between two, as created by "Christian" doctrine, than my next year-and-a-half at the little community in the high plains above Albuquerque, New Mexico.

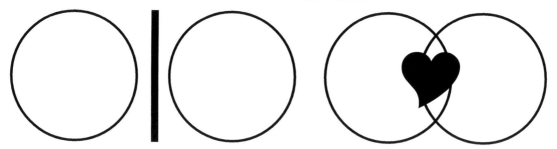

Two divided, then one out over the other with the Father's heart connecting.

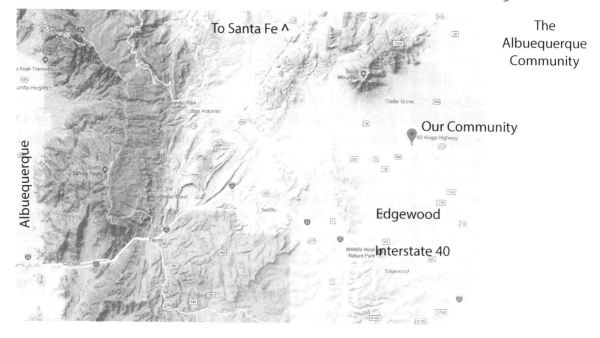

The Albuequerque Community

Our Community

Albuequerque

Edgewood

Interstate 40

10. Heading to New Mexico

July 1979 - December 1980

The Albuquerque Community

During the Bowens Mill Convention, July 1979, I spoke with some of the ministry regarding my leading to be part of the Albuquerque community. Visions were sought which confirmed that leading. Because Jimmy had returned to Oregon, I caught a ride with someone down to Citra for a short visit. Then I bought a week-long Greyhound pass and spent the week zig-zagging across the states on my way back to New Mexico.

The Albuquerque group had purchased 80 acres of dry scrub seven miles north of the town of Edgewood, New Mexico. When I look at the map now, I see no relationship to what the area was then. There was no other house within three miles of us, and Edgewood did not have any real stores, let alone a Walmart Supermart as it does now.

On the opposing page is a map showing the approximate location in relationship with the Sandia Mountains, Interstate 40, and the city of Albuquerque in the Rio Grande valley on the left. 60 Kings Highway seems to be the right spot, but I can hardly tell. No house you see now existed. The street view was taken during April or May, the only time there is a hint of green anywhere.

The adobe house being built was not visible from the road, blocked by a slight rise in the land. It was maybe 150 yards back down a dirt lane that never muddied because it (almost) never rained. The 80 acres were slightly rolling, covered in sparse tumbleweed and the occasional tuft of grass or other weeds. Nothing with a woody stem grew. There was no well or water anywhere near. We got our water with a 300 gallon tank on a small trailer from a place in Edgewood. The property was as opposite from the green paradise of Oregon as one could get.

On the next page is the layout of the adobe house as it was when I arrived, on the left, and then the rooms and walls I added over the next few months on the right. This is a rough guesstimate.

The walls were adobe blocks 10" thick and the roof was southwestern style, almost flat behind a small parapet with rain channels running through for the half dozen or so times it actually rained a bit. Halfway down the lane towards the house there was a cow shed and a chicken run next to each other. To the left of the house was pitched a large green army tent used for storage. The outhouse was already in place to the right and a bit back from the "Boy's Room" and a makeshift shower was set up behind the house. There was a propane stove in the kitchen, otherwise there was no other modern convenience.

But, hey, I loved adventure and this was new and exciting. At no point is a young man deprived with the lack of plumbing, electricity, or anything such.

The three elders in the fellowship when I arrived were Pepi Navarrete, her sister, Helen Rodriguez, both Hispanic, and a sister from Arkansas, Judy Jones. Pepi was the leading elder, although she never lived at the Edgewood "farm." Pepi's husband was not a believer; they lived in the city of Albuquerque with their three children, Tony, Reici, and Roseanna, around my age and a bit younger. Pepi and her children were part of the move fellowship and came out to the farm two or three times a week. It was a forty-mile drive.

Helen, Pepi's sister, did live at the farm. She shared the "Girl's Room" with Judy Jones and her three girls, Jeanie, Susie, and Sarah, who were on the younger side of teenagers. The "Other Room" was occupied by Cherri Kidd, the niece of Judy Jones, who was in her early thirties, along with her son, Chris Kidd, about six or seven years old. In the "Boy's Room" were a young man my age from Denver City, Texas, Richard Hernandez, and another young man from Canton, Ohio, Doug Brown, who was courting Reici Navarrete. There were also two young men, teenagers, there for the summer, who were Rodrigues cousins of the Navarrete's. Pepi and Helen's mother and father were also in the fellow-

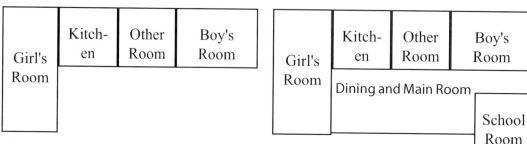

Girl's Room	Kitch- en	Other Room	Boy's Room

The house as it was upon my arrival.

Girl's Room	Kitch- en	Other Room	Boy's Room	Utility Room

Dining and Main Room

School Room	Our Room

The rooms and walls I added.

ship and also lived in Albuquerque. They came out each Sunday for the main service.

As you can see, there were basically two family groups, those related to Sister Pepi and those related to Sister Judy, plus the three of us young men unattached. I would continue to know Judy and her girls and Cheri and Chris Kidd at Blueberry in later years as well as Richard both at Bowens Mill and Blueberry. Richard would be my best man at our wedding.

I joined the young men in the "Boy's Room." The community now consisted of twelve individuals, from age 6 to age 40 something. I was 22.

I will divide my time there into the second six months of 1979, the first six months of 1980 and the final six months of 1980. These were three quite different times for me.

The First Six Months

The first six months of my time with the Albuquerque fellowship was mostly wonderful. I fitted right in and felt at home.

Life in community falls into a simple rhythm. Richard and Doug had jobs off the farm, so they were gone during the day. The ladies did the cooking, and I led the two Rodriguez boys, first in pouring the slab for the addition on the east side of the house, and then in building the adobe walls. Building with adobe blocks is a great idea, one I would use in certain situations. We bought the adobe blocks themselves, but made the mud for the joints from the wind-blown silty dirt on the high end of the property.

I have never eaten better in my life than I did when Cherri Kidd and Judy Jones were the cooks. Because this was mostly an Hispanic community in New Mexico, we ate lots of Mexican food. I learned to enjoy hot peppers – I had no choice. We ate lots of pinto beans.

The Navarrete's had made an agreement with a local grocery store to pick up their barrels of thrown-out stuff each week and replace them with empty barrels. Tony brought the loaded barrels out to the farm in his pickup once a week. It was mostly vegetable waste along with yogurt containers, etc. About half was fine for cooking, the rest went to the chickens. This fresh food made a huge difference for our diet. Cherri and Judy were quite creative with it.

At the end of the summer the Rodriguez boys returned home for school. Around the same time, Roseanna Navarrete moved out to the farm, joining the women in the "girl's room." I remember Doug working some with me, but Richard continued working out most of the time he lived there.

My dad had sent me a letter asking if I could come home for a couple of weeks to help him put the roof on a barn he was building. I flew home in September to do that. It was a good time working with my dad. When I returned to the Albuquerque community, however, I felt as if I were returning to my real home. Roseanna said she was worried that I would not want to come back. I said that this was my home now.

And so Roseanna. Roseanna was everything a young man might desire in a young lady, good-looking and attractive, but most of all, Roseanna loved to talk – to me. I had not talked with girls since first and second grade. Roseanna and I became friends.

The Navarrete's were talkers. When we visited in their home in Albuquerque for a meal, they all talked non-stop through the meal. My family never talked at meals; it was not part of their culture. This was very different for me, but I enjoyed it, at least for the first several months.

We had good services. The Navarrete's and others came out from Albuquerque, or we drove into town to their house. Of course, once our main room was usable, that's where most of the services were held.

We put a roof with skylights on the addition. Then we built the front wall of what became our main room and roofed it. This wall was framed and mostly filled with windows. At first the main room had just a dirt floor, but later I poured a concrete slab. Once the outside was done, I began the long process of plastering, sheetrocking, and painting the interior. At this point I worked mostly by myself.

In October, most of us in the community, along with the Navarrette's, piled into a couple of cars and drove to the Bowens Mill convention in Georgia. I think Cherri and Chris stayed home to tend the place.

Then, sometime in the fall, Doug and Reici decided they were not meant for each other, and Doug returned to Ohio.

In the move fellowship, young men and young women are to remain just brothers and sisters. Any closer friendship was to be witnessed to by the elders first and then closely covered. If a young couple wanted to marry, they must first "walk out a year." This time together, never alone, was not engagement. Engagement came after the year and after it was witnessed by all that this union was of the Lord. I mostly agree with this practice. It gives the couple time to get to know one another without the intru-

sion of sexual feelings. And it allows a couple the chance to discover if they are not suited for each other. It is painful to end a time of walking out a year and to part ways in the view of the whole family, yes, but not devastating like a divorce.

It became apparent that Roseanna and I were more than "brother and sister." We asked the elders about walking out a year. Pepi suggested that we wait until the Lubbock convention in December where we could talk with the ministry of the move first. This was difficult for us.

One time, most of us in the community piled into Richard's large car to drive to Edgewood for something. I happened to swing into the back seat next to Roseanna. Soon, I felt her hand creeping over onto mine. This was nice. Then, after we arrived home, I was the first into the house. Roseanna came right behind me before anyone else. She put her hands around my neck and kissed me. This was very nice. At this point I was "in love."

Roseanna and I spent too much time together. We were asked to back off, but we did not. Finally, the elders called us into a meeting, and Pepi said that she was no longer in favor of talking to the ministry about our relationship, that it should cease. This was impossible for either Roseanna or me.

At that same time the Lord began to speak to me in a certain way. This voice of the Lord would become utterly familiar to me over many years.

The Lord said, "No." This was just a whisper, a knowing inside. A deep wrenching feeling that something was not right.

I rejected the thought utterly.

The "No's" continued, slowly growing louder. I refused them all.

The Flesh

I have two points of move doctrine I want to bring into view because they are pertinent to my time at the Albuquerque community. The first is the doctrine of "the flesh" and the second is "submission."

Pepi was very sharp. She was a strong woman, with a non-supportive husband and with Sam Fife's drive against "the flesh" and disregard of others as her example. I have never had a defense against an angry woman. Pepi "raked me over the coals," more than once. I remember once I was on a ladder trying to teach myself how to mud sheetrock when she came from town. As I heard her voice upon entering the house, I could not move. I was trembling and frightened inside.

Sam Fife and the move had one answer only to internal human difficulty – *"Die, brother, die."* But of course no one ever explained how we were to accomplish such a thing. The reason they did not was because the idea of the human soul "dying" is simply absurd. It's not real, and no one has ever done it. Nonetheless, when *"Just die, Daniel,"* was thrown at me, I thought it was the truth of God. Because I always woke up the next morning, I became more and more confused.

Pepi said that we are friends only with Jesus. We are not "friends" with anyone else, just brethren in the Lord. The result of such thinking, then, creates relationships of form only, and not of heart.

I would refer you to the list of things Sam Fife taught that I also teach now, and the list of things that Sam Fife taught that I teach against.

Sam Fife believed he had restored the missing ingredient, that is, the teaching of the "cross" to the church. He had done nothing more than re-invigorate the cross of Constantine, a cross of unbelief, a cross meant to hack "the flesh" endlessly.

Now, we had the Spirit of the Lord moving among us. We had genuine Christian love. We generally moved in good order together. But there was an unholy trinity, one might say, in our doctrine, common to all Nicene Christianity, that worked always against the truth and against individuals on the inside where it counts.

The first was applying Jeremiah's statement to the believer in Jesus – **"Your heart is deceitful above all things and desperately wicked."** This fixed belief meant that we could never know Father by heart and we could never know one another heart with heart. Yes, Christ was in there somewhere, but the heart of each one was "known to be" evil. We did sing, over and over, **"Create in me a clean heart, Oh God."** But we never once believed that we had received such a thing from God.

The second was the curse of the serpent in the garden – *"You have a life not Christ."* And so this belief, that, *yes, Christ is in us, but so also is a life not-Christ. And that other life "has to die" before the Christ-life in us could ever be truly known,*

The third was that *the will of the Christian and the will of God were utterly and perpetually opposed.*

There was no peace between God and the individual. This belief was pure Calvinism, though no one knew that. This meant that to be "led by the Spirit" was to go contrary to one's own self. This was the doctrinal position out from which "submission to the elders" grew.

We were taught at the Albuquerque community that it was God's will for us to submit to the elders, regardless. Now, this was something Sam Fife had taught, but it was not a belief held by any of the other ministry in the move fellowship. Others were clear that if you were asked to do something you considered to be wrong, then "submission" was not of the Lord.

Nonetheless, this grappling with "submitting to the elders" was a huge deal, something I did not come to terms with successfully during my time in New Mexico.

But, as you can see, calling your own heart and your brother's heart "evil" is to drive out any knowledge of Father with us, Father at home. Believing that we have a life not-Christ that must yet "die" meant that we could never really know Jesus Sent into us, now our only life. In some ways, though, the worst of all was the human will always at war against God's "will." This kept us from knowing any actual and personal relationship with the Spirit.

The belief in an evil heart is anti-Father. The belief in a life not-Christ is anti-Christ. And the belief in a war of wills is anti-Spirit. And these three have ruled in God's church for nearly 2000 years.

Now, none of this is real. These are all just mental ideas that cannot prevent the Lord Jesus from living as each one who belongs to Him, nor can they prevent the Spirit from moving among us. God was with us because of the Blood of His Son, not because we *"had it right,"* as we imagined. What these false ideas did, however, is they prevented us from knowing the glorious Salvation in which we already lived.

But the other thing they did was prevent us from ever knowing one another. There was good relationship and Christian love in the move, but, for the most part, no friendship. The idea of knowing one another's heart or asking someone what they were feeling deep inside, those ideas never existed. We were lonely ships passing each other in the dark and in the fog.

In December, we went to the Lubbock convention, held during the Christmas break. This was my first Lubbock convention. Pepi did not talk with the ministry about Roseanna and me.

The Second Six Months

Roseanna and I were now in a quiet and muffled rebellion. We tried not to spend too much time together, but we could not let our relationship go. The "No's" inside continued. Slowly, they began to limit my ability to speak. This was not a problem at first because Roseanna had always done most of the talking.

I must confess that I have never really looked at this situation with the eyes of an adult and with the care over a community of precious brethren. Roseanna and I had created a real difficulty for the three elders of the community and for all the others as well. I am feeling a bit ashamed of myself right now, something that is right to feel from time to time.

I was wrong in my conduct, and I would ask those who lived there with us to forgive me.

From my side of things, I had wanted to be married since I was twelve, yet I could not talk with any girl. Roseanna talked with me, joyously and comfortably. She was very attractive to me. Emotionally, I could not draw back. This relationship filled an empty space inside of me. I held to that deep emotional sense, even against the ever-growing voice of my spirit saying, "No."

This relationship was not the whole of our life, however, and so I want to continue with life at the Albuquerque farm.

Because there were so few of us, we became close. Once, probably in January, we went up onto Sandia mountain to play in the snow and to look out over the crest to the city of Albuquerque below. This was a good and fun time.

Sometime in here Lester Higgins came through. He shared his word of Christ our life, but he did so in sorrow. I knew he was speaking the truth, and I longed to know what it meant, but such a word was far away from me. I could not know it. He went on, and I never heard him again.

During this time period I worked for a couple of months framing houses with a crew of men in the area just to the west of us at the base of Sandia mountain. This job was okay; I do not now remember why it ended.

I finished the "school room" in the addition first. A family from Clovis, New Mexico had sent their two children, Matthew and Naomi Sanchez, of junior high age, to the community for school. Roseanna taught them as well as Chris Kidd and Sarah and Suzie Jones. Sister Judy was not much on formal education.

Richard and I, then, shared the new bedroom in the front right corner of the house.

Cherri Kidd's mother was an elder at the Blueberry Community in northern British Columbia. In February, for reasons not shared with us, she and Chris headed north to Blueberry. Their leaving left a big hole in our community.

Once, as I was quietly working, minding my own business, a strange thought entered my mind. I thought, "These other people are just like me inside." That was the most astonishing thing I had ever imagined. It was so foreign and so absurd that I immediately threw it out. I did not know or understand other people. When I learned that I was Asperger's, the official definitions explained that my "problem" was an inability to read "social cues." That's only a little bit true. Most people don't bother to know other people inside their bubble of self, and most don't care. Most succeed because they are gifted at pretending they know something when they are actually bluffing completely. Asperger's are no good at pretending and are among the few who begin to wonder about the possibility that other people are real.

But things were not going well for me. I was confused and lonely. I was clinging to a relationship with Roseanna that the elders and the witness of my own spirit were against. At one point I remember trying to explain something about myself to Roseanna. She understood it wrongly and shared how she understood it with the elders. Up until then, Sister Judy had been somewhat sympathetic towards me, but now her face was hostile. No one asked me; such a thing was not done.

The relationships of the community were becoming strained. I thought for sure that it was all my fault. Then, probably in March, an older couple with a young son came to visit from the Lubbock community, George and Freddie Young. They were thinking of moving to the Albuquerque community and wanted to check it out. They had lived for some years in the move communities in the jungles of Columbia in South America.

Brother George was a wonderful man, filled with a vision for the community and many good ideas. He was like a breath of fresh air to me. I worked together with him to rebuild the engine of Sister Judy's 1968 Mustang. That was the only time before or since that I enjoyed working mechanics. He had the idea of building houses on the front of our property next to the road and selling them as a way of earning an income.

But Brother George also knew things about the community and the relationships among the three elders that I knew nothing about. When he asked me for my view of things, I discovered that my growing sense that something was wrong was not something wrong with me. That there was, actually something quite wrong with the functioning of the community. I had become discouraged, so this knowledge was a tremendous relief.

The Young's were there for a couple of weeks before they went back to Lubbock. They did not return.

A young woman, Mary, from the small move fellowship in Denver City, Texas, came to live with us at the farm around this time, however. She was a fresh addition to our strained community.

One day in early April, Judy and Helen had gone into town for an elder's meeting with Pepi. Long before we expected them back, Judy came hurling down the drive in a trail of dust. She slammed to a stop, got out of the car, and shouted to her three girls, "Pack your stuff." Within an hour they were gone, following Cherri to Blueberry. They must have flown because Judy left her Mustang in town until she could get it later. Someone drove it back to the farm for us to keep.

I do not know why Judy left. I do know that Pepi was a very controlling person, but I do not know any of the particulars. I learned later that after she arrived at Blueberry, she spent time with the leading ministry there, Brother John Clarke, one of the apostolic ministries of the fellowship, expressing her concern, particularly for Richard, Mary, and myself. Judy was firmly convinced that the Albuquerque community should be closed.

Then, also in April, several piled into one car and we went to the April Bowens Mill convention. At this convention I slept in an addition to the men's bathroom that had been built, but into which the plumbing fixtures had not yet been installed. It served as a "men's dorm" for the moment. The result was that I hardly slept since the bathroom on the other side of the wall was used through the night by men talking.

After the convention, Pepi wanted to leave right away. I asked that we wait one more night, so that I could sleep in order to be able to drive. She refused; we left that afternoon with the intention of driving through the night since we had three or four drivers. I was too sleepy, however, to take my place at the wheel except for less than an hour each time, maybe, before I had to trade with someone. It was a long and strained drive home. Finally, somewhere in eastern New Mexico, we simply had to stop alongside the road so that all could sleep. The result was that, in the end, the time Pepi thought we would save was wasted.

Helen was now the only elder at the farm. Helen was much more quiet of a person than her sister, Pepi. Helen would have sided with Pepi, of course, but I never had any difficulties with her. My memory of my relationship with Helen is neither good nor bad. But having just one elder was not a good situation. Nothing was shared with us, but one day, probably in May, another elder showed up to be part of the community, a Sister Hilda from McAllen, Texas. She was cheerful and strong, but we knew little about her.

Roseanna had continued at the community because of her teaching obligations. But in early June, with her task completed, she moved back to town with her family. Matthew and Naomi Sanchez returned home to Clovis. I would know them in later years because Matthew became my brother-in-law.

The Final Six Months

There were now just five of us at the Albuquerque farm, Helen Rodriguez and Sister Hilda were the elders, and then Richard, Mary, and myself, their "flock." A dull numbness settled over our community experience.

I want to bring in a few more things that were part of my life at the Albuquerque community that spanned more time than these last few months. First, early on, I had taken on the care of the farm animals. We had a couple of cows and a flock of chickens. We also raised a pig for meat.

Sometime in the spring we prepared to butcher the pig. I had helped in the butcher shop at Graham River, so I had some idea of what to do. Nonetheless, I needed Richard to help me and since he worked out, Sunday was the only time we could do it. For that reason, even though the Sunday service was in progress, Richard and I were released to begin the job.

Pigs are smart. They know when their time is up. Richard wanted to do the job there at the pen; I wanted to do it up at the house so that we would not have to drag a heavy carcass up there. I tried to kill the pig behind the house by shooting it in the brain. It's hard to kill a pig with a bullet because their brain is not where you think it should be. The pig took the bullet and ran. I ran after it with a knife, and with Richard running behind me. The pig, with us behind, ran right by the large picture window filled with astonished faces looking out wandering what on earth we were doing. Finally, back behind the house I managed to grab the pig and kill it with the knife. Needless to say, the experience was awful and lessened my enjoyment of butchering.

But the cow stall was a place of refuge for me. Whenever I needed a retreat, I would go there and sit in the hay against the wall with the cows. Only there could I find peace.

Also, probably in the spring, we had a bonfire and a picnic outside in front of the house. All the time we were around the fire, enjoying the food and talking, I felt that something important was missing from our experience. Only later did I realize what it was – there was no sound of water running over rocks. In fact the nearest running water of any kind was the Rio Grande, 50 miles away and dry several months of the year.

It rained a bit in April and May. For a few weeks the land turned a slight shade of green. Our property was situated just so that any thundercloud dropping rain would move across to the south of us or to the west of us or to the north of us or to the east of us, but never over us. And when it did rain, the top quarter inch got wet. Just beneath of that, the dirt remained dry dust.

By the summer of 1980, I could no longer bear to lift up my eyes. It was brown everywhere. There was no water. I never want to live in a land without water again.

There had been a small garden behind the house the summer before. I enlarged it, and we added another garden in front of the house. I spent long hours working in the garden, all by hand. I double dug everything and made raised beds in both gardens. Planting the garden was fun. I remember that Roseanna was still there for that. We had to water by hand, making trips a bit more often out to Edgewood to fill the water trailer.

I dreamed of having a hose with water coming out. You have no idea just how valuable such a thing really is. I would have watered everything all day long.

We had also heard that the move fellowship had started a college with one of the branches being at the Blueberry Community. I imagined that I would never have the opportunity to go to such a thing, but I thirsted for knowledge so deeply that I dreamed of offering my services as a builder just to be near such a wondrous thing.

The last six months was a time of great personal sorrow for me. I wanted to stucco our adobe house. Pepi asked if I had ever stuccoed before. I said, "No, but I can quickly learn how on the back wall." (I had never mudded sheetrock before, but that task had come earlier.) She said, "No, you can't, since you don't know what you're doing." This was the only time in years of experience that "not knowing what I was doing" ever stopped me from being successful in any construction task.

We wanted to build a small adobe shed in order to raise some rabbits. Pepi said, "Not until all the money comes in for the entire project." Before then, as I had worked on the house addition, money had been donated, a bit at a time just as we needed. Now, all donations ceased.

I put everything into our garden. Sometime in the late spring, Pepi announced that they could no longer justify the time and effort to bring the barrels of fresh produce out to the farm. With Judy and Cherri gone, our eating became very plain.

I had two large rows of chili peppers growing in the back garden. They were thick and green and loaded with growing peppers. When they were big enough, we harvested a few. They had no heat. Helen said to me, "It's okay, Daniel. It's okay." No heat in the peppers meant they could not be eaten. Eating the peppers as fresh food was unknown. All of that bountiful harvest went into the compost.

I grew a nice bed of Swiss Chard. I love Swiss Chard. When it was ready, I brought some in to Sister Hilda. She had never heard of Swiss Chard. I explained to her carefully how simple it was to prepare, but it did not show up on the table that evening. The next morning I found the Swiss Chard in the compost bucket. Nothing else was said, but we ate no Swiss Chard. For years after the memory of that Swiss Chard thrown out always brought tears of sorrow to my eyes.

The truth is, in spite of all my work, we ate very little from the garden. I cannot blame Helen or Sister Hilda, for that was all they knew.

For six months we ate pinto beans, breakfast, lunch, and supper. Once in awhile we had liver, the only protein because it was cheap. The truth is, if one had to eat only one kind of food of necessity, then pinto beans are a great choice. I did enjoy my last plate of them as much as the first.

Mary became very sad because she had no companions, only two older ladies who were both elders. I sorrowed for her. I wanted Richard to help me with some of the work, but he always had a job. During that summer the job he had ceased, and he spent the next few weeks at home. Now I had plenty of help but we had no money, so it benefitted nothing. Richard's meagre earnings had been all we had.

I do not remember what happened that pressed me beyond measure. But something did. There was to be a meeting in town that evening. Everyone else was in town; I was to come in later in Judy's Mustang. Again, I don't remember the circumstances, but the rift between Pepi and I had become complete. I was ready to call it quits. On my way into Albuquerque that afternoon, I realized that I could simply keep on driving. Judy wanted to sell her car; she would have no problem selling it to me. I could go home to Oregon.

I was caught between two all the way into town. Going home to Oregon meant not knowing God. Community meant knowing God. My decision was firm and final.

But I did not go to the Navarrete house, rather to someone else's house to drop off the Mustang. I did not want to go to the meeting at the Navarrete's. I communicated that to Roseanna on the phone. Pepi came to get me. I submitted quietly and climbed in her car. All the way to her house, my heart longed for her to ask me what was wrong. She never said a word; I assumed, rightly or wrongly, that she did not care.

One day in late August, Pepi came out for an elder's meeting. After closeting themselves together

for an hour or two, the three elders called the three of us non-elders, Richard, Mary, and myself, into the meeting. "We have no money for the community," Pepi announced, "and we have decided that you all will go out and get jobs to earn it."

Richard and I got jobs with a carpet cleaning company in Albuquerque. Mary also announced finding work in Edgewood. Pepi immediately chewed her out for her arrogance. She was too "immature" to go out to work. I knew how devastating this blow was to Mary, how wrong. But Richard and I were gone most of the day; we did not know the lonely months she now suffered.

Mary, oh Mary, please forgive us for the great wrong we did to you.

I lasted only a couple of weeks cleaning carpets. The job was contrary to me in more ways than one. I then found work with a construction crew framing houses in Albuquerque. Richard stayed on cleaning carpets for awhile until he got a job working with Mr. Navarrete installing carpet.

The one bright spot through this time was my friendship with Richard. It was a forty-five-minute drive each way to town and back. We had much time for good fellowship. Contrary to move doctrine or experience, we became good friends and remained so for years.

Below is a picture of Richard and me together.

I was not sleeping well. I wondered if part of the reason was that I was eating stuff not good for me, specifically Dr. Pepper's. But natural health was considered "of the devil" in the move. Pepi assured me that we could eat candy bars and drink coke and God would bless the food to our bodies. I thought why not get the banana and the orange juice right next to it, but I dared not say such a thing. I was not able to stop drinking Dr. Pepper's.

Sometimes it was more convenient for Richard and me to spend the night at the Navarrete's on foamies on the floor rather than the long drive back to the farm. That did not last long. The furnace in the house going off and on kept me awake. Because I could not sleep, I had a really hard time at work.

Relationships became more strained.

Roseanna and I still related together in hopes of things working out. One day through this time, however, I was in their house for a meal. My lack of talking at the table had become, in their minds, a fleshy bondage. Roseanna wanted to talk to me before the meal, so we sat in a private room together. She insisted that I talk with her, that I say something, or our relationship would be over. I cannot tell you how much I want to say anything, just one word. But no matter how I strained, no word came out. I could not speak. The inward "No" had become impossible.

Roseanna rose up angrily and left the room. I could do nothing. Our relationship was over.

My relationships with the men on the construction site were not good. One day I had enough and quit. Pepi got on the phone with one of the move ministries who advised her that I needed to go back to work. She insisted, and so I submitted, humbled myself, and asked for my job back. It was just a few more weeks until the Lubbock convention.

One final note. My mom and dad came down to New Mexico to visit me at the Albuquerque community. I had a good time with them; in fact, this was the first time that I actually conversed with my father side by side as adults and the first time he actually shared with me things about himself.

Helen returned to town before the Lubbock convention. Mary and Sister Hilda left. Both would return to their home towns. Richard and I were the last ones at the Albuquerque farm, for a couple days, I think. Finally, we boarded up the door and drove away. Our community had failed.

We spent a couple of days at Richard's home in Denver City, Texas before going on to the Lubbock convention.

It was there that I observed the faces of Pepi, Hilda, and Helen after they had spent a session with the leading ministries of the move fellowship, including John Clarke. I do not know what was said to them, but the Albuquerque community was closed down. From their faces, I got the idea that messing with God's people was simply not the thing to do.

Pepi Navarrete

What can I say about Pepi Navarrete? I have known many bullies in my life, male and female. Female bullies are different from male bullies; Pepi left me far more "shredded" inside than any other before or since.

I also know this, that having only women elders in charge was out of balance. Having only men elders would be imbalanced on the other side. God gave mothers and fathers to families because both are needed. In my experience women "in charge" have been more controlling than men.

But I do not pretend to know or to judge what Pepi was inside. I know she loved the Lord; I know she moved in the anointing of the Spirit; I know she believed that she was moving in the love of God.

I have never looked closely at this time before. I never knew that my deepest sorrow was for Mary. I had not realized just how much difficulty my infatuation with Roseanna was causing everyone.

Where is the blame? I place the blame entirely upon a wicked theology, Nicene thinking made hyper by John Calvin, a theology that keeps Father far away from our hearts, a theology that keeps us from knowing Jesus now our only life, a theology that prevents us from walking in the confidence of our Salvation, our every step embedded in God's tender regard for us. – **It is an enemy who has done this.**

But my Father is with me now, and with Him, I have the authority of His Mercy Seat, that is, my own heart.

And so, as I shared in the last letter, there is no question in my mind that Pepi loved the Lord. Of course she did. And that is all I need to draw my heart out over hers right now just enough to seize her into God and into His throne.

"Father, You and I together draw Pepi Navarrete into my heart, a heart I now share fully with You and You with me. You and I together, Father, draw Pepi into love, here just above the Blood of Your Son sprinkled fully upon me. Father, I love Pepi, with Your own out-poured love, and I set her and You together completely free of me, that You might rise with her into all newness of life.

"Pepi belongs to You, Father, and with the Lord Jesus, I give You and her place to meet together in my own out-poured soul, set forth for her. I break all darkness and the ignorance of Your Salvation, and I release Pepi into the glorious liberty You have given to me. She belongs to You, and in joy, I see her returned back to me as a dear friend forever.

"And Father, let us not leave out Helen and Sister Hilda, Judy Jones and Cherri, and especially Mary, and all the children. You and I together, Father, draw each one of them as well, by name, into our shared Hheart. And we release each one into the knowledge of the JOY of Your Salvation, the only place they live or have ever lived.

"And Roseanna. Father, I thank You that I live in Your forgiveness for not hearing Your voice in my heart. Father, I wronged her. Roseanna, I ask for your forgiveness as well. Father, I go back with Jesus to those moments. I see Him living there as me, sharing all things with me, responsible for all that I am and was. I place my desire for a woman's love and all my loneliness and inability into You, Lord Jesus. You were sharing Yourself with me, yes, but I did not understand or know what to do.

"Father, I do not know about drawing Roseanna into my heart, for she does not belong to me, yet I do know how much You care for her and that You utterly carry her through all as well. I release her into You, Lord Jesus, into Your most capable hands. You are her life and her Salvation.

"Father, I ask that You seal all these things inside my heart, that You finish all You intend inside of me, that You heal the broken places and make smooth the rough ways. Father, I believe that I have received all that I ask. Thank you, my Jesus, thank You, with all my heart."

Maps and Pictures of Bowens Mill.

Below: **The Tabernacle at the Ridge**

Above: **The Ridge Office.** - My second favorite building I built, with me in front.

Below: **An Outline of the Bowens Mill Property.** The non-highway boundaries of the property are approximate. It was, I believe, about 480 acres.

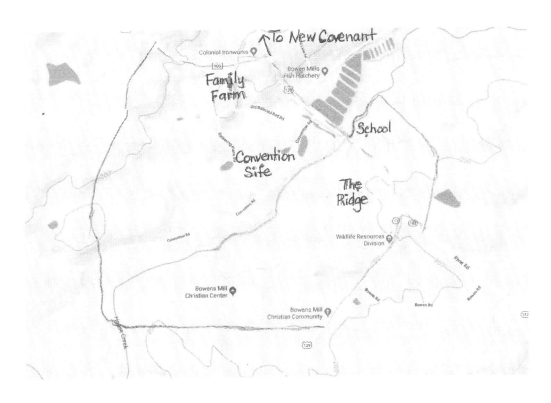

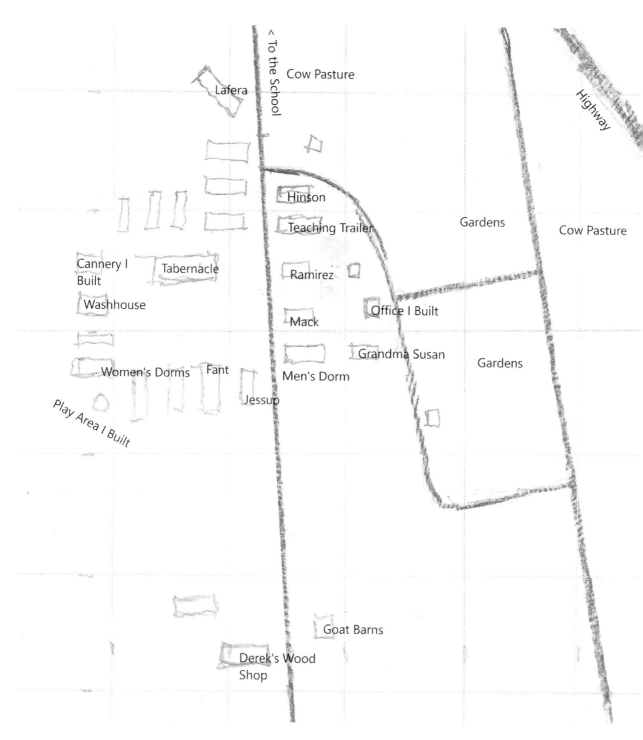

A Rough Outline of the Ridge.

11. Back to Bowens Mill

January 1981 - September 1982

I Give You Thanks

I have always had an odd notion in my awareness of myself. I do not know if it is shared by others or if I'm just weird. I have always had the idea that I WILL BE giving an account of my life face to Face before the Almighty.

Now that union with the Lord Jesus has turned me completely around, I see what that means from a different viewpoint. Giving an account does not disappear; on the contrary, giving an account of our life is what we do every moment. There is only one question – how do we call our life? By Christ? Or by loss and ruin and failed ambition?

I now understand the judgment of God, that **every knee should bow and that every tongue should speak the Lord Jesus**. It means that every individual person, including you, dear reader, will give a detailed account of your life, just as I am doing, you will bring every moment into the Lord Jesus, and you will give thanks.

Every hidden thing will be brought out for all to see and all will call themselves by Christ in that moment, against all memory of accusation and regardless of any wicked or deceitful action, and all will give thanks. Those who give thanks now are glorious beyond all conception, kept utterly inside of Father's Heart.

"Father, I give You thanks for my time with the Albuquerque community. I give you thanks for every moment there and for each one with whom I interacted. Father, I give you thanks that I have been able to set forth this time of my life for all to see, in spite of any present emotional awfulness and sorrow. I give You thanks that You have sealed my heart in You.

"And Father, I give You thanks beforehand for the road just ahead. I could not travel this road, I could not give an account except You, my Father, were utterly with me in all things, as You are."

Returning to Bowens Mill

Before we went to the Lubbock convention, Pepi suggested to me that I consider Bowens Mill as a destination after the farm closed. At Lubbock, I met with an elder from Bowens Mill by the name of Claude Mack. It was arranged that I would catch a ride back to Bowens Mill and join the community there. On the drive, as we entered Arkansas, I saw sprigs of green grass coming up across the fields as far as the eye could see. I wept for the beauty of green.

I arrived at Bowens Mill in the first week of January, 1981. I was 24-years old. This would be my home for four-and-a-half years. I had simply followed where I was directed.

In my letter, "Into the South," I gave you a picture of the original Bowens Mill buildings as they appear today. In this letter, I want to give you two maps; the first is the larger Bowens Mill property. "Bowens Mill" had become three different communities living in conjunction with each other: the Ridge, the Family farm, and New Covenant, two miles to the northwest. The second map is the Ridge

There had been two purposes in the people who had arrived at the Bowens Mill property from the start. On the one hand were the many coming from the Sapa, Mississippi care and teaching community who desired to continue with that ministry. On the other hand were those who came to be part of taking care of the newly-built convention center and who did not wish to live in the stricter environment of a "deliverance" community.

Each of these three communities functioned as their own unit, but we all gathered together twice a week for the main services. The elders of the three communities also met regularly to discuss common issues, including the larger property and the school. And so the Bowens Mill property itself became divided by use into four distinct areas, the Ridge, the school (the original buildings across the road), the convention site, and the Family farm.

I am dividing my time at Bowens Mill basically into three parts. The first is from January of 1981 until September of 1982, a time of precious anointing and fruitful ministry. The second is from October of 1982 to December of 1983, a time of growing loneliness. The third, then, is from January of 1984 until June of 1985 during which I discovered a new song for which God had created me, yet in the midst of great difficulty.

The Ridge

On the south side of the road from the original Bowens Mill buildings was a small slope up for a couple hundred yards and then a flat space for another couple hundred yards before dipping down again. On this "ridge," there had been an old CCC camp building in great disrepair. This building was "redeemed" and turned into the Tabernacle of what then became the Care and Teaching community at Bowens Mill, commonly referred to as "The Ridge."

The Care and Teaching community focused its ministry on those who had various mental or emotional needs, providing them with a structured environment, that they might be restored to a sound mind. The number of people needing some sort of care at any given time might have been between 10 and 20. The majority at the Ridge were there either to minister as caregivers or were family members or just chose to live in that community.

When I arrived in January of 1981, there were a little under one hundred people living at the Ridge in rows of trailers lined up around the Tabernacle. At that time there were only two fixed buildings, the Tabernacle and a washhouse just behind it.

The map on page 92 is an outline of the Ridge, my home for the next several years. Again, the outlines of things are approximate. There were more trailers than I have shown, I do not have an exact layout to copy.

I have placed the names of people in some of the trailer locations. The primary elders at the Ridge were John and Bambi Hinson who spent about half their time here and half their time at the Citra community. Then there were Jim and Joyce Fant, originally from Greenville, Mississippi, and Claude and Roberta Mack as well as Roberta's mother, Susan Jacobsen, from California. There was Abel Ramirez from Mexico, Margaret Crowson from Texas, and Jim Messick from Maryland who moved there with his wife not long after I arrived.

The Ridge provided a three-month teaching for all new-comers called "the Basics," taught by Jim Fant. Brother Jim was a southern gentleman of great dignity and worth. The teaching time took up the whole morning, so I was on the work schedule only in the afternoons and on Saturday. Because I reacted to the great change in climate from all-dry to all-wet, I came down with the "flu" a number of times the first three months and missed quite a number of teaching days. Brother Jim thought I should sit through the teaching a second time in order to receive what I had missed. For that reason, I spent my first six months at the Ridge in the teaching trailer listening to Brother Jim teach "the Basics."

There was an interesting distinction of "doctrine" held by Jim Fant and John Hinson versus the rest of the ministry in the move. Those two believed and taught that we are secure in our salvation, whereas Buddy Cobb presented the "God" of John Calvin who was ready to cast off anyone at the drop of a hat. In contrast, the Ridge environment was much more strict and disciplined whereas other communities moved in a more real level of grace. This strictness was ostensibly for the sake of those in need; the problem is that it becomes a theology or way of thinking in itself.

I learned many good things from Brother Jim, but the most important was his statement, repeated often, "Justify God in all things." That line strengthened my own heart in the seed God had planted in me at age fifteen – to give thanks. It would bear critical fruit in the years ahead.

Immediately upon my arrival at the Ridge, I was given a bed at the back of the men's dorm trailer, on the bottom bunk. That would be my bed for the next 4 ½ years. There were about a dozen men living in the men's dorm after my arrival. We would have up to 15 in there at the most, but twelve was still crowded. The trailer was twelve feet by eighty, not new. In the back bedroom where I was were three bunks, that is, six men. In the middle room was a bunk, open to the hall. In the front room was another bunk. Someone slept on the couch in the living room and there was another bed in what had been the kitchen. I was given a small closet next to the front door.

In the front room were David Troshin and Peter Honsalek. Peter was the dorm example at that time. He was the cousin of the Mack girls; Sister Susan was also his grandmother. David Troshin was – how shall I describe David Troshin? I would bear with this man for four years. He was in-part a child, yet utterly conceited, yet simple, yet cunningly deceitful. He was, to put it mildly, a difficult man with few if any redeeming qualities. He was originally from California, having connected with the move through the same group as the Mack's. But he was at the Ridge for care; otherwise he would have been out on the street or in prison. I walked closely with and worked with this man for four years, yet nothing bore fruit and no real connection was ever made. You will understand more of why I am getting side-tracked here as we go forward. But David Troshin received a sizable monthly disability income from the government, and his money had bought the trailer, so he had the front bedroom and bath. I must add that this was at least one redeeming quality in David, that he was always generous, and that generosity was reasonably real.

In the middle bunks were Lebron Tucker and Mark Santora. Lebron had been at the Sapa farm. He was a tall, strong, good-natured man who had bad epileptic seizures often. Mark was from Jacksonville, Florida. He was also tall and strong. He had been in a car accident as a teenager and had become stiff, difficult, and often angry. His parents had sent him to the Ridge as a "last hope." Mark was a handful. He conflicted with David Troshin more than any.

Around fifty different men spent time living in the men's dorm during the years I was there; I cannot remember them all. I will name a few more as time goes on, those with whom I was most involved.

Peter Honsalek was walking out a year with Patti Landis, from southern Florida, so after a few months he stepped aside from being the dorm example and moved to a smaller men's trailer. The elders chose John King, the son of Margaret Crowson, to replace him. John King lasted a month before he was ready to call it quits and leave the Ridge.

Right next to our trailer on the north side, parallel to us was a much smaller trailer in which lived Claude and Roberta Mack. Then, directly behind our trailer, in the same "row," was a smaller trailer, an Airstream, in which lived Susan Jacobsen, Roberta's mother. In the trailer with Sister Susan were Patti Landis, and the three Mack girls, Lois, Jessica, and Maureen. Lois is less than a year younger than me, so when I arrived, she would have been 23, Maureen was 18 and that would have put Jessica at 21.

The "Mack girls" seemed to me to be quite out of my league.

The trailers were mostly surrounded by pine trees throughout the community. There were plenty of open spaces as well. The setting felt sheltered and warm. We had two meetings a week with the other two communities, Wednesday evening and Sunday morning. Those meetings were held over the years either in the school building across the road or in the Family Farm or New Covenant Tabernacles, or in the large convention Tabernacle. I remember the various meeting places well, but just not when. Because there were over three hundred people in all three communities, the preaching was varied and good. Because Bowens Mill was the convention center three times a year, we had many leading ministries stopping by to preach in the regular services.

The Ridge Tabernacle was too small to hold the larger gathering. For us, it was crowded, with one aisle down the middle and a row of tables on each side. We had all three meals together in the Tabernacle as well as additional Ridge meetings through the week.

I also want to mention a sister who, though not an elder, was very much a part of the life and "flavor" of the Ridge and that is Laurie Pettis, not yet married to Don Pettis when I first arrived, but their marriage, I think, was my first experience of a move wedding. Laurie was blind from the medical practice in the early fifties of putting pre-mature babies into a high-oxygen tent. This created many blind children and was soon brought to a severe halt. Laurie was gifted in singing and in piano playing and many anointed songs flowed out from her. She often led us in rousing worship and often was asked to sing duets with another blind girl at the Ridge.

There are a few more things that will give a further perspective on our life at the Ridge. They had a number of milk cows, so I was soon part of the milking team. The Ridge also had a large goat program, overseen by Roberta Mack. The wash was all done by the sisters in the wash house behind the Tabernacle, so we had to put our names on every piece of clothing. The Ridge had large and bountiful gardens, with a number of the men working in them. A few of the men maintained regular jobs outside of the community. The children would all troop down to the school house across the highway each morning and return in the middle of the afternoon.

Although the sisters did most of the cooking, there was a rotating shift that included the men on Sunday mornings. I was part of the Sunday cook crew on occasion.

Finally, there was the nightwatch. Because the Sapa community had been much more a "deliverance" community, and because it was so large, they had instituted a nightwatch. In that same thinking, the nightwatch was maintained at the Ridge. That meant two men spent the night awake, mostly sitting in the Tabernacle, but making regular rounds throughout the community buildings. Married men were not part of that duty, so we single men served one night a week on nightwatch. We would sleep, then, through the morning of the next day. Nightwatch was a regular, mildly unpleasant part of my life until I started teaching school in January of 1984. There were at least a few times when having a nightwatch did forestall difficult situations. During the nightwatch, I spent much time in many and varied Bible studies.

My First Construction Tasks

Abel Ramirez was the elder in charge of the men's dorm and the men's work. In the same line, Brother Jim was the teacher and lead elder; his wife, Sister Joyce, was in charge of the kitchen. Roberta Mack covered the women's dorms and the goat program. Claude covered those men who did maintenance tasks, electrical and mechanical, and Jim Messick was in charge of the gardens.

Because I was in the men's dorm and a builder, I immediately connected with Abel Ramirez during my afternoons. Abel was a wonderful man, in his mid-thirties at that time. He was gentle and patient, caring and anointed to care. I was soon at work constructing a small carpenter shop out on one of the entry lanes.

Because I was a builder willing to take the initiative on any task, I was soon marked, however, for the building needs at the convention site. A few weeks before the April convention in 1981, the Ridge elders agreed to release me to lead the construction of a large building for nursing mothers and little children at the convention site, just across the road from the large Tabernacle. A couple of other men from the Ridge, probably including Lebron Tucker, who was a good construction hand, joined with me, but at the same time, I worked with men from the other communities. We had ten days to build the entire building from start to finish. We succeeded, having it ready for little ones and mothers the day the convention started. In fact, men from elsewhere in the country came in the evening before to lay the carpets.

It was while we were building the nursery that I discovered a wonderful gift. I have never been much for "praying," my time on my knees being spent thinking about everything pressing me. But it was there on my knees, thinking about an impossible construction dilemma that the simple answer came to me. This would be a regular occasion through the years. The Lord faithfully anointed me to lead these construction crews.

I don't remember things well enough to give a full chronological layout, so I will approach this account more thematically. I would return to more construction at the Tabernacle site in February of 1982. Meanwhile, at the Ridge, I was given the task of constructing a "cannery" in May, situated directly behind the Tabernacle on the downslope. The women elders had already created the design. The front part was a large storage room filled with shelves for jars of food. The back part, overlooking the woods below, was the canning kitchen. I remember working with Glenn Fant, the younger son of Jim and Joyce, building sliding windows for the cannery. The floor of the cannery was to be vinyl tiles. I had never laid tiles. I told Brother Jim that I was not sure how to do it. His response was immediate and cheerful, "I have every confidence that you will do a great job." What a wonderful difference that was in contrast to my experience at the Albuquerque farm.

After the cannery was completed, I constructed a child's playground on the downslope between the two women's dorms. It had a slide and swings and a center gazebo. I made it mostly out of branches, having pealed off the bark. I remember little Angela Gearhart as one of the children playing there; she was always cheerful and bright. Sadly, the playground lasted only a couple of years before it was rotting away in that humid climate.

And it was humid and HOT and muggy. Chiggers were everywhere and other unmentionable critters. Any foray into the woods meant chiggers under your skin eating away. Some of the men in the dorm would scratch until they became bloody. I learned that utterly ignoring them meant they caused much less trouble. There were no air conditioners anywhere, just fans. It was hot in the back of the trailer with just a large window fan right next to me. I had to learn to sleep in the noise and heat. I'm sure it got well above 120 degrees inside the trailer on a regular basis. One just learns to live with it.

In September, I was given the task of building a front office. Again, this design was created by Roberta and Joyce. One side would be the main community office, the other side would be the financial office occupied by Carol Breeze, who kept the accounts for the community. Across the front of both rooms was a foyer. In the center of the foyer, I built a brick enclosure for the wood stove. I did not know anything about cabinet construction, so I built all the desks and cabinets like framing a house. I built a lovely little wooden desk with a locking lid for Sister Carol. This office was my second favorite building of all I have built. It was ready to be painted when I flew home in December to visit my parents. Adele Ramirez and Nancy Jessop picked out the paint colors. I was horrified at what they chose. When I returned in January, it was painted. To my utter astonishment, the awful colors they had picked worked wonderfully well together, increasing my enjoyment of that building.

Dorm "Example"

By the end of June, I had completed the "Basics" and John King had had enough of being a dorm example at the Ridge. When he left, the elders asked me to be the dorm example. Brother Jim told Abel, "I think we've got the right man this time." I would be the dorm example for the next four years, longer, I suspect, than anyone else. It was a task that battered the hearts of many.

BUT – not while Abel was over the men's dorm. Once I had settled into life at the Ridge, and was no longer in the teaching sessions, this next year in the community was good and memorable. As the dorm example, I was "in charge" in the dorm. I would report regularly to Abel whenever difficulties arose with the men. Abel always treated me as an equal with him in ministry. We shared much, heart with heart, in our care for the men in the dorm. My limited times in prayer for the men were anointed and fruitful. I walked in peace and wisdom and in the anointing through this time.

David Troshin was our primary difficulty in the dorm. He aggravated everyone, especially Mark. David loved to fart, to say the most irritating things

to everyone, to evade work, and especially to shave. If we did not keep an eye on him, he would be shaving his face three or four times a day. Nonetheless, each of the other men had their own issues.

In October, Richard Hernandez came from Denver City, Texas, to join with us at the Ridge. He had the bottom bunk opposite me in the back room. Richard would be at the Ridge for about three years. He soon joined with Jim Messick as his lead helper in the gardens. Our friendship continued, but not as it had been. Because my task was to share with the elders all the going's on in the dorm on a daily basis, I could not develop close friendships with the men, just a brotherly and working relationship. Because I was not an elder, I did not have a close relationship with those men either. While Abel Ramirez was my covering, this was no problem at all. That next year was one of the more successful and good times of my life. I learned much, working and walking with men in their various levels of difficulty. The Lord anointed me in that task.

A Word from God

Once the wrenching of my heart from my experience with Roseanna Navarrete had passed into the distance, my desire to find a wife continued. While I was building the little carpenter shop one day, a pretty girl by the name of Lois Mack walked by. She look intently into my eyes and smiled at me quite cheerfully. That happened more than once over the next few months – but later, she caught another fellow's eyes and no longer looked at mine.

Then, an energetic tomboy of a girl, with her hands deep into goat problems or butchering or whatever adventurous task, caught my eye. Her name was Jessica Mack. It's not that she showed any interest in me, but that I admired her.

One time that first summer, Roberta Mack organized an outing one Sunday afternoon for several of the young people, a hike past the fish ponds and down to the Ocmulgee River. Her three daughters were along as well as Peter Honsalek, Patti Landis, and myself. There were also a few others I no longer remember. This was a good time in my memory. I didn't talk much, but it was good to be out of the men's dorm and with girls and boys around my same age. I remember inspecting an abandoned stone house along our way.

Maureen was a quiet girl who did not smile much. I had taken little notice of her in the light

The Mack family.

From left:

Maureen
Jessica
Lois
Roberta
Claude

of her two older sisters (who all continued, in my imagination, to be entirely beyond my "reach"). I remember brief conversations with her on a couple of occasions.

One day in October I had a dream from the Lord. This was probably the most God-filled dream I have ever known. In my dream, I was sitting on a bench waiting for an elder's meeting. I was in trouble over something and had to wait for my turn to give an account, not a comfortable feeling. In my dream, Maureen came up to me with kind gentleness on her face. She expressed her concern for me and said that she wanted to know me better. There was complete acceptance in her stance towards me.

Then, as I was awakening from the dream, I saw first, Lois's face and second, Jessica's face. I was fully awake, then, when the Lord spoke His word to me, "Man looks upon the outward appearance, but the Lord looks upon the heart." I knew immediately that the Lord was referring to the story of Samuel bypassing the older siblings and choosing David, the youngest. That word resounded all through me. I knew that God had chosen Maureen for me.

A short time later, I shared that dream with Brother John Hinson.

Before continuing, I must give an account of John and Bambi Hinson. I highly regarded Brother John and Sister Bambi; both were profoundly anointed of the Lord. Yet I also learned to hold them at arm's length. They were both great encouragers,

yet their exuberance seemed to me over time to be outward only. When asked to bless the meal, Brother John would pray only four words loudly, "Thank you, Lord, Amen." I picked up that practice from him.

Once, after I had been dorm example for awhile, Brother John shared in the Ridge Tabernacle that anyone desiring to be trained in ministry should come to see him. I was soon at his door, where I was received with exuberance.

EXCEPT – nothing ever came of it. This hollowness that was Brother John Hinson would be the final factor in my time of great difficulty and in my contention with God, coming up in the third chapter of this season at Bowens Mill.

I shared my leading concerning Maureen with Brother John. He received all that I shared exuberantly, as was his wont. He suggested, however, that we say nothing at all to anyone, not yet, but that we give it time to settle. I agreed fully.

Several weeks later, however, he came up to me in the drive in front of the newly-built office, put his arm around my shoulder, and said to me, "I shared your leading concerning Maureen with Claude and Roberta Mack. They asked Maureen, and she expressed that she had no interest at all in you. So, I guess that's that."

This betrayal of trust was a terrible blow to me, one that could only grow in its immediate disconnection. Certainly I was hurt by Maureen's response, but far more by the cavalier attitude towards my own heart, when I had shared in complete trust.

Yet such an approach was part and parcel of Ridge eldership practice, most of which was guided by John and Bambi.

Needless to say, once I thought I was interested in Maureen, all ability to speak to her vanished from me. I saw her many times a day over the next nearly three-and-a-half years. She passed by the dorm trailer on her way to the Tabernacle. Time and again the Lord arose in me in joyous witness when I passed her. One time after a difficult night-watch and after milking early in the morning after, I passed through the kitchen on my way to bed. I felt awful, emotionally and physically. Maureen was alone in the kitchen, preparing breakfast for the family; her back was turned to me. As I passed her, saying nothing, without cause, joy leapt in my heart, and I went to my bed in the dorm in the life and joy of the Spirit. This happened, unsummoned by me, so many times.

Yet I could not talk with her, and I never saw her smile through these years.

I did not know what to do.

From Motels to Kitchens

Once the office at the Ridge was finished, in February of 1982, I returned to working at the convention site in a big push to prepare more lodging before the April convention. This time I worked in conjunction with George Hawkins, a wonderful southern country man who lived in a house at the convention site with his family. For the most part, it was George and I working together on two "motel buildings." These were long two-story buildings with four bedrooms on each floor in motel style. We mostly completed one and then went on to the other. During this same time we also built a cabin with money provided by a particular move group. That would be their cabin during a convention.

I really enjoyed working with George Hawkins. He was funny and light hearted. We worked well together as equals. One of the neat things I added to my construction knowledge was that I got to put in the whole electrical wiring system in both motel buildings. A brother who lived near the communities was an electrician, and he gave me good advice on what to do.

Now, back at the Ridge, through this winter,

Derrick Jessop, who had a bit of money, (around $40,000) had completed a training in cabinet making off the farm. He wanted to invest his money into a cabinet shop at the Ridge. Peter Honsalek, who was also a builder, worked with him to build a new woodshop across the ravine, next to the goat barns. The little building I had built then became the mechanics shop. This lovely new woodshop was small, just 20' by 40', with a wood floor. But Derek had purchased a full array of high-quality woodworking tools. Derek was a stickler in the use of his shop. He required that everything happening in it be done his way. I had to "test out" on all the tools to his satisfaction before I was allowed to use them. Obviously, this rankled; nonetheless, I came to greatly value Derek's procedures and simply loved the hours I spent working in his shop.

The final couple of weeks, then, before the April convention, were a huge push to get everything completed in these two motels before the convention started. Earlier, because the sawdust floor had become unacceptable, a crew of men had poured a vast concrete slab for the convention tabernacle. I was not part of that job. Now, a new platform and sound booth were being completed as well. For the motel rooms, we needed three bunk beds per room. That makes 48 bunk beds, if my calculations are right. I created a design that enabled me to mass produce them. Derek, though not liking it, surrendered his shop to me for this massive assembly-line project.

Let me share something about myself. I have never had normal male stamina. Recuperation from hard work always came slower for me than it did for most men. I worked hard, yes, but at a certain point, my body would collapse, and I could do nothing at all for a couple of days except lie in bed. This would happen every now and then through the years.

There were two days to go, ninety-six people coming to the convention needed beds in which to sleep. The foamies were all purchased and waiting. I was working on the bunks mostly by myself, putting in long hard days, going back and forth between Derek's shop and the convention site, directing the work there. My body gave out. I could no longer continue. I dragged myself back to the dorm and lay down in the middle of the living room floor. I could not move. Yet I had this great responsibility upon me. I lay there for a bit, then I called upon the Lord, drew something I did not know I had from deep inside, got up and went back to work. Somehow, by the Lord's anointing, I had the strength, not only to finish the bunks and get them in place, but also to oversee all the other things being completed at the convention site.

In April, Brother Abel shared with Richard and I that he wanted us to attend the Mexico City convention. Abel was big on experiencing the reality of other cultures, something that fitted well with move communities all over the world. Richard and I decided to go. First, we drove down to New Orleans where we spent the night in the home of an elder there, Betty Burke. Then we flew from New Orleans to Mexico City. We were in Mexico City for two weeks, including the convention time. We stayed in the home of the leading elders in the Mexico City fellowship, a man and wife, last name of Naranjo; I do not remember their first names.

A young lady from a community in northern British Columbia called "Blueberry" was spending several months in the home of this couple in order to learn Spanish. Her name was Elisabeth Roes. Richard and Elisabeth hit if off right away and spent the time forming a happy friendship.

I really enjoyed my time in Mexico City. It was very different. We visited the central cathedral and drove over to Puebla on May 5 for the Cinco de Mayo parade where the battle happened. During the convention time, with other people coming in, Richard and I moved over to another young couple's home. We had the servant's room on top of the flat third floor, accessed by a narrow and high spiral staircase. This was pretty cool to me.

I could write a separate chapter on this visit to Mexico and all the neat things we got to experience, but I will refrain.

After returning home to the Ridge, my next task was to build a two-room addition to the Mack trailer. I spent a couple of months working on this addition for Claude and Roberta including a work room in the back for Brother Claude and an office in front for Sister Roberta. I built a work counter, shelves, and a desk. I sided it with cedar siding.

Through this time, Derek was talking with me and with Joyce Fant about his desire to use his shop and new trade to build a really nice kitchen for the Ridge. The old kitchen was a catastrophe, designed to turn every task into far more work than necessary. The job of designing the layout of the new kitchen was given to me. This would be my first design; I was 25 years old. What a joy that was. You see, I am a designer, that is, an INTJ on the Meyer's Brigg personality scale. I always think efficiency, how to make every job flow smoother.

I designed a really cool kitchen, but I will refrain from putting that design here. In the old kitchen every movement conflicted directly with another movement. In my kitchen no worker ever crossed paths with another. All tasks followed a smooth flow from one function to the next. And when the kitchen was completed and in full use, all my ideas worked seamlessly. Forgive me for my boasting, but that design was one of my best accomplishments.

Of course, we had to rip out the entire kitchen before we could start. I had charge of the construction zone while Derek put together the design and construction of the cabinets themselves. I think the ladies used the cannery kitchen to prepare the meals through this time. We rebuilt the walls; I remember a lot of attic work, but not what it was for. As we had the places ready, Derek brought in the materials to install the cabinet bodies.

During this time, however, Abel and Adele Ramirez announced their leading to move, first to El Paso, and then to Ciudad Juarez in order to lead the brethren there towards starting a community in Chihuahua state. They left that September. I had no idea of the loss their departure would be to me.

To the left is a picture of Abel and Adele a few years after this time.

12. A Season of Loneliness

October 1982 - December 1983

Working with Derek

After Abel and Adele Ramirez left for Juarez, my circumstances changed accordingly. But those changes came gradually. In fact, it was only much later, as I pondered over and over what went wrong, that I began to see the wonderful distinction that had been my life while I walked together with a man who treated me as an equal in the Lord versus all the other times.

And so, this "Season of Loneliness," began slowly, right after Brother Abel left. But before delving into the "loneliness" part of things, I want to give a layout of my work and experiences through the next several months.

Once the general construction work on the new kitchen had been completed and the cabinet bodies installed, the focus now turned towards the visible woodwork, the cabinet faces, doors, and countertops. Through the winter months, Derek and I worked together on these things in his shop. Derek taught me cabinet making in a well-tooled shop, one of the loves of my life. Derek had his ways, but I learned to adapt to them. To be honest with you, I look back now and treasure his gift to me, not only what he taught me, but also himself.

I remember that Peter Honsalek had been helping Derek up until this point. So – this must have been the time of his wedding with Patti. Maureen was one of the bridesmaids. It was one of the more gallant weddings of many at Bowens Mill while I was living there. Peter then became involved in the school and was no longer working with Derek.

Derek and I had purchased a huge pile of oak 2 x 8's for the cabinets. We cut all this down to make door panels and face frames. We used cypress for the countertops. This was a mistake, but we did not know that at the time, and they were beautiful. The wood was too soft, however, and soaked up dirt and grease. A couple of times after, on nightwatch, I scrubbed them down with steel wool, re-sanded, and then re-oiled them. Their beauty was worth it, but they could not last.

Derek and I together made a beautiful kitchen, still in use to this day.

By March we had completed that part of the task and the kitchen was back in full use. Now, Sunday morning dinner prep was a breeze. Everything went smoothly.

My attention turned, then, to the walk-in cooler and freezer off the back of the kitchen. This was quite a project, one on which I worked mostly by myself. I built thickly-insulated walls, floor, and ceiling, installed full metal sheeting inside, and built a thick oak-framed door with commercial-grade clasp and hinges. Claude helped me install the compressor system. I built removable cypress shelving that could be taken out and cleaned. You had to pass though the cooler to the door for the freezer. It was similar to the door into the kitchen, but cypress instead of oak.

One day, while I was working on the shelving deep inside the muffled freezer room, I overheard strange sounds from the women in the kitchen. I also heard a distant, thump, thump, but it was too muffled for me to give it any heed. I stuck my nose out, however, to see what on earth all the excitement was about. As I came out of the thick-walled cooler, I heard the noise as of many freight train engines going right over the top of us. I saw with my own eyes rain water coming in the open window on one side and going straight across the room to go out the open window on the other side.

The mighty roaring ended as quickly as it had started. In complete astonishment, I went outside to see what terrible damage had just occurred. Brother Claude met me in front of the Tabernacle, and we walked around the trailer park together, seeing the destruction, and hoping we would not find mangled bodies.

The tornado had removed a huge gum tree, on the other side of the washhouse, taken out the clothes lines, and then lifted up to remove the roof from the wash house. It's massive tip was right above the tabernacle where I was working, but not on the ground. It removed the upper part of the tall pines alongside the tabernacle, went right over the teaching trailer where Brother Jim was teaching his morning class and came back down to the ground just beyond the Hinson trailer where it turned the small cowshed into toothpicks. It then proceeded on the ground, in full view of the astonished students and teachers at the school, removing huge pine trues, throwing them high into the air and slamming them to the ground.

As Claude and I walked through the trailer park, we saw a miracle. Every tree and branch that would have crushed a trailer still stood. Every one of the many trees that came down were in-between the trailers. Only one trailer was slightly dinged and another one damaged a little bit. That one was the only trailer that had insurance and the insurance company paid for rebuilding their entire trailer, something the owners were asking God to accomplish for them.

No one was touched. The brother working in the cow shed had forgotten a tool and was busy getting it when the cow shed turned to tooth picks. Dozens of people were in those flimsy trailers or working on the grounds, and no one was touched. This is a grace upon brethren walking together in community that is not found in most other contexts.

Sometime through these next few months, Derek became discouraged with the constraints of life at the Ridge. He and Nancy moved back to San Antonio, Texas, taking all of his wonderful tools with them, though the shop building remained. The Ridge had only a few inadequate tools to replace them and working in that shop now became to me an empty shell.

Reassessing Everything

Claude Mack is my father-in-law, the grandfather of our children. They have always called him "Papa." He and Lois will be here in our home again this Thanksgiving.

When I married his daughter, absolutely the best thing I have ever done in my life, I was, in one sense, binding myself to "Bowens Mill."

I have always known that the Lord did something special for me during the deliverance times at Blueberry through 1987-88; that is, He removed from me most of the difficulty inside towards my

time at Bowens Mill. But only now am I seeing the full impact of what that means.

In essence, God's wedding gift to me, through the months before my friendship with Maureen began, was the miraculous removal of bitterness from the inside of me regarding my years at Bowens Mill. As I am writing of this time period now, I see the contrast. Writing about my childhood through my time at Albuquerque has brought great travail accompanied by gentle healing. I suspect that writing about my time from Blueberry on will be the same.

But for Bowens Mill, I do not find those same wounds inside. Neither was my time there as much of an issue during my years of healing with John Eldredge. What would my marriage and the raising of our children have been like if God had not given me such a wondrous gift? I have no need ever to know.

I am so deeply grateful to a Father who is good all the time.

As I look at the account thus far, it seems little more than an outline of what I did. That's partly because I had no close relationships during this time. Nonetheless, I loved community, and the Ridge was a godly Christian community with love and regard for one another paramount. Yet it was during these years that I began to say to myself, "I love community; it's just people that I can't stand."

My relationship with Claude Mack has been the most difficult relationship over time in my life, a relationship of close proximity beginning in December of 1980 until now. My dear wife has insisted absolutely that, regardless of anything, her father is to be treated in all honor and with the highest respect. I have always agreed with her, being always strengthened by her resolve.

Having written about the Ridge thus far, I find myself reassessing everything. God's removal of all hurt from me was, in a sense, a negative, that is, the negation of something that would have been harmful. I find the opposite happening inside of me now, that is, the addition to me of a realization of the value and goodness so many experiences, and primarily, people from this time really are to me. I am a wealthy man, and my treasures are increasing daily. You see, that is the "power" of an endless life, that all things that belong to me will return again, each in its season. I can lose nothing, but only gain forever.

Up until my time of deliverance at Blueberry, I

knew only bitterness and grief regarding the time at Bowens Mill after the Ramirez's left. From that time of deliverance until now, I have known mostly an empty slate regarding the things I will share in this letter and the next. But now, completely separate from any design of mine, I am discovering the arising of neither bitterness nor blankness, but instead, abundant treasure and life everlasting.

And so, dear reader, I contend with you that, as I share of these difficult things, as I must, you will not cast any aspersion upon anyone, regardless. More than that, I do believe absolutely in "the dealings of God," in their season and time.

God was after something on the inside of me that He had to remove for me to know Father and to share Father with you now. God proved the full completion of that removal in a Bowens Mill Convention in late March of 1997. Let me give that thing a Bible name – "Korah," that is, "Christian" rebellion. I witnessed "Christian" rebellion in another again just recently. When I am pressed beyond all measure, it is there that I KNOW that the removal of that thing from me is the greatest work of God in my life, a value beyond all measure.

Writers of great literature, Tolstoy, Cervantes, Shakespeare, Austen, Tolkien, are counted as timeless writers because of how they take an individual human and press that person by circumstances beyond all measure. It is there, as with Hamlet, at the point between play-acting and real life, between sanity and insanity, that the human soul can be opened up for all to see the depths inside. Few scenes in literary history are more piercing and impactive than that moment when Natasha Rostov of *War and Peace* sinks to her knees in the chapel in utter despair, and finds not only the Lord Jesus there, but also her true self.

And so I want to draw a straight line of the hammer of God upon the heart of a young man, from September of 1982 until March of 1997. I want to show you the blows, the pain, and the deliverance. Clearly, I am an epistle of Christ, written by the greatest Author in the universe, a God who wins our hearts for His dwelling place.

Yet in setting forth my soul for you, dear reader, I am expecting to win the same removal of "Korah" from your heart as well, and that for Father's sake, that He might live inside of you without hindrance and in all overflowing JOY.

"Touch not Mine anointed and do My prophets no harm." - "Touch not Mine anointed and do My prophets no harm."

Claude Mack

After Abel and Adele Ramirez left for Juarez, Brother Claude became my "covering" as the dorm example. This was somewhat convenient, since he lived next door. His front door and ours were maybe thirty feet apart.

Everything that Abel was, Claude was not.

Up until writing these accounts, I had always placed Claude in the category of the "bullies" in my life. I suddenly realize that is completely incorrect. A "bully" is one who gains a perverse pleasure, a stroking of conceit, through manipulating and abusing others. That was not Claude Mack at all. Claude was a military man, and he practiced only what he believed was his duty.

So far in this account I have resisted the inclusion of anyone else's "story," which would not be mine to give. Nonetheless, because Maureen and her family are entering my story through this time, it is right for me to place Claude's history just a bit.

Brother Claude was born in Brownfield, Texas in 1932, but grew up in nearby Seminole. That would have placed him as an adolescent through WWII. By the end of high school, then, Claude signed up for the U.S. Navy. Claude is a very diligent man, greatly self-disciplined, and he gives his full attention to duty. These qualities meant that he rose in the ranks to become the Chief Petty Officer (the highest rank a service man can attain), serving on three different aircraft carriers that played a significant role in the Vietnam war. Claude's primary skill, besides running a "tight ship," was electrical maintenance.

While Claude was stationed in Hawaii in the 50's, he met a young woman who had come from San Francisco to work as a Sunday school teacher by the name of Roberta Miller. They married in 1956, and their first daughter, Lois, was born less than a year after my birth, followed by Jessica, and then Maureen in 1962. Only for Maureen's birth, they were stationed at the naval base in Albuquerque, New Mexico – and yes, there is a naval base there in the high desert. They moved to Oakland, California, then, in 1964.

During Maureen's childhood years, Claude was away on-ship much of the time. This was the height of the Vietnam war. When Maureen was just three, she went with her mother and grandmother, Susan Jacobsen, to hear Sam Fife preach for the first time. While Claude was at home, then, he would have participated in the move fellowship services.

Claude retired from the military in 1972, when I was fifteen and Maureen nine. He and his family soon moved to a small Christian community near Marlette, Michigan. They then moved to Sapa, Mississippi, a year later. At Sapa, first Roberta and then later Claude were set into the ministry by John Hinson. For five years, Claude and Roberta, along with their three daughters, were a significant part of the Sapa Deliverance Community as well as a couple of smaller communities sponsored by Sapa. When Sapa closed in 1978, they hitched up their trailer and drove it to Bowens Mill, finally parking it in its spot at the Ridge sometime in 1979.

At the time, I knew none of this, of course. All I knew was an iron man of firm discipline, of little display of emotion, and of no interactions I would have called friendship.

When I shared with Abel concerning the doings of the men in the dorm, it was our ministry together towards them. When I shared with Claude the same things, I was speaking to what appeared to me a blank face. Then, when I had done my duty, that was it. Everything was now in the hands of "the elders."

I did not at first realize there was any difference. In fact, I was mostly oblivious to the human person inside. It would take years for me to comprehend the role Abel played in my life and the severe reduction that came to me when he left. All that I knew was that things started not working out, things started going all wrong. I had no idea why.

Nonetheless, the question before me now is this. Can I value Claude Mack as he is and as he was without requiring him to be different? If I have the right to place the Lord Jesus upon all that I am and upon every moment of my life, then so also does he. Indeed, my continuing relationship with my father-in-law has always been at the contending heart of God teaching me Christ as us.

"Father, I thank You that from the start You have contended directly with me that if Christ Jesus has entered into union with me, then He has also entered into union with Claude Mack, that if Christ lives as me, then He lives also, just as much,

as Brother Claude. Our differences of expression, though outwardly great, are nothing more than differing expressions of Your own Person, our dear and good Father.

"And so Father, I do again as I have done, yet now at a deeper level of personal understanding. I draw Claude into my heart, just as he is, embedded now inside of Your Love shed abroad in me. And there, Father, I release Claude into You, that he and You might arise together into all life and joy, utterly free of me.

"Yet, Oh Father, I am willing for You to do much more than that. While I am not able to do such a thing, I know that You are well able, and that You do all things well. Father, I am willing for You to return Claude Mack back to me as my close and dear friend forever. I am willing, my Father. Let it be to me according to Your word."

A Conception of "Ministry"

The move of God was NOT a "cult," and I will resist any attempt to brand it as such. It was little different than any other close Christian experience, the same thing, just intensified. I found the exact same "cultic" elements in every other Christian setting since, though Christian "cultism" is nothing compared to the normal cultic practices of the world. The public school political structure was far more cultic than anything Christian, far more destructive, and with far fewer redeeming qualities.

Everyone wants to blame this or that for problems. There is one problem only – humans. And there is one reason why humans are the problem, and that is the universal rejection of the knowledge of God, even including Nicene Christianity.

One element inside the move fellowship could be called "cultic," however, and that is the ordering of "ministry." Give people a false role to play based on human ability, tell them that moving in this role is "God's order," and you will place everyone into the spinning of false stories of self, a "this-is-me," that is not Christ.

Essentially, Brother Sam established an "order" in the move fellowship based on 1 Corinthians 11:2-16, a passage that has no relationship with the Old Testament, but comes right out of Aristotle, one of those problematic pieces inside of Paul's letters that we cannot know and that should be left entirely on the shelf. God's kingdom arises from beneath; it does NOT create a top-down hierarchy of "authority over." Tie that together with the Calvinist's deceitful translation of Hebrews 13:17 into **"obey those who have the rule over you,"** and you have the recipe for the creation of a natural aristocracy, an ordering into which people must place their self-story. (The writer of Hebrews actually said **"have confidence in those who are restoring word into you."** In other words, connecting you with the Lord Jesus, not with themselves.)

This issue is such a big deal in my own life story that I must begin to address it here.

Out from his own personal need to stay protected, as I shared earlier, Brother Sam established an ordering of ministry. Apostles covered elders who covered all who were not "ministry." Because we humans always take things in directions God does not intend, this ordering did more damage to those who were elders than to any other. Having such a place "above" the regular "body members" creates inside a twisted story of self that will take a great work of God to unravel.

You see, it's only now that I understand these things. It was only confusion through my years in move community. I am writing this part now, after Thanksgiving during which Claude and Lois spent a few days in our home. I was astonished as I watched my father-in-law laughing and smiling over his great-grandson (Gabriel) on the video phone. I never saw him do that once with his grandchildren. And then I understood why. While our children were little, Claude was still functioning as an elder in move community. At the present time, he is not. The Claude that I saw this Thanksgiving was real; Claude's outward expression that I knew for years was not. Instead, he operated inside what he thought was "expected" of him by God. This false expectation, then, creates a human persona that cannot be true.

Nonetheless, even though the structure of "ministry" would work the same separation into an elite "aristocracy," as it always has among humans, the move fellowship was filled with Christian love and the Spirit of God. One thing Brother Sam insisted on was that ministry must always be corporate. That togetherness brought a measure of balance.

I observed at close hand the same authority structures in the public school system and realized that it is normal for humans to be utterly corrupted by such a false story of "I am in charge of you." The world is far more cultic than anything inside Christianity.

Yet it would be upon this anvil of ministry "above you" upon which God would strike His greatest blows upon my heart, the bulls-eye towards which the arrow of God passed through my life to hit that one thing inside the human soul that will keep us from ever knowing Father.

As a young man in my twenties, I was outwardly mature and capable. Inwardly, however, I was very needy. I did not understand people, though I always moved in maturity towards others. Inside, though, I spent so much of my time spinning great fantasy daydreams in my mind. My mind moves very rapidly, and its only outlet was to escape the frustration and loneliness by creating fantastical mental stories. Of course, I was always the "ruler" in my stories.

David Troshin and the Dorm

I can portray this time of aloneness for me only in context, that is, life in the men's dorm. It was, for the most part, a miserable place to live. Since I was "in charge," and since my role was to report daily to the elders all the "goings on" in the dorm, I could never be in a normal relationship with those who lived there.

One time, after a contention with someone in which I did not act as well as I should have, I was called into an elders meeting. One of them told me, "Daniel, if you want friends, you have to be a friend." This statement was so disconnected from my reality that I had no idea where to place it. And I did not understand. You cannot be friends with those whom you are reporting "for their good." And none in that circle of elders had any idea of being a friend to me. I lived in this fog of disconnection for three years.

Then there was David Troshin. David had to be accompanied always; if not, he would do something bizarre that would aggravate the most "spiritual." David had a wonderful way of getting under one's skin, of discovering every religious desire in others to "set him straight," all of which was a complete waste of effort.

Since I was "in charge," I took the larger part of being with David to services, etc. Others would take their turns, but preferred not to. We would have a wonderful service; I would be lifted up into the joy of the anointing, and before we got home, David

Troshin always succeeded in dragging me down into "the flesh."

I noticed something strange, over the years, that I could not comprehend. When we sat down in a row for the main services, wherever they were held, the row in front of us and behind us and to each side of us would fill up, but the row in which David and I sat never did unless there was nowhere else for latecomers to sit. Then, when I was in the audio booth, running the sound system, I noticed that when David was with anyone else, the rows filled up normally. It wasn't him; it was me. What do you do with something like that, something that happens consistently for years? I did not know that this was a typical reaction to Asperger's.

An Asperger's is very different outwardly than what they are inwardly. Their problem is that they know only what they are inside. They have no idea how other people see them. And other people see Asperger's as harsh and arrogant. But that "harshness" is coming from a totally different cause than with most.

Of the fifty-some men who passed through that dorm while I lived there, almost all of them left further from the Lord than when they came. These men found themselves caught between David Troshin and Claude Mack. David made life miserable for everyone, and Claude, the "authority" over the dorm, could not express human compassion. He was a military man, demanding explanations for "bad conduct," explanations that could never satisfy him.

Men would run to get away from this impossible combination.

More than that, the Ridge was the strictest community in the move fellowship. I saw close hand one of the reasons why God hated the old covenant based on human performance. The directive given towards people was not "know Christ your life," but rather, "submit to the covering and follow the order." It was believed fervently that what people needed was to "follow the order," that this kind of performance would make them "right with God," and thus they would be made whole.

I observed the opposite result. First, those who gave themselves to "submitting" created such a false story of self. They became religiously and humanly fake. I observed such human fakery closely for years. I cannot tolerate it nor any of the false ex-

pectations that create it. Then, as people "put on a show" for the elders, their true needs, deep inside, are covered over. All people are REAL deep inside, and that realness wants to know the Lord Jesus alive inside their hearts. But external expectations of performance will ALWAYS force people to turn to fakery in order to be "like Christ" in the eyes of those who are "above" them."

Then, when they disappear from the community and you never hear from them again, you have no idea why. They had seemed to be doing "so well." Law cannot ever impart life.

I am not subject to fakery; I never have been. That's part of why I was sometimes charged with being "unsubmissive." Yet I have always respected authority and always submitted in what was right and always given myself to the needs of others with all my heart in the only ways I knew how. Always, other humans look upon outward appearance to define one another, and always the Lord looks only upon the heart.

You see, I am now able to take the delight on Claude Mack's face toward his great-grandson, Gabriel – my daughter Johanna's son, that is, the real Claude, and impute that same knowing of him through every moment of my interaction with him over the years. Doing that turns everything around and gives me great compassion for a man who was caught also in a false story he did not understand.

Through this time, however, I understood none of these things, but stumbled forward only, in a fog of hurt, confusion, and loneliness. [And please don't join me in any "pity party." I certainly felt sorry for myself more than most. I can only laugh at such folly now. Yet I must present to you as accurate of a picture of my life as I can.]

Charlie & Wassel

Two men in the dorm through these years were friends to me, and I count them as friends today, though both are with the Lord, Charlie Jones and Wassel Tschiniak. Both of these men were a bit older and, in their own ways, a bit stronger than I.

Charlie was a builder and worked off the farm through these years, running a construction business doing work mostly in the town of Fitzgerald. Charlie was strong and filled with exuberant joy. I did one job for him, building a porch addition onto a house in Fitzgerald, one that needed a tricky roof design. Typically, however, we were not together that much since our daily lives took us in different directions.

Charlie was always sharing how the Lord led him here and led him there, how the Lord said to buy this tool or hire this man, and how the Lord always prospered him. And indeed the Lord did. My own story was the opposite. All I ever heard from the Lord was "No." When I tried to buy a screwdriver, the Lord said, "No."

I learned a critical principle of God through this relationship. God does lead two people side by side in very different ways. What God is leading you to do is NOT what He is leading your brother or sister next to you to do. And imposing my definition of "God" on others must always be false – and must create only falseness in others.

When Charlie moved into the dorm, he took the bunk above David Troshin. Charlie had been a sergeant in the army and, although he was always easy going, he had a firm line drawn. One time David crossed that line and Charlie beat him up. That got Charlie in trouble with the elders, but such a thing bothered him not at all. In complete contrast, David treated Charlie with utmost respect from then on and was actually half decent for the next week or so.

Because I had to be always firm with David to prevent him from doing really bizarre things that served always to aggravate others, he often threatened me with his weird twisted notions of "getting back." I paid no attention to his threats. I now know that was unwise.

Nonetheless, I must close out my account of David Troshin with his end. A few years after my family and I left the move communities, a man visiting the Ridge during a convention reacted typically to David by "setting him straight." This time, David did more than say, "I'm going to poke you." He followed the man and did "poke" him – with a kitchen knife. His threats were actually real. The brother died. I know nothing more of David Troshin's story except my assumption that he would have been taken to a hospital for the criminally insane.

In-between writing the two parts of this letter, I felt a reluctance for some time to come back to this topic. That reluctance is my disgust for the four-and-a-half years I spent with this man. My testimony has always been, "All of His ways concerning me are perfect. He has never led me wrong; He has never not led me." This is the only chapter of my life for which I see no redeeming qualities. David Troshin was a dead weight that dragged so many men down. Few reached into him as closely as I did. All I found inside was self-centered gibberish; I could not find a heart.

"Lord Jesus, I do not understand David Troshin or the years of my life through which he was my burden. I can find no purpose. Can I draw David Troshin into love within my heart? I can do it, Lord Jesus, because I know that You are true.

"And Lord, I have to accept that my drawing of David Troshin into Your love in me will not affect him at all, in the foreseeable time. He is willfully and dumbly set against responding to any such thing. Yet David Troshin comes out from You every moment, Lord Jesus, and You have always carried him.

"Lord Jesus, I forgive David for the yuckiness he has always been to me, and I forgive those who allowed this man to continue to do so much damage to so many. And Lord Jesus, I forgive You for placing this man in my life for so many years.

"David Troshin belongs to You, Lord Jesus, and You will triumph in his life. I know that the day will come when he, with sound mind and heart, will give You thanks for all things."

Wassel Tschiniak was an entirely different matter. Wassel's mother was from Latvia. He was born in a ditch in Poland as she fled before the Red army driving into Europe. He made his way to Chicago as a young man and did well as an enforcer for the mob. He and Charlie were about the same age, huskiness, and strength, not that big, but much stronger than they looked.

Wassel got saved and joined the move fellowship where he became an elder and a traveling ministry. For a few years he was the leading elder of the Ware Farm, just outside of Boston, Massachusetts. Wassel could preach up a storm, though he repeated himself over and over to do so. Yet in the press of "ministry," he would break, sneak out, and get stone-cold drunk.

Buddy Cobb removed Wassel's "ministry" role from him. If he wanted to continue in the move fellowship, then he needed to go to the Ridge for help. Wassel showed up at the Ridge not long after I was the dorm example. Wassel was big-hearted and generous. He befriended me more than any other did. At times he could be trusted; he was willing to take David Troshin off my hands more than any other was. Yet at other times he could be a sneak.

Wassel always had to be watched closely when he went to town. Once, he went with me into a drug store. I knew I had to watch him every second, but for about two seconds my back was turned. When I turned around again, he was gone. Immediately, I raced out of the store to find that he had already downed an entire bottle of cough syrup he had snatched off the shelf. One time in the dorm, I found him quite drunk. There, out from the bottom of his soul, he expressed his hatred for those who had stripped him of his "ministry."

Yet Wassel's immaturity had hurt so many people; he should never have been put into such a false position in the first place.

I liked Wassel, and I know that our friendship will be restored in goodness and truth.

My Time in the Word

I did very little reading during my years at Bowens Mill. There was neither time nor place for it. I did read *Fearfully and Wonderfully Made* and *Into His Image* by Dr. Paul Brand through this time. Dr. Paul Brand had a large impact on me, in my knowledge of God, one that continues to this day. You cannot but gain from spending time in his books.

As an aside, while Derek Jessop was still living at the Ridge, I borrowed a set of books from him and read them all. The author was Immanuel Velikovsky, and the books were *Worlds in Collision*, *Earth in Upheaval*, and *Ages in Chaos*. I was massively affected by these books and have adhered to their basic premise all the way through. Nonetheless, this was not a topic that could be raised in move conversation. Velikovsky's premise was that early humans, in their record of events, were telling us the truth, including the Biblical accounts. Yet that testimony presents a history of the solar system that is VERY different from what most today suppose.

Today, I am convinced by much scientific evidence that Velikovsky had it right. The universe is electrical, and the solar system known by humans before the flood was utterly different than what we see today. More than that, the scenario of Egyptian dating used by historians is false. In order to have an accurate understanding of Bible history, one must draw Egyptian history forward 600 years. Moses led the children of Israel out of Egypt at the destruction

of the old kingdom, and Solomon's "Queen of Sheba," was Queen Hatshepsut of the middle kingdom. When you do that, so many things in the Old Testament line up with known human history.

This is a critically important understanding God gave at that time, one which will be essential to know in the years ahead as the solar system once again goes "haywire" and most will totally freak out. But, I will include no more of that here.

I continued my habit of writing out verses and books of the Bible in endless word studies. The hours of nightwatch each week lent themselves to that task. I remember doing a complete write-out of the Song of Solomon using Watchman Nee's book on the subject as my reference.

This was my mid-twenties, when my mental capacities were slowly nearing their peak. I did hide God's word in my heart as a matter of course, but I also toyed with figuring out Bible prophecy with my mind. I did not know then that Isaac Newton had already done that – and no one cared.

Nonetheless, in my mental enthusiasm, I decided that it would also be a great plan to write a single gospel, pulling in the wording from all four. I was walking from the Tabernacle to the dorm, happily imagining how much fun that would be when I found myself confronted by a bony finger sticking itself in my forehead, so to speak, and the harsh words spoken into my spirit, "What are you doing to My word?" This was the same One who had come upon me in fear in the Prince George bus terminal.

Needless to say, I dropped my plans like a hot potato. From then on, I stopped any attempts at "figuring out" the Bible. I sought only to plant all that God speaks into my heart, to know what He speaks, but not to know what it has to mean.

During my years at Bowens Mill, I attended fifteen different conventions including one at Lubbock and one in Mexico City. Move conventions were always deep spiritual experiences that worked profoundly inside of me.

I took on the task of transcribing the series of teachings Sam Fife preached in Hollywood, Florida just before his death, titled "The Hollywood Series." These were six messages of about two-hours' length each. I listened to the tape recording during the night watch hours and wrote them out word for word. I connected with one of the traveling ministries who was staying at the Ridge at that time, Sister Janet Myers. Since I had no typewriter, she had a relative of hers type out the transcriptions, and they were turned into little booklets.

I also developed a series of teaching booklets from these messages. I gave them to Brother Buddy at New Covenant to see if they could be useful for the fellowships. I had put many, many hours of work into this; it was for me a labor of love and joy. After a convention a number of weeks later, Brother Buddy was in the front seat of a car pulling away from in front of the Ridge Tabernacle. The car stopped, and Janet Myers in the back seat rolled down her window. She beckoned to me, and gave me all of the study booklets I had given to Buddy Cobb to peruse.

Janet Myers said to me, "These aren't of any value. Brother Buddy says that Brother Sam was teaching deception." Then, they drove away.

Long before I left the Ridge, I had lost all heart. This was the moment it was crushed.

What on earth do you do with something like that? Life continues, but the fog only increases.

Seven Years of Word

From the summer of 1977, when I heard Sam Fife preach on "The Mystery of a Man with a Maid," on tape at Graham River Farm, until the summer of 1984, a probable ending point for this seven-year season, I listened to quite a number of words preached by Brother Sam. The majority of those words were on tape, but a fair number were in person before his death.

The words on tape were as vivid to me as the words in person, and through all of them my heart was wide open to God in the heavens and I received from my Father His Word deep into my heart.

One word that lives inside me even now is Brother's Sam's teaching called "Christ is a Corporate Man." He said, "Christ life is corporate life. it has never been anything but corporate life and it never will be anything but corporate life." Union with Christ has taught me the balance, that Christ life is also completely personal to each one of us. Yet I hold to Christ also as Community even until now.

Two other words that implacted me deeply were Sam Fife's word on Abraham and Mt. Moriah and his word on jacob, "I Will Not Let You Go." Wrestling with God until He causes me to know Him is the story of my life. But in his word on Abraham offering Isaac, Brother Sam spoke of a test God would bring into your life, a choice between everything you ever wanted and knowing God. I know now that God does not "test" us, rather, He proves Christ to us. Yet this is the pattern of my life.

Further Experiences

My parents were planning to fly to Michigan that August of 1983 to visit with their brothers and sisters living there. It worked out for me to borrow a car from a sister in the community and drive up. Three other fellows went with me, two of whom I dropped off along the way. The third, Teddy Hsueh, went with me all the way to Detroit. I was glad for that, Teddy lived on the outskirts of the move; his wife lived at the Ridge. Teddy was streetwise and tough and Detroit was not safe.

We stayed in the Christian community in Detroit, however, all of whom were African Americans and very much part of the move. My parents flew in, and we spent the night in the community house coming and going. They were received as at home.

I learned something important while visiting with my Uncle Charles in Michigan. His daughter, a cousin much older than I, had Down Syndrome. She was short and fat and of very little mind. Yet she was also all heart. When we arrived, she raced out of the house with wide-open arms to greet mom and dad, whom she remembered. Once inside, she soon had her head on my mom's lap, weeping, "I miss my mommy," who had passed on not long before.

At the Ridge prior to that time, I had walked for a short time with a young man who had completely "flipped out." He needed constant watch, 24/7. We were not able to help him. All those who were "mentally ill" at the Ridge had the same overwhelming quality of pure selfishness. At no point could anyone else's needs or concerns enter into their picture.

My cousin was the opposite, mentally retarded, but big of heart and filled with love for others. The two "mental conditions" are opposite. My cousin had a brain problem; the mentally ill at the Ridge had a heart problem – absolute self-centeredness. I am convinced that in the resurrection many of those who were Down Syndrome now, when they are restored to full minds, will have hearts larger than most. They will be seen as the real humans.

After spending time with our relatives, I returned my parents to the Detroit airport and then proceeded back to Bowens Mill by myself. If you will look at the map, you will see that a straight line from Detroit to Bowens Mill passes within 500 miles of Gettysburg. To be within 500 miles of Gettysburg and not go there was entirely impossible, so I headed east.

As I passed through the Canton, Ohio, area, I determined to find Dan and Joanne Kurtz. You understand that, as a young man, I did not ask for directions or warn people I was coming. I remembered "Uniontown," and in Uniontown, I found a Mennonite Church. Sure enough, someone there knew of the Kurtz's, and so I spent the afternoon with them. It was over four years since I had last seen them. We had a wonderful visit together. Then, I spent an entire half day at the Gettysburg battlefield site before driving on back to Georgia.

Through the next few months I continued working, mostly by myself, on more jobs associated with the kitchen, including a second full kitchen on the back porch for milk processing, etc. Working by one's self in construction in community becomes a very lonely experience.

I want to add two more experiences before this chapter is completed. Both of them likely happened in 1983, though I did not record them when I cast the outline of my autobiography twenty years ago. The first was the first dream job of my construction career, and the second was a wondrously fun community "fishing trip."

I had dreamed for years of building a house of my own design. That chance came when Brother Woody Crossin, moving up from south Florida to serve as a caretaker at the convention site, asked me to design and build their home, the one standing right at the corner where you turn in towards the Tabernacle. My designs until then, except for the Ridge kitchen, had been partly fantasy; this one had to be real. I turned to a brother who lived at the New Covenant farm, Nick Shipsky, to help me get the bathrooms right. I designed a story-and-a-half home, with an upstairs in the roof, but with dormers.

I could not be released from the Ridge for the normal time it would take to build that house, however. Neither were any of the other builders on the different farms able to take the time. Thus it was decided that we would all gather and build the thing in one weekend. I would be in charge.

Twenty-six men gathered on a Saturday morn-

ing to construct the house, most of them professionals. We had framers, sheetrockers, painters, plumbers, and electricians. In order for this to work, however, everything needed to flow. The brothers at the convention site had already built the foundation and floor when we arrived, so we started with the walls. The stairs were in place before all the walls were up and all upper deck work could go up and down the stairs.

We would have finished in two days if everyone had been there both days. As it was we came close. I did little of the work; most of my time was spent coordinating everything. I absolutely loved it; it was so much fun. Sheetrockers and painters, plumbers and roofers, all doing their stuff at the same time. It was heavenly.

I would get to do that twice more, the next time being bigger and far more glorious, but that comes in a future chapter. I was certainly held in much higher respect by those men from then on.

Sometime in here a neighbor in-between us and New Covenant had a large fish pond he wanted drained in order to rid it of frogs and turtles. He offered to the move communities to catch the fish in the pond as the water drained. Many people from the three communities were gathered that Saturday around the banks, eager to process the fish. Someone brought two long, two-man fish nets.

I got the end of one of the nets with Darryl Cobb at the other end. I think it was Richard and Wassel on the other net. We started at one end and worked our way forward in conjunction with each other. When we got to the end of our first run, we each had a few turtles in the nets, but no fish. We knew the fish were there, but they jumped right over the nets. We tried again, doing it differently each time. After awhile we were coming up with hundreds of small fish in our nets through each pass. The people on the shore put the fish into large barrels to be carried to the different communities. Everyone was having such a lark. It was one of those great experiences one stumbles across through life, just like the disciples on the Sea of Galilee.

Then, sometime near the end of 1983, I was busy with a chain saw, clearing some brush along the drive into the farm when Jim Fant came walking up to me. He asked me a question that would change my life and set me on an entirely new course. But that must await the next chapter.

13. A Song in Great Difficulty

January 1984 - August 1985

Finding My Song

A number of people from the Ridge were teachers in the Bowens Mill Christian school across the road. I had been invited on a couple of occasions to come down to a classroom and share with a class on this or that topic of my interest (mostly geography). For some reason I felt wrong about it inside and so declined the opportunity.

In late December, 1983, on a Saturday, as I was cutting brush out of a hedgerow along the lane into the Ridge, Brother Jim Fant came walking up to me. Brother Jim was the principal of the school that year. "Daniel," he said to me, "A teacher in the school has just needed to pull out this Christmas break. We need an English teacher for the tenth grade. Let me know by supper if you want to do it, you will be starting on Tuesday."

On January 3, 1984, I stepped into my first classroom. And in that room, with four eager tenth grade students, I found my calling in God. I was 27 years old.

My first four students were Glen Mosher from the Ridge, Dina LaFera and Ben Hawkins from Family Farm, and Andrea Knight from New Covenant. I was their English teacher. As I write these words, I know such profound joy and gratefulness.

I had found the singing of my heart. I loved working with young people. I loved books and curriculum and lessons. I loved teaching literature and grammar and writing. I loved the whole concept of teaching as an art and a skill. I loved every part of this new-found song; I had no idea before how much these things meant to me.

But most importantly, the classroom gave me a place. Behind my desk, I was the "teacher." I knew my role, and I could function as the "teacher" in that role. I cannot express how important this is for Asperger's. If I don't have a "place" given to me by others, then I have no idea how to function. In this place, then, teenage girls talked to me as their teacher. I did not know it then, but it would be

friendly and cheerful girls talking with me in the classroom setting, both here and later in college at Blueberry, that would coax me out of my defensive autistic shell bit by bit.

Since I was teaching only one class a day, I continued in my other functions at the Ridge. However, in March, there was a need for someone else to take on the 9th grade history class, so I added that to my day, and then by May, a third class opened to me. I don't remember which that was. Before the end of the school year, I signed up to teach full time for the year 1984-1985.

I was 27 years old and had never been to college, but I am the kind of person that tackles a challenge like this with all enthusiasm. Many of my students counted me their best and favorite teacher. I don't think it was because I knew what I was doing, but rather because I enjoyed their youthfulness and I cared.

Winding Down

For three years I had given myself wholeheartedly to the Ridge, to its needs and concerns. Then, beginning with my first class in January, 1984, I slowly attached my heart to the school and teaching, and disconnected it from the Ridge. This slow process covered most of that year.

In order to lessen my load in the men's dorm, the elders at the Ridge added Richard Hernandez and Charlie Jones as "co-examples." I was still the lead, but I could rely on them to cover many of the responsibilities. I am sad to say that I did not spend a lot of time with Richard through these years. We remained friends, but our lives unfolded in very different circles. The dorm was little more than a place to sleep. Someone else took on the milk cows, so I no longer had that task as part of my day.

Besides finishing the Ridge kitchen by August, a two-year job, I took on a number of remodeling tasks, including wallpapering in trailers and a couple of weeks spent under the Ridge Tabernacle, shoring up the floor with new supports. Much of this time I worked by myself. Contrasted with the joy of the classroom, working by myself became very lonely. During the summer of 1984, I also helped in the construction of two more cabins at the convention site, including the Dallas cabin.

Sometime in the middle of the summer of 1984, I made myself report on David Troshin's unacceptable behavior, as was my responsibility. I was tired of giving these endless reports, and the utterly blank look on Brother Claude's face, I interpreted as the statement of a profound "I don't care." Something snapped inside of me. I remained the dorm example until I left the Ridge the next June, but I never reported again. The men in the dorm could do whatever they wanted, I no longer cared.

A Twelve-Year Course

When I left the Ridge in June of 1985, I was leaving the move-of-God fellowship, deeply angry with God. Although the classroom remained my joy and my refuge, all other parts of my life became difficult. I will include more good things regarding my love of teaching, but through the remainder of this letter, I want to describe the great press of God squeezing me from every direction.

I now understand the necessity of God's dealings with me; I certainly did not understand it then. As I look back now, I see that God was preparing me for a most confusing experience with Him during the April 1985 convention. In that convention He would begin a work inside of me that would not be finished until twelve years later, sitting in the same place in the same Bowens Mill Convention Tabernacle in late March of 1997.

When God spoke to me in late March of 1997, "Son, you passed the test," I did not perceive everything God meant by that statement as I understand it now. Nonetheless, in recent years, as I will share with you later, these most difficult years of experience showed themselves to be the most important thing God has ever taught me. And as I set forth my soul for you, for your sake, I am convinced that God will use my difficulty for your blessing, that you will gain from Him the same thing He gave to me.

I fear God. – And I would suggest to you the immense value of possessing such a quality.

I will approach this final year more thematically than chronologically. I warn you that I must open myself up, in doing so, and share less attractive things. But I believe that God is using this present task of sharing my life story in this way, bringing the Mercy Seat of God into every difficult place. I am encouraged that this is part of my task in the turning of the ages and in the release of the knowledge of God into all the earth.

I began this account stating that God has no good reason to choose me; I have always been self-centered and self-willed. Yet God has chosen me contrary to reason. Part of my purpose is to show you why I make such an indefensible claim.

Contending with the Word

I have always contended with God concerning His word. And the word, whether preached or written, has always been central in my life. I have usually been unsuccessful at any "doing" of the word; nonetheless, I have never left off contending with God face to face regarding what He says.

Here are three short passages that were of great importance to me through these years, they held my heart and gave me something to keep hold of through the stinging blows.

Moreover He called for a famine in the land; He destroyed all the provision of bread. He sent a man before them—Joseph—who was sold as a slave. They hurt his feet with fetters, he was laid in irons. Until the time that his word came to pass, the word of the Lord tested him (Psalm 105:16-19).

Then Jacob was left alone; and a Man wrestled with him until the breaking of day... And He said, "Let Me go, for the day breaks." But he said, "I will not let You go unless You bless me!" ... And He said, "Your name shall no longer be called Jacob, but Israel; for you have struggled with God and with men, and have prevailed" (Genesis 32:24-28).

I am the man who has seen affliction by the rod of His wrath. He has led me and made me walk in darkness and not in light. Surely He has turned His hand against me time and time again throughout the day. ...He has besieged me and surrounded me with bitterness and woe. He has set me in dark places... He has hedged me in so that I cannot get out; He has made my chain heavy. Even when I cry and shout, He shuts out my prayer. He has blocked my ways with hewn stone; He has made my paths crooked - - - (Lamentations 3:1-9 and on).

And yes, Lamentations 3 was the most comforting Scripture in the Bible for me through these years, for this is a description of my life and these words showed me that God was in my affliction. Like Jacob, I wrestled with God concerning His word; as with Joseph, the word of the Lord tested me through fetters and irons until the time it would be fulfilled. And with Jeremiah, I wept. – You know, I can be melodramatic at times, but I am telling you the truth.

There was some contention regarding the word in the larger arena of the move. I now understand that this contention was actually caused by Buddy Cobb. Except for the conventions, however, Buddy Cobb had little direct involvement in my life. I will not bring him into resolution until the last chapter of my years in community, Blair Valley.

Nonetheless, when Buddy Cobb told me, through Janet Myers, that Sam Fife taught many things that were contrary to the truth, he was referring to all the things I learned from Sam Fife that I now teach to you. And all the things Buddy Cobb retained from Sam Fife in his own teaching are the things I speak against all through what I teach now. (See the list at the end of Chapter 9, "Cutting the Covenant.")

Everyone looked to Buddy Cobb and trusted his apostolic leadership and the anointing of the Spirit that truly was upon him. In that context, that was the right thing to do in the Lord. God is not after the ideas we hold in our heads, but after the condition of our hearts. But what Buddy Cobb taught does not come into this history until those final years when I had surrendered all my objections and believed and taught the same as he.

Nonetheless, many still held to those things Sam Fife had taught; whereas others embraced the pure Calvinism of Buddy Cobb with all gusto.

There was a couple living at the Family Farm who were both elders, Tony and Maridel Tudelo. I had only a public and indirect relationship with them, nothing personally close. Nonetheless, they figure somewhat in this discussion and so I will bring them in by name.

A wonderful Bible teacher by the name of Ernest Watkins, who lived at the Hilltop Community in northern British Columbia, spent a couple of weeks at the Ridge giving a Bible teaching. Most of those at the Ridge attended his sessions, along with a few from the other communities. I believe he was teaching the history of Israel.

Well, Tony Tudelo was one who attended the Bible studies. Brother Ernest was good at raising questions without getting himself involved in any debate. Tony Tudelo loved to debate on the side of "you sin, you go to hell." Few other preachers magnified the flesh as much as he did. As he stood in the Bible study to proclaim his "sin and death" message, Brother Jim Fant, who was also there through the teachings, could not keep quiet. He rose to his feet as well to assert that God by His grace keeps us, regardless of our difficulties.

The problem was that Sam Fife had preached both words. Under Buddy Cobb, however, "God keeping us by His grace," was no longer in favor. Now it was up to us to "hear and obey."

Another wonderful Bible teacher was Don Stockbridge, who lived at the New Covenant community. He had a gift to open up the Bible stories of the Old Testament as a view of Christ our life and the wondrous goodness of God.

I ran the sound system and taping of the services through most of my years at Bowens Mill. When Tony Tudelo stood to preach his "gospel of sin and death," I was tempted to turn off his microphone. I did not, however. Nonetheless, after his messages, I always felt further from God. Acting from "the flesh" is the only result I have ever seen coming out from such a word. When Don Stockbridge set before us the beauty of Christ revealed in His kingdom, however, I was so enthralled that I was convicted of whatever "sin" might have been dragging me down. The fruit coming out from such a word was always to life. I made note of this great contrast, but I did not understand it.

Through this time a couple of Christian Jews, who had anointed ministries, connected with the move and preached in the conventions. One of them was Art Katz from Minnesota; I do not remember the name of the other.

Nonetheless it was the other Jewish brother who preached in a convention in 1984 that placed a great question upon my heart. He started his word with Solomon's pessimism and lack of faith in Christ. **"Better to go to the house of mourning than to go to the house of feasting, for that is the end of all men; and the living will take it to heart"** (Ecclesiastes 7:2). Yes, we can draw wisdom out from Solomon's words, but ONLY as those things are RULED by the gospel of Christ our life.

This brother was mightily anointed of the Lord, and his word was right in line with what Buddy Cobb preached. I was caught in the anointing and power of his words as he opened the heavens to us. Basically, his premise was that we must mourn over our sin and our falling short and that the only way out is to "hear and obey." Nonetheless, God pours out His Spirit upon all humans, regardless, and this man was strong in his humanity and thus in the Lord.

As part of his word, the brother shared an experience he had. He enjoyed mountain climbing, and one time he had scaled a mountain in Switzerland. In all his experiences, he knew God with Him, and so he had my full attention. A storm came up and night fell. He could not see his way to safety, yet he was huge on God with him and he with God.

The brother heard God speak to him, "Walk down the mountain." And he obeyed. He walked straight forward, every step in God, until he was in safety at the bottom of the cliff.

When he finished his word, I was transfixed and mesmerized. I was utterly overwhelmed. I looked at all the people getting in line for hot dogs after the service, and I could not understand. I handed David Troshin off to someone else and went straight home. I got on my face on the floor beside my bed. How could I know such a God? How could I ever do such a thing? If such "hear and obey" was required of me, if God were behind such an impossible barrier, what hope had I? Yet I contended with God there on the floor, for not ever knowing Him was impossible to me.

Teaching Full-Time

When I was doing something I loved, I had the tendency of taking on too much. When that happened, I would scale back just a bit until I was comfortable in full engagement. For the 1984-85 school year, I took on seven classes. That meant no off-period, not even lunch. For a while I supervised the lunch room as well and ate with the students.

First period, I taught 11th grade American History, the same four students I started with in January, along with four 10th graders and one 12th grade student. At the same time, I oversaw two 12th grade girls taking American government, Andrea LaFera and Michelle Gibbs. I will only give you some of the names, but please understand, these young people were most precious to me. (And I do have my lesson plan book, so this is not all out of memory.)

Second period I taught American Lit to 10th and 11th grade students. Third period was almost my favorite. I taught 8th grade English to two cute, smart, and cheerful girls, Angela Gerhardt and Christi Knight. I had so much fun with those two.

Fourth period I taught World History to the 9th grade class, along with some of the 10th graders, those who were not in American History. Fifth period I taught standard English to a mix of 10th, 11th, and 12th graders. Sister Ruth Mosher, my mentor through this time, was teaching a creative writing course that included the more capable English students. Finally, in the last period of the day, I taught boy's carpentry skills. The students then went home at 3 PM.

These students became my life, and all my energy and thought was devoted to them. I continued sleeping in the men's dorm at the Ridge and eating supper there in the Tabernacle. Breakfast I skipped because I was at my desk by 6 AM or so, preparing for the day, and one of my students from the Ridge, Janet Lee Klingbeil, made a lunch for me each day for the noon meal. I was too exhausted to do much school work from 3PM until supper, but in the evenings I felt better. After supper, I came back down to the school and worked on grading student papers, often until 10 PM.

The weekends, of course, I was at the Ridge, continuing to work there on various things. One thing we did was to pour a huge concrete septic tank for the Ridge community in the sandy bank just below the wood shop. But I did not like the weekends. Monday was always my favorite day because now I was back in my classroom for the week. This was my sentiment all the years I taught school in move communities.

I had no formal training in classroom teaching nor any experience of it prior to stepping into the classroom. I must have had a knack for it, though. We used the ABeka curriculum (which I do not recommend for a number of reasons), so I always had the text book to fall back on. I learned more than I realized at the time about teaching and learning, by practical experience. Nonetheless, one question that grew in me over the months was – How do you teach kids to think?

Let me share one experience that explains Asperger's perfectly. I had taken on too much, so someone else took my place overseeing the student lunch hall. I then ate my lunch in my room, which was located as a wing at the back of the main community hall that you see in the picture in Chapter 7, "Into the South." Nonetheless, the older girls liked to come into my room during lunch hour where they were free to chat easily among themselves and with me. I owe so much to the talkative girls who were now in my life; as I look back now, I see that their friendliness to me was a gift of God. Besides Dina LaFera, there was also her sister, Andrea LaFera, of Italian talkativeness, along with Michelle Gibbs, Sharon Stafford, Rachel Stansbery, and others.

You see, they did most of the talking. I wasn't much good at talking back, so I was pretty much limited to smiles and, "Is that right." But one day, I was out with them among the student desks. Andrea LaFera, a senior, was, as I think now, more mature in her expression, and so I was able to visit back with her. Meanwhile, Michelle Gibbs, seeing my empty chair behind my teacher's desk, went over and sat down in it. Instantly, I lost my "place." I no longer had a connection to meaning or purpose. I was adrift in a sea of chatting females, and all I could do was hold my breath and hope that nothing would be required of me. When Michelle bounced back up from my chair and came back around my desk, instantly, my place and purpose as "the teacher" came back to me, and I breathed a great sigh of relief.

I had no idea of it then, but this is a symptom of Asperger's.

Sister Ruth Mosher, who lived at the Ridge with her husband, Bruce, and a whole passel of cute girls, younger and older than Glen, their only son, was the other high school English teacher. She was my mentor through this time, and I learned a lot from her. Only Glen was in the grades I taught. During that year she led her creative writing course of the more gifted 10th through 12th grade students in creating a class yearbook. They wrote a short piece on each student and teacher in the school as part of their creative writing. On the next page is the one written of me, I believe it was by Dina LaFera, one whom I carry close inside my heart. Along with it is my picture. You can see that I was skinny as a bean pole.

Maureen and Sheila

Maureen taught first grade. In fact, Maureen was teaching school before she graduated from high school. Her picture and the writeup for her by the creative writing class are also on the next page. You can see how beautiful she is. Yet she was not talkative, and I could not talk with her.

And this was the word of the Lord that tried me through these years. The witness arising in my heart that Maureen would be my wife did not cease. Yet there was nothing outwardly. I attended many weddings while living at Bowens Mill. Over and over, I would watch a young man win the joy of his heart and be married, but I was incapable of doing the same.

But I cannot talk about the agony of my non-relationship with Maureen through this time without bringing Sheila Gerhardt into the same picture. Sheila was a tenth grader in my classroom, twelve years younger than I. She had been in one of my classes in the spring, and was in two of my classes through this full year. Sheila was incredibly cute, very intelligent, and talkative. Sheila loved to chat about anything and everything, and she didn't mind chatting with me.

As I think about it now, I realize that Dina LaFera fitted the exact same description. The only difference was that Dina lived at the Family Farm, and so I saw her only at school, whereas Sheila lived at the Ridge, and I had known her and her family since I moved there. And as I said, I now realize that both Dina and Sheila were a wondrous gift from God to me. But Sheila was the only one from whom I gained any kind of friendship through my last year at the Ridge.

The Gerhardt's lived in a trailer in the row to the left of the washhouse, their mother, Bonnie, who worked as a nurse in town, Sheila, Angela, whom I had in 8th grade, and Gary, who was a good tag-along little brother. The dad wanted nothing to do with the move; I believe they were divorced. During this time, Maureen had her bedroom with them in their trailer.

In May, at the same time that I first had Sheila in my class at the school, I worked at remodeling the Gerhardt trailer. Part of my work was in Maureen's bedroom. I must confess that, in my loneliness, I did look through Maureen's picture albums. I went no further than that. At the same time, I began to enjoy

Mr. Yordy may come across to some folks as being an austere person, but with one look at those twinkling, mischievous blue eyes it's a dead give away of a very fair person. He has never lost the "joy of learning.," and he never fails to strike a spark of interest in those who have him for a teacher. Impartations of grace have made him popular with his students, as he is easygoig and is able to enjoy good times without forfeiting his place of authroity. A mild, forbearing teacher who remains outsoken in his deeply held convictions, many will remember him as the one who sauntered into their lives and hearts in his gentle, dignified way.

DANIEL YORDY
American History/World History
English 10-12/English 8
American Literature

MAUREEN MACK

An oasis in the midst of an arid, desolate wasteland, Miss Maureen is an everpresent source of comfort and solace that her stdents have come to rely heavily upon.

She mingles yet remains distinct because of her serene, charming and graceful ways. Her silken repose creates a pool of tranquility about her.

Her elegance is due to her personality, and her patience enables her to be an excellent teacher with a calming effect on her little, energetic students.

Sheila's company. Like I said, she was bright, bubbly, and very talkative.

The thing is, I was becoming ANGRY with God. Why did God continue speaking to me about Maureen while, apparently, saying nothing whatsoever to her? This had been going on for three years, now. I was getting fed up with the agony. Nonetheless, my regard for Maureen did not diminish. Through the cold mornings of the winter time, I went into her classroom early each morning and lit her gas stove so that her classroom would be warm. When I ask her about it now, she says that she just thought someone lit the stoves in all the classrooms. She did not know that I was doing it for her.

My friendship with Sheila fitted into that emptiness. Although I certainly felt enamored of her, I never considered her as a "future companion." She was way younger than I; neither did we share the same values. I must defend myself here, though, by asserting that nothing improper, either in word or

in touch, ever occurred. We remained only friends, no matter what emotional trauma I felt.

There is no further experience for me to share regarding Maureen through this time. She was a closed door to me for seven long years.

A Great Press

The months from September 1984 through May 1985 were marked with two extremes, my love and joy for teaching and for my students on the one hand, and the entire "move" – "Ridge" – ministry structure on the other hand. I continued at Bowens Mill until the end of the school year only because I wanted to continue teaching and "Oh, I quit" will not open any doors.

By October, I had separated my heart completely from the Ridge. I was still present there when not in school, but I did not care. Then, by the end of 1984, I had separated my heart from the whole concept of a hierarchy of ministry. Let me give you the particulars. Now, these things were a big deal, yes, but they are also representative of a whole slew of little things.

More than that, I lived through these months in an intense disagreement with God. If you had asked me then, I would have claimed that, most of all, I had separated my heart from God. That was not actually true, however, for God had long since sealed me out from the valley of decision.

My workday began at 7:30 in the morning, with the arrival of students at the school. I went non-stop, no breaks whatsoever, until 3 in the afternoon, seven-and-a-half hours. Besides that, I put in around four hours each day of prep time, for a total of over eleven hours a day. I loved it, but it was exhausting. In contrast, with all the breaks and a long lunch, etc., a typical workday for most of the men at the Ridge was under seven hours. Because I was brain-dead in the late afternoon and because I was faced with a few more hours of work in the evening, I sometimes took a nap in my bed in the dorm before supper.

One day, not long into this regimen, David Troshin found me napping during "work time." He gleefully went to Brother Claude to inform him that I was not "following the order."

A question had been growing inside of me for some time, a question that would continue to grow until I screamed it to God at the top of my lungs during the April 1985 convention.

– Why don't they ask? –

Not asking was part of move doctrine and practice and part of their definition of "ministry."

Now, this is the part where I will place a shadow of bitterness upon the page. I am free to do so, because I now understand exactly what God was doing for me and how important all these things would be for you, that I would have this word of Christ our life to give.

Sam Fife had taught that an elder is anointed of God, that's why they're elders. They hear from God, and they move as Christ towards those who are not elders. On the other hand, those who aren't elders are not elders because they are not yielded to the anointing, which means they are primarily "fleshy."

More than that, John Hinson had taught the ministry at the Ridge that an elder never apologizes. God is speaking through them; to apologize is

to allow their role to appear to be "not God." This view, that non-elders are flesh, was more prevalent in the move than I knew at this time. Nonetheless, I watched various ones of the elders rebuke non-elders for their ideas and feelings as if the elder was "of God" and the non-elder was only "of the flesh." Even Jim Fant, who was a man of grace, was caught in this absurd definition.

Buddy Cobb taught that ministry needs to have the word of the Lord; they need to "discern." And when they speak, they speak the penetration of God into the fleshiness of the non-elder.

To ask would be to cater to "the flesh." The terrible thing is, they were wrong more often than not, and the few times they were right in their guesses made them imagine that they were always right.

Another concept peculiar to the Ridge was that John Hinson taught them that the eldership is always one. If one elder says something, even in private, all the elders are one with that statement or action. Thus an elder can never be "wrong."

Now these were godly people who loved the Lord and moved by the Spirit. I am not speaking of anything inappropriate or immoral.

Claude Mack did not ask. He came in, with David hovering gleefully behind him, got me out of bed and ripped me over the coals in full military regalia for napping during the work time. I could never stand against Claude Mack, though he was small of stature. Neither do I ever defend myself in such situations. I am typically unable to speak, and it usually takes me hours and days and months to finally figure out what on earth just happened.

In that moment, all connection to the Ridge or to its authority in my life ceased out from my heart. I did go to Brother Jim Fant and shared that experience with him. This was one of the few times when he broke with the norm in disagreeing with another elder.

Napping in my bed was no longer an option. To compensate, I found a small easy chair and put it in the back corner of my classroom along with a small table on which sat a coffee maker. Since I started work by 6 AM, I could make my coffee in my classroom. Then, in the late afternoon, I could nap sitting in the easy chair. Understand, this nap was vital to my ability to maintain the full load I was teaching.

A couple of months later, word got around to

the elders of the three communities that Daniel Yordy had an easy chair in the back of his classroom. This was too "fleshy" to allow.

You see, every one of those elders had their own living rooms with their own easy chairs in which they sat most evenings in quiet and comfort. I had just the men's dorm, a dozen men with a living room that would sit only four or five, one of whom was always David Troshin, who made sure that no one could be comfortable there.

No one asked me; they just told me to get rid of the chair.

For about five months, I napped in my teacher's chair, with my head on the hard desk in front of me. I became immured to it, for that was the only way I could maintain my class load and the love and joy of my life, my care for my students.

A couple with a long history in move community, but who were not elders, Jeff and Nancy Nalley, had moved to the Ridge just before I started teaching school. Their son, John, was in my classroom. One evening, I stopped in their home after supper to visit. I felt so secure and comfortable in a family living room and home. But after a bit, Jeff said he had to prepare for his one class the next day; it was time for me to leave. I walked on down to the school in the dark. The contrast between his warm home and my lonely desk that night was a bit much.

The Agony of Disrespect

Of far greater agony to me, however, was the disrespect shown to the young people in the communities. This was not just a "move thing," for I have seen the same in public schools and in other Christian schools.

I was twenty when I became a part of this fellowship of Christian communities; I had come in by choice as an adult. Now, for the first time, I was on the receiving end of the teenagers growing up, not by choice, under the doctrine of *"die to your flesh."*

I will give three instances that are reflective of an ongoing climate of disrespect that was a normal part of treating teenagers in move community schools. This would be one of the three primary reasons why I chose to leave that fellowship. I saw the same practice looming over my own children, and I would not have it. Again, my children assure me that Maureen and I are different, that this is the same way most Christian parents raise their children. It's how most

humans raise their children; it's certainly not peculiar to the move.

I had been directing the after-school work of two young men who lived at the Ridge, Bobby and Chip. I had both of them in my ninth grade class at school. But when I started teaching full time, I was no longer there to do that. The elders then asked Jeff Nalley to step into that role. Within a few days Bobby and Chip were coming to me in utter desperation. Jeff was treating them like dirt, accusing them of all sorts of things and not trusting them or what they might say or do at all. There was little I could do, but they kept coming, getting more desperate. I had the opportunity to observe and was aghast at the things beings spoken against them.

It's not that they had it easy with me; I did make them work. But I also respected and enjoyed them as persons, and they knew the difference. I went to Brother Jim and shared their dilemma with him, with evidence. Brother Jim was an honorable man, and Jeff Nalley was soon assigned to other tasks. Sadly, this kind of conduct was all too common, elders or non-elders.

I had Janet Lee Klingbeil from the Ridge in two of my classes. She also was one who often found refuge in my classroom during lunch. One day, one of the elders in the school, Maridel Tudelo, accused Janet Lee of some wicked thing. Janet Lee was completely innocent, but Maridel would not hear it. She persisted and I think she took it to the larger three-farm elders' meeting. Janet Lee was beside herself with distress, something she was free to share with me. Her mother was one who had struggled with mental issues in the past. I do not remember the outcome for Janet Lee, but she was stronger than her mother and came through it okay. Again, this type of treatment towards the teenagers was all too common.

It is not wrong for me to be angry over this kind of stuff. I know that it distresses our Father.

That he might turn the hearts of the fathers to the children – that he might turn the hearts of the fathers to the children – lest I come and strike the earth with a curse (Malachi 4).

The third occurrence happened just after the April Bowens Mill convention. Sheila had attended a young people's gathering after the convention and was greatly touched by the Lord. Her heart softened, but as she basked in this new-found desire to know the Lord the next day, while working in the kitchen at the Ridge, one of the lady elders came through. This elder remembered some minor infraction Sheila had committed prior to this experience. She proceeded to rake Sheila over the coals without any modicum of respect or compassion. That was the final straw for Sheila, she was gone from the move, at age 16, just a couple of months later; I doubt that she has ever looked back.

It was also just one more of those final straws for me. Again, these are three examples of things these children struggled with on a regular basis.

Rock Bottom

I must back up a couple of months prior to the April convention to share with you my rock-bottom experience during this time. But in order to do that, I must bring in another aspect of life in move community.

Brother Sam had moved as a mighty deliverance ministry. When I get to Blueberry, I will share with you Jane Miller's story. Sam Fife had prayed over her for deliverance in the mid-sixties and set her free from multiple schizophrenia and out from a padded cell for life. The tape of her deliverance became a classic in the move.

Sapa had been a deliverance farm, but deliverance there was a ministry practiced in private and only with the elders. At Blueberry, Sister Jane made deliverance a ministry of the whole family.

I think that the ministry at the Ridge did conduct deliverance services a few times in the privacy of the Hinson trailer, but I knew nothing about it. Brother Jim taught that we had to stand for our own deliverance in refusing to heed demonic voices. A great emphasis was placed, rightly, on singing praises in the midst of spiritual assault.

At the time, I rejected absolutely the idea that any "demon" might have anything to do with me. I was too much "in control of myself" to tolerate such "nonsense." Nonetheless, as I shared earlier, I lived for fifteen years, from the time I overdosed on LSD at age 16, with unending torment gripping me in the gut. A wonderful word preached or a revelation from the Lord would relieve that torment for a few days, but back it would come, never having lost its grip. Part of my reason for spending my days in fantasy worlds was to escape this torment. Nonetheless, I have never been one to come under control to anything. No hypnotist could affect me.

During my hardening of my heart against God through these months, I had a desperate encounter with demons.

A young man from Juarez had come to stay at the Ridge. In my mind he was ugly, and in the dorm I saw his obnoxious side. But he was a great lady's man, and he soon tacked onto Sheila. We had a gathering at one of the other communities, and there I saw him, sitting in the row next to Sheila, and they were chatting merrily.

I went home in a cloud of darkness. I was bitter, and I hated the man. I went to sleep with my heart filled with hate. When I awoke in the night, my jaw was clenched so tightly I was in pain. At the same time, something let loose inside, other persons inside my bubble of self, screeching their mockery at me. I was well aware that I was at the door of "mental illness."

The truth is, however, all my "disconnection with God" was in my imagination only. At that moment, I grabbed hold of Jesus with all my might and sang, "The Blood of Jesus," over and over. It did not take long before, "Pow," they were gone. I had looked again into darkness and rejected what I found there.

The young man did not remain long and was soon gone, probably by the April Convention.

A Very Strange Convention

During that convention of April, 1985, I had an ongoing and very puzzling experience with God. It is something I have long pondered and which I am still placing into my understanding.

I was angry with God regarding Maureen. I was finished with the Ridge. I wanted nothing more to do with the move. Yet I continued for my students' sake and because I was determined to finish the school year.

That doesn't mean that I did not have a relationship with God or that I did not continue in grace and in good conduct. It does mean that I was having an ongoing series of angry conversations with God over all the inequities I saw in community as devised by Sam Fife, Buddy Cobb, and John Hinson. I was in community because community has filled my heart all my life. But something was missing, and I did not know what that was.

I wept over what community ought to be. Another elder by the name of Paul Putnam had moved to the Ridge several months before, with his wife,

Helen. He was a good man who wanted to be life and help in the lives of people in need. I saw the same sorrow upon his face as he realized that his heart was not shared by others. "Follow the order" was the only answer allowed. I thought about pouring out my concerns to Brother Paul, but I did not.

Again, through the months leading up to the April convention, I had engaged in many "fleshy" arguments inside my "carnal" mind regarding all that I thought was "wrong." I was in distress, and I was finding no answers.

Then I sat down in the convention. It seemed to me, in word after word, that I was the one who had written the script for what God wanted to say through this convention. Preacher after preacher shared out from my arguments against God, giving my "solutions" to the congregation as God's solutions. I was flabbergasted. How could my fleshy agony be God speaking?

But something yet remained. The biggest thing of all. That Saturday evening, I walked home after the service alone. As I crossed the bridge over the creek, I paused and turned up to God. I raised my fist in anger against Him. "What about this?" I cried. "What are You going to do about this – about precious ones struggling in loneliness and despair and no one comes, no one asks. People are dying in this community, God," I cried, "and the ministry does not see."

You see, I was not the only one in this same distress. It was, in fact, "normal" for the Ridge.

The next morning, the last service of the convention, a Sunday, Brother John Hinson, the leading ministry of the Ridge, got up to share. His first words were, "God came to me in a dream last night and told me that people are dying in my community and I am not paying attention." The dream and his interpretation were much more detailed than that; it was an experience of the finger of God coming against someone who has placed himself over others in the church. It was everything I had yelled against God.

I was utterly astonished, to say the least. How could God pass from my angry words to His hand in the visions of the night against a leading ministry in the move?

I do not think more highly of myself than is right. And what is right is that I have failed at everything. Nonetheless, this was a mighty piece of evidence in

God's years-long campaign to persuade me to trust the it is He who is speaking inside of me.

Yet at the same time, He has also caused me to know that every time I think I am "right" about someone else's "problem"; I am always wrong. Embarrassingly WRONG.

It is in writing these things, however, that I can see so many things falling into their place, as they have been all along, a straight arrow shot of the dealings of God in my heart.

The issue of God and the serpent, the issue of Moses and Korah, the issue of David and Absalom, the issue of Christ with those who go forth in His name is – how do you respond when those who are "over you" in any way do what you think is wrong?

This convention marked the beginning of a twelve-year assault of God against that thing inside of me that could not remain – contempt. Or, as Gene Edwards puts it in *A Tale of Three Kings*, "What do you do when someone throws a spear at you?"

At the end of twelve years, in the same part of the same convention Tabernacle, God spoke to me, "Son, you passed the test." I can now see that, here at the beginning of the hammering of God, beating and beating the mercy seat of my heart into its shape, my Father was showing me, "My son, I am with you, part of you, even in your greatest agony." God's real test is completely different from what they all claim.

Sadly, nothing came from John Hinson's dream, at least nothing that I knew about.

Preparing to Leave

Sometime through here, maybe in April, I received a letter in the mail from Sister Judy Jones whom I had known at the Albuquerque Farm. In that letter, she invited me to come to the Blueberry Christian Community, where she was an elder. She also set out the possibility of my enrolling in the college the move fellowships had recently started, Covenant Life College.

I knew I was deficient in the teaching craft, and I longed to learn in a disciplined way. I put this invitation out there in front of me; nonetheless, I wanted nothing more to do with the move. The letter did, however, smooth over my request to the elders to return home to Oregon.

I had also heard from my mom. Dad was declining in health, and she needed help at home, particularly in putting a new roof on our house. She said that she would pay me for my time.

When I shared with the Ridge elders that my mom needed me at home for a season after which I was thinking about college at Blueberry, they were fully agreeable with my leading.

I asked my mother if she could see to sending me my wages for replacing the roof so that I could buy a car and have the means to get home. She sent me about $2500, and in May, I bought a Toyota Corolla station wagon from George Hawkins for $1500. I also went to town and purchased an Alpine tape deck and speakers, giving me a top-notch sound system for my car.

Because I had been teaching American literature, a desire to read all the great books had been reborn in me. Someone from the New Covenant community had given me an entire set of the Great Books, and I had begun with reading *Moby Dick* by Herman Melville.

I built boxes for all my stuff to prepare for the trip home. I had a lot of stuff.

Of course, I did not want to drive straight home. I wanted to spend time with Richard in Denver City, Texas, and then see parts of the country I had not yet seen. I got me a large road atlas and began plotting my meandering trip across the country. There was a problem, though. I wanted to go through places I had not yet been. The question then was, where have I been?

The solution was obvious – color in every single US county in which I have passed since I was twelve. I spent some happy hours down in my classroom, remembering the exact routes I had gone and filling in all the counties.

And so my most peculiar hobby began – I collect counties. Every time I plan a trip, I pull out my map of all the counties of the US and, if I can, chose a route that takes me through counties not yet colored in. At the end of most every trip, I get to fill in a bunch more counties.

I was still lonely, and I wanted Sheila to go with me. I wasn't thinking straight, of course, but God was with me even though I was trying my best to exclude Him. I finally found the courage and the moment to ask her. She laughed in a silly way and kept on chattering about a totally different subject. So much for that. Sheila left the Ridge the day after

school was over; she moved up to be with some relatives in Maryland.

I stayed on to be part of the graduation of the senior class, three of whom I had taught. It was a very good time, a good closing of my new-found joy of teaching school.

Another brother at the Ridge, Claude Savard, also wanted to go on up to Blueberry. He asked to ride with me at least as far as Oregon. He agreed to help me replace the roof on my parents' house. We loaded my little station wagon full, inside and on top, said our "Goodbye's" at the Ridge, and headed down the road that would eventually take us to home in Oregon.

A Sad Failure

I must share here one of my many failures in life. During this time of "trying to escape," I lied to Brother Jim Fant. In fact, that lie was probably the last words I spoke to him while he was a godly covering over me. This was a man who treated me with kindness the entire four-and-a-half years I walked with him. And the wisdom he imparted to me fills my present relationship with God. There is a time, entirely inside of the Lord Jesus, to be utterly ashamed of one's self and to weep tears of Godly sorrow. This is one of those times.

I was finished with "the move," and as I was preparing to leave, I bought a music tape that contained "Christian rock" music. The elders had heard of this and brought me into an elder's meeting.

There I was, sitting in the elder's meeting – Jim and Joyce Fant, Claude and Roberta Mack, Susan Jacobsen, Paul Putnam and others, brothers and sisters in Christ of high regard and of poured out lives. Brother Jim said to me, "I heard that you have bought a music tape of rock music. I am very disappointed; could you explain yourself."

I felt like a dear caught in the headlights. Then I remembered that there was one good song on that tape, a song that had been sung recently by a sister in the fellowship. I said, "I got it in order to enjoy that one song." I lied. – Why did I lie?

I could claim that I lied because I was embarrassed and did not want the elders to think that I was a "fleshy" person. But that would be just another lie. I lied because I wanted to control Brother Jim's thoughts towards me.

"Oh my Father, and Brother Jim, forgive me. What I did was cruel and wrong." I know now that rebuilding trust with Brother Jim Fant will be a joy in my future, even in the resurrection.

The Mercy Seat

You can see the bitterness that would fill my heart for the next three years until God removed it from me during the deliverance time at Blueberry. I now see God's good purpose for it.

Nonetheless, I cannot just open up this difficult time and then "go my way." Everyone must be drawn into the Mercy Seat; everything must be released into goodness. The shaping of God's heart to fit yours and the shaping of your heart to fit God's is the only truly meaningful thing happening in your life. It is my continual covenant with God that He will take from my life and cause you to share Hheart with Him.

"Father, I now know that the removal of Korah from my heart is the greatest gift of Your hammering that You have given to me. Yet You, Father, were with me there in my cries and in my agony. My distress was already being shaped by Yours."

What kind of a God shares fully the agony of the human soul, Heart together with heart?

[Note: as I look through the pictures of each of my students, speaking their names out loud, I realize that Sheila is simply one of them. More than that, each of these are now in their early fifties. I have only heard news of a couple through the years and seen only a couple since I taught them in school. Nonetheless, they each remain a part of my heart, and I will place them, with all confidence, into the Heart of God.]

"Father, You and I share Hheart together, Your Mercy Seat, the throne of heaven. The Blood of Your Son, the Lord Jesus Christ, is sprinkled here upon my heart, as You say it is. Father, I draw each one of these who were my students at Bowens Mill, each one by name, into Your Love that You share with me, inside of me. Father I know that You also carry each one of them. Father, I place Your seal upon each one, that You would capture their hearts, that You would keep them with power into Your arising. I thank You, my Father, for I am confident that You have done all that I ask.

"Father, I also ask You to cleanse me from any wrongness found in my needy connection to Sheila. Thank You, Father, that the Blood sprinkled upon my heart cleanses me."

"And Father, I pray for John Hinson, along with the ministry at the Ridge, although many are now in the heavens only. Certainly they made mistakes, as I have made mistakes. Yet You turn all our mistakes into unending goodness. Father, I give You thanks for the role John Hinson played in my life. I give You thanks for the testimony of Christ that he was to me.

"Father, I am astounded and amazed that You shared all of my agony with me, in every moment and through every step. I am astounded and amazed that You have always placed Yourself beneath of me, that You have always lifted me up.

"And each one who contributed to that agony of this time, Tony and Maridel Tudelo, Claude Mack, Darryl Cobb, Jeff Nalley, the young man from Juarez, I place each one and all others into You, Father, into the Love that fills my heart to overflowing. Father, they are free of me to arise into Your joy and peace.

"Father, You are good, all the time.

14. A Time of Reset

June 1985 - August 1986

Resetting Bowens Mill

Reset – okay. That's just what happened as I finished writing the last chapter. Bowens Mill has reset itself inside of my memory. What did I gain most from writing the last letter? First is the realization of how much I loved my students in the Bowens Mill school and how much joy teaching them was to me.

And second is writing these words: "This was a mighty piece of evidence in God's years-long campaign to persuade me to trust the it is He who is speaking inside of me." I have been so very slow to believe that it is, in fact, God who has always been arising inside of me with the understanding of His word, just as He promised me from the start.

Truly, truly, the dark hole inside that has been my memory of Bowens Mill is now filled with love and joy, with memories of good things and with a completely different perspective of the difficult things. This is so wonderful.

My sharing of this next period of time, a transition between Bowens Mill and Blueberry now proceeds through two points of view. First, I must show how I saw things then, but second, I must also show how things really were. I imagined that God was not with me when, in fact, He always has been. I thought He was against me when He was always for me. I did not then understand the truth.

The Trip Home

My younger sister, Jenelle, was attending Oral Roberts University in Tulsa, Oklahoma at this time, and so Tulsa became our first destination. I am ashamed to say that prior to this time, my younger brother and sister hardly "registered in my radar." They were much younger than I and in my self-centered pursuit of my own interests, I had hardly noticed them.

I was having an electrical problem with the Toyota Station wagon. As we were approaching Ida, Oklahoma, the car died. We walked up to a nearby farmhouse. When the farmer came home, he offered to pull our car down to the nearest Holiday Inn motel and then come get us the next morning to pull the car to a shop. The first mechanic we went to could not discover the problem, so he sent us on to an expert in "foreign cars." It took this guy about ten minutes to find and fix the problem, and we were on our way. We certainly felt taken care of by the Lord.

We spent a couple of days with Jenelle. She was learning to be a news video tape editor. ORU was it its height at that time and she showed us all around the campus. After that we drove on to Denver City, Texas.

We spent a couple of weeks with Richard Hernandez. Denver City is an oil town with an oil refinery. Richard owned a small home in the town. During our time with him, we made two different trips to Carlsbad Caverns in nearby New Mexico. We absolutely loved exploring the caves.

When we left Richard's, we drove on to Albuquerque. I had managed to spend all the money mom had sent me, so I had to ask her to wire us more, which we picked up at the Western Union in Albuquerque. We also spent the afternoon visiting with Pepi Navarrete in their home. We had a good visit, but no one mentioned the community experience at Edgewood.

We headed north from Albuquerque into the upper Rio Grande Valley in Colorado. We attempted to cross over the continental divide above Silverton on a gravel road. We made it almost to the top, but had to turn around because of snowbanks and because people coming over the top were telling us that the bridge was out in the valley below. Driving my little car through water was not a good choice. We had to go back down, then turn north and then west, so that we could come at Silverton from the north, 150 miles of detour when we had been just 10 miles away. Nonetheless, the road coming into Silverton from the north is one of the most amazing feats of engineering a road through rock cliffs I have ever seen. It was breath-taking.

We headed towards San Francisco, winding just a bit to pick up more counties. We spent time in the Redwood forest before heading on up to my parent's home in Lacomb, Oregon. Claude Savard made the statement later that one needs to travel with Daniel Yordy if one wants to see a view of America most people miss. I had a good time traveling with Claude, but I had no contact with him before or since. He was a good road companion; I remember spending hours explaining to him everything I had learned from Velikovsky. I don't know what he made of that.

Claude spent a few weeks helping me replace the roof on our house. Afterwards, mom gave him some wages for his trip on up to Blueberry. I drove him up to Vancouver, British Columbia where he caught a bus for the trip north. We did manage to drive around the Olympic peninsula in Washington state on our way.

Back with My Parents

I had taken a long time driving home because I NEEDED a prolonged break, a time of enjoyment with no obligations.

When I arrived home, my dad was 67 years old. He had been slowing down gradually, with Parkinson's disease, for the prior several years. He was still able to walk around a bit, with mom's help, at that point. Within a few weeks, he went down another notch, and from then on could not walk at all. He would spend the next seven years either lying in bed or sitting in a wheel chair. He was fully aware of everything around him, but he could not speak.

I want to talk about my now "adult" relationship with my mom and my brothers and sisters. I was 28 years old, but I had never really connected with any of them as an adult. In my youth, my only thought was to head down the road, and I did not then have any real relationships with my family. In fact, it was only now that I had the capacity to consider other people, just a little bit, the first fruit of teaching in the classroom.

My brother, Franz, had sold his pig farm in Nebraska and moved with his family back to Oregon. They were renting a house on the south side of Lebanon at this time, one which Maureen and I would rent later on. I read a book once on the difference in children growing up either as the eldest, the youngest, or the middle child. The eldest is a perfectionist and believes that his parents had gone soft when

the others came along. That describes Franz. The youngest has no hankering to head down the road and is there for the parents over the years. That describes my younger brother, Glenn. And the middle one is heading out to find life elsewhere; that describes me.

Glenn was the only one still home, although he was engaged, at that point, to be married to Kim Foster. Glenn had the room upstairs next to my room, which I had moved back into. Glenn worked for a dairy farmer whose farm was just down the road next to Larwood Bridge. He would have been 19. Sadly, I did not make much connection with Glenn through this season.

I do not know, even now, how to call my relationship with my mom. It remains a puzzle to me. It is a relationship of comfortable mother-son fellowship combined with a seemingly impassable disconnect. As I realize it now, I think my mom and I were so much alike. Mom was not Asperger's, but the trait had come to me through her family line. I have learned, of course, that inherited autism is a spectrum, and the line between what is Asperger's and what is not, is unclear. Mom was not quite Asperger's, I was just. In some ways we were like ships passing in the fog and in other ways we were very comfortable together.

On the one hand, if there is anything I would do differently in my life, it would be those difficult elements in my relationship with my mom, but on the other hand, even if I were to redo those places with what I know now, I'm not sure anything could have been different.

I would not have survived over many years and in many ways if not for my mom. Yet in reference to her, I will be least kind to myself as I give this account.

My mother, Rhoda Yordy, was one of the greatest women of faith and devotion I have known in my life. In those things, my wife, Maureen, is very much like her.

When dad became confined to bed, unable to care for himself, my mom asserted that she could learn to do anything a nurse would do to meet his needs. She fed and cleaned him, turned him in bed, and, with my or Glenn's help, got him into a wheelchair for a bit each day so that he could sit in the living room and enjoy the sunshine.

My mother devoted herself to caring for my

father, 24/7, for seven years, with no break except my wedding at Blueberry. Besides that, she tended the garden, kept the homestead, and bailed her children out of every need we managed to stumble into. And through all, her profound relationship with the Lord Jesus in grace and joy only grew. And my brother, Glenn, with his wife, Kim, cared for her for the rest of her days.

But this is an account of my life, and so we must come back to my anger with God. When I left Bowens Mill, I instructed God as clearly as I could that I was taking back charge of my life and that He could go mind His own business. To my great consternation, God didn't seem to get the message.

I was planning not to go to church; I wanted nothing more to do with any of it. But arriving at home, to my horror, I discovered that mom had brought a church into our living room. What could I do to escape church in our living room except give the lame excuse of going to church somewhere else? My sister Frieda and her family were attending an Assembly of God church in Albany at that time, so for awhile I went there.

Mom had offered her home with its large living room and beautiful yard and view to a brother who lived up Roaring River Drive by the name of Dennis Cline. Dennis pastored a small group of several young couples and mom. After a few weeks I gave up and started attending services with them. Dennis was several years older than I, a wise and anointed man with a pastor's heart. Slowly my heart began to relax in the goodness of services with them.

Working for Tim and Frieda

Jimmy Barkley was no longer in Oregon at this time. Once I had finished roofing the house, I was slow to go out to find construction work. I knew that if I got a job full-time in construction, then I would need tools, etc., and soon I would be in debt. I wanted to be free to move on, so I chose, rather, to have less income during this time.

Tim and Frieda had purchased a property on a hillside near Jefferson, Oregon, not far from where my sister Cheryl has lived with her family all her married life. They were attempting to build a house on the property with mom's assistance. Mom made an agreement with me that she would pay me to work on their house as well as continuing to work on my parent's home. Apparently, dad's retirement money was sufficient for all that was needed. Mom

lived comfortably, but she was very frugal towards herself.

Tim and Freida's house was already half constructed, with the frame and roof done. They were staying in a small travel trailer with their children, April and Ryan, next to the construction site. My task was mostly interior work, including building them a nice oak kitchen. This was the largest part of my work for them. Tim had a radial arm saw that I used for most of the cabinetmaking. I knew how to make kitchen cabinets, now, and, as I think about it, I remember that I made them a beautiful kitchen.

Until I started college in the fall of 1986 at Blueberry, these two houses were most of my work during my time at home.

My days were not packed, however, and I did take it a bit easy, sometimes working just five or six hours in a day. You see, my newly awakened desire to learn and to read the works of great literature had discovered the wonder and joy of used book stores in Albany and Portland where I could get hardcover books for 1-2 dollars. I came home with many boxes of books over time.

I spent a lot of time reading. I read Tolstoy and Cervantes, Homer and Fielding, Hugo and Dickens (again), the list is endless. I built a large book shelf for all my books, filled it, and kept on buying and reading. By May I had over a thousand books. I do like books.

God used two of those books in particular, however, in order to set me up for the great clash with God that would come to its head during the deliverance time at Blueberry. And as I see now, God was very specific in His determination towards me, that I would know His ways, even though at the time I thought it was all confusion.

The first book was *The Hunchback of Notre Dame* by Victor Hugo. The second was *The Brothers Karamazov* by Fyodor Dostoevsky. Let me explain the seasons of literature which I was not aware of at the time. Up until around 1850 a full belief in God and Christianity was simply assumed by all writers. From the end of WW1, say 1920, most literature contains no assumption of God or Christianity; there is no "rebellion" because God is not assumed. The majority of writers from around 1850 to 1920, however, placed God and religion into their stories in order to rebel against Him and in order to lead their readers into rebellion. The worst of these is Thomas Hardy, whose books and movies I refuse to consider. But the most powerful in impacting the reader is Fyodor Dostoevsky.

With *The Hunchback of Notre Dame*, the problem was stupefying injustice committed by "Christian" officials. I don't know that I have ever been moved so powerfully in anger and grief after reading a book, in the feeling of hatred against "those who should have known better." My heart was in such convulsions that I imagined I was close to a heart attack. But it was Dostoevsky in *The Brothers Karamazov* who raised more poignantly than has ever been portrayed by any other the great challenge against God, that if He is so good and so powerful, then why the hell does He allow such horrifying things to happen to innocent children. By God's intention, that same rebellion seized hold of my heart.

God cannot answer such false accusation until He has brought it out front and center.

In the Crucible

I have titled this period "A Time of Reset." From dropping Claude Savard off in Vancouver until the next sub-section, which is attending the Shiloh Convention in February, is just seven months. In this portion, I want to share how my obstinance of heart against God turned into a once-again eager running back into move community.

A group of young people who were attending a YWAM, Youth with a Mission, training session in Salem, Oregon, came to our home to be part of the service with Dennis Cline. They were required as part of their training to participate in differing local services. It was about 35 miles from Salem, but somehow they had heard of Dennis.

[As an aside, later on, Dennis Cline became the pastor of the Albany Vineyard church and has played a prominent role in the outpouring of the Holy Spirit in that area.]

One of the young men who came I had known as a boy at Graham River Farm. I visited with him, and with that connection, I began to go up to the YWAM in Salem to attend some of their gatherings. One of the young ladies had also caught my eye, a further reason to attend the YWAM teachings. It turned out that she had devoted this time entirely to the Lord, so nothing ever came in that direction.

Through this time, Richard also came through Oregon on his way up to Blueberry. He spent several days with us.

There was another young couple who attended Dennis's services, David and Theresa Newman. They were not much older than I, and I went often to visit with them in their home, about halfway to Lebanon. I fellowshipped often with them and with Dennis and his wife, Anne, in their home as well as in church fellowship throughout this entire time period. These were good friendships and times of fellowship.

Between enjoying Dennis Cline's services and the Spirit-filled teachings at YWAM, and good fellowship with the Newman's, my heart slowly began to soften towards the Lord.

It is a decently long drive home from Salem, a time to ponder. As I slowly began to thaw, I also began to notice that there was a word planted inside of me, as a child in the womb, a word I could never escape. I wept much over that word, yet I was unwilling to touch it.

Bit by bit, my heart began to weep over a knowledge of God I did not possess, over a word of the revelation of Jesus Christ planted in me, a word that seemed to have no hope of fulfillment. By November, I was in great spiritual distress, unable to remain in spiritual lethargy and unable to reconnect with the vision planted in me.

One afternoon, in that distress, I picked up once again *I Looked and I Saw Visions of God* by Annie Schissler, laid on my bed, and read it through.

As I read her vision titled "That Most Holy Thing," which I have included many times in my letters, I was seized with an overwhelming horror. God was doing and about to do mighty things in the earth and I was not part of them. The horror was so great that I rejected my hardness of heart and determined to reconnect with the move.

Here is that vision.

THAT HOLY THING

As I entered His presence, He showed me something so impressive and frightening that I feared greatly. Although He specifically told me not to fear, even so, I could not feel completely at ease, for in almost unbearable pain and in great love, He tore open, as it were, His own spiritual form or body. Even though He had told me to look at it, I feared to and wanted to hide my eyes, for after this great tearing open of Himself I could see within. There I beheld something so terribly perfect in its holiness, that even the word perfection seems to sully it in my memory. This living something was very much a part of Himself, yet it seemed as though He were bringing forth, in a tremendous beginning, a new being from His own person. It was the same beginning in God that He had shown me several days before, in "The Place of a Beginning". For long eons He has waited to manifest this most Holy Thing which He is about to bring forth.

The tremendous, radiant perfection - the holy glory of this beginning that He showed me - was so far beyond expression and so filled with holiness and God-life, that I felt greatly perturbed, and trembled even though He told me over and over again not to fear. It was something too high, holy and perfect to look upon.

When He said, "The hour has now come," it seemed that He was about to explode, not in an explosion of terrible, destructive violence, but rather a pacific explosion. Then He came forth, as it were, in this explosion, and it was tremendously sweet. From this sweet, explosive breaking forth, He extended Himself over all; that is to say, He desired to manifest Himself, pouring this forth upon those of His own ones who were waiting upon Him. To me it seemed so imminent that it appeared to be right now, yet I know it was not at this moment in our time. Wherever He broke forth in this manifestation it began to extend, and the wonderful glory and ineffable sweetness of that perfect thing that He was bringing forth made such an impact upon my being that it greatly troubled me; because I could in no way understand the vision.

And here is my comment in the margin. – "This vision is to me one of the most important. I read it first 39 years ago, and it has wielded an enormous influence on my knowledge of God and the pursuit of my heart. Based on this vision, I have contended with God over many years, that He would place this Holy Thing, His very Heart, inside of me. It is from this vision that I draw the phrase, 'sharing heart with God.'"

You see, God was proving to me His determination which He Himself had placed inside of me to know the revelation of Jesus Christ through His Church, regardless. Nothing expresses the intense determination of my heart more than this vision.

The first step, then, after regaining my senses, was to begin again to drive up to Portland to be part of the move services there. I was no longer visiting at YWAM. The second step was to write a letter to the Blueberry eldership applying for enrollment in Covenant Life College.

The Shiloh Convention

I was much too eager to rush back into Feast of Tabernacles' life to wait to hear back from Blueberry. So in February I drove up to Fort St John, to that area that held the magical memory of my time at Graham River Farm.

I never told anyone I was coming, and I had never been down the Blueberry road. As I drove north on the wintry roads, I was so excited. Blueberry is only about four miles down a side road to the east from the Alaska Highway. I turned down that road and promptly ran into a snow bank. Randy Jordan soon came along with the tractor and merrily pulled me out. He had been snowplowing.

My connections at Blueberry were Judy Jones, one of the elders, and Richard Hernandez. I soon found them and stayed for a couple of days with Richard who had a room in the cabin of Judy's sister, Joanne Branham. I met with the two main ladies involved with Covenant Life College at Blueberry, Charity Titus and Delores Topliff. It seems my application to the college was accepted.

I was so eager to start that Sister Delores agreed that I could do a full course of self-study on Russian history that would be accepted as college credit, while I waited for September to come. At the same time, they pointed out how important my construction skills would be in meeting the many needs of the community there, enlarged as it was with young people coming to college. I agreed to move there permanently in May, with the understanding that I would return to Oregon for several weeks in the summer to be part of Glenn and Jenelle's respective weddings.

I was there only a couple of days, and so I will not describe Blueberry to you, not until I arrive there for school in the next chapter. Richard and I then drove over to the Shiloh Community to attend the last convention that was held there. They had just remodeled their large Tabernacle, even though that community had declined quite a bit in number from its peak of 200 members. It was so wonderful to be back into a word of the revelation of Jesus Christ and the power of a third feast anointing.

We stayed in a large room next to the Tabernacle that was used as a food processing place above their root cellar. It had been converted into a dorm for the convention visitors. A brother about our age who had lived at Shiloh for many years showed us all around the community and told us many stories.

Again, I will not describe Shiloh further until it becomes that most precious place for us, Blair Valley.

Richard and I also drove into Graham River and visited with the family there. Most I had known at Graham River were gone; there were maybe thirty people remaining, including Eli and Marty Miller and most of their large family as well as Harold and Mitzi Witmer. In my conversation with Brother Eli (who had participated in several of the conventions at Bowens Mill while I was there), he shared that he was planning a ministry trip throughout Oregon, Washington, and Idaho and wondered if I would drive him around. That was exciting to me, so I readily agreed.

After dropping Richard back off at Blueberry, I returned home to Oregon.

Confrontation

I was not aware that God was preparing a great vise in which to squeeze me in His confrontation with me, this great contest between my determination to know God and my own folly and conceit. I was self-willed. And I fought with God for many years, trying to get "my way" without any success ever.

I was too impatient to start college and so I considered enrolling in Linn-Benton Community College just south of Albany. I could hear the Lord saying, "No," quite clearly, but I was not to be deterred. One day, I was driving with my sister Frieda into Albany. I was thinking of "storming the breach" through all God's objections and just enrolling at LBCC, regardless.

As we were driving, Frieda was telling me a story about someone whom God had confronted and told them that He would take their life if they chose

to go down a path that would take them from Him. That was not the first time I had heard such a thing. God had spoken the same thing to Sam Fife when he had sought to use the apostolic anointing in the wrong directions. "Don't turn away from Me again, My son."

Freida asked me, "Do you think God would do that, take someone's life to keep them from going in the wrong direction?"

Except I didn't hear Frieda, I heard God through her, and I knew that God was telling me exactly that, that He valued my commitment to Him too much to lose me to darkness. That He would take me to Himself if I went down that path.

Needless to say, that was the last of any thought of LBCC.

Brother Eli flew down to Portland, and I picked him up there. We drove up to visit the small move community in Kettle Falls, Washington. There I met Don and Martha Howat and their three small children, members of that community. I really enjoyed my time there. We made stops at a couple of more places where Brother Eli shared before returning to Oregon.

Along the way, I poured out all my distress over my experiences at Bowens Mill. Brother Eli took it all in stride, but I'm sure it didn't help him.

Back home, Eli shared a word with Dennis Cline's group, again in my mother's living room. He then asked to borrow my car for a visit he needed to make in Eugene, Oregon. When he returned, he was quite sheepish. Someone had driven into the back of my car and crushed in the hatchback door. My insurance covered it, however. When I got the insurance money, I decided to fix it myself, so I bond-oed and painted it. It didn't look good, but now I had the money for my return trip to Blueberry.

During my trips to Salem, I had reconnected with Larry Jensen who was living with his parents in a double-wide trailer on the east side of Salem. I did not spend much time with him, but towards the end of April, I spent most of a day with them. Larry and his two younger brothers still lived with their mom and dad. John Jensen was still a boasting fleshpot, and Larry still treated his mother like dirt. It was then, as I was listening to Larry's many stories about all his "accomplishments" that it dawned on me that he was making much of it up. That realization gave answer to so much confusion from our time together as kids. I think that Larry did not know that making up stories was not what really happened.

BUT – the significant part of that visit was when Larry's youngest brother was insisting on buying a waterbed for his bedroom. John Jensen said, "No." And so the argument began. It went on for maybe twenty minutes during which time they were on their feet hollering in rage at each other. John Jensen's roar went all through me. "I WILL NOT HAVE THAT BED IN MY HOUSE!!!"

And so, I packed my stuff into my car to head back into Christian community. I put brackets on my large bookshelf and tied it on top of my car, loaded full with books. I roped it down with a tarp over it. I was by myself, so every cranny inside was filled with books and the few other things of my possession.

I explained to Denny Cline and all the others there where I was going and why. I said all my "Goodbye's" and headed north on I-5.

As I drove north from Salem, suddenly I heard the words inside my spirit, firm and unmistakable, "I will not have those books in My house." "Phooey on that," was my initial response. I kept driving.

Past Portland, "I will not have those books in My house." Past Seattle, the urgency grew, "I will not have those books in My house."

As I approached the Canadian border, however, the urgency became a mighty roar. "I WILL NOT HAVE THOSE BOOKS IN MY HOUSE."

I broke, turned around, and drove back home in utter humiliation.

I had to explain to everyone, including Dennis and Ann Cline, what God had required of me. I spent a few days selling some of the books back to the used book stores at a loss. I gave most of the rest to my brother, Franz, but kept just a few that I thought would be "OK."

I no longer needed the bookcase. I packed my few remaining belongings back into the car, and with my wings clipped, my hair singed, and my tail between my legs, so to speak, I drove back up north to Blueberry.

Blueberry and Weddings

It was now springtime when I arrived at Blueberry, the snow was gone and green was beginning to appear. They were busily readying the gardens for planting, though school was not yet out. I stayed for a couple of days with Richard, but then I was invited to move into the home of Victor and Nancy Raja and their two girls, Freda and Ruth. I would live with the Raja's for the four years I was in Covenant Life College.

There was a need for a new greenhouse, and so I was soon busy building it in the garden space just below the Raja cabin. Brother Roger Henshaw was over that project. Brother Roger was an older gentleman who had been a machinist most of his life. He and his wife, Bertie, had opened their two-story home for a number of college students. After about a month, the greenhouse was ready for service, and I headed back to Oregon for Glenn's and Jenelle's weddings.

Jenelle's wedding came first, in June. She was marrying a young man she had met at ORU by the name of Jim Hall. We rented a wedding ceremony house and yard in Salem. It was a very gallant occasion. I believe Dad was able to come. He would have been confined to the wheelchair with a sash tied around him to keep him upright.

Jim was a news camera operator. A few years later, they filmed news videos on board an aircraft carrier during the first Iraqi war. Jim also got the chance to film Boris Yeltsin in Moscow for a news interview.

Jim and Jenelle remained in Oregon, however, after their honeymoon, to attend Glenn and Kim's wedding in July.

Glenn had known Kim Foster for several years. Kim lived with her parents and younger sister and brother at a farmhouse less than a mile west of the dairy where Glenn worked. They had a huge and abundant grape arbor just outside their kitchen door. Glenn was like dad; Kim was always the only one for him.

Glenn and Kim had their wedding in Kim's grandparents' yard, filled with flowers, not far from her parent's house. It was funny because Kim's parents were the same age as Glenn's brothers and sisters and mom was the same age as Kim's grandparents. Our family has long generations from my great-grandfather, John, on. I think that Dennis Cline conducted their wedding; I'm not sure if he did Jenelle's as well.

Glenn and Kim now live in northern Minnesota,

and I stay with them when I visit my daughter at the Upsala, Ontario, community.

Once Glenn and Kim were married, Jim Hall went down to their new home in Los Angeles. Jenelle stayed a bit longer to pack up all her things to take down. She asked Dennis Cline if she could borrow his small pickup to carry her stuff, and she asked me to drive her down to LA and then return the pickup to Dennis.

So, in the first part of August, I drove Jenelle down to Los Angeles with all her stuff in the little pickup. When we had unloaded, I did not stay long. I headed back north towards home.

EXCEPT. Hey, I had a five-on-the-floor nicely-powered little pickup and the never-before-driven (by me) California Highway 1 unfolding in front of me. Oh, heavenly joy. A thousand feet down on the left to the Pacific always in view. A thousand feet up on the right. A VERY winding paved road in and out and a nicely-powered five speed on the floor.

I was able to keep up with a high-powered sports car. I think the guy was amazed. Then, it was another passage through San Francisco and on home. It wasn't long before I was in my Toyota Corona and heading back to Canada.

Return to Blueberry and College

I did not understand my drive to Blueberry.

All the way back, every mile, I heard, "No." It was not nearly like the loud roaring of the May attempt, but it seemed real. God seemed to be saying to me not to return to Blueberry. This made no sense to me. I could not turn back. My heart agonized the whole way, and even after I was back in the flow of Christian community, I did not sense the Spirit for nearly two weeks.

This was the second time that I kept driving in spite of the seeming "witness" inside against it. The first was my first trip to Bowens Mill.

All the way up, all I could think of was the lethargic misery of not-knowing God that would be my lot if I turned back.

If I had turned back, I would never have known the power of God in His church. If I had turned back, I would never have become a full classroom teacher.

If had turned back, I would never have married my dear wife, Maureen, nor known our four pre-

cious children. If I had turned back, I would never have had the wondrous word of Christ our life that I now share with you.

I did not turn back, but I did not understand.

The command of the gospel is to put the Lord Jesus Christ upon myself, upon all that I am, with no regard to the flesh, what it is or does.

In 1986 I drove out from my parent's home in Oregon to drive up to Blueberry, a distance of about 1100 miles, four different times inside of six months. The first time up, I was filled with excitement and joy. The second time up, I was battered by the refusal of God and turned around before half way. The third time up, I drove in humility and peace. And the fourth time up, I drove under a cloud of unclear questions and confusion.

I know that many of the times I heard "NO," it was truly of God, saving me from a wrong or terrible direction. I have heard such a "No" even since I have been writing this present word, this time regarding a direction one of my children wanted me to help them take. It has always been deeply humiliating, especially when I have presented the direction to others as a great idea and must then tell them that God has told me, "No."

Yet there were times, I think, when the "No" I perceived might have been the emotions of Asperger's. When I left the move communities in 1998, I set my heart against regarding all such feelings of "No." This was necessary to keep hold of my sanity.

Nonetheless, Blueberry was my most blessed experience in God and in Christian community, and Blueberry was my most difficult experience in God and in Christian community.

Here is the truth. – **The way of man is not in himself; it is not in man who walks to direct his own steps** (Jeremiah 10:23). – And then – **God ALWAYS leads us inside of triumph** (2 Corinthians 2:14).

The greatest mistake is to place not-Christ upon the course of one's life, to make the false assumption that "I" was ordering my own steps. If God had not wanted me at Blueberry, I would never have been there. Since I was there, Christ Jesus living inside of and as me was also there.

You see, the great issue and turning point of this time, and indeed of my life, was reading the Annie visions in November 1985. In many of her visions she saw the Lord offering to believers the opportunity to enter into a next place of knowing God. She saw, however, that many refused to enter and thus God pressed them again with entering that next room in God. But when they continued to refuse, God removed His offer from them. They would never ever know what they had chosen to refuse.

To be offered a wondrous dimension of knowing and living inside of God, and to fail to enter, is to me an inconceivable horror. The fear that I might have done so is intolerable.

And therefore, my personal response to the truth Annie saw in her visions comes out from 2 Corinthians 2:14, one of the ruling verses of the Bible.

Here is my confession of Christ. "All of His ways concerning me are perfect. He has never led me wrong; He has never not led me."

The reason I drove every mile that final time up to Blueberry, refusing to heed whatever uncertainty that seemed to be pressing against my way, was this determination fixed in me, to know my Father, regardless.

Did I suffer loss? Undoubtedly. To know my Father as I do now is to have long ago accepted restraints pressing me in from every direction.

He has led me and made me walk in darkness and not in light. Surely He has turned His hand against me time and time again throughout the day. ...He has besieged me and surrounded me with bitterness and woe. He has set me in dark places... He has hedged me in so that I cannot get out; He has made my chain heavy. Even when I cry and shout, He shuts out my prayer. He has blocked my ways with hewn stone (Lamentations 3).

I am writing this account because I must place the Lord Jesus Christ upon every moment of my life, regardless of all my pain, confusion, and darkness, regardless of any crying of the flesh.

I do not believe in "what if's" nor do I regard anyone who asks them. God is – end of story. I will include only one "what if" inside this entire account, but only to place the Lord Jesus into the deepest point of my heart and life. That "what if" will be "What if we had stayed at Blair Valley."

"Lord Jesus, I must have You inside of every moment of my life, carrying me inside of Yourself. Therefore, as I regard this moment of great contradiction as I arrived at Blueberry in August, 1986, I see You alone, utterly with me, carrying me inside Yourself and expressing Your intentions as me.

"Lord Jesus, Your ways concerning me are perfect. You have never led me wrong; You have always led me. I place all the great angsts and contentions of my life utterly into You. You utterly intended me through every step and in every moment.

"Lord Jesus, I know that it is when I am feeling my worst that You are most carrying me. And I know that You and I together cause me to know my Father as His Heart intends from the beginning.

"Lord Jesus, You are my life; I have no other life."

There are no easy answers. Placing the Lord Jesus Christ upon all that you are will cost you everything. Yet we count all things as loss that we might KNOW Him.

Larger Blueberry Layout

I have placed the white letters just above each location.

A. The foot bridge over the Blueberry River.

B. The Raja cabin where I lived for four years.

C. Our Tabernacle

D. The School Building - Covenant Life College, and where I taught for seven years.

E. Sister Charity and Sister Sue's cabin.

F. The location of our first little house of our own after Maureen and I were married.

G. The former location of the Henshaw/Deardorff cabin.

H. The Austin cabin

I. The new shop building that we built in 1992.

J. The location of the original old barn.

15. Blueberry and College

August 1986 - August 1987

Framing Blueberry for Me

I was part of the Blueberry Community for more years than any other of my community experiences. There I knew my greatest achievements and my greatest failures. There, I tasted the greatest power of God in His people and the deepest shame of humiliation.

I realize now that I must slow down the pace of this account. For you to know the word of Christ coming through me now, you must walk with me through these years. I hope that you will be amazed at the goodness of God and rejoice in the beauty and glory of His Church; I hope that you will share tears with me and wonder at the hand of God contending with the heart of a man.

I can easily divide my time at Blueberry into three distinct parts. First was my four years of college, truly among the best years of my life. Second was the next three years during which Maureen and I were married and our son Kyle was born. These years were, shall I say, confusing. And third was when we returned to Blueberry from Oregon for another year-and-a-half. Only one word fits my perception of this time – grief.

I have re-written this introduction several times. My memories of Blueberry draw me in more than any other time period. I had not remembered how much I had loved Blueberry at the beginning. In fact, I saw, in a flash that the time of grief was separate from my first seven years. Set free from the grief, the confusing time diminished in its relationship to the love.

Yet I am all turned inside out. And as I progress forward in this account, I am experiencing every human emotion at mildly traumatic levels. Because I place the Lord Jesus Christ upon myself, upon all that I am, I know that the end of this passage IS a wide open door. My writing of these times is the costliest thing I have done in my life. I do it for Father's sake.

I have called Blueberry "the womb of the church," and indeed, that's what it was for me.

The Blueberry Community

The history of Blueberry is relevant to this story, and so I want to share a brief outline.

There was a fellowship in southern Ontario under the ministry of Tony Materick with whom I had worked briefly at Bowens Mill. In this fellowship were several Dutch families, along with a few formerly Mennonite families. Former Mennonites included Alvin and Marie Roes and Elmer and Mary Gerber and their families. On the Dutch side were Kars and Minnie Kiers, and John and Mary Katerburg, among others. I will not include names not relevant to my own experience, however. John and Mary's daughter, Martha, was my student for five years.

When Sam Fife began preaching community, the first communities to form in Canada were Hidden Valley, begun first in southern BC, and Graham River Farm, Shiloh, and Headwaters, to the west of the Alaska Highway. This was the early summer of 1972. At the same time, God was speaking the same thing to the group in southern Ontario. In the late summer of 1972, Elmer Gerber and Kars Kiers drove up together to Fort St. John to look for property for another community. They were advised by the brethren already there to find property to the west of the Alaska Highway, but they did not witness to that area for them. Instead, they found a section of land on the north side of the Blueberry River, four miles east of the Alaska Highway. They both heard God speak to them, "This is the place." From having sold their farms in Ontario, they purchased that property and prepared to build a Christian community there.

Alvin and Marie Roes came to Blueberry in the summer of 1973. They had a string of children, all of whom I met, but their older ones remained in Ontario. Moving with them to Blueberry were Shirley, Ruth, David, Elizabeth and Rachel. David was around my age and Elizabeth a few years younger. The Roes's mean a lot to me and became part of the joy of my life.

There were others that joined with these three families. When I arrived at Blueberry, however, only the Roes's remained from that original group. Kars and Minnie had moved up to Headwaters and the Gerber's had moved over to the Hilltop community. My family and I would join with Kars and Minnie Kiers as well as Rick Annett, also from southern Ontario, and his wife, Shirley (Roes) at Blair Valley, the last of my community experiences.

Then, when the Hidden Valley community, which had moved up to a property south of Dawson Creek (where I had attended my first convention in 1977) closed down shortly after that, a number of people from Hidden Valley moved to Blueberry. John and Nathel Clarke were two leading ministries in the move fellowship. I remembered having laughed harder and longer the first times I heard Brother John preach than just about any other such. They had gone from Hidden Valley to Blueberry with their children, John Mark, and Nadeen, Martin, and Anne Lincecum, already, in June of 1977, before the convention I attended.

Some that followed the Clarkes to Blueberry in the fall after that convention included Charity Titus, Edie Dwyer and her son, Bryan, Sue Sampson, Dave and Norma Smilie, among others, as well as Randy and Martha Jordan who came a bit later.

By the time I arrived at Blueberry in 1986, there were around one hundred people living in the community. A number of other families had moved to Blueberry through the intervening years. That number, however, included somewhere around twenty who were there as students coming for either college or high school. There were two types of students, those, like myself, who were not only attending school but who were also part of the community. For us, our work in the summer was counted as covering the costs of attending school. Then there were several who came only for the school time. These paid a small fee each month for room and board. There were no tuition costs.

To understand the layout (map on page 132), you must picture that feature of land in the taiga regions of the globe in which the layout consists of flats, then slopes up to more flats and so on. The greenhouses were on the flat that was just above the Blueberry River, then there was a small slope up to the flat on which the School and Tabernacle were situated along with several of the cabins, the washhouse/shop, and the old barn. A number more of the cabins were on the long steeper slope up, with the Austen house and Clarke cabin at the top on a bit of a flat before the road went on up to the larger flat above the river valley.

The ridge to our west was not common, that is, it was a complete ridge, going up steeply from behind the Henshaw cabin. The road going up between the Austen's and Clarke's became quite steep, matching the less-steep upslope from the root cellar. Thus the entire range of community buildings was in a hollow, with the ridge to the west, the crown of the valley slope above us to our north, and the Blueberry River below us to our south and east. All of the cabins were within sight of each other and of the two central buildings. I would guess that the Austen house was maybe 75 feet higher than the Tabernacle.

The vegetation was mostly spruce and poplar trees; with poplar trees intermingled with grassy areas throughout much of the family area. There were a few spruce as well, but most of the spruce was up on the higher slopes or along the Blueberry. The Blueberry River itself was not that large, comparable to Crabtree Creek back home. It was too large to just walk across. The soil of the benches was loam that became deep mud when it rained.

Most of the cars were parked on the other side of the river and to arrive at the community, everyone had to walk down the road between the ridge and the river and past the spring from which we got our water before arriving at the first buildings. You could drive to Blueberry from the other direction over several miles of dirt roads. The decision was made not to put in a road bridge because had they done so, the road through the middle of the community would have been accessible to the public and therefore legally owned by the province.

Covenant Life College

I arrived back again at Blueberry in August of 1986. I was 29 years old. The first college courses started in September. I loved college. I was at Blueberry on a student visa. With a letter of enrollment from the Blueberry school, it was an easy thing to get a student visa at the border. Then, Mr. Wenham, the immigration officer in Dawson Creek, renewed the visa as needed for seven years.

The primary motive for the creation of a full college inside the move fellowship was the fact that all of the communities and fellowships throughout the move each had their own school. Thus the need for teachers educated inside of a Christian and Feast of Tabernacles viewpoint was very great. Discussion concerning a college had begun soon after Brother Sam had passed on and by the spring of 1980, when I was at the Albuquerque farm, the idea was known by all.

Covenant Life College is registered with the state of Alaska with its base at the move community near Haines, Alaska. The college, while designed to maintain the high standards that would be expected of any college, was also designed to be flexible in a number of ways. One way is that there were a number of branches of the college in differing places. The first branch of the college to start unofficially, in the fall of 1982, was in the fellowship in Brussels, Belgium. In August of 1985, Maureen flew to Brussels to begin her first two years of college there. I was aware that she was planning to do so when I left Bowens Mill that June.

The primary branches of Covenant College began in September of 1983, at Haines and at Blueberry. Charity Titus was the head of the college at Blueberry and Delores Topliff moved to Blueberry with her two boys, Andrew and Aaron, from the Shiloh community, in order to be one of the main teachers in the college. Shirley (Roes) Annett began college the first year it started at Blueberry as well as Luann Larson and Patrick Downs, who lived at Hilltop. Then, at the same time Maureen went to the Brussels branch, her sister, Lois Mack, also began at Blueberry and thus was a fellow student with me there, one year ahead of me.

I was part of the largest single group passing through the Blueberry college at the same time, around ten individuals at the start with some going elsewhere and others coming in so that ten of us graduated together. During these years, the college was a primary focal point of the community, in spite of the fact that there were only about twenty to twenty-five students at any one time.

The Raja's

Victor and Nancy Raja, their two daughters, Freda and Ruth, along with Mike Pelletier were my home and family through the four years I was in college. Victor and Nancy were from the Montreal area and had been part of the Headwaters community from early on. Their two older boys had been among those young people who were not happy at

Headwaters. At the time I stayed with the Raja's, the older boys lived and worked in Fort St. John. Both Victor and Nancy were elders.

Victor was from southern India, a Tamil, dark of skin. His heritage was out from the Pentecostal revivals in southeastern India including from the ministry of Smith Wigglesworth. Victor was a cheerful and intense man, but maybe a bit narrow-minded. Nancy, on the other hand, was of Scottish decent, a mother to me, most certainly, but maybe a bit brash in her expression. Freda and Ruth, then, were half Scottish and half Tamil.

Freda started college that same year I did; she was several years younger than I. I do not know why I forget, except that I close things off to protect myself. But Freda was most definitely the dearest sister to me as a sister in all my community experience. Ruth was a bit like her mother and was much younger, just in grade school when I first arrived at Blueberry. The whole family welcomed me into their home as a son and brother. And I was most comfortable and glad to be part of their family.

Let me add this perspective regarding Nancy Raja. When I moved into their home I was basically ignorant of how to live with others, especially females, in a home. Nancy, without being overbearing, though always definite, took me in hand, so to speak, and prepared me in such ways of doing that would make me much more suitable for a wife than I would have been. Brother Victor corrected me only a few times and in mild ways, one of which was to take me out to the outhouse after I had used it to show me that the ladies do not like finding the toilet seat up. That was the last time I did such a thing. What I mean to say is that Nancy Raja filled the place of a mother to me much more substantially than I have thought about before now. Thank you, Sister Nancy, I am deeply grateful even if I am limited in showing it.

Mike Pelletier was from the Boston, Massachusetts area. He had arrived at Blueberry in June, the same as I. Mike came early to take charge of the bee and honey program, which was his primary work through all the years he was there. Mike had also come to be an English teacher, and so he and I took most of our courses together. Mike did not start teaching the first year, as I did, and when he finally had his own class to teach at Blueberry, he discovered that classroom interaction with kids was not for him. Nonetheless, he graduated with the same

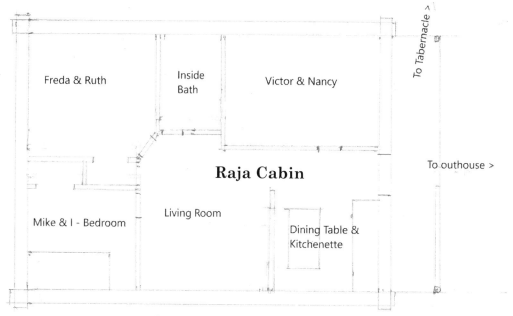

Freda & Ruth

Inside Bath

Victor & Nancy

To Tabernacle >

To outhouse >

Raja Cabin

Mike & I - Bedroom

Living Room

Dining Table & Kitchenette

View to gardens & greenhouses

degree as I. We were the same age; we got along well together. We had similar interests; we argued a lot. But in the end, we never really became close friends. That doesn't mean anything against either of us; it's just the way it was.

The First Semester

On the next page is a drawing of the School, a place in which I spent much of seven years of my life. The school and Tabernacle were matching in the roof line, outward size, and the placement of the bearing posts. I will include a drawing of the Tabernacle in a bit. Both buildings were two stories, but only up from the first inner row of posts, making the upstairs thirty feet wide inside instead of fifty. The upstairs of both also had an outer wall of only maybe six feet in height, so the buildings were not overly high. In the upstairs of the school were the primary grades; it was open with dividers except for the far end, which was the "gym," ten feet by thirty feet enclosed with a higher roof line. The gym was sometimes used as an additional college classroom.

In the downstairs of the school, there were only a few fixed walls, with only the science room being entirely closed in. There were also a few half walls. The classrooms were separated only by heavy, but movable dividers. Charity Titus could see and hear

most of what was happening in the school from behind her desk, with no obstructing view. The floor was strong vinyl, and the ceiling was tiled. The outer walls, posts, and beams were all rough solid spruce, however. The outer walls were six-inch square stacked spruce beams with fiberglass pressed in-between.

Even though I did a lot of construction work at Blueberry, nonetheless, especially for these four years, the college was my life. To know me, you have to go with me into this building and experience things as they meant to me. More than that, again, to a reader all these whom I mention are just names; to me they are precious beyond measure. I do not believe you can know me through these years without some idea of the Blueberry family. God calls each of us by name.

Because the dividers did not reach floor or ceiling, the entire atmosphere of the school was a quiet hubbub of learning. The high schoolers had their own classes separate from the college classes, but both used the same rooms as we moved around by our schedules. The center of the school was the open study area with the classrooms around the edges. This was one of the best applications of the pattern of home, "private edges – common core," that I have experienced.

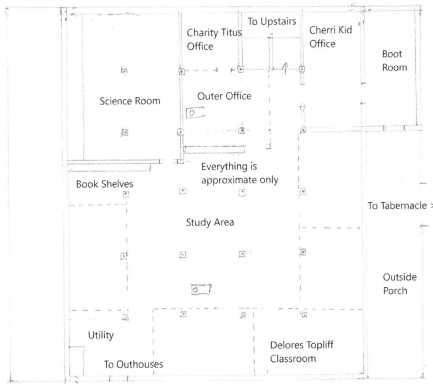

Charity Titus Office

To Upstairs

Cherri Kid Office

Boot Room

Science Room

Outer Office

Book Shelves

Everything is approximate only

Study Area

To Tabernacle >

Outside Porch

Utility

To Outhouses

Delores Topliff Classroom

The college was designed to be flexible in another way as well. Because we often had teachers coming in from outside of the community, the semester was divided into a series of one-week, three-week, and nine-week blocks, or whatever was needed. We took only one course in a three-week block, which was very intensive, but we could take two or three courses in a nine-week block. I loved college, I loved disciplined study, I loved almost every topic on offer. And so I basically crammed in every single class I could. I got the college in trouble with the Alaska authorities because I got high grades in too many courses. But I am a fierce learner, and I thrived on almost too much.

More than that, having taken courses in other secular and Christian universities, including three years of graduate courses, I can state with certainty that almost all of the courses offered at Blueberry were at least equal to, in academic rigor, and often better than what was offered in secular colleges. Two courses at Blueberry, those taught by Moselle Clarke, were actually graduate-level courses, and, in my experience, equal to the best-taught in any graduate school.

School for us did not start until after the Septem-

ber convention, typically held at Shepherd's Inn. Attendance at both the fall convention, and the winter convention in February was counted as part of our schooling. So, when I look at my transcript, I see that my first semester was much less than normal for me. The year started with Brother John Jeffries from the Haines, Alaska community, one of the traveling ministries, teaching a two-week block on Church History to all the college students.

Then, we started our first longer block, with much smaller, specialized courses; that is, only three of us were focused on English, the rest were focused on the sciences. I took three courses, Old Testament Survey, held in the science room with all the students in attendance, western literature, taught by Delores Topliff with Mike Pelletier, Terry Miller, and myself, and then World History, also taught by Sister Delores, but with several of the science students as well.

Terry Miller was from New Orleans, sharing similar interests with Mike and I, although he was a bit slower. Terry was also a builder; later I would teach him the entirety of a construction degree program. So – I spent more time with Terry Miller, in classes together, teaching him construction courses, and working with him in the construction jobs in the community, than any other person during my first seven years at Blueberry. Terry's slowness aggravated me, and I have apologized to him since. He told me he did not remember that, he only remembered that I was always there for him. It's a symptom of my limited autistic thinking that I never thought of Terry as a "friend." When I think of it now, I realize that Terry Miller was one of the best friends of my life.

Delores Topliff was part of my life more than any other teacher in the school. Later, I would build her a new home. Delores was a strong woman who had raised two fine sons by herself at the Shiloh community, in what became a difficult environment over the years of early wilderness community. She was a great-hearted and enthusiastic teacher, but, the best way to say it would be that when she was a round peg, I was a square hole and when she was a round hole, I was a square peg. We didn't always fit, and when we didn't fit, it felt to both of us, probably equally, that there was a bit of hammering going on. Then, Delores also oversaw my teaching practicum.

It is important to me to place Sister Delores in my life. At the time, since she was an elder, I imagined that the difficulty was her fault. Over a period of eight and a half years, I experienced many difficult things with Delores. Now I realize that we were similar in not fitting. We just saw and responded to things so differently, and neither of us knew how to place the other. Yet never once did I experience anything of unkindness from her, and I hope that I never disrespected her. But I cannot write this account, I cannot bring the Lord Jesus upon every moment, unless I can look Sister Delores in the eye and know that we are nothing more than a couple of silly and bumbling humans, learning by every hard way to love one another. I saw Delores last at my daughter, Johanna's, wedding. – Just now, in writing this, for the first time ever, I can look right through the outer shell and see Sister Delores's heart. Her heart is and was always good; her heart is filled with Jesus. Every difficult thing now falls into goodness.

To make the school work, all of the education students, except the first year, also taught at least one course in either grade school or high school. Since I had taught successfully at Bowens Mill, I had my own eighth grade English class right from the start. We used Sister Delores's classroom. My students that year were Amos Deardorff, Howard Wallace, David Mailman, Deborah Austen, and Martha Katerburg who lived at Evergreen and came over to Blueberry every day with other students and teachers who also lived at Evergreen. I taught these five, with Rachel Martin who would come the next year, every year for five years. And I was part of the graduation of all six.

Finally, I must talk about some of the girls in the college who were my fellow students, three in particular, Monica Rotundi, Lena Pacey, and Laura Weitz. All three were a few years younger than I. Monica and Laura started college this same year, but Lena had started the year before with Kathy

Lewis, Jennifer Hanna, and Lois Mack. Monica was from Graham River, and I had worked with her dad and brother and visited in their home a number of times. She was quiet and small, but she came to me often through all four years of college to get help with her work. The terrible thing is (I say that with a smile) that she graduated with a higher GPA than I and would have been valedictorian.

Lena Pacey and Laura Weitz, on the other hand, though quite different from each other, were outgoing, talkative, and friendly. Both of them zeroed in on me, almost as their "ministry" one might say, to coax me, step-by-faltering step, with cheerful friendliness, out from my autistic shell. As I realize it now, I owe quite a lot to these two, and Monica as well. Thank you for helping me to know how to relate with girls and to be much freer in my expression than I could have been if I had not known you. The truth is, they gave me the gift of being able to become friends with Maureen.

At the end of the first semester, Brother Joe McCord, one of the apostolic ministries in the move, who lived at the Lubbock, Texas community, taught a week-long course titled "Current Events in the Light of Daniel and Revelation." Brother Joe was the watchman on the wall for the move fellowship. In his teaching, he expounded on the role of the Rothschild's and international banking. Nonetheless, his vision was the revelation of Jesus Christ through us, His church. During this teaching, I sensed in Brother Joe an anointing approaching that which I had known through Brother Sam Fife. The only other ministry I would see that level of anointing upon would be Sister Jane Miller.

Trying to Understand Myself

As a mildly autistic man, I carry inside myself all the griefs and all the joys of my life. Things that happened thirty years ago are still here, when I consider them, as if they happened just a few days ago. Thus I have had to learn how to place and hold all the noise of my life in the midst of the present goodness of Christ.

This is not a quality to be "delivered from"; it is the quality from which I draw all good things to share with you. I share nothing that does not come out from grief and joy together. How else could we know the Heart of a God who carries all, in all His grief and joy as well as theirs, close inside Himself?

Now, I reference myself as Asperger's, yet at the

time, I knew nothing about such a thing, nor did anyone else. But I didn't know a whole lot about people, either. When I wrote above that I see into Delores Topliff's heart for the first time, that's an incredible thing for me. Neither did I know myself in relation to other people. I had no idea that I was smart; the idea had never before entered my mind. All I ever thought was that school was easy if I liked the subject and to be avoided if I did not.

One of my problems was that I talked TOO MUCH. In every class. That is, I had the eager answer for most every question any teacher asked the class, and I was always making connections with what was being taught, and thus often raised my hand to share. Too much, too often. By the time I got to graduate school at Lubbock Christian University, I had learned to BITE MY TONGUE nearly half the time. That was so hard, but I did my best. Only when I took graduate courses at the University of Texas, in my late fifties, was I finally at peace in responding in class only occasionally.

I was oblivious. I was in my narrow little zone of absolute fascination with whatever was being taught, and I was so eager to connect with it. I thirsted for disciplined understanding, and I made large and constant connections with nearly every topic on discussion. I can understand now why people did not know how to fit me into their normal understanding of things. As I think now, I can remember so many instances, and I can remember the great patience in which every teacher in the school bore with me.

Please forgive me, I had no idea of anything beyond my blinders. Now, when I read the experiences of others who are Asperger's, I see that we are similar.

And those who are Asperger's share the same story, that others see only the outward shell, but we see only our passion and intent inside our shell, with no idea at all of either the existence of the shell or of those "others" out there. It is completely untrue that Asperger's do not feel care about people; our problem is that we, having felt too much, have disassociated from some of that in order to maneuver through all the "noise" coming at us. We care as deeply as any, we just don't always connect with it in normal ways.

All my years in community, I poured myself out for others because that is what I was. All my effort came out of one thought only, the desire to meet the needs of the family. I chose against myself and for others all the time and carried those needs of the community that fell within my sphere as my own personal responsibility. But I had zero idea of an outer shell that other people saw, a shell that appeared to be something I was not.

I do not say this as any excuse for anything I did or said that might have hurt other people. If I did, I was wrong, and I ask you to forgive me.

Inside this line of thinking, then, I want to share two experiences that happened in my first year of college. Sister Charity and Brother Victor asked me to sit down with them as they wanted to share some things with me. Sister Charity started talking and soon she said, in regards to my construction work on the Tabernacle, "You know that you do not submit."

All I could do was blink, like a deer caught in the headlights. I had no idea of her words. I had chosen against myself in that job to submit to John Austen who was covering my work. I had done two things on my own, however. I had been asked to close in the outer porch entry in a very temporary manner. Knowing that there is no such thing as temporary in move community construction, I had made it slightly more permanent. And I had designed the back stairway to be safe, whereas the former stairs had been incredibly unsafe. I had done both for one reason – my love for the people who would use these things.

Then Brother Victor said, "You have sequestered yourself in the school, you should be more involved in the work of the community so that you can relate more with other people."

His words were simply the opposite of my reality. When I worked in the community, it was always and only with the same couple of men. I had almost no interaction with anyone else. Inside the school, it was the opposite. There, I was in continual relationship with all kinds of different people of both genders. In the school, I knew community; in the construction work, I knew mostly loneliness.

But I respected people too much to give answer or to defend myself. Defending myself in such a place is not in the design by which God made me. I gave no answer to either, for I could not understand them. Nonetheless, I highly regarded everything said to me, though I did not know what to do with it.

Then, sometime during the first semester, I was messing with the photocopier in Cherri's office and it stopped working. Ashamedly, I gathered my stuff and went to class. We were sitting in Sister's Delores's literature class, when Sister Charity came wheeling in (Sister Charity was crippled by arthritis and always in a wheelchair), having made her rounds elsewhere, and announced, "Somebody has messed with the photocopier. No one is allowed to make any changes on the photocopier."

When I had the chance, I went to her in her office to apologize. The moment I did, she stopped me and said, "Oh, Daniel, please forgive me. I did not know that it was you, if I had I would not have done that."

Her words were like a healing spear going all through me, for I had lived for years under the idea that no elder ever apologizes. More than that, as I think about it now, I have never known anyone in any context of my life, who was "over me," to apologize personally for a thoughtless word or action. Anyone, that is, except five different Blueberry elders over the years, Sister Charity, Gary Rehmeier, Dave Smilie, Nathel Clarke, and John Clarke.

And so right from the start I was caught in a great contradiction, my great respect for some of the wisest, most anointed, and kindest people I have known and the confusion coming to me through some of what they said. Both of these things would grow and grow, respect and honor inside of confusion and confusion inside of respect and honor until that moment, in October of 1996, when the clash between the two had become so overwhelming that all I could do was pack my family into our little car and drive away in complete and utter failure.

The Blueberry Family

The Blueberry Family was the most wonderful group of people I have known. I will share names and families more specifically, however, at the start of the next chapter.

On the next page is a drawing of the Tabernacle. This was our family center, a place of mighty deliverances and wonderfully anointed services, a place of laughter and the joy of sharing one another's lives, the place of eating meals together, the place where Maureen and I were married. This was a good, good place.

I loved the fellowship around the tables as we ate together, and the wondrously anointed services in that same room, the same as I did at Graham River. I loved the laughter, the honesty, the sharing together, the cheerfulness, the sobriety. I loved the worship together, the intensity of poured out praise towards God. There is a quality of reality that comes out from dedication and commitment to God and to one another that is simply not known in any other setting.

I want to share two experiences that showcase family life in community, things that meant a lot to me. Then I want to comment about a quality of Church life that most Christians do not know and do not believe.

Near the end of December, between school semesters, in temperatures way below zero Fahrenheit, most of the older young people of the community, students and non-students alike, planned to have a sleepout in the empty greenhouses. There were around twenty of us gathered there that evening, sitting on the bare growing beds, all bundled up for the cold. I'm sure we had a heater of some sort going, so it wasn't too bad. No elders had joined us, something that should have been more common, but was not. Someone suggested that a fun thing to do would be to go around the group, one at a time, having each who wished to share fun stories about that person.

Elizabeth Roes was the second one chosen. Elizabeth is funny, from a family who laughed and made dry jokes all the time. She was a beloved sister to everyone. And so some began to share funny stories about Elizabeth.

Then it was Brian Dwyer's turn to share about Elizabeth. Brian, a few years younger than I, factors large in my life through all these years, but I will share more of him later. Brian loved Elizabeth as a brother loves a sister in the purity of Church life. As he began to share, something changed. Brian talked about what Elizabeth meant to him, how she had befriended him when he first came to Blueberry, how she had helped him to know how to live and to love.

When he had finished, we all knew that something holy, something purely of God had come upon us. We continued around the circle, from one to the next, with each one speaking of the good things of Christ they knew in whomever we were speaking to. It was such a strengthening, such an honor of one another, such deepest of joys. We con-

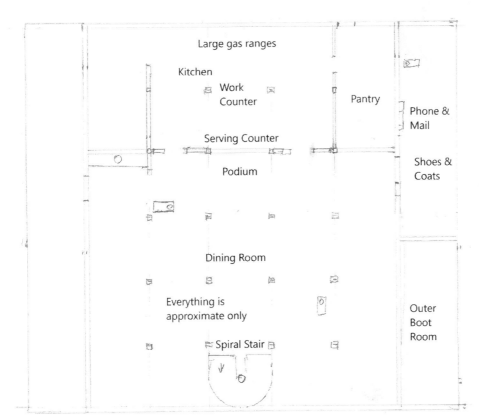

Large gas ranges

Kitchen

Work Counter

Pantry

Phone & Mail

Serving Counter

Shoes & Coats

Podium

Dining Room

Everything is approximate only

Outer Boot Room

Spiral Stair

whom I counted as my best friend. Their story of walking out a year I will hold until the next chapter.

I want to define a quality of life inside of committed Christian community inside the Spirit of God, and that is of brother-sister love and regard for one another. There is much to be said for submitting to a godly order of walking together under the covering of an eldership and inside of the fear of God and the earnest desire to know Him. And so, young people, growing up in the community knew ONLY a brother-sister relationship. Any kind of "romance" or physical touching (except for welcoming hugs) was simply not allowed, not even when two were walking out a year. We were not teenagers, but in our twenties. Each one of us had chosen this way of life as our own.

When I say that I loved Freda Raja or Monica Rotundi as sisters, or that Brian loved Elizabeth as a sister, that is not a "platonic" love, nor anything remotely connected to romantic thoughts and as far away from anything "sexual" as one can get. I am speaking of true Christian regard for one another out from the Jesus of our hearts. That doesn't mean that there were not sexual indiscretions in the history of the move; it means that those things were rare and isolated and not a part of our lives.

I am not a fighting man, and I typically do nothing more than delete words that are spoken against me. But when words are spoken in mockery against the reality of Christian love inside of committed Church life, I am not myself. I will fight the one who mocks God in such a way; I will silence their contempt.

tinued until after midnight. When we were done, most of us abandoned the thought of spending the night in the cold except for Richard and a couple of others. We walked to our cabins in a hushed sense of God among us.

This was community as I knew community must be.

Then, two or three times, Cherri Kidd invited me of an evening to her home next door, in the upstairs above the Rehmeier cabin. Rachel Roes lived with her as well as Chris, who was in sixth grade, and not yet in my own classroom. Elizabeth was there as well as Richard Hernandez and Brian Dwyer. We played Pictionary together; I think at least three times, maybe more. I have never had so much fun in outward expression in the laughing together over a silly game. I had never been involved in this fun way with people my age in community before. Sadly, these kinds of times did not continue; I do not have an explanation why.

Elizabeth was not a student in the college, and so I did not have much more involvement with her, except that she was close friends with Richard,

Jesus is real, and He really does live in the hearts and lives of those who are committed to His revelation through His Church.

The Second Semester

Through my second semester at Covenant Life College in the spring of 1987, two courses were being offered for the "upper level" students, "Child Growth & Development" and "Reading in the Content Area." I could not stomach not being involved in anything on offer, so I persuaded Sister Charity to allow me to enroll in those courses. Thus I had Charity Titus as my teacher for "Child Growth & Development," and "Philosophy of Christian Education." I have sat under many teachers in eight years of college and graduate school, the two best teachers in every way were Charity Titus and Dr. Hannel at Lubbock Christian. I counted it as one of the great privileges of my life to sit in her classes and learn from her clarity and wisdom.

Moselle Clarke taught "Reading in the Content Area," which, with her other course later, were the two courses typically found in graduate school. It was from Moselle that I began to find answers to my big question when I taught at Bowens Mill – "How do you get kids to think?"

I had only one course with Sister Delores this semester, the second half of Western Literature. In that course, we were assigned a research paper on literature. – Let me explain something about the grading at CLC. By rule, a perfect paper, or a larger assignment, was a 97. That means that a 98 to a 100 meant that you not only did a paper that fulfilled all of the objectives, but that you went way beyond requirements. Needless to say, I went enthusiastically "way beyond" on most larger assignments. This semester, I did a huge paper for Sister Moselle, which I still have and value, and I did a way-beyond presentation of my analysis of literature.

The premise of my literature paper boiled down to this – that humans are wicked by nature and that all literature, except that which is clearly Christian, is "of the devil." Mike and I even argued with Sister Charity over C.S. Lewis, whose works she loved. I am very grateful that we did not win that argument.

While there were many valuable discussions of literature in my paper, I now reject its premise. You see, we did not know that we defined God and man by John Calvin, out from the arguments and definitions of the serpent in the garden. We did not know

that all are sustained by the good speaking of Jesus every moment, nor that all creation groans with eagerness towards knowing the God out from whom all things come.

That does not mean that the evil one is not involved in every area of human expression, especially in modern culture. It means that man is the image of God, regardless, and that knowing God and knowing the human are something that only happen together.

Of course, you can see the irony of God towards me, as I swung on the pendulum from the extreme of trying to bring a thousand such books to Blueberry all the way over to calling all of it by the devil. Nonetheless, God was doing something important inside of me through all these questions and issues. I will keep that until the next chapter, however.

Juliann Ingram

When I left Bowens Mill, I closed myself utterly to the idea that Maureen would be my wife. I had hurt so much, I had become so angry against God, that I had to reject and even become hard against that hope, even though I knew it was still what God had spoken.

It wasn't long, then, in the first semester of classes at Blueberry that I noticed a beautiful, smart, and friendly blonde-headed girl in my classes by the name of Juliann Ingram, even while I saw the she was noticing me. We soon became good friends. I liked Juliann, a lot. I was able to visit with her. Juliann was from Wisconsin; this was her second year at Blueberry.

By springtime, Brother Victor was urging me to go to the elders and ask them and her parents (whom I had met when they came to the February convention) about walking out a year together. Actually, he counseled me in that direction several times, "She's quite a prize," he said.

I went to Sister Charity and shared with her what God had spoken to me about Maureen and where all that had seemed to end. Sister Charity assured me that such was not any "requirement" of God upon me, that I was free of that. She expressed her favor towards a further step in relationship with Juliann.

Except I could not. I wanted to, but the witness inside that this was not the Lord for me eventually brought an end to our relationship. Juliann returned home that summer, not planning to return. Sister Charity actually took my side and believed that Juliann was in the wrong. She spoke wonderful consolation into me.

I thought deep and long about hopping in my car and driving to Wisconsin that summer. Juliann's mom ran a small school; they owned a lovely country property. It seemed that everything I wanted was there, waiting for me. Yet I also knew, a second time, that if I drove away from Blueberry, I would never make it to Wisconsin, that God would take me to Himself rather than allowing me to go a different way.

Summer Work

The primary construction work that I did through the summer of 1987 was to build two high pole barns, 30 feet by 80 feet for hay for the cattle. The Blueberry community had invested a lot in a cattle program as a means of income for the family. These two pole barns were up on the flat above the river valley, one just north of the family buildings up the slope. This one ran east to west. The other was to the east, in the cattle loafing area, a building that ran north to south.

Don Howat had moved to Blueberry with his family in the fall of 1986. Slowly, he would become my covering in the construction arena, but since the cattle were John Austen's department, most of the work this summer was done under his direction. Nonetheless, in this and in other jobs, I had begun to work with Don Howat, pictured here..

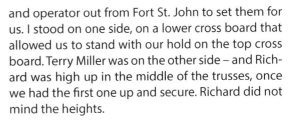

Don Howat would become the most important person in my life in the Blueberry context, and, with Rick Annett, the most important person to me in the move. Our walking together will unfold through the next several chapters.

We set the poles and connected them together with a cross board, maybe twenty feet up. Then we built a whole series of large trusses to my design. When everything was ready, we had a massive day (or maybe two) of putting the trusses on top of the cross boards. Brother John had rented a large crane

and operator out from Fort St. John to set them for us. I stood on one side, on a lower cross board that allowed us to stand with our hold on the top cross board. Terry Miller was on the other side – and Richard was high up in the middle of the trusses, once we had the first one up and secure. Richard did not mind the heights.

The crane operator would lift the next truss up, Terry and I would grab each end, while the crane lifted the top up towards Richard with a special board I had made, a board that had nails already driven in it above and below. All Richard had to do was slam the truss up against the nail underneath, and then hammer down the nail already in place, while Terry and I nailed the bottoms. Then we were ready for the next truss. We did both roofs in one or two strenuous days.

Before we finished each set of trusses, we nailed diagonal boards as braces, I think on both slopes on both ends, to keep them upright until we could come back to install the roof boards and tin. That night a freak wind storm went all across the Peace River region, all the way to Edmonton, with small tornados appearing in places. This was an extremely rare event.

Then next morning, someone breathlessly asked me if I knew that my trusses were lying broken on the ground. I coated myself against the driving rain and trudged up the hill to see. The first pole barn, the one running east and west, was fine, the freak wind had passed through parallel to the trusses. But when I got to the pole barn next to the cattle barn, there were all the trusses, twisted and broken on the ground.

I thought through very carefully regarding our bracing, something we had done last minute at the end of a hard day's work. My conclusion was that we had indeed braced the trusses sufficiently even for any normal winds. But this freak storm, something that had happened only once before when I was living at Graham River, with the winds hitting the trusses head on, was something no one could have planned for. I was my fiercest critic, and I had to satisfy myself that it was not a stupid mistake.

Nonetheless, we had to spend a couple more weeks rebuilding those trusses, re-hire the crane and operator, and do it all over a second time. The second time worked, and we were able to finish the tin roofs.

The next school year at Blueberry, "A Season of Deliverance," coming up next, would be one of the most remarkable and momentous years of my life. And that season would turn into the next at the start of my third school year with the most wonderful experience that has ever happened to me.

"Father, I thank you for the goodness of Your people in Christian community, and especially the family at Blueberry. I give You thanks, regardless of anything, for the opportunity to have been a part of the lives of each one, and they a part of my life. I know that all that belongs to me of truth, will return to me in its time. I can lose nothing.

"And Father, I ask forgiveness of, and extend Your forgiveness towards each one, in all favor, as I cast my mind across their faces and their many interactions with me. I place You, Lord Jesus, upon every one of them in my seeing, and upon every moment of my time there. You have always been all that I am and all of those who are my brothers and sisters inside of You."

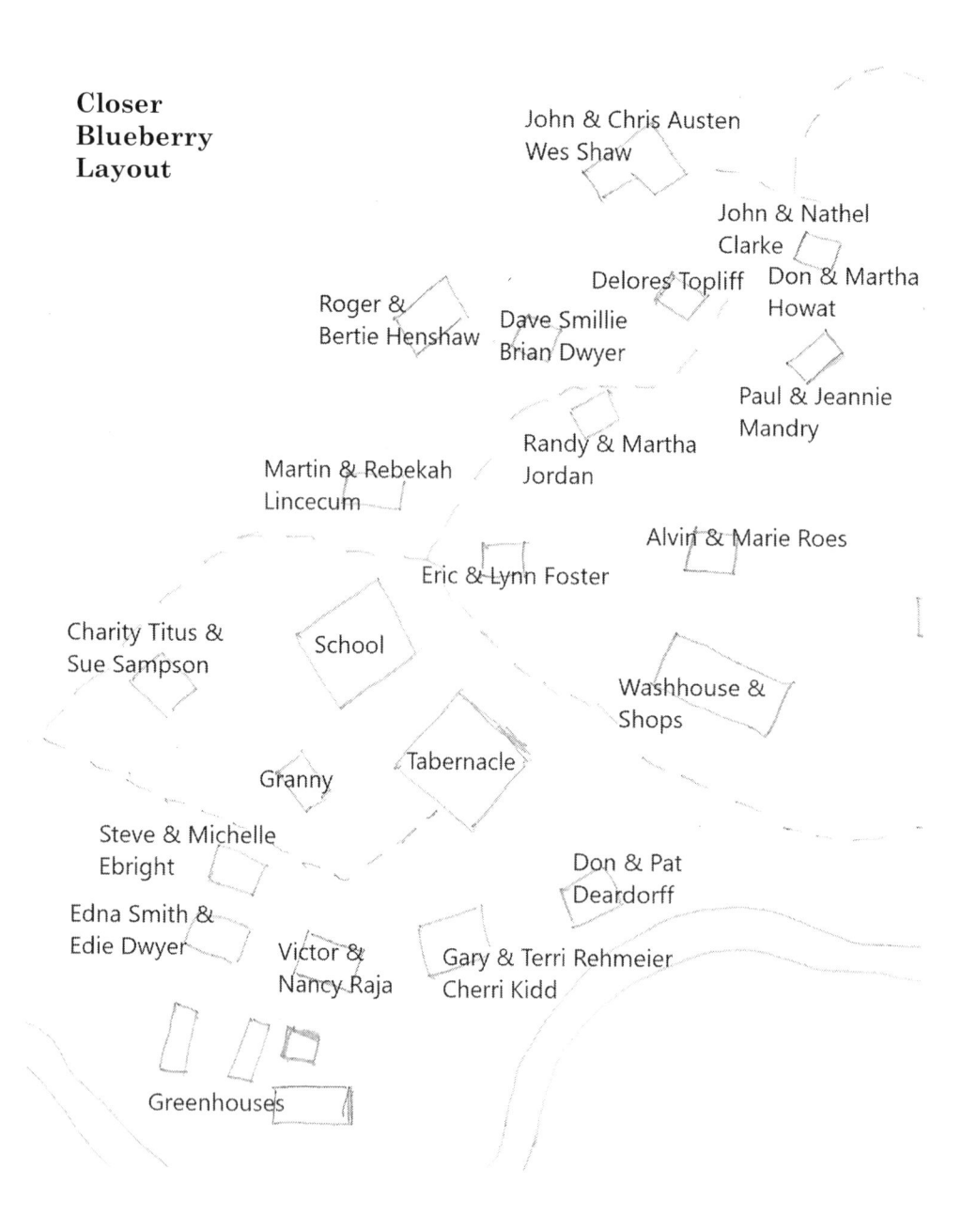

Closer Blueberry Layout

16. A Season of Deliverance I

September 1987 - December 1987

The Blueberry Family

I want to take the time to place many of those with whom I lived and worked and worshipped. I will start that with a new addition to the Raja home and to my, now ninth grade group of English students, Rachel Martin. Rachel was the sweetest, kindest, bubbliest, and most helpful girl I have known. Rachel had grown up at the Shiloh community. Her mother was First Nations, I think from a group in southwest BC. Her father was European. Her family was leaving Shiloh and the move, but Rachel wanted to continue in a community school, so she moved in with us, sharing Freda and Ruth's room and adding bright joy to everyone's life.

On the previous page is a more close-up map of the Blueberry Community, showing who lived where. Families and individuals came and went, people moved from one house to another over the years. For that reason, I am placing people where we remember they lived at the time Maureen arrived at Blueberry in August of 1988.

Let's start with Judy Jones and her sister, Joanne Branham, both of whom were elders. They, with parts of their families, left Blueberry that first year and returned to the states. Sister Judy had been a good and cheerful friend to me all the time I had known her. Joanne Branham's daughter, Cherri Kidd, remained at Blueberry with her son Christopher as well as her younger brother, Jason. Judy and Joanne's mother also remained at Blueberry; we called her "Granny." Judy's oldest daughter, Jeannie stayed; she had married Paul Mandry from New Orleans, who also started college at the same time as I. Cherri Kidd was always the secretary of the school and for Sister Charity through the years I lived at Blueberry. Christopher was in my classroom for five years as well. You can see several of these names on the cabin map.

Let's continue, then, in the area around the Raja cabin and work our way up the hill. Gary and Terri Rehmeier lived in the bottom of a larger, two-story cabin to our east, with their four children, Jesse,

Wendy, Angela, and Steven. Gary was one of the elders; he had charge of the logging company, called North Star, which belonged to the Blueberry Community, and so he was out from the community much of the time. Some of the men worked full time under him and others part time. The logging company wages provided a good amount of income for us. Terri was a nurse and midwife; she would play a brief, but significant role in our life, in the birthing of our two older children, Kyle and Johanna. Cherri and Christopher lived in the upper floor, then, with an outside stairway access. Rachel Roes had a room with Cherri all the time I was in school.

Many singles, whether college students or not, lived in the homes of most every family in the community. There were NO dormitories, thank God. Dormitories are just wrong. One of the psalmists said that God places the solitary in FAMILIES – not in dorms.

To our west were two cabins. Edna Smith lived in the one closer to the greenhouses. I think that Edie Dwyer shared one of the bedrooms in that house through these years. Both of them were elders. Sister Edna was a long-time English teacher in the public schools in west Texas, and then in the communities. These were older single women. Sister Edie covered the washhouse and food drying house.

In the other cabin were Steve and Michelle Ebright and their four children, Joy, Stephanie, Micah, and Johnathan. Steve often worked out under Brother Gary, he was a laid-back, easy going man. Michelle was a mainstay in the kitchen. I count her as an equal in my life to my older sister, Frieda; they were of a similar age. When I think of the worship of God in the church, it is Michelle's face in the praise services that comes to my mind. Joy became one of my students who was most precious to me, one who filled her name simply and always.

Granny, of course, I have mentioned. I do not actually know her name, she was "Granny" to the whole community. She always had college girls sharing her home with her.

Charity Titus and Sue Sampson shared a cabin just to the west of the school building. Both were from California and elders of the community. Sister Charity was the oversight of both high school and college, whereas Sister Sue was the oversight of the primary school upstairs. She also taught courses in the college. As I said, Sister Charity was strongly arthritic, with twisted fingers. Sister Sue took care of her home needs, but everyone served to wheel Sister Charity back and forth from home to school to Tabernacle or wherever she needed to go. The Monday evening elder's meetings were always held in their front room.

The cabin to the east of the Rehmeier's, just south of the washhouse/shop and sandwiched against the Blueberry River, belonged to Don and Pat Deardorff and their children, Lorna, Amos, David, Anita, and Karen. Lorna was college age and went to the University of Alberta at Edmonton through this time to become a nurse. Amos, David, and Anita were each in my classroom and a major part of my life. Don and Pat were not elders, though they were leading adults in the community. Don was the math teacher in high school and college, a brilliant man and gifted teacher who laughed and joked all the time. The Deardorff table in the dining room rang out in hilarious laughter regularly, such that everyone would turn just to enjoy their laughter. Amos liked to play trumpet. I had a trumpet, so I sold my silver trumpet to Amos. I cannot picture Anita except either with a mischievous grin or just a big smile.

All the houses above the main road were situated on small flat spots going up an ever steeper slope. Alvin and Marie Roes lived in the cabin just above the washhouse with their daughter, Elizabeth. Alvin was an elder and covered the vast farming part of the community across a number of sections of land which Blueberry had acquired over the years. Cheryl Mailman lived with him; her son, David, was in my class. Ken Geis also stayed with them for a while. Ken was a part-time college student around my age and everyone's friend, a jokester.

Just above the Tabernacle was a little cabin which, when Maureen arrived in the fall of 1987, belonged to Eric & Lynn Foster. Eric was my age and started school at the same time as I, but after he married Lynn, who had been living at Shepherd's

Inn, he pulled away from school classes and devoted himself to the fieldwork as Brother Alvin's second. Lynn was Maureen's good friend through the years; we couples knew one another in goodness and in sadness.

Before continuing, I must mention two couples who married in these first two years, but had moved elsewhere before Maureen arrived. One was Rohn Ritchie, whom I had known at Graham River. Rohn was the community mechanic, working under Wes Shaw's oversight. A brother and sister, Andrew and Mary, had moved to Blueberry from the states. Andrew was a blacksmith. Rohn and Mary married and then moved up to Whitehorse in the Yukon, to be part of the move fellowship there. Then, David Roes married a young lady who had lived at New Covenant while I was at Bowens Mill. I think they were in this little house for a bit, but they then moved on up to Alaska.

Straight north of the school was Martin and Rebekah Lincecum's cabin. Martin was Nathel Clarke's son; he worked full time with Gary Rehmeier in the logging business. Martin was a highly skilled big equipment operator. Rebekah was one of two sisters who had come to Blueberry from one of the Alaska fellowships. The other sister was Sarah Gregg, who lived in the Henshaw cabin. They were of college student age, but were never part of the college.

On up the hill were three cabins on about the same level. Up against the ridge to our west was the two-story house of Roger and Bertie Henshaw. These two were an older couple, leading adults in the community, though not elders. Roger had been a highly skilled machinist and was the community's small-item maintenance man. Sister Bertie was the community book keeper all the time I was there. Actually, Sue Sampson was the "treasurer," and Bertie worked under her. I spent a lot of community money buying building materials in Fort St. John. I knew that if I forgot the receipt, I would be in trouble with Sister Bertie. At the same time, Sue Sampson always "went to bat" for me in money requests to the eldership. With Roger and Bertie was another elderly lady, Sister Elsie, as well as many college students. Their upstairs was filled with young ladies. Their home was always an open door, with people in and out all the time. One did not knock, and Brother Roger greeted everyone coming in with great cheer.

I must also mention a family of siblings, the Hanna's. The Hanna family had lived, first at the Peace Valley Farm, and when it closed, at Shiloh. The whole family had "left the move" and returned to the states. Their oldest daughter, Jennifer, however, had chosen to return to community and to school at Blueberry. Eventually, her whole family followed her back, but at this time, just her first two younger brothers, Eric and Fritz. Nathan would follow a bit later. These three all married daughters of Blueberry. I knew Jennifer as a fellow classmate, but I spent more time with Fritz, since he was often part of the construction team. I have no idea where any of these four lived until after Eric and Fritz were married.

Kay Wallace from Portland, Oregon, also lived somewhere with her two sons, Howard and Michael. I just can't place where they were until Kay and Dave Smillie were married.

Then, facing each other on each side of the road going up the hill were Dave Smillie's cabin and Randy and Martha Jordan's. Dave Smillie's wife, Norma, had passed away, I think of cancer, prior to my arrival at Blueberry. His home was filled with college students as well as Brian Dwyer, who had his bedroom in Brother Dave's home the whole time I as at Blueberry. Dave was an elder, but I don't remember that he carried responsibility for any particular area. Randy and Martha were not much older than I, they had three small children. Randy was a highly capable machinist, welder, mechanic, and metal worker. Randy and I did not actually work together, but our work often fitted together on the same projects. I remember passing Randy on numerous occasions and being lifted up out of sorrow into gladness just by his kind smile. Martha was the covering of the kitchen through these years, very capable. We ate really well at Blueberry.

On up, at the steepest part of the slope, on the west, Delores Topliff's cabin was carved into the slope, but to the east, Paul and Jeannie's cabin was perched at the top of the long grassy run down to the butcher shop and washhouse. Delores was an elder with her focus mostly inside the school; she always filled her home with college students. Paul and Jeannie were just starting their family.

At the top of the slope, above the Henshaw and Topliff cabins was John and Kris Austin's large two-story house. Their children were Deborah, Rebecca, and Paul, each of whom I had in my classes in the school, and then three younger girls, Elizabeth, Abigail, and Karen. The Austin's were a big part of my life and a big part of the community. You will find few people more poured out in service to God's people than John Austin, with Kris as his match. John's father, Paul Austin, had been the CEO of Coca-Cola, and thus his mother held significant amounts of money for John's and his children's inheritance. In John Austin's entire mind and world, that money belonged to the Blueberry family, with no thought otherwise. Nonetheless, before his mother would release some of that money, she required John to build a nice house for her grandchildren. So, yes, their house, though still a log cabin, was a bit nicer and larger than the other dwellings. Nonetheless, to John and Kris, that was just a good reason to fill their home with people. Wes Shaw had one of the rooms in the downstairs. Judy Patterson and Gail Young, both teachers in the primary grades, shared a room. There were lots of others as well. Like the Henshaw home, the Austin door was "wide open," you never knocked. Their living room was everyone's living room.

John was an elder, and his project, towards which he directed some of the money, was the beef cattle program, a main part of the work and income of the community. The larger chunk of money established the North Star logging company, which Brother John soon released to Gary Rehmeier, never once thinking of it as his. Of truth, I have never known two young men of higher regard than their sons, Paul Austin and Jesse Rehmeier.

Then, last but not least, was the cabin of John and Nathel Clarke, situated on a bluff overlooking the Mandry cabin, and the grassy slope down, right inside the juncture of the two roads coming up the hill. John Clarke was one of the apostolic ministries of the move and he and Nathel spent probably half of each year traveling around the world to minister. When they were home, however, they moved only as two of the elders in the community. Brother John was an anointed minister, yes, but his greater anointing was in wisdom and counsel. The elders often yielded to his kind wisdom, although such was never required.

Brother John had been a Pentecostal pastor in Coeur d'Alene, Idaho. Sister Nathel Lincecum had been a part of the same group in California with Charity Titus and the Smillie's'. I do not know the story, but she moved to Brother John's church with her children, including Nadine, Martin, and Anne. Sister Nathel introduced Brother John to Sam Fife; the two were married before coming up to the Hidden Valley community in British Columbia. John Mark, Brother John's younger son, had passed away of cancer before I arrived at Blueberry. His passing was an incredible loss to everyone in the community. I do not know anything of Brother John's older children. Roger and Bertie had also been part of Brother John's church in Idaho.

I don't know how the Clarkes fitted everyone in, although their cabin had been added onto and was a bit larger than it shows on the map. Nonetheless, they made room for Don and Martha Howat and their three small children when they moved to Blueberry, as well as others. Rick and Shirly Annett also stayed with them for a time; Rick was one of the elders while he was there. I stayed friends with Rick and Shirley, even after they moved to Evergreen; we would share life together at Blair Valley. Don Howat was also an elder and the covering over the building needs in the community, and therefore my oversight and companion in the construction part of my life. Brother Don was just like Abel Ramirez, in that he always treated me as an equal. I would thrive in my construction experience through the years we worked together.

Someone, in reading this account, might think that there could not be so many wonderful people anywhere, that I must be exaggerating. I am not exaggerating; the Blueberry family was the finest group of people I have ever known. To have been part of their lives and they part of mine is an incredible gift of God.

The School Year Begins

The fall semester of 1987 began with a one-week block taught by Brother Buddy Cobb, who was the leading apostolic ministry of the move fellowship. He titled his teaching, "The Plan of God." Brother Buddy was tremendously anointed of God, he wove Scriptures together constantly, and he was very convincing. Nonetheless, his whole "Plan of God" made no sense to me whatsoever. Brother Buddy taught in the Tabernacle so that those who could attend during the day would have room; and in the evening, the whole dining room was filled for his teaching. We had one paper for our grade; most of my fellow students just repeated what he said and got an A. I am convinced they had no idea

what they had written in their papers. I can't do that, however, so I got a B, which was a low grade for me.

Nonetheless, this assignment marked a beginning in my life. I will not include a section on "the Bible and I" until the next chapter, but this moment is an important shift for me. Brother Buddy's position was that God had proven His love to us, yes, but far bigger than anything such might mean, God EXPECTED us now to PROVE our love for Him, which could be only by perfect hearing and perfect obedience. And so God's entire "plan" was a series of performance requirements from one group of people to the next, something everyone else had failed in, but which we were now called of God to do.

Inside of this grandiose "plan," there was no motive or purpose or heart, no original desire of God for creation other then – "Do what I say right now." I did not know it fully then, but when I read John Calvin's *Institutes of the Christian Religion*, I was reading the exact same argument and the exact same strange and disorganized arrangement of innumerable verses, with the Old Testament equal with the New. I did, however, understand that Buddy Cobb was Calvinist, though I never dared suggest that, for I would have been told I was WRONG without thought.

As I considered how I must write my paper, I knew that I must begin with God as Father and God as Love. Thus I attempted to place Brother Buddy's "plan" out from such a motive. In other words, God used this difficult assignment to plant in me the knowledge of the source and motive of God for creation.

But there were two other great dilemmas that arose for me in this week of teaching. First, these brethren in the northern communities had sold everything, and paid every personal price, in response to a word of the revelation of Jesus Christ through His Church, a word of LIFE. Brother Buddy clearly had no thought of such a thing in his teaching. At one point in an evening teaching, Sister Charity herself raised her hand to ask a question. I do not remember her exact words, and so I will put it this way. "Many of us have embraced and believed in a word of Life, where does that fit in what you are saying?"

Brother Buddy had a quick answer, "We'll get to that later." Only he never did.

But then he made a statement, "No ministry in this move has ever taught that the manifestation of the sons of God would be prior to the resurrection of our bodies." The problem is that I remember. I knew he was not speaking the truth. So I went home that evening and pulled out the Hollywood Series booklets that I had transcribed. It did not take me long to find Brother Sam's exact words saying what Brother Buddy was claiming had never been said. I was distraught, and so I took that booklet to Sister Charity in her office in the school the next day to show her this fact of history. But she stopped me immediately. Again, I don't remember her exact words, but it was a very earnest impartation to me that we do NOT speak evil of a leader of God's house, as God makes very clear in the Bible – **Touch not Mine anointed and do My prophets no harm.**

And so, just over two years after, this great contest God had started in me between rebellion and respect was now taken to a very practical next step. Here's the deal. Doctrine is NEVER the issue; the issue is always the heart. The issue is always how you treat other Christians, especially those who are "over you" in the Lord, for that IS how you treat God Himself. Sister Charity's words were the salvation of God to me; I closed my mouth.

My Fall Semester Courses

The school year of 1987-1988 was my jam-packed year. I took 25 credits of courses in the Fall and 28 in the Spring even while teaching a high school class every day. I had come to college to learn, and I fiercely loved doing so. Part of how I managed was how I ordered my time. Because of the needs of the college students, the community had our main service on Saturday evening. This left Sunday morning free for doing school work. I never did any thinking work after supper, only reading. So, while most of my fellow students took a break in the late afternoon, I did not. When I left my afternoon class, I sat down immediately and did most of any assignment. Then I would let it sit until the afternoon before it was due. At that point, I would look at it fresh, revise and finish it, and go to bed early, even while my fellow students were up into the wee hours trying to get it done last minute. At the same time, I would save the biggest assignments for Sunday morning. From Friday supper on, I did not think about school work once, until I arrived at the school early Sunday morning with my cup of coffee and a clear mind. In that condition I could get a lot done in short order.

I am not sharing all of the courses I took, of course, but I am sharing a number of them that were of great importance to me, not just academically, but for my life. In both semesters of this year, I took New Testament Survey taught by Ernest Watkins, who lived at the Hilltop community. A lot of Bible went into me as I sat and absorbed Brother Ernest's teaching. Then, I had three courses this semester with Sister Delores, English Composition, History of Education, and History of the English Language. Each of these three were of great importance to me and in each, Sister Delores excelled as a teacher. My big project for the history of the English language was a layout of the flow of words into English as a bulletin board. That bulletin board stayed for a couple of years, there to the left as you go out the back door; I still have all its faded pieces.

I want to introduce Peter Bell to you now. Peter Bell had moved to the Evergreen community with his family so that he might finish his degree at the Blueberry College. They never lived at Blueberry, but I visited with him and Barbara and their children at Evergreen many times. Peter had married Barbara Beebe of the Upsala community. I just watched a video of my grandson, Gabriel, not yet two, dancing in the Tabernacle at Upsala to her father, Ted Beebe, now in his nineties, playing the piano as dear Sister Dot Richie from Graham River, Rohn Richie's mother, watched him adoringly. This is our heritage; it is the goodness of God.

Peter Bell was also an English major, and so he joined with Mike, Terry Miller, and myself in Sister Delores's many classes. Peter loved linguistics as I do, and we could talk for hours in sheer delight over the nuances of language and how it works. Peter had a wonderful chuckle that added a sense of delight every time something interesting was said in class. Peter will play a large part in my story over the next many years.

The college course that changed everyone's life and the life of many of the communities across the move, however, was Sister Jane Miller's "two-week" block titled "Spiritual Warfare," which we "took" in November of 1987.

Sister Jane Miller

Sister Jane Miller's college course was set up in the larger dining room in the same way that Brother Buddy's course was set up. Theoretically, this was a "college course" and through the first week, Sister Jane did teach several hours each day. The core of her course was her own life story.

In every other respect however, this was no "college course." Let me explain the heart dynamics of this family of people I have described in this letter. We were a people who had sold everything, who had committed our lives to God and to one another at great cost for years. And we had done so because every person in that place thirsted after the living God, that we might know Him, and that we might be the revelation of His glory. This was no "Sunday-go-to-church" congregation of people. We knew the demonstration of the Spirit and power, we were determined to know God in all fullness.

From the moment Sister Jane started to teach that Monday morning, everything was different. All other work of the community had ceased. The school was closed. Only some of the sisters made our meals quietly in the kitchen, right in full hearing of Sister Jane. Every person in the community was crowded into that dining room with many also from Evergreen and Hilltop. We college students had the tables in front as we listened to the most anointed woman of God I have ever known.

Sister Jane Miller's story is relevant to my life and to this history, thus I will share it briefly with you.

Sister Jane had grown up in west Texas. While still a girl, once, when using the outhouse, she was frightened by a spider. That fear grew inside of her through her teenage years. Then, when she married Dick Miller and they had several young children together, in the difficulty of raising little children something snapped inside of her.

Jane Miller became what is called, "schizophrenic," except she was far more than most, many very different personalities raged inside her person. Medical professionals at Tulane University in New Orleans attempted to treat her, but were not able to help. They advised Dick to divorce her and to marry again so his children would have a mother. They told him that Jane would spend the rest of her life in a padded cell.

What they did not know was that deep inside her heart, Jane Miller knew and loved Jesus. Outwardly she was only whatever demon was playing her at the moment, but inside she called upon Jesus to save her. In response, the Lord Jesus sent her Sam Fife. This was, I believe, 1965. Sam Fife had pa-

stored a church in New Orleans that followed him into the move of the Spirit coming out from his receiving a revelation from God through George Warnock's *Feast of Tabernacles*. And so Dick Miller brought his young wife to the gathering of that fellowship in New Orleans. I knew later some who were there, including Purcell Coalwell, who taped on a cassette recording the entire times of deliverance prayer.

With the elders of the New Orleans fellowship, Brother Sam cast the demons out from Jane Miller. This time took a few hours, all of which was recorded. Brother Sam required of each demon to speak before he sent it away, so that Jane could know that this voice inside of her was NOT her and was NOT God. Each one spoke back with a very different personality. The university doctors, when they listened to the tapes, heard each of the differing personalities they had dealt with.

Jane Miller was set completely free into a sound mind and the joy of Christ. The doctors at the university could not deny the miraculous change, and so they used the tapes in their teaching for a few years.

But Jane faced again the same fears that had overwhelmed her as a young mother, and in her weakness, she fell back again into the horror of all those voices. Her husband, Dick, asked Brother Sam to please come again for his wife. Sam Fife agreed and prayed to set Jane free a second time. He told her this time, however, that he would not do so a third time. She herself would have to stand against all those voices.

And so Sister Jane did. And in standing fiercely inside the liberty of Christ against all the wailing voices of fear and accusation, Sister Jane became one of the most anointed ministries in the move. I had listened to her deliverance tapes as part of the "Basics" under Brother Jim Fant at the Ridge. Listening to her share the same story, now through an anointing that came closer to the open door that rested upon Sam Fife, carried a mighty impact into every single heart listening to her in the Blueberry Tabernacle.

Sister Jane continued her teaching for several days; nothing else happened in the community. She taught about the realms of darkness, similar to what Sam Fife had taught, which we had also listened to at the Ridge. But now it was more personal and real, and through Sister Jane's words, the Spirit of God was touching the deep heart's cry of everyone hearing her, the cry to be FREE.

An Outpouring of Deliverance

After the teaching was over, Sister Jane was gathered in the Science room with all of us college students. The others of the Blueberry family were carrying out necessary tasks, long neglected. Nonetheless, some of the more "desperate" shall I say, non-students were also there with us. One of those was a sister, a wife of the community, who had been communicating privately with Sister Jane. It was late afternoon.

Sister Jane began to pray for this sister, with all of us gathered around, singing the praises of deliverance. She prayed for a couple of hours, while we continued to sing. The sister came completely free, filled to overflowing with joy and grace. Our deliverance practicum had begun.

The next morning, I came up onto the school porch at the same time as Sister Jane. As we walked into the school building, I said to her, "Sister Jane, you are going to pray for me before you leave because if you don't, I will crawl into your pocket until you do."

Some of the dividers had been moved back and we were now gathered in the central area of the school. A chair was set out for the one to be prayed for and we all gathered around to sing praises while Sister Jane prayed. Some of the other elders were there as well, sharing in the prayers of deliverance. There were many tremendous praise leaders in the Blueberry community, including among the students, and so the leading of praise simply passed from one to the next.

Meanwhile, I sat on a bench, partly watching, all constricted inside, waiting with desperate hope for my turn. You see, I did not understand anything, but, in spite of all the good things of God I had known and experienced, still the torment of fear from the overdose on LSD gripped my insides every day. As I sat there, I heard my Father speak to me words unbidden by me. First, He cast my mind across the dark years of my youth when I had used drugs and during which I imagined that I was not "saved." "Son," He said to me, "Even through those dark times, you were still My son." This was the first time that idea came to me. It did not take me long to realize just how important that bit of understanding was.

Then, sometime in the afternoon, Sister Jane called me up to the chair. At the same time, she motioned to Brother Victor Raja to take the lead in prayer, while she stepped into the background. I did not like that, but there was nothing I could do. They prayed over me for deliverance, somewhere between one and two hours. When my time was over, although I felt great relief, I had not come clear. During the times of prayer, those who saw visions shared their visions with whomever was praying so that they could pray in the knowledge of the Spirit. Then, after each time of prayer, different ones shared those visions with all. One had seen a vision of a great black panther inside of me that was the ruling power over whatever lesser things held influence in my life.

You see, none of this was "theology." My fear was real, and our cry for deliverance was real. As far as I am concerned all the theologians who know so much can take a hike. They know nothing at all. They are all those who go rushing by the wounded, blessing them in their passing, but never ever "demeaning" themselves by getting down into the pit with those who are suffering and waging war, together with God, until this dear one is FREE.

Those who say that a Christian "can't have a demon," are cruel beyond measure. Nonetheless, as I have come to know since, the only true weapon in our possession is Christ our life, that Christ is all first before anything not Christ could ever vanish away.

The next morning, I had to drive into Fort St. John to make some construction purchases, a trip that was unavoidable. I went by myself; before I left, the whole family was gathering into the Tabernacle. Again, everything was shut down and the entire Blueberry family, with others from Evergreen and Hilltop were joined together in this outpouring of deliverance.

I was NOT free. And all the way into town God contended with me more explicitly and personally than He had ever done before. "Will you surrender all that you are to Me, My son." I knew, then, that deliverance was no "panacea," there could be no escape from a face to face, heart with heart confrontation of God with me. I was in complete agony until that moment when, on the return trip to Blueberry, I said quietly, "Yes, Lord." The agony lifted and the peace of God flowed all through my heart.

It was still early evening when I returned home to Blueberry. As soon as I could, I was back in the Tabernacle where the mighty prayers and songs of deliverance were continuing in full flow as they had been all day. Everyone gathered around the one being prayed for, one of the elders. Most of the elders sat in the chair for their own time of deliverance, at one time or another, even as they shared in the prayers for deliverance for others. This time, I was fully free inside the joy and wonder of God among His people.

Picture, if you would, the dining room at Blueberry, a carpeted floor, with the tables rolled away and some chairs arranged across the back of the room. In the front center, about where the podium usually was, there was a chair, and the one being prayed for sitting in that chair. Around the chair were gathered Sister Jane, Sister Charity, Sister Barbara James who was staying at one of the other communities at the time, as well as some of the other Blueberry elders. Sister Jane led the prayer, while the others stood with her. All around them was the entire family, young and old, all on their feet, all of us singing the praises of God inside a mighty flow of the Spirit of God. Those who saw visions were typically in the background in silent prayer, but would come to share their vision with Sister Charity who would then share with Sister Jane the wisdom that the Spirit of God was giving.

We sang and prayed from 7 to 9 PM, until the sister stood from the chair, filled with overflowing JOY.

Then the door into the Tabernacle opened and a man whom we did not know stepped in. With him was his daughter, a young woman named Delynn, in her late twenties, painfully skinny. Upon her face and from head to foot was the specter of death. Her dad had been in communication with Sister Jane, and when he learned that God was visiting His people in power, he put his daughter with him on the plane and they had flown from Philadelphia to Fort St. John that day, arriving at Blueberry, finally, at 9 PM.

Sister Jane gently greeted them and directed them to sit down in chairs near the front. She wanted Delynn to rest in the praises of God before she prayed for her. Then, Sister Jane turned to Granny and Sister Elsie, the two little old ladies in our family, not to pray for their "deliverance" for such a thing would have been disrespectful. Rather, we gathered around these two in order to honor them with the blessings of God.

Around 10 PM, after visiting personally for a bit with Delynn, Sister Jane drew her into the chair in the center. As she did, something happened inside the heart of every single one of us in that room. Delynn was under the power of a dark spirit of anorexia, but in that moment, the determination of God gripped our hearts. We would see her FREE, and we would pay whatever price to do so. All that we could give, however, were our voices, and so we sang WITH ALL OUR MIGHT. Some had been singing all day.

Every individual in that family drew close, from the littlest to the eldest. I had my eyes on my students, and, I saw even them calling upon Jesus and commanding demons to come out. If the hearts of two seventh-grade boys in particular were so caught in the outpoured love of God, you can be sure everyone else was even more so. At a certain point, during the time of prayer and praise, Sister Jane motioned to us to be quiet. Then, she turned towards Delynn and commanded the demons to speak. She did this to show Delynn that these voices were NOT her.

One thing demons hate is being exposed. They choose always to remain secret and hidden, so that their masters imagine that the demon's voice is nothing more than their own thoughts. But something else terrifies demons far more than being exposed, and that is the Blood of Christ in the mouth of believers in Jesus. It was clear to everyone, including Delynn, that it was NOT her speaking, but a demon. The demon said that he gained power over Delynn through the music she had listened to. At the present time, I would suggest that to be only partly correct.

Just before midnight, Delynn came completely free. She stood to her feet, pale, but radiant with joy. All of us had lost our voices by then. But the JOY that filled the heart of everyone was palpable and thick. Sister Jane lifted her arm and slowly swept it around to honor the family of God and as she did so, such a glory came upon us as I have never known before or since, the Shekinah glory of God.

This was November, when the daylight is short and the night long. Before the sun rose in the morning the Tabernacle was packed full again, with more coming from Evergreen and Hilltop and a whole bunch from Headwaters. The dining room was filled with people, there was no more room for any chairs. Because so many thirsted after the living God and longed for the power to be FREE, a decision was made to have two different chairs going at once with the family split evenly in great circles around, singing the mighty praises of God.

And so the prayers of deliverance continued. In the early afternoon, I needed to step outside to use the outhouse behind the school. When I came back in, everyone had gathered into one circle because the need of one individual was so great that Sister Jane wanted everyone focused on her. The press prevented me from at first seeing for whom they were praying. When I finally saw, I was SHOCKED to my core.

Let me explain. I am NOT an easy believer. I always REQURE evidence, either valid historical evidence or hands-on scientific evidence or what God ACTUALLY says in the Bible. When I am certain of the evidence, I give myself wholly to what is true, but not before. Concerning "demons," in spite of the mighty experiences over the prior several days, I was still very much a skeptic.

There on the floor, writhing in agony, was the sweetest and dearest young girl I have known in my life, one of my students, who had brought such joy to everyone. Only it was not her. Behind what sort of looked like her face was an aboriginal mask, an ancient, twisted, and dark thing. In that moment I knew that I was not looking at this dear girl. I knew her; this was not her. Then, when our prayers had finished their work and she was herself again, she was, if that could be possible, more ebulliently sweeter and joyous than she had been before.

Something clicked inside my heart-mind connection, and I knew, from then until now, that demons are real inside the human experience, as familiar to every individual person as our own breath and thoughts, bringing torment, fear, and confusion to all their masters who imagine that, by playing with their pet demons, they might gain some advantage.

Continuing On

The mighty deliverance times with Sister Jane continued day after day. More and more people, each one of whom I knew personally and loved, came free into the glorious liberty of Christ. Complaining and muttering vanished from our midst. The earnest determination to know the living God only increased. Even after Sister Jane went on to other communities, with this new and mighty outpouring of the Spirit of God touching people's lives and establishing community families everywhere inside the love and joy of Christ, the same Spirit of deliverance prayer and praise continued on with the Blueberry family, month after month, for years.

I want to bring in another impactive course taught by Sister Charity, and that was "Family Life," which she taught as a three-week block that December. I can only say again just how much wealth I received into myself from Sister Charity's wonderful teaching. There was a high point for me in this course, a personal moment of God's goodness to me.

As part of studying "family life," Sister Charity assigned each of us to write a paper on our remembrance of how our parents had raised us. As usual, as soon as class was out at three in the afternoon, I sat down to write my paper. As I was writing, out from my mind, how my parents had raised me, I wrote these words, with no thought of what they actually meant.

"I know that my dad loved me and gave himself wholly for me."

I finished my paper before supper. At first I hardly noticed, but slowly, bit by bit, a lightness arose in me, a joy unspeakable and full of glory. By the time I walked over to the Tabernacle for supper, I was walking in the clouds, filled with a peace like I had never known before. I was amazed and astonished, but it was not until I was eating my supper that the realization hit me of what had happened that afternoon.

As I wrote those words, I was forgiving my father.

This is hard for me to understand. My father never once did even the slightest thing to warrant the bitterness I imagined that I held against him. He was the kindest and most generous of fathers. As I have raised my own children, I struggled with the same impossibility he knew, that he could not share of his own personal life with us, and I understood. Yet not once did anything but love and honor ever come towards me out past my father's own inner difficulty. My bitterness was nothing more than my own twisted, hurting, and confused rebellion.

A few months later, I had a vivid dream. In my dream, my father came to me, spoke forgiveness to me, and held me close to the comforting of his heart. When I shared that with Sister Charity, she made sure I knew that it was just a "vision" of what was true, and not actually my own father coming to me in the heavens for real. I accepted her understanding, though I secretly did not believe it. Neither do I believe it now. I accept that it really was my own dad, imparting what had always been his heart to me.

I will continue this "Season of Deliverance" in the next letter. Because there is so much more I want to share inside this one year of time, this has become a two-part chapter.

17. A Season of Deliverance II

January 1988 - September 1988

The Spring Semester

The entire year, from September of 1987 until the end of August, 1988, was inside this same season of deliverance, yet we have covered only four months. The remaining eight months, however, contain so much that is of importance to my life and to the deliverance of God. Deliverance times did continue after August of 1988, but they stood in second place to something far more important to me.

In other colleges, the courses I took were peripheral to my life. At least half of the courses I took at Blueberry were central to my life and to my knowledge of God. Besides the second semester of New Testament with Brother Ernest, I also took "Learning and Evaluation" from Sister Mozelle and "Understanding the Adolescent" from Sister Charity. Both of these courses were key to my knowledge of how to enable my students to learn.

From Sister Delores, I took "Library Skills," more English Composition, and "Writer's Workshop." I will share more from these in a bit. Second to Sister Jane's role in my life, however, was a "Speech Workshop" in March, conducted by Bill and Bettie Grier from the Whitestone Christian community in Alaska. Bill and Bettie were leading traveling ministries in the move. This Speech Workshop meant so much to me and to others.

Continuing Deliverance

Before we get to the Speech workshop, I want to share the experience I had, probably in February of 1988. After Sister Jane had gone on elsewhere, the services at Blueberry continued in similar levels of anointing and power. It was a season of wonder.

In one such service, during the praise, there seemed to come upon each one personally, and thus all of us together, the same levels of anointing for deliverance we had tasted with Sister Jane. I found myself so caught into God. – But in that place, suddenly, I saw those eight long hours of terror when I was sixteen, lying on my bed overdosing on LSD. The moment I saw that, something let loose inside of me. I felt as if a huge swarm of hornets were swirling around in desperate anger just above and back from my heart.

I shot my hands up into the air and cast myself utterly upon the Lord Jesus. As I did so, I felt a great snap or pow as that angry horde left me, with the sensation of their departure right behind and above my voice box.

Most every day for fifteen years, in spite of all the deliverances and revelations of God, that tormenting fear had gripped my guts. From that moment until now, I cannot remember such a thing, what it was or meant. I know of it only as something that was once true, but it is utterly gone from me, never to return.

I want to explain how this all works. You see, a natural health practitioner knows that, if someone has a significant health problem, cancer, say, you cannot just start treating that condition. Rather, other health problems are sitting on top of that larger problem, one might say, and those less significant problems must be dealt with first. To treat the large problem without removing those lesser issues, could jeopardize the life of the patient.

It is the same for God as He brings spiritual healing to us. The terror of being lost was the larger issue inside of me. But God could not remove that until He had first touched and healed some other things in my life, including forgiving my father. Once those "lesser" things were healed and gone, then God could break the greater thing without destroying me.

The same thing is happening as I write this account of my life. Except this time, it is the final little things that God is bringing such wondrous healing to, filling up all the remaining crevices of my memory with joy and goodness. I could never have given an account like this before, not until so many much larger things had been healed, even all through this present season of speaking Christ my only life.

Speech Class

Bill and Bettie Grier had been leading ministries in a move of the Spirit called "the Walk" under John Stevens. In that fellowship, they lived in a community with their congregation in New Hampshire. Then, in 1980, they, with most of their congregation, switched over to being part of "the move." (That sounds silly, I know, but what else do we call what God is doing among His people.) Most of that congregation then moved up to Alaska to a property southeast of Fairbanks. Their community was called Whitestone, which also held a branch of Covenant Life College. Bill Grier had been accepted as an apostolic ministry of our fellowship, but his wife Bettie was certainly his equal.

Apart from being strong and leading ministries, Bill and Bettie both were speech teachers. As such, their speech team in the high school at Whitestone won the Alaska state speech competition over and over. They often went on to the national competitions and won the best high school speech team in the nation more than once. What I mean to say is that for eight jam-packed days, from dawn to well-after dark, we were immersed in one of those wondrous experiences in life that come seldom, but which were my privilege to be caught in.

All the college students were in this eight day course, as well as a number who were not students including Brian Dwyer and David Randolph, a brother about our age who had come to Blueberry that spring from the Yukon. The course itself was held in the science room, but we practiced our lines all over the school and throughout the community. For eight days, the whole community was caught up in our speech practice.

Bill and Bettie alternated as they taught us speech fundamentals and practiced us in various impromptu speech exercises. They worked together perfectly, back and forth, through this whole time.

Now, let me tell you, speech, and acting on a stage and "performing" in front of people was NOT me. I would almost rather have gone to the dentist! So, when I had to stand in front of the class to give a little prepared spiel and NOT be distracted, while everyone hooted and hollered (that was the drill), was bad enough. Except that Mike Pelletier and Ken Geis had been assigned to be my chief distractors, which Mike fulfilled by climbing on my back and Ken by blocking between me and my audience in every ridiculous pose! Needless to say, I did not do too well on that exercise. (I am laughing as I write this.)

Each of us was assigned two major things. First was a two-page reading, which we were to perform in front of the class for a major part of our grade. This reading had to be memorized, eloquent, and fully expressive, that is, we had to be the characters we were expressing. I chose a piece from *Roots*, when the older slave couple learned their daughter would be sold away from them. I had to speak the dialogue of five different individuals, the narrator, one white and three black, four of them Southern and all highly emotional.

The second was a reader's theater presentation of *The Great Divorce* by C.S. Lewis, which we would present to a packed audience on the last evening of the course, that is, the end of the seventh day. My part was the dead Anglican priest, living out from his theological intellect, come out from Hades to view a distant heaven. My conversation was with a human, played by Lena Pacy, whom I had known when alive, coming out from Christ to convince me that intellectual theology was worthless and that we should just love Jesus for real. My character was not persuaded.

Again, this was not something I did, yet there I was, being coached by two of the best as well as by several of their top students from Whitestone who had come to assist.

To explain what this great press was for all of us, I want to focus on Monica Rotundi; indeed we all were focused on Monica Rotundi because, for some reason, Brother Bill went after her with everything he had. Monica was a little mouse of a girl, bright and warm certainly, but acting outwardly in this way was harder for Monica than for any of us.

Monica's personal reading was from the Jesse Owen story when his mother had to cut a tumor out of him herself, because they could not afford a doctor. Brother Bill made Monica repeat her piece over and over in front us, never accepting her performance because it was not good enough. Bill and Bettie were fierce, but they were also anointed of God and knew exactly what they were doing. They together were master creators. All of us wanted to protect Monica, but we did not dare. And the worse thing was that Monica's personal presentation was to be given to the whole audience. She also had a part in the reader's theatre presentation of *The Great Divorce*.

Then, as we were rehearsing the reader's theater (which means that you are expressive as the character, but you remain standing in one spot without moving around as one does in acting). As those of us who were ghosts arriving up out from hades, Monica was sitting behind me in our "train." She lost it, in full panic mode. I wanted so much to comfort her, to tell her it was okay. But Brother Bill was nearby, and when he saw Monica panic, he became too angry to speak. He called Bettie over, and she said, in stern command, "Monica, snap out of it."

To my compete astonishment, Monica did. She went completely to peace. Let me tell you this, though, such an approach is almost always false; this time, with these two, it was true. When Monica gave her Jesse Owen's performance the next evening to the entire crowd, she did it better than any time of practice. She had us all completely mesmerized.

I gave my presentation from *Roots* to the class in the Science Room the afternoon before our final presentation. This was difficult for me, but I had worked hard on it with help from Whitestone students. So I stood and did the best I could, not knowing how it would be received. Brother Bill was sitting just in front of me, but Sister Bettie was in the back corner behind the teacher's desk. When I had finished, Brother Bill was in tears. He stated that he had been unable to mark my points because he had been too deeply moved. They had to rely on Bettie's marks for my grade. I did not expect this, but his response planted something deep inside of me that would change my teaching career.

We performed *The Great Divorce* to a packed house. I remember that Sister Jane was also there, having been ministering in a nearby community. Lena Pacey and I had practiced our characters together quite a bit. When I spoke my lines in what I hoped was an Anglican intellectual voice, the whole audience laughed, including Brother Bill. This was amazing – I had made people laugh. Wow.

Someone had taken a video of the performance, and so in our final day of the course, which was a debriefing of what we had experienced, we watched that video together in the science room. This was the first time in my life I had seen myself on video. I was astonished and overwhelmed; it was almost too much for me. I had never before known that I had an outward appearance that people saw. As an Asperger's individual, I had been completely oblivious to such a thing, something typical of us. This was a major moment in God bringing me out of my bubble of happy but hurtful oblivion.

One more element of this speech experience lodged itself in my mind. David Randolph and Kathy Lewis had done their personal presentation together, a piece from *The Lion, the Witch, and the Wardrobe* by C.S. Lewis. And so I heard this line from the white witch, over and over as they practiced and presented, "Go to sleep, go to sleep, go to sleep." Of course, in the presentation, that was the voice of the enemy. I took the meaning of that false voice to heart and have stood against it consciously from then until now. It's not part of this story, but I can show you just how much those words rule over the lives of too many believers in Jesus, "Go to sleep, go to sleep, go to sleep." Pure and perfect rest is Christ; 'go to sleep' is the enemy.

Monica was never the same after this experience. From then until now, she was much more expressive and free towards others outwardly. The same was true of me, but mostly inside the arena of my teaching classroom. My older son and daughter, Kyle and Johanna, will tell you that, while I am not typically expressive outwardly, in two places I am, in my reading out loud to them and in the classroom. This is a gift both Monica and I owe to Bill and Bettie Grier. Thank you.

Issues Coming out from Writing

I took three writing courses this semester – four, actually, if I were to count a Vocabulary study I did on my own. You have read some of my homework from the English Composition course, my character descriptions of Henry Miller and Sam Fife. (That's funny, two more opposite individuals could not be found.)

We also took a Library Skills course that consisted primarily of a field trip to Edmonton and the writing of a research paper. My choice of topic was "Lexicography," or the history of the writing of dictionaries. I am weird, I admit, but this topic was absolutely fascinating to me. In fact, before I took Sister Delores's course on the History of the English Language, I had never thought before that the English language had a history. A great love for something I had not known awakened in me then, and continued on in this course – What are words and why do they mean what they mean?

There were only several of us in the van trip to Edmonton. I know that Mike Pelletier and Kathy Lewis were along, and I think that Lois Mack and Terry Miller were as well, and, of course, Sister Delores. I don't think Peter Bell was on that trip. There might have been a couple of others. We had a wonderful time together.

The primary purpose of our trip was the library at the University of Alberta in Edmonton. Except that Delores had gotten permission for us to access the graduate library, not the regular college library. I like books; I like libraries, I have never seen such a wonder before or since. The entire college library at the University of Houston (where I have taken my students several times) was the same size as the regular college library at Edmonton. The graduate library was more than twice as big, five full and large floors, crammed with books. To give a for-instance, in the history section, every monarch of England occupied a seven-to-eight-foot width of shelving, floor to ceiling. I had learned in my study that the first person in English history to write down a list of English words was a guy by the name of Wynken de Word, in the 1400's, just as modern English was coming out of the fusion of Norman French and Anglo-Saxon. How on earth could I find books on Wynken de Word? Yet there were two whole books just on this one obscure fellow whose only claim to fame was that he wrote a list of words!

From writing this paper, I learned that there is no such thing as any "original" definition of any word. A word means only what the one using that word intends in that context and moment, and it means nothing else. And so all dictionary writers simply take various sentences in which authors or speakers use a particular word and deduce what they mean by that word out from context clues. That's why you have several definitions for each word, because different individuals meant something different when they used it. Let's not get sidetracked, however.

I'm not a big-city person, but I liked Edmonton. We did a lot more than just visit the library. We spent a few hours in each of two other places, the Royal Alberta Museum of Natural History and the Muttart Conservatory, "botanical gardens in pyramidal biomes." Both places were wondrous, especially the gardens. This was northern winter and snow covered the ground outside, yet we walked in tropical and subtropical vegetation all around us.

The other course I took with Sister Delores was "Writer's Workshop." One of the assignments I did would be a critical milestone in my life and of utter importance to the revelation of Jesus Christ through us, His church.

The first assignment I did in that course, however, was a short story which I titled "Conflict with Conscience." During my first times up to Graham River, back and forth, my friend, Andy Wyatt, had found a home with my parents for a few months. During that time he decided to join the army to serve the Lord as a chaplain. My dad counseled him against such a thing, explaining to him that the entire institution was only about killing and nothing else. Andy went anyhow, but returned from boot camp several weeks later, a broken man, though holding an "honorable discharge." I remembered Andy's story in full, for he had told it to me. Then, at Blueberry, I learned that Eric Foster had done boot camp at the same Fort Dix in New Jersey. From Eric, then, I learned all the outward details, the buildings and drill inside of which Andy's story took place. My story is a true story, then, of just how anti-Christ the militaries of this world really are.

The other big assignment in this writing course, then, was to write a play. Since we had just completed the Speech course, I had a much better idea of how a script for the stage should read. I chose *A Tale of Three Kings* by Gene Edwards. As my assignment, I turned the core of that story into a play that could be presented on the stage.

I believe I had been introduced to Gene Edward's books while living at Bowens Mill. John Jeffries had started his course on Church History at the beginning of my college experience with *The Early Church* by Gene Edwards as our initial text book. I had gone on, then, to read *A Tale of Three Kings*; both books marked some deep understandings of God and His ways inside of me. I recommend that you obtain and read both; both are critical to your life in God as well.

That action of turning *A Tale of Three Kings* into a reader's theater script meant that I immersed myself in the meaning of David's life and his conflicts with Saul and Absalom. David demonstrates for us the utter refusal of "Christian rebellion." The story of Korah in Numbers 16 is the most explicit portrayal of Christian rebellion in the Bible, but David is the one who shows us the opposite, first towards Saul above him and then towards Absalom, a wannabe' below him.

The great question of Edwards' book and of David's story is this. What do you do when someone throws a spear at you? Not what do you feel, but what do you do? Before you will ever be a part of the revelation of a God who humbles Himself as He steps into His creation, you will give God your answer to that question, not with words, but in the hard reality of life. And, of course, David's response from beginning to end was, **"Touch not Mine anointed and do My prophets no harm."**

What I mean to say is that these things did not go into me as ideas, but as the very Seed of God planted in me, and I pondered them in my heart for the next few years until they had become the proof of my own life, keeping me inside of confusion and grief.

Some Days of Sadness

Two sadness's happened in my life through this Spring semester. The first was Richard's story, which is mostly not mine to tell, except that part relevant to me. Richard's friendship with Elizabeth was enjoyed and witnessed to by everyone. They had walked out their year and were approaching and preparing for a wedding. Then something happened inside of Richard, and he began to doubt his up-coming marriage with Elizabeth. I don't know what was truly going on inside of him, or even, in the long run, if the Lord wasn't using this time to challenge Richard's commitment (something He would also do with me).

I do know what Elizabeth has shared with me, that the next few months became difficult for her and her family as Richard was unable either to let go or to commit. And, as Richard's good friend, I was sometimes caught between.

Sometime later that summer, then, Richard was hammering a fence staple into a post. The staple ricocheted off the post and went right into Richard's eye. Since Terri Rehmeier was a nurse, she knew what to do and that was not touch the thing all the way into the emergency room in Fort St. John. Richard lost that eye, and the losing of it was agonizing pain. He has worn an eye patch since.

Not long after, Richard finally ended his relationship with Elizabeth and went away, eventually ending up at the community in Detroit Lakes,

Minnesota. This was a great sadness for everyone, something no one understood, including, I think, Richard himself. After coming up to be my best man in our wedding, Richard eventually ended up back at his home town of Denver City, Texas.

Then, one day, near the end of the school year, John Austin came up to me just outside the Tabernacle with sadness on his face. "Daniel," he said, "Brother Victor has been killed in a car wreck."

I want to back up a bit, now, and share some more about Brother Victor and my relationship with him in our home. I mentioned that Brother Victor had prayed for me at the beginning of the deliverance times. A few days later, however, I found him at home instead of in the deliverance and, in fact, I did not see him there very much. I could see that he was deeply troubled by something, but I did not know what.

Then, over the next several months, Brother Victor began to share with me as a confidante some troubling things about his disagreement with some of the elders. I had no idea what he was sharing, and it became a bit of a weight to me, even though he always treated me with kindness. Eventually, his speaking against become so troublesome to me that I shared of it with Brother John and Sister Nathel. During that time Brother Victor shared a word in the services from one of the prophets – **"the winter is come and we are not prepared".**

I do not and did not know what was troubling Brother Victor. As I look back now, I see him for real and I know his heart. I do not know if what troubled him was what would eventually trouble me just as much, but I do extend my heart out over him, that he would be comforted, even now. Death causes no separation in the spirit; neither is death any sort of answer for us. It is a time of waiting.

We did not have money for expensive materials, but Terry Miller and I designed and built a beautiful coffin for Brother Victor. Andrew, the blacksmith, made nice wrought-iron hardware for it. After the burial service, Brother Victor's older son came up to us and expressed how much the thoughtfulness that went into the coffin meant to him. It told him that his dad had been loved.

Shock and Agony

Brother Victor's death was not the only shock I was to experience as that school year came to a close however. One day I was busy taking off my outside shoes and putting on my inside shoes before entering the dining room, a daily ritual, after which I stood back upright and found myself looking right into the eyes of Claude Mack. And right next to him were Roberta and Maureen Mack. This is where we say – OMG!

Though I was stunned, I greeted them briefly. Then, over the next several days, it seemed to me that, whenever or wherever I was doing something, I would look up, and there was Maureen, entirely by coincidence, yes, but I felt as if I could not get away from her.

Maureen had done two years at the Covenant Life College branch in Brussels, Belgium, then had spent a year back at the Ridge, teaching in the school again, and was now planning to finish her final two years of college at Blueberry.

All I could think of was the pain of God not speaking to her, the agony I had lived in and then rejected when I left Bowens Mill. (God does have a sense of humor in His dealings with our sometimes tricky hearts.)

Maureen returned to Bowens Mill with her parents after a week or so, but I was left, then, through the next two months, planning to leave college, Blueberry, and the move, for I could not bear to return to that awfulness.

What God will do to get right at the core and heart of a man is overwhelming. I was in agony, rolling around in my mind, over and over, the impossible scenario of a return of what life had become for me at Bowens Mill and my inability to stay. Until one day, God spoke to me.

I don't quite remember how His voice came to me and so let me paraphrase it in present words that show what I heard. "My son, do not be afraid. Be of good cheer, for I am with you. My Spirit is good, and I would never do anything to torment you. What happened for you at Bowens Mill will not happen again."

Even though I did drive down to Oregon to spend a week with my mom and dad, I was at peace in my return. I had no idea what would happen or how, but I knew that God does not play games with us, but He is good all the time.

An Awesome New Project

As our second school year ended, it had become clear to Terry Miller and to Delores and Charity, that teaching school would not be part of Terry's future. But Terry was deeply earnest in his desire to learn and to complete his college degree. The thing that did interest him and towards which he had some aptitude, was construction, house design, and woodworking. There was, of course, no such courses offered by the college.

Terry's dilemma came to me in two complimentary ways. First, I cared about Terry, and it did not sit right with me that he should be excluded from his desire to learn in a disciplined way. And second, the idea of creating an entire college degree program, a construction degree, and designing and teaching all the courses in it was like me being let loose "in a candy shop" with endless "cherries on top."

Whenever an idea like that comes to me, I run with it with all my might. And so I penciled out the degree program as well as the initial courses. I took my ultra-bravado proposal breathlessly to Charity and Delores and to my utter amazement, they agreed. In fact, the entire construction degree program was included in the next Covenant Life College handbook and someone at the Haines, Alaska branch signed up to teach there the courses I developed.

This was FUN – designing and teaching full college courses. And they were. I gave to Terry over the next three years a fully credible degree program in construction. We started together in the fall of 1988 with the first of four semesters of Architectural Drafting and the first of four semesters of Applied Construction Techniques. I treated every scheduled classtime with Terry as if I had a room filled with students in a regular college. We started at the correct time and continued for the set period. Since Terry lived at the Austin's through this time, we set up a drafting table in their half-attic, which was open to the living room below. I went up there with Terry every class time for two years, going through every objective I had penciled out for the course. There were quite a number of other courses as well, including four semesters of kitchen design and fine woodworking.

I have not thought about it until now, but now I realize just how much this time with Terry meant to me. It was much more than my own arena of fun, it was an imparting of myself to my brother in the goodness of Christ. And as I think of it now, there is no question but that I received back the same from him in return.

The Summer Work

I worked construction on all Saturdays and any days there was not school. I worked on almost every building in the community over the years, either remodeling or adding on or building anew. I had remodeled the little cabin just above the Tabernacle for Richard and Elizabeth, but when Richard left, that cabin would go to Eric and Lynn Foster. Later on, it would be Maureen's and my first full home.

This summer, our primary project was a portable camp unit for the logging business. We made it in sections that could be taken apart, put flat on a truck, and transported to the next logging site. Part of the job was to assemble it for the first time, a central hallway between two modular bunk houses. My design worked, but it was a bit clumsy. They used it for several years until it was no longer easy to put back together. If I had done it again, I would have changed my design just a bit.

Then, when I returned from visiting mom and dad, we started a brand new cabin for Dave Smillie. His old cabin was too far gone to remodel it, so we tore it down. Brother Dave's new cabin was my first double-walled project, two layers of insulation all the way around to make it much easier to heat through the long winter months. We continued working on it even after school started – there were a number of men on the construction crew who were not students, and I continued to direct them as I could. The roof was on before it got too cold, so we were able to continue working on the house through the winter.

In August, I took part in a major college course held in the upstairs of the school where we had lots of room with all the dividers moved away. The course was on using *The Writing Road to Reading* to teach children to read. This was a very meaningful course for me, an innovative method of learning to read by phonics, except with the children writing the sounds before they learn to read them. My wife has used this method to teach many children to read, and it is the only approach I would recommend to any mother teaching her own children.

A young lady came to college at Blueberry that year, in time to be part of this summer course, by the name of Noemi Maldonado. She was from Lawrence, Massachusetts, but before that, from the Dominican Republic. The thing about Noemi is that she had three younger brothers, fairly close in age, and all out of high school. These three brothers had

no idea of allowing their beloved sister to travel far away without them accompanying her to make sure she was safe and provided for. The three brothers were Dani, Ezekiel, and Paul Maldonado.

And so these three fellows became a big part of my life. They were the most generous, kind, and giving young men I have known. Dani wanted to learn building, and so he joined my crew right away. Paul wanted to work in the fields with big equipment, so that's the direction he took. Ezekiel wanted to do both, so he worked with Dani, Terry, and I only some of the time.

I mentored Dani Maldonado through the next five years, but when I returned to Blueberry in 1995, I worked under him. We became good friends. Although Noemi returned to Massachusetts after she finished school, her three brothers stayed, eventually marrying daughters of Blueberry. Dani and Ezekiel still live at Blueberry with their families.

Positioning Ourselves

As I am writing these several letters covering my college years at Blueberry, I have found myself back in that same feelings I knew then. There, inside that mind, I think about the confusion and grief that are yet to come. And there, inside that same mind, I seek to give answers to all of that, yet I find no answers, but only a return of the same voices of condemnation I once knew.

In order to know this word of Christ that I share, it is necessary for you to walk with me inside this mind through these first four years at Blueberry, and so we will continue, knowing that we are utterly carried inside of Jesus, regardless. I am, in part, giving an idealistic view of my Blueberry experiences, but only in part – for they were indeed real and true. Nonetheless, all of these things were found inside a way of thinking, that is, Nicene theology, that always left Father Himself out in the cold and resulted in our own hearts alienated from God and from one another.

Then, once this narrative has taken us past graduation from college, we must change our view. That is, at that point we will interject the present mind of Christ, here and there through the narrative, so that we might see all things clearly, and not only as I saw them then. Even so, my personal view as it was then remains of vital importance.

As we work our way, now, through my second two years of school at Blueberry, keep in mind that

I have once again immersed myself in my present mind into the thinking and feeling of those days.

༄

I wrote the last little bit a few days ago. As I have continued working on my account of Blueberry, I have been in communication with some who lived there with us in order to get some of my details right. In that communication, the thought was conveyed that some of the elders whom I knew through these years, who lived/live at Blueberry, might want to read my story. At first thought, this sounded great, but soon that thought plunged me into horror.

I will not try to explain things yet, not until I have finished the next letter, which will take us to graduation from college. After that, I have inserted a letter titled "In the Womb of the Church." I wrote the first part of that letter this morning, yet I was writing it in fear. I will keep some of what I wrote, but I must have time to bring my Father into this conflict inside of me, knowing that He shares all things with me, and that He is inside of Christ inside of me, reconciling all to Himself. Our travail together is for the sake of each one whom I have named.

When I do write this critical explanation, then, I must be able to write it in the full joy of Father with me, so that you might receive life and not the confusion into which I have fallen momentarily. This present confusion, however, is an essential part of the placing of Christ Jesus upon myself, upon every moment of my life. I know that once I have passed through these next few months and have completed that portion of my story that was inside the move of God fellowship, I will know the strength of God poured out in me as I have never known.

I want to give you briefly the three opposing issues of which I will write more in "In the Womb of the Church," so that you won't be as confused as I was living through these years.

The first issue is the gospel of the serpent that looks for and finds sin in the flesh instead of Christ our life. Because we had no knowledge of Christ our only life, deliverance became just ever more of "getting rid of" in order to "someday know Christ." Out from this false way of thinking, so many dark things were spoken into me over the years, words that brought only death. When I speak of standing firm against all the wailing cries of accusation, it is these voices against which I must stand.

The second issue is the dealing of God with my own heart, that I would not accuse or find fault against others or against myself. If I had done so, I would have become a blackness that none of these precious brothers and sisters in Christ ever were. This is what God meant when He said to me, "Son, you passed the test."

The third issue is God's commission upon my life as a pathfinder, a mapmaker, one of the spies sent into the good land of Christ, that I might carry to you the wondrous and rich fruit of that land as well as the outlines of the giants and fortified cities that are found inside of Church life.

So many, upon leaving the communities, as Jesus put it, pulled up all the good wheat and threw it away in their vicious effort to root out all the tares. Indeed, very much inside the precious seed God gave me to carry out of these years of darkness and confusion just ahead are to be found these same brothers and sisters, dear to my heart, who spoke such awfulness into me.

You see, here is what was happening to me from the fall of 1987 on. Bit by bit God was bringing me out from my autistic shell where I had been safe for many years. I was oblivious to the fact that I had any outward appearance or that these "others" would see only that outward appearance. I could tootle along inside my zone, with all my blinders on, giving myself with all bold confidence in doing the things I loved to do, yet without any repercussions coming back through my impervious shell.

I have begun to trace this "stepping out" of that shell and will continue to do so, until that moment, just after college graduation in May of 1990, when I found myself blinking in the glaring light, now fully out in the open, with NO protection at all.

I now know exactly why God made me the way He did and why God set the exact course for my life as He did. And in knowing, I am humbled to my core, and I place my forehead upon the ground in worship of a HOLY and a MIGHTY Father.

God is good all the time. Father and I together synergeo all things towards goodness.

Giving Thanks

"Lord Jesus, I want to place You, now, upon every moment of these four years of college at Blueberry. And I want to do so by giving thanks.

"Lord Jesus, I thank You for each individual person in the Blueberry Community and in the school whose lives became so precious to me. I thank You for all their contribution to me and for the joy of being a small part of their lives.

"Lord Jesus, I thank You for all the college courses and teachers from whom I learned so much. My life and teaching was greatly enriched by them.

"Lord Jesus, I give You thanks for the mighty times of deliverance, both in my own life as well as having the privilege of being part of such an outpouring of Your Spirit. I give You thanks for the Church at Blueberry and how much I learned of what Church life is and means.

"Lord Jesus, I give you thanks for each thing that was difficult or disturbing to me through these years. I know that You carried me through all, that it was You proving Yourself in my life.

"I thank you, Lord Jesus, that I can place You upon every moment and circumstance You were living me through. You did not always intend the difficulty, but You always intended me and You always intended my brothers and sisters in Christ with whom I walked. Lord Jesus, together with Fa-

ther, You and I turn every moment, good or difficult, into the outcome of goodness through our confidence in the victory of our Holy Spirit."

The New School Year

On the afternoon before the next school year began, I went into the school to pick up my schedule from Sister Charity. As I left her office, scanning over the courses I was enrolled in, I noticed a sister there also looking at her schedule. On the spur of the moment, in this environment that was fully safe for me, I did something very, very brave. I asked her what courses she was taking.

What happened next was the most wonderful thing I have ever experienced in my life.

The picture below is of the teachers in the Blueberry Christian School. Those I mention frequently from the front left are Don Howat, Delores Topliff, Don Deardorff, and Charity Titus. Yours truly is on the upper right.

18. Friendship with Maureen

September 1988 - May 1990

The Best Thing Ever

Maureen Mack arrived back at Blueberry at the end of August, 1988, flying up with Jill Shapiro from Hollywood, Florida, who was also coming to college at Blueberry. Jill would become an important part of our lives, eventually marrying Ken Geis. To my consternation I continued to find myself next to Maureen unexpectedly and often. At the September convention at Shepherd's Inn, in the large meeting tent they had pitched for the convention, I sat down in a row near some seats that had been saved – by, of all people, Maureen, Cindy Dix (our daughter, Johanna's, mother-in-law), and Jill, who came in just before the service started and sat next to me. I had no idea what on earth God was doing.

Then, on the evening before school began, I went into the school to pick up my schedule from Sister Charity. As I left her office, scanning over the courses I was enrolled in, I noticed Maureen standing there also looking at her schedule. On the spur of the moment, in this environment that was fully safe for me, I did something very, very brave. I asked her what courses she was taking.

What happened next was the most wonderful thing I have ever experienced in my life.

MAUREEN MACK TALKED TO ME.

We talked, back and forth, about the courses we were taking – and then, to my utter astonishment, we kept on visiting for maybe twenty minutes. As we went into the bootroom, preparing to go to our respective cabins, Maureen paused and said something to me that was like a mighty spear piercing all through my soul.

"Daniel," she said, "I've been really bothered by how I treated you at Bowens Mill. I want to ask you to forgive me."

Forgiving her was the easiest forgiveness I have ever granted. I walked home in a daze of joy and wonder – "Maureen Mack talked with me." She tells me now that she also walked home in the same daze of wonder – "I talked with Daniel Yordy."

It had been seven years since God had spoken to me that Maureen would be my wife, seven years of being unable to speak to her; it would be two more years before she would walk down the aisle to stand by my side. But our friendship had begun, and I was filled with the joy of God's goodness and great generosity to me.

My Fifth Semester of College

The fall semester of 1988 was a lighter load of college courses for me. It began with a one-week block by Ernest Watkins on the life of David. Then I took "Twentieth Century British Writers" with Sister Delores and a classroom management course, which has been, at times, my least successful part of teaching (including getting a B for that course.)

Because of this lighter load, I was able to fill my time up with adding a second high school class, which was an eighth grade geography class that included Paul Austen, Jesse Rehmeier, Chris Kidd, and Ruth Raja, whom I would also teach each year for five years. I really enjoyed teaching them geography, and I developed, in my estimation, a very good course. (My students remember it as a highlight for them.) I gave them a similar task to what I had done when I was their age, that of writing to the embassies of various nations to ask for information on their country. Jesse Rehmeier received a wonderful package of propaganda from the then Soviet Union. I also devoted a large amount of time to teaching the construction degree program to Terry Miller.

My Friendship with Maureen

Visiting with Maureen on the day before school began was an open door for me. Over the next couple of months more opportunities to visit together arose. Maureen lived in the upstairs of Roger and Bertie Henshaw's cabin, so I found good reasons to go visit with Brother Roger more frequently. The twinkle in his eye told me that he knew I had an ulterior motive, especially since I used those visits to greet Maureen in passing.

After a couple of months, Maureen went to Sister Charity to pour out her consternation with the whole business of our "non-relationship" over the years. She was astonished when Sister Charity replied that she knew all about it already.

The truth is, as Maureen tells me now, she had resisted coming to Blueberry for school all through that summer for the same reasons I had struggled, that a return to the difficulty of a "non-relationship" with me was more than she wanted to accept. That sounds strange, but it does describe our situation. The truth is, it wasn't that God had not spoken to her through those years, it's that she had avoided "hearing from God," and with good reason. I was a closed shell outwardly prior to the fall of 1988. In fact, as I look back now, I realize that God brought Maureen back into my life just as soon as I was free enough inside to relate normally with her.

Sister Charity took our situation to the Blueberry eldership, and they devised a special "dispensation" for Maureen and me, which they termed a "covered friendship." You see, the typical pattern of only a brother-sister relationship until a couple began "walking out a year," would not have worked for us because of our involvement in college. More than that, our developing relationship, I think, required time, and Sister Charity was wise enough to see that.

A "covered friendship" meant that I could visit at the Henshaw's without "seeing Roger" as my excuse. Maureen and I would sit on the couch in their living room and visit together. This was slow-going, because neither one of us was an "exuberant" talker. I must admit that I was secretly pleased at the shocked expressions of some of those who lived at the Henshaw's as they passed by seeing Maureen and me together like that for the first time.

By March, the elders agreed to a small increase in our relationship, that is, to something they had invented, separate from the broader and more strict move-fellowship order for brother-sister relationships, that is, a "covered relationship." This was not quite walking out a year, but it allowed us a bit more time together.

Then, in May, after having written to Maureen's parents and having received a favorable reply, I went to the elders' meeting to ask about our walking out a year. They must have already discussed it, because Don Howat said, with a grin on his face, "Well, why don't you get out there and ask her?"

I went immediately and found Maureen just leaving the school. "Maureen," I asked her, "would you walk out a year with me?" "Yes, I will," she replied. That sounds like a simple thing, but for me it was a miracle of God.

Let me describe, now, what "walking out a year" meant. First, it was not an engagement to be married, that would come only after the year was completed and the Lord had confirmed, through visions and the witness of the eldership and family, that this joining was truly of Him. But it meant that we would sit together in the mealtime and services, and that we would be together in any community activity, including going to town, etc. The restrictions were that there would be no touching of any kind, and that we would never be alone together, but always within sight of a responsible adult.

This seems "restrictive" in a day when everything goes, but it is a practice that I agree with fully. By not allowing for physical "sensations," we were free to know one another as real people. The woman who walked down the aisle to stand by my side had become my best friend. But for some, it meant that the discovery that a relationship was not going to continue could happen without undue hurt or shame. In fact, through these years at Blueberry, we watched three such separations happen. It was emotionally difficult, of course, but there was no shame or undue hurt as is normal all through a careless world.

And so my friendship with Maureen grew slowly, even as completing college was an important task for us. And from May on, we were together much of the time.

Spring Semester of 1989

The spring semester started with Sister Ethelwyn Davison teaching a one-week block on praise and the tabernacle of David. Then, besides several practical courses about teaching, I also took "Early American Literature" with Sister Delores.

During this semester, the entire high school staff agreed together to lead the high school students in a speech workshop and presentation, drawing from what we had learned the year before from the Grier's. Paul Mandry, a fellow college student and teacher, was given overall charge of this program. I was assigned several young men as my charge in practicing them on a speech presentation.

David Deardorff was one of those whom I coached. He wrote his speech about some of his experiences growing up at the Shiloh community. David was different from the others. There was a depth of untapped quality inside of him. With the others, I practiced them in expressing themselves outwardly, but I believed that was not right for David. I wanted him just to know his lines. This distressed David such that he complained to Sister Charity, but I defended my decision.

Then, we had an entire Saturday night meeting devoted to the high schoolers sharing their speech with the whole family. David's speech was to be the last one. I might have had something to do with that, but the Lord had far more. Just as I knew would happen, the moment David started speaking, that depth of being and anointing inside of him came out. No "posing" could have matched what happened. There was not a dry eye in the place, and no one would have been able to present after, if David had not been last.

Not that I had much to do with it, but David Deardorff's presentation was a highlight of my teaching experience.

The Bible and I

I am finally beginning to understand the meaning and purpose of God through the years of my life, and especially through these critical years at Blueberry. The most important thing for me in my outward life, of course, was my friendship with Maureen. But inwardly, the most important thing was my relationship with the Bible.

God created me with a desperate, desperate need to know what the Bible actually says, through all the years of my adult life. Part of that need came from my Asperger's vulnerability, which, in spite of it's more difficult parts, was a critical gift of God to me. I needed to know God for real, and I could not pretend to be what I was not. I am a word man, and God had put His Bible in my hands. I have not and will never rest until I know His Word all through my being.

As I have shared, hearing the words, "the Bible says," was always overwhelming for me. I trust no one. I have a Bible; I will know, for myself, what God says.

Now, I have added a chapter titled, "In the Womb of the Church." That next chapter is necessary because my experiences at Blueberry became very confusing to me once I was no longer in college, and especially after we were married and our son, Kyle, was born.

In this chapter and the next, I am including three topics, "The Bible and I," "Services at Blueberry," and "My Identity." In each of these topics, I will cover the entire time of my college years at Blueberry. And I can lay these things out only because I finally understand what it all meant, and what God's incredible purpose for me was.

As I shared, I did not do any mental school work after supper, just the reading of a text when it was assigned. That meant that most of my evenings were free to do what I loved doing most – writing out Bible verses in endless word studies.

First, I did a massive study of the book of Revelation. I took every key word or symbol in John's vision, and, using *Strong's Concordance,* I wrote out every verse in the Bible containing that word or symbol. Remember that I had long since abandoned the practice of "figuring out" what these things mean. What I wanted was to KNOW what God says; I did not have to know what it meant. Writing out a verse, word for word, is a wonderful way to see those words and to ponder what was actually being said. This study filled many notebooks with verses.

Strong's Concordance is a list of the English words in the King James translation, but I had run off with a different kind of concordance that had been my dad's, a Greek New Testament Concordance, which was matched to Strong's numbering, but which included all the occurrences of the Greek word, regardless of the several English words into which it had been translated. I chose many key Greek words of the New Testament and wrote out every verse, in order, containing that Greek word. Among those words that I chose were apocalypse, life, God/Jesus, Paul's references to himself in any way, lie, death, grace, logos/rhema, salvation/saved, and so on. As I wrote, then, I looked carefully at the context clues, to determine, from the text, what God might have meant when He used that word in that place.

As I did that, I began to notice something terrible, something overwhelming, something I had no idea how to place or handle. You see, no dictionary ever defines any word except by the study of context clues. And the context clues I found in the text, as I wrote these verses over and over, were NOT the same as the "received" definitions that had come to me out from Christian theology and preaching.

What do you do with that? The little boy who said, "But the emperor has no clothes," was most likely Asperger's. Now I was that little boy – but how on earth does this fit?

Let me give a for-instance. In writing out every verse in the Bible in which the word "grace" is found, I found NO context clues indicating the meaning of "unmerited favor." That definition is imposed on the Bible; it does not come out from the Bible. The biggest, however, was the word "salvation," or *soteria* in the Greek. What does it mean? I was satisfied that I did not know. Except that Brother Sam had given me the license to throw out "go to" heaven as having anything to do with salvation. My word study found NO VERSE allowing anyone to place "go to" heaven as the goal of the beleiver.

Think of a kaleidoscope. Every time you turn it, the colored crystals line up in different formations. Very often, the same Bible verses were appearing before my eyes throughout my different word studies, yet in a slightly different arrangement, depending on which word I was writing. Then, think of Nicene theology in a similar way, that is, as ways of explaining how different verses fit together.

I could not find any match between what I was seeing in the Bible and received Nicene definitions. Certainly there were innumerable similarities, but NEVER a match.

I did not know what to do. All I knew was that God did not say what "they" claim He said.

Here is another example. Since "hear and obey" was the core teaching now in the move fellowship, with Sam Fife no longer around, contrasting the words *logos* and *rhema* had become a favorite topic of some preachers. "*Logos*" was supposed to be the "written word," and "*rhema,*" the "spoken word," that is, God speaking personally to you. So, I wrote out every verse in the New Testament with *rhema* and *logos* in it. It wasn't true. *Logos* refers to spoken word more often than written, and *rhema* refers to written word as often as spoken.

I did not know what to do with this massive disconnect; finding fault with the ministry of the word was not inside my sphere.

Through these years, God was bringing me out from my autistic shell through both deliverance

times and my college experiences. At the same time that He was doing this, He was planting the beginnings in me of the present word I now share. What would be my anchor? I desperately needed an anchor, and for me, that anchor could be one thing only – the key gospel verses. But what were they, for nothing in all the Christianity I had known was giving those defining verses to me.

I could not have told you at the time, but my heart was found in John 14, beginning with verse 23 – "**My Father and I will come to you and make Our home with you.**" This was simply the best and only possibility for me, though I did not know how such a thing could be. I noticed the words, "**You shall be with Me where I am**" – matched by "**You will know that I am in the Father.**"

I did a study of the word "image," and in that study found this definition, that an image (or idol) was a visible representation and dwelling place of an invisible spirit being. I secretly read 1 John, knowing that, in actuality, 1 John was heresy by all Nicene Christian theology – God Himself dwelling inside of me. (The remainder of John 14:20 and Ephesians 3:19 were simply not visible to anyone, including myself; that is, no one I had known or read could see those words except as something far in the future and utterly meaningless to us now.)

I did not understand what any of this meant, but, somehow, around the middle of my college years, soon after my full deliverance, one verse came into me to become the ruling verse of my life and of all my desire – **conformed to the image of His Son** – Romans 8:29. This I wanted with all my heart, though I had no idea what it meant or how on earth it could happen to me.

And I also could not have said it at the time, but the one line that defined "image" for me and that would undergird how I would receive everything God says in the Bible was this one line. "**He who has seen Me has seen the Father.**" (The doctrine of "the Trinity" is one of those many things that simply have no relationship with the actual words of the New Testament.)

Interestingly, I also did a different kind of study of the book of Hebrews through these years. Hebrews is a sentence nightmare. And so, as a grammar teacher, I wrote every small phrase in Hebrews as its own complete sentence. This required some doing, but in the process, another verse came into my knowing that I KNEW must rule how we are to know what God says – Hebrews 10:19-22. I had no idea what it meant; I just knew that if it were true, it had to rule.

Services at Blueberry

My study of the Bible, however, was never isolated from the mighty movings of God by His Spirit in the midst of the Church. By my involvement with those services, I knew the demonstration of the Spirit and power, right along with the word. For that reason, even though I am a word man, I never separate Word from Spirit or Spirit from Word, for they must never be separated.

I do not remember which service happened when, and so I will simply share some of the highlights together. In one service, prior to Brother Victor's death, for I distinctly remember his involvement, we had a communion and foot-washing service. In fact, this was one of only two communion services I participated in within that fellowship, something I regret, even though our breaking bread together daily is the true "communion service."

The entire service of probably three-hour's time was devoted to this communion and foot washing. The anointing of God upon us was palpable; there was such meaning and sobriety. I remember washing Brian Dwyer's feet, something that will gain more meaning in just a bit. I remember John Austin and Victor Raja both washing my feet. Knowing God in the midst of His Church as we humbled ourselves to one another meant a whole lot to us.

In another service, at a later time, as we sat quietly waiting for someone to stand up to lead praise, Sister Edie Dwyer, Brian's mother, got up from her seat, went over to another person, got down on her knees in front of them and asked them, before all the congregation, to forgive her of some wrong she had done them. In that moment, something extraordinary opened to us, and without any planning or direction, over the next two to three hours, one by one, many got up, knelt before another person, and, in tears, asked forgiveness. Again, I remember doing that to Brian. This was one of the holiest times of my life experience.

And in another service, again as we were waiting quietly for the praise to start, Edie Dwyer stood at her seat and spoke aloud a thanksgiving. Again, something extraordinary came upon all of us and for the next two to three hours, without any planning or direction, this one and then that one stood and spoke mighty thanksgivings. This was a most incredible time. When the Spirit is free in the Church, amazing and real things happen on a regular basis.

Another time, Brother Gary Rehmeier was there for a service; he often was not, since he had to work the logging company. But he got up to lead the praise. For some reason, he was all excited in the Spirit, and that same Spirit was upon everyone. As we sang praises, we soon began to dance, as was our wont. Except this time we felt like celebrating. Brother Gary soon stopped us and said, "Let's get rid of the chairs." They were soon gone and we began to dance together in circles, small and large, singing the praises of God in all joy – for two or three hours.

These services stood out, yet they were only representative of many spontaneous movings of the Spirit of God in the midst of the Church. This is normal Church. There were always anointed prophecies in the praises, and the proclaimed giving of thanks through the preaching of the word, and responses of joy and faith. There was always praying and singing in tongues, always spontaneous, always filled with the Holy Ghost and power, all through the years I was at Blueberry.

Indeed, I lived inside the womb of the Church and there, God marked me deeply with His finger concerning His Desire for His people. The covenant I had entered into with God at age 22, that I would know Him, and that I would walk with a people who know Him, remained my embraced reality. In fact, I shared that very thing, as I had experienced it (as found in "Cutting the Covenant"), in one of the Wednesday-night sharing services. I remember Sister Nathel Clarke getting up after and expressing how much that meant to her and to us all.

In another sharing service, I shared about the rivers of my childhood, the rivers of Oregon, and how the Columbia River was not one, but many, as in RIVERS of living water flowing out of us. And so John 7:37-38 was also coming into my knowing as a verse that must rule all things. Sister Charity shared with me later how much my sharing of that metaphor had meant to her.

And let me say this also, a whole lot of this flow of the Spirit in liberty came out from Sister Charity Titus, in her utter devotion and commitment to the revelation of that Spirit in power in the midst of our gathering together.

Visiting Other Communities

Through my college years, I often visited the nearby communities, specifically, Evergreen, Hilltop, and Shepherd's Inn. Evergreen community was about five miles to the east of Blueberry. In fact Blueberry owned property on both sides of Evergreen, which we farmed. Evergreen was very involved with Blueberry because students and teachers in the Blueberry school lived at Evergreen and came over to Blueberry daily. Among them were my good friends, Peter Bell and his family, and Rick Annett and his wife, Shirley, who had moved to Evergreen after Shirley had graduated from college in the spring of 1987.

Then, Hilltop was another community, maybe four miles further to the east and north of Evergreen. In fact, the road going by Hilltop and Evergreen continued on over to connect with the road coming up from Mile 73, at the small town of Buick. This would be a road I would traverse a number of times since the Blueberry trapline (coming up) could be accessed by the road going on north from Buick. The Hilltop community consisted mostly of people who had come up from the move fellowship in Houston, Texas, including Patrick Downs, who had also graduated from college in the spring of 1987 with Shirley. I had become good friends with Patrick.

I visited with Patrick at Hilltop a number of times through the years. Since it was a bit further, I typically went Saturday evening and stayed the night through Sunday. This way I got to be a bit more part of the family there in service and in meals. Patrick and I got along great and had many wonderful conversations together. He taught in the school at Hilltop and was part of the cow-milking program. Hilltop was one place that had copied my design of benches from Graham River. In fact, there were families from Graham that had moved to Hilltop.

Something amusing to me was the different expressions of "not being worldly." Blueberry did not have any curtains in the dining room, but we had sheetrock on the ceiling. Hilltop, however, refrained from being "worldly" by not having sheetrock on their dining room ceiling, but they had curtains on the windows. God's people can be silly sometimes, but the motives were sincere.

Then, I visited with Rick and Shirley at Evergreen two or three times, until they moved on up to Whitehorse in the Yukon for a season. I also went over a number of times to spend time with Peter and Barbara Bell. In my visits to Evergreen as well, I often joined the whole family for a meal in their dining room. I connected with Peter most of all, for we shared so many odd intellectual interests. Peter was always great fun, and we laughed a lot. Usually, I drove my Toyota Station wagon and, when the roads were dry, went the five-mile dirt-road over. When the roads were wet, however, I had to drive out to the Alaska highway, down to the Aiken Creek road, and then up to Evergreen on gravel.

One time, for some reason, I borrowed Brother Alvin's car to drive over for a visit to Evergreen, I think I was going to see Rick and Shirley – this was after Brother Victor had been killed, probably later that summer. A mile up the Aiken Creek Road, Brother Alvin's car died. I learned later that the timing belt went out. There was nothing to do except to leave the car and walk back home to Blueberry in the dark. It was nine miles, a mile back to the Alaska highway, four miles up, and then, four miles back down to Blueberry.

Needless to say, both bears and bulls on the road were very possible. In order to place my concern, though, I sang praise songs all the way back. It took me about two hours, but I remember the last mile as if I were floating in the heavens in the joy and praises of God.

Since Shepherd's Inn was on the highway, at Mile 72 on the way into town, stopping there was a very common occurrence through these years. Brother D and Sister Ethelwyn lived at Shepherd's Inn through this time, so I visited with them in their home a number of times. Ian and Isabell Still and Harold Witmer from Graham River also lived at Shepherd's Inn. Sister Ethelwyn had started the Shepherd's School of Music and many came to Shepherd's Inn to go through her program. Maureen's sister, Jessica, was one who did that, and she came to Blueberry as well, during the day, to take a few of the courses on offer there. Sister Ethelwyn was mightily anointed of God in praise and in the word, and her students were "out of breath" to keep up with her.

One night a week, the School of Music put on a special presentation in the restaurant dining room. Many came out from Fort St. John just to enjoy that music presentation. In fact, after Maureen and I were walking out our year, we had dinner there with her parents. I remember how hard I forced myself to eat as slowly as I could. It was agony, but I persevered. When I had finally finished my plate, I looked up to discover that Sister Roberta had hardly started! So much for my relationship with my future parent's-in-law.

Sometime in 1989, Mike Pelletier moved elsewhere and Michael Wallace came to share the bunk-bed with me. At that time, Michael was still younger than the students I taught. I'm not very good at relating with younger kids, and so I did not develop a significant relationship with Michael. I only hope that in some way I was a blessing to him.

In fact, his mother, Kay, whom I had known from the Portland group, came to me during these times, as she was in the process of making her will. She asked me if she could put me down as the one who would become the guardian for Michael should something happen to her. I agreed that I would.

Thankfully, nothing did happen to Kay, but I would like to extend that care in the Spirit towards Michael even now, these thirty-some years later.

The Summer of 1989

My relationship with Don Howat in the construction work had grown slowly. At this point in time, we worked together most of the time. Don was the elder, and technically the oversight, but I was the designer and builder and, for the most part, Don worked under my direction. It was a good back-and-forth relationship, however. Don was a bit older, stronger in Spirit and wiser than I, and because he treated me as an equal, I flourished during my years with him. I yielded to his wisdom, and he yielded to my abilities.

We mostly completed Dave Smillie's house before moving them back in. We didn't complete everything inside, which some thought was "wrong." But in the north, outside work can happen only in the short summers. Inside work can be left to the long winter months. The building needs of the community required us to take full advantage of the summer months for outdoor construction.

Sister Delores Topliff's cabin was the next on the list. It was literally rotting and falling down, past the place of being habitable. You see, her cabin was carved into the bank of the hill, and thus more subject to damp. While I was designing her a

new home, and while her old cabin was being torn down, then, we turned to a remodel of the drying house, where much of our food was preserved for winter use. I enjoyed designing Delores's new home. She was always big-hearted towards others, and so I made it fairly large, with a steep roof-line and dormers, allowing a number of rooms to be in the upstairs. She had earned a fair bit of money herself doing handwork on the side and we had access at that time to government grants for the rebuilding of derelict homes. Thus we had the money to do a half-decent job.

We widened the site, and thus had to put in a heavy retaining wall, about three feet high, to keep the slope from sliding down against the house. Slumping earth is a powerful force. At the same time, the move community habit of no foundations simply would not work here. More than that, foundations in the far north region of permafrost are a continual problem. An attached porch can go up three to four inches in relation to a house each winter, and then back down in the summer. Permafrost can spit posts right out of the ground.

Don and I chose to drill holes down below frost level, maybe seven feet deep and pour concrete pillars around rebar set in each hole as the foundation of this house. We rented a two-man digger, which was a lot of hard work. I helped with most of the holes, and through the process, put my back out worse than it has ever been out. I did not want to spend a few days in bed. In the service that evening, as I stood up for the praise, I realized that my back was about to throw me to the floor in writhing agony. John Austin had gotten up to speak, but I put my hand up and asked if the elders could please come and pray for me. They did, and as they prayed, as I stood there, my back went into place, sound and whole.

Then it rained, hard, the next day. And muddy water filled all our newly-drilled holes up with slime. We had the "brilliant" idea of using the outhouse slurry pump tank to pump out the mud. The result was that we caved in the large tank. We eventually got the holes cleaned out and the cement poured. Through July and August, then, we built the frame, as frames go, fairly rapidly, again, with double walls. But I was planning a trip down to Oregon again, in August, and so I asked Brian Dwyer to head up the team to get the new blue tin on the roof while I was gone.

That August, then, Maureen and I drove down to Oregon for her to meet my parents, with Nancy Raja and Freda and Ruth as our chaperones. What a wonderful gift that was, for Sister Nancy, who was a good mother to me the four years I lived in her home, to meet my own mother and for all of them to see where I grew up.

One thing I remember in that trip is that I took all of them up to the top of Snow Peak with me. We drove most of the way, but then had to get out of the vehicle and hike the last mile or so. Sister Nancy did not brave the rock peak itself, maybe a hundred feet up, but the girls all went up with me. The lookout building was no longer there, but we could see the whole Willamette Valley in one direction and the snow-covered peaks of the high Cascades in the other direction.

This was August, the best time for me in Oregon, when the blackberries are ripe. I like blackberries, especially when you funnel them off the hard-spined vines straight into your mouth. I also remember us all going down to Crabtree Creek and swimming in the swimming holes of my youth. I was so thrilled to share these things with Maureen and the Raja's.

To the right is a picture of Sister Nancy with Frieda, Ruth, and Maureen in front of her on the lawn of my childhood home.

Sister Delores had been in Portland, visiting, when we drove through, and we invited her down to mom's house for the day. We have a picture of all of us sitting out on the patio deck, with Delores telling us stories.

When we returned to Blueberry, I went right on up the hill to see how it was going on Sister Delores's new roof. They were just finishing it up. Brian, as always, was doing an impeccable job. It was a tough roof line, and he was the best to have done it right.

As I looked up at these fellows, including Terry Miller, finishing the roof, my eyes opened and I saw something I had never seen before. I saw how badly I had treated those who worked with me in construction.

Regarding our relationship with God, shame is an enemy, but when it comes to how we treat one another, seeing one's self from a distance and being heartily ashamed of one's actions, is a gift from God.

For the first time in my life, the idea that how we work together was of equal importance to getting the job done entered into my knowledge. It would be several years, then, before it worked its way into the practice of my heart. But that is a later story.

Bryan Dwyer

I want to introduce here my relationship with Brian Dwyer over the 8 ½ years I lived at Blueberry. Brian was just a couple of years younger than I. His work was primarily in welding, machine operation and metal work, along with Randy Jordan, but Brian helped us out in construction from time to time. Often, when there was large equipment work that we needed done, it was Brian who did it.

Brian did everything methodically and impeccably. A job that covered me with mud from head to toe would see no mud on him above his boots, in spite of being in it all day. But on almost every job where we interacted, his way of doing things and my way of doing things were opposed. Brian was never bashful about telling me that I was doing it wrong. Whereas I was never bashful about doing it my way anyhow. And, of course, I had the crew and the responsibility for the job, so we almost always did it my way, to his consternation.

We never found agreement through all those years on how anything was to be done. And sometimes our clash became something that either Dave Smillie or Don Howat had to intervene to bring us to peace. Yet we were never hostile against one another, just over how something should be done. Brian thought everything should be done by the book; whereas I did it however it worked best for me in the moment.

As I think of it now, I realize just how much Brian's seeming "obstinacy" was a gift from God to me. Because my bright and enthusiastic ideas were challenged so often and with such ferocity, I had to think more deeply and more carefully. We had clashed the summer before on the kind of chimney I had bought and brought home for Brother Dave's cabin, which was Brian's home as well. And so, when I looked up and saw that Brian was completing the difficult roof task so well, something I had worried about the whole time I was down in Oregon, something clicked in me, the idea that different could actually be a treasure. You have seen that thought coming through many things I have shared; we can both thank Brian for that gift.

I can't say that we ever became "friends," but we learned to respect one another deeply, and I count Brian as one of the most important people in my life. He will return to this narrative more than once as we go forward.

The Trapline Cabin

Before bringing in the outline of both my and Maureen's final year of college, I want to go forward to November and to the design and construction of the trapline cabin, my favorite in all my construction career and knowledge.

Brother John Austen had purchased a trapline for the Blueberry Community, the south end of which was situated around fifty miles north of Buick, British Columbia. It was accessible by a windy dirt road from one side and by the railroad running through on the other side. In fact, the train tracks were less than a mile from where we built the cabin. The road was nearby because of the existence of a fire watchtower, which was manned through the summer months.

Steve Ebright would run the trapline, at least for the first couple of seasons, but he wanted his family to be out there with him. For that reason, we built the trapline cabin slightly bigger then normal, so they would have a nice home and a place for the children to homeschool.

I designed a cabin 20 feet by 30 feet with a steep-pitched roof and a larger flat dormer in the center facing south. I put large windows in the living room and in the dormer above, which would be the school room so that the winter sun would shine brightly in. At one end was a covered porch, then the door opened into the kitchen to the left and

the dining table to the right with a stairway going right up in the center. Upstairs, the center room had a high ceiling with the window wall seven foot tall. The two outer sides, then, were large bedrooms fully inside the slope of the roof. Steve and Michelle's bedroom was in the back left corner downstairs.

Although I would not study *Patterns of Home* until years later, this little house, when completed, incorporated each of those ten patterns of home perfectly. That was entirely happenstance, but it also explains why I loved that little cabin.

I designed a double-wall as well, with a framed inner wall and then the old logs from the Topliff cabin as the outer wall. The rafters were made with an OSB beam, 16 inches wide, and thus could hold twelve inches of fiberglass insulation as well. This cabin would be snug and warm.

Eric Foster, Steve Ebright, and Tim Kiezebrink, from the Upsala community, braved the first drive up with a large truck loaded with the logs and other building materials. Meanwhile, Gary Rehmeier, John Austen, Don Howat, Terry Miller, Dani Maldonado, and myself went into Fort St. John and climbed into the engine of a freight train heading up to Fort Nelson. That was quite an experience, two hours standing up in the very front of a locomotive through the Canadian wilderness. This was something the railroad often did, dropping people off wherever they needed. We returned the same way, but on the return trip we all rode back in the caboose; again, a pretty cool experience.

We had the structure nearly finished in just a few days, enough to be lived in, although the interior was not nicely finished. Coming up to finish the interior is a story that comes in a later chapter. There is something about the wildness and remoteness of the Canadian wilderness that is planted deep inside of me.

My Final School Year

I will include a brief overview of my final year of college here, but the final two sections, "My Identity" and "Graduation," are in the next chapter.

The school year began with a one-week block titled "Salvation" taught by Tom Rowe from Atlanta, Georgia, one of the apostolic ministries of the move. I had done my study of the word "salvation" prior to this. Again, we had one assignment, a paper summing up what we had learned, and again, I got a B because I could not just repeat back; I cannot write things except they make some sense to me. Nonetheless, this course made me think deeply about what God might mean by what He says.

Through both semesters of this year, Maureen and I took a course on learning Spanish, taught by one of our fellow students, Leslie Cedeno, from Mexico City. It was just the three of us in the course, and we had a lot of fun together. I cannot hear or speak another language, but I am good with the written word, and thus I have some idea about the Spanish language.

In December, then, a new chapter of my life opened; Sister Delores allowed me to team-teach her college Geography course with her. She even gave me much space in the shaping of that course, which I realize now was very great-hearted of her. My enthusiasm in something like that, to shape and mold it, can be very focused, and I am often oblivious to other people. Nonetheless, we taught a wonderful course together. Maureen was in the class, so now I would be marrying one of my students. I remember that Barbara Bell's brother, Tim Beebe, was also visiting from Upsala and was able to take that course with us. We had a full class in Sister Delores's room.

Sister Marlyss Johnson from the Covenant Life College branch in Haines, Alaska, came to Blueberry for the entire spring semester to teach two courses, both of which I signed up for, "The Gospel & Epistles of John," and "General Geology." I enjoyed both of her courses; nonetheless, for a reason I don't understand, I did not always connect fully with her as a teacher.

Let me explain. After conflicting in my own heart with what Buddy Cobb taught at the beginning of my second college year, and after continuing through the times of deliverance, I slowly began to adopt what Buddy Cobb taught as my own. You see, Brother Buddy continued coming through the northern communities twice a year and so we continued under his strong influence. I knew that I was twisting some gospel verses to do so, but I had begun to define most everything by his Calvinist theology.

And so, as I was "coming out from" my autistic shell, I was "coming into" a way of thinking that I had two lives in me and that God expected me to live in one life and not the other by the performance of "hear and obey," something I had no ability to do

whatsoever. Now, I will position Brother Buddy in my life in the closing chapter of my season of the move of God fellowship. God wanted me entirely inside of an anointed, Bible-based understanding of that entire way of thinking – that He might bring me to despair before bringing me to Himself.

And so, Sister Marlyss included in her teaching on John some of the "life" stuff we had received from Brother Sam. I got in trouble with both her and Sister Charity because I had the effrontery to contend with her on that "problem," that is, why was she teaching contrary to Buddy Cobb!

Then, in our geology course, my one science course, we took two significant field trips. The first was to a huge open-pit coal field in the northern Rockies of Alberta, near the BC border. This was quite an experience for all of us. The second was a field trip up the Peace River valley to the gorge below Williston Dam to see the coal seams in the rock. On this trip, as we were driving along the Peace River, Sister Marlyss made a comment about geological things we were observing. In my logical mind, I could see the probability of a completely different explanation, and so, as was my wont, I expressed that opposing viewpoint.

This was in a confined vehicle with several people together. After "correcting" her, I could, for the first time, see what I had just done, as an observer. I knew, then, just how cruel my "logical corrections" could be. This moment was a significant part of my coming out of that shell of oblivion inside of which I had remained safe over many years. The truth is, it also changed how I responded in such situations.

And so, Sister Marlyss, I ask you to forgive me for my unthinking cruelty, and I want to thank you that, in your forbearance towards me, you helped me to drop some of my blinders and to begin to see that other people were, indeed, real, and that my words did affect them, sometimes painfully. Thank you for the good heart of Christ inside of you.

I also took a course in this final semester titled "The Christian Teacher," taught by Sister Janet Randall from Evergreen. I realize now that some things expressed in this course helped shape the awful false identity in which I would live until God brought me into the Lord Jesus, my only life. And so I will bring those things into the next chapter.

19. In the Womb of the Church

Including March 1990 - June 1990

The single most unpleasant experience you and I have ever endured is when our mother's body decided it was time for us to leave the womb. At that moment, that which had been so protective and comfortable suddenly became our great enemy, forcing us out with pain and even violence into the cold cruel world. "Get out of here; this is no longer where you belong."

This pressure of travail is not only a metaphor of God, but the best way to frame, not just my own experience, but for you to understand what God would take you through as well.

Being expelled from the womb is one of three metaphors I will use to understand the next eight years of my life. Then, these next two topics follow right after the topic of "My Final School Year."

My Identity – (and Whispers of Darkness)

In my layout of this time period, November of 1988 says this, "Sister Jane comes again; I receive a greater deliverance." Then, in the entry for January of 1989, it says, "I am prayed for again for further deliverance." The difference between these two entries, separated only by three months, is critical.

The time with Sister Jane could easily be called a completion, which means that the "deliverance" prayer in January of 1989 was the first of many desperate attempts to become something different than how God made me. Why? Because, obviously, *"there was something wrong with me,"* or so I had begun to imagine.

When I read the stories of others who are Asperger's, I see the exact same struggle and difficulty that I endured, and the same responses to it from others. I am so glad that no one knew anything about "autism," however, for this sect, like many evangelical and deeper truth sects, would have seen the autism as neither Christ nor human, but a "demon to cast out." Yet, it is pointless to ask – What if? Very simply, it is God who made me and not I myself, and He is the one who directed my path entirely for His good purposes.

Up until around 1988, I was just me, tootling along inside my blinders, inside my mildly autistic shell, seeking God and giving myself to the family in the only ways I knew how. I was one person in my identity. But through my college years, by some of the things spoken into me and by the general force of Nicene and Calvinist doctrine, I was becoming two, or even three. I would not become one person again, in my identity, until 2008, a period of twenty years.

During my first year at Blueberry, the concept of the four "humors" was a bit of a fad, passing around inside the family – which one are you – sanguine, phlegmatic, choleric, or melancholic. That is, until the elders decided it was distracting us from Christ and asked that it cease. I fitted completely all the definitions of a melancholic.

I was sitting on the porch of the school one day, visiting with Sister Charity, and I mentioned that I was a melancholic. She said to me that Jesus was not melancholic, therefore I could not be like Him so long as I remained as such. The terrible thing is that I believed her, that I must be something different from how I found myself to be in order to, somehow, become like Jesus.

Before continuing, however, let me draw a very severe line. Through all the years I lived in move community, any correction that came my way, concerning specific shortcomings in acting towards other people, was good and wholesome. Certainly, I didn't like such corrections; no one does. Nonetheless, even if such corrections may have been partly off-based, they did not affect my identity in any debilitating way.

That statement from Sister Charity, that I could not be "as Christ," so long as I remained the "way I was," is a fundamentally different kind of word, a word that goes to the core of one's being with the speaking of not-Christ. And so began the speaking of "not-Christ" into me – *"Christ is not your life; you have a life not-Christ."*

Nonetheless, nothing has ever come close to me through my entire life except that it was Father with me, carefully shaping me for His purposes through those circumstances and preparing my heart to know Him. You see, it was twenty years of living inside the delusional horror of *"there are two lives in me"* that gave me the great incentive to run with all my might into Christ my only life the very moment I saw such a wondrous thing.

My purpose is to set a distinction between the good things of God shaping my identity, even inside of painful difficulties, versus the speaking of not-Christ into me with all the confusion that it brought.

Basically, Asperger's meant the whispered view towards me that "there is something very wrong with Daniel Yordy." A view that was never overtly spoken, but was acted out from by others, especially the elders, only on occasion, actually, but always leaving me with no idea why.

I realize now that a shift came, somewhere midway through my college years until by the time of my graduation, I felt at times that I was looked upon and treated out from a certain suspicion. I never understood why, nor do I to this day.

Yet through these same years, God was also performing a critical "cutting away" inside my identity, the story I told myself about myself. I was intelligent, yes, even intellectual, but that was not my identity. I was melancholic and even obsessive, but that was not my identity.

My identity was that I was all alone, a frightened little boy inside, hoping that someday I might become real. And inside of that frightened loneliness, I clung to those things that were familiar to me. More than that, succumbing to sexual desire in my own bed created a tremendous underlying sense of shame and guilt.

Rebellion is nothing more than standing forth with a hard forehead in a desperate clinging to a fake identity. I was not rebellious outwardly, regardless of what some may have imagined, but God was after the root deep inside of me, the need to cling to things of identity that were not real.

I mentioned having read Fyodor Dostoevsky's *The Brothers Karamazov*, which had planted the question of rebellion and accusation against God inside of me prior to coming to Blueberry. During my first year at Blueberry, Sister Barbara James gave a series of teachings on the life of Job. God gave me

some profound answers through Job and through her teaching regarding giving thanks in the midst of suffering in contrast to accusing God.

But I still had some books and some tools towards which I believed God had told me "No," but that I had kept anyway. My friendship with Maureen, however, was something God used to get His knife right at my core. And so, at the beginning of that friendship, and in the midst of this deliverance time, I gave all the rest of my books and tools away, as to the Lord. I gave my tools to Terri Miller and most of my remaining books to the school. (I did retrieve most of those before I left move community, thank God, one of which was my wonderful Webster's 1926 Dictionary.) But I had a large set of books on American history which I perceived to be "beyond the pale," one might say. And so, in great agony of soul, I went through the process of putting those books into the stove and burning them.

I now know that the problem was never either books or tools, but rather my identity. God was after the rebellion deep inside of me common to all. (You see, identifying one's self as an "elder" or an "apostle" is no different. Those become false identities that always take the place of Christ.)

There were two other confusing things Sister Charity spoke into me through these college years, things that struck against the core of my identity. In the "Family Life" course, I had raised my hand to share that, in all my years I had never once heard my mom and dad speak an ill word to each other. She immediately corrected me, that such a thing was impossible. When I insisted, she became stern, that I was wrong in my perception of my parents. Then, in "Understanding the Adolescent," I wrote in a paper that through my teenage years, there was no one to guide me; that I looked for help, but no help came. She called me into her office and explained to me that I was reading my life completely wrong, that there was most certainly "help, but my problem was that I had refused it.

I had no idea what to do with these "corrections," but they buried themselves deep inside with the whispers that "there is something terribly wrong with me."

I want to share a couple more things that were central to my identity through these years, from 1988 through 1993. First, I'm not any good when it comes to personal "prayer," nonetheless, I sought the Lord with dedication as my "prayer." Brother Alvin Roes would get up early most mornings to go into the school to pray before the day began. For awhile I joined him. But being on my knees did not work much fruit in my knowledge of God. And so I took my "prayer time" in a different direction.

Following is a terrain map of the Blueberry Community and the area straight to the west, which was "crown land."

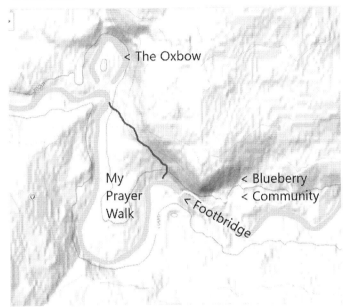

The Blueberry family, as well as the college students as a group, would sometimes hike over to the other side of the Oxbow to have a picnic on the grassy slopes above the quiet water. Once, we went over the top of the Ridge, but usually, we hiked along the river past the footbridge and along the base of the Ridge just below the blue line on the map. That blue line is not a path, however, but rather the boundary of what became "my prayer walk."

Starting soon after Brother Victor died, I often went over to that tongue of land of a Sunday and walked its meadows and woods, and along the creek all the way around, speaking in tongues and seeking God, at least in the stance of prayer, even though my mind is too energetic to stay long with "prayer." Yet that was the intention of my heart, and so I brought my mind always back to my longing to know the Lord. These times were just during the summer months, of course.

If I were to list the things most precious to me in my years at Blueberry, this time and this place would be near the top of my list. I came to know its paths and the layout of its woods and meadows and terrain. I am an explorer, you see, and my heart is all tied up in the land and its shape. Living in Texas all these years has been, in that dimension, a quiet sorrow.

Another thing I hold is the love of growing things. I always had my own little garden growing up, next to my mom's larger garden. In move community, because the shared meal together was the center of our life and the communion of Christ, we did not grow any vegetables in private plots near the cabins. And in the early years of move community, growing flowers was considered to be entirely "of the flesh." Thankfully, that absurd thinking was disappearing during the eighties. In fact, at the Ridge at Bowens Mill, I had created a series of flower gardens around the men's dorm trailer. But since raspberries grew in the cold north and since they were not grown in the community gardens, I was free to create my own little raspberry garden. I also grew some peppermint and other herbs. I spent much happy time shaping the bank below the Raja cabin into terraces, walled with stacked stones. The bank itself was maybe six or seven feet high with a moderate slope. My terraced garden was at three levels, maybe five by eight feet in size. My raspberries even bore a bit of fruit while I still lived at the Raja's.

Since my terraced little garden was just inside of the view out the Raja cabin windows, Maureen and I were free to sit there among my raspberries and herbs to visit. This is a small thing, but it goes deep into my heart. I remember sitting there sharing with Maureen that my commitment was to knowing God and to community, and that would never change. I thought at the time that we would never have a "house of our own." That was not true because I did not yet know the Lord as He is, but the rest was true.

On the next page is a picture of Maureen and me sitting in front of my little terraced garden. The Raja cabin is behind us on the left of the picture, and we are facing towards the greenhouses.

"Contrary" to God

I want now to come to the final semester of

ened to do anything. As an Asperger's man, I am left with the disability of being unable to pretend. When I perceive that others whom I respect "expect" something of me, I short-circuit inside, my mind goes blank, and I am like a deer caught in the headlights. To act the way it seems they think I should act is far outside of my ken; neither am I able to respond with any words.

I must insert here a line from Galatians 6, from the Jesus Secret Version. – **Whatever indeed a man might sow, that also he will reap. For the one sowing into flesh will reap decay and rottenness; the one sowing into Spirit, however, out of Spirit will reap age-unfolding life.**

school and to a course that added greatly to my confusion, "The Christian Teacher" taught by Janet Randall. But to explain the dark things that came into me through this course, I must explain a bit more concerning the doctrine that had become the strong center of what Buddy Cobb taught in the move.

Brother Sam Fife had taught that Christ is inside of us. Even though I know that Brother Sam had a personal relationship with Jesus, nonetheless, this "Christ" was us as mature sons of God, separate from Jesus. But Brother Sam had also taught the exaltation of the flesh, common to Nicene Christianity, that the "flesh" was opposed to Christ and typically triumphant over Christ. And that only "the anointing" AND the "covering of the ministry" enabled us to walk in Christ and not in flesh.

And so I saw the elders as anointed, which they were, and therefore as Christ to me.

But then Buddy Cobb increased the meaning of *"you have a life not-Christ."* And so, Romans 5:10, **we are saved by His life,** became a requirement of obligation that we *"get out of our own life"* and *"get into Christ life."* And there was only one way we could do that, and that was "hear and obey," successfully and consistently.

I was just no good at that; the elders seemed to be very good at that; and so I was left very confused. I did not "hear," and when I thought I heard, I typically short-circuited inside and was too fright-

When you sow not-Christ into people's hearts and lives, then not-Christ is the ONLY thing that will be reaped. Planting words of not-Christ into the Christian is the central practice of Nicene Christianity, resulting in the continuation of Adam's delusional world of death contrary to the redemption of Christ. The move fellowship was no different, except in one way; in the move fellowship, everything common to Nicene thinking was amplified in our lives.

It is not my purpose to judge to condemnation, but to life. Nonetheless, judgment to life, in its going forth, must sometimes be severe, especially towards a placing of one's self "above" God's people as a "vicar" or a go-between of "Christ." Those who speak not-Christ into others are not, by that, acting as ministries of Christ Jesus, but of the destroyer.

There were many good things in the course Janet Randall taught, but four not-good things marked themselves deep into my identity.

First, Sister Janet clarified a teaching that was common in the move, but that became much more defining for me, since I was, at the same time, stepping out from my autistic shell of protection. That teaching was that God's will and my will were utterly and irreconcilably opposed and that I would be doing God's will ONLY when I was opposing my own will.

It is this teaching that threw me into years of terror, of living frightened out of my wits.

You see, the words of Jesus, **"Depart from Me, for I never knew you,"** were words I held deeply personal to me, words that I MUST NEVER hear. And so this schizophrenic doctrine of *"there are two lives in you"* and *"you must hear and obey Christ life (which is not your life) and refuse to obey your life (which you will never actually accomplish)"* created in my identity of myself, a third little guy, this "me" that must "choose" running back and forth, desperate, confused, and afraid.

This horror is the driving essence of the words of the serpent in the garden, but I believed, with all my heart, that it was the "gospel of God."

We were also given the assignment of writing an essay about how God spoke to us to be classroom teachers. I wrote that God had never actually "spoken to me" that I was to be a teacher, rather, that, upon stepping into the classroom, I had found an environment and a task which made my heart sing. Sister Janet made it clear that if God had not "told me" to teach, then I had no business being a teacher. – Yeah. What do you do with that?

Third, we were given the assignment to write a Bible study on a selected topic from a list of "Christian teacher qualities." Part of the clear instructions was that we were to develop a meaning of our term ONLY out from what the Bible says, and not from what we knew in Christianity and, specifically (these were the exact instructions) that we were even to disregard what might be taught by the move ministry. I chose the word "conscience," wrote out every verse in the New Testament containing the Greek word, *syneidesis*, and then wrote an extended definition of that word using ONLY the context clues I found from every passage where it occurred.

The problem was, very simply, that the New Testament teaches nothing about choosing between good and evil, but that our consciousness is either ALL good or ALL evil, with no mixture of the two. I got in trouble with that one, in spite of the assignment directions, because what I wrote contradicted what Buddy Cobb taught on the subject. This dilemma was significant to me, for I had committed my life to submit to the ministry of the move and to the word that they taught.

Finally, Sister Janet instructed us to spend the next couple of days between classes, carefully seeking to "hear," obeying what we heard, and then reporting back what we learned. In the next service, then, as we were waiting for someone to get up to lead praise, a time often filled with singing, the thought that I should get up to lead the praise came strong into me. It arose from my heart, but getting up to lead praise was not inside my safety zone. I struggled, but I remembered our assignment, and so, with my heart beating strongly, I got up to do just that. It went okay. The Blueberry family was enthusiastic in praise, and they cheerfully supported me.

But back in the classroom, I was again rebuked before all. "That is NOT what I meant."

This is a very important twist that I must somehow convey to you, for this underlies all my confusion through the next three years. It's very simply this, that if another had felt to get up to lead praise, that would have been appreciated and honored, but since it was me, or so it seemed, the only motive there "could have been" was arrogance and self-promotion.

Now, Sister Janet, if she were to read this, would have every reason to be deeply hurt. I intend fully to bring a balance, to separate her as a dear sister in the Lord from my perception of things at that time. That balance will come in a bit, but for now, I want to leave this stark and direct, for this is, indeed, how I heard these things that became fear in my life.

I can share these things clearly with you now, but then, I did not understand at all. I perceived an underlying accusation against me coming through, not only in these responses, but in other responses from elders and from eldership "decisions" toward us, a seeming charge that I was arrogant and self-promoting. This charge was never spoken to me directly, not until the last year I was at Blueberry, in 1996, but it seemed to be the unspoken basis of many responses towards me.

I was very confused. Not only was I innocent of this charge, regardless of any outward autistic inability, but I admired these elders and had committed my life to submit to their direction and to the things they taught me. I trusted them, and I trusted and believed their responses to me.

More than that, our year was coming to an end in May, and Maureen and I were looking towards marriage. At the same time, I found myself no longer inside the protection of being oblivious to everything. I was about to step into being a husband and a father, of raising my family, within the underlying horror that there was something TERRIBLY wrong inside of me, a horror that was not true at all.

Graduation

I will share only briefly of our graduation from college; it marked a milestone and a significant change in my life. There were ten of us who graduated on May 27, 1990. – Paul Mandry, Gail Young, Mike Pelletier, Maureen Mack, myself, Jill Shapiro, Peter Bell, Darlene Symes, Freda Raja, and Monica Rotundi.

Our graduation was a major formal occasion. The dining room was packed. We graduating seniors gave a presentation (which became long and boring). Then, Brother John Clarke and Sister Charity Titus gave us our diplomas.

In fact, in looking at the picture of Sister Charity giving me my diploma, I see the full expression of honor and joy towards me. I graduated Covenant Life College with a Bachelor of Science in English Education.

It would be a huge mistake if you were to gain the impression from some of the things I must share, that I was mistreated in any outward way or that my time at Blueberry was not, for the most part, a sharing of life together with a most precious family of God.

As I look at the pictures of our community times and the first years of our children in the communities I see joy and goodness. Our children had a happy childhood, and as I look across the faces of all,

including the elders, I see nothing but a precious and kind group of people.

I also see many whom I have not mentioned at all, which is sad, but I cannot include everyone and everything, at least not until we share our lives again in the resurrection.

Regardless of any difficulty, real or even imagined, I lived in and have come out from a wonderful heritage, indeed, I have lived inside the womb of the Church.

Positioning the Next Eight Years

It is not possible for me to present my life through the next eight years without honesty. At the same time, I will not give an account that allows accusation against anyone. My problem is that when I am immersed in writing any of these chapters, I find myself inside of the feelings and fears of that time. That cannot be otherwise. Yet for both my sake, the one giving an account, and your sake, as a reader, and especially for the sake of all these who belong to Jesus, what I hope to do in this letter is to cast guy wires, one might say, out over the void, so that we might hold onto these critical understandings as we pass across the turbulent waters.

In "A Season of Deliverance II," I gave three issues that seem to work against each other, but which are vital for our safe passage. Let me state those again briefly.

The first issue is those words of a theology of separation, of a mighty wall of opposition between the heart of a believer and the Lord Jesus Christ, words that dig in deep to create the fear of the evil one that "God is far away from me." The second issue is the true dealings of God in a person's life, including why these contrary things are happening. And the third issue is the critical task of coming through this passage with the good things of God intact. And those "good things" very much involve the individual brothers and sisters who were part of my life.

Writing the first chapters of Blueberry was one of the hardest things I have done – not the writing, of course, but the re-living. It plunged me into all the emotions and fears that would come later in my Blueberry experience. This was wonderfully of God, however, because I had to face everything again, things I have never looked at. Yet to place the Lord Jesus Christ upon every moment, as the gospel commands us to do, has been to find a healing in me at depths that had never been healed before.

It required me, not just to forgive, but to see the goodness of Christ in those whose voices had become harsh accusation to me.

Writing the first chapters of Blueberry turned me inside out in convolutions of pain and healing over almost a month before the Lord Jesus completed that healing. In the midst of that agony, I awoke in the night enveloped inside the full fear I had lived inside of through these eight years ahead, that is, from June of 1990 to August of 1998.

I arose, went to my computer and wrote the next short section. I will leave it as I wrote it.

The Stakes

I am fleeing for my life, carrying precious seed. Even before finishing "A Season of Deliverance," I am frightened out of my wits.

Nonetheless, it is for your sake, dear reader, as well as mine, that I must pause in this desperate run out from death and into life in order to place everything into its place through the present eyes of the Lord Jesus Christ, through eyes of fire.

The stakes could not be higher. It is death, close at hand as well as behind us, or life, beckoning ahead, for me, for you, and for all creation.

The picture inside of which I am finding my only way out of this plunge into icy waters is the picture of Eliza, the slave girl in *Uncle Tom's Cabin*, as depicted by Harriet Beecher Stowe. Indeed, I find that picture on a recent edition at Amazon. The fear that is upon her face is exactly what I am feeling right now.

Behind Eliza is enslavement under a regime of horror. Beneath her feet are the icy waters of the St. Lawrence River as she leaps from one block of ice to the next. And in her arms is her precious child, of greater value to her than her own life.

Yet here in this land of glorious salvation, inside of life and joy and love, I know beyond all question that it was never me. It was always Jesus, my Savior and my life, carrying me inside His arms, through the cold and the night. Never once could the fear have touched me, though I was frightened beyond measure. The icy waters were no threat to me, though I nearly slipped into them. And if I came out of this run, frozen inside without any hope or any ability to know that God loves me, carrying intact that which God had placed inside of me, that is His

doing as well.

Do you wonder that I have no connection with anyone who would blither that Jesus is not my life, that He is not Savior and all Salvation?

When God said to me, as I climbed up the shores of the other bank, "Son, you passed the test," He was not speaking of me, but of Jesus, yet He was speaking of me, for Christ is the only life I am (Galatians 2:20).

～

Let me now explain why this picture from a story became so vivid to me in the night. The dogs of slavery were the voices of the hard doctrines of Nicene Calvinism spoken into me, that I was contrary to God and that it was my fault. The icy waters of the St. Lawrence were the bottomless pit of my finding fault, of speaking against, and of blaming myself or others. The distant shore of Canada was our precious union with Christ inside of which I now live. And the "baby in my arms" was the precious word and truth of Christ which God was giving me through every day of this "run."

UNCLE TOM'S CABIN
HARRIET BEECHER STOWE

This is an accurate picture, and these were the stakes.

"They Lied to Me"

My writings through the year 2014 represented a beginning of healing for me, coming out from the transformation that took place when I read "Sealed in the Midst of the Storm" into audio in May of 2013. Writing the first chapters of my book, *Musings on Union*, in late 2014, was my first foray back into the pain of my Blueberry experience. I wrote Chapters 3, "Double or One" and 4, "One and One," out from the first real healing God worked in me, though certainly not the last. If you were to read them, you would see some of what I hope to convey again in this chapter.

Just prior to starting *Musings on Union*, in September of 2014, I wrote these words in my book, *The Feast of Tabernacles*. ~ "They lied to me. They lied to me. When they told me that You were far away from me in my distress, when they told me that my mistakes meant I was in trouble with You, they lied to me. And all those years of heartache came from something NOT TRUE. You are so close; You are my life and my breath. You are bound to me in perfect Covenant Bond forever. We walk together in all ways as one." ~

Let me divide very carefully between the "voices" and the individual people who belonged to those voices. In doing that, I am not claiming that I "imagined" all these things. Rather, I am separating between Christ living as the individual persons who were ministries over me in the move fellowship and the ideas they believed were true, which they spoke with sincere hearts.

Let me use Janet Randall as an example. I wrote what I shared above, then I felt a disquiet inside until I understood the difference. You see, I must place myself with Father beneath her. That means I honor her as the Lord Jesus, but not as a "ministry over me." Some of what I heard from her may well have been only my perception of things, but not all.

Nonetheless, the Lord Jesus intended Sister Janet in those moments just as much as He intended me, though He did not intend our false thinking, yet He carried even it inside Himself. Then, the moment I see the vast divide between words and ideas and fears versus the precious brothers and sisters in whom Christ dwells, I am free. I am free to love; I am free to look back through the pictures of this time and see only joy and goodness; I am free to honor each one as the Lord Jesus Himself, even those who did speak wrongful things to me.

This is the true judgment of God.

Setting out the Issues

Let me expand on what God was really doing in my life, why He made me the way He did, and placed me in the exact circumstances that He chose. Indeed, my life is and has always been perfect, regardless of anything outward, and carefully directed by my Father for His Desire, that He might be made known through me.

Again, the first issue is the gospel of the serpent, from which we are escaping. The second issue is the true dealings of God in our lives. And the third issue is carrying intact the precious word of Christ AND the precious people whom God gave us, all the way through to the other side of the darkness.

I am placing these three issues, then, across the eight years of my life from June of 1990 to August of 1998. And this is as critical for you, dear reader, as for me. The icy waters of death over which we are fleeing are CONTEMPT for other Christians, especially towards those who are "over" us in the Lord, the very reason Adam chose to defy God.

God created me the way I am, including with an Asperger's disability, and God placed me into the move of God fellowship and into these particular Christian communities for a very specific purpose. And my heart is bowed upon my face before my Father, that He would set such determination and purpose upon me, regardless of all my searing inabilities.

Nonetheless, the place for sharing the whole picture must be at the end of this narrative. Here I will place only my overall Blueberry experience.

The problem, essentially, is the fall of the Church into Roman darkness, in the imposing of the words of the serpent in the garden upon every gospel truth, and thus creating received Nicene "theology." This "Roman darkness," then, was first made hyper by John Calvin. And when I looked closely at John Calvin just a few years ago, I was overwhelmed at the stark sameness between that and what Buddy Cobb taught in the move fellowship. It is a weaving of all the gospel "truths" into a pattern that is contrary to God and to Paul's gospel of our glorious salvation inside of Jesus.

And so my use of the two metaphors, one, of the womb becoming hostile and driving out the baby, the other, of Eliza fleeing across the St. Lawrence bearing her precious child, is an escape, not from the move of God fellowship, but from the gospel of the serpent in the form of Nicene theology, a theology that placed upon me one outcome only – **"Depart from Me, for I never knew you,"** that is, the slavery of corruption.

And I was always running towards one place only – **"And My Father will love him, and We will come to him, and will make Our home with him."**

Yet it was not death that was as the hounds baying at my heels, but death was that which lurked right beneath my feet. Death would be my own false choice.

DEATH, the death of which Adam ate and then turned and vomited forth upon God's creation is CONTEMPT – hating God by hating other people.

The great issue of this period of my life would not be the word God was giving me; it would not be the people of the communities; it would not be the false theology of the serpent; it would not be reaching the other side. The great issue of this period of eight years was the purifying FIRE that is God, removing out from my heart all the root hairs of contempt.

Touch not Mine anointed and do My prophets no harm. - Touch not Mine anointed and do My prophets no harm.

Whatever you do, "say, think, or feel" towards the least of these My brethren, you ARE doing it to Me.

And in spite of many of the things that Brother Buddy Cobb believed and taught that were contrary to Paul's gospel, still, it was he who planted inside of me the greatest gift from God beyond "Christ alive in my heart" – and that is a genuine, true, and deep fear of God.

Here inside of the love of God, it is then the fear of God that keeps us "on top of the ice" all the way across. Indeed, we flee across the death of contempt and into God All-Carrying with all determined boldness as our escape from any thought of **"Depart from Me"**

What I mean to say is that the most important aspect of my life through these years is that finger of God working in my heart, teaching me to impute no blame at all.

Placing Myself into Jesus

As I go forward, now, in sharing with you the next three years of my life, I realize that some might perceive in what I must write a strong "accusation against." That is not my intention, but I cannot show you from whence comes so much of what I share in the present time except I take you with me through this difficult path.

More than that, if any of those who were elders at Blueberry or ministries in the move read this account, the answer of the goodness and kindness of the Lord Jesus through them to me would be a very simple, "Please forgive me, Daniel, I was wrong." And with great joy, it all becomes part of walking together inside of Christ; it all becomes rivers of living water.

Nonetheless, I do not feel here, in this chapter, to draw anyone into the love of God poured out inside of me. Rather, the right thing to do here and through the next three years, is to place myself utterly and entirely into the Lord Jesus.

I was at times treated badly and without cause, and especially as a false word spoken into me. It is right and necessary for me to say so and to declare my just innocence inside the Lord Jesus.

"Lord Jesus, I place myself utterly into You, through these three years from mid-1990 to mid-1993. You carried me inside Yourself through every moment. Lord Jesus, I know that You have filled my heart with your glory through my entire life. I know, now, that my heart was good, my heart was filled with Jesus in every moment of my confused agony.

"Lord Jesus, I know that You intended me out from all goodness in every moment. And though You did not intend any wrongful thing, nonetheless, You bore the brunt of it, allowing just enough of the awfulness to pass through Your mighty wall of protection to share Your own suffering with me, that my heart might be shaped to fit our Father's heart.

"Lord Jesus, I declare now and know that I was never alone, but that You were living in me and as me, that You were extending to me precious things that would become the center of my knowledge of Father.

"And, Lord Jesus, looking out, now, through Your eyes, I see each one of my brothers and sisters through these years, and especially the ministry that You placed in my life for that season, calling them each by name, and I see their hearts, longing to know You, just as much. Whatever mistakes they may have made towards me, You also were carrying them through those instances. I find, even now, Your great compassion already poured out in my heart.

"Lord Jesus, You and I together turn every mistake, those made by others as well as those made by me, into the result of goodness and blessing towards me, yes, but even more so towards each one of them.

"You are good, Lord Jesus, all the time, You sustain all things by Your good speaking, and You do all things well."

Below are pictures of John Clarke and Charity Titus speaking at the graduation. Then, the group with whom I graduated are, from the top of the staris down, Monica Rotundi, Paul Mandry, Gail Young, myself, Maureen, Mike Pelletier, Frieda Raja, Peter Bell, Jill Sapiro, and Darlene Symes.

20. Marriage and Family

June 1990 - August 1991

Caught in a Vice

Graduation meant that college was behind us, and so Maureen and I asked the elders for visions to confirm our marriage. At the same time, I had been planning another trip down to Oregon. I hoped to spend a few weeks with mom and dad. I also wanted Maureen to come with me, which would require someone else as a chaperone.

At this point of time, it seemed to me that the elders were presenting a blank face towards our relationship, and towards me in particular. It is true that I am not expressive outwardly in many situations. But at the time, I had no idea why I was receiving this blank response, nor did anyone talk it through with me.

The evening before I was to leave for Oregon, John Austin came to me with the visions they had received for our marriage. The visions were strongly positive, but he told me that there was not a witness to Maureen going with me on this trip and neither did the elders believe that it was God's time for us to be married. I left early the next morning by myself, in my Toyota station wagon, heading into a very lonely month.

My own son was caught in a bit of a vice in the few weeks before his marriage last summer. When he came to me for understanding, I was able to share with him that this was God's best time in his life to get right at things inside of him that God wanted to touch. I was able to share that with my son because that is exactly what God was doing with me.

I could not have defined then what God was after in me; if I had tried, I would have gotten it completely wrong. And so I was caught in the grip of a vice. I wanted to be married; I wanted to spend my life with Maureen. Yet that goal now seemed unreachable, even though it was so close. I did not understand.

I must mention the Pacy family, John and Carol Pacy, who lived in Aldergrove, BC, not far from the US border. I have shared how much help Lenna Pacy had been to me in befriending me and teaching me to be more at ease in social settings. Her younger sister, Ruth, also lived at Blueberry through this time. They had lived originally here in the Peace River area and then in the Yukon with their parents and older brother, where they had connected with the move fellowship. The Pacy's had a home in a rural suburb of Abbotsford, a street of houses, each of which had a five acre lot. This is garden country, and their place was lush and green. In the back of their acreage was a goat barn with a loft above that was made into a bedroom.

I had already begun stopping at the Pacy's on my way down to Oregon and back up, as I did this time as well. This was a quality of life that I found only inside the move fellowship, that anywhere you went, you were at home. I always felt at home with the Pacy's and loved the privilege of spending a day or two with them now on my occasional trips through. They were always welcoming and great fun. I was always refreshed by my time with them.

I don't remember anything of my time at home except that I was pressed with the dilemma of this unexpected blockage in my great hope of finally being married. I will share more concerning my relationship with my mom in upcoming letters, however.

The Summer of 1990

And so I returned to Blueberry and to the summer work with nothing resolved.

The two main projects for summer construction were to complete Sister Delores's house so that she could move back into it and to build a small building for Mike Pelletier to have a place to process the honey. We built the bee shop on the slope between the root cellar and the old barn. It had two rooms, the front room as the work space and the back room which contained a large piece of equipment used for processing the honey. Mike's bee program was becoming very productive, and we were able to sell a fair bit of honey. I remember on this project my growing relationship with Dani Maldonado in the construction work.

I had designed a too-big house for Sister Delores. Through the summer, the elders decided that it should be split into two homes. We removed the stairway and added a different front entry to the upstairs where it was level with the slope, just below the Austin cabin. The upstairs would become its own separate home. The advantage, then, was that it would be much simpler to complete the downstairs first as its own unit. One problem was that the upstairs bathroom was right above the downstairs dining table. I raised the bathroom floor with a double frame and wove fiberglass between the now completely separated floor and ceiling. It worked; no one below ever heard any sounds from above.

At the same time, Don Howat shared with me that the elders were concerned about how long it was taking to complete Sister Delores's house. Some had suggested that if it was not done by the end of the summer, then something else would have to happen. What, I don't know, but I took that need seriously and gave myself as much as I could to finishing the downstairs.

By the first of August, I was fed up with the indecision regarding our marriage. In talking with John Austin about it, he suggested that, if I meant business, then I should say that to the elders. And so Maureen and I went to the elders for that purpose. We told them that we believed it was time for us to be married. When they saw our resolve, they agreed. Nonetheless, their faces still seemed blank towards us.

Now, I suspect that part of their hesitation was that they thought that I would run rough-shod over Maureen. They thought that because they did not know Maureen. In spite of her true gentleness and kindness, Maureen is a fierce lioness. People who don't know her, give her their full respect immediately. The idea that I would "control" Maureen is absurd, neither has there ever been such a thought in my heart.

I don't remember exactly what Maureen said, but she had had enough. She told them that our marriage was and ought to be a happy occasion, and that they should be excited. I could see that some were a bit taken back by her fierceness, but it was Don Howat who saved the day. He rose and applauded us with joy, allowing the other elders to smile as well.

And so, even though there was much contending with God and He with me through these weeks of impasse, in the end, what God wanted of me was that I be definite, a very good thing.

New People and New Places

In order for the remainder of the summer to make sense, I will include the families that were moving to Blueberry at this time, and the many moves being made by different families from one living place to another in the community.

I do not know who came when, through this summer, or the year before or the year after, so I will start at the top and work my way down the hill. First, David Randolph and Lenna Pacy were married and they had a small wooden home trucked in. Maureen tells me that it was Lenna's parents' first home in Buick, BC. It was put into a little hollow just above the Clarke cabin. Then, across from them, on a flat spot just above the Austin cabin, a single-wide mobile home was placed for Philip and Carolyn Bridge and their two school-age daughters. Carolyn Bridge was the sister of Barbara James.

Another family moved to Blueberry from Smithers BC through this time, Jim and Shirley Mancha and their son, John, and three daughters, Rebekah, Michelle, and Stephanie. Rebekah was enrolled in the college where she would be in the courses I taught, and I had John and Michelle in my high school classes. The Mancha's would eventually move into the upstairs of Sister Delores's house as their home. Where they stayed before that, I don't remember.

Meanwhile, we turned two of the rooms in the upstairs of the Tabernacle into living spaces. Roger and Bertie Henshaw felt that taking care of a large home filled with young people was becoming too much for them. They moved into one of those rooms, and Sister Edie Dwyer moved into the other. Don and Pat Deardorff had agreed to become the caretakers of the Henshaw's large house and so they moved up there with their children. That left their cabin between the shop and the Blueberry River available to Don and Martha Howat, and so they were preparing their move into it.

Because our marriage was confirmed and Maureen and I were free to set a date, we were given a large room in the back corner of the Austin's down-stairs as our first "home." Since that room was now empty, I moved up to it as my living place, having spent four good years as part of the Raja fami-ly. Not long after that, however, Sister Nancy Raja announced that she and her daughters, Freda and Ruth, would be leaving the community and moving to Fort St. John. This was overwhelming to me, for I believed strongly in community. I still do, but not as the fetish it had become to me then. I remonstrated with her, but they were quite set.

When Brother Victor had been killed, Nancy had received a decent insurance settlement that had al-lowed her to buy some nice furniture for our cabin and then that made it possible for them to move comfortably to town. She soon found a job at the health food store in Fort St. John, where Maureen and I were customers whenever we went to town.

Before the Raja's left, however, a seemingly mi-nor incident happened that marked a deep shad-ow against my heart. You see, we had begun dis-cussing the need for a new washhouse and shop to replace the old building, which was nearly derelict. Because Don was the oversight of the construction, not all the elders knew how much of that responsi-bility actually came out from me. Sister Nancy had been the oversight of the old washhouse, and so Brother John Clarke wanted to meet with her in the upstairs of the Tabernacle, in the little sitting room just above the spiral stairway, along with someone from the construction crew (he probably thought Don Howat) to discuss what the design of a new washhouse might be.

As I arrived for this discussion, I overheard Broth-er John say, regarding me, "What is he doing here?"

At the time, of course, these words were just an-other nightmare entering into my confusion. But let me answer his question now. "I am here, Brother John, because I love this family as much as you do and because I carry their needs in my heart just as much as you."

This was the simple truth, but I could not have said or even thought such a thing then. I did not understand.

Another incident with Brother John happened several weeks later, in the preparation time for our wedding. Brother John asked to visit with me to dis-cuss the actions and responsibilities of being mar-ried. I highly respected Brother John, but I did not

know what he wanted of me. He asked me several times if I had any questions, but no thought could enter my mind, no matter how hard I tried. We spent awhile in awkward silence. I suspect this was one of many autistic moments that was interpreted as "conceited pride."

The Raja cabin was then opened to Martin and Rebekah Lincecum to prepare it as their new home. That meant that the "Lincecum" cabin, just above the school, was now open to another new family to Blueberry, William and Charlene Brown. William was African American. He had been a fine chef in top-notch restaurants, and he also loved to gar-den. He soon took oversight of the food produc-tion in the Blueberry gardens. William had lots of good ideas, and he was given much liberty in his approaches to gardening. One of these things was that, through this time, Blueberry became certified organic. A number of the elders, including John and Nathel Clarke, were natural-health conscious, something unusual in the move fellowships.

Some singles moving to Blueberry through this time whom I also want to mention (I cannot bring in everyone), included Donovan Van Gorkom from Smithers. His dad made high quality custom hiking boots in a shop in Smithers. Donovan soon went to work with the NorthStar logging company. Then, Sir James Barlow came to Blueberry from northern Ireland. He was a proper English gentleman and a great friend to Maureen and me. Lester Flowers, originally from Peru, also came to Blueberry as a college student.

In late August, then, new building projects were added to our already large obligations for that sum-mer. The Lincecum's wanted their cabin remodeled before they moved into it. This was very disconcert-ing to me because I had done a lot of work remode-ling it already while I still lived there. All of that was to be torn out and replaced. It's not that I was not willing to bear that loss to me, but my difficulty was that it was not really necessary. I was laboring under the "threat" concerning Sister Delores's cabin being finished even while all my crew was pulled away to work on the Lincecum cabin. But Martin worked out with North Star and thus brought in tangible money to the community, and Sister Nathel was his mother, so that's the way it would be.

At the same time, Don Howat had begun work on his new cabin to get it ready for their move. Meanwhile, I continued plugging along by myself trying desperately to get Sister Delores's house finished under the obligation I had perceived.

One day, I was working on the table saw which we had set up in the upstairs as our "shop." Don Howat came up and stopped me. I had felt some friction towards my refusing to drop this job and to help with the two new jobs. Please understand that this is part of Asperger's. When I see an obligation as I felt then, I wear blinders in my pursuit of that obligation. It is very, very difficult for me to "switch paths," one might say.

Don stopped me and said, "You know, Daniel, I would like it very much if I could sit in my living room and look at the shelves on my wall and say to myself, 'Daniel built those shelves for us.'"

Don's open honesty and regard won my heart. I relinquished the need to finish Sister Delores's cabin and spent several days working with the others on the Howat cabin. I even helped some on the Lincecum cabin.

Finally, another mobile home was set up just to the west of the Brown cabin, just below the Deardorff house. This was occupied by Lloyd and Colleen Green just moving to Blueberry with their school-age son and daughter.

Our Wedding

Maureen and I were very happy in our planning for our wedding together; nonetheless, many difficulties continued to press against us. As I watched my own son going through his pre-marriage dilemmas, I thought how glad I am that such a time, nine years for me, is long gone into my past.

After communicating with my brothers and sisters, we hoped that we could set a wedding date in the first part of September since that was the best time for them to break with their obligations to come up to northern British Columbia. Dave Smillie and Kay Wallace were planning to be married that summer as well, however, and they preferred mid-September. Weddings are a big deal in community, and Blueberry was having lots of them through these years; so a couple of weeks were needed between. We submitted, putting our own needs second. Somehow, all my brothers and sisters were able to arrange things. They would all be coming with all their families. Lois lived at Blueberry and Jessica came up from Lubbock, Texas where she now lived. Claude and Roberta would be driving up from Bowens Mill.

I had waited so many years for this, and having all my family come to visit me inside of community was a big deal to me. We both wanted our wedding to be a memorable time, a family time, a time filled with community. We wanted a morning wedding, so that we would have time in the afternoon for family and a non-stressful exit before the evening was late.

And we wanted a wedding in which most everyone had a part and where the Lord Jesus held the place of honor.

Let's go straight to our wedding day, exccept for one thing. To prepare for our new home, I asked Terri Miller if he would build a bed for us to my design as his wedding gift. He readily agreed, and it was in place when we returned from our honeymoon.

Maureen and I were married on September 29, 1990, a Saturday.

All my family was there. Franz and Audrey, with their four children; Frieda and Tim with their two, Ryan and April; Cheryl and Dave with their three children; Jenelle (Jim did not come thus she was by herself); and Glenn and Kim with their first little girl. Even more than that, Mom had hired a nurse to take her place full time for a week, and so this was the only time in seven years that she left dad to another's care.

On Thursday evening, two days before our wedding, we had a pre-wedding sharing service. My own family were all there for this. Different ones got up to share about our lives and to bless us. As I look through our wedding pictures, I see so many sharing and even dancing in joy. I then got up and shared about the word God had spoken to me nine years before, that Maureen would be my wife, and how the fulfillment of that word had seemed so impossible for so many years. I concluded my sharing with this statement, final and absolute in my heart. — "Now I KNOW that God does what He says He will do."

Our wedding began at 10 AM on Saturday morning. Freda Raja sat behind the guest-book table. Richard was there as my best man, along with my brother Glenn. This was the first that I began to see Glenn as I should have always seen him, as a brother highly regarded. We stood at the front with Brother John Clarke who was to marry us.

Ken Geis and Mike Pelletier were our main ushers. Then once everyone was seated, all the high

Above from left: Lois, Jessica, Maureen, me, Richard, and Glenn.

Below top from left: Jessica, Lois, Glenn, Jenelle, Frieda, Franz, and Cheryl.

Bottom from left: Claude, Roberta, Maureen, me, and Mom.

school boys and young men sang a choral song together up front.

Patrick Downs played his violin and another sister a flute, while Howard Wallace played the piano as Jessica, Maureen's maid of honor, and then Lois, came down the aisle to stand opposite us. Once they were up front, Laura Weitz joined them as they sang a song of praise. [I will not apologize for all the details; this is my story, and this was the best day of my life.]

Then Donovan van Gorkum stepped forward to play "Come, for the Spirit cryeth, 'Come'" on his silver trumpet as Maureen came down the spiral stair case, and then as Brother Claude brought her down the aisle.

When I walked my own daughter, Johanna, down the aisle to Matthew Schneider, I saw myself in him, and remembered the supreme joy I knew. Tears streamed down my face both times. That this precious woman wanted to be part of my life was more wondrous than anything I had ever known.

After Brother Claude gave Maureen's hand to me, we sat down on the front row. First we had a time of praise. I had asked five to lead the praise, Jennifer Hanna, Dani Maldonado, Ken Geis, Sister Sue Sampson, and Leslie Cedeno. After that, Brother John stood and shared a good word, about fifteen minutes long (short by move standards).

Then, Maureen and I went forward with our attendants for the first part of the marriage ceremony to the giving of rings. At that point, we had Claude, Roberta, and mom join with Maureen and me for a brief communion service of bread and wine together ministered by Brother John with Richard assisting. This was one of the ways I wanted to bring the Lord Jesus into our wedding. While we took communion, however, all the young ladies in high school and college, or of that age, had gone up front and sang a choral praise, a song of communion that Mike Pelletier had received from the Lord for our wedding.

Finally, all the elders gathered around us to pray for us and to bless our marriage. Brother D and Sister Ethelwyn were there as well. I see Rick Annett in that picture, who would become such a dear friend to us. When the blessing was finished, Brother John Clarke pronounced us man and wife. We were married.

As I look through the pictures, I see all the wonderful people who were part of our lives and of this most wonderful day. I see such joyous giving towards us. And to see all the members of my own family there at Blueberry as well, this was truly God's bounteous gift.

After our wedding we went outside for pictures while the Tabernacle was being rearranged for our wedding feast. After the dinner, there was another sharing time, with Don Howat as M.C.

Of course, I had to carry Maureen into our new home up in the downstairs of the Austin's. Except I picked her up too soon, going all the way up the back way with outside stairs. I did make it without dropping her. We had a quiet time in the Austin's upstairs, opening some presents with friends and family before we changed for our departure.

We had a relaxed afternoon and were able to say goodbye to everyone before driving out in our Toyota station wagon for Dawson Creek.

Our Honeymoon

The Blueberry family was very generous to us for our honeymoon and new home, giving us probably over $2000. More than that, actually, because more money had been given for our wedding and $400 for our rings. That was great, because I could get a $350 diamond ring for Maureen and a $50 gold band for me.

I had reserved the honeymoon suite in the larger hotel in Dawson Creek for our first night, and then two nights with a regular room in one of the better hotels in Prince George, set up inside as a tropical resort. In my mind, though, a honeymoon was an excuse to visit communities and brethren whom we would never get to see otherwise. Maureen was in agreement. Tropical beaches or exotic locations meant nothing to either of us. It is people whom we love.

On Tuesday, we drove to Smithers, BC., to the little move community there, just outside of town. We visited at the Smithers community for a week. This was where Milton and Bonnie Vereide lived, two leading ministries in the move. They were gone on a trip, however, so we were given their home to stay in. We arrived after dark. When I got up in the morning, I opened the curtains. Maureen looked out the window and said, "There's a mountain outside our window!" And so there was, and wondrous mountains on the other side of Smithers as well, all covered in snow.

Smither's is a picturesque little town. Dan Ricciardelli was also an elder at the Smithers community, and we had good times getting to know him and his family. We enjoyed sharing meals with the community. Brother Dan insisted that we spend three days just visiting sights in the area. We visited the town of Smithers, stopping at the Van Gorkom boot shop. We drove as high up onto the snow covered mountains west of Smithers as we could. The rest of the week we did what we liked better, I helped Dan on construction work on their Tabernacle and Maureen chatted while she cut the hair of most of the ladies in the community. Sister Janet Myers was also visiting at the time, so that was a special treat for us as well.

We went on next to Prince Rupert. I had hoped to have our one "expensive" meal in a seafood restaurant overlooking the ocean, but, strangely enough, even though Prince Rupert is a major port, its not really a sea town because several railroad tracks run right along the edge of the water all the way around. Bummer.

On our way back inland, then, we turned north and drove up to Telegraph Creek. That summer, another family had visited Blueberry, Mark Stevens from Telegraph Creek, with his three daughters and younger son. His two older daughters, Sola and Kimberley, were staying at Blueberry for school and were at our wedding. They very quickly became as daughters to Maureen and me.

Mark Stevens had acquired an incredible property twenty miles west of Telegraph Creek on the large shelf just above the huge Stikine River canyon and just at the base of a large mountain to the north, blocking the northern winds. The deep canyon below meant that all cold air would drop down. Mark had maybe fifty acres of cleared pasture land with their newly built home on one side.

We had a wonderful time with them. To my utter amazement, we went out to his garden and picked strawberries. This was the second week of October; Blueberry was covered in snow, and we were further north!

We drove on north from there to Whitehorse, in the Yukon, and spent a night or two with Jim and Kate Buerge. It was so great to connect with them again. Then we went on further north into the Klondike country to spend three nights and two days with Del and Virginia Buerge on a farm meant to be a community, but with only them there at that time.

I am glad we spent this time with Del and Virginia. Del was a workaholic, yes, and he had a dim view of spending one's time as a teacher (which was not real work to him.) But they were good friends, and we had a wonderful time with them. Del had made a productive farm of his property, including a small orchard that actually produced fruit. While we were there, we helped them butcher chickens. Yeah, we got to gut chickens on our honeymoon! It's just good to be real and to be part of other people's lives.

On the way back to Blueberry, we went swimming in the Liard Hot Springs, with snow covering the ground all around. That was fun.

The Winter Months
When we got back to Blueberry, our first home, one large bedroom, was all ready for us.

The downstairs of the Austin cabin, was, by itself, larger than most of the other dwellings in the community. It had a large entry, three large bedrooms, a front room that included both a kitchenette and a living room, and in the back corner was a large wood furnace that heated the entire building. While we were there, the interior stairway remained in place, though the people who lived upstairs rarely used it now.

Along with Maureen and I in the back bedroom, two other newly married couples shared this home with us. In the front bedroom were Eric and Rachel (Roes) Hanna, and in the middle room were Fritz and Sarah (Gregg) Hanna. The two, of course, were brothers, and had been part of the community for longer than I.

Our living situation there was adequate and fine. But it was not comfortable for any of us couples. It's hard to begin a life together trying to share space with two other newlywed couples. All of us were looking forward to any other space opening that could become our own private homes.

By November, Maureen knew that she was carrying our first child, to be born the next August. We both knew that it would be a boy. This was a very big deal to me, yet I knew how incapable I was in all my inability.

It was a wonderful thing, though, to find that in so many areas important to family life, Maureen and I shared the same views and outlook. We were both interested in natural health, and thus began our marriage from then until now, in the pursuit of such understanding and practice. And so, I had read about barley grass, that drinking fresh barley grass juice daily would be of wonderful benefit in the healthy development of a child. Maureen claims that I said that drinking barley juice made the child smart, so if she didn't drink her barley juice and if Kyle wasn't smart, it would be her fault. I remembered saying something similar as a joke. Anyhow, I kept a box of barley grass growing in the one sunny window we had in the downstairs and made barley drink for Maureen every morning.

The trapping season does not start until mid-winter. There was talk of completing the interior of the cabin before the Ebright's went back out that did not include me. This was very distressing to me because I loved that little cabin, and I had remembered making an agreement to complete it. I confronted John Austin on this exclusion, and he suggested that I take my concern to the elders. Maureen and I did, and they agreed that we would go out together to lead a crew in finishing the cabin.

And so we made the long wintry trip by road this time up to the trapline cabin. Maureen was there for just a couple of days before returning, while a larger crew of men then came out. We did a beautiful job on the interior, putting in kitchen and bathroom cabinets, a plywood floor, and wood paneling on the walls. We sheetrocked under the sloping roof. This was another time where Brian contended with me on how something should be done, that is, that he should do the interior paneling instead of me and that I should do the outside chinking instead of him. This is one time that he won, but he was harsh, and Don Howat did speak with him afterwards.

Because I was no longer taking college courses, I was able to teach more in the high school. More of the community children now became my students. I can best define the classes moving through by the three Austin children whom I taught. I had started with Deborah in eighth grade, and then Paul Austin in eight grade two years later. Now, I had the group in-between those two which included Rebekah Austin, David Deardorff, and Joy Ebright. The group younger than Paul Austin, (whose class now included John Mancha) became my students as well, that would include Anita Deardorff, Wendy Rehmeier,

and Stephanie Ebright. I name most of my students because they were all very special to me and continue to be so.

For the spring semester, Sister Mozelle Clark agreed that I could team teach "Learning and Evaluation" with her. Again, I can't do anything like that without seizing it "whole hog." I laid out the whole course. Sister Mozelle said that she took a deep breath when she saw my intense excitement and gave me great room. Thank you Mozelle, I understand now how much you gave to me.

I loved teaching college, and I loved teaching about teaching.

In March, Paul Mandry, who had been heavily involved in the school, moved to Fort St. John with his family. This became a difficulty for some in the community because the elders, and especially Brother John Clarke had instituted the typical move practice of breaking off all contact with "those who leave" and forbade any of their close friends from visiting them in town.

That is not my story, however. The fact that Paul's history courses now needed a teacher was, and so I stepped into teaching history in the high school as well.

Kimberley and Sola Stevens were in my classes, (with other students coming in for their final high school years as well, too many to include). This is a good ministry, however, to provide a school for the final two years of those who had been home-schooled otherwise. Always, their eleventh grade year was struggle, but their final year of high school was excellence. Maureen and I also sent two of our children to a move community school for their last two years of high school.

Through this year, I finished the construction degree program with Terry Miller so that he could graduate in the spring. I had also included Dani Maldonado and Fritz Hanna in some of the classes with him, particularly woodworking and cabinet design. One assignment Terry did in woodworking was to make a beautiful podium out of birch for the services, light of weight and on wheels, in contrast to the prior one which was heavy and hard to move. I see that Terry's podium was there for our wedding. It was indeed a work of art.

Then, that May, the first group of students I had begun to teach at Blueberry graduated from high school, including Amos Deardorff, Deborah Austin, and Rachel Martin. Most of them had been in my classroom for five years. They were my joy and great reward.

Our New Home

Because the Mandry cabin was now vacant, Eric and Lynn Foster moved up into it. The little cabin just above the Tabernacle was now available. The elders agreed that it would belong to Maureen and I and to our soon-coming family.

This new cabin had a second small bedroom and so Maureen and I, almost together, thought of one of the funnest things (in my mind) we would do in our new life together.

Kimberly Stevens was a bright and fiercely independent girl. She was determined in her school work, but she had poor, even hurtful, experiences with move practices in her childhood, through the difficult season when their mother had died of cancer. Kimberly was not rebellious, in fact, she was very kind and giving. But she stood for herself against those who liked to exercise authority and so was always getting in trouble, both in her home situation and with many of her teachers.

Maureen and I did NOT see her in that way. We saw an incredibly wonderful girl whose independence was not to be squashed, and our hearts wept for some of the stuff being imposed upon her. So – the very moment we knew this newly opened cabin was ours, we asked Kimberley to come up and speak with us. We sat down formally, pretending to be serious (something I'm not very good at). To our delight, we could see that Kimberley thought she was in trouble again.

Then we asked, "Kimberley, we want you to be part of our home and family. Would you come and share our new home with us?"

The expression on Kimberley's face was worth good money. She became as one of our daughters and so remains to this day. We got to see her here in Houston just a couple of years ago, as she was stopping on a fly through. Kimberley has always made Maureen and I so very proud.

I had remodeled this cabin already, a couple of years earlier, thinking it would belong to Richard and Elizabeth. It didn't need any major changes. I wanted to build a new set of kitchen cabinets for it, with oak-plywood fronts, but I would do that through the summer months. There were a few things that I asked the elders about, that would help make it a nice home for us to move into. Since I was taking a much heavier load in school, I also asked if Don, Dani, and Terry could be given two or three days each to help me do that work.

The elders said, "No."

When I had remodeled this cabin, I had put in a larger window meant for a bay window to be built. That bay had not been installed. I loved growing things and sunshine coming in during the long six months of icy winter. Sister Nancy had a bay window in her living room filled with flowers. There were others in the community. But my request was denied as being unnecessary, even "fleshy."

Other things were denied as well and we were told there was no time for this, that "other pressing needs" in the community meant no time was available for my home. Sister Nathel Clarke came over with Don Howat to help me simplify my requests for the cabin. She scowled and spoke critically of its layout, then left.

In the end, all that was agreed was that Terry Miller could give a couple of days to make the second bedroom more private for Kimberley.

In all my years in community, this was the single most painful thing ever done against me. I had worked many, many hours making almost every dwelling place in the community better for those who lived there. I had built Dave Smillie a beautiful home, yet he never thanked me for it, not once. (Sister Delores did thank me for her new home, something that meant very much to me.) And I had done all that work for others for one reason only, because I loved them.

The summer before, we had dropped everything to do a major remodel on Sister Nathel's son's cabin, and Brother Don had spoken those meaningful words into me. Now I was starting my family, Kyle was soon to be born. This was our first home. I felt truly that I had been kicked as hard as could be kicked.

I will not hide or try to explain away this offense. More and more, over the next couple of years, my strength as a husband, father, and provider in the community was being stripped away from me by a continuation of this type of treatment. Having stepped out of my autistic shell, I was very vulnerable and unprotected. The deep sorrow and helplessness of this important moment would work grief all through me for the next ten years and would mark its pain on the early lives of our children.

The one thing I must do here is to stand up for myself. – And that is what I must do in placing the Lord Jesus upon myself in that moment. – You had no right to disrespect Maureen and me in that way. – The claim that this was counteracting my "fleshy sinful nature" is, itself, hostile against the Salvation of Christ Jesus. – As you treat the least of these whose hearts are filled with Jesus, so you ARE treating Him.

Having said that much, I will leave it there.

Nonetheless, in the present, I extend my forgiveness, with all my heart, over those whose decision worked such hurt in me. I now understand that they did not realize what they were doing. Even more than that, I recognize and honor the Lord Jesus who filled their hearts with His Person and glory, just as much as He filled mine.

A Garden of Peace

Through this time, the North Star company had acquired the teardown job of a large shop in Fort St. John. Our reward was to have all of the materials for the buildings we were planning to build the next year at Blueberry. Others had charge of this job and it became frustrating to many because the leaders did not know how to lead a crew of men, staying focused only on what they were doing. It was many hours of long hard work, with a crew of maybe twenty men to tear down that shop. And again, Brian found places to contend with me over how I was trying to do something.

Then, with the job maybe two-thirds done, Mike Pelletier, Ken Geiss, and I were taking down a high plywood wall. It was maybe thirty feet wide and sixteen feet high. Mostly just the studs, but some of the plywood was still on. Whether it was too heavy for us or not, I don't know, but much more than that, it was top-heavy. There was a split moment when we all three knew that we could not hold it. In that moment, Ken slipped to the side and Mike twisted between the studs where there was no plywood. I also made a split decision and saw that I had no options. The side was too far to my right and in front of me was plywood. (This was not their fault, I'm glad the other two were unhurt.)

And so the wall came down hard on me. I knew how to handle such a thing, and so I made it roll across the curve of my back, but it stretched out

my spine and drove the claws of my hammer into my side. I was not badly injured, but that was it for me. The logging company's insurance paid for my chiropractic needs. Others finished the job while I returned home to rest and recover.

Both Graham River Farm and the Shiloh Farm had dwindled down to just a few people by the time I visited them in 1986. Both were closed completely by 1988. The properties were owned by the move fellowship and the buildings remained. Through this year of 1991, I believe, Brother D and Sister Ethelwyn Davison were led of the Lord to return to Graham River with the Shepherd's School of Music. A number of students and teachers who had been a part of that school went with them. This included two families that would become more involved in our lives from then until now, Steve and Cindy Schneider and Lee and Claire Wilkerson. Maureen, especially, was close friends with Cindy (Dix) and Claire.

The problem the new Graham River faced was that prior to their return, one of the young men who had lived there in his teenage years, went across the ice one winter when no one was there and lit fire to the two big barns, the school building, and the Tabernacle, burning them to the ground. Because of that, their first "tabernacle" was the largest cabin, which happened to be the former Davison cabin where I had also lived.

At Shiloh, one of the families had remained for a few years, farming and caretaking the land. Before the end of 1990, they also had moved out to Fort St. John. Because of what had happened at Graham, the regional eldership gathering had decided to maintain a caretaker presence at the Shiloh property, with different ones taking a week or two at a time.

That July, Maureen and I agreed to spend a week at the Shiloh Farm as the caretakers. We had no obligation, just to be there in order to be sure that everything was watched over. We drove over by ourselves. It's a long drive into Shiloh on gravel and then dirt roads over rough terrain. A two-story house just to the north of the large Tabernacle had been made into the caretakers' cottage.

Our time there at Shiloh became a dream in my memory. It was the height of summer. Everything was green and abundant. Flowers bloomed everywhere. Stepping aside from the intensity of Blueberry, with time just to ourselves and nothing required of us was close to the most delightful week of my life. We spent our time exploring everything. Maureen, of course, was large with our new baby, so we did not exert ourselves. Shiloh had been a large community with many buildings spread over a much wider area than Blueberry or Graham. It was situated in a broad valley, about a mile wide between two ridges on either side over 1000 feet up. It was isolated from everything and the feeling that valley gave was of wild but gentle protection. In the north, it only takes a few months after buildings are abandoned for the forest critters to move in, so it felt like we were exploring a strange ghost town.

It was for us that summer a garden of peace.

Our Son Kyle

Let me share now about our preparation for the birth of our child. We had been perusing a list of names, and I was calling out every ridiculous name to Maureen just to be silly. I wanted the name to include my own dad's name, Emerson, however, and so we needed a first name to go with it. Maureen had our daughters' names in her heart from her childhood, so this was partly my choice. At that point, we did not actually know by fact that it would be a boy. Suddenly my eyes lighted upon the name "Kyle," and I said, "Kyle Emerson." Both of us felt in that moment that Kyle was telling us what his name was already. (We were to learn later that "Kyle" was one of the most popular names chosen in British Columbia in 1991!)

We took preparation for Kyle's birth very seriously. One large issue for us was the question of vaccinations. I was neither opposed nor for doing such a thing to our child; I simply did not have enough information. This was a question others had as well, and so we gathered a number of studies and articles, both pro-vaccination and anti-vaccination, all of them written, supposedly, on the basis of "science." We made the firm decision to let the facts decide for us.

We were astonished at the difference between the two types of articles. The anti-vax articles were filled with sound argument and provable/disprovable scientific and historic evidence. The pro-vax articles were filled with hot air, contempt, and the mighty claim of "evidence, evidence, evidence," as if repeating that word over and over would actually produce something that does not exist.

Our decision was simple and clear. More than that, in the years since, I have seen only these descriptions of both sides of the issue, except for one difference. The pro-vax argument, while continuing to contain only hot air, has become far more contemptuous and hostile than it was then.

More than that, our children have never known any of the many man-made childhood problems that come out from the vaccine needle.

Terri Rehmeier, the nurse in the community, had much experience with childbirth. We planned to have our first baby in the hospital in Fort St. John. But Terri gave the two of us a full course in pregnancy and childbirth which was invaluable to us. At the same time, Rebekah Lincecum agreed to be Maureen's helper in the hospital, and so she worked with us in preparing Maureen for the pain in labor, teaching Maureen how to breathe and hold herself steady.

You see, Maureen was determined that Kyle would not begin his life stoned out of his mind, which is what happens when the mother takes pain killers for the birth.

On the fifth of August, a Monday, Maureen began to indicate labor. It was slow at first. We drove out to Shepherd's Inn with Rebekah Lincecum and spent the night in the trailer of a brother by the name of Roman, who graciously gave us space. That way, we were only a half-hour from the hospital should we need to go quickly.

The labor was slow, so we went on to the hospital the next morning, a Tuesday. The hospital staff suggested that we not commit to the hospital until later, but that we should spend the day in town, doing things until the birth pangs increased.

(I would spend quite a number of stressful days in the Fort St. John hospital over the next several years. I must say here that, in spite of its hospital feel, most of the nurses and doctors there were wonderful and always treated us with care and regard. Because Canada is a single-payer system for health needs, everything was taken care of for us. All they needed was our basic information.)

Our doctor for Kyle's birth was supposed to have been Dr. Watt. Maureen had kept several appointments with him prior to this time. He was away on these days, however, and so Dr. Umadaly stepped in for Kyle's delivery.

Maureen's labor increased slowly through the day. As evening came on, we were walking around the block near the hospital. We paused on occasion and Maureen put her arms around my neck to wait out the pains. A First Nations lady was not far from us. The woman was clearly drunk, tall and stocky. But she came up to us with compassion on her face, put her hand on Maureen's shoulder and blessed her in the name of the Lord. "God is with you," she said. We returned to the hospital in awe of the grace of God that always surrounded us.

After Maureen was admitted to the hospital, Rebekah stayed with her through the night, but at a certain point I went to the family room and slept on the couch. We went into the birthing room around noon the next day. It had been a long haul for my slip of a wife. Rebekah was her help, coaching her to breathe. I stood just behind her, utterly useless. In fact, at one point the doctor thought I had fainted, but I had just stooped to change the praise tape in the tape player.

Kyle was born just after 5 PM. Except – the cord was around his neck, and he was quite blue. After all that, and suddenly the doctor was running out of the room with our little baby in his arms and with all the nurses at his tail. We waited in the grace of God until they returned. Our little boy was fine; I was a dad.

I took Rebekah home that evening; we left Maureen to rest quietly with Kyle. The next day I returned to town. I had little money when I went to the flower shop, so all I was able to buy was three red roses in a tea cup. That Wednesday had seen the birthing of several babies in that wing of the hospital. As I carried my few roses into Maureen's room, shared with other new mother's, I saw vast flower bouquets and balloons everywhere. At first I felt a bit ashamed of the little I had to give, but then I remembered that every one of those other mothers had screamed for drugs in the pain all alone. I may have been useless, but I was there for her, with Rebekah.

Maureen told me that the others had asked her what was wrong with her, how could she have been so quiet.

As I looked at my precious wife, holding our wonderful little boy, two things awoke inside of me. First, was the realization that women are stronger than men. But much more than that, I realized, for the first time, just how deeply I loved Maureen. Yes, Asperger's take awhile to connect with their true feelings.

Kyle will be 29 years old this summer. It would not be possible for parents to be more proud than we are of him. And that same love I felt for Maureen that day has only grown deeper and more true.

Note

In drawing this letter to a close, I find that I am yet unable to bring a complete resolution inside the Lord Jesus to the difficulties shared here. I have not had the courage to say what I said in "Our New Home" in all these years before now, only the healing God has brought me through writing about Blueberry thus far gave me that courage. It is right that what I have said in this letter should stand as it is. When I start the next chapter, I will place things into God.

21. Inside the Press

August 1991 - May 1992

Justifying God

Giving an account of one's life in the presence of God is a terrible thing. It could not be done except we know how utterly embedded we are inside of Father's Love. You see, there is also the realization that every person with whom one has interacted will also be giving an account, and their account must include you and your actions and responses towards them.

The shadow of darkness first entered God's creation with the accusation against God that His words are false. Every offense of angels and humans since has been an extension of that same accusation. God will answer every single accusation against Him through Jesus, the Word He is continuously speaking, proven faithful and true.

When Paul said that every knee will bow and every tongue will speak the same word that is Jesus, that includes giving thanks for every moment, circumstance, and person in one's life. This giving of thanks is central inside every giving of an account from every created being. God requires that every accusation ever uttered be shown to be false by the good speaking of Jesus and to be recognized as false by the one who so foolishly spoke it. That's what "every knee bowing" means.

If I have done wrong, if I have offended any particular person, I willingly confess my wrong and ask forgiveness.

But the accusation against the Lord Jesus Christ, that one who belongs to Him and whom He carries inside Himself, is "evil," and that a heart in which He dwells in Person in all glory, is also "wicked," this accusation is the "gospel" of the serpent, mocking the Atonement of the Lord Jesus, the very revelation of our Father.

I said in the last letter. "You had no right to disrespect Maureen and me in that way."

I knew that I would have to write those words from the moment I started writing about Blueberry. And the terror of that necessity is what flung me into a month of turmoil, for I was hearing the same voices again speaking the same words against me and the same devastating blows struck against my heart.

There is not and was not bitterness in my heart, only grief. The bitterness I had known at Bowens Mill and Albuquerque was long gone from me. And I do justify God in all things, that He alone is right and true, and have done so. I recognize clearly now God's purpose in my life. It was not He doing something to me, but rather, I know now that in all these things, it was my Father bearing the brunt of the assault, carrying me closely inside His heart, though I knew it not. And in seeing His wondrous purpose, indeed, His intentions to share Hheart with me, I bow my face upon the ground and I give Him thanks.

God is good all the time.

Nonetheless judgment in no way ends with forgiveness, but continues into the imputation of the goodness of Christ. Yet it goes even further, for in seeing those whose thoughtlessness caused me such grief, I must also recognize that not only are they also filled with the Lord Jesus, but that the love of God is already poured out in their hearts towards me, whether they know that or not.

And so to judge that which was wrong, I must go under with Father, in lifting them up and in recognizing in humility the great love coming always from them to me and the costliness of that love.

Understanding Myself

I have been sitting here pondering what it was that went wrong inside of me. It would be impossible, I think, to grasp the dealings and intention of God with me unless I am able to rightfully capture my growing internal split. That's really what it was, a split taking place between the mental theology of my head and the Jesus of my heart.

You see, I was fully attached to both, and no matter how much confusion the theology of my mind created for me, it could never take me away from my faith in and desire to know the One who lived inside of me. I suspect that if it had, my confusion would have ended and you would never have heard of me.

That was never a possibility; in the end, a theology of separation could never appeal to me no matter how dramatically it was preached, nor how much I imagined it to be correct. I needed life and life is Jesus. I knew that by the Spirit; I knew that in my heart. But I did NOT know it in my head.

It is a dangerous thing to trust, even to trust good people. I have been pleased to see independence of mind in my children and always encouraged it, for there are many pied pipers anointed mightily by the Spirit of God. Even good and sincere people, who are genuine and true, still can live inside a theology of the serpent and not inside of the salvation of Jesus, for that is all that has been known.

I can trace for you in the present time the beginnings of the word I now teach as the key verses of the Bible became rooted in my understanding. But I had no real idea of what they meant; I had nothing "figured out." All I did was hold the word closely inside my heart.

Meanwhile, I held the elders at Blueberry in the highest regard and trusted their anointing and wisdom. That was not wrong; and I received much from them of great value, much of which shows itself through all I have written.

In some ways, my friendship with Maureen through my last two years of college had placed me into a steady, ongoing outward involvement. And this outward involvement was showing to me my Asperger's inabilities. Yet not completely to me, but rather, it was my perception of what others seemed to see in me.

What were those inabilities?

I can't get ahead of my story and bring in the many things that I will share when I get to my fifties and first discover that my life-long difficulties were shared in full by many others. I must remember how I perceived things then.

One problem I had is that I have to understand something to see how it all fits together, before I can talk with others about changes that might be made. People would give me their designs, all measured to the inch – except they would leave out

the thickness of walls, or something like that. Their plans could not actually work. I had to have plans that could work before I was able to talk about what changes needed to be made.

You see, building a house is very real and very practical. If it won't work, it won't work. And people in their dreams and ideas are not practical. Then, I would try to explain why I had something a certain way in the design. But I would also take all their ideas and complaints, think about them long and hard, and then discover how I could alter the plans to make their desires work. Of course, sometimes that was not practical.

Here was the problem. I did not know I was doing that and I could not have told them that's how I thought. What they saw was an outer shell that was not me and of which I knew nothing.

Think of an autistic person and realize that autism is a spectrum. I was both high-performing autism and with a reasonably high IQ. You are aware that an autistic person gets very involved in the thing they are obsessed with. Other things are kept at a distance as they are focused on the patterns they are creating. Then, when someone intrudes and messes up their patterns, it's like great noise pushing its way in, it's like fingernails scratching on the chalk board. It's very confusing and disconcerting.

Even now there is one arena in which I go all haywire inside, and that is if I am driving and someone else is looking at a map and trying to give me directions. Think about the fingernails scratching on the blackboard; that's what it feels like inside my mind and through my nerves.

And so sometimes I would hold onto my ideas tightly like a little boy grasping his toys.

This is NOT a demon; it's a disability. I know well the difference between the two. But if someone is blind, you don't shout at them that they have a demon, and if they would just get with God, "rise up into Christ," they would be able to see. When someone has an internal physical disability, however, Christians can be very cruel.

Everyone expects God to heal an autistic person as if that's all God could do. Few see the Father revealing Himself as He is through them as they are. But those who are able to do such a thing, are able to see God as they never before understood God to be. There is a depth of ability to know inside an autistic person that can be found only by reaching deep inside of them. If you are wise enough to do that, you will learn things you never could have known.

Then, I was very uncomfortable in social settings. One of the worst things for me was to come to the dining room and hear, "Sit wherever you like." Instantly, I no longer had a place to sit, for I did not know where my place was. One of the most wonderful changes in my life, then, was when I came into the dining room with Maureen and heard that statement.

HA! I know where my place is. I will sit next to Maureen!

But family activities in the swirl of games, etc., these things make me very uncomfortable because I have no idea where my place is or how I fit. I was comfortable in my role only in two settings, the construction site and my classroom.

And I have never been able to counsel personal things with my students. I cannot draw from them their concerns or engage in a back and forth on personal matters or even on controversial topics in the classroom. It's a wild and unsafe place far beyond where I could go. My safe response was always, "Is that right."

For reasons unseen by me, however, I perceived that the elders whom I trusted believed that there was something wrong with me, that I held some sort of hard shell of conceit against God.

Here is an absolute law of reality, however, one that cannot be altered.

What you plant, that's what grows. If you see sin, sin will increase. If you look for demons, demons will show up everywhere. If you root out flesh, flesh will be cropping up in every direction. What you seek, you WILL find, and you won't find anything else.

That's what was happening. We were looking for demons as the cause of our incredible "belief" (that is, unbelief) that God was displeased with the "fleshy" people of Blueberry. (This is not something I would begin to understand until 1996.)

There was a young man come to Blueberry. He was odd; he did not fit the profile. And over time, he did not seem amenable to change. He was not becoming like the preferred personality that being "like Christ" has to be.

So, in one of the many deliverance times we continued to hold, he went up for prayer. I felt to go up and share the prayer time over him with John Austin and Gary Rehmeier. And we prayed up a storm, even pushing on him, trying to get these "demons" to let go so that this brother could become something different. Nothing happened at all.

This experience really bothered me. I began to realize that maybe we were trying to "cast out" his human personality as God designed him. At this point in time, I know that is exactly what we were doing. This brother didn't "look like" Christ "ought to look like," and so we could not see Christ revealing Himself through him as he was.

I am searching for how it was that I defined my world from deep inside my human beliefs and desires. And to do so, I must become honest. And I really can't convey my reality unless I successfully describe my personal view of things at that time, so please bear with me.

The community was our world and our life. We were all committed to the community as to the Lord, with all our hearts. For the most part, this involvement was good and joyous and conveyed many blessings unknown by those who have never lived in such a setting.

But inside the community there was a definite class structure – those who were elders and those who were not. The elders, of course, were not overbearing. They were anointed of the Spirit in wisdom and love, and they gave themselves to the needs of the family more than most.

I wanted to be an elder. – There, I've said it.

As humans, God created us like Himself, including with the desire to belong and to advance in place and role. I didn't want to be an elder in order to be "superior." I wanted to be an elder because I wanted to belong, to be part of this group of people who represented to me everything I longed to be in my life. In all my years in community, I rarely felt that I belonged.

But even more than that, I had known from my youth, deep inside my depths, a word, a desire to speak for God up from my heart, to teach that word in the anointing. Although I shared fairly often in the sharing service, this longing ache deep inside was unfulfilled until November of 2008, actually. It was only then that I had something to share.

I carried the ache of that voice, but no understanding of the gospel, no real words to give form to the groaning of the Spirit inside of me in words that could not be uttered.

In my high regard for the elders, I saw a number of wonderful examples of Christ in an outward and expressive manner on a daily basis, Sister Charity, Brother John Clarke, Sister Sue Sampson, Brother Gary Rehmeier, Brother Don Howat, and so on.

I wanted to be like them; I wanted to be part of them. I wanted to belong.

But I could not. And for reasons I could not understand.

And so from, say, 1988, until the summer of 1998, I was caught in the grip of a great and unrelenting agony. What was wrong with me?

I came truly to believe that there was something terrible, something nameless, something so contrary to God that must be in my makeup, something horribly wrong with me.

And this belief was not my fault or the elders' fault or the move's fault. The fault was the serpent in the garden and how much we Christians believed he spoke the truth, especially since AD 311 when a psychopath took the cross of Christ and turned it into an instrument of violence to hack people's flesh into pieces, and everyone called it "God."

And so everyone imagines that "the cross" means that we have to put our flesh to death, somehow, and that we're always getting "off the cross" and always must make ourselves "die," a Sisyphean exercise that cannot happen because it's neither real nor true.

That was my continual dilemma, for I always got up the next morning, and it was always still me pulling on my pants. No one knows what "die, brother, die," means, they just use it to distinguish difference of place. In fact, in all my years, I have never observed the cross being presented in that way, either behind the pulpit or to me personally when it was not that person, the "ministry," wanting to get me to submit to them, being convinced that I was or we were – not.

BUT – let me qualify that statement again. You see, this path of imposed schizophrenia I am setting before you, and by "imposed schizophrenia," I mean not the split-mind that comes from demons, but the split-mind that comes from fervently be-

lieved Nicene theology, this path can lead only to one place for me – a complete mental breakdown by the end of 1998 – UNLESS.

And that "unless" is three men through the years of my life, three elders, Abel Ramirez, Don Howat, and Rick Annett, who never once placed that false cross upon me, but always lifted me up with encouragement. It was that memory of my successful days with them that I held to as everything else inside was going all haywire. It was my memory of my times with those three men that enabled me to retain my weak grasp upon sanity.

One final thing. I watched a Dutch language television show recently that included an autistic boy just discovering his autistic dad who was behind bars falsely charged with murder. The boy was very bright, however, and he loved his version of patterns. But when people intruded into his space, it felt to him like noise, an unending increase of painful, screaming noise. His acting out was solely his attempt to silence all that painful noise.

My own limitation was not nearly as bad as this boy's, but the meaning was the same. You can see, in my writing, the piercing memory inside of which I hold most every moment of pain in my life. My season of deliverance did bring a resolution of sorts to the difficulties I had known at Bowens Mill and Albuquerque. But from 1988 on, as I was slowly coming out from being oblivious to everything, there was no resolution.

And so event after event, word after word, face after face, gathered itself inside of me as voices of ever-speaking noise that I could not silence. Again, I know what bitterness is, and I described it for you in my time at Bowens Mill. This was not bitterness; it was grief.

You see, at the very moment that God began my season of healing, in December of 2001, every wound of my life was right there as if it had just happened yesterday. Keep that disability in mind, then, as we go forward through these next few years.

I do believe I have given sufficient foundation so that many of the things I must share will have meaning to you. You will have some idea of the why.

More than that, I am absolutely convinced that this path was utterly my Father with me, for the things I know now, that come out from Father and I walking this path together, fill my writing with understanding I could never have otherwise.

And all the way through, I walked in the deep and utter knowledge of the grace of my Savior in which I always lived.

Two Massive New Projects

Although there were always any number of small work projects ongoing inside community life, two specific construction jobs would now fill these two next years at Blueberry, the new washhouse and the new shop. In fact we built them almost simultaneously, going back and forth between the two.

Brother John Austen had received another significant sum of money from an inheritance. This time, he wisely reserved some of it for each of his children. (I suspect this is what he was counseled he should do.) But there was still over $100,000 which he freely gave to the community needs. This bought a new tractor for the fields and a very nice band-saw mill to replace the aging sawmill located above the high gardens.

It also provided around $50,000 for the new shop and washhouse. In other words, we had the resources to build them right so that they would last. Indeed, much of this good resource we then directed into the foundations of both buildings, for this was sandy river bottom, and a building as heavy as the shop would sink and break and tilt in every direction otherwise.

I designed and drew up the plans for both buildings through the spring or early summer of 1991. In all my designs at that time I was laboring under a handicap that I hope to be free from when my season of designing community returns back to me.

That handicap was this. Building a building was a big deal. It took lots of gut effort and skillful diplomacy in every direction. I had the knowledge and the gut; Don Howat had the wisdom and the diplomacy. More and more, we walked together in this role. And in that walking together we shared a lot of commonality of purpose and much good fellowship.

But, not only was building a building a big deal, but a community of this size contained so many and varied small needs, needs that would never get a space unless a space was made deliberately for them. And so my handicap was that I tried to fit into every plan I drew a space to meet all sorts of different needs in the community.

For instance, Brother Roger Henshaw was a machinist and the handyman of the community. He had many tools for his trade and work. But Roger never had a room of his own where he could set up all his tools and work in an efficient space all his own. If I was to design a shop building, then a nice little room just for Roger must be included. Then, Sister Terri Rehmeier was the nurse of the community. Yet always before, any such needs had to be met in her living room, with her nursing implements stuck here and there through her family's belongings. If I was to design a center work building for the community, then a room made specifically as a first-aid station just for Terri, must be included.

And so I designed larger buildings with lots of different spaces in order to accomplish many space needs inside this one construction job to which we had put our shoulders. In an ideal situation, I would not do that, I would design a series of smaller buildings, fitted comfortably together, like a French village, with each one unique to its need. There can be some combination, but not as much as I put into the shop and the Graham River Tabernacle coming up the next summer. Nonetheless, it is my conviction that a healthy community provides a workroom for each person in their interests and giftings that is their space alone, though it can adjoin the larger community space by the pattern of "Private Edges – Common Core."

Part of my relationship with Don and others beginning through this time was the searching together for those things needed to make community life successful in the natural. Such a pondering had not existed when the communities started and so much that was formed worked very poorly and inefficiently. Many community spaces were almost anti-human, which was considered "holy" in the first years, a way of thinking that some of us had rejected, especially since we were the ones crawling under derelict buildings, trying to shore them up.

In fact, sometime through these years, and I can't remember where it fit, John Austin hired a large track-hoe dump truck operation to come out and dig the dirt away all around the back of his house and all around the root cellar which had been built into the slope above the old barn and buried not that many years before. This earth against wood was not working, in spite of some effort to seal the wood. And so, rebuilding the root cellar inside and out and constructing hundreds of small crates for its use is another of my many projects fitted in somewhere. In fact, we had to get the root cellar insulated in with a double wall before the snows came (whether in 90 or 91, I don't remember). So I was given a large crew of men to do that job on a Saturday. The ground was soppy wet, and we worked in mud all day.

I had put Brian on the one task that most needed to be done right, and that was the insulated skirting around the bottom. So Brian had to work in sloppy mud almost to the top of his mud boots all day. We got the job done well, but at the end of the day I looked at Brian. You see, I was covered from head to foot with mud as well as every tool in my pouch. Brian had not one speck of mud above his boots nor on any of his tools!

You can see that we were very different.

We tore down the old washhouse/shop in the center of the community and located the new washhouse basically in that same spot. Don and I decided that we did not want to do a repeat of the poured cement pillars as we had done with Sister Delores's cabin. Rather, we chose the foundation style of driving large creosote logs straight down into the ground. We purchased those logs from somewhere and hired a big pile driver out from town to drive them into the ground. We had considered carefully where a large water line was going through, whose location had never been marked. We believed we would miss it, but we were wrong, the farthest back piling cut it apart. Brian had to dig that out, then and re-splice the water line around the building.

When I was leveling out the tops of the driven logs, then, this was another time when Brian had to come along to tell me I was doing it wrong. I always respected Brian and never thought to do that to him, so I never understood why my ways of doing so aggravated him. I was doing it the best way, however, even though it was not by the book, so I ignored him and kept on.

Once the washhouse pilings were in place, ready for the building to be constructed on them, we left that project for the next summer and turned to the foundation and floor slab of the shop. This project was a bigger deal. The shop would be forty feet wide and ninety feet long. I made it two full stories with further spaces inside the roof with dormers as

the third floor. The shop had three large bays, 30' by 30' as their base size, but with a ten foot space at the back that would serve as tool and work bays. Each bay was divided from the other with a large roll up door, with large rollup doors at either end. This way a large logging truck with a load could be driven in one end, be entirely inside with the doors closed to be worked on, and then driven straight out the other end. To the furthest bay, however, we enlarged it twenty more feet on the east side so that a large grader could be driven in through another rollup door on the side and be completely inside of a heated space. The concrete slab beneath where the grader would sit had to be much thicker and stronger to hold its great weight.

All the large beams and roll up doors that we needed for this project, and all the planks for both shop and washhouse, we had obtained from the shop we tore down in Fort St. John. I designed the building partly to fit these components.

The new shop building was located to the east of the washhouse, just inside the road curving up the hill towards the root cellar and across from the old barn. This was silty river-bottom land. I was not fully confident in my engineering knowledge, and others were less confident, so we employed an engineer out from Dawson Creek to determine what our foundation must be so that the shop would not move. He sent out a test driller to get a core sample of what made up the ground beneath. Maybe ten feet down through soft sand there was a several foot band of watery slush at the level of the river.

So, Don and I drove down to Dawson Creek to see the engineer and get his recommendations. As we sat there, he looked at the core sample details, then he reached up, pulled a book off his shelf and opened to a chart, the very same chart I had taught Terry Miller from my own construction books. He put his finger on the lowest number and said, "You have to design the foundation to fit this load level," so much thickness per pound of weight sitting on it. He also drew out for us a basic sketch of how the footer, stem wall, and slab should fit together and how the rebar should be structured. That was it, $1500 to know which book to pull off the shelf. – Oh well. It was worth it, however, for now we were free to build the right foundation with confidence.

But – I still had to design it all myself including calculating the differing weights throughout the whole building.

Constructing this large foundation was a huge task, but a lot of fun. Brian and/or Randy dug out a deep trench all the way around with the backhoe. Our foundation wall would be five or six feet tall, all underground, with a thick and wide footer beneath of it. We constructed and assembled forms all the way around. We bought big bags of cement from Edmonton and trucked in loads of sand and gravel. We filled the forms with rebar as we built them up. We hired a concrete mix truck to come out and sit beside the job site. Randy would fill its hoppers with cement and gravel, the operator ran the mixer, and we received the pouring concrete all the way around. Once the side walls had dried, we filled the space again all around them and packed the dirt with thumpers, similar to a jack hammer. When the ground was once again even with the tops of the walls, we were ready to pour the slab. "We" included myself, Don, Dani, Terry, John Austin, Brian, and quite a few others not normally in the building crew assisting with this job.

One issue in designing our new shop that concerned Don and me was that the move communities had a long history of woodstoves in shop buildings burning the shops to the ground. We did not want a woodstove in our new shop. For that reason, that prior winter, Don and I had visited a large personal shop next to the home of a trucker in Charlie Lake, just north of Fort. St. John. This man had installed a hot water heating system inside the slab before he poured it. That meant that, at 30 below zero, he could drive his ice-covered truck into the shop late in the evening and find it dry and warm by early morning. Because the heat was coming up from the concrete, the entire building was easily and inexpensively warm. Don and I had this man carefully explain every part of his system to us. We also obtained pamphlets on this heating style.

We then put in an entire hot-water under-slab heating system for the new shop. Randy constructed the metal pipe hubs where all the lines would come together. Once this was all in place, with the rebar (and triple rebar layers under where the grader would be parked), we were ready to pour the slab. We also asked Tony Cobb, from Dallas, Texas, to come up and help us with this large pour. He was one of those who had come to Citra to help pour concrete while I was living there.

So, with Brother Tony's help, we poured a large and beautiful concrete slab for the shop floor. I did some research on finishing the slab and learned that raw linseed oil was best for new concrete. The next spring, after it was fully cured, we spread two coats of raw linseed oil on it before we began any construction. This made it the best shop floor I have known. Sweeping sawdust with a large broom meant no dust at all left behind on the first pass.

And so, before the winter came, both foundations were in place. And the shop slab and foundation were all one piece; no part of it could budge without all of it shifting together. But because it was so large, such a shift would never happen.

The School Year

This school year had begun before those foundations were complete. I had a full teaching load this year, though I was no longer teaching Terry Miller. I had the history classes as well as English in the high school, probably two English classes. I attempted to use the *Writing Road to Reading* to improve the spelling in one group. That was the class with Paul Austin, Jesse Rehmeier, Chris Kidd, and now John and Michelle Mancha. I learned from that experience that, while that full phonetic approach was great for children learning to read, it did nothing to improve spelling skills for high schoolers. I appreciated teaching the full range of world history as well. I believe that it was the next year, however, that I taught Church history as a full-year course. This exercise gave me the broad and specific grasp of the movement and patterns of world history that I so much appreciate having.

Then, this year I was given the wondrous privilege of teaching two full college courses all on my own, one in the fall semester and one in the spring. In that fall I taught The History of the English Language and in the spring The History of Education. I tell you what, for both of these courses, I applied more design principles with more effort and carefulness than any design I had ever done before then. Oh, this was heaven for me. I think that my students enjoyed two wonderful courses. I had maybe eight to ten college students per course; even Sister Sue Sampson enrolled in and took my History of the English Language course. That was fun for me.

Rarely in all my life did my heart sing in the joy of doing than it did in the teaching of those two courses. As I remember back now, overall, this was a good school year for me.

Our Home & Kyle and Kimberley

Let me place Maureen and I together with our little boy, Kyle, along with Kimberley in our little cabin. It was a good little home which we remember with fondness. By the next summer, Kyle was talking and running around, before he was one, so I have to separate that away and just remember him as an infant. At this point, now, I have Maureen to help me remember.

But one thing that we did together took place in the summer a month or so before Kyle was born. You will remember that I love few things better than exploring the wilderness, preferably in a vehicle–hiking relationship. I had gone before with a number of college students to a place called Sikanni Chief Falls. I wanted to take Maureen there now, with Kimberly and Sola for a picnic, probably on a Sunday. To get there, you drive north up the Alaska Highway past Pink Mountain and across the Sikanni Chief River. Then you turn west on Mile 171 road for several miles until the road ends. There, you hike about a mile along the high bluff above the river until you arrive at the rocky area in full view of the falls. Here you were just above where the water went over the edge. Before, we had hiked down to the bottom of the falls which were about 100 feet high, but Maureen was pregnant, so we did not try that. If you want to see pictures of the place, Google Search – Sikanni Chief Falls. You must understand how much I love the wildness of the north. I even gasped looking through these pictures for I recognized the rocks. And yes, I went with Kimberley and Sola to that breathtaking view out over the top of the falls that you see in the pictures. We went there several times over the years.

Enjoying this day together, taking Maureen, Kimberley, and Sola, into a wilderness experience that I loved, is a happy memory for me.

We had a happy little home together. Kimberley was helpful and kind; she never responded to us as she had to others because she had no need to protect herself. Maureen and I always treated her in the highest regard. And Kimberley was great friends with little baby Kyle. It's a bit sad that he was too young to remember that friendship.

Because I was now part of Maureen's life, I enjoyed all of her friends coming to visit. Maureen just naturally drew people in and made a place for them inside her friendship. And so many more of the sisters in the college and community became a part of my life as well. Our home was always a place of refuge, not in "rebellion against," but in the receiving of Christ. And, of course, many came just to hold and play with Kyle.

Having a son was a big deal to me because I have always known that we, each by ourselves, meet with God face to face, and that such an answering is utterly real. And I have always known that no relationship with God can ever be imposed, but must always arise from within, in a joining of heart with Heart. I am convinced that God must meet with each of my children and they with Him inside of their own hearts, that nothing true can come any other way.

Inside of this certainty, however, I also knew just how inadequate I was, and how my own limitations made me incapable of giving to Kyle all that he needed to grow up inside a personal knowing of God. And so I held my son, close to my heart, with tears streaming down my face, and I covenanted with God, that He would be and do towards my son what I could not be or do.

God is a keeper of Covenant.

We had a dilemma in the layout of our house, and that is that we had a small wood stove right in the center of a fairly small space, a stove that burned hot continuously through the long winter months. As Kyle began to crawl, I considered building a fence around that stove, as some have done. We did not have enough space, however, and I was also convinced that no fence would keep a determined little boy out. The probability that he would burn himself badly on that stove was pretty high.

And so I chose to implant inside of him the understanding that "stove" equals "pain." I would let him get near the stove, and then whack him, either on his rear or on his hand as he reached out towards it. It's called corporal discipline, the inflicting of a lesser pain in order to prevent a far greater pain.

It worked. Kyle seemed to be a fast learner and soon we no longer needed to be concerned about the stove.

When Maureen and I took the course to become foster parents here in Houston (which we chose not to complete), we were presented with the philosophy from the state, that corporal punishment is evil. The vicious hypocrisy of this claim was overwhelming to me. You see, the state, along with the general public, will condemn in great self-righteousness, the paddling of a twelve-year-old boy for disobedience. But when that boy turns eighteen and he disobeys the state, the cruel punishment inflicted upon him without mercy by both state and public is ten thousand times worse than a simple spanking. This is true evil.

That being said, such care for one's children works only inside of a general environment of respect for their person and tender regard and attentiveness towards them, that they know they belong and are deeply loved. This truth will mean a whole lot in the growing up of our children.

That December, Maureen and I drove down to Oregon with Kyle to visit our family and for mom and dad to see their new little grandson. Dad could not respond, but I know that he was aware and got to hold our boy named after him. We took a roast of moose meat with us. I remember how Tim and Dave, my brothers-in-law exclaimed over how good that moose roast was. While we were all seated in the upstairs larger room, visiting, Kyle was sitting on one of my knees. Without warning, the little guy swung down and bit my other leg just as hard as he could. I have no idea what inspired his little mind to do that, but boy, that one hurt!

My Dad's Funeral

I must insert two things that happened in the early months of 1992. First, after our trip down to Oregon in December, I had invited Glenn and Kim to come up to Blueberry for the convention the first of March, which they did. They had two children at this point, their son, Alex, was around Kyle's age.

Partway through the convention, Glenn received a call from Mom in Oregon. Dad had passed away. Glenn had not been there to help Mom get him up. She was doing chores outside when Dad gasped for breath, but could not breathe. Glenn took it hard, blaming himself for not being there. He and Kim left to return to Oregon right away. Dad was seventy-four years old.

A few days later, I flew down to Oregon by myself for my Dad's funeral. It was a good time in Oregon with my brothers and sisters and mom. We had a brief memorial service in the funeral home in Lebanon. Dad was buried in the Lacomb cemetery on a grassy slope overlooking the Beaver Creek Valley about half a mile south of Lacomb.

There was a growing animosity between my two brothers, however, Franz and Glenn. This prob-

lem will factor into my life story and so I will share more of my brother, Franz's, growing disability in later chapters.

I think there might also have been a bit of a conflict regarding "blame" and "responsibility," along with Mom being caught in-between. Understand that, at this time in our lives, my brothers and I were very limited in our ability to communicate together and most of what we said to each other had to go through Mom.

Glenn and Kim now lived in the downstairs of our house and Mom was in the upstairs as its own apartment. When everyone else had gone home and it was just Mom and I, I felt some need to "correct" Mom regarding her handling of an issue, which I no longer remember. I waxed eloquent in the anointing, showing her the "error of her ways." Mom listened to me quietly and patiently. When I had finished, she shared the reality of the situation with me.

I was completely and entirely WRONG, and the shamefulness of my self-righteous posturing was clearly evident to me. This was a very important moment in my life, for it showed me the fallacy of assuming "knowledge" that God, in fact, never gives. If God does not remember our sins, how could He inform His "prophets" of things He does not know?

Nonetheless, this definition of "discernment" and "correction" was deeply embedded in move-of-God practice. God was making sure I was hit hard with the reality of its falseness. I would be hit hard many more times ahead until my Father succeeded in burning all of that wickedness from my own heart.

Kyle and Surgery

Kyle was born with one eye turned in. Thankfully, in Canada, all medical costs were covered by the government and the hospital system is big on putting the needs of children at the top.

In February of 92, we began to take Kyle to the hospital in Fort St. John regarding his "lazy eye." They had us keep a patch on the good eye so that the brain would be forced to connect with the "lazy eye" and not cut if off from its knowing. The staff in Fort St. John also connected us with one of British Columbia's leading pediatric ophthalmologists, Dr. Cline from the Vancouver area. Dr. Cline included children from remote areas in his practice and would travel where needed to perform surgeries.

Kyle was scheduled for surgery in April. This was overwhelming, especially to Maureen, that our baby would be placed under sedation and a knife put to his eye. The day before the scheduled date, however, Maureen received a phone call from Dr. Cline. He shared with her that he had Kyle on his mind all day during his surgeries and wanted to see Kyle early in order to know for sure that surgery was necessary. Dr. Cline's concern brought complete peace to Maureen. Indeed, I don't think we have ever connected with a finer medical practitioner in our lives than Dr. Cline.

Dr. Cline did operate on Kyle's eye on April 24, at the Fort St. John hospital. The surgery was a success, but a second surgery would be needed, which would then take place in January of 1993. In between the two surgeries, we continued with the eye patch so that Kyle would learn to use both eyes. The second surgery was also exactly as Dr. Cline intended, and thus no more was needed. Kyle uses both eyes, though they remain somewhat independent of each other.

The Russians and Graham River

Let me begin with the Russians. I'm not sure, but I think that it was 1991 that the Russians came to the Peace River Country. I'm not sure of the dates, but I will place this experience here that included many instances over time. They were actually German Russians, whose families had moved from Germany to Russia under the invitation given by Catherine the Great. Many German Mennonites had also moved to Russia to be farmers at the same time. In fact there are over two million ethnic Germans scattered throughout Russia.

The story of these brothers and sisters in the Lord can be found in a book titled *The Siberian Miracle* by Peter de Bruijne. That is their story, of course, but through the years of 1991 to 1992, my story in community was connected just a bit with theirs. To be honest with you, this book is one of the most important that I would recommend you read. There is truth in it that is vitally needed for all Christians in our world today as tyranny re-imposes itself everywhere.

This story is of two pastors, father and son, both named Victor Walter, in their struggle to be the church together in community inside Communist Russia. They won this struggle in the late eighties, just before the Soviet Union came apart, and the

KGB allowed the entire church, who had been living in community together outside of Vladivostok in far eastern Siberia, to emigrate together to Germany. Because they were German, they were recognized automatically as German citizens, but they did not feel comfortable inside a highly populated and worldly society. After about ten years there, they sought to immigrate to Canada, to the Peace River region, which is very similar to Siberia. They could not immigrate as a group, but all the families did manage to immigrate separately.

The older Victor had passed away before they left Russia, so it was the younger Victor Walter who brought them into Canada. They purchased two separate farms along the Halfway River on the road to Graham River and began to build two separate, but related Christian Communities on those properties. Their liaison in British Columbia was a brother named Boris. Boris knew of our communities and had visited them before this. Victor Walter visited Blueberry with several of the men and Boris, probably in the early summer of 1991. He came to request aid from our communities and from Blueberry in helping them build their new communities.

In the end, the Blueberry elders agreed just to send Don Howat and me over to give them what construction and design advice we could give. At the same time, Amos Deardorff chose to live among them for a period of time, maybe two summers, to help them set up their farming operations. These were good people, but very legalistic and their attitudes towards women we did not share. It was wise that we did not become too involved, though we helped them with good suggestions.

Another thing that happened in this spring of 1992, then, before the school year was over, is that Brother D and Sister Ethelwyn asked Don Howat and I to come visit them at Graham River and give them suggestions as to their construction needs there. Of truth, Don and I worked together like this to help brethren at Evergreen and Hilltop as well. We had become a recognized team together. And so Don and I spent a weekend at Graham River.

Brother D and Sister Ethelwyn had the cabin at the end of the row above the gardens, that had once been the Herman cabin, and onto which Steve Herman had built a greenhouse, which was still functioning. That's where Don and I stayed, but all the gatherings for meals and services were in the former Davison cabin in that same row, where I had lived with them years before. Some of the interior walls had been removed to make it a larger and very comfortable place to gather. There were maybe twenty or thirty people now living at Graham, most of them involved with music and praise. They had restored a number of the cabins and had added onto them.

The problem was that they were growing rapidly, many people from all over were asking to move to Graham River and to be a part of the Shepherd's School of Music. And, of course, the original Tabernacle and school building were no more. The brethren at Graham wanted our advice regarding how to meet their need for a larger Tabernacle.

As we walked the community grounds and through our discussions together, it came clear that a large project would be difficult for us to help on, since we had full obligations back home. Graham River at that time did not have dedicated builders who could have tackled such a project. In the discussion, however, I remembered my wonderful experience at Bowens Mill when a large crew of men gathered together and built the Woody Crossin house in one weekend.

I suggested that this might be the solution to their need, that they might send forth a call to all the communities for many to come together at Graham for an extended weekend (four work days) and, with all the materials already gathered, raise their new Tabernacle in one great community effort.

Brother D and Sister Ethelwyn became very excited about this possibility. It wasn't long at all before they made it official and asked the Blueberry eldership if they would agree to release me to design their new Tabernacle and for Don and I to be released to plan and prepare for this great gathering that would number 65 men, to raise their new home in four days.

I was now caught in the expectation of the four most glorious days of my work life. At the same time, I was becoming comfortable in this new role that Don and I shared together and how we were now becoming known throughout the area communities.

The second half of this chapter will cover the next seven months, June through December of 1992, a time filled with an extraordinary number of things. And now, for the first time, I see God's determination towards me, not just through these months, but all the way to October of 2011, and all I can do is place my face upon the ground before a holy and a mighty God and worship Him.

To my utter astonishment, everything makes perfect sense, and all of it is good.

I must also place inside of anything God might be doing in my inward person the wonderful blessing to Maureen and me that was every person at Blueberry towards us. to do that, I am including a few more pictures of our graduation and wedding.

All the students in the college. Frieda Raja is on the far left and Terry Miller on the far right.

On the left: Brother Claude giving me the greatest gift in my life. Above: Martha Jordan, a picture of out-poured love, and representative of many others.

Below: Taking communion. This picture includes a good shot of Brother John Clarke, who married us.

22. Glory Against Shame

May 1992 - December 1992

This chapter is just a continuation of the last. I will not bring things into resolution until the end. The problem with God is that there is no escaping His determination once He has set it upon you. I have spent years kicking and screaming and can testify that there is no escaping the bony finger pointing right at one's forehead. What I mean to say is that I don't really want to write this chapter, for it should be titled "Glory inside of Shame." Yet it will not leave my mind and so I will escape it in the only way possible, by placing it out into the light into whatever the Lord intends to do with it.

The Summer of 1992

From May through July, we put up the outer structure of the washhouse and started the new shop. By the end of July we had weathered in the washhouse with the roof on and doors and windows in place. Maureen and I were planning a trip down to Bowens Mill and Texas in August. We must have finished the large structure of the shop with its high walls and large heavy beams after our return. We would not finish the interior of either one until the winter months.

I was at the center of those two jobs, with several men helping, especially when we got to the shop. Nonetheless, they were not my main focus through those months. Rather, I devoted much of my time to designing and planning the Graham River Tabernacle. I spent more time at Graham, visiting with the brethren there about their needs for a new Tabernacle. Bill Alter was the elder with whom I spent the most time. He had moved up to Graham from Arkansas with his family to be part of the Shepherd's School of Music. Bill did have some construction knowledge.

I was given much liberty in designing the new Tabernacle. I designed it as an L-shaped building, except we would build only the larger rectangle first, forty by sixty feet, with an L of forty by forty being added later. It was two stories with a large steep-pitched roof, at a 45-degree slope. The bot-

tom story would be mostly underground, with the west wall at ground level. The ground there was sandy loam on top of river rock, and so draining a basement would be a simple thing. A forty-foot-wide building meant that the third floor would be twenty feet high in the center.

The design was, bottom floor, a 20' by 40' foot root cellar, with the other 40' by 40' area containing a utility kitchen, laundry, and storage. We planned for underfloor heating like the shop at Blueberry, but we also put one wood stove in this area. The main floor would be a well-laid-out kitchen above the root cellar and a 40' by 40' dining room. The upper floor inside the roof would include a living apartment above the kitchen and the remaining area for the Shepherd's School of Music. That part would be open but with dividers as needed. My goal was to meet many different needs of a community all in one building project.

Overall, it was a simple layout. I designed it to be double insulated. But I did it better this time than before. The main wall was 6" thick and then a 6" space with an outer frame that just hung there without carrying any weight, upon which the siding could be fastened. Inside that 6" space, we could wrap the entire building in 6" of fiberglass, with only the glass of the windows not being inside that blanket. And I did put in lots of large windows, especially in the dining room.

I designed beams of plywood and floor joists and rafters made with OSB sheeting cut at 16" strips with a 2x4 on each side, like an "I" beam. The rafters could then hold 12" of fiberglass with a 4" airflow space above it. I made special care to design the plumbing and electrical connections to fit into an accessible vertical and horizontal chase so that the main pipes and wires could be easily added to or worked on.

But drawing the plans was only one-third of my job. I also created an exhaustive materials list. That means, every single board, plumbing piece, etc., in its exact dimensions. I drew complete layouts of every wall, etc. We were also planning for a cement floor in the basement and a large septic tank outside. Every single item in every part of this large building I drew out and dimensioned, metal, wood, pipe, wire, concrete, caulk, etc. You see, when 65 men gather to put up the building in four days, there can't be any hindrance to the constant smooth flow of work. Everything must be on paper in front of them so they can just DO.

And so, as I planned and drew, I also built every single part of that building in my mind's eye, fastening everything together in my imagination, step by step, so that I would not miss anything. That was the third part of my task, then, to layout an exact order of construction tasks hour by hour through four days. In order for everyone to keep working at full blast, every task had to be coordinated.

I divided the work into eleven different crews, each with a crew leader. That way I only directed eleven men, and they directed the several in their crew. I will share more of that when we get to those four days in September. By the first of August my plans were mostly completed and I gave Don Howat the materials list for the brethren at Graham River to purchase and bring to the building site. Don would take the materials list out to Graham, while Maureen and I were gone, and help them in obtaining everything needed.

Our Trip to the South

Because my mother no longer had dad to care for, she was free to come visit us at Blueberry. She came up in June, when everything was green, and spent six weeks in our home and in the community. Kimberley had returned home after she graduated, so Mom stayed in what had been her room. After that, it became Kyle's room. Kyle would turn a year old in August, it turned out, while we were in Texas.

Maureen's grandmother, Susan Jacobsen, who was one of the elders at the Ridge, was having her 90th birthday celebration to be held at Maureen's uncle's place, Stan and JoEllen Miller, just outside of Stephenville, Texas. This would be a large gathering of her entire family, all of Sister Roberta's siblings and all their children. This was a chance to celebrate the godly heritage Grandma Susan had given to all.

We drove down to Oregon, taking Mom back home, and then up to Seattle, Washington, to board a flight to Atlanta, Georgia. One wonderful aspect of living in community was that there were no bills back home needing to be paid. All of our needs were met inside the community and thus it was much easier to travel with little money than it is now when we seem to be earning far more money but are tied down to all the bills. Claude and Roberta, who had returned to Bowens Mill from Graham River for the summer, picked us up at the Atlanta airport and we drove on down to Bowens Mill. We spent a few days visiting there at the Ridge before heading for Texas.

While at Bowens Mill, I received a phone call from Don Howat. He had gone with Dural and Ethelwyn into Fort St. John with my list and they had priced everything, It came in at well over $100,000. Don told me that the normally placid and calm Brother D was "hyperventilating." But Don is a diplomat, and he was able calm them down and get them focused back on faith and on God's provision.

At that point I suggested that we do the construction in two parts. Just complete the basement now, with a temporary roof on it and all the ground work finished, and then, in a couple of years, we could do the second floor and the permanent roof. This phased-down plan would still cost maybe $60-70,000, so it would take great provision from the Lord to be able to keep our plan for four days in September.

Grandma Susan would be traveling to Texas with Claude and Roberta. That meant that Maureen and I, with Kyle, would drive ourselves in Grandma Susan's little Toyota. I needed some dental work done, so Brother Jim Fant suggested a dentist he knew back in Greenville, Mississippi, who would do the work for a reasonable cost.

It was a beautiful drive across the South. I always try to stay off the freeways in the South in order to enjoy the country roads and the lovely landscapes. On our way out of Georgia, however, I had a strange experience. I was just driving when I felt a profound "snap" in the back bottom part of my brain, right at the junction of the cerebellum and the brain stem. I did not know fully what it meant, but as time went on, I noticed that a familiar connection inside my brain was no longer happening. This is hard to explain, yet when I raised the issue with the Doctor of Psychiatry at the University of Houston, who is an expert in Asperger's Syndrome, I learned that this disconnect at middle age is indeed common among Asperger's.

It was as if the thinking/dreaming part of my brain slowly began to drift apart from the acting/doing part. This had some pluses, for I soon began to sense that my overwhelming internal drive was no longer so powerful. I could relax a bit more. But, as you will see, it was not too many years before this disconnect would become problematic for me and for my family. Now, I have no idea what actually happened inside my brain tissues on this drive to Mississippi, or if it had anything to do with anything. Nonetheless, the passage of my life from strength to no-strength turned that August of 1992. I was thirty-five years old.

As we approached Greenville, we passed through a dark and fierce thunderstorm, with rain dropping as sheets and no visibility. That was a bit scary. The dentist in Greenville was highly contemptuous of anything in natural health. To him, mercury fillings were God's gift to mankind. He did a poor job on my teeth, the two he worked on would have to be pulled within a few years. I'm sure the new mercury did not help my brain disconnection.

We drove on to the Miller home outside of Stephenville, Texas. I finally got to meet all of Maureen's aunts and uncles and cousins. Peter and Patti Honsalek were there; they had lived and married at Bowens Mill during my years there. It was a good time of celebration. Grandma Susan could still get around well at that point, four years before she passed. Her godly life had passed on to generations of off-spring.

When we returned to Bowens Mill, a friend of Maureen named Susan, whom she had known in Brussels, agreed to drive us back up to the Atlanta airport. On the way, however, we wanted to make two stops in the Macon area. First, we visited with Andrea and Dina LaFera. They were not walking with the Lord at the time and were a bit wild, but they were dear to us. When we left, Susan had to go back in to retrieve something she had left. She told Maureen and I later that she overheard a friend of theirs, who was also there during our visit, asking Dina about Maureen and I. "Wow, they are real people, aren't they?" And Dina answered, "Yes, they are."

We then visited Charlie Jones who was in a hospital in Macon having just had knee replacement surgery. It was good to connect with him again.

We flew on back to Seattle, and then returned to Blueberry before the end of August.

The Next School Year Begins

Many things were happening back at Blueberry, besides the start of the new school year. First, we finished the construction of the shop, with a completed roof and all the doors and windows in place. That way we could work inside to finish it during the winter months.

At the same time, money had come in from all over for the new Graham River Tabernacle and the brethren there were busy purchasing everything needed and ferrying it across the Graham River. The water was low, so they were able to tractor a wagon across the ford. I had planned for the brethren at Graham to dig out the building site and to pour the footer prior to the great gathering. Because this building was sitting on solid river rock, the foundation was relatively simple.

At the same time, people from all over were communicating their desire to come and be a part of this great endeavor of providing a new Tabernacle for the family at Graham River.

Something else that had happened this summer, however, was that this next school year of 92-93 would be the seventh year for many of us on student/work visas. That summer, Mr. Wenham, the immigration officer in Dawson Creek, had let us know that our time on temporary visas must come to an end. A number of us at Blueberry would have to leave Canada by June of 1993. We received this as from the Lord, being grateful for the graciousness that had always been extended to us by the Canadian authorities.

Nonetheless, the only thought anyone had at Blueberry was that it MUST BE God's will that we all find a way to immigrate and to return to Blueberry. Those whose visas would expire in 1993 were Maureen and I, Don and Martha Howat, Mike Pelletier, Laura Weitz, Terry Miller, and Sister Mozelle Clark. And so every one of us except Laura seemed to be caught in this great enthusiasm and need that we must immigrate because we were "part of Blueberry."

To immigrate, then, one must have a way of earning an income that did not take jobs away from Canadians. So we were attempting to come up with any number of "business" ideas that might work. I have since learned the Canadian immigration system well and now know that most of our ideas were just a waste of time. In fact, of all of us, only Maureen and I did immigrate to Canada, and that was by an entirely different reason – which is a later story.

Another family, the Franklins, had moved to Blueberry that summer. The husband, whose name was Alan, was an elder, and they also were interested in immigrating to Blueberry, and so were part of this ongoing discussion.

The school year began before the time planned for the raising of the Graham River Tabernacle. My teaching load was much less this year, maybe about half of a load. That way I could give more of my time to the completion of all the building projects. Paul Austen, Chris Kidd, Jesse Rehmeier, and John Mancha were all seniors this year. Paul, who had been short all his life, grew a foot this year and became as tall as Jesse.

These were mature young men. Nonetheless, the exaltation of "the flesh" had grown inside the move, and the common view of teenagers was that they were almost entirely of the "flesh," and thus could never be trusted. At the same time, almost the entire school faculty were single intellectual women, the type that gravitate towards teaching college.

We planned a wonderful project for the start of the school year. We would put on a series of survival training sessions, some of which would be given at the Oxbow. Different ones in the community would teach different types of skills. I suggested to the school faculty that the seniors be given some responsibility for this occasion and that they be allowed to teach a session as well. My suggestion was counteracted immediately and completely. "NO!"

The problem is simply this. Yes, intellectual single women have much to give, but they have no knowledge of young men. The thought is only to control their every move out from an unsettled and misguided fear. It was a good project, yes, but as I watched those four young men, denied responsibility of any kind and almost neutered in their need to be respected, my heart groaned for them. That, and other similar things through these years after my graduation caused my heart slowly to disconnect from the Blueberry School. By the end of this school year, I would be done with this particular all-controlling version of schooling.

The education council of British Columbia had devised a new approach to education. There is an entire story of their attempts to bring the move community schools under their control, and how our principled stand for freedom caused them to rewrite the law down in Victoria, the capitol, in order to allow schools like ours to remain free. I will not share that story in detail. Nonetheless, in this new approach to BC education, there was an interest in making the schooling experience more practical and hands-on for the students. I saw this as a way to more truly integrate our practice of education with our community life style. Everyone else saw it as the intrusion of the devil.

I bring this in here because I will have much more involvement with BC education in coming years as well as my own attempts to devise a better way to teach middle school children, including my own, later on.

The Graham River Tabernacle

And so we come to the four days of September, 1992, and the gathering of 65 men to build the first part of the Graham River Tabernacle. I will describe the plan first, and then the experience.

I had chosen eleven men to be the leaders of the eleven crews. I gave to each of these men a complete layout, hour by hour, of their crew's tasks through each of the four days. Reality would change the timing of that layout, but the ordering of tasks would remain similar. It would be my role to keep everything flowing together.

I had two main framing crews and a third, small-project framing crew. A young man from the Ridge who was an experienced framer had come up with Claude and Roberta; he led framing crew 1. My brother, Glenn, came up with his wife, Kim, and their children. Glenn led framing crew 2. Then, Dani Maldonado was the crew leader for the small-projects framing crew. He would do things like stairs and bays, leaving the two main crews to alternate with each other in the raising of the walls, the building of the second floor, and the construction of the roof.

Don Howat was the leader of the electrical crew. Tony Cobb came up again from Dallas; he led the concrete crew, a big crew because they were also forming and pouring the large septic tank. Bill Alter led the saw crew. He had lists of every board to be cut in order and he and his men did nothing but saw everything to length. The framing crews assembled only. Another brother from Graham led the materials handling crew. Their job was to get all supplies to where they were needed at the moment they were needed.

I forget who was the plumbing crew leader, that crew would also install the underfloor heating tubes. David Miller, Sister Jane Miller's son, along with Terry Miller (no relation), led the cabinet construction crew. They were set up with good shop tools in a nearby shed. They would have the cabinets ready for installation the moment the space was ready for them. Del Buerge had come down from the Yukon to be part of this time. I think he worked with Dani Maldonado. That crew would also do the construction of the outer false wall and the outer sheeting. There was a crew for insulation and sheetrock. That makes ten crews. I had eleven, but I don't remember the other one.

On a prior work occasion, we had done two meals a day. I suggested the same for this project. We would start at 7 AM and work for two hours. Then we would have an hour for a huge and hearty breakfast from 9-10 AM. At that point everyone was hungry, and we chowed down. That large breakfast, then, carried everyone until late afternoon for a wonderful dinner after which we worked a couple more hours for a ten-hour work day. This system works great, with less time spent on meals and better eating as well. Sister Ethelwyn led a large crew of sisters who were all really good cooks.

All of my crew leaders were experienced and professional men, and so all the willing helpers had good guidance in their work. I was thrilled to have my brother Glenn there as one of my crew leaders, participating in a wonderful community experience.

Our four days were Wednesday through Saturday. Most would remain Saturday night for a worship meeting in our finished building on Sunday morning. All the crew leaders had gathered on Tuesday afternoon to go over the plan together. I had a blackboard and began to explain the layout of the work to the crew leaders. Brother D stopped me however, and apologized for not having started the meeting with prayer. I was a bit embarrassed as he prayed, placing all of this great gathering into the Lord. You see, I was a "get the job done" sort of guy. Nonetheless, Brother D's gentle correction lodged itself deep inside of me, and I gained from it the great importance of placing everything into such faith-prayer.

By supper time on Tuesday, all the men had gathered to be ready to get started at dawn. After supper, in the twilight, Don Howat and I walked together down the airstrip for a ways and then back. During the day, he would work under me, but otherwise, Don was my strength. We talked about the coming days, and Don encouraged me greatly in strength and in the Lord. The truth is, that time with Don was as important to me as the whole project experience.

Let me describe the flow of the work on the first day. Remember that there were sixty-five men on this work site. The concrete crew began the forms for the septic tank right away. The saw crew had already started sawing. The cabinet crew began their work in the improvised shop. The electric crew were working out the main line to come underground from the generator. Meanwhile the two main framing crews were positioned on opposite walls from each other. As the materials crew brought them their boards, the crew leaders unrolled their drawings for each wall, the long side walls first. All they needed to do was place the boards where the diagram showed, nail them together, and raise the wall. Then, the two crews took one an end wall and the other the first inner bearing wall. After that, while one of them built the second bearing inner wall and the other end wall, the other crew began setting the joists on the one side of the floor above. As the crew beneath finished the remaining lower walls, they came behind the crew on the joists, and sheeted the newly laid joists with plywood.

Just as soon as the first twenty-foot bay was covered and it was safe beneath, the plumbing and insulation crew came in to install their work. And as soon as heating pipes were installed in the first twenty foot bay, the cement crew switched over to installing the rebar and pouring the slab. You see, the concrete floors would have to be poured and then have time to dry before further work could take place in those rooms. We did include an ingredient that made the cement dry more quickly. I was very glad to have a professional like Tony Cobb overseeing that difficult work.

By noon my carefully laid-out time plans were no longer in sync with the reality of the job flow. I was at the height of my construction skill and experience, and this was what I was made for. My task was to replace that time schedule, to circulate constantly from one crew to the next. I knew more about what each crew and even each individual was doing than they did. My task was to be sure that each thing needing to be done was completed so that the next crew could start their part.

The anointing of God came upon me, and I walked in a knowing of all things in this construction task. It was seldom that anyone had to pause for the lack of knowing what to do next. It was seldom that any crew was blocked because something was not yet ready for them to do their part. I remember only a bubble of grace and of joy, of knowing and wisdom and direction. It was glory to me, the best experience of my building career. There were, of course, many problems and even some contentions, but those were all worked through in good order.

By the end of the fourth day, a Saturday, everything was coming towards completion. The septic tank was finished and covered over and the roof was on. The sheetrock was mudded and the cabinets were being installed. A number of the men kept working late into the evening, but before Saturday was over, we were finished with all we had intended to do.

That Sunday morning, we all gathered inside the new dining room, which, for the present time, was the space that would become the root cellar. We ate a breakfast made in the newly completed utility kitchen. The electric lights and the piped water were all working. And we worshipped God together. Such an anointing came upon us; we knew that God had done a mighty thing in our midst, in this wondrous flow of community work. We knew that we had tasted together of a glory yet to come.

Darkness and Shame

Let me include another factor in my life experience through this season of Blueberry that had begun several months before. Lloyd Green was a few years older than I, a strongly self-assertive man who had definite ideas about how work in the community should be conducted. Lloyd was very good at presenting himself as "the expert," and Don Howat and all the elders seemed to be excited about what he could bring to the work flow of the community.

Lloyd wanted everything discussed and fully "planned" by experts. What people don't realize sometimes is that work does not happen just by planning, it happens by gut, by getting in under the responsibility of the job. Things don't go by

"plan," decisions have to be made on the spot by those who have the heart to bear the load. I was very good as the primary community work leader, which at that time was mostly construction, especially with Don as my oversight. I would often show up at the job site early before anyone else and, as I walked the site, I would draw out from my gut the flow of the day. My heart was given utterly to the needs of the community, and I would bear any weight on my part that was needed.

In order to establish his own place, Lloyd would have to sabotage my hands-on role and wrest my place in the community work from me. I don't think the elders understood that. I'm not sure what was in Don's mind. Everything of the construction work came out from me, but it went to the elders through Don. To some, I think my role might have appeared small. Lloyd was not a doer, but a planner and even a conniver. Getting under the weight of an individual job did not seem to be in his sights. But I had no ability to express that. I had no ability to convey to anyone the reality of the work and my role in it. And my stuttering attempts to explain seemed to some to be nothing more than a petty attempt to control on my part.

In the weeks leading up to the Graham River Tabernacle experience, Don had been sharing with me a new direction for the community work at Blueberry that the elders were considering. Only two of the men elders participated in that arena of work, Don Howat full-time and John Austin part of the time. Lloyd's ideas of the leading men to sit down together and to plan out every detail of every project before the men went out to do that work, was to be the new order.

Other non-elders who would be part of this planning team would be Brian Dwyer, Randy Jordan, Philip Bridge, Sir James Barlow, Roger Henshaw, Lloyd Green, and Steve Ebright. Don assured me with great faith that I, also, would be part of that team.

I do not know fully the sense of the elders towards the Graham River Tabernacle project and towards the new role Don and I were finding as other communities looked to us for leadership and advice. I know that some had expressed disagreement and that Blueberry's participation in the Graham River project was not wholehearted. Again, I perceived that some, by knowing only my outward shell and inability to socialize and communicate, thought that my stance was one of conceit and self-serving.

But of my peers, those listed above, with all their many good qualities and skills, there was none with the aptitude and the heart to get under the load all the way through and to make the big construction needs of the community actually happen. Yet to explain this reality in a way that could be understood and received was far away from my abilities.

A few days after I had returned to Blueberry from the Graham River project, Brother Roger Henshaw, who was considered as a deacon, took me aside in the dining room to share with me the decision of the elders. He said that the elders had determined that I was not ready to be a part of this new "planning" team.

Roger was gentle and kind, of course, but he was not an elder. Where was Don Howat? I did not know. I did not know what this could mean. The idea that this new approach could actually produce good results was not real. My complete exclusion from the planning process after years of all the construction planning coming out from my own heart and gut was outside of my ability to comprehend. I knew what it was like to work under others and I hated it, because all you did was stand around most of the time watching them do all the work, and giving no directions to anyone. When I led the job, I always had my eye on everyone's progress and was ready with the next task for each the moment the prior task was completed.

I was not to sit with my peers to discuss the work I had carried all these years. Yet I would have to fit under the "plans" created by men who, except for Randy and Brian, did not do any of the work. To say that I was thrown into a great agony of confusion and humiliation would be an understatement. It was Don who had encouraged me to believe that I would be part of this; where was he?

That evening, Sister Barbara James was there for another deliverance service at Blueberry. Deliverance services were seeming to become the "solution" for every apparent lack in the community because we did not know Christ our life. I was sitting with Maureen in the back of the room. At a certain point Lloyd Green came by and beckoned me to come upstairs with him. We sat down in the sitting area at the top of the spiral stairs. Lloyd wanted to "talk" with me.

Maureen was disturbed by this and she went over to Don Howat to inform him what Lloyd had done. He assured her that I would be fine.

Lloyd presented himself to me as the spokesman for the elders. I was already confused, humiliated, and deeply wounded. Lloyd's "appointed task" was to explain to me why the elders had decided I was not mature enough to participate in the new order for work, most of which would now be coming out from him.

I was now in the hands of the most powerful psychopathic bully I have ever experienced in my life, and I had no defense. He began by ridiculing and mocking my role in the Graham River project, making it seem little and meaningless. He was very skillful at taking any word I attempted to use in my defense, twisting it back against me with even greater ridicule. Lloyd mocked me in every conceivable way. He mocked my upbringing and my dad. He mocked my Mennonite background. He belittled my role in the community and in construction. He made fun of my place as a husband and a father.

I had no defense. Don did not come to help me.

After about forty-five minutes, he was finished. I don't remember my stumbling walk home through the snow to our cabin. I do remember crawling into bed, and, even as I drew the covers over me, so I also drew darkness over me so that somehow I could hide my shame.

You see, Lloyd was speaking, not as the elders would ever have sanctioned, but, nonetheless, entirely out from their decision that I did not belong with my peers and that my years of pouring out my life for the needs of the community were not to be honored.

From that moment on, for the next ten years, the years of the birth and early lives of our four children, the bottom-line of my self-story would be one phrase, over and over, "I am so ashamed of myself."

Do not ever imagine that calling people "flesh" is benign or that you do no harm. The death that you sow must be reaped, and how many will suffer before it comes back to you again?

A Word from God and Near Death

I stumbled through the next couple of weeks, mostly in the school, in a daze of hurt and confusion. I waited for Don to come and explain things to me, but he never did.

Do not think, however, that I am so easily defeated or quenched. I had set my heart from age 22 to know God and to be part of a people who know God. I have never once thought to take my heart back ever since, regardless of all my searing inability.

I did not understand things then, but I had no need to be concerned about the new "order" for the community work. Creating a complete plan with all the details filled in before a job is started is unreal. Certainly, I made a detailed plan for the success of the Graham River project, but if we had followed my "plan," it would have become an unmitigated disaster. We would have been nowhere near finishing, and all the men leaving would have counted it as a terrible experience.

The simple problem is that those who plan are not those who do. And the requirements of actual reality meant that I continued to be the source of all ongoing construction do-ing regardless. There would be sadness inside that experience for me, however, some of which I will share in the next chapter. Of truth, of all the men at Blueberry, only two could lead a large task on the spot as I did,. Bryan, of course, when he wanted to, and the other was Dani Maldonado, who did step very capably into my role after I left Blueberry and made me very proud to have been a teacher to him.

I want to step aside from that particular diffculty, now, and bring in a much more important issue through these three months of October through December, and that would be the future and direction for Maureen and me and our family.

As I said, the press to "immigrate to Blueberry" was very strong. Don and I were busy planning what business we could start that would enable us to immigrate. For awhile we entertained the idea of the bandsaw mill and starting a wood business. When we dropped that idea, Alan Franklin from England asked if he could take it on as his way of immigrating. We freely gave that idea to him while Don and I looked at other ideas. I lighted upon the idea of starting a seedling and plant nursery using the greenhouses. None of us knew anything about making a production business successful, of course. We had no idea that the majority of any business is selling and if you're not in the business of selling you're not in business at all.

But none of that was the issue for me. The thing that disturbed me deeply was that I was becoming aware of a growing lack of witness towards immigrating to Blueberry. In saying that, I am not speaking of inward hurt, even though that was certainly a factor, but the growing realization in the Spirit that Maureen and I did not belong at Blueberry any longer. It was not God's place for us.

But I still wanted to immigrate to Canada.

Meanwhile, talk had begun among the regional elderships about a restoration of the Shiloh community, but with a new name, named after the small creek that flowed through that valley – Blair Valley. Sometime in October, this hope of a new community starting was shared with everyone.

I continued laboring intently before God, that He would show me the next step for us. I could not walk in my "prayer walk" area because it was covered with snow. So I walked the road across the Blueberry footbridge and up the hill, in intercession before God for His direction. I remember this as a burden of many weeks, and of much placing myself before God to know His ways. Some of those things I will share in the next letter however, since this season of God with me would overlap into the first five months of 1993.

It might have been in October or November. I remember walking up to the phone in the bootroom of the Tabernacle, but before I could reach up, a word from God rose up out of my spirit. I had, just before, raised the question again to God about our immigration. I heard, "Immigrate to Blair Valley." His words to me were in all singing joy and peace. Such relief, such hope and direction. I shared it with Maureen and she witnessed to those words. Afterwards we shared it with the Blueberry Eldership, and they also witnessed.

We had a new and exciting direction, filled with possibilities.

Nonetheless, life continued at Blueberry, and I remained crippled and grieved in my soul. I weakened physically as well. From the time that large wall fell on me, to this day, in fact, I have had a frequent pain in my right side, in the liver area, where the claw of my hammer had gouged, though it had not penetrated. I have never known what that pain meant, nor has any doctor been interested in or knowledgeable of such a thing.

I don't remember when, through the course of these months, but at a certain point, with advice from others, I determined that maybe I had gall stones. I went through a gall stone cleanse, using large quantities of olive oil. It was horrendous, but I did pass quite a few greenish stones. That did not solve the problem, however.

Then, it was always difficult, if not impossible, for me to switch my mind from a teaching-school mind to a construction-work mind in the same day. Because I was no longer teaching full-time in the school, I experienced a lot more back and forth. Nonetheless, it was a switch I could no longer make. On a new morning, yes, but not halfway through a day. And so I began to know unproductive time, something new for me in my community experience.

Finally, by December, the grief of my heart had become sickness in my body. I had shared what I had endured with Sister Charity, but other than assuring me that the elders were NOT behind Lloyd Green's actions, she had no word of Christ for me.

I became very sick – pneumonia. We were not against going to the hospital, but it was, for me, only a last resort. I wanted to believe God for healing. It became difficult to breathe, a weight pressed down on my lungs. I could hardly breathe at all lying flat in bed, so we constructed a plywood ramp against our little couch so that I could sleep in a sitting position.

This continued for a few days. I was not getting better. Claude and Roberta came by for a day, but they were experiencing some difficulty with each other and their contention in our little home increased the pressure against me.

Several of the sisters who were not elders, including Kay Smiley and Michelle Ebright, came to pray for me. They prayed with such joy and hope. I was greatly blessed and for a little while seemed to be doing much better.

Then several of the men elders came into our little home to pray for me, John Austin, Dave Smillie, Don Howat, Alvin Roes, and maybe Wes Shaw. These are all precious brethren and I honor and respect them. That afternoon, they were in the full regalia of "move elders," something I would not come to understand until several years later.

They spent maybe twenty or thirty minutes praying "at" me. Their prayers included my deliverance from "what was wrong with me" that so obviously was the cause of this continued sickness. John Austin was pressing hard against my chest. I

was afraid to ask him not to do that because I did not want him rebuking my words as a demon. But I had to because I could not breathe. God is always kind because he accepted my request and removed his hand.

When they finally left, there was only one thought in my mind, "Do they even think I am a Christian? Do they even think that I also love Jesus?"

Early the next morning, Brother Alvin drove me on icy roads to the hospital emergency room in Fort St. John. All the way in, I rejoiced in the Lord, that He was keeping me in all goodness. Dr. Watt, whom I had seen before, was there. His diagnosis was quick, and I was placed immediately on an IV with powerful antibiotics flowing into my system. I did not know that I was almost dead.

Don Howat had come into town that day with his family. In the late afternoon, he stopped by the hospital to see me. He did not stay long, but I learned later what happened after he left. Don went out to his car and told Martha and their children that I was near death. Together that little family prayed for me. All I knew of it then was that a few minutes after Don left my hospital room, a darkness lifted off of me, and life was now free slowly to return.

Antibiotics are destructive to the health of the body, but they are always better than death. Dr. Watt had to use the most severe at his disposal to save my life at the last minute. I was three days in the hospital, and when I returned home on Christmas Eve, I continued in a weak state.

Nonetheless, through these last weeks of 1992, I continued to seek the Lord concerning His direction for us. Part of my cry was the growing realization that we did not belong at Blueberry. Where did we belong? Where was there a place where Maureen and I could fit and be a part of family life in honor and respect?

Inside that expectation of God, He spoke to me again, another word rising out from my heart in such overwhelming joy and wonder.

"Blair Valley will be your home."

This was so good, except for one small problem. "Blair Valley" did not yet exist.

Placing Jesus within the Press

One should never take on any sense of "responsibility" towards a psychopathic bully, for such false thinking will do nothing more than increase the power of the dark spirits behind it over you as the victim. Whatever Lloyd Green is or does, he belongs entirely to the Lord Jesus Christ and not to me. When his time of giving an account comes, I will receive him, without question, but not before. Rather, I place him entirely and only into my Savior.

Deliverance from that experience did not begin for me until 2014, and only as the Lord led me, in my mind's eye, to KICK Lloyd Green right out of my life, full stop, with both feet in the chest. This was the doing of God and the first time that I could consider any part of Blueberry without unquenchable pain.

At this time in my life, however, I know exactly what God was doing and why, for the issue is far bigger than I have known before. And in that knowing, I bow myself before Him in awe and worship. God is good and wise all the time.

The elders at Blueberry are a different matter, however. I must place the Lord Jesus Christ upon them regardless of their lack of understanding and theological perversity. It is right for me to do that with two in particular at this time, and that is Don Howat and John Austin. Others will come later.

I know that they believed they were moving in the "wisdom and counsel of God." I know that Jesus lives in their hearts and that they love Him and are committed to His glory. What they did not know was how contrary their theology was to the gospel of our Salvation or how devastating their words and actions could be in the lives of people they did not fully regard.

"Lord Jesus, I give You thanks for Your involvement in my life through Don Howat. You gave so much to me through this good man, so very much. I do not know what was in his mind when he did not come to help me. Nonetheless, I freely forgive him with all my heart.

"Lord Jesus, I give You thanks for Your involvement in my life through John Austin. He has always been a faithful and devoted expression of Your love. I know that he did not know what he was doing. I know that You carry him all the way through the darkness and into life.

"Lord Jesus, I place You upon me all through these months. I know that You never intended the wrongful things, but that You always intended me in spite of them. And I know that You and I together turn whatever was harmful into unending goodness for others that many might also know Father with them. Lord Jesus, I know that Father's purpose in my life passed through these difficult things to become great and precious treasure in my heart, for You have turned what was evil into Your keeping power in my present experience now and forever.

"Lord Jesus, You are so good. You have always been the only life I am. And You were there carrying me tenderly inside Yourself, even though I did not know what that meant."

I complete this letter in great sorrow. I cannot yet give resolution. I know that peace will come in its time.

"Father, I know that my desire to cry right now is Your desire to cry, for the disrespect we sometimes show to one another hurts You even more. And You are so good, my Father, to cause us to share Your heart that we might be life and goodness to others just as You also are life and goodness to us."

23. Return to Oregon

January 1993 - December 1993

Such Peace

Such peace has come to me, such incredible peace. After writing the last letter, I knew the deepest sorrow and I wept. But slowly through the day my sorrow turned into a peace beyond understanding, the pure knowing of Father with me.

After reading the last chapter, you now realize why writing about Blueberry was difficult for me from the start. Indeed, it was only through the last few weeks of trying to put off writing the last chapter to "some distant point in the future" that I began to understand that it was indeed shame that became the story of my life, a shame that would work its crippling effect in both body and soul until it had stripped from me any strength I once knew.

At the same time, I continue astonished to discover so little in my time at Blueberry that was anything other than goodness and blessing in interacting with wonderful people. The shame robbed me even of that memory through all these years.

I want to apply a bit of hindsight now, in order to place everything into God and into a true perspective. Two things of importance were happening with me. One was the conflicting stories of self that I knew regarding myself, a conflict that showed itself clearly in my first attempts at writing and that would not be resolved until the week before I sent out my first *Christ Our Life* letter in November of 2008.

My real struggle was inward with the argument of the serpent, coming through the theology of the word preached, that Christ was not my life, and that I had a life not-Christ. All through these years, I knew the development of two opposing stories. On the one hand, God was planting His word as Christ inside of me and my knowledge of the grace of God always grew, even though it seemed to grow slowly. But on the other hand there was the fear that was engendered by the false belief that there was something terribly wrong with me.

I would know both stories intimately and through great pressure and in every imaginable relationship situation.

But the other reality governing my life through all these years was God's unbelievable intention towards me. This was a passage through which I must pass in order to have what I presently possess in order to share life with you.

How could I now divide for you between life and death, by the fine cut of the knife, if I did not know both in all closeness. That which is destructive so easily appears to be life and that which is life-giving so easily appears to be destructive. When a reader speaks words to me that are destructive, but that they imagine to be "Christian," having known such words through their entire Christian experience, the separation between the false and the true cuts through me like the finest and sharpest of blades.

I know the difference. And I know the difference because of this incredible path upon which God walked with me. And because I never spoke against, but honored even those who were not always treating me right, I am also able to bear with that cutting in the present time and to show to the one speaking the wondrous goodness of Christ our only life.

School and Writing

The spring semester of 1993 was my last in the Blueberry school. I taught there for seven years. I don't remember much from this final semester. I see from my layout that I must have taught College Geography again, this time as the sole teacher. At the end of this school-year, I saw my second five-year group, including Paul Austin, Chris Kidd, and Jesse Rehmeier graduate from high school.

The desire to write had been with me since I was a teenager, but having something to write had not yet come. Probably because of an ongoing conversation with me regarding that desire, Paul Austin told me that he wanted to help provide for that newly awakening direction for my life. Paul bought me my first word processing-typewriter, a Sharpe, I believe. It was an electric typewriter, yes, but with a small screen that would show a line of text before it then printed it onto the page. That way I could see my words before the typewriter printed them accurately.

This was one of the most precious gifts to me anyone has ever given. I placed it on our little dining room table and began to write. I had two books in my heart at that time; one of them I titled "The Unveiling of Jesus Christ," and the other, "The Great Story of God." In the end, these two merged into one volume, which I would complete through 1994. I will share more of that in the next chapter.

So my first thoughts in those directions began to appear on the little screen in front of me.

One thing I do remember from that semester that I must include was that Lloyd Green taught a class in the high school, I believe it included Anita Deardorff, Wendy Rehmeier and Stephanie Ebright. His classroom was next to mine and I could hear his words to them as my own students were studying. I heard, but could hardly believe, for he spoke in a quiet undertone such contempt and rebellion against the elders to those girls. He was very good at presenting a different face publicly, but it was not just towards me that his words brought ruin and loss.

God with Me

As I said in my last letter, do not think that any difficulty could separate me from my ongoing relationship with God or my desire to know Him by His word. And so I want to include a number of things that won't be connected by any sequence of time.

First, through this season, I had a most extraordinary dream. I will give words now to that dream, words that are accurate, but which I may not have known then. In my dream, I found myself entirely inside of Jesus and I found Jesus entirely inside of me.

Union with God had been a growing topic in the move through the early 1990's. John Clarke had preached on it. In fact, it had been Sam Fife's view of our entrance into the Holy of Holies. Nonetheless, such a life was always presented as something to be attained, yet remaining now just beyond our reach.

In my dream, I KNEW that very union with Christ now. And inside knowing that union, I knew NO consciousness of sins.

When I woke up, it was not long before the theology of "sin in the flesh" and all the terrible feelings that come with it, came rushing back in. Nonetheless, I knew that what I had known in my dream was real. I shared that dream with the family in the sharing service. I presented what I knew in that dream as our goal, rather than our present reality as I know it now. Sister Sue Sampson got up after and shared how much that vision of our union with Christ meant to her. Sadly, we did not know that it was already and entirely true.

I had another dream in which my dad came to me and held me in his arms and comforted my heart with peace. When I shared that dream with Sister Charity, she cautioned me that it was just a good vision from the Lord and not really my dad. I appreciate fully her purpose, for those who seek to communicate with the dead will be caught in their own vanity by glorious but false spirits. Nonetheless, I still think it was actually my dad coming to me in the heavens.

At the same time, through these months I wrestled with the call of God upon my life in deep groanings. I would read the first several chapters of Ezekiel or the first several chapters of Deuteronomy and my spirit would groan with a knowing beyond what my mind knew. I never tried to make anything mental out of those times, I just held them before God.

I was troubled by how easily I forgot what God speaks in His word. And so, through these years, many more times than once, I would press my Bible against my chest and, in great tears before God, I said, "Oh my Father, if it be possible, write this Word upon my heart so that I might never forget what You speak."

God was also speaking to me about my role towards His people, but in cryptic ways, which means I really had no idea what He meant. Of truth, what God means can come only out from an utter rest inside of knowing our already completed union with the Lord Jesus Christ.

I read the book, *Pass Me Another Brick*, by Charles Swindoll, concerning the meaning of Nehemiah's story. God spoke things of great meaning to me through this book. In fact, you have read my referencing those things many times through my letters. Maureen and I both read *How You Can Be Led by the Spirit of God*, by Kenneth Hagin, which gave us a very different view of walking with God, in liberty and joy rather than the obligation and falling short that was the common view of the move and, indeed, of most of Christianity.

I pondered the meaning of community inside the anointing of God, often in the services, and God began to show me some things about His ways that could shape a new Blair Valley community. If you have read my text, *Symmorphy V: Life,* you will have received many of those things fully developed that were then coming to me in beginning form.

It was in these early months of 1993 that God planted in me a vision for the community of my heart. With the words, "Blair Valley will be your home," I took that to mean that, just as my Father had brought Maureen to me, so He would bring to me a people who would know God together with me as I had covenanted with Him to do. In myself, I was as incapable of the one as of the other.

At the same time, God was speaking to me from a different point of view, that which I had learned in my study of the lives of Saul, David, and Absalom – what do you do when someone throws a spear at you? Except in getting my full attention, God had included the strongest example of Christian rebellion in the Bible, even more than Absalom – Numbers 16 – the rebellion of Korah.

"Who do you think you are, Moses? God speaks to all of us, not just to you."

This finger of God would only increase against me through our time in Oregon, this agony of seeing shortfall in those whom God had placed over me in my life. How would I respond?

Continued Sorrow

There were darker things, however, that seemed to conflict with these wondrous things I was beginning to perceive in my relationship with God. Again, these are not connected by time, for I have no idea what happened when.

Eric Foster was driving a logging truck for the NorthStar company. He had pulled off the Alaska Highway to check his load. A pickup was driving by containing a man and his teenage nephew. The driver did not see the corner of Eric's truck and hit it head on. Both of those in the pickup were killed. The police determined that Eric was not at fault, and Gary Rehmeier must have connected in some way with the family in Fort St. John who lost their son.

Out from that experience, Brother Gary preached a word to the Blueberry family that sums up the kind of "God" we believed we lived under, the attitude of the eldership towards the family, and the dark belief of Nicene Christianity under which we all have labored. You see, we were preached at and exhorted so often that we who were not elders were NOT measuring up to the word or to the requirements of God. We heard so often that we were fleshy and unsubmissive. I would not really understand this attitude until 1996 when I sat with them as an elder.

Brother Gary shared about how this young man who was killed was taken in a moment. There was great sobriety upon his words. He shared about another young man in a move community in Peru who had "rebelled against the elders" and had left the community, who was then killed by some accident only a few days later. The insinuation was clear; if we did not get with it and be obedient to God and submissive to the elders, then we could expect a like punishment from God.

That sounds starker, maybe, than Gary preached it, but it is much better to reduce things down to what is actually being said so that those things can be clearly seen. And I in no way "blame" Gary, for he was sincere in what he thought God meant. Nonetheless, this was the clearest example of using God as one's whip that I have heard.

Through these months, Sister Charity spoke several more things to me that were dark (in the midst of all the good things). One time, little Kyle was running excitedly around the dining room with Maureen trying to catch him. Sister Charity warned me, "You have to get control of him, Daniel, or else he will be lost." I can say to you now that I have stood against that word all the way through and if you would know my son now, you would know just how false that dark prophecy really was.

As we were all preparing to leave Blueberry, with the Howat's going back to Washington state and Maureen and I to Oregon, Sister Charity said to me, "God isn't doing anything in the Pacific Northwest." I will show you how God proved those words completely wrong through both Don and me.

Then, in counseling with Sister Charity, she spoke dismissively concerning my mother, indicating that she was not mature in God. I knew this was not true, and I will say now that my mother was more mature in God than Sister Charity. God's measurements are very different from the human definitions found among those who see by outward appearance.

Again, I am NOT sharing these things to disparage Sister Charity, for I received more goodness from her than just about anyone in my life. In fact, I am convinced that Charity, after she passed into the heavens, sought out my mother from her driving desire to know the truth of Christ. But that is a topic for a later chapter. The reason I am sharing this is to show this gauntlet of God pressing against me, words that would sink deep inside that caused me to run and run and run with all my being into the knowledge of God.

Partly because I seemingly had not been honored in my work in the community and partly, probably, from Lloyd Green's influence, some of the young men whom I had taught in school now began to mock me just a bit in the work times. I did not understand this and bore it only inside of increased sorrow and shame.

Because the shop and washhouse were not getting done, the eldership decided that we should have a large work weekend with all the men of the community, including those who worked out, all working inside one or the other of those buildings, putting in the insulation and the sheetrock or plywood sheeting on the walls. As I had said, the proposed "planning" system was not real, and so, I led this whole project as well.

My problem was that I had begun feeling a physical weakness, including the pain in the liver area. I had gone to the hospital, but it was a different doctor than Dr. Watt. I shared about doing the gall bladder cleanse and was informed that such a thing was stupid and unreal. They took x-rays and told me that my intestines were plugged a bit, basically, that I was full of crap.

This diagnosis added to some of the contempt I was feeling from some. The continued physical weakness prevented me from doing much physical work that weekend, and so, I felt a sense of "we neither want nor need you, Daniel," coming from some.

Don did have me meet together with Randy and Bryan concerning finishing the shop. I shared that I was sensing that my time in bearing the construction needs of the community was coming to an end. They did not understand what I meant.

My point is this, slowly, there came the growing sense of sorrow that I no longer belonged at Blueberry. This was the doing of God, for His purposes were far greater.

The February convention was held at Blueberry in this early part of 1993. During this convention, the ministry of the move considered more specifically the reopening of the former Shiloh farm as a new Blair Valley Community. At that point, several different elders from the area had expressed a leading, that God was speaking to them about being part of that new endeavor. Maureen and my leading to Blair Valley was also considered as part of that discussion, but we did not know yet who the other people were.

After the convention, Wes Shaw asked Maureen and me if we would spend a few days with him at Blair Valley as he was taking a care-taking stint there. We leapt at the chance to spend more time there inside the present speaking of God. It was early March, with long nights and short days still, and a few feet of snow everywhere. We stayed in the same caretaker's house.

For some reason, however, both Maureen and I felt uncomfortable inside, not for any outward reason, but something inside our spirits was troubled. On the way back to Blueberry, Wes shared that he was one who was planning to be a part of the new Blair Valley, which was why it had been Wes communicating with us concerning our leading. This was a shock to us, yes, but both Maureen and I felt immediately a disconnect, that something was not right.

Even as the various families did move to Blair Valley to begin the new community that summer of 1993, with Wes Shaw among them, we continued to feel troubled. We had no outward reason to think that way, but even though I continued to believe that Blair Valley was God's destination for us, the present sense was a very strong, "Not yet."

By May, we knew that Maureen was carrying our second child.

Preparing to Leave

Our plan was simply to return to Oregon and to live with Mom, with the hopes that we could continue to work on an immigration business possibility there. She had plenty of space for us in her large upstairs "apartment" in our house. And so that's the direction of our face the last couple of months we were at Blueberry.

A couple at the Evergreen community hired me to draw a set of plans for a new house they wanted to build. They had the funds to do it right, and so I was able to charge what such a job was worth. This income helped provide for our move back to Oregon.

My brother Glenn had acquired a Chevy Step-Van which he had begun to fix up for his welding work. However, mom negotiated with him that she would pay him to give it to us. Glenn had completely rebuilt the engine – it ran on propane. He had put a heavy steel floor throughout and a heavy-duty bumper. He had painted it blue and installed two nice seats that Franz gave him for us.

Sometime in May I bussed down to Oregon and drove back up with our new Blue Van. I planned carefully how everything would fit and we loaded it with all of our stuff. We set up our mattress, however, so that we could sleep in the van on the way. We positioned Kyle's car seat just behind Maureen and strapped it to a steel bar.

I am sharing two pictures of our Blue Van as we

were preparing to leave. This van will factor much in our lives through the coming years. I loved it a whole lot, and I miss it very much.

Brother Claude is saying goodbye to us; the Dave Smillie cabin is behind him and our cabin on the right. Then, the school is on the right and the tabernacle on the left in the lower picture. The cabin in the distance was the Ebright cabin; it would become our home as well in a few years.

Before we left, however, the family at Blueberry put on a special occasion, a banquet, for all of us who were leaving at the same time. They had prepared a large table in the center of the dining room. The rest of the family ate their regular dinner, but William Brown, who had been a chef at a top-notch hotel, cooked us a many-course meal and Sir James Barlow, who had served as a waiter in a fine restaurant in Northern Ireland and who conducted himself as the finest of the English aristocracy, served us. It was a meal for which one would have gladly paid $100 a plate. When we were finished, different ones of the family shared what each of us had meant to the Blueberry Community.

Don and Martha Howat would be going to Sequim, Washington, where Don's brother lived, Terry Miller to the Lubbock, Texas community, Mike Pelletier to his home state of Massachusetts and Laura Weitz to her home state of Wisconsin. I'm not sure where Sister Mozelle was headed, though she did end up in the Atlanta area.

And so we drove out together, Maureen, Kyle, and I, to a new adventure. Seven years of Blueberry were behind me; I was 36 years old.

Back Home at Mom's

I loved the trip down in our van. I loved sleeping along the road and then climbing right into the driver's seat while Maureen and Kyle remained in bed. We spent a couple of days with the Pacy's in Abbotsford. We have a hilarious picture of their goat chasing Kyle. We arrived back home in Oregon the first week of June and to the bedroom that had been mine through my teenage years.

Having Maureen now sharing my own home as hers was just wonderful to me. Showing little Kyle all around, splashing in the mud puddles, playing in the yard where I had played, was such a joy.

I set myself right away towards developing a business for immigration to Canada. I had chosen the nursery and gardening business because it featured high on the list of preferred businesses for Canadian immigration and because I have always loved growing things. Our living costs were low, we added little to utilities, and we ate out of the gardens and out of mom's pantry. Mom agreed that I could spend a few months devoting myself to this potential business.

In Oregon, gardens can't start until the first of June because April and May are just too wet to even work the ground. Mom had moved her garden from the old, worn-out garden area to the space just to the east of the house, right on the other side of the yard fence. Just to the north of the yard and driveway, in the same open field, I prepared a space for my own garden. I was ambitious, and I made it large. I kept the diagram of it, where everything was planted, for many years, but I don't know if I have it still.

I dug out three rows of raised beds, running east and west, with nine beds in each row, and each bed maybe 3 feet wide and 15 or 20 feet long. The ground was sloped gently down and faced Buzzard's Butte across Crabtree Creek. I planted a lot of stuff, and this being Oregon, my garden grew abundantly.

By July, Maureen and I were taking produce from the garden to a farmer's market in Lebanon each Saturday. We were beginning to experience "business." We sold lots of raspberries, a few green beans, and not much else. I built several lovely herb boxes out of cedar wood and offered them for sale with herb plants in them. None sold. We were off to a very slow start.

Glenn and Kim with their three children, now (their second daughter, Jessica, had been born), lived in the main part of the house. Glenn operated a welding shop in the barn I had helped dad put the roof on years before. He had a steady flow of work. Frieda and Tim, with their two children, April and Ryan, now lived in a house in Canby, Oregon, about fifty miles north of us.

Right off the bat, we started having Sunday morning services in the main living room of the house – Glenn and Kim's living room. It was Mom, Glenn and Kim, and Maureen in attendance, with Frieda coming down often, along with April and

Ryan. Maureen led the praise and I shared the word. They all took the things that I shared very seriously and were open to Christian community.

During this summer of 1993, Dan Ricciardelli visited us with his family. Dan was a traveling ministry in the move and he shared the word with us who were gathered at Mom's. They spent several days with us, during which we hiked the Silver Creek Falls park. While they were with us, John and Nathel Clarke also came through. I drove all of us up to Gresham to the Rutledge's, but could not find their house until the evening was mostly gone. There was time, then, only for Brother John to share briefly with the group gathered there. It was not one of my better attempts at navigation.

My Family

I am brought up short in the present moment regarding my natural family. At the present time we are scattered all over the continent. We have little face-to-face connection, and I am not a long-distance communicator. All have known great wounds; not all are walking closely with God. Some followed me into move community – and then I left the move! Although there is understandably some bitterness, I also know that there is a genuine love among us.

Yet I ever remember the covenant my dad made with God in tears concerning me, and the faithfulness of God in keeping that covenant. My mother, continuing in her own family traditions, had made a beautiful quilt for each of her children. Mine might have been the first; I took it with me when I first went to Graham River, and it was my bed cover until Maureen and I were married. In its old age it became a favorite outing blanket for my children. But Mom did not stop with her children; she continued right on to make a quilt for every one of her grandchildren as well, each one unique and beautiful, twenty-six in all over many years.

My mom is one of the greatest women of faith and faithfulness that I have known. It is not possible that she did not pour her heart out in the expectation of God for each one as she spent weeks and months crafting each quilt as her work of love and her covenant with God for her children and her grandchildren.

My sister, Frieda told me that she and her children followed me into move community because she saw the change in me and knew that it was God.

You are My Son, today I have begotten You. Ask of Me, and I will give You the nations for Your inheritance, and the ends of the earth for Your possession (Psalm 2:7-8). I have the right to be a son of God, for Christ Jesus is the only life I am. I have the authority from God to lay down my life for the sake of those whom He has given to me.

I would honor my father and my mother. And I would covenant with God for the sake of all who belong to them, many more than twenty-six when you count those whom we have married and our own grandchildren as well. It is my right and my authority, that they would see the proof of Christ in me as God returns us back into Christ Community in the present season, and that each one would run into the Lord Jesus Christ in all fullness as the gates of Tabernacles are flung wide open. Let any cost fall upon me, for my Father shares all with me.

Many Moves

Franz and Audrey had returned to Oregon several years before and were renting a house on the south side of Lebanon. They had taken a principled stand in Nebraska regarding homeschooling at a time when it was illegal. Franz was charged and went to trial, but he sent Audrey and their children to Oregon where they would no longer be subject to such false law. Franz defended himself in court and won. His case was written up in newspaper accounts and helped change the law in Nebraska for other families.

The place Franz rented had a small shop and a large yard area. He had started a bee business that included making and selling wooden bee boxes and frames as well as raising bees for honey. This would be his livelihood for many years – Snow Peak Apiaries.

Prior to our return to Oregon, a disagreement had arisen between Franz and Glenn regarding mom's property. To mom, it should go to Glenn and Kim since they had remained at home to care for her and dad. Yet Franz also felt a claim to the property, since he was the eldest and had helped dad to build the first parts of the house.

We did not realize at the time, but Franz was beginning a slow decline into a mental disability that made him see things darkly. Frieda believes it might have stemmed from the accident in Michigan, when Franz had been badly battered as a boy. Glenn was still in his twenties and did not take kindly to some of the ways in which Franz moved. A reciprocal animosity had begun to grow between them.

And – I am sharing Franz's difficulties through these years because they did color many of our decisions and because I intend to bring these difficulties to a very specific conclusion inside the Lord Jesus much later in this narrative. In sharing these things, however, I place my brother entirely into the goodness and grace of God, and any difficulties there may have been, I see only as resulting in the goodness of God. Nonetheless, through this time, I did not understand his disability and held him responsible for his confusing actions. Should not our oldest brother know better? I am so glad that I no longer see it that way.

Glenn and Kim made the decision to leave Oregon and all the promise of continued contention far behind them. This was a big deal, for Oregon was all they knew, and Kim, also, was very close to her family who lived just a few miles away. They made the decision to move to a Christian community in Detroit Lakes, Minnesota, that was part of the move fellowship. I handled much of the communication with the move ministry and with the Detroit Lakes eldership. The visions that were sought were confirming, and so Glenn and Kim prepared to move with all their belongings.

This would mean, then, that the property and mom's house would go to Franz and his family, now four children, Jason, who was in his early twenties, and Rachelle, just a couple of years younger. Then Nathan and Camilla were quite a bit younger. In fact, Nathan spent more of his childhood and youth calling that place home than I did.

And it would also mean that Maureen and I would need to find a place elsewhere. Mom chose to come with us and leave Franz and Audrey free to make the place their own. So, we went to see the man who owned the house where Franz and Audrey had lived. He readily agreed that Maureen and I could rent it at $500 a month.

And so, while Glenn and Kim were preparing to move to Minnesota, Franz and Audrey were preparing to move out to the house in Lacomb, and Maureen, mom, and I were preparing to move to their house in Lebanon. I do not remember the timing of any of this, just that it all took place in August. I am very glad that we had our Blue Van; it was a workhorse.

Glenn had built a large trailer onto which he loaded all of his work tools, etc. He pulled that with his pickup loaded full. Then, he asked me to drive his Bronco, also filled with stuff. I might have also pulled a rented trailer. And so, in the midst of all these moves, I helped Glenn and Kim in their move to Minnesota. I remember stopping at a rest stop along the way, somewhere in Montana, and sleeping in our vehicles.

The brethren at Detroit Lakes had found a mobile home in the nearby town that Glenn and Kim could rent. They would be a part of the community as much as possible, however. Glenn soon found work at a manufacturing facility. They were well-received by the brethren there and fitted right into the family life.

Glenn bought a train ticket for my return, and so, I hopped on the Amtrak passing through Detroit Lakes and took the northern route across the prairies and through the Montana mountains. I really enjoyed the leisurely trip with comfortable seats and the liberty to walk around, including going to the dining car. It was much better than the bus. Seeing the Rockies via the train track route was awesome as well. This was one of so many treasured experiences God has given me.

Upon my return to Oregon, we settled into our new home on South Main Road in Lebanon. This would be our home for almost two years. The pictures are as it is today, mostly the same.

Country Herb Gardens

Let me begin by describing our new home. This was a good home for us, filled with blessing and many good memories. The front wing out towards the road was a large living room with an alcove on the left that became my office. The living room was one room with the dining room, whose window you see in the right side picture as the middle window, towards the back. Then, the last window is a small downstairs bedroom. In the left side picture, the wing in the back is the large kitchen and the bathroom, with an enclosed porch entry. The back roof had been enclosed as two bedrooms inside the low slope, accessed by a steep stairway. Maureen and I took the one on the right and we put Kyle into the one on the left. Mom took the downstairs bedroom.

Behind the house was a separate garage with a nice workroom on the side closest to the house. The yard was large and closed in with a solid double-high block wall along one side and a thick row of trees on the other side. Inside this large area were several apple trees, rose bushes, a grape vine and a large garden area. One difference is that we did not have a fence along the road, which was not a good thing. But we felt very tucked in and protected. A nice grocery store was just down the street and a smaller-sized Walmart was only a couple of blocks behind us. We were still in town, but the houses were thinning out and countryside was not far off.

Mom agreed to continue to support our living costs while I worked on starting a new business. On the one hand, I had a wonderful space for the business. Because our space was part of the rental shop next door, it was zoned commercial. I had plenty of room for gardens and several greenhouses with a good shop and work room right in the center. One drawback, however, was that my large garden was still out in Lacomb and we had to drive out to Franz and Audrey's place now to work and harvest it.

In August there was a move convention in Vancouver, British Columbia. We attended with mom; my sister Frieda also came with us and probably her two children, April and Ryan, who were now young adults. This was the first time they participated in a move convention with the power of a third feast word and the strength of the praise. Brother D and Sister Ethelwyn were there, and I remember in particular the profound word that she shared.

My business idea was to set up several greenhouses and to grow plant starts for sale, primarily herbs. I called it Country Herb Gardens. I tackled creating a business with all seriousness. I researched writing a business plan and sought council from local business-minded people. I spent about a month creating my business plan. It is well-executed and is one of my favorite creations. I took all the legal steps necessary.

My brother had conducted his business entirely without any contact with the city officials. I wanted to "submit to the elders," so I applied for full zoning recognition. They had some requirements, however, including that I must put in a concrete driveway so that customer traffic would not carry gravel out onto the street. All this went into the business plan.

Part of my preparation for business, then, was that I enrolled in Linn-Benton Community College to take courses on plants and the nursery business. I don't remember all that I took, but one course was Botany, which study I enjoyed very much. Another part of our research was trips up to the Portland area to see similar nursery businesses and to

connect with various suppliers. I found a specific type of greenhouse that was brilliantly designed. A single one would cost around $8000, but it would start us off in strength. So – that also went into my business plan.

What I needed, of course, was capital, specifically $16,000, which would be sufficient to begin well. So, with that in mind, Maureen and I, with Kyle, flew down to the October Bowens Mill convention. Maureen remembers that Frieda also went with us. We counseled with Brother Buddy Cobb near the beginning of the convention. He connected us with a sister in the move who would look at my business plan and who could possibly connect us with capital. Meanwhile, Brother Buddy asked for visions to be sought for our new endeavor. We shared the business plan with the sister and then enjoyed the continuing convention.

I remember that Kyle, just past two, found several girls older than he, whom he could entice into chasing him across the lawns. He had great fun with their enthusiasm.

At the end of the convention, we spoke again with Brother Buddy. He gave us the visions and told us, rather abruptly, that they were negative and that the sister had said, "It will not work." And so, that was the end of that.

When we got back home, I canceled my enrollment at the community college and began to look for a construction job to support our living.

I do have some regrets, of course, for I would have loved to have obtained that greenhouse and to have worked that business plan. Nonetheless, my heart was set on immigrating to Canada, on the one hand, and I had no idea of the importance of selling, selling, selling, on the other hand. The truth is that a successful business in Oregon would have its success by fully-developed connections in Oregon. You don't just disconnect such a business there and then re-connect the same things in Fort St. John. A successful Country Herb Gardens would have meant our remaining in Oregon. That may have been a good thing, but it would not have taken me where I will go, into the knowledge of Father with me and of a people who know Father with us together.

Working for Terry Williams

To search for work, I went down to a local temp service and signed up with them. The gentleman who counseled me fitted me immediately with a man by the name of Terry Williams who did construction work and who hired all his workers through this temp service. And so, by the first of November, I was working full time for Terry Williams, mostly framing houses. He was a wheeler and dealer and preferred to be "the businessman," and so quite soon I was his crew leader.

I would work for Terry Williams for about four months. It was a bit brutal, hard work on the one hand, but the guy did not know how to speak without using cuss words, a minimum of one per sentence. And then, he was a "bang it together and get on to the next job" kind of contractor, a big ego and a little mind. One job we did was his own house which he was constructing about halfway to Lacomb. I started taking the time to make the end of his roof trusses straight. He shouted at me with curses to stop wasting time and bang it together. His facia board, then, was as crooked as a dog's hind leg, but he did not care.

It was income for us and it was reasonable for me for a couple of months. But more on that in the next chapter.

Because my spare time was no longer engaged with planning a business, I turned that time to developing the book I had long hoped to write.

Johanna on Her Way

Meanwhile our first baby girl was well on her way. The due date would be at the end of January. We both wanted a home-birth this time. For one thing, connecting with American hospitals was expensive and difficult. But we both had embraced a natural lifestyle fully and wanted a purity for our children. We connected with a local midwife with the thought of preparing for a home birth.

After the first meeting with this midwife, however, Maureen felt that the fit was not right. And so, before the end of December, we communicated with the Blueberry eldership and they gave us a green light for Maureen and Kyle to come up and for our baby to be born at Blueberry with Sister Terri Rehmeier as our midwife.

And so we made plans for me to drive Maureen and Kyle up the first week of January, but then for me to come back home to continue working.

24. Finding Myself

January 1994 - March 1995

Johanna's Birth

As I am writing this, our daughter, Johanna, just brought forth her second child, another little boy, Konrad Martin Schneider. He was born at 11:45 PM at home, in the midst of Christ Community, at the same time and in a similar way in which Johanna was born.

In the beginning of January, 1994, I drove Maureen and Kyle up to Blueberry, a distance of around 1100 miles. I had taken time off from work, so I could not stay long. Steve and Michelle Ebright had moved up to the downstairs of the Austin cabin, where we had first lived after our marriage. They opened their home to Maureen and Kyle for their stay at Blueberry.

While Maureen was at Blueberry carrying Johanna, she spent time with her good friend, Cindy Schneider from Graham River, who was also at the same place in carrying their first child, a little guy named Matthew, who would be born around the same time as Johanna. We have a picture of Johanna and Matthew in their mommy's tummies, right next to each other.

While Maureen prepared for Johanna's birth, I drove back to Oregon and continued working for Terry Williams in construction. During this time he hired two other fellows who were aggressive in taking a leadership position in his business. I continued as the lead, but I was now working with several men who were quite foul in their expressions.

My sister Frieda, along with her two children, April and Ryan, made plans to go with me back up to Canada. They had become interested in the Shepherd's School of Music at Graham River and wanted to check it out. We left on a Sunday morning for the long drive up to Blueberry, arriving there around 5 PM on January 31.

Maureen had woken up at 5 AM and had been in early labor all day. She was fervently praying that we would arrive before the baby would be born. Right around the time we arrived, she knew that Johanna was on her way.

We had supper with the Blueberry family. Right after supper, the contractions began in full earnest. I had designed a nice nursing station in the back corner of the new washhouse and that is where we went. Terri Rehmeier would preside over the birth, and Rebekah Lincecum was also there to help. The main room of the washhouse was spacious and comfortable. By about seven or so, members of the family began to fill up that room, altogether around fifty to sixty people. They sang praises as in a deliverance service, filling the birthing room with the singing of God.

All through Maureen's labor, they sang. I went out for brief times to sing with them. I remember Jennifer Hanna and Sister Barbara James, Donovan Van Gorkom and Dani Maldonado with his brothers, their faces in the light of the Lord. All through that evening they sang the praises of God until Johanna came into the world at 11:45. It wasn't quite as difficult a birth as Kyle's, but it was difficult enough. Nonetheless, when it is over, there is such joy. Johanna was the cutest little girl you could imagine. And little Konrad is quite the guy as well.

If it could be, I would see all children born into this world in the singing of the Church.

I had taken at least a week off. We could not return until Maureen had a few days to recover. Meanwhile, we went over to Graham River so that Frieda, April, and Ryan could visit. They all felt very welcome there and liked what they saw. In fact, Ryan decided to stay. I would guess he was around twenty at the time, around the same age I was when I first went to Graham. Ryan soon caught the interest of a young lady named Heather, who was attending the music program. They were married a few years later and, in fact, Ryan lived in move community for around fifteen years, both at Graham River and then later at the Lubbock community.

After a week, we returned to Oregon, minus Ryan, and I went back to the construction job.

More Transitions

Having a new little baby girl was a lot of fun. Kyle was about two-and-a-half, the big brother. Mom enjoyed her new granddaughter.

Meanwhile, my work situation was becoming more difficult. While I was gone for a week, Terry Williams gave the leadership position to the two new men. They gloated over their now superior position over me. This was all inside the dealings of God with me. The question is always how do we respond.

I remember one incident very clearly. We were working on a two-story roof. Those two fellows were putting the gable rafter on the overhang while I was nailing plywood on the back part of the roof. They called to me to come help them. I had done what they were doing many times with just Jimmy and I, so I said, "You don't need me." After a bit, they did succeed. Then, the larger one came and stood on the roof above me. He positioned himself to have the advantage. He said to me, very tensely, "When we say come and help, you come and help!"

I realized that I had been wrong. "I apologize," I said, "I was wrong." This was not what he was expecting. The tension slowly dissipated, and he went back to work, having accepted my apology.

Then in mid-March, Terry Williams sent me back to that house to do some interior trim work by myself. It took me a lot longer to complete the job than he expected and I did some of it wrong so that the other guys had to go back and redo that part. The next day, at the end of the day, the two guys were waiting for me with my final check. Williams did not have the decency to fire me himself.

It was humiliating, but the work environment had become impossible for me. I was so relieved I no longer had to return. I was home, then, about a month before I found another job.

Let me explain my mother and I. One problem was that we were so much alike; another problem was the idea I had latched onto that some of my so-called "problems" came from how my parents had related with me. Mom was not expressive. She was often misunderstood and had learned to keep her thoughts to herself even as a child. When I showed my mom some building plans of a house I had designed, she was able only to point out some faults, without any word of encouragement or praise. Again, I imagined that this lack in my mother had contributed to my present difficulties.

One of my own children, now, is much like my mother, prickly, or so it seems to me, and like I was towards Mom, expressive against me in putting me in my place. And so I did towards Mom during this time, shutting her up very meanly when she tried to contribute her thoughts towards our situation. This happened a number of times. In my frustration, I was unkind. It is clear to me that the Lord is showing me in the present my own wrongfulness back then, with a reversal of roles.

I am afraid that Mom began to think that she could not be at home with me. I cannot say "with us," because Maureen is always giving and kind. That March, Mom flew to Minnesota to spend a couple of weeks with Glenn and Kim at the Detroit Lakes community.

While Mom was gone, Maureen's sister, Jessica, was coming through, on her way from British Columbia to Texas (or vice versa). She spent a couple of weeks with us and her niece and nephew, Johanna and Kyle.

Having services together had been a sporadic thing through all the comings and goings of the prior few months, but by April, we were back to having regular Sunday services. Frieda and April would come down to our home each Sunday.

During her visit to the Detroit Lakes community, Mom made the decision to move there to be a part of the community and to be close to Glenn and Kim with their children. In fact, except for these few months when Mom was with Maureen and I, from the time that Glenn and Kim were married, Mom was with them or nearby for many years, and then in their home through her final years.

Tim and Frieda agreed to drive Mom to Minnesota with all her stuff in my blue van. This was around mid-April. Mom had been given a bedroom in one of the homes in the community. It would be over a year-and-a-half before we visited her there and saw her situation.

I so appreciate Glenn and Kim in their years of service to our mother. And I am ashamed, in the Lord, regarding my own lack towards them and towards her. Expressing myself out from behind my own difficulties has been an impossibility to me, even now.

"Lord Jesus, I know that the love of God has been poured out to full measure inside my heart, whether I 'feel' it or not. Lord Jesus, I was so wrong in my treatment of my mother and some of the hurtful things I spoke to her. Please forgive me. I place my mother, even now, into that love of God shed abroad in me, I draw her into that love, that she might dwell in peace and joy inside of You. And Lord Jesus, I ask that you honor and bless Glenn and Kim for their faithfulness to Mom over many years. May they know Your close goodness even now.

"Lord Jesus, I thank You that You carry all my lacks and inabilities inside Yourself, inside that same love of God poured out. I thank You, that, as I continue in confidence inside of You, we together are turning all that was difficult and even hurtful into goodness and blessing for the sake of others."

"And Mom, I would still be unable, even now, to work through my own outward difficulties into a proper caring relationship towards you. This is my fault, alone. You have always stood by me in my needs and given so much to me over many years. I am confident in the resurrection that the day will come when I can return to you manifold what I could not give in my present inability. Indeed, our hope in Jesus is our entire hope."

Before the end of April, soon after Tim and Frieda had returned the blue van, Frieda showed up at our door, needing a place to stay. A difficulty had arisen between Frieda and Tim, and Frieda felt the need for a season of separation. That difficulty does not belong in this narrative, however, only my ongoing relationship with my sister. I am so grateful that within a few years they were back together again, inside Christian community, and have enjoyed the continuation of their marriage inside the Lord until this day.

We gave Frieda the downstairs bedroom that had been Mom's. April came a few days later, to share that room with her mother.

I have always had a good relationship with my sister, Frieda. It's not that I haven't had a kind relationship with my other siblings; it's just that Frieda was always the easiest one to talk with, the one who seemed to understand me best.

I Write a Book

A number of topics inside this two-year time in Oregon are spread out over a year's time or more. For that reason, I will share these things topically, rather than chronologically. The first is the devotion of my non-working hours, and that is, my new-found joy of writing.

I first titled my book *The Unveiling of Jesus Christ*; I had also titled it *The Third Man*. If you were to peruse it now, you would see that it is very similar to much of my published writing; nonetheless, as I look through it now, I see ways of thinking that are contrary to the faith in Christ in which I walk now. The three "men," in my layout, were first, Adam, then Jesus, and finally the sons of God at the end of this age. My purpose was to show the common thread through all, and how you and I are called now as the second witness of Jesus Christ in proving Adam and the serpent to be false.

I wrote the chapters slowly over nearly a year's time. I alternated between fictionalized accounts of the Bible story with chapters explaining the truth of the revelation of Christ as I understood it then. You would find a lot of similarities with what I teach now. Nonetheless, I also understand now what was missing and what I was seeing wrong.

By this time I had completely embraced, in my mind, Buddy Cobb's viewpoint and teaching. I was not wise enough then to understand how the knowing of Jesus in my heart stood in contradiction to that mental theology. If you want to know what Buddy Cobb taught, then read John Calvin. Their teaching was almost identical. John Calvin made Nicene theology hyper; Buddy Cobb made Calvinism hyper.

Nonetheless, God was teaching me and dealing with me all through my first foray into writing His word. And so I must share something of critical importance that God worked into my knowing through this time.

Korah's rebellion, in Numbers 16, became a chapter in my book, and in writing that chapter, God made the issue of rebellion very real to me personally. "*We all hear from God, Moses. Who do you think you are?*" Korah was right; he and many others in the camp of Israel did hear God speaking to them and leading them. That was not the issue.

The issue was a simple one, the same issue from the beginning, arrogance in self and contempt towards others versus humility in self and respect towards others.

Yet the real proving of God is our response towards those who are "over us" in the Lord, especially when they get it wrong or perform beneath our expectations.

During this study, I discovered a little statement Moses had made in his sermon to Israel forty years after Mt. Sinai. Moses told them a secret that they had not known for forty years. He shared that all of them would have perished back then – except that he had placed himself before God for forty more days that God might spare their lives. And God had given him what he had asked for.

Moses, through his outpoured care for them, saved the lives of two million people. Korah was alive only because of Moses; he was disrespecting the man to whom he owed his life.

Here is a more accurate rendition of Hebrews 13:17. **Have confidence in those who are leading you, and yield to them as they watch over your souls, as they restore word to you; that they might do this with joy and not grief, for that would be unprofitable for you.** Of course, the Calvinist translators phrased it contrary to the Greek wording as "Obey those who have the rule over you, for they watch out for your souls." But that is how I knew it and received it.

God writes His word upon our hearts, according to the gospel. There are few words found in the Bible etched more deeply upon my heart by the finger of God than these words of David, **"Touch not Mine anointed and do My prophets no harm."** When I hear anyone speaking against any minister of Christ, regardless, all I want to do is get far away from them in horror in the same way Moses cried out in fear when he heard Korah speaking those awful words.

God taught me something else along these lines. One Saturday morning, as we were preparing to go out, I had thought to myself, in a boastful way, that I had not had a traffic ticket in years. I felt pretty proud of myself. But as we left home, I became aggravated with something. As we turned onto the street that went by the high school I had attended, I pressed the gas way too hard. There was no one on the streets that morning – except one, a cop who nailed me with a speeding ticket. We did not have the money, but I had to pay it anyhow. From then until now, any time the thought has come to me to boast in something of myself, I have always turned it towards giving thanks for God's good grace to me.

Again, if you were to read the chapters in my first book, you would find the same things I teach now. I had one thing horrifically wrong, I included a chapter of the cover being taken off and Christ being seen as filling us with all of His glory. What I could not believe was that this is true now; I imagined "someday" only.

Nonetheless, writing these things and placing them out in book form was central to God's intentions, for He needed me to carry the truth of Christ into utmost despair inside that whole arena of Nicene thinking.

One further thing in regards to my writing. The little typewriter that Paul Austin had given me was too small to hold many chapters of a book in its memory. So we went shopping for something bigger. A full computer was out of our price range, but we found a larger electric typewriter with a larger screen and memory and full word processing software. I could store my chapters on a floppy disk, and about a third of a page would appear in the screen. This new typewriter cost about $450. I advertised my smaller machine and it sold immediately for $150, a very good price. This meant a lot to me because I was able later to tell Paul that I had recouped the majority of what he had paid, and thus my new typewriter continued to be his gift to me.

This new typewriter would be my writing machine for four years, until I replaced it with my first computer. We had no television, and most of my spare hours were spent on writing the word.

Yoder's Woodworking

After a month of recuperation from my prior job, I went looking for a new job. I saw an ad for a cabinetmaking position, which interested me very much, and I drove over to Tangent, Oregon, about halfway between Lebanon and Corvallis, to interview for the job. Warren Yoder was a young man just a few years older than I. He was a Mennonite, and therefore a man of peace. I seemed to him to be exactly what he was looking for and after only a few minutes, I was hired.

Warren Yoder was the best boss I have ever had,

and the year I spent working for his cabinet business was the most enriching and meaningful to me of all such construction jobs. Warren needed an assistant cabinet installer to work with his main installer, Amos Stoltzfus, also a Mennonite. I worked with Amos for a year, again, the most meaningful work relationship in my life. I showed up with my tools the next day and went right out with Amos to an installation job.

As a woodworker, I know how to take the initiative as well as how to fit myself right with the lead of another woodworker. Within a couple of hours Amos knew that Warren had found the right man to assist him. On my side, I was to learn so very much about, not just cabinetmaking, but fine woodworking and supreme quality as well. It would not be possible to find two bosses so opposite as Terry Williams and Warren Yoder.

Warren had started his cabinet business in his twenties. On his first job, he made a mistake and there was a minor defect in the final installation of the cabinets. He negotiated with the customer for a lower payment to compensate for that defect. This really bothered him and so he re-thought his philosophy of work. From that time on, he charged a high price and then installed only the highest quality of work. This philosophy meant that if a mistake was made, you simply redid the job until it was perfect.

This was a wonderful philosophy to work under. You see, when I (or anyone) made a mistake, which was not infrequent, all we ever heard from either Warren or his foreman was, "Oh, okay. Well, just do it again." Once I wiped out an entire sheet of laminate that had to be re-ordered. Again, "just do it again," was all I ever heard. The result of such a response was two things. First, we made fewer mistakes and second, I learned what quality workmanship really is. Quality workmanship is not "doing it right." Quality workmanship is doing it again, patiently, until it is right.

Warren rented two large bays in a warehouse. In the first bay, the raw materials came in where his saw man cut them into pieces. In that same bay, another man constructed all the cabinet doors. Then, in the second bay was the assembly benches, the loading area, and then the finishing area. One man was hired to assemble all the cabinets and another to do all the spraying. There was also a foreman who oversaw all the in-shop work and filled in the

more complex tasks. Only two of the men were not of a Mennonite background.

Warren had his office in the second bay. His role was to find the work and interface with the customers. The foreman did most of the drawing. Warren was very meticulous in how everything was to be done. Nothing was left to chance. Everything was drawn out. When any cabinet was not rectangular, that is, if there was any angle at all, the layout would be carefully drawn first to full size on a sheet of particle board and both the measurements and the assembly happened on that drawing. For that reason, everything always worked out perfectly in the installation.

And that's what Amos and I did. Each kitchen job was assembled first in the staging area to make sure everything fitted perfectly together. Then Amos and I would disassemble the cabinets and load them into the truck. We would drive to the worksite, unload the cabinets, and begin the installation. The majority of the time, Amos and I were installing. In-between installations, on occasion, we would work at various jobs in the shop. There I sometimes did cabinet or drawer assembly. Having all the best tools and setup for building cabinets was a dream.

Most of the jobs we did were in the Corvallis area. There were enough wealthier people there who valued fine custom woodworking in their homes. Of truth, we were artists, and Amos and I installed many beautiful kitchens, bathrooms, and other woodworking. Oak was the most common, but we did a lot of maple cabinets and some cherry. We fitted everything perfectly to the walls. Warren did not allow any trim or caulk to fill in unnecessary cracks. When we installed cabinets onto crooked walls, our joints were seamless. I have not known anyone else to work in that way.

The Howat's and the Clarke's

As I shared, Don and Martha Howat had moved to Sequim, Washington at the same time that Maureen and I had moved to Oregon. Maureen and I went up to Sequim at least three or four times during these two years to spend a few days each time with them. And Don and Martha came down to our home with their children sometime during the summer of 1994.

During our first couple of visits, Don and Martha were staying in an apartment at his brother's place.

Later, they found a house with a small acreage on the slopes a few miles north of Sequim, which is situated above the Juan de Fuca Strait on the north side of the Olympic Mountains.

Don is very outgoing, very joyous, filled always with overflowing faith in God, and welcoming and inclusive towards everyone. Within a short time of his arrival in Sequim, he had become the center of a gathering of believers who did not fit into the established churches. They met for services in the home of one of the couples, probably around twenty to thirty people. Maureen and I participated in the services every time we visited.

Don and Martha were like a fountain of living water to these brethren and their meetings together were times of great joy in the Holy Spirit. As I think now, I remember distinctly five different couples. There were others as well, and their children. I was often able to share the word when we visited. Don and I both had a heart for God's people and we were careful in what we shared, that it would be in such a way that they could receive from us in joy. In fact, we talked about that. Don shared with me that God had sent the two of us out because we would not dump "movism" on His people in the way that too many in the move did. We shared only as much as they were able to receive in their own connection with Jesus – and that was quite a bit.

I remember one visit in particular. We were gathered together in one of the homes. We had a good praise service together, then I shared a word, after which Don shared. Meanwhile, a visitor sat in the back of the room, a young man. We could see that there was a shadow on his face; he was not receiving from the Lord. Before the service was over he left. The sister in whose house we were visiting was one of the leaders of this new little group. She went out to speak with this young man when he left. She came back in and shared with us what he had said, that we were just following ritual and form and that it wasn't the Lord. She said, "That might be something we should think about."

Don responded immediately, gently but firmly. "No we should not," he said. "We have moved in faith in God, and we cannot allow darkness to cause us to doubt the presence of God with us." I learned much from that God-filled response.

When Don and Martha came to visit us, then, he spent awhile sharing with me, imparting to me the need to be confident in the Lord and in the ministry of Christ. Don's words to me of confidence in God meant so much to me; they more then made up for that brief season when he, for whatever reason, had been unable to help me.

John and Nathel Clarke visited with the Howat's a number of times and to share with their little group. Away from Blueberry, they were very encouraging in their ministry to others. On two more occasions, they came down and visited with us on their way to the South.

I learned an important lesson during their first visit with us in June of 1994. Maureen and I had some deep concerns for which we needed counsel from the Clarkes. At the same time, Frieda and her children also needed to counsel with them concerning the difficulties they were facing. I did not communicate this need to the Clarkes, and they arrived late in the evening, having to leave early the next morning. We had waited, imagining that they would have a sharing service with us before we could all have time to counsel with them. As it turned out, Maureen and I had only a short time with them and Frieda and her children none.

My lack on this occasion was so very sorrowful to me. I learned, however, the importance of asking and of communicating your expectations clearly in such situations. I'm sure that if they had known, the Clarke's would have arranged for more time with us. – You have not because you ask not.

Even More Transitions

During the first part of June, Ryan had returned from his visit at Graham River and moved in with us. He slept on the couch in the living room.

I must bring in now the issue concerning my brother, Franz. During these years in Oregon, Franz had become involved with some other Christians who understood the darkness of this world and who moved in a deliverance ministry towards people escaping from Satanic ritual abuse. In this ministry, Franz learned of the incredibly dark ways in which numerous power people in business and government moved, including the performance of Satanic ritual in certain spots throughout the Willamette Valley and on the top of specific hills.

Much of what Franz shared with us was true. However, we did not understand at that time the mental disability that had begun for him. Now that I do understand it and know as well the great difficulties inside my own soul, I have nothing but compassion for him. At the time, however, my only thought was that our older brother should know better.

The point is that any visit we had with Franz and his family always veered entirely into hearing him share all sorts of dark things going on all around us. Somehow, he was losing the confident connection he had once known with the Lord Jesus.

One time after Frieda had come to stay with us, Tim must have communicated with Franz because when I went out next to the home place, needing to pick up something, Franz stopped me in the driveway. He spent several minutes telling me how wickedly I was moving and how, if Tim went to hell, it would be entirely my fault.

I did not respond, but I was very hurt by his words, for they held no connection with the reality of the situation, as is always the case when people are moved to speak "Thus saith the Lord" in a corrective manner. I was able to talk it through with Frieda, however, and came to peace.

There is no question, however, that I should have moved in more clarity and grace towards Tim through this time than I did. On my part, I gladly take upon myself whatever offensiveness I might have been. In whatever way I was wrong, I do ask forgiveness.

That June was also the 20th year reunion of the class of 1974 from Lebanon Union High School. We attended the inexpensive gathering, but did not have enough to pay for the formal meal at the main gathering. For that reason I did not see everyone, but I did see my friends, Andy Wyatt, Tim Steele, and Tim Greiner. I had become something very different from all of them, however. I invited Andy to come by to visit with us while he was in Oregon. He agreed, but did not come; I don't fully know why. Yet the wholesomeness of my family life was unmistakable to everyone.

When we took our children to a restaurant on occasion, people would comment to us in amazement at how well-behaved and wholesome our children were.

And on that note, yes, I took Maureen and the children exploring up in the mountains as often as we could. We even had a service in one of my favorite spots, just Maureen and I with the children. In fact, during this time, I had become interested

in the small vale beneath the two waterfalls on the southern slopes of Snow Peak and we spent a number of times exploring and hiking this area. Kyle and Jo were not always appreciative, however, of their dad carrying them through thick brush and across streams and up onto great rocks. We did have picnics as well, and good times along the rivers and streams of my youth.

Meanwhile, that July, Tim had found a different residence, and Frieda, April and Ryan moved back up to their home in Canby. That August, they went with us again to the convention in Vancouver, British Columbia. Frieda, especially, was much blessed by her time there. She visited with D and Ethelwyn and thus applied for her and Ryan to enroll in the Shepherd's School of Music. Frieda and Ryan drove up in their own car that September, and I followed after with all their stuff in my blue van. That included the piano that had been in our home growing up, a piano originally bought for Frieda, which now sits there in the cold north, probably unused, all these years later.

Ryan was glad to return to Graham. He had connected well with Bill Alter, one of the elders there, a good man with whom to work. I think that Heather had caught his eye by this time as well. Frieda fitted right in and thus began with several courses in the music school. I did not stay long, but returned back home and to my job at Yoder's Woodworking. April continued, however, at their house in Canby.

Christian Renewal Center

Sometime that July, Maureen and I were driving down the main street in Lebanon on the north side of town. I glanced at one of the houses along the way, a small brick house, and saw a sign, "New Beginnings Fellowship." The name intrigued me, and I was always willing to check out any new thing God might be doing. So we attended their next Sunday morning service.

It was a pleasant little Spirit-filled group, led by a young pastor and his wife, named Lou and Rhonda Mimone, who were out from the Assembly of God. We attended that little group quite often over the next few months and visited a number of times with the pastor couple.

The Mimone's had connections with a place near Silverton, Oregon, called Christian Renewal Center, having attended their gatherings on prior occasions. Christian Renewal Center was staging a

Thanksgiving get-together, a long weekend with around 100 people sharing together in a community type experience. They invited us to attend with them that November of 1994. And so we did.

This Thanksgiving at Christian Renewal Center was a primary turning point in my life.

Christian Renewal Center is situated on a south-facing slope just above the North Fork of Silver Creek before the creek enters Silver Falls Park and flows over the Upper North Falls. The road enters at the bottom of the property, which means you drive up a gravel lane through fir trees with an occasional house or lodge along the way, up to the main lodge in the center of the property. As we drove up that lane, there were banners spaced every so far, and written from one banner to the next was "Holy, Holy, Holy is the Lord of Hosts."

My heart was caught in God.

Here is a quote from their website. "CRC was founded in 1970 by Pastor Allan and Eunice Hansen and is now being carried on by Tim and Julie Hansen. Christian Renewal Center has been the fulfillment of a life long dream of providing a place of spiritual refreshment for people thirsty for more of God."

Lou and Rhonda Mimone had a room in a lodge further up the slope, but Maureen and I, with Kyle, now 3 and Johanna, just 10 months, were given a room in the downstairs of the main lodge. Since the lodge was built on a slope, our south wall was level with the ground, but the main floor above was level with the ground on the north side. Above the main lodge was a cabin in the woods belonging to Allan and Eunice Hansen. And below us on the slope was a rose garden and in that rose garden was a prayer hut, an A-Frame building, overlooking the slope below down to the creek.

All who were in attendance ate our meals together in the main lodge, and there were sharing times and service times and times of thanksgiving together. It was community, and Maureen and I came alive, for we were right at home. The Mimone's did not have the same view, and it seemed to us that they observed things from a distance.

There were several lodges, cabins, and chapels on that wooded slope. We had a number of services in a round chapel surrounded by trees. The Hansen's had invited in different Spirit-filled ministries from the local area to share in the various services. There

were times of great praise and of good things in the Lord. One who shared was Pastor Swan of the Silverton Episcopal Church, who was a Spirit-filled man. I really enjoyed what he shared and visited with him a bit concerning my book. Later I mailed him a copy, and he was kind enough to reply that there were some good things in it.

But it was the people that Maureen and I enjoyed, God's people, from many different churches and backgrounds, all of whom loved Jesus and upon whose faces was the light of the Lord. As I looked across their faces in the worship, my heart was deeply moved. "Your Church, Father, Your Church. Who will care for her?"

One thing I loved at CRC was the plaques all over of words of God and grace. On the entrance to the rose garden was a plaque that said, "I come to the garden alone while the dew is still on the roses." I knew the song – "He walks with me and He talks with me and He tells me I am His own and the joy we share as we tarry there none other has ever known."

And so I went to that prayer hut a number of times through that weekend. (These pictures are from the CRC website.) Inside, it was about 8 feet by 8 feet. There was a chair and a desk in front of the window, a cot to one side, and an electric heater. And in that prayer hut, I talked with God, and He talked with me. I knew that these precious people belonged utterly to God, and yet they did not know His fullness. I knew that God had placed a word inside of me that His people needed more than they understood.

But I also knew that until that word was pure and utterly of God, He would never enable me to give to her the things He had planted in me.

And so I covenanted with God, there on my knees in that prayer hut, that He would accomplish His purposes in me so that the Word that His Church, His precious people all over the world, so desperately need will be there for her in the time of her affliction.

As I arose from that prayer hut, God took me into the worst years of my life. I had no idea that His answer to my covenant with Him, a God who answers by fire, would bring me back to that same wooded hillside two years later, in November of 1996, shattered and broken, having failed utterly in all things.

I must add this note, however, that the layout, purpose, and functions of Christian Renewal Center lodged deeply inside my heart. This experience provided me with a model of an aspect of Christ Community that I have carried until now.

Expanded Services

I also shared my book with Lou Mimone, the pastor of New Beginnings Fellowship. He did not care for anything I had written and shortly after, he closed out that little church.

My niece, April, had connected with a young man in the Canby area named Jacques Potter. He had come with her down to our home several times for the services. During our time in Oregon, we had also gone up to Portland a few times to visit with the only remaining couple in the move fellowship that had been in Portland, Lee and Tommy Rutledge. In our visits at this time, we decided to have services together at April's house in Canby, partway in-between us and the Rutledge's, who lived in Gresham.

From December through May of 1995, then, we had services together each Sunday. Typically they were at April's in Canby, but sometimes they all would come down to our place or we would all go up to the Rutledge's. We were able to buy a lovely acoustic guitar for Maureen to play as she led the praise. It was the six of us, along with Kyle and Johanna. And so, through these months, I was practiced in sharing the word every Sunday. At the same time, my little "congregation" looked to us for pastoral care and counsel, and the Lord gave Maureen and I a heart of wisdom.

In these services I gave a series of teachings on what I

would later call "The Two Gospels." In that teaching you will find many wonderful things similar to what I share now. My problem was simple, however; I had the "two gospels" switched. I was teaching the false and repudiating the true. Nonetheless, my focus was on union with Christ; the difference is how union happens. I thought it was by our performance.

Meanwhile, through these months, I continued working on my larger book, *The Unveiling of Jesus Christ*, now in it's third draft.

Amos Stoltzfus

I was continuing to work with Amos Stoltzfus installing beautiful custom cabinets. I want to share a bit about my working relationship with Amos. Amos was a few years older than I, around Don Howat's and Jimmy Barkley's age. We worked so smoothly together. Amos was the lead, but he did not "have to" be. When we tackled a job we both went at what was next to do. I guesstimate that maybe forty percent of the time I followed his lead and about forty percent of the time he followed my lead in a smooth back and forth. Then, maybe twenty percent of the time it was clear to me that the decision was all his as the superior. I had worked with Jimmy in a similar way, but not so instinctively as with Amos.

Amos and I did some beautiful work together. It was astonishing to me some of the difficulties we faced and how Amos would come up with the right solutions. One time, the cabinet would not fit through the passage into the house. We had to saw it in two and then piece it back together. After we had finished, no one could ever discover that we had done that.

One time, however, Amos and I ran into a very knotty problem installing cabinets in a house. The owner was there and had become very distressed because we were not finding the solution. Amos stopped and called Warren. When Warren arrived, I watched one of the most amazing displays I have ever seen. He came in, inside of the peace in which he always walked. He spent a brief moment looking at the problem, then went over and spoke quietly to the owner. Afterwards he came to Amos and me and said, "Do this and this." Then he left. His counsel was perfect, the problem was solved, and the customer was thrilled.

Amos and I had a reasonable personal relationship as well. Amos was a sceptic of most everything, so I could share only a little with him of my life. But as long as he was producing the topics, we had good conversation.

In December, Maureen and I wanted to attend the convention in Lubbock, Texas. I asked Warren for the time off, but, after looking at his job calendar, he said, no, that there was too much work needing done. I submitted to that as to the Lord, and so Maureen flew down herself with Kyle and Johanna to the convention. Warren did give all of us workers with our spouses a very nice Christmas dinner at a fancy restaurant.

Then in the spring of 1995, Amos had a week's vacation. During that time, I continued installing cabinets as I had before. EXCEPT – nothing went right. I made mistake after mistake and took way too long to finish a job. This experience was key for me later on, when I had to know why I was anointed of the Lord when I worked with others, in order to counter the awfulness created in my mind from endless failure by myself.

One time as well, when I was working by myself, I tracked mud into the home of a customer and into the entry of a business in Corvallis with whom Warren worked. This was the only time Warren corrected me. He asked me to go back and apologize. He was completely right, for it was his good reputation upon which I had tracked mud. I humbled myself and apologized to both parties I had wronged.

In March, Warren brought in some "experts" to review his work procedures and to give him advice on how to improve efficiency. This troubled me just a bit, because I know that if he had found a way to hear things from each of us, his workers, he would have received better advice for free. The experts told him that he had too many workers. I would have told him that one way he was losing money was his allowing some to work overtime at pay-and-a-half. Not only was that work more expensive, but then these same fellows made more mistakes and worked more slowly during regular hours because they were worn out. Another simple thing would have been a ramp for the truck, so that loading and unloading would have taken a fraction of the time.

One day at the end of March, I rode out to a job in the truck with Amos. All the way to the job and all through the workday there was a great peace and anointing of the Lord upon me. When I arrived back at the shop, Warren told me that, because of a slow-down in work, he was laying off me and one other. That was my last day as a professional cabinet installer. Yet, because of that great peace all day, I knew that it was of the Lord.

Finding Myself

I have titled this chapter, "Finding Myself." I want to explain briefly what that means to me.

The Word God speaks, as He speaks it, is the most important thing to me in my life. I look now at *The Jesus Secret II*, and I weep over how much I love His word. And I love above all things that God has planted His word in my heart according to the covenant I made with Him.

But next to that Word is God's precious Church, His people all across this earth, and especially His people together in committed Christ Community.

When I was twenty years old, I heard a word preached concerning God's people and concerning those who would nourish her in her hour of greatest need. I had no idea how I could be part of such a thing, but I wanted to, with all my heart.

"Finding Myself" means three things, then. It means writing the Word, that I might see, with my eyes, the truths of Christ flowing across the page. It means teaching the Word to God's precious people, though in a small and limited way. And it means a heart for God's Church all across the earth in her time of greatest need even as we see it now unfolding in this year of our Lord, 2020.

For this I write; for this I live.

25. Into God's Shattering

April 1995 - August 1995

I have remembered so many things, including the writing I did through the 1990's, only through the unresolved pain. Just as I have realized the goodness of my time in the Blueberry community as I have written this account, so I realize that what I wrote then is a lot more in line with what I write now than I have remembered.

Of truth, to say that I had "adopted" Buddy Cobb's teaching is not accurate. Yes, I had drawn those things into my mind, and they influenced what I wrote, but I still continued with the things God was teaching me out from the key gospel verses that had already become my determination. The result was great conflict between the two inside of me, a conflict I could not resolve.

More Friends

Not long after we had moved to the house in Lebanon, a man about my age, named Dennis, connected with us. I think that he had known the Troyer's. Dennis was a chiropractor, but also a lonely man. He visited with us many times through this time period, including attending some of the service times. He was in our home at the same time that Don and Martha Howat visited us. I got in an argument with him regarding our assurance of faith in Christ, having mentally embraced Buddy Cobb's teaching that it's an easy thing for us to damn ourselves. I would love the opportunity to tell him I was wrong.

Dennis was a very practical chiropractor and taught me much on how to put my back into place by myself by pressing on the bones of the back of my skull, thus relieving the muscle tension and allowing the vertebrate to slip back into place. Little Johanna was a bit plugged up. Dennis simply pressed gently on the flap of skin between her thumb and finger and in a few minutes, the pipes opened wide! Dennis would be one of many who followed us into move community, in his case a visit at Blueberry for a few weeks in the late summer of 1995.

My mother had many friends in the Lord throughout the area. One sister that visited while Mom was still with us in Lebanon was Virginia Martin. Virginia continued visiting with us even after Mom went to Minnesota, just for fellowship in the Lord. After awhile, though, the things I shared became too much for her. She wrote us a letter saying that she would not continue visiting with us. Maureen and I valued her friendship too much, however, and so we shared that we needed that friendship, and I resolved to be more careful with what I said. Virginia agreed and continued occasional visits with us, while we also visited in her home out in the McDowell Creek area.

Then, in August of 1994, Maureen had signed on with Avon in order to earn a little extra money. We had purchased a small Ford Fiesta sedan from Glenn and Kim before they left for Minnesota. Although much of the time Maureen walked our neighborhood with the children to sell to her Avon customers, she also had this car, while I drove the blue van to work. One of Maureen's customers was a lady named Katie Bracken who lived just a few blocks away from us. In the spring of 1995, Katie came over to our house, saw some tapes of my teaching sessions, borrowed them, witnessed to the word I shared, and became a life-long friend.

Katie Bracken was a tall thin woman, maybe ten years older than us. She suffered from an auto-immune disease and should have died more than once. She could not work, but had successfully persevered until she was accepted on Social Security disability. She was exuberant and filled with faith and joy, however. She adopted our children as her own niece and nephew. Katie immediately became a large part of our lives.

Katie, then, introduced us to a number of people in Lebanon who did not fit into regular churches. These people had been reading Gene Edwards. We fellowshipped with them, and I shared the things I could. They received little, however, that was outside of their theological comfort zone. I lost some because I used an Old Testament passage to speak of God with us, that they had assigned to the present nation of Israel contrary to Paul's gospel. I lost others because I dared to suggest that we could walk with no disconnection from God, that is, without sin.

It is the same in the present time. People are really committed to a tiny and faraway Jesus and to a someday salvation.

Last Months in Oregon

I signed up for unemployment benefits after I was laid off from Yoder's Woodworking in April. At the same time, I thought it would be good to get my own small woodworking jobs. I contracted to build some cabinet doors for someone and enlisted Yoder's Woodworking to do the part for which I did not have the equipment. Virginia Martin's husband had a woodshop and tools, and I visited with them about my own woodworking business. At the same time, I worked a few weeks for my brother, Franz, in constructing bee boxes in the shop he had set up in dad's barn.

The problem I faced was that any money I earned had to be reported and was thus removed from the unemployment check. This made it pointless to earn extra money without obtaining a full-time job. The point is that I did not seek for a full-time job, but what I did try to do seemed to go nowhere. At the same time, I had begun to feel the effects of physical weakening in my body, just a bit. A forty-hour work week was beginning to be all that I could do.

Through April and May we continued with the services at April's in Canby and our fellowship with the Rutledge's. One of the traveling ministries of the move, Gary Snow, from the community in northwest Arkansas, came through with his wife, Shelley, and shared in our service.

Jacques and April came separately to us regarding their relationship. I shared good counsel with Jacques and Maureen with April. In the end, they decided to go their separate ways. I communicated with Jim and Joyce Fant at Bowens Mill, and they agreed to receive Jacques for a season at the Ridge. He flew down and spent a few months there. We have no more knowledge of him after he left Bowens Mill.

Meanwhile, April talked with us about the community in Lubbock, Texas, where Maureen's sisters lived. We spoke with Stan Martin, one of the elders there, and he welcomed April to their community and agreed to help her find a good job in Lubbock. Sometime in the summer, then, April closed out things in Oregon and moved to the Lubbock Community. Frieda also went down to Lubbock this summer to join her daughter in that community.

In May, Virginia Martin was diagnosed unexpectedly with a brain tumor. We visited her in her hospital room in Salem. Meanwhile, John and Nathel Clarke had stopped by for the third time. Virginia had returned home, so we all went to see her at her home in the McDowell Creek area. John and Nathel prayed for her, for the Baptism of the Spirit as well as for healing. Later, Virginia did receive the gift of tongues while she was alone worshipping the Lord.

Virginia lingered until December. We were visiting with Frieda in Lubbock when we heard that she had passed on; it was quite a shock to us.

A Decision I Made

Why did I do it? I have asked that question often over the years, being able to place my decision into God only now. Let me give a bit of a background for this momentous decision.

On the one hand, sometime that spring, we heard news that Wes Shaw had left Blair Valley and moved permanently back to Blueberry. Up until that moment, I had held fiercely to the word God had spoken to me regarding Blair Valley and our desire to immigrate. Nonetheless, immigration was going nowhere, and we continued feeling a blockage concerning Blair Valley. We did send them gifts of money on occasion as we were able. The very moment we heard that Wes Shaw was no longer at Blair, the blockage we both had felt lifted instantly and the joy of Blair Valley as our home returned to us in full.

In the other direction, our time in Oregon also seemed to be going nowhere.

We had been introduced to the multi-level-marketing craze during this time. I had attended one, Primerica, and found it to be lots of hoopla and little substance. The main sister of the group in Lebanon, with whom we had connected through Katie, came over to our home and told us that God had spoken to her that His solution for us was a phone-card MLM that we could sign up for under her. It did not take much thought to perceive that this was a Ponzi scheme with just enough substance to make it legal.

After studying that particular MLM, I knew in my heart that it was immoral, regardless of all the hoopla. This was a strong test, however, because my former eighth grade teacher, Mr. Philips, had signed onto it early and become a millionaire. We had bought our car insurance through him, and he offered to help me to become rich as well.

I preferred to know the Lord.

Then, the brethren in Lebanon also confirmed to us what Franz had shared concerning the dark practices that were prevalent in Oregon. One of the places where dark things happened was Champoeg Park, on the Willamette River north of Salem, not far from Canby, where the charter was signed that made Oregon a state. We had visited there not long before and enjoyed the big trees along the wide river. This bit of information troubled us deeply. It was becoming hard to see the green hills around us with this knowledge.

I thought that maybe we could move to one of the communities in Alaska. I had never had a leading towards Alaska, but this seemed to be our only way back to northern community. And so I wrote a letter to the elders at the Sapa Community in Alaska, not far from Copper Center on the road from the Yukon to Anchorage. It was here that the Johnson's from the Portland group had moved. They soon replied, excited that we felt to move up to be a part of their community.

The moment I read their letter welcoming us to their community, I knew that it wasn't the Lord. I had to write a letter of apology back. Later on Sister Lee Fife, whose daughter also lived at the Sapa community, shared with Maureen and me that we should know what God was speaking before we ever presented such a "leading." She was completely right. The problem was I just never heard God telling me what to do. No matter how much I tried to hear God for direction, I have usually (though not always) gotten it wrong, even to this day.

Then, while I was driving with my family up to Canby, the Lord did speak to me in the way that He so often has, not with direction, but with a word of life. He said to me, "Son, do not fight giants I have not placed before you."

I had been deeply concerned by the rumors of dark things in Oregon, even though the dark things did not actually affect us.

Nonetheless, immigrating to Blair Valley was what God had put in our hearts, yet that seemed to be more impossible than ever. We had a list of qualified trades for immigration, and cabinetmaking was at the bottom of the list.

One afternoon in May, as I was mowing the lawn, the thought came into my mind, whether from the Lord, I do not know, that maybe we could obtain a work visa to teach in the school at Blueberry, thus enabling us to return where we would at least be close to Blair Valley. We called Brother John Clarke with our leading, and he soon replied back that they had sought visions and that the visions were positive.

We set ourselves to return to Blueberry.

At the same time, we had been in communication with Dural and Ethelwyn at Graham River concerning the completion of the Tabernacle project. They hoped to do it during July of 1995. And so I was busy preparing for that project as well. We hoped that it would be a similar occasion as the first time, with many men gathering over a four-day period.

Returning to Blueberry seemed to us to make it much easier to be part of the second Graham River Tabernacle raising.

Returning to Blueberry

And so we did. We said our goodbyes in Oregon. Amos came by to help me load all our belongings into the blue van. He was a good friend, but he felt troubled about our decision. Claude Mack came down from Graham River to help Maureen drive our car up.

I had purchased a small trailer to pull behind the blue van. When I loaded it with stuff we had left out at Franz's, the tongue folded up under the weight. We rented a U-Haul trailer instead.

Mom had left quite a few of her and Dad's things with us, that is furniture and household utensils, including the couch and recliner Dad had bought in the early 70's, both of them the best I've ever sat on. We still have the couch in our living room, though it has spots tattered by our cats. I simply wore out Dad's recliner a few years ago. It remained my comfortable connection with Dad for many years.

We continued to stop at the Pacy's place when we could on our many backs and forths. Meanwhile, I had found that the Canadian immigration and customs office at the Aldergrove crossing was much more congenial to us than other crossings had been. They had consistently and peacefully given me what I asked, and this time was no different. With the letters from the Blueberry School, we were able to obtain a two-year volunteer work visa, a visa that required us to be at Blueberry only.

And so, with Claude's help, we drove back up to Blueberry with all our belongings.

We Came to the Wrong Place

I had been a part of Blueberry and its culture for seven years. Maureen and I had been part of many occasions of welcoming visitors or new arrivals. It was often made into a grand occasion. All the way up, and especially as we drove north from Fort St. John, we imagined the joy of our welcome in returning as a family to Blueberry.

We parked in the parking lot on the other side of the river and walked across the bridge and up the roadway to the community. As the four of us walked into the Blueberry community, however, I felt an immediate horror all through my being, growing stronger each step along the way.

We had come to the wrong place.

That feeling did not lift from me for one moment for the next year-and-a-half. Yet what could we do? Our visa placed us only at Blueberry; we had no other choice.

No one was there to meet us. We came to the Tabernacle. We saw almost no one, there were no signs of welcome. Finally, we saw John Austin and asked for help in bringing some of our things across. His response was, "Oh, I thought you were coming tomorrow."

We were given one large room in the upstairs of the Deardorff cabin, where Maureen had stayed during her two years of college. Within a day or two, Maureen and I sat down with Sister Charity on the front porch of her cabin. I shared with her that we had come to the wrong place. She paused, breathed deeply, and after a moment said, "Daniel, have you considered Blueberry?" She stated that Blueberry had given us so much, and it was our time to give back. That wasn't really the point, for I always gave freely, but I did not understand.

I shared with her that I very much needed a successful community experience. She said that I needed to die. I had no idea what "die" meant. But I respected and trusted the ministry of the move; I did not know that they also had no idea how someone was to accomplish any actual "dying," a concept that exists only by being unwilling to believe that God is telling us the truth.

We asked to see the visions that had been received for our return to Blueberry. When we read them, we were shocked to the core. They were not positive to us. The strongest of them showed a couple who arrived at a place wearing backpacks. Through all the time they were in this place they never removed their packs nor ever felt at home. The other two were similar, showing clearly the same sense I felt immediately on our return, that we had come to the wrong place.

Through the first couple of weeks, I did simple construction work under Dani Maldonado. We built a new outside stairway for the Austin upstairs. It was good to work under Dani, not carrying the construction responsibility myself.

Just a few days after we arrived at Blueberry, then, Katie Bracken flew up to spend most of the summer with us. We were at Blueberry a few weeks before we went on over to Graham River to prepare for the Tabernacle-raising part 2. Katie accompanied us to Graham.

Graham River Tabernacle Part 2

Soon after the first of July, Maureen and I, with the children and Katie Bracken, went over to Graham River Farm. This time, we stayed in the home of Ken and Natalie Womack; Ken was originally from Houston, Texas. The Womack's had five children; their oldest daughter enjoyed Kyle and Johanna and played with them through these days. Of course, Claude and Roberta Mack, as well as Ryan Louden, were also living at Graham River. They had a wedding during these days, and so Katie got to enjoy a move wedding.

I had communicated with the elders at Blueberry concerning the Tabernacle project and their role in it. I requested the use of some of their shop tools so that we could build a nice kitchen for Graham. Soon after we arrived at Graham River, we learned that the Blueberry eldership chose not to be a part of meeting this need at Graham River. I do not know why and therefore will not speculate, but neither their men nor the tools would be available. Gary Rehmeier did agree that the brethren at Graham could use North Star's large motor boat to ferry the supplies across the Graham River, which is at its highest through June. Steve Schneider, Lee Wilkerson, and many of the other brethren at Graham worked hard and faithfully to carry all the boards, sheets of plywood and sheetrock, and other supplies across the torrent.

We were at Graham more than a week before the scheduled time. I was given the school cabin, now empty for the summer, as a place to work on the plans and design. I was having a hard time connecting myself with the project. I could not get my mind around it. I simply did not have the support that I had enjoyed the first time. Don Howat was not there, and there were few of the men planning to participate who knew anything of construction. I found a copy of *Jane Eyre* by Charlotte Bronte on the shelf and read it for the first time instead of working on the plans.

Meanwhile, Brother Milton and Sister Bonnie Vereide were visiting at Graham River for this occasion. One of their children lived near Sequim, Washington, and we had attended services when they were ministering there. Brother Milton Vereide was a man of great faith and honor, and I always highly valued his words.

We had a sharing time in the dining room, in what would become the root cellar when the upper parts were finished. I was discouraged and my eyes were cast down. I heard Brother Milton speaking and realized that he was speaking directly to me. I looked up and, one of the few times in my life, I looked straight into his eyes. Brother Milton spoke into me such words of strength and faith and courage. When he had finished, I was once again able to connect with and give myself to the project.

Only around forty-five men were available for the project this time, even though the work was as much as the first time. Since the family at Graham River was much larger than before, about half of those men were from

Graham River. None were professional builders, and only Bill Alter was skilled somewhat in construction. I leaned heavily on him, a good thing for me, but he was not able to fill Don Howat's role.

Nonetheless, I planned the project to proceed in a similar way as before and on the days chosen in mid-July, we began. The first thing that happened was the careful removal of all the roof tin from the temporary roof. We would use it again for the final, much higher and steeper roof. Things had to move well and quickly so that there would be no risk of rain on the now exposed second floor. It was not until the second day that we had the second floor walls up and the third floor joists and sheeting installed. As usual, I had the stairway put in place as soon as the walls were raised so that it was easy to carry the materials up.

I had designed a twelve/twelve, or 45 degree pitch for the roof slope. That meant large and long beams and rafters, all made out of plywood and OSB, and it meant a high center ridge beam twenty feet above the third floor. We had scaffolding, yes, but this was a big deal, and I did not have professionals who could take charge of that part. For that reason, as the first beams and rafters went up, I had to be at the center of the work, directing everything and taking on the most difficult tasks in setting the big beams.

I was under an enormous pressure with everything resting on me and with little experienced help, yet with forty-five men to direct and to

keep busy. My stomach was all tied up in knots. I had to sit in the outhouse without finding relief. When the first rafters were finally set on the south gable, I looked up at them from the ground and saw how high they went. I was stricken with my own folly, that I had designed something absolutely absurd.

Sister Ethelwyn was standing nearby, however, and I went up to her and asked, "Well, what do you think?" She turned to me with her great enthusiasm and said, "Daniel, I LOVE it." That's all I needed to hear; I was able to continue.

Nonetheless, by that evening, although most of the rafters were in place, the roof was behind schedule. As soon as the third deck had been sheeted on the second day, we had set up some less adequate tools in the second floor to begin the kitchen cabinets. At the same time, all the interior work of electrical wiring, plumbing, and insulation, etc., was proceeding. The problem was simple and overwhelming. The roof HAD TO BE DONE, and the roof was way behind schedule.

By evening I was considering the hard reality of shutting down all work beneath the roof, sending half the men home, and taking full charge of that high roof myself. The roof had to be done. Yet that evening, while it was still light, a man came across the Graham River in the boat. He was from the Smithers group, and knew the Vereide's. I had met him when we visited Smithers on our honeymoon. This man was a builder, and not just a builder, but a man who loved high roofs and difficult tasks. His name was Dan.

When I met him I asked, "Dan, are you here for the job?" "Sure am," he replied. "Will you take the roof," I asked. – "I would love to."

In that moment, I knew that God's favor was with us. And so Dan took the roof, took charge of all the men working up there, the heights, and the careful installation of the tin. In fact, I had been planning to build a high scaffolding on the end in order to put the last sheets of tin on the overhang. Dan did it himself, without the scaffolding, clambering down a ladder hooked on the peak.

Meanwhile I was free to devote my attention to all the work going on underneath, including the kitchen cabinets. I did not need to give any more thought to the roof.

Nonetheless, after four days the work was not done. Some of the men who had come from elsewhere went back home, but all the men from Graham continued with me. The full work project continued for two more days for a total of six days this time before everything was well-enough finished and the Graham River family could use their new facilities.

I have included two views of the Graham River Tabernacle during construction.

The kitchen was only partly done, however. I really wanted to stay for one more week. Although many of the Graham River men had to return to their other duties, I still had enough men to keep the momentum going, and I know that one more week would have seen the kitchen completely finished to my plans.

I asked the Blueberry elders for that extra week at Graham River. John Austin came right over with their reply. "No, there is too much work needing done at Blueberry, you must return now." This was one of the hardest moments of submission in my life, but it was to such that I had committed myself. And so Maureen and I, with Kyle, Johanna, and Katie, returned to Blueberry the next day.

The kitchen was never finished, one of the many sorrows of my life.

Back at Blueberry

The job the Blueberry elders needed me to do right away was to design a new home for one of the families at Blueberry. This would be an almost complete rebuild of their existing home, using very little of the original. I tackled the job, but soon discovered a disagreement between this couple and John Clarke. The disagreement could not be resolved, and the two weeks I spent on the job were a waste of time. I was given another task that came to nothing after a week, through no fault of mine. And then a third task that also came to nothing. Four weeks back at Blueberry and I had accomplished nothing, all from circumstances entirely separate from me.

I certainly imagined at the time that this was God's response to Blueberry's response to the Graham River project. Neither I nor anyone else can really know that, however.

Soon after our return, Brother John Clarke got up in a service to share the chastisement of the elders upon the Blueberry family. The problem was that we were fleshy and un-submissive to the elders. I was astonished at the difference in him, for in Oregon and Washington, he and Nathel had been wonderful encouragement to everyone. This made absolutely no sense to me.

In August we moved up to the small apartment in the top of the washhouse. This was larger than the room at the Deardorff's and was quite cozy for us. It was our home for two months.

Many Who Followed

Meanwhile, through this summer, we had more visitors from Oregon coming up to spend time at Blueberry. Dennis drove up in his small camper pickup to spend a few weeks with us. He saw me slip and fall on the washhouse stairs, putting my back out badly, and was right there to help put it gently in place again. He also worked on the muscles of Sister Charity's back, which allowed her spine to snap back into place, giving her much relief.

Tommy Rutledge came up for a few days, but soon returned to Oregon disappointed. In the next summer, 1996, Katie Bracken's sister, Nancy Chaney, with her husband and three adolescent children came up from Oregon in their motorhome to spend a few weeks at Blueberry. In actuality, sixteen people followed us from Oregon into move community, whether for short or for long. Half of that number were members of my own family.

Having precious believers in Jesus, including my own family members, follow my lead is a deep concern to me. Look at my two headings above – "We Came to the Wrong Place" – and – "Many Who Followed."

I am compelled, then, to place here a caution, something I have only come to understand over many years.

I have had one pursuit in my life, one direction alone in which I am going. That one pursuit is best expressed by the covenant I made with God when I was 22, that I would know God and that I would walk with a people who know God. More than that, the thing I wanted most out from the Bible was to know in full John 14:23, that is, Father with me at Home in my heart.

From the day I gave my heart back to God at age nineteen until this morning as I am writing this chapter, that one pursuit has never deviated or turned aside, regardless of all my searing inabilities and all the roughness of my outward shell. Some might imagine that I went here and then there, that I "left the move," etc. etc. I have certainly imagined the same.

I now know that is untrue. – But, what I must do over the next several chapters, until August of 1998, is to show two things. First, I continue to place all the brethren in the move and all my experiences into the love of God towards me. And second, without damaging your honor as a reader towards God's people, I must show you why and how the move fellowship, by 1998, was no longer part of my pursuit of the knowledge of God, and why I would never suggest to anyone now to visit most of the move communities.

I now see my time in that fellowship as being a spy sent into the land of Christ to find the good fruit that is there as well as to experience the full measure of those things that are not of Christ so that I might show both to you.

When I read now the letters that Mom and Katie Bracken and others wrote to us through this time, I see two things. First, I see their own positive and strong interaction with God leading them and the joy and desire in their hearts to be part of Christian Community. Walking with Jesus and learning of Him was their continual expression. They were not "following me," per se, but were walking with God in full faith. Second, however, I see that what convinced them and drew their hearts was the love and life that flowed out from Maureen and me to them, beyond what they had known elsewhere.

Here are some things Katie wrote to us several months later. When Katie left Blueberry at the end of the summer, she returned to Oregon, disposed of all her things and business there, and moved to the community at Detroit Lakes, Minnesota, where Mom and Glenn and Kim were living. Her words were a great strength to us.

"I, deep in my heart, miss you and your family (Maureen and I). You, all of you, mean so much to me, to my life in Christ. I'm here in community because of you guys. You have large quantities of Jesus seeping out of you everywhere you go." – Then later, "Thank you very much for the wonderful visit and fellowship. Of all the people God has used in my life, you, your family, has had the most powerful impact on me, my spirit and my walk. Through you God gave me new hope and a new vision. Words cannot express the wonderful deep work God has accomplished in me since meeting you both."

This, then, is my present consternation. Not everyone in any fellowship is connecting with God in the same way, nor does everyone possess the same desire to bless God's precious people with life and joy. And the terrible thing is that among those who become leaders in the false hierarchy of "authority over" that is the church in this age of the ignorance of God, more than half are not connecting with God in the only way I must. And even those who move in "authority over" with a true heart, are easily swayed by those who have a different view of God and of service to others.

I led my family and friends into a structure of church that operated contrary to God in many critical ways. Then, three years later, I "left the move," while they were still in it.

This seems to me to be an inexcusable action, one of which I must give a full account. Nonetheless, I do not condemn myself, for I did not yet know Father with us as I know Him now. At the same time, just as I also place the Lord Jesus Christ upon every moment of my life and give Him thanks in all, so also must they.

And so I will continue to weave these thoughts through the next several letters. Regardless of how I place Jesus upon all the circumstances of my life, I have no intention of connecting any reader with

that particular fellowship as it has remained. I ask God to give me the right words to show you why.

Sorrow Towards Blair Valley

We quickly learned upon our return to Blueberry that the attitude of the elders towards the group now living at Blair Valley had flipped. When we shared our continued leading to join that family, we were told it wasn't the Lord. Different ones of the elders said dark things to us against Blair Valley, just in passing. These things confused us very much. One time I was entering someone's home and a new sister at the community, from Holland, was coming out with her husband. She proclaimed loudly to me, "Blare, Blare, that means a loud noise. Why would anyone call a place such a name." Her husband saw the pain upon my face and quickly led her away.

At that point, we had no understanding of this unexpected reversal.

Nonetheless, we asked for visions for our leading to Blair Valley so that we could begin the lengthy process of all that is needed for an immigration application. One thing we needed was letters of welcome from the family at Blair Valley. The visions were wonderfully positive, so much so that the elders had to accept them, although Brother John counseled that they showed a barrier. We saw no such thing in the visions; nonetheless, we had committed our lives to submission.

That October, we finally were able to visit the family at Blair Valley and spent several days there. At that point, there were three families at Blair, Bob and Connie Newman with their several children, Kars and Minnie Kiers, an older couple, and Rick and Shirley Annett. The Newman's and the Kiers's had come to Blair from the Headwaters community and Rick and Shirley, after their years at Blueberry and Evergreen, had spent a few years in the fellowship in Whitehorse in the Yukon before coming to Blair.

Our time at Blair Valley was so wonderful, but I will share more of our visits there in the next letters. The important thing here is what we learned.

There were two problems at Blair Valley. The first problem was that Kars Kiers was a strong-headed Dutchman, who had no problem putting everyone in their place, with his way being the only right way. Kars was, in short, a bully. Now I say that inside of the fact that I walked daily with Kars Kiers, he and I, for a year-and-a-half. That was a good time for me, a time of great peace, and Maureen and I counted Kars and Minnie as friends.

The other problem was Wes Shaw. Basically, Wes did little to support the needs of the family at Blair because he always found concerns to devote himself to away from the community. At the same time, he was an easy target for Kars. When Wes returned to Blueberry, he gave his side of things to the eldership. I'm sure there was some truth in it; I also suspect that it was neither complete nor completely accurate. Nonetheless, the Blueberry elders sided entirely with him.

Again, it is not my place to share the failings of others except that Maureen and I were caught right in the middle of all this, as in the jaws of a vice.

Meanwhile I had gotten up to share in the sharing service a word concerning what God had taught me through the story of Moses and Korah. Let me share here what I meant, as I understand it now. I shared that the elders, in their care over us, paid a price before God for our sakes, just as Moses had for the children of Israel. I shared that sometimes, just as then, we do not know what things they bear for our sakes and that we need to honor and regard them no matter what outward difficulties we might be going through. I believed that with all my heart and walked fully in it.

The truth is, I am still convinced that I owe much of my present knowledge of God to the price paid before God, sometimes unseen in the darkness, by Brother John and Sister Nathel, Brother John Austin and Sister Edie Dwyer, Brother Gary Rehmeier and Sister Charity, and by all the others. We have no idea how much we owe to many who have gone before.

What I shared was well-received by the elders, but not so much by the family. Michelle Ebright said to me, "That's Old Testament, Daniel." She was completely right as well. I was in the hand of God's determination towards me, most certainly, but I did not yet know the wondrous joy of our already completed Salvation.

Some final notes, then, inside this topic included first the sorrow of my connections with the brethren in Oregon. Basically, I was told that by coming to Blueberry, I was completely cut off from all that and my care for them was no longer of God. I walked into the dining room one day and Brother Dave Smillie came up to me and said, rather forcefully, "What's your problem, Daniel, you need to be married to Blueberry." He did apologize to me a few days after for saying that. Nonetheless, I could not change the sense of disconnection that filled me.

Sister Nathel had come to me, and, speaking out from the good times in which we had known her and Brother John in Oregon, shared with me that she wanted to be a personal help to me in the Lord, and that if I had any need, I should feel free to come counsel with her.

And so, one day in September, Maureen and I walked up the hill from the washhouse to the Clarke house at the top. The Clarkes were getting ready to leave on a ministry trip that day, but Nathel had said she could spend a bit of time with us. We were so discouraged, caught in things we could not understand, and helpless to change our situation.

You see, I cannot know for sure, but I don't think that it ever entered anyone's mind that what I felt inside could actually be the Lord. Everything was framed only in "What is wrong with Daniel Yordy."

We sat down in the Clarke's living room. Nathel left Brother John to finish the final packing into the van and came in to talk with us. I did not share much before she began to respond. For the next fifteen minutes, Nathel rebuked me in great anger. I have no idea what she said, I was too confused. Maureen clung to my hand. When she was done, she went out, got into the van, and they drove away. Nathel is a good woman, and this was not at all at the level of my experience with Lloyd Green. Nonetheless, this was the second worse moment I endured in my years in move community.

Maureen and I stumbled back down the hill to our little apartment, keeping each other upright. We did not understand, and we had nowhere to turn but to the Lord.

The Issues of God

As I am writing this, the deep sense is growing in me that Maureen and I walked through all these things inside a bubble of absolute Grace.

I must address my brief experience with Sister Nathel and with all the elders through these months. The false words spoken into me have sat in me as a deep underlying strata of grief for the twenty-five years from then until now. But as I have finally shared them with you, I look inside and see no grief at all. This is one of the most profound experiences of salvation I have known.

Sister Nathel, in later years, sat with Brother John across from Maureen and I in her daughter, Ann's, living room here in Houston and personally apologized to us for how she had responded to us, not just that time, but both of them asked forgiveness for their incomplete "covering" of us. Maureen and I gave them our heart-filled forgiveness with all joy.

Nonetheless, that one-time experience with Sister Nathel is not the issue for me, for that grief is gone forever and only joy remains. Here is the greater contention. – "We Came to the Wrong Place" – and – "Many Who Followed."

After writing that portion, I spent more than a day carrying inside a great condemnation of shame and grief such as I have not known for several years. I placed that condemnation entirely into the Lord Jesus sharing Himself with me; nonetheless, I pondered its full meaning and allowed it to run its course until the sweet revelation of God's intentions showed itself to me.

When I look at several letters written to us by dear ones precious to us through these years, I see that they all had known a life and love flowing to them personally from Maureen and I that lifted them up in respect and honor as their hearts told them Jesus really is.

I realized that is all I have ever wanted to be or do as a minister of Christ, to lift people up into the joy of their salvation, into knowing just how much they are valued and honored. I have never, never understood any other approach to God's precious people. And this is the great press God is taking me into through the year of our Lord, 1996.

I did not "lead" anyone into any "wrong" place. When I look through especially Mom's and Katie's letters to us, I see them engaged clearly with the immediate presence of the Lord Jesus, even through the difficult circumstances. It was He who led all of these inside of His path for the unfolding of their lives, and we know that God always leads us and that He ALWAYS leads us in triumph.

The sorrow of condemnation I felt was that I was unable to continue showing to my family members and to all these dear to us the joy of their salvation in the love and light of Jesus. I could not because I did not know that joy myself, because I cannot maintain long-distance relationships, because of the crippling pain and grief I have carried through these years, and because, without the move communities, there has been no place of fellowship and connection.

All of these issues will be very much a part of the unfolding of my life story from August of 1998 until today. What I hope to impart here, then, is God's true issue in my life.

From November of 1994, when I required of God that He would make me a vessel through whom He could give His Word to His precious Church, until today, over twenty-five years, I have carried in my heart before God through many tears and much travail, not seeing how it could be, that God would establish through me a place for His people, a provision of the true gospel, of the life of Christ, of lifting up, of loving one another with pure hearts fervently.

And I will not let go until He does.

26. Becoming an Elder

August 1995 - May 1996

The Pure Seed Company

The issue of income is a big deal inside the arena of Christian Community. Many of the communities in the states simply saw everyone working at completely separate jobs out in the secular world. This approach is not healthy for the life of community, however; neither was it an option for the wilderness communities in the north. And so the need to earn an income was increasing in the discussion and attempts of the communities.

William Brown, the brother in charge of the gardens, had come up with a plan for a business that could be conducted almost entirely from within the community experience. That business idea was to grow and sell potato seed, but not just regular potato seed, rather, to provide organic and specialty potato seed. By the time we returned to Blueberry, this new business endeavor was in full swing and the Blueberry community was fully committed to it. The business name was The Pure Seed Company.

Brother Alan Franklin, an elder, the brother from England, was working with William in starting the seed-potato business. William's primary focus was to go small, developing potato starts in a greenhouse lab and specializing in organic specialty potatoes only. Brother Alan persuaded him to go big as well, and thus twenty acres of potatoes were planted in the Blueberry property on the other side of Evergreen, just for the Pure Seed Company.

As August continued and the potatoes grew in the fields, the excitement towards the Pure Seed Company grew among the family at Blueberry. I have never seen such a concerted witness and effort of heart coming from a community family towards such a project as I was part of now.

During the month of August, I helped Dani rebuild a small building in the greenhouse area into a seed-potato development lab. William Brown had gotten a huge chunk of money as a grant from the government and we put a lot of it into this lab. Nonetheless, this was again a study of the fallacy of

"saving money" by using an old building. We saved nothing, and when we were done with all the work converting it, it remained an old building. It would have cost the same and have gone more quickly if we had torn it down and started from scratch. Nonetheless, this was a pretty cool lab/greenhouse with lots of high tech equipment.

School was beginning in September, and I was lined up to teach some college courses. Nonetheless, I was not given the liberty to develop my own course, but rather handed the exact layout by Sister Delores. That wasn't really the problem, though, rather that experience caused me to realize that nothing inside of me could go back into that school. I shared that with the elders; they did not understand, but they gave me the freedom. Instead, I turned my focus towards The Pure Seed Company.

Then, that August, we were sitting in the dining room for dinner. There were not a lot of people there, many were busy elsewhere. There was a sense of quietness resting upon us. Awhile later, a pickup drove by with several of the field-crew men on the back, on the way past and on to Fort St. John. The sense of doom grew. We soon learned that the field crew, on their return from the fields, coming down the steep ravine, had found Alan Franklin lying off the road next to an overturned three-wheeler. He had come down the hill too fast, with no brakes, his three-wheeler had flipped, and he was killed with a broken neck. The difficulty his family went through after that is not a part of my story; I say that not meaning to be indifferent, but rather to be kind.

I would not learn until the following spring the great pressure that Brother Alan's death placed upon William in that now he was carrying both sides of the Pure Seed Company himself. But William was up to the task, or so it seemed, and he was extremely positive concerning the wonderful prospects for the company. He was very confident in sharing with everyone how many tons of potato seed would come out of that large field and how much money would come into the community from the sale of those potatoes.

We all got excited. Many put all their effort into the things needed to make the seed potato business successful. Altogether, from August through October, we spent around $250,000 coming from government grants, from many family members, some giving a lot with some pitching in their little bit, and from various community and North Star reserves.

[Some might imagine that spending this much money on a business to support over 100 people is "greed" or "wasteful." But that's only because they do not rightly judge their own situation and all the millions spent on the infrastructure and services they enjoy every day. Think of all the facilities you use in your own town; then think of how much all that costs, all for your support and benefit.]

The hearts of the Blueberry family, in giving themselves in excitement towards this endeavor, were true and good.

Two major things were needed to handle the seed potatoes. On the one hand we needed a state-of-the-art storage system and packing facility, along with large crates to hold the potatoes and a forklift to handle the crates. On the other hand we needed some significant pieces of equipment to harvest and process the potatoes.

Our own root cellar was not adequate to handle the tonnage of potatoes we imagined were coming in. Neither was there a constant electrical power source nearby. The closest power line was on the side of the Blueberry property next to the Evergreen Community. There was a house on one side of the road and a former farmyard on the other side. It was there that the large potato storage building was built. The outfit from which we purchased the Quonset style metal building erected it on the site and sprayed it with a thick interior of insulation. This building had two rooms, the back larger room where the potatoes were stored and the front room where we would process and pack them for shipping.

With others helping, I built the large crates, about four-foot cubed, for potato storage and the woodwork needed in both rooms. Bryan helped me with the installation of the heating-cooling system that would hold the temperatures throughout the entire large storage room at a precise point year-round; that is, the seller installed the computer and heater/cooler equipment, and Bryan and I made the rest of it work by his specifications. Then, Randy designed a potato harvester and a potato washer and he and Bryan constructed those. These were large pieces of equipment. We leased a forklift from Edmonton.

We harvested the potatoes in September. The school closed for those days and the entire family was out in the fields along with the potato harvester. It was quite a day. The potatoes were loaded into the crates and I helped run the forklift into the storage unit, stacking the crates three or four high, with air spaces in-between.

Except at the end of the harvest, only about half the tonnage we had prepared for came out of the fields.

Of course, in a business like this, all the production expenditure happens in the fall of the year, but sales do not happen until February through May. Thus all your investment has to sit and wait for the time of sales.

The most important business question, in fact, the only thing that makes investment and labor into a business, is – Who are our customers, where are they, and how do we connect with them? Some thought was given to reaching the customers, but, in the end, not nearly enough.

Further Steps

During the time of the harvest, Maureen and I moved into a cabin that had become available for us. This was the former Ebright cabin, behind the former Raja cabin. It was a full three-bedroom, and since we needed the use only of two bedrooms, we agreed that Jennifer Hanna would live with us in the third bedroom.

Jennifer Hanna was a few years younger than Maureen. We had a good time with her sharing our home, although the relationship was never as close as it had been with Kimberley. Jennifer had her own solid life and was often busy elsewhere.

In October, Maureen and I with the children spent about a week at Blair Valley. This was a wonderful time. We renewed our friendship with Rick and Shirley Annett and just loved their little cabin. We got to know Bob and Connie Newman and their children and spent much time visiting in their home, one of the larger of the old cabins, restored.

Typically, in our visits to Blair, we stayed in the upstairs rooms of the cabin that Kars and Minnie Kiers had restored. They were very kind and hospitable. Sitting and sharing life with them would become a significant part of our own lives. I also took a box of organic seed potatoes with us and gave them to the Blair family for their own gardens.

In late October, I asked the elders if I could share with the Blueberry family the teaching I had given in the services in Oregon, the teaching that would become "The Two Gospels." They agreed that I could have a week or so of an extended morning devotion time to share that series. What I shared was well received. In fact Brother John Clarke was in attendance in some of those meetings and was greatly impacted by what I shared.

In the first part of December, I was asked to come to the elder's meeting. When I had sat down in that circle, Brother John Clarke said that the Father ministry of the move had agreed with him that I should walk out a time as an elder. This is a similar concept as walking out a year, in that I would move and function as an elder for a year or so, and, at the end of that time, as the Lord proved Himself through me, I would be set in as an elder by the apostolic ministry of the move by the laying on of hands with prayers and prophecies.

I did not expect this, and I was, of course, overwhelmed.

Brother John shared that they had based this decision on three things. First was the way I had moved in Oregon, not just in faithfully holding services, but in the pastoral care for those whom God gave to us. This had been reported in part by Gary Snow. Second, the sharing of the word in the anointing there at Blueberry that all had witnessed to. But third, and most important, was Jennifer Hanna's report to the elders concerning the environment of our home when the doors were closed and we were alone. She had shared that there was only kindness and peace in our home, with full respect towards the elders, regardless, and never any speaking against.

Before I could be recognized as walking as an elder, however, I needed to visit with the Apostolic ministry of the move so that they might connect personally with me. The next place and time they would gather would be the Lubbock Convention near the end of December.

To Lubbock and Detroit Lakes

Maureen and I prepared for a trip to Lubbock. At this point, Ryan Louden also wanted to move to the Lubbock Community to join his mom and sister there. Frieda's belongings also needed to be transported down. We made arrangements to use the large Blueberry van for our trip. We loaded the van with Frieda's stuff at Graham and headed south with Ryan. This was winter time, but the Lord favored us with no wintry weather and no snow or ice on the roads all the way down and back again.

We attended the convention in Lubbock. During that time, I met with the Father ministry of the move, Buddy Cobb, Joe McCord, Tom Rowe, John Clarke, and Bill Grier. I knew each of these men personally and had sat under their teaching for years. These were simple and good men, filled with the love of God and faithful in service to God's people over decades.

The meeting with them was little more than their asking me for my perspective and then sharing wisdom and encouragement with me. Nonetheless, when I left the meeting with them, I was now recognized throughout the move as walking as an elder.

Ryan remained permanently at Lubbock and became an important member of that community for the next several years, working with Stan Martin in his sound-system business.

Because Detroit Lakes, Minnesota, is not far off the route from Lubbock back to Edmonton, Maureen and I stopped there on our return trip. Although we had good roads, it was winter time and the land was covered with snow. This would be the first time we would see the place to which Mom, Glenn and Kim, and Katie Bracken had come.

At Detroit Lakes, we stayed in the house belonging to Roger and Jenny DeHaan, as they were away on a trip. We had a good time visiting with Glenn and Kim and with Mom and Katie.

The Detroit Lakes elders and family were good people, of course, but somehow there was not the same care that is found in some of the communities. And so Mom had been given a single room in the basement of someone's house. It seemed to me that she felt kind of lost, that she didn't fully fit or feel at home. Mom was one who would make the best of it in her trust in God, but I was not happy with where I had sent her.

As an elder, I was fully free, now, to share in the regular services, and so I ministered the word that Sunday in the Detroit Lakes fellowship. I don't remember what I preached, but it was a good word and they were greatly blessed. They also gave me the offering, a few hundred dollars. This was a pleasant, but unexpected blessing.

We then drove the long wintry miles back to Blueberry.

Katie wrote us a letter soon after our visit, however, that best expresses my sense of unease concerning this place to which Mom, Glenn, and Kim had come. She shared that the elder's held a "natural family" sentiment that gave greater favor to those in the "in-families," and non-related people were treated not quite the same. This is one of the "giants in the land" that must always be guarded against. Katie's need for a special diet was not honored; she was told to just eat whatever was served and "God would bless it." Had she followed this direction, she would have soon died. She shared with us that Glenn had found no friendships inside the community, and that Mom was quiet and withdrawn, feeling misunderstood.

Again, this did not mean that they were not walking with the Lord Jesus and seeing Him in every moment of their lives.

A Low January

This is a chapter of my life towards which I have prepared carefully inside of God, that He would give me the right words to share. I cannot impart to you the meaning of His words to me in March of 1997, "Son, you passed the test," without conveying to you the deep press in which I found myself through all of 1996. Nonetheless, I cannot share that press with you without also holding each individual person involved in the highest regard.

And so I write this chapter and the next inside a deep peace that has come out of fear and trembling before God through the past few months, knowing that giving an account for 1996 must come.

We are in no game; we have been seized in the determination of a holy and a mighty God who desires with all His heart to reveal Himself through a people given utterly to Him. Neither do we ever set ourselves against His anointed ones, for those who do such a thing never want to know Father with them.

Driving two thousand miles into southern lands and then returning again to the cold north in the darkness of January is a shock to any immune system. In fact, people becoming sick after returning from Lubbock, that is, a winter convention, was common.

Both Kyle and Johanna came down with a high fever. Maureen and I were both committed to the natural approach to health, convinced that, except for immediate emergencies, the world's medical system is based on a non-scientific paradigm of control. But whooping cough was happening elsewhere that January, and Johanna got much worse. She was not quite two-years old. Her fever went to 104. That evening, Maureen applied first a homemade salve and then crushed garlic to her feet and wrapped them in plastic and socks. The next morning, to our complete amazement, her temperature had dropped to 99 and she was fine. Garlic gives tremendous strength to the body's own immune system.

Then Maureen and I both came down with a fever. The gist of the story is that it was not until probably January 29, that I first sat in the elder's meeting as an elder.

The Elder's Meetings

Most of the things discussed in the elder's meetings were personal and private and not to be discussed elsewhere. I have no intention of violating what is proper in this account.

Nonetheless, I must share the larger picture as well as those things that directly impacted me that can be shared with a larger audience. Yes, all things will be unveiled as each one gives an account of their own life. But that is the point. Each one will share, in all honesty, only those things pertaining to their own life story. This is the only Godly way by which all things will be made known.

The elder's meetings were held in Sister Charity's front living room. The room was not large and we were close together, though not uncomfortably so. The primary elder's meeting was held each Monday evening starting at seven and typically lasting until around one AM. I took the chair nearest the front door, right next to Wes Shaw. It seemed that most sat in the same spot each time, though this was never a "rule."

In the elder's meeting were John and Nathel Clarke, when they were home, which through this particular year was well over half the time. Then Charity Titus and Sue Sampson, who lived with Sister Charity. Then Delores Topliff, Edie Dwyer, Gary Rehmeier, John Austin, Dave Smillie, and Bill Vanderhorst, a Dutch brother who had moved with his wife to Blueberry from Ontario while Maureen and I were in Oregon. Then Edna Smith, Alvin Roes, Wes Shaw, and myself (that is not in order of where each one usually sat). Six women and eight men.

I testify that I was sitting among the most loving, the wisest, and most anointed group of shepherds over a church of Christ that I have ever known. I felt absolutely privileged to be among them and cherished every moment.

Two primary types of things were discussed and decisions made in the elder's meeting, first things pertaining to the ordering of the community, to the work and to life together, and second, private things concerning individual needs. My layout in *Symmorphy V: Life*, 11.3 Building Shelter, of how the governmental meeting of a community should be conducted is drawn from this experience. The things needing to be discussed were presented quickly by each one and written down by that evening's moderator. Then the moderator would lead the discussion, working through the list until we were done. Each one that shared, did so concisely and with great respect for the others and each one listened to the things shared by each with all honor and regard.

Decisions always had to be unanimous. If one elder was not sure in their hearts concerning any decision, it was put on hold until the Lord would make things clear.

At the same time, there were many more impromptu elder's discussions. Often, after a meal, one would say, "The elder's need to gather," and we would join with each other in a corner of the dining room as the family was cleaning up, in order to make a decision needed in that moment. I must confess that, after observing such meetings as a non-elder for the prior nineteen years, being one of those who stood up to gather with the elders was rather a heady feeling, at least for the first few times.

And I must say, with all affirmation, that sitting and gathering with the elders, hearing and seeing how they conducted themselves towards each other and the great care and wisdom towards every member of the family was for me a rich treasure of learning the power and reality of God in His Church.

Many, many good things that I have shared with you in my *Christ Our Life* letters through the years have come out from what I heard and learned there.

Nonetheless, in order to rightly convey to you the great crisis of soul in which I was soon caught, I must develop the story step by step.

The Potato Business

One of the first things discussed that February was the potato business. John Austin had temporarily served as the elder covering The Pure Seed company after Alan Franklin had died, but he was also heavily involved in the cattle program and this was calving season. I volunteered to take on the potato project. This was accepted by the elders, and so I became the elder covering the work part of The Pure Seed Company.

That did not mean that I superseded William Brown in his role, for most of it belonged to him. It meant first, that the needs of the potato project went from William to the elders through me and vice versa. And second, I took on the task of handling the potatoes as we got them ready for sale. In that role, I served under William.

In that task, a young man named Michael Kuntz, who had worked in the gardens during the summer, now worked full time with me. When we needed more help, Fritz Hanna joined us as well.

And so I began what became a deep friendship with Michael Kuntz over the next several months. Michael was in his twenties, a bright and outgoing young man. He had fallen in love with Deborah Austin through that prior summer and at this point they were walking out a year together. That summer soon after we had returned to Blueberry, a young man had foolishly attempted to drive his jeep across the creek at Ted's Gate. He succeeded only in sinking it to the bottom in the mud. Randy had to pull him out with the tractor to everyone laughing. That young man turned out to be Michael Kuntz. It's not that he was dumb, just adventurous and daring.

Michael and I shared many interests and our work allowed us to chat most of the time. Nonetheless, the primary topic that concerned us was how can we earn a living inside of Christian Community. This was a major concern and our discussions were extensive, varied, and from the heart. I don't know that we came up with many answers, but we did search out the questions, which is the first step, and we discussed many possible answers.

Meanwhile, Michael and I began to prepare the potatoes for sale. The plan was to sell potatoes in two ways to two different markets. One way was in large bulk to potato farmers, and the other way was in small bags to home gardeners. There was a gardening show in Victoria, BC, coming up in March, which William planned to attend in order to present The Pure Seed products to the gardening public. One of the things we did, then, was to fill a couple of crates with small bags of seed potatoes of many different varieties, each nicely labeled in preparation for William's upcoming trip.

We would get a crate of dirty seed potatoes out of the large storage room with the forklift, and bring it into the front processing room. There, we had a layout of washing and sorting equipment into which we would dump that crate of potatoes. After washing them, we went over each one, rolling them as needed, in order to find and throw out the bad ones. There were quite a few with defects.

William did have several potato farmers lined up to buy seed from us, and so we also prepared those larger orders.

In March, William went down to Victoria with his family and all the bags of potato seed we had prepared. All of their expenses for the trip came out of the Pure Seed Company operating fund. At the gardening show, however, he was allotted a space at the end of a run and most of the huge flows of people did not find their way to his table.

William returned with a few hundred bags of potatoes unsold, and now crumpled. He had sold only a few. At first I did not quite understand this large pile of bags that we would have to re-bag before they could be sold again.

Not a Viable Business

Meanwhile, before we could deliver any seed potatoes to farmers, they would have to be inspected by government agents. In fact, the seed potato business was centered in Edmonton, Alberta, and so this was a common enterprise in that larger area.

Except, our potatoes did not pass inspection. First, only after the inspector came out did I discover that it is against regulations to wash seed potatoes. BUT – if we did not wash them, we would have

been unable to see and remove those with defects, either knicks or small bits of rot on the surface. BUT – that didn't matter anyway, because even though we had carefully gone over the potatoes, the number of defects in the top of the large crates being inspected were way above the limit required to sell as prime seed.

William said, with all enthusiasm, that that would not be a problem. We would just lower the price a bit and find farmers who wanted to pay less for potatoes that had not passed the inspections. He did find buyers and so potatoes began to flow out of our building.

Soon into April, however, as I walked through the storage room looking at all the crates remaining, the enormity of the situation slowly dawned in my realization. You see, up until that moment, I had trusted William implicitly, as had everyone else. For the first time I had to break that trust and begin to assess things myself with a cold eye.

You see, farmers in the north country have to get their potato seed in the ground by the end of May. To be successful, the ground would have been fully worked the fall before so that planting would be the only thing needing to happen on the fields in the spring.

By mid-April more than ninety percent of the potatoes were still in the storage room. They were simply not going out to buyers. I shared that realization with the elders and so they commissioned me to search out the problem and to find any possible solutions. I took on that responsibility, then, including Michael in our search as much as possible.

By this time William Brown seemed to have retreated into himself and thus the primary task of continuing the seed potato business and discovering the extent and causes of the problem now rested on Michael and me.

I went to Fort St. John to visit with the government agents with whom William had set up this whole endeavor and through whom he had received the grant money – around $75,000. In the various conversations with them, they talked about "Bill this," and "Bill that." It slowly dawned on me that they were speaking of William Brown and that the face he had presented to them was not a face we had ever known in the community.

Now, I do not want to lay a "blame" on William Brown. He had wanted to start small, but the enthusiasm of Alan Franklin and the whole community had pressed him to go big. Once committed, then, he simply kept on the show of what we wanted to hear. The truth is, he was overwhelmed after Alan was killed; the problem was that he did not share that fact with anyone.

Bit by bit, over time, I began to understand the reality. A seed potato business cannot exist in the British Columbia portion of the Peace River region and especially as far north as Blueberry. For that reason, no license to grow seed potatoes was ever granted to anyone in BC, that is, until William came along and talked them into it. Seed potatoes grown in our neck of the woods cannot ever pass inspection, unlike those grown in the gentle soils around Edmonton. More than that, William's original idea was to grow small amounts of high-valued specialty potatoes. As a business that could have worked. It would have required less than half the money that we spent on the larger business, except that the BC agricultural officials were not willing to bring potato inspection to BC for what was to them only a few bags of potatoes.

The thought comes to me now that we could possibly have negotiated to take our much smaller amounts of seed potatoes to Alberta for inspection there before offering them for sale. That thought did not come to us then; nonetheless, it was much too late for that. We had drained the funds of every other part of the community and many family member's life savings as well. All of that money was now at risk. In the end, none of it would ever come back.

The other side of the problem was that we just did not have customers lined up ahead of time to buy our seed potatoes. After the harvest was in, everyone relaxed. I guess we just expected that William had the selling under control, yet the layout of any "plan" he had was not generally known.

They did not sell. The only small bags of specialty potatoes that sold were those few that went in Victoria. Almost ninety percent of the harvest remained in the storage building. The money that did come in barely covered the cost of planting the twenty acres.

Yet there was another significant problem as well. The old root cellar at Blueberry was in a very poor condition. Of the potatoes that would be put in there in the fall, around half were thrown out as rot in the spring. That fall, all of our eating potatoes would come out of the crates in the new wonderful storage unit. BUT – because we were going to make "so much money" from selling them; all through that winter, I brought only the cast-offs back to the kitchen for the family to eat. This was not well-received, but it was accepted because of everyone's great hope.

Many tons of large and good potatoes became fertilizer that June.

John and Nathel Clarke had been away on a ministry trip through this time. Near the end of May they were on their way back. The elders asked me to bus down to Prince George and join with them there. That way I could share all I had learned of our dilemma on the trip back up to Blueberry.

I did that. It was a good ride back with them, but very somber, and with much prayer.

Blair Valley and Immigration

Through 1996, I want to stay closer to chronology. In March, Maureen and I spent several days at Blair Valley. This was soon after the February convention. This time, Eric and Lynn Foster and Sister Barbara James were there with us as well. We all went along with Sister Barbara, who had planned a time of prayer and deliverance with the Blair Valley family. This picture is Rick and Shirley Annett in their little cabin with Johanna tucked between.

Except for one strange thing, we again experienced a wonderful time of peace and belonging there at Blair Valley. A number were prayed for and received much joy and healing from the Lord.

That strange thing was that at a certain point, Sister Barbara James wanted to counsel with Maureen and me. We were in our bedroom in the upstairs of the Kiers's cabin. Maureen and Barbara were sitting on the bed, and I was sitting on a chair against the closet doors. In that conversation, Barbara shared with Maureen about me and about my problems and my responsibility in God. She did not address me, even though I was right there listening, but only spoke about me. Yet the things she was saying, though real to her, had no meaning or connection to me. They simply did not fit. This felt very strange to both of us.

And – the moral of the story is – don't make up stuff in your head about other people and call it "God." God does not share with anyone what He Himself does not remember. Paul said that only the spirit of a man knows the things of a man. The only thing anyone of us knows is ourselves, and all judgment we create concerning "other people" cannot be anything more than our own analysis of our self. But, as I have shared, asking was not a policy of move ministry.

Now, I bring in this incident because our ongoing relationship with Sister Barbara over the next few years would create some great puzzles for me.

Through this time, however, Maureen and I were slowly piecing together our immigration application package. One of the things we needed, for instance, was full chest x-rays to determine that we had not ever had tuberculosis. Kyle and Johanna (and Katrina) are full Canadian citizens, and thus had no need to immigrate.

We had dropped the pretense of starting a business as our means of immigrating. Rather, we relied on letters from the Blair Valley community giving us a house and full support. In other words, we were basing our immigration on provision in poverty and not on material wealth.

A Growing Disquiet

Many things discussed and said in the elder's meetings were outside of my "comfort zone." I had no idea concerning Asperger's, nor why certain things, particularly talking about other people's private business, was overwhelming to me. But I would come home from the discussion, often around one in the morning, and sit in our rocking chair, rocking back and forth, for nearly an hour before I was able to go on to bed.

I am very slow to understand what things mean. And the truth is, as I share with you the meaning of my distress, mostly in the next chapter, I understand these things fully only now. At that time, I went, in the end, by the instinct of my gut, not actually knowing what any of it meant.

Before continuing I must raise the question – Was the great loss that The Pure Seed Company became the "judgment of God?" The answer is an unqualified, "NO!" The "judgment of God" is the cross of Christ – "It is finished."

God's answer in any circumstance is to give thanks, and to turn, together with God, all such difficult things into the end result of good, by our expectation of God and by speaking good grace into every ongoing moment.

The problem was that we trusted the "anointing" separate from sound business sense. And inside of that trust, we left much of the business stuff with one person who, as it turned out, was in over his head. Yes, Philip Bridge, a professional accountant, did work with William on the business plan, but he was not an elder. And our system of governance inside the move communities seemed to work against the kind of common-sense managerial approach required for a successful business.

In fact, the North Star logging company was successful only because after initial difficulties when it started, the wise decision was made to separate that business completely from the community governance and to place it entirely under the management of Gary Rehmeier. But North Star operated outside of the community, whereas The Pure Seed Company was inside our life together.

As I think about it now, I think that William's original idea could well have worked. And that, with an investment of maybe $150,000, a sum that would not have placed stress on anyone, we could have created the smaller specialty seed-potato business, including maybe $40,000 being spent on establishing viable marketing channels. But all this is hindsight.

Before finishing the rest of 1996 in the next chapter, I want to remind you of that issue set before me by God back in April of 1985, that became a twelve-year path of the dealings of God inside of me. Here is what I wrote in Chapter 14 "A Song in Great Difficulty."

"I now understand the necessity of God's dealings with me; I certainly did not understand it then. As I look back now, I see that God was preparing me for a most confusing experience with Him during the April 1985 convention. In that convention He would begin a work inside of me that would not be finished until twelve years later, sitting in the same place in the same Bowens Mill Convention Tabernacle in March of 1997."

Later in the same chapter, I wrote – "This convention (April 1985) marked the beginning of a twelve-year assault of God against that thing inside of me that could not remain – contempt. Or, as Gene Edwards puts it in *A Tale of Three Kings*, "What do you do when someone throws a spear at you?"

And so I have titled the next chapter as "What Do I Do?" And I would suggest to you, dear reader, that this is the most important answer of the proving of Christ in you as well.

Completing the Chapter

My wife has found her calendars on which she recorded her activities for many years. She did not include some of the things I was doing, but she did jot down most of what we did together as well as her involvement with the children and with her friends. These calendars are filling in some of my missing pieces.

At the same time, I have been reminded of the very real hurts many who lived in these communities experienced, some of which were devastating. My choice to forgive, to embrace, and to extend all redemption is not a flippant or an easy thing. I do so now because of the Salvation of God coming through me. Nonetheless, healing only comes with resolution; continuing to blame only increases one's own injury.

I am convinced that every conflict ever experienced between two humans will be resolved, most usually with both on their knees towards one another (**every knee shall bow**). Things said to me may have hurt me, but even if only in my own internal accusations and fear, I also hurt others. Nonetheless, none of us are innocent except in God; all of us have done overt acts of injustice or spoken cruel words of hurt, and we will be on our knees before the one whom we sinned against until that one releases us.

This is God's justice, and no human will escape. It is a River of Life.

Before establishing the balance we must have, then, I want to add two more things that took place during the early months of 1996 while I was first sitting among the elders.

Two Late-Winter Experiences

There was a really cold stretch through this time. I was asked to watch the North Star Logging Camp for a few days because it was too cold for machines or men to work. The camp was situated to the east of the Alaska Highway, much further north. I drove a new Suburban up, so I felt quite safe. It was one hundred miles north from the Alaska Highway on a snow-covered logging road, fifty miles on beyond the closest other buildings where there may have been people.

Through this time of year the days are short and the nights are long, with the sun rising around 9 AM and setting around 3 PM. It was likely colder than -40 F. The logging camp was a series of trailers, including one in which was a large diesel generator. My job was to check all the buildings once a day and to check the oil in the generator every other day. I stayed in one of the bunks. The freezers were filled with good food, and I could eat whatever I wanted.

I found a book in one of the bunks, *The Frontiersman*, by Allan Eckert, the story of Simon Kenton, a significant figure in the settlement of Ohio and Kentucky. From this story I learned the meaning of a blood covenant and I read the account of Simon running the gauntlet set for him by Shawnee Indians, only to fall at the hand of the last old lady in his way.

This picture of the gauntlet, in which a man runs for his life between two rows of Indians striking at him from both directions, is a critical picture of our run into the knowledge of God-in-us and we-in-God, for we have always had enemies, both demonic and human, trying to stop us or to divert us by any means possible.

More than that, this picture described how I felt through this time. I loved the experience of sitting among the elders, and I moved in full integrity, but I still felt inside that we had come to the wrong place. More than that, I wrestled with the fact that "moving in the anointing," which seemed so easy for many, seemed at times almost impossible for me. The conviction that there was something terribly wrong with me had begun during my last year of college and had only grown more difficult ever since.

And so through these days, all alone in the bitter north, far from any human help, I walked the boardwalk outside, back and forth, shouting at the top of my lungs. "God, what is wrong with me. God fix me. God, if it be possible, save even me! God make me to be anointed like all these other people."

I never heard a word. I did not know! I did not know – that He had already answered all my cry inside of the Lord Jesus Christ.

One other thing that happened during these late-winter months was that, as I was sitting waiting for an elder's meeting to begin, one of the elders arrived with a note for me. The brethren at Graham River had called, needing my help.

The note said that the front window wall of the Tabernacle I had designed, the one facing the gardens, had shifted. They had braced it immediately, but they needed to know how to fix this problem. As I read that note, the realization struck me that I had made a great error and that, indeed, my grand design was quite capable of falling down, even to crushing people inside the building.

Here was the problem. I had designed the building originally to be an L shape, and we had put in the foundation for adding the short leg of the L. In that larger design, the forty foot window wall facing the gardens continued on for at least twenty more feet with enough solid wall to brace it. However, we did not build that further wall, which meant my window wall did not have enough sold wall in-between the windows to prevent it from shifting. It could easily collapse, and only the strength of the roof kept it up.

As it turned out, I was able to give the brethren at Graham the advice they needed, and the problem was fully resolved. Nonetheless, I was shocked to the core, a sobering up that I needed, most certainly, but that also ended my youthful self-confidence.

A Life-Saving Balance

What do you do with abuse of authority in a Christian gathering? Where is the balance between respect and justice, between honoring those whom God has anointed and protecting those who are being hurt?

I have used the phrase from David several times in this narrative, that is, "**Touch not Mine anointed and do My prophets no harm.**" Both Jesus and Paul brought this same principle into the New Testament by stating it this way – "**Do not speak evil against a ruler of My people.**"

I can safely assert concerning anyone who believes in Jesus, that the primary intention of God in your life is to shape your heart to fit His, that He might share His compassion through you, even towards those who offend. A second intention of God towards you, then, is a necessary companion of this first intention, and that is to remove every vestige of contempt for others from your heart. And the removal of that contempt must include the removal of contempt for those individuals who positioned themselves in some way over you and who abused that position.

At no point and in no way, however, does God's removal of contempt from our hearts ever remove justice. Even forgiveness cannot remove justice.

There are few actions more wicked inside the church than when those who are anointed and who are in a place of leadership, use "God" as their whip to assert control over other believers in Jesus. And one of those whips in the hands of such people is "Touch not Mine anointed." Another one is, of all things, "Bloom where you are planted." These statements can be true when the one showing you the kind intentions of God towards you places him or herself beneath of you in all honor and regard. In the hands of abusers, they become great weights of despair.

My terror through these years was that the God I wanted to know with all my heart was against me and that I was in trouble with Him. This teaching is the greatest of all Christian evils.

This is 1996; two years later, I will make the decision to leave that fellowship because of the false actions and the false teachings of some of the individuals named in this chapter. And a significant element in our decision to leave was to protect our children from a false use of authority.

This gauntlet in which we are caught is no light thing. And in showing the mercy and kindness of God through me towards my brothers and sisters in Christ, imputing just innocence to them in spite of their wrongful words and actions, I am in no way condoning those actions and words.

You see, if we stand against wrongful actions done by others, yet we ourselves possess hearts filled with rancor and bitterness, and we ourselves do wrongful things against others without thought inside our own spheres, then our "standing against" is an equal crime with those who abuse God's people for self-exaltation. We accomplish nothing but more destruction.

True judgment comes only through those who impute the just innocence of God, especially where it is not deserved, as Jesus did upon the cross. Yet that judgment, by its very nature, pierces like a sword, and requires the one receiving it to humble themselves and confess, "I was wrong," and even to say, "What I did to you was wicked."

It is certainly my hope that some, in reading this account, will be moved by my forgiveness extended freely towards them, to repent of the wrongful things of self-exaltation they have done or even continue to do.

I must extend this critical and life-saving balance a bit further.

Abusing one's authority is not a move community problem, nor is it a Christian problem. Abusing authority is a human problem. One of the most important pieces of understanding God gave me inside the public school and inside a Spirit-filled Christian school, is that the exact same elements of abuse and the arguments supporting it were found in those two realms, just like they existed in the move communities. And thus it is incorrect to say, "Well, it was that 'cult.'" The world is always much worse.

Now, I do not want to bring in here things that ought to unfold through the flow of this narrative. But I do want to draw one line of distinction.

Most who abuse places of authority inside the Church still love Jesus, more or less, and still can be good and kind. Of all the people towards whom my own attitude has changed through my giving of this account, my father-in-law stands at the top, having passed from the "worst elder" in my experience, to my realization that I, also, was wrong and to my ability to see his heart and to extend compassion and understanding.

BUT – there are a few who are vicious religious abusers. They are anointed of the Spirit, they hold a place of authority, but their actions and intentions are wicked. Part of the heart of wisdom God wants to share with you is the ability to distinguish between these few and the many.

Consider the enormous difference between my placement of Nathel Clarke and my placement of Lloyd Green. I receive Nathel as a friend forever with all joy, but I do nothing more with Lloyd Green than to place him into the capable hands of my Savior. I have no further thought towards him. I do not know him – yet I do know Sister Nathel well, that she loves Jesus.

So, here is the balance. Abuse cannot be allowed to continue inside any fellowship, especially abuse of authority. Abuse that is not stopped will destroy the lives of many.

BUT – if those removing the abuser have contempt remaining in their hearts, and not the imputation of the just innocence of God, then all you have going on is a power struggle, one set of abusers removing another set of abusers.

"Touch not Mine anointed," does NOT mean allowing abuse to continue. It does not mean submitting to that abuse. It does not mean that the hurt caused by the abusers is anyone's fault but theirs. It does not mean that you should not point out wrongful teaching that drives fake wedges between precious believers and their Father. And it does not mean that you should not warn others concerning that abuse. The hard reality is that allowing abuse to continue makes you part of it.

What "touch not Mine anointed" does mean is that we neither hold contempt in our hearts nor speak against that person. Saul was an abuser, anointed of God, but David did not strike against him. Yet neither did David remain under his abuse, nor did he 'sugarcoat' or excuse it. But then, of course, David was caught doing a similar abuse and had to repent of it.

Allowing abuse to continue makes one a passive part of the abuse. Striking against the abuser, however, out from the same heart of disconnection from God, and with the same contempt and desire to hurt, makes the original "victim" an equal abuser, with an equally twisted self-story that will come to open confrontation inside the presence of a holy and just God.

And so I want to reference again the picture of Eliza found in Chapter 20, "In the Womb of the Church." The slavery she has escaped is, in my case, the Nicene definitions of "God" and of "salvation," that is, the gospel of the serpent. The dogs are the voices of elders and apostles. Eliza is me. The babe in her arms is the precious word of truth and the knowledge of God which I carried. The distant shore is my present knowledge of our wondrous union with Christ.

BUT – the icy St. Lawrence is the death of falling into my own speaking against, my own joining the abusers by abusing them. And that is one of the primary issues of this narrative.

I am no victim. All my life has been ordered of my Father, and I see the Lord Jesus upon me inside every step. I justify God and give thanks inside of and for the sake of all.

UNCLE TOM'S CABIN
HARRIET BEECHER STOWE

27. What Do I Do?

May - October 1996

Understanding Myself

I had forgotten about the pain. I used to say, "Sticks and stones may break my bones, but words are the only thing that can hurt me."

I'm not speaking of that grip in my gut that came into me when I overdosed on LSD and that left me fifteen years later in a moment of glorious and powerful deliverance, a pain I have never known since. Rather, I'm speaking of an autistic pain that throbs between heart and brain, a pain sometimes caused by other people's words, things I cannot understand and am powerless to counteract, words that strip from me my own power and self-respect.

You see, over the last seven years, I have known little of that pain, not like it was so much of the time and especially through this year of our Lord, 1996. Even as I was preparing to write this letter, however, something was said to me that, in the scheme of things, was minor, but in the moment, it recreated that same throb of great pain. God orders my steps, and writing this narrative opens to me all the emotions of that time that they might pass from me forever.

And so I have borne this autistic pain as a regularly occurring internal suffering from age nine until today. It is NOT caused by demons, but rather by a disability of the nerves. Only in the last seven years have I known to place it with my Father and Father with it, sharing all things with me. Whenever I do that, which is always, the pain vanishes, and I know what I have always wanted to know – Father with me.

Someone might say, "Hey, Yordy, if you were truly 'of God,' you would be healed of all that stuff." BUT – if God had healed me of that pain at any point along the way, I would not know my Father now. Consider an oyster and a grain of sand. That sand hurts, and so the oyster coats it with salve, but it continues to hurt, and so the oyster continues to coat it until it becomes a pearl of great price, the entrance into the city of God.

The pain I have known all through my years has caused me to reach desperately for what God actually says in the Bible towards everything and to find the precious truth of Christ which I now share freely with you.

If I had the choice between being healed of the pain and never knowing Father with me as I do now versus bearing that pain over many years and knowing Father with me now, it would not be a choice for me. My choice was made when I was twenty-one and twenty-two; I have not revisited that decision since.

Let's return now to 1996. A number of great issues arose through the months of May through July in various discussions of the elders, the governing body of the community in both things temporal and things spiritual. These issues are of paramount importance to my desperate decision in mid-October, and so I will go carefully through each.

Most everything from May through October served only to increase that pain.

Issue One: The Potato Business

The first issue was how we should handle the disaster of the potato business.

During the September rush to complete everything for the harvest, Randy Jordan and I had spoken with certain family members concerning a special investment that would be repaid first upon the sale of potatoes in the spring. We needed this money to finish the potato storage unit. Two couples and one individual agreed to invest their savings under these promises. We gave them our word that their money would return in the spring. Randy went as far as to assure them that, if not, he would personally go to work in Fort St. John in order to return their investment.

Brother William was asked to come into the elder's meeting to share his side of things. That is when I learned the difficulty that had come for him with Brother Alan Franklin's death. Yet I knew enough about actuality to realize that William was still living inside his dream, somewhat disconnected from reality. I shared that with the elders when he left. We had no desire to lay any "blame" on William, however. Nonetheless, we had to decide how to proceed.

Since I was the covering over the potato project, I shared a role in this particular discussion. I was very concerned about the commitment that Randy and I had made to those last investors.

I presented my conviction that we should sell enough of what had been purchased in order to pay back those to whom we had promised a return by May. My conviction did not seem to be shared by anyone else. "Embrace the cross" would be their response to them. In fact, when Randy presented his intention to go to town to work in order to pay those loans back, he was spoken of as immature in the elder's meeting, that this problem had nothing to do with him.

I had become convinced that maintaining a seed potato business in our area of British Columbia could not work, because the potatoes would never pass inspection. More than that, the effort and dedication that it would have taken to turn it back to William's original idea was nowhere to be found. And so, even though I spoke only occasionally and briefly, I did hold to a negative position throughout the discussion.

In the end, Brother John Clarke announced that he and Gary Rehmeier would take full responsibility for the ongoing business dilemma; everyone breathed a sigh of relief. It was never discussed again. I know that sometimes optimism is better than pessimism in business, but I also know that most everything was lost and nothing was paid back.

Issue Two: God's Order for Church

Soon after the issue of the business disaster had vanished, the issue of "the order" for the community was raised. Sister Nathel thought that, on particular occasions, the women should be allowed to wear pants. Sister Delores felt that women should never be allowed to wear pants.

This question then opened up, ostensibly, to review the entire order for the community, which parts we continued to believe were God's established order, and which parts might be altered. And so, as elders, we spent two entire days, separate from the regular elder's meeting, discussing this issue of God's order for the Church at Blueberry. Afterwards, we took the discussion to the family, and spent two days in the Tabernacle, with many giving their input.

In the end, after four days of discussion, no conclusion was made. AND – to my utter astonishment, we hardly went beyond the topic of women's clothing.

I do not mean to make light of things that were believed strongly to be of the Lord by some at that time. Paul is very clear in Romans 14 and 15 – it's not what you do that counts, but that you do it in the expectation of faith, that God is with you in all things.

Nonetheless, this experience raised a huge question inside of me that would percolate until I was finally able to do something about it several months later. That question is – what is God's order for His Church as presented in the New Testament? That is, what are the New Testament commandments of God by which Christians should direct their lives?

At the time, one BIG New Testament commandment was very pertinent to me, and I wondered that it never arose in all the discussion for "God's order for His church." Here is the King James version. **And be ye kind one to another, tenderhearted, forgiving one another, even as God for Christ's sake hath forgiven you** (Ephesians 4:32).

I had the silent idea at the time that any discussion of "God's order" should begin here.

Issue Three: Writing

Through this time, I wanted to continue to write, this new-found joy of my way of knowing God. In the elder's meeting, I put that topic into the list and when my turn came, I asked if I could have two mornings a week given to writing.

The problem was that no ministry in the move wrote anything. The only writing was the transcription of sermons preached, put into booklet form. Thus, there was no context for anyone to think that writing was anything other than "of the flesh."

Sister Delores shared that years before she had taken up writing, but God had told her no.

I asked that the elders hold my request before the Lord to see what He would speak now. A week or two later I put my request back on the list. When it's turn came, I asked it again. No one responded.

After a few minutes of awkward silence, the moderator went on to the next topic.

I did take some time to write, regardless, but the bigger question that arose in me through this experience was the question of hearing from God. Did anyone actually listen to the Spirit or did everyone just assume already? The elders claimed that they "heard from God." What did that mean? How did that work? Were they actually "hearing" or were they also operating out from group thinking and pre-judgment?

I did not have any answers, but I pondered these things deeply. If I was going to be an elder "hearing from God," I had to know the honest and real meaning of such a thing.

Issue Four: Abuse & "Rebellion"

An issue had arisen at the neighboring Evergreen Community that came into our discussion in the elders' meeting partly because Brother John Clarke, with Bill Grier, had been asked to go into the community to resolve the difficulty.

A couple from England, man and wife, whom Maureen and I had known briefly at Bowens Mill, were living at Evergreen. It seems that they had gathered with some others who were not elders and were teaching them to live in Christ as them rather than just submitting "blindly" to the elders. Two close friends of ours at Evergreen were part of this "rebellion."

And so Brother John and Brother Bill went into the community and "set everyone straight" from behind the pulpit. Basically, they shared that all should either submit or find somewhere else to live. What they did not do was sit down with any non-elder to hear from them.

At the time, all I heard was what was shared by Brother John and Brother Bill and what was discussed among the elders. Only later did I hear the larger picture, of which we did know a part.

There was a brother at Evergreen, who had also lived at Shiloh, who was a pedophile. Now, most of the time, he was a dear brother in the Lord, desiring to walk in the grace of God. And I know that to be true. Nonetheless, on occasion, he would abuse a young boy. Afterwards he would repent, and when the action came before the elders, earlier at Shiloh, and now at Evergreen, he would express great remorse and desire to find the grace of God.

Surely the power of God in us for redemption is greater than any action of weakness. Indeed I teach, with the writer of Hebrews, that we walk in "no consciousness of sins."

The problem inside this unbalanced way of thinking goes in two directions. First, if Christ is living as this brother, regardless of his momentary evil actions, why can't he continue inside the grace and kindness of God from within a jail cell, just as much?

That is the lesser question, however. The far greater question is – what about the little boy? When justice is denied such a one, the only result is an increase in the internal abuse, a ripping apart that cannot ever be healed in this present season.

You see, a little one, having experienced such abuse, feels that somehow, this was his fault. When the adults in his life, those who claim to be protecting him as his covering, do nothing about it, that sense that "this is my fault" goes far deeper and becomes permanent.

Indeed, the action of continued injustice against that little boy by those who should protect him, then becomes equal to the original wickedness.

You CANNOT hurt people. And you CANNOT allow such a one to remain. If the law requires it, then the law must run its course, for that is the only place that grace can be real.

It was only a short while later that our friends heard the rumor that their own boy was "next." They did the only right thing they could do. They packed their bags immediately and went to Fort St. John, leaving the community and the move.

In the end, all that Brother John and Brother Bill accomplished was to add their ignorant fervor to the same abuse.

But let me bring in my own moment of "rebellion" into this same picture. The agony inside of me was growing, without resolution. And the primary reason for it is coming up in the section titled "Disrespect." Yet through all this time, regardless of the maturity and grace in which I moved, I still felt, every day, that sense that we had "come to the wrong place." In my distress, I came up with the idea of a move to the Lubbock Community. I shared this with John and Nathel.

Shortly after, in the elder's gathering, both Brother John and Sister Charity expressed, in cryptic ways, that God was "not having His way." The meaning was clear to me, that I was "on the precipice of rebellion and departure from God."

I was incapable of taking the thought any further, and so returned to a greater confusion.

My Summer Work & Experiences

All of these issues are arising during the ongoing course of my days, and so I will turn here to the layout of my life through this summer.

In May, William had also indicated a retreat from his oversight of the Blueberry gardens. In the elder's meeting, Sister Charity expressed her concern for the gardens, for they were no longer producing enough food for the family. There were many reasons for that, and not all of them were known. In fact, the garden production was falling way short.

I love to garden. And so I volunteered to become the oversight of the gardens. The elders agreed. Through this entire growing season of 1996, I was in charge of the Blueberry gardens, a fairly large enterprise.

Working with me were Michael Kuntz, Deborah Austin, Judy Patterson, who was in charge of the greenhouses, and a girl from England. When the work required, many others helped out for short times.

Katie Bracken returned to Blueberry from Detroit Lakes this summer again and spent more than two months with us before her return to Oregon. At the same time, her sister, Nancy Cheney, came up with their family to visit us at Blueberry. I remember working with them in the gardens harvesting peas. After they returned to Oregon, the Chaney's eventually connected with the move fellowship and small community near Kalispell, Montana. They lived there for several years as part of that fellowship. While the Chaney's were at Blueberry, Nancy introduced us to the world of essential oils and the Young Living company, a quality we have enjoyed since.

Working in the gardens was a wonderful "aside" for me, where I could find some peace inside the turmoil of everything else. Nonetheless, Michael and I took seriously Sister Charity's expressed concern and devoted our hearts and much discussion to understanding the Blueberry gardens, to discovering why the production was much less than it had been in the past, and to come up with some possible good solutions to the problem.

We soon discovered that part of the problem with the gardens was a pervasive attitude in the elders and in many of the family at large that elevated the field work as superior to the gardens. Blueberry was big on farm production and vast acreages and a much larger crew of men were devoted to the production of grain and hay. Most investment money for big equipment went their way, with the garden receiving only a little bit. In fact, we did not have access to a tractor, even though the gardens occupied many acres of ground. If we needed tractor work, one of the young men who worked the fields came in and did it his way, with no regard for our needs.

Reality was clear, however. The entire production and all the income of money from the sale of grain and cattle was only enough to pay for the ongoing expenses of those two parts of the community work. We ate little of the beef from the cattle lot and none of the grain from the fields. All of that had to be sold in order to pay for next year's work. Only in one way was there benefit, and that was the training of many of the young men in the community.

For all practical purposes, the fields and the cattle program were little more than a fetish. When the issue was brought up in the elder's meeting (by me, I think), the only response was that God had spoken to us to do these things and that if we stopped doing them, we would be disobeying God. Meanwhile, the garden program that existed solely to feed the family limped along with inadequate support.

I will not bring in any further garden experiences, nor of the practical discussions in which Michael and I engaged and the conclusions we came up with, except to share the ending of this particular sad saga in my life. Indeed, I am remembering so many different things, but I must limit myself only to the more important. And so, before arriving at the gardening "conclusion," I want to share some other experiences through this summer.

First, the little cabin in which Maureen and I lived had limited plumbing facilities, mostly just a couple of drains. We purchased a twelve-volt pump, run on a battery charged by the community generator which was run only during the day. In order to have piped water to the kitchen and bathroom, however, I took on the job of tunneling in the soft sand under our house. I dug a hole on the back side of the cabin and then proceeded horizontally, carving out the sand and carrying it out to a pile behind the house.

It was actually a pleasant job, lying on my side in the sand in the cool under the house. But one day, as I paused in my work for a breather, I was just minding my own business, thinking my own thoughts. In that moment, words came out of the heavens, and I knew it was God speaking to me. The words were, "Son, you have a sectarian heart."

This caught me completely by surprise, for such a concept was not an issue inside my present life experiences. Yet as I lay there in the sand, wondering, my time back in Oregon came afresh to me. I looked at my attitude of "movism" in my responses to many, and I could see clearly. I replied to God, "Yes, Father, I see that You are right."

This seemed to be a little thing at the time, but I am discovering just how BIG those little things from God have been in the intentions of God through me. This issue will grow and become a factor in our decision to leave move community. Yet it has continued to grow, and out from those few words from God has come my continual expression of receiving into our care all who believe in Jesus all across this earth, regardless, sharing our Savior's heart with Him.

In fact, I could see at that time that God's concern came right out of that agreement I had made with Him, on that wooded hillside in Oregon, during the Thanksgiving season of 1994, that He would prepare me for His entire church.

We have many pictures of Kyle and Johanna playing outside in the yard in front of our house. Kyle turned five that summer, making Jo now two-and-a-half. It is important to note that they had a happy childhood, filled with joy and good experiences.

I continued on occasion to caretake the North Star logging camp during times when the men were at home. This summer they were logging on the slopes overlooking one side of the Blair Valley, several miles north of the community. There was no road connection from the logging camp to Blair Valley, however. My only task was to make sure everything in the large camp was okay. I stayed in one of the bunk buildings and cooked my meals out of the plenteous supplies in the freezers and pantries.

I enjoyed this task, and it provided some income for us. I was alone some of the days, but on two dif-ferent occasions, Maureen and the children came up to join me. We had a great family time together hiking and exploring in the logging areas.

Then, sometime in mid-summer, Brother Gary Rehmeier asked me to stop by his house because he needed to talk to me. He would be along in a little while. So I sat and waited for him in his North Star office in the wing added to the front of their home. When Gary arrived, he said to me, "I have heard that you are not meeting your obligations in the gardens, that you are often not showing up. I had been planning on chastising you, but on my way here, I passed Michael and Deborah and asked them. They told me that they knew nothing of that, that you were always there working with them. (You see, the gardens were scattered over a large area and when I was working in one, it seemed to some in other gardens that I was "not around.")

Then Gary said, "You should be grateful that I passed them on the way, or else you would have been in trouble."

I was indeed grateful that I was not, once again, "raked over the coals" with no opportunity to present another side of things. Nonetheless, my thought was, "No Gary, you are the one who should be grateful that you did not sin against me with false accusation." I would never say such a thing, for it is disrespect. I am not moved to disrespect others, even if they are disrespecting me.

Finally, later in that season, maybe in September, I asked for the opportunity to share with the eldership some of the things Michael and I had learned in why the gardens were not producing well and some of our thoughts as to how we could resolve those problems.

I had not spoken long before one of the sisters interrupted me. "I don't remember anyone asking you to make any changes in the gardens," she said.

I was absolutely stunned and had no words to reply. Had Michael and I not carried the concern expressed by Sister Charity in our hearts for the prior four months. And was there no interest towards the hearts of two brothers in the community who had carried the needs of the family before God in seeking His answers for us?

I do not have the gift of words in such situations. And so it passed, and nothing came of the things to which Michael and I had devoted ourselves for months.

Issue Five: Disrespect

The issues I have shared thus far were little more than a background hum. Through the rest of this letter, I will share the real dilemma in which I was caught.

Previously I mentioned concerning coming home from the elders' meetings without understanding what was bothering me, and sitting there rocking back and forth for nearly an hour each time before I could go to bed. For the first few months I did not know why I felt like that. I did find it shocking, however, to be part of discussions of people's private concerns and of our making decisions that rightfully belonged only to them. In the way I am made, such a thing is immoral. Yet this was the practice of all eldering in the move from the start. I could not reconcile my sense of wrongness with the respect in which I held these brothers and sisters with whom I now sat.

Sometime around the beginning of the summer an incident occurred that first began to clue me in on what it was that was really bothering me.

Prior to the start of another regular elders' meeting, several of us had gathered, but not yet all. In fact, Sister Charity was still in the school and had not yet come. The few that were together included Sister Nathel. Two college-age sisters in the community stopped by and asked about gathering in one of the homes for a time of praise while we were in the elder's meeting. You see, the elders had earlier established an order that during the elder's meeting, when no elders were out among the people, all who were not elders should remain in their own homes. The idea was to make sure that no fleshiness would break out while elders were absent.

To Sister Nathel and to me, this sounded like a wonderful and reasonable request, and so we gave our permission to the sisters to do just that. A few minutes later, however, Sister Charity came in. We shared with her what we had decided.

"No," she said. "That is not allowed. The only reason they want to do it is fleshy rebellion."

To my amazement, I saw a shadow of great discouragement come across Sister Nathel's face. We submitted, however, and sent word to the sisters to tell them that our decision had been revoked, that they all needed to stay at home. Nonetheless, I knew that Sister Charity's pronouncement against these two sisters was untrue.

I was gaining a first understanding of some of the real psychology operating under the sometimes blank pronouncement of "hearing from God." From that time, I began slowly to understand what was really bothering me. Now, this thing is huge in God's path for me, and so I must develop it fully. At the same time, what I share now comes from pondering these things over many years. I knew then what I now understand clearly, but mostly in my gut, and only a little in my rational understanding.

In all the communities in which I had lived, there had been an undercurrent sense among those who were not elders, an "us versus them," with "us" being the non-elders and "them" being the elders, as in "why did they make that decision regarding us." This was always understood to be a part of the "rebellion of the flesh." Nonetheless, there is no escaping such an underlying pattern of thinking when a hierarchy of "authority" operates as the order of any group.

I had learned, over the years, not only to accept brethren who saw things differently than I, but to value those differences. My regard for Brian, for instance, had only grown. In fact, Brian had come to the end of his move community journey through this time. I will not bring in his story, however, except that he left Blueberry in grief. We touched hearts briefly, as he was leaving, and knew that we cared for and respected each other.

It took me a few months, however, of listening to the elder's conversations, and how they framed their words, slowly to realize that the "us versus them" did not come from the non-elders in the community, but from the elders.

As I said, I had grown to love and respect the non-elders in the community equally with the elders, seeing Christ as them. We had worked together, laughed together, wept together, and worshipped God together for years. To hear these same precious people spoken of as "fleshy" and "rebellious," was just wrong, contrary to everything we had learned from God.

I am not making this up, however, for as time went on, I heard it stated clearly that *we elders are elders because we are anointed of God and walk in the Spirit. We are the true firstfruits. All "those others" who are not elders are not elders because they don't walk in the Spirit, but in the flesh. They will never be firstfruits because they are always fleshy and rebel-*

lious. Rather, they are our cross that God has chosen to give to us that we might be perfected by bearing with their fleshy rebellion. And yes, I heard these very things expressed over time.

A proposal was made that we should have a communion service, like the one we had enjoyed together several years earlier. Sister Delores and others were opposed to such a thing, however, because the college students, especially, were "fleshy and rebellious," and having a communion service with "such sinfulness in our midst" would "offend a holy God."

In this and other discussions I heard the expression of a profound belief that the responsibility for the kingdom rests upon "our shoulders." And that righteousness (whatever that means) in the church was entirely our responsibility, that God would depart from Blueberry if we did not keep these fleshy non-elders firmly inside God's order and holiness.

The wife of one of the elders, who herself was not an elder, had expressed an interest in attending some Spirit-filled services in Fort St. John, given by a ministry not in the move. The elder husband hoped that another one of the elders could steer his wife away from such a thing. I had a good relationship with this sister, and so I volunteered to speak to her.

I did so, sharing gently with her that we should not be seeking any word outside of what the move ministry was giving us, for such a thing always leads to "leaving the move." I think she was moved by my tender regard and agreed to drop that interest. I went away feeling awful and ashamed, however, for what I had done as an "elder" was more than the good practice of sharing wisdom, but rather, fully inside the box of "control." In fact, I think that it was shortly after this experience that I heard God say, "Son, you have a sectarian heart."

As time went on, I began to perceive a definition of what "being an elder" meant that was very different from anything I had known. It was expressed in one small way or another, that I would have to perform well in this way, in walking in the Spirit myself and in keeping the fleshiness of the non-elders under control. I would have to take on a persona and an action that simply was not inside of me. By September and October, this contention had become a great tearing inside, for I was realizing that I would be set in as an elder only if I learned to be

and to practice something I was not. In order to be an elder, I would have to pretend in a manner that was far beyond my abilities.

Nonetheless, in spite of saying all this, I do not want you to imagine that there was not also much love and care, wisdom and giving expressed at all times through each of the elders. God's people are always a mixed bag, including you and me. We do not cast anyone as "false" simply because they err as humans, for otherwise we condemn ourselves.

Issue Six: Managing the Work

I must now set out that story-line in which the great proving of God came for me. By the beginning of June, with the collapse of the Pure Seed Company, the men elders gathered to discuss how the work of the community could be better ordered. In fact, it was Wes Shaw who carried this concern the most and who put all this together.

And I will say this about Brother Wes. As non-elders, we had always carried a dim view of Wes Shaw and wondered why he was an elder, for he often seemed to be serving himself at the expense of others. As I sat next to him inside the elder's meetings, I realized that there was a side to Wes that those who were not elders rarely saw. I saw, at times, the expressions of a good heart and began to appreciate walking together with him.

And so, by Wes's incentive, we gathered together as men elders in Brother Gary's North Star office to discuss a new approach to the community work for the men. Brother John Clarke was at home and thus able to be a part of this discussion. Our hope was to make everything fit together, both the ongoing plans for the potato business, as well as a number of other business ideas, along with all the ongoing work of fields and cattle, gardens and construction.

Our plan was that each one of us as elders would take on a different role. Yet we also included a place for a number of men who were not elders, including those who had been recognized as deacons, an office that had little practical meaning. Wes Shaw agreed to be responsible for all the sales and interaction with the public for various community endeavors. Brother John Clarke agreed to meet with the group of men who were not elders in order to shepherd them in their discussions and decisions. I agreed to take on the educational side of things, to create ways in which the education of college and high school students could fit better into the overall community work. Others agreed to take on different specific roles.

The biggest issue, however, was the practical management of the regular work of the community, including construction, maintenance, and firewood. We needed someone hands on, and with Don Howat not here, none of the elders fitted that ability. John Clarke even suggested that we persuade the Howat's to return so that Don could take on that role. Meanwhile, I had taking a firm stand against my being fitted back into the construction part of the work.

We finally decided that Randy Jordan would be the man for this central management task. Bill Vanderhorst agreed to be Randy's covering and sounding board as the work manager. So we called Randy into the men elder's meeting and shared with him the role we hoped he would agree to take. But Randy was cynical, and he expressed his concerns. He shared that we had attempted similar things in the past and then the elders had not engaged as they had promised and he and others had been left "holding the bag" so to speak, and had received the blame for the ensuing failure of the "great new plan."

Different ones assured Randy that this would not happen this time. He agreed to consider it.

When Randy left, however, some expressed "concern" for Randy, that he was being grumpy because things didn't go his way. They were speaking of a "Randy Jordan" I had not known.

Randy agreed, and so our new management system for the community work went into play. And, in fact, Wes Shaw's heart to make this plan work was strong and essential for any ultimate success. EXCEPT, Wes then expressed the need to go to New England for several weeks. We did state in the main elder's meeting how important his presence at home was to this endeavor, but he insisted. Because he was an elder, it was just assumed that he was "hearing from God," and so we agreed and away he went.

I was astonished, because I had known many times when non-elders, including myself, had to change their plans, even to personal loss, in order to fit the needs of the community. More than that, Brother John Clarke had cancelled his normal involvement with traveling around the world with the father ministry of the move to all the far-flung groups, so that he might devote himself to this particular community need this summer.

To make a long story short, however, the only elder among us who did any part of what we had committed ourselves to do was Bill Vanderhorst, in working with Randy. It's not that anything "unraveled," for no other part of our plan happened except that part laid upon Randy, just as he had known.

This, then, is the context in which God intended to prove Christ in me.

I Will Not Speak Against

My distress only increased. Something I must add about the autistic pain is that I am also compelled to hide it from others. I now know that is also part of Asperger's.

One time, before I was married, I was walking up the hill at Blueberry, with my coat drawn tightly around me, hunched over, with the pain written all over my face. Don Howat appeared out of nowhere and saw my face. "Daniel, are you okay?" he said. But the moment I saw him, I replaced the pain with a different face, "I'm fine," I replied.

This is different from the pretending of a false story of self. Rather, as an Asperger's man, it was impossible for me to have someone see that pain and think that there was something terribly wrong with me. I could bear the pain, for I walked with God in grace. What I could not bear was being treated with condescension, for I was powerless in the face of such a thing.

The difficulty I was feeling inside had begun to weigh heavily on my relationship with Maureen and the children, that is, Maureen had become quite distressed by my emotional absence from them. In early September, I found a note on the headboard of our bed one day in which she said that she could not continue with me unless something changed. There is nothing more awful to me than the thought of losing my dear wife and children.

I went to counsel with Gary Rehmeier concerning the note. When he had read it, I said, "I am a broken man, Brother Gary."

"No you are not," he replied. He went on to explain to me that we cannot know ourselves, that only others who are anointed of God can know what we are. "You are the proudest man I have ever known," he said.

I was too numb inside at that point for his words to cause further harm. Nonetheless, I walked away from his house with no hope and no word of Christ towards me. I apologized to Maureen and wept. Maureen shares with me now that her heart was turned back to me. I wonder, very often, why this wonderful woman continues to love me, for I know I don't deserve it. Yet I am so very grateful that she does.

Nonetheless, the proving of Christ in me would be found primarily in my heart attitude towards Brother John Clarke. I had watched him move in such wisdom and gracious anointing over the years. I had seen his expressed care for people. I had gained so much from the word that he shared, including times of great laughter. I had watched him submit to the decisions and concerns of others; I knew of the great personal losses he endured for the sake of God's people.

The truth is, I could also say the same things about Sister Charity Titus and my words would stand all tests of proving.

Over the months, as I continued to ponder the psychology operating inside the elder's gathering and the question of "what do they mean when they say, 'hear from God,'" I could see that the other elders bent their thinking to the influence of Brother John Clarke, Sister Charity, and Brother Gary. I could see the result, not of "hearing from God," but of defining "hearing from God" as being, "what would Brother John or Sister Charity or Brother Gary say."

I have realized since that ultimately it was not three, but rather Sister Charity, who, as I know now, was simply the most controlling person I have known. Her "control" was always benign, always with a true heart for others, always for their sake. Yet I have known few people who believed more thoroughly that "God with us" meant her keeping tabs on what everyone in the community was thinking and doing. I don't know of any direct personal harm that went from her to anyone, especially not to me. She believed that she was fulfilling God's purposes and moved only out from faith. Nonetheless, it was Sister Charity who was "in control."

I am saying this very carefully because, in spite of these things, I know that both Brother John and Sister Charity, who both have since passed on, loved Jesus and God's people, and gave themselves utterly for our sake with true hearts.

After Wes Shaw had returned to Blueberry later that summer, the men who were not elders, who had been gathering together as we had set out, had come up with some thoughts, which Wes then shared in the elder's meeting. But what they had thought up was not well received. Brother John Clarke said to him, "Who are these guys you're talking about?"

I watched Wes carefully fit his words to a full respect for Brother John. "Oh, just some of the brethren who were talking about various needs." I was fully aware in that moment that a direct answer would have been, "That group of men, Brother John, that you stayed home this summer for the sole purpose of shepherding them in their meetings." Such a thing could be said, but only in private and in all graciousness and honor. That was not an ability given to me, however, and most who would give answer directly would be following Korah's example.

Then, sometime in August, Randy grew discouraged with trying to carry responsibility for all the work with little support. A few of us were gathered in the outer office in the school discussing the situation. It was John Clarke, Wes Shaw, Dave Smillie, and myself. During this discussion, John Clarke, along with the other two, expressed a discouragement that included the belief that the primary fault of the difficulty lay with Randy.

I am very often an observer, rather than a participatant, in situations such as this. It was clear to me that most of the blame lay upon Wes Shaw and John Clarke and that the only thing Randy deserved was a deep apology followed by meaningful gratitude. Yet, in spite of being a somewhat analytical "observer," I did not rationalize my own response. Rather, what I did came out of the depths of who I am, out of Christ Jesus living as me. I regarded no blame or censure against Brother John in my heart. I imagined no words of "correction" or any such mindless folly.

The words of these men caused me only pain and sorrow, but I regarded nothing against them or against myself. Instead, I allowed God to be God, regardless. I allowed God to be God in Brother John, in Wes Shaw, in Dave Smillie, in Randy Jordan, and in myself. That does not mean, however, that my deep sorrow did not increase, for that, also, is the travail and proving of Christ.

Issue Seven: The Final Straw

In September, after the Shepherd's Inn convention, Brother Buddy Cobb gave a series of teachings for elders. Elder's spouses could also attend, and so Maureen went with me. There were always good things to be learned from Brother Buddy, but at the same time, it remained the same exhortation that if we didn't "get it right" we were "in trouble with God."

Through the first of October, Maureen and I went again to Blair Valley to spend several days with them. Rick and Shirley Annett were rebuilding a house they had chosen, which was situated not far from Kars and Minnie. Maureen spent her time working with Shirley, Connie, and Minnie. I spent my time working with Rick; we were able to move the project well along, including installing some large double-pane windows I had brought over from Blueberry. They would have a lovely view out of their dining area towards the woods.

When we returned to Blueberry, the topic of discussion was our now glaring need for food. In spite of all the care and effort we had put into the gardens that year, they had produced more poorly than ever. And, of all things, we were running out of potatoes available for eating before the winter had hardly started.

We discussed purchasing several tons of potatoes just for the family which we would put into the old root cellar in the community. As I thought about the problems with that old root cellar, I realized that it would be foolish to buy the eight tons we needed only to have half of them rot and thus have to replace them with another purchase of four tons in March or April. That approach would still mean two trips to Edmonton for potatoes.

On October 14 or 15, some of the men elders and some of the men deacons were getting together to discuss a solution to our potato problem. I shared my thoughts first with Randy, and he agreed with me fully. I do not remember all who were in this meeting, but there were more than Randy, Wes Shaw, Dave Smillie, and myself.

In the discussion, Wes Shaw stated that we should get all eight tons now. Randy suggested that half would rot, and thus, that we should purchase only half now and the other half in the early spring. Wes objected, saying, "No, that's not a good idea." I then spoke in agreement with Randy, for it was my thoughts he was presenting.

Not long after that, Wes Shaw and Dave Smillie cornered me in the dining room after a meal, wanting to talk with me. I sat down opposite them at one of the tables. Wes took the lead, with Dave Smillie giving full support to him in his facial expressions.

There was an unnatural fervor in Wes's face and eyes as he spoke to me. He rebuked me for siding with a non-elder against an elder in any discussion. Brother Dave's face expressed full agreement. Wes said to me, "I love the family far more than Randy can, that's why I am an elder." The implication was clear, by agreeing with Randy, I was joining his "lack of love."

I was registering Wes's words, but they were simply moving on by me. This was another of those few times when I looked straight into someone's eyes. To me, knowing what I knew, I saw only a religious madness dancing in those eyes.

I went straight home and told Maureen, "Honey, we must leave."

That evening, I shared with the elders that my family and I would be leaving Blueberry. Brother Gary said, "We do not understand, Daniel." "Neither do I," I replied.

In order to have some finances, I took on another five days of watching the North Star camp. The announcement of our leaving was made to the family while I was at the camp. Different ones came to help Maureen pack our stuff. Then, I picked up Maureen and the children and they spent the last two days at the camp with me.

It was a few more days of packing our stuff, then, and getting our little Ford Escort worked on. It was four of us in our little car, including a car seat for Johanna in the back. We loaded what we could into the trunk and in-between spaces. I made sure there was a spot for my large electronic typewriter.

We did not know where we were going, but I could no longer stay in a place where I did not belong and among people with whom I could not agree. Most of our stuff we simply left in our little cabin, along with our blue van in the parking lot. I told the elders that I would return in a few weeks to deal with our things.

The next morning, Tuesday, October 22, we went to the morning devotions. The elder's were meeting, so none of them were there. They had asked Philip Bridge to lead the devotions. He gathered all the family around us, and they prayed for us with great blessing and encouragement.

By noon, we drove out the road to the Alaska Highway; Blueberry was finally behind us. I was almost 40 years old.

I could not pretend to be something I was not. I could not be an elder. I had failed.

What I Did and Do

There is something in the human heart that runs far deeper than addressing wrongfulness or bringing justice. Deeper than all human action, there is the bottom line of – what about God?

In all things, is God just and true? Or has He, somehow, abandoned His claim that He directs our steps and that He is with us always? And if God has "failed," do we then take matters into our own hands, setting forth our own limited and selfish judgments, practicing the very same hurt against others for which we are accusing them?

Justify God in all things and find Him right and true. For it is only when we place ourselves only inside of a God who is good all the time that true justice could proceed from our hearts.

I have believed this and walked in this all my adult life, regardless of all my agony.

I must address my brief experiences with Gary Rehmeier and Wes Shaw. Gary, of course, knew only himself, for that is all we can know. He knew nothing of me because he never asked. He saw only my autistic pain and the shell I had erected to cover that pain, and he judged what he saw by his own knowledge of himself.

Yet I have always highly regarded Gary, who has since passed on, and received much good in the Lord from him both as an elder and as a person. More than that, I recognize the love of God poured out in his heart towards me. And I did not and do not judge him falsely in return.

If one had taken a poll of the Blueberry family as to who expressed the love of God in caring for others more, I have no doubt that Randy's score would have rated high and Wes's low. We had walked with the man for years and had seen him so often assert himself over us for his own benefit.

But Wes was so full of his own untrue story of self that he was unable to comprehend that what he said to me was a lie. Had he been by himself, that

would have been bad enough, but Dave Smillie's full support made me know that this same self-exalting madness had become the self-story, to a greater or lesser degree, of many of those gathered in that elder's meeting.

Yet I know that inside of Wes there was indeed a true and good heart.

And so, with all my heart, I receive Gary and Wes, and all those involved in our lives during this difficult time, as the Lord Jesus Himself. I place the determination of God towards me upon my every moment through this season of shattering.

I justify God and find Him right and true in all things. God is good, all the time. All of His ways concerning me are perfect. He has never led me wrong; He has never not led me.

I am not a victim. I place the Lord Jesus Christ upon every moment of my life with the full awareness that in every moment, I walked with God, no matter what I felt or knew.

I am a redeemer together with the Lord Jesus Christ, and we together seek and save all that is lost. Forgiveness is not towards those who made us happy but towards those who did us wrong. Yet, with Father, I go way beyond forgiveness.

God was in Christ, reconciling the world to Himself, not imputing their trespasses to them (2 Corinthians 5). No one ever did more wicked action-against than the Pharisees who conspired to put Jesus on the cross and who then stood there mocking Him. But Jesus, in spite of His very human agony, was no victim; rather, He was the expression of God's Heart. And the sword of His mouth cut through all those wicked actions with **"Father, forgive them, for they do not know what they are doing."**

I know many who have passed through similar difficulties and worse, who know only how to be victims, thus making themselves the same as the ones who did them wrong. I do not make light of anyone's pain, for it is real and it is awful. And God requires all justice for every single moment of hurt. But I place myself as an example of Christ before you; MAKE those who hurt you so badly to be your best friends forever by the power of redemption that is God through you.

By this we have known love, because He laid down His life for us; and we also are committed

to laying down our lives for our brothers and sisters. – Receive one another in just the same way that God inside of Christ received you.

As God has received you, imputing just innocence to you in all things, so you receive each one who offended you, imputing the just innocence of God to them.

This is the Salvation of God.

My Brethren

It would be wrong of me if I did not leave you with a full picture of what these brothers and sisters, whom I observed and with whom I participated inside this gathering of elders, meant to me.

Brother John Clarke was as a father to many, the best kind of father. He was the greatest example in my life of leading by wisdom and by deferring to others. He was always gentle and kind. John Clarke cared about people.

Sister Nathel Clarke was an intercessor. She and Brother John prayed for all those God had given to their care constantly across their many miles of travel. When she sat across from Maureen and me and asked for our forgiveness, I saw a true woman who cared more for us than for herself.

Sister Charity Titus took me under her wing through all the years I lived at Blueberry. She was a mother to me and the wisest and most influential teacher I have ever sat under. She cared about everyone in the community, that all would be safe and loved. She cared about God, that His presence would be known in our every gathering together.

I know that even now Sister Charity has joined with my mother in continued watchcare and prayer over me.

Sister Sue Sampson always encouraged me with blessing. She always supported me and made sure I had what I needed in all my work. She was an example to me of joy and confidence in God.

Brother Gary Rehmeier was a man of strength and exuberance. I always admired him; I always enjoyed it when he led the congregation in enthusiasm. Brother Gary sacrificed his life for the sake of the community, that we would be provided for.

Brother Alvin Roes was a man of much prayer and faithfulness to God. I have rarely known one of such quiet and earnest commitment. Yet he always had this unexpected way of making everyone laugh. When I think of Brother Alvin, I think of the same dedication to God by his example inside of me.

Brother John Austin was an example of earnest giving to all of us. He poured himself out, his strength and all his resources, for the sake of the Blueberry family, always. There was never a time, never a difficulty, never a cost, where Brother John was not right there, ready and willing to meet someone's need.

Sister Delores Topliff included me in her heart in spite of all my prickliness. She always treated me with kindness. She made sure to thank me for constructing her new home. I can trace much of the solidness of my English- teaching ability to Sister Delores as my teacher over many years.

I have mentioned those who were the most influential in my life. Yet all who were elders at Blueberry blessed Maureen and me with the goodness of Jesus through all our years in that fellowship.

I regret nothing. I value every relationship. I value every gift given to me by these elders who gave their lives that I might know the living God.

I am a wealthy, wealthy man.

28. A Proof of Christ

October 1996 - April 1997

Back and Forth

When we drove out to the Alaska Highway after leaving Blueberry, we turned north and drove the long wintry road to Blair Valley. We stayed at Blair Valley about a week. I continued to help Rick work on his and Shirley's cabin. Maureen taught school to Kyle. We visited more with the three families there. It was again a time of peace, a chance for my turmoil to dissipate.

When we left Blair Valley, we headed south towards Oregon. We had little money, but just enough for this trip.

It was necessary for me to write the last letter out from the clarity by which I understand everything now. Nonetheless, at the time I did NOT understand most of the perspectives that I placed around those events. My descriptions are accurate, and what I share is what I knew in my gut. But I really did not understand.

You see, being an elder seemed to me for many years to be a "next step" in my desire to know God and to walk with a people who know God. At this point in time, I assumed and understood only that I had failed. Readers of the last letter might say "But Daniel, you did not fail."

Understand, however, that I had zero idea of the words God would speak to me six months later, nor any part of what they meant. I simply had not measured up, not been able to fill the role I had wanted to fill. And I stumbled confused and blank inside through the next few months.

We spent a couple of days near Vancouver, not with the Pacy's but with their daughter, Ruth and her husband, Ricky Singh, who lived several miles away. They had both lived at Blueberry where they began a relationship, but were married back in Vancouver. I remember us all watching *Anne of Green Gables* with Megan Follows while we were there. We were enraptured with the story and it became one of our family favorites. We also visited John and Carol Pacy during that time.

We spent a couple of days at Sequim, Washington, with the Howat's before driving on down to Oregon. There, we connected with Katie Bracken and stayed with different ones of her family. Katie Bracken had returned to Oregon after visiting with us at Blueberry during the summer, and was living with her parents in Hubbard. They had turned an old storefront into their home. They offered us their small motorhome, parked outside on the street, as a place to stay for a night or two. The motorhome was not comfortable for us, especially with a train whistle nearby several times a night.

The only thing we knew to do was to drive back out to Christian Renewal Center to see if we could stay there for several days, while we figured out what we could do. We arrived there for supper on November 4. The Hansen's greeted us warmly; in fact, this was very much a part of their ministry, providing such a place for Christians like us for a time of respite.

We spent a week-and-a-half at CRC, using it as our home base while we attempted to establish ourselves somewhere in Oregon. The problem, of course, was that mom lived in Minnesota, and there was no more place for us to go in Oregon.

Sometime in this summer of 1996, Mom, Glenn and Kim, and their children had all moved to the Christian Community on the east side of the state, north of Duluth, called Meadowlands. Mark and Cindy Alesch were the leading elders at Meadowlands. Mom had gotten her own single-wide mobile home and they parked it right across from the Tabernacle. Glenn and Kim had a larger single wide parked a short distance away, now part of the community. I would see their new situation a few months later.

The Hansen's gave us one side of a cabin "duplex." It was dormitory style, but more than adequate as well as quiet and in the woods. We joined the staff at CRC for meals in the main dining room. We were able to help out a bit with some of the work, at least in the kitchen.

The only thing I knew to do was to try to get

some construction work. I waded through all the requirements in Oregon to be a contractor; I even found someone who was willing to loan me some tools. Meanwhile we visited with Katie Bracken about finding a place to live together with her. We looked at different possibilities.

We went down and visited with Dave and Cheryl, my sister, and then out to the home place to visit with Franz and Audrey.

After a couple of weeks, neither Maureen nor I felt that Oregon was the right place for us. We gave up and drove back up to Sequim and the Howat's. On the way we stopped at the woodworking tool show in Portland, Oregon. That was a memorable experience for me; it gave me lots of ideas to dream about for my own woodshop, something that has not yet materialized.

We spent a couple of days with a young couple named the Killam's who were fellowshipping with Don and Martha Howat. While we were there, Milton and Bonnie Vereide were visiting and we enjoyed their fellowship.

We drove on up to Vancouver and stopped again with Ruth and Ricky Singh. You see, I had to go on back to Blueberry in order to pack our stuff out of our cabin and into the blue van. So Kyle and I caught a bus up to Fort St. John where we got a ride out to Blueberry while Maureen and Johanna stayed with Ruth and Ricky.

Kyle and I stayed in Fort St. John for a few days with Peter and Barbara Bell, our good friends from our college years who were living in a mobile home near Charlie Lake. Then, Kyle and I took our blue van with a load out to Blair Valley. When we returned to Blueberry, I backed the blue van up to the front of our cabin, and with some other help, undoubtedly the Maldonado brothers, we loaded all of our belongings into the blue van. Kyle and I then drove it out to Shepherd's Inn on the Alaska Highway. We received permission from the elders there to park it in their staging area behind their back row of trailers. We went on back to Fort St. John, then, and bussed back down to Vancouver.

EXCEPT – while Kyle and I were at Blueberry, we picked up our mail. Lo and behold! There was a large package from Canadian Immigration. Our immigration had passed the first part, and we were scheduled for an interview in the Buffalo, New York Consulate on January 28, 1997.

How would we get to Buffalo, New York by then? This required a complete change of thinking. The only real possibility was for us to drive on down to Bowens Mill where Maureen's parents lived, having returned from their time at Graham River. I could work there to earn money for our plane tickets up to Buffalo. The simple problem, however, was that we had no money to get to Bowens Mill.

Back with the Singh's in Vancouver, Maureen and I obtained our passports and the medicals we needed for immigration. Maureen learned that she was carrying our third child, Katrina Dawn.

After leaving the Singh's, we went on to Sequim, Washington, where we spent a week with Don and Martha Howat in their oddly shaped house, and with their three children. Don connected me with a job for a few days installing insulation in a store that gave us a bit of traveling money. Don is always a great encouragement. I was able to share in the services with the fellowship that gathered in their home. Monica Rotundi, whom I had known from early Graham River and then in college at Blueberry, was living in Sequim and fellowshipping with the Howat's, so we got to visit with her as well.

When we left the Howat's, we drove on down to Portland, Oregon and spent the night with John and Tomi Rutledge in Gresham. While we were there, although we had not raised the subject, John and Tomi handed us an envelope containing $1000, more than enough to take us all the way to Georgia.

When we left the Rutledge's, we connected with Katie Bracken again. We spent the next couple of nights, however, with Clara Lou, Sister Bertie Henshaw's sister, who lived not far from Stayton, Oregon. We spent the nights there, but visited with my family during the day, as well as Katie's family. Finally, on December 9, we headed south into California.

Heading South Again

I had only a few more counties to go before I would have all counties in California colored in on my "county collecting map." I already had all counties in Nevada. So we headed towards the gold rush country in the Sierra Nevada. Maureen was not too thrilled over the extra hours of riding with the kids, but we got the counties.

We found a Holiday Inn in Stockton. While Maureen and the children were bedding down, I wandered out and found a store where I picked up a bottle of wine. I had not drunk alcohol in over twenty years, except for two communion services at Blueberry, but at this point in my trajectory, I needed some form of emotional consolation.

And so while Maureen and the children slept, I drank a bottle of wine. At this point in time, my presence in the Blueberry elder's meetings just a few weeks before was current. I had arrived at the pinnacle of my hope of twenty years; I was sitting among brethren at the forefront of the kingdom of God in the earth. Now here I was, drunk in a motel room in California.

How are the mighty fallen. Except I don't fit that line, because I certainly have never been "mighty." But David also said that wine is appropriate for times like this, and so eventually, my self-pity drifted off to sleep.

I must bring in here part of what I mean when I reference "my searing inabilities." As I looked at all this back and forth, and all these precious people who helped us and blessed us, I realized that I have never communicated back with any of them. Some we have never seen again. Communicating long distance is outside of my ability. Facebook is a nightmare to me, filled with "exploding landmines." I cannot even keep communication with my own family, except when I'm coming through. This is wrong, but it is also outside of my ability.

Recently, when I once again stopped with my brother Glenn in Minnesota, he said to me, "Daniel, you are always welcome here." I can't tell you how much that meant to me, that I am received in spite of my lack. And, the thing is, I am completely normal when face to face with people and am always kind and respectful. It's just long distance that becomes a great mental barrier to me.

My failures are significant and real. I can place them into the Lord Jesus now, but I knew nothing of that wondrous part of our salvation in 1996.

From Stockton, we drove into San Francisco. We visited Fisherman's Wharf and drove down Lombard Street, the one that winds back and forth. Then we drove over to Oakland and found the house in which Maureen had grown up and the school where she had attended through fifth grade.

We drove on to Modesto, then, and had supper and spent the night with Maureen's Aunt Miriam and Uncle Al before driving on down to Los Angeles to spend a couple of days with my sister Jenelle.

At this point, Jenelle had divorced from her marriage to Jim Hall. She had her own apartment somewhere just south of the city center, I think. I have not had much opportunity for visiting with Jenelle over the years. We have always lived far apart. I was very glad to know her better, even if only for a short while.

While at Jenelle's, we all went to Disneyland. Kyle enjoyed going on rides with his Auntie, but little Johanna was not impressed. We had her in a stroller, but she put up quite a fuss until I found an Eeyore. She grabbed Eeyore ferociously and quieted down. That would be one of her favorite toys for some years.

From southern California, we drove towards Lubbock, Texas. I had borrowed a couple of books from Jenelle, one of which was *The Client* by John Grisham. From the moment I read the first page, I asked Maureen to drive, for I could not stop reading until I had finished the book. I have been reading Grisham ever since. Then, I took much extra time collecting counties in New Mexico, and so we did not arrive at the Lubbock community until 1 AM on December 15.

We spent a couple of days at Lubbock, visiting with Maureen's sisters, Lois and Jessica, as well as my sister, Frieda and Tim. Tim had been living in the community for some time. He demonstrated his love for Frieda by agreeing to live separately for a short time and to win her love again. Their marriage was fully restored, and they were together at this point in one of the homes in the community.

We drove on, then, to Bowens Mill, arriving there on December 19. Maureen's good friend from her youth, Alison (Meffin) Robeson, who now lived in Australia, was visiting at the Ridge. Maureen got to spend most of two days with her before Alison and her children flew back to Australia. They were like two girls again in the joy of one another's company.

Back at Bowens Mill

We spent the next several months at Bowens Mill. I will no longer go into the detail that I have thus far in this chapter. We had a good time while at Bowens Mill and visited with many whom we had known, both from Blueberry, from Brussels, and from Bowens Mill.

All accommodations at the Ridge were full when we arrived. We had told Claude and Roberta we were coming before we left Oregon. They then arranged with the convention site and the fellowship in Dallas for us to use the Dallas cabin at the convention site. This was a cabin I had built in the early 80's. It was much improved since then, with a full bathroom and kitchenette. We moved into this cabin on our second day at Bowens Mill.

This was the Lord's kindness to us, because it allowed us to be involved with the different communities without obligation. The cabin was bare, but adequate. We made it our home for about two-and-a-half months. The center was the living area, kitchenette, bathroom, and on either side were rows of bunks curtained off into little "rooms." We only needed one side for the four of us, so we closed off the other side and did not use it. The cabin had a large front porch and was surrounded by trees and quiet.

We were not alone, however, for there were several other homes on the convention site not far from us, but blocked from sight by the trees.

I soon found paid employment, while Maureen often went to the Ridge with the children during the day. In January, Kyle began attending the kindergarten at the Bowens Mill School across the road where both Maureen and I had taught. We typically ate the evening meal at the Ridge with the family there.

We took the opportunity to visit with many different people at the three communities, including friends Maureen had known while she was at school in Brussels. One of the families at Bowens Mill had started a coffee and lunch shop in Fitzgerald called Tony's Just Coffee. It was a delightful place, in the rooms of a converted house. We often went there with different ones.

Michael Kuntz and Deborah Austin were married at Blueberry the first part of January. As part of their honeymoon, they came down to Atlanta where the Austin's were from. Maureen, the children, and I went up to their wedding reception at Deborah's grandma's, the wealthy and "formidable" Mrs. Jean Austin. It was so good to connect with Michael and Deborah again.

Soon after we arrived, I got work with Paul Weaver at his sawmill and wood business, just across the highway from the Ridge. Daryl Cobb worked with Paul as well. Paul had a nice bandsaw mill. I helped handle the logs going on and the boards coming off. I love watching a log turn into beautiful boards.

I worked with Paul for less than two weeks. I must share one incident. Daryl Cobb was on the forklift with a load of wood intended to go into the kiln. I was standing at the back of the kiln while Daryll drove in with the load. Daryll was coming pretty fast only to discover that the machine had no brakes. His face was aghast. I saw the wall of boards coming straight at me. I judge such situations and react instantly. My judgment this time was that I could not go up and I could not go down. My only thought was that I would be crushed against the back wall.

And yet it stopped! An inch from my chest. From fast and unstoppable to – nothing.

I have indeed known the grace and keeping power of God, in many more ways than one.

Then, before our trip to Buffalo, I got a job with Chris Hawkins from Family Farm, the son of George Hawkins with whom I had worked on the convention site years before, doing construction work in town. I will share more of that in a bit.

Immigration

Meanwhile, we had used our remaining money from the Rutledge's generous gift to purchase plane tickets from Atlanta to Buffalo, New York. We left on a Saturday, driving up to the airport early. Kyle and Johanna stayed at the Ridge with their Grandpa and Grandma.

It was winter upon our arrival in Buffalo. We found a Days Inn not far from the airport where we would stay through our time there. This was Saturday evening, but our immigration interview would not be until Tuesday and our return flight was on Wednesday. We had a quiet evening together on Saturday night. I remember our only choice for food nearby was an Arby's; we have not eaten at Arby's since.

Sunday morning however, we wanted to attend a church service somewhere. I like different, as you have probably guessed by now. Leafing through the long list of churches in the yellow pages showed little that interested me, until I arrived at the title "The Church at Buffalo." "Sound's interesting," I thought.

So, after calling the place to confirm our visit, Maureen and I took a cab there for the service. It was in a room in an office-building, and it was filled with Chinese people and a sprinkling of Europeans, but probably no more than fifty people in all. "Interesting," we thought. The service was lively, but different. I was busy working my mind, trying to figure out what group this might be. Before the service was over, I had determined that it was a Witness Lee group. They were definitely believers in Jesus, regardless of their uniqueness.

One of the elders of this group was a European man, married to a Chinese woman, Tony and Olivia Lyons. They introduced themselves to Maureen and I after the service and invited us over to their home for dinner. After dinner, we spent a couple of hours visiting with Tony and Olivia; it was a wonderful time. God's people are unique, and they are found in every setting. Later that afternoon, Tony drove us back to our motel.

On Monday, Maureen and I bussed up to Niagara Falls. It was winter and the falls were ice. It's a fantastic picture, totally different from the normal summer view of the falls. Then we walked across the bridge into Canada. Our visas were still current, though we were just going over for a couple of hours. We went up to the top of the Skylon tower, a circular restaurant overlooking the Canadian side of Niagara Falls. We decided to splurge and ordered their top quality salmon dinner. I have eaten a lot of potatoes, broccoli, and even salmon in my life, but we have never eaten anything as good. After our excursion, then, we took the bus back to our motel.

On Tuesday, January 28th, we bussed into downtown Buffalo to the Canadian consulate for our immigration interview scheduled for 9:30 AM. To me, being fifteen minutes early is "being unacceptably late," so I'm sure we were there waiting an hour before. Our interview did not happen, however, until 11:15.

Our interviewer was a Canadian lady, probably in her mid-thirties, very professional. She went over part of our application with us, asking questions. She asked about Blair Valley and the people there. We were immigrating on the basis of our welcome at Blair Valley only, typically not enough, but our two children were Canadian, so that was a large factor. Her interest in the interview, however, seemed to be to know who Maureen and I were. It wasn't long before she said to us, "Welcome to Canada."

We left the Canadian consulate in a daze of joy and wonder. How could it be? We were immigrated to Canada. Only long after did I realize that she was assuming that we still lived in British Colum-

bia, which was technically correct, for all our stuff was still there. I think she made her decision partly based on our long-term commitment to living in Canada.

Nonetheless, that was just the first part of a long process. She specified that we should wait until our next child was born to complete the process, which would then include a trip back down to the border at Aldergrove, BC, because the final step of immigration happens only when crossing the border. We were completely free, however, to live at Blair Valley until we got our final papers.

Our lives had become new again.

Grandma Susan

Just before our flight up to Buffalo, Maureen's grandmother, Susan Jacobsen, had suffered a stroke and was taken to the hospital in Fitzgerald. She was ninety-four years old. Maureen's mom, Sister Roberta, spent the first day and night in her room with her. Even while Maureen and I were flying up to Buffalo, Grandma Susan's several sons and daughters were arriving or on their way.

That evening, while we were back in our motel room, Sister Roberta called to say that Grandma Susan had left to be with Jesus.

Several of Grandma Susan's daughters had been in the hospital room with her. These were godly women of great respect, in their fifties and sixties. I know Aunt Miriam and Aunt Irma were among them. They were singing praises with their mother. Then she closed her eyes to rest while they sang. Suddenly, Grandma Susan opened her eyes, looked up into the corner of the room, and with great joy on her face and arms lifted up, she said, "Jesus," and left.

Though her body remained, it's hard to say that she actually "died."

Maureen and I did not arrive back at the Ridge until late Wednesday evening. By that time most of Roberta's brothers and sisters had arrived. We got to visit with them for the next few days. There was sobriety, certainly, but no grief. Grandma Susan had walked with God her whole life, and all her children had grown up inside of the power of the Holy Spirit. This was, in fact, a time of joy.

On January 31, all of little Johanna's great aunties held a wonderful birthday party for her. Jo was three years old; it was a celebration of joy.

Grandma Susan's graveside service was on February 5; she was buried in the little cemetery at the edge of the Bowen's Mill property, right down from the Ridge. That evening we had a memorial service for her at the Gathering Place, the three-farm community worship place at the convention site. Many shared, both family members and people of the community, for Grandma Susan had given a heritage of God to us all.

Building Walnut Cabinets

Upon our return from Buffalo, I went back to work with Chris Hawkins. Chris was much like his dad, George (who had earlier passed on), very friendly and talkative, and good to work with. Chris did construction contract work, and he loved walnut on the side, walnut trees, logs, boards, and making things with walnut.

Chris had secured a large remodel job in the house of one of the wealthiest men in Fitzgerald. I don't remember his name, but he made big bucks most every weekend running a large gun show around the southeast. He paid us cash, with which he was overflowing. The man was "new rich," which meant he wanted the most extravagant home in Fitzgerald. But he wanted appearance more than value, so it was always a contest between his exhortation to slam it together and our desire to do quality work.

Chris had sold him his reserve pile of beautiful walnut boards to be used to build a fantastic office in the man's basement, along with a secure

show room for his guns. That was my part of the job, while Chris handled all the rest of the remodel work. Chris's job was difficult, because the wife would say, "Do it this way," which he did, only to have the husband come by and say, "No, do it this way," which he did, only to – yes, on and on.

The office and show room were not in the wife's domain, so I had to struggle only with the impetuosity of the man. Nonetheless, I made him a beautiful set of walnut cabinets for his office. I have included a picture of it, with Kyle and Johanna visiting with me.

I worked on this job all the way up until we left to return to Canada, the first week of April.

In the third week of February, we went to the Georgia coast with Claude and Roberta for an outing. While there, we visited St. Simon's Island and walked with the children along the beach.

Kyle had begun his guitar-playing career in kindergarten, and so we attended two performances of his class playing their little guitars.

On the first weekend in March, Maureen and I drove up to Atlanta with the children to spend the weekend with Peter and Patti Honsalek. Peter is Maureen's cousin. He was doing well working as a house painter and running his own company. Peter had a house design software program on his computer, and so I spent a few happy hours drawing my thoughts for our home to be at Blair Valley while Maureen visited with Patti. Maureen and Patti had lived together with Grandma Susan when I first moved to the Ridge.

We spent several hours at Stone Mountain, just outside of Atlanta. We took the gondola ride to the top and then hiked down the rock mountain back to our cars. It was a memorable experience. That evening we watched our first John Grisham movie, *The Client*, which story I had just read. This was the second edge-of-your-seat experience in my enjoyment of Grisham from then until now.

An Intense Study

Even though I have not always mentioned my continual relationship with the Bible. my intense study that I might know what God actually says in His Word had not slowed down. I continued writing verses and chapters and books and reading from cover to cover around once each year.

My strength was continuing to abate. At this point in my life, working a forty-hour work week was all I could do. If I were to survive at the job, I could not do anything physical in addition. This was a bit distressing for Maureen, since the only way I could earn money was to rest through all the non-work hours.

So, through February and March, sitting in our bare cabin on evenings and weekends, I hammered away at my electronic typewriter in my pursuit of knowing what God says.

The big question for me was – What is God's order for His church, according to the New Testament?

I begin at Matthew, turning page after page, and typing out every verse that was any kind of command or instruction. For my first time through, everything was ordered by the books of the New Testament. This was not sufficient to give understanding, however, and so I set myself to retype all those verses a second time using the printed out pages as my study reference.

And so I organized all the New Testament commandments into categories. One category was commandments to be righteous, another was those to love, a third was the "follow Me," commandments, a forth was "give thanks – do not be afraid," and so on. I spent many fulfilling hours on this task, and I still have that second set of pages in my file cabinet.

In this process, however, I discovered a specific set of New Testament commandments that required their own category, for they were fantastically different from all other gospel commandments – and that is the "Be Just Like God" category. And inside that category of commandments to us as believers in Jesus to be just like God was a New Testament verse that I had never noticed before or heard preached on in my life, a verse that fitted itself into my heart in this incredible exercise God was pressing me through, that of changing my definition of God.

Receive one another in exactly the same way that Jesus receives you (Romans 15:7).

Granted, I still was defining so many New Testament things by the Calvinist definitions preached by Buddy Cobb. Nonetheless this verse lodged itself in my heart. I did not know what it meant or where it fit, but I knew that it spoke of something not found in any definitions of Christianity I had known up until then, something that sang inside the desire of my heart to know God and to walk with a people who know God.

Bowens Mill Convention

Because of the upcoming convention, the Dallas fellowship needed to have their cabin free so that it could be prepared for their use during the convention. For that reason, Maureen and I, with Kyle and Johanna, moved over to the Ridge, to Grandma Susan's now empty airstream trailer, about ten days before the convention.

This year the "April" convention was to be at the end of March. Glenn and Kim Yordy, with their children, came down from Meadowlands over a week before the convention in order to spend time with us and to visit the communities in Georgia. Glenn, who is also a builder, went to work with me for a few days, to help with the remodel job.

A couple of days before the convention, Tim and Frieda Louden arrived from Lubbock. It was a mini Yordy reunion, though mom had not come.

The convention ran from March 26-30, ending on Easter Sunday (which we made no note of, as was the custom in that fellowship). It was a regular convention, filled with mighty praise services and much preaching of anointed word.

About midway through the convention, Brother Ernest Watkins got up to share a word. In his word, he gave an illustration of a mafia story he had read.

A young man had grown up in the mafia and now wanted to take his place as a crime boss. The older men agreed, but on a condition. They asked him to fly to St. Louis to take care of a small "job." At the airport in St. Louis, however, the young man was seized by federal agents and spent a few years in prison. When he was released, he came back to New York.

The young man sat down with the men who had sent him to St. Louis. They all put their guns on the table. He asked them, "What went wrong? What did I do that got me caught?"

They replied, "We were the ones that informed the FBI." As he reached for his gun, they asked, "Do you want to know why?"

"You see, you were asking for a place of trust among us. We could not give it to you until we knew that you would never speak of our affairs to the police. You did not; you passed the test. Now, before you shoot anyone, tell us, which nightclub or casino would you like to run as your own. We now know that we can trust you."

Brother Ernest's point was that sometimes we think that what is happening to us means one thing, when all along, what God was doing in our hearts was something entirely different.

At this point, in the anointing of the Holy Spirit, all my failure at Blueberry and in the eldership came up before me. And in that moment, I heard the words, not in my mind from Brother Ernest's illustration, but in my spirit from my Father. – "Son, you passed the test."

And in that moment, I knew that what God meant was that regardless of all my failure or the shortcomings of anyone else, I had justified God and found Him right and true, and I had not blamed others or myself.

From then on, the importance of this moment in my life has grown in my understanding. The first thing that it did in me at that time was the realization that God is different from what I had understood Him to be and from what I had heard tell of Him, and that God's purposes are not the same thing as what has been preached.

I lived in a theology that claimed that to "please God," we had to hear Him speak and to be sure to obey. "Pleasing God" was entirely inside the arena of outward performance. In that arena, I had failed and continue to fail completely.

But my Father's words to me opened my understanding to the fact that what God is after is the heart as His dwelling place, and that He must remove contempt from our hearts before He could ever show Himself to us.

In writing this account, I have realized the connection of this twelve-year arc, from the April convention of 1985, to the March convention of 1997, sitting in the same part of the Bowens Mill Tabernacle. At the beginning, the issue was John Hinson, at the end it was John Clarke.

Would I find fault with them or would I justify God and find Him right and true in all things? This is the proof of Christ.

Now, let me carefully define what I mean by "the proof of Christ." I don't mean me; I mean Jesus. It is Jesus who proves Himself in me to the Father. It was Jesus, my only life, all the way through. It was He alone, inside my heart, who caused me to be what the Father desired.

I could never have known, and if I had known, I certainly could never have done.

Christ Jesus is my life; I have no other life.

On Sunday, Maureen and I sat down with the Father ministry to share with them our intention to return to Blair Valley. Again, it was Buddy Cobb, Joe McCord, John Clarke, Tom Rowe, and Bill Grier, all of whom we knew well. They blessed us in our going. I asked about my position of walking as an elder. They assured us that they knew of no reason why that would not continue. Brother Buddy stated that it would be the life and blessing in the community at Blair Valley that would affirm my being set in as an elder.

That afternoon, Maureen and I, Tim and Frieda, Glenn and Kim, and all our children went to Shoney's in Fitzgerald to enjoy their buffet. They would return to their homes on Monday.

Returning to Blair Valley

Through the next two days, we packed our things and said our "Goodbyes." On Monday afternoon, Michael and Deborah Kuntz came by to visit with us. On Tuesday, the family at the Ridge put on a "going away" celebration for us.

We left Bowens Mill on April 2, heading north. It was springtime in the south, with flowers blossoming everywhere. We stopped at Chickamauga, near Chattanooga, Tennessee. I wanted to tour the battle site and Lookout Mountain.

At that point, however, Maureen began to experience some difficulties with her pregnancy. We spoke on the phone with a sister at the New Covenant community who was a medical doctor. With her advice, we decided that Maureen should not continue on this trip in the car. We spent the night in a motel there in Tennessee. While Maureen rested in the motel room the next morning, I took the children on a tour of the battlefield. Then we drove back down to Bowens Mill.

The next day, Maureen saw a doctor in town and received an ultrasound. Little Katrina was just fine. The physical stress of sitting in a moving car, however, was not a good idea.

So – Maureen decided to stay at the Ridge with Johanna and her parents while Kyle and I drove up to Blair Valley, to prepare a place for her. They would fly up to Edmonton together in May when Maureen was feeling stronger.

So, on April 5, Kyle and I headed north again. This was a special time of several weeks to spend with my son, in both the long drive up to Blair Valley and then working on our home together, getting it ready for the girls to come up. Kyle was five, and would be six in August. He was a very aware little boy and remembers all these things well.

But, hey, I was behind the wheel of a car, with many days of no obligation, just me and my boy, so we did a zig-zag route on our long trip north. I had been enthralled with Simon Kenton's story in the opening up of Kentucky and Ohio, so it was Kentucky where we did the most zig-zagging.

First, we hiked through Mammoth Cave. I did not find it as impressive as Carlsbad Caverns because it was just a large rocky "hole" with no limestone formation. Then we went to Boonsboro, the site of Davy Crockett's fort. Both of us were really impressed with this fort. It was like a community, with the wall around it, and various village craft workshops against that wall all the way around, all of them facing the interior plaza. I still hold that concept in my mind for one part of a "teaching community."

Then, after driving through Simon Kenton's part of Kentucky, we ended up at Abraham Lincoln's birth place. Kyle and I walked the path through the woods to see the little log cabin where Lincoln was born. At this point, I still believed the tales I had been taught all my life. As I tried to explain to Kyle what it all "meant," I teared up and could not speak. A great sense of worship arose inside of me, as great as anything I had known in an anointed worship service.

I was appalled, and I began to ponder what on earth that meant. It would be about three or four years, yet, before I learned of the falseness of the Lincoln cult, who is the "patron saint" of "God bless America." But having experienced the power of the demonic that rules the entirety of that dark religious cult, I was backing swiftly away from it.

We headed on north, then, in a reasonably straight path to Meadowlands to see Mom. By Indianapolis, the ground was dusted with snow. This was a fascinating study, because Spring was past at Bowens Mill when we left, and as we drove north to Minnesota, we went back through the opening of springtime, bit by bit, all the way to full winter in Duluth. We stopped in Madison, Wisconsin and explored the state capitol there. It was a beautiful and impressive building.

We arrived at the Meadowlands community, less than an hour's drive north of Duluth, Minnesota. At this time it was a vibrant community. The lead elders were Mark and Cindy Alesch. Mom had her own trailer, a single wide, just across from the Tabernacle. Kyle and I stayed in her trailer for the three days we were there. The community was not large, maybe thirty to forty people in all, so, even though Glenn and Kim's trailer was on the other side of the building area, it was just a short walk.

I was so pleased. As we sat in the dining room and watched the flow of the family together, I saw my mother honored by all as the grandmother and matron of the community. I was especially thrilled to see how Cindy Alesch blessed mom as well as Glenn and Kim's children. They had come to the right place.

I realize now that my difficulty with my mother was only when she was trying to live "with me." Every time I visited her, including this time, we spent long hours sharing together in good conversation and in the fellowship of Christ.

I realize now, maybe for the first time, how much I miss my mom. I think that's a good thing to realize. Sometimes we take mothers for granted, or at least I did.

Meanwhile, we were in communication with Maureen by phone several times. She was missing us, but feeling better. She had obtained plane tickets for their flight up in May.

On April 12, Kyle and I crossed the border into Canada. We were headed straight across the diagonal to Edmonton, and then on to Blair Valley, shown in the map on the following page..

Above: **Blair Valley Tabernacle.** This is after I added the new siding/insulation. The old Shiloh Tabernacle is on the right.

Below: Map of the Blair Valley property and the roads in.

I have placed the white letters on or just above the locations.

A. Our original Gundy bridge

B. The steep slope going up.

C. The steep slope coming down.

D. The Gundy Road did not then exist on top of this ridge.

E. The northern point of our fields and property.

F. The center of the community buildings. The location of the Tabernacles shown above.

G. The southern point of our fields and property, two miles from the northern point - E.

H. The high ridge to our east.   I. The high ridge to our west.

J. The winter road out. (The letters continue in the sketch on page 286.)

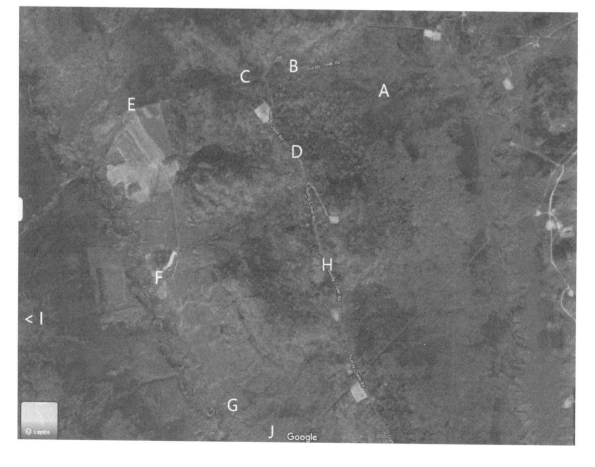

29. Peace at Blair Valley

April 1997 - December 1997

Into Blair Valley

Kyle and I turned left at Mile 120 on the Alaska Highway onto a gravel road heading directly south. The road stayed on the top of the ridge for ten miles; to our right was the valley of the Gundy Creek. We passed two ranches down in the valley, the last one near where the road turned west and we dropped down towards the Gundy, still ten miles to go. After wandering another mile or so we came to the Gundy Creek. The original bridge across the Gundy had been wiped out a few years before. While Wes Shaw was at Blair, he had Randy Jordan come over, and they put a new bridge across the Gundy (A) for access to Blair Valley.

After crossing the small bridge, we meandered slowly upward until we came to the steep ridge that separated the Gundy Valley from the Blair Valley. Here the road went up sharply and then turned steeply to the north as it angled up the side of the ridge (B). Near the top it turned west again. As we came over the top of the ridge, we saw the road ahead dropping steeply down into the valley of the Blair Creek. It's quite an exhilarating ride down that steep hill (C). The brethren who had built the Shiloh Community had simply followed the seismic line straight down the slope. (See the map on the left.)

At the bottom of the ridge, the road continued west across the northern fields of the Blair Valley property (E) before turning south again. We drove a mile through hay fields on either side, with the Blair Creek looping to our right. In the center of the property we came to the wooded area interspersed with lawns in which the original Shiloh buildings had been constructed (F). The pastures of the Blair Valley property continued on another mile (G), but we turned to the right and followed the lane in amongst the cabins.

We were home.

We passed Rick and Shirley Annett's cabin in the woods on our right (K), and then Kars and Minnie Kiers's cabin (L). We drove a little further and came to a stop at the building now used as the Blair Valley Tabernacle (M). This was the building where Richard and I had stayed when we came to the 1986 Shiloh convention, above the root cellar, right next to the large old Tabernacle (N). Rick and Shirley, Kars and Minnie soon came to greet us. It was April 16, 1997, and we were home.

I loved the Blair Valley community with all my heart and still do. There is no painful memory from our time there; the only difficult question is why we left. But that question is for another chapter. I do feel like crying, however, for our loss is truly great.

I want to describe for you the land, the buildings of Shiloh as well as those of Blair, and the brethren who shared Blair Valley as home with us.

First, Bob and Connie Newman were no longer living at Blair Valley. We had heard at Bowens Mill that they had moved away, back down to the states. This was quite sad for Maureen and I. I had hoped to teach school to their teenage children. The company of the Newman family would certainly have added goodness to our life together. I will share more of why they left at a point when it best fits.

Look again at the map of the larger property inside the Blair Valley on the previous page. The property is most of two square miles, running north and south, the area that is cleared, mostly on the eastern side of the Blair Creek, but a small portion on the western side, accessible only by a ford. The majority of the acreage is vast fields across two miles north and south, once partly grain, but now almost entirely hay and pasture. The bottom of the Blair Creek is wooded as well as the part of the property going up the slopes of the ridge to the east, a mix of poplar and spruce trees.

The valley itself is bounded on its eastern and western side by ridges about a thousand feet up (H & I). The flat on the bottom is nearly a mile wide, giving a sense of both spaciousness and bounded protection. High green ridgetops were always in any view while outside.

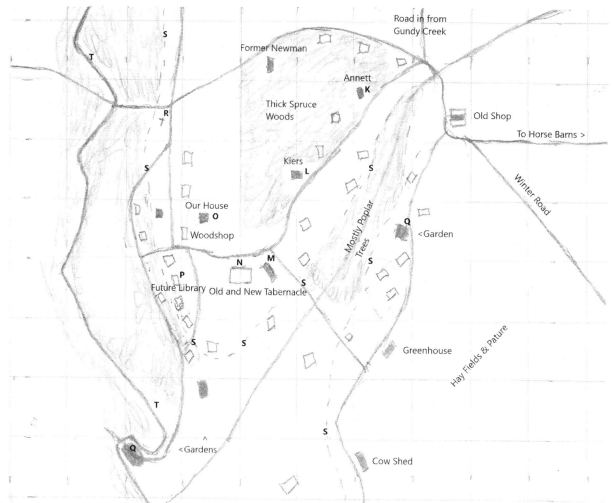

In trying to make this sketch clear in the printed book, I am including two kinds of identification. First are the written words and second is a continuation of the lettering from K to T. I name most of the letters in the text. Here are the few I do not indicate.

P. The cabin that I later turned into our library.

Q. The garden spots.   R. The spring where we got our water.   T. The Blair Creek

The building area in the center is spread across a wide area. Above is a map showing the old buildings of Shiloh, a few of which we were using. I have darkened those, the "Blair Valley" buildings. Note that sizes and positions of everything is approximate only. Also disregard the scale lines needed for drawing everything in.

Cabins were built wherever anyone felt like without a sense of togetherness, though Shiloh was not nearly as spread out as Headwaters had been. From our house to the old shop or to our cow barn was about a quarter-mile walk. Our house, the

Kiers's house and our Tabernacle were reasonably close. The buildings we did not use, which were many, were derelict and filled with squirrel debris and old things left behind. Walking through them always felt a little haunted.

The dotted line (Marked S all the way around) represents the edge of the level area where the slope dropped down, either to the seasonal creek down through the middle or to the Blair Creek on the left. The slightly darkened area shows the woods (Thick Spruce Woods). There were a few scattered trees elsewhere, but not many, mostly open grass fields. Views in different places and directions were stunning. The roads were all dirt and would turn to mud whenever it rained.

Kars and Minnie had insisted on keeping the whole area beautiful, which included NOT using the roads when they were wet. I agreed fully. Minnie had flowers around her house and around the Tabernacle, and regardless of the insides of the derelict buildings, the outsides were all clean and neat except for around the old shop.

I would like to give you a real sense of how beautiful this valley and community building area was to us, but I cannot without taking you there, so I will leave the description at that. Pictures don't really do it justice, for they could not capture that sensation of wonder one felt.

The Kiers's and Annett's

Kars and Minnie were probably in their seventies. They had been teenagers in Holland when the Germans invaded. After WWII, Kars served for a time in the Dutch East Indies, in the failed attempt to keep it from becoming independent. They told us some stories of these times, but nothing of the atrocities. In fact, the Dutch did as badly to the Indonesians as the Germans had done to them. Kars and Minnie had immigrated to Canada, where Kars farmed in southern Ontario before they connected with the move in the late 1960's.

Kars and Minnie did have several children, but they were long since grown and wanted nothing to do with move community. We may have met a daughter, but I don't remember any other, except Kars' brother who came from Holland to visit.

Kars and Minnie were very hospitable, and we always felt welcome in their home. Minnie tried her best to give it a Dutch feel inside and even outside with tulips during the summer. We spent many good times visiting with them in their home and around the dinner table at the Tabernacle. At the same time, they were set in their ways and were not always open to other people's ideas. Whenever a conversation ventured into areas that did not interest them, their expressions of disapproval ensured that it ceased.

Rick and Shirley Annett were probably in their late forties at this time, a few years older than Maureen and I. Shirley was one of the daughters of Alvin and Marie Roes and had lived at Blueberry

with them. Rick was from the same part of southern Ontario as the Roes's. Rick and Shirley had married before my time at Blueberry.

Rick was laid-back and easy-going. The problem with calling Rick a "dear friend" is that you will find hundreds of people lined up to call him their "dear friend" as well. Rick made you feel warm and accepted; his expressed friendship was always genuine. Shirley was like her dad a fair bit, not as talkative in general conversation, but with a dry sense of humor, always coming up with something funny with a dead-pan face. Shirley was efficient and business-like. I think she kept the books. By trade, Rick was a barber. He also played the piano and led our praise services. Rick and Shirley never had children.

Working on our Home

When we first arrived, Kyle and I stayed in the upstairs of the Kiers's cabin. Right away we started working on our new home (O).

Maureen and I had our hearts set on the former caretaker's cabin and when we had shared this earlier with the Blair family, they had agreed it would be ours. We had great plans for it that would take a couple of years to complete.

On the next page is a picture of our cabin; this is while Kyle and I were working on it. It is plain, yes, but we hoped to make it more comfortable over time.

I had drawn out a complete plan for both upstairs and downstairs. As you can see, the upstairs wall was only five feet high, with the pitched roof going up from there. We really liked the compact feel of that style. In order to have a place for us to live, however, I left the downstairs alone and worked only on the upstairs, turning it into our home for the time being.

I took out the inner stairway (which was in a poorly-chosen place) and put it to the side of the house up to a landing and cut a doorway into the side of the upstairs. Then our bedroom and Kyle's were on that side, with the living room in the middle behind the upper window in front, put in later. I built a little kitchen in the back center, where the final stairway would be. On the far side, then, were Johanna's (and Katrina's) room in the front and a nice-sized bathroom in the back corner.

The downstairs, which would later contain a larger kitchen, and living room, etc. (by our plan), I

once a week, we used a gas-powered pump to fill a larger tank from the spring just up the road from our house and then pumped it into each of the four tanks as well as down in the cow barn. That gave us a somewhat pressured water-flow inside. To our system, however, I added our 12-volt pump. We also had a propane hot water heater next to the bathroom. A tank of propane would last us about a month. I would heat the water in the late afternoon, then shut the propane off again. That

left as it was, with the woodstove in the middle. We used it as storage and as Maureen's laundry room. In the back corner we piled our winter's supply of firewood, which meant that it was dry and right at hand. In the front behind the right window, I had my office. I found a nice teacher's desk from the old tabernacle and placed on it my electronic typewriter.

None of this was in place, however, when Kyle and I began, so we had to remove all the old walls and start anew. Kyle was just five, so he mostly played while I worked, but he helped me when he could. We worked hard but were not nearly finished when it was time to go get Maureen and Johanna in Edmonton.

My strength was waning, but when I mentioned to the Kiers's that I needed to take a day off to recuperate, they expressed disdain. Nonetheless, they left me free to order my time and work as I chose.

Let me add a few more details about our home. When we heard that the Newman's were leaving Blair Valley a few months earlier, I had asked Bob if we could buy their solar panel and battery set-up, which we did. We now installed it on our house. I had asked Randy Jordan to make us a steel pole that would easily swivel, which he did. That way I could turn it through the day to follow the sun. This gave us 12-volt DC power for our home.

In the top part of the roof slope above the bathroom area, I placed the large water tank that had been in that house. All of us, including the Tabernacle, had such a tank as high up as could be. About

way we had hot showers that evening, and Maureen would have reasonably warm water for laundry the next day.

We also had a 12-volt picnic cooler for some foodstuffs and 12-volt lights as well as my tape-player for music. I set up a real washing machine in the downstairs for Maureen. We used the small community generator to run it on wash days. Then the clothes were hung to dry either out back during the summer or inside the downstairs during the winter. Laundry was still hard work for Maureen, but much better than what it had been for the mothers in the early communities, that is, all by hand.

Maureen and Johanna Arrive

Because we did not have our new home ready for Maureen and Johanna's arrival in mid-May, we moved over from the Kiers's to a little house just across the road from us, on the edge of the slope. Wes Shaw had fixed up this little cabin for himself, and the Annett's had also stayed there until they could move into their new place. It was tiny, but cozy. The bed in the back corner was a tight fit and the children slept in the loft, accessible by ladder. It would be our home for a few weeks.

It turns out that soon after Kyle and I had headed north, the Mack's decided to take a trip to visit relatives all across Texas. So, after several days of rest, Maureen and Johanna went with them. They were gone to Texas for more than two weeks during this time. It was great for Maureen because it gave her a chance to visit with sisters, aunts, uncles, and cousins on both sides of the family before she left for the northern wilderness. They returned to Bowens Mill a few days before their flight up.

In the middle of May, Kyle and I drove to Edmonton the day before, spending a night at the Hilltop community with Patrick Downs on the way. We picked up Maureen and Johanna at the Edmonton airport. We were back together again. After spending the night with brethren in Edmonton, we drove back to Blueberry that evening. We went on to Blair Valley the next day, arriving to a cold evening, but a warm welcome with a turkey dinner made especially for Maureen and Johanna's arrival.

We stayed in the tiny little cabin on the edge of the slope while we continued to work on our new home. We completed and moved into it in phases over several days but did not spend our first night there until June 8. We were home.

Life at Blair Valley

Let me now give a general sense of life at Blair Valley through this first summer. I will begin with our Tabernacle, the heart of the community.

The original building that was our Tabernacle had been built by Shiloh, right next to the large old tabernacle, with a root cellar below ground and a food processing facility on the main floor. The building had no second story, and we were hardly conscious of the root cellar beneath of us as it was heavily insulated. It was a long rectangle. On the north end were the stairs down, a small office space, where we had a solar powered setup to run the phone, and then the main entry on the east side. The larger center was split down the middle with a kitchen on the west side and the dining room on the east side. Both were comfortably sized for our use. They had carpeted the dining room, so it felt quite homey. The windows had lovely curtains. On one end of the dining room was a couch and living area, on the other side was the piano and a space for the service and in the center was our dining table. The kitchen had both a propane stove and a propane refrigerator. It was also comfortably laid out. Then, on the south side was a large room that had been the school room when the Newman's had been there, but which was not used now.

We ate dinner and supper together in the Tabernacle each day. Breakfasts were at home. It was six adults around the table, plus little Johanna and

Kyle. Bob Newman had shot a young moose the winter before and they had canned most of it. It was wonderful meat and lasted us for most of the first year at Blair. The root cellar beneath was filled with last year's crops, cabbage, potatoes, onions, beets, and carrots. Minnie was a wonderful cook, and Maureen and Shirley as well. We ate well, just as we had at all other move communities.

We had worship services on Wednesday evening and Sunday morning. I often shared in the services, as did Minnie, Kars, and Rick. Shirley shared only occasionally and Maureen not at all. Rick played the piano and led the praise. Eating together and worshipping together are what Christ life is all about and our fellowship was warm and good.

Kars had been a farmer and then in charge of the gardens at Headwaters and Blair Valley. When I asked to share the gardening, he was hesitant, but then he agreed. I took charge of the little garden across the gulley, while Kars continued over the greenhouse and the root crops in the gardens down along the creek. You can look at the map above to see the locations of these. I have made them a darker shade. In my part of the garden we grew the broccoli, cabbage, peas, and other aboveground crops. There were tomatoes and cucumbers in the greenhouse, and carrots, potatoes, and onions in the creek-bottom garden. Around the greenhouse was a field of chives, planted by Shiloh, but that now grew of its own, and along the path to the lower garden there was a large stand of rhubarb that also continued each summer on its own. Minnie made tremendous rhubarb pie; Kyle still remembers it as his favorite. He and Johanna would snap off the stalks and eat them raw.

When we arrived, there were still a number of horses up at the horse barn area. Bob Newman and his sons were cattle and horse men. We chose not to keep them through the next winter, however, for we had no use for them. They were sold later this summer. We also had a few beef cattle, including one angus milk cow that would give birth later in the summer. But I wanted chickens, and so early on, I received permission to order a small flock of new-born chicks from Fort St. John. I think Kars and Minnie expected them to be white meat chickens, but I don't care for standard white chickens. They only looked disapproving, however, and did not say anything, when they discovered the chickens were all red or black and white. We kept the little chicks in our downstairs until they were old enough to be out in the grass. I built a wired hutch for them that I could move along the ground so they would have fresh clean grass every few days. Little Johanna loved reaching in and picking up a fuzzy chick to carry around.

During the spring, I also worked with Rick some in cutting down poplar trees along the edge of the slopes and dragging them into piles with the tractor. Next year's firewood had to be cut at the beginning of summer so it would have a few months to dry out. We would then saw and split the firewood in the fall, just before the snows came. The firewood we were using now had been cut and split the summer before.

When Sister Barbara James had been at Blair Valley the year before, she had advised the family not to distinguish between elders and non-elders in the governance of the community. They had followed this advice to good fruit. Rick, Kars, Minnie, and I were elders, and Maureen and Shirley were not. To have discussed anything about our life together without those two would have been wrong. So we had our governance meetings every Monday evening, up in our house, so that Maureen could be near the children in their beds. We called them family meetings instead of elders meetings. I was deeply struck with the difference. There was NO "us versus them" at Blair Valley, something that felt wrong in all other move communities. We conducted our family meetings with the same level of respect for one another that I had known at Blueberry.

We enjoyed a number of visitors through our time at Blair Valley, families coming to visit as well as ministries. The problem, however, was our road – twenty miles of dirt road in, some of it quite steep. If there was any rain, then whoever was in, was in, and whoever was out, was out. Sometimes when we went to town we had to stay overnight at Shepherd's Inn or Blueberry because it rained and the roads in were impassable. And so most visitors kept one eye on the sky to the east and would leave abruptly at the slightest hint of a rain cloud. This quick departure of some left us all feeling a bit disconcerted.

One visitor this summer, however, was Sister Janet Myers. She stayed with us for several days, a true mother in the Lord. When the rains came, she just laughed and used the phone to cancel her scheduled meetings elsewhere. She had come to be with us, regardless. Brother Dural and Sister Ethelwyn came to minister; we had a communion service while they were there. Elisabeth Roes/Kroker also came for a few days with her children to visit Shirley.

One final thing was the pressing need for income. There were twenty sometimes impassable miles to the highway, and it took two hours to get to Fort St. John. We were not farmers or cattle ranchers. Kars and Minnie had their pension income, while Maureen and I now received child benefit payments from the Canadian government, which amounted to a reasonable sum, actually, several hundred dollars a month. The Annett's had no income, however. The point is that I came up with the idea of starting a magazine and obtaining an income from the sale of subscriptions. I shared this idea at the family meeting, and we agreed to consider it. We would actually launch a much smaller version the next year, which I called "Times of Refreshing."

Katrina's Birth

Meanwhile, Katrina's due date was coming closer, she would be born on July 27. From the time Maureen arrived at Blair, we went out to Blueberry and to town regularly to prepare. We had chosen a hospital birth this time.

Maureen and I had always read to the children from the time Kyle was old enough to look at a book. This practice, however, increased at Blair Valley. There were no other distractions, and so, I would read, with Johanna in my lap, and Kyle and Maureen on the couch. I doubt that you will find two children who had more books read to them than Kyle and Johanna. This summer, in the weeks before Katrina's birth, we started reading the Laura Ingalls Wilder' books, interspersing them with many other books over the months.

The old tabernacle was a large building, between our house and the Blair Tabernacle. The Shiloh community had put large sums of money into an almost complete renovation not long before the community had closed. The one thing they did not renovate was the roof, and so it leaked. The "new" floor was rotten and caved in. The upstairs had been the school, a long hallway with classrooms on each side. One of these was the library filled with school and reading books. The books themselves were not being dripped on, but the room was damp and the books uncared for. This was quite distressing to me and I did what I could to protect and order them. I pulled so many good books out of this collection to read to the children. One of my favorites was *Along Came a Dog* by Meindert DeJong.

Because of the road conditions, we went out from Blair Valley ten days before Katrina was due. We stayed at Blueberry with Eric and Lynn Foster mostly, but also with the Bell's, who were able to purchase a house in Fort St. John through this time. Even when we spent the night at Blueberry, we usually went into town during the day. The week Katrina was due was Fort St. John's fair time. We spent a couple of days visiting the fair. This was great, because we were finally connecting with Canadian people and events, something we had no experience with before. Maureen's doctor for the birthing was at the fair as well; in fact he was at the fair with his daughter the morning Katrina was to be born and had to be called to the hospital.

Katrina Dawn Yordy was born on July 27, 1997 in the Fort St. John hospital. It was the easier of the four births. Many friends from the communities and from town came by to visit Maureen in the hospital, including the Annett's. We did not return to Blair Valley, then, until the end of July.

It often was that both the Annett's and the Keirs's were out from Blair Valley as well, sometimes at the same time. We did enjoy the summertime at Blair, the days it was just Maureen and I with the children. The first week of August was Kyle's sixth birthday. During that week, when it was just us, we had a hot dog roast in our yard and then Kyle and I went "camping." Kyle liked eggs and pancakes, so that was his birthday treat.

Blair Valley was a wonderful place for the children. They liked to play in the ditch down the road, coming home all muddy. We often went down to the Blair Creek to watch the beavers or to play in the water. The cold water did not bother the children. One time, however, I remember that Kyle ventured too far out into the water and could not swim. I leapt in to rescue him. Kyle often helped Maureen hang laundry. And there were so many places to explore. One time we hiked through the fields to the original trapper's log cabin that was on the property before it became Shiloh.

To Lubbock and Back

Meanwhile, Maureen's sister, Jessica, had walked out a year with Matthew Sanchez at the community just on the northern outskirts of Lubbock, Texas. Matthew had been in our school at the Albuquerque farm when I lived there. He had set himself to win Jessica's heart. It took some years, but he was patient. Their wedding date was August 23, and, of course, Maureen would be the matron of honor.

So, we planned a trip all the way down to Lubbock, Texas. Little Katrina was just two weeks old, but Maureen braved the trip for her sister. We left Blair Valley August 10, but spent the night at Shepherd's Inn, this time with Doug and Meri Witmer, both of whom I had known at Graham River. Meri was Sister Ethelwyn's daughter, and I had milked cows and worked in the butcher shop with Doug. They had a large double-wide set on a full basement on a small property right next to the Shepherd's Inn property. When we stayed with them, we had the downstairs as a guest suite. We always felt so comfortable and welcome in their home.

We had to stop in Prince George for part of the immigration process. Then we headed east to Jasper National Park, which was beautiful, then down through the Rockies on the road connecting Jasper to Banff National Park, which was even more beautiful. We have a most wonderful picture of Kyle and Johanna sitting on a stone wall looking out over Lake Louise, one of the most picturesque lakes in the world.

Nancy Cheney, Katie Bracken's sister, was living with her family in the Kalispell, Montana area, near the move community. We spent the night with them before continuing on. We managed to fit in a trip to the top of Pike's Peak before arriving in Lubbock on the 16th.

Tim and Frieda, as well as April and Ryan, were living at the Lubbock community at this time, so we got to see them. Frieda made Maureen's dress for the wedding. We were there a week before Matthew and Jessica were married in a lovely ceremony. We left for home three days later.

We drove through Santa Fe, New Mexico and enjoyed the southwestern shops, including the church with the "miraculous stair." I was in my "county collecting mode," and so, I swung over to Los Alamos. That's when our little Ford Escort first began to show symptoms of trouble. We limped along up to Alamosa in Colorado. After spending the night in a motel, I had a mechanic work on it. He "solved the problem" for about $400. The car seemed to be fixed, so we drove on through the Colorado mountains and across most of Utah. Then, I took another side-trip to acquire another out-of-the-way county, and then the car started acting up again. We made it back to the freeway before it stalled out completely. There we were stranded alongside the road in the middle of nowhere. It wasn't long, however, before a trucker stopped and invited us all to climb into the front cab of his truck for a ride to his home in Pocatello, Idaho. He promised to come back the next day to retrieve our car. We spent that night in his home, which did not feel entirely comfortable though he was very helpful. While he went back to pick up our car, Maureen remembered that friends of their family lived in Pocatello, so we called them. They invited us to stay in their home until our car could be fixed.

The trucker continued to help us. He took our car to a shop. We were in Pocatello for a week. We had to ask my mom and Maureen's parents to wire us money for the car repairs. Matthew and Jessica happened to be coming through on their honeymoon, so we spent time with them. We went to the Pocatello zoo. It was not until the 3rd of September that we finally headed north again, with the car seemingly fixed. Driving through Missoula, however, something serious happened in the engine. It still kept running, however, and we made it back to the Cheney's by evening.

We were with the Cheney's, then, for four more days. The car did start the next morning allowing me to drive it to a repair shop. When they took the engine apart they discovered that the front main bearing was gone and the driveshaft had been "flapping in the breeze," so to speak. How it got us through those miles is something only the Lord knows. But now it was toast.

We visited at the community, called Meadowbrook. I shared in their Sunday morning service, and they generously took up the offering for our needs. The next day, we moved over to the community and stayed with Walt and Doris Koslosky. We were there four more days. The big question, of course, was how do the five of us get back to Fort St. John with all our stuff?

In the end, Doris Koslosky offered to drive us to

Shepherd's Inn in her mini-van. Another sister from the community went along so she would have a companion on the way back. They were both very friendly and kind. We had a wonderful time on the road with them. We spent the night in Edmonton and did some shopping. This is when I first found the Lee Valley tool store in Edmonton, one of my favorite places. We were finally back at Shepherd's Inn on the 13th. Doris dropped us off with warm hugs. The brethren there gave us the use of a motel room for a couple of nights. The road to Blair Valley was impassible.

We went into Fort St. John the next day for Maureen to see the doctor. She was fine, but this had been a lengthy ordeal with a new-born child. It was the 18th, then, when Merlin Samson and Don Rutherford, two brothers from Shepherd's Inn, finally drove us back out to Blair Valley with all our stuff. We were home. All this way, Maureen and I felt carried by the Lord, that we could not find a way, but He carried us, through many helpful people along the way, all the way home.

Preparing for Winter

In the north country, frosts begin in August, but it usually doesn't snow until the end of September. October is usually alternating rain and snow, however, before winter begins in earnest by its end. Because of our isolation, preparing for winter was a bigger deal than at the other communities.

The biggest job was getting the logs that had been stacked the year before cut up into firewood for the winter. This time, the logs were down at the far end of the southern field. We first sawed them into firewood length with chainsaws. Then, we used a borrowed hydraulic log-splitter to split the poplar into stove-sized pieces, which we would stack on a wagon. At the end of each day, we would pull the wagon load of firewood back to the community with the tractor and stack it at the four places that needed firewood, the three houses and the tabernacle.

One day, I was working with Rick chain-sawing the logs into proper lengths. I was accustomed to "taking charge" of work projects and I always think efficiency. Rick was sawing and I was stacking, but Rick was not being "efficient" in his approach to the job. I stopped him and said, "It will go quicker if you do it this way."

Rick paused for a moment. Then he said, "You know, Daniel, this is me, this is the way I like to do it."

Rick's words went all through me. Rick was my friend, and I honored him. This was a turning-point for me. I was ready for the Lord to take from me my need to "control" the flow of work. Of course, as I think now, I realize that I have seldom had a crew of men to direct on any job since then, though such had been my whole work life for the twenty years prior.

Then, near the end of the job, we had one more day's work to finish the pile of wood and have it all back near the buildings. But I was completely worn out, and I could not work the next day. When I shared with Kars that I needed a day to recuperate before we returned to finish the job, he was not impressed. "Sons of God" are supposed to move in great faith and are supposed to "keep the flesh" obedient.

So Kars persuaded Minnie to go with him the next day to prove what "sons of God" do. (And I'm saying it this way to position the narrow place God was taking me into.) They worked hard and almost finished the job. I felt bad, but I hardly had the strength to move. Before the end of the day, however, Kar's back went out bad. It would be a couple of months before he would be able to do any physical work. This is something I long pondered, how that attitude so often leads to that outcome, how "manly strength" as the "proving of Christ" by strong elders, so often resulted in such loss.

And so, I must come back to my relationship with Kars Kiers, and, in fact, his relationship with all the men at Blair Valley. Kars was a bully, and he would insist on his way, with strong religious overtones, most of the time. At the same time, he would often speak very demeaning things to others, including to Rick. I had not realized until now, but Kars's practice of speaking down at Rick had caused great distress for him and Shirley.

Yet Kars did not overtly speak that way to me. Let me share part of the reason why. Sometime during this summer or fall, I was talking with Kars outside, the two of us together, I think about halfway between our house and the tabernacle. I was sharing with Kars an idea I had for the community. Kars shut me down with contempt, but I stopped him. (I learned this approach from Sister Charity, actually.)

I said, "Kars, Kars. This is not the issue. Look at me. The issue is you and me, our relationship together. Whenever you share any idea, I listen with eagerness and respect. But when I try to share my idea, you respond to me in this way. The idea is not the issue, the issue is you and me. I need you to respect what I share, whether you think it's a good idea or not."

I don't know what went on inside of Kars, of course, but that was enough to mostly end his attempts to bully me religiously. I did have to say the same thing again the next spring, but that again sufficed until Maureen and I left. At that point, the bully in Kars did get in the last kick. But that comes later.

But Kars had been really hard on Bob Newman, refusing his desire to somehow provide for his family in that setting as being "not of God." I know that Kars could be awful. In fact, while we were still living at Blueberry, I had seen Bob and Connie come to counsel with Brother John and Sister Nathel more than once. In the end, it was Kars's bullying that had first driven away Wes, and then Bob and his family. The problem was, of course, that Kars could never see that; to him it was always them abandoning "God's will."

Now, as winter approached, it was Rick. When they shared with Maureen and I the shamefulness Rick was being subjected to, I wanted him and me to sit down with Kars and address this wrongful practice. But Rick disagreed. I can only say that confronting people in that way was not in his makeup. It's not in mine either, but bullies must be dealt with and there is only one way to do that, by showing them the relationship instead of the "issue."

Meanwhile, Rick and Shirley had racked up some expenses both for constructing their home and for a complete and costly overhaul of their vehicle when the engine had gone out. They had no income, and so their debt was on credit cards. They needed to work in town in order to pay it off. One day in October, in the family meeting, Rick and Shirley announced that they were planning to live in town to work through the week, but that they would be home every weekend and were still part of the community and of our lives. This was quite a blow to Maureen and I, and we did not witness to it nor agree with it. Nonetheless, it was not in us to impose ourselves upon them, and so we gave them the respect of making their own decision without interference from us.

I did raise a different possibility. The community owned a trapline that we were not using as well as some large farm equipment up on the hill by the horse barn. I suggested that we sell the trapline, which would have provided more than enough to pay off the Annett's debt as well as give us money to find some way to earn a living.

Rick, Kars, and Minnie were against such a thing. Let me try to explain why. There was a belief that we were "preparing a place for God's people" in times to come. In fact, one summer before we arrived at Blair Valley, a man from Edmonton had driven into the property. He said to the brethren there, "Do you know that God has reserved this place for His people in times to come?" "Yes, we do know," they had replied.

And so to sell anything for the sake of the present people of God seemed to be against that vision. What was not realized was that not selling those things would mean that the entire property would be lost to community.

Even though Rick and Shirley did come out faithfully every weekend as they had promised, their absence through the week left a hole in our community life. Now it was just Kars and Minnie, and Maureen and I, with our three little ones as the "community."

It is only now that I am finally understanding God's wondrous purposes in our lives. At that time, I did not understand at all.

Other tasks I did before winter included, first, that I began to build an insulated second wall around our Tabernacle to make it much warmer inside while burning less firewood. As part of that job, I put on a lower skirting as well as a new large front porch at the main entry door.

There was also the harvest of the gardens and food preparation for storing. We set a day to all help butcher the male chickens for meat. The hens we would keep through the winter for eggs. For that reason, I created a "chicken" room in the cow shed, building a wall of hay bales to keep them warm, alongside the room that the several cows would also keep "warm." The two rooms would be cold, but they remained above freezing. We might have put in some auxiliary heat for the coldest days, I

don't remember. The hens did lay eggs for a while, until it got too cold.

Then, we asked Randy Jordan to come over for a few days from Blueberry to help us put a snowplow on our tractor. He did that, and gave us a crude, but effective way to keep our winter road open whenever it snowed. Once the roads were covered in snow, the route over the ridge and across the Gundy Creek was impassable. At the same time, we were able to plow out an ice road across the marshy ground going south down the valley until our road connected with a well-kept gas-well road which went east past farmsteads to the Alaska Highway just north of Wonowon.

Final Immigration

We had one more trip before the end of the year, however, and that was to finalize our immigration to Canada.

Kars and Minnie had purchased a newer vehicle and given their pickup to the community for general use. It was now our only vehicle, except the blue van, which, although I could use it around the farm just a bit, it had little power for the steep hill slopes in and out.

So, we all five piled into the farm pickup and headed south to Prince George on November 20. The starter went out on the pickup in Prince George, and we stayed an extra night with some friends there and got it replaced. We did not know, when we drove down through the day, that our tail and break lights were not working.

We crossed the border into Washington state in the late afternoon and headed to Whidbey island for the ferry crossing that would take us to Sequim and the Howat's. It was dark, however, as we approached Anacortes and the highway three-lanes-wide was packed with cars in rush hour. Suddenly police lights went on behind us. I was in the left lane and could only pull over to the left. Maureen rolled down her window. A very red-faced policeman came up to the window and screamed obscenities at me, right across Maureen and the children. I did not reply.

In the end, he did not ticket us, but instructed us to drive no more after dark until we got our lights fixed. He drove behind us to the nearest motel, just outside of Anacortes. It was early evening, so, after we put the children to bed, Maureen and I turned on the television to find *The Godfather* just starting. This was the first time we had seen it and we watched it all the way through. Stark, but impressive, to say the least.

The next day we crossed the ferry and drove on to Sequim. They were having a service that evening, so I had the opportunity to share a word. We visited with the Howat's but spent the night with the Killam's. The next day, Mr. Killam slid under the pickup and saw that the wire running to the lights had been broken. He pieced it back together and our problem was solved.

We went on that day to the Rutledge's in Gresham, Oregon, and spent the night with them. The next day we met up with Katie Bracken. We went to a mall together where Johanna wandered off and got lost. We spent awhile in frantic searching before Kyle hollered her name and she stood up from a lady's lap who had found her and was waiting for us. We spent that night back at the Yordy house with Franz and Audrey. The next day we visited with Glenn's wife, Kim, who had come to Oregon for a visit. We also spent part of the day visiting with Cheryl and Dave.

The next day was Thanksgiving. We all gathered at Franz's for dinner and a family get-together. The next day we were back at Sequim with the Howat's. Marlyss Johnson was visiting Sequim, and she shared a word in the service.

In the late afternoon of November 30, we crossed the Canadian border again at Aldergrove. We took our immigration papers in to the same man who had been kind to us over many years. He said to us, "You are the kind of people I like seeing immigrating to Canada." He signed and stamped our papers with a flourish.

We were landed immigrants to Canada.

That night we spent with Ruth and Ricky Singh before heading back north.

Without Hope

For some reason we took the route into the Rockies and Jasper Park instead of through Prince George. I like driving roads I've never been on before. On this trip through the Rockies, Maureen and I listened to a tape of a sermon that Dan Ricciardelli had preached at a Bowens Mill convention that year. Brother Dan's topic was "hope."

In order to set the stage, I must explain to you what "hope" meant to me by that point in my life. What Dan taught about hope went deep into me. I witnessed to it in my spirit. I had a significant problem, however; I did not really know what hope was, for I had lost any hope I once had.

My hope in the move of God fellowship for over twenty years was that, through the years of the dealing of God, of walking under His hand, of living in Christ community, of submitting to the covering, of commitment to a Tabernacles word, that I would become a manifest son of God, part of the firstfruits of Christ in the ending of this age of human folly, and part of the arising of a new age, that I now call "the Age of Tabernacles." My understanding of that calling and vision had grown at that time to include a real hope of entering into union with God.

The problem was very simple. None of that was happening. My eldership role was going nowhere, Blair Valley had suffered a significant loss with the Annett's in town most of the time. My physical strength was vanishing.

I remember one of our times at Sequim, that Sister Barbara James was there. She is wonderfully anointed, in praise and in word. We had one of the most wondrous praise times of my life that evening. But she had preached a word, common to the move, in which she warned us that if we allowed any weakness of our flesh to gain an upper hand, then it would keep us from connecting with God. She said that allowing inadequacies to continue meant that they would rule our life and not God. And this idea came inside a constant preaching of hear and obey, and do not do anything unless God tells you to do it.

I have never known a life of "hear and obey." Such a way of living has always been far away from me. And now the tiredness of my body and the inadequacies of my person seemed to stand against any hope that God might one day make me like Jesus.

To put it very simply, we believed that salvation was OF US, and not of God, and that if we did not "measure up," then, we might "go to heaven," but God would not include us in the revelation of Jesus Christ.

I did not measure up in any direction. I drove back home to Blair Valley without hope.

I am determined to share with you somehow the beauty that Blair Valley was to our family, especially in the summertime. Except for the picture of Johanna sneaking a baby chick, these are all in the summer of 1998.

The top picture of this first set is Johanna sneaking a baby chick out of the pen. In the distance is an unused "Shiloh" cabin, situated directly in front of the Kiers's cabin to the left.

In the middle is our home in the summer of 1998. You can see the flowers and a nice yard.

The bottom picture is our backyard showing the view north and two empty "Shiloh" cabins.

In the top picture of this next set, the children are playing along the path from our house to the Tabernacle. You can see the silver roof of the Blair Valley Tabernacle above Johanna's head. To the right of it is part of the old Shiloh tabernacle.

The middle picture is from the ridge slope to our east, looking down towards the community buildings area. We were enjoying a picnic from this splendid view.

Then, I have a picture of our family, taken not far from our house, with the trees that stood at the top of the drop to the Blair Creek bottoms, on the west side of our house.

Above: Kars and Minnie Kiers

Below: Rick and Shirley Annett

30. A Valley of Decision

December 1997 - August 1998

A Dark and Cold Winter

I added up the nights we spent not at Blair Valley from the time we arrived in mid-April, until we returned as landed immigrants in December. One-third of all nights were spent elsewhere, and only two-thirds at home. After our return on December 3, we no longer went out except for trips to town. There would be (almost) no trips afar for the rest of our time at Blair.

This was good.

Only now, as I am laboring inside of God over all these memories, placing myself back into a time that has held the biggest unanswered questions in my life, I see everything lining up into the goodness of the Lord Jesus Christ. But I must divide carefully between the clarity with which I now see and the complete absence of understanding through which I lived in these months.

These next eight months at Blair Valley would be a time of even greater peace outwardly. I now know that God made it so in order to take me through the process of changing my mind without pushing me into insanity. I did know at that time that a complete mental breakdown was just a nudge away.

It has been observed in Christian history that a pursuit of the knowledge of God over many years can lead to a mental breakdown. I know now this is only because of the evil definitions we Christians have given to God, to salvation, and against ourselves.

I was aware of this "Christian" experience of seeking a God who always seems to be "against us" at this time; indeed, I was living in it. Yet I knew no way out.

The winter of 1997-1998 was dark and cold. The nights were long; the days were short and dim. Snow covered the ground for six months solid, with the promise of mud following after.

When we arrived back from the border, I had hardly any physical strength. I had only a few chores, however. One was to walk over to the cowshed once a day to check on and water and feed the animals. One was to fill up the water tanks around once a week. And a third was to keep the fire going in our stove and in the Tabernacle. I also carried out our potty bucket to the outhouse once a day. Then, anytime it snowed, I traded off with Kars to spend a day driving the tractor and snowplow all the way down our winter road, several miles to the gas-field road, and then back again, plowing snow all the way. This was actually quite a beautiful task, through the wooded winter landscape, making our road smooth and clear.

Beyond that, I had no strength of mind or body to do anything else. So I sat in the downstairs of our house behind my desk, and wrote. I did not know God, but I wanted to, and the only way I knew how to know God was to write my way into knowing Him, and so I have continued until now, over twenty-two years later. I love to know God so much and His Word is so very beautiful to me, that I doubt I will ever stop, not for a few trillion years, at least.

I must describe the setting to you. I had the decent large teacher's desk with my electronic typewriter on it. I know it was powered, and we did have a small inverter for it, but I also remember some difficulties with adequate power. My "office" was divided by a "wall" of blank studs with nothing on them. The firewood stack was just behind me. The wood stove just in front. It was warm in our home and easy to keep heated. Although I did have to come down the outside stairs regularly to stoke the stove, having dry firewood right there at hand was an incredible blessing. Plus, because the entire floor of our living area was heated from beneath, we had no cold corners whatsoever.

The open studs and the walls all around were rough and bare. I did have a nice window facing south towards the old tabernacle, which was my view across the snow-covered way. But January and February are long, cold, and dim months. I grew up in Oregon; I love green and growing things. I was becoming weary of so many long months without any garden greenery.

I had the teaching I had given in Oregon and then again at Blueberry on tapes. I transcribed those tapes and typed out a rough version of a booklet I called "The Two Gospels." Then I worked and worked on it, to make it succinct and well-written. When I look back now, I see two things. First, I see that I was writing then so very much of what I am writing now, even bringing into view a relationship of union with God. And second, I see that I had the "two gospels" switched. I was calling "another gospel," the "true," and what I now know as Paul's gospel I called the false.

The terrible line in my book was this – "when we come into union with God." That is something no human will ever do. Salvation begins when we accept a Jesus who first comes into union with us, taking into Himself all that we are, including our sin and our shame. But I had zero knowledge then of such a thing. What I did know was that, in teaching a word that was in line with what Brother Buddy Cobb taught, I was deliberately and knowingly twisting verses, especially Paul's verses, to make them fit this view of "the gospel." I knew I was doing it, and I hated it. I just had no idea what I was missing.

And that's the point. Over these months, I became fully aware that I was missing something HUGE, right at the center of the gospel. But I had no idea what that "something" was.

On a different note, besides occasional hunters coming over from the other farms to our moose-filled valley, our only visitors through this time were Russel and Marina Stendhal. They were missionaries in Columbia, but had been somewhat connected with the move for several years now. They shared in a service and visited with Maureen and me a bit in our home.

And yes, we did have moose, lots of them, coming in close to eat from the few large round bales of hay still sitting in the fields. (Our neighbor paid us to allow him to process and take the hay for his own cattle operation.) Some moose would come right into our back yard.

A Very Quiet Word from God

I can describe for you the setting and the state of my mind, but I could not cause you to know

that setting truly unless I could take you back there again to see and to understand. You would be stunned by the miles of impassible wilderness to get there and the isolation amidst the grandeur surrounding our home at Blair Valley. The Kiers's house was not in view of ours, and thus we seemed quite alone.

I want to add an experience that happened during this time that contributes to the sense I hope to convey. As I said, Rick and Shirley came out faithfully every weekend, usually arriving Friday evening and returning to town on Sunday evening. This might have been in late December before our winter road was accessible. Anyhow, they came out from town one Friday evening and attempted to cross the high ridge from the Gundy valley. They had chains on a four-wheel drive for the task. They called in from Wonowon to let us know they were on their way, but a few hours later they had not arrived.

It was nearly fifty below zero. After I visited with Kars, I bundled up into the pickup and drove up over the ridge. I had to put on chains, but I made it over the top and down the other side. Understand that at these temperatures, a difficulty on the way meant certain death. We had to know that Rick and Shirley were okay. On the shallow slope up, just before the road climbs steeply and then turns abruptly at a 45 degrees to climb up the steeper slope above, I saw their tire tracks coming in. I saw where they had turned around and driven back out, choosing not to risk that steep climb that night. I knew that they were safe.

I turned the pickup around and headed back up the slope. I made it around the bend and halfway up before one of my tire chains broke apart. I stopped and carefully eased my way back down a bit. The chain was in pieces. I would not make it up the hill with only one chain, indeed, to try meant a high risk of getting stuck and thus stranded at fifty below. It was just three miles to home where my wife and children were anxiously waiting for me, but it might well have been a thousand. I thought carefully. We were just opening the winter road and I might have been able to come in by driving maybe fifty miles around, but I had not been on it before. I was not familiar with the way and at fifty below and at night that seemed to me a senseless risk.

So, I had only one recourse. I turned around and left my wife and children there alone in that cold valley with only an elderly couple as their help, and

I drove the two-hour drive into Fort St. John. I did stop at Wonowon to call and let them know what had happened and that I and the Annett's were safe. In Fort St. John, I stayed again with Peter and Barbara Bell, our good friends. I would not be able to purchase new chains until Monday, however.

Peter and Barbara always had a room for us in their downstairs. There was a family room down there as well. To pass the time, I put on the movie, *Dr. Zhivago*. In this movie, a man abandons a wonderful wife and two children, just as the Communists are taking over, in order to adhere to a prostitute. His decision was so wrong to me; indeed, I do not see it as a "love story," but as the worst form of betrayal. Then, he was taken away from St. Petersburg for a while. The point came in the movie when the man was wading through deep snow in cold winter, trying to get back to his "family." At that point, I shut the thing off and have never looked at *Dr. Zhivago* again. I cannot express the horror I felt, with my dear wife and children, one hundred impassible miles away through bitter cold, and I could not get to them.

I did get chains on Monday and drove safely back to Blair Valley. Everything was fine, of course. Kars and Minnie expressed strong disapproval over my decision, but their alternative, of daring the risk by being a faith-filled MAN of God, or something, was so silly to me that I gave it no mind.

It was in this setting, then, that I was sitting at my desk one wintry day, feeling all through my heart and soul NO HOPE AT ALL. I did not know God; I did not know His Salvation. I believed that with all my lacks and inabilities, I was incapable of being part of that vision to which I had committed my heart years before.

And in that emptiness, I heard four words inside my spirit. They were so quiet, so incongruous, that I almost missed them. Nonetheless, those four words remained in my memory and I knew that it was God who had spoken them.

He said to me, "Give My people hope."

I had no idea what that might mean, for not only did I not know what hope was, not only did I know no hope at all, but the idea of me giving God's people anything was simply inconceivable. And so I left those words there in my memory, not understood, but knowing God had said them.

Brother Buddy and Brother John

February convention would be held at Blueberry this year. Kars and Minnie volunteered to stay at Blair so that Maureen and I could go out with the children.

Because Kars did not have a good relationship with Brother John Clarke, he turned us as a community to Brother Buddy's counsel, and so Maureen and I also now looked to Brother Buddy as our primary "covering."

I had sent an email to Brother Buddy the summer before concerning my idea of our earning an income at Blair through creating a magazine. (And yes, we did have email capacity over the wireless phone at that time. Minnie would print out all the emails and bring us ours.) My purpose in sending the email was just to visit with him about it; I was not yet ready to present it to the Father ministry for a decision. Nonetheless, I received a quick reply back in which Brother Buddy stated that he had mentioned it to Brother Joe and Brother Joe had said it would not work. At the same time, I visited with a brother while we were in Lubbock who had run a print shop. He expressed immediate contempt for my idea and refused even to discuss it. This is something I have never understood, for I have always treated other people's personal leadings and sharing of the vision of their hearts with utmost respect.

My reply to Brother Buddy was not entirely respectful and so I felt bad about that.

At the Blueberry convention, Brother Buddy preached at least twice. Regardless of which Scriptures he used or which angle he took, however, it was always the same hopeless Calvinist rendition of *"salvation is up to you hearing and obeying and generally proving to God that you are getting it right."* (And when I say, "salvation," I do not mean "heaven after death," but rather being like the Lord Jesus Christ inwardly and outwardly.)

This time, Brother Buddy, using Jesus' words about "God alone is good," began to say, that, in fact, Jesus Himself was e--. Except he did not quite finish his line because Brother Eli Miller, sitting right behind him, said very loudly, "Careful now." That was the only time such a correction happened like that. It was very much on point.

I shared my booklet, "The Two Gospels," with Brother Buddy at the beginning of the convention.

At the end, I visited with him again about it. He said to me, "This is right on." He meant it to be an encouragement to me, but it did feel a bit hollow.

They had scheduled a general elder's meeting to be held at Shepherd's Inn right after the convention. Maureen and the children returned to Blair Valley, while I stayed for that gathering. I must admit that I took great pleasure in seeing the shock on Brother Gary Rehmeier's face when he came in and saw me sitting there. I suspect he had believed me to be completely washed out. But, as I have said, he never really knew me.

Brother John Clarke stood to share in this all-community elder's meeting. This was 1998. The outpouring of the Holy Spirit that was known as "The Toronto Blessing" had occurred a few years before. I knew and had visited with brethren in Oregon, including Pastor Dennis Cline, who had gone to Toronto as soon as they had heard that God was moving among His people. They came back mightily blessed, with renewed vigor and that same anointing now flowing in their churches. It was clear to me that this experience had brought them much closer to the Lord Jesus and into a life of holiness and earnestly seeking after God.

Brother John started talking about the "Toronto Blessing." He called it "an outpouring of devils." This was absolutely overwhelming to me. Jesus said, "Listen, you can say anything you want against the Father or against Me, but do not call the Holy Spirit 'a demon.'" I have read stories of people doing just that, in speaking against an outpouring of the Spirit, and then falling over dead. (And it's only those who hold to the serpent's gospel that imagine that laughing out loud in the joy of our Glorious Salvation – and in "church" no less – is "of the devil.")

My distress included the fact that I knew that precious brethren were walking more closely with the Lord Jesus as a result of that experience. This was sectarianism at its very worst.

I drove back to Blair by myself. Most of the way back, I churned over Brother John's accusation. I was very angry, but I did not know God's answer. I felt that my anger was "wrong" however, especially after what God had taken me through the year before. Even though I was very bent out of shape inside, I did surrender my anger to the Lord before I arrived home. I know now that Jesus was sharing His anger with me. When I feel the same way now, I hear Him say to me, "Your anger is just and right, for it is My own feelings that I share with you. Nonetheless, can we take our shared frustration and place it inside Father's love?" And every time I hear Him say that to me, I know such joy and peace.

But I did not know that then. And so, from then on, Blair Valley became a valley of decision for me.

A Long and Slow Process

The next few months became a long and slow process of coming to terms inside with my commitment to the move of God versus my commitment to knowing God, two commitments that were becoming irreconcilable inside of me.

In a chapter coming up, I hope to set out the reasons for leaving the move as I understand those reasons now. Here, I hope to convey a bit of what and how I knew things then, which was NOT knowing any part of Father with me; that is, I lived in a very Christian hades.

Let me share my mental state first. I had no idea then of "Asperger's." All I knew was that in certain areas of life and expression where other "anointed" people excelled, I short-circuited inside. I could not function in social interaction in the strong ways needed to be a "successful elder." And actually, my fragile mental state continued even after we moved to Fort St. John and did not begin to dissipate until the end of the year.

I did NOT understand my life, not at all. It was a confusing mess of good things surrounded by awful things, of ability surrounded by failure. Yet my sharp memory, still retaining all the pain from all the years, also remembered the good. And so through these months, I brought to the forefront of my mind my time with Abel Ramirez and with Don Howat, and now, even, with Rick Annett (and far more so after we moved to town in August). I remembered that I experienced continual success in the anointing and in my creative work while I walked daily with them, but only loss and failure through the years in-between.

I did not know what that meant. But I held to those memories, that maybe I was not insane. And it was that memory of my time with these true brothers, and especially Rick's ongoing friendship towards me, that held me on an even keel through this entire year of weaving through confused murkiness on the edge of the precipice.

And because our life at Blair Valley was generally good, I faced no present difficulties that would overwhelm me as I worked my way through this conflict of commitments.

I was coming to realize that I could walk with God or I could walk with the move, but I could not walk with both. Yet I did not know God, not really, neither did I know of any answer for the vast hole I perceived at the center of my knowledge of the gospel. I knew the Bible, and I knew that it says many things that my theology did not acknowledge and that my theology disregarded many things that God actually says.

And worst of all, I KNEW that to say, "God loves me," was "evil deception." The "true word" was, "God loves me – BUT…," with some version of "I MUST" following the BUT, which always stood far larger than God ever could be.

One day, on a weekend, we were all gathered in the dining room for the day. I was playing a game on the floor with the children, the ladies were in the kitchen visiting merrily, and Kars and Rick were sitting on the couch in conversation. It was this conversation that opened me to understand a significant part of my dilemma. They were talking about "those brethren out there," and how "fleshy they are," and how "far from God they live," and how "they need to come under the covering and die to their flesh to be righteous (like we are)." The problem was not Kars saying these things, but Rick agreeing with him.

Now, I do not say that Rick was doing anything more than being agreeable, for he sees that issue now as I do. Nonetheless, some fifteen years later, I observed some brothers whom I know well, still in the move, chatting together on Facebook, exclaiming how those "fleshy Christians out there just don't measure up to our righteousness in God." (They might word it slightly differently, but that's what their words mean.) I could not believe they were continuing to spin this so false a story. I do not know how people can lie to themselves.

And that's a big part of my problem. I can only go so long living in what I know to be a lie about myself before I cave in before God to seek His answer. I am woefully incapable of pretending to be something I'm not.

I knew in that moment that Amos the prophet was completely right, "**Two cannot walk together except they be agreed**." I was no longer in agreement with this move attitude of self-righteousness always expressed as contempt against God's precious people whom He had chosen not to lead into the "move." It was bunk, and I could not comprehend how people can live in such falseness.

One day, I was out with Kars and Kyle behind the old shop. There were all kinds of metal things piled all around, including non-working tractors. Kyle had climbed up into a small tractor and was happily turning the wheel and pushing the levers. The thing had no value, and Kyle was bothering nothing. Nonetheless, Kars strongly rebuked him and ordered him to get down. The fact that I was standing there seemed to mean nothing.

This occasion touched another great disagreement inside of me, the same thing that had caused Maureen and I to open our home to Kimberley, to rescue her from such false religious treatment. I knew that there was no way I could protect Kyle from Kars through years of growing up inside his sphere. In my mind, a father protects his children from evil and from shame, end of story. Maureen and I were both in full disagreement with how most in the move treated any who were not elders, and especially the children. Most children who grew up in move community do not remember the good (which was much, actually), but count it only as a curse.

I had tried to share the vision of my heart for a community of Christ, for a place of refuge where precious people can come, if only just for a season, to be strengthened in the love of Christ and in the knowledge of God. What I shared hit only a blank wall, and I soon realized that it would not happen in that context.

I had always disagreed with the flavor of our version of "community" in the move. It seemed to me to fit neither the gospel nor what I knew to be true and real in my heart. Again, I was reckoning with the profound disagreement between myself and the move. I was realizing that the disagreement was substantial.

At the same time, however, I was not setting myself up as "the one who has it right." I had it wrong. The difference is that I knew that I did.

It is only now, however, as I have been pondering these things the last couple of days, that I felt my Father inside showing me that the issue was commitment. I saw that God honored my commitment to the move and, in fact, gave me a safe path by which I could let go of that commitment without also losing my unassailable commitment to know Him and to walk with a people who know Him. This is one of the greatest miracles in my life.

But to "leave the move" is a BIG DEAL, with great repercussions. This was not a light or easy decision. And how would I support my family? Construction or any other kind of hard physical work was no longer possible.

During these months, through my reading of the Bible, and even through other's preaching, a story had become vivid and real to me in the Spirit of the Lord. The story is in 1 Kings 13. A prophet had been sent by God to speak to the wicked King Jeroboam. God had told the prophet not to eat or drink nor to turn aside until he had spoken and then returned to Jerusalem. But another prophet heard of this and came out to meet him on the way. This other prophet said to him that "God" had told him that it was now okay to turn aside and to enjoy himself. But after the first prophet heeded this other word, he did not make it back to Jerusalem, but was torn to pieces by a lion on the way.

God spoke to me to immigrate to Blair Valley. We had followed that leading and God had opened all the doors all the way through. God spoke to me that Blair Valley was our home, and it was. Maureen and I both loved Blair Valley in spite of its isolation.

In April, Sister Jane and Brother Dick Miller visited us at Blair where they ministered wondrous grace and blessing to us and then spent a few hours with Maureen and me in our home. We were much blessed and encouraged by Sister Jane, and, in fact, she was always on the "commitment to God" side of my life.

Then in May, Sister Barbara James came to visit us and to minister. During her time at Blair, she stepped aside with me, wanting to counsel me in particular. "You can't stay here," she said, "Not with just the Kiers's. Entering another winter all by yourselves will be too much for Maureen and the children. In fact, it would be dangerous."

She was to me as that second prophet turning me aside from what God had spoken to me. Yet I knew that her words were right and true. From her counsel, then, I formed the decision inside that we would leave, how or when I did not know. Yet at the same time, this story of the prophet who heeded someone else, claiming to be "God speaking," haunted me for many years. I believe that the Lord Jesus will resolve that agony through this narrative.

Times of Refreshing

I must add something during these late winter months. I was determined to rescue the books from the upstairs of the old tabernacle, before the snow melted and the leaks became greater. And so I selected a nice little cabin, not far from ours, cleared out all the interior walls, and built bookshelves all around and through the center. Then we carried all the books over, a couple thousand or so, and placed them in order in our new library. Kyle and Johanna enjoyed this task with me. We loved our little library, and reading lots of those books to the children continued.

Two other things began for me in March of that year, one is the first writing which I began to send out to subscribers, a printed several-page letter that I called "Times of Refreshing."

The second is my decades-long quest to discover and to resolve my physical difficulty. My wife and I have always inclined towards natural health. We have made use of the medical system for emergencies, but not for health. In fact, we were seeing a wonderful naturopathic doctor during these years, Dr. Pontius in Quesnel, British Columbia.

When I first began experiencing physical weakness, I read about the teeth and how they are critical to health or to ill-health. I finally understand my difficulty fairly clearly, and it is wonderful to know now that I was right on target concerning my teeth. My teeth were filled with mercury fillings from my childhood. I knew that the mercury must be removed.

While we were still at Blueberry, I had gone to a regular dentist in Fort St. John to have three mercury fillings removed. He did so with no protection for me or for him. I knew this was madness as the same mercury on the floor would cause a hazmat shutdown of a building. I found a dentist in southern Alberta who believed in a natural approach to dentistry and who was against mercury fillings, but his cost was beyond my reach.

I asked the local move ministry for financial assistance. They would have helped with a local regular dentist but chose to contribute nothing to natural dentistry. Though I knew these brethren well, the masks I saw on their faces troubled me deeply.

And so I turned to my mother, who was always willing to help. After receiving the cost for the trip and the dental work from her in March, I took the bus down to High River, Alberta, south of Calgary. This was a quiet and good time for me. I got a motel room for three nights. I went to the dentist for my appointments. He removed two teeth, one of which was the bad one destroyed by the dentist in Mississippi and replaced some of my mercury fillings. In-between, I walked the little town and spent time in their library. I could not check out books, so I sat and read *Jamaica Inn* by Daphne du Maurier for the first time. The dentist did not do all the work needed in one go, as it would be too much for my poor mouth, so I came back again later that summer. By the time he had finished, all mercury was safely removed from my mouth.

Also in March I formulated an idea for a reduced version of my "magazine" which I would call "Times of Refreshing." I wanted to write some articles and include other things written by brethren in the area communities, which I would then send out to paying subscribers throughout the move. I wrote to a sister who had been a part of the Shiloh Community and who was well off. She had expressed an interest in helping us in establishing ourselves at Blair Valley. She sent a check of $1000 for my endeavor. Kars and Minnie assumed that the check was only for Blair Valley and not my magazine idea, but I held my ground, and they conceded half of the money.

I gathered a list of addresses from all across the move and sent out a few hundred letters offering a subscription to *Times of Refreshing*. I received back maybe one to two dozen paid subscriptions. And so I put together my first volume. I asked Brother Ernest Watkins and Brother Dural Davison to write an article each. I included a little poem by Terry Miller as well as some of my own writing. I was not comfortable with how Brother Ernest and Brother D worded things. I wanted my newsletter to be NON-sectarian, and so I assumed editorial license and changed the wording to make what they shared receivable by anyone. I realized later that this probably contributed to some of the blank faces towards my endeavor that I began to see.

In this task, Maureen and I took a couple of trips out in order to get both *Times of Refreshing* and *The Two Gospels* printed and bound. I had offered my booklet for sale in the letter going out and some

had ordered a copy. We took one trip to the Staples store in Grande Prairie, Alberta. That was an enjoyable family time. When we were in a print shop in Fort St. John, I noticed a picture of Abraham Lincoln with a statement supposedly his beneath. I did not yet know how dishonest the story spun about the man really is, but the words were good.

"I will prepare myself until my time comes." – I received those words as the Lord speaking to me and was encouraged by them.

The people who sent money for *Times of Refreshing* had purchased a year's subscription, and so I persisted in sending out monthly or semi-monthly issues even after our move to Lubbock, Texas in 1999. It was a limited but important step in my writing career.

I want to talk about another issue that was troubling me, what I called "the dance of faces." I was becoming frustrated with the practice of wearing different expressions for different people. More than that, when I observed those brethren who were trying so hard to follow Brother Buddy's teaching, I did not care for the twisting that I saw in their faces. I saw Wes Shaw in town and was again deeply troubled by the expression of his face.

I was disturbed by the slow realization that our relationships together as believers were not through Jesus, but rather, through the "covering" and our participation in the move. I was disturbed by my own limited attempts to pretend that I was "anointed" or "in the Spirit." In fact, putting on the face of "I'm in the Spirit, brother," was a move practice from the start.

The Summer of 1998

In May, Kars's brother came to visit from Holland for several days, along with his granddaughter. Afterwards, Kars and Minnie planned a trip to the Netherlands. They left by the end of May and were gone for two months. Maureen and I had Blair Valley to ourselves, through the week. Of course, Rick and Shirley continued to come out most every weekend, which was always wonderful.

Blair Valley was so beautiful to us this summer. The flowers, the herbs, the green.

I was feeling stronger as warm weather and green came. I continued building the second wall along two sides of our Tabernacle. I filled it and the space between the outer wall and the original wall with insulation taken out of the old tabernacle. I tore down buildings in order to obtain the lumber and siding that I needed.

At the same time, I took on the task of running a grader behind the tractor, making our dirt roads smooth and nice all through the camp. I even went over the ridge, making the Gundy Creek road nicer. This was an unnecessary, but enjoyable task.

I also tended the gardens and took care of the animals. Maureen, of course, had full time work in taking care of our three wonderful children. She had taught Kyle and Johanna school all through the winter months as well.

It Is Time to Go

During this time alone in the stark and gentle beauty of the Blair Valley we worked our way to the decision that we must leave. It was not a question of leaving Blair Valley, but of leaving the move. Maureen tells me that it was very hard for her to leave Blair Valley, but it was I who could no longer bear to live inside of pretending, for that was all I could perceive regarding the vision that we held.

I believed that I had to produce something in order, somehow, to please a "God" who was very hard to please, in order for Him to decide that I could be part of His firstfruits. And I knew that I was incapable of ever accomplishing such a production.

No one is capable of pleasing God, of course, and all the vain effort of determined Christians to do so is the most difficult thing for our Father to bear, for in every moment of effort, we are refusing to know Jesus as our life. I am astonished when I witness the same brethren, now decades later, still pretending that someday they will get it right. At this point in my life, I could no longer live in that lie.

I had come to a complete end of trying to be a "son of God," or to become as Christ myself before God. In my knowing that I was missing the key point of the gospel, I made the firm decision that what I needed was Someone Else to help me. I needed a Savior, Jesus, to be and to do what I could not. In fact, through these months, I made a firm and final decision that I would know only Jesus, though I did not then know Him well. In fact, I asked God to make Jesus as real to me as Abel Ramirez or Don Howat or Rick Annett ever were.

God designed me to need two entirely different environments, however, and I do best going back and forth between these two environments through the week. I love solitude, and the isolation of Blair Valley met that need. I loved to sit along the creek and watch the beavers swim lazily through the water. I loved hiking with my wife and children, gathering medicinal herbs, which grew everywhere, for our "medicine cabinet." I loved no sounds except the wind in the trees and the calling of the birds. There were few sights more beautiful to me than to watch the storm clouds beating against the ridge to our west. I loved the wildness, the protection, the grandeur.

Yet I am made for the classroom as well, and for the dynamic interchange of ideas with the faces of young people responding to me. I must have both, and I was not doing so well with the absence of that social interaction in which I could function – my classroom. If I had had a classroom at Blair, even with only a few students, then I may not have chosen to leave.

I settled on the one way I thought that I could succeed in providing for my family, and that would be to become a public school teacher. The Peace River country had its own community college called Northern Lights Community College. The main campus was in Dawson Creek, but there was also a large campus in Fort St. John. Northern Lights had a program that would connect students with the teacher certification program in British Columbia.

I made plans, then, to enroll in Northern Lights Community College in Fort St. John with the hopes of becoming certified as a teacher. Of truth, my sights were not set on teaching in the large public schools; rather, I hoped to find a teaching spot at one of the First Nations schools scattered across Canada.

Maureen's sister, Lois, came up to Blair Valley for a week's visit near the end of July. While she was with us, we attended the country fair outside of Fort St. John. I have loved few things in life better than doing interesting things like that with my wife and children. We also hiked up the east slope of the Blair Valley to a high bluff overlooking the community, where we had a picnic.

The Kiers's returned from Holland while Lois was still with us. We enjoyed hearing the stories of their visits. Then we took Lois to the airport in Fort St. John and returned to Blair Valley.

Right after we got back, something quite scary

happened. You see, Maureen was pregnant again, and our hike up the eastern slopes of the valley was a bit steep in spots. Without going into details, Maureen had a miscarriage, and the hemorrhaging would not stop. The ambulance for our area was situated at Pink Mountain, an hour away, but it was run by brethren from Headwaters. Minnie got on the phone and had them coming as fast as they could. We discussed whether we should take Maureen out to meet them on the long road into Blair Valley, but Minnie felt that Maureen should not move until qualified medical help was present.

I loaded the children into the pickup and we drove out, passing the ambulance on the way. They picked up Maureen and began the two-and-a-half-hour drive into Fort St. John. At Shepherd's Inn, they met an ambulance from the hospital and transferred Maureen. The children and I waited anxiously in the hospital emergency room. They were just in time; Maureen was still with us. They soon treated her, and then the doctor told her to get an herbal tonic to rebuild her blood.

This, of course, is a huge difficulty in living in such isolation. Nonetheless, the Lord kept us, as He keeps us now, and without Jesus carrying us, proximity to emergency assistance avails nothing. Maureen was weak and tired, but was back to normal within three weeks.

I visited with the counselor at Northern Lights College, and she connected me with the student loans that would support us while I went to school. This was a simple and easy process. At the same time, with Katrina's birth, we now received around $1800 a month in child benefits from the Canadian government. Brother D and Sister Ethelwyn had an older brown and large Ford Station Wagon they were no longer using that was kept at Shepherd's Inn. They sold it to us for a reasonable price. This car served us well over the next couple of years and, despite its age, did not give us any major problems.

In the family meeting at Blair Valley, I shared with the Kiers's and Annett's that we were moving to Fort St. John and that I was enrolling in the community college in order to obtain teacher certification. Kars asked, "Have you discussed this with Brother Buddy?"

"No," I replied. Immediately a mask came across his face and Minnie's. With that one act, we were no longer part of the move, and we no longer had a relationship with them. We were now "*in the flesh, walking against God.*"

Lee and Claire Wilkerson came over from Graham River to help Maureen and me pack and load our things into the Blue Van and the station wagon. Meanwhile Kyle and Johanna went over to Graham River to spend a few days with Steve and Cindy Schneider and their children. We have a picture of little Matthew Schneider, around Jo's age, a few feet up a spruce tree, holding on for dear life, with Johanna just beneath him hollering at him to get on up the tree. Meanwhile, Katrina was just learning to walk during these days.

Maureen went out first in the station wagon, probably driven by Rick. I would follow later with the Blue Van. We had found a townhouse in Fort St. John which we had rented, using the money from the student loan.

As I drove the Blue Van out, Kars and Minnie followed behind me in case I had any difficulties. They also needed to go into town. I stopped on the gravel road partway out to the highway, needing to fiddle with something on the van. Kars got out to help me.

I had offered the use of the Blue Van to the community to carry the water tank around, providing the community purchase a simple connecting hose that allowed me to fill the propane tank on the Blue Van from a regular propane bottle. I think that's what I had to do then. When I was finished, Kars insisted that the hose belonged to Blair Valley and not to me. I had been clear, in offering the Blue Van, that the hose would be my payment.

Kars was so sharp and hard, his words to me so cutting, that I did not contend with him, but allowed him to win. I said to him, "Kars, I am still a Christian; I still believe in Jesus." I do not remember his words, but they were savage, that since I had rebelled against God in leaving the covering, I was no longer ---.

I drove the rest of the way into Fort St. John feeling as if I had been kicked savagely in the gut with no wind left in me.

This was late August; we had left Blair Valley and the move. I was 41 years old.

Resolving the Issues

I have carried only one disturbing "what if" through the years since. – What if we had stayed at

Blair Valley? What would God have done for us in revealing Himself to us, both in provision, in healing, and in the knowledge of God?

I have never had an answer to that question, of course, and over time, the question itself has quietly subsided. I will address it again in the chapter after next, "Why Did We Leave?" Yet the question itself would remain as the haunting whisper of my heart for many years.

Kars and Minnie, Brother John Clarke, and Brother Buddy Cobb have passed on in the years since.

I have no need to "place" Brother John Clarke and his statement that triggered in me the conflicting realization that I was no longer in agreement with the attitudes and theology of the move. Several years later, here in Houston, Brother John and Sister Nathel apologized personally to Maureen and me. They had also apologized publicly to all the brethren in the northern communities, as they themselves left Blueberry and the move. In fact, the Clarkes afterward connected with Bill Johnson in Redding, California, and others in that move of the Spirit, as did many who left the move through these years.

Kars was never a real problem to me. The few times he spoke against me were isolated. Nonetheless, in writing this account, I have come to realize that Blair Valley really was all about Kars and Minnie. Everything else circled around them and their religious prejudice. By making it impossible for other men to express themselves equally at Blair Valley, Kars had made Blair Valley impossible. Yet I have mostly fond memories of Kars and Minnie and of our fellowship around the table. I forgive them freely with all joy and place the Lord Jesus upon their every moment and interaction with us. I receive Kars and Minnie Kiers as Jesus Himself. I receive them as my close and dear friends forever.

Before I close this letter out, however, I must place Brother Buddy Cobb and the entire move of God, with its ministry, into the Lord Jesus Christ carrying us all the way through. It was God who placed me into the move fellowship and under their covering and ministry, and God does all things well.

Prior to 1998 I would not have done well in my relationship with God separate from the support and environment of move community. I could have remained a Christian, certainly, but being a "Christian" has never interested me. I must know God and

Jesus Sent into me. In the process of our leaving through these months of 1998, God weaned me, so to speak, of this dependency on the move. From that time forward I have adhered utterly inside of me to seeking the knowledge of God. Nothing since has presented the slightest distraction.

The truth is that I owe Brother Buddy a lot. He was an anointed minister of Christ and of the word and his faithfulness to the churches can be matched by few others in history. I sat under Brother Buddy's preaching more hours than any other in my life. He pressed me into Romans 7 for years, right where God wanted me to be, right where I would come to despair in myself and any ability to get it right or to please God. Part of my knowing the word so well comes from Brother Buddy, and yes, I do oppose the majority of what he taught. Yet when I speak specifically against the false, I know its subtlety well because of Brother Buddy. At the same time, you could find good things all through what I share that also came to me through him. I even sound like him sometimes when I am reading my letters into audio.

Brother Buddy was a good man who gave his all in what he knew. The fact that he was deceived just makes him the same as every other minister of Christ in the world laboring inside of Nicene Christianity, ignorant of Paul's gospel.

I receive Brother Buddy as the Lord Jesus and bless him with all my heart. I draw him into the love of God poured out inside my heart and there release him into the liberty of Christ. Though he no longer has an earthly body, that means nothing, for my blessing towards him lifts him up inside of Jesus right now. Thank you, Brother Buddy, for pressing me against the wall, for without your role in my life, I would never have found the salvation that is Christ for which I have yearned, the Jesus who is the only life I am.

And having found all I ever wanted, I am able to open the same door to you and to all in the move of God fellowship who sought God with tears all the years of their life.

It was God who took me into the move of God fellowship. It was God with whom I connected through all my years in community. And it was God who led me out, for His purposes and in His timing. God is good all the time; Jesus does all things well.

31. The Move to Fort St. John

August 1998 - April 1999

The Next Eight Years

These next eight years, from August of 1998 to August of 2006 stand as an in-between time in my life. In August of 1998, I was numb and frozen inside, filled with a million unhealed wounds and unanswered questions. I was basically just trying to survive one day at a time. In August of 2006 I heard the most wonderful words that have ever come to me across the pulpit, and in that moment, my thirsty soul was fully ready to receive those words as the very River of God.

I have penciled in six chapters to cover these eight years, plus three explanatory chapters including the next one, titled "Why Did We Leave?" Through the first half of these years the task was to receive the gentle healing of God and the second half was to re-awaken my desire to know the living God.

I made firmly two critical mental positions that would carry me through the slow unraveling of all my hurt. The first was towards "hearing from God" and "seeking His will." – I refused. I refused to vacillate any longer over the issue of "will, will, what is God's will?" I refused to entertain any "check" or to seek any "peace" or "lack of peace." This was not throwing God out, but the opposite. I determined that I would live in the expectation that God alone directed our steps. I have not altered that determination from then until now.

The second is that, in leaving the move, I took EVERYTHING I had heard or believed or taught and put it all on a shelf in the far recesses of my mind. I kept one thing only, the grace of the Lord Jesus inside my heart. Everything else went onto that shelf. You see, I knew that God had spoken to me and revealed Himself and His word to me over many years. I knew that I had received many things that were truly of God. My problem was that I also knew that I held many ideas in my theology that were contrary to the gospel and that I had heard many things that were not of God. And I simply had no idea which was which.

I made a covenant with God concerning everything that had come into my life, every understanding I had received, the true and the false, that God Himself would bring those things back off that shelf in His time, arising inside of me in present revelation. And that if God did not bring something back off that shelf, then I would know it no more.

God is a keeper of Covenant.

Our House in Town

You can see the townhouse into which we moved in the picture on the top of the next page, probably on September 1. This would be our home for eight months. This was a nicely apportioned home. The street level was living and kitchen area; the upstairs was three bedrooms and a bath. Then, there was a full and open basement beneath. The laundry and storage were downstairs, but also a large corner for my office.

One of the first things that I purchased with the student loan money, in September of 1998, was my first computer. I was finally on the Internet. I built a nice little computer desk, having plenty of space in the basement for such construction work. I still use the same desk now.

Maureen homeschooled Kyle and Johanna. Little Katrina was much more active at this point. She was the mischevious one. She would see me heading for my chair and run to leap into it first, laughing while I lifted her out. She would sit on the stairs up next to Kyle and scream loudly, just so I would get after him for messing with her, even though he was not.

The wide spaces of Canada meant that it was normal for children to grow up in isolated places, and so education in the provinces was always geared towards meeting the needs of everyone. For this reason, homeschooling was much more prevelant and supported by provincial education. There was a nice educational building available for our use, with a craft room and library. We also made

Our Home

extensive use of the Fort St. John library, right in the center of town. Spending our time wandering among rows of books or sitting and reading this or that was becoming a trademark of our family.

There was also a large gym/swimming pool available for the children. We enrolled Kyle and Johanna in swimming classes, and thus they learned to swim well.

Since we were no longer "in the move," we also bought a television set. I still continued to read many books out loud to the children and Maureen, but we also began to enjoy many good family movies together. Watching good family movies together was a shared experience and would be an ongoing and wholesome part of the fabric of our family.

At the same time, we enjoyed connecting with real Canadians in Canadian life on a regular basis. Our outing became Subway, at least until we tired of Subway.

I want to add here a large book I checked out from the FSJ library and read all the way through, *The Sovereign Individual*, by William Rees-Mogg and John Davidson. I responded to the liberterian approach to understanding human life found in this book. Because I had the Internet, now, you can be sure that I searched widely to understand the world. In this search, I connected this book with a man named Bill Bonner, whose writing I enjoyed. I bring this in, because this connection will take me, after we move to Lubbock, to the most important source in the present time for my understanding of this world, and that is LewRockwell.com.

Fall Semester at Northern Lights

I began college a second time at Northern Lights Community College. My path forward was not clear, so I just started at the beginning. Among the courses I took this fall were a first year Composition course, Canadian History, and Physical Geography. I also started with a computer course, but soon dropped it since its slowness drove me bananas.

My geography teacher was Wim Kok (pronounced Vim Coke). I see that he is still teaching geography at that same college, these many years later. Wim Kok was one of the three or four best teachers in my educational experience. I loved geography as a subject, and I loved how Wim Kok taught it. I learned so much. He would explain things in such clear detail on the board, starting on one corner and working his way across, filling the entire large whiteboard with clear and complete explanation.

I learned something interesting about teachers in secular colleges. Those who have a "Christian" base teach real things, things that mean something or are useful. Those who do not have a "Christian" base have replaced such thinking with Marxism. These teachers have nothing real to teach and leave you with useless and empty so-called "ideas." My "English" teacher was one of those, but I was just being introduced to the role of Marxism in college education and was not in a position to be overly bothered by it.

On the other hand, Wim Kok had a Catholic background and my Canadian history teacher was Mormon. Both of these saw the world as practical and real and imparted useful understanding. I had also signed up for an introduction to Sociology course. The teacher was a Marxist lesbian feminist up from Victoria. She saw her role as the one who would break these young people away from their "false ideology." I saw her as one who wanted to be the high priestess of a new religion in the minds of these students. Needless to say, it was not long before I dropped that course as well.

But I love college, both as teacher and as student. And so, in wandering these "halls of learning," I noticed two things on the bulletin boards. One was a contest by the local radio station that offered $2500 towards schooling costs for writing three to five Canadian short stories, which they would then read over the radio. I applied to this contest and was accepted. I wrote a great little story set in the Peace River country, drawing from a true event, but expanding on it with an historical fiction approach. They liked that one. My second was similar, but just okay. For the third one, I wanted to write a story about First Nations people. I thought I could interview some in order to get the basis for my story. However, I ran into a massive internal block that shut me down. Though I worried myself against that block for several months, in the end, I could not write that third story. This puzzled me deeply; now I know of it as Asperger's. The result was that I received only half the money. Being unable to finish what I had agreed on troubled me deeply, however.

Then, I also saw a notice regarding an election for a student member of the educational council of Northern Lights College. I got someone to nominate me and, lo and behold, I was "elected." (I doubt that very many students voted, and I may have been the only nominee.) And so, I became a full voting member of the governing body of Northern Lights College. This also paid for my entire tuition for the year. Now, I was 42 years old at this point, more than twice the age of most of my fellow college students.

This meant that once a month, starting in October, I rode with the administrator of the Fort St. John branch, Casey Sheridan, down to the main administration building of the college in Dawson Creek for the meeting of the educational council. These were several individuals, including the college administrators from each branch, myself as a student representative, and several others involved with the academic side of things. We would make

the final decisions regarding courses offered, etc. This also gave me an hour's time each way for conversation with Mr. Sheridan, which was awesome. I did raise the issue of the Sociology teacher pushing her religion in the classroom. He thought that was wrong, but I'm not sure he understood I was speaking of Marxism. Of truth, I did not understand that whole arena either.

This was a remarkable experience for me, coming on the heels of being an elder in the move and sitting in the decision-making meetings in that context. There were a lot of similarities in how the governing meetings were conducted. But there was also one large difference, and that was the policy-management approach to governance. As the educational board, we set the policies, but it was the administrators who worked those policies without our "micro-management." If there was a disagreement, that would be addressed only in terms of "were the policies followed or not." Otherwise the manager was free to manage as he or she saw fit. I pondered these things deeply, since I had come away from move community governance with some troubling questions. I attended about seven of these meetings, from October to April; they were a rich experience for me and gave me an important new view of education.

Then, a ways into the fall semester, a new course was started called "Portfolio Development." I enrolled in this course since it seemed to be geared towards my goals. In this course, we were trained in how to express in concrete terms what we learned through life experience. In this way, we could obtain college credit if our learning matched specific college courses. My hope was that I could skip many of the required courses to obtain a second bachelor's degree, and maybe even bring in many of my Covenant Life College credits. I could see two-plus years towards obtaining a teacher's certificate, but not five.

This was not easy for me, however, because to describe my learning, I had to go back through my years in community, most of which caused me great pain for which I had no answers. No healing could yet start, not for three more years. At the same time, I still talked too much, and that made things even more difficult for me. In this course, we took the Myers-Brigg personality test, a very reasonable approach to different human personalities. I came out as an INTJ; that is, introverted, intuitive, thinking, judging. This personality type is one of the rarest. BUT – this was the extraordinary thing; as I was reading about the life experiences of INTJ individuals, I was reading about me. Other people were like me! This was the first time I knew such a thing.

I want to include one experience at Blueberry that I read about in the Myers-Brigg literature. Before we moved back down to Oregon, in 1993, I had drawn up a set of plans for the remodeling and expansion of the school building. In my mind, my ideas in the plans were there ONLY for the purpose of providing a starting point for discussion. But when I asked Sister Charity if she and Sister Delores could talk with me about their ideas for this plan, they refused. I pled, but they refused. Then, when we returned in 1995, I discovered, to my horror, that they had followed my plans completely. This was part of my reluctance to enter back into teaching in the Blueberry school. Those lines on the paper were just starting points for discussion, they were NOT meant to be the final plan.

The reason Delores and Charity had refused to discuss the plans with me was that they believed that my mind was set and that I would refuse all their ideas. I never thought that way, ever, but all I could surmise was that there was something terribly wrong with me. Now, I was reading that INTJ people were just like me, needing to set out a clear possibility in a plan before being capable of discussing it, and had experienced the exact same reactions from other people. For the first time the thought that I might be "normal," just different, was hovering around my consciousness. As I said, there could not yet be any healing, but at least some form of mental stability was coming into view. Being INTJ is not the same as being Asperger's; it carries its own set of difficulties in life.

Through all these experiences, then, I thought about the thinking processes taking place inside the Blueberry elder's meetings. I began to realize the meaning and extent of what can be called "group think," that is, how we define our world by how we perceive the most influential people in our world would define it. "Group think" has the power to blind people to things others outside the group see clearly. This was indeed a factor in my separation from the Blueberry eldership.

Different Fellowships

There were quite a number of people living in Fort St. John who had once lived in the move communities. Some of these were still connected with the move, including Rick and Shirley Annett, but others wanted nothing to do with the move, including our good friends, Peter and Barbara Bell. Maureen and I maintained our friendships with many on both sides of this divide.

We began attending a small home fellowship with the Bell's. This was led by a father and son pair, the Wilson's, who had lived at Graham River in the early years, but had "left the move" before I arrived at Graham in 1977. After a couple of months with them, Maureen and I switched over to a larger Spirit-filled church, called Christian Life Center. There were a number of former "movites" attending there. The Lord was with us in both gatherings, but in neither did we find what we really needed. Of course, we had no idea what we really needed; we just knew what wasn't.

The Meaning of Friendship

I want to bring in the critical things God was taking Maureen and I through inside of this topic of friendship. It is clear to me now that, inside God's intentions, Fort St. John was simply a transition point for us; no fulfillment would happen there in any part of our lives – except one.

First, leaving the move was an overwhelming experience of identity. For 21 years, I had identified myself by the move. My entire relationship with God had been in terms of move-of-God practice and theology. Now we had broken from that identity. Even inside God's great care for us, this was overwhelming.

The Wilson's who had left Graham River years before had the opposite experience. Brethren from the communities (all of whom themselves later "left the move") came to them in town to rebuke them for their iniquity and rebellion in "departing from God."

Then, at Christian Life Center, I gained an insight into a massive phenomenon that was part of the fabric of Fort St. John, something I had never considered or known existed. In 1998 it was now twenty-six years after the communities had first started in 1972. For twenty-four years (and continuing even until now, in 2020), the Christian brethren in Fort St. John, of whatever denomination or outlook, had been receiving an unending stream of broken, hurting, and confused people leaving the "farms" and moving into Fort St. John in an attempt to rebuild their lives and their sanity.

Deliverance services for "move demons" were not unknown.

This was a terrible, but true aspect of the move-of-God experience, one which we had kept ourselves ignorant of, because of our "religious superiority." This is not the only view one should have of the move communities, but it is a vital view, nonetheless.

You see, from the time we left Blair Valley until now, I have never left off my determination to be a part of a Community of Christ, the community of my heart. Now, I was gaining the first definition of a community with whom I would walk. That definition is this – "People WILL BE more blessed in their going then they are in their coming." Indeed, I practice this definition of Christ life every time a reader unsubscribes from my letters. Though I feel normal human hurt, nonetheless, I bless them in their going with all my heart. They belong to Jesus and never to me.

The problem we were experiencing, however, was that even those who had "left the move" still practiced the same things for which Maureen and I had left, that is, this favorite human practice of manipulating and controlling other people. I was beginning to realize, right from the start, that these things were not "move problems," nor Christian problems, but human problems.

At Blueberry in particular, an effort towards me was to "fix my problem," by getting me to acknowledge my problem and then to change my performance. I never connected with their definitions of "my problem" because those definitions did not fit, and even if they had, I was utterly incapable of pretending the change they wanted to see. As the prophet said, "**Can a leopard change his spots?**" And as David said, "**It is God who has made us and not we ourselves.**"

But now I had entered what would be a very strange three-year time-period in my life, in which different ones made very direct effort to alter my identity. I never understood any of this, and it made finding my way through the murkiness even more difficult. Nonetheless, I see now that it was through these experiences that God enabled me to understand human identity, the false and the true.

In the home fellowship, I was sharing the vision and dream of my heart with the younger Wilson, who was the leader of that fellowship. I did not understand it fully myself, of course, and so I said, "I want to start a Bible school for God's people."

Before I had any chance to share what I meant by that, or why it was so important to me, he replied with all assertive correction. "God is NOT doing that anymore." This is a practice of disrespect that I have never understood. The brother had left the move, but the worst practices of the move had not left him.

We had reason to attend one of the convention services at Shepherd's Inn. We needed to connect with some who would be there, including Gary Rehmeier. (About what I don't remember.) One of the sisters from Blueberry needed to talk with me. We sat down together, and she proceeded to counsel me with all concern that I had abandoned my family in order to pursue my interests (in going to school at Northern Lights.) There was no room in her heart for asking me or for hearing a different understanding. I was going to school so that I could eventually support my family. School, however, took much less of my time than full-time work would, and I was more "with my family" then most men. Her "ministry" to me resulted only in greater sorrow.

In fact, I had stopped at the Blueberry school during our move to Fort St. John in order to retrieve my books and filing cabinet with my school papers that I had left there, including my large Webster's 1926 dictionary. Sister Charity had said to me, "I hope you find what you are looking for." I did not respond to that; I was not looking for some sort of "zen" or other revelation nor any "place of recognition." I just wanted to support my family. People like to read into other people's lives without asking, just assuming they actually know.

AND – the truth is, although I have not found a long-term way in which I can support my family, I have found all that I ever wanted in knowing Father-with-me.

This "abuse of identity" against me will continue through the next two years, even after we moved to Texas. Here, however, I want to set against it the opposite. And that opposite was found in Rick Annett.

The Lord Jesus Christ proved Himself to me through Rick Annett, that our bond of friendship together, he and Shirley with Maureen and me, had nothing to do with the move or anything outward, but was fully out from Jesus in our hearts. Very simply, Rick and Shirley continued their relationship with us, just the same as it had been at Blair Valley. And through Rick, I came to know the deepest meaning and value of friendship. I am not speaking of any large actions, rather, just the joy of sharing one another's lives. In fact, the topic of "friendship" finds its place in my guide for Christian Community, *Symmorphy V: Life,* entirely out from the proving of Jesus to me through Rick Annett.

Now, as I said, Rick and Shirley had not "left the move," and so Rick was unwilling to continue regular services with us as that would not be sanctioned by the move ministry. This is why we attended Christian gatherings elsewhere. Nonetheless, we visited with them in their apartment, and they in our townhouse often and regularly. Rick and Shirley, of course, knew Peter and Barbara well, having lived in the same community with them at Evergreen.

Very simply, Rick accepted me and valued me as I was, with no shadow of any need for me to change in order to fit any prejudiced definitions of "Christ." And here's the wonderful thing. I can copy towards you what Rick was towards me and be more "like Jesus." To learn of Christ does bring a change in us, entirely in the arena of how we regard and care for one another.

Rick, you gave me the most valuable gift any human can give another – friendship.

And it was Rick's continued friendship towards me that enabled me to safely maneuver along the precipice of a mental breakdown until I was safe enough to leave it behind. Because of Rick and Shirley, Maureen and I did not know the awful breakage forced against most others who "left the move."

The Spring Semester

In the Spring Semester, I continued with Physical Geography and Canadian History. Getting a Canadian view of Canadian history and interaction with the U.S. was especially important as it enabled me to know that Americans can be deluded about themselves and their view of the rest of the world. I also added a second course with Wim Kok, titled "Resource Geography." This course was at the 400 level and thus came through the University of Northern British Columbia. I really loved learning from Wim Kok and wrote one of my more memorable papers in this course, a study of the Three Gorges Dam in China.

I also started a business course, but soon dropped it as impractical. I took an Anthropology course on the relationships between First Nations and the governments of Canada. I really liked this course as well. I wanted very much to learn more about these hurting people and hoped that I might teach in one of their reservation schools. It is with sorrow that I say that this was not God's path for us.

The Annett's and the Dickout's

By January, I no longer had an interest in attending the fellowships in Fort St. John, for I was not finding anything I needed. Maureen did attend sometimes with the children. Instead, we began the bright part of our experience in Fort St. John. Dan and Ann Dickout, whom I had known in my early years at Graham River, before they were married, were now living just outside of Charlie Lake, a few miles from Fort St. John. They were attending Christian Life Center where they often led praise. Dan and Ann Dickout were wonderful praise leaders, deeply anointed of God. Dan made a living teaching piano and other musical instruments; he had a studio in town.

Anyhow, by January, we started going out to Dan and Ann's home each Sunday afternoon with Rick and Shirley as well. We would have dinner together and then spend the afternoon fellowshipping together and often in singing and praise. These times with the Annett's and the Dickout's were of great value to Maureen and me. Dan and Ann's children were a bit older than ours, but they played together in the downstairs.

This was 1999, and many were getting ready for "Y2K." I don't remember my reasoning, but I had determined for myself that nothing would actually happen. The Dickout's and many others were getting prepared, however. This was also a few years after Riverdance had wowed the world with a new style of Irish dancing, and two of the Dickout children were learning Irish dancing and were willing to show their steps for us.

By the middle of March, we knew that Maureen was carrying our fourth child, James.

No Options

The primary concern for us was how I could support us with a decent-paying career.

Sometime in February, some ladies from the British Columbia teacher oversight visited Northern Lights College concerning the teacher preparation program. I visited with one of them concerning my desire to become a teacher as well as my previous education and teaching experience. When I asked about proving out some of my Covenant Life College credits through portfolio development, her entire demeanor towards me changed. Her face turned red with deep hostility; in fact, it was clear to me that a demon had filled her call against me in that moment. "NO credits from any Christian college will ever be accepted," she hissed.

I realized in that moment that, even if I did go through an entire program of five years of school at the undergraduate level, I still might not be accepted by these virulent Marxists. In their possessed minds, Christians are "people of hate" out to destroy children's lives.

I was interested at the time in linguistics and the idea of getting a master's degree in Linguistics from a Christian university and becoming a Bible translator with Wycliffe translators appealed to me. I looked in that direction for a while but found no real peace. That direction would never have supported us, nor fulfilled God's intention for my life.

And so, by March and April, it became clear to me, not that God was closing doors for us in Fort St. John, but that He was not opening any.

Leaving Canada

Meanwhile, my sister, Frieda, along with Tim, Ryan, and April, were all still living at the Christian community on the outskirts of Lubbock, Texas. Maureen's sister, Jessica and Matthew Sanchez also lived there. Maureen's other sister, Lois, had a little house in town.

Since I had the world on the Internet, I began researching Christian graduate schools in Texas. I discovered two things. First, that every school in Texas, Christian and non-Christian, offered teaching certificate programs, easily accessed. And second, that a master's degree program just might accept my entire bachelor's degree from Covenant Life College. This would allow me to obtain a teaching certificate AND a master's degree at the same time, AND in one-and-one-half years, not five.

I did not want to go to Texas. All my time in the move, it was Texas this and Texas that. The last thing I wanted was a "Texas driver's license."

Even more than that, we had gone through so much to be immigrated to Canada. I did not want to leave Canada. At that time, Canada was much freer than the states. In Canada, the Canadian government had demonstrated fear of both the people and the provinces. In fact, the provinces often made decisions together without inviting the Federal government. One did not fear the Canadian government. The U.S. government, on the other hand, is overwhelming in its power and tyranny over the people and over the states. The idea that we live in a "free country" is simply absurd.

But by April of 1999, there just seemed to be no other path. At the same time, some of the brethren in the move fellowship in Lubbock had connected with a natural health practitioner named Dr. Hall who was doing great things for people. This connection presented me with the possibility of treatment and cleansing that might help me regain the energy I needed to support my family.

We decided on a "temporary" trip to Lubbock, being able to stay with Maureen's sisters or mine for a short time, in order to take advantage of this health program. At the same time, Lubbock Christian University had a master's degree program that also provided teacher certification. Our thought was that we would go to Lubbock for the summer and then see if God opened that door for us or not.

This was definitely a clear path forward. In fact, it was the only path forward visible to us.

And so, with definite sorrow, Maureen and I prepared to leave Fort St. John and Canada and to return to the states. In fact, a large part of my thinking was that Maureen had followed my lead faithfully through all these years, and now, maybe it was time for me to make a choice for her, so that she could be part of her sister's lives as well. For Maureen and the children's sake, I was even willing to don the "sad title" of being a "Texan."

We were in a monthly rental position with our home, and so we could leave just after school was out, at the end of April's rent. When we had moved to Fort St. John, I had sold our solar power setup to an individual who had property just north of FSJ. He had allowed me to park the blue van on his property, since we were allowed only one vehicle at the townhouse. I was very relieved to retrieve the blue van, which I loved deeply. It started right away, even after months buried in snow.

We divided all our belongings into two parts, the larger part would go into the blue van, which I would leave parked again at Shepherd's Inn. The smaller part would be fitted into and on top of our Ford Station Wagon, along with places for all five of us to tuck into. I fitted a lot of stuff into the station wagon. When it was half full, I took it to a shop to be worked on. The mechanic rebuked me severely for weighting the car down too much. Except I was only half done. You see, I needed that vehicle to serve us, not the other way around. And it did serve us well.

We did not need to go straight to Lubbock, however; so we turned our direction towards Meadowlands, Minnesota where we hoped to spend a couple of weeks with mom and with Glenn and Kim and their family.

I parked the blue van at Shepherd's Inn, with their permission. We said our goodbyes to the Bells, the Annett's, and the Dickout's, which was more sorrowful to Maureen and me than leaving Canada. We headed east towards Winnipeg.

In Winnipeg, we spent a night or two with Elizabeth (Roes) Croker and her children. Her husband was out on a job. It was great to connect with Elizabeth again. She was as filled with cheer and laughter as always.

Soon after we left Winnipeg, we crossed the border into Minnesota. We had left Canada behind us, a loss we have borne with sadness from then until now.

32. My Reasons for Leaving

Respect Requires

My respect for God's people with whom I walked requires me to set forth my reasons for leaving the move of God fellowship and that covering under which I had walked for twenty-one years. Then, I must also add my reasons for leaving Blair Valley and finally, for leaving Canada.

Through the last two chapters, I have attempted to limit things partly to my thoughts and feelings through this time. Now, however, I must give you the full meaning as I understand things in this year of our Lord 2020.

The covenant I made with God when I was twenty-two years old remains unchanged from then until now, that I would know God in this life and on this earth, and that I would walk with a people who know God. Not a day has gone by from then until now that I have not held this commitment and vision in my heart, regardless of all my ins and outs.

Why Did We Continue?

There is a different question that must come first, and the answer to this question God has now shown me, and indeed, it is the deepest answer for all other questions.

A casual reader, going through my account of the difficulties and pain God took me through from 1990 on, might well raise the question, "Why on earth did you stay in such an environment for years? Why did you not leave earlier?"

The answer is commitment.

In the Headwaters Convention, in February of 1978, God spoke to me "You can trust this ministry; I have sent them." I do not take a word like that as an absolute. What it means to me now is that for this season of my life, this fellowship and this ministry were God's chosen environment for me to walk, in order that I might know Him.

I committed myself to that word and that ministry at great cost over many years.

As I was writing the chapters on Blair Valley, the Lord showed me that it was my commitment that He honored in giving me a godly way of transferring that commitment from that which is outward to the Lord Jesus inside of me, and through Him, to all who belong to Him.

The outward structure was necessary for me until it wasn't. But think of that. What if I had just said, "Phooey on this," and gone my way. If my commitment to God inside the move fellowship meant so little to me, then it would have continued to mean little anywhere else.

The unwillingness to commit one's self to God's people, even to continuing through great costs, is an unwillingness to commit one's self to God. As John said, "**We cannot say that we love God if we do not also love our brothers and sisters.**"

Love is not a feeling; love is a commitment.

God never violates the integrity of our persons. God gave us the season of peace at Blair Valley because He honored Maureen and me and gave us the place where we could separate from that fellowship inside the integrity of our own hearts and for very specific, personal, and godly reasons.

And in saying that, a time that has held the most difficult unanswered question for me is now filled with the Honor of God.

Reasons for Leaving the Move

From the time I first read the Bible through, at age nineteen, I chose one verse in the Bible as the desire and direction of my heart. That one verse was John 14:23. **If anyone loves Me, he will keep My word; and My Father will love him, and We will come to him and make Our home with him** (NKJV).

This desire of mine, to experience the Father and the Son coming to me and making their home with me, has been the primary motivation behind how I have walked and how I have studied the Bible.

By the early months of 1998, the teaching of the ministry of the move, apostles and elders, had removed from me all hope that I could know the only thing I wanted to know. This was a profound and existential removal of hope.

I had no idea that, by leaving the move, I would come to know this one thing that I wanted, but there was no question that remaining in that fellowship would never bring me to the one place I will go, knowing my Father at home in my heart through Jesus Sent into me.

Through all the writing I have done over the last fourteen years, I have made one claim only regarding myself or what I share. That one claim is that I have found what I always wanted, Father at home in my heart.

The second reason I left the move fellowship was that I was quit with a "Jesus" far away from me. I needed a Savior, close, personal, and real, the One upon whose breast I always lean my head. From that moment on, I have rejected any thought that I would ever be a son of God in myself. I cannot ever please God myself, and in leaving the move, I quit all idea that I ought to do such a thing.

As you can see, those first two reasons were closely related. I will also place the next two reasons for leaving the move together.

The third reason I left the move of God was that the vision for community that I carried in my heart for all those years was rarely my actual experience. I now understand the reasons why the order and philosophy of the move communities never answered the cry and longing of my heart.

However, at that time, there was a very large issue inside the wrongful definition of community, with which I could no longer walk in agreement. That issue was the self-righteous sectarianism of the people, ministry and non-ministry, who were part of that fellowship. God took Maureen and me to Oregon through 1993-1995 in order to open my heart to His entire church.

My final two reasons for leaving that fellowship were personal, towards me and towards my children. The truth is, losing the community, rural, and agricultural environment for my children to grow up inside of is the single greatest loss we suffered in leaving the move. Yet I count the integrity and honor of their persons to be more important. And I knew that, had we continued in the definitions of that sect, my children would have experienced wrongful disrespect of their persons. That happens everywhere, yes, but it is different when it's coming from "God" in their minds, rather than God being their refuge.

For my children to grow up imagining that God disrespected them – that would not be!

The final reason I left the move of God fellowship was for my own sake. I was riddled with unhealed wounds. I was numb and frozen inside. I was hurting at every point. I was on the brink of mental and nervous collapse. I continued in this way on the inside of me for two years after we left, before any kind of healing could even begin.

I believe that I have given a complete and honest account of my decision. And in all these things, it was Maureen and I together, though I realize now that she followed my lead each time, always faithful to me beyond what I ever deserved.

Blessings from Being in the Move

There were two different things operating inside the communities of the move-of-God fellowship. One of those things was people, operating as humans do, with every practice of manipulating and conniving, thoughtlessness and disrespect that all humans are so capable of doing, inside the context of the intensity of daily togetherness and out from a theology that painted God, humans, and salvation in the false manner of Nicene Christianity.

Operating equally and in conjunction with all the problems that are humans, was the other thing in the communities, and that is people, filled with Jesus, of great value and regard, stumbling through life together, and in all their difficulty, learning what it means to love one another.

I was no different than any, neither better nor worse. Yet having passed through those years, I have the same choice that every other human has in the present moment. I can call every moment, circumstance, and interaction with others by the Lord Jesus Christ and find each to be a blessing of life. Or I can call every moment, circumstance, and interaction with others by not-Christ and find each to be a cursing of death.

Since Maureen and I left the move, it has always been in my heart, not only to keep all that God had taught me through those years, but to draw any good thing of Christ from my experiences with all the brethren in the move into my present rejoicing inside of Jesus.

When I chose to live in Christian Community in 1977, I did so carrying a vision inside of the community of my heart. When I left the move in 1998, that vision was NOT one of the things I placed on the shelf. Rather, I have walked every day before God from then until now in the expectation and hope that God will raise up around me, somehow, that Christ Community of which I would be a part.

You might think that I have sent out these letters over the last twelve years to give God's people hope. That is not quite correct. I have sent out every single one of these letters in order to call forth that Community of God's precious people that I am determined to know. If you have received good things from what I share, that's part of the overflow of God.

And so, as I entered into the rest of knowing my union with Christ, sending out my first *Christ Our Life* letter at the same time, I determined to draw out from my years of experience in move of God community all the good things of Christ that I knew. And I determined to draw out from those same years of experience a clear outline of the giants in the land and how we are well able to defeat them. I have considered myself to be as Caleb, sent into the land of Christ to spy out both the good and the destructive, and to tell God's people, "Let us go up and take the land, for we are well able to overcome."

They said: "We went to the land where you sent us. It truly flows with milk and honey, and this is its fruit. Nevertheless, the people who dwell in the land are strong; the cities are fortified and very large... Then Caleb... said, "Let us go up at once and take possession, for we are well able to overcome it" (Numbers 13:27-30 – reduced).

I want to list a number of incredible qualities that I now possess out from my years of being a part of the move of God fellowship and Christian community.

The most important thing I gained was from Sam Fife, and that is my relationship with the Bible. The first thing Sam Fife did for me was to obliterate all the structures of thinking and definitions from Nicene Christianity that are not the gospel and that prevent Christians from seeing what God actually says. Then, in its place, he taught me the massive importance of "the words that I speak to you are Spirit and they are life," knowing the life of a Spirit-empowered Word.

Sam Fife gave me "permission," one might say, to regard the huge powerful statements of the gospel, things not part of most Christian thinking, like being filled with all the fullness of God, setting creation free, and overcoming death. He imparted to me a profound understanding of God's metaphors of bringing forth life and of the Tabernacle of Moses and the Feasts of Israel. But most of all, Sam Fife gave me a taste of the opening of the heavens and the piercing voice of God coming through out from the depths of His being. The echo of that voice, knowing that God Almighty maintains a personal relationship with me in power, reverberates all through me to this day.

To know God and to know His Word – this is the greatest gift of my life.

I will continue, now, without trying to rate "importance."

I think of all the wisdom imparted to me from so many over all those years, but especially from Brother Jim Fant and Sister Charity Titus. I absorbed the things they taught me probably more than they realized. There are some things I teach that are original to me, but it would be impossible to divide most of what comes through me as coming from one or another.

I must make something as clear as I can. When I speak of "running the gauntlet," or the picture of "Eliza fleeing the dogs of slavery across the icy St. Lawrence, carrying her child in her arms," I do NOT mean that the move of God or any of its people are part of that opposition. On the contrary, the thing I was escaping was the gospel of the serpent, and inside the precious treasure held tightly in my arms, close against my heart, is every single brother and sister, precious beyond measure inside of Jesus, with whom I interacted inside of Christian community.

Yet I am in no way "superior." I love the story that Dr. Paul Brand shares at the beginning of *In His Image*. He tells of working in the operating room with his Indian students and seeing on their faces the face of his own instructor when he was a young doctor training in London. He quizzed them after, wondering how on earth they learned the expressions of someone they had never met. "Oh no, Dr. Brand," they replied, "that is your expression we have learned."

Here is the truth. You might have found a lot of wisdom through the things that I share, but you would be wrong if you imagined that was coming from me. What you will discover instead is that you have sat in the classroom of one of the wisest people I have known; you have been taught by Sister Charity Titus.

To be able to carry to you such treasure as I received, not just from her, but from many through all the years of my move of God experience, is to me a reward beyond all measure, a reward I certainly did not earn.

A third area containing many things of great value is the hammering of God upon me over so many years and in so many places. Christian community was the anvil and God's Word was the hammer, and I was caught in-between.

One of the greatest gifts ever received by anyone is the gift of the removal of rebellion from one's heart. Nothing in any regular church would have ever accomplished such a thing in me, only move-of-God Christian community.

But with that hammering of God, shaping my heart to fit His, though I knew it not, came the opening up of myself, out from my disassociated shell, that I might know how to relate with other people and how to understand my own humanity.

Just like Much Afraid in *Hinds Feet on High Places*, I carry as great treasure every place of stumbling and pain inside of relationships with other people in the family of God. These gems I possess may seem of little value to those who have not walked in such a path, but they have no idea just how wealthy I am.

A fourth area is all the many wonderful things I did and experienced all through my years in the move of God. All the many and varied construction tasks that I did and learned to do, all the different courses I had the privilege of teaching in school, even before I was trained to do so, all the many wilderness and work and life experiences, that I would never have known in any "regular" life, I tell you what, these things are invaluable. And because I live inside the power of an endless life, none of these things are memories only; all things that I love to do and to participate in WILL come back to me again, in their season.

Finally, I want you to understand the meaning of the text that is dearest to my heart of all that I have written, *Symmorphy V: Life*, a handbook for Christian Community. If you have gained anything by reading of my years in Christian community, then know that every line in that text, every suggestion and perspective, comes out from intense care to set before you a real and true vision of the Promised Land of Christ, brethren, walking together in love.

What you find in that book is the Community of my heart, not just unharmed by any of the giants and fortified cities inside years of difficulty, but rather strengthened and made clear by all. You will find a full appraisal of the giants, yes, but an even more real setting forth of the Lord Jesus Christ as Community, as the revelation of Father, all the good fruit and blessing that is Christ Life.

It was twenty-one years of walking together with other believers in Jesus in the move of God, all the joy and all the pain, that gave me all that you find in that text, and I would not trade any of it for anything less. I have taken all the straw of my life, and I have woven for you gold.

I must pause and marvel at the undeserved wealth of my life, the majority of which came to me from my years in the move of God.

Reasons for Leaving Blair Valley

When we left Blair Valley and moved into Fort St. John, I felt at different times that I needed to give a reasonable explanation of why we left. The reason I gave was that we just were not able to find any way to support ourselves in that isolated place. And that statement was entirely true, though it was not, of course, anywhere near the entire answer. The nice thing is that it seemed to be satisfactory to all.

The problem in me then was that I could have shared a dim view of why we left the move, but I had no idea, really, of why we left Blair Valley.

And in all the twenty-two years from then until now, that question – Why did we leave Blair Valley? – What if we had stayed? – has haunted my heart with a measure of despair every day.

Writing these chapters has turned all that entirely around. God has not answered my question; instead, He has shown me that His proof of Christ in me was always the only thing happening.

It was clear to me as we worked through the decision to leave Blair Valley, that the community of my heart, a non-sectarian place that received all of God's people regardless, with wide-open arms and with no obligation, would not happen at Blair Valley in that present context. Blair Valley was mostly about Kars Kiers, and Kars Kiers was mostly about the narrowest religious and sectarian aspects that blemished that fellowship.

You see, the bottom line of all my hope towards our arriving at Blair Valley was that God would now bring forth a community that answered all the cry of my heart for real, for life, for being a blessing to others, to God's people all across the earth. The bottom-line of my HOPELESSNESS was not "move doctrine," then, but the deep realization that such a community was not and could not happen there.

Heart despair is why I left the place, though I never left the vision.

God's Purpose for Us at Blair Valley

Writing these chapters on Blair Valley inside the flow of God's dealing in my life and placing the Lord Jesus upon every moment has given me a perspective of God's purposes that I have never seen or known before now.

Let me explain. There is an awesome comparison between the Feasts of Israel and the development of a baby in the womb. And the truth is that on the fifteenth day of the seventh month of pregnancy, that is, the day that Tabernacles begins, the child is first able to live outside of the womb. Nonetheless, God's design is for the child to remain another month-and-a-half in that place so that it might be fully strong when it does come forth. And, in fact, the first day of the ninth month is the feast of dedication, added later.

I now see that God's intentions towards me inside the move-of-God context were completed at the end of March 1997, when He spoke to me, "Son, you passed the test." But I was in no way ready to "leave the womb," so to speak.

Then, as I wrote about our time at Blair, God showed me the honor and respect that He extended towards me in giving me peace at Blair Valley inside of which I could work through the decision to separate from that fellowship, that had been as the womb of the Church to me, without any loss to the integrity of my heart and person.

I am in awe at the goodness and kindness of our Father, and I give Him all thanks.

Reasons for Leaving Canada

We had gone through so much over so many years to be immigrated to Canada. Our immigration status remained current for one year after our departure, and then we applied for and received an extension for a second year during which we could have returned at any time.

Except – we had absolutely no means to do so nor any place to go in Canada where we could support ourselves. The last day, in April of 2001, when our immigration status ceased, was a very sad day for both Maureen and me.

Now, as I have written this account, the answer has become simple and clear. God opened no other doors for us in Canada. And so we submit our hearts to His hand in all joy and goodness.

The Question of "What If?"

I have never set aside the word God spoke to me concerning the fulfillment of the Community of my heart, that our home is at Blair Valley. Nonetheless, I have been more than willing for God to plant us in such a community in a different place, at least for the time being. Because I live inside the power of an endless life, it would be no surprise at all if I were to find myself inside of a wondrous Community of Christ back in that valley in northern British Columbia during the Age of Tabernacles.

Nonetheless, I carried a return to Blair Valley close in my heart for many years, but especially, the bringing forth of a Christ Community as I was able to describe in *Symmorphy V: Life*. This fact of my heart-desire posed a problem to some and was at the center of the identity issues God would take me through over the next couple of years after we left Canada.

I want to point you towards the two letters I wrote in the early months of 2013 that express this vision that I thought about most every day from our leaving Blair Valley on – "My Vision I" and "My Vision II," found in my book, *Gathering to Life*. And as I said, I would have gladly accepted the same thing anywhere else that God would place us inside His peace.

Through the seven years from the summer of 2013 until now, the years of Symmorphy, I have known a release from that particular location for the Christ Community I am anxiously ready to move into today, the very moment God raises it up.

But let me go back to the troubling of my heart as we left the place God had called "your home." As I wrote out the story of the prophet in 1 Kings 13 who was torn apart by a lion because he had disregarded God's instruction, the Lord asked me how I would place such an interpretation now. The answer was simple and clear, I would throw that interpretation right into the dung heap where it belongs right along with all of Satan's use of Bible verses to tempt us not to trust in Jesus.

And the moment I knew that, the question "WHAT IF" vanished from my heart and I know it no more. There is no need for a non-answer to a non-question.

Yet there is another, deeper question that underlay that now-vanished question of "What if." That deeper question is the security of being covered versus the sense of "flapping in the breeze," now that we have no committed relationship with any ministry or fellowship.

Covering is important; it's how local fellowships connect together. When I was "under the covering" of the move ministry, I had a place and connection everywhere I went. I was able to be a "ministry" during our time in Oregon, raising up a little fellowship, because of that sense of connection, purpose, and covering.

The fellowship in Lubbock, Texas, under Pastor Gary Kirksey, where Maureen and I will find much help and the beginning of healing, held a similar understanding of covering for the safety of the church as was found in the move. This is not a sectarian issue.

Yet I am presently "on my own" and have been so since we came to Houston. I looked for some connection here, but God opened none to us. I KNOW that great blessing and a knowledge of the presence of God comes inside of commitment to one another inside the context of the local church, a commitment that includes a place of safety and protection found under that ministry of God that He places with heart-care over His Church.

My present lack of "covering" has troubled me all the years we have been in Houston. I have even felt uncertain that our place here was "God's will."

My question of leaving Blair Valley, the Lord Jesus answered with – "Because I respected you." But the answer to this question of covering, and of, "are we, maybe, in the wrong place?" He answered in an opposite manner – with stern rebuke.

And I feel as Jesus did in Hebrews 5:7, on His face before God, that God might save Him from death. The death God would save me from is the death of a lack of absolute CONFIDENCE in Christ, that He alone directs my steps out from His own heart purposes.

If I lack confidence in God in one small and hidden area, how can I impart true confidence to anyone?

"Lord Jesus, You are well-able to direct my every step and I am confident with all certainty that You have done so, through every day of my life. We did not "stumble" into Houston, but You placed us here and You gave us no outward connection with Christian brethren here, for Your purposes and desire. Jesus, You are absolute Lord over every moment and day of my life, and I place myself absolutely into Your Confidence, filling my heart with glory."

It is this confidence, then, that is and will be a covering for many, a shelter from the storm, a place of safety and belonging.

A Life Made Whole

Our daughter, Katrina, who just turned 23, has bought herself a travel trailer that she hopes will be her own home. Katrina is the head of the heritage program at Jesse Jones park and is becoming known throughout the arena of Texas heritage. Her spunk and determination make Maureen and I very proud.

When Katrina first put the trailer onto her pickup, it weighted the pickup down more than is safe. She drove it around, but when she came back, it seemed that the weight of the trailer was beginning to pull the pickup apart. In difficult driving situations, such an imbalance of weight could have resulted in the trailer pushing the pickup in directions Katrina would not want to go.

Then our son James, who will be 21 in October, borrowed torsion bars and an anti-sway bar from our neighbor across the street and installed them on the trailer/pickup hookup. These bars pulled up the trailer and pickup even with one another tightly. I drove the unit back home from an outing to Waco and was pleased with how safe it felt. I was driving one unit. When I turned or when I braked, I never felt that the trailer was anything other than part of the pickup.

As I finished writing the chapters on Blair Valley, that image of the trailer weighting down the back of the pickup came to my mind as a clear picture of how my life has been.

Let me explain. The trailer is that large and heavy portion of my life that was my years in the move of God and in Christian community. The pickup is my life since we left that fellowship and we are now in the cab, being driven forward by the power of Christ our only life. My adult life has been two large parts, the first part resting as a heavy weight upon the second part. Most who left the move tried to unhitch and cast off the "trailer" of their move experience from their present life. I am convinced they are doing nothing more than deluding themselves.

The connection between the trailer of my years in the move and the pickup of my present life was our leaving Blair Valley and Canada. That connection has always been weak inside my heart, and sometimes it seems that the years of difficulty might push our present life in wrong directions because of that weak connection.

The picture of James installing the torsion and anti-sway bars, pulling up the trailer and pickup even with each other, now one tight unit, came to me so strongly as God honored me with Himself through this weak point of my life.

And in that moment, I felt that the two large parts of my life have come fully together as one. I feel whole, complete, and put together.

Now, as I am looking forward to writing the second half of my adult life, I am filled with anticipation of the joy of Christ my life entering my experience.

Every particle of my years in the move fellowship is fully complete, fully inside of Jesus, fully filled with blessing and joy.

And I realize now that until this has happened for me, until that weak connection of our leaving Blair Valley was lifted up into the strength and honor of God towards me, then I suspect that any foray into a community experience might well have resulted in being pushed by hidden emotions in directions I would not want to go.

"Now I am ready, even so come, Lord Jesus. Place Maureen and I into that community of my heart where we will know God and where we will walk with a people who know God. Let it be so; it is so."

Bearing Precious Seed

When the Lord brought back the captivity of Zion, we were like those who dream. Then our mouth was filled with laughter, and our tongue with singing. Then they said among the nations, "The Lord has done great things for them." The Lord has done great things for us, and we are glad.

Bring back our captivity, O Lord, as the streams in the South. Those who sow in tears shall reap in joy. He who continually goes forth weeping, bearing seed for sowing, shall doubtless come again with rejoicing, bringing his sheaves with him (Psalm 126).

Let me share with you two paragraphs in the first chapter of this narrative.

~~~ So, if you are willing to entertain my foolishness for just a bit, we together must ask the obvious question – Why in God's good name would He, in fact, pick such a bumbling failure of a man as this unknown "Daniel Yordy" to speak the revelation of Christ as He is to His church?

I am writing this account of my life for two reasons. First, it is my intention to prove to you that God has no good reason whatever to speak to His church through me – and many, many good reasons why He would not. And second, it is my responsibility to lay before you how God has taken me by the hand, step by faltering step, and led me into His own heart, that here, hiding entirely inside the heart of my Father, I might show that heart to you. ~~~

I hope, at this point in the narrative, that I have proven beyond all question that God has no good reason whatsoever to give such a treasure of word to one such as I.

Yet He has. And my heart is overflowing with tears of goodness and joy. For nearly twelve years, now, I have sown this word in tears, this word of the Community of Christ that I carry in my heart FULFILLED.

Doubtless, I will come again rejoicing, bringing my reward with me.

And my reward is you, dear reader, found in all the joy of Christ your only life through every moment and circumstance through which you have walked. You are my treasure and my joy, that Jesus would prove to you that you have always been His revelation.

33. Gone to Texas

May 1999 - February 2000

Meadowlands

We arrived at the Meadowlands community north of Duluth, Minnesota, in the first week of May and spent more than two weeks there.

Meadowlands was a small community but blessed of the Lord. It was still part of the move at this time, but Mark Alesch shared with me a few years later that he and his wife, Cindy, had felt a growing discomfort towards recent move teaching, very similar to the things I had become concerned about. By the mid 2000's, they had separated from the move. Mark and Cindy Alesch purchased the main part of the property and made it into a place of accommodation. Glenn, my brother, purchased the smaller part of the property across the road, and he and Kim built a home there.

Here is the property now, as Alesches Accommodations - https://www.alesches.com/. They have made the interiors of the homes very nice for guests, but the outside is much the same as it was in 1999.

Maureen and I were received at Meadowlands without thought that we had "left the move." This was unique in move community; people who "left" continue to be viewed as "outsiders." We were welcomed into the life of the community, and the hearts of the brethren were open to us and to anything the Lord would share through us.

We were given a full apartment in the downstairs of a large building that had three living units in it. Glenn and Kim had the other end of the building, both upstairs and downstairs as their home. At this point they had four children. Maureen and I, with our three children, had just the downstairs on the side facing the shop. The floor above us was another apartment. Mom still had her trailer at this time, situated right across from the Tabernacle. A family from the Ridge, Robert and Rachel Klingbeil, had the trailer where Glenn's had lived. The Alesch's older son, Kevin, and his family were also living there at this time. There were several others, but I don't remember all.

I had agreed to build a new kitchen for Glenn and Kim's apartment during our stay at Meadowlands. Kevin had a beautiful woodshop right across the drive from our front door, where he made furniture and other things for sale. He had top-notch equipment including a heavy shaper and a large power feed sander. He gave me free access to all his tools. Glenn also had tools and his own workroom, so that is where I did most of the work.

I built and installed a lovely oak kitchen for Glenn and Kim during these two weeks. It was a really fun project. At the same time, our children and Glenn and Kim's children, of around the same age, had a wonderful time playing together. We had good visits with mom.

The thought to stay at Meadowlands did not enter our hearts, but it would have been awesome if the Lord had pointed us in that direction.

Lubbock and Mexico

We drove on from Meadowlands, then, to Lubbock, Texas, arriving before the end of May. We stayed for a few weeks with Maureen's sister, Lois.

Lois was renting a cute, but very small house, situated in the back yard of another larger home. We walked into the backyard filled with flowers and greenery in order to arrive at this little house. Lois's house had two small bedrooms, so it was a squeeze to fit all five of us in with her. The children were scattered on couch and floor.

I soon made an appointment with Dr. Hall. One of the sisters in the community, Patty Jordan, was his assistant. He gave me a full diagnosis, using an advanced form of muscle testing, that is, judging my body's response to vials containing medicines of various frequencies. And yes, I am convinced this is a full scientific approach, in contrast to the pseudo-science of pharmaceutical medicine. It is based on how the body works, not on the drugs to be sold.

I signed up for a trip to Mexico in June. Dr. Hall conducted his treatment in a house in Juarez since he could not do it legally in the U.S. So, I flew down to El Paso to join a number of other patients; I remember that Ryan was also along on one of these trips. We stayed in a motel in El Paso and went over each day to a house in Juarez that Dr. Hall rented. There, he hooked each of us up on an I-V and inserted our differing treatments into that I-V. We sat around with our I-V's, visiting or reading, and drinking LOTS of water. Dr. Hall kept tabs on how we were doing and changed our treatment as needed.

What I received was a healing process, resetting the various functions of my body into a healthier state. At this point, all mercury was gone from my teeth, so I no longer had that particular silent killer in my mouth. At the same time, I had made use of lacquer thinner abundantly all the years I was a cabinet maker, as well as spraying lacquer with little protection. What happens is that your liver removes and sequesters all those toxins very successfully for years – until that moment when poisoning the body has become too much for it, and then it quits. My liver was filled with toxins and my adrenal glands were almost entirely shut down.

Dr. Hall determined that I needed a second round of treatment, and so I went with another group of folks down to El Paso and Juarez a second time. It was my mother's goodness towards me, woefully undeserved, that paid for all of this.

I was helped to some extent. In the next year, I would do a full Young Living Essential Oils cleanse. At that time, I thought that this second cleanse was what helped me. I understand it differently now. The cleansing I received from Dr. Hall was as a foundation that the Young Living cleanse was then able to build upon. The fact that I felt much stronger for the next several years came from both treatments together.

Part of my problem was also a yeast infection. And so Dr. Hall gave me a diet that I "ought to" follow in order to counteract the bad yeast. I made some changes, but to switch to a yeast-free diet in everything was too much for me at the time.

In the present day, I live by a far stricter diet than what Dr. Hall gave me. I have an incentive now which I did not have then. When I eat poison now, it means I cannot write for two or three mornings. I hate not being able to write, so I refuse to poison myself (most of the time). For instance, just a small amount of sugar in a bit of dessert means no writing for two or three days. I don't eat sugar. I enjoyed some ale last Sunday afternoon, but that meant that I could not write at all on Monday and Tuesday mornings. I do such things very seldom, for I do love to write.

No sugar was the biggest part of the anti-yeast diet. I wasn't quite ready for that then. Now, I no longer eat any wheat or similar grain, in fact, I seldom eat starches. If I had been able to embrace the diet I practice now, my energy from then until now would have been better. By the time I did begin my present diet, however, my emotions had been too battered by the world to be able to function in it anymore. But that is for chapters coming up.

Lois went on a trip, then, and the owner of the little house preferred that we did not remain. So in July, we moved into Matt and Jessica's house, Maureen's sister, at the Lubbock Farm. They had a two-bedroom house, and so all five of us had one bedroom. That is, Maureen and I had the bed, and we inserted the children into various places on the floor around us and on the couch.

Yet here we were, back in a move-of-God community farm. At this point in time, Tim and Frieda were renting a house in town. Ryan and Heather Louden, and April continued in the community. April was preparing for her wedding with Ben Lewis, the younger brother of one of the sisters with whom I went to college at Blueberry.

We did not attend services in the community, however; instead, we began attending Lubbock's largest Spirit-filled church called Trinity, with Pastor Gary Kirksey. The praise at Trinity was just wonderful, and Pastor Kirksey was anointed of God with the word Maureen and I needed to hear. The first time I went up for prayer, when the invitation was given to all to be prayed for by the elders in front, I was simply overwhelmed by the brother's prayer of blessing and goodness into me. I had not heard such words for years, having been accustomed to prayers "against the flesh," that I understand now as prayers of cursing.

A brother in the community was working at a large cabinet and millworking shop in town, called Hunters Millworks. With his introduction, I applied for a job and was hired. I worked for Hunters Millworks for about a month.

This was the place where I was told, right off the bat, "This is the way we like to do things here. This works for us." Which actually meant, "We are NOT interested in any suggestions you might have to do things better." And, of truth, I have never worked in a more inefficient setup than this large cabinet shop. Everything was laid out and every practice along the way was designed to increase greatly the amount of work needed to do a simple job. I used this example in my writing course for years, all the extra calisthenics we did in order to accomplish any task. I won't bore you with a description here, however.

In the end, the foreman asked me to go into the glue room and spray glue onto an assembly. There was no gas mask for my use. I went to the boss and told him that I needed a gas mask for health safety. He refused. He said that if all the others sprayed toxic fumes without protection, then he wasn't going to change things just for me. I did not have the money to buy my own gas mask at the time, so, I had no choice. I do not place myself in unnecessary danger for anyone. It is not in me to accuse, however; so I called the next day and said that I was not really the man they needed for the job.

And the truth is, the toxins from this whole task of assembling cabinets were working against what I had gained from my trips to Mexico, and I could not afford to re-do my physical difficulties.

A Door Opens

We had come to Lubbock "for the summer." Meanwhile, we had placed before God the question of my acceptance into the master's program at Lubbock Christian University, whether He would open that door for us or not.

In July, I applied for the Master's in Secondary Education Program at LCU. I went for an interview with Dr. C.W. Hannel, a wonderful west Texas gentleman and educator. Dr. Hannel had taught and been a principal in public schools for years before becoming the dean of the Graduate Education program at LCU and its main teacher. Dr. Hannel was willing to accept my bachelor's degree from Covenant Life College with no further requirements, but on a probationary status. My work in class would prove out the validity of my education.

My acceptance into the master's degree program meant that we were eligible for student loans and that God had swung a door wide-open for us.

Presently, I have sixty credits at the graduate level in Education and English, basically enough for a doctoral degree without the dissertation. I have only ever gotten A's; at this level, I am unable to mess around. The truth is, I count this training in the discipline of my mind as one of the greatest gifts of this kind God has given me in life, second only to my knowledge of the Bible. My writing to teach, including the *Symmorphy* texts, is possible only because of this training. When the Jesus of our hearts is our only life, then a trained mind serves as an important and God-given servant.

One other thing happened this August before school started, and that was my niece, April Louden, was married to Ben Lewis. Ben was living in the Lubbock community while obtaining a degree in architecture from Texas Tech. April had been close to her cousins growing up, and so Sarah Zehr and Rachelle Yordy, Franz and Audrey's daughter, came to be her bridesmaids. Cheryl, Jenelle, and Mom were also there.

First Semester of Graduate School

I began the first semester of graduate school at Lubbock Christian University, then, in August. LCU is a Church of Christ college. I had no knowledge prior to this of that particular denomination. They were all wonderful people. I had no evidence through all my time there, however, that they were born again. I'm not saying some weren't. It's just that there was no indication of a personal knowledge of God as is found in any Baptist church. They were very sectarian, however, meaning "we are the only true church." The college did accept non-Church-of-Christ students, but not teachers.

Of course, I am speaking of the college as a whole. The graduate program in which I was involved was wonderful for me, and I was not required to participate in any part of campus or church life. Most of my teachers were superb, and I rate Dr. Hannel as one of the three best teachers in my educational experience.

My transcript says "Trimesters," but in actuality, the program was divided into four equal time periods, fall, winter, spring, and summer. And so I began with "Integrating Educational Technology," that is, using computer technology in the classroom, and "Administrative Theory and Educational Leadership." I believe Dr. Hannel taught that second course. You see, in order to obtain a Texas teacher's certificate, I was enrolled in the "Secondary Education" program. However, the majority of my fellow students were wanting to obtain a Texas principal's certificate and were in the Administration program. Because both programs ran concurrently and some of the courses were the same, I simply took all the courses required for both certificates.

Because I was now set for completing the master's degree program at LCU, and because the student loans gave us a living we could count on, our decision to remain in Lubbock was complete. For that reason, I took several days off from my college courses in order to bus up to Fort St. John to get and drive back our blue van with all our stuff. Kyle went with me; he was now eight years old.

We had a good, but long trip up on the Greyhound bus. This one finally had movie screens, which helped pass the miles. We were not long in Fort St. John. We did go out to Blair Valley with Rick, just to see the property again. Kars and Minnie had left Blair Valley just before winter came the year before, soon after Maureen and I had moved to Fort St. John. They were now living at Shepherd's Inn. A few months after our visit at this time, the move would sell the property to the neighbor who had run the hay fields. It went for around $250,000, very little for a property that valuable to us.

We pulled the blue van out from behind Shepherd's Inn and began the long drive back to Lubbock. When pulling into a convenience store in Wyoming, I forgot about the stuff on top of the van and my upside-down wheelbarrow wiped out their awning. We were very blessed to still have British Columbia insurance on the blue van, and they eventually paid the bill, over 10 grand.

Then we headed on down through Colorado on Interstate 25. You see, I had two considerations. First, I needed propane fuel, which was hard to find. I imagined that the main freeway and the big cities would have propane; I did not realize that the truck route across the flat great plains was more likely to have propane. Second, I was shooting for the final two counties in New Mexico, which I could get if I angled across the northeastern part of the state. What I did not figure on was the immense climbs on I-25 with the heavy load in my one-ton van. (We were carrying several tons of load.)

As we were trying to go up one such climb near Pueblo, the transmission of the van went out. I don't

remember how we got to a motel, but the problem was that it was Friday evening. There was nothing open, no garages to look at the van or rental places to obtain another truck. We would have to wait until Monday morning. After getting a motel room, we got on the phone with Maureen and her parent's and my mom. Both my mom and Maureen's parents were able to wire us money, enough funds to get us back to Lubbock come Monday.

It was not feasible for us to have the van worked on in Colorado, especially since I needed to get back to school. For that reason, after a quiet but dull weekend in the motel, on Monday morning, we rented a large U-Haul truck. We moved a large amount of the stuff from the blue van to the rented truck and hooked up a hitch on the back of it to which we attached the blue van. I abandoned New Mexico, and instead, we headed east across the great plains towards the Texas panhandle. We arrived back in Lubbock late that evening, and I was back in the classroom the next day. Meanwhile, we had to park the van in the back of the community property until we had the money to get a different transmission.

James Is Born

Sister Barbara James was living in the Lubbock Community at this time, one of the leading elders. Brother Joe McCord, one of the father ministries in the move, also made this community his home. Meanwhile, Jessica was also carrying a child at the same time as Maureen, but then Breanna, Matt and Jessica's only child, was born early. For that reason, Sister Barbara came to us with an unusual proposal. She had convinced the elders in the community to offer Maureen and me a home, even though we were not "in the move" nor officially part of the community. In fact, as she shared this with us, she said that she had gotten them to agree that we were not bound to the community, and that we could, in fact, continue our attendance at Trinity Church.

We were family, and in the minds of some, that was sufficient.

On page 324 is a map of the Lubbock Community as it is now. It's mostly the same, no new buildings, but with a few of the buildings from back then now gone. The building with the tin roof closest to the main road is the Tabernacle where services were held. Because everyone worked out on different schedules, this community shared only a meal or two a week together, on the weekends. The larger tin-roofed building nearer the center of the loop had been the school. There were not enough students for them to maintain a school, however, and so this building was empty. It did have a small library, which I made use of. It was here that I found my first Agatha Christie book, and so Hercule Poirot became an important part of our family tradition.

Behind the Tabernacle inside the loop were twelve homes, all the same, most of which were two-bedrooms, but some had a third bedroom added. On the far right, between the loop and the cotton field, at that time, were spaced about four double-wide trailers. The bright silver building on the back side was a shed and then another double-wide across from it. In the southwest quarter, you see three houses. The first belonged to Stan and Jan Martin, the second was Joe and Ellen McCord, and the third belonged to Roy and Kathy Mears.

Matt and Jessica had one of the regular houses. The one in the front, nearest the Tabernacle was empty and so that was offered to us. At this time, it has been removed as well as two others. They were not well-built and have taken a lot of work to maintain over the years.

At the bottom of the map was a barn that had been turned partly into a small wood shop. Dan Ricciardelli and his family were living at Lubbock at this time, and the wood shop was his, though I was free to use it as well.

Kyle and Johanna made good friends among the other children in the community. Through these months, Maureen homeschooled them.

James was due to be born mid-October.

Maureen and I talked about her busing up to Blueberry to have James, so that he would be a Canadian citizen. Even if she had him at the hospital in Fort St. John, it would all be paid for. I tried to make that happen. The more I worked on it, however, the less peace I felt. In the end, it seemed to be impossible for us to accomplish.

We wanted a home birth with a mid-wife, however. A few years earlier, a couple now living at the Lubbock community had a bad experience with a home birth, and some were reluctant for us to plan such a thing. We persisted however, and they sought visions. Brother Joe McCord shared the visions with us, and, although some were still dubious, he encouraged us greatly that we would be

blessed of the Lord in going ahead with a home birth. Maureen connected with a Lubbock mid-wife who was also a Christian. (Lubbock is a very Christian city.)

James Allen Yordy was born on October 17, 1999, on our bed in our own bedroom. The quiet peace of a home birth is worth an enormous amount. Besides the midwife and me, April Lewis was also in attendance to help Maureen, along with Roberta, who had come over from Bowens Mill with Claude for this time. Although the community was not gathered as the Blueberry community had been when Johanna was born, James's birth was attended by much prayer. Everything went fine. And so all of our children were born into community.

James was a large little guy; now he is the tallest of our four children. James is the same height as my dad, and Johanna is short, like my mom. It's a funny thing, thinking about the genetics that create one's children. James and Johanna, the two J's, seem to us to be much the same, and Kyle and Katrina, the two K's, are similar in a number of ways as well. At this point, however, Maureen's slogan became "four and no more." Our family was complete.

A Great Downturn

A problem was developing in the minds of some of the brethren in the Lubbock Community. You see, every Sunday morning, Maureen and I with our four children, headed out from the community in the Ford Station Wagon, on our way to Trinity Church. As we were going out, we passed others on the road coming to church at the farm. This did not sit well with some, that we would be by-passing the community church on our way to some "Babylonian" church (and yes, it was still thought of by some in that way).

I think that Sister Barbara continued to speak up for us, but it was Brother Stan Martin who shared with me that this "arrangement" was not working out. By the first of December I caved in and we began attending Sunday services again in the Lubbock Community Tabernacle.

I had been blessed and helped at the Trinity Church. Pastor Gary Kirksey was God's provision for Maureen and me all through the three years we lived in West Texas, completely the best choice of a pastoral guide for us. Returning, now, to the condemnation of the move services was not good at all. I very quickly became discouraged and was going downhill emotionally and spiritually. Healing had not yet begun for me and more hurt was not in my interest.

Kyle has shared with me that, even as an eight-year-old boy at this time, he was deeply disturbed by the agony and pain that he often saw in my face.

Meanwhile, besides going to school at LCU, I got a part-time job with the Lubbock School district as a substitute teacher. This meant that I would get a call on any early morning and be assigned a spot at any junior high or high school in the city. Because the program at LCU was for practicing teachers, the courses there were all in the evening. This, then, was my occasional job for the next several months. I did not like substituting. You walked into a class-room filled with rowdy kids with no real plan in front of you nor any list of names. When you don't have their names, you have no authority. Some days went okay, but a few were nightmares. I did one stint of several days at the disciplinary school for the Lubbock School District. There, no student was ever allowed to talk, and police were present to back you up. The thing is that I did enjoy that one location, not so much because the students were quiet (I don't like too quiet), but because I had a heart for these kids caught in a system they could not comprehend. Plus there I had all the student names on a chart in front of me.

I was not made to be a substitute teacher.

At the same time, I did a number of construc-tion jobs for the community, for which I was paid. One of those jobs was to install a basement under an addition they were building onto the back of the house next door. Y2K was coming up, and the com-munity wanted a place where long-term survival items could be stored. This was all concrete work, including a concrete floor on top of the basement.

Meanwhile, the Lubbock convention came around, again at Christmas time. And the thing is, Mom and Glenn's, and Frieda and Tim were all still in the move. So, we attended the first couple of servic-es at the convention, which was held in a large hall in town, as many came from all over. Brother Buddy Cobb was one who preached during those services I attended. This did not work for me; I was plunged back into the despair I had known before I left the move. I did not attend any more of the services.

Then, soon after the convention, Brother Stan Martin informed us that the community now need-ed the house we were in for a family that wanted to be part of the community. He gave us until Feb-ruary to find another place to live. In the moment, such a thing is discouraging, but because the de-cision was forced upon us, we now had hope for a better place.

Finding Another Place

Maureen and I went looking for a used mobile home we could purchase and place on one of the mobile home parks in the city. We could in no way rent a regular house, not with student loan mon-ey. At the same time, we could soon own a simple mobile home and have no more payments on it. We found a dealer, Quality Lands and Homes, just north of the city. The owner took us back through their rows of single-wide mobile homes for sale. As we walked down the row, I glanced at the one on the end. Instantly, there arose in my heart the thought, "That is our home."

Sure enough the man was very agreeable to us and offered to let us make monthly payments, and he would personally carry the loan with little inter-est and no bank involvement. This was a gift from God. It was a 14 X 80 foot single-wide, older, but in reasonable shape. In fact the name on the trailer in metal letters was "Blair Valley."

We soon found a spot at the back of Applegate Trailer Park on the south side of Lubbock, the most "treed" lot of any we looked at. In January, they moved our new home, the first one we "owned," into its place at Lot 326 in Applegate, and we made the move out from the farm.

Sometime through these months we had re-placed the transmission in the blue van, and it was now working for us. We were finally (almost) free of the move, and this is now the first environment for our family life that I can look back at with fondness, other than the solitary family times at Blair Valley.

We immediately returned to attendance at Trin-ity Church, and the gentle Spirit of the Lord there was free to begin the slow process towards that time when healing could actually start for me.

The Winter and Spring Trimesters

Before finishing this chapter, I want to include a bit more regarding the environment of the gradu-ate program at LCU, which was shaping my life in a large way, including my courses in the winter and spring trimesters.

I love school, and I love the topic of education. By this point, at age 43, I had finally learned to limit my contribution in the classroom, at least to what would be reasonable.

The graduate program had the top floor of the education building; I believe the downstairs was undergraduate education courses. Because we had our classes in the evening, we seldom saw other students. At the same time, some of the teachers also worked at the Education Service Center which supported all the public schools in Texas Region 17. A number of our courses were held there, including the technology course, since they had the setup.

Since I was also taking administration courses, I was obtaining a wider view of Texas public education, which I appreciated. In the winter trimester, I took Action Research and Educational Law. I always think about how to improve whatever I am doing for better results, but the Action Research course taught me to do that systematically in the classroom. My writing course later on would be greatly improved by knowing these things. Educational Law was held at the Education Service Center. I enjoyed understanding Texas law.

In the spring trimester, I took Instructional Theory and Curriculum Design, both at the LCU classrooms. The second was taught by Dr. Hannel; from it I learned how to develop educational courses, something I already loved to do. You can see the fruit of that course in my *Symmorphy* texts.

But more than just a wider view of public education and a better understanding of classroom teaching, I was also being presented with a completely different view of teaching and learning than what I had known in move community. The most wonderful aspect for me was that there was no concern whatever about "the flesh." These were children, created in the image of God, to be loved and nurtured and taught. Teaching was no longer about what the teacher did, but what the students learned. Of course, Jesus also said that it's not what goes in that counts, but what comes out, that is, outcomes.

What that means is that if the students aren't learning, that's my fault as the teacher, and I need to change what I do until they ARE learning. When I returned to teaching in a Christian school here in Houston, I discovered to my horror that they had the same philosophy as the move, that what counts is what goes in, and if the students don't produce, then it's their fault. This philosophy gives lots of room, then, for really shoddy teaching practices.

More than that, inside the limitations of the public school classroom, public education in Texas is a finely honed enterprise, with dedicated professionals at all levels who produce the best results one could hope to find, again, inside the box in which they are required to work. And in Texas, and especially west Texas, the majority of those who work in the schools are Christians.

The jaded view of public education I had received from move prejudice was solidly disproven. There are things very wrong with the whole system, but those things have nothing to do with teacher dedication or teaching effectiveness.

To be free to teach children with joy, without viewing them as "evil" (something I had never done anyway, which had gotten me in trouble more than once), was a wonderful new way of seeing education for me.

My Anger Is Just and Right

In this narrative thus far, I have been careful to see each person with whom I interacted through the eyes of Jesus and as a redeemer. I realize now that I will, in the ages to come, look at our time together in this present age, face to face with each person, and we will work our way through to a full restitution in the joy and honor of Christ. I am satisfied that I will not be ashamed of what I have written concerning them in this account.

More than that, my regard for each person is true, and the love of God abounding in my heart embraces all, regardless.

You can see, however, how eager I was to get us moved into our trailer at Applegate trailer park, our final direct disconnection from the move. I had not thought about the meaning for me of the graduate courses until now, but as I was pondering all that was going on inside, I saw the first entrance into my mind of a different view.

I became angry, and my anger is just and right.

Let me explain. On a recent trip sharing this word with others, a certain brother stated openly to many, "It doesn't matter if what I teach turns out to be deception; I'm still going to keep teaching it until the Lord shows me otherwise."

To the brother speaking, this must have sounded like a noble and reasonable thing to say. I, however, heard it as it stands in reality. – "I will lie to you, and I don't care."

Living inside of lies is anathema to me. Walking into a store filled with people wearing face masks is unrelentingly disturbing to me, for everyone is lying. Living under dishonesty was the root agony that caused me to flee with all my might into Christ my only life, the very moment I knew that I could.

But to lie to you about God and about your salvation, the very thought is a mindless and biting horror entirely outside of my ken.

For twenty-one years the ministry of the move of God fellowship lied to me about God; they lied to me about myself; they lied to me about Christ; and they lied to me about salvation.

And I lived for years in God's definition of hades as a result, frightened out of my wits.

Here is the problem. For argument purposes, let's say they lied about half the time. The other half of the time, they spoke the truth to me out from the Spirit of Christ. It's as Jesus said, the wheat and the tares growing side by side. The terrible thing is that they had no idea which was the truth, and which was a lie – and, of course, neither did I.

If you cannot speak Christ to God's people, then it is better not to speak at all.

Those who would be a ministry of Christ should consider spending maybe forty years on their face before God in tears, with their Bible wide open and their heart held in His fear, before they might have something to share.

You don't lie to God's people.

We are in no game. It's not a question of life OR death. We have been only in death, and our escape is into life. – **Narrow is the gate and pressed in is the way by which you are led (out of death and) into life and few find it.**

Sometime in the fall of 2000, two years after we left the move, I had an experience with God that I will share that finally made healing possible. But it was another year after, in December of 2001, before actual healing began, and it was terrible.

I cannot share this season of healing, continuing from then until now, apart from anger.

Look at those people inside the way being led into life; you are looking at a bunch of angry people, angry against lying and angry against death. Certainly, somewhere halfway through, their anger is being placed more and more into indescribable joy, but it remains, and it is fierce.

God gave me the experience of November-December 1999, ending in listening to Buddy Cobb one last time, to show me the ridiculousness of that whole Calvinist awfulness, and the horror of living under it. And it's the same thing in every Baptist and Pentecostal and Roman church.

I cannot share the healing of God apart from this anger, but I will leave it now as a foundation for an occasional expression of that anger going forward. It is the anger of God, the anger against hurting His people with lies.

34. A Time of Transition

February 2000 - July 2001

It has been several weeks since I wrote the last chapter. I'm not quite sure why I feel reluctant to "leap back into the fray." Part of it might be that the next six years feel rather bleak. It's not that I was being sidetracked; I was simply trying to support my family. Nonetheless, the path the Lord led me upon seemed to end, by June of 2006, in a bleaker and more hopeless place than before.

I could call these 'the wasted years," if I did not believe in Jesus. It seems, in the present moment, a bit harder to me to place the Lord Jesus upon every experience of these years and to receive with joy each person with whom I interacted.

Yet my measurement is the Lord Jesus Christ, and He does all things well. As I walked through our house just a moment ago, where we have lived for eighteen years, now, the longest time in one place in our lives, I felt such gratefulness, that this place has indeed been our home.

Our Life at Applegate Trailer Park

First, below is a picture of our trailer at Applegate as it is now. I did add that second trailer to our lot, making it my "shop." The trailer on the top side of the picture was not there; we were more isolated. And yes, that is the most treed trailer lot in Lubbock. It looks better approaching from the road, however, rather than Google's top-down view.

It was our home and a good place for the children. The children were in two small bedrooms on the left and Maureen and I were all the way to the other end. The living room was fairly large, so I had a space for my computer desk in the back corner of it.

Our children were and are very creative. We enjoyed good children's movies together, but they did not watch "television." Rather, their creative energies went into making forts inside and out, and all kinds of artistic expressions, especially dressing up in different types of costumes. When I look at the pictures of our family life in the trailer, I see lots of creative happiness. At the same time, I continued to read books aloud to the children and Maureen regularly.

Because there were few other trailers in the back corner of the park, we felt fairly safe. Only once was something stolen, Johanna's bike parked behind the trailer. Nonetheless, we were careful about their safety and trusted God in keeping us.

During this time, we continued in attendance at Trinity Church and fellowshipped with a number of people whom we met there as well as people we had known from the move. In June, we joined a weekly home group that was part of Trinity led by Erwin and Lisa Hyatt. We had wonderful times fellowshipping with those gathered in their home. Then, we connected with an older couple who had been in the move and had once lived at the Lubbock farm, Gaye and Ronnie Herrin. They were no longer in that fellowship, but still walked in the life and knowledge of God they had known in the move. We would often visit with them in their home, and because they continued in connections with people from the move, including Barbara James, we had further relationship with move people through Gaye and Ronnie. This was a good transition mix for us.

Besides continuing with substituting for Lubbock ISD, I also connected with a family from Trinity, named Owens, who needed cabinet work done in their home. In March, I built and installed a new vanity for their bathroom. By June, I turned my blue van into a "shop." I installed a power box and a heavy line to plug it in. I had a work counter and just enough room to use a small table saw. I did work on the ground outside, of course, but had a dry and lockable place for tools and materials. I then did another set of bathroom vanities for the Owen's.

During the spring months, I found that I could apply for a larger amount of money in the student loans. We did that and used the extra money partly to work on our trailer and for our health. We continued to use Young Living Essential oils, and I was able to do their complete cleanse. After a few weeks, I had begun to feel much better and was able to work better for the next several years.

Franklin Graham held a crusade in Lubbock in April of 2000, which Maureen attended with Kyle and Johanna. Through the service, Kyle kept telling his mother that he wanted to go home. Then, when the call was given, towards the end of that time, Kyle suddenly stood to go down to the front. Soon, Kyle was the only one of few remaining, a little eight-year-old boy alone. At that point, Johanna wanted to go down to join him, which she did; she was six. Both of them gave their hearts to the Lord in that service.

Doors that Close

Trinity Church also had a full school. The primary grades were at the main church building, while the high school was in a large building several blocks away. Trinity Church had purchased a large empty shopping center and converted it into their high school and annex for church socials, etc. During these months, the church itself was flooded and needed extensive repairs. For that reason, Trinity had their regular services in the annex of the other building, in a very large room. This continued environment of spiritual wholesomeness and life was slowly thawing me out inside.

Because I was substitute teaching, I also applied to substitute for Trinity Christian High School, and did fill in there a number of times. I applied to teach fulltime as well. At the same time, Trinity Church offered a pastoral mentoring program for which I applied. I wanted to learn a fresh way of being a "leader" of God's people.

I never heard back from either one of those applications. As I look at this transition time, the four years between Blair Valley and Houston, I see that it was a series of finding several closed doors, and then, presto, the one that opened. This pattern would occur several times. By summer, however, it became clear why Trinity Church itself was not God's path for us.

The Summer Trimester

The summer trimester at LCU was a high point for me in the graduate program. Because teachers were not in school, the courses were held during the day. The four courses I took were Learning and Human Development, Instructional Leadership, Principles of Supervision, and Content Area Literacy. Much of our time was at the educational services center and included various courses by which we were certified as instructional leaders in Texas public education. I enjoyed being a colleague of equal standing with professional educators.

Content Area Literacy was taught by Dr. Hannel in our building on campus. This was an important class for me from which I gained much, the teaching of reading while teaching other subjects. I knew how to teach writing because I had slowly learned to write. But I could not grasp teaching reading because I never really learned to read. They told me what the letters were in the first months of school, and I have not stopped reading since. A more recent job, however, taught me the fundamentals of teaching reading.

A major paper I did for Dr. Hannel was titled "Writing Across the Curriculum," about teaching writing inside the different school subjects. In move community, I enjoyed teaching all the subjects in the humanities. But at this point, teaching students to write well was becoming my focus and interest.

CityView Fellowship

Pastor Gary Kirksey was an anointed pastor who sought the Lord inside arenas of the charismatic movement closest to the Feast of Tabernacles. A subsection of the charismatic movement, including John Osteen, had been influenced by George Warnock's little book, *Feast of Tabernacles*. They did not take what they learned into sectarianism as Sam Fife did, but still there was much knowledge of the life of God revealed in His church that was known by many, including Pastor Kirksey. Part of Pastor Kirksey's interest was to connect himself and the church with a "covering" of leading charismatic ministries. Otherwise, Trinity Church was just on its own, so to speak. Pastor Kirksey had no interest in any formal or legal arrangement, rather a spiritual covering of life and of interacting with other mature ministries. This interest of Pastor Kirksey was not shared by many of the elders of Trinity Church.

We found the services held over at the annex to be wondrously anointed of the Lord. Then, one Sunday morning, it happened. The service began as it always did, but somewhere halfway through, the Spirit of the Lord began to lead us in a different direction than what the bulletin said, and Pastor Kirksey followed the Spirit. This was the last straw, and the church elders gave him the option of resigning or being fired. He chose to resign so that he could say goodbye to the congregation the next Sunday.

A few hundred people in the congregation, however, wanted to remain with Pastor Gary and his wife, Marsha. They rented rooms in the Sysco building (the owner was part of the fellowship) and the next Sunday four hundred people gathered there (out of Trinity's congregation of around 1200). CityView Christian Fellowship was launched. Maureen and I did not attend that first service, but we went for the second service, which was at the Lubbock Civic Center because the gathering was too large for the other place. CityView was now our home church.

A young ministry couple who had been pastors at Trinity, David and Colleen Eppler, also came with Pastor Kirksey to be part of the new pastoral staff. Colleen had been the praise leader at Trinity, one of the most wondrous praise leaders, of an equal with Lori Pettis or others I had known in the move. Sadly, she did not continue long as the praise leader at CityView, but became the oversight of the children's ministry. Maureen and I took our turns (be-cause we had kids) teaching Sunday School under her direction.

I want to share an experience I had one Sunday morning at the CityView fellowship sometime in the fall of 2000. The services at CityView were very vibrant and life-giving. We even began to dance in the Spirit. Some would slowly dance through the aisles with bright-colored cloth banners as we worshipped. A few times (probably in the next year), Johanna was invited to dance her graceful ballet moves in the front, near the praise leader. She was so beautiful and anointed of God.

This was a good fellowship of people who loved Jesus and who drew us into life. In fact, Pastor Gary soon instituted a meal together once a week before the Wednesday service, thus moving us in the direction of Tabernacles.

Then, in a service, Pastor Gary called many to come down to the front in a time of repentance and dedication to God. In spite of all the goodness of God, I had continued in distress deep inside, still frozen emotionally and locked into too much hurt. I went forward and lifted my hands up to God. I prayed in my own heart, "Father, I repent of ever having listened to Buddy Cobb." Something lifted from me in that moment and for the first time, I could say, "God loves me." Do you see that period after "me."? Up until that moment such a statement was "blasphemy" in my mind. God loves me, BUT – I MUST, is how I had thought it should be.

It might be strange to you that, in spite of my knowledge of the revelation of Christ, I could not know "God loves me." At that time in my life, being able to sink into such a knowing still seemed radical. It would be another year before healing could actually start, but God could now begin to soften my heart against all the pain.

Fall Courses & Student Teaching

That fall, we enrolled Kyle into the Trinity School for his fourth-grade year. He was now nine years old. Maureen continued to home school Johanna and Katrina. We had enrolled Johanna earlier in a ballet program (Katrina was too young, she would take ballet later in Houston). Johanna really enjoyed this and was so very graceful in her dancing.

In the fall semester, my primary task was student teaching. I took two courses as well, Administering Special Populations and Ethics. I will talk about Ethics first. The Ethics course was strange, mostly because they didn't really know the Lord. I am looking at what I wrote for the course exam. Here is a bit.

"You suggested in class that we contemplate what would be our position if we discovered there was no God. Would we stay moral? I found such a request incredible. For all of my adult life I have sought to walk with God. I have heard His voice; I have received His rebuke. I have seen His power and His glory. I have seen His sovereign hand in my life and in the lives of others in incredible ways, I have experienced physical miracles, I have seen Him deliver people from powerful oppression. Every day, I consider His claim on my life, every day I cry out to Him to direct and help me. I am sorry, Dr. Patty, I don't want to boast in myself, but to consider that God may not exist is beyond me. If God ceases, we cease. … Where God is present, there is true goodness, where He is absent goodness is not. Doing good deeds apart from the presence of God is sin that will result in death. …Love is God. Love is not a gift from God, but it is the presence of God Himself."

I did not yet know our precious union with Christ, but as I read through the rest of the essay, I find much that I teach now the same.

I applied to student teach at O.L. Slaton Middle School that fall of 2000 and was assigned to Greg Reeves who taught advanced English to the brightest junior high students. This was my first venture into the public-school arena as a teacher. Greg Reeves was a great choice for me, partly because he specialized in teaching writing.

The initial core of my writing program that I developed over the years came from Greg Reeves' approach in his classroom. I have changed and adapted it, yes, but I give full credit to him for some of the initial ideas. He also taught the students archetypes, which was the first I had heard of such a thing. My enjoyment of bringing the archetypes of story into the classroom and into the present word of Christ began here as well.

I love teaching. And I love kids. Much of the time in student teaching, I watched Greg Reeves teach and assisted him as needed. As part of my "training," I also taught the full lessons several times. This was my first experience with teaching non-Christian young people. I found that my love for them was equal to my love for the young people in move community schools.

I remember attending a school assembly with our students gathered with the rest. In fact, a number of our students stood on the platform as part of the presentation. They were "wild and worldly." Yet all I knew in that moment was just how much God and I loved them. I was free to see them through Christ, with no tentacles of seeing through accusation.

My last day of student teaching was November 3. When I announced that my time with these young people was finished, I received a surprising and gratifying response. I seem to have won a place in their hearts.

Graduation and Winter Trimester

Once I had successfully completed the student teaching "course," I was eligible to take the Texas Test for Teacher Certification and the test for teaching English. I did that, and thus became a certified Texas public school teacher. I immediately began applying to teach in several different Lubbock area schools.

At the same time, I had completed all the courses for the master's degree in Secondary Education. I finished the degree requirements with a significant written exam covering all the courses that were part of the degree. I then prepared for a formal graduation in December with my colleagues.

I did not have a teaching job yet, and so I continued with student loans and with enrollment in courses that would also allow me to obtain Texas Principal Certification. In the winter trimester, I took two courses, The Principalship, with Dr. Hannel, and an advanced writing course designed for school administrators.

Meanwhile, mom was coming for an extended visit in order to attend my graduation. Our trailer was decent and livable, but it could use improvement. So, I began some extensive remodeling. Eventually, I re-sheeted all the floors with plywood and new flooring. I started with the children's bedrooms and re-did their bathroom vanity as well. Mom would have the girl's bedroom while she was with us.

During this time, I purchased a small trailer from the trailer park owner. I sheeted it with a new plywood floor to make it my wood shop and put a storage room in the back. I moved it over to our site with the blue van and parked it perpendicular to our trailer on the western side. This made our yard feel more protected. I built a porch in front of it at the same height as the floor inside the blue van. That way I could back the van up against the porch and it was all one even floor. Now, I had a "three-room" shop. Things were tight, but it was a good space.

At the same time, I was thinking in terms of trying to make a living doing my own construction projects. I was not hearing back from any of my applications to teach. Of course, it was mid-year, and most districts hire in the early summer. So, I obtained credit with Home Depot and purchased a number of stationary woodworking tools. Besides a table saw, I obtained a chop saw, a drill press and a bench sander. I set all these up in my new shop.

I felt a little hesitancy inside about purchasing all these things, but I ignored it and pushed ahead. I needed to support my family, and I had to find a way to do that.

Mom came for a couple of weeks. Our graduation was held at the LCU auditorium. This was one of the most controlled such events I have experienced. We all wore cap and gown. As a group of students, however, we very much wanted to be able to say a bit to honor Dr. Hannel, who had done so much for all of us. Our request was turned down. My colleagues then selected me as the spokesman and as the one who would share. I again approached the school administration. In our minds, this was our graduation. Alas, they did not share our belief. Request denied. Needless to say, it was not a meaningful time, except for obtaining a master's degree, something I needed to do out from the way God made me.

The better part of the graduation was that mom and Freida and Tim, with April and Ryan were all in attendance, as well as Lois and Jessica. We made it a good family time together.

The Spring Trimester

In the spring trimester, I took two final courses, two of the most meaningful courses I have taken in my life. The first was Exceptionality and the second was Administration Internship.

The Exceptional Children course was about working with special needs children of every kind. We had an LCU instructor for this course, but the heart of it was taught by James Harris, head of spe-

cial education in one of Lubbock's more difficult inner-city schools. James Harris was also the head of Texas Teacher's Certification for the whole state, so his signature is on my Texas teaching certificate. James Harris was the most impactive teacher I have known in my life. He was given only about half the class time, but he packed so much practical experience of working with needy children into the time he had. We also went to his school for a field trip.

The thing I learned so powerfully from James Harris was that you do NOT judge children by how they are acting outwardly. The little boy who disrupts your class just might be going home to a drunk father who vomits on him and beats him every night. The little girl who seems withdrawn, and not doing her work, just might be hungry and scared. Every outward action is coming out from some hidden inner pain or defense. The outward problem cannot be addressed until the inward difficulty is known. This real-world understanding was so refreshing after some of the narrowness I had been taught in move community school.

My task in "Administration Internship" was to shadow a working school principal through the course of his days and to record many different aspects of his job. For my internship, I chose Robert Guerrero, of O.L. Slaton Middle School, because I was familiar with him and his school from my time there as a student teacher the previous semester. What a rich experience this was.

Mr. Guerrero was a superb principal, with his hand always on the "life-blood" of his school, one might say. Regardless of what he was doing, every bell-time between classes, he was out in the halls, greeting students and being seen as part of their lives. I would join him first thing in the morning as he greeted kids arriving at school. During the day, he went back and forth between mundane tasks and dealing with spontaneous crises.

I followed Mr. Guerrero through a number of days and recorded everything he did. He was very willing to have me shadow him and gave me much good understanding. I have a very large notebook filled with documents from that internship. I also interviewed other Lubbock principals as part of this assignment and attended a school board meeting for the Roosevelt ISD.

Once I had completed the Administration Internship, I was eligible to take the Texas State Principal's test, and thus I obtained a Texas Principal's Certificate. On paper, I was qualified to be a principal in any Texas school.

These courses were my last at LCU. I had taken courses there equaling 45 credits, 30 towards the Secondary Education degree and 15 towards the administration certificate. Through this time, I continued looking for a teaching position in some Texas public school.

Directions of Fellowship

Let me begin this section by stating that, once I had a connection to the Internet when we moved to Fort St. John, I most certainly continued searching to understand this world in which we live. While we lived in our trailer at Applegate Trailer Park, I found an important website that would shape much of how I presently understand things, and that is www.lewrockwell.com.

I had much to draw from in my own understanding of human action, having lived in a subsistence environment for years. At the same time, you will have ascertained that my strong inclination, inherited from my own father, was towards liberty. Each of my children, when they turned 18, were shocked when they next asked me if they could go out. My response each time was, "Why are you asking me?" It did not take me long reading the Lew Rockwell website to realize that the writers there were sharing the same conclusions I had come to, both in how economics actually works and the value and importance of liberty.

Liberty-first is the mother of peace, prosperity, and order, whereas order-first is the mother of chaos, poverty, and war.

My thinking about the kingdom is shaped partly by Lew Rockwell, whom Kyle and I had the privilege to meet here in Houston, and many of those who write for his website. You will find that thinking all through what I share. Lew Rockwell is the first news website I read every morning, and I always turn to them first to shape my basic understanding of world events, although I am by no means limited to their understanding.

Once CityView had become established, Pastors Gary and David began a leadership training class for members of the church who wanted to be more involved in the fellowship. Maureen and I attended these training sessions, held in the Sysco building.

Erwin and Lisa Hyatt, in whose home we had been a part of a weekly "cell group," felt to stay with Trinity, so eventually we switched from their group to one which we held in our trailer. An older couple shared oversight of this gathering with us.

As I sat and listened to the teaching on church leadership from a different perspective than in the move, I had so much to ponder. This was a leadership without condemnation, without putting people "into their place." It was a leadership into joy and the knowledge of God. The mighty edifice built inside of me by my years in the move, however, would take time to be re-built, and so I simply pondered these things deeply.

I must bring in again our continued fellowship with Ronnie and Gaye Herrin. We visited often in their home, and after a time, began having regular "counseling" sessions with them. There was no question that I was still "ripped apart" inside from our time in community and in leaving community. Yet I continued to believe God that "Blair Valley was our home," for He had spoken those words to me.

And so our counseling time with the Herrin's became very sad to me. They were good friends with Sister Barbara James, and so, I'm sure that they had her view of me. It seemed that my profound faith in God and the vision He had placed inside my heart was not in their picture. Instead, they interpreted the cry of my heart concerning the vision of a Community of Christ as the fetish of a man who was filled with himself and who had little connection with God. – That is how it seemed to me, whether actual or not.

If they had told me that God had filled my heart with a vision of Himself, but I would have to wait patiently until it was His time, that would have been such strength to me, for it would have been in agreement with a God who had always shaped my heart for Himself. But such a view was not found in move philosophy. And so their counsel to me was for me to "let go" of that vision as "not-God," and to get on with the present program. This part of their counsel served only to increase my confusion and pain, for it required me to agree that I was never connected with God on the inside of me and that He had not filled my heart with His understanding.

The last time I saw Barbara James was probably in the spring of 2001. I came home one day and she was sitting in our living room, visiting with Maureen and Lois. I walked through and sat down. In any social setting, I always wait for the other person to recognize me before I respond; being the first to greet another feels like presumption to me, something I don't do. Barbara James did not look at me or greet me or even recognize my presence in the room. She continued visiting with the others and then eventually left.

I realize, of course, that I cannot know what another person is actually thinking and that I then project my own inadequacies upon them. Nonetheless, that last picture of Barbara James and "move ministry" was one of "we do not know you and we know that God is not in you." Again, I'm not accusing Sister Barbara of any such thing; I am sharing what I felt inside.

Directions of Work

Through the first few months of 2001, I did a number of different construction jobs. I worked on the home of a sister from the move, Linda Green. I installed a new tiled shower for her, the first time I had worked with bathroom tiles. I contracted with another couple from CityView fellowship, the Woodard's, and built an entire kitchen for them. It was fun to build a kitchen, but I was not pleased with the final result. You cannot do fine work without fine tools, and my inexpensive tools did not do well enough.

By February, however, we came up short on money for our living expenses. We had lots of bills to pay and nothing to pay them. Out of the blue, a family from CityView handed us a check for $2000, more than enough to cover our needs. At the same time, others were providing for Kyle's monthly bill at Trinity School, which was not cheap.

In April, I found a job with a local construction company, another hard-driving man similar to Terry Williams in Oregon. I could just barely endure a forty-hour week of hard construction and was soon completely worn out for anything else. I worked for this man for a month. Near the end of this time, I was building cabinets in his small shop behind his house. It was Friday afternoon, and I was worn to a frazzle. In my tiredness, I began making small mistakes in the cabinet work, mistakes that would need correction. Realizing these mistakes would continue, I went in to see the boss, who happened to be home. I told him what was happening and why and that come Monday morning, it would be

an easy thing to fix those mistakes. I asked to go home a couple hours early. He agreed.

Then, on Monday morning, when I arrived to continue the cabinet work, the boss and his foreman were waiting for me. Both of them chewed me out for the mistakes I had made. I did not answer; I do not defend myself. When they left, I took about fifteen minutes to fix those mistakes; they really were no big deal. Nonetheless, I do not work inside such disrespect, but neither do I place blame on anyone. I finished the day, and that evening I called the boss and told him that my physical weakness prevented me from being able to fulfill the job. I did not return.

Also in April I connected with another job, an educational editing job. This will take some explanation. This was 2001, and lots of investment money was flowing into new ways of doing things. A company named Edison was moving into education, a private company using public money to do a "better job" at educating kids. This larger company started a subsidiary called Edison Extra, which focused on running summer school programs. Edison Extra had contracted with the state of Missouri to put on summer school programs in several districts throughout the state.

The state provided a certain amount of money for each student who completed summer school. This money then went to Edison Extra who would put on the program and hire local teachers. Edison Extra packed their summer school programs with lots of kids by offering a large number of valuable prizes.

A brother in the church, named Ron Wood, who had been hired as the accountant for Edison Extra, came to me with an additional need that they had. They had found educators to write courses in all subject fields for the summer program. Those courses would be given by local teachers in each district. But the course syllabuses needed editing, and Edison Extra hired me to do that.

I loved editing these course syllabuses. They were a mess, some much more than others. Educators don't necessarily know how to write or how to think. I had to straighten out a lot of confusing directions, as well as to correct poorly written text. I did art, language arts, science, sports, math, rocketry, Spanish, and so on. I was paid per page, and I can do that kind of work very fast. In fact, I am partly made for educational writing and editing. I was making more money per hour than I ever had before.

Then, soon after I had quit the construction job in May, Ron Wood asked me if I would go to Missouri with him to help train the teachers in the various school districts on Edison Extra's approach to teaching these courses. And so I flew to Missouri several times, both to Kansas City and to St. Louis, always routing through Dallas or Austin, usually accompanying Ron Wood. The first place we visited was Neosho, in southwestern Missouri, then two school districts in the Kansas City area, one in the St. Louis area, and one halfway between.

On one of the flights home, I was stranded in the Dallas airport because of storms and had to spend the night on an airport-supplied cot along with hundreds of other people.

The man who ran Edison Extra, Larrie Reynolds, tackled every problem by throwing tons of money at it. I am the kind of person who requires carefully thought out plans that can work. Needless to say, there was not a real connection between him and me. I just went with the flow, but did not always care for the results. At the same time, although I am very comfortable teaching things I have developed over time, I'm not very good at spontaneous presentations. I did my best, but I don't think Mr. Reynold's was pleased with my performance.

Then, in June, as the summer schools began, I spent a week in Raytown, near Kansas City, helping to supply the teachers with everything they needed. The summer schools were packed with kids, all hoping to win one of the ten-speed bicycles or other cool stuff. After that, however, Mr. Reynolds did not keep me on to continue the editing work, though I sent him letters explaining what I could do for his business success. I am convinced he had no idea how much what I did was worth to Edison Extra in turning poorly written and confusing syllabuses into something easy for any teacher to follow.

Another Closed Door

June is also the month when all the school districts of Texas are actively looking for new teachers to fill the openings in the next school year. There is always a shortage of teachers – why, I would eventually find out. I went to a job fair in Lubbock. All the big school districts in the state were there, looking for teachers. I connected with the Fort Worth representative and filled out the application for that district.

Fort Worth ISD was interested in hiring me, so I drove to Fort Worth a couple of times by myself to interview and to look for a home for us. By the first of July, I had signed a contract to teach for Fort Worth ISD. I was presented with an eighth-grade English classroom in an inner city junior high. It all looked bleak and difficult to me, but this was what I had worked towards for the last few years, so I bravely continued. Then, in mid-July, that position was no longer available. I had signed a contract, so the Fort Worth administration was trying to find me another spot.

Meanwhile, towards the end of July, we drove down to Fort Worth together, Maureen and I with the children, to look for a new home for us. We found one for sale in Azle, Texas, just outside of Fort Worth, that seemed to be ideal for us. It was an older blue house with a new master bedroom suite added on. It was shaped very oddly and uniquely. It had a carport with a room that could be a shop as well as a small barn and two acres of land (filled with nightshade and other weeds). It seemed to be in our price range and the owner was willing to work out a deal with us to buy it.

This was not a "purchase," more an "intent to buy" that we signed with him. Meanwhile, the house needed some work done to it, so he agreed that we could stay overnight in the house while I began that work.

Now, Maureen and the children loved the house initially. I did as well, though I had a check inside that it really wasn't the Lord's provision for us. I liked my plans for the place, however, and so we persisted. That first night we stayed in the house, in the new master bedroom suite, Maureen and I both woke up at the same time, sat up, and looked at one another in horror. "This is NOT our home," we both said almost at the same time.

[In later years, the Azle area would become a place of contention over fracking, which poisoned all the water, including the ground underneath the blue house, along with leaks of poisonous gas in places.]

At the same time, the Fort Worth district was not finding another spot for me. We agreed mutually that we would go our separate ways.

We drove home shocked and discouraged. It was only a couple of weeks before the school year would start, and I had no teaching job, no way to support my family. It was three years, now, since we had left Blair Valley, and other than my continuing in college, every door we had sought to step through had closed tightly against us.

Placing Jesus Upon

I wrote the first paragraphs of this chapter a few days before I actually began to write the text. When I did begin to write, I was astonished at the great calm I felt inside regarding giving this account of my life. It was as if everything had settled out through the intervening weeks, with all the pain from my whole life until this time finally placed into the full rest of Christ.

Nonetheless, there are several things in this chapter that I must bring into resolution, placing the Lord Jesus upon all things, and giving Him thanks.

The first is my attitude towards Lubbock Christian University, outside of the Graduate Education program. I did not realize that I have not forgiven the college administration for the bad experience of our graduation. That lack of forgiveness had shown itself once a year from then until now when I received the yearly alumni magazine from LCU. That is, I would gleefully toss it into the trash can next to my chair.

I would ask the administration of LCU to forgive me for my bad attitude. I was wrong.

Then, in this particular chapter of my life, only one episode brought me deep nostalgia as I wrote about it, and that is my time at O.L. Slaton Middle School in both student teaching and interning with Principal Guerrero. The truth is I love working with students, especially at the middle school age. Even though one's connection with young people in the public schools is much less than in the communities, only one hour five days a week, still being their teacher means a whole lot to me.

By 2009, I would no longer have the stamina to handle junior high kids; college students are much easier, for they require no babysitting. But the loss of working with those children is one which I carry inside the promise of an endless life, that what belongs to me will come back to me in its time. I will know middle school children in my classroom again, in the joy of being human as the revelation of God forever. I know that it is true.

I have never "gotten away" from the move, for we have visited family members back in the communities many times until now. Yet my final experiences with Sister Barbara and with the Herrin's would close out any spiritual relationship I had with that fellowship. It was a closing out in grief and loss, found inside the profound belief that my heart was bad.

And so I now place the Lord Jesus Christ upon that grief and loss, upon all my confusing interaction with move ministry and philosophy. I know that He carried me through every moment and that Jesus does all things well. I give Him all thanks.

And I bless Sister Barbara James, along with Gaye and Ronnie. I know that their hearts were good and filled with Jesus towards me. I draw them into my own heart, into the blood shed for us sprinkled there, and release them into all that the Father is inside of and through them.

God is good, all the time.

35. The Vision and I

November 1994 - August 2002

I have left my heart out as I have shared the events of our life from leaving Blair Valley through our time in west Texas. In the last letter, I shared:

~~~ If they had told me that God had filled my heart with a vision of Himself, but I would have to wait patiently until it was His time, that would have been such strength to me, for it would have been in agreement with a God who had always shaped my heart for Himself. But such a view was not found in move philosophy. And so their counsel to me was for me to "let go" of that vision as "not-God," and to get on with the present program. This part of their counsel served only to increase my confusion and pain, for it required me to agree that I was never connected with God on the inside of me and that He had not filled my heart with His understanding. ~~~

I can honestly say that, regardless of all my outward anything, my own experience all the years I was in that fellowship was with a personal God shaping my heart for Himself, something of which I was constantly aware. I did not know Him very well and I knew myself less; nonetheless, it was always God Himself contending with me.

And from that moment when God planted a seed inside the heart of a twenty-year-old boy, concerning the revelation of Christ through Christ Community and a place of refuge for God's Church in her hour of greatest need, that vision has never departed from me, no matter how it has been battered along the way.

When I was twenty-two, I made a covenant with God that I would know Him and that I would walk closely together with a people who know Him. Anyone who would think to turn me aside from that covenant is wasting their time.

Yet now, over forty years later, I am more by myself than ever and the vision I have labored over in tears for decades remains yet unfulfilled. Yet I find no more reason to turn aside from it now than I ever have, for the vision of God is life forevermore.

When we arrived at Blair Valley, I carried in my heart a vision for a Community of Christ different from what I had known in the move. I hoped that God would fulfill that vision there, as He had said to me, "Blair Valley is your home." A large part of my hopelessness in February of 1998 was the realization that it would not happen in that context. Nor did I have any idea how it might happen.

The change had come for me in November of 1994 when God showed me the face of His precious Church at Christian Life Center in Oregon. And it was there in that prayer hut on the wooded hillside that I placed myself before my God, that He would prepare His word in me for her sake.

From that time on, even as we returned to move community, I have labored over the meaning of that vision, how it might be fulfilled.

Now, if you want to know what I mean by "my vision of a Community of Christ," then read *Symmorphy V: Life*. Everything I wrote from August 2006 until November of 2017 was so that I would be able to write that text. And everything I have written since I completed it has been so that I, with others, would become what is written there.

From the day we left Blair Valley until this day as I am writing this chapter, twenty-two years later, I have carried that vision of a Community of Christ in my heart in the expectation of God, that He would fulfill that Word which He alone has planted inside of me. I have carried it with many tears and through many lonely places.

More than that, for the first half of that time, I could not consider my place in that vision anywhere else than upon the Blair Valley property, for God had said to me, "Blair Valley is your home." I just wrote the following line in my chapter, "Sent as Kingdom."

~~~ The picture of earth together with air, then, is the largest and central meaning of the Kingdom of God. And the best earth word that describes such a thing is the LAND. I cannot express the ex-

tent to which "the land" expresses the deepest longing and love of my heart. And "the land" meant the most to me when we lived at Blair Valley. ~~~

With my brain, I can conceive the fulfillment of that vision for me in any place, so long as I know God placing us there. And if that is God's interim, I am more than content. BUT – not with my heart. My heart sings only when I consider the fulfillment of the Community of my heart inside the land that is Blair Valley.

Now, as I have shared the details of my life with you, I do have a strong memory of things, yes, but I also have much documentation, transcripts, letters, college papers, calendars, photographs, and so on, all of which give me many specific details. And Maureen has provided many things she remembered that I did not.

At the same time, while we were still living in Lubbock, I began penciling out my autobiography in a month-by-month chart. I communicated much with my mother during our visits with her and by letter concerning many of the details, and thus had that all laid out before we moved to Houston.

But as I was considering the next chapter of my life, "A Season of Healing," I realized the importance to me to set forth a structure of my grappling with this vision inside, what it meant and how it could be fulfilled. And, as I said, I was simply unable to consider the vision being fulfilled anywhere but at Blair Valley, even for years after we had left.

Basically, I was being asked, out from move philosophy, to take all my experience with God inside of me from November 1994 on, all the travail, all the expectation of God, all the seeking to know His meaning, and chuck it all out as nothing more than a fleshy fetish. This was not a "fetish," it was God inside my own heart.

Into Blair Valley

There were four arenas of difference concerning a vision of community between what was beginning to form in me upon arriving at Blair Valley and what had been my experience in move community. In actuality, these heart ponderings began through 1996, the worst year of my life. Those four arenas of difference would be (1) the life of the community, (2) the attitude towards one another, (3) the governance of the community, and (4) the method of provision for community needs. In fact, it was our

experience at Blair Valley that gave me my present view of community governance, and that was all adults included in the general decision-making, no "elite" group deciding for everyone else.

The truth is, from the time I left the Blueberry eldership in October of 1996 on, my eyes were opened to the deliberate elitism being fostered by the elders everywhere in their thinking of themselves. And the more evidence I saw of such an awful thing, evidence I had never noticed before, the more appalled I became. I will share my final experience with that elitism in a chapter coming up, after we moved to Houston.

Because I am a practical man as well as a dreamer, the need for provision is the issue that shaped most of my thinking and discussion with others from 1996 on.

It was Sister Ethelwyn Davison from whom I first heard the vision of a teaching community. I suspect that she received that concept from the Lord while they were living at Shepherd's Inn and conducting the Shepherd's School of Music there. The school put on an evening "dinner and a performance" once a week for several years. Many would come out from Fort St. John to eat dinner while enjoying the singing and music put on by the students and faculty.

When the School of Music moved out to Graham River, that was no longer an option; Graham was too far for town people to drive out. Nonetheless, Sister Ethelwyn shared over time her continued thinking in the direction of community provision coming from providing a place of "respite" for outside visitors.

This concept, of "worldly" people coming into the community for a short time, was NOT in move philosophy and most did not receive it. And it was this part of my vision for community that was instantly ruled out by Kars and Minnie Kiers with no further discussion.

You see, the idea of a teaching community, a place to which people could come for a short time of refreshing and then return home strengthened and renewed, sang all joy inside of me. Indeed, that is exactly what our brief experience at Christian Life Center was all about.

Because I am a dreamer, as well as a practical man, I dreamed of my vision of a teaching community through all my steps at Blair Valley. And in leaving Blair Valley, I dreamed of returning there someday soon with the provision to make it happen. I purchased detailed maps of the Blair Valley north and south and poured over those maps. I walked the paths of the property, dreaming of such a Community of Christ, and where its buildings would be placed. And I poured over those maps and those steps in my mind's eye for years after.

I am an obsessive and unrelenting dreamer, a dreamer of very practical realities.

God gave me the key to how we should relate together in community while we were at Bowens Mill in the early months of 1997 – **receive one another in the same way that Jesus receives you.** I shared this at Blair Valley, and indeed it was received well, including being the core part of how I persuaded Kars not to disrespect me. Nonetheless, it did not become the general heart of the community; neither did I have the ability to make any real changes.

Finally, the life of the community then became a significant part of my decision to leave the move, that life being JESUS and Jesus alone, our Savior and all Salvation. I wanted nothing more to do with a "christ" or any "christ-life" without Jesus Himself in Person.

Early Times of Refreshing

I have shared about my first letter that I began to send out in the spring of 1998, while we were still at Blair Valley, which I called "Times of Refreshing," specifically from Peter's words in the first part of Acts, that times of refreshing will come from the Lord as God restores all things.

My *Times of Refreshing* letters went through three distinct phases. The first five letters were written while I was still in the move fellowship. The problem was that I had contracted a year's worth of issues with those who had purchased subscriptions. When we moved to Fort St. John, I had sent out only those first five. In my mind, I owed my subscribers a total of twelve issues.

At the same time, when we arrived in Fort St. John, I soon purchased a regular computer and thus "retired" my large word processing typewriter, a unit which did use floppy discs for storage. I no longer have any record of most of my first issues, however. Yet now I find buried deep in my saved folders, issue Number 6, which I wrote in December

of 1998, while still in the fall semester at Northern Lights College. I wrote and mailed out the remaining six issues, then, over the next year, not finishing my obligation until after we had arrived at Lubbock.

Thus the second phase of *Times of Refreshing* was those I wrote during this time of transition. The third phase was a complete series of another twelve letters, which I wrote and sent out in 2004, coming up.

Now, I am the kind of person who must have everything working together in perfect harmony and purpose. Much of my writing through the years has been to discover how God is such balance and harmony. Those who have followed my writing from the start know how I have rejected a "God" who knows or does evil, out from the clear teaching of the New Testament. Yet I have always been appalled at the persistent belief, among all Christians I have known, that God "knows" evil. I could not stop writing about it until I understood the harmony and purpose of God in all goodness.

And so, in my present mind, the development of the vision of Community growing inside of me works seamlessly together with my continuous laboring over the education of children AND my attempts to understand myself AND my love of designing homes AND Maureen's and my love of natural health and aromatic herbs AND ---.

I just went through all my early folders which I managed to retain as I went from one computer to the next over the years. I printed out all relevant documents that would show a progression of my thinking from December of 1998 through October of 2003.

I want to take you, now, across that path, up until our final month in Applegate trailer park. Then, I will update that path as we go through the chapters of my life from then until now.

The Word and I

I have two documents in hand, both of which I wrote in December of 1998, while living in Fort St. John and attending college at Northern Lights. The first document is issue Number 6 of Times of Refreshing, with an article titled "For There Are Three Who Bear Witness." The other document is a paper I wrote for the Portfolio Development course I was taking at the time, titled "Request for Credit and Portfolio."

I want to describe and even quote from these two documents and explain how they are intrinsically tied together.

Of truth, this is the central purpose of writing this entire account of my life, to set forth the relationship between the Word God speaks in the Bible and me, all the way through, so that I also might know God-with-me.

In the *Times of Refreshing* article, I use the courtroom metaphor and into that metaphor, I place the challenge against the word God speaks spoken by the serpent. And then the determination of God to prove Jesus, all that He speaks, faithful and true. This is the same place and context, then, inside of which I wrote *Symmorphy I: Purpose*.

Then, if you were to read through the article, you would think, "Hey, this is the same thing Daniel teaches today." You would be mostly right, but entirely wrong.

Knowing now our precious union with Christ and defining everything by the ruling verses of the Bible, it is the easiest thing for me to show the difference.

In the previous chapter, "A Valley of Decision," I made this statement. ~~~ "Yet I did not know God, not really, neither did I know of any answer for the vast hole I perceived at the center of my knowledge of the gospel." ~~~

I know that "vast hole" so clearly now, here it is. Let me quote, first, and then alter the wording.

~~~ God stands accused of lying. Satan was His first accuser, but Jesus triumphed over Satan. Today, it is you and I who accuse God of lying when we fail to believe what He says. What does God want of His people? Two things: first that they maintain a relationship with Him whereby they truly hear and understand what He is speaking, and second, that they believe absolutely that what God says must be fulfilled in them in this life. ~~~

On the surface, it appears as if I am focusing on God and His Word, but in actuality, this becomes the same Nicene exaltation of self, making it all about the human and not about God.

Let's try the same thing as I would write it now. I have underlined the altered words.

– God stands accused of lying. Satan was His first accuser, but Jesus triumphed over Satan. Today, it is you and I who accuse God of lying when we fail to believe what He says. What does God want of His people? Two things: first <u>that they rest in their relationship with Him whereby they hear God speaking them through the good-speaking of Jesus</u>, and second, that they believe absolutely that what God says <u>is already completely</u> fulfilled in them in this life. –

The first paragraph positions the issue correctly, yet leaves the Christian in unbelief, rebellion, and death. The difference is one thing – confidence that God is already true. That is the "vast hole" I was missing, and it is the entire difference between all life and all death. You see, the second rendition is all about God fulfilling all things through us as He now wishes.

However – what a careful researcher would see is that the entire context of what I teach now is all there, including what God actually says about the key issues, in contrast to all Nicene theology. What I was missing was the how. "*MUST BE*" versus ALREADY IS.

In the end, my first rendition is the same as the serpent. "You shall be," as a replacement for God's "You are." I would not truly know the difference until 2008.

Except for the "HOW," I taught the same things then that I teach now. Thus I can know for myself with all certainty that from my early thirties, when **"conformed to the image of His Son"** became my ruling verse, until now, I have taught the same word all the way through. The only change that is needed is a simple one, from "shall be someday" to "I am." I was not able to see that it has been all one word until I have written this account.

Then I look at my portfolio and I see that I was grappling with the issue of understanding myself equally with the issue of knowing God and what He actually says.

We can't know God without knowing ourselves, and we can't know ourselves without knowing God. This is God's riddle, set clearly in place all through the Bible. God is known by a Man; man is God-made-known.

I did not know myself. I did not know that I was smart, all I thought was that some things were easy and fun. I did not know how others perceived me. I did not know the harsh outer shell I wore. I did not know these "others." I did not know that they were like me. And move philosophy taught us that God is completely replacing us with something different. That what I am was unacceptable to God; that He required me to be something else.

Writing this portfolio, a description of what I know and can do, was the first time in my life that I considered myself as God made me. It was a startling and even frightening experience. I did not know what to do with what I found.

Here is something I wrote in that paper. – "I am the kind of person who does not do something timidly. If I am interested in something, I will spend hours designing my own versions of it. I have always been willing to tackle large and difficult projects, even with little experience. I do the job well, the experience comes, and I remember what I have learned." – You see, I was 42 years old and I had never before thought things like this about myself.

Yet if you had asked me then if there was a match between all that God speaks, and my own human qualities and attributes, I could not have seen such a thing. I did not know that God intended to bring these two things together, His Word and my life, and make them one. And, dear reader, God is doing the exact same thing with you.

Jesus and I – and My Heart

Then, in 1999, after our move to Lubbock, I have a piece titled "Personal Profile Statement" and then a list of many verses titled "Jesus Way," all of which I typed out in full, not copy and paste. – "Knowing Jesus, knowing myself. I would have told you then that these things are far apart; I did not know they are two sides of the same thing."

Then I have three more documents all pertaining to my vision of a Community of Christ, which I was now calling "Times of Refreshing." Even before James was born, I was using what I was learning in college to lay out an ordered description of this "place of refuge" and "Christian renewal center."

Then, I have the first of several renditions of a *Times of Refreshing* issue in which I lay out "my vision" very similar to how I wrote the same thing again in *Gathering to Life*. I don't think I ever sent that issue out.

Finally, I have a document, written in November of 1999, titled "Thoughts on the Mission Statement," referencing my vision of a teaching commu-

nity. Here is part of one of the paragraphs.

– A group of Christians, seeking to be the temple of God, will have this attitude and expression: the temple is the place where God and men can meet. It is a place where God is willing to come, because of both the blood and an atmosphere of respect for His ways, but it is also a place where lost or searching people are willing and able to come, either because they have a hope to meet with God, or because they simply feel welcome in an environment of hospitality and openness. … The temple is NOT for the pillars and the walls; it is for God and others. –

You can see here the same context of thinking into which the latest things God has taught us about being the Mercy Seat can appear, that is, our entire lives being the place where our Father can meet together with others and they with Him.

Doing What I Can Do

I can write the entirety of the vision in minute detail, rooted in practical human realities and coming out from every Word God speaks. What I CANNOT do is make any of it happen. This great inability was as distressing to me then as it is now.

To compensate for my inability, then, I have done two things, all the way through. First, I placed my confidence in God, that He does what He says He will do. And second, I wrote, or at least, at that time, I tried to write. I can write. And if I can't do anything else, then by the grace of God, I will write my way into being part of the revelation of Jesus Christ through His Church.

The next document is larger, running from July 6, 2000 into November. It is titled "Times of Refreshing Journal," the same concept as the "Student Teaching Journal" about my experiences each day working with Greg Reeves in the classroom, that I wrote for college during the same months. In it is also two large letters that I wrote to Peter Bell.

The journal starts with these words. ~~~ I want to commit myself to spending at least ten minutes every day writing about Times of Refreshing (a term I now used to mean my vision of a Community of Christ serving as a Christian renewal center). My topics can range from personal feelings, things the Lord shows me, doctrinal issues, structural or practical issues, hopes and dreams, frustrations, doubts, faith, or anything else that comes to mind. ~~~

~~~ I thought this morning, Blair Valley and Times of Refreshing are the only things I know that clearly fulfill and answer everything I find in my heart – the desire to be a part of something bigger than myself, the desire to see God manifest in His people, the desire to be involved in a river of life, the desire to be a teacher and administrator of an instruction facility, the desire to do and live in beautiful woodwork, the desire to find purpose and meaning and direction outside of the narrow deadly confines of sectarianism, the desire to get my children to a country setting. ~~~

Then I have an itemized cost list of how to turn Blair Valley into the community of my heart.

At that time, however, because I did not know Christ my only life, I did not have the same drive to write daily as I do now.

Here is the entry for October 1, 2000. ~~~ Lord, do it. Enable me. Make me to know Your will. Make me to understand Your word and Your ways. Lord, I ask it in faith, believing. Your will be done… I need to keep writing. ~~~

What I want you to see is twenty and thirty and forty years of my same contention with God for the same vision fulfilled.

Letter to Pastor Gary Kirksey

Next, I want to share most of a letter I wrote to Pastor Gary Kirksey, dated October 28, 2000, a few months after City View had begun.

~~~ Dear Pastor Kirksey,

I have wanted to communicate with you for some time. My wife and I had attended Trinity for about a year. When you began City View, we visited and felt the Lord would have us continue as a part of the new church. We have especially appreciated the word you have shared over the last year. Several times we felt your sermons were meant just for us. We want to thank you for being a channel of God's ministry to our lives.

We have been a part of an apostolic fellowship for many years. We separated from that particular fellowship two years ago because of philosophical differences. Yet we continue to desire to be a part of what God is doing in the earth, but in the broader context of the full body of Christ.

As I have been reading Peter Wagner's book, *Churchquake*, I am excited both at the confirmation

of our experiences over the years, and the confirmation of the direction God is now taking us.

I am presently completing a Master of Education degree at Lubbock Christian University, with a teacher's certificate. I taught for several years in Christian schools, but I did not have a state certificate. I will obtain a teaching job in a local secondary school soon. However, teaching in the public school is an interim step for me, a way to support my family in the meantime...

Part of the goal I believe God has placed in my heart for some years now is to establish a Christian renewal center/School of ministry with a unique emphasis that is partly described by what I read in Peter Wagner's *Churchquake*. I am working on a pamphlet describing the vision God has put in my heart. As I see it, it will be a several-year process to establish such a thing. I believe in covering and would appreciate your insight into this endeavor. One of my strongest concerns is that whatever this school of ministry, etc. becomes, it must be plugged into the city-wide local church as well as the body of Christ world-wide. It will not become an entity unto itself.

I would enjoy an opportunity to visit with you more about this topic and to hear what is in your heart concerning the things I have mentioned whenever you might have time.

Thank you again for the things God has done in our lives through your ministry. ~~~

Note: This "pamphlet" I mention to Pastor Kirksey I have also printed out. It is a complete layout of "Times of Refreshing Center" as I was learning such layouts in my college courses, with mandate, mission statement, and so on.

Knowing Jesus and Teaching Kids

Through the early months of 2001, my focus turned towards my thoughts concerning the education of children. Through all the years our children were of school age, I have labored over my conception of childhood education. And the thing is, inside a context created by someone else, I can do a lot. But what I cannot do is bring forth that context myself.

Yet my waiting upon God in expectation of faith saw my children raised and gone. The urgency they provided is no more, but my vision for the regular school part of a teaching community remains.

It was the courses I was taking in the graduate school that were inspiring many of my directions of thinking. I can't hear anything that I am not immediately applying to my knowledge of God and of Community. I have a document I wrote for "Advanced Writing," dated January 11, 2001 and titled "Definition of Experiential Education." It lays out the thinking of learning by doing valuable things rather than deskwork only.

Then, I have more business brochures, my unending effort to start a business of my own that would provide for my family, and, if successful, provide for the beginnings of a Community of Christ. At this point in time, my business thoughts were in the direction of woodworking, having my own shop and woodworking business.

Then in March, I am writing about Jesus as the Lamb of God and laying out a list of chapters for a book on being a son of God. I did not write that book because I still did not know Paul's gospel.

Then, in April, I wrote "Rationale for The Interesting Academy," my first name for a school of my own.

This is not a symptom of "going from one thing to another." Rather, it is the harmony together of all things that I love and do, yet all still in vision form only, waiting upon God.

Teaching Kids and Knowing Jesus

When I travel while drinking coffee, my brain seems to open to new ideas and possibilities. For that reason, much of my time in the back and forth of the job with Edison Extra in Missouri, through May and June of 2001, I was thinking up all sorts of things.

I have a document titled "Yordy's Guide to Self-Study," and another titled "Exploring the World through Projects," the beginning conceptions of my Project-led Learning Guides.

I love teaching kids, and I love the joy of a child learning through doing something important to them, and I love the entire spectrum of education.

Then there is the "Yordy's Guide to Self-Directed Learning," followed by "Freedom Learning Center: Business Research Plan." This was my second "school name," always part of a larger Community of Christ.

At the same time I am writing these things, however, I am also writing "Essential Truth." Let me include all of that document here.

~~~ 1. The heart of the Christian life is knowing the risen Jesus as our close personal friend. The thing that made Jesus different, that drew His disciples to Him like a magnet, was that he really liked people, all the time. He delighted in people - not condescendingly, but at their level.

2. We can only be to others what Jesus is to us. If we are distant to others, it is because Jesus is distant to us. We can love others unconditionally, only when we are living in the close, personal love of Jesus ourselves. As I know that He delights in me, I also can delight in others.

3. We will only ever be a full and established version of what we are now. If we are not being a blessing to others now, we will not suddenly become a blessing to others at some distant point in the future.

4. Community, though blessed of God, carries this great danger – that we will restrict ourselves to loving only those who love us and greeting only those who greet us. The heart of the Church's mission, our mandate, is to be a blessing to whomever the Lord sends, even to those who will never give anything back.

5. The reward of the believer, the crown we receive at the end of our life's work, is the glory of those who have been blessed by us. "For you are our joy and our crown."

6. Obedience and righteousness are the fruit of the presence of God; never the other way around. We do not seek obedience and righteousness so that we might obtain the presence of God. We seek the presence of God and out of His presence comes obedience and righteousness.

7. The presence of God is obedience and righteousness. God created each of us as unique individuals; no human model can show me how I am to be like Christ. I am holy when I am filled with the presence of God and unholy when I am not. To be filled with all the fullness of God is the earnestly sought goal of the believer, not as some distant event, but as the grit of our daily experience. ~~~

Again, you can see the missing ingredient of the gospel of our Salvation, already finished, not coming someday.

This is then followed immediately by a pamphlet for a new business idea, an educational editing service. Of truth, I have earned way more money per hour doing educational editing and writing than any other task for money, though it was always while working for someone else. None of my own business endeavors ever went very far.

And every one of these many things is an essential part of the Community of my heart.

What you have in this book, then, is the life of an incapable man, filled with dreams, but unable to make any of it happen, yet a man who will NEVER let go of God or of His Word or of the Vision God has planted in my heart.

Conclusions

The urgency I feel writing this chapter is to set forth and even to understand for myself the bridge between the revelation of Jesus Christ and the experience of community, as I knew both in the move of God fellowship, the bridge between that and this present word I share as it brings forth the practical expression of the Christ Community of my heart. I feel that this urgency is that of my Father's, that He would prove out the unchangeableness of what He speaks, of what He actually says in the gospel.

Much that is believed about our salvation and about God in Nicene Christianity is not found in the gospel, and the key verses of our salvation are not found in Nicene theology. That is a powerful statement, and true, and absolutely devastating. And the purpose of God for the entire path of my life is to search out the meaning and distinction of this great contrast between the two gospels.

I rejoice in God increasing my understanding of what He means by what He says day by day in directions I never knew before. But what I cannot have is a God who changes what He speaks from one season of my life to the next.

I must have a God who speaks the same word in me as I share with you in *Symmorphy V: Life* and *A Highway for God*, now in my early sixties, as the word God showed me of Himself in my early fifties, of a God who carries all.

And I must have the God of my early fifties speaking in me the same word that I find in my early forties as I labored over our relationship with God and with one another, not knowing at all how any of it would be fulfilled.

And I must have the same God of my early forties, this time I am writing about now, speaking the same word inside the same vision then as He spoke into me in my early thirties as I made the absolute decision to ground all my thinking on the ruling verses of the Bible, the same verses out from which I think today, and inside my love for community and college at Blueberry.

And I must have the same word in my early thirties that God spoke into me through Sam Fife in my early twenties, a word and a God I embraced with all my heart in covenant bond.

And I must have the same word preached into me by Sam Fife in my early twenties BE the same word that entered into me at age seven when I asked Jesus to live in my heart.

But more than all of that, I must have a God who is telling me the truth. I have written this chapter so that I might KNOW that it is true.

There is a further reason for this chapter. The three years coming up, 2006, 2008, and 2011, that are the mightiest years of my life, as God gave His "HOW" to me, as Jesus said, first birthed by Word, second by Spirit, and third the knowing of Father, the importance of these years can be known only in the context laid out in this letter and the last.

The wisdom and philosophy of the move, and the voices of all those good people speaking into me, denied any thought that it might be God-with-me. *"Know your place; it's clear that God has not anointed you. Stop all your silly imaginations that He will do what you think."*

In 2008, I stood against those voices for nine months solid as they wailed against Christ my only life every day. And at the end of that season they vanished from my mind, and I heard them no more.

In this chapter, then, the connection between the two parts of my life is made complete. Now, starting in the last months of 2001, I can begin to trace out the arising of a new knowing of God, of myself, and of Salvation. Same word, yes, but all sorts of verses that had been shoved into the background by unbelief and false theology can now come into the singing of my life.

You cannot and will not and should never try to come into union with God, by any means whatever. God, your Father, has already come into union with you through the Lord Jesus, now the only life you are. Believe that He is.

36. A Season of Healing

August 2001 - August 2002

A Door Opens Wide

In the first week of August, I found an ad for an English teaching position available in a school district called Three Way ISD. The school, which turned out to be the smallest by population in Texas, was located in the cotton-ginning tiny town of Maple, Texas, right against the border of New Mexico, truly in the middle of nowhere.

This would be a two-bit, low paying job, and I was frustrated that it was the only thing available. I made an appointment for an interview with the superintendent of the district, Dr. Tom Alvis, and drove by myself out into the empty cotton plains to the school.

Dr. Tom Alvis was a small man in his early seventies. He had been an honored Texas school administrator for many years. In my first moments with him, it was evident to me that he loved Jesus and was filled with the Spirit, not from anything he said, but from the light upon his face and the welcoming cheerfulness that always flowed out from him.

We chatted for a bit. He looked at my credentials and commented on the fact that I had a principal's certificate. It was a good interview, and I returned to Lubbock in some hope. The next day he called; I was hired. School would be starting in a couple weeks, and, of course, Kyle would be in fifth grade there and Johanna in second grade.

I was soon driving out by myself, in order to be prepared before classes began. It wasn't long into my time that I discovered that Dr. Alvis had hired me as "the principal," which I had not realized. I would also be teaching high school English.

Let me define that role. This was a small school district, fewer than ninety students with all grades in one building. Although Dr. Alvis was the superintendent, and his wife, Geneva, the district secretary and school counselor, he also fulfilled the public and "political" functions of a principal, whereas my actual role would be more that of an "assistant principal." Nonetheless, for that year, I was the one who signed my name on everything as the principal.

Even when school started, I continued to drive out, with Kyle and Johanna now, from our home still in Lubbock, for several more days.

Living and Teaching at Three Way

Because I was also the principal, my pay was higher than the other teachers. At the same time, Three Way was one of those West Texas schools that provided homes on the school grounds for many of the staff. Tom and Geneva Alvis had been staying in a house in the front, alongside the road, but gave it to us, and moved to a home behind the school. There were four houses in a row next to the road, ours was the second. Then, there were a few more homes on the back of the school property.

The school and its buildings are long gone from Google maps, but the plan of the walls can be seen in the lines on the slabs still remaining. I include a map of the school and other buildings, once located a couple miles north of Maple, Texas. The Baptist Church across the road is still there and in use.

Frieda and others helped us to paint and clean our new home, and when it was ready, Maureen and the little ones moved out with us – on Labor Day, September 3. Our home was three bedrooms, with a large master bedroom on one end, an office space in front of it for my computer, a bath, and a bedroom for the boys. Then the living room, dining and kitchen, with another bath and the girl's bedroom on the other end. There was a small, enclosed back porch. Our yard had a fence all around of solid roofing metal buried into the ground. This was to keep out rattlesnakes. Thus our space was safe and enclosed. There was a tree in our backyard, one of several on the property.

There was no rent for us, and our utilities were electricity only, at fifty dollars a month. For this reason, we were reasonably well off through our time at Three Way. Of course, I had to start paying off the student loans.

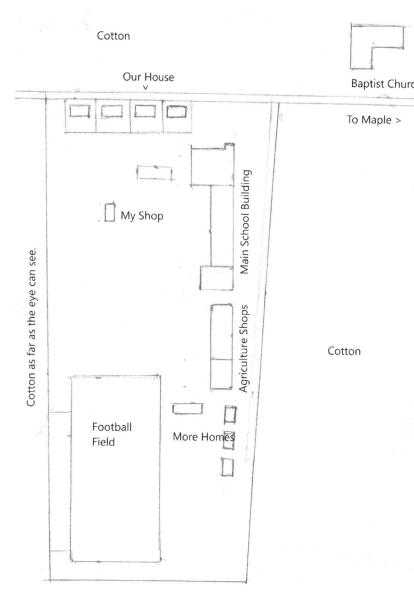

Cotton

Our House

Baptist Church

To Maple >

My Shop

Main School Building

Cotton as far as the eye can see.

Agriculture Shops

Cotton

Football Field

More Homes

My four English classes did not start until late morning and then into the afternoon. Thus I typically spent the first few hours of the day in the Principal's office near the center of the school, just inside the side entry doors. The school was a 'well-oiled machine,' and so I typically had little to do except walk the hall on occasion. Only the more difficult disciplinary cases were brought to me from the lower grades, just a few times through the year.

Mr. Alvis took care of all the public relations and dealings with suppliers, thus the non-teaching staff answered to him, while I interacted with the teachers.

I had a nice large classroom, back from the main hall and right next to the library. I don't remember the order in which the grade levels came into my classroom, but I taught a class of seven ninth graders, ten tenth graders, six eleventh graders, and just two of the eight twelfth graders. The other six seniors were taking advanced English via a live Internet connection from a teacher in the "nearby" Sudan school.

I put our trailer up for sale and soon found a buyer. We had felt a growing discomfort the final few weeks we were in the trailer park, with people moving nearby us that seemed unsavory in their conduct. I got a decent price for our two trailers together, and thus we soon had no obligation there. Then, we found out later that the family who moved into that trailer experienced a series of burglaries inside their home. God had protected us in His grace.

I loved the short walk from our home to my classroom and office in the school. In fact it might have been just a hundred yards from our front door to the front entry into the school.

The students in the school were about 60% Hispanic and 40% white. Some of the white students were children of the local cotton farmers whereas most of the Hispanic students were children of the farm workers. Many families, including ours, had children scattered through several grades. There were other teachers who also lived on the property and had children throughout the school grades.

I have the school yearbook for that year and so I can look at the pictures of everyone involved. Kyle was in fifth grade with Mrs. Smith, who lived at the end of our row of houses. She had five other students besides Kyle. And Johanna was in second grade with Mrs. Viera along with five other students as well.

I had twenty-five students, which I will not name except for two families, Heinrich and Rodriguez. Kara Heinrich was a senior, actually not in my class, who was, one might say, the personality center of the student body, well-liked by all, an intelligent and wholesome Christian girl. I had her brother, Canaan, in my tenth-grade class, and there were Heinrich's in the younger grades. The Heinrich's attended the Baptist Church just across the road, and so we visited there on a number of occasions. Then, I had Rigo Rodriguez in my ninth-grade class. His older brother, Robert, was a senior, but not one of my two seniors. Those two seniors were Chase Cannon, whose dad had a large cotton farm on the way to Lubbock, and Amanda Kingsley, the daughter of one of the high school teachers. I mention Rigo, because he was just a great kid, always helpful. In fact, I hired him to work for me for a few weeks after school was out.

Because these were small groups of kids, in primarily a Christian environment, this was a wondrously good first year of public-school teaching for me. I enjoyed my students and, I soon learned, they also appreciated me.

You see, my tenth grade class had not liked their English teacher the year before and so one of the girls persuaded the others to fail their state test so that the teacher (and the principal) would get a savagely low mark in Texas school ranking. That taught me that the state test does NOT determine how much the students know; it determines how much they care. (Through my public-school years, my students always did well on those tests.)

I wasn't long into the enjoyment of our new home and my new role before I began to hear a terrible rumor. I refused to believe it at first, but finally, Dr. Tom Alvis confirmed that it was true. The Three Way school district, with fewer than 90 students in pre-kindergarten through twelfth grade, was too small for the state to justify its continuance. For that reason, the state had asked Dr. Tom Alvis, who had been retired, but who was very capable at handling such a thing, to be the superintendent for the final year of this district, and to oversee its choice of which neighboring school district to which it would then become a part.

This was so very sad, because one could not have found a more ideal living/teaching situation.

This was how Three-Way was formed, however. In the sixties and seventies, three small rural school districts had closed out their schools and come together to become "Three Way."

On a final note, there was a nice block building not far behind our house that had been used as a shop. Mr. Alvis gave me permission to turn one corner of that building into my own little shop. So this was very nice; I had an enclosed space with a garage door that locked and a concrete floor for my shop tools.

September 11

I was settling into my role as teacher/principal, and getting to know the students and the flow of the days by September 11 of that year. – And this is one of only two world events that I will bring into this narrative, the only such events that had any affect on my life.

That morning was a school morning like every other, with me starting the day in the principal's office (without all that much to do). The high school science teacher was Mary Ferguson; she was also the "home" teacher for the seniors, and so her classroom was always filled with them in and out through the day.

That morning, she came to my office and said, "Mr. Yordy, you need to come and see." I followed her back to her classroom where all the students were glued to the large TV screen mounted on the wall. The first of the twin towers in New York City was pouring out smoke. We watched while the second tower was hit. At this point, schoolwork was not important. Then, however long after, still before my classes would start, I watched the first of the two begin it's eleven-second collapse at free-fall speed. I am a man of years of practical experience, including working with steel and concrete. Within four seconds into the collapse, my brain was informing me with all clarity, "I am watching a controlled demolition." Even before my late-morning class, the name of Bin Laden was being sounded on the news, before any criminal investigation could even begin.

Both buildings had collapsed the same way by the time my first English class began, with my regular classes in the afternoon. I did the same thing four times that day for my students. First, I explained the purpose of "terror" as a strategy, and that is to get the targeted people off kilter so that they will do predictable and stupid things in response. I then drew a map of the Middle East four times that day, moving on the assumption that the news casters were not wrong in their assigning blame on Bin Laden. I explained that if it were he, then his goal would be to draw the US forces into Iraq, in anger, and thus the American empire would be subject to destruction. I was not prophesying, but simply stating clear geo-political strategy.

Dr. Alvis then invited all students who wanted to gather with him for prayer around the flagpole. Many joined with him to pray over the next several days. This was not considered a problem in rural west Texas.

Of course, in that setting, we had a state-of-the-art Internet connection, and I had a reasonable amount of spare time. I had to know what on earth had happened. So I spent many hours online researching the facts, even for several years after. Within a couple of days, I read an article written by a professor of engineering at a New Mexico college explaining why it was clear that this was a controlled demolition and calling for an investigation into how those buildings had been wired for such a straight down and rapid drop.

On Monday of the next week, however, I found another article written by this same professor. In a robotic tone, he recanted of everything he had said in his prior article, stating that he was wrong, that it was only a natural collapse caused by the small fires.

The moment I read that, my blood went cold, for I knew what it meant. Then I read more articles of teachers being called into their principal's office and fired on the spot for daring to "explain" things to their students, even though the "official" story had not yet been spun.

In that moment, I knew that, in leaving the move fellowship, I had chosen to be momentarily deceived. You see, I had entertained the thought that maybe the world wasn't so bad after all. I had even voted for George W. Bush because I had believed what he said about good relations with all countries, including Russia. When I read the New Mexico professor's recantation, I knew that I had been wrong, tentacles of power reach everywhere.

And so I researched that event more than any other before or since, so that I might know the difference between actual facts and the impossible story pushed by the government. But that is not the topic of this narrative, and so I will leave it at that, except for one point. One of the first things I searched out was who were all these people who had come into power with George W. Bush. There were four Gentiles visible at the top, but almost every person right underneath of them were the sons or grandsons of the same Communist Bolsheviks who had sailed from New York City to St. Petersburg in 1918 to wreck such awful terror and death on the Russian Christian people. And that is a statement of fact, over and over.

It was learning this, above everything else, that returned me fully into the knowledge of this world that I had gained from Gary Allen, in *None Dare Call It Conspiracy*, and other similar texts I had read and sermons I had heard preached in my early years in the move. For the next ten to fifteen years, I will read more than a hundred pages of news on the Internet almost every day. I have never found the actual facts of any continuing event to counter that basic understanding.

Back to Our Life and Work

Because we did have a number of debts, besides the student loans, Maureen found work at the local cotton gin in nearby Maple, where she served as the dispatcher for the scales. Farmers would call and schedule their cotton to be picked up by the gin trucks, get weighed, and then unloaded. Maureen's job was to oversee and keep record of all the movement of trucking and weighing. Maureen's boss was named Marvin McCaul.

Maureen's job became twelve hours a day seven days a week, then, during the heaviest part of the harvest. And so her parents, Claude and Roberta Mack, agreed to come from Bowens Mill to Maple, Texas around the first of November to take care of the children while Maureen worked the long hours at the gin. The house in the row next to ours was empty. We set up a bed there for them. However, there was little other furnishing in that house, and so Claude and Roberta spent most of their time in our home, continuing until the cotton season finally closed after Christmas.

This was not an easy thing for me. My relationship with my in-laws was cordial and respectful, but not good. It seemed to me that they were set in their mind-set of being "the elders" and thus did not always submit to the flow of our home. Again, this was never anything outward, just a sense of strain for me on a number of occasions. Nonetheless, we were very grateful for their time with us and their input into the lives of their grandchildren.

All the time we lived at Three Way, we continued in Church attendance at City View in Lubbock. It was about an hour's drive, which we drove each weekend. Because of the lengthy trip, we usually spent the day in town, and often Saturday night. Lois had bought a house on the south side of Lubbock, not far from where our trailer had been, so there was always a place for us to stay. We often ate at our favorite place to eat through our children's growing up years, Souper Salad. We continued, as we were able, with the leadership training and with continued fellowship with brethren who also attended City View.

Sometime near the end of 2001, Maureen and I were able to purchase a better family vehicle for our needs. We were staying at Lois's over a weekend, planning to go looking at used car lots on Sunday afternoon. The evening before, I was feeling unsure about this step and raised my concerns to the Lord. That Sunday morning, the devotional for the day read, "The Lord gives blessing, with no sorrow added." We went out in peace and soon saw a large green family van, a Dodge Ram. Sure enough, it was available for a price within our budget and the bank agreed to give us a car loan. Our new family vehicle had a large carrying capacity and was very comfortable. I was able to sell our old Ford station wagon to some people in Maple who specialized in buying fixer-upper's.

In west Texas, high school football comes a close "second" to church. And so football was a big deal at Three Way. The football field in the back corner was very nice and kept green and watered. Typically, the principal was the one who ran the loudspeaker at the football games, but I am so very grateful that Dr. Alvis knew that I was not made for such a thing, and so he just stepped into that role. And he was good at calling the names of each player as they did this or that in an enthusiastic way, over the loudspeaker. The whole area turned out for the games, with much hoopla. Our young men were very good sportsmen and usually won, both football and later basketball. Little Rigo Rodriguez, though in ninth

grade, was as skilled as his older brother and the two of them were often at the center of leading us to victory in both sports.

This was my home, and I was very quickly committed in heart to my students. Nonetheless, this was a first to me, to sit there in the bleachers and watch my own young men so very determined to strike visiting young men and knock them to the ground. My heart wept inside as I watched it. I remember walking home from those games through the dark in the Spirit of the Lord, crying, "Oh Father, there has to be something else, something real upon this earth."

John Eldredge and Heath Ledger

Johanna had been involved in ballet up until we moved to Three Way. She was scheduled to perform in the Nutcracker Suite with the Lubbock Ballet in early December, so we kept her in practice. At the same time, such ballet groups always have a problem finding boys willing to fill young boy roles in the Nutcracker, and so Kyle had agreed to participate. He also was trained for his role. I really liked that, for it taught him how to present himself with dignity to girls.

The week of the ballet, Maureen was planning to stay in town, at Lois's with her parents. I returned to Three Way by myself. Before I left Lois's house that afternoon, however, I saw a book on her shelf titled *Journey of Desire* by John Eldredge. The very name of the book demanded my attention, so I pulled it off the shelf and read these words.

~~~ "There is a secret set within each one of our hearts. It often goes unnoticed, we rarely can put words to it, and yet it guides us throughout the days of our lives. This secret remains hidden for the most part in our deepest selves. It is the desire for LIFE as it was meant to be. Isn't there a life you have been searching for all your days? You may not always be aware of your search, and there are times when you seem to have abandoned looking altogether. But again and again it returns to us, this yearning that cries out for the life we prize." ~~~

Myy heart was gripped fiercely by these words. I told Lois, "I'm running off with your book!" At the same time, I had picked up a movie to watch titled *A Knight's Tale*, with Heath Ledger.

I was at home alone, then, for the next few days. I opened *Journey of Desire* and began to read.

How can I explain such an experience, lasting over months, even into 2003?

John Eldredge is a Christian psychologist based in Colorado Springs, Colorado. I have never known anyone who understood ME all the way through. As I read his books, John Eldredge took me back through event after event in my life, all the way from my childhood to our leaving the move, and opened to me every place of pain and hurt, and in doing so, John Eldredge gave me the answer that sang for real all through me, an answer that healed, an answer that rang true to the gospel, an answer that was the opposite of every specific "answer" I had been given in the move.

But this was no simple thing. For the extent of my hurt was beyond understanding. I know that, if not for John Eldredge, I would have died before now from the grief.

Every page in his books was like a sword going all through me and on every page, I wept. Time after time I was on the floor in tears before God as His ANSWER came into untold numbers of raw and open wounds.

And the first time I was on the floor was this word, coming into me for the first time in my life – My heart is good. My heart is good; my heart is filled with Jesus. – When that knowing pierced into me, it was like oozing sores of deep, deep hurt discharging onto the floor.

Let me explain. I am hyper-sensitive, and I remember everything through my life, every cutting word that hid its pain inside my soul. Then, at the same time, I had lived under a theology for years that told me that I had to "hack away" at myself because I was evil. The truth is, more than half of my hurt was self-inflicted.

In contrast, I have rarely known someone to open himself up to the reader in the way John Eldredge does. And what he does is take the reader through every episode of life to show you that God intended you, but not the hurt. That it was not your fault.

To take the overwhelming weights of shame from off my human soul was no little thing.

Through all of it, of course, it was Jesus, coming to me through John Eldredge's words and stories, showing me that it was always He, carrying me with honor through all. One of the more terrible moments for me was when John Eldredge took me into the locker room at Lacomb Elementary School and Jesus said to me, "It was not your fault. – You were not at fault."

Probably on the second evening alone, then, I watched *A Knight's Tale*. It's mostly a silly story, but good, and I was on the edge of my seat throughout. Then it came to the climax, when all of his companions tell William Thatcher, played by Heath Ledger, to run for his own sake. He had been pretending to be a knight so that he could compete in the jousting tournaments throughout England and France, but he had been found out and was about to be arrested and broken. William Thatcher listened carefully to each one with full respect, but torn inside. When they had finished urging him to run, he paused, and then said with great fervor and certainty, "I will not run. I am a knight."

Those words again went all through me like a spear thrust. I stopped the movie. I was gasping for breath with great sobs. I had run away. I had run away from the eldership; I had run away from Blair Valley; I had run away from the move. Or had I? Or was it that I had not run at all, but only into God? I did not know. I did not know what it meant, only that the line just tore me to pieces. Indeed, I know now that I was running a gauntlet, as I have described in earlier letters, and that I was almost dead from the blows. Yet I also know now that I did not run, but that I have never veered aside from the covenant I made with God at age 22, that I would know Him and that I would walk with a people who know Him.

Yet no answer to that great tearing of heart came to me at that time.

I will go on to other topics, but I spent nearly three years with John Eldredge, and I count him to be one of the dearest of friends in my life. I have not met him, but he shares himself openly in his books. I did write him a letter and received a good and lengthy reply. After *Journey of Desire*, I read *The Sacred Romance*, then *Wild at Heart*, then I read all three again, still weeping on every page. Then I read them all again, adding his fourth book, *Walking with God*. On the third time through, later in Houston, I wept not as often.

The healing was slow, it was deep, it was terrible, it was day after day, and it was not completed until writing this autobiography.

And I really don't care what anyone thinks or says. All the way through, it was Jesus showing Himself to me through every difficult place in my life. And all the way through, the answers I received from John Eldredge were the answers of God towards every human difficulty.

My heart is good; my heart is filled with Jesus.

Continuing with Life and Work

With our new family van, we took some vacation time to drive to Carlsbad, New Mexico, where I took my family through the same wondrous experience of the caves that I had enjoyed years before. On our way home, we drove through Denver City, Texas, and found the home of Richard Hernandez, but he was out on his job of driving truck. I had spoken with Richard twice during our time in the Lubbock area. I had wanted to drive down to see him, but he said both times, "No, I will come up." Except he never did. That was a sorrow I could only bear quietly.

By the beginning of 2002, the steps needed to merge with another school district were well under way. Maureen's cotton ginning job had ended in January, so now, Mr. Alvis offered her a part time job as a remedial teacher with the school, with very decent pay. She did that through the remainder of the year. I do remember picking the little ones up from a babysitter in Maple on occasion.

Because I was the principal, I was invited to attend and be a part of the monthly school board meetings, probably starting in September. This was my third foray into governance, and I enjoyed it very much. Marvin McCaul, who managed the cotton gin, was also the head of the school board. As superintendent, however, Dr. Tom Alvis led the meetings. I was free to participate in the discussion, although, along with Mr. Alvis, I did not have a vote. I learned this about education in Texas, that it is very efficient, and that money cannot be wasted. Of course, schools in Texas do not have to deal with activist teacher unions.

A lot of our discussion, then, was pertaining to negotiations with two neighboring school districts, Morton and Sudan. Morton was closer, but Sudan was wealthier. In the end the local voters would decide between the two. And in all this discussion, we had a close and practical look at much school law and due process.

In the vote that spring, the community chose to merge with Sudan, which also meant a forty-minute bus drive twice a day. Again, the board discussion continued with the practical aspects of merging Three Way and all its assets with the Sudan district. Sadly, they neither needed nor wanted any part of the school facility. They did hire some of the teachers from Three Way.

In the picture below, I am at the school board meeting; I was now 45 years old. Dr. Tom Alvis is at the head of the table.

Let me share a number of additional experiences that were part of my role as teacher/ principal, not in any actual order.

I was reading *The Fellowship of the Ring* out loud to my two seniors (as part of their British literature), and so when it came into the theaters that fall of 2001, we made seeing it a field trip. In fact, when the trailer for *The Fellowship of the Ring* came out earlier, it was likely the most watched movie trailer ever, for millions of people were highly suspicious of what they would do to the beloved story. I was one of the first to watch it the moment it appeared.

This was an agricultural community and very involved with county fairs. In fact, the school had a large and well-equipped agricultural and farming shop as part of its facilities and curriculum. That is now the only building remaining on the property. The agriculture teacher found two goats for us, one for Kyle and one for Johanna. I was greatly disappointed when he brought them home, however, for they were Boer goats, scrawny and wild. They were not at all like the goats Maureen and I had known when we were children. Our own children could never connect with them as pets.

Kyle did show his goat in the county fair in Muleshoe, though it was not of the quality of the other goats in the show. However, Three Way also put on their own fair, and so a judge came for it. Since our goats were the only ones in the contest, Kyle got first place for his and Johanna second place. They received ribbons and an ornate belt buckle. They had their ribbons pinned on their wall for years.

One of the farmers gave Johanna some chickens that ran around in the back yard, and we had a rabbit for Katrina.

In the spring, I went with a bus load of students as their oversight to a school quite a distance away for the annual academic competition. I remember watching the new Pixar movie of *Joseph* with the students on the bus on the way back, hearing God speaking to me all through it. (Johanna's teacher took them all to watch *Monster's Inc.* in the theater, which I thought was a terrible idea by the name – that is, until I watched it myself and loved it.)

In April of 2002, Maureen and I were invited to be part of the Junior/Senior dinner which took place at the County Line restaurant on the north side of Lubbock. A number of other teachers and spouses were included as well. When I look at the pictures of that event, I remember it with much fondness. This was a good time.

I was accused of racism, two different times. This is when I was so glad for Tom Alvis, for he was wise and anointed of God and helped me through these things. The first time I was at fault, not for "racism" but for insensitivity towards some students. The difficulty was resolved by my apology. The other time was neither racism nor our fault, but Mr. Alvis and I were able to work it through. The thing is, when I was confronting any out-of-control student, it was always a white male on the other side of that confrontation. Hispanic boys are very peaceful and always easy to work with, though they get themselves in trouble just as much.

We had a student body that was majority Hispanic, so obviously, a majority of difficulties would be with Hispanic children, and the school board was all white. Nonetheless, at no point did I ever know anything but deep respect and care for every student, regardless, coming from Tom Alvis, from myself, or from the school board. Certainly, in the grind of the day, we sometimes say things we should not, but which "group" a student was part of never entered my mind.

Dr. Tom Alvis was towards me the same as Abel Ramirez and Don Howat had been, sharing wisdom with me and encouragement in the Lord, while giving me full liberty and respect.

A New Season of Writing

Meanwhile, I continued to write. And with the wondrous new knowledge that my heart was good, my heart was filled with Jesus, my understanding was at a new level of knowing God.

Near the end of December, I wrote, "My life is forever changed. I have found Jesus anew."

On February 14, 2002, I sent the letter to John Eldredge with this opening paragraph.

~~~ Dear John, I want to thank you so very much for the books *Journey of Desire* and *Sacred Romance*. I have sought to walk with the Lord for over twenty-five years and in that time I have never read something that has changed my life as much as these books are doing. I am reading them the second time and still, page after page penetrates my heart and resonates deeply with the years of longing to know the Lord and the countless experiences of deep disappointment. I lost my breath when I saw your chapter title, "The Wildness of God." I had never put wildness together with God, even though

I have lived in the Canadian wilderness for many years, but I immediately knew it was so. I love to watch a storm beat itself against immovable mountains. I also know what it is like to be caught in the grip of overwhelming disappointment, knowing that a loving Father is in control, justifying Him in spite of the confusion, yet not understanding why. Your books put words to things I've felt inside to be true, but which my past "theology" seemed to contradict. Jesus has been using your books to make Himself profoundly real to me as never before. I am grateful. ~~~

I went on to share with him my vision for a Christian renewal center and community of Christ, a vision similar to what he shared in his books concerning the Church.

I wrote two long letters to Pastor Gary Kirksey through these months, sharing with him concerning my difficulty with my in-laws, not as people, but as "move elders." I shared some of the difficulties of my community experience and my present vision for a community of Christ.

The most important writing, however, is that I began this story of my life in the early months of 2002. All the chapters concerning my experiences at Graham River that are found in *The Great Story of God,* and that were then transferred to this autobiography, were written at this time. Although I added things for this larger story, there is very little change in wording.

I needed, so very much, to get that first vision and experience of community down on paper.

The first chapter of *The Great Story of God*, "Unquenchable Desire," is found here: https://christrevealed.info/story/unquenchable. If you are interested, you could read through that again, knowing that I wrote most of it in February-March of 2002, during this season of healing.

A Sad Closing

And so the school year came to a close. There was a finality about it because Three Way would be no more. I had known it only for one year, but most of the seniors had spent their entire school lives in its halls. It was such a place of peace for me and for my family. God could begin healing there because there were no further hurts being added.

Once the vote had chosen Sudan, that school district now "owned" everything that belonged to

Three Way. The superintendent and principal from Sudan came to a school board meeting to discuss the transfer. Sudan wanted only the newer computers and distance learning hub, everything else was superfluous and was to be disposed of.

We had the graduation of Three Way's final graduating class in the school cafeteria/auditorium. Once that was finished, the disposal of things began in earnest. All the houses were put up for sale to be trucked away, except that the teachers were free to remain in their home until such time as they had found another place to live. The library was opened up to people wanting the books; I was able to make off with a large number of books. We had an auction during which I purchased filing cabinets, school desks, and other things we could use for home schooling.

The school was a very nice building, but to the Sudan school district it was only a liability that would cost them money to maintain without any value to them. Their long-term plan was to demolish it. The thing is, and I have groaned over this for years, if I had been able to offer them $250,000 for the grounds, the buildings, and everything in them intact, they would have grabbed the offer immediately. We would have had a perfect site for a community and school with a strong Internet connection by which we could have made a living.

Yet I had no money, and everything is now gone from the site, and I know it wasn't the Lord for us. I had an appointment with God coming up just four years later, and that appointment was in Houston, not Maple.

The local community did NOT like their school being gone, however, and so they tried to negotiate with Sudan to keep the building going, partly so that the local boys could continue using the beautiful, maple-floored gym. There was also a desire to turn one of the classrooms into a long-term display room for Three Way's history and many sports trophies.

Sudan agreed to this, though it was an agreement that did not last.

Because I was a woodworker, Dr. Alvis asked me to bid on doing the cabinet work for the display room, which would be down by the cafeteria in what had been the kindergarten room. I bid a decent price, which made Mr. Alvis flinch, but which the school board accepted without question.

Nonetheless, it simply meant that I would be making 10-12 dollars an hour instead of the 3 dollars an hour that was typical in my bids in Lubbock.

At the same time, I hired Rigo Rodriguez to work for me in my cabinet shop and in installing the cabinets with glass doors in the new display room. This was a first for me, because Rigo did not always measure up to my "construction zone" requirements. I had to pause and say to myself, "No, he is more important than the work."

I would still receive my monthly paycheck through August, so this job was a significant amount of money towards our next move.

Several of the teachers from Three Way were hired at Sudan, but they did not need an assistant principal or an English teacher. I made an effort to be hired there, but did not feel a witness that it was the Lord nor find any door opening in that direction.

We continued to live at our home on the Three Way property, however, and Kyle was enrolled in Sudan for his sixth grade year. They graciously allowed us the home for as long as was needed.

A Wrong Direction

Meanwhile, I was continuing to work on my ideas for a different kind of school, which I called project-led learning. I am convinced that junior high school kids, from seventh to ninth grades, have no business being forced into a school desk and assembly-line routine. They ought to be doing valuable things with their hands, with learning tied loosely to their work.

There was a young couple in Lubbock whom we knew through City View fellowship named Jared and Dana Squires. In fact, Maureen and I had become friends with several young couples, something unusual for me, a big plus of being married. Jared and Dana had become interested in a particular type of approach to Christian education that was a hybrid mix of homeschooling and classroom. Students would attend class two days a week to direct their learning, and the remainder of their time, they would work at home. This would give them a focused education without the expense of full-time private school. While sharing with Jared concerning my own ideas of a school I would like to start, the suggestion came that I might be the principal of this new school they were starting called Kingdom Preparatory Academy.

And so they hired me. Jared and Dana had formed a non-profit and thus had a "school board." I presented my ideas to this board and they were well-received, although they did not really fit with the model the Squires were using. I started driving into Lubbock, then, before the end of June, to work on getting the new school set up. The Squires had negotiated with a Lubbock Presbyterian church to use the upstairs of their teaching building, which was no longer in use. Part of my job was to get this place set up for school starting in August. In fact, I donated quite a few of the books I had obtained from Three Way to this new venture.

Tim and Frieda were back at the Lubbock community at this point, in one of the homes. I spent the nights with them through the week, so that I did not have to drive the long distance every day.

The Squires had begun to advertise for Kingdom Preparatory Academy. They had prepared, with the help of other families, a float for Lubbock's big parade in July. And so Maureen and I with our children walked beside the float through the parade, handing out pamphlets. I was not feeling well at all, and so part way through I had to ride in the vehicle rather than walk along the front of the crowds. Of course, the hand-pumping political part of a principal's job was entirely outside of my ken.

The problem was that the parade started in a poorer part of town and ended at Texas Tech. For that reason, through the first half of the distance, we were giving the pamphlets to children who would never be eligible for the private school, and when we got to the wealthier section, we had no more pamphlets.

This reflected a serious issue with me, one which I argued with Jared over. Most Christian schools test all incoming students with the bar set at achieving a standardized test score above the 50 percentile. That means that ONE HALF of all children are always ineligible for every Christian school. Although it's falsely called "maintaining a high standard," it really means, "we don't want you in our school if you are stupid or have any learning limitation."

In my mind, a Christian ministry was meant to serve all, regardless of where they began. And I would much rather teach special ed kids, actually, then the smarter ones.

This approach to schooling was popular among Christians in Texas at that time, so there was a large conference held in Marble Falls, Texas, which Jared and I attended together. I was getting my first taste of the mind of "Christian schooling" in America, and I was not overly impressed. That is, there was so much hoopla that this new approach to schooling was going to "save" America. Yet, the truth is, it retained so much of what is wrong with schooling in general and it held no appeal to me.

Jared was the kind of person that was quiet and listening, easy to have a conversation with, yet never revealing his true thoughts. (Richard Hernandez was like this as well.) In contrast, I have always been too trusting and thus, with such a person, I most definitely talk too much. On the long trip home, I not only expressed some of my concerns about excluding children, but I also talked about events in America, including 9/11. I explained how the George Bush family was, in fact, one of the most powerful organized crime families in the US.

Several days after our return to Lubbock, Jared and Dana asked to have lunch with Maureen and me. Jared said that he had come to the agonizing realization that he had made a mistake in hiring me. My thoughts concerning the US government, my inability to play the crowds in the parade, and some other things I had said, had persuaded him to offer me a lesser role in the school, something he held out because he was an honorable man.

Even though I turned this new situation down, the Squires did pay me what they had promised for my summer work, which now gave us plenty of funds for a move. Yet it was now the beginning of August, and suddenly, I had no teaching position, again, just a couple of weeks before school would be starting.

A Trip to Houston

As we knew that my job at Three Way would end by summer, I had been looking around different school districts in the Lubbock area, in the hopes of finding an English teaching position. Most of them paid the same as at Three Way, but without a home in which to live.

Thus while driving around the Lubbock area, we looked for a place to live. But I just could not bear it. I can survive without mountains, though I don't like it, but I cannot live without trees. The only trees in the Lubbock area are inside the city. The point is that I was just not connecting with West Texas anymore.

That first of August a single English position opened up on the state-wide teacher hiring website. This was in a district called Sheldon ISD in Harris County, just to the east of Houston. Because an oil refinery sits inside this district, it was one of the wealthier in Texas and offered a much higher salary than schools in West Texas.

I looked at Google maps and determined that there were TREES in this school district. I also looked at house listings in the area. When I clicked on the first house in the list and a picture of it opened on my webpage, I gasped, for the thought rose strongly in my heart, "This is our home!" But I was not yet hired.

So, I filled out the application and immediately received an invitation to come down to Houston for an interview. School was starting, and they would hire anyone who was qualified.

Kyle went with me in the green van down to Houston. We spent the night in a motel just on the east side of Interstate 610. We went out to C.E. King high school for the interview the next morning. It was the principal of the school, Frances Baccigalopi, and the director of curriculum, Vicki Giles, with whom I interviewed. Vicki Giles had been an English teacher and then the head of the English department before becoming part of the administration.

It was a pleasant interview. Tthey hired me on the spot and sent me to Human Resources to sign a two-year contract. We were moving to Houston!

My last service at City View in Lubbock had been quite strange, however. just before Kyle and I went to Houston.

I had seen Jared visiting privately with Pastor Gary. You see, I had crossed the line. You can't really be a Christian educator in Texas without being a supporter of the Republican party and a flag-waving adherent of "God bless America."

In that last sermon, Pastor Gary was preaching on the death of Moses and Joshua stepping into the new leadership role. At a certain point he looked straight at me, and, although I know that sometimes I imagine such a thing, this time, I am convinced he was intentionally addressing me. He said something along the lines of "Moses is dead, it's time to move on." Maureen also remembers this.

I knew in that moment that God was taking us elsewhere.

Closing this Chapter of My Life

I must bring this time at Three Way into the Lord Jesus, and place Him upon every moment and circumstance.

I was planning to draw you an outline of the rooms of the school, but then I saw that I was holding to a sentimental attachment to "what might have been." It would have been nice if the Three Way property had been God's place for us, but it was not, and so we leave it.

Yet "leaving" Three Way was a wonderfully new experience for me, that is, to regret leaving a place, the first time and only time I had such regret in my life. As I think now, however, I do have one regret. Probably because I was so emotionally fragile, we had little private interaction with the other people on the school property or in the Maple area. It would have been nice to have had different ones over for dinner, and especially Tom and Geneva, but I don't think we ever did. We should have gotten to know them much better; they were wonderful Christian people.

I have a couple of regrets towards Kyle through this time that I want to place into the Lord Jesus. He had wanted to join a baseball practice group, and I was, in fact, driving him there. But I could not bear the thought of his being humiliated if he did not "measure up" (as I had been as a boy) and halfway there, I turned the car around and we went back home. I tried to share why with him, and he always respected me, but I doubt that he understood. On another occasion, he was attempting to help me attach the blue van to a horse trailer. He was not doing his part right, and so I hopped out and chewed him out. He was just ten, the poor little guy. I felt so ashamed afterwards. He tells me now that he does not remember it.

But Kyle, I want to ask your forgiveness for the many times I failed at being a good father to you. I wanted to be, but I did not always know how.

Lord Jesus, I thank you for this time we had at Three Way. I thank you for Tom and Geneva Alvis and their goodness towards us. I thank you for my good experiences in that school. And I especially thank you for John Eldredge and his great gift to me.

And Father, I am sorry that I was not able to be what Jared and Dana needed. That was entirely my fault. I pray that you bless them with all Your goodness. And thank you so much for Pastor Gary Kirksey and what he meant to us through this necessary season of healing

I place you, Lord Jesus, upon every moment and memory of our time at Three Way. All of it was You in me, and all of it was good.

37. The Move to Houston

August 2002 - July 2004

As I finished posting the last chapter, there arose in me the sense that our time in Three Way was much more important than I had understood, and that I will know more what that means as we go forward in our present lives. This makes me very glad, for we all loved our brief time there.

At the same time, as I have written this chapter, I realize that God gave me three years of peace and family happiness, from our arrival at Three Way to the late fall of 2004, before He took me back into the press in preparation for the most wondrous word God has ever spoken into me. And so, a big part of my purpose in this letter is to give you a flavor and sense of the joy of our family. As I realize now, our time with our children growing up was the best time of my life.

School Begins

As soon as Kyle and I had returned from our trip to Houston, we started loading our blue van with all my tools and anything else that would fit into it that was not needed for Maureen and the children. They would remain at Three Way until I had found a place for us to live in Houston. Now, we say, "Houston," because that is our address, but the Sheldon ISD is outside of Houston city limits, which borders on the district's west side.

There was a training time for new teachers beginning several days before classes started, so I drove down in the blue van by myself as soon as possible. A tire blew out in the late afternoon as I was entering Waco. Since there were duals on the rear, I could keep driving, but I had several tons of weight and had to get the tire fixed. I found a truck shop open that was able to put on a new tire and thus arrived in Houston late that evening.

I think on the second day of the teacher training time, I was visiting with some other teachers about my living situation, with my family remaining in west Texas until I could find a place. A lady sitting opposite from me perked up and offered me a room in her and her husband's home for the inter-

im. Their last name was Rogers; they lived north of Sheldon ISD in Atascocita.

I found a storage rental place and unloaded most of what was in the blue van before driving on up to Atascocita to spend the next several weeks staying with the Rogers. I felt very welcome and comfortable in their home and had a nice bedroom. It was not a long drive to the school, maybe twenty minutes with traffic.

I was now teaching English in a large public high school. My year began reasonably well; my experience at Three Way helped greatly to prepare me. I will share more of my new teaching experiences in a later section.

I really enjoyed my time with the Rogers; they were friendly and comfortable. I spent around five weeks with them. Besides teaching school, however, my first task was to find a home for us so that Maureen and the children could come. They continued living in our home at Three Way. When school started, Kyle began sixth grade at Sudan, while Maureen taught Johanna at home. Then, my second task was to find a church that was similar to what we had known in Lubbock.

I drove by the house for sale that I had first seen when I searched the Internet. It was located in a quiet neighborhood about a mile southeast of C.E. King High School. But I did not think we could get a loan to purchase the house, and I preferred something more in the countryside with a couple of acres. So I drove all around in my big blue van looking for a home. I found a nice double-wide on a large country lot north of Dayton. I found another empty property southwest of Dayton that I could easily purchase as the note was carried by the developer. I ended up at a mobile home seller in Porter. Then there was a lot of running around trying to find the right mobile home and to put it all together. Needless to say, none of it seemed right, but I was getting acquainted with northeast Harris county.

I visited a number of churches, including a Methodist church with the Rogers, but even though I rejoice in worshipping with other brethren, none were like City View. I will share one experience, however. On a drive from Dayton to Atascocita, I passed an "Apostolic" church. I thought, "This sounds interesting." And so I visited there one Sunday.

It was a Pentecostal church; it was also good that I sat in the back row. The praise was anointed of the Spirit, and then the preacher began. His sermon was "Jesus only," that we are to be baptized in the name of Jesus only. I'm willing to listen to anything the Bible might say, so I paid attention to his verses. I could see his point, but I also knew the many verses he ignored. Believing something radical out from the Bible is no problem to me, but the heart of the speaker is. And it did not take me long to identify the heart of this preacher. He exulted with joy over the fact that all the millions of Christians in the Houston area, who imagine that they love Jesus, were all going straight to hell because they had not been baptized in the name of "Jesus only."

At this point I was ready to leave straight away, but I dared not, because it also seemed probable that he would nail me as an apostate before I could escape. So I endured the rest of his sermon and fled the place as soon as it was safe to do so. It doesn't matter what his Bible verses were, his darkened heart against God's precious people told me everything.

I was not feeling successful in finding a home for us, and this was rapidly becoming a problem because, although I love some solitude, I love being with my family more.

On Labor Day weekend, Maureen flew down by herself, leaving the children with her sisters, in order to be part of choosing our new home. I was still with the Rogers, and it was nice to share my new experiences with Maureen. We did look at the several different places I had scouted. We wanted something larger, so that each of our children could have a bedroom, but it had to be within our price range. Larger houses in our price range, however, had something wrong with them. One was rotting. We also looked at that first house I had seen while still at Three Way, at 7914 Fernbank Drive. The problem with the house on Fernbank is that it had an incredibly poor interior design, though it was definitely big enough.

We finally agreed to pursue a loan, believing that this house was ours. After Maureen flew back, I connected with the listed realtor and applied for a loan. Because of my two-year contract as a teacher with Sheldon ISD, we were approved. We then went through all the steps needed to finalize the purchase.

Meanwhile, the Roger's daughter was returning, and they asked me about finding another place so that they could use the room I was in. They were very kind and gracious. Meanwhile, Vicki Giles, the head of curriculum at C.E. King, had also offered me a short-term stay in a spare room in their home. Vicki Giles and her husband lived in a nice sub-division just northwest of Crosby. And so I spent the next two weeks in their home. They were a bit more formal and less conversational then the Rogers, but I was quite comfortable in their spare bedroom.

I continued through all the steps of securing our new home. When those steps were in the right place, around the first of October, I moved from the Giles' into that empty house with a foam mattress in what would become our bedroom. I continued to teach school every day, through this process.

Our New Home

Our new home was still not ready for Maureen and the children to come, so I went right to work on it. I was feeling much stronger than I had at Blair Valley, and so I tackled the first part of a complete remodel with enthusiasm. On the next page is a rough floor plan of how it was when we bought it, followed by the front of our house nearer to the time we bought it.

As you can see, the previous owners had done a lot of work to it, first turning the garage into two bedrooms and then enclosing the patio as one large room added to the house. This made it large like I wanted, but because the resulting interior layout was so poor, it remained in our price range. Yet it was sound and comfortable. In fact, the owners had just installed new floor tile and bedroom carpets and gotten a new paint job in order to sell it. Of truth, they should have saved most of their money.

There were several big problems. First, the kitchen was tiny, and all traffic went through the kitchen. If you opened the fridge door, you could not open the oven and vice versa, and no one could pass through if either were open. Then, the "dining" area was narrow, with the step at the back of the garage

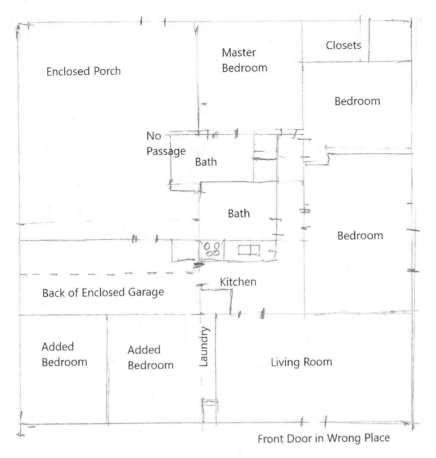

Enclosed Porch

Master Bedroom

Closets

Bedroom

No Passage

Bath

Bath

Bedroom

Back of Enclosed Garage

Kitchen

Added Bedroom

Added Bedroom

Laundry

Living Room

Front Door in Wrong Place

I drew up a couple of new floor plans, and Maureen chose the one that I then built over the next three years. But the messiest job was removing the brick wall inside the house and opening up between the narrow and useless "dining area" and the large but cutoff back room. I did that work and then cleaned the whole house before Maureen and the children came.

I became quite eager to make everything as nice as I could before they came. One thing I did was to buy a large above-ground plastic swimming pool from Academy and set it up in the back yard. I told no one about it.

Then, when our new home was ready enough, I took a Friday off from school and flew to Lubbock. Maureen and the children met me there and we rented a large Penske truck. Brother Claude also flew into Lubbock to help us with the move. After driving out to Three Way, I asked Canaan Heinrich and his younger brother, as well as Rigo Rodriguez if they would come help load our stuff into the truck. They were all farm boys, like the young men at Blueberry, and were energetic helpers. It was with sadness then, that we drove away from what had been a

running down the middle, even though they had tiled everything. Then, the two bedrooms still had the garage's sloping floor, and the large backroom was cut off from the house by the back wall of the garage, which was still brick, with only a small door as passage.

lovely place for us in Maple, Texas.

But we were heading to a new home, and that was good. Little James was almost three years old. We put his car seat in the Penske truck with me. That is his first memory, riding with his dad to Houston in the big yellow truck. Claude, Maureen and the other children came behind in the green van. Of course, each of the other children also got their turn in the big truck. After a long trip down, we arrived at our new home on Fernbank Drive, around the middle of October. I had such fun enticing them into the back yard where the children immediately leapt into their new pool. We unloaded and returned the truck, and I continued with teaching school on Monday.

The First Year at C.E. King

There is not much to share with you concerning anything through the school year in the first two years I was teaching at Sheldon. I had the same students every day, around 140 of them, each of whom I saw only once a day, and things were pretty much the same all year long. And I taught the exact same thing, pretty much, several times in a day.

But I will give you just a sense of my first year of teaching.

The school itself was large and sprawling, housing around 1100 high school students. A former elementary school on one side had become part of the high school, even though it was two separate buildings. Down the street, on the other side of the student parking area, was the large junior high school, also called C.E. King.

This first year I had both tenth and twelfth-grade classes, regular English. I also had a group who needed special help to pass the state tests. And most everything is oriented towards passing those tests, all year long, because there is no other option. Yet the skills of test-taking, which are different from the skills of reading and writing, are skills never used in any other life activity.

I connected with two fellow English teachers in particular. One was Mrs. Wilson, a kind older black woman who was a Christian. I was always welcome in her room when no students were around, and I often went to her for advice. The other was Mr. Leahy, not Christian, but very friendly. Mr. Leahy shared with me all the places we could enjoy as a family in the Houston area, including the Thanksgiving fireworks near the Galleria and Dickens on the Strand in Galveston.

I began the development of my writing course in earnest with my seniors. I used the assignment I had watched Greg Reeves take his students through, a "Remembered Event" paper, which I now call "Personal Narrative." The difference for him and for me is to have them write, then mark and comment, then re-write, and re-write again if needed. Most teachers just assign a paper, mark it, and go on, without the students continuing to work on that paper until it's right and until they know how to make it right.

In Texas education, the state mandates the objectives for student learning, everything a student must know or must be able to do for each grade level in each subject. These objectives are universal and sound. The content, including how those objectives are to be met, is left to the discretion of each individual teacher. In fact, at C.E. King, we were encouraged not to teach the textbook, but use it only as a resource. Developing one's own teaching material was normal. This was the same philosophy that had been in the Blueberry school. It's also the only way I think.

I had around two dozen students per class. My teacher's desk was in the front corner of the room. I stood in front of the whiteboard as I taught – I like using the board, but I sat at my desk where I could observe everyone while the students did their work.

When I was in high school in the early seventies, we did not talk while the teacher was talking. It was just not done. At the same time, if a policeman had been stationed inside our school, most of us would have refused to come. We were Americans and independent, yet, even though we were worldly, being quiet during instruction was normal respect.

By 2002, students not talking while the teacher was giving instruction was an unknown. At the same time, because of the false reaction to 9/11, police with guns patrolled the school. It was a completely different world. The one thing I lack is the ability to keep students quiet. For the first three years with Sheldon, I did manage to keep a relative flow between my teaching and their chatting. And I do like a lively class. The one thing I do not allow, however, is disrespect. For that, Texas law backed up the teacher. If a student cussed or spoke with disrespect, they would be taken into custody by the police and a judge would fine their parents $500. The students knew that, and so things typically remained smooth.

My first days with any new group of students are always stiff, because I am stiff outwardly. They soon learn my respect and care for them, however, and things become much smoother. I did make a huge mistake, though, with one of my seniors, a girl. I sometimes made thoughtless pre-judgments, a defect I did not lose until in my first semester teaching college several years later. The seniors had written the first draft of their "Remembered Event" paper, and I was marking them. One girl had written many pages more than I had required, a wordy and sentimental account of the death of her best friend. I was feeling tired and frustrated when I got to her paper and so I wrote, without thought, "This is way too wordy, cut it down." (If I faced the same situation now, I would explain to the student very gently how her story would become so much more powerful and real if she was able to say the same things, but with fewer words.)

Needless to say, my comment greatly angered this girl, and rightly so. She kept a glaring hostility against me until the end of the semester, and then got transferred to another teacher's class. Overall, however, I had a decent relationship with my students through the year.

Family Life & Home Schooling

Because my pay was nearly adequate, Maureen homeschooled the children. Kyle continued his sixth-grade year, Johanna was third grade, and Katrina was in kindergarten, learning to read. Maureen is a superb teacher of first-reading. Little James busied himself with pestering his sisters.

We had started using a reading-based curriculum while still in Lubbock, called Son Light Curriculum, a system I would definitely recommend for homeschooling, especially in the primary grades. This approach to schooling made use of a large number of books in every subject for each grade level. We purchased all that we needed for the children.

I continued to read lots of books to the children, school-based stories or others. Our evening time was always special, gathered in our new living room, with either me reading a book out loud, or us enjoying a good family movie together. I read the entirety of *The Hobbit* and *The Lord of the Rings* to them through this time.

That Halloween night, Maureen's Aunt Jenny was visiting with us. After I had gone to bed, they heard something bang against the front gable of our house. It was dark and after all, trick or treaters were coming by. The next morning, however, we discovered that some of my seniors had found our house and plastered raw eggs on the front and tee-peed our front yard and tree. While our own neighborhood has always been safe, the neighborhoods around the high school were not. Gangs were prevalent, of all three races, white, black, and Hispanic. Nonetheless, that was a one-time event.

Still in October, we happened upon a fellowship that was meeting in rented rooms at a local high school called Fellowship of the Nations, with Johnny and Sarah Brady as pastors. We visited on Sunday morning. There were around a hundred people in attendance and we were very pleased that the teaching and outlook was similar to City View in Lubbock. We believed that we had found a church home. In that first service, we saw a black family sitting on the front row with a string of children the same ages as ours. Something inside Maureen said, "I would like to be friends with that lady." We did not see them again in that fellowship, however.

And so we began attendance at Fellowship of the Nations where we continued for several months. Pastor Johnny had a good word; his wife, Sarah, led the praise. The praise was not at the level of worship we had enjoyed before, however, but the fellowship was good.

During Thanksgiving, we went to the fireworks just north of the Galleria. We hiked up with crowds of other people and enjoyed the display very much. By Mr. Leahy's direction, we attended our first Dickens on the Strand in Galveston the first week of December. Inside a roped off several block area, everything is Charles Dickens and Victorian England culture. This first time we were not dressed in Victorian-like outfits, a mistake we never made again. The streets were filled with displays and entertainers and booths selling all sorts of cool things. The stores of the Strand were all open, providing their own fun family time.

Maureen's sister Lois often came down because she enjoyed our children as an important part of her life. She spent several days with us through our first Christmas in Houston.

In the spring we went to the large Harris County and Houston public library book sale in downtown Houston. This began a family practice we all loved, that of carting home boxes and boxes of used books at reasonable prices for our growing home library. Each of the kids got to fill their own box. Our back yard is larger than normal, with plenty of space for the children to build all sorts of different forts over the years. There was a large tree in the middle that the children loved, especially Johanna. You see, all through her growing up years, Johanna believed that a tree had one purpose – for her to climb to the top. We also hung a swing from one of its branches. That Christmas I got each of the children their own different-colored large rope to swing in the tree.

Right from the start, I was determined that we would have a garden in our back yard. I love to garden, but I also wanted my children to know where their food comes from and to know the meaning of gardening. I chose a space in the back yard that had decent sunlight and created two rows of raised beds around 3' wide and 12' long, a total of eight in all. I use the principles of "square-foot" and "no-till" gardening, and will only garden with those approaches. We purchased a truck load of "compost" for our new garden. Of course, it turns out the 'compost' was only half-composted wood waste that would take a few years to break down. I also created a small herb garden and a garden bed just off the back porch along the fence. There I put in a nice lattice work using metal posts for pole beans and cucumbers.

We would garden for several years, but all through, our garden here did poorly. I don't know fully the reasons why. Green beans, sweet potatoes, okra, and cucumbers grew well. But carrots or beets or squash produced nothing at all. And none of it did as well as my gardening in Oregon and in British Columbia. This was sorrowful to me because I had so longed for abundant gardening through the long winters in the far north.

In January we found a local home school group and went to one of their meetings. There were some whites there, but most were black. We were pleased to see that the family we had observed at Fellowship of the Nations was part of the group. Their names were Joe and Kim Rideau. They lived not far from us and our families became friends all through our children's growing up years. Their oldest daughter, Joy, was Kyle's age, their oldest son, Byron, was Johanna's age, their daughter, Faith, was Katrina's age, and their younger son, Josiah, was James's age. They would later have another little boy, while we stayed with four.

There was another couple with their four children, Henry and Delia Dibrell, who also lived not far from us. While they were watching their kids at the YMCA, Maureen found herself in conversation with Delia. They both felt a connection of deep friendship. I'm not good at maintaining relationships over years, but Delia and Kim have continued being Maureen's best friends here in the Houston area.

We met formally with the homeschool group once a month, but did many different "educational things" and field trips together regularly, especially through the summer. We went together to the Museum of Natural History, the Houston Zoo, and PE. The children were able to present their different projects at the formal group meeting. Kyle got involved in learning to cook international cuisine, and of course, Johanna and Katrina have never ceased loving to make costumes and dressing up in different cultural expressions. Because the girls were studying China, we visited Chinatown at one point, and Jo and Katrina persuaded me to buy them Chinese outfits for their presentation to the homeschool group.

There is a park in north Harris county, just outside of Humble, on Spring Creek, called Jesse Jones Park. They were putting on a Texas Pioneer Day that Maureen had discovered in her search for activities. As we enjoyed the heritage events and walked the paths of this park, we felt such peace. Recreating how settlers lived in the 1800's included many things we were accustomed to in the wilderness communities. We knew this was something we wanted our children to be involved with. It would not be until a few years later, however, that we became part of the volunteer group at Jesse Jones Park and participated in the historical reenacting.

It was always important to me that my children experience many different things, and even more than that, that we experience them together as a family. Not long into our time in Houston, we signed both Katrina and Johanna up with a local ballet school, and we found a young lady named Bethany Millican, who attended a Baptist Church just down the road, who gladly taught piano to Johanna.

Working on Our Home

I worked on remodeling the house part time through the school year, but with school out during the summer months, I spent most of my time on that project. The biggest deal was a new kitchen, which I built in the spring and early summer of 2003.

During this time, while Kyle had his own room, Johanna, Katrina and James shared the other room, all in the older part of the house, which I did not yet tackle for remodeling. Kyle's permanent bedroom would be in the front corner of the house, and therefore it was the first room that I finished.

I could not build a new kitchen, however, until I had put a level floor across the whole area that had been the garage. And I could not build a level floor until I had placed a steel beam to carry the heavy weight of the back side of what had been the garage roof. I bought a long slab of steel nine inches wide and sandwiched it between two 2 X 10's and bolted them together. This was more than enough to carry the weight across a twenty-foot span. I remember Brother Claude helping me install that steel beam after he had driven with us to Houston, before returning to Bowens Mill.

Below is a rough sketch that shows the new rooms of our home.

Through the winter months of 2002-2003, I removed a lot of the ceramic tile from the sloping floors of the two "bedrooms" so that I could have extra tiles for later needs. I then framed in a level floor at the height of the step-up at the back of the garage, just a bit higher than the adjoining former kitchen. I widened that floor, then, into the large room at the back, with a step down to the continuing tile floor.

This area now turned into a larger dining room and kitchen, and a bedroom for Kyle. I made the floors out of white pine boards we purchased at Lowes. They were all white pine, but the kitchen boards I chose were softer – which was a mistake. Although I glued them down, they shrunk and the glue broke and from then until now, we have squeaky floors. I had made it my mis-

sion while living in northern BC to eliminate all the squeaks in all the floors upon which we lived. Now, however, I find the same squeaks strangely comforting, a reminder of "home" to us.

By early spring Kyle was moved into his new bedroom, Johanna now had her own room, the space for the new kitchen was ready, and so I began to build it. There is a covered porch on the back side of our house, where I set up my shop tools, and I had the large space that also served as our "school room" in which I could assemble the cabinets. Because the front bedroom of the "garage" had contained the washer and dryer, there was plumbing already to the space, which I could then use to connect the kitchen sink. We moved the washer and dryer to a "utility" space near the back door.

Because I had only low-grade shop tools, I crafted the kitchen out of white pine boards, which were soft and easy to work with. At the same time, Lowes had nice wide-paneled boards made of white pine

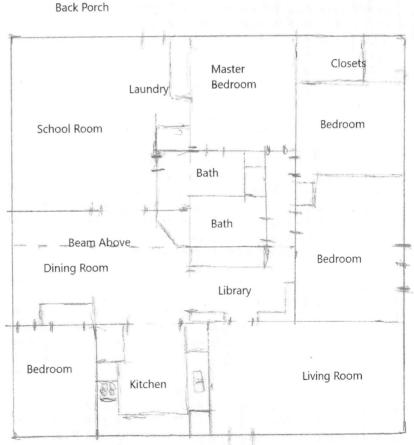

Back Porch

Laundry

Master Bedroom

Closets

School Room

Bedroom

Bath

Bath

Bedroom

Beam Above

Dining Room

Library

Bedroom

Kitchen

Living Room

Door in Better Place

glued edge-to-edge. I would use these for the cabinet doors. I designed my own style for the kitchen, drawing from all I had learned previously. It is a style that I would definitely use again.

The kitchen was finished and ready for use by the middle of the summer, everything except the doors and drawer fronts. As we moved into our new kitchen, we then moved the former kitchen cabinets to just inside the back door for the utility area, with a deep utility sink installed in front of the washer and dryer.

Because I had a solid decent-paying job and thought that we could fold the cost of remodeling the house into a future re-finance, all the purchases for the remodeling work were put on credit cards. This was the time when obtaining further lines of credit at low interest rates was easy. I'm sure you can guess at how all that turned out.

With the old cabinets gone from the central passage room of our home, I was then free to turn that space into our library. And this was really cool, because if one were to draw house plans from scratch, one would not place the library at the main junction of the house. Since this was the only reasonable use of that space, our library now became the center of our home, something I have loved immensely.

I built a set of display cabinets with doors and a counter, of the same style as the kitchen, but with attached bookshelves on top. Then I built nice bookshelves on the two other walls of the space. I would guess that these shelves hold around a thousand books, the heartbeat of our home. But, I built lots of bookshelves elsewhere as well; we had bookshelves filled with books in every room of the house. I do like books.

On the next page are pictures of the kitchen and library before the doors were installed.

At the same time, we turned the large room in the back corner of our house into our "school room," with bookshelves as well. In the far back corner, I had my garden center. I built a lovely little gardening bench where I grew starts for the garden in the spring.

I planted a concord grape vine where an old tree had been cut down and the stump had rotted. We built a nice trellis for the vines, which grew well enough and have produced grapes each year ever since. It's too hot here in Houston for Concord grapes, but I wanted my children to know the joy of eating grapes off the vine and so have insisted each year that they all go out and eat to their fill. I taught them to swallow the grapes the same way I had done when a boy, pop off the skin first, and then swallow without biting into the seeds.

Meanwhile, Maureen had found a job with a care-giving business, who placed her with an elderly lady in Pasadena, named Ruth Fleming. Although she filled in full time through June of 2003, from then until the summer of 2004, she worked only on weekends for most of the time. Miss Ruth was a larger lady, warm and loving, whose husband had made his money in the oil business.

A Transition of Fellowship

In March of 2003, Maureen and I attended a Retreat with the brethren from Fellowship of the Nations. This was a time of wonderful spiritual renewal and fellowship for us. At the same time, this church had the same style of cell-group meetings we had known in Lubbock, and so we had joined one and met with them weekly.

During that spring, the church had signed an agreement giving them an option-to-buy on a large property not far from our home. This was a large monthly payment that did not yet pay on the principle. Pastor Johnny knew that I was a builder and designer and so he asked me to walk the property with him to look at possibilities for construction of the fellowship's own church facilities.

I drew up some possibilities for them, but then I saw the new "plans" for the church complex drawn up by an architect. My vision and the Brady's vision for the new property were worlds apart. I was designing a community of Christ. The official new plans were nothing more than a grandiose church complex, something I wanted no part in. In the end, it was all too expensive, and they had to drop the option to buy and lost the money that had already been paid.

One day in July, I woke up with the realization that Fellowship of the Nations was not God's place for us. The word was going nowhere, and I was not connecting with God in the praise. I don't believe in going to a church where I experience no personal connection with God. I had shared with Pastor Johnny that I had a vision of God fulfilling His Word in our lives. He asked me what I meant. I pointed to Ephesians 4 – **Till we all come to the unity of the**

faith and of the knowledge of the Son of God, to a perfect man, to the measure of the stature of the fullness of Christ. He challenged me with a hard forehead, "What are you claiming that means?"

I am not able to give answer to such hardness, and so I went my way. Even those who know the Spirit of God are typically hostile to the idea that God would fulfill His Word in our lives now and not after we "go to" heaven.

I received an email from Pastor Johnny saying, "I thought you were with us for the long term." I replied by saying, "I thought we were too, and I was surprised myself when the Lord showed me that our time with Fellowship of the Nations was over." I did not receive a reply.

Meanwhile, Henry Dibrell, the husband of Maureen's good friend, Delia, had gotten a post as assistant pastor at the Assembly of God Church in the Heights. We visited there in July and liked it. We attended regularly for about a year. When I look for it now on Google Maps, however, I discover that the church is entirely gone and the space where it sat is filled with high-value new homes.

I received more from the pastor at this Assembly of God church than I had at Fellowship of the Nations, but the praise services remained a disappointment. I do expect God to speak to me inside the flow of the anointing in every service I attend. If that's not happening, something is missing. But – for these months, the Lord did speak to me occasionally through this pastor's teaching and it was a good place for the children.

In May of 2003, on Mother's Day, we attended a service with the move of God fellowship group here in Houston. Their meeting place was just inside of the interchange between I-10 and Beltway 8 on the far other side of Houston. We had known family members of some of these brethren in the farms in British Columbia. It so happened that John Mancha, one of my students at Blueberry, who had also been in Lubbock while we were there, attending Texas Tech, had also just moved to Houston and was visiting this move fellowship that morning as well.

It was great to connect with John again. He soon after married Crystal Garner, a girl who had grown up at the Hilltop Community in BC. They have made their home in Houston, and we have visited with them occasionaly through the years.

That service was Mother's Day. There was a traveling ministry of the move there for the service, an Hispanic woman whom I had never known. She was clearly anointed of the Lord in the way I was accustomed. The elder then called for a time of prayer for the mothers in the assembly. Except, he wanted to begin with all of us praying just for this sister who was ministry before praying for those mothers who were not ministry. She came up front and we all prayed a blessing upon her. The elder who led the service prayed a wonderful prayer of blessing and encouragement, honoring this "mother" in the Church and her years of faithful service.

Then it was time to pray for the "non-ministry" mothers, including the elder's wife and Maureen. They all gathered in front, we laid hands on them, and the elder led the prayer. His prayer was all about their flesh, and how they needed to stop walking in the flesh and to start walking in the Spirit. There was neither encouragement nor blessing in his prayer. I was, to say the least, appalled. This was the normal way of thinking across the move, however, as I had seen. Making the 'clergy' a special group always brings forth such a false distinction.

The Second Year – Middle School

An eighth grade English teaching spot had opened up at the C.E. King Middle School, just down the street from the high school. The school administration asked me if I would like to fill that spot, which I agreed to readily. The truth is, I like teaching eighth graders the most.

And so my second school year with Sheldon ISD was at the Middle School. Again, I had around 140 students, over six class periods and all eighth graders. I taught the exact same thing, then, six times in a day. This was nice in that it was much less prep work. I liked my students, and they liked me as well, mostly because I enjoyed and respected them, but also because I was the only teacher whom they ever had who apologized to them when I was wrong.

I taught them reading and writing. I read two books to them through the course of the year, *Holes* in the fall and *Bud not Buddy* in the Spring. Both are great choices for teaching literature. I do not remember the name of the principal that year, but my oversight was Mr. Applegate, one of the assistant principals. It was Mr. Applegate who observed my teaching that spring, gave me a high mark and approved me for a second two-year contract at the end of that school year.

One amusing anecdote from this year was that I was standing in front of my classroom door as the next group of students were coming to class, chatting with a neighboring teacher, who was one of the coaches. Just as the bell started to ring, a larger young man, who was on the sports team, came running around the corner, dropped to his side and slid into the classroom like sliding into home plate. The coach said, very sternly. "Act your age." This amused me tremendously, because, you see, that twelve-year-old boy was most definitely "acting his age," something I always enjoyed.

For some reason, I had not connected much at a personal level with my students during the first year at the high school. I did connect with many at the Middle School, however. One was a young girl, of a similar brightness and personality as Kimberley Stevens at Blueberry, who suffered much in an inadequate home situation. Not long into the year she shared with me that she was hoping to find a non-abusive place to live.

This need sparked something in my heart, and so Maureen and I signed up for the foster parent training program at Depelchin Children's Center along Memorial Drive. We attended all of their training sessions and fulfilled all the requirements to be eligible for taking in foster children. In the training, however, it became clear to me that the state was an inflexible tyrant and had no thought of mercy or consideration. When we were told to discuss around the table why "spanking" a child was child abuse, I pointed out that when the same child turns 17, if that boy disobeys the state, they will punish him in horror and without care for years. It's called hypocrisy. A small amount of pain for disobedience now is far better than the shattering pain without mercy inflicted when one disobeys the excesses of the state. (For the record, I would never consider spanking any child not our own.)

Other similar things concerning the inflexible nature of the state were said, however, enough to give me pause. And so, as we considered the final step, having our home inspected for compliance with state requirements, I balked. We would have been required to change many things that were part of our own children's growing up years. We were more than willing to take needy children into our home and hearts, but to allow the state to have jurisdiction over our home – Maureen and I both said no.

Nonetheless, going together to the full training to be foster parents, even though we did not take it to completion, was a rich experience Maureen and I shared together.

In January of 2004, because I was a teacher in the middle school, we enrolled Kyle there for the second half of his seventh-grade year. I did not teach seventh graders, who were on the other side of the building, so I did not see him often, but he had good teachers. In fact, when he told his English teacher, Miss Carroll, that he had come from Maple,

Texas, she told him that she was from Maple as well. In fact, she was Marvin McCaul's niece. Her husband was also a teacher and coach in the school, and both looked out for Kyle. Kyle also signed onto the theater program at the school and we attended his performance in the plays.

Continuing with Home & Family

In August of 2003, Lois came down again to celebrate Kyle and Katrina's birthdays. We had a big party in the back yard. The Rideau and Dibrell children were all there. In fact, our children spent much time at the Rideaus, and their children spent much time at our home, all the years of their growing up. Below is a picture of our children at Christmas of 2003, in front of the faux fireplace and brick wall of our living room.

After a year of teaching Johanna piano, Bethany Millican went on to college, and so Bethany's mother, Chris Millican, became Johanna's teacher. We enrolled Katrina with Chris as well. In fact, Claude and Roberta helped us to pay for a nice little regular piano for the girls which we placed in our living room.

With this continued connection with the Millicans, we visited the Baptist Church a number of times. It was a good church, and all there knew and loved the Lord; Mr. Millican was the praise pastor. We took the children there for their Vacation Bible School, and Kyle also became friends with Samuel Millican, around his same age. In fact, Kyle often attended the Baptist Church functions by himself, just to be a part. It was only gradually, however, that he noticed a little girl growing up in that church, by the name of Shelbie Stephens.

I continued working on the house. I completed the doors and drawer fronts for the kitchen and library and began a remodel of the bathrooms. I got up into the attic and sprayed insulation all through it, thus lowering our air conditioning costs considerably.

The garden improved somewhat across the seasons, and it continued to be a main feature of our family life. In Houston, we gardened three seasons, spring, summer, and fall, with fall being the most productive. Even in the slightly cold months of December and January, we were preparing for the spring gardens. Houston winters, that is, days experiencing slight freezing, last around two or three days, once or twice each year.

The care-giving business Maureen was working for closed out in early 2004, and so Maureen was able to switch her working agreement directly over to Miss Ruth and her daughter, Sandra Wilson. Starting in May of 2004, Sandra Wilson asked Maureen to take the night shift, and thus she had a bed in which to sleep and got up through the night only when needed. Maureen took care of Miss Ruth for several years, and enjoyed working for her and her daughter. Because Maureen was at home during the days, needing only a nap in the afternoon, she continued homeschooling the children, slightly easier with Kyle no longer at home.

To be honest with you, I know of nothing more valuable to me in life than our times together as a family, going to different places and experiences together in our comfortable green van.

Putting Things into Place

As I conclude this two-year portion of my life story, I realize that it was almost entirely a good time, a time of healing and refreshing, a time for the re-awakening of the agony of Desire inside of me to know the living God and to know the meaning of His Salvation. The key that would unlock all that for me was still missing, however, and so from my point of view, I was still very much groping in the dark.

"Thank you so much, Father, for the goodness of this time, for our new home here in Houston, and for our family life together. Thank you for the completion of this season of healing and for that time of the re-awakening of desire in spite of the agony about to come through which it would be birthed."

However, in July of 2004, the pastor at the Assembly of God church in the Heights included in his sermon a rant against the Iraqi people, accusing them of being evil because they had met "our kind love and our true American desire to help" with violence.

The thing is, I was reading the personal accounts of Iraqis who had welcomed the Americans but had soon come to know the horror into which their country was thrown. I don't know about you, but when I hear such lying from a pastor, such desire to wrap an ignorance of reality around one's self in order to maintain blindness towards the wicked violence of the criminals who run the American state, it's always Solomon's words that come front and center to me.

"Do not consent to run with those who shed innocent blood…"

Ignorance of fact is no excuse. Many who give their agreement to the slaughter of thousands of innocent people and the ruin of millions of lives will find their time of giving an account to be far more distressing and confined than they expect. The forgiveness of God comes first, most certainly, but forgiveness cannot ever remove justice.

Anyhow, the moral of the story is – that was our last service in that church.

Nonetheless, "I thank You, Father, even for the experiences of church in this world that were proving inadequate for the cry of my heart to know You. There is no question that Your answers come only in response to the great agony of THIRST that You also place inside our hearts.

"I bless all those in the Fellowship of the Nations and in the Assembly of God Church in the Heights with whom we interacted. Fill them, Lord Jesus, with the knowledge of Your glory and Your tender compassion towards them."

39. Re-Awakening of Desire

Before – 2004 – After

Re-awakening to the Vision

In spite of all the other stuff going on in our lives, don't ever think that I left off seeking to know the Lord and to understand what I was missing in my knowledge of the gospel. The bigger changes will come in the next chapter, but by 2004, my season of healing with John Eldredge had come to its completion.

Although we continued in church attendance, especially for the sake of the children, it had become clear to me again, that the church in this world was simply not offering what I required from God.

And so I continued to write, and I continued with my *Times of Refreshing* letters, the second volume. I do have all twelve of the issues of this second volume in my computer. The first is dated April 5, 2004 and the twelfth is dated September 5, 2006, so these letters covered a span of two years. The second and third letters are dated May and June, while the fourth was not until August 5.

I mailed these to an address list that included some who had subscribed originally to *Times of Refreshing* and to which I added some in the homeschool group as well as some others. I may have sent out forty or fifty such letters each time.

The larger article in the April issue of *Times of Refreshing* begins with the following statement. ~~~ "God has laid upon me the necessity of sharing with others what He has taught me over the years. I find myself faced with the accountability of 'to whom God has given much, much shall be required.'" The article is an attempt to place what I later on called the second, third, and fourth most important verses of the Bible, filled with all of God, rivers of Spirit flowing out, and casting down all accusation, upon the certainty of Isaiah 55, that God will accomplish all that His word means in our lives on this earth. ~~~

Then the second article is "Thirst." I placed that into my book, *The Great Story of God, with* very little change in the wording. When I look through it to

quote an important line, however, I want to bring in most everything. And so I would suggest you read it in order to understand the desperate cry of my heart continuing in the spring of 2004.

Here is one line. ~~~ "All the years I have walked with God a question has haunted me, pursued me, found me out every time I managed to build a 'safe' place for myself. Is God doing something in the earth and I am not a part of it? To be honest with you, I can think of nothing more horrifying." ~~~

The May issue was all about knowing a Spirit word, of our need for the Holy Spirit to show us what God means by what He says – **"The Spirit gives life."** The June issue continues with the importance of a Spirit revelation and the levels of the anointing in the calling of God. In this issue I introduce to my new readers the concept of the Feast of Tabernacles, that God has so much more for His people.

My purpose in this bit is to show the deep agony of heart that was re-awakening in me, that I would not be found anywhere else but inside of God and inside what He is doing upon the earth.

Our Family Life

Before recounting the monumental and disastrous fall semester of 2004, I want to share about our transition of church fellowships in the summer of 2004, giving a further picture of our home and family life through this time. I also want to outline some major changes in my thinking that came through this year.

First, in June, Kyle, who was twelve going on thirteen, had the opportunity to visit his grandparents, Claude and Roberta Mack, at the Ridge in Bowens Mill. We dropped Kyle off at the airport and he flew to Jacksonville by himself where his grandpa picked him up. He enjoyed a good time with them before returning home the same way. Although we had left the move fellowship, we still wanted our children to have some continuing experience of community and of the anointing of God that is simply not found elsewhere.

The pace of remodeling work on our house was slowing down. I began re-building the bathrooms. We painted the dining and living rooms. I did not record an exact schedule of what we did when, however.

I had noticed a "Church on the Rock" on the by-pass going into Baytown. We had visited a similar church in Lubbock and knew it to be a good Spirit-filled fellowship. Awhile after we stopped going to the Assembly of God in the Heights, we attended the Baytown Church on the Rock and liked it. The pastor was Tommy Meekins and his wife, Barbara. Their son, Jeremy, led the praise. Jeremy Meekins was a wonderful praise leader, and this was the first time in the Houston area that we could freely worship God in the songs that were sung. Jeremy was slow and contemplative and preferred songs of worship.

The children, especially, fitted right in, and the brethren there welcomed our children, who were bright and inventive and who loved the Lord. This was not a large church, maybe 50 to 75 members. We would attend here for more than a year. In the end, however, we found little depth there, and thus this final "church" experience for us through this part of our time in Houston proved empty as well.

Great Changes of Understanding

I know that much of what I am sharing in this section took place across the span of 2004, just not when. In fact, now that I know Father-with-me, I understand better the causes of changes inside of me. I realize now that writing the article "Thirst" through March of 2004 opened thirst back up inside of me. I had separated myself from the word of the revelation of Jesus Christ, not by cutting it off, but by simply placing it on a shelf until the Lord brought, as I understand it now, the necessary healing. By this point, my time reading John Eldredge had completed its good work in me.

The result was that through these months of mid-2004, the seed God had planted in my heart through Sam Fife slowly re-awakened inside of me with deep groanings. But I had separated myself from the present teaching of the move and would not look in that direction. I spent time searching on the Internet such terms as "sons of God," "manifestation of sons," "feast of tabernacles," and so on, hop-

ing to find people who taught the same word that filled the cry of my own heart.

I want to include some pieces that I wrote through the early months of 2004 that display what I mean. First, I wrote this.

❧

I would like to share briefly what God is speaking to me at this present time and what He is presenting to me. I am in an unusual place, by God's design, I am convinced. For twenty-one years I lived by sitting under the anointed preaching of the Word. That Word was my life. For six years, now, I have been waiting on God to give me the things that I knew were missing in my life. That is not completely true, because these last six years I have also relaxed. I know that I needed to relax for God to heal my heart, but I also know that the anointing that I long for comes through intense commitment.

I find that the Word that I long to sit under once again is not available to me at the present time. Some might say, "Well, you need to go here, or, you need to go there." I have done that, and what I know I need to live is not there, including the move. God has to put me into this kind of a place before He can begin to convince me that I need to be strong and of good courage, that I need to be convinced of Him as David was, that I need to place myself before Him until He brings out of me the word that I know I need, and not only I, but God's people as well.

❧

Then, here are some excerpts from a piece I wrote titled "Why Return to Christian Community." I include a fair bit, because I need you to see my heart's cry through these in-between years.

❧

Am I a people person? Yes and no. Yes, in my propensity to find life paths that are filled with people. At present, I spend my days interacting with 140 teenage kids. Before I was married, I was driven, almost, to seek out people, to be with people, to establish relationships with people. I enjoy solitude as well, though. I realize now that my inclination to spend my evenings with people, whether partying before I was converted, or fellowship and Bible study after, was driven by a deep loneliness, a loneliness that did not abate until I married Maureen. An amazing thing happened, though, when my wife walked down the aisle; the loneliness vanished and does not exist until I have spent more than one night and day without her.

But the present. Why am I no longer driven to seek out relationships with other people like I once was? Partly because I am fully content and without loneliness in my own home and partly because of the pain I have received over recent years from such seeking of relationships. But when I look at the "friendships" that have not worked out in recent years, I realize that there was no possible compatibility of heart between them and me. Unless two hearts are centered on the same vision, they can share no meaningful relationship.

But am I a people person? There is much evidence to argue that I am not. I no longer seek out other relationships. I have always been ready to go right after a formal event, like a service, is over. I hate to sit and chitchat. The other day my colleagues at school (all women) were standing in a circle on duty, chitchatting. My mind immediately closed it out and I was somewhere else. I have always been like that. I am not comfortable, at all, in informal social gatherings, I never have been. A formal social gathering, where there is a focus and a purpose – say a speaker, I love to be a part of, with intensity. But the moment it switches from formal to informal, I am gone.

When I am in large gatherings, especially the preaching of the word, a deep angst, an exquisite agony creeps into my heart. It is not demonic, though sometimes the anointing is greater. The angst is most strong when the word has penetrated my heart most deeply, and I have to get by myself before God. I cannot imagine engaging in the empty talk so many of God's people are able to do after hearing such a word.

My greatest lack in relationships is my unreasonable fear of confronting people with what I feel about something, especially those in authority when I am in disagreement with them. The only time when I do not have that fear is when I clearly have the position of leadership and I have a clear purpose. In the past, I would be abrasive in that role, but I believe that is gone. I have 140 eighth grade public school students with whom I interact daily to prove or disprove anything in that.

I am definitely not a loner, and I most clearly have a heart for other people. I refuse the definition that because I do not and will never connect with

idle talk and because I feel very out of place in informal social gatherings and will always do so, that I am therefore not eligible to enter a calling that includes constant heart to heart relationships with people. And be careful in judging personality types. What seems to some to be weakness, could be the very quality necessary to carry the day in the path God has set before an individual.

[Note: At this point in my life, I had neither heard of nor considered Asperger's.]

I know Christian community. I have lived in six separate communities over a total of eighteen years and have spent significant time visiting many others. I have moved in many different aspects throughout the heart of community, including leadership. I spent most of my time working within the community; I went out to work very little. I know how Christian community works. I know its strengths and weaknesses, its ups and downs. I made a careful and deliberate decision to separate myself from the communities of the move, and looking back now, I realize that it was just in time. I was closer to being spiritually comatose than I knew. It has taken God six years since to rescue me and to heal my heart.

But now that I find myself restored and whole inside, I come back, once again to the reasons I lived in community in the first place. And that is what this paper is about.

The first and foremost reason for me to desire a return to community, in fact, the overriding reason, that alone is sufficient to bring a return is this. There is a presence of God upon community that does not exist elsewhere. People go to church, God moves, and they think it is exciting, and so it is, but in a godly, faith-filled Christian community, the continual presence of God and of the anointing upon the service and upon individuals is far, far beyond. From the beginning I have known that. I have left communities several times, broken, hurting, and confused, but I have always gotten up again and returned. Why? Simply this. Enduring all the discomfort of community in the midst of the presence of God was far preferable to me than the ease and comfort of life apart from community, but with only the tiny, occasional trickle of His presence, if that at all.

I miss His presence so badly I could weep. When we visited the little community north of Houston

[Note: I will include this experience in just a bit], yes, there were oddities, yes, we instantly reacted to the less pleasant aspects of immature Christians and "group expectations" in community. But, oh, when we gathered together to worship and seek God, the river of His presence, the joy and light on the faces of all, the freedom of worship and of sitting under anointed word, was so, so wonderful.

I would rather know the river of His presence, and I say that, in spite of the present weariness of my body.

There are other reasons for considering a return to community. A second is our own needs, physically and spiritually. In order to have the land and life we want we will have to share it with others, it will come no other way. Sitting and hoping for an unexpected jackpot will not bring it. Really hard times are coming, we need neighbors to whom we are connected both physically and spiritually. We are walking through a battleground; we need fellow soldiers walking along side of us. This is a real and pressing need, a need that gets only lip agreement from others, but nothing more, apart from committed community.

A third reason is my own heart's ambition. The word that is in me and the calling to ministry I have on my life can find true expression only from community. The word I would preach must both lead to community and flow from community. That may not make sense, but I know it is true. Apart from community as a base, the ministry I carry as a burning desire in my heart, will never come to fulfillment, it will remain forever, only a "what if," hollow and empty.

A fourth reason is our children being part of a larger story. We left community partly for our children's sake, that is true. But I have no intention of ever re-entering move communities. I will share later what kind of community is in my heart, certainly a community that will be significantly different than what we have known. When we talk about our children, let's hold an "ideal" community in our minds, whatever that is. When I see the tiny, little lives lived by the kids I teach in the public school, I am aghast. I want my children to know a larger picture, to understand and be a part of the great story of God. To be a part of something radically different from the shallowness and banality of this world. I want them to experience so many different parts of

life, things they only get to read about now, farming, animals, missions, ministry to others, but more than anything else, anointed praise. I want them to know the value of land, the beauty of sloping hills and streams of water. I want them to know the wildness of the country. I hate the confinement of city life.

A fifth reason is me, who I am, being able to devote my entire life to what I believe in. Oh, my sweet wife, in all of these things, I have not included you, but then, you have a nature that builds community wherever you go. Let me, in this paragraph, finish about myself. I am a builder, a designer, a dreamer, a farmer, a teacher. I have for so long given my strength to things I do not believe in. Every day in the public school, I see good reason that the whole thing be abolished. Yet, I must give my support to it, because that is the only way I can get my living. It is endlessly debilitating to devote one's self to something entirely contrary to one's heart. (Not that I am not pleased to, by it, bring home what my family needs to survive.) My vision for community would engage all of me in every way. My deepest desire is to devote my life to teaching the Word to people who long to grow in the grace of God.

❧

Note: I did not send the above piece to anyone.

Bill Johnson & the Spirit Out-Poured

I have noticed a marked difference between those who "left the move" after the deliverance times with Jane Miller and those who left before. I will share a brief experience with one who "left before" in the next chapter. There is often a bitterness expressed from them.

Those who left after the out-pouring of the Spirit through Sister Jane were not "leaving," but rather, going on to know the Lord. Many of these brethren, including Sue Sampson, Mozelle Clarke, and Janet Randall, who had been my teachers at Blueberry, gravitated towards the ministry of Bill Johnson of Bethel Church in Redding, California. Many visited his church and, even if they lived across the country, attended his conferences and listened to his good teaching.

But some did move to Redding to be part of his church and school of ministry. My niece, April, with her husband, Ben, moved there and April attended and graduated from the Bethel School of Ministry. Katie Bracken moved there, and eventually, Michael and Deborah Kuntz.

Bill Johnson had gone to Toronto during the out-pouring of the Spirit there in the 1990's, as had Dennis Cline. That experience changed his ministry, and through him affected many who continued seeking God in the Spirit even as they "left the move."

When I first arrived in Houston, before Maureen and the children came, I had seen a flyer advertising a "Holy Spirit revival" at a church called Victory Christian Center in northwest Houston, with Tony Krishack, pastor. I attended and found the same type of experience that had been known as "the Toronto blessing." It was a wonderful service, and I received much from the Lord. We visited there a few times after as a family, but it was a bit too far for regular attendance.

At the same time, it seems that in those realms, the Spirit is an end in itself. While that's wondrous, without a word of the revelation of Jesus Christ, such a continual experience cannot satisfy me. And yes, there was much wondrous laughter in the service, as there ought to be among those who rejoice in the joy of their salvation.

Through 2004, I read Bill Johnson's book, *When Heaven Invades Earth*, and was much blessed by it. I knew it contained a part of what I needed in order to be a part of the fullness of Christ. Maureen and I listened to some of his teachings on tape.

Then there was a conference put on at the Humble Civic Center called something like "The Holy Spirit and Fire." We attended during this time period, primarily because Bill Johnson was in attendance, and we wanted to hear his word. It was a strange event for us. Bill Johnson shared early on, and that was entirely of the Lord. But this was a conference put on by others to which he had been invited.

Todd Bentley spoke. Half of what he said went in one ear and out the other. Maureen and I found nothing "wrong," but not much that was meaningful, either. At the same time, I just could not connect with the praise. It all sounded good, but there was not a flow into which my spirit could rejoice. Then someone else got up to share; I have no idea who. Immediately, I knew that something was wrong. I motioned to my family; we got up and quietly went out the door. It is not my place to say that Jesus was not speaking to different ones according to His purposes in their lives; it's just that I cannot remain

inside something contrary to my own spirit.

In fact, Maureen went again with Kyle, but also got up quietly and left for the same reason.

I share this experience, not to place Bill Johnson with things "not right," but actually to distinguish that, inside the realms of the out-poured Holy Spirit, as in all realms, there is much that is good, but always some that is not right.

Sons of God Community

In my Internet search, I found a Christian Community called "Sons of God Christian Community" about halfway to Dallas, near Crockett, Texas. I communicated with the brother who oversaw that community, and we went up for a visit on a Sunday. The first time was probably in early 2004.

This was a very interesting experience for me, but not so much for Maureen. We attended the service, shared meals with the community in their dining hall, and visited in the home of the lead ministry. I spent most of my time there visiting with the head elder, while Maureen conversed with some of the sisters who were not "ministry." That's what gave us two very different perspectives, though I was not ignorant of what she was seeing. I saw and enjoyed the community side of things; whereas Maureen saw the legalism under which the sisters lived.

They were a Spirit-filled group with a partial understanding of the revelation of Jesus Christ. I was freely invited to share in their service. I had long talks with the lead ministry (I do not remember his name and their website is gone), and we found much common ground of understanding.

Then we went up again in the fall of 2004. I know it was then because I remember what I shared, things I was also writing in *Times of Refreshing*. We went up on a Saturday, planning to spend the night. We had a wondrous praise time, everyone dancing in a circle in the joy of the Lord. Again, in spite of a measure of legalism, there is an anointing found resting upon life together that is simply not known elsewhere. [This is what I referenced in the piece above.]

I was hoping to speak in the morning service, but the brother spoke a long time, a word very similar to Buddy Cobb's. I got up to share anyhow, because I felt that my word was important, "The Treasure of the Heart," which I had written in July. I saw a longing for the grace of God on the faces of many while I shared. And some came up to me afterward expressing how much it meant to them. I saw such a wistful longing in their eyes. We stayed for most of the day, visiting, before returning home to Houston.

After that, Maureen insisted that we were not visiting there anymore. My love of leaping into adventure had to be tempered by the goodness of having a wife and children who would have to make such leaps with me.

Trying to Start a Fellowship

I wrote a letter to different families in our home school group, including the Rideau's, expressing my desire for a fellowship of Christ. We invited different ones to our home for times of sharing. No such connection ever came to me from them, however. I do not have the gift of drawing people into something.

Here is a description of the fellowship I was seeking. I believe I sent this out in my *Times of Refreshing* mailings.

༅

The Fellowship of Jesus
A Different Approach to Church

The Fellowship of Jesus will be a group of simple-hearted Christians who would rather be a part of what Jesus is doing than anything else in this world.

Our Mission will be:
- To so give ourselves to Jesus and to His Spirit that He can change us into His image and mold us together as one body that He might triumph through us over His enemies.
- To present everyone who belongs to Jesus faultless before the Presence of His glory with exceeding joy.

We Believe:
- God will do what He says; He will fulfill His word in this earth – and in us.
- God is doing something awesome in the earth, and He wants us to be a part of it.
- God is inviting us into what He is doing, and His invitation requires of us commitment and a forsaking of every lesser destination.

We Preach:
- A vision of the unveiling of Jesus Christ and the resurrection from the dead.

- How God is preparing us as His sons and changing us into the image of Christ.
- What it means to overcome the accuser for one another.
- What it means to love one another in the glory of Christian community.
- The necessity of extended worship and the presence of God upon His people.
- The great story of God as it comes to its climax and our role in that story.
- The coming destruction of the world system and the total defeat of our enemies.
- That the power of God is greater than the weakness of man.
- That your heart is the precious treasure and the very throne of Almighty God.

At The Fellowship of Jesus, you will hear a word that will challenge you, shock you, stir you, lift you up out of your American lifestyle, and birth in you a vision of the revelation of Jesus Christ.

You are welcome if you are:
- Thirsty and hungry.
- Longing for the glory of God.
- Determined not to be left out of what Jesus is doing for anything in this world.

༅

The cry of my heart at this time is clear, but I was never able to make anything real happen. At the same time, you can see the seemingly slight adjustment that is coming into how I understand what it means to be "like Jesus."

Preston Eby & Reconciliation

In my search on the Internet for the word I carried in my heart, I found that word, over and over, being taught at various levels of understanding by anointed ministries in the Church.

But I had a big problem, for all of these brethren teaching the vision of my heart, planted in me through Brother Sam, were inside the "ultimate reconciliation" arena. The primary person whose website I found was Preston Eby. And most of them I found on Gary Sigler's website – *Kingdom Resources*.

Now, I had known that Preston Eby and Sam Fife had ministered together in the 1960's, after which they parted ways. And even though neither mentions the other by name, I am fully aware that they are speaking of each other when they point out what they "disagree with." Preston Eby believed in ultimate reconciliation and Sam Fife did not. Sam Fife preached a structured order for the fellowships, and Preston Eby disagreed with such a thing.

Other than those two things, however, Preston Eby and Sam Fife teach the same thing. To know what Sam Fife taught, minus the sectarianism, then read Preston Eby, minus the ultimate reconciliation.

Eternal damnation was not preached in the move. It was assumed, yes, but only as an unimportant side issue. Brother Buddy taught that God was well able to save, even after death.

But I had a problem. My problem was that I will not know anything that God does not say in the Bible, and I will hold to all that God speaks in the gospel as He speaks it and as He means it.

Nonetheless, I am always willing to hear any presentation of "what the Bible says." I always judge carefully against what I know God says, and I always search it out in Scripture until I know a thing to be true or not. So-called "heresy" has never bothered me, especially when I hear orthodox preachers saying all sorts of non-Biblical things, and when I see BIG things in my New Testament that nobody includes.

Among all those teaching of the same vision of the revelation of Jesus Christ through us, His Church, I carefully chose Dr. Stephen Jones as the one whose books I would order and study. I did that through these months. I spent much time in "Creation Jubilee" as well as my Bible. I also studied Preston Eby and others on-line. I bought other books as well, including *The Jerome Conspiracy*.

Here's the thing. I don't care what "Christianity" says or "believes" about anything. I care only about what God says in the Bible, and I have found the two to be opposed so many times.

I studied what was taught carefully, and I studied my Bible even more carefully. At the end of that study, I agreed with Stephen Jones and Preston Eby, that the Bible does NOT teach unending damnation in torment.

Now, this is an account of my life and the word I share, not a "doctrinal study." Some might say, "Well I believe, end of discussion." Such a claim is absurd. You and I are quite incapable of creating what is not and de-creating what is, no matter how hard our "believing" forehead might be.

And so, if you believe otherwise, then I chal-lenge you with that statement – the Bible does NOT teach eternal damnation, but rather, a bounded time of purifying in judgment. Either my words are true or not. Only the Bible itself will show you; definitely not some preacher. And in searching out such a thing, it is always good to read from both sides. The true will always show itself to those who are actually seeking Him.

The simple fact is that my decision was based on one negative and one positive. The negative is that the word "eternal" has no place in our Bibles. The Greek word is *aeon*, meaning, an age of time. It was Jerome who stuck "eternal" into the Latin Bible because of his fascination with pagan torment in fire. No one in the first two hundred years of church history knew anything about such a thing as "hell-fire." It came in only through the Latin theologians.

The positive is Paul's gospel, which, according to Paul, stands above everything else found in the Bible. Paul's gospel alone enables us to understand the very cryptic things written in John's vision, a vision that no one in the first two generations of the Christian Church knew anything about. And Paul taught very clearly what God's end game is – all restored back to Father – God all inside of all. In the end, the entire doctrine of eternal hellfire is based on one idiom no one can translate accurately, *aionos aionos*, in John's hard to understand vision – and on nothing else.

I will go no further, except to say that, while this new understanding would never become the focus of what I teach, it did alter my understanding of God. I have no interest in knowing what God does not mean, and every interest in knowing what He does mean.

For the first time in my life, the possibility that God does NOT know evil could begin to shape my knowledge of the Father.

More Times of Refreshing

The August 5 issue of *Times of Refreshing* was on the treasure of the heart, that your heart is good, and on glory versus shame, that God speaks well of us. The September 5 and November 5 issues were about the Feast of Tabernacles, which you have read, for they became Chapter 2, Applying the Feasts, in my book, *The Feast of Tabernacles*.

I did not send out the next issue until March 5, and it's on the same topic, God filling His House, the Church, with His presence and glory. I did not write another issue, then, until December of 2005, so I will include my concern in that issue in the next chapter.

Natural Understanding

Then, also through 2004, two elements of natural understanding came into my picture.

Soon after I was on the Internet in our townhouse in Fort St. John, I came across a website by David Talbot, a disciple of Immanuel Velikovsky, who was attempting to make Velikovsky's ideas more current. His website was about the planet Saturn as it was before the flood of Noah. That website eventually disappeared. Then, in 2004, I saw a link to a "Velikovsky" website on a news page I frequented. I followed that link and so was introduced to www.thunderbolts.info, shortly after it was created.

What had happened was that David Talbot met a man named Wallace Thornhill, who was a student of the great electrical universe theorists of the twentieth century, including Kristian Birkeland and Hannes Alfven. As Talbot and Thornhill conversed, they discovered that they were studying the same thing. And thus the thunderbolts website was born.

Almost every weekday, five times a week, the Thunderbolts website posts a new article titled "The Picture of the Day." From 2004 until now, I have read most of them, early in the morning.

I never liked astronomy in school or as any personal interest, but the electrical theory of the universe fascinated me. I do not accept ideas, however, that are not proven out by much demonstration of evidence. And so I set myself to know the evidence of an electrical universe. I bought the books and studied the website until I was fully assured that it is reality. When I mention it in my teaching, I am well-versed in what I am sharing.

Then, in December of 2004 was the massive earthquake just off of Thailand, and the tidal wave that destroyed so many. In searching out the reality of earthquakes, I found this website – https://ds.iris.edu/seismon/index.phtml. You see, I have been swayed in the past by grandiose claims of the end times, including the claim, on a regular basis, that "earthquakes are increasing."

Once I found the seismic monitor, I determined that I would know the facts. And so, from December of 2004 until this morning, I have looked at the earthquake map nearly every day. I have learned that earthquakes are not "increasing." What happens is that there is a rhythm. For a while, earthquakes are small and infrequent, then for awhile they reverberate around the ring of fire. Then they are quiet again. The claims that "earthquakes are increasing" happen only on the upswing. You never hear anything from these guys when earthquakes are low.

The pattern that is happening here is that by my forties, I was done with believing hype, whether Bible hype or science hype or world events hype or "God bless America" hype, or any other hype. I need facts and evidence. I need things that can be proven or disproven, demonstrated either true or false. And that very much includes "what the Bible says."

Placing Jesus Upon

I know that I repeat myself, but as I am writing these accounts, the knowing of the straight arrow of the word through the days of my life is so very important to me. I could not live with the imagination that any part of my life was not found inside of God and inside of His determination through me.

"Thank you, Lord Jesus, that you have always kept my heart close inside of Yours. Thank you that You have never left me alone, regardless of all my ins and outs. Thank you, that the very moment I was healed enough, You placed in me again that awakening of great thirst to know You and through You, the Father."

"Thank you, Lord Jesus, that You were so faithfully preparing my heart for that moment when the heavens open wide to me and You become the very fabric of my life."

Now, I can begin the next chapter with the most disastrous semester in my teaching experience.

40. Into the Furnace

August 2004 - July 2006

The Fall Semester of 2004

I had leaped out of the "frying pan" of the move only to now find myself in the "furnace" of a godless educational system. Yet I was never outside of God's hand and heart. God was taking me straight to what He knew was coming towards me two years later, and I needed to be ready, that is, I needed to be more desperate than I knew was possible.

The 2004 school year began with great promise and excitement for me. We had a new principal at the junior high, named Donna Ulrich, who was one of the best principals I have been privileged to work under. From her came a sense of excitement and energy for the new year. I would be teaching eighth-grade English, again, but this time, my room was in the upstairs with all the other English teachers.

I had taught the whole year's curriculum in the prior year, so this was a first for me, that I would teach what I had already taught, which meant that I could make good improvements without having to "wing it," like I usually do.

I prepared for classes, and was excited that I knew what I was doing. At the same time, I was asked to mentor, just a bit, a first-year teacher who had her room next to mine. School started and the first couple of weeks were awesome. (I taught regular English and Kyle was in AP English continuing with Miss Carol.)

Then, before the end of the second week, I saw a notice on the board outside the school office, asking for anyone who had a Texas administrators license and who was interested to apply for a new administrative position in overseeing the creation of a new disciplinary unit for Sheldon ISD, called DAEP, that is, Disciplinary Alternate Education Program. This possibility caught my breath, and I went straight to Miss Donna with it. (In the south, all women teachers are called "Miss," regardless.) She encouraged me to apply.

And so I did, and in a short time learned that I had received the post. Suddenly, my eighth-grade classroom was no longer my job, now I was engaged with something new and exciting. In fact, I was an administrator with Sheldon ISD.

There are two types of "disciplined" students, and when I say "disciplined," I mean those who have done something that requires more than detention after school. The first type is those who have violated school regulations to such an extent that the administration feels they need such discipline. And the second type is those who have broken the law, but not enough to be sent away to juvenile prison. This second type is in the disciplinary unit under the supervision of a judge.

Up until this fall of 2004, Sheldon ISD had sent its disciplinary students to the High Point facility, just down the street from our home. They had to pay for this, however, at a much higher cost than what any student brings in from the state. The Sheldon school board had decided to attempt an in-district disciplinary unit that would save the district money.

Most of the students in the new disciplinary unit came from the high school, but there were a few from the middle school as well. The facilities for the unit were an unused section of the middle school jutting out into the parking lot from the special education area.

When I look on Google maps, I see that, after building a brand new high school, Sheldon ISD turned the high school where I taught into a junior high and sold the middle school where I taught to the Methodist Church. Nonetheless, the picture from the street is still when it was a school building, so here it is.

The DAEP unit itself had an outside door as access, but the students came in through the side entrance. In order to keep them separate from the regular school kids, however, the DAEP was held in the late afternoon – evening. The hall through the side entrance connected with a hallway angling in from the main hall in the school. You then went past a small office, through double doors into a larger room that was, in fact, a complex of rooms all as one unit. The larger center room could hold maybe twenty students in desks. On either side were two small rooms, four in all. On the outer wall, next to the DAEP entrance were bathrooms for the unit.

My job was not to teach, but to oversee and administer. Each student was focused on their own laid-out work in front of them. As time went on, we were able to place quite a few on computerized courses. Other teachers from the high school were paid extra to come in the evenings to work with the individual students; there was never any group teaching.

A policeman was assigned to the DAEP as his full workload. Sadly, I do not remember his name, but I worked with him all the time through this semester. He was a great choice because he was honest and true and shared my care for the kids. I will call him, "Terry" because I want to regard him as a person. He was a short, but well-muscled man, similar to Charlie Jones at the Ridge in a number of ways. At no point did I deal with the students without Constable Terry hovering in the background.

Let me describe my students in the disciplinary unit, most of whom had broken the law, and many of whom struggled to cope inside a system that they could not comprehend or escape from.

I will start with the most difficult, the only student I taught in the public school that I would call "irredeemable" in the present time. He was Hispanic, which was unusual, because most Hispanic boys are easy going and congenial. He was a bit large and muscular. His crime was dealing drugs. His mother worked in the school cafeteria and he would often beat her. When he first came in front of me, Constable Terry was immediately behind him. I challenged him and saw like a serpent slither across his face and body with all hostility against me. I did not challenge him again, because doing so was pointless. When he acted up, which was often, I simply suspended him and sent him home. That meant he would be hauled before the judge and his mother fined another $500. He simply did not care.

I had a young black man, a twelfth grader, whom I liked very much. His problem was that his stress level was very low, and he would turn violent easily.

I had no problem working with him, but I had to deal with his mother more than once. She went into attack mode any time any teacher or policeman attempted to bring correction in the young man's life. The anointing and grace of God helped me there more than once.

I had a ninth-grade Hispanic boy who was likely the biggest pain-in-the-rear of any student I have taught. He was defiant and disrespectful just all the time. I would have classed him as "beyond the pale" as well, EXCEPT – I had him in my classroom the next year, and I saw a broken hurting boy who did not know how to survive in a world that always seemed to be violently against him. I hope that I brought some care into his life, but that's for later in this chapter.

I had a young man from the middle school, a special ed kid, who was happy-go-lucky and no harm to anyone. He did like to fantasize and to play tricks on his teachers, however. One day he had a bunch of stuff crammed into a jar, nothing of consequence. But he told his teacher he had made a "bomb." Sanity left the public school system after 9/11, however, and so this was treated as a great "crime."

There were a couple of girls who had stolen. The list goes on; I don't remember all. I will share a couple more in the next section, however.

Because my job was in the evening, I had the mornings at home, which was awesome. I was able to do more writing, but I also worked on my gardens and some on the house. And I was at home for the children's home school. Because my job was in the evening, however, my mind did not function as well on the job. I had no problem whatsoever working with the students, but my mental capacity to tackle instructional writing and development was limited.

Of the two little rooms on the far side of the unit, one was my office and the other served as an overflow room for the computers when we had more students. On the side nearer the two entrances, Constable Terry had his office, and the other room was for storage. Because I did not "teach," I spent a fair bit of my time in my office, with the door open. I was always fully aware of the students, however, and walked out among them regularly, as did Constable Terry. In fact, we worked very well together, in full harmony, through this entire semester.

But because my mind diminishes in the evening, I did spend much of my non-engaged time on the Internet reading world news, which is my wont. I suspected, though I don't know for sure, that all Internet usage on school computers is monitored. I can't not read, though, and I do not waste my time on officially "approved" websites. Nonetheless, this was a failing on my part, one that may have struck against me, again, I do not know. If it had been morning time, I would have worked on developing a better curriculum for the DAEP. Mornings at home were mine, however, and I would not be using them as unpaid work for the public school.

For a short time, I allowed snacks during their break time. The high school principal came through, and that practice ended abruptly.

The principal of the high school was my primary oversight. I do not know his name. I did not connect well with him, and, since Donna Ulrich was just down the hall, I went often to her for advice and direction. She was always very helpful to me. But as time went on, I began to realize that administration requires a political ability, that is, the ability to make people believe things that aren't true, and to manipulate other power figures for your own agenda. I was slowly sinking into the realization that I had no ability in that entire arena.

Nonetheless, on the practical side of administration and working with the students, I was quite capable and did well. In fact, because I was now an administrator with Sheldon ISD, I had a place at the table in the administration building when the

disciplinary unit was under discussion. I attended a couple such meetings during this semester. At this point in time, Vicki Giles, the lady who had hired me, was now an assistant superintendent. In the year after I was no longer with the district, she became the superintendent and served well more years than most. In fact, she was superintendent still when our daughter Katrina graduated from C.E. King High School. I will bring her in again at that point. I count it an honor to have had some small relationship with a woman of such respect and competence.

Then, because I was an administrator, I could also sit in the decision sessions for special ed students and sign off as the administrator. At one point, I was asked to sit in on a decision meeting for a student over at the High Point unit. I think it was because no one else was available, and I had the afternoons free. The student's mother, regular teachers, and special ed teachers were there, and I was the "administrator" for the session.

The boy in question was autistic. That didn't mean anything personally to me, however. But I sat there listening to his mother talk about her son. Slowly, an awareness began to grow in my understanding that she was talking about me. This was quite a thought; one which I had never considered. Nor did I take it as anything consequential. I was a highly trained teacher and administrator, how could "autism" have anything to do with me? Nonetheless, the thought of such a thing had been planted in me, and there it rested.

Then one day, probably in October, I was called over to the High School principal's office. He was very angry, and his anger was directed against me.

"I have heard rumors," he said, "whispered around the school, that there is a man in the DAEP who respects and cares about students. That is NOT what discipline is for. I want their time in the DAEP to be miserable. I want them to hate it. The purpose is for them to stop acting up, to stop breaking the rules, and do what they are supposed to do in the regular classrooms. You will make it awful for them."

Discovering What I Am Not

I can testify that I am NOT a politician.

You can imagine that I was quite shaken by this. Shortly after, however, I was asked to go with the high school principal and Miss Donna up to visit an established DAEP unit in the Splendora, Texas high school in order to see and learn from how they did things.

I rode in the back seat with the two principals in the front. They were talking together the whole time. The high school principal was driving and as soon as he hit the freeway, he was 20-30 mph over the speed limit. Sure enough, flashing lights stopped him, somewhere north of Humble. He got a ticket for speeding. When we arrived at the Splendora High School and went in, the first person we met was the constable connected to the DAEP there. And the first thing he did was show her the ticket and ask her if she knew the policeman who had written it. She did, and like any skillful politician, he talked her into seeing that it was annulled.

You have to understand that such dishonesty is simply overwhelming to me. They showed us their program, but before our time was over, the high school principal got a call saying that a bomb threat had been made against the school and that everything was shut down and the police were all over the building. We hastily drove back to C.E. King.

I stumbled home that evening, torn to pieces inside. I sat down in my chair, Maureen sat in my lap and held me, and I sobbed in great distress.

How can you punish children for "breaking the rules" and then play such a cynical game with the rules yourself?

The "bomb" threat was a prank, and the high school student who thought it would be funny to pull that prank was soon sentenced by a judge into my DAEP unit. He was an intelligent, studious, and good-mannered boy who had made one foolish teenage mistake that would ruin his life.

It was conveyed to Constable Terry and me that it would be a good thing if we could press the criminal Hispanic boy into a violent action against us so that he could be found guilty of a larger crime and shipped off to a state facility so that the district would no longer have to pay for his expense. We talked about that request together and both agreed that it was, to us, immoral, and that we had no intention of complying.

The older brother of the ninth-grade Hispanic boy whom I called a "pain-in-the-rear," came into the unit for a couple of weeks. This young man was a senior and the leader of the Hispanic gang in the school. This young man carried himself with dignity, and he was a natural leader of great respect. The thing he did not respect was the falseness of the school system that bound him and others to a dance they did not comprehend. Nonetheless, his presence in the DAEP was a great help to me because I easily enlisted him to corral his little brother and make him behave.

A mother brought her son into the DAEP to talk with me. The judge had just assigned him to the disciplinary unit. This kid was bad news from the get-go, and she did not like her choices. I pointed out that, by state law, she could home school her son. She thought that would be a great idea, but what I did not realize was that such would not be an option since he was under the jurisdiction of the judge.

About a week before school was out, in December, I was informed that my time as an administrator was over, and that I was being replaced by a "battle-ax." It was several years later that I woke up to the realization that the kid and his mother probably conveyed my advice to the judge, and that I was most likely penalized for that reason. That was frightening to me when I realized it until I then remembered that it was years in the past and good riddance anyhow.

The last week was gloomy, but on the last day of school, as the parents were coming by in the late evening (around 10 PM) to pick up their kids, I forget what happened, but there was a great scafuffle, I think some were getting too excited, and Constable Terry had to take police control of the group. That meant that the parents had to wait outside for awhile until things were settled and then take their kids as they were released one by one. Well, like kids, like parents. So that did not work very well, because the parents were more out of control than the kids.

There was no saying goodbye, and the unit closed under someone else's control. When everyone was finally gone, I went home that last day of DAEP, feeling kicked by a horse.

Just a few days ago, my son, Kyle, who was attending school as an eighth grader in that same building at the time, reminded me of something I had not fully realized. He said, "You know, Dad, your respect and care for those kids made a bigger difference in their lives than you might know." I know that that is true. And whatever I lost in the view of Texas public education, I would far rather gain in the lives of a handful of confused and hurting teenagers.

Family Times

In the fall of 2004, we went our first time to the Texas Renaissance Festival, which Mr. Leahy had also pointed us towards. Although the children were dressed up in "Lord of the Rings" elven/ranger cloaks that the girls had made, Maureen and I did not dress the style this time. Again, that was a mistake we did not make the next time. It is so much better to be part of the flow and entertainment rather than just an "observer." The Renaissance Festival had replaced all things Christian in Medieval times with pagan custom, and so that was disappointing because it was untrue.

The first weekend of December 2004 was our second time at Dickens on the Strand as a family. You can see that we went all out in joining the style of the event. This picture represents the most important thing in my life. Whatever difficulties I might have been facing in my work life, our family life together was far more important to me.

Let me bring in here first Kyle's experience in the middle school in the fall semester. He continued to perform in the theater class, and was again a leading character in the school play. At a certain point through the year, however, a girl in his class who was a bully targeted him with a terrible false accusation to the assistant principal, who happened to be Mr. Applegate.

Kyle was very shaken by this, but I counseled him to be fully respectful to Mr. Applegate, to accept whatever fault might be his, and to trust Mr. Applegate. That's what Kyle did, and thus Mr. Applegate was free to find the truth of the situation and that the charges were false, made just to hurt Kyle.

This kind of stuff is common when you place foolish children together so many hours. And I do not believe in teaching your child to endure such nonsense. For that reason, we together made the decision that Kyle would return to homeschool for the remainder of his eighth-grade year. By Texas law, we did not have to inform the school district, but because public schools often violate the law concerning homeschooled students, we knew from the Texas Home School Association exactly how to write a letter to the school, and so there was no problem.

The Spring Semester of 2005

The school had signed a two-year contract with me, so they had to keep me employed until the end of the 2005-2006 school year. In the spring, they moved me back to the high school, to a classroom in the adjoining former elementary school. I was given two groups of students, first, four classes of ninth-grade students who had failed the state tests and who needed special work to enable them to pass, and second, a class of high school seniors taking AP English, the smartest students in the school.

Come to think of it now, in spite of the deep discouragement under which I had been cast, these two groups of students in this semester were by far my favorite groups of students in my time with Sheldon ISD.

Not long after the semester began, however, there was some sort of scandal, and the high school principal was gone, replaced by a woman who had been an assistant administrator in the district. Now, I have worked under many highly competent and wonderful woman bosses in my life, some who will be coming into the picture as we go forward. This woman was not one of them.

But – let's start with my seniors. There was a sadness in this group of students. They were the smartest and most capable overall of any I have taught. Every assignment I gave they returned to me completed at an A level. But it was, in part, like teaching to empty shells, as if a light had gone out in them. They were finished with the absurdity of what school has become and were simply filling in the time until it was behind them.

Two young ladies, however, sat near my desk and soon developed a good conversational relationship with me. They were very literary-minded, and we found similar interests. Except – they were Gothic, with the chains and spikes and black leather persona. This was an extraordinary thing I discovered, that typically this type of student, though small in number, were among the most thoughtful and conversant in literary things than most other students. I always liked my "Gothic" students.

There was another young man in this group, a tall, thin, black boy from a poor but Christian home. I have a reasonably high IQ, but this young man's IQ was way beyond mine. Every paper he handed in or response he gave was not just brilliant, but literary and fluid, bringing in meaning and connections be-

yond what anyone else could see, yet doing it naturally and without effort. There was nothing I could teach him, nonetheless, I was incredibly honored by him when he brought his application letter to Harvard Medical School to me for help. I was even able to give him a few pointers. Sure enough, he was accepted out of a poverty high school on the east side of Houston straight into Harvard without anything in-between. Yet he was an example of the gentleness and humility of Christ.

I really liked my four groups of ninth graders who had failed the state test in English Language Arts. Many of them were special ed students. I enjoyed my seniors, but I liked teaching these students best in all my public-school experience. I had them only three days a week, however, and another teacher, who was proficient in teaching reading, had them two days a week. So my load this semester was reasonably light.

The principal of the school told me that none of these students would pass the state test, regardless, but that we were just to do our best. The problem is that most teachers think that filling their minds with more content knowledge was the way to help them pass. I know that teaching test-taking strategy is the way they pass the test. And it's not hard to weave content knowledge with testing strategy.

My own mental ability is geared much better towards breaking complex things down for less gifted students to understand rather than teaching to those with capable minds. This group of low-performing students had their own sets of personal problems, but I really enjoyed them all.

All ninth-grade teachers were to teach *Romeo and Juliet* this spring. When we had completed that teaching, all the other students hated Shakespeare and thought he was boring. My less-gifted students loved *Romeo and Juliet* and thought Shakespeare was cool. What I did was to explain a scene, read some of the text, point out Shakespeare's dirty jokes, show how his writing was ultra-current and hip. Then, we would watch one act at a time from Leonardo De Caprio and Claire Dane's *Romeo and Juliet*. And the truth is, Shakespeare in his day was like that up-to-date rendition rather than the dull performances most choose to put on.

My students understood and enjoyed Shakespeare; for most of the rest, he was immediately forgotten as irrelevant.

I also found a way to bring into their study some of the exciting things I was learning from the Thunderbolts Project.

Two-thirds of my students passed the state test, beyond anything the administration expected. At the end of the year, when I was informed that the district would not be renewing my contract, I pointed out the high passing mark of my students. The principal assured me that was because of the other reading expert. I knew that they learned little from her, for they told me that she confused them. But such could never be argued, so I held my peace.

(Forgive me for any self-boasting in this part. What I want to share is not my "cleverness," but rather the joy and meaningfulness of these two groups of students that I continue to hold as great value in my heart. I found greater depths of character in both groups than in the normal run of high school students.)

Before the end of the semester, I visited with Constable Terry again about the DAEP unit. He told me that the discipline was neither more nor less than mine (and I had kept a tight discipline, there was no looseness), but that my replacement, while ruling stringently, had no other care or thought for the students. Constable Terry was not pleased with the direction the DAEP unit had taken.

When the school year was finally over, and I had stumbled through all the complicated things teachers must do to "close out" the school year, I went home without any remaining strength. I was sick for a week, with another week needed to slowly recuperate. I loved working with my students, but the entire political arena of the public school was becoming more than I could bear.

Our Trip to Meadowlands

I believe that it was during the summer of 2005 that my work on the house stalled out. I was becoming physically weak again, a slow downhill slope. Part of the contribution to that was that I had bought the materials to build two canoes for my sons as their Christmas present, but this required a lot of painting with fiberglass resin. Then, weeds from our garden had spread throughout the yard, and I attempted to be rid of them by spraying Roundup Ready all around. I am certain that these two blasts of chemicals pushed my liver back over the edge.

At the same time, we had rung up a fair amount of debt in remodeling our home. And any new project, even if it was seemingly small, racked up ever more cost. I was halfway through working on the cabinet doors for the two bathrooms when, because of the pressure from these two sources, something disconnected between my mind in the front part of my brain and the working in the back part. I will try to explain that a bit more in an upcoming chapter.

The point is that I suddenly stopped working on the house, unable to continue. I would do more work on different parts of the house as we go forward, but those were brief enthusiasms that ended as soon as that project was done.

We had planned a trip to Meadowlands for this summer, to visit mom. In fact, most of my other siblings were also planning to visit with mom this summer, a family reunion. In July, we loaded up our green van and headed up I-45. I even obtained a cartop carrier to carry our stuff. The green van had always had a problem with over-heating when loaded, however, and soon up the road it became much worse. Finally, at Madisonville, I realized that it was simply too loaded down. Rather than return home, however, I rented a storage unit there, just off the freeway, and we made the hard decisions of what stuff we did not need, including the cartop carrier. We were able to continue, but with some difficulty.

Our trip plans included a stop in McAlester, Oklahoma. Cindy Dix, who had married Steve Schneider, and whose little boy, Matthew, was Johanna's age, was from McAlester, and her parents were elders in the move in the small fellowship there. They were living at the move community in Upsala, Ontario, just north of Duluth Minnesota, at this time and often came down to Oklahoma.

Cindy's parents, Ray and Jan Dix, owned two houses side by side. One was their home, and the other was where the fellowship had their meeting place. We stayed in a bedroom in the back part of the fellowship house. We probably arrived on Friday and stayed the weekend. There was a brother there who looked at our green van, and with Steve Schneider's help, was able to make it work better. We had a great time visiting, and I was able to share a word in the Sunday-morning service.

Then, at this same time, Peter and Barbara Bell were in the process of moving from Fort St. John down to the states. They had been awhile in Tulsa, Oklahoma, but had settled in Kingsport, Tennessee by this time. Peter was visiting again in Tulsa by himself while we were driving through. Tulsa was not on our route, so I drove up on Sunday afternoon to spend a few hours visiting with Peter. We, as usual, had a great time together, talking non-stop. I shared with him my change of thinking concerning the redemption of all. Peter expressed full agreement with what I shared.

Meanwhile Maureen and the Schneider's had planned an outing for that afternoon that included some rock climbing. Steve Schneider shared years later that as he watched Johanna with Matthew, and especially when Johanna was being herself, that is, climbing up the rocks, the Spirit of the Lord whispered to him that God meant them for each other. The truth is, I was sensing the same thing, even at that point. Neither one of us gave an indication of that, however; Matthew and Johanna would have to find their own path towards each other.

We drove on up to Meadowlands, then, without any more problems with the van. Tim and Frieda were there, and Cheryl had flown in. Jenelle had married again, a man named Eric Frederico, and they had two little children, Grace and Sean. Sean was the youngest of all mom's grandchildren. The Frederico's had all come as well.

We had a wonderful time. Our children and Glenn and Kim's children were around the same age, and they had great fun playing together. Mom's trailer was no longer there; she had been given a cozy house just behind Mark and Cindi Alesch's house. I spent many hours sitting in her comfortable living room, just she and I, conversing together. We had more in common than I had once known.

I shared the word in the Sunday morning service, and it was well received by all. In fact, Eric Frederico said to me that he was especially moved by what I shared. I was so blessed as I saw my mom in the midst of the family, and the place of honor she was given, especially by Mark and Cindi. Mark shared with me at this time that he was no longer connecting with the word Buddy Cobb was preaching. The community was still "in the move," but not for much longer. We returned home to Houston much refreshed.

The Final School Year Interrupted

In August, then, while I was still teaching at C.E. King, we enrolled Kyle and Johanna into a Christian school that we had seen often, right next to Beltway 8 about six miles from our home, called Family Christian Academy. Johanna was in 6th grade, and Kyle was in 9th grade. Kyle would complete all of his high school years at Family Christian. Because Maureen was also working, we could just afford the private school costs, which were lower there than most.

There is little to share about my final year of teaching at C.E. King. I was back in the regular English hallway with six groups of tenth grade students. That did make my workload simpler, because I again taught the same thing six times each day. At the same time, I had a homeroom group first thing each morning for a short time, a mix of all four grade levels. We were supposed to be student advisors, etc. during this time.

This school year was interrupted, however, by a major adventure. By the third week of September, Hurricane Rita was headed straight for Houston, gradually increasing to a Category 5 hurricane. Category 5 is not to be messed with, it will flatten everything in its path and kill many of those foolish enough to remain at home. By Monday, the 19th, all of Galveston county had been ordered to evacuate. Beltway 8, just beyond our back fence, was packed with a slow-moving exodus. Already, the immensity of evacuating seven million people was showing.

As teachers, we were not dismissed from our posts until Thursday. All the millions of people living south of us had to pass before our turn to evacuate came. At this point, Maureen had purchased a little blue Chevy Prism for her work vehicle. We boarded up our windows and doors and loaded our essentials into the Prism and the green van and split the children between the two vehicles. Maureen followed right behind me. I thought to avoid the massive choke of vehicles on Beltway 8, and thus we drove up to Crosby and took the route north through Huffman, and thus over to route 59, heading towards Lufkin. I was mistaken, however, for this was the entirety of Baytown heading north. We drove for nine hours. Once we finally were on the 59 freeway, there were not three lanes, but five, for the two sides were used as lanes as well. The other side of the freeway was empty, however. We stopped at the Walmart near Porter and got into the long lines using the only restrooms available to thousands of people. The movement on the road was go a bit, then stop, go a bit, then stop.

I was listening on the radio to the official news and began to realize that we were heading into a terrible bind. First, Rita had shifted its direction, and was now moving just to the northeast of Houston, with Beaumont, Texas on its hardest side. We were heading straight for where the hurricane would pass. Then, it was announced that our route was not "official" and so the state would not be sending in gas trucks for these hundreds of thousands of cars trying to get to Lufkin. Except we WERE on the route the state had earlier told us to go. I now saw that we would spend the night alongside the road somewhere, huddled together in our two cars, out of gas, and with a Category 5 hurricane going right over us.

I said to Maureen, "Forget it." We whipped over to the empty side of the freeway and drove home. Nine hours up became forty-five minutes back home. To my amazement, a gas station not far from our home still had gas. We were able to fill up both vehicles. Back home we turned on the TV to watch the path of the hurricane. It had not yet arrived. Saturday morning, then, the 24th, the outer winds of Rita began passing over us. Without hurry, we got into our vehicles and drove straight west to San Antonio on I-10. This was one of those surreal experiences in life. The city of Houston was empty. The freeway, the widest in the world, was empty.

This is what I learned. A hurricane comes onshore at only several miles an hour. We were driving away from it at 70 mph, with no traffic. And we knew the exact path of the hurricane and could easily avoid it. I will never be caught in such a foolish rush of crowds again, if I can help it.

All the way to San Antonio, the sides of the freeway were littered with empty vehicles that had run out of gas. Many had stayed the night in their cars. The officials had opened the east bound lanes to be used by the exiting traffic, called "contraflow" (they did it late and did not do it at all on 59), and so, even though we were the only vehicles on the road, I went to the other side so we could go 80 mph on the opposite lanes, just for fun.

In San Antonio we had been invited by Linda Kaufman to stay in their home for the evacuation time. Miss Linda had been Linda Friedman at

Bowens Mill, and had been one of Maureen's main teachers in the school and her mentor as Maureen began teaching. Sid and Linda Friedman had even lived at Blueberry for a period of time, before I arrived there. Sid had passed on since then, and Linda had remarried to a man named Al Kaufman who lived in San Antonio.

We were welcomed with open arms into their home. Miss Linda's two daughters, Debbie and Miriam, also lived nearby with their own families. We had known both of them in their growing up years at Bowens Mill.

Al and Linda Kaufmann were Jewish, and although she remained a Christian, she was also very involved with the Jewish community and synagogue in San Antonio. We had long and interesting conversations with both of them. At times, I sat and visited just with Al. He was very interested in my teaching experience but expressed prejudice against minority students. We observed their daughter, pushing her own children to be the top students in their classes. Miss Linda spoke much of the Jewish people and their culture.

On Sunday morning, we attended the church in San Antonio pastored by Max Lucado. He ministered the word, and, because Miss Linda was acquainted with him, we got to meet him personally.

We were invited to the gathering at the Synagogue, probably on Monday evening. This was a unique and different experience for all of us. Different ones spoke on different topics and I remember some sort of skit that they put on. By the end of the evening, however, I was struck by something very wrong. Afterwards, Maureen went with Al and Linda, but I had all the children with me. I felt such strong concern, however, that I had to stop the car in order to share with my children what they had just experienced.

You see, the entire identity of these people, expressed through every different part of the presentation, and including in all that Miss Linda had said, was that "We are the special ones, we are the good ones – AND everyone else hates us." I said to my children, "We have never identified ourselves by what our German forefathers suffered, but only by our life in Jesus now." I had never heard of such an anti-identity in my life. I was so burdened that my children would know that our entire human identity was Christ alive and new in us every morning.

When we returned home, we found that Rita had pretty much missed the Houston area, though Beaumont was devastated, as well as Lufkin, where thousands of people had fled.

Homestead Heritage

I want to include two things here before briefly recounting my depressing final year of public-school teaching.

In my Internet searches, I had found a Christian Community, called Homestead Heritage, just north of Waco, Texas, that put on a great presentation to the public on the Thanksgiving weekend. We spent two days there, that Thanksgiving, spending the night in a motel. This community had a completely different relationship with the public than anything I had known in move community. There "beliefs" and private practices were of no interest to me, but their public involvement was of immense interest. I will explain briefly, but if you are interested, you could study their public involvement on their website.

Most every craft and work that the people of the community did, including the older children in their school, was orientated towards teaching the general public, and giving a wide customer base a place to come and to enjoy the good fruits of the community, both in purchasing hand-made items and in signing up for any of the many craft training sessions they give throughout the year. Most every single aspect of homestead and farmstead life as well as school learning was on display, and very often, the young people in high school were the ones presenting to the public and we were buying their work.

This even included their English work, of all things. Customers could purchase nicely bound copies of things written by high school students. And I can assure you that because their schoolwork had such value, they did a tremendous job with it. Their pottery was especially magnificent, and I would have bought Maureen an entire kitchen set if I had been wealthy, I did get her a lovely hand-crafted serving bowl. I bought something for each of the children, including old-fashioned dresses for the girls made by students in the school. In fact the girl who made those dresses was the one who sold them to our girls.

There were many different store and craft fronts to visit and special presentations for the Thanksgiving visitors. We went into a tent where the choir

from the community sang lovely gospel songs. I was impressed, and what I saw there made a huge impact on my vision for Christian education and for the life of godly Community.

Then, through that fall semester, as part of our children's homeschooling, we decided to sponsor a child in another country, through World Vision. We chose a girl in Albania, about Johanna's age, named Anxhela Idrisi, and set up a schedule to send her money each month for her education and for nice things she could not have afforded otherwise. Though we have not had the chance to see her in person, Anxhela has become as a daughter to Maureen and me, and we share her life with her to this day.

Anxhela wrote to our girls, at first only through World Vision, but after a few years, we switched over to sending her money directly, once a month, and communicating diretly with her. We were able to help her afford musical training and a better education. Today, Anxhela is married with two lovely children, and is a schoolteacher. It is so good to be part of her life.

My Final Year in the Public School

The first semester of the 2005-2006 school year was almost survivable. There was little that was meaningful in it, however. My inability to control my class was growing and I could not keep them from talking, especially the African-American girls.

I will share three incidents with students. First, Hurricane Katrina, in devastating New Orleans, sent a number of inner-city students our way. I had one young black man who was rather vicious. I had to kick him out of my room more than once. One day, he threatened violence against me. I stood in front of him and said, "Great, awesome. Hit me, hard. That way, I get two years off, fully paid, and you go to jail." He did back down. Amazingly, I met him a few years later, now out of school, working at Jiffy Lube, and he greeted me as if I were the best teacher in his life!

The young Hispanic boy, Rodriguez, I think, who had been such a "pain-in-the-rear" in the DAEP, was now in one of my tenth-grade groups. Except this was different. He had come to know that I cared about and respected him. And so he found a place of refuge in my classroom. All his other teachers flunked him and kicked him out of their rooms. But quite a few times he came, then, into my classroom, even though it wasn't his period, and sat in the back of the room. I was glad that I could give him a place of peace inside a world that was violently confusing to him, a world in which he could not function.

Another young Hispanic man was in my classroom, eighteen and old enough to be graduated, but still in tenth grade. His name was Jonathan. He was a great young man, very polite. He loved to dance and was a "ladies' man" and carried himself very respectfully. But he was not gifted academically, and all his other teachers gave him F's. I knew he wanted to be a welder. So, before the end of the year, I sat him down and said, "Jonathan, you're of age, you can't be forced to sit in school any longer. Stop coming back. What you need to do is take a break, then study how to beat the test and get your GED."

He followed my advice. I saw him a year later in Lowes. "Mr. Yordy," he said to me, "I did what you said. I got my GED, and now I've been hired in an intern program to be a welder."

You can be certain that I had come to know the deep faults underlying modern schooling. Through this time, I read John Taylor Gatto's books on why modern schooling fails children. His reasons are real and not false like so many public-school critics. Changing the content of what is taught changes nothing. Requiring more "disciplined" student work changes nothing. Yet I had arrived at the same conclusions independently.

Sometime this year, John Taylor Gatto was speaking in Houston. I went to his lecture and had the chance to meet and briefly visit with him.

My final semester was at the bottom. The school administration was forcing all the teachers to follow an external "apply the objectives" program that had little relevance to classroom teaching. We had to go to lots of "professional training sessions." I was so tired and limited in the ability to keep my students quiet. I often took off days "sick," in fact, I had many sick days stored up and through this last semester, I used them all.

My first period class was bright and talkative, and the most difficult for me to keep quiet. One morning, one of the new "impose the objectives" administrators observed my teaching in that first period class. That was one of my weakest mornings. I could hardly teach that morning, and I could not get them to stop talking. The lady stormed out of my classrooms to file her official assessment of me. When I received it, it went straight into the trash. I was not interested.

The thing is that when the state test results came back, although the high school overall had done poorly, and the school was edging into the danger zone of being "looked at" by the state, my student test scores were the highest among the English teachers and among the highest in the school. That fact, of course, had no bearing on my employment.

The principal had all the teachers in the school gather in the auditorium after the poor test results. A former superintendent spoke first, and said some cruel things against all of us. Then the principal got up to speak. She ordered all the "elective" teachers to stand up, those who did not teach the courses that were tested. As they were standing in the midst of hundreds of teachers, it took me awhile to process what I was hearing. For some strange reason, the principal decided to blame them for the failure of the school. She spent several minutes treating them very cruelly without restraint. I was absolutely shocked.

I was only one of dozens of teachers who were not offered a further contract that year. I did not care. It had been all I could do to make it to the last day, and I was ready never to return. At least, on the final day of work, they processed us first, and though it was humiliating, I was soon gone. I went home, and all my defenses collapsed. This time I was sick for over two weeks, with another week to recuperate slowly.

The thing about this experience, however, was that, although it was hard, I had no personal connection to the public school, and thus it carries no painful emotions into the present.

Yet I had failed, even more than before. You see, I had set myself to support my family by teaching school, and we had borrowed nearly fifty thousand dollars to enable me to do that. And we had been paying on those student loans. Yet my failure, now, to provide for my family brought me to a level of hopelessness, this summer of 2006, that was, in some ways, greater than the hopelessness I knew in 1998.

Here is one "what if" that gnaws at me sometimes. If I had known about Asperger's as I know now, I could have gotten a clinical diagnosis fully paid for by the health insurance from the district.

I had also purchased disability insurance, which would have paid me a two-thirds salary for the rest of my life. – But I give thanks, that Jesus does all things well.

Searching for a True Church

Christmas of 2005 was our last time at the Church on the Rock in Baytown. Maureen and I loved the praise worship there, but the word that was preached was something entirely different. You see, Tommy Meekins had been a gospel singer. And in the present time, he was a leading figure in the Baytown Christian arena. His role as pastor was, one might say, a side task. But I have no interest in judging the brother, but judging the word he shared was another matter.

I tried. For all the months we attended that church, I really tried to hear God speak to me, even once, through what was shared from the pulpit. I never did. Well, I sort of did, once, but I think I was stretching it. How could we keep attending a church where there was no personal word coming from God? By the end of 2005, I could no longer do so. At the same time, in our distress, we had asked the pastor for counseling. His response was simply to ask if we were involved enough in the church programs. That was the last straw for both of us.

Through the first half of 2006, then, we visited a number of churches, including the big Grace Church on the south side of Houston and the big Church in The Woodlands. We went several times to the Grace Church, but I did not care for it. For one thing it was too big.

Basically, we did not go to church, then, through these months. We did have some sharing times at home, however.

Through this whole school year, however, I was at a dead-end place concerning the vision of my heart, and concerning my desire to know the Lord as He really is, at least, that's what I thought. Time and again, when I was driving by myself, I wept before God. "Who will speak for You," I cried, "and for Your heart?"

I did not know the central truth of the gospel and I knew I didn't know, and I wept much over my great ignorance and over the ignorance of God throughout His Church.

In March, we heard that a sister we had known at Bowens Mill, Diane Stockbridge, had passed away, in San Antonio. She had been a close friend of Linda Friedman/Kaufman and Miss Linda invited Maureen and I to the memorial to be held there.

Prior to this time, Sister Nathel Clarke's daughter, Anne, had moved to Houston with her husband, Juan Giron, and their three boys, Kyle's age and just older. We had visited in their home and were able to leave Katrina and James with them for this trip. Kyle and Johanna stayed with friends. Katrina and James had a great time in the Giron's swimming pool.

We saw Don Stockbridge at the memorial, who, though once a traveling ministry in the move, had left that fellowship. His word had been one of the most precious to me, but somehow, his experience in leaving the move had left him empty and broken.

Then, we were again visiting with Al and Linda Kaufman in their home. Linda's two daughters were there with their husbands and children. Another sister who had spent a short time in move community was also there.

During this weekend visit, Miss Linda filled the conversation with how great the Jewish people are. She shared her concern with me that all this talk about Jews "needing to be saved" was just wrong. Such a good and wonderful people had nothing to be "saved" from.

We were gathered in their large family room after the memorial. I was conversing with the sister who had once been in the move. In the conversation between just the two of us, I shared that, in spite of the things I now disagreed with, God was truly among us in the community. One of the daughters, who had lived at Blueberry through my first year there, overheard me saying that. She began to rebuke me, and all other conversation in the room stopped. Every eye was on me and my responses. The sister stated that she had sought God on her knees through her time at Blueberry and had never had any experience with any God. She said that no one in move community ever had any experience with "God," and that the people who went into such a way of living were already psychologically deficient, that's why they were so easily fooled.

I answered gently, and in great kindness, in attempting to defend myself. Afterwards Maureen said how proud she was of me. But the thing that got me the most was the eyes of all the family members on me, the gleeful joy to see how I would respond to such a strong accusation.

Now, I am including these things because this is an account of my life, and this is one of those several things that I must place out where I can bring the Lord Jesus into a full forgiveness inside my own heart. I have never been treated with such disrespect as a guest in someone's home anywhere close before or since. I have not considered a revisit since.

Yet, I am being careful to give only my own personal experience, and not to draw any larger "conclusions."

Bringing All into Jesus

This time period, then, is one of two, during our years in Houston, that I must bring fully into the Lord Jesus Christ past my own emotional objections.

Let me begin with the DAEP first. Was I at fault? Most certainly. I should have spent my time working on curriculum for the students instead of reading Internet news and I should have been more careful in what I said to the students. I was not wrong, however, for caring for them and treating them with respect.

"Father, I thank You for Your complete forgiveness towards my own inadequacy and foolish mistakes. Even more than that, I thank You that You share even my mistakes with me through Jesus, and that we together, in speaking good grace together, can turn all these difficult things into goodness and blessing for others."

In the remainder of my public-school experience, the truth is, I simply did not have the strength or ability needed to function well in what the district was paying me to do.

"Lord Jesus, You were there, carrying me through every moment. And I place You, in all Your precious Person, upon every nuance of my inadequate and faltering humanity through this time. I am so grateful, Lord Jesus, that in every moment of my life, I lived inside of You, though I knew it not."

"Oh, Father, I think about the more than five hundred young people that sat in my classroom through the four years I taught in Sheldon ISD. I know that Your Holy Spirit is always flowing out from me, bringing life into others, whether I see

anything or not. And Father, because You brought every one of those children into my life, I have the right in You to bring every one of them into Your heart. Father, You and I together hover over each one, sending our shared Holy Spirit into their lives right now. Father, bless each one of them, lift them up into Your knowledge. I thank you, Father, that You share Your heart with me."

"Lord Jesus, I thank you for our time at Church on the Rock in Baytown and for the good experiences our children had there. I bless Pastor Tommy Meekins with all my heart, and draw him into Your love shed abroad in me. I pray that right now, You would bless him with a measure of knowing You beyond what he has known and in goodness and joy.

"And Lord Jesus, I pray that you would bless Al and Linda Kaufman and their family. I freely and with all joy forgive them for any difficult experiences I may have known. They are precious to You beyond measure, and to me as well. Lord Jesus, I release them from all my emotional difficulty into Your liberty, that they might find their place inside of You."

"Father, I see now the wondrous path upon which You were leading me, into great purpose. I see now that everything You took me through was critical towards preparing me to hear that most wondrous word when You opened the heavens to me and poured out into me what I had sought with tears through all my years."

Disgruntled Agreement

In the third week of July, Maureen read that Darlene Zschech, a wonderful praise singer from Australia, would be singing at the Sunday morning service at the BIG church in Houston, the largest church in North America. I did not like the big church in Houston; I did not like big churches at all. And I had successfully resisted any attempt to drag me to the big church prior to this point.

This time, however, Maureen was insistent. I thought, well, it can't hurt. So, on July 23, 2006, I climbed into our green van with Maureen and the children, and, compliant but disgruntled, I pulled out of the driveway, heading into Houston and to the big church I did not like.

Lakewood Church. Above: the south side, facing I-59.

Below: Like the mountain valleys of my youth. We sat in the upper left of this picture our first time there. Usually we sat in the bottom section, just behind the main front section, near the white X.

40. The Time of the Jesus Secret

June 2006 - December 2007

Lakewood Church

We arrived at Lakewood Church that morning, just off of Highway 59, halfway between downtown Houston and the Galleria. We found a place to park and joined the flow of hundreds of people into the building. Lakewood church had been a former professional basketball stadium now converted into a church.

Where to go might have been confusing to us, but we were guided by welcoming people all the way through. We ended up on the southern slope, looking down at the thousands of people below and on the slopes all the way around, more than twelve thousand in this service, the largest of four each weekend.

It was just like the mountain valleys of my youth, vast slopes of saints all around and on the valley floor below, worshipping God together in the full anointing of the Holy Spirit. The praise service was wonderful, led by several together, although Darlene Zschech was the primary worship leader that morning. It was the kind of praise that I could join freely, worshipping God with all my heart. The prayer time was living and personal. Victoria Osteen spoke for about ten minutes. She is a fiery Pentecostal preacher as strong in the Spirit as many I had known in the move.

Then Joel Osteen shared his word. Joel is a small, Texas man, about the same height as his lovely wife, Victoria. Joel is an optimistic man who sees the best in all and can't really help that he smiles all the time. He is very unassuming. He has shared many times that he had no thought of stepping into his father, John Osteen's, place nor of ever being a pastor. Yet the hand of God clearly set him there. For that reason, he states, he never tries to give God's people anything more than what he is, as God has taught him.

That morning, Joel's word was on the value of natural health and eating organic when possible. This was not a common topic for him, but one which Maureen and I loved. To say the least, I was enthralled with Lakewood Church and have loved it from the first moment there.

The next Sunday, Joel completed his teaching on healthy eating. Afterwards, we stopped at the Whole Foods grocery store on Kirby and Alabama, right across from a large Borders bookstore. We had shopped here before, but now it was "on our way." We saw lots of people that must have been at Lakewood. Afterwards, we ate our Sunday dinner at the Souper Salad on Gray and Dunlevy, on our way towards home. And thus, the pattern of our Sundays for the next seven years was set.

Joel states that if you come to Lakewood three times, then consider yourself a member.

August 6, 2006

August 6 was our third Sunday at Lakewood Church. I was 49 year's old. I do not remember anything about that service in particular, or where we sat, or what Pastor Joel's word was about.

But before I share what happened on this momentous day, I want to place before you the man that sat in that service that morning.

I have been an incredibly vulnerable man from my youth, knowing that of myself I am LOST, knowing that I have no ability whatsoever to figure anything out. For that reason, every time I found myself assailed, which was often, I reached in all desperation for the only thing I knew to be true, what God actually says in the gospel. When I was 25, God rebuked me strongly about trying to figure out what Bible verses mean with my mind. From then until now, I have only hidden what God actually says in my heart, weeping often that somehow, He would write those words there for real.

But then something terrible began to happen inside of me as I hid in my heart what God actually says with no need to know what it means. A haunting whisper began that grew slowly over time saying, "This word I have hidden in my heart so that, in my overwhelming desperation I might know the living God, this word is not in agreement with the 'correct' ideas in my mind or with what is being preached all around me or believed as 'Christian theology' among Christians. I became convinced that there was something terribly wrong with me, and so I applied myself earnestly to 'believe in' the 'correct ideas' being preached into me.

Alas, I had no success at all. And so I came to that cold and lonely place, in February of 1998, when I had no hope whatever that I could ever know my Father or please Him or do His will. I KNEW that I did not know the gospel and I had no idea that I ever could.

Yet as I stumbled forward, hurting from a thousand unhealed wounds, I determined one thing only, that Jesus is my Savior and that I will know nothing else. Then I did something even more desperate. I set aside everything else, every word planted in my heart and every idea found in Christian preaching. I had no more interest in being a 'Christian,' but only that I might know my Jesus, close and real, carrying me through the darkness, through a way I did not know.

Then, slowly, in His gentle kindness, Jesus brought the first great level of healing to me, beginning with the most wondrous thing - "My heart is good. My heart is filled with Jesus."

Before long however, I was thrust back into that great contradiction whispering inside between what God actually says in the gospel and what all Christianity teaches. You see, it is a dangerous thing to plant God's word in your heart in the desperate hope that God will cause His word to be what He means. For such a word planted in that way burrows deep and sends forth powerful roots even as it hides, almost as dead and unknown by you, until that moment when it springs full-grown into your consciousness.

Because, you see, I still had no idea what any of it meant or how I could know my Father that I might live.

If you had looked around the Christian world that Sunday of August 6, 2006, I don't know that you would have found a heart more filled with Gospel word as God actually says it or more convinced that he does NOT KNOW what any of it means or more desperate to know what God does mean by what He says. I think you would agree that God had 'set me up' and that every step of my life had brought me directly here.

This was the kind of man who sat there that morning, as a garden soil dug deep and made ready for the most far-reaching Seed of Life God would ever plant inside of me. It might have been in an exhortation, that Joel spoke that six-word phrase that was familiar to him and the Lakewood congregation, but which I had never before heard or considered.

"Speak what God says you are."

I can hardly express the wonder that happened in me the very second those words entered my consciousness, for I saw, in that moment their far reach and the wondrous gospel meaning that they carried. I was now oblivious to everything else as all the word stored up in my heart for decades leaped up to meet together with all the Word of my Father coming out from the heavens now flung wide open to me.

Hope long deferred gripped my heart with excitement and all I could think about was getting home to my desk and to my wide-open Bible so that I might see and know what God says I am.

I want to show you what I mean by the RULING verse of the Bible. From my early thirties, I had determined that Romans 8:29 was my ruling verse and that the covenant God had entered into with me would RULE how I understood every verse in the Bible.

Conformed with the image of His Son - we shall be like Him as we see Him as He is - transformed into the same image.

As we began our drive home, I shouted to God inside myself. What am I? Who do You say that I am? And God answered my cry through His ruling verse and through the Covenant by which He had bound Himself to me. "In my finished state, as I am in completion before God, God says that I am just like the Lord Jesus Christ."

Before we arrived home, I was already formulating in my thinking how so many New Testament verses, of so many different types, would read if they were speaking of me in my completed state, just like the Lord Jesus.

Nothing else could exist for me, at least for the next few hours after we arrived home as I rushed to my computer desk and opened my Bible to the book of Matthew. Before 1:30 that afternoon, on August 6, 2006, with my heart seized in astonished excitement, I typed the following words onto my computer screen.

I follow Jesus. I am a fisher of men.

I am blessed because I am poor in spirit; heaven's kingdom is mine. I am blessed because I mourn (with those who mourn); I am comforted. I am blessed because I am meek; the earth is my inheritance. I am blessed because I hunger and thirst for righteousness; I am filled.

I am blessed because I am merciful; I receive mercy. I am blessed because my heart is pure; I see God. I am blessed because I am a peacemaker; I am a son of God. I am blessed when my enemies assault me; heaven's kingdom is mine. I am blessed when people say terrible and false things about me and persecute me; I rejoice and am thrilled. I possess an incredibly great reward in heaven as a result.

I am the salt of the earth. My neighbors are blessed by God and kept from evil because of me. I am the light of the world; I set my light where all can see it; I give light to all around me. People see my good works and give glory to my Father.

I am perfect in the same way my Father in heaven is perfect. God's will is done in me as it is done in heaven.

❧

You can be sure that at this point I was soaring in the heavens, filled with overflowing joy, for every aching longing I had ever experienced over decades, that I might know God and His Word, was being answered a thousand-fold. I would never return to my former way of thinking or knowing again.

Family Times

Before continuing on with the unfolding of my new joy, I want to bring back in the context of our family life through this time.

In the first week of June, while I was still overwhelmed with sickness from escaping the public school, Maureen's parents and aunt and uncle, Werner and Erma Honsalek (Erma was Roberta's younger sister), were both celebrating their fiftieth wedding anniversary, to be held together in Lubbock, Texas. Our green van was continuing to have minor difficulties, and so we rented a minivan for the trip, which was much cheaper than even a minor breakdown. I didn't do too well on the trip, but we made it.

We had a wonderful time with family at the joint celebration. The Honsaleks and Macks were all there, and many more. We got to visit with Tim and Freida again. In fact, it was during this time that April shared with us her leading to attend Bill Johnson's school. They went to California not long after, and April gained so much from the Lord in that wonderful school of Spirit Ministry.

Brother John Hinson was the key speaker at the anniversary celebration. His word was filled with life and power, as usual, and yet, in the end, saying little of consequence. It was good to see him again at a personal level, however.

We arranged with Claude and Roberta for Johanna to spend a few weeks with them at Bowens Mill, just as Kyle had two years earlier. And so Johanna left with them for Georgia; Claude and Roberta would then bring her back to Houston. On our way back, however, we all stopped at Uncle Werner and Aunt Erma's home, just south of Dallas. They were and continued to be missionaries to Brazil and Aunt Erma worked in the library of Christ for the Nations, where their son, Tim Honsalek, Maureen's cousin, also taught music. We would visit in Werner and Erma's home a number of times through these years. Uncle Werner had a large miniature train setup that he loved to show our children.

Johanna reminds me that she forgot her suitcase at the Honsaleks, and we had to retrieve it. She went to Bowens Mill with borrowed belongings, but it would be a wonderful experience for her. In fact, she would write about one of her adventures there when she arrived in my English classroom at Family Christian.

Meanwhile, without telling Jo, we planned a complete remodel of her room. I went all out on this job, building her many wall shelves for all her many books, and a writing desk, a little project table and a lovely hope-chest/window seat placed under a nicer new window. We painted everything two shades of blue trimmed with white, but leaving a number of things as clear varnished wood.

When Claude and Roberta brought Johanna back, sometime in late July, they knew what we had done, but Jo did not. It was such fun to blindfold her and bring her into her new room and then watch the joy and wonder on her face.

In July, I drove Kyle to the Greyhound bus station and put him on the bus for McAlester, Oklahoma. He was not quite fifteen. A move community in southern Missouri put on a week-long youth camp each summer, which Matthew Schneider and other young people from Upsala came down to enjoy. Kyle would get a ride with them and others from the McAlester fellowship. Kyle would attend these camps each summer, with Johanna after this first time, for several seasons.

Through the Spring of this year, Brother John and Sister Nathel Clarke made the monumental decision to leave the move of God and their leading place in that fellowship. Before they left, they stood before the gathering of many people from the BC communities and apologized and asked their forgiveness for any way they might have failed them as a covering of God towards them. Now, much of all this would be their story to tell, and not mine, so I will share only what I understood as they shared personally with Maureen and I, here in Houston.

John and Nathel had come to realize that the word of the gospel, which had become for them a view towards union with Christ even before Maureen and I left the move, was opposed to that impossible obligation preached by Buddy Cobb, that God is against us, and that He requires perfect obedience from us to prove that we actually love Him. After some time of speaking with Buddy Cobb, joined by Brother Tom Rowe as well, they realized that Brother Buddy would never hear them and that his teaching would only continue to dominate the move.

Soon after John and Nathel separated from the move, Tom Rowe did as well, along with many of the brethren in the Atlanta area. John and Nathel found a home in Creston, British Columbia along with others formerly from that fellowship who had made their homes there. A few years later, Rick and Shirley Annett would also move down to make their home in Creston. Many of these brethren, including John and Nathel and some from the Atlanta group found a good connection with Bill Johnson and have enjoyed the good teaching of Bethel Church until now.

You can be sure that two apostolic ministries separating themselves from the move at the same time and for the same reasons caused quite a stir across that fellowship. Some who remained were deeply offended by Brother John's apology.

Later in August, after Lakewood had become our home church, John and Nathel came to Houston to spend several days in their daughter, Ann's, home. Ann and Juan Giron lived on the other side of Houston from us, about an hour's drive. They were also attending Lakewood Church, and we had visited with them before. Juan and Ann have three really fine boys, close in age, with their youngest around Kyle's age, all three born while they were still living at Blueberry.

John and Nathel visited privately with Maureen and me in the Giron's sitting room. They apologized to us and asked forgiveness of us for any way they had failed us. Maureen and I gave them our full forgiveness with all our hearts. This was truly a gift of God coming with the wondrous new word of living in the favor and goodness of God which we were now hearing.

We went out to eat at a Chinese buffet with the Clarke's and Giron's. During our time together, Sister Nathel, especially, spoke words of blessing and Christ into Maureen and I. Indeed, this was how we had known them during our time in Oregon. We went home that afternoon in joy.

A New Faith in God
Before continuing with our history, I want to share more of this wondrous knew way of knowing God and His word that continued to pour through my fingers onto my computer screen. –Speak what God says you are – God says that in my completed state I am just like the Lord Jesus Christ, thus every word concerning Christ in my Bible is God speaking of me.

It did not take me long to work my way from Matthew to Revelation, many pages of wondrous confessions of faith. Yet as I look back now, through much hindsight, I know that my present life began when I got to Colossians. Colossians 3:3-4 & 9-11, in the NKJV, says this.

For you died, and your life is hidden with Christ in God. When Christ who is our life appears, then you also will appear with Him in glory. - You have put off the old man with his deeds, and have put on the new man who is renewed in knowledge according to the image of Him who created him, where there is neither Greek nor Jew... but Christ is all and in all.

And on my page I wrote these words among the many coming out from this brand-new book.

"Christ my life. Christ is all in me."

This was not the most explosive moment of my life mostly because I had no idea what on earth had just passed through my lips (for I had learned long before to shout the word of Christ out loud). Nonetheless looking back, I know that something very deep was sealed in me at that moment, the greatest Seed of Christ my Father has ever planted into me.

Having completed Revelation, I had just begun to write out from my new joy, and so, through the next few months, I wrote in rough form what is now *The Jesus Secret*. I meant, of course, the mystery of Christ, but that sounds so old and already religiously defined. A mystery is a secret and Christ is Jesus, hence the Jesus Secret.

Now, here's the thing, this wondrous new flow of what God actually says in the Bible now made real in me through the speaking of my mouth, completely separate and even beyond what Joel Osteen taught, was also joined with the simple and clear words of the favor of God which Joel spoke into us each Sunday.

Simply this, God says that He speaks all good words of heavenly blessing into me. But I had learned over many years to hear endless words of accusation and condemnation against myself and to speak them constantly in my own mind. In fact, in the move, the general prejudice was that since you are always contrary to God, you need to live a life of continual "repentance" defined as always speaking against yourself, but with nothing ever to replace "you." To speak blessing and the favor of God towards yourself could only be "of the devil."

And so Joel Osteen, through his simple teaching over and over, saved my life and my marriage by teaching me to stop the anti-Christ self-cursing and see myself inside the goodness and favor of the Father. Maureen became much happier over time as well, and we were able to treat each other with greater kindness than before. Our lives became much more peaceful.

It would take five years of sitting under Joel's continual teaching of this one most important principle of the Christian life for my mind to change completely and two further years to seal it permanently. I can say truly that from the summer of 2013, when I knew that God's season for us at Lakewood Church was complete, I have never once thought any wicked accusation in my mind against the Lord Jesus, that He has failed in His ability to join me utterly with my Father. And it is Joel Osteen whom I thank for the beginnings of that wonderful gift.

In August, I also wrote the 12th and final issue of *Times of Refreshing* and sent it out, dated September 5. I was still processing what I was learning, for I didn't really know what it meant. This issue was filled with much more goodness than anything before.

A Strange Day & a Terrible Night

After leaving the public school, we still received my full pay through the month of August. By September I was still so shattered inside from that whole experience that I simply was not ready to find other work. Instead, I cashed in my Texas educator retirement, which was several thousand dollars, more than enough to carry us for a few more months until I could find my feet under me once again. Because I was no longer receiving an ongoing salary, however, we pulled Johanna out from Family Christian and back into home school for the first semester of her 7th grade year.

Through this time, Maureen continued spending most nights at Miss Ruth's in Pasadena. She had a bed there, but was on call and got up often through the night. She would nap some, then, at home during the day, but also had much of the day to work with Johanna and Katrina on their schooling and to teach James to read.

The problem was this. That August, we had signed the girls up with a free charter school, named K-12, a public school that was entirely online. We received many boxes from them, containing a computer for the girls and all kinds of things for educational projects. We set everything up in our schoolroom and the girls went to work, with Maureen helping to guide them. The curriculum was set, and the instruction was all online. This seemed to be an awesome and simple solution for our situation.

Except it wasn't. You see, the charter school did not understand that in a normal classroom, about half the time is actual instruction and the other half of the time is spent coaxing the children along. And so the girls were hit with twice the load as normal school. On the one hand, it was too much for Katrina in 4th grade, but too boring for Johanna, who was missing all her friends at Family Christian.

A family member misunderstood our situation, and (I assume) determined that I was somehow abusing my family. This person turned to a 'Christian counselor' whose method was to break families apart so that "change" could come.

It was a strange Sunday, sometime in October. As we approached the main entrance to Lakewood Church, we noticed armed police mounted on horses. They were positioned just behind two rows of people lined up on either side of the flow of people into the church. These people were positioned on public property just beyond the church property. They had large placards that they waved at Maureen and I and our four children as we walked to Church to worship the Lord Jesus and bullhorns through which they shouted at us. The placards were of Pastor Joel with devil's horns forking us all into hellfire and other similar things. and the shouts in our ears were that we were all going to hell if we went into that Church.

I had never experienced anything even close in my life. Maureen and I put our arms out to keep our children close and passed through. The elders of Lakewood Church were standing on the step up that marked church property, welcoming all the people passing through that gauntlet with us into the joy of the Lord. When we came into the vast auditorium, I marveled, for the congregation was singing the one song, the only word that counts. "The Blood of Jesus washes away our sin." And they were singing it in the worship and anointing of the Spirit of Christ Jesus.

As Jesus said, **"They have hated Me without a cause. - If they have hated Me, they will hate you also."**

On top of that strange experience, I drove home carrying a premonition in my heart that the day was not over. Later that afternoon, there was a knock on our door. When I opened the door a hard woman, a "Christian counselor," stepped into our home, having already determined that my family needed to be taken away from me.

· As this woman sat in our living room, she accused me of being an abusive father and husband. It was as if I was guilty simply because I was a man. The plan was that Maureen and the children would go live with the family member who had brought her, the children would all go into the godless public school system, and they would all be much bet-

ter off. Meanwhile I would be left to fend for myself without my precious wife and my dear children.

The thing is, that God did give to me the very best friend. Maureen told them, "NO!" And that they needed to leave.

They did soon leave, and that evening Maureen went on down to Miss Ruth's. I gathered my four children next to me on the couch and held them close and wept over them. I did not sleep that night, in fear that this cruel woman would go to the authorities with her accusations, that I still might be in danger of losing our precious children to awfulness.

That all passed, of course, and I soon returned to the joy of that word of the Jesus Secret that was now pouring through me onto the page. But I knew quite clearly that the devil had come against me with great wrath, knowing that his time was short because I was learning to cast him out of my heavens.

Although I forgave this family member, though there was never any recognition or apology for the horror intended against us, I still find myself quite angry, and I know that my anger is right and just.

"Lord Jesus, together with You, I place our shared anger into our Father's love, that Father Himself might carry this family member all the way through the darkness and into knowing You as life. And I receive this person now as You, without any consciousness of sins, made clean long ago by Your Blood. Thank You, Lord Jesus that You are such a wonderful Savior."

Concerning the other woman, I don't know her, and I leave her in the very capable hands of our Savior far away from me.

We did continue with the K-12 program until the semester ended in December. What we did not know was that Johanna had been paying attention to Pastor Joel's teaching on the favor and expectation of God. The thing is, God does what He says.

Family Christian School
Through this fall semester, Kyle was in his second year at Family Christian Academy. We had attended some of his events, and Johanna's the year before, and met their teachers, including Robert Anderson, the principal of the school. That December, we attended a "field day" of games and fun activities that

was the last school day before Christmas break.

When Johanna got home, she pulled out her school clothes and said, "Mom, I'm going to iron my clothes because I'm going back to school!" Maureen asked her why she thought that. Johanna replied that Pastor Joel said that when God speaks to us, we are to take a step in faith.

Later that afternoon, Kyle came home to announce that one of their favorite teachers in the school, a Mr. Garcia, had resigned to go on to other things and that the school was looking for a teacher to take his place.

I updated my resume, filled out the application, and went to the school to see Mr. Anderson. This was a Spirit-filled church, and it did not take long in visiting together to know that we shared much of Christ in common.

To put it briefly, I was hired, and would step into Mr. Garcia's classes when school started again in January. My pay would be much lower than in the public school, but with a wonderful benefit; all our children, including Kyle, could now attend without any tuition required.

Our two younger children had to be tested for placement; they tested well at the grade levels they had been. And so Johanna would complete her seventh grade back at Family Christian, Katrina would be in fourth grade with Miss Mathis, and James first grade with Miss Lentz.

Family Christian Academy is a large attachment onto Family Christian Church, all one building. The school had a full and very nice gym on the side facing the beltway. Below is a picture from the front. The entrance on the left is into the school; the en-

trance on the right is into the church. This would be my workplace as a teacher for the next two-and-a-half years. I was now 50 years of age.

Before the end of December, however, we rented the cabin at Village Creek State Park and spent a lovely weekend there. I have not brought in our love as a family for camping in Texas State parks. We began when Kyle was 12, in August of 2003, just he and I went camping at Martin Dies State Park as a father-son time. I wanted to share with him that all the things going on inside him were perfectly normal and human, that I also had known them, and that Jesus was inside of him inside of all that. On our way home, we watched the first *Pirates* movie together at the theater, just the two of us. It was all a great shared experience. We went back to Martin Dies Park as a whole family the next year. That time we all went out onto the lake in canoes. But I will not include all our camping trips, just a couple.

Back in the Classroom

As I will develop my experience at Family Christian and my relationship with those brethren as we go through the semesters, I want to keep this first semester fairly brief.

A quick description of the interior of the school will suffice. When you enter the big school doors, there is a hall to your left which is the primary grade classrooms in the downstairs as well as a stairway going up to a similar set of rooms that were most of the middle and high school classrooms. If you went straight on towards the back from the entry, the hall was wider and culminated with the gym. On the way back to the gym was first the school offices to the left and then the school cafeteria. On the right were the large entry doors into the church sanctuary. We teachers had a devotion time in the sanctuary before school each morning. All the way across the sanctuary and up the stairs on the other side was a large youth room that was the classroom for several of the high school classes and a meeting area for middle and high school chapel each Thursday morning.

This was all brand new to me this January of 2007, and I do not remember all that I taught that first semester. My classroom was in the upstairs after the hall turned to the right, about half way down, near the math and science rooms. I do remember a large group for eighth grade Bible class, US History with the seniors that year, and a drama class as an elective chosen by students from seventh grade to maybe tenth. These were the only seventh grade students I have ever taught. I was able to teach them a bit, but I am definitely not a drama teacher. Since I was simply taking on most of Mr. Garcia's courses, and since there was another full-time English teacher, I did not teach English this semester.

I love to teach, and I connect with my students after they discover I'm not the gruff person they first imagine, still, I do not remember now that much of consequence from these first classes.

Just before the semester began, a number of the middle and high school teachers rode up to Dallas to attend a Christian teacher's conference at a large Christian school there. It was a great time to get to know my new colleagues, although I will not share any more names until the fall semester. I rode in the front with Mr. Anderson who was driving, and we fellowshipped together all the way up. As I said, we had much in common in the Spirit. On the way up, however, Mr. Anderson said something that imprinted on my memory. He was talking about the tendencies of the world and said, "We live in a day where people call evil good and good evil." These words would come back to haunt me.

Soon after school started, I learned that I was required to lead the children in the pledge of allegiance. I went straight to Mr. Anderson and said as gently as I could that I could not in good conscience participate in such a thing. I was not about to share how I view the practice of teaching little children to take their hearts that belong only to Jesus and to swear them with a binding oath of their mouths to the kingdoms of Satan in this world. Something about "millstones" and "necks" got my attention long ago. You see, I am a timid man, I don't try to control other people, I know Jesus does all things well, but most of all, I had to have this job to provide for my family.

Mr. Anderson replied that the school required this in order to teach respect. I was free not to par-

ticipate, thus I always stood and placed my hand on my heart but did not speak the false words. Nonetheless, it was clear, right from the start, that I was not a member of the cult of "God Bless America." This would be the agony inside of which I would work for the next two-and-a-half years, caught every day between the wondrous word of Christ my life, now rising inside of me, precious brothers and sisters who loved Jesus and walked in the Spirit, and the grotesque exaltation of this world as if it shows us "Jesus."

And so I began my time at Family Christian feeling as inside of a straight-jacket. I was filled with wondrous knowledge of Christ and accurate knowledge of this world, but no one was interested. I found these students had been taught never to think critically, but only to regurgitate what was put into them. I did insert good things from *The Jesus Secret* whenever I could, but those things could go only a little ways. And I did attempt to throw "monkey wrenches" into the gears of their imaginative fictions concerning this world, but, especially this first semester, I received mostly mockery in return.

I remember speaking of our being made perfect just like the Father, as Jesus said, and a seventh-grade pastor's son hurling back, "You don't believe that, do you?"

Now, before continuing any further, I must position both Robert Anderson and my time at Family Christian into God's intentions towards me. Before I arrived at this chapter in my life, I recognized that there was unresolved anger in my heart towards both of these. Then, before I inserted this paragraph, I had finished writing about my first year-and-half at Family Christian. I could then see some of that unresolved anger in my choices of wording.

This is a good thing and the glory of giving an account of our lives inside the presence of a devoted God. As we place the Lord Jesus upon everything and ourselves inside of Him, we find that we are then free to give thanks in and for the sake of all, and to place our own normal human reactions into the love of our Father.

As my daughter, Johanna, reminded me of the private grief Robert Anderson has carried in his personal life through all these years (as is true for all, in one way or another), so my heart melted towards him. The last thing I would want is for any reader to hold Robert Anderson in anything less than the highest regard as a dear brother who loves Jesus and who has carried in his own life the suffering of Jesus for the sake of others.

At the same time, however, it is my task before God to give a clear accounting of the path from whence comes this Word I share. Much of that includes my own internal pain towards things that hurt and confused me. I expect God's enabling presence that I can share this path even while carrying these precious brethren into joy.

The Summer of 2007

In July, Johanna was old enough to attend the Missouri summer camp with Kyle. I put them both on the Greyhound bus heading for McAlester, where they would again ride with the Schneiders and Dix's to the camp. A few hours later I got a call from a concerned Kyle saying that their bus was late into Dallas and that they had missed the next bus and were stuck in the Greyhound terminal in downtown Dallas. He informed me that Johanna was "having a meltdown." I told him to stay put and I would call Aunt Erma.

It wasn't long before Aunt Erma picked them up and took them to her house for lunch. Meanwhile I also called McAlester, and someone there agreed to drive down and pick them up. Aunt Erma met them on the northwest side of Dallas, and they were on their way again. Kyle wrote about this adventure in his "Remembered Event" paper in my writing class, so I know it well.

Johanna's sister-in-law, Luanne, a few years younger than Jo, wondered that Johanna has always seemed to her to be a part of her growing up years, even though they lived a thousand miles apart. The stops in Oklahoma on the way to the summer camp in Missouri were a reason for that.

I had become interested in making a living online so that I would not have to be subject to the worlds of employment, something that would be inside my expertise. I saw an ad for a copywriting course from American Writers and Artists in Florida. I purchased the course for a few hundred dollars and completed it. It was worth every penny in teaching me how to write to sell. The amazing thing is that God "wrote" the gospel perfectly to the things they taught (or maybe the other way around), to persuade people to buy into something that carries great benefits, but mostly meets their deepest needs.

I loved this course and what it taught me and now waited until I could know just how to implement it. I would also turn and draw much from it in my own teaching of writing. Even now, when I peruse the AWAI website again, my heart is drawn to that whole arena. I know, however, that it will not bear fruit in this present season, and that is part of the story going forward from here.

Our First Years at Lakewood

Our lives through the next seven years, and through these several chapters of my narrative, take place inside the context of our attendance, most every Sunday, at Lakewood Church. Even though this is talking about fewer than seven hundred hours of actual time, I equate this environment as being as impactive upon my life and the life of my family more than any other, save Blueberry.

The only reason Lakewood Church does not have a chapter or two of its own is that outwardly, it was pretty much the same all the way through. Because the impact of that environment on our lives as a family, and upon the development of the present Word of Christ which I teach, was so great, however, I hope to keep the power of that environment inside the Holy Spirit fresh and current through this season of time.

Joel Osteen taught me to HOPE IN GOD far beyond what I had ever known was possible.

The original Lakewood Church had been nearer to our home for many years, but had grown too large for the facilities that had been John Osteen's church. When the city needed new tenants for the then unused Compaq Center, a basketball stadium, Lakewood Church agreed to lease the facility from the city. While we still attended, the city asked Lakewood if they wanted to buy it outright for a very reasonable price, which they did.

After leasing the new facility, the congregation signed for a remodel of around $100,000,000. That sounds like a lot, but it's not really. Everything had to be re-built to hold a large congregation that grew to around 45,000 people. That included a four-story addition for classrooms. As a builder myself, I was very pleased in my interaction with the building, that choices had always been made for enduring quality and never for outward show. You can't have bathrooms used by thousands of people each week needing to be re-built every few years, for instance. Yet the feel of the building was always comfortable, but simple. (These things are important to me, personally.)

The huge parking lots that had been used for the big games remained accessible to Lakewood Church. There were large lots, two levels underground as well as others above ground in different places. For the first couple of years, we parked our green van in an above-ground lot for big vehicles. Our path was partly above ground, and then underneath to eventually join with the huge flows of people coming up from beneath and entering the main entrance of the church.

This walk from and to our car was a really special part of my life for seven years. Little James had wheelies on his shoes, and so he grew up wheeling back and forth along this way. Maureen and I walked together hand in hand while our children walked in front of us chatting and laughing merrily. And we walked in such hope coming and going for I never attended a service there (almost) in which God did not speak to me profoundly both through the praise and through the word shared. There were times when my connection with God inside the anointing of the Spirit upon those services was greater than anything I had known before, sometimes almost more than I could handle.

It's a very simple equation that Jesus made quite clear. - We find what we seek. - If someone declares that they did not "find God" there, well, nothing more needs to be said.

Now, because I want to bring Lakewood Church fresh and living, into each of these five chapters, I will leave a description of the service itself for the next chapter.

I want to finish here, however, by expanding a bit more on our trip home each Sunday, for again, as I said, the going to and coming from Lakewood Church was central in the goodness of our family life together.

We left every service in the joy and expectation of God. We drove the few blocks to Whole Foods. On Sunday afternoons, Whole Foods set out free samples of different foods for sampling, fruits and olives, cheeses and chips. Our children would race on ahead, browsing on all the good things while Maureen and I gathered the groceries we purchased from there. An environment of wholesome foods carries a sense of God in itself, but even more in the joy of the service we had just left. At the same time,

the people who worked there were odd, a bunch of hippies, so I felt right at home, as did our children.

We then drove on down Alabama and turned left on Dunlevy until we came to Souper Salad. We ate there most every Sunday for years. In fact, we found out later that the owners thought of us as their special Sunday family and our absence on occasion was a little less joy for their week.

Often, though, we would eat first and then spend a couple of hours in the big Border's bookstore right across from Whole Foods. There are few things that we did as a family that I loved more than our many times in bookstores. Borders was twice as big as Barnes and Nobles and had many more comfortable places to sit and read. Johanna and Katrina each read more than one book, just across our times at Borders. Only James turned out not to be a reader; he is very hands-on instead and prefers a tool in his hand, not a book. There was plenty to occupy him in these stores as well, however, including taking people up and down the elevator or standing at the entrance to hold the door open for customers going in and out.

Our journey home took us down Allen Parkway and the city parks along Buffalo Bayou. We often stopped and walked the parks, especially in the spring and fall months. Our favorite park was the smaller Sam Houston Park, tucked between Buffalo Bayou and the tall buildings of downtown Houston. Johanna dubbed it "Hobo Park," because homeless people sometimes sat on the benches inside the park. The park was a grassy slope down to a small lake filled with ducks. There were walkways lined with huge and marvelous Live Oak trees, the kind that boys like me want to fill with treehouses. Around two sides were set historical homes and a small church that had been preserved from an earlier Houston and had been placed here. These buildings were not open to the general public, but we enjoyed a guided tour two different times.

Here is what I mean to say in all this, that the joy of living in the expectation of God and the joy of family life together combine seamlessly, hand in hand. And so God gave of Himself so richly to Maureen and me, and our hearts overflow with gratitude.

My First Book

In order to fit everything in, I will place here my continuing work on *The Jesus Secret* and not bring in my teaching experiences through the fall semester until the start of the next chapter.

Through the summer of 2007 until December, I worked to turn my mostly finished book, *The Jesus Secret*, into an actual printed book I could hold in my hand. First, I sent copies of the rough draft to three individuals, my sister Jenelle, Katie Bracken, who was in Redding, California at this time, and Kay Smiley, who had moved with her husband Dave Smiley from Blueberry to Florida. I asked them to mark it for me and comment in the margins. Asking people who don't know how to edit was not the best avenue, however. Jenelle helped the most, in pointing out wording I had used that treated people in a shallow way. I absolutely did not want to do that, so I was very grateful for her corrections. I have slowly learned to edit those things out before they show up on my page.

Katie did not quite understand what I was doing, I think, and wasn't able to add anything. The one thing she did not connect with was the back and forth meaning of **"abide in Me and I in you,"** that this relationship is reciprocal, not one-sided. When I had written those words out from the definition of "abide," I knew that this was against everything believed about Jesus and us, but I also knew it was what God actually says, and so I persisted.

Katie Bracken continued to communicate with us through these years, especially with Maureen and Kyle. I did send her a few of my early books, but she was quite ill through this time and has since passed on. I have no doubt that if she were hearing my present understanding of the Glorious Salvation in Whom we live, she would receive such knowledge of Christ Jesus with all joy.

Kay Smillie was writing comments for a bit that seemed to show her enjoyment of what I had written, then suddenly she wrote in the margin, "This will not work," and that was the end of her assistance. I take her words as meaning, "Since we are NOT like the Lord Jesus, speaking Christ has no meaning, and will not transform anyone." That would be typical "move" reaction. I emailed Kay, but she replied to me that (my paraphrase), "I have no time to consider what you are saying about Christ in me. I have enough concern dealing with anti-Christ in me." She wrote that she wanted nothing more to do with anything I might write.

I asked a sister I knew through Family Christian to draw for me the cover for my new book, a way to represent the resurrection of Christ.

I then found a Christian editor online, a young lady named Emily Sather, whom I hired to carefully edit the book. I might have paid her $600 overall. Emily Sather was the perfect choice because she never corrected me or what I taught, but she marked how I worded things heavily, and even rejected how I argued things at time. I embraced 95% of Emily's correction because I write for readers to know Jesus, and if my poor wording prevented that, I would have failed in my purpose. In fact, I re-wrote my opening pages with very different approaches until she was satisfied.

Because I set myself to embrace and implement most of Emily's corrections, many on every page, in the end, she became my final writing teacher, one might say, and the one I learned the most from. Thank you, Emily, for your kindness and help. Such an approach to editing I have found since is very rare. From then on, I applied what she taught me to the flow of my writing until many of those problems no longer show up.

Once Emily had found and corrected so many mistakes, I went through it again myself and found many more. Then, I sent it to my friend, Peter Bell, and paid him around $300 to do the final proof. Peter is very exact and meticulous, and I was astonished at how many tiny little mistakes he found that Emily and I had both missed, almost on every page.

I don't take any of my books through this process now because it would cost a lot more money than what I have. If I did have the means, I would take all of them through this same edit; it would serve only to make them more readable and accessible.

Through these transitions, I had a local Christian print shop print it as a book with a cover, but three copies cost me $35 each. Finally, when it was all ready, I hired a Christian book printing company I found online, located somewhere in the mid-west. I paid them around $750 to print and ship me 100 copies of *The Jesus Secret*.

If I remember correctly, this final process took place through the Christmas break and by the beginning of the spring semester of 2008, I had 100 printed copies of my first book in hand ready to give away.

A New Metaphor

What I did not know was that God had just begun to blast me as a Saturn Rocket out of Christianity in this world and into living and walking only inside of Jesus. And the picture of a Saturn Rocket, powered by three phases of fuel blast in order to break free of the pull of earth's gravity, came to me only as I wrote this chapter of my life. Again, I had always thought of myself as a desperate and incapable man stumbling from one mistake to the next. I had no idea.

The second stage of the rocket will fire in February 2008, coming up next, and the final stage in October of 2011. And if I might mix metaphors, all three came through the agony of travail, as of a woman filled with Jesus crying to give birth in the face of the dragon, that is, me, as the little guy being thrust out of the womb into a brand new and glorious world unlike anything I had imagined in the darkness.

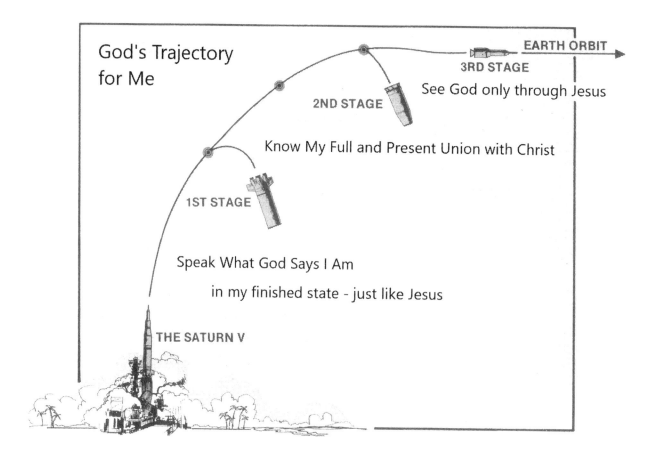

41. Discovering Christ My Life

August 2007 - June 2008

This diagram I found, depicting the three stages of a Saturn Rocket breaking free from earth's pull, describes perfectly what is happening with me. The first and largest part of breaking free from Adam's death was speaking what God says I am. I never confused this with any idea that I was "accomplishing something" by doing this. Rather, I knew that God was changing my thinking until I came to believe and to know what was already true. Nonetheless, this practice has made the entire Bible and all that God speaks in it an integral part of my own being.

The second rocket blast is the topic of this chapter, but in order to set the stage for the mind-blowing thing that happened to me in February 2008, I must first share the growing disconnect between myself and the version of Christianity believed and practiced at Family Christian. Before I do that, I will share my own experiences with the courses and students I taught across this 2007-2008 school year.

A New School Year

At the end of the previous school year, the high school English teacher had gone elsewhere, and so I became the English teacher at Family Christian. At the same time the Rideau's had seen all of our children vanish from the home school group and into the Christian school. Miss Kim was a good teacher, and so I encouraged her and gave my recommendation. Mr. Anderson hired Kim Rideau, then, as the middle school English teacher, and the four Rideau children followed our four into the same classrooms. This was great, since I then had Joy and Byron in my classrooms with Kyle and Johanna. Katrina could continue to share classes with Faith, and James continued being friends with Josiah. Miss Kim also took the drama class and did a much better job than I. Johanna had Miss Kim this year as her 8th grade English teacher. Meanwhile, James was in second grade with Miss Rita Borny and Katrina was in fifth grade with Miss Sneller.

This school year I taught 9th grade English, 10th grade English, and a combined 11th and 12th grade English with American literature. I also taught architectural drafting as the elective course, and I taught world geography to the 10th graders.

The pastor of Family Christian was Nathan Hyman. He had taken on the pastorship from a man who had started both church and school together. Although the church existed separately, its primary purpose and ministry was the school. Pastor Hyman and the elders of the church were the board over the school; nonetheless, the school felt as an equal to the church and not a sideshow.

Robert Anderson, who lived on the next street from our home, was the principal. John Bohacek served as the assistant principal, but also worked more as the 'principal' over the primary grades. I had Mr. Bohacek's two older daughters in my classroom, Erica and Haylee. They were both intelligent and outgoing natural leaders.

Rita and Jean-Francois Borny were both teachers in the school. I had their two older daughters in my classroom, Samantha and Serena. Miss Rita taught second grade and Mr. Borny taught high school science. Miss Sue Cannon was a small and friendly black woman who taught high school math. Mr. Valentine, whose last name was unpronounceable, was from Nigeria. He was hired prior to the start of the 2007-2008 school year to take Mr. Garcia's place (since I had moved over to English), as the high school Bible and US history and government teacher. Then, the middle school teachers were also part of our upper-level regular meetings, including Kim Rideau and Miss Hernandez who taught middle school social studies and art.

Three different "races" working together was simply normal, at least in the Houston area, and no one thought anything about it. We had a good number of black students through all the grades, as well as Hispanics; I knew of no distinctions one way or the other from anyone. The Rideau children especially fitted right in and were loved by all in the school.

All teachers gathered each morning in the main sanctuary for devotions. Then, the upper grade teachers met together with Mr. Anderson once a week. The entire middle and high school gathered for chapel in the large youth room of the church each Thursday morning.

My Classes and Subjects

I will begin with the 10th grade class this fall semester whom I had for English and Geography. These 10th grade students were my 'homeroom' class, and so Maureen and I arranged to take them all to Dickens on the Strand with us the first week of December.

I had blanked over this part of my life, and, once again, as I look back, I discover just how much I loved these young people God had brought into my life. I won't bring all of my students at Family Christian into the narrative, but this group was special, and I had them all at least three times over two years, English and Social Studies.

There were nine 10th graders. Samantha Borny, a studious and cheerful girl whose parents both taught in the school, Ashley Bouse, whose mother was the school secretary, Kaylee Faina who was smart and independent, one who didn't fit in other people's boxes, Larissa Hernandez, whose mother also taught in the school, Joseph Williams, who was a fun, happy-go-lucky boy and who was good friends with Kyle, Bishoy Agaybi, eager and pleasant, who was from Egypt and whose family had been Coptic Christian for centuries, Chad Steiger, a quiet and earnest young man, and Ryan Thomas, a tall African-American who loved sports. Finally, there was Joey Sneller, whose mother also taught in the school.

We prepared long before the trip, our third or fourth time to the Dickens festival. Maureen and I took all the students around to various used clothing stores and Maureen, Johanna, and Katrina had a lot of fun helping each one create a reasonable "Victorian" outfit. We spent most of the day in Galveston, enjoying all the sights and being part of the "Dickens" presentation. The students loved it; many of them had never had an experience like that before.

I had this 10th grade group study *Hind's Feet on High Places* as a literature study later in the year. I had taught from it before more than once. I did not read out loud to them, but gave them some time to read it in class. One day, as I was reading the chapter quietly at my desk, along with them, the Spirit of God was flowing over me with understanding and tears, as the Lord always has every time I have read that book. I said to my students, "God is speaking wonderful things to me as I am reading this; let Him speak to you as well."

In both 9th grade and 10th grade English, I read aloud *All Quiet on the Western Front*, a chapter each Thursday, and then we watched the movie after. This was a good choice because it showed that the millions of Christian young men who joined Germany's armies in WWI did so fully confident that they were serving God, the cause of Christianity, and the country God had chosen, equal to or greater than the same thing in the American young men. Since history is always written by the winners, you don't have an accurate view of WWI or of its fully intended anti-Christian outcome.

I had loved teaching geography at Blueberry, and I enjoyed teaching a similar course to this group of students. Two geography issues were current at this time, peak oil and global warming. I studied both and found that peak oil seemed to be a valid concern, but that man-made global warming was without scientific or logical basis. I layed out both for the students. Of course, the earth is cooling dangerously now, but I was mostly wrong on peak oil which seems to have faded away as an issue. Both were interesting studies that combined science and geography.

The 9th grade class was the largest group in the upper grades and was considered the 'rowdiest,' often getting in trouble as a group. The obvious leader of that class, Kai Ordonio, a native Hawaiian, was NOT a troublemaker, rather the opposite, and often served to get them back "out of trouble." The thing is, I love students of that age and their liveliness and rarely found for myself what the fuss was all about. I remember studying Shackleton's incredible story of survival with my 9th grade group, but I can't remember if it was in English or if I taught them a social studies class.

In that 9th grade group, Kai was warm, intelligent, and generous to all, including me. Josiah Grier was smart, but sometimes religious. He soon figured out how to ask me exactly the right question in class that would send me down a 'rabbit trail' and relieve the class of any work for several minutes.

He employed his craft successfully for most of two years, but I did not mind. I love rabbit trails (a side topic that catches my enthusiasm, but which has nothing to do with the current topic of study) and am convinced that students gain more from them than from rote learning. Haylee Bohacek was probably the source of much of the trouble this group got into. She was as smart as her older sister, Erica, but did not care for the fact that everyone expected her to live up to Erica's 'example.' I really liked Haylee, however, and always enjoyed her leadership in this group, even though it was different from her sister's. Brendan Farias was another young man in this 9th grade group. He was the only student at Family Christian with whom I ran into more than the usual difficulties, but that will not come in until next year. Then, two other girls with whom I had some connection were Paris Weber, who was impacted by my teaching of English more than I knew at the time, and Catie Buell, who was almost a 'Gothic' and fit the good temperament I had come to know them to be.

Mr. Anderson agreed that I could teach drafting and house design as my elective. This proved a popular choice for many from 9th grade to 11th. Our first project for the year was to build the sloped drafting boards each student in the course would need. I remember watching Bishoy Agaybi's face just come alive in this hands-on and actually useful 'classroom' work and grieved much inside that there was so little of it in modern education. Two in particular from ninth grade who took this class were Gabby Voronov, a young girl for whom I cared deeply and sort of "looked out for," and Emmett Brown, who was not gifted in academic study, but who was brilliant beyond the others in every assignment I gave on drafting and home design. I encouraged him much to look at a career in architecture, but I don't know the outcome.

My problem, however, is that I was beginning to gravitate at this time to my one joy of teaching writing and to the growing dislike of teaching most other subjects. And so through the year, mostly in the second semester, I slowly disconnected in the enthusiasm of my mind from teaching drafting. The more that I disconnected, then, the harder it was to get my drafting students to do their work, and the harder it was to get my students to do their work, the more I disconnected. By the end of the year, the drafting period was little more than a study hall.

This was entirely my fault, but it will be a few years, yet, before I discover why.

My final class this year was English for the combined group of 11th and 12th grade students. This combining of the two grades, then, went back and forth between American and English literature from one year to the next. This year was American literature. And this was the first time I had my son, Kyle, who was in 11th grade, in my own classroom with other students. I will share more of what that meant to me in the account of the next school year.

The three seniors in this group included Jess Farias whose mother taught one of the primary grades. Jess was the "life of the party," always the center of attention, though Erica Bohacek was the true and anointed leader of the high school. Kyle's grade level included Joy Rideau, as well as Chey Wilshire, who had also been in our homeschool group before coming to Family Christian for high school. I'll also mention Cassie Zurovec in this group, whose younger sister, Jenna Zurovec, was in the same grade level with Johanna. Jenna and Johanna have been best friends from sixth grade on.

There were a lot of smart and outgoing kids among them. I enjoyed working with them, but they were often a challenge as well, requiring me to flex to meet them at their level. The book studied in American Literature is *The Scarlet Letter* which I had not understood until I read it again in my late twenties. I had them read only portions and read a number of the chapters out loud, while explaining the real meaning of the story. Then, with this group, I brought my writing course a significant step further towards what it eventually became. This group was a good laboratory for me to prove out what worked and what did not. I also included a unit on writing sales copy out from what I had studied with AWAI. Some of their sales letters were pretty convincing.

A New Agony

This fall semester was the same time period through which I was engaged with the long process of finishing my first book. Through this fall semester at Family Christian, however, a new agony arose inside of me. I was filled with such words of joy, and I could not share them with anyone. I knew without question that there is no such thing as word flowing in without the same word flowing out to others.

I had fitted some of the confessions of faith into my Bible class lessons and they were well enough received. These brethren knew the meaning of spiritual things. But there was always the impassible barrier of a Jesus faraway and someday. The truth is that I myself did not know or understand the real meaning of those words that had seized my heart in such hope.

How do I share this word? I had three possibilities, all three of which came to almost nothing. The first was my book, *The Jesus Secret*, mostly complete, but not quite ready to hand out. And the second way was personally sharing this word with individual people who might receive it.

The third way was that I got myself a little digital voice recorder and in the early morning hours while my family was asleep, I recorded a total of twenty-one teachings, three groups of seven each. These were all unscripted and rough, right out from my heart and out from the agony of having nowhere to share this overwhelming word that now filled me to overflowing.

You see, my great burden was two-fold. Writing *The Jesus Secret* in no way satiated my burning desire to know God by knowing His Word sent into me. In complete contrast, it increased that agony manifold. My purpose in these early morning and lonely recordings was to understand the joining of this new-found joy of speaking in confident faith what God says I am in my finished state, just like the Lord Jesus, and all the word God had planted in my heart over many years, Word that I knew was of Him.

I put these twenty-one recordings onto CDs and attempted to get people to listen to them, but they didn't. I had my family listen to them, but that also hit a wall halfway through and we could not finish. I transcribed them all into written form, but my wording was very rough.

I did not know that God had not yet released His Word through me, not until my experience with Jesus in February of 2008 became my knowledge of the Bible. And that is the first time I have seen February of 2008 coming up, set against February of 1998, and I bow my head in wonder before a holy and a faithful God.

I worked a lot to improve the wording of those three sets of seven lessons each, and they eventually became the core chapters of each of the three parts of my book, *Our Path Home*. The first topic was the meaning of the first four most important vers-es of the Bible for our lives today. I titled that "The Goal of the Believer," then changed it to "Journey's End," and ended up with "Home as It Really Is." The second topic was "What Is Man?" That is, what does it mean that we are conceived out from God. And the third was about what it might mean that we are being "Transformed into His Image." You can identify those twenty-one early recordings scattered through Our Path Home because they are stiffer or blockier than the other chapters.

My First Websites & The Jesus Secret

Through these fall months I created my first two websites, dyordy.com and thejesussecretsociety.com. I had to go with "society" because someone else already owned "jesussecret.com." I did little with the dyordy site at this point and worked mostly on the Jesus Secret website as a sales page for my book. I wrote a decent sales copy page following all the things I had learned from the copywriting course. Sadly, this website sold none of my books.

Before we arrive at the momentous and life-changing thing Jesus did to me in February of 2008, I want to share my sending out of the 100 copies of *The Jesus Secret* that I now had in hand. This giving away took place over several months, but the majority in January and February.

I sent copies to individuals I had known in the move, including Rick Annett and Joe McCord. These were the only two sendings that bore fruit. Rick shared with me the profound joy and victory that speaking the Jesus Secret brought into his life. I would not know of it for several years, but Brother Joe did begin to draw from my books now and then to share good things in the word that he preached. These two, however, were the only responses I received back.

I gave copies to different ones in the home school group and among my colleagues at Family Christian. I don't think that those who did read some from it really understood what it was about. I visited with Sue Cannon often, sharing the Lord in fellowship with her. She always responded in receptive joy, but as I look back now, I realize that was probably more her way than any actual understanding of the things I shared.

I sent copies of my book specifically to John and Nathel Clarke and to Joel Osteen. With them, I included a personal letter, each of which I want to share here.

~

January 22, 2008. Dear Brother John and Sister Nathel, we hear the news of you from Ann. May the Lord bless and strengthen you during this time.

I want to share my book with you as my gift to you. This is more than a book, but rather the experience of thirty years, drawn with all my heart into what God is speaking to me today. As I finished the last page, I saw that everything I have ever gone through was for this, and I heard the Father say to me, "Well done, good and faithful son." I never felt more blessed and filled with joy in my life.

Much of the good in those thirty years of experience came through you, and I bless you for it. My hope, Sister Nathel, is that you will read my book aloud to Brother John. Read it with my blessing and thankfulness.

My heart has never left the word God first birthed into me in the first two years I was in the move. In leaving the communities, I asked God to sift out what He had not spoken from what He had spoken. There is no way in this world that I want to lose one iota of what was God speaking; I want everything that was not God speaking gone. I think you will see, as you go through *The Jesus Secret*, that sifting.

This is my anointing; this is my gift; this is the purpose of all the glory and all the agony of my life – the Jesus Secret. And now, as I see myself going forward, my task is to get this book into the hands of as many of God's dear people as I can.

My prayer is that the vision that God Himself birthed in you will be re-strengthened as you go through this book. I know that you rest in His joy over you.

~

March 11, 2008. Pastor Joel, my family and I have been attending Lakewood for over a year and a half. I must admit, I avoided Lakewood for the first few years we were in Houston. I thought a "mega" church must be all about production. When my wife insisted we visit, I loved it. 2006 had not been my worst year in life, but it was close enough. Within a couple of months of sitting under the word you teach, I was able to say truly that 2006 was the best year of my life so far. 2007 was much better and 2008 has started off with a knowledge of His presence like I have never known in my life.

The key for me was a statement you make over and over; I think it is also found in your book, *Your Best Life Now*. "Speak what God says you are." I am the kind of person that takes a word like that all through the Bible to see what God really says. And so I wrote down every statement in the New Testament that describes me on this basis, that I will be just like Jesus when I see Him as He is. I put all that together in this book I am sharing with you. Yes, much that is in this book is drawn from over 30 years of seeking God and walking with Him, but the spark that drew it all together was the word you spoke into my life. Thank you.

I also want to say that, yes, I have sat under "deeper teachings" for years. But my knowledge of "deeper" truth did not help me because God was far away. You have taught me to believe that He is for me, that His favor is upon me. You have taught me to draw near to God with full assurance of faith. All deeper teaching, as important as it might be in the long run, is useless without the foundation of trusting in God as you share like I have never known before. I soak in every word you teach, and I will value it for the rest of my life. Thank you.

I would like to share this book with you, *The Jesus Secret*. As I finished the book, God showed me that everything I have gone through in life was for the writing of this book. I do not know how far God will take it. I hope it will be a blessing to many.

~

Understand that Joel receives hundreds of communications like this every day from all over the world. He likely has staff members who go through them and give to him only what is most pertinent. Whether my letter or book made it to Joel, I do not know. But I always leave all those things in the hands of my very capable Savior.

Now, in spite of some repetition, I want to include a total of four of these letters. The next I gave personally to Bill Johnson along with a copy of my book; which circumstances I want to share. Also you will notice that the letters to Joel Osteen and Bill Johnson came after the incredible thing Jesus would do with me in February, though I include them here.

Sometime in March, Bill Johnson was ministering at Victory Christian Center, and so we attended that service. I was determined to give Bill Johnson a copy of my book with this letter I had written.

Bill Johnson shared in the service, both word and prayers of healing. When the service was over, Pastor Tony hustled Bill Johnson through a side door right in front of me, in order to escape the press of people who would want to attach themselves to this "man of God."

Now, this was quite different from the move, which did have many godly qualities. In the move everyone had personal access to the ministry and saw them daily as part of the family if you lived in the same community. Brother Sam, Brother Buddy, and Brother Joe knew most everyone personally, thousands of people world-wide.

As I saw Bill Johnson disappearing behind that door, with my heart pounding, I did one of the bravest things in my life. I got up off my seat on the front row, in front of hundreds of people, and followed them through that door.

I joined them in Pastor Tony's office and gave my book to Bill Johnson, asking him to look through it if he would, pointing out the letter to him I had included. He received me with great kindness, but also a tinge of sorrow. "I have stacks of books like this in my office, given to me with the same request," he said. "I can't promise that I will be able to look at yours."

I left all that in the Lord's hands. Here is the letter I had written.

∽

March 12, 2008. Dear Pastor Bill Johnson, you do not know me, but I have been in a couple of your meetings here in Houston. You are also acquainted with a number of people I have known for years, John and Nathel Clarke, Tom Rowe, and others. You may also know Katie Bracken in your congregation as well as my niece, April Lewis, who recently enrolled in your Bible School.

Reading your books, a couple of years ago, helped set me on a journey that culminated with the writing of this book, *The Jesus Secret*. I believe it dovetails very well with the word God is speaking through you. I hope it will be a blessing to you.

God is moving in the earth to fulfill the New Covenant, in its entirety. We are becoming like Jesus as we see Him as He is. Great power is issuing forth from the Father, not just to cause us to be a witness of Christ in power, as important as that is, and not just to fulfill every word of the New Covenant, as

exciting as that is, but to bring to completion now in our lives the original determination and intent of God, our complete union with Christ.

It's happening and it must happen in this age, on this earth, in our lives.

It is my prayer that God will use my book to bring many into the determination of God. Please take a few minutes to leaf through it. If God quickens anything to you, it might be of some value to you to spend more time with it. I pray that you are blessed by *The Jesus Secret*.

Thank you for the word that you teach. My wife and I receive your podcasts and gain much life and encouragement from them.

∽

Though I eventually gave away all copies of *The Jesus Secret*, I received no return response from anyone except Rick Annett. It was a wall of silence.

A Growing Disconnect

My relationship with my students in the classroom and the content I was teaching them was one thing, existing separately from my growing disillusionment with the worldliest church I have ever known personally and with an approach to "Christian" education that kept all the destructive practices and philosophies of modern education while retaining little of the excellent instructional methods that are common in Texas public schools.

Now, the Lord has just shown me something incredibly wonderful. I had thought up until now that all my work through these years, literally thousands of hours, on a different approach to teaching children, that all of it has come to nothing. And so I have borne it with great sorrow until now. Yet now the Lord shows me the obvious, that such is not possible, that all I have labored over with tears will return to me fully formed in its season, for I can lose nothing. At the same time, this entire milieu of my concern with a different way to educate young people, from 1999 until 2015, is essential to the environment in which the Word of Christ is being formed inside of me. And so I will include some of these things as of equal importance with everything else taking place in my life.

I find a great jealousy arising inside of me, that I would impart to you, as completely as I can, the preparing of this wondrous path into all the knowledge of God. With all my heart, I would have you know from whence this path comes. Nonetheless, this is not a diatribe concerning "not loving the world," nor a treatise on education, and so I must carefully weave these things as they fit with my on-going life experiences of affliction, goodness, and glory.

This environment into which God had placed me was perfect and critical to all that God was working inside of me. I do NOT want anyone to think that this was not a wonderful group of Christian people who loved Jesus, who walked in the Spirit, and who knew the power of the Holy Ghost coming upon them on a regular basis. These brethren represented God's great dilemma and travail over His people all across the earth, and they treated me with all kindness and respect, including and especially Mr. Anderson. They are good people filled with Jesus.

Nonetheless I was once again plunged into an environment with which I did not agree, and God moved with me inside of these many contradictions with much grace and with much inner sorrow. Some of the contradictions fit more into the next chapter. Here I must start with Mr. Valentine and chapel.

Mr. Valentine's philosophy of education seemed to be that teaching is all about the teacher and all the "important" things the teacher was presenting to the class. The students were left then with the task of discovering what they were expected to learn. The work they were given did not relate sensibly with what was taught, but again, the students were responsible for producing what the teacher expected even though they had no idea what it was. And when they did not, they failed and the problem was their fault. They simply were not applying themselves as they ought.

This caused great difficulty for the students. They had no idea what Mr. Valentine expected. Erica Bohacek, who "applied herself as she ought" beyond almost any other student I have taught, was barely making a D. Kyle, who is today an effective college instructor, was receiving F's, and others were struggling much more than he. And yet they were exhorted that this was their fault. Such an approach to teaching, of course, always reduces student learning even among those who love to learn.

The problem came when I tried to raise the issue with Mr. Anderson and with the gathering of my colleagues. When I suggested to Mr. Anderson

that he and I sit down with Mr. Valentine and gently share a more effective way of teaching, Mr. Anderson would not consider it. In the meeting with my fellow teachers, which included Mr. Valentine, I shared that if my students were not learning what I thought I was teaching, I would take that upon myself and alter how I taught until they were learning successfully. Sue Cannon immediately contradicted me and told Mr. Valentine never to think that way, that if his students did poorly on his test, that was entirely their fault. And so I could only keep my mouth closed.

This "teacher-centered" approach to classroom instruction is all too common in Christian schools. In fact, I got in trouble over this issue at both Bowens Mill and Blueberry. So what if your brilliant display of classroom teaching was 'of God,' if your students did not learn a thing, what have you actually done? Jesus said that what goes in doesn't count, but only what comes out. What is the actual fruit of your teaching inside your students bound against their wills to the desks in front of you? Some teachers don't consider such questions.

Another method of classroom instruction used by some at Family Christian and in other Christian schools is text-book centered teaching. The ABeka curriculum is like that, driving the classroom moments with rigid control. Others simply say, "Read the chapter and answer the questions." Thankfully, this method was discouraged at the Blueberry school and in most of Texas public education. It is an approach I never "rebelled against" but never implemented, ever.

Kyle graduated from four years of sitting under these approaches and philosophy of education with great sorrow, counting the educational side of his teenage years to be almost a complete loss. At the same time this great contradiction created for me one of the greatest presses I have passed through in my life – in the next chapter.

Let us now go to chapel. Chapel very quickly became more than I could bear.

Don't get me wrong, there were mighty movings of the Spirit upon the students in these chapel services all through our time there. The Lord touched many and there were times of great dedication to the Lord. But Nicene Christianity is all about mixing Christ with that which contradicts Christ, to equal measure.

I sat there listening to grown adults telling these children, all the way down to 12 years old, that if their neighbors went to hell, IT WAS THEIR FAULT. There was a continual tension between the Spirit of God drawing the students to worship the Lord in a wonderful anointing and the exhortation that if they were not coming to the front - especially you on the back row - then you are in rebellion against God.

Then there was Mr. Valentine who, as the Bible teacher, also oversaw the chapel times. Mr. Anderson was there, but he played the drums in the praise and let Mr. Valentine officiate. Both Mr. Anderson and Mr. Borny were men of the Spirit and very often the genuine flow of the Holy Ghost would proceed out from them as well as out from Erica Bohacek, but they did nothing toward that which so contradicted the Lord Jesus.

To Mr. Valentine, the law was fully equal with the gospel. That is theory only, however, for wherever there is any percentage of law, the gospel goes quiet and cannot speak. Again, there was much gospel known apart from Mr. Valentine, but it did not come through him.

'I' Disappear

On Thursday, February 21 (or the 14th), I attended another typical chapel meeting. Again, Mr. Valentine shared the message, and again he pounded law into these children contrary to the gospel of Jesus inside them. And again, as I stood at the back of the chapel room with the other teachers, in great agony of soul, I also did what I always do.

Let me explain. Although I knew nothing of Asperger's, I have always possessed the agony of too much feeling assailing me and I have always possessed the answer to too much pain and noise, the ability to disassociate, that is, to separate myself into another "mind" that does not hear the awful things. This ability is only partial because I remain fully aware of the outer reality, but I am protected from it. Since I had begun to speak what God says I am, this other "mind" was no longer a fantasy world, but rather the Person of the Lord Jesus.

And so as I stood there hiding inside of Jesus from Mr. Valentine vociferously pounding anti-Christ into these children, the most extraordinary thing happened to me.

"I" disappeared, and Jesus was the only One remaining.

I knew, in that moment, my full union with the Lord Jesus Christ, even as we had looked towards such a thing at Blueberry, exactly what I had known in the prophetic dream I shared while there in 1995. Yet I also knew, instinctively in that moment, that it was never "I" who had come into union with Christ as I once falsely imagined to be our obligation. In complete contrast, it was Jesus Himself who has actively and presently come into union with all that is me.

I rushed from there to my computer once again, and this time, typed "union with Christ" into a Google search. That very afternoon, I found www.christasus.com and began to read with all earnest excitement. This website included the writings of a number of those who had followed Norman Grubb and who taught our full and present union with Christ. A man by the name of Fred Pruitt was a primary teacher in this group, and right off the bat I connected with his spirit and his wonderful explanations of the gospel.

This is meant to be an account of my life and experiences and not any foray into Christ-our-life teaching. But I want to set here my experience. I have surrendered my heart and life to God at ever deeper levels and in three different ways all the days of my life. And that surrender has been proven out inside of difficulties greater than is common to most Christian experience. There were the gentle surrenders when I sought the Lord, and He came to me and showed me His kindness towards me, beginning with asking Jesus into my heart at age seven. There were the desperate surrenders with the bony finger of God pointed straight into my forehead attended either with a mighty and holy fear resting upon me or that implacable, "No, no, no," that did not cease until I had broken before such an uncompromising God. And then there were the Covenant surrenders when I bound God to myself, that He might never let me go.

No surrender I have ever experienced comes anywhere close to the greatest surrender of the Christian life, the surrender to a Jesus who comes into union with me.

To surrender to Jesus all of my sin, all of my shame, all of my sinfulness, all of my stupidity, all of my endless and humiliating mistakes, that all of these now belong only to Him, and never to me again. That from this moment on, Jesus is utterly responsible for me, for all that I find myself to be including all that I do and say – This is the greatest surrender of the Christian life.

Nonetheless, I had now become dangerous to the evil one, and the last thing that accusing voices want is to be shut out forever. From this moment on, for the next nine months, I came under spiritual assault greater than I ever knew before or since. I will unfold that experience as I go forward through these months.

Fred Pruitt & Union with Christ

One thing I must again emphasize is that Family Christian was where I worked, around forty hours a week, but it was not my home or my fellowship. Community, of course, had been all three, and thus, much more intense, though its rewards were also much greater. Here is most of a letter I wrote to Fred Pruitt before the end of February.

⮑

Fred Pruitt, my name is Daniel Yordy. I have been reading your web messages the last few days and have emailed Linda Bunting. She suggested that you might be willing to swing by Houston to meet with us during your trip to Texas in April. I'd like to briefly share with you my history as an introduction.

After reading *Rees Howells: Intercessor* and being deeply moved by the book, at the age of 20, in 1977, I headed north into the Canadian wilderness, seeking a deeper experience in God. There I found a move of the Spirit led by Sam Fife, a ministry who taught a sonship message of overcoming death and going on to the fullness of Christ. For the next twenty years, I was part of that fellowship, living for most of that time in Christian community. Sam Fife was killed in a plane crash in 1979 and the ministries who led that move of the Spirit eventually led it in a direction I could no longer agree with. My wife and I left that move of the Spirit in 1998 and eventually ended up in Houston, Texas where I am presently teaching in a Christian school.

However, in leaving that move of the Spirit, I did not want to lose anything God had taught me through those years, but I did not know the dividing line between what God had taught me and what had been tacked on by man. So I placed myself before the Lord, first to bring healing to my life and second to reveal His truth to me. God is doing just that.

In the summer of 2006, we started attending Lakewood Church with Joel Osteen. In spite of the megachurch status, I was surprised to find just the word God knew I needed. Joel Osteen said something that sparked a fire in me. He said, "Speak who God says you are." I'm never satisfied until I know the totality of what something like that means in the Word, so over the next few months I wrote out every description of who I am in the New Testament, gradually turning it into the material for a book. Last fall, that book became *The Jesus Secret: Who I Am*. It is a guide to speaking who God says we are, which I have practiced since I started writing it.

The word that has changed me the most is this: "Christ is all there is in me; I am complete in Him." Every time ill-feeling and despair would sit upon me, I would speak that over and over. It takes no time at all for the ill-feeling to vanish and to find myself in full faith in Jesus. Anyway, last week, the Lord began to speak to me on a deeper, more intimate level than I have known. He showed me that I was to lean upon Him and trust Him utterly. Last Thursday morning, I was in a difficult setting [the chapel service above]. I closed my eyes and envisioned Him, casting myself fully upon Him. But instead of leaning upon His breast, I found myself disappearing into Him and He into me. I knew, more clearly than I had ever known, that I was one with Him.

Meanwhile, over the last few years, I have been looking on the Internet for people who were hearing the same things God has been teaching me. I had found Gary Sigler's Kingdom Resources and have my own website posted there. But Thursday evening, I came across Christasus.com and began reading. I have been so blessed and overwhelmed with joy as I find the same word in you that has become so precious to me. When I read your words, I open my book and read mine and find them saying exactly the same thing, over and over.

So, yes, I would like very much if you were able to visit us here in Houston next month. I may have a small group that would like to listen to what you have to share, but whether or no, my family and I would welcome the connection.

⮑

Fred Pruitt did come to Houston that April with three other brothers traveling with him sharing with small groups on our precious union with

Christ. They were sharing at a sister's home on the north side of Houston on a Saturday afternoon, and so Maureen and the children climbed into our van with me and we attended that sharing time. All of the brothers with Fred shared a bit to the several people gathered as well as the six of us. Fred shared last and longest. It was a new and fresh word to me, and we enjoyed the fellowship and a light meal together after.

I invited them to come and share in our home the next morning, a Sunday, and, since they had nothing else in their schedule, they agreed. We also invited them to share Sunday dinner with us, so before they arrived, I rushed to pick up a couple of rotisserie chickens and tubs of potato salad from Kroger's.

The four of them sat in our living room with the six of us. At this point, James was nine, so that was conceivable. Fred Pruitt shared last and the longest, a wonderful explanation of union with Christ and Christ living as us. I noticed a stark difference, however. I had expected a great and sober anointing to be resting upon such men carrying such a word, but only Fred's words came into me through the Spirit, the others were just nice men sharing nice things. We had good fellowship and dinner together, however, and as they left, I gave each one a copy of *The Jesus Secret*.

I then ordered several of Norman Grubb's books and started to read his primary book, *Yes, I Am*. After reading a couple of chapters, however, I hit a wall dead on. There was no Spirit anointing upon or any present knowledge of "**My words are Spirit, and they are Life,**" within Norman Grubb's writing. His words were primarily mental ideas. I cannot know God in that way, so I stopped reading and gave away most of those books. I do not draw anything that I teach directly from Norman Grubb, nor from most of those who follow him, for there is little Spirit-knowing in their understanding.

Two of those who knew Norman Grubb, however, had received full immersion into the Holy Spirit before they had met him, Dan Stone and Fred Pruitt, and thus through what these two wrote, I received much word as Spirit and as life.

The important thing here is that through the next few years I spent much time reading Fred Pruitt's articles and gained much immediate confirmation and understanding of the truths of our precious union with Christ that I continue to share today all through everything I write.

Continuing at Lakewood

When God spoke to me to "Give My people hope," He had no intention of leaving me on my own to figure out what that might mean. On the contrary, when the time came, God put me under a man who taught me to hope in the expectation of God most every Sunday for seven years. I think this way, that 350 times, and, one might say, in 350 ways, Joel Osteen taught me to HOPE in God.

Do you understand why I regard this man as one of my dearest friends in life? And like reading John Eldredge, to hear and watch Joel Osteen is to know him personally, for all that he shares comes out from the goodness and expectation of God in his own personal life.

Next, I want to share a bit more about the ministry at Lakewood and the order of the service. I will describe more in upcoming chapters because I want each of these chapters to be known as inside our time at Lakewood. The Lakewood church ministry was primarily the Osteen family. Joel and Victoria were the lead pastors, joined by Joel's brother, Paul, a medical doctor by profession, and Joel's sister, Lisa Comes. Paul and Lisa often shared the word in the Wednesday night services, some of which we attended. Their mother, Dodie Osteen was viewed by all as the 'mother' of the church. Dodie Osteen's incredible and determined faith in God impacted everyone, but especially her children.

Then, Marcos Witt served as the assistant pastor as well as the pastor of the full Spanish service held every Sunday afternoon, soon after our service was over. Marcos Witt had grown up in a missionary setting in Mexico. He was a gifted singer, widely known across Latin America as a prominent gospel singer. When Joel was not present of a Sunday, Marcos Witt was typically the one who shared the word. Pastor Marcos always had us laughing in the joy and goodness of God.

The praise times at Lakewood were led by several together. The initial praise leader was Cindi Cruse-Ratcliff. Then a black brother and sister had joined the Lakewood staff soon after we started, Da'dra Greathouse and Steve Crofford. These two were wonderful praise leaders; in fact, they all moved together back and forth in the flow of worship. Much of the time, another black brother also joined in leading the praise, Israel Houghton, an Emmy-award-winning gospel singer. You might know some of his songs, including "I Am a Friend of God." More than once, Israel and Steve or Steve and Da'dra would sing back and forth to each other in the leading of the praise as is common in southern African American worship. I loved those times.

The praise songs chosen at Lakewood were songs anyone could freely join with, unlike the strange non-sing-able beat all too common elsewhere. There was a large supporting orchestra behind the main platform, but their sounds did not dominate as is the case in many modern churches. It was always a rich Spirit-anointed river of life flow of worship, always lifting me up into the Spirit where God often spoke incredible understanding to me.

I will share more of a typical service in the next chapter.

Withstanding All Assault

When Sister Jane Miller first taught me that many dark things pressing against me, things I once thought were "just me," that those things are demons, unclean spirits whispering untrue words, I was forced into a life of spiritual warfare. I did not want to fight, but I wanted to be under false feelings and lying accusations even less. And so, when a false spirit made me feel cut-off from God, I attempted to oppose it. In the end, only a gentle surrender into God arising from within my own spirit, broke the hold of darkness against my mind.

But I did not like to fight; fighting is not what I want to be doing, or so I thought. Yet living un-

der demons pissing all over me was worse. And so I fought, and over years I learned to fight, and I learned what things were truly of my human person and what things were false and not of me at all. I fought against demonic assault against me, the lying inside, the dark feelings, the "I-am-in-trouble-with-God" sensations without letup, really, from 1987 to 2013, twenty-six years.

I DO NOT allow demons to piss against me.

Yet I had not known spiritual warfare like that which came against me from the moment I knew my full and present union with Christ. For nine long months, from February to November of 2008, I endured every screaming voice wailing its accusations against me. The words came in the voices of those I had known, preachers of Nicene theology, elders and apostles in the move. It was not those persons, but the words were those they had spoken, now in the form of unclean ruin relentlessly assailing my mind and heart every day.

"You have no right. – You are moving out of your place. – You blaspheme God. – Who do you think you are? – You are the proudest man I have ever known. – You are unsubmissive."

And through all these months, I spoke the words of the Jesus Secret – Christ is my life; I have no other life. Christ is all there is in me.

I spoke those words, not as a chant, not in order to "make something happen," but because they are TRUE and because they are the ONLY place I WILL live. – You see, I have a desperate, desperate need to live; death, that is, not knowing Father-with-me at home in my heart, is not an option for me.

42. Out of the Furnace

June 2008 - May 2009

The last chapter ended with "withstanding all assault." This chapter begins with "withstanding all assault." I cannot express too greatly the relentless awfulness that assailed me through all these months, the crying, wailing voices of accusation and despair. Yet none of these voices were on the inside of me, as I had once known them. My own speaking of Christ my life was on the inside of me and all these voices were outside. They were close, they were all around, but they were NOT me, nor did I ever give them heed, not for one moment.

Now, all these voices were of three larger types of accusation. The strongest in my ears was that I had no right, that I was exalting myself against God. The second was against Jesus, that these words I was speaking were not actually He in my heart and mouth, that they were just words and that speaking Christ personal as me was gross hypocrisy, for such claims are visibly untrue. And the third was against myself, that I am a failure and a loser, that I so fall short of God.

I would not hear them, and I kept my ears closed against the screams against me by speaking the Jesus Secret without fail. Christ is my life; I have no other life. Christ is all there is in me.

The Summer of 2008

This June, Maureen's mother, Roberta Mack, was celebrating her 80th birthday. Sister Roberta had been diagnosed with cancer some years before, but had continued in faith in God and it had not progressed. At this point, however, the decline was showing itself, not outwardly, but in weariness. Maureen and her sisters wanted us all to celebrate this time with them at Bowens Mill. This would be our last trip in the green van. We drove along the Gulf Coast through Mobile, Pensacola and Tallahassee on our way to Bowens Mill. We stopped to enjoy the white sands of the Florida beaches.

When we arrived at the Ridge, Sister Roberta was still doing reasonably well. She and Claude were no longer in their little trailer. They had a small double-wide across the way from the teaching trailer, about half-way between the Tabernacle and the top of the slope down towards the school. Right behind their trailer was a nice large single-wide with a sitting room porch added on. This is where we stayed, in the large master bedroom with the kids in the rooms on the other end.

We had a good time visiting with Claude and Roberta and with Maureen's sisters and Matthew. Our children were good friends with Breanna, but had not had much time to spend with her during their growing up years. These several days at the Ridge were an adventure they shared with Breanna. I gave copies of *The Jesus Secret* to Claude and Roberta and to Jim and Joyce Fant. I was able to share life from the present word of Christ with Jim and Joyce, and I shared a devotion with the whole family at the Ridge that was well-received.

I liked the fact that my kitchen was still going strong, fully enjoyed by the family. At the same time they had added two wings to the front of the dining hall to allow for bathrooms and for a nicer family area beyond what had been a crowded and narrow dining room.

I have one memory from this visit that embarrasses me even now anytime I think of it. I had just watched and enjoyed the silly animated movie, *Surfs Up*. I suggested that the family watch it in the family area of the tabernacle, which we did of an evening. The problem was that it was not appropriate in that setting, and by the end everyone but Claude and Roberta had left. Yet I have learned to place the Lord Jesus upon such foolish mistakes, for He shares everything with me.

A Business Idea

On our way back to Houston, we headed towards Dallas first in order to visit with Uncle Werner and Aunt Erma Honsalek. While we were in their home, Uncle Werner gave me his entire set of the *Great Books of the Western World*, from Homer through Freud. I had owned this set before, given to me when I was teaching at Bowens Mill, but I had sold it when God turned me around and forbade me entrance to Blueberry with all those books. Now, God returned it to me separately from any false identity in me, and I have enjoyed using those books as an important resource all through my writing.

On our way home from Dallas to Houston, driving south on I-45, I was thinking.

Let me explain. I love to drive, for driving keeps my brain quietly occupied in such a way that I am then free to think about anything and everything. At the same time, driving in the early part of the day, while drinking coffee, inspires my mind into seeing things clearly.

I wanted to start an Internet business so that I could support my family from home without needing to tie myself to employment situations that were hostile to my heart and strength. Along with the copywriting course I had taken, including a second course that was even more useful than the first, I was reading Michael Masterson, the author of both courses, and his sound approaches to business.

And so, as I was driving, three things came together in my mind, (1) my desire to teach teenagers, (2) the things I was learning from Michael Masterson, and (3) my desire to apply what I had learned from the copywriting courses. What I saw, as they came together, was "Micro-Business for HighSchoolers," an online course designed to establish teenagers in a business of their own inside of which they would learn many practical things as part of their schooling. It became what I would call, "business-driven learning." I excitedly hammered out the details of this potential business in my mind on the rest of the drive home.

This online course would be massive, extending over a full school year, as a full high school course, with teaching and practice. And from day one, it would guide the teenager in the start-up and expansion of their own money-making business. Every facet of business expertise including business math and writing, marketing and Internet, production and practice, writing a business plan, and so on, every skill was to be developed step by step, even while the business had begun.

In other words, the motivation to learn would be the successful making of money through the student's own business. Here is my one-line de-

scription. ~~~ Micro-Business for HighSchoolers is a nine-month course - always updated - that leads teenagers through the process of developing real-world businesses, while they master many of their high school learning objectives, and bring profit and value to their world. ~~~

I went right to work on writing this course as soon as we were home. It was too big of a job just for me, and so before school started, I had hired three other writers through an online freelance website to help me in writing specific lessons. I obtained funding for this endeavor through a new credit card, expecting that it would pay for itself as well as support my family.

By the time the fall semester at Family Christian had begun, the first parts of Micro-Business for HighSchoolers were completed and the business idea was well on its way. At the same time, I would write about the spiritual side of this experience in my first *Christ Our Life* letter.

My Classes for 2008-2009

I was moved to another classroom for this year, the one nearest the front main door in the upstairs. This year I taught eleventh and twelfth grade English, British Literature. The group we had taken to Dickens on the Strand were now the eleventh graders and my son Kyle and his class were the seniors. Then, I taught tenth grade English and world history, and ninth grade English and geography. The ninth grade group included my daughter, Johanna. I must have had another class, but I don't remember what it was.

Mr. Anderson was suspicious about my beliefs concerning world history, that America was not the apex of God's dealings with mankind, and so he stood outside the door, unknown to me, through my world history introductory session. He must have been satisfied because he allowed me to continue.

I really appreciated having Kyle and Johanna in my classroom, for those two saw a side of their dad that they would not have known otherwise. I am very good in the classroom with teenagers, but my abilities there are not duplicated anywhere else.

The prior spring, I had asked Mr. Anderson about using a different set of books for my English classes, books that would have been much more useful to their learning than the ABeka grammar books. He did not grant my request, but proceeded to buy the ABeka stuff anyway. I brought one of the grammar books to the start of each of my three classes and read a couple of lines from the first chapter. "We are required to use these books," I said, "and so we have." That book went back to the book closet and there they sat on the shelves.

The thing is, I wanted to teach these students how to write and filling their time with a grammar book means they would never learn to write.

I enjoyed teaching British Literature; it allows for such a variety of study and enriching projects. I had taught my writing course the year before to my upper level groups. For that reason, this year I took them through writing a short story. This was an incredibly fun task, an exercise which taught me a lot about teaching writing. And after helping them work their stories to completion, I had some awesome stories. The best one was a western, written by Chey Wilshire. I encouraged him to consider a career of writing stories.

I took the ninth grade group through my writing course. The best writer I have ever taught was the young black man from C.E. King who went on to Harvard Medical School. The second best writer was my daughter, Johanna. I have tried to convince her of that ever since, but she won't believe me. She claims she doesn't "like to" write.

I read *Watership Down* by Richard Adams each Thursday to the ninth and tenth grade groups. That's a long book. My son, Kyle, has assured me that it was, in fact, a "horror story," but that all my students were entranced by my reading of it. It's not a horror story to me, except when I watch the animated version of it. Nonetheless, it is one of the best portrayals of true leadership in world literature.

With my juniors and seniors, I read some out from the British Literature pieces we were studying. I also pulled out my poetry folder from teaching poetry in the Blueberry School and taught the upper grades a poetry writing unit. Again, this was a tremendous experience for them and for me.

Mr. Anderson questioned Josiah and Kai, who were in my tenth grade world history class, as to whether I was actually teaching them substance. You see, I do not teach rote learning, the memorization of endless and soon-forgotten facts. I teach the story and meaning of history and the student work

is always writing essays. Grading essays is a lot of work, but it's the only way real learning takes place. Josiah and Kai gave Mr. Anderson proof that I was, in fact, teaching them from the book and assured him that they were learning more from me than any other teacher they had.

This underlines, then, a growing problem for me through this school year. I teach by how young people actually learn, and not by the rote, "fill their heads with facts and quick answers to a simplistic worksheet" method, like the popular ABeka curriculum requires. At the same time, I respect my students and treat them as real persons. I had between 40 and 50 students who had never had a teacher like me. It is they who will say that they learned more from me than any other teacher. They were not accustomed to a teacher who respected them and who taught them to think critically and not just accept what they were told.

A black girl in the tenth grade group had borrowed a book from my desk. When I needed it in class, I could not find it. She assured me that she had returned it, but since I did not see it, in my frustration, I basically "accused" her of losing it, in front of the class. When they left to go on to their next class, in the quiet of waiting for the next group to come in, I paused long enough to discover that, indeed, there it was, among some other books on my desk, just as she had said. In my consternation, I sat down immediately and wrote her a note, "Teneshia, I did find the book on my desk. I apologize for saying those things to you. I was wrong. Would you please forgive me." I asked the first young man coming in to take it over to their room and give it to her.

I learned later that she cried after she read the note. The thing is, most teachers just don't do things like that, especially towards a black girl who was sometimes a trouble-maker.

I have learned only recently that at least two of my students at this time, Paris Weber and Jenna Zurovec, Johanna's close friend, had both hated English and school prior to my being their teacher, but have now devoted their lives to teaching. It is always an astonishment to me, but I have found the same report from many over the years.

Hurricane Ike

School had been started for only a few weeks when Hurricane Ike headed our way. Hurricane Ike was huge in size, but not as powerful as Hurricane

Rita had been. Ike was a Category 2 when it came on shore at Galveston. School had closed down and everyone was at home. The officials instructed the people to sit this one out, since it was not destructive like Rita might have been and the millions of people trying to escape in their cars would guarantee a greater disaster. The people along the coast were asked to evacuate, however, but 80 some people on the Bolivar Peninsula to the east of Galveston chose to ride it out. They were on the side of the heavy storm surge hitting the coast, for the eye came right over Galveston. All the buildings on the Bolivar Peninsula were washed away, and all those people died. But the mainstream press never reported it anywhere, although alternate media did the very next day, with pictures of bodies scattered across wet fields. It was years later before I found the written confirmation that the alternate media was right.

We boarded up all the doors and windows and sat it out. A Category 2 is severe, but the roofs of the homes throughout the southeast side of Harris County mostly stayed on. The only problem areas were along Galveston Bay, where the storm surge broke the houses. Josiah Greer's family lost their home, but most of the other student's homes were fine.

Our roof sustained a small amount of damage. At the same time, the electrical power went out for everyone and no one had power for a couple of weeks. The school remained closed for this reason. In the mad rush of preparation for the hurricane, however, I had bought a generator from Home Depot. Thus we were able to keep our refrigerators going, and were basically fine.

What I did not have, however, was Internet connection with the several free-lance writers who were working with me on my "Micro-Business for HighSchoolers" course. For that reason, I drove over to San Marcos, Texas where I could rent a motel room for a couple of nights and have Internet hookup. It was late in the evening as I approached San Marcos, and I was driving too fast. I tried to slow down, but I was weary and before I knew it, my speed had gone back up as I went through one of Texas's many little towns who make their money just this way. I was stopped by a cop and given a ticket. The thing is, though, I was grateful because the experience woke me up and may have saved my life.

In the motel room, I continued working with my writers and on the Micro-Business course. Because the topics of the course varied considerably, from accounting to understanding business, to practical shop tips, and so on, I had found three writers with differing skills. One was a college shop teacher from Michigan. One was a lady from Tennessee who had insisted she was good at writing general business concepts, and the other was a lady from California, named Karen Corey.

Of the three, however, only Karen, who was skilled with accounting and similar topics, sent me material that was at the standard I required for my course, with only a normal amount of editing on my part. The man from Michigan, who was a shop teacher of all things, could not write anything practical. After a few useless pieces, I paid him and let him go. The lady from Tennessee I had asked to write about such things as finding a good business idea and finding market niches, etc., her stuff was half usable. That is, I could re-work them a whole lot and end up with something useful. When I suggested that she improve what she sent me, she became angry. Before long, I had to disconnect from her as well; it was taking me more time to fix her pieces than to just write them myself.

Karen was great, though, because her part was entirely outside of my expertise and she seemed to be in it for the long haul. I put her name with mine, then, as the authors of the course.

Once we got back to school and things settled out from the hurricane experience, we had the insurance adjustor look at our house. Maureen was with him when he came, and, because of her graciousness, people always respond positively with her. Sure enough, the adjustor marked our house as needing a new roof, paid for by the insurance company.

I still had some strength at this time, and so I chose to do it myself rather than hire a contractor. This way I could spend more money on the roof, adding insulation, and rebuilding a section to fix a leak that had started prior to the hurricane. I then hired some of the young men from Kyle's class to work on the roof with me after school hours. I hired Kyle, of course, as well as Aaron Pierce and Daniel Smith. Chey Wilshire also helped us for a day or two. The young men had a great time working with me on our roof, but they did find that I am a very different person when I am running a construction crew, much more of a driver than when I am in the classroom. And so the hurricane did benefit us with a new roof.

War Continues

Through these first months of school, the internal war to stand in Christ my life against all the wailing cries of accusation continued full on.

I want to continue just a bit with the spiritual environment that Lakewood Church was for me through these years. There was always an anointing resting upon every part of the service. Even when they put on a carefully planned presentation for special days, like Mother's Day, etc., and everything was choreographed, still, all things remained in the anointing of the Spirit throughout. I suspect a lot of prayer was behind everything.

After praise and prayer, Victoria spoke for about ten minutes. As I said, she was a woman of power in the Spirit. I didn't agree with everything Victoria shared, but she is the only speaker I have ever heard who presented **"filled with all the fullness of God"** as a reality for the believer.

I want to share an experience that probably happened a couple of years ahead, but which describes that open heavens into which I often entered partly inside of the anointing resting upon Pastor Victoria. Arriving at a particular Lakewood service, I felt a weight of discouragement. During the praise service, it seemed to me the entire congregation was under the same discouragement. As Victoria came out to present her exhortation, she must have sensed the same thing as well. I don't know what she had planned for that morning, but it must have been set aside, because she strode across the stage and spoke with an authority as great as what I had known through Sister Jane Miller. Victoria commanded the demons to leave the house of God, with strength. As she did, I sensed thousands of dark spirits flee that auditorium in that moment, and we returned to the full knowledge of God with us.

It was this same spiritual environment of authority in God inside of which I was being kept through these beginning years of a new understanding of God and His word.

Now, I did not understand myself at the time. Only recently have I begun to realize what I was actually doing through these months of assault, indeed, through the seven-year time period that we attended at Lakewood Church.

Through these seven years, from the summer of 2006 to 2013, I cast down my enemy. Filling my house with Christ began in August of 2006, however, and was the cause of that all-out assault of the evil one against me, an assault that reached a fevered pitch in February of 2008 when Jesus showed me that He had already come into full union with me.

And so I have learned to fight, not because I wanted to fight, but because I wanted to live, that is, I wanted to KNOW Father-with-me above all else. Through these nine months especially, as I realize it now, I have "slain my thousands," and I have "slain my ten thousands." Yet I most certainly had help, an army of mighty angels taking down every powerful, familiar, and desperate demon ordered to insert its words into my sphere. There were no survivors.

A New Mailing List

Through these months, I had set up an email program on my computer that I could use to manage a mailing list and to send out bulk emails. I put the sign-up form on my dyordy.com website. At the same time, I asked Gary Sigler if he would put a link to my site on his Kingdom Resources page, which he did. As a result, through these fall months, a number of people signed up for my not-yet-begun *Christ Our Life* letter.

Among the first to sign up were Rita Robertson in Wisconsin, Bill Wilkerson in Virginia, and Bonnie Morris in Arizona. Bonnie Morris had her own website, "A Bridge Builder," listed with Gary Sigler, and I had been in communication with her, as well as some others who wrote things similar to what God was teaching me.

At the same time, I was in communication with Fred Pruitt and the Christ as Us brethren, and a number of those signed up on my list.

Christ Our Life Begins

The day came, then, in November of 2008, when the relentless spiritual assault that I had known for nine months broke completely, and I knew it no more. Yes, there would be short times over the next few years when I would sink into discouragement, but at this point in time, I had won a place inside the knowledge of God that I have never left since.

With great joy, I wrote and sent out my first *Christ Our Life* letter on November 16, 2008. Because it speaks to everything I was experiencing at the time, I want to share portions of it here.

∽

Although I have had this list for some time, it is only now that the Lord has released me to send out the first letter. The Lord took me through a time of proving my faith and brought me through into a most pleasant, flower-filled meadow of rest in my union with Him. I have never known a more delightful joy.

When the Lord first shows us that He is our life, that we have no other life, that He fills every part of our human self and that every part of us, including the ugliest parts, He carries in Himself and has always carried in Himself, when we first come to that understanding, it is so foreign to everything that has ever screamed at us, from our own mind, from the pulpit, from Christian "theology", from do-good others, that it takes many months for the whole thought processes of our mind to change.

Last summer, I started building an Internet publishing business in an attempt to support my family in a way I am able to do, with the hope that we can somehow get to a country property. Focusing many hours a week on business takes one's mind "away from the Lord." Then, in August, school began again, and I found myself once again in the desperate place of needing God to come through for me on a regular basis. I disagree with most of the Christianity that is presented in the school where I teach, yet I see Christ certainly visible in the brethren with whom I work. I am not a bold man, nor confrontive, and the situation the Lord has created for me to walk through is not easy. I do not speak, nor would it be the Lord if I did, yet I am very distraught over many of the things I believe are in open opposition to the Lord Jesus Christ, yet made to appear "Christian."

That is the setting, but what I want to share with you is the truth on the inside of me. Always in the past, if I FELT rebellious, or angry, or frustrated, or far away from God, I believed that I was "in the flesh," and that I was, in fact, far away from God. At the same time, I once believed that if I FELT mightily anointed, with joy welling up in my soul, that I had now entered His presence.

It is easy to see how absurd that notion is. Is Jesus my life only when I FEEL a certain way? Does my FEELING bad indicate that He has departed from me? When I FEEL raunchy, does that mean He has removed my sin from Himself and placed it back upon me? When we look at it this way, it is obvious that we do not determine truth by what we see with our eyes, but by what God says.

But then we get into the hard press of life. I feel un-anointed; yet I desperately need God's help to survive the day. My Christian brethren assure me (through their devotional statements and prayers) that I am "in the flesh, in the carnal mind." All the old arguments that weighed against me for years crowd into my mind. "Give it up, Daniel, you know God is displeased with you. You're in rebellion, trying to do something that isn't of Him."

Yet, I will not. Jesus is my life. He lives His life in all of my humanity. All of these ill feelings that seem to work against me, He carries in Himself. He is simply sharing with me the agony of His people. I groan and weep over the false teachings being presented to my own children. I grieve over the idolatry being mixed with the Holy Spirit of Christ, knowing that innocent people are being murdered right now, today, on the other side of the world, as a result of that idolatry.

It is enough for me to say that Jesus lives in me – in all of me, in all of my humanity. And those raunchy parts of myself He has always carried them utterly inside of Himself – He carried them all to the cross long ago, and He has never offered to place them back upon me. It is faith. It is believing against the sight of the eyes and the feelings of the human.

And so I have believed that Jesus is my life, that I walk in utter union with Him, He in me, and I in Him, without regard to any feelings or circumstances whatsoever.

Hold to that belief! Hold!

And then the darkness passes as if it never was, and it dawns on me that I walk in a garden of peace, with a delight of oneness with Jesus that I have never known before. The joy of knowing that an unending discovery of Jesus in me and me in Jesus lies before me. Jesus, as He is right now, lives His life in my life, as I am right here. And I? I am hid with Christ in God. I no longer seek His will. I live in His will with all confidence of joy.

Jesus is my life; I have no other life.

⤙

As you can see, my letters were much shorter at the beginning than they are now. Writing this much once a week was a full measure for me then, especially since my primary focus was classroom teaching.

You will find the first several letters, written through November, December, and January, two per chapter, in *Our Path Home*: "Home As It Really Is," Chapters 5. "Christ is Personal," 8. "The Exchange," 10. "Between Two Ages," and 13. "All His Ways Are Perfect." In addition, some of the early letters are also sprinkled through "Who Are We" and "Into His Image."

A Miss-Step

Even as the joy of Christ my life was increasing, my struggle with the environment in the school that seemed to me to oppose the wondrous gospel of our Salvation, only increased. At the same time my physical strength was declining. I could still manage a full 40-hour work-week and meet all my teacher requirements, but just barely.

And so, as the end of the semester approached, I became very eager to separate myself from that environment and to devote my time to my Internet business, to get it off the ground and bringing in what I believed would be a good income for us. I do readily acknowledge that the needs of Kyle and Johanna were not in the front of my mind as they should have been.

I loved my students, and I loved to teach, but I cannot bear with Christian opposition to Christ. Let me give some examples.

I will first include an experience I had with a student. Brandon Farias was a young man in my tenth grade class. I had always perceived something blank inside his expression, although he was a "teddy bear" to his classmates. One day, Brandon challenged me in class. His stance was open disrespect, but his tone was quiet and absolute control. I love teenagers in all their antics, but I do not allow disrespect.

I told him to leave my classroom and to go see Mr. Anderson. He refused. I said that I would call the police (the option in public school and in college, but not here.) He laughed at me and refused to move. He mocked me and dared me to do it. What I perceived in him was not a dark thing sitting upon him, but rather, the full control of the human over a spirit of rebellion. By the hand of God in my own life over many years, I could not be in the same room with such awfulness.

Immediately, I stepped outside the room, but not beyond where I had a full view of my students to be sure they were safe. I motioned to a nearby student to go bring Mr. Anderson. Mr. Anderson came quickly and escorted Brandon out of the room. I was now free to return to my classroom and to continue teaching.

Afterwards I asked Mr. Anderson if I could sit down with him and Brandon to talk through this difficulty. Mr. Anderson said, "No." Now, I cannot know his reasons, but it seemed to me that there was no "walking together" in the experience or ordering of this school. It seemed to me that I was given no place in any larger ministry to these young people.

Then, in the high school teacher's meetings with Mr. Anderson, on one occasion, Sue Cannon exhorted us all that the devil was going to win over us if we did not get more serious about "walking with God." I gasped in astonishment when she said that, for all I knew was Christ Jesus filling us with all of Himself, as the Bible says.

On another occasion, Mr. Anderson exhorted us with that meaningless phrase, "Step out of the way so that Jesus can be seen in your classroom and not you." – If Jesus is in me, and I step "out of the way" (something no one has ever done or could do) then Jesus must also vanish.

The worst moment, however, was in the morning all-teacher's devotions. Mr. Bohacek was sharing the devotions that morning. He waxed eloquent about the American soldiers in Iraq who were such examples of "Christ" to us. I bit my tongue, for I was close to rebuking him openly for such horror in equating killers with Jesus. Yet that is how these people saw the world, and how they defined "Jesus."

In fact, Mr. Anderson had brought some military men into the school to speak with the older male students. I had Kyle come to my room so that he did not have to become a target of the U.S. military. This was truly an act of placing evil in front of children and calling it "good."

I became very angry with Mr. Bohacek and Mr. Anderson. Here is what I wrote.

↩

The other morning, I was feeling angry about some things my Christian brethren had said. At the same time, the old familiar voice whispered to me that I was in a "state of rebellion" and that I "needed to submit" to these brethren, that unless I did so, I could not be under God's "covering." I refused; I was not about to let my anger go, because it was right and just.

Then, I thought, "No, Jesus is living His life in me. This feeling of anger is Jesus, sharing His frustration over lies that bring destruction and darkness. The moment I thought that, Jesus spoke to me. He said, "Will you love these dear brethren, in spite of our anger, with My love." I said, "Yes, of course, Lord." Immediately, all trace of the anger vanished, swallowed up by God's love through me.

This is a terrible thing! God's love does not displace His anger, it swallows it up. That means that His anger is carried inside of His love. Yes, all expression of God's anger is surrounded by and works for the purposes of His love. But it is still terrible.

Yet it is also a wondrous thing. Now, I could continue to love my brethren, beyond the anger, with God's love. Yet, I had not diminished myself in any way. Self was swallowed up in one with God. I knew that Jesus was living His life in me.

↩

And so, in December, I submitted my resignation to Mr. Anderson, that I would not be returning in January and that I hoped to spend more time on developing my Internet business. Part way through the Christmas break, however, Mr. Anderson invited me over to his home. He shared with me that he had been unable to find a replacement and he asked me, in humility and kindness, if I would consent to return in January and finish out the semester.

I told him that I would. It was a humbling experience, returning when I had told everyone I would not be back, but I am well used to such things by now, so it wasn't that big of a deal. My students were thrilled that I would continue.

The spring semester of 2009 continued much the same as before, yet I was becoming more weary, and the physical requirements of the full teaching job were becoming more than I could fulfill.

I must insert here that, through the prior months, the engine in our green van went out, and we sold it for scrap, as it would have cost too much to repair. I needed a vehicle to get to work, and so the Rideau's offered us a red Buick LeSabre they had acquired, for $1500 paid monthly over time. This was a tremendous blessing to us. The Buick was strong and comfortable, but it had lots of peripheral problems and was not suited for any long drive.

Sister Roberta Mack

In February, Maureen received an urgent call from her dad that her mother, Roberta Mack, was declining rapidly because the cancer was spreading.

Maureen bought a ticket, but it was timed too late, for February 23. Sister Roberta passed on February 22, 2009. From Atlanta, then, Maureen rode down to Bowens Mill with Aunt Jenny and others of Roberta's siblings flying in.

I realize now that two eulogies must be part of this narrative of my life, the first for Maureen's mother, Roberta Mack, and the second for my own mother, Rhoda Yordy, who passed on a few years later.

I first saw Roberta Mack at Bowens Mill in June of 1978 when I had chosen her Bible studies to attend. There was something earnest and deep inside of her, in seeking to know God, that drew me. Of truth, I thought to myself later, when God first spoke to me that Maureen would be my wife, "like mother, like daughter." I've never had a moment since when I thought otherwise.

Roberta was devoted to God and to knowing Him her whole life. With Sister Ethelwyn Davison and Sister Charity Titus, Sister Roberta was an example of a life poured out for God's people on a daily basis for years and years like none others I have ever known. She never flagged in her devotion to the people at the Ridge, to their needs, and to her care for them, not once in the thirty-one years she gave her life there, at Graham River, and with us.

Sister Roberta was a heritage of God that impacted the lives of hundreds of people, but especially her daughters and grandchildren. Yet it was a very sad thing to me that, in her final days, she knew sorrow, for the vision to which she had devoted her life with all abandon had not been fulfilled in her. She never knew the joy of an already completed salvation.

The children and I took off several days from school, and rented a vehicle to drive to Bowens Mill for Sister Roberta's memorial. I had signed up for an economy car, but when we arrived at the car rental place, they did not have what I had ordered, and so they upgraded us to a Toyota mini-van at no extra cost. This was awesome. We went a more direct route to Bowens Mill than we had the summer before.

When we arrived at Bowens Mill, we again stayed in the 16' wide single-wide set behind the Mack's home. This was a very comfortable place for us. Brother Claude was subdued and sorrowful, but he was a man of faith in God. In fact, I think at this time he was free to be more real as himself than he normally was. All of Roberta's brothers and sisters were at Bowens Mill as well, having flown in from Texas, California, and Oregon.

There was an open casket visiting time at the Funeral Home before the burial service. The chapel room there was filled with both relatives and brethren from the community, everyone standing and visiting quietly while different ones walked by to view the open casket.

After Maureen and I with the children passed by for one final view of Sister Roberta, we also stood among the guests to visit. This was the last time I saw Buddy Cobb. He passed me in the viewing room, though he did not acknowledge me. He paused to speak momentarily to John Hinson, standing right near me. I don't know if he spoke for my sake or not, but the gist of his words to John was this: "No one can know God unless they are submitting to authority under the covering." His words were quiet, but hard.

It has been my typical experience, when visiting move community since we left, to feel an environment of condemnation all around me, partly because that's how it always was and because I knew full well that was the attitude towards those who had "left the move," and especially towards someone like myself, who had become "deceived into imagining that I could live in union with Christ now."

This was the end of February, 2009, twelve years after God had spoken to me, "Son, you passed the test," and twenty-four years after God had begun this great contest with me concerning my attitude towards leadership in the church.

I had shared *The Jesus Secret* with a number of different people in the move, including Jim Fant (who had also passed on a few months before Sis-

ter Roberta), and some of the traveling ministry. Now, here I was, having won full victory into the joy of knowing Christ Jesus, now as my only life, faced with five men who stood as leaders in the church, yet in opposition in one way or another to Christ and towards me, Claude Mack, Buddy Cobb, John Hinson, Robert Anderson, and John Bohacek.

And so I was hit, over and over through this time, with the biggest question of all. IF – Christ lives as me, in all that I am, and has done so all my life, and regardless of all my fault, does He not also live as each one of these men, regardless of their lack of knowing Him as He really is?

Here's the thing. The work of God in me through the first twelve years of this confrontation was complete. Never once did I hesitate. In every present difficulty, I deliberately placed the Lord Jesus Christ upon each one of these men, and saw them as Jesus to me, regardless of the pain and confusion it brought to me.

Oh, I certainly struggled with all the wherefores and the why-hows, but never with the doing. If the salvation of Jesus means so very much to me, how could I withhold the same salvation from anyone? Yet I continued in agony with the great contradiction that, if Jesus is living as these men, then why do they not know Him, why do they persist in so much anti-Christ thinking?

We had a memorial service at the Gathering Place, a building built at the convention site specifically for the regular services of the three communities. I also shared in this memorial service concerning what Sister Roberta meant to me, and especially the great gift of her daughter. What I shared was well received by all.

Sister Roberta was buried in the little cemetery on the Bowens Mill property, just south of the Ridge, right next to her mother. I saw several other grave stones there of people I had known when I lived at the Ridge, including Brother Jim Fant's.

Because we had the larger mini-van, we had room to load a number of things that had belonged to Sister Roberta that Claude wanted to give to Maureen, including quite a few books.

Difficulty Increases

Upon our return, there were about three more months to go to complete the school year. The truth is that, for Kyle and Johanna's sake, I am so very glad that I agreed to remain. The religious environment of the school was getting as difficult for Kyle, especially, as it was for me.

At this point, I had become physically and emotionally weary to the point that I had to choose not to do some of the teaching requirements. In such a contest, I always chose for my students and dropped certain "school" duties.

It was my students who always gave me the strength I needed. One time, before school started, I had my head on my desk, too weary to even think about teaching that day. Chad Steiger walked first into my classroom and sat down at his desk. I raised my head as he came in, and instantly, I had all the strength I needed for the day. But when the last student left my classroom, I dropped again, wearier than before.

I could not bear the chapel times, and so did not attend. Mr. Anderson corrected me, however, and said that I was required to attend. I submitted and did so. Of truth, he was always gentle and kind to me.

Nonetheless, one Thursday morning, when I was in my classroom during chapel time, Kyle came into my room and asked if he could wait out the chapel time with me. This was so thrilling to me, that my son would flee the religious nonsense of others and find refuge with his dad and with the Jesus I know. This is not common.

One time, in the chapel service, when there was an especially strong anointing (which there often was, in spite of the hostility of word), I felt to prophesy. As I spoke, the Spirit of God came upon me and my words in great power. No one spoke after, until Mr. Borny, moving in the wisdom of the Lord, connected what I spoke to the students as the Lord speaking to them.

Because of this evidence of the anointing upon me, I was allowed to share with the students in a chapel service. I don't think I did so well with that, however; I think I talked too long.

Here's something else I wrote during this time.

❧

The other night, I was hit with all the discouragement and despair that is so familiar to me. In my mind, I had every reason to quit. Who was I kidding? I am alone, cut off from fellowship, maybe because

God has cast me off. I'm a jerk, a loser. I decided to wrap myself in despair. I did not call on Jesus.

I tried, but I could not. Jesus laughed out of my heart, throwing off the darkness, "You silly boy, you belong to Me." Joy and faith and hope flooded me, filling me full. The darkness vanished as if it had never been.

❧

The end of school finally came. At that point, I knew that I did not have the strength anymore, physically or emotionally, to sign a contract committing myself to a 40-hour work week. I have productive days, yes, but I have too many weak days to satisfy an employer.

Graduation

The graduation of Kyle's twelfth-grade class was a very good occasion, especially since he was chosen by his fellow students as the "King" for homecoming and all the attendant honors. Kyle was also the vice president of the student council this year.

In fact, I would sit in the cafeteria and marvel at my son, at his graciousness as he went from one group of students to another, joining briefly with the conversation of each group in full harmony and welcome. And Kyle always had a heart for the Lord. When he was old enough to "go out" on his own, it was to church services that he went, at churches I knew nothing about. I supported his choices fully, for I have always believed that it is Jesus with whom my children must connect, and not me.

Yet the graduation was bitter-sweet for me. Even though I was so relieved that the time at Family Christian was over, I found that disconnecting from my students there became very strange. Some of these children had never had adults treat them as real and valuable persons in themselves, though they had lived in a Christian environment their whole lives. And many of them attached themselves to me in what felt like a "stickiness," one might say. Their apparent "need" of me became very uncomfortable.

At the graduation, however, Robert Anderson spoke of "honoring those to whom honor is due." He used George W. Bush as his example and spoke harshly against those who "dishonor" the American government by not believing the official account of 9/11. Yet my knowledge of the facts told me that he was honoring those who had no honor at all. Of truth, the words he had spoken to me at the start, "We live in a day where people call evil good and good evil," had come full circle and were, in fact, a description of his own untrue view of this world.

My Departure from "the Furnace"

All through these months, I struggled over this contradiction in my brethren at Family Christian between their sure knowing of the Lord and their false connections to this world. I pondered John's exhortation, "**Do not love the world nor the things of the world**," knowing that it was true, even while also seeing that Jesus was, in fact, carrying them inside Himself in all that they were.

Throughout my entire time in that place, I grieved much inside, for I knew that the wells of salvation and the knowledge of God were to be found inside of me, if anyone was interested. Yet no one was. A man filled with the knowledge of God passed through their midst and no one noticed, and I could do nothing more than weep in sorrow.

In spite of the fact that so many American brethren worship the beast and give their hearts and the hearts of their children in binding allegiance to it, they still belong to Jesus, and He carries them all the way through the darkness and into life. I have long since become settled inside regarding this great contradiction. I don't say that I have all the answers, but that I am at peace.

Two years later, when Josiah Greer and Kai Ordonio were graduating, they got after me, insisting that I attend their graduation. Maureen and I did go, to our great regret, for the U.S. military was given greater prominence than before.

Before continuing, I must share that I had finished this letter in a way that left me unsatisfied; then, I wrote large chunks of the next two letters. This time of my life, from, say, January of 2009 until January of 2011, is a period I have not understood, and for that reason, have not considered it up-close. A conversation with my daughter, Johanna, plunged me back into my failure that I had no idea where to place. And that is the reason for this long gap in writing these chapters.

God used this two-year time period, that also marked the steady first-growth of the word I share, to bring me into the full outward understanding of my own inadequacy and failure. And so, after I had written these portions of my life story, I grappled

in agony with things I have not understood. And as He always does, the Lord Jesus brought me to such peace and to such pure understanding, and I give Him thanks, for all His ways concerning me are perfect.

Now, I will continue presenting this two-year time period, but with an understanding of joy that I have not had before this moment.

I did not belong at Family Christian Academy, and neither did Kyle. Yet that is where God put us for this season for very good reasons. Think of the womb in the hours before the birth; the womb must become the enemy of the baby, for the baby no longer belongs in that place. Yet to the baby, it's all confusion and pain. – "You don't belong here; get out."

By placing us into that pain of not belonging, God enables our heart's cry reaching out in desperation to know Him as He is, contrary to all the darkness of the church in this world. If God did not put us into such a place, we would sit in our ignorance and never know that there is LIFE we have not yet tasted. A baby that will "not be birthed" can only die.

I did not belong with these people; they were my brethren, and I loved them and saw the Lord Jesus in their lives. But they were not going where I must go nor living in that which I must know.

I now also understand the critical importance, in the path God has set before me, in my firm and continual choice to look at these leaders in the church who stood in such opposition in my own perception, and to see them and to call them as Christ Jesus living as them and carrying them all the way through. I will show you what I mean in the next few chapters.

I have left out many sharp details of "not belonging" in this account. One that stands out was a mother coming into my classroom demanding that I apologize to her and her daughter for daring to suggest that the U.S. government might be lying.

I always humble myself in such moments because I have no ability to "defend myself," but even more because winning the heart of a dear brother or sister is always far more important than any foolishness of "being correct."

And so I place Robert Anderson and John Bohacek, and all the brethren and all my students at

Family Christian, inside my heart upon the blood sprinkled there and in the presence of my Father, and I set them completely free of me and from any offence or grief I might have known. At the same time, I ask God for life for them, that, as He gives me life inside of Jesus, so He would give that same life to them as well, regardless.

When I left Family Christian at the end of May, I would never again find myself inside such an environment of this world that could be only a great furnace to me. And it is with joy unspeakable and full of glory that I now know God's intentions through all of this.

43. Shaping a New Path

March 2009 - May 2010

This chapter includes a number of things taking place through the last year we were at Family Christian, things unrelated to any difficulties of mine. Besides covering the next year of my life, this chapter is also an attempt to share my reasons for writing and the first year and a half of sending out the *Christ Our Life* letters, thus I go back and forth on differing topics.

Family Life

So much of this account is about me, but when I look through my wife's calendars and pictures, what she recorded is about the children, our visits with family and friends, and our many pets.

As I look through these years thus far, I see that I have left out many things we did together, things that were part of the children's lives. Yet a home and yard filled with happy and adventurous children watched over by a loving wife was very much my environment. I want to share some of this briefly with you, though I will not try to place what happened when.

All four of our children are musically inclined. We had continued the girls in piano lessons through these years. Katrina also expressed an interest in the violin, so we bought her one. It did not take her long with a violin teacher, however, to discover that maybe she did not want to play a violin after all. Johanna continued advancing in her piano studies. We took her up from one level of teacher to another, until she was learning under a master pianist who lived in the Kingwood area.

Johanna was so brilliant on the piano. I could listen to her for hours and never tire; her music was to me like the sound of water running over rocks, the most beautiful sound I have known. She played the piano formally in the graduation ceremony for Kyle and his classmates. People coming in were stunned to see that the classical music they were hearing was coming from a ninth-grade girl. It was one proud dad sitting there beaming.

Kyle loved the guitar. He participated in the praise leadership in the chapel services and had begun to lead the praise at times. James took to tooting on a trumpet and soon switched over to the French Horn, which he played for several years in school bands and orchestras.

We went to various parks as often as we could, including overnight camping trips to state parks on a regular basis. We went to the Renaissance Fair a second time, but this second time, Maureen and I rented "medieval" costumes as well. It's just so much fun to be part of the presentation rather than just a gawking onlooker.

Our house was often filled with girls, Johanna and Katrina's friends from school. I look through all the pictures and see joy and kindness and sharing, and my heart is glad in the goodness of God.

Kyle went out for track during his four years of high school. Johanna also joined track, but only in her eighth grade year. We went to their track meet near Angleton, Texas that year, but Kyle then participated in a major state-wide track meet in Waco in the fall of 2008, the first semester of his senior year. His grandpa, Claude Mack, had been a sprinter in high school as well. Kyle placed fourth in the state meet, and his record is still on the walls at Family Christian.

In March, James was injured at school. Another boy had jumped on him in gym class and broken his collar bone. Maureen and I took him to the emergency room at the children's hospital in the Houston medical center. We waited all night, that is, Maureen did with James. I went home for a few hours of sleep through the early morning. I returned, then, and James finally had his appointment later in the morning, having suffered without help the whole night. After taking x-rays, the doctor told us that there was nothing they could do. When we mentioned seeing a chiropractor, they laughed as if such a thing is ridiculous. They gave James an expensive sling, charged us $1500, and sent us home.

We then took James to our chiropractor, now that we had clear x-rays. Two visits and maybe $100 later and he was all better again with the pain gone and the slight fracture able to heal. The difference between the scam and the real was pretty stark to us.

YGuide

Besides working on "Micro-Business for High-Schoolers," I also started a website in the fall of 2008 which I called "YGuide" at yguide.org, which no longer exists. I had come up with the idea since my time at Lubbock Christian University as an expression of my desire to create my own approach to self-directed education, the Yordy Guide to Learning History, etc., becoming "Y"-Guide. Except the YGuide website was my attempt to give form to a community of Christ in the expression of every part of "village" life.

Following is a portion of the front page of the website, similar to how it was in its beginning. I signed onto Clickbank affiliate program and filled many pages with ads for e-books on the various crafts found in each of the categories. I did make some money from people who bought a black-smith program and a grape-growing program. I also wrote a number of articles on these topics which I posted at ezinearticles.com, some of which are still there.

⤷

YGuide – A Homesteading Community and Journal

The delights of strong and healthy children, warm and inviting homes, the aroma of herbs, the cackle of chickens, the richness of the soil, shaping wood into beauty, tinkering with machinery, the comfort of a full and well-stocked pantry, the beauty of growing things.

Dream of a simple life, of the increase of the fruits of the earth and of your labor. Share with others from your abundance.

The Homestead – The Herbarium – The Wood Shop – The Healthy Home – The Home School – The Farmstead – The Garden – The Metal Shop – The Home Office – The Home Studio

⤷

I developed this website through 2008-2009, adding other things to it. I did not continue with it aggressively, however, partly because most items were not worth the money asked, though a few were. My main drive turned elsewhere, then, by the late summer of 2009.

A Sad Outcome

I must conclude the outcome of "Micro-Business for HighSchoolers." In order for my course to be complete, I advertised for a business-minded writer on a free-lance website. I needed someone who could look at the entire package with a business eye and think through all of its parts to tell me if there was anything missing, or if any part might be made better. A lady from Dallas assured me that she could meet my requirements, and by her resume and reviews I believed her.

After signing a contract with this lady, I sent her my stuff, including the outline for the entire course. I instructed her that I did not want her to do any editing of small mistakes, as I was not paying her for that. (It was a rough draft, full of all the little mistakes that you fix only AFTER you know it's what you want.) I asked her to look across the whole course to give me her thoughts.

What I received back was small edit corrections as well as personal ridicule for having those small mistakes in my writing. When I asked her for what she had agreed to do, an overview with a business mind, she replied that she could not possibly do that. I paid her and said that I had no more work for her to do. (All three of these individuals who did not produce for me together cost me hundreds of dollars.)

Then, as I continued working with Karen Corey in completing and polishing the first three months of the course, I went onto the AWAI website and asked for a copywriter to write the sales landing page for an ad I planned to place on LewRockwell.com, a site read by the kind of people who might want this learning experience for their children. I wanted a fresh and different mind to come up with the argument that would convince people to buy. I hired a lady from the Midwest who had graduated from the AWAI program and paid her six hundred dollars to write my landing page. It was okay, not quite what I had hoped, but good enough.

We launched the course when we were one-third complete, offering it to parents who wanted to purchase it for their teenagers. I believed that we could stay ahead of any students with course creation as they progressed. I then purchased a month-long ad on LewRockwell.com for another $600. This might have been June of 2009. During that month thousands and thousands of people clicked on my ad and went to the landing page that offered to them "Micro-Business for HighSchoolers." Thousands looked, and not one expressed any interest at all. Not one.

Then Karen Corey in California, who was the one truly useful participant in this project and who enjoyed being part of it, sent me an email that she was not able to work for a time because she was in the hospital with pneumonia. She seemed to get better, and wrote a lesson or two more for me. And then I never heard from her again; no one responded to my emails. I do not believe that she "quit." My only conclusion was that she had passed away.

If you were to look at all my course, and all the work I did on it you would see that it is beautiful, that it is brilliant, and that, in the right context, it would benefit teenagers tremendously and be a far superior way to focus the final years of high school – business driven learning. But what I did not know how to do was make it able to support my family.

Christian Connections

In March of this year I came across a website blog by a brother in England named Chris Welch. To my astonishment, I read in his latest blog of his desire to see the word taught by Norman Grubb on union with Christ merged together with the word taught by Sam Fife and the move on the revelation of Jesus Christ, the very thing I had begun to do.

I was very timid, and it would be several more years before I could see my writing as anything more than my own desire to know the Lord expressed through rough drafts shared with a small number of people. I certainly did not view myself as anyone of consequence in the larger picture of the Church. Nonetheless, I sent Chris Welch an email inviting him to look through the slowly accumulating articles on my website at dyordy.com. He replied cheerily, appreciating greatly what he found there. It turns out he had been in the move there in London for a short while in the early years and had known John Clarke and others.

This was a milestone for me, in connecting with Chris Welch, for he soon started posting things I had written on his blog and sending more readers my way. I was filled with excitement, for this con-

nection brought good fellowship and interaction with others inside the word I was writing at that time. I gained new subscribers to my *Christ Our Life* letters.

Not long after I began communicating with Chris Welch, he convinced me to sign onto Facebook and join the fellowship there. When I did that, I was quickly "friended" by many of my Yordy cousins with whom I had not had much connection before. This was a wonderful benefit. Facebook, however, puts me out into a very "unsafe" place, and so I had to take occasional breaks from that flow of conversation.

Then, through an article posted on LewRockwell.com, I connected with a pastor in Oregon who promoted Christian community. On his website, he enabled connections with people of like minds to get together. Through these connections, Maureen and I contacted a couple living in The Woodlands, just north of Houston. Their names were Sandy and Richard Roberts. This would have been in the fall of 2009.

We visited with Sandy and Richard in their home a number of times over the next year and found much in common concerning the vision of Christian community. Sandy, especially, loved all we shared about our experiences in community. Although they expressed an eagerness towards being a part of a small gathering of people on a rural property, in the end, it seems, as is so often the way, that actual commitment with all of its costs was not quite in their consideration.

It was Sandy who said to me, "I don't believe in 'leadership.'" Yet as I pondered that statement, I realized that, in gathering together in community, saying such a thing would be an act of taking control.

Meanwhile, I wrote an article on the topic of community and the need we have to gather together in rural places. I then received an email from Fred Pruitt explaining to me why such things as Christian community and homeschooling have nothing to do with Christ as us. I replied with the question – if Christ lives as me, than how would the things that I valued not be of Him. I also said that I am not following him or Norman Grubb. I received a second email, a bit sharper, rebuking me for instructing him on union with Christ. Although this exchange was overwhelming for me, Fred's words were not personally hostile or controlling.

In the fall of 2009, I invited Fred again to our home, as he was coming through Houston accompanied by two other men who had been with him the first time. I also invited John and Crystal Mancha to that meeting with them. We received them gladly and any difficulty there might have been was put into the goodness of Christ. The sharing felt a little rushed to me, however; again, not the kind of impartation I expected from those who purported to know the living God. John Mancha did say that he enjoyed it, however.

Nonetheless, I was struck by one of the other brothers saying that "Christ as me" means we have no need of any gifts or anointings of the Holy Spirit. This ignorance of the nature of God and the construction of the human was astonishing to me. Although I continued email communication with Fred from time to time, and continued to gain much understanding reading his articles, I knew that I would not know God as I wanted from those connections.

Also, a couple of those from the Norman Grubb connection who were on my mailing list posted letters of mine on their blogs. One sister posted "Practicing the Presence of God," which sent many readers my way. Another brother asked to post an article, but told me that he had removed every occurrence of "Jesus" and replaced it with "Christ." At the time, I thought only – "Well, Christ as you." Once I understood what it really meant, several years later, I would have graciously refused.

Bonnie Morris of Arizona communicated with me more often than any other reader. She replied to most of my letters with warm encouragement and blessing. I had connected with her through her website, *A Bridge Builder*, but she closed that down. Because I believe in corporate ministry, I asked her if she wanted to post her articles on my website, and so I made a section just for her articles, with a link so that readers could communicate directly with her.

My Writing

Why did I write and continue writing the *Christ Our Life* letters, almost all of which found their place into one or another of my books? What was my drive and purpose? What did I hope to gain from this endeavor?

My first reason was that I was fed up with a "Christian theology" that denied the biggest verses of the gospel and gave them no place. I was fed up with the discovery, over and over through the years, that the definitions of "what the Bible says" that are considered "orthodox" were simply not supported by what the Bible actually says, in particular the non-Biblical concept that salvation is all about "going to" heaven. I was fed up with the practice of twisting verses to "prove" doctrinal points, even when those verses are pointing to something else, something more glorious than anyone considers.

Nonetheless, I approached the Bible by the practice of NOT forcing my own definitions upon it or of attempting to "figure it out." Rather, I hid the words of the Bible in my heart over decades, that those words might be what they are inside of me.

And so, through these first few years of writing, the great issue of "how do I know that I am right" hit me regularly, not so much from others, but inside of me.

Yet here's the thing. I find so many BIG things in the gospel that no one knows, no one teaches or fits into their way of seeing anything. What is that? Why are verses central to Paul's gospel thrown out as "heresy?" Why are verses twisted so badly to say even the opposite of the words? How could Buddy Cobb preach over and over on the jeopardy of the gospel from Hebrews 3 and NEVER look beyond the "IF" to see what God actually requires?

My heart ached to know the Word, what God actually says, and what He means by what He says. This is the first reason why I could not stop writing. Yet I never imagined that I would know the Word by any intellectual "prowess." God had so forged in me His meaning of "**the Words that I speak to you are Spirit and they are life**," that, since my twenties, I have never considered attempting to know the Bible intellectually. The fact that I remember things does not signify an intellectual approach to Scripture.

The second reason I wrote was that, in and of myself, I am utterly lost. I cannot find my way; I cannot save myself. When I write, I hear Jesus singing in my heart, and I am determined to know Him inside of me as real to me as Don Howat or Abel Ramirez ever were. The only way God has given me to know Jesus Sent into me is to write. And so if I write endlessly, it's because I love to be with Jesus.

The third reason I wrote was that I was becoming aware, not so much mentally, but in my heart, of the extensive accusations against God found in

Christian and human thinking, that *He knows evil,* that *He "punished Jesus" instead of "punishing us,"* that *He is responsible for terrible things happening in people's lives.* I had found those who demonstrate that God's judgment is for a season and not forever, and that it carries great purpose coming out from love. But then many of those same people wanted to claim that *Satan did not "fall," but that God created him evil in the first place.* They use a couple of lines from Scripture to make this savage accusation against God, not realizing that they mean, then, that all evil must come through Jesus.

As I said, this agony in my heart was not so much known to me mentally, but I became deeply disturbed. And so I found myself with a great need inside to know how everything in the Bible can be true in an entirely different way than by the definition of a "God" who "knows evil" and who brings forth hurt out from His own being.

The fourth reason that I wrote, which was the reason that I dared to send out my letters to other people, not an easy thing for me, was that I had to do something to call forth the community of my heart, to gather together those precious holy ones who would be part of the second part of the covenant by which I bound God to myself, that I would walk with a people who know God.

Often, as I sent out my letters, I was hit with the autistic fear of stepping "out of my place." I endured much pain, simply over the thought of "exposing" myself to ridicule. But I sent my letters anyway, out from my determined faith in God, regardless. And in sending every letter out, I believed what God says, that as I "cast my bread upon the waters, so it will come back to me."

During my final months at Family Christian, I read through the Annie visions, *I Looked and Saw Visions of God,* for a third time. This time, they became brand-new to me. The first two times, although they had presented to me a glorious vision of knowing God, yet they had also seemed to place that vision far away from me. As I read them this time, I saw union with Christ throughout, and the vision of knowing God seemed right at hand.

Yet, in reading them again, I was struck, as I had always been, with the awfulness of being given an opportunity by God and then failing to enter into that opportunity such that God removes it and never offers it again. In my desperation, I looked across

the years of my life, and I said, "NOT SO." And thus I wrote this line, "All of His ways concerning me are perfect. He has never led me wrong; He has never not led me." You see, I cannot have anything God offers me of Himself to be lost to me. I cannot have such a thing at all.

And so, I did not write for others, and I did not even write "for God," as if human endeavor could benefit Him in some fleshy way. I write always for myself, that I might know God, and that somehow, by His grace, I might walk with a people who know God.

The Progression of Christ Our Life

Several years ago, I created a list of every *Christ Our Life* letter I sent out in order, with the dates. Then, when my last computer cratered and the hard drive froze up, that list was one of the few things I lost. I no longer know the exact order in which I wrote the progression of letters from January of 2009 to August of 2011. I will do the best I can, then, to piece it together.

I did not assemble any of my letters into books until after I self-published *The Kingdom Rising* in late 2012. For that reason, I did not write through this time with any final "book" in mind.

For the first several months, my writing bounced around without following any specific series. I would often write in response to questions or comments coming from different readers. Rita Robinson in Wisconsin often asked me questions concerning things that I said that countered things she had heard in ultimate reconciliation circles. Bill Wilkerson of Virginia was deeply drawn to what I taught and asked a number of deep questions. One of Bill's questions, probably in the late summer of 2009, sparked my first series of letters on a single topic, and that was "The Life of the Age to Come."

At the same time, I received a number of antagonistic responses. Such responses always bothered me immensely, like a grain of sand under an oyster's shell. I cannot leave such responses alone, but I must coat them with truth and coat them with truth until I have written a gentle response of Christ and thus resolved in my understanding the issue that was raised.

The single most important such antagonistic response came through my Facebook correspondence with Chris Welch. Someone had seen on my website the statement, "God sent Jesus to make us just like Himself." They challenged Chris that, "the Bible says no such thing," and that we ought to go only by the Bible "like the Bereans."

I can tell you that this REALLY bothered me, especially since few people are more "Berean" than I and since most who say, "The Bible says," really don't know what it says. Yet it was this agony that birthed in me the concept of "the most important verses of the Bible." And so I wrote my response and sent it to this brother. Rather than responding to "what the Bible actually says," he replied with a list of doctrinal talking points, wanting my response. I did not reply.

In the fall of 2009, I began the series of letters that would form part of *The Great Story of God*. Readers who had connected with me through Chris Welch really enjoyed this series on the meaning of story. Then in the spring of 2010, I wrote the series titled "The Unveiling." My purpose in writing this was to bring my understanding of what God says concerning the revelation of Christ in the closing out of this age into my present knowledge of union with Christ.

YGuide Academy

Upon leaving my teaching position at Family Christian Academy at the end of May, 2009, I was no longer emotionally or physically able to meet the requirements that any full-time employer would have for a forty-hour work week. I was then 52 years of age. From that time until now I have not had a full-time job.

I left Family Christian intending to devote myself to creating an online business that would bring in money passively 24/7. Thousands of people all over the world were doing just that, and I was certain that I could do the same.

Yet it seemed that "Micro-business for High-Schoolers" would not be that business, at least for the moment, and so I set it aside. Don't imagine, however, that any discouragement ever remains with me long. Give me a few weeks and I'm back at it again, "knocking on new doors," expecting something to open. As Alexander Pope said, "Hope springs eternal in the human breast."

And so, sometime in the middle of the summer of 2009, I must have been driving long distance somewhere while drinking coffee, because that's where all my best ideas come. This time an idea

came to me, an idea that is so beautiful to me and into which I poured my heart and soul and countless hundreds of hours of work.

You see, I love teaching middle school kids the best, even though they take more emotional energy than any other group. At the same time, the schooling needs of my children, who were now back to homeschooling, were pressing on me. But I had long since come to the conviction, as you can see since my time in Lubbock, that chaining middle school children to desks all day and to rote busywork, filling out meaningless worksheets, is a crime. It is child abuse.

Children of that age, especially, need to be DO-ING something they love with their hands.

To make a long story short, I decided to create "Project Guides" for project-led learning that I would offer to homeschooling families as well as use for my own children. The first one I wrote, as a trial guide, I wrote with Katrina in mind, and that was "A Project Guide for Raising Rabbits."

Here is part of a brochure I wrote before the end of July, 2009.

⤸

Project-Led learning weaves the learning objectives of schooling into a range of projects that are interesting and valuable to the life of a middle school child. With all of their hearts, middle-school-age children want to explore the world in which they live. They want to make things, to work with their hands, to experience things. A child wants to fix a car, build a go-cart, cut mommy's hair, make a dress, build a dog house, grow some funny looking gourds, plant some flowers, ride a horse, spend a day deep-sea fishing, work a sail-boat, build a canoe, go fishing with Grandpa, show a steer at the fair. Discover what project-led learning can do for your eleven to fourteen-year-old child.

Project-led learning bridges between the structured elementary years and the character- driven high school years. It turns the junior high years from a time of boredom and frustration into a time of wonder and excitement. Raise rabbits, make candles, create a movie, read great literature, build robots, play a cello, go out for little league baseball, repair a car engine. And all the while, learn reading and writing, math and science, history and art!

⤸

I proposed a series of Project Guides written specifically for individual homeschoolers. My hope was that once these were written with individual children in mind, they would be useful to many. And so I started with a boy in New York who wanted to grow a garden, build a greenhouse, and enter his pumpkins in a fair. In actuality, his mother paid me to write ten project guides for him, one in each category of learning.

Then a girl in Florida wanted a project guide for studio dance and another for growing herbs for fragrance. A boy in Illinois wanted to study nature at his local park. A boy in Washington state wanted to train his dog and to go camping in the woods. A mother in Florida asked for a project guide to teach her son how to "submit to the elders in the church." I compromised by writing one called "Visiting the Elderly," which is a superb project. I also wrote "Raising Chickens" for this young man.

I wrote "Martial Arts Karate" and "Playing Football." I wrote "A Microscope in the Garden" for the boy in New York. Then I wrote "A Microscope & the World of Bugs" for the boy in Illinois. Another boy wanted to build a computer, and a boy in Australia wanted to fix small engines. I wrote several versions of "Design and Build Backyard Structures" for different boys. I made this a "math" guide, that is, designing and measuring.

I wrote "A Sewing Business," "A Woodworking Business," and "A Metal Smithing Business." The list continues. In all, I wrote for maybe eight or ten different homeschooled kids, several different guides for each, boys and girls, in the differing categories.

I put a lot of work into these guides. I spent time at Border's Book Store, flipping through books on various subjects in order to choose the best for that age of learner. I searched the Internet for the right articles and videos. If you would like to see three updated versions of these project guides, you can find them at the following link. – www.thelearningconservatory.com

Just click on "Project Led Learning" on the right. Then, "Natural, Physical, and Scientific Projects." You will find the link to a guide on each of those pages.

At that time I called my school "YGuide Academy" and put all the arti-

cles about this way of homeschooling on a website of that name. I advertised in various homeschool outlets and wrote articles for a homeschool website for a year. I also got some of my clients through homeschool articles that I posted on ezinearticles.com.

A Peculiar Love

Again, I am bringing our regular weekly service at Lakewood Church one piece at a time through these several chapters. When the account is finished, one could take each of these descriptions of Lakewood services, put them together as one service, and multiply that by the around 350 times we attended there.

Here, I want to show you the paths we walked to and from church, that is, about 700 times over seven years. You will find mention of the second path many times in my writing; I now realize just how much this path holds a place in my heart.

The thinner solid line going up from the center of the church was our walk for the last four years. The larger dashed line to the right shows the path of thousands of people underground. The dashed line up shows the flow of hundreds of people using the sidewalk. I drove in on the left of the church in the picture, dropped off the family, and then parked the car at the X at the top of the picture..

We would sit down right after the service ended and wait until the rows behind us were cleared. Then we went up the steps inside the auditorium to the second level. There we crossed the flow of hundreds of people heading towards the main

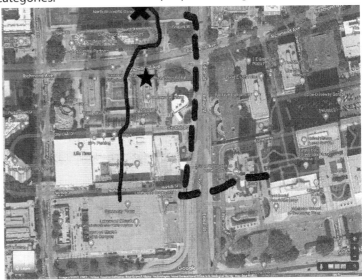

Our Children's Schooling

Kyle turned 18 this August; he was now an adult. The first time after his eighteenth birthday that he asked me, "Dad, can I go out to –?," I replied with, "Why are you asking me? You're an adult, do what you want, just let me know on your way out the door." The shocked look on his face was one of the best enjoyments of my life, something I got to experience twice more with Johanna and Katrina. (James was another matter, but that's several years ahead.)

From his enjoyment of playing guitar at Family Christian, Kyle also had an interest in recording music, and thus, audio engineering. The best audio engineering college program in Texas just happened to be South Plains College several miles west of Lubbock. And so Kyle applied and was accepted into South Plains College. We arranged with Lois that Kyle would rent a room in her home. Before the end of August, Kyle packed his stuff and ventured back to Lubbock and to college.

doors and the dashed lines out. We left the church building through doors on the north side and crossed a covered parking area that was not part of Lakewood parking. We crossed a little-used street and then entered the grassy area with fountains of water as you see in this picture. We then crossed a slightly busier two streets and on to our car. When we left, we took two right turns and encountered no Lakewood traffic.

I placed a star on the map at the top of the large glass building which is on the left in this picture. If you had stood on top of that building at the Star most every Sunday afternoon for four years, you would have observed hundreds of people streaming down the sidewalk on one side, and each Sunday, the same one family walking alone through the green grass and bright sun and fountains of water. I loved that path, for Maureen and I would walk together arm in arm, with Kyle and Johanna ahead of us, also walking arm in arm and chatting merrily together, and ahead of them Katrina and James would run and alternate between scrapping and walking together visiting. And coming out from Joel's exhortation each Sunday, we walked this path filled with the hope and expectation of God.

You see, we loved all those other people and blessed them with all our hearts. We were just going a different way.

Because I was not working full time, we lived primarily on the good salary Maureen was bringing home caring for Miss Ruth in Pasadena. We could not afford any payments for our remaining three children to continue at Family Christian, and so we planned to home school them for the 2009-2010 school year. Johanna was in tenth grade this year, Katrina in seventh, and James in fourth.

I had created reading lists of books in differing categories that I thought should be read by a young person at each grade level. Johanna was a reader, and so I put her into a schedule of working through reading those listed books she had not yet read. I also bought her a large college textbook on world history. What I did not know, however, mostly because I was oblivious, was that this school year became a sad time for Johanna. She had been close to so many friends at Family Christian, and now she was alone in her room every day.

I ask forgiveness of Johanna for my thoughtlessness. Nonetheless, in looking at the path of her life,

I realize just how necessary this year was for her, for the Lord Jesus was switching her heart towards the path He had for her, which was very different than for our other children. You see, Johanna was born in the praises of Christian Community in the wilderness.

Katrina had expressed an interest in raising rabbits, and thus I wrote my "Raising Rabbits Project Guide" with her in mind. We were not able to get rabbits until the summer of 2010, however. Katrina also liked nature as well as sketching and drawing. I wrote the "Drawing Sketches Project Guide" for her and directed her through its exercise. I had her study and draw the things of nature in our back yard. Katrina also went through the literature reading I had listed out, even though it started at the eighth grade level. She tells me now that she did not read *Oliver Twist* because she did not understand it.

Katrina had found math frustrating and difficult, and so we skipped math for this year and the next. My theories were proven right when she returned to a formal classroom in ninth grade and suddenly understood and did well in math. When you try to force things on children when their brains are not ready, you succeed only in making them hate to learn.

James soon excelled at looking like he was doing something while doing nothing at all. Of truth, I had read some of the arguments for "unschooling" and agreed with them, at least for a year or two scattered throughout the school years. The fruit of doing nothing academic for a whole year would come when James went back into the formal classroom in the fall of 2010.

In actuality, I am very glad that all of my children experienced different kinds of schooling back and forth through all their school years, public school, Christian school, and homeschool. It gave them a full sense of distinction and difference, that there are many things in life. In complete contrast, those who grow up in only one setting imagine that is all there is, an untrue fiction. Our children experienced as much of the variation of life as we could give them, and I see the fruit and wisdom of that path in their present persons.

More Family Things: Spring and Summer 2010

In May of 2010, I won the lottery! Somewhere around $3500, if I remember rightly. To celebrate we went down to Academy Sports & Outdoor Supplies and purchased a large family tent, a campsite kitchen and propane stove, cots, and other camping supplies. Then we headed into the hill country towards Pedernales Falls State Park. We passed through Brenham on the way and toured the Blue Bell ice cream factory as part of the children's homeschooling. We splurged in their ice cream store afterwards.

We arrived at our campsite after dark and tried to set up our new tent, not knowing what we were doing. At that moment the clouds dumped heavy rain upon us. We gave up and drove down the road to the first motel. After a great night in a cozy motel, we returned to our campsite and a sunny morning and finished setting up our tent correctly. We might have spent two nights there. We hiked the Pedernales river, clambering over the rocks around the falls. I even spent time myself swimming in the warm water.

After our time at the park, we drove north to Longhorn Cavern State Park. We spent several hours there, touring the caverns and the large historical rock fort and eating our lunch in the park restaurant. This was a worthwhile place to visit.

Then, on the way back home, we angled southwest to the Bastrop area. We had found a lady in that area who had rabbits for sale, the specific breed we wanted to get for Katrina. We spent a couple of hours at their beautiful rustic place in the countryside, in their country home, and toured their little "farm" in the woods. We purchased two rabbits for Katrina, a male and a female, and drove on home to Houston.

I had seen a notice of summer courses on learning nature being offered at Jesse Jones Park to school-age children. We had visited this park several times and loved the heritage environment there. So I went early in the morning and got in line in my car – I was not the first – and I signed up Katrina and James to participate.

They both went to their respective classes that June and loved it completely, especially the canoeing down Spring Creek. Our connection, then, to Jesse Jones Park and all its activities was cemented into place and continues until now. The park has been Katrina's place of employment for several years.

Sometime in May or June, Maureen and I took our YGuide Academy brochures and project guides to a home school fair in Conroe, Texas. We stood behind our table, giving out brochures to those few who came by and discussing the concept of "project-led-learning." There were no takers.

More than that, even though I advertised on homeschool websites, and even though many visited my page of completed project guides at $14.95 each, few bought. Eventually I came to the conclusion that trying to make a living off of homeschooling families was a narrow field indeed.

Nonetheless, my problem was never my ideas or the market, but always my inability to make people feel comfortable and thus willing to buy.

Yet I place all that I am into the Lord Jesus. My long hours of work over months did not result in an income for us, nor did it seem to fit the needs of very many homeschooling families. I know that my ideas are worthwhile and that my project guides are of great value. Yet I have carried all this inside as a great loss. It was when I began to write this chapter of my life that the sorrow returned to me, and then the Lord showed me that all my work was of great value to Him and would become valuable to many in the future.

"Thank You, Lord Jesus, that I belong utterly to You in all that I am and that You belong utterly to me in all that You are. Thank You, that those things that seem to be loss to us in the present time, are only gain forever inside of You.

"Thank You, Lord Jesus, for the goodness of Your gentle hand always upon my life."

44. Aspergers and Bankruptcy

June 2010 - September 2011

"Look Me in the Eye"

In late June of 2010, I went together with my family to the Barnes and Noble at Gray and Shepherd, down the street from our Sunday-dinner Souper Salad. I was fifty-three years old. As usual, everyone quickly scattered through the rows of books. I went into the upstairs of this store and turned down an aisle between two book shelves. At the far end of the aisle, on the bottom row of the shelf running perpendicular to this aisle, I saw a book.

Now, it might seem an "extraordinary" thing to you that I saw a book in a book store. Nonetheless, what I saw was a picture of a twelve-year-old boy with his eyes squinted tightly shut. I could not do anything but run down that aisle. When I was close enough to see the title of the book, I read, "Look Me in the Eye." With a picture like that under those words, I could not do anything else but grab that book, buy it, and begin to read.

And what I read, in that book, was the story of my own life. You see, when I was a twelve-year-old boy, the most awful words I could ever hear was some stern man commanding me, "Look me in the eye." I never did; I could not.

In actuality, *Look Me in the Eye: My Life with Asperger's* is the autobiography of John Robeson. John Robeson is my same age. Outwardly, the course of his life was very different from mine; inwardly, our life was identical. In his teenage years John had known some abuse; I had known none. Yet the things he did and the reasons he did them in his teenage thinking were identical to mine. Then, in his twenties, his love of designing patterns took him into becoming the stage designer for the rock band, KISS, with Gene Simmons, whereas my love of designing patterns took me into designing and building Christian community, very different outwardly, but identical inside in our thinking and all our approaches to what we did. And we were doing these things through the same years, for we were about the same age.

From beginning to end, this little book described all the love and passion, hurt and confusion of my life. It answered every unanswered question, thousands of them, even questions I did not know were there. Such profound relief, such joy, to know that I am not WRONG, that there are other people who experience the world in just the same way I do.

Asperger's is a sub-group in what is called "the Autism Spectrum." It is typically an inherited condition, rather than the medical injury that is most of today's autism, abusive injury coming from the vile practice of injecting loads of toxic chemicals straight into the bloodstream of infants. Asperger's is also called "high-performing autism."

If you met me face to face, you would at first not think me any different from anyone else. Nonetheless, if you were to walk with me through daily and public circumstances, it would not take you long to notice my autistic peculiarities. And if I did not point those things out to you, it would not take you long to define me as so many have.

In July, we purchased tickets and attended the circus at the large Reliant Stadium as a family. Before the show started, the performers were rehearsing inside the rings, while crowds of onlookers pressed close to watch. Maureen and the children pushed through the crowds until they were against the dividing fence in order to watch the rehearsal. I did not. I feel very UN-comfortable in such public and exposed settings, and so instead, I backed up all the way against an outer fence with no one behind me. From this protected place I could enjoy my children's enjoyment from a distance. Then, just before the show began, we went up into the stands to find our seats. You see, I had a ticket with a seat number on it. Then, I found the seat with that SAME number and sat down. Instantly, I was completely safe; I was now in my place where I was "supposed" to be.

This had been my norm all my life, yet all the way through I had puzzled and agonized over "what was WRONG with me," and other people as well, reacting to my responses in the way that all who are Asperger's experience. As I stood there in my temporarily almost "safe" place, and when I sat down in the chair where I BELONGED and all thought of exposure vanished, in both instances I marveled and said to myself. "I am Asperger's. This is Asperger's. Many other people are the same as I. I'm okay; it's all right. I am free in Jesus to be what He made me to be."

I purchased several more books on Asperger's over the next while and connected with some Asperger's things online. Several months after this, while I was teaching college, I attended a gathering of Asperger's with Maureen at the University of Houston, in a program overseen by Dr. Katherine Loveland, professor of Autism Research. As I listened to those others who were Asperger's sharing of their life experiences, I heard my own life experience in theirs. There was a real sense of belonging for me. Nonetheless, I had two problems. The first was internal; you see, I was a highly educated professional, a college instructor and a literary man; most Asperger's don't do well in school. This was a bit hard to put together. The second was towards Professor Loveland. It seemed to me that we were "specimens for study" to her.

I have not continued these connections, for there is no fruit of Christ through that avenue. Nonetheless, I have learned something very important through my study. Those who research and write "about" Asperger's as a field of study mostly don't know what they're talking about. If you read official stuff, don't take it as complete reality. In contrast, everything I have read written by people who are Asperger's just sings as truth to me.

One of the most important things I have read is this, and I paraphrase. "Many think that Asperger's people have no feelings or empathy towards other people. This is opposite of the truth. Asperger's carry a deeper empathy towards the hurts and sufferings of others than most, but the problem is that they feel TOO MUCH. For that reason, in order to cope with life, they learn at an early age to compartmentalize their feelings, and to disassociate from them to a certain extent, so that they will not be overwhelmed." And so I did and do.

The responses of zealous Christians towards the autistic can be brutal at times. Even at Lakewood Church, one of the children's pastors had an autistic son. He shared one time about their love for their son and all he had learned caring for the child. He brought the boy out onto the stage as a blessing. This was all wonderful, but I thought to myself. "No sir, that boy is not in your life so that you can discover healing from God to 'fix' him. That boy is in your life to show you Christ Jesus through him in a way you have never considered."

In fact, that experience inspired these words written in October, 2011. – "If we want to know the way into the fullness of Christ, we had better go looking for people who never get it right, for people who are crippled and maimed in body and in soul; we need to follow the blind. If we want to know God, we better find a Down syndrome boy and ask him to tell us the secret; we better find an autistic girl and learn what makes her sing."

Asperger's as How I Function

The question here is what does being Asperger's mean inside this time period and in how I approach and write about God and the Bible?

Asperger's includes the following qualities: (1) an obsessive mind, driven to see patterns; (2) a deep vulnerability and inadequacy, a deep sense of peril – this quality creates blinders around the mental drive, it also causes the 'blocking out' of other people as unsafe; (3) an inherent, even compelling need for honesty; (4) a profound empathy, a deep sensitivity that becomes way too much, and thus requires the practice of disassociation.

Please understand, I did not make myself this way; rather, I am only discovering how God designed me and His purposes for my design. Thus, in sharing these things, I am not boasting of myself, but only seeking to understand myself as God made me, and thus to become more comfortable with His purposes.

To people in general, I am a strange mix of contradictions, seemingly empathic and seemingly disconnected, seemingly kind and seemingly self-centered, even harsh. To bullies, I seem an easy target, yet they are always astonished to discover that they never had the slightest hold on me. To God, I am always in great need of salvation, and, having found my Salvation, I will never let Him go.

Yet it is towards the Bible that all of these qualities come into play, as well as the kind of mind, both the brain-mind and the heart/gut-mind, God gave to me. Intellectually, God gave me a reasonably high IQ, at the bottom of the level required to see and understand the larger picture and where things fit. But my mind is also literary and tends towards story; I can do math, but I don't like it. At the same time, I have a practical side, specifically in construction, and thus I am driven to see how things fit together.

And that's the key word – driven. My brain goes non-stop, and I spend much of my time doing things that calm it down. I HAVE TO understand the world and how everything fits together. And I remember many things, not photographically, but rather, things that interest me. At the same time, the sensitive vulnerability carries all hurt. Even through the years of the "The Season of Symmorphy," coming up, the very thought of Blueberry caused only severe and sharp pain that could not be viewed.

Consider the three places where I feel completely safe, where I "belong." First is my home library and my easy chair where I read or watch stories. Second is the classroom, where I am the teacher – this extends itself to writing. And third is the construction site, where I fit things together to create places where people can belong.

Yet look at this balance between a mental drive that never slows down and a desperate need to find safety in an unsafe world, along with a requirement for honesty. You see, I cannot treat the Bible intellectually, for how could my brain ever place me into the salvation of God? It is my desperate vulnerability, then, that requires me to find and know a Personal Savior, both in my heart AND on every page of the Bible. My requirement for honesty is what causes such pain inside when I hear preachers abusing the word or what the Bible says about God. I have never been able to ignore any challenge to what God says, for I must worry that thing for months until the Word God actually speaks has become my only dwelling place.

This is an obsession, driven relentlessly. I must know God; I must know Father with me at home in my heart by every word that He speaks – and I cannot really say "or I will die," for there is no thought other than the obsession.

My Project Guides
I continued writing the project guides for individual homeschoolers and putting them for sale on

my website into the summer of 2010. I did get to meet one of those students and her mother, who lived in Katy, Texas, at an event in a state park both of our families enjoyed. They were Sufi Muslim, from Indonesia, and they were wonderful and caring people. I looked up "Sufi" afterwards and was astonished at the similarity it shares with union with Christ. The thing is, Jesus is Savior, not ideas of the mind.

I can include this regarding Asperger's; the thought that having the 'correct' mental ideas might 'save,' a delusion held by many Christians, is only absurd to me. Only a Person saves.

Nonetheless, I found that writing each next project guide became harder and harder. It was like trying to swim through, first thick syrup, and then becoming as wet concrete. There came a moment when my ability to put my mind around one more project guide vanished as a snap, as a great gulf. The "wet concrete" had become a "brick wall" in my mind. I was unable to finish all the guides I had agreed to write for the girl from Katy, but her mother was very understanding and was happy to support me, regardless.

Myy great intention to provide for my family through an Internet business came to nothing.

Another School Year for the Children
In the fall of 2010, Johanna was looking at 11th grade, Katrina 8th grade, and James 5th. Homeschooling under my direction had not proven very productive for them. Only Katrina wanted to continue with her self-directed studies.

We enrolled James in Royalwood Elementary School, a public school several blocks from our home. James was born in October, like I was, but whereas I started first grade at 5 going on 6, we did not start James until he was 6 going on 7. For that reason, he was in the older segment among his classmates, and a bit bigger than most of the other boys. This made me very comfortable, for he would not be a target for bullies. More than that, James has always carried himself in a way that such difficulties would never be an issue.

We met James's teachers; they were good Texas women, primarily Christian, and that would be true whether African or European American. It did not take long to discover the results of a year of "un-schooling." Although his mother did have to stay on top of his getting his homework, done, typical for any boy, still, he was better off in the classroom because of the year's break.

James would spend the next four-and-a-half years in the public schools of Sheldon ISD.

Each one of our children is quite unique, and I love pondering over their similarities and differences. Johanna did not fare so well in the isolation of homeschooling and more than that, having seen me in the classroom, and then comparing that outgoing and expressive "me" with the "me" at home that was incapable, I realize only now how hard that must have been for her.

My first problem is that younger females terrify me. I can talk personal things only with Maureen and that only sometimes. I can converse freely with my boys about every sensitive topic, but when it comes to personal issues with my daughters, I leave that to Maureen, for I am scared witless, that is, it is venturing out into a very unsafe place where I do not belong. In fact, it's too far out there for me even to consider such a venture. But that does not answer the heart-need of a teenage girl.

I titled this chapter "Asperger's and Bankruptcy," but I could have also titled it "My Season of Failure," not as different from all the other chapters of my life, but where failure became intensely personal.

Johanna always got mad at me when I tried to share some understanding concerning this world. She did not want to hear it. In the opposite direction, however, Johanna had me wrapped around her little finger and knew that she could get me to do or buy for her anything she wanted. "Daddy, could you get this for me?" Saying "No" never entered my mind, that is, if I could afford it.

That brings the thought of Cracker Barrel. We enjoyed many times at various Cracker Barrel restaurants as a family. We would first eat their good home-style meals. Kyle and Johanna often sat together at their own table. They grew up being very close friends. We would play checkers or the little triangle peg-jumping game while waiting for our food. Then after we ate, we would wander together through their country store, always ending up at the stick candy display each time. Each of us would pick out two or three choices of stick candy flavors; I made sure they all learned to like horehound. Then we would sit in the rocking chairs out front, sucking on our candy sticks.

I left out the fourth place where I was safe; I was safe going out with my family, doing such pleasurable things together. I was safe when one of my little ones held my hand and said, "Daddy."

But I still could not talk of personal things with girls, nor intrude myself into their lives. And so Johanna also objected to "Christ is my life; I have no other life." At least, that's what it seemed to me, a continuation of her antagonism towards my talking about this world.

Later in the summer, after Johanna had set her heart on going to school at Upsala Christian Community, I drove home from somewhere, just me and her in the car. Somehow our conversation had become prickly, and I was feeling very defensive. She wanted to tell me how difficult being at home alone was for her, but I did not know that. Her frustration with me and my inability provoked in me only a tighter clasp of my own blinders and inability to connect.

I foolishly imagined she was attacking me, and so I said, "Christ is my life; I have no other life." But in her teenage girl's need, she heard only a dad who was shutting her out. She got out of the car angry and in tears. I did not know what to do.

I did not understand any of this until my recent visit with Johanna in Canada, where she shared of this and I could hear her freely.

Johanna, I do not use my searing inability as any excuse; I was wrong. I ask you to forgive me. And I think you know that I have always loved you deeply, and that I have always covenanted with God for your sake.

We were visiting with Sandy and Richard in The Woodlands. Sandy gave our children the task of sorting through a large number of coins. Many of these were Canadian coins, which she then offered to the girls, knowing they were Canadian.

Johanna took the Canadian money and said, "What will we do with this?" Maureen answered her, "Maybe you can give it to Matt when you see him at camp next time." And then, without thought, the words flew out, "Or maybe you can spend it when you go to school up there." And in that moment, Johanna grabbed hold of that thought as from the Lord and would not let it go.

Johanna went to the youth camp in Missouri again in July, where she visited again with her friends come down from the Christian community in Upsala, Ontario. At the same time, she applied for and was accepted into the school at Upsala Christian Community, about a hundred miles northwest of Thunder Bay, which is on Lake Superior. A number of the people there knew us well. Johanna is a Canadian citizen, so that was never an issue.

Now, I have never done anything in my life that demonstrates more my profound trust in God than to allow my daughter to return to a move community and to be again part of "the move." To release her utterly into God, that He directed her steps, and that He alone kept her, this was not an easy thing for me, yet it was also never a question. It was always the only possibility.

And so Maureen and I placed our precious daughter into God our Father, and released her to leave home far away for her last two years of high school. And somehow we also knew, both of us, that Upsala was different, even though we had never been there, that the family and ministry in that community would receive her with kindness, in ways that were not the same in all other move communities I had known. We could not have agreed to anywhere else.

During the first part of September, we drove Johanna to the large airport in Houston to put her all by herself on a plane flying to Toronto and then to Thunder Bay. Our Jo was just sixteen. Johanna is very intelligent, but she can also be oblivious like her dad. We stood there watching as our little girl went through security and then to where she would go either left or right to her gate. She turned the wrong way and vanished from our sight!

And in that moment I discovered that I had married a Lioness. My wife would not be turned aside. She persevered and persevered before every obstacle until they allowed her through to find her daughter and bring her safely back. She insisted until they had placed Johanna on another flight the next day.

When we took Johanna to the airport again the next day, she was now focused. Her flight went well and she was welcomed back into Christian community in the wilderness. I must also mention that Kim and Joe Rideau wanted to help provide for Johanna's school costs, and so they paid her living of $100 a month for the first school year. Later, Johanna was able to earn the money to pay her own costs.

Katrina wanted to continue the homeschooling another year, and so it was just she and I. In my mind things went better, and I really enjoyed overseeing her learning. We sat together each day and went through her various studies. I laid out for her the work for the day, and then left her to do it as she wished. Her studies continued basically as before.

Meanwhile Kyle continued at South Plains College near Lubbock, staying with his Aunt Lois.

Bankruptcy

In September of 2010, the money that had been available for Miss Ruth to be cared for in her own home ran out. Maureen had a good relationship of friendship with Miss Ruth's daughter, Sandra, one that has continued until now. At the same time, of all the people Maureen has cared for, Miss Ruth was the most kind. And so it was very sad to everyone involved that Miss Ruth had to go into a nursing facility for the duration. She did not last long there, but passed on a short time after.

Maureen had lost her good job, and we now had no income. The expectations had all vanished, the hammer had swung home, and we were now faced with a terrible reckoning. I'm sure an astute reader will have picked up on a whole lot of spending of borrowed money. Here I must give a full account.

We were scrambling to pay the bills. We looked for and found help from a number of directions. Lakewood Church helped us a bit, and Sandy and Richard Roberts were very generous to us.

After about three weeks, Maureen did find a new care-taking job through an agency, assisting an elderly couple, Art and Mary Kleiderer, in their home, which was several blocks south of the Lakewood Church area. At the same time, I also looked for part-time work, and so, even though it was late in the season, I did apply for a job as an adjunct, that is, a part-time instructor with Lone Star College. I had no idea of getting such a job, however.

Even though we were late on one mortgage payment, nonetheless, we were somehow able to pay all of our bills.

Yet these weeks without income had thrown us into reality, for we had been "robbing Peter to pay Paul," as is said, for sometime now, finagling our finances somehow to keep up with all the payments, which were low on each, and thus nothing was being paid off.

It had to stop, and so we found a bankruptcy lawyer, and managed to put together the $1000 he required. We could do that because the moment we signed a contract with him, we no longer had to pay any of our many bills, other than ongoing utilities.

Here is reality. From the time we left Blair Valley, from September of 1998 until September of 2010, twelve years, our living had cost, on average, $1000 more each month than our income. Now this did include the three years of living on student loans, and I do not include the mortgage on our house in this overall calculation. With the student loans, although I did make many payments, I was also able to obtain long periods of forbearance in which they allowed me not to pay without placing me in default.

The majority of the burdensome debt, however, came from my many attempts to provide for my family through self-employment, starting with the cabinet-making tools I bought while we were still at the Applegate trailer park in Lubbock. I never really paid any of that back, and further attempts only increased that debt in sizeable increments. I also got too excited buying stuff for my kids, especially at Christmas time.

Yes, I wore blinders, always HOPING that next time something would work out.

The worst though was the money I borrowed from my mother. When Franz and Audrey took our home place and made it their own, they paid mom an agreed upon "mortgage" with a monthly payment. In 2005, then, Franz's bee business, Snow Peak Apiaries, was doing well enough that Franz could get a new mortgage that also allowed him to expand his business. Land values on the west coast were going up and up. With that new mortgage, he was able to pay mom the remainder of what was due to her, about $80,000.

We had so many high-interest bills at that time, and so I asked her if we could borrow $40,000 from her to pay off those high-interest bills and then pay her a sizable monthly payment in return. At the same time she sent us the money, our furnace/air conditioner went out and we used a few thousand of that to replace it, though we got a tremendous bargain through one of my students at C.E. King. We did make the payments to mom for several years, through our time at Family Christian,

but then we just did not have the money and so I stopped, again, hoping that my Internet business would provide for all.

The truth is, I did not include this fact in my earlier chapters because I am ashamed of it. Sometimes it's good to be ashamed of things, at least for a bit.

Bankruptcy is deeply humiliating. We had to give an account of every single item we owned. That's when I discovered that we had over three thousand books. I'm sorry, but I do like books.

Not long into this process, I woke up one night and, for the first time, realized the awful thing I had done. You see, when I speak of "being oblivious" or "wearing blinders," I'm not speaking of something incidental, but of something complete. I did not know; I had not seen.

As I lay there in the awfulness of having borrowed nearly $150,000 from other people and then spent it, never to return, my precious knowledge of union with Christ seemed to be entirely inadequate. And so I spent that night trying to pull the old familiar darkness of shame and accusation back upon myself.

In this season of failure, I failed at that as well.

Let me share what union with Christ means to me. It means one thing, that Jesus is an integral part of my life, that every moment is He sharing Himself with me. And inside of all my inability, Jesus remains Himself, real and alive, living inside my heart.

By morning, Jesus Himself arose inside of me in all joy, "My son," He said to me, "I carry you, even in all your failure, even in this."

From the time I began writing the *Christ Our Life* letters in November of 2009, this level of Jesus saving me became a regular occurrence. I know Him, and no one could ever take from me the joy of a living Savior arising every moment.

Sure, I experienced times of discouragement through these years, times when I did not send out any letters for a week or two, but they never lasted long, and they always ended abruptly in the joy of my Savior singing inside of me.

Jesus is real, and He really is my life.

Into the College Classroom

Then, on an incredible day, September 22, 2010, I received a phone call from Beverley Turner, the

Dean of Developmental Education at the Montgomery Branch of Lone Star Community College, located in The Woodlands. She said she had my application and resume and asked me to come for an interview the next day, a Thursday.

Beverley Turner was an older, gentle woman, almost like the Mennonite women I had known (if she was Christian, it would have been private in that setting). The interview went well, and I was hired to teach developmental writing. Of truth, Miss Turner was the "best" female boss of my experience, similar in many ways to Warren Yoder.

This was late in the semester. The reason for their need to hire me was that a number of students had applied late, and thus needed a late-starting developmental writing course. Developmental reading and writing are considered pre-college courses, and thus my Master's degree in education qualified me for that position. To have been hired to teach regular college composition, I would have needed eighteen credit hours in graduate level English, of which I had only three. Nonetheless, I much prefer to teach struggling students to write than to deal with those who already can.

I stepped into the college classroom again on Monday, September 27, 2010. The Montgomery Branch was just past The Woodlands off of I-45, about a 50 minute drive from home. I had the red Buick, with all of its problems, for this drive.

On the next page is the front main entry of the college. I did teach in the building on the left for a couple of months. That was the English Department this first semester and where I had the interview. My first classroom, however, was in a temporary classroom module, located to the back right, next to the cafeteria. In the spring semester, all English courses would move over to a new building just finished to the left of this picture. The developmental reading and writing courses were their own department, but they were also tucked into the English part of things.

This was so exciting to me, having a college classroom in which to really develop my writing course. I had around twenty students, of varying ages, some just out of high school and some much older, come back to school to gain a better job. These were students who had not done well on their writing entrance exam and thus needed instruction in writing to do well enough in their regular college courses. Miss Beverley had given me her own syllabus to copy and change for my own use; I had done so with a quick layout of my approach. The developmental writing course has a lab component, making it a 4 credit course, and thus I had sixty classroom hours into which to fit my writing course. This was absolute fun.

The difference with teaching college is very simple. These were adults, and they needed no baby-sitting, neither did they talk while I was teaching (except a few fresh out of high school, and only a bit). Basically, you condensed what would take a year in a high school classroom into, in this case, twelve weeks. I went up to The Woodlands two times a week for my one course. The down side of teaching college, however, is that the college students are in for one semester and then gone. There is no real ongoing interaction with them outside of the course itself. For that reason, there is little to share about any interaction with people in this part of my work life.

A Time of Humiliation

Before I got the college instructor job, however, Sandy and Richard Roberts had offered me a job building kitchen and closet cabinets for their home. They were remodeling it to prepare it for the market. They planned to sell and find a more rural place to live as they continued to talk about "community." This was a big job that would provide us with some income, and so I tackled it. I had only the simplest of power tools, however, and only my back porch in which to work.

I had contracted with the Roberts to be finished by the end of October. Because of gaining the teaching job, however, my work slowed down a bit, and the finish date was being pushed back. They were patient and understanding. The problem was that they also had a deadline for the sale of their house.

Sandy and Richard did have some strange ideas, including not wanting anything to do with the Holy Spirit. Maureen and I went with them to a Bible study put on by some others whom they had connected with through the same 'community' website. We rode with them to Bryan, Texas for that get together. The brother was teaching from Ezekiel, and he seemed to have no knowledge of Paul's gospel. We did visit about community with this group, but it seemed that we were on different planets.

I drove home in complete humiliation. I was 54 years old and still subject to public, autistic humiliation. I was in pain. I cried out to God in deep desperation, "I didn't mean to be this way, God. I didn't mean to be."

By the time Richard came down a couple of days later to pick up the materials I had purchased with his money, I had humbled myself. I accepted the money he offered and my wrong and asked his forgiveness.

In seeking further relationship in the Lord with all of these, we found no knowledge of the Spirit, nor any perception of what I teach.

Persevering with the cabinet work became more difficult for me. Again, I was feeling the mental disconnect that made it feel like swimming through thickness to keep at the job. I confess that at times I chose to write my *Christ our Life* letters when I should have been working on the Roberts' cabinets. I have never tired nor ever known any disconnect in writing to know the Lord.

Time went on, and I was not finishing. It was into November, and, as I was installing the first parts, I think they were not satisfied with the results. It is difficult to do fine woodworking without high quality tools. I really should not have taken on the job. I knew I was not meeting their needs, but I could not face it, so I put blinders on and kept going forward. In that state I am unable to communicate; I can only plow ahead, refusing to see outside of my narrow path. I do that because I feel very unsafe.

Sometime near the end of November, I took up a load of bedroom closet cabinets to install. Not long after I started, Richard came home from work to talk with me. He informed me that they had decided to hire someone else to do the job, someone who would do it much more quickly. He doubted that this new contractor would want to use anything I had done. He offered a much smaller sum of money than what I was expecting to earn. I had been counting on this pay for our living, and so I remonstrated with him, but it was final.

Then, I had entered the college classroom with a bit of a poor attitude towards these college students. I had pre-judged that they "should have" learned to write when they were in school, and that it was "their fault" that they had not. This was not a strong attitude, but it did show itself in comments I made from time to time. At a certain point, I realized that I was completely wrong. There were any number of reasons why these older students needed help learning to write better and most of them were not their fault. I apologized to them for my attitude and have not carried that self-righteous view of others since.

Sometime in October, then, a teacher of developmental reading had to take time off for health, and so Miss Beverley asked me if I would take on that class. This would be on the same days on which I already taught. And so I stepped into the middle of that classroom. I did not at first connect well with this group; they were accustomed to their former teacher and were resistant towards me. At the same time, I knew little of how one might "learn to read," as I have said before. This was also before my self-righteousness had come to its necessary end. These students seemed quite immature, even though they were older. In fact, one was a young police officer who was acting like an adolescent.

I became angry with this group one day and said some unkind things. One of the young ladies, a strong-forehead sort of person, filed a formal complaint with the appropriate authorities in the college. This was frightening to me, but Miss Beverley helped me with perspective. During the next class session, I shared with them that I had not slept well and was under some stress. I said that I was not offering that as an excuse, that the comments I had made were wrong. I asked for their forgiveness. After this semester was over, the same young lady who had made the complaint wrote a comment of how much she appreciated my stance and how much she had learned from me.

In November, a pickup ran into Maureen's blue Prism and totaled it. She was not injured, but now we had only one car, the somewhat unreliable Buick.

Maureen and I went before the bankruptcy judge in December. This was a very somber occasion. Our lawyer was with us as well as a number of other people in bankruptcy with their lawyers. We went through the process; it is not designed to make anyone feel very good about themselves, but there were no snags either. When we left, we had no more debts – except the student loans, which cannot be bankrupted by decree of congress contrary to the U.S. Constitution.

This was a low moment for us, but we were free.

Also in December, while I was feeling quite low, Bonnie Morris shared with me that a ministry from Phoenix, named Rick Manis, whose messages she had really enjoyed, would be sharing in a little Pentecostal church in northeast Texas, called Life Tabernacle Church. At the same time, a sister who lived in Longview, Texas, had been in communication with me concerning what I teach. And so I took Katrina and James with me for this trip. We spent a night in the home of the sister in Longview and had good fellowship with her, then we went on to Life Tabernacle Church Sunday morning. While we were sitting in the pre-service "Sunday school" time, an older lady began to speak in the anointing of God. I said to James and Katrina, "Listen carefully, for you are hearing a mighty woman of God." They had already recognized it.

Rick Manis had a good word; I visited with him a bit, though no long-term connections were made. But then I also had the chance to visit with the older lady who knew the Lord in such power. It turns out that this church was the first church in Texas to receive the outpouring of the Holy Spirit right after Azusa Street, when her own parents were young.

I drove home from this experience much lifted up and restored by the Lord from the lowness of the prior couple of months.

Learning from Pastor Joel

Pastor Joel always started his sermon with a silly joke. Thus, when we opened our Bibles, we were laughing. This worked well, as it came naturally from Joel. Then, Joel had one basic message, and that is to be confident in God's presence and favor in our lives. Yet each time he taught his primary message, it was always fresh and new and anointed of the Lord.

On a number of occasions, Joel shared about how God enabled him to deal with criticism, his nicer word for the onslaught thrown against him by so many. I embraced what he shared into myself, for I needed such help. Joel shared that when God gives you a path to walk, there will always be opponents, but to counteract them, we should gather around us those who see what God is doing and who support and encourage us in that path.

Pastor Joel said two things, one often, and the other in every service, that were as an open door for me into the heavens, enabling me to receive whatever God might be teaching me through Joel's illustrations and stories. The first was – "in all that God intends for you," and the second was, "you don't have to attend here, find any Bible-based church where you are comfortable." Those seem like little things, but in the Spirit, I knew they were huge. In the Spirit, Joel was saying, "You are not tied to me, but go with God as far as God would take you."

At the same time, Joel was never political. In fact, he did not usually share on political Sundays, leaving that to others. I learned to avoid those Sundays. The absence of any politics in Joel's word left me free to enjoy hearing from God.

I would sit there in that anointing, hearing God speak to me through Joel's words, things far beyond what was even in Joel's mind, let alone those sitting around me. And when God is free in any service, He will speak different things to every person there, according to their own walk with Him. You see, because I was also writing the *Christ Our Life* letters all through this time, the word I heard from God in the Lakewood services was always an extension of what I was writing. In fact, I marveled so many times that when I wrote something in a letter going out early Sunday morning, that same topic and those same verses would be the center of the service that day at Lakewood.

As I have said, the thing I learned the most from Joel Osteen was to stop speaking all the endless curses against myself in my mind and to walk in confidence in the goodness and favor of God.

At some point during these years, Pastor Joel offered to hold a baptism in water service. Many signed up, and so Joel had his work cut out for him. Nonetheless, we placed our two youngest on his list, and so Pastor Joel Osteen baptized Katrina and James in water.

Through 2011

In January of 2011, the new building for the English Department was completed, and so we all moved over to it. This time I had two full developmental writing classes, on the same days. This made the long drive cost effective. I always arrived an hour before my first class started; I need that quiet time to be ready for my students when they arrive. On more than one occasion, however, problems with the Buick made me almost late.

Other than that, this semester went quite smoothly such that I have little memory of it. Each time I went through my writing course, however, I made continual improvements, removing things that did not work, adding new good ideas that fit, and adjusting everything to be more effective in the outcome of those students leaving my course, knowing how to write well.

Through this time, I reduced some of the stuff we had. I sold the two canoes I had made for the boys, which had not really worked out all that well for them or for me. I sold the generator I had bought for Ike, it was too big and I had no place to keep it. I sold a number of other things, some of which I regret, specifically my drill press and the potting bench I had made. I was no longer gardening, so it seemed to be unnecessary. I reduced our continuously increasing selection of books by around 1000 books, some to used book stores, but many I sold through Amazon.

The biggest thing for me, however, was that I also sold the Blue Van, for $500. The Blue Van had quit running well in 2006, and so I had parked it in the back corner of our yard and used it for storage. As it was pulled out of the yard, I was very sad. The buyer would not let me talk him out of the sale,

however, and so it went. That van was the single most meaningful possession to me in my life.

Maureen had also taken on a job caring for an elderly woman in The Woodlands, named Mrs. Dotson, two nights a week. That was a long drive in the Buick, an unreliable car, especially at night. At the same time, she had to drive me up to teach college and then come back to pick me up after the day's work. This was simply putting too much on my dear wife.

Meanwhile, Claude had been keeping Grandma Susan's little 1980 Toyota running, barely, and offered it to us. Not knowing better, we accepted it. He came with it but then returned to Bowens Mill. We now had two cars again – except the Toyota was in worse shape than the Buick. It worked for a while, but it needed oil added almost daily. At a certain point, while Maureen was driving through Spring on her way to The Woodlands, the motor froze from low oil, and that was it.

Claude wanted to come fix the Toyota, rather than just letting it go for scrap. He came in May and spent several weeks with us working on the little Toyota under our back porch, trying to rebuild the engine. He spent several hundred dollars; we helped as we could. In the end, he was not able to make it work.

My relationship with my father-in-law was cordial, but as time went on, there was a growing strain. I will not share the circumstances, but an incident happened in which he came towards me in all the "correcting power" I had known of him when I was under his eldering at the Ridge. I could not have that, however, and so I said, with strength, "Sir, no sir." To my astonishment, Claude did an about-face, saying nothing.

I did not see this as any sort of "triumph," and as an Asperger's, this was really "out there" for me. I went to bed right after, feeling very unprotected. As I lay in bed, I saw, in my mind's eye, Brother Claude with Brother Buddy behind him, and all the condemnation I had known from them. I looked straight into the eyes of Jesus, again in my mind, and I said, "Jesus, You are my life, and You share all things with me." Immediately, all the horror of condemnation pressing all around me vanished, and I could sleep in peace.

Probably before Claude left, Maureen and I had found a lovely, red 2007 Toyota Corolla, for which

Maureen qualified for financing. This was the best car we have ever had, well-built and faithful. It served Maureen and us well until it was rear-ended in May of 2018. After Claude left, we then sold the 1980 Toyota for a couple of hundred dollars and sent the money to Claude to pay for some of what this whole thing had cost him.

I taught my writing course during the summer block. This was more concentrated, about four hours each day, covering only a few weeks. My course works well, however, as it has distinct components that can be fitted to the times available.

Johanna remained in Canada through the summer. Maureen made a surprise visit to spend several days with her in her new experiences. At the same time, Kyle had returned from his time in Lubbock, not having quite finished his associates degree in audio engineering. Lubbock had "closed" to him as it had to us.

The Progression of Christ Our Life

I gained two new readers of my letters who communicated with me through this time-period. One was Annalize Mouton, a Dutch woman from Cape Town, South Africa. The other was Dennis Rhodes of Western Australia. Both of these have maintained their own websites over the years where they have sometimes shared things I have written, and both continue to read my letters. At this time, they were new to union with Christ and to speaking Christ our only life. I hope that I was able to answer some of their questions.

Through this years' time, I wrote my first series on "Union with Christ," the chapters of which folded into my book, *The Unveiling*. I also continued writing letters that would end up in either *The Great Story of God* or *Gathering to Life*. For the most part, the order of their writing is unimportant.

I also wrote "Eating of Christ," one of my favorites, in the spring of 2011 in response to a question sent to me by Rita Robertson. Then, the last letter of this time period, written in September, 2011, was "Knowing God."

I also want to add a question sent to me by my sister, Frieda, sometime during this year, in response to something I had written in *The Great Story of God*. She asked me – what about Genesis 3:22? – **Now man has become as one "of Us," knowing good and evil.** – Doesn't it say that God knows evil? The

moment I read her question, I knew exactly what I would find when I looked at the Hebrew words of that verse. Sure enough, the Hebrew words say, **"man became as one who knows good and evil."** That Hebrew word is one of the most common, used many hundreds of times throughout the Old Testament. Never do the translators ever find the need to insert the words "of Us" as part of its translation except here.

Yet Jerome, and all translators since, driven by a desperate need to line God up with the serpent's lies, have inserted *"like US – knowing good and evil."* Understanding this served only to increase the sense inside of the wrongness against God that fills so much of Christianity, this need to define God by the words of the devil. My burden to remove from God all accusation that He knows evil would be a foundation for the wondrous vision of God that came upon me on October 2, 2011.

Placing It All into Jesus

This was definitely a conflicting time for me, with some very low points of humiliation. How could I "pretend" to be someone who knows the Lord and who shares that knowing with others, and yet be this incapable, even to going bankrupt because I had wasted other people's money?

I now know that God sees things quite differently from how we see them. And God needed to remove from me the last vestiges of self-righteousness, because He was about to show Himself to me in a way I had never known. Even more than that, God was going to take me into a place inside of Him where few hve been. No presentation of "ME, MYSELF" could remain. No thought that "I" was anything but unrighteous in myself and an utter failure, even towards God, was required, and that the cross would mean to me a wondrous "good riddance" towards any false claims humans make towards God.

You see, some of my siblings had also gone bankrupt, and I had harbored a "holier-than-thou" attitude towards that fact deep inside. Now that I had also passed through this debilitating point, along with all the other wonderful things God had arranged to increase my knowing of humiliation, all of that was gone. I have not once raised "myself" before God since December of 2010. I am more than content to know Jesus as the only life I am.

As Paul said (my paraphrase), "I count all of myself in all my so-called 'achievements' to be nothing more than dog crap, compared to the wonder and beauty of knowing Jesus in the power of His life and in sharing a death already finished."

"Father, I thank You that You so faithfully removed from me any thought of separation from You, that I could ever 'stand on my own.' Father, I give You thanks inside of all the difficulties of these times, to turn every moment to goodness forever. And I do see the wonder of Your Hand, and Your intentions in my life, not to diminish me, but to re-move from me that which diminishes and to set me upon a place of wonder in knowing You."

I have closed this chapter in mid-September, 2011, including God's intentions towards me through this season of my life. Then, in late September, I received an email that struck me with hurt and anger as great as any I have known in my life and changed my life forever and the lives of many others as well.

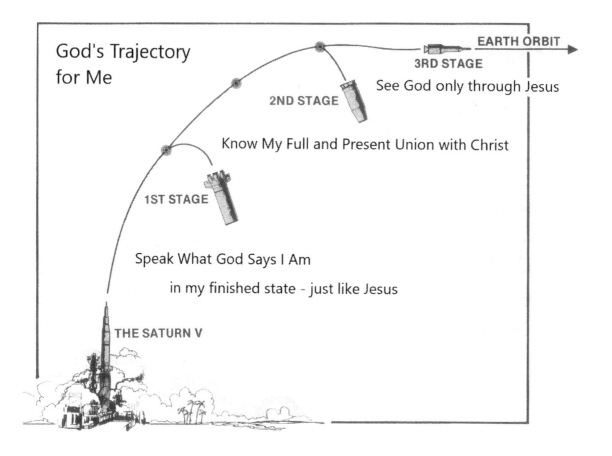

God's Trajectory for Me

EARTH ORBIT

3RD STAGE
See God only through Jesus

2ND STAGE
Know My Full and Present Union with Christ

1ST STAGE

Speak What God Says I Am

in my finished state - just like Jesus

THE SATURN V

45. A Vision of God

September 2011 - August 2012

A New School Year Begins

In August, a new school year began. Katrina chose to go to C.E. King for her high school years, and so I ventured back into those halls again to enroll her in the school. James was in sixth grade, and was now enrolled in C.E. King Middle School, and so I made my way back into those halls as well. This was not easy, but the Lord and I worked through all the conflicting emotions. Kyle did not continue with school right away after his return, but worked for a time at a Ruby Tequila's Restaurant in midtown Houston.

Johanna began her senior year at Upsala Christian School. Barbara Beebe, who was the principal of the Upsala school asked me if I would teach my writing course to Johanna and to Matthew Schneider, who was in her same grade, as he wanted to learn to write better. I agreed to do so and thus was as an English teacher to those two through the whole year, even though it was long-distance.

Meanwhile, I had two new college groups taking developmental writing at Lone Star College. This was now my fourth time through my course in the college classroom and it was becoming more effective. Being immersed in teaching writing had inspired me to believe that I could make it my online business, and so I created the website www. thewritingconservatory.com. In fact, I became all excited about making use of this website with my college students. I signed them all up onto it on the first day of school and immediately it crashed. I was not able to make it useful to many all at the same time, although I maintained it as a resource for my students. Matthew and Johanna were able to use the website as part of my teaching them as well.

Under an Arrogant Christ

On September 20, 2011, I received an email from a reader. Only now am I realizing the great importance of this moment. Let me set the background first.

I had written my letter, "Knowing God" (found now in *Gathering to Life*), and sent it out on Sunday, September 18. This letter was several things. First, it was the most anointed letter I had written up until that moment. Second, it focused the whole purpose of my life and the intensity of my heart – to KNOW God my Father. Third, even as I wrote it and sent it out, I knew that I was still reaching, that I still had not fully entered into the knowing of God with me that my heart longed for. Yet, fourth, it expressed quite clearly the agony and desire of my heart at the time. And fifth, it served as the "bait," that is, talking about Asperger's, that drew an awful response. And so I must share a bit from it, the portion that sparked the horrifying email I received two days later.

᠆

From "Knowing God." ~~~ Some people have a problem with my talking about Asperger's and autism. Someone wrote to assure me that "Christ is not Asperger's." Others say, "Well, it's just how we 'see' things." Technically, that's true, but the problem always comes in that, according to them, ME, as I am right now, cannot be Christ. And for me to KNOW Him, I must alter myself, get away from myself, whatever.

If Christ is not my Asperger's, then I have no hope. If I have to alter my emotional difficulties in order to know Him, then I can never know Him. If I have to be something other than what I find myself to be, then where do I turn? You see, I have decades of knowing that "voice" and all the horror of frustration, all the endless agony that it produces, all the numbing hopelessness. It is not Jesus, though it comes through sincere and good people.

And it's not just Asperger's. Every one of us is afflicted with a weakness appointed to us by a Father who does all things perfectly. All of His ways concerning us are perfect.

To deny our weakness is to pretend. Christ is made perfect in our weakness.

All of me, in all of my ups and downs, my ins and outs, my fears and distresses, I am always and totally fused together with the Person of the Lord Jesus Christ and He with me in an intimate union of the complete immersion of my spirit into His Spirit and His Spirit into my spirit. His consciousness is inside of me, my consciousness is inside of Him, and we walk together in an utter sharing of life.

I went through great emotional and physical difficulty on Friday (in the middle of writing this piece). I was greatly distressed, weeping over my gross inability to fulfill the reality that is in my heart – and to provide for my family's needs. I felt as if all I long to see accomplished was nothing more than my fleshy fallen ambition and that it could never ever be.

The next morning, when I felt a bit better, I heard the Lord nudging me inside, "You passed the test." Do you see how foolish it is for us ever to judge ourselves? What had I done that He approved of?

Simple. In all of my weakness and inability, I saw no shadow of separation inside myself between me and Jesus. I looked at my center and saw Jesus. I knew, with no shadow of thought otherwise, that He is my life and that we are joined together in perfect communion, soul to Soul. I knew that He shares all things with me that I am. I knew that I share all things with Him that He is. I knew that we are joined in a perfectly fused union. I knew that ME, in all the distress of my weakness and anger and inability and despair, He carries ME inside Himself, and He walks in intimate union with that very me.

Then, I can best describe what happened next by quoting from the next letter I wrote and sent out on September 25, "Christ versus Superman I. Please bear with me, for in some ways, this is the most important moment of my life. I must convey to you its full impact and meaning. These quotes also show the close and ongoing relationship that I had come to enjoy with the Lord Jesus since February of 2009.

After posting my letter, "Knowing God," on my website of a Sunday, I received an email response that arrived the following Tuesday morning. The email came from a brother who has sent me many email responses over time, the great majority of which have been sharply critical. In the majority of

those emails there was no personal communication, no fellowship of Christ from one heart to another, just jab and poke.

Finally, nearly a year ago, he sent me one that was too overwhelming for me. It is my responsibility before God to stay free from controllers, and so I removed the brother's email from my list and erased all his subsequent emails without opening them. I hope to justify that decision through this letter.

However, the subject of this recent email said, "Hello Daniel." I am always a hopeful optimist, ready to believe the best, so I opened the email and read the short paragraph that was there.

I do not write these letters to be read, per se. Rather, I write them to know the Lord Jesus Christ more fully than I do. As I write, I hear Him singing. Yet to send out what I write is to open myself up to pain and sorrow. I bear that pain, though I don't want to, because of the love in my heart for those dear ones who also hear Him singing in their hearts when they read and because I know that a stopped spring soon grows stagnant.

I read the email twice, eyes blinking, knowing I had made a terrible mistake, but not wanting to read it wrong. I was already feeling weak, but I headed to my college classes in great pain and turmoil of mind and emotions, knowing from long experience that the pain and turmoil would not lift for at least 48 hours. God orders my steps and all His ways concerning me are perfect. I give Him thanks with joy for all things.

On Thursday morning, as I awoke, the Lord spoke a verse into my heart: **Blessed are you when they revile and persecute you, and say all kinds of evil against you falsely for My sake. Rejoice and be exceedingly glad, for great is your reward in heaven...** (Matthew 5:10-11).

I realized that what I had thought was my own pain was really the Lord Jesus Christ, sharing His suffering with me for my glory. It was then that full peace finally returned to me.

However, from the time I read that email until now, the desire to speak against the issues raised in the email has not left my mind, issues that I have watched destroy so many dear people whom I love, along with the desire to shine the light upon the darkness until God's people can see most clearly the pitfalls that press so closely to the path of

Christ. It is my hope that some, at least, will escape those pits of darkness because of what I write.

But I did not think I could actually write until the next Sunday morning for two reasons. One, the subject matter is too dark and too filled with human suffering to walk lightly into. And two, it is a delicate and difficult thing to separate between a brother and a string of emails which he has written. I do not judge the brother; I do not possess the wisdom to do so. He belongs to Jesus and is in very capable hands. However, I do judge the email and the things said in it. And I judge those things with all the ferocity that is in me.

My anger is right and just. Yet anger must always be carried inside of love.

～

Now, when I included the email in my book, *The Kingdom Rising*, I stated that I will never read it again. I have kept that commitment, even though I have edited and then read the chapter many times since. However, as I prepared to write this chapter of my life, I thought that maybe I should read it for the purposes of sharing my life story more clearly. After pondering my reaction, and thus remembering the things it said, I chose against that idea. And so I include it now, sticking it in at the last minute so that I don't have to skip over it more than is necessary.

You see, I must have you understand the violence and the ferocity inside of me to this day against this wicked, wicked definition of the Lord Jesus. It was four weeks and four letters after I received the email and read it twice that this anger and violence continued in me. In fact, in the fourth letter, sent out on October 18, I included these words.

From "The Mystery of the Holy." ~~~ "I am nowhere near finished with this topic. It burns as a fire inside of me hotter and hotter. I will speak for those who cannot speak for themselves; I will build a shield around the defenseless to protect them from the torture of well-meaning Christians." ~~~

I do try to be nice when I write – what I really meant was "from the torture of the arrogant 'Christ.'"

Here, then, is the email I received that changed everything for me. I will not read it again, for my anger is God's anger carrying the hurt He knows against all who accuse Him of being evil, who place their own perversity upon the Father.

～

I decided to write this only because your desire for the fullness of Christ seems to great. I hope it really is. Your insistence to put a name Asperger's above the name above all names.

Some like the name cancer or autisms or one of many they parade around today and wear them like badges of courage to define who they are and how they over come in spite of their given name. Christ

Well I like the name of Christ and know that in Him I have been made new and in Him there is no Asperger's or cancer or poverty or any other thing of the fallen man. And our life has been made new in Him and by resisting all that would tell us otherwise. I love you brother and believe you are on the right path but for some reason continue to believe that something beside Christ is your real life and who you are. Don't need to respond I can hear it now an excuse for why you are the way you are instead of the truth that you have been made whole in Christ and that is the truth end of sentence.

～

This "Christ" as expressed in this email, was the so-called "Christ" that I had known in my carnal mental darkness for years, standing high above me in his arrogance, demanding of me something I could never produce, a "Christ" who was no savior at all. Of course, it was this same false 'Christ" that drove me into knowing only Jesus my Savior when I left the move fellowship.

The dark anointing upon the words of this email placed the power of that false image as I had known it for years back upon me. But the assault against me that I heard was "Shame on you, Daniel, for being autistic. Get out of your autistic self and get up into pretending like you have never pretended before, and then call your pretending, 'Christ.'" Even now the hatred in me against this wicked definition of "Christ" burns just as fiercely as ever.

In my agony during the next couple of days, I reached for the only solace I have ever known, and that is the words of my Bible, God speaking the gospel of His salvation to me. I opened to one place, 2 Corinthians 12, and I studied what Paul actually said until it was written upon my heart. – **And He said to me, "My grace is sufficient for you, for My power is brought to full perfection and completion inside of your weakness." Most gladly,** therefore, I will boast inside of my weaknesses, so that the power of Christ may rest, dwell, spread as a tent over, and abide upon me.

Then, I wrote "Christ Versus Superman I" by that weekend, and I wrote it in anger for by that time, God had resolved much of the hurt. Then I wrote a long email to Dennis Rhodes in Australia, who was one that could appreciate my frustration. Often, I can express myself more personally when I am writing to a specific person. Much of my email to Dennis then became a large part of "Christ Versus Superman II," which I sent out early Sunday morning, on October 2, 2011, just before we went to the Sunday morning service at Lakewood Church.

Seeing God as He Is

I must somehow convey to you the meaning of what happened to me next. To do that, I must bring in two threads, one concerning my thinking, and the other, a central part of my experiences with God through the seven years we attended Lakewood Church.

Over the prior few months I had been pondering the walk of the Atonement, and had begun to consider the meaning of a Man on His face in the mud under a cross He could not carry. I had been wondering how it is that in seeing this Man, we were seeing the Father. And I had been placing before my eyes the fact that Jesus alone shows us what God is like. At the same time, I had been teaching that you and I were inside of Jesus as He carried us through death and into life. Nonetheless, I had not put all these things together; they were just the beginning of thoughts.

Then, inside the anointing that was upon the Lakewood Church services and the liberty I felt in the Spirit to hear God speaking to me as He would, Sunday after Sunday, I experienced many times over the years moments of the heavens opening to me and the Father showing me things of Himself inside the context, both of what I was writing at the time or of what was being said in the service, particularly by Joel, and often out from both words together.

This opening of the heavens and the voice of my Father coming into me may not have been quite as strong as it was for the seven years I experienced the same thing listening to Brother Sam Fife minister the word, whether in person or on tape, but it

was with much greater understanding, because in my early twenties, I could hardly believe God was speaking to me. At this point, having embraced the speaking of Christ, I knew that God was telling me the truth.

More than once, this seeing, this entrance of the knowing of God into me, was so profound that I could not keep myself from expressing outwardly in tears in the praise service. – And that is not something I readily did as an Asperger's man.

Now, I do not remember which of the many things coming out from the heavens onto the pages of my letters that came during these times of great anointing. – Except here – October 2, 2011.

As I had rejected the above-you "Christ" over the prior couple of weeks, and held firmly to the Christ who shares all my weakness with me and who carries me inside Himself all the way through, so I was pondering that morning, inside an open heavens, the real meaning of what I was seeing.

And in that moment, I saw God, my Father, through this stumbling Man, God carrying me inside Himself through His incapable Son, all the way through a way neither Jesus nor me could ever go. In that moment, I saw that the weak human Jesus alone shows us God, and that this God is NOT above me, but beneath of me.

God was beneath my feet – carrying me!

I have never accused God of arrogance from that moment until now. And, of truth, the more I speak of a God who is meek and lowly of Heart and who thinks more highly of others than of Himself, the more all the words of the Bible sing together for joy inside my heart.

I remember that walk to our car right after the service, through the green lawns and by the fountains of water, basking in the wonder and goodness of a God who carries me. And I have been on a mission from then until now to change your definition of God to a God who knows no evil or hurt, to a God who **covers all for all, hopes all for all, believes all for all, carries all for all.**

The next morning I began writing "God Is Beneath Your Feet," the letter that changed the whole course of my writing and the anointing upon it from then until now.

On page 454 is, again, the diagram that I shared in Chapter 40, "The Time of the Jesus Secret."

On August 6, 2006, I began to speak what God says I am in my finished state, just like the Lord Jesus. This was such a lift-off into a knowledge of God and of Jesus inside of me that I had longed for all my life, but had never known. On February 21, 2009, the Lord Jesus showed me that He had entered into union with me and that I existed only inside of Him. I have not seen myself as separate from Jesus since.

And on October 2, 2011, my Father showed me that He walked beneath of me, carrying me and Jesus together all the way through. My Father showed me that Jesus alone is His image, that He has no other image through which I am to know Him, that the walk of the Atonement is not something God "did"; it is the only visible expression given to creation of God as He IS. I have never known my God in any other way or lived anywhere else since.

A Facebook Fellowship

My relationship with Chris Welch seemed to have grown through this time. I often included things he wrote in my letters as well as out from the correspondence between him and me. As I had shared, Chris had persuaded me to enter the Facebook world and to join with him in sharing union with Christ with many.

Then, Chris was facing a particular need and he gathered together a number of people inside of a Facebook private chat room in order to share that need and that we would pray with him. He included me in that sharing, along with some others who were reading my letters as well as others whom I had not yet known. When he created the private chat room, he was thinking only of a short-term thing, except, once the sharing began, it just continued. In fact, the sharing and fellowship among a couple dozen people continued for about three years.

I often shared things in the FB fellowship, as did many others. It was an experience of strength and blessing to me. Yet, at the same time, there were no "rules" inside the sharing, and often people would post, not just a link to another article, but the entire article itself. Sometimes these other articles contradicted our wondrous union with Christ, bringing back in the old story of human performance, a story that always fails.

At the same time, I had introduced Chris to my understanding of the world, and to knowing about the wicked men who control things behind the scenes. He had pursued his own study of the topic and was putting many things he had found in that study on his main Facebook page without explanation or discernment.

Both of these things bothered me, but I did not have to spend time with all of that, and so I put it all into "Christ living as them," and continued with my enjoyment of that fellowship.

Continuing in School and Writing

The spring semester of 2012 would be my last at the Montgomery branch of Lonestar College. The reason is that I did not fully understand that, as an adjunct instructor, I was not in any way "employed." That meant that I did not have a spot in any upcoming semester unless I secured that spot well in advance. The dean did not just pencil anyone into another session.

In February, I took the adjunct certification course at the Montgomery college, several sessions over several weeks. It was very similar to things I had learned in graduate school at Lubbock Christian University. I had hoped that this would raise my standing in the college. But then, the entirety of Lonestar (several other branches besides Montgomery) decided to merge the developmental reading and developmental writing into one course. To be prepared for that new course, I would need to take some further training being offered.

Because of some circumstance I don't remember, I missed that further training time. But it was only later that I discovered that because I had missed it, I was no longer eligible for teaching again in the fall semester. I had taught my course five times, at this point, and it had become quite effective. I remember one girl, Cynthia, who said to me in class, near the end of the semester (and I paraphrase), "Mr. Yordy, I always hated writing in high school. I never understood it and no one taught me. But now that I have taken your course, I know how to write and I actually enjoy writing."

Through this school year, I was also developing *The Writing Conservatory* website hoping to obtain an income from it. I obtained written permission from all sets of students over these two semesters to use bits and pieces from their writing on my website and in the course. I even used a couple of complete Personal Narratives as examples. In fact, you can see a comment written by Cynthia as well as others at www.thewritingconservatory.com – Action Writing through Personal Narrative.

In the next chapter, I hope to explain just a bit what my writing course had become.

This spring semester, I took Johanna and Matthew through writing a short story, something I had done at Family Christian, only now I knew better what I was doing. Both of them were excellent writers, but Jo is one of the best writers I have ever read. For some reason, I have never been able to convince her of that; maybe when she is older and her children are grown, she will pick up the pen again.

Meanwhile, from my first letter written to bring down that awful image of an above-you "Christ," "Christ versus Superman I," my *Christ Our Life* letter writing became much more focused on a complete series that would be the size of a book. My topic was the kingdom of God, but my purpose was to know God as He had shown me that wondrous day in October. You see, it takes time for things to come clear and for all the necessary verses to find their place.

Through these months, then, I progressed through the chapters of what would become *The Kingdom Rising*. I remember my chapter "Repent of Augustine" causing quite a stir on the general Facebook feed, since Chris Welch posted all of it on his site as well as on Facebook.

It was in writing the three letters, however, "Defining God Defining Man," "The Weakness of God," and "The Foolishness of God," that I worked my way into understanding the strong distinction between two images of God, either Jesus or the serpent, as well as what God means when He says, "great." This included a description of God that has formed all subsequent writing. Here is that description as it finally became by the time I had completed "The Kingdom Rising" series.

~~~ God always reveals Himself through weakness, swallowing up into Himself all that we are including our sin and rebellion, becoming us in our present state, limiting Himself by our weakness. Thus, carrying us inside Himself, stumbling and falling along the way, He arises out of death into life, ascending on high, and we inside of Him. ~~~

There was an additional turning point in my writing that happened as I came to know God only in this way, a verse that stuck its nose, so to speak, under my tent, a verse I did not understand at all, but that has wanted to put itself onto my pages as I write, unbidden by me, from then until now. That verse was 1 John 3:16 – **and we also ought to lay down our lives for the brethren.** I allowed this verse to push itself onto my pages without having a clue as to what it meant until it took me into Jesus upon the cross in Psalm 22, in June of 2019. But that's a later story.

Rhoda Marie Yordy

On May 4, 2012, my mother, Rhoda Marie Yordy, passed away into the next season of her life with Jesus. She spent her last few months in a care home in Hibbing, Minnesota, a good place. Let me share just a bit of her last years.

After we had visited Meadowlands in the summer of 2005, the community closed. Glenn and Kim had purchased the forty acres across the road and there Glenn built a house. At the same time, Mark and Cindy Alesch had arranged to purchase the main part of the property from the move fellowship. Mark and Glenn continued to work together in the construction business.

Glenn had built a space for mom in their new house, and when it was completed, they all moved over. That was mom's home, then, for a few years. In fact, earlier, Johanna had come down from Upsala to spend time with her grandma and aunt and uncle. Through 2012, then, Glenn and Kim knew they could no longer meet mom's needs and so put her into Guardian Angels Health and Rehabilitation Center in Hibbing for her last several months.

We had been planning a trip up to Upsala for Johanna's graduation, and thus we came up to Meadowlands, probably at the end of May, 2012. I will describe that whole trip in the next section. All of our siblings were not able to come to Minnesota at that time, and so we planned for a family memorial service for the next summer, when all could gather in Oregon and we could put mom's remains in the cemetery plot next to Dad's on the green slope just south of Lacomb.

The care home was having its own memorial service for mom and for a couple of others who had also just passed. Maureen and I with our children, and Glenn and Kim with their children all attended this service at the care home. This home was beautiful and mom had been well taken care of. Members of the staff shared with us how great a blessing mom had been to them, that, even though she did not speak, her smile always filled them with life and joy.

Mom did not have the outward gifting of some of the sisters I had known who moved in a mighty faith and anointing; I am thinking of Sister Charity and Sister Ethelwyn. Nonetheless, I now see that her faith in God inside her sphere was as great as any. Mom never looked elsewhere, for her hope was always utterly in the Lord Jesus Christ. And she always imparted that same faith to each one of us, in spite of her inability of expression.

Over the years, mom had labored over a quilt for each of her children and grandchildren. Mine was the first, and Jenelle's son, Sean, was the last, twenty-six quilts in all, I believe. Each of our children keep their grandma's quilt as a prized possession. I have no doubt that mom's faith in God in tears was also poured out for each in the making of their quilt.

Johanna's Graduation

Johanna's high school graduation from Upsala Christian School was set for June 9, 2012. We had only the red Toyota Corolla for the trip, a great car to drive, but a bit small for five people and all our luggage. I drove most of the way, with Kyle in the passenger seat. Maureen endured the center of the back seat in order to be between Katrina and James and thus keep the peace. We hoped to visit with as many Yordy and Handrich relatives as we could on the way up and on the way back, thus we planned a fairly long trip.

Our first stop would be with Arlene Litwiller Sutter, my Aunt Ada's (dad's older sister) oldest daughter, in west central Iowa.

As we were driving north through Missouri, past Kansas City, I heard the voice of my Father, unbidden by me and unrelated to any other thought, quiet, but unmistakable, "Son, because you have honored My word, I will honor you."

I have often thought of these words, for there has been no outward fulfillment of them, that is, not as yet. Nonetheless, before the end of this narrative, I hope to show you that God has done what He says in my life, not in an outward manner, per se, but with greater value to me than I could ever have hoped.

What I thought was my stumbling through endless unrelated experiences, I now see as God's incredible preparation in my life. The next two chapters of this narrative will contain a series of related and very specific difficulties. I now realize that God spoke this word to me beforehand, the right word at the right time.

We had a wonderful visit with Arlene. Afterwards, we drove straight west to the northern suburbs of Chicago to spend the night with Deborah Coleman, the younger daughter of my Uncle Orvin (Dad's oldest brother). Deborah is married to an African American man. I had remembered her as a girl, just a bit older than me, in one of our visits to Michigan when I was a boy. She shared that she had always wondered about me and the direction my life had taken. She has been reading my *Christ Our Life* letters since.

From north Chicago, we drove up to Neenah, Wisconsin, arriving there late morning. We met with Rita Robinson, a sister who has read my letters and books from the start and has communicated with me much over the years. We gathered in the home of her cousin, Marie, and Marie's husband, Richard Williams, along with a couple of others who wanted to hear what I had to share. We all sat on their couch and I shared a word of Christ our life, the first time I was able to share with eager hearers. After the time of sharing, we ate at a restaurant, with good fellowship together. Then Rita took us to visit her home where we met her husband, Wayne.

This was an unusual thing for them, that a "ministry" would take the time to share Christ with them. As we were leaving the Williams' home, Marie insisted on giving us an envelope which turned out to contain a generous amount of money. Maureen and I were overwhelmed with the goodness of God. The truth is, we did not really have enough to cover the cost of the trip; now we did. Thank you, Richard and Marie, for your great generosity.

We drove on that afternoon to Meadowlands, north of Duluth. We stayed there a couple of days, visiting with Glenn and Kim and their children, and Mark and Cindy Alesch. While we were there, all the Yordy's gathered in the downstairs of the Tabernacle one evening, and I read aloud to them Johanna's short story. The truth is, it was just inside the "horror" category of story. Because I read with expression, the story had full impact on all listening.

We finally arrived at Upsala a couple of days before the graduation. This was my first visit to this community, although Maureen had spent several days here the summer before. We were given Johanna's room. She had lived with Ray and Paula Brumbach through the second year she had been at school. Paula was one of Jo's teachers in the school. We had a most wonderful time in their home. They received us in all the joy of the Lord, and we spent hours in good fellowship.

The Upsala community was divided into three small communities, the West Farm, the South Farm, and the North Farm, just a few miles apart. You can see their locations on the map. Each community had its own mealtimes together, but all three gathered for services and for school. The South Farm was the largest of the three; this was where Johanna was living; whereas the school was up the road a mile or so, as part of the North Farm.

Above is a layout of the South Farm, which I use as a model in my book, *Symmorphy V: Life*. The land slopes down from the gardens to Lang Lake, and thus the lake is in the view of any north-facing windows.

We gathered with the family in the Tabernacle of the South Farm for mealtimes. This was a wonderful family of people, much closer in their expression to what I had envisioned community should be. We visited with John and Gerry Kiezebrink. Their daughter, Kittie, had stayed with Dan and Joann Kurtz at Graham River years before, at the same time I was there. We visited with Dot Richie. She had also been at Graham River, though her husband, Bill, had since passed on. Steve and Cindy Schneider, Matthew's parents, were living at West Farm; we had a meal with the family there.

Ted and Eloise Beebe lived at the South Farm as well. Ted Beebe is a highly skilled musician, piano player, and composer. He had taught Johanna on the piano, taking her to a higher level of classical piano playing than she had known before. Barbara Bell, the wife of my good friend, Peter, was Ted and Eloise's daughter. Their oldest son, Paul, lived there with his wife, Gaye. Paul made his living manufacturing fine wood-working knives, chisels, and gouges, which he sold through Lee Valley Tools. His little shop was right there on the way to the Tabernacle. Then, their second son, Eric lived with his wife, Barbara, at the West Farm. Barbara was the principal of the school, and Johanna's main teacher.

I love community, and I loved being back in its expression at Upsala. The elders there had chosen against some of the poorer practices of the move and had even taken a firm stand against some things Brother Buddy taught. It was a wonderful place for our daughter; she is very much a wilderness girl.

The graduation was held in the Upsala town community hall, a public building. The move communities often rented it for larger services. It was a very comfortable accommodation, not far from the West Farm. There were five students graduating, including Johanna and Matthew. Jo and Matt had become good friends during their two years of classes together, but as yet, Johanna, at least, had no thought of a romantic inclination. Because I had been one of the Upsala school teachers, as well as the dad of one of the graduates, I was given a speaking part in the graduation ceremony. I also was able to pray a prayer over them in the anointing of union with Christ.

Johanna was not ready to return home, however. She wanted to spend at least another year at Upsala, being part of the family and working in the larger community to earn some money. So the rest of us continued on our visits with family on the way back. We drove into northern Michigan and spent the night with my cousin, Carl Yordy, Uncle John's youngest son. On our way down to Ashley, Michigan the next day, we made two stops. First we drove over to Fairview and spent a couple of hours with Rosemary, the daughter of mom's sister, Donna. Rosemary was the only one from the Handrich side of the family we were able to visit with on this trip. Afterwards, we stopped at the Fairview Cemetery and found the gravestones of my two brothers, David and Thomas. Then we drove over and found Yordy Road. This really impressed Kyle and we took a picture of him standing in front of the sign.

We had supper with Arlyn DeBoer, the older daughter of Uncle Orvin, and sister to Deborah Coleman. Afterwards we drove on down to the Yordy farm, now owned by my cousin, Wallace, Uncle John's middle son. We spent a couple of days with Wallace and Jean. They were not living at the original farm, but in another house down the road. The next day was a mini-Yordy reunion because of our visit. A couple of Uncle Charles's children were there, though I never knew them well. Also, John David, Uncle John's oldest son, drove up with his family. John David Yordy was a professor at Goshen Mennonite College in Indiana for many years and then became the president of the college.

Our last stop on the way back home was in Bloomington, Illinois, with Mary Salter and Phyliss Litwiller, two more of Aunt Ada's daughters. We spent the night with them and had such a wonderful visit.

These visits to all the Yordy/Handrich relatives really impressed Kyle, especially. All of my family are warm, generous people, always quick to laugh. But many of them have had one thing or another to do with education. Kyle came back home with the realization that, "I come of a family of teachers."

After we returned, Kyle enrolled in San Jacinto Community College for the summer term, hoping to finish his audio engineering associates degree.

From Kingdom to Covenant

All through this trip, I had continued writing the final chapters of what would become *The Kingdom Rising*. In fact, it was during my early morning hours in the home of Ray and Paula at Upsala, that I wrote, inside a beautiful anointing, one of the most important chapters of my career, "Filled with God." I would use from this chapter again and again whenever I return to this topic in future writing. Indeed, it was after writing "Filled with God," that my focus of faith began to switch from "Christ is all there is in me," to "Father, You fill me with all that You are."

After our return home, I set myself to turn *The Kingdom Rising* into a printed book, my second. At this point, technology had advanced in the book publishing business. A couple of years earlier, I had sent a PDF copy of *The Jesus Secret* to a print company in Boston, Massachusetts. They charged $75 to put the PDF into what is called a "book expresso machine," that is, a large photocopier that prints and binds a single copy of a book when it is ordered. This way, I paid only for one copy at a time, whenever someone ordered *The Jesus Secret*. At the same time, this print shop mailed the copy directly to the buyer.

At this point in time, however, Amazon had begun their own similar print business with a subsidiary called Create Space. Amazon has since switched all that was Create Space to Kindle Direct Publishing, which is basically the same thing. With Amazon, however, you simply upload the PDF yourself, right into their computers, at no cost. Then, you order a proof copy or two from them and upload again until the print copy is exactly what you want. In all, to publish a book through the Amazon website costs me only the proof copy cost, from five to fifteen dollars total. Then, a printed copy is made only in response to someone ordering it.

On August 14, 2012, *The Kingdom Rising* was published and available to all on Amazon.

Meanwhile, after writing about the Kingdom, the outward expression of God in the earth, my heart interest turned to the Covenant, the inward binding agreement between God and us.

More than that, I had been pondering for some time the meaning of the walk of the Atonement. My idea, then, was to combine three things, the New Covenant, the Walk of the Atonement, and the furniture of Moses' Tabernacle, particularly the Altar of Incense.

Now, through these years, I was very connected to communication with others, particularly Chris Welch and Bonnie Morris. Bonnie did not join the Facebook fellowship group, but she responded with blessing to almost every letter I sent out.

Now, understand, I am very impacted by "what people say." And so being in an environment of regular communication with others regarding the word God was giving me to write was both a blessing and a distress. The distress came when there was contradiction of the word of Christ our life, not direct contradiction against me, but rather a general expression of the old way of thinking attempting to insert itself into the present word of union with Christ. And by "old way of thinking," I mean expressions of disconnection from God, of the obligations of performance, and of harsh words spoken against people who love Jesus, but who are not "with us." The worst for me, however, were statements coming out from the accusation against God that He knows evil.

As an Asperger's man, however, I never feel any obligation to come under the manipulation of bullies. When someone sends harsh or argumentative words my way, I simply erase the email without responding and never look at an email from that person again. I do not "hide"; rather, I follow Nehemiah's example, that I have a job to do, and I will not be turned away from that task to meaningless and lifeless discussions.

The first letter of "Covenant" I wrote as a challenge, and it did cause a bit of a stir in circles beyond me. Then I set myself to explore and to know the meaning and reality of Jesus' walk, beginning with Gethsemane and ending with the Resurrection and the sprinkling of His Blood upon the Mercy Seat of heaven. Please understand that this was much more than any "interest"; it was a burden and

a cry deep inside of me to KNOW the living God through KNOWING Jesus Sent into me.

What It All Means

As I have written this chapter, I have found myself sealed into a certainty of knowing God's hand upon my life that I have been unable to know before now. I do not exalt myself. The practice of waving the flag of "Oh look at God upon MMMEEEE!" has always repulsed me. I have always believed that those who shared out from "God upon me" were sincere and true, and I always received them as from the Lord. But as an Asperger's man, I could never think that way of myself. Rather, I only ever thought of myself as a desperately vulnerable man, stumbling from one bed of hurt to the next through all the course of my life, longing to know God my Father.

But having finished this chapter, I now can know, with all quiet certainty, that my life has always been God's intention, that I am a vessel set apart for His purposes, and that He has ordered my construction and the circumstances of my life solely for His Determination towards His Church and the revelation of His glory.

And I know that the words Jesus spoke to Ananias concerning Paul are also His words concerning me. – **Go, for he is a chosen vessel of Mine to bear My name... For I will show him how many things he must suffer for My name's sake"** (Acts 9:15-16).

I did not invent myself, neither did I order my steps. And so I rest in peace, knowing that I am not "putting myself forward," something utterly abhorrent to me.

At the same time, I KNOW that my life is nothing more than a pattern for you, for your sake, dear reader, so that you might also place the Lord Jesus upon all the days of your own life, so that you might also KNOW with all quiet certainty that you have always been seized in the grip of the All-Carrying One for His purposes just as much as I might have been, just as much as Paul was.

If it isn't true for the least and for the littlest in God's house, then it cannot be true at all.

46. Sealed in the Storm

September 2012 - December 2013

My college teaching had just been part time, bringing in around $1000 a month towards our living. Now, I was not bringing in anything. Rather, our income came from Maureen's two jobs, weekdays taking care of a couple in their home, and then two nights a week with a lady in The Woodlands. This job allowed her to sleep, some, but she had to be ready to help whenever she was called. This was not easy for her, because it meant that she was not available to Katrina and James through this time period of their lives as much as she wanted to be. And taking care of elderly people includes a number of quite unpleasant tasks.

My inability to provide for my family was very distressing to me. I tried to get an adjunct teaching position at both Houston Community College and the nearby San Jacinto College, but I never heard back from either one. Teaching part-time in a college classroom was something I could do, but full-time work was beyond my physical and emotional strength.

This sounds questionable, but other Asperger's men of the same age also experience the same shutdown physically and emotionally, including the inability to maneuver through all the political stuff that successful employment requires.

Yet if I were not weak, I could never have justified taking the time to write as I have done and through writing, to know the Lord. This is a great contradiction to me, for I would never say, "Well, I can't work because I have to write." Rather, it is that, "Since I cannot hold a full-time job, then I will use my time to write with all my heart as I am able." Yet my writing was not bringing in any provision, and thus I continued in great distress, not knowing the answer to our need.

My Vision

In September of 2012, John Gray, an African American man and a fiery speaker, preached a word at Lakewood Church titled "Lazarus Come Forth." We did not know it, but this was John Gray's intro-

duction to the Lakewood congregation. He would become the assistant pastor to take Marcos Witt's place. The word John Gray preached, however, marked a deep path in my soul. Here is what I wrote in "My Vision I" found in *Gathering to Life*.

～

Last weekend we listened to a brother by the name of John Gray share a word at Lakewood Church. The brother was hilarious, but inside the laughter, he drove home an incredibly important truth concerning the Word of Christ and how He brings forth God's purpose. He pointed out that when Jesus first heard that Lazarus was sick, He spoke a word – "This sickness will not result in death." That word, as the Author of life and reality, went into the tomb where Lazarus would be placed and was there, waiting for him before his dead body was laid there.

Then, Jesus waited until Lazarus had died and was buried four days before arriving at Bethany. When Jesus stood before the opened grave, He stood there as the Finisher. He spoke, "Lazarus, come forth." The word that He had already spoken as the Author responded to this word which He spoke as the Finisher, and Lazarus could not remain in the grave.

Great excitement stirred inside of me as I pondered that word. Then, early the next morning, God brought this word home to me, personal and real. For eighteen years I have carried a word inside of me, a word I have never let go of, holding to it by faith, knowing that God does what He says. But outwardly, by the sight of the eyes, that word has been dead for 14 years. God spoke to me, now, in late September, 2012, "I will finish the word I have planted in your heart."

～

I continued with an overview of the meaning of Blair Valley to me and of the word of community I have carried in my heart since we left there. More than that, I presented in "My Vision II," a calling forth of a return to that property in northern British Columbia. I made that call out of faith in the word of God to me and out of the desire and purpose of my own heart.

The vision that I shared caught the interest of many readers, yet in the end, nothing came of it. Blair Valley remained as far away from us as ever.

Putting Together My Books

I like books, and making books is fun. And so, having in hand *The Kingdom Rising* inspired me with the thought that I had a whole lot of stuff written, all of which could easily become books. I had written several short series of letters as well as others that just stood on their own.

First, I transferred *The Jesus Secret* to Amazon; that was on September 6, 2012. Then, I penciled in the several short series I had done into the outline for four other books. Next, I looked at all the many solitary letters or small groups of letters that were not in a larger series, and just stuck them in here or there where they seemed to go.

I began with my short series on *The Great Story of God*, and added a number of other articles that fit. This book was published on September 27. I merged together my two series on "The Unveiling of Jesus Christ" and "Union with Christ" into one volume and inserted a number of other related articles, with *The Unveiling* published on November 27, 2012. After that, I went back to my earliest articles and wove them into the three series I had spoken into my digital audio recorder just after I had first finished *The Jesus Secret*. These then became my book *Our Path Home*, published on December 4. For this text I wrote some new articles to make it flow better.

My final short series were "The Life of the Age to Come" and "Eating of Christ." Besides those, I had a number of disconnected articles on the topic of Christian Community. I put all these together into what would become *Gathering to Life*. However, that text needed several more chapters, and thus I did not finish it until March 2, 2013.

None of these books were laid out in the order in which they were written, as I have done most of the time since *The Kingdom Rising*. My books do not read smoothly like most Christian books one can buy. My purpose, however, is not to write popular literature, but to know the Lord. More than that, my books remain rough drafts. I cannot afford to take them through the editing process in the way that I did with *The Jesus Secret,* though I would, for editing only improves the clarity with which readers can perceive what I share. Yet rather than redoing any of these books, I write a new book that goes back through the same topic, but inside the present word of Christ.

I sent copies of all these books to Rick Annett, who was still living in Fort St. John at this time and asked him to give copies to different ones of the brethren there, which he did. Chris Welch ordered copies for himself and posted on his website a picture of himself rejoicing as he held my books in his hands. But I have sold very few books. I have given away way more than I have sold.

Because I now write with a full book in mind, I lay out the topic into an outline of chapters and then typically write one book at a time. It is my great hope that, not long after this account of my life is in your hands in printed form, I will have published a total of 24 books, although I have a number of others that could also become books. I am very much in favor of Solomon's "prophecy" – **Of the writing of books, there is no end.**

Anguish over the Word

I do not write just to write. I write to know the Lord through KNOWING what God means by what He says to me in my Bible, and to know it as Jesus written upon my heart. And so I often write in anguish, that God would cause me to know His Word.

At the same time, I do not write out from my head. Rather, I start with a thought that pulls in a Bible verse, and I start writing about what the words of that verse say. As I continue, then, other verses arise from my heart, having been planted deeply there over many years. I do not search out "the next verse"; rather, it comes to me, often unbidden.

For thirty years, I received word into myself through others, much word from many directions. Now, my purpose had become to bring forth from my own heart the agony I felt from God over the Word that was buried deep inside. I have always distressed over dishonesty towards what God actually says in His Word. To me, then, to write is to live, to know God by knowing the reality of His words now written all through me.

I would read "what other Christians say" that contradicts what God says in the Bible, or twists it contrary to the context or puts verses into the wrong places or is contrary to our precious union with Christ or that accuses God of evil in one way or another or is illogical and pointless or is NOT what God is doing in us in the completion of this age or is entirely of the evil one in a rejection of the gospel. Very often, my writing is a response of great distress, in the burning of my heart against that which opposes Christ, yet is so readily and thoughtlessly spoken by Christians.

Through August, I had written on "The Altar of Incense" and "Gethsemane" in *The Covenant*, two chapters that marked themselves deeply inside of me. But then, around the first part of September, Chris Welch posted some things that just contradicted Christ living as us, a truth he had seemed to support. These things included speaking against other ministries of Christ who "had it wrong," not to clarify the truth, but to demean them. In fact, in the summer of 2011, I had written my letter "Strange Fire," in response to someone writing on Chris's feed words of accusation against another coming out of *"Hey, my accusation is Christ as me!"*

So I emailed Chris asking him why he would say such things in light of our belief in union with Christ. I received no response, which I interpreted as his forbearance towards my foolishness in thinking that I should correct him. Nonetheless, I was thrown into great distress. Was I hearing from God or was all my writing just a bunch of nonsense?

In that agony I wrote the first half of "God of the Cup" having no intention of sending it out. Yet, after a couple of weeks of not writing, I looked back at what I had written and realized that if I wrote a conclusion, it could be a valid expression of this great contention of "Truth, truth, who's got the truth!!!" This letter, "God of the Cup," is one of the most important I have ever written and is, if you will receive it, the same Mighty God contending with you.

Here is just a portion of what I wrote. ~ God is not under my control. I do not have Him figured out. I cannot define Him; I cannot explain Him. All I can possibly ever do is bow my head upon the ground in silence before Him. To one He says, "Speak," to another He says, "Shut up." To one He says "Go here and go there," to another He says, "Sit down, you aren't going anywhere." And He WILL do the very opposite of what you want, and He will ask you to bow in silence before His right to order His creation as He sees fit. ...God does what He wills with His own and He asks no man's pleasure. ~

I sent that letter out in late September, and then I was able to continue writing the next chapter of my outline for *The Covenant*.

Sometime during these months I received an email from Kathy Macdonald of southern Ontario. Kathy had been introduced to my writing by another reader and was deeply moved by my letter, "The Altar of Incense" in *The Covenant*. Kathy had been in deeper truth circles for many years and was anointed by God to understand. Her emails to me were long and were filled with some of the deepest encouragement I have ever received. She did not "puff me up," but rather confirmed in ways I could receive that God was indeed speaking to His church through me. I was very slow to accept this thought, but Kathy continued to encourage me in this way over the next few years.

In December of 2012, my outline of *The Covenant* presented me with two chapters, "A Heart Throne," and "The Mercy Seat." A question concerning a "new age" writer had come up in communication with a reader. As part of that conversation, I looked briefly at a second "new age" writer as well. In this man's writing, he talked about drawing people into "love" inside your heart. He was not drawing them into God inside his heart, making it only twisted. Nonetheless, because I have God inside my heart, I knew that such a practice could be true.

The first thing I did was to draw my Asperger's into my heart to give thanks for all of it. That was a first and a mighty revolution in my life. But I also then presented this practice as something we do towards others, for their sake. I felt concerned, for was this a "new age" practice? And so I placed the fear of God upon my explanation of "practicing the Mercy Seat," that this is something we do ONLY for the sake of others and ONLY to set them free from ourselves. Yet it was this December of 2012 that the concept of "practicing the Mercy Seat" first entered my life.

Meanwhile, Chris Welch had added a brother named Rich Novek, and his wife, Linda, to the Facebook fellowship. Chris had been communicating with Rich inside the topic of our union with Christ. Because I was a writer and a teacher of writing, Rich asked me to edit a short book he had written and to help him publish it on Amazon. He offered to pay me a reasonable sum for this work, so I took it on.

I am very good at using Adobe InDesign to create books; it did not take me long to lay it out. Nonetheless, there was also a fair bit of editing to do, both in grammar mistakes and in poor word choice. I worked my way through his book; some of it was good, but some of it contradicted our precious union with Christ. At one point he said something contrary to the clear gospel teaching on the Atonement, and so I altered the wording to make it closer to what God actually says. Rich discovered that change, however, and required me to put it back to how he had it.

By the time I was finished with this short book and we had published it, I realized that editing Christian writing was not for me, for things that people say in typical "Christian" terminology that speak against Christ and against our Salvation bother me way too much to endure. Nonetheless, I was intent on practicing seeing Christ as my brother, and so I continued to do toward Rich and Chris.

Rich and Linda Novek lived in Weatherford, Texas, just a few hours from Houston. In January of 2013, Maureen and I drove up to spend a weekend visiting with them. Another sister named Joan Reilly, who was a reader of my letters and part of the Facebook fellowship, was also visiting with the Noveks. Joan was supporting Rich financially, and had been the one who sent me the payment for working on Rich's book.

We had a wonderful time fellowshipping with the three of them. Rich and Joan both drew much out from me, and I was able to share freely. While we were there, Rich put together a conference video-call on his computer with Chris Welch and Annalize Mouton, similar to the Zoom meetings we now enjoy. It was great seeing them live and hearing them speak.

In our conversations together, Rich and I both shared about our desire to travel around to share the word with small groups. We suggested the possibility of going on a ministry trip together. This was very exciting to me, for I do much better when I am with someone else. After we left their home, when we were sitting at a gas station, Maureen encouraged me with her blessing towards this trip. She knew how much such a thing meant to me.

A Time of Clarification

In February, I switched my email service to Constant Contact, which I have used since. Starting with the announcement of our "Upcoming Trip," sent on February 4, 2013, I now have an accurate record of when I wrote each letter.

During the month of February I wrote the first version of my small booklet, "The Ten Most Important Verses of the Bible." I had been pondering the meaning of "ruling definitions," how we hold certain key definitions deep inside, things we hardly ever think about, and that all our thoughts go in the directions those definitions require. I wanted to make the key verses of the gospel to be my own ruling definitions, and I wanted to round their number out to ten, rather than my previous eight. I completed "The Ten Most Important" in the first part of March.

Many of the things that were being posted inside our "union with Christ" fellowship on Facebook continued to really bother me, however. Then Annalize Mouton posted some articles that, to me, contradicted union with Christ by placing the obligation of dishonesty back upon God's people. I don't usually respond immediately to things like that; this time I did. But I wrote harshly, in a way that was deeply offensive to Annalize. In fact, I wrote my first version of the letter, "Union with God FIRST," in that same harsh tone.

I was caught between two, between my "being right" and the heart and friendship of a dear and precious sister in Christ. There was no question that the heart of my sister was far more important. It took me a few weeks, however, of humbling myself and of kind entreaty before I was able to bring my offensive action towards Annalize to a resolution.

I was continuing to publish Bonnie Morris's occasional articles in her part of my website. Many of them were very good, and some I even sent out as my regular letter. Nonetheless I sometimes found that which seemed to me to contradict the joy of Christ Jesus as our all-Salvation. Through all this time, however, she continued responding to what I wrote with wonderful enthusiasm, for God indeed seemed to be speaking to her through my little bit.

Sometime in late 2012 or early 2013, one of Bonnie's private statements to me seemed so contrary, that I was quite bent out of shape by it. In my consternation, I used her quote, without referencing her, but as something I was correcting. I was not yet cleansed from an occasional bit of sarcasm escaping through my fingers.

Soon after, I received a reply from Bonnie in which she stated, coldly and directly, "You had no right to publish my private words to you." She was absolutely correct. Again, I was faced with a choice of what was more important to me, my "pride" or Bonnie Morris's friendship. I wrote an immediate response to her of deep apology. I shared with her that her friendship was more valuable to me than anything. I sent out a correction to all my readers, apologizing for my offensiveness, and I removed those lines from the webpage and even from my audio.

Bonnie willingly forgave me and continued her almost weekly encouragement, something I needed very much.

Rich Novek and I were planning a ministry trip together that would be a series of stops in Florida and Georgia. We wove together visits with people of his connection with people of my connection, about an equal number. My sister, Frieda and Tim, were living in the Tampa Bay area at this time, near their children, April and Ryan and their families. I hoped to spend time with them while we were in the area.

Then, unexpectedly, Rich's vehicle, which we were planning to use for the trip, needed extensive work. He emailed me, stating that, because of the difficulties, we would have to reduce the length of our trip. He included a reduced list of stops. All of his connections were on this list and none of mine. I responded in the cheerfulness of Christ, suggesting an alternative plan which would include some of my stops. Something else happened and again there was a need to reduce the length of the trip and again, his new plan removed all of my stops.

When I saw that, I knew I was dealing with a man who had no thought for others. I realized that I would be under the control of a man who would expect me to fit into his arena without any consideration of the word or ministry coming through me. I do not subject myself to such things. I sent Rich a kind email, taking the fault upon myself, that I would be unable to make the trip at this time.

After I announced to my readers that I would no longer be making this trip, I received emails from both Annalize and Kathy sharing that they had not witnessed to my involvement with Rich Novek, but

had been waiting on the Lord that He would make that clear to me, which He did.

Sealed in the Midst of the Storm

From February of 2013 on, my letters became the series that I would title *Through Eyes of Fire*, which was my first study of the book of Revelation inside the present word I was sharing. While writing this series large changes of understanding came to me. God used this study to affect a significant change in my life and in my knowledge of Him.

Not long after I had disconnected from Rich Novek, my next outline topic was Revelation 7, the sealing of the saints, an article which I wrote through the week of May 19th. I completed that article, titled "Sealed in the Midst of the Storm" and read it into audio on Saturday, May 25, before sending it to my readers the next Sunday morning. In that letter I had written the following prayer out from the words "**I will write on him the name of My God**" in Revelation 3.

⁓

"Father, You say in Your word that I am transformed by the renewing of my mind. You say that You write Your name, the very New Name of Christ upon my forehead; You speak of my being sealed in my forehead before the storm hits. Father, You are speaking of the gospel of Christ; You are speaking of the Cup that turned to Joy in Jesus' heart. Father, Your word is Your will for me. I ask according to Your will.

"Father, I ask You to write Your name, 'God,' upon my forehead as the visible evidence that I am filled with all the fulness of God, according to the gospel. Father, I ask You to write Jesus' new name upon my forehead in all that You mean by Your metaphor, as the proof that Christ is indeed my only life. Father, I ask that You write the words, 'New Jerusalem,' upon my mind, as the sign of Your Spirit flowing out from me as rivers of living water.

"Father, I ask You to seal my mind utterly in You, that I am no longer susceptible to any thought, any vibration, any energy that is not flowing out of You through me. Father, I ask that, from here on through, I will see all things through seven eyes of Fire, through the lens of Your Spirit, that I will walk knowing as You know and seeing as You see.

"And Father, having asked according to Your will, I keep the Word Jesus spoke. I believe that You have given me, that I have received in all fullness all that I have asked."

"Thank you, Father, that Your name is there, in neon lights, upon my forehead. I will never again be conscious of any other name. Thank you, Father, that Jesus' new name, the name of the victorious, ascended Christ, covers my forehead, my face, my whole body. Thank you, Father, that my mind and forehead are utterly sealed into you, that I have the mind of Christ. Thank you, Father, that I am Your Jerusalem, the city of David, and that Life is always flowing out from me.

"Thank you, Father, that I see all things through eyes of Fire, through Your eyes. Thank you, Father, that my judgment is true, for I am never alone, but I see always through You, who always fills me full.

∽

As I spoke this prayer out loud into the audio, my life forever changed. Prior to this moment, I had been assailed upon occasion by times of great discouragement and frustration with God and with my inabilities. At times I went a couple of weeks without writing anything, just wallowing in discouragement. During these times I had allowed myself to believe that I was "cut off from God." Every time, however, the Lord would arise in me and restore my heart to joy.

On May 25, 2013, this all came to an end. From then until now I have never known a moment when I chose to believe that God was "far away from me." From then until now I have not known a week when I did not want to write out from Jesus singing in my heart. I am a man who has wallowed in self-pity for decades. There is no question that God fulfilled His word in my life, sealing me into Himself, as I spoke this prayer out loud. God does what He says He will do.

Our Final Time at Lakewood

After this experience inside of God at the end of May, I realized that two changes had taken place inside of me specific to general Christianity as it is known. The first realization was that the word was no longer satisfying my deep cry to know the Lord. It was still a good word preached by Joel Osteen, but my season under that word was coming to a completion.

The second realization was not so much towards what Joel was preaching, but rather towards Nicene Christian speaking in general, the speaking of words contrary to the good-speaking of Christ, words of unbelief. This included things that others said in the services rather than from Joel's messages of encouragement. I began to groan inside over the agony of the true words of our union with Christ not being declared.

This agony has only increased. I simply cannot bear to hear words preached contrary to Christ, the agony is too great. If you would scan through my chapter "Sealed in the Midst of the Storm," you will see that this quality is very much a part of that letter. I wrote these words just prior to the prayer. – "Do we weep over the limitation of Christ? I have wept over the limitation of Christ for many years and now more than ever." ~

By mid-July, I knew that our time at Lakewood was complete. Lakewood had been our home church for seven years, the place where our children grew into their teenage years. They had always attended the main services with us rather than going to the children's or the youth services. Maureen and I wanted them to be in the word and Spirit of the Lord, and, of truth, they preferred to be there as well.

For seven years, Joel had taught me to stop speaking curse against myself in the story of my mind. At the completion of those seven years, God sealed me into a mind that will know only Him. That doesn't mean I am no longer human; it means that I always place my human foolishness into God, that He shares all that I am together with me. I never separate myself from my Father in any moment's thought.

But there was an additional reason why our time at Lakewood came to an end that July. You see, Joel preached one line in many different ways, and that was to put our hope and expectation in God, in the certain knowing that God's favor surrounds our way in all things.

Sunday after Sunday, for seven years, I would leave the service in great hope, believing with all my heart that now was my time, that God was about to fulfill my desire by taking us as a family into a Christ Community in a rural setting as I now knew community should be. Yet nothing ever came of that expectation. When nothing came from writing "My Vision" concerning a return to Blair Valley, I became quite discouraged.

I could no longer endure that yo-yo, between encouragement and discouragement every week. What I did not understand at the time was that I was turning my expectation of God into one direction only, into the fulfillment of the Community of my heart. I was not applying it to my family's everyday life. It would not be until the summer of 2021, eight years later, before God would change all of that, but that is for a later chapter.

Nonetheless, I love Joel and Victoria Osteen and their ministry to God's people. From then until now, whenever I drive by Lakewood Church on the freeway, I bless them with all my heart out from the Spirit of the Lord.

Mom's Memorial

My sister, Cheryl, planned for us to gather at her house in Oregon on July 27th, a Saturday, to have a memorial service for Mom and to place her remains in the plot next to Dad's in the Lacomb cemetery. We did not have the money for us all to go, and so I flew by myself from Houston to Portland, Oregon, a few days before the memorial.

The last time I had been in Oregon was in November of 1997, almost sixteen years earlier. Oregon had held a powerful emotional place in my heart, and I was not sure how I would react in revisiting it. I arrived at the Portland airport around noon. It would be a few hours before Frieda and Tim's flight would arrive and Sarah, Cheryl's daughter, would pick us all up at the airport.

To fill the time, I took the bus into downtown Portland to visit again Powell's book store, a place I had loved to visit in earlier years. I looked for a locker to store my stuff, but there was none. I asked a guard and he said, "No, we have not had airport lockers since 9/11." My thought was to say, "I guess the terrorists won, then," but I did not. There was a fierce desire in his eyes that would have loved to take me down. So I climbed on the bus with all my stuff. I enjoyed my visit at the book store and ate at a nearby restaurant before returning to the airport. I had never really liked Portland, however, and in comparison to Houston, it went down a few more notches in my estimation.

Back at the airport, Frieda and Tim soon flew in, and we rode together with Sarah down to Albany. We dropped Frieda and Tim off at the motel where they were staying and went on to Jefferson, Oregon, where Cheryl and Dave have lived their whole married life. They have a small but comfortable home on a large town lot with lots of fruit trees and vines. Jenelle had already arrived with her two children, Grace and Sean. I shared a bedroom with Sean, who was around 10, a nephew I had hardly known.

I had thought that I would borrow Cheryl's car to visit my old haunts on Roaring River and Crabtree Creek, but once I was at her home, I realized that I no longer felt any emotional bond to those places and I chose not to stir such a thing up again. I spent the next few days visiting with Cheryl, Dave, and Jenelle, and with Tim and Frieda. We had not seen each other for years, yet we are family, and very comfortable together. We had some good and long conversations.

Glenn and Kim had chosen not to come to the memorial. Glenn simply did not want to face our brother Franz. In fact, we did not know if Franz would come to the memorial or not.

We had a wonderful memorial service at the Lacomb cemetery. Franz did not come, but all of his children were there with their families and all of those I have already mentioned. We gathered in a circle around mom's grave for a time of sharing. Tim Louden, especially, had some really good things to say. I shared some good things as well, and prayed. Some expressed to me afterwards how much my prayers meant to them.

After the service, we all went for dinner to Franz and Audrey's, the home place where I had grown up. Franz came out and joined us for the meal, which was set up on the patio and yard. Audrey suggested that we not go into the house in order not to put undue pressure on him. After dinner, Franz and Audrey took us on a tour to see all the changes they had made in the gardens and between the house and the road, which were extensive.

The biggest thing was that Franz had built a large shop next to the road for his bee-box-making business. By this time, however, he was no longer able to work the business. They had put in many garden beds and fruit trees throughout to be ready for times of difficulty. During our tour, Tim connected with Franz and walked with him, visiting, and keeping his mind off of the animosity he felt towards the rest of us.

And so I must share with you here concerning my brother Franz. I can do so out from the goodness of Jesus carrying all.

During the years after he returned to Oregon, Franz had connected, as I have shared, with those working in deliverance ministry towards Satanic abuse victims. During that time he had learned of many dark things taking place, yet Franz had no sufficient counterbalance in the truth of Christ.

The result was that Franz began to write terrible emails to different family members, though he never wrote one to me. I do not know what all was said in these emails except that he denounced the person to whom he was writing as well as all of us, including me. As I shared, it was Frieda who helped me to place Franz into the realization that he was injured and ill.

Franz had become very dark. His children were not able to continue working for him. His business had ground into nothing. They were on the verge of losing the property to foreclosure.

Franz had come out onto the patio deck when I arrived. I greeted him warmly. He was not outwardly hostile, but there was a sad grin on his face as he said something curt against myself and against Joel Osteen. I did not respond, but Audrey apologized to me later.

I remained at Cheryl and Dave's for a few days more. We pondered much about our brother, Franz. Audrey had been connecting with Bill Johnson's ministry in Redding, California, and asserted strongly that she expected that God would restore Franz to a sound mind.

After I returned home to Houston, then, in a continued communication with Audrey, Frieda, Cheryl, and Jenelle, Audrey asked for our response to their letting go of the home property. I responded for all of us. I wrote to Audrey that, while it was sad to us that we would lose the property, we supported her absolutely in whatever decision she felt was right.

Soon after, the bank foreclosed and Franz and Audrey had to move out with all their accumulated stuff. Audrey moved in with their son Jason and his family in Newberg, Oregon, but Franz was not willing. He stayed in the Lacomb/Lebanon area living out of his vehicle.

As I had considered this account of my brother, I had thought that I would place before God, here in this chapter, my determination to contend with God in the resurrection for Franz's sake first, that I would be the one to break through the gates of

his hades and draw him out into the kindness of Jesus. That was not something I was able to do while Franz was still alive, but I was ready to commit myself as soon as I was able.

Franz passed on a couple of years later. I did not go to his funeral because we simply had no money for me to do so, and I do not know the details of his sadness. Nonetheless, my relationship towards my brother changed dramatically in January of 2021, but that is for a later chapter.

I will conclude this part by placing the Lord Jesus upon my limited relationships with my brothers and sisters. Although I would spend a number of times over the next few years in Glenn and Kim's home in Minnesota, this was the last time I saw and visited with my other siblings face to face.

Frieda had been on my mailing list and had read my letters for a while, but in November of 2016, she unsubscribed. Every "unsubscribe" is emotionally difficult for me, and thus I pause and bless that person in the Lord. Frieda's "unsubscribe" was the most difficult of all. I know nothing of her reasons and will not speculate.

After this visit to Oregon, Cheryl read my letters for a while, but ceased doing so after a couple of years. To my amazement, Jenelle has continued to open all of my letters to this day. I know that she sees the world in a very different manner than I do. It is my hope, however, that she receives some goodness through what I share.

After the memorial service, I thanked Tim for what he had shared and for taking Franz under his care during our visit. I had observed that there was something in Tim against me, not necessarily an animosity, but definitely a reserve. I know that he had been offended with me during the time that he and Frieda were separated, yet they had come back together again, just as I had hoped. I have always held Tim in high regard and looked up to him since I was a boy.

I think, though, without knowing for certain, that there is also a blame towards me for leading them as a family into move community, and then bailing out myself soon after. As I have shared, this blame is certainly understandable and even justified.

Yet I know that the day will come when they will give thanks in turning their experiences in move community into utter goodness, together with the Father, and when that time comes, the abundant goodness flowing out from their time in move community will bring blessings to many. I know that Jesus carries each one of us every step of the way and that He does all things well.

By the authority of the Lord Jesus which He shares with me, I speak overflowing goodness into the lives of each one of my siblings, not only that they would know the Lord, but that through their giving of thanks, multitudes of people will be abundantly blessed.

Back to School

This summer, Maureen's time of taking care of her present clients came to an end. At the same time, a friend had asked her to care for her mother, Melba Turner, in Kingwood, Texas. This new job meant more pay and would last for several years. Miss Melba, however, could be difficult at times for Maureen.

At the same time, Katrina became an intern for the summer at Jesse Jones Park, the place we had often visited. James wanted to be an intern as well, but he was too young.

In August of 2013, we prepared for a very different school year for several of us. First, Johanna was returning home from Canada. She rode down with her stuff in the vehicles going from Upsala to the Missouri summer camp. I rented a small SUV and drove up to the Missouri community with James to get her and her stuff. We enjoyed driving through the mountains of Arkansas on the way there and back. We stopped at some really cool folksy stores in the Ozarks.

This was the first time I had been to the small move community in southern Missouri. It was not a comfortable experience for me, and I was very glad to leave the move behind me once again.

So Johanna was back home, except she didn't want to move back into her old room. Instead, she wanted the room with the patio doors. She had money from working at Upsala, and so she paid for new French doors going out onto the patio as well as new flooring and a complete redo of the walls with new paint. She bought some really nice old-fashioned furniture as well.

Johanna wanted to become a hairdresser. The nearby college, where Kyle was attending, had the better cosmetology program, but Johanna had set her heart on attending Kingwood College, about twenty miles away. This would cost more and be further to drive, but I helped Johanna work through all that enrolling in college for the first time takes, including a number of visits to councilors and the registrar.

Johanna would attend Kingwood College for two years, from which she received an associate's degree in cosmetology. It's a beautiful campus, and I had reason to visit there a number of times. At the same time, because Maureen was also now driving to Kingwood, this proved to be an added provision of the Lord.

Through this same time, Kyle had been floundering a bit in his pursuit of an audio engineering certificate. He had completed all the required courses except for one, which was already filled to capacity. So Kyle had no certificate or way forward. I knew that Kyle needed a nudge into a clear direction. Kyle's grandpa, Claude, had been an electrician, and I had observed that Kyle carried some of Claude's good qualities. I pointed him towards the electrical construction program at San Jacinto college. Kyle already had all other courses needed, and so he would be able to complete the electrical certificate in a year.

Kyle latched onto that direction and soon found himself under the teaching of an older gentleman, Mike Elder, who became a great mentor to him. Kyle also arranged study groups that he might help other students to learn what was easy for him. His path was soon set towards his electrical license and towards teaching.

Kyle was still working at a local Taco Bell while attending school. One day in November, a young man near his same age, named Will Fonder, came into the restaurant and struck up a conversation with Kyle. The two connected and became close friends to this day. And so Will became a part of our family. He was from Fredericksburg, Texas and was teaching junior high English at a local school, while finishing his master's degree. Will is the kind of guy that is easy and good to converse with, and so he and I had many long discussions on teaching writing.

This fall, Katrina began her 11th grade year at CE King high school and James began his 8th grade year at CE King middle school. Katrina continued immersing herself into the drama program and choir, and James into the band program. We attended all of their performances. I always appreciated that Kyle also attended the performances of his brother and sisters. Soon Will was joining us at times as well.

Meanwhile, my own career was going in two directions at the same time. First, I applied for teaching as an adjunct instructor of developmental writing with the Cypress-Fairbanks branch of Lonestar college. I was hired to teach two courses of developmental English at the small Fairbanks branch in northwest Houston, about a forty-five minute drive from home. I taught my writing course for two semesters in this building, a time and place I enjoyed very much.

At the same time, I was thinking that teaching college-English full time would be something I could do. I was not qualified, however, unless I obtained fifteen more credit hours in graduate level English, for a total of eighteen. (I already had three from LCU.) I found that the English graduate program at the University of Texas at Tyler was right for me. Most of the courses offered were online, which meant I could work at home.

I applied to the Master's of English program at UT Tyler and was accepted, again on a provisional basis. I justified obtaining student loans so that I could afford this step by the rationale that I would be able to pay them back with a better paying full-time job teaching college.

At the same time, we clearly needed a second vehicle, especially for Johanna to drive to her school in Kingwood. For that reason, we went looking for a Suburban. We found an ideal one for just $6000, a red 2004. Johanna had the money to buy it that August and then I paid her back when I got the student loan. Our Suburban was my favorite vehicle that we have owned; it carried all of us plus one more, with lots of stuff, and it was very comfortable to drive.

I enrolled in three courses for the 2013 Fall Semester, "Bibliography and Research Methods," "Studies in Victorian Literature," and "Teaching Poetry Writing." The poetry course was not online, however, but at the Tyler campus. I wanted that course, so I drove up to Tyler every Thursday afternoon for the evening course and then back home again. It was a 3 ½ hour drive each way. I would get home after 1 AM. To make this all work, I rented an economy car from the local Budget rental each Thursday morning, returning it, then, on Friday morning. I spent the long hours of driving listening to my audios of *Through Eyes of Fire*, which I had put on CD's.

The poetry course was actually an introduction to poetry at the graduate level. The instructor, Theodore McLemore, had no idea why it was listed as "Teaching Poetry Writing." I really enjoyed this course and Mr. McLemore, even though he was semi-hostile to Christian thinking. The two large assignments I did for him are among my favorites. The first was a compendium of poems that I selected, weaving explanations through them out from all we had been taught. The second was a large research paper, forty pages long. My first choice, a layout of a poetry writing course, was turned down. I then chose to do a paper on the Anglo-Saxon poem, "The Seafarer."

Dr. Karen Sloan taught the other two courses, both online. I gained the most from the Bibliography and Research course, for it gave me what I needed for the next job the Lord had for me. For the last part of this course, we listened to the lectures of a leading U.S. professor of literary criticism. This professor was brilliant, one of the most astute teachers I have ever heard. The most amazing thing about his lectures was that, after listening for several hours, I realized that he had not said one thing that had any meaning.

The Studies in Victorian Literature course was a different matter. It did not take me long to discover that I had inadvertently wandered into a dark Marxist religious cult that by this time had occupied all college English departments in the United States. I had to maneuver through stuff that was quite offensive to me, but I managed to hold my own. When the instructor wanted us to denounce a particular character in a novel, I swung back with the realization that he was Asperger's, like me, and that, as an autistic boy growing up in a world he did not understand, he had no help. This silenced the "three-minute hate" which is part of Marxist ideology and practice. I did manage to get an A in this course.

From Through Eyes of Fire to The Two Gospels

Writing *Through Eyes of Fire* contained many momentous experiences for me as God gave me clarity of understanding in a number of basic issues that would rule all my subsequent understanding of God's reality.

After "Sealed in the Storm," I worked with the issue of how a God of love requires justice of all, that all things stolen in the darkness must be restored. A reader questioned some things I said, and so I doubled down and wrote the chapter "Restitution." Writing this chapter fixed my understanding that has continued until now. Inside this issue was the contention over "Lucifer." Some readers did not like my use of that name. My argument is, who cares what you call him, but he must be named, for we must know that our enemy is an individual and limited person. Yet from this time on, I have used mostly "the serpent" or "the evil one."

Meanwhile, Bonnie was writing things to me that were just contrary to my relationship with God my Father through Jesus. I worked for weeks on an article which I hoped would refute forever all reliance on self for salvation. That article is titled "Hear and Obey."

Then, Chris Welch continued writing things against other believers in Jesus, including Joel Osteen. At the same time, a reader sent me a piece denouncing Billy Graham. I wrote the article "Two Women or One?" as a direct pleading with Chris Welch to understand that if Jesus can save him and me, then Billy Graham or Joel Osteen is no problem to him. Those who denounce "sin" in others, are, in fact, exalting their own self-rightness.

Understanding the story of self in our human consciousness came through these chapters. I had chosen not to write on any topic in John's vision that I did not yet know through Paul's gospel. For that reason, I skipped many things. But suddenly, I saw that the scroll of Revelation 5 and 6 could be one thing only, the letter of Christ written upon our hearts. For the first time, the enigmatic things of John's vision began to come under Paul's gospel in my knowing.

Kathy MacDonald continued to send me long and deeply encouraging emails in response to the things I was writing. I wrote "Time to Hear" in response to one of those emails. Writing "They Sat on Thrones," and "Judgment to Life' were milestones for me, followed by a transformation of my understanding of everything in the chapter "Appearance versus Substance." Much of Scripture is based on

this principle, and yet the church has never understood it.

I completed *Through Eyes of Fire* and had it as a printed book by October 20. Meanwhile, I had already started writing *The Two Gospels*. My purpose in writing *The Two Gospels* was to discover what God actually means by basic gospel terms, beginning with – What is Paul's gospel? I did not yet actually know the answer to that question.

I was writing *The Two Gospels*, then, through October and November, when the darkness of the Marxist cult that ruled the thinking in the UT Tyler English department began to bother me such that the contention entered into my chapters. Whatever I am going through always impacts what I write directly. I wrote this in the chapter titled "God." ~ "Why would I bring Karl Marx into the question, What is God? (That is, why would God have me fuming over Marx while I'm trying to know Him?)" ~

We were using a short story by Mark Twain in the Bibliography and Research course, and thus a long quote from Twain shows up in the chapter "Travail." I am convinced that God placed me into this arena to cause me to hit up against these very issues first hand. The truth of God must fit into the contentions of humans in this world and it must give full answer to ALL.

The fellowship inside the Facebook thread was continuing inside the anointing of God despite of some of the contentions taking place. I now know that Annalize in particular felt an unease towards Rich Novek, but when she tried to share, Rich and his wife came out with strong words against her. I stepped into this contention with gentle words of seeing one another as the Lord Jesus, and Rich apologized. Still, I was skipping much of the flow of conversation because it was much too "noisy" for me. Yet I often inserted some of what I was writing.

Kathy Macdonald had joined this fellowship group, but Bonnie Morris did not. There were a number of other readers of my letters in it, as well as a number who were not readers, people Chris Welch had connected with and brought into the fellowship.

Then, Chris Welch "corrected" a sister inside the fellowship in, apparently, a harsh manner. This was a sister who had known Norman Grubb and who did not accept anti Christ-as-me nonsense. She immediately left the fellowship. I did not read any of this, but rather, I came back in to read some very dark comments being made by Rich Novek, things I had heard in the move being spoken against people who "left," things I absolutely HATED.

In response, I wrote the letter, "Church," in a much stronger tone than how it appears in the final version. The truth is, I was referencing Rich Novek's actions, not Chris Welch's, for I had not read any of his involvement.

I have run out of space in this chapter to include what happened next, and so it must await the next chapter, "Time to Turn Around."

48. Time to Turn Around

December 2013 - May 2015

A Most Difficult Break

Chris Welch interpreted my letter, "Church," as a direct correction of him. This was not entirely true concerning that letter, but it was true concerning "Two Women or One?" Nonetheless, as I look back through "Church," it is easy to see why Chris would assume I was speaking of him. However, in my mind was only my experiences from the past.

If I had to walk through this same thing over again, I would respond in the same way.

Here is the gist of what I wrote. ~ When a corrector begins to "correct" others in a fellowship of believers, those who truly know the Lord are simply amazed. It is so plain that this corrector is talking only of him or herself, yet foisting their own judgment of themselves upon others as if the problem is the others and not the false self. Let me give the absolute law of all church. Whatever you do, say, see, feel, or do to others you ARE doing it to Me." Notice the "doing to." Church is doing things with each other; not-Church is doing things to each other. ~

Then I wrote this ~ I cannot be in the same room as scorn. When I see scorn, not as human foolishness, but as deep-rooted theology, then I can only get as far away as I can as fast as I can. It is not any judgment of others; it's simply God. ~

In speaking of scorn, I was speaking of Rich Novek's words inside the Facebook fellowship, as I shared in the last chapter. The entrance of those words would require my exit from that group.

I received an email from Chris Welch. This was mid-December. There was no personal reference in this email, no asking of questions for understanding, no human sorrow. It was simply scathing accusations based on assumptions I did not recognize. Receiving this kind of response from a man whom I thought believed in union with Christ and with whom I had a relationship of ministry, was, as you can imagine, overwhelming to me.

I replied immediately, attempting to connect with him as a person and assuring him that I had no knowledge of what happened in the group between him and the sister.

Shortly after, I received an email that Chris Welch sent out to a large group of people, some whom I knew and many whom I did not. This was not an email to me; I was just added as a recipient. I did not read the entire email, nor do I remember it well. But it was about me, how I was false and how the ridiculous things I taught were false.

I have rarely experienced something more frightening to me than to be publicly denounced as a false teacher by a brother whom I had thought was a friend.

As I laid down in my bed soon after, I faced a ring of demonic personages, just outside of my sphere, but pressing in close, screaming every curse of condemnation against me. I did not regard them, but I reached up, in my mind's eye as it were, and I took Jesus' face in my hands. I said twice, with all fervency, "Jesus, You ARE my life. Jesus, You are my LIFE!"

In that moment all the darkness vanished and I knew only the closeness of my Savior.

It is not my purpose either to justify myself or to lay any blame upon Chris Welch. In giving an account of my life, I must share only how I perceived things at the time, what I did and why. I know firsthand that his account of this circumstance is very different from mine.

The insertion of vitriol into the Facebook fellowship, completely separate from me, had already persuaded several members to remove themselves. I also removed myself from it, only to find that Chris had put me back in immediately after. I think he did the same with some others. Then, even more left, for the Spirit of the Lord no longer seemed to be inside that connection.

I wrote a much stronger email to Chris, treating him with respect as a person and as a brother.

Nonetheless, I was specific concerning his accusations against Joel Osteen, that they were without purpose and had no part in union with Christ. Before sending this email to Chris, however, I first shared it with Kathy MacDonald and with Annalize Mouton. I very much needed their input and covering. Their responses back to me were wonderful and encouraging. In fact, this whole episode had left them feeling much the same as I.

The email I received back from Chris in response to this final entreaty was again void of any personal communication. Rather, the words in it were the full expression of what I would call religious bullying. In essence, it seemed that Chris's "anointing" was the lead, and I would find a place in God only by submitting to his "superior" ministry. He said, concerning his words against Joel Osteen, "I call it like I see it." You will find me referencing that line on occasion from then until now.

I then wrote him a final email. In it I asked him to remove all reference to me from the front of his website, though I left him free to keep my articles that were scattered throughout his blog. I also stated that I would not open any further emails, so there was no point in sending them.

Chris sent two or three more emails to me, packing harsh words into the subject line. I simply deleted them. I do not give bullying any place in my life. In order to prevent him from inserting himself into my Facebook pages, I unfriended him on Facebook.

It is my intention to share here all my further interaction with Chris Welch rather than bring it back into future chapters.

Cutting off religious bullying as I did is not typically an easy thing for most people. And so Annalize Mouton received several long emails from Chris Welch. She shared some of them with me, wanting my response. Through all this, I also kept Kathy MacDonald in the loop, for I needed both their anointings.

I would describe the emails that Annalize received as filled only with religious manipulation, an exaltation of "my (Chris Welch's) anointing" and how important it is to everyone. I did the best I could to strengthen and encourage Annalize and advised her to cut off any communication with Chris. Again, that's not easy for most. Finally, a few months later, I received another email from Annalize, sharing with me another email sent to her from

Chris Welch. At that particular time, I was feeling overwhelmed, and so I did not open it.

Some years later, I was going back through things and I found that unopened email from Annalize. I opened it and read this further email that Chris Welch had sent her, longer than the others and much, much worse.

This is another one of those places where I greatly sorrow over my searing inability, that I was not able to be the strength and help to Annalize when she needed it. Please forgive me, my dear sister.

Then, sometime in 2019, I think, I received an email from Chris. This was over five years later, and at this point, my knowing of Father with me was much greater, and so I thought, "Why not," and opened the email. It was just a short paragraph. Chris began by calling me stupid. I believed that what he meant was that I was stupid for cutting off those who would seek to control me or the word I must share. Then he went on to threaten me, something along the lines that I would be punished by people. He concluded by speaking what seemed to me to be a curse against me. At this point in time, I was not deeply affected by these things, just the normal sorrow of the Lord.

Finally, just a few months ago, as I was preparing to write this part of my account, I ventured back onto Chris Welch's blog. I had not looked earlier to see if he had removed me from the front of his site as I had asked, but I saw that he had. My curiosity always gets the better of me, however, and so I clicked on the link that would take me to my articles posted on his site. They were all still there.

Then I noticed something awful in the list and clicked on it. There I found the emails I had sent to Chris in personal and private confidence, including those for which I had asked Kathy and Annalize for their witness. Arrayed against them were Chris's emails to me, which I had not opened. The introduction to this set of emails was an invitation to the reader to judge between him and me.

I was aghast; I certainly did not continue reading. If I had known in December of 2013 that my private emails to Chris were made public soon after, it would have been more than I could have borne. The Lord protected me by my not knowing. Nonetheless, I could see that the threat Chris made in his last short email to me was not to be disregarded. I am well aware that my sharing of this circumstance could lead to further recriminations. This is part of why I stalled for four months in writing this account. Yet I know that no weapon formed against me can prosper and that I am utterly safe inside my Father sharing all things with me.

Lord Jesus

"Lord Jesus, the sorrow You bear for Your Church is very great, no matter how confident You are in being the Salvation of God. It is such a privilege, Lord Jesus, that You want to share that same sorrow with me, that I might know You in all things."

Since Chris Welch wounded me inside the present word that I share, I find it harder to place him into the love of Jesus inside my heart. Yet I want to be part of Jesus so much that I am willing to do such a thing, no matter what I feel.

Rich Novek, on the other hand, was one with whom I had very little connection, not enough to be troubled by personally. Soon after, the man did go on to commit ungodly acts against those closest to him, but that is not part of my story.

"Lord Jesus, I place Chris Welch and Rich Novek entirely into You. You are such a capable Savior and You know what You are doing. I never knew Rich Novek, but I thought I knew Chris. Lord Jesus, I forgive both, and I release both from any obligation to me. Lord Jesus, You carry me always, including all my distress and limitation. I know that You keep me, even now."

"Lord Jesus, I forgive Chris Welch and I bless him inside of You with all out-poured goodness. I ask that he would know You, Lord Jesus, and run with all joy into Your humility."

A Second Semester at UT Tyler

I signed up for two more courses at UT Tyler for the Spring semester. Two courses at the graduate level is still considered "full-time," plus that was all I needed for my purpose of gaining fifteen more credits in five additional English courses. I had been rubbed raw, not only by the offensiveness of Marxism, but by its underlying threat of violence, which was about to get much worse.

I took "Composition Practicum" and "Studies in Composition." Both courses were focused on how to teach the first and second-year college composition courses, that is, how to teach writing. The problem was that the Composition Practicum was not online, but at Tyler only, and thus I rented a car and drove up once a week through this second semester as well.

Dr. Hui Wu, the dean of the graduate English department, taught the online "Studies in Composition." This course was primarily reading various educators in the field of writing and their take on teaching writing. The practicum course was on the actual teaching of college composition.

It was the practicum that became terrifying to me. It was taught by a younger lady, a full Marxist-feminist. It came clear right away that all my views on teaching writing would be challenged and struck down. By the third session, I felt that I was in danger of being called out as the enemy, as a white male Christian capitalist, all of which was true. You must understand that this is very frightening to me. I simply could not return. I wrote an email to the college department that handles student concerns, but there was no response. An older white man cannot be in the "victim class." I could not drop the course because then I would have to give back the entire student loan. And so I drove up to the fourth session, casting myself upon the Lord the whole way up, but still quite afraid.

When I arrived in the classroom, Dr. Hui Wu entered as the replacement teacher. Apparently the previous teacher had to resign because of illness. I would never wish such a thing upon anyone, but I knew that God had intervened on my behalf. Dr. Hui Wu was one of the best teachers I have ever been privileged to sit under. Although all my classmates continued to push Marxist ideology, Dr. Wu did not. And so I was able, not only to finish the courses I needed, but to learn a whole lot that is useful.

My Writing Course

The spring semester of 2014 would be my last semester of teaching developmental writing in the community college. After this semester, they wanted me to teach in a branch much further from home, and just one course, not two. It simply wasn't practical.

I did make some attempt to find a full-time position teaching college English. The problem was that I now knew the extent to which Marxism rules the English departments in most universities, and I was still in shell shock one might say. The Lord opened no doors in that direction.

At the end of this final time I taught my writing course, a young lady in her early thirties came up to me and said what I had heard so many times. "Mr. Yordy, I always hated writing because I did not understand it. You have taught me to write, and now it's my favorite thing."

Developing my writing course was the work of many years and of equal weight as building the Graham River Tabernacle. For that reason, I want to share briefly how it had become.

Through the semester, I had my students write two major papers. The first was a personal narrative and the second a simple informative essay. For both of these papers, I required three drafts. I made the first draft EASY, and then taught them how to make it more effective, one piece at a time.

Student writing is incredibly boring, primarily because of the lack of action verbs. My main purpose for the narrative was to give them something to write that they already knew well and then to teach them what I called, "Action Writing."

Writing the second draft was the most work. I used a clever device that worked every single time. After they had all turned in their second draft, I came back the next time and "threw" it back at them, rejecting it utterly. They had not done what I required! This device was actually in my lesson plan, but disguised. Always they came back with far better second drafts.

I used rubrics for every draft, a clear explanation of what I would grade in each draft and how many points it would receive. They knew exactly what I wanted. And then, when I marked their papers, it was clear to them exactly what they were lacking, things they must, then, fix.

I always held my breath as I waited for the third draft, hoping that my teaching methods were effective. I was never disappointed. The students themselves were amazed at how well they had written their narratives. In fact, I told them that if I forgot I was reading a student paper because I was lost in their story, I would not mark anything, but just put a 100% on the top of their paper. That happened several times over the semesters I taught my course.

My principle of teaching was to teach them inside what they were writing and then to have them keep redoing it until their paper was effective. They always knew, then, exactly what they had done to make it effective. Everyone who did all that I asked got an A – AND left my classroom knowing how to write effective essays for their other classes.

I loved teaching this writing course at the college level and was very sad when that season came to an end that May of 2014.

Beginning The Feast of Tabernacles

As I continued the remaining chapters of *The Two Gospels* following the devastating experience that came out of writing Chapter 10 "Church," I wrote in great sorrow, especially the letter, "Face," which actually came right after the worst part of the interchange with Chris Welch. That letter begins thus ~ You are free of me. You most certainly do not need me or anything that I write in order for Jesus to continue living you all the way into life. You belong to Him; He lives as you; He always leads you in triumph; and He most definitely does all things well. ~

I wrote this whole chapter as my rebuttal of the practice of controlling and manipulating God's people for one's own self-exaltation. I might suggest that you read "Face," in light of where it fits in my story. I count it one of the most important letters I have written. ~~~ "What happens when you correct the corrector?" ~~~

By March 7, I had finished the last chapter of *The Two Gospels*. Writing the second to the last chapter, Chapter 20 "The Two Gospels," was an overwhelming experience for me, however. Yet as I realize now, it was so necessary for what is coming next.

Here is what I wrote, and I bring this in because this is a critical moment in my determination to write my way into knowing the Father at Home in m heart.

⌒

Okay, I have finally pulled this booklet titled "The Two Gospels" written by this Yordy fellow in 1996, but not completed and printed until early 1998. I am speechless. I had no idea. – There is almost no difference between that little booklet and the gist of what I write now. Same verses, same truths, same view of most everything. All except one thing. One thing that brought me to the loss of everything.

I have not looked back at this booklet since I left move community in late summer 1998 numb and frozen inside. Please bear with me, this is very difficult. I can share now only out from a "stream-of-consciousness" sharing of my present very real search to understand how a man could speak the same things from the same verses with a view to the same end and one speaking be darkness and death and hopeless loss and the other be light and life and unending joy.

I cannot convey to you the highest importance and greatest value of one thing alone in all the truths I have ever heard or shared. This one thing, that Jesus, my Lord and my God, drank His Father's cup, drank me, all of me, into Himself and then allowed the Father to send Him back to walk this earth again, planted now as me in all I find myself to be. Oh, oh, oh – how utterly I can cast myself into Him.

In 1996 it was all about me making it somehow into a God so far away. In 2014 it's all about Jesus carrying me all the way to the full knowledge of the Father. To know that my own gross inability to fulfill any requirements, even of the gospel, cannot remove me from Salvation nor prevent me from walking right now in full union with God.

Again, I am feeling pulverized right now, this is not easy. There is almost nothing in this booklet to refute. Yet it brought me into utter despair.

↜

As I considered the meaning of this chapter, "Time to Turn Around," I realized God's purpose for my life and for the way He made me.

As an Asperger's man, I have known a lot of internal pain, but few things give me more pain than to listen to someone lying about God and His Word. From that moment on, I am incapable of rest until I have found God's answer to that lie, from His Word and by His Spirit. Conversely, if it is a lie that I have held in my mind, and I hear the truth spoken contrary to that lie, again, I am incapable of rest until I know what God actually says all through His Word and what He means by His Spirit.

Satan lied about God, right from the start, by accusing God of knowing evil. All Christians agree with the devil to the extent of all translators falsifying the wording of Genesis 3:22 to lie to all Bible readers that even God agreed with the devil in supporting that horrific accusation.

Sometime through these months, Kathy Macdonald sent me an email asking this question. – Why did Jesus have to die? My answer to her then was incomplete, a fact that really bothered me.

My answer now is very simple and clear. – Jesus died because that was the only way He could convince me that He was serious about winning my heart. More than that, for me to walk out from my imagined prison, I have to have a vivid picture of all the falseness GONE, taken far away from me by Someone who loves me so. In short – Jesus died for me.

Notice that inside this present answer there is no shadow of that hideous accusation that God knows evil. The removal of that shadow did not come quickly.

Consider the table at the bottom of this page..

The box on the left is all Nicene Christianity, utterly opposed to the box on the right. Christians read what I write and they recognize how Biblical it is, but they do not recognize the God of whom I am speaking, a God who does not know evil.

Jesus told us clearly that after the first generation of the Church, Satan would enter with his own words planted into Christian thinking, and that both words would grow up side by side looking the same. That is the definition of every teaching I have ever heard in all the realms of Nicene Christianity. People see mighty things in their New Testaments and they draw near to God. Yet they keep their knowledge of the truth entirely inside the box of a God who knows evil.

Then, when the question came, "Should we pull out the tares." Jesus said, "No." – "No, lest you pull

A God Who Knows Evil (and good)	A God Who Thinks No Evil
All the Bible verses and all the gospel truths read and understood inside this accusation. All theology and all patterns of truth directed by and containing the shadow of this accusation.	All the Bible verses and all the gospel truths read and understood inside this Love. All definitions and all patterns of truth directed by this Love with no sense of shadow.

up the wheat with the tares." You see, that's what always happens anytime someone discovers that God is actually telling us the truth. They grab what they perceive to be tares, yet half of what they grab is wheat and out it all goes.

Because of the way God made me, I am just as much in agony when I discover the root of a tare as I am when I see a root of the wheat also being pulled out. I am incapable of rest until I know the full separation between the fine root hairs of the wheat from the fine root hairs of the tares. And I MUST know the difference out from what God says in the Bible and by His Spirit.

I MUST know every Bible verse and every gospel truth removed from the box on the left and known only inside the box on the right, full and intact as God means it.

Please understand, this is no mental endeavor or self-appointed crusade. This is DESPERATION inside of all agony. I cannot live without knowing Father at Home in my heart. And this desperation also includes the driving need to know what all those lies really are and from whence they come. I can find no rest until I KNOW, all through my knowing of God, a vast wall of separation between the lies and everything my Father speaks in His Word. I have to have a Bible that does not present to me a God who knows evil. I have to have a Bible in which every Word is God telling me the truth, in which every verse fits the wondrous knowledge of Christ my only life.

And I have no peace until I do.

In February of 1998, inside my great hopelessness, I imagined that I was missing the key point of the gospel. When I looked back to that moment for the first time, in March of 2014, I was shocked to discover that I was missing nothing. Instead, it was one tiny little lie sitting there inside basically the same truth I teach now, turning it all into despair.

That little lie was that all this so great Salvation was up to me, that I am the one who has to connect with God. When I KNEW, in February of 1998, that I was incapable of doing such a thing, I was honest towards God for the first time in my life. I thought I was in darkness; I did not know that God had just turned on the light.

My next writing project was my favorite of all my earlier books, *The Feast of Tabernacles*. Yet this was a

Sam Fife/move of God topic, requiring, for the first time in my present writing, a return to the use of the Old Testament.

It was God's time for me to remove the Old Testament and its patterns from the box of "*a God who knows evil*" and to know it all inside of a God who does not.

I was completely astonished as I looked closely at all the Old Testament verses I was using to teach the feasts and journey of Israel. Not once did I ever have to twist or bend any Old Testament reference to make it "fit," a practice common to most. Rather, I found that the exact phrasing of Moses' words fitted perfectly with our present understanding of our precious union with Christ and of the revelation of Christ through us His Church.

Sometime in March, I received an email from a new reader in Cape Town, South Africa, by the name of Karen Leigh. Karen had grown up inside the Jewish environment, but had drawn towards the Lord all the way through. Nonetheless, she was versed in the Jewish understanding of the Old Testament. Over the years, she has corrected me when I pull out of "what I know" when, in fact, my "remembrance" was incorrect. Because of her desire to know the Lord inside her questions, I was able to clarify this practice of using the Old Testament to know the Lord Jesus Christ our life.

Then, in the first week of April, I wrote "Seeing the Invisible One," one of the defining moments in my walk with God. You see, at this point, I had already pondered what would be the main point of this whole study, not the actual Feast of Tabernacles itself, but rather, The Day of Atonement, one of the most important chapters I have ever written. I knew already what the critical moment would be in the pattern of the Feasts of the Lord, and that would be that moment when Aaron would turn around inside the Holy of Holies.

I want to include here the main part of "Seeing the Invisible One," for it is critical to this time in my account. In fact, it comes out from what I had discovered when I found the one thing that was wrong in all my former thinking, the little lie that defeated me.

⸏

You and I cannot and will NEVER connect with God. The very idea is rooted in practical atheism, the denial that God is God. God, this God who already fills us full, connects with us. God is God. He alone can be God. You and I cannot make Him visible; He alone makes us His image. God conforms Himself to us. God knows how to do that; we don't.

What is our part? Faith. How is faith expressed? Three things: 1. Speaking Christ our only life. 2. Asking all that God speaks and believing that God is, right now, revealing Himself through us. That He IS!! As in IS!!!!

Did we get that – IS!!!!!! As in "I AM." Thus, 3. Giving thanks for all things, that all things ARE God through us. **All things are of God** (2 Corinthians 5). – **God works all in all** (1 Corinthians 12). All things are God through us.

Every individual trying to connect with God lives in denial of the Lord Jesus Christ and His redemption. The Blood – never consider sin again. The Cross – never consider sinner again. The Resurrection – consider all that you are, spirit, soul, and body, as Christ alone, Christ your only life. Then, turn around, turn around, turn around, turn around, turn around, turn around, turn around.

You cannot sit down upon the throne of heaven without turning around. You cannot be the Mercy Seat in the earth, God revealed, without turning around. God, in all things you presently experience, is now going out through you. Give Him thanks. – Salvation Revealed. You are already fully connected to God.

⤿

What was it, in my own walk with God, that had begun to press me towards the concept of "turning around?" I now know that it was the entrance of 1 John 3:16, insisting on inserting itself over and over into my writing, that turned my thinking towards God now coming through us.

it was now time for me to turn around, to be in all confidence the entrance of God into my world through my weak humanity and through utter trust in Him. I was now ready to move every tiny aspect of the redemption wrought by the Lord Jesus out from the box of a God who knows evil and into the box of a God who does not. And to do so in answer to Kathy's question – Why did Jesus have to die?

In May, I wrote "The Form of God" and saw the Ekenosis truly for the first time as God now coming into our world through us. Right after that, God established in me the true meaning of redemption.

Jesus did not die "for God"; Jesus died for us, for our sakes.

In July, then, I wrote "The Day of Atonement," working into my own knowing the certainty of turning around. This was then followed by "Thinking Like Jesus," that is, without consciousness of any separation from God, followed by the first entrance of "sharing Heart with God." I was now ready for the next great shift God was about to give me in my knowledge of the Father.

Dr. Claudia Sheets

In June I was no longer teaching college. At the same time, I was still reeling from my escape out of the religious Marxist hate-cult that rules today's colleges. Maureen then came across an interesting advertisement offering a writing business for sale. She convinced me to look into it, which I did.

Maureen and I drove up to Murchison, Texas, not far from Tyler, to visit with the owner of this business, Dr. Claudia Sheets, and her husband. We had a great visit with them in their home. We had no money, of course, and thus buying the business was impractical unless I was working inside of it and the transfer could take place slowly. Dr. Claudia agreed to give me a trial run writing for her.

The business was ghost-writing doctoral dissertations for graduate students in the field of education attending a particular college in Florida. These educators had completed all their course work, but because their gift was not in writing, they were stalled in the completion of their degrees. In any other arena this would be called "cheating." I justified my participation in this business by the realization that these are people who are superb educators, but who may not be skilled at writing. All humans are gifted in some things and not in others, that's why we need one another.

A doctoral dissertation in education has three parts of about equal length, around 30 pages for each part, the proposal, the literature review, and then the actual experiment with its statistical results. Dr. Claudia offered me the opportunity to write the middle part, that is, the literature reviews. Of truth, my course work at UT-Tyler had prepared me well to do this very thing. I enjoyed it, and I was good at it.

At the end of June, I received my first pay check from Dr. Claudia for doing a trial two-pages to her satisfaction. She had agreed to pay me $75 per double-spaced page. Of course, writing the literature review was only the second half of the task. Finding the right research articles in the many educational journal databases and weaving them into my pages was the first half of the task.

My first large literature review in July was "After-School Remedial Reading." This was my first introduction to how to teach reading. This was followed by "Educator Professional Development," and then, "Character Education in Junior High" in August.

Here's the thing. I have counted each one of these literature reviews as equaling a three-credit course at the graduate level. And yes, each was that much work and learning for me, even though I spent about thirty hours in each study. The thing is, I do work about three times as fast as the normal graduate student. But I do so only in short spurts, entirely dependent on how much sleep I get.

Even while I was still teaching at Family Christian, not getting enough sleep had begun to be a problem. Now it was pervasive. I did well to have two mornings a week in which I could write. When I had such a mind, everything was clear to me and the flow just poured through my brain. But when I looked at the same stuff after not-enough sleep, nothing made any sense and I could not see any part of the picture. I could make four to five hundred dollars on a morning I had enough sleep, and zero on all the other mornings. And so, I embarked on a quest to improve my ability to sleep well enough, a quest that went nowhere.

As of this summer of 2021, I do know what has kept me from sleeping, that is, sinus membranes that are out of kilter and hurting, especially when I am lying flat. I now solve that problem by sleeping half of the time sitting up in my chair. In 2014, I had no knowledge of this.

Another School Year
Kyle had completed his electrical training at San Jacinto College in the summer of 2014 and then was accepted into the electrical union after which he was hired by Wayne Electric as an apprentice electrician. At first, Kyle worked on a new sports arena at the University of Houston, but by September, he switched over to working in a new hospital building in the Houston hospital district. This was a long-term job.

In October, Kyle and Will Fonder leased an apartment together about four miles away, and thus Kyle left home a second time. He and Will were in and out of our home quite often, however.

Johanna began her second year at Kingwood College in the cosmetology program. Katrina was now in her final year of high school at C.E. King, continuing in theater and choir. James was in ninth grade and thus had moved over to the high school. James joined the high school marching band, playing his French horn. Maureen continued her long hours of caring for Mrs. Melba Turner in Kingwood.

I wrote three major literature reviews through these fall months. In September, I wrote "Concussion in High School Sports." This was outside of my box, partly in the medical field, and thus a fascinating learning experience. Then in October was "Job Satisfaction," and my first literature review for teaching writing, "Writing Blogs." And I include most of these because learning is very important to who I am.

Tabernacles to Union
I finished *The Feast of Tabernacles* right around the time of Tabernacles, in October. I was astonished at the fact that after writing that entire book, I still had little idea what God means by the fulfillment of Tabernacles in the life of the Church. Only three chapters were devoted to Tabernacles, and those were only a vague outline. This lack was something I pondered deeply.

Around that time, I received a question from a union-with-Christ brother in the Netherlands concerning the issue of "responsibility before God." I wrote a letter in response, and then three more to finish my response. This direction of writing then became my series, *Musings on Union*.

Near the end of October, I had a dream that was profoundly of the Spirit. Let me share what I wrote in "Double or One."

⁓

In my dream, I saw Charity Titus and my mother (both of whom have passed on) sitting across from each other at a little restaurant table. I knew that Charity had purposefully sought out my mother (who had visited at Blueberry and knew Charity) in order to reconcile with her. As I greeted them, Charity stood (there was no more wheel chair) and spoke words of present encouragement into me.

Part of what she said to me was that, even though she had not understood my outer shell, she had always deeply admired me and seen a depth of the grace of God within me.

Then I awoke. In my awakened state, Charity Titus came to me, as I sensed in my spirit, and said to me: "Daniel, I was so wrong in how I perceived you and how I treated you. Will you please forgive me."

I willingly and with all my heart forgave her. And in so doing, I understood that Charity is right now in the heavens, focusing her intercession and the believing of Jesus inside of her upon the victory of Christ through me right now upon this earth, through Daniel Yordy, and that she has joined deliberately with my mother for that very purpose.

You have no idea what it means for me not only to say that, but to know that it is true.

In that one moment, Charity Titus passed entirely out from the pain and confusion, fear and vulnerability, and became part of the strength and joy that fills my heart and propels me forward.

I am so glad. I am so very glad.

That had to happen first, before I could ever consider what happened next. A few days later, in the middle of the night, as I was standing in the strength of my spirit in warfare against the remaining voices from that time, I faced Lloyd Green once again (see Chapter 22, "Glory Against Shame"). I kicked him, Jesus and I, just as hard as we could, with a full kangaroo kick in the chest, right out of my life.

I stood up for myself, and Jesus stood up with me for us.

꩜

You see, all the healing God had taken me through up until this moment was extensive, but it had not touched the pain that came with any memory of my time at Blueberry, memories that came quite frequently. This moment, when Sister Charity came to be my present support and when I removed the awfulness of the experience with Lloyd Green, was now the beginning of healing towards Blueberry, a healing that would not be complete until I finished my account of that time in this text.

Was that actually Sister Charity and my mother? I believe that it was.

I continued to write *Musings on Union* from October through March. Yet it seemed that I was in a "holding pattern," waiting on something, I did not know what. Of truth, nothing stood out in my writing through those months. I understand it now as a deepening and strengthening of those things the Lord had taught me while I was writing *The Feast of Tabernacles*.

It was while I was writing this series that two new brothers began communicating with me. The first was Ed Carter, from Nashville, Tennessee. Ed responded enthusiastically to everything I wrote and asked me good questions, some of which became chapters in *Musings*. Another brother named David Wenger, from Ohio, also began asking me some really good questions through this time. My response towards David's questions always came from the depths of my spirit.

Our Family

The first weekend of December, we all dressed up to attend Dickens on the Strand in Galveston, as was our wont. It was, as usual, a whole lot of fun.

This time, we rented a room at Commodore on the Beach, a curved hotel overlooking the ocean. This way we could enjoy both days of the festivities. I bring this in, however, just for the chance to share one of my favorite family pictures with you.

Then, during Christmas break, Katrina and I drove the Suburban to Abilene, Texas, to visit Abilene Christian University. Katrina was interested in pursuing theater in college and this was a choice of such a program at a "Christian" college. We spent two nights in a motel. The streets were covered in snow. Katrina did her tryout for the drama program and we toured the university. The roads were very icy as we returned back to Houston; I had to drive really slow. Neither one of us felt a witness to pursue the Abilene school any further. I did really enjoy this time with Katrina, however, a bright warmth against a cold direction.

By the end of the semester in December, Maureen and I had come to the conclusion that the public school environment was no longer the right place for James. And so we pulled James out of C.E. King High School to be homeschooled. I did set James up with some work at home, but James is a hands-on young man and never took to academic work, that is, no more than was necessary to endure the school classroom.

We connected James with three things. First, I enrolled him into a homeschool orchestra program. I drove James up to Spring once a week so that he could play his French Horn in the orchestra. Second, we enrolled James in a two-day-a-week homeschool co-op at a church facility in Kingwood. James took a number of interesting courses offered there. James became good friends with a classmate named Will O'Farrell, a friendship that continues to this day. Finally, James devoted one day a week to volunteer work at Jesse Jones Park. In fact, through this time, James became the park's most frequent volunteer. He earned the Presidential Volunteer Award.

As you can see, I was now committed to a lot of driving of James to far distant places, a task that would continue until the summer of 2016.

In January, Dr. Claudia raised my pay to $100 a page, which meant, basically, $100 an hour. This was really nice, to whip out 30 hours of work doing something I enjoyed and receiving a check for $3000. Nonetheless, my struggle with not-enough

sleep only increased. I lit upon the idea that maybe my problem was our mattress. We did need a new one, and so I convinced Maureen that we needed to buy an organic foam mattress for $3500. In my mind, if I could sleep, paying this off would be a cinch. Once we had signed to buy, however, I knew that I had pressed too far. We may have been better served with "natural" foam at less than half that price. Nonetheless, that is our mattress until now and it is comfortable. But it did not improve my ability to sleep. And so writing literature reviews became more of a struggle.

In January, I wrote "Reading Engagement for African American Boys." I really enjoyed that one. Then a second "Writing Blogs," which had to be totally different from the first, for there could be no plagiarism. In fact, I cannot ever use lines from any of these papers elsewhere, for they are owned by the person who paid us. What I learned is mine, however, and if I needed to, I could draw from what I wrote so long as it is entirely re-worded.

After a number of lesser topics and some gaps in time due to my lack of good sleep, I wrote "Teaching Reading and Early Literacy" in May. This was a milestone for me in learning about the teaching of reading, something I value very much.

Waiting on God

I want to convey to you the meaning of this "holding pattern" I had found myself in, especially as I finished *Musings on Union* in February and March of 2015 and turned it into a printed book. I knew that I was waiting on God for something that was not yet clear.

The idea that both the Father and the Son lived in Person inside of me was increasing to me as something I did not know anything about, but wanted to know very much. What does God mean by living inside of us as another Person, His Person inside of our person? I thought maybe this could be the topic of my long-awaited *The Jesus Secret II*, but that idea did not develop.

I continued to write the present word, which I called "The Song of the Lamb," but I did not really have an entire book in my mind. I knew that something else was needed.

Then, in the first week of May I wrote what would become one of the great turning points of my life and of the knowledge of God, the letter, "Sustained."

In that letter I wrote that, if Hebrews 1:3 is true, **sustaining all things by the word of His power**, then it MUST define everything that exists, that is, that Jesus actively and immediately sustains all things by His good speaking, that all things come out of the words that are Jesus every moment.

Let me place the importance of this moment inside of this "Time to Turn Around."

The knowledge that every created thing, both physical and spiritual, is coming out from the good-speaking of Jesus every moment is not found in any Nicene thinking. And it ought not to be found there, for then, by the accusation that God knows evil, we would have had to place the "evil natures" of humans and angels as coming out from Jesus. And so God did not give me the truth of being sustained by the good speaking of Jesus until after I had removed all shadow of evil from my definition of God, and especially, from my definition of our redemption.

When I wrote "Seeing the Invisible One" in April of 2014, I possessed then a beginning view of the meaning of living "turned around." Then, when I wrote "Sustained," in May of 2015, God completed in my own life the entirety of living turned around. From that moment on, I have had no thought of "going into" God. In all things, I know only a fully completed Salvation entering my world through me.

Two other things happened with readers during these early months of 2015. The first is concerning Bonnie Morris. Bonnie had never really connected with the meaning of "Christ as us." Yet by the end of *Musings on Union*, she finally understood what it meant and seemed to be "on board." In fact, I had sent out one of her letters in my *Christ Our Life* email in August of 2014, titled, "So Great a Faith." This was an excellent letter of encouragement in Christ.

At this point, I was still reading Fred Pruitt's writing on occasion. I always marveled at the truth in what Fred shared and how close it was to what I was sharing. Sometime in early 2015, however, Fred wrote something that I did not witness to as being from the Lord. I mentioned that to Bonnie and she said, "Please send it to me to read." I found myself very reluctant to do that, but I did send it to her.

Meanwhile, Bonnie had been writing a little booklet on natural health and she asked me to help her put it into book form through Amazon. I had done that and it was nearly ready to publish. I put quite a few hours working on Bonnie's booklet for no pay. Then, I received a note from her saying that she had changed the whole thing and no longer needed what I had done. But she did want me to go back into the Amazon workspace and make her a new cover page. As an Asperger's man, this kind of thing is very difficult for me to process.

At the same time, Bonnie sent me another letter to post in her portion of the dyordy.com website. When I read through this letter, I was stunned, for there was no speaking of life in it. It was placing obligation upon God's people only. It seemed to me (and I have no knowledge if this is true or not) that Bonnie had reacted to the wrong spirit in Fred's letter by chucking out the whole idea of our union with Christ. Then I looked more closely at a number of Bonnie's letters that were already on my site and was horrified to find that there was no speaking of Christ, but rather much obligation, a yoke no one can bear.

I replied to Bonnie, "Please forgive me, Bonnie, but I find that this present letter does not fit the truth I am sharing on my website. Also, I'm not feeling well; I'm sure you will be successful at creating the cover page yourself. Thank you for having compassion on me."

I am very sad to say that Bonnie's good encouragement of me over several years ended. I received nothing more from her except an occasional letter that she mailed out to many, things I could not read. When I finally closed out my dyordy.com website, her pages vanished as well.

"Lord Jesus, bless Bonnie right now with all our poured out blessing."

And yet, from these experiences with both Chris Welch and Bonnie Morris, I realized that I could not attempt to share ministry with anyone who had not first proven a continued commitment to the word of our precious union with Christ, to the word of the revelation of Christ through us, to the word of a God who knows no evil, and to the humbling of one's self before God and His people.

It was time to turn around.

Then, at some point during this chapter of my life, I received a strange envelope in the mail. This envelope contained a money order written to me for $100. There was no communication with it. The letter was postmarked somewhere in Kansas I had never heard of, and it came every month from then on. In the second or third such check, there was a very brief note stating that the sender expected no reply, not even to say "thank you." The name on the address label was "Bill Horton," but sometimes it was a "Mrs. Horton," and sometimes it had a Nebraska postmark. So I had no idea who this was, man or woman, Nebraskan or Kansan. It was not someone on my mailing list.

Yet the checks continued month after month.

Finally, while I was sitting in the church parking lot in Spring, Texas, waiting while James practiced with the homeschool orchestra, a most wondrous idea came flooding into me, the answer to how I could know this big question that was only continuing to grow inside of me.

What is God doing living inside of me, His Person inside of mine? What is He up to?

And in that moment, a new season of my life began.

48. The Season of Symmorphy I

April 2015 - July 2016

A Grandiose Idea

As I sat in my car on April 23, 2015, waiting while James was practicing his French horn with the homeschool orchestra, I was meditating on the Lord. I wanted to know what it means to have another Person living inside of my person, and I needed a new approach to how I would write about such a thing.

The idea came to me that I could write a college-level textbook, and that the discipline of such an endeavor would give me the form I needed to shape the direction of the words flowing out from my heart. And the topic of that first textbook could be only one thing – God's purpose. – What does God want out from this whole thing?

But I don't think small, and when I get really excited about something new, ideas flow into me like rivers. I had pen and writing pad, and before the hour was over, five different textbooks had taken shape in my mind, with the first four already outlined chapter by chapter.

Basically, I wanted to cover the topics of all I had written before, not as a re-write, but as something brand new. The first text would be another look at *The Ten Most Important Verses of the Bible*, only at a much deeper level of exploration. The second text would be a second look at the meaning of Bible words, with the same focus as *The Two Gospels*. The third text would be *Kingdom* and the fourth *Covenant*. The fifth, which did not take form right away, would be Christian Community, that is, *Gathering to Life*.

Yet all of them would be simply a means of KNOWING this incredible topic, John 14:20 & 23 – You inside of me and I inside of you, that other Persons, Father and Son, are living inside of us, what that means, and what They might be up to in this incredible reality. You see, in my Christian experience, I have never heard anyone raise this question or hardly any mention being made of John 14:20 & 23. It's as if those two verses don't exist.

I was so excited, off like a dog after a rabbit.

Let me defend my choice of format. I greatly value my years of education, particularly at the graduate level, culminating in my then present work of spinning out literature reviews for doctoral dissertations. I value a disciplined mind; I love working with the minutiae of words and their definitions. I require clear thinking.

None of this is "the carnal mind." That is, when the mind is a servant of the heart, and when the heart desires to know one thing, that is, the Father, then a disciplined mind is just a tool in the hands of the Spirit of God, the only teacher. More than that, I don't even come close to the IQ and the discipline of thinking of the writer of Hebrews or even of Paul, yet I write out of the singing of Jesus in my heart, just as they also did.

I rushed home and opened several college textbooks on my desk, going back and forth until the format I wanted became clear. At UT Tyler, I had done a fair bit of on-line college work, and so I also studied what would be the best low-cost online teaching program for me. I chose Moodle; it's free and easily worked.

I was going full speed ahead with all enthusiasm, and so it took me only several days to pull all this together into a place where my new Bible school, Christ Revealed Bible Institute, could begin. In fact, I created the www.christrevealedbible.institute website on April 27, 2015 and soon had Moodle up and running inside of it.

Since a college course has 30 sessions of 1.5 hours each, I had divided my first textbook, "The Purpose of God," into 27 chapters of content, with one chapter for introduction, one for review, and then the final exam. I then apportioned those 27 chapters to the ten most important verses of the Bible. My primary purpose was to take these verses all apart, to look closely at the Greek, and to understand them much more than I had before. I started writing the lessons as soon as I could.

On May 23, I sent out a letter titled, "Yes!! – Another Bible School." It reads the same as what I just wrote thus far. Now, the life-changing word, "Sustained," went out on May 10, so I was too busy working on the first course, "The Purpose of God," and had skipped a week. My thought was that I wanted all of my readers inside the Moodle school, and that I would not post the lessons I was writing on my regular website, which, at this point, was www. christrevealed.info.

I invited my readers to enroll in the Bible school and join with me inside the fellowship.

By the end of May or the first of June, my "grandiose idea" turned into the purpose of God for my life. I had skipped parts of the introduction, knowing that I wanted it to be at a high level of form, something that would come later. I had written about God's heart and purpose and then had taken apart the Greek wording of Romans 8:28-30 in Chapter 3. I was now working on the center of Romans 8:29, the defining verse of the entire Bible.

In that center, being made just like Jesus, I pondered this Greek word Paul had invented, a tidbit of information I had found in my *Little Kittle Theological Dictionary*, the word "*symmorphos*." Always before, the mental rule forced upon this word and its English counterpart, "conformed," was that we were one thing right now, but at some point, far in the future, we would become something entirely different. More than that, God expected us to try our best to become something different now, even while knowing that we cannot, not really. And yes, this is the Nicene meaning for the center of the "gospel."

I was deeply bothered by that definition, though it was the only one I knew. So I thought, "Inventing a word, okay. Paul just stuck two common word parts together in a new way, something English does all the time" (as in "tele" and "vision" or "micro" and "phone"). Then I thought – "Okay, so what English words do the same thing with 'SYM.'" And that, of course, is extraordinarily easy. Here, then, is what I wrote, with understanding flowing into me with overwhelming power.

~~~ "Symphony" does not mean one sound becoming another sound, but many sounds woven together. "Synchrony" does not mean one time becoming another; it means two things sharing the same time. "Sympathy" does not mean one feeling becoming another feeling; it means two people sharing the same feeling. Symmorphos does not mean me, now one thing, becoming some other form, it means two people, Jesus and I, becoming one form. It means utterly braided together. ~~~

Anglicizing Greek words when translating the Bible into English is a common practice; William Tyndale had no English word when he translated Luke's account of Gethsemane, and so he simply turned the Greek word into English, and thus "agony" entered the English language. Baptism, presbyterian, eucharist, are more examples of the same practice.

By the end of the next chapter, "Covenant Core," I simply continued the tradition by turning *symmorphos,* the word at the center and heart of Paul's gospel, the defining word of all the intentions of God All-Carrying, into symmorphy and symmorphosed – formed together with, having the same form, being fashioned together. Not long after, my first text changed in title from "The Purpose of God" to *Symmorphy I: Purpose.*

This was the end of the school year, however, a year of completion for both Katrina and Johanna, and so let me bring that in before we continue with Christ Revealed Bible Institute.

Completion for Katrina & Johanna

The end of May marked the completion of Katrina's high school years, all of which had been spent at C.E. King High School, in the same buildings where I had taught. After four years of returning into this school for Katrina, I had become fully reconciled to it.

Katrina was in the top ten percent of her class, and so, prior to graduation, the school put on a special dinner for that group. Maureen and I attended with Katrina. After the dinner there were various presentations.

Superintendent Vicki Giles was participating in the dinner and celebration. This was the lady who first hired me at C.E. King and in whose home I had spent a couple of weeks. She had been superintendent for eight years, which means she was good at her job. This was her last year with Sheldon as well. After the dinner I spoke briefly with Dr. Giles. For a moment there was a recognition of knowing one another in a shared connection of love for children and for teaching. She spoke well of Katrina. The moment was not to be prolonged, and so I returned to my table. But I have treasured that sense of a shared professional love ever since. I see now that Vicki Giles is an instructor and dean at Houston Baptist College, teaching Curriculum and Instruction. I do envy her, just a bit, though in a good way. I know that my own season inside those realms will return again.

We attended Katrina's graduation in the huge auditorium used by many districts, the same place I had attended the first year I taught at C.E. King.

Through this summer, I had my final literature review for Dr. Claudia, but I was not finding any clear-thinking mornings enabling me to work on it. Weeks went by and it was not finished. Meanwhile, Dr. Claudia had found a buyer for her business, another lady, and was in the process of transferring all the work over to her. To my amazement, she showed extraordinary patience towards me and allowed me to keep trying to complete it.

Johanna had more coursework in her cosmetology program through the summer, but completed it by August and received her associate's degree. Meanwhile she had chosen to return to Upsala, Ontario that August in order to teach in the Upsala Christian School. Johanna is, at heart, a wilderness girl.

James had the opportunity this summer to spend a couple of weeks with Maureen's cousins and Aunt JoEllen Miller in Stephenville, Texas. He managed to go flying off a dirt bike and broke his collar bone, so we had to work through that over the phone. He was well-taken care of.

Christ Revealed Bible Institute

Around twenty people signed up for the first course in Christ Revealed Bible Institute, the text that became Symmorphy I: Purpose. I was still writing it. As I completed each chapter, I would upload all of its parts including assignments. Then, the "learners" would go through it and post their responses in the forums. This way, different ones could read other's responses and share back and forth.

Some of those who signed up did not participate. This was astonishing to me, for my website is my living room. Why would people sign up and then not visit with those gathered together? As an Asperger's man, this was a difficult puzzle to me.

Around a dozen people did participate, and about half of that inside every chapter. This small number, however, made a wonderful fellowship. Ed Carter joined with me as a mainstay in the fellow-shipping. He is fun, talkative, and welcoming. Joan Reilly, whom I had met in our visit to the Novek's, participated fully. Her expression of the things God was teaching her through the lessons I had written was heart-filled and very encouraging. Lida Lindeque, from South Africa, was a regular participant, one who encouraged me very much as well. Andrea, from Austria, was new to this word. Several of the others shared good things with her as we went forward. Susan Ryan from Canada also shared some as well as Annalize Mouton from South Africa.

A couple of brothers whom I had not known signed up and participated for a little while, but they soon vanished. One I had to remove because his posts were not of the Spirit.

Meanwhile, I was no longer sending out what I was writing to my larger email list of nearly 180 people by this time because the lessons of Symmorphy I: Purpose were supposed to be reserved for those inside the Moodle course. I sent out two letters in June and one in July, encouraging people to join us inside the online Bible Institute. I don't remember anyone else joining with us. Finally, by the first of August, I could no longer bear with the many not being able to read the wonderful things the Lord was giving me to write.

I placed all the lessons on my regular website for all to enjoy. On August 2, I sent out the first part of several lessons in Chapters 3-7 in my Christ Our Life letter with links to the website. At this same time, I was converting Christrevealed.info to the present CMS form called OCPortal (now called Composr). By the end of August, I was sending out complete lessons in the regular email post.

At the same time, I was reading the lessons from Symmorphy I: Purpose to my family each Sunday morning, gathered in the living room. Will Fonder joined with us for these sessions and was much blessed by the word I was sharing. He and I continued to have many good and long talks. At a certain point, however, he no longer came. I think that the word had filled his ability to receive. I am confident that it is continuing to work inside his heart.

Through October, however, just past halfway through the course, the participation inside the Moodle learning platform diminished and finally ceased. "One Day in Gethsemane," sent out on October 18, was the last good involvement together inside that small fellowship. I do not have the ability to keep a gathering going, to keep everyone encouraged and involved. I am a good teacher, but someone else must gather the students and keep them in front of me. This lack is very sad to me, but I place it utterly into my Father's hands, for He shares all things with me.

Although the entirety of Christ Revealed Bible Institute is still there, nothing of any consequence has happened inside of it since.

The Next School Year

Johanna flew up to Upsala in August to begin an exciting new chapter of her life as a school teacher. She began her first school year with two students, one in grade 5 and the other in grade 6. She would teach these two grades for the next three years.

Katrina was determined to enter a good drama program in her first year of college and thus cast her eyes on Lamar University in Beaumont, Texas, as it had been her high school drama teacher's school. We made a family trip of it in August, going to inspect the campus. We were given a tour of the campus and of the drama department. It was a lovely place and seemed a good choice to us. We did not know how we could pay for it, but we were hoping.

I had shared with Katrina more than once how I trusted her that her understanding was good and that we would support whatever her decision was. Not long before school was to start, she shared with us her realization that the Lamar campus was beyond our price range and that she had chosen the local San Jacinto Community College, which had a decent theater program at its central campus in Pasadena. She could remain living at home and the Pell Grants would pay for the costs of her college tuition.

I gave Katrina the use of the Suburban, and she began to drive down to Pasadena for her first of two years of college.

James continued in the homeschool orchestra in Spring, the homeschool co-op in Kingwood, and one day a week doing volunteer work at Jesse Jones park. The orchestra teacher also conducted training sessions once a week in Katy for those who lived over there. James and I both wanted him to have more involvement, and so we often drove over to Katy, an hour's drive to the far other side

of the Houston area, a second time a week for that practice session. All of this had to be coordinated with Katrina's use of the Suburban, and so I was quite busy driving my kids around.

We added two things to James's schooling, however. First, Katrina drove the Suburban into the back of a stopped semi that crushed in the front metal all the way around. The insurance company totaled it, but I loved that Suburban and, because the engine and frame were not affected, I took less money and kept the vehicle. I gave the job of rebuilding it to James as part of his schooling. He did an excellent job, and we got to keep the Suburban for a while longer.

Then, I signed James and myself up to a cave-exploring Meetup group and we joined their meetings a couple of times at a rock-wall gym about halfway to Katy. James was too young for them to accept his presence with them on an actual spelunking expedition, and so we stopped going. James did discover a love for rock wall climbing, and so we stopped there a number of times. He continues that sport to this day.

In September, I finally completed my last literature review for Dr. Claudia Sheets. At this point the transfer of her business to the other lady was complete. Part of the reason it took me so long was a blockage I felt towards giving my mind towards secular topics. I confess that writing *Symmorphy I: Purpose* was a distraction. It's very hard for me to do both.

I now had no more income. Maureen continued to provide for us by long hours caring for Mrs. Turner who was not an easy person to assist.

September 29, 2015 was also our twenty-fifth wedding anniversary. Katrina wanted to surprise us and so "conspired" with our other children to prepare a "treasure hunt" for us. First, our hunt took us to a lovely (and expensive) French resturant in The Heights, then to a symphony orchestra presentation, and finally to a gathering of our children at the water wall near the Galleria. It was a really special occasion.

Participate in Ministry

Through this summer and fall two other brothers connected with my website and what I share. One was Bayila Dalaky from northwestern Nigeria. I communicated with Bayila a number of times over the next few years and sent him a number of my books. At the present time, Bayila no longer has good access to the Internet, which is sad, for he is a good friend and I had hoped he could continue to be involved with our present fellowship.

The other brother was Christopher Küttner of Germany. Christopher had been searching the Internet for a soundness of truth. In that search, he had come across some of the ministries of the move. He did an Internet search on some of those names and thus found my website. He decided to critique me on the basis of what I wrote about "the antichrist." What I shared about that topic rang true to him as sound, and so he continued reading and not long after began to communicate with me by email. Christopher connects with the breadth of my understanding of this world with an intellectual mind, but he also has a heart that longs to know the Lord.

Another sister from North Carolina, Rachelle Ross, began to communicate with me by email a bit. She had been searching to know the Lord and had witnessed to an article of mine posted on some other website. Finally, in August, she typed in a Google search on "what is eating of Christ." That search took her straight to my website and my article "Eating of Christ," which is found in *Gathering to Life*. What she found on my website was a real and broad table of that for which her heart was longing.

Meanwhile, Rita Robinson of Wisconsin and Karen Leigh of Cape Town, South Africa, continued regular email communication with me, although they had not joined into the Christ Revealed school. Dennis Rhodes has also been a regular communicator with me.

My inability to maintain a living fellowship inside of Internet long-distance sharing meant that I was now back to just sending out the lessons of *Symmorphy I: Purpose* as my regular *Christ Our Life* letter.

On December 20, I sent out a letter titled "Participate in Ministry." I want to quote a bit from it to give an understanding of how I felt about the word God was giving to me. (I have reduced and thus pieced this rendition together.)

~ Ever so slowly, I have accepted a mantle of "place" from the Father upon my shoulders. I have been able to do that only because of those of you who write to me out from a confirming prophetic

spirit encouraging me to believe that God is, in fact, sharing His word through me. It is you, my readers, who give me "place," and you do so only as you hear Jesus speaking to you from your own heart as you read or listen to what I share.

Last spring, I began to sense that the season of how I had been writing was changing into a new approach to the Word of Christ. I knew that I wanted to write about living together as one person with the Father, but to write in a specific and disciplined manner.

Writing these lessons in the course, "The Purpose of God," and in this format, writing that comes out from my discovery of what this wondrous word, Symmorphy, really means, and how we are connected utterly together as one person with the Father, through every word that is Jesus, has just electrified my life. I may have known life before, but now I know that snapping of electricity and the exploding of glory as I write every lesson. I am simply astonished when I complete each one. I sit here in overwhelming awe and wonder.

For now, God has limited and confined me to one expression only, to sit here in front of my computer screen and to write. And in this limited place, God does one thing for me, He opens up His Word to me, filling me with the joy of Jesus singing in my heart. Yet part of my gift from God is that I become obsessed with what fills my heart, and I pursue that obsession with unflagging zeal.

That brings me to the title of this letter: "Participate in Ministry." It is my conviction, born out of absolute enthusiasm, that I should write these five [Symmorphy] volumes, making them available, not only online, but also as hard copy "textbooks." And, besides writing, to make what I write more known, that many more who long to know Jesus as He really is in them, will be able to find it.

My job is to establish the Spirit WORD that is Jesus Sent, connecting each of us as one person together with the Father, and connecting us together as one body, walking in love, the revelation of Father forever. My job is to prepare a highway, a straight path, so that those rushing into Tabernacles and the Father rushing into them, might connect together freely and truly without any hindrance or blockage.

Someone from Kansas, a reader whom I do not know and who is not on my mailing list, sends me a check for $100 every month and has done so for around two years now. I deeply appreciate that gift and use it to cover the present costs of the websites and to send out a few books to those who ask. Sometimes it has gotten us out of an immediate financial hole.

If 15-20 people were to take on themselves the same ministry from the Lord, committing to sending a set amount each month, then $1500 + a month would be sufficient provision for me to show my wife that my time spent writing is indeed contributing to our family's needs. This is what I want to do. And I am asking of you to help me.

⤶

At the end of the letter, I asked my readers to consider setting up regular monthly donations through PayPal. I sent this letter out just as I drove north again to Canada, making the trip still caught in the dilemma of my providing nothing for our family's needs.

Another Trip North

In December James spent a couple of more weeks with the Miller cousins in Stephenville. This time, he shot a deer, which he brought home for us to process. That was quite a job. He had also agreed to go with them on a medical missionary trip into northern Mexico the first part of March.

Johanna had waited to make her final decision of where to live, but now she wanted to move all her stuff up to Upsala. She flew down and we rented a small Budget truck into which we loaded all her things. Johanna and I then drove the truck up to Canada together, leaving on December 28. I had forgotten that it was winter in the north, and so we had to stop at a thrift store in northern Minnesota for me to buy a winter coat. That was not the last time I had to do the same thing. On our second night on the road, Johanna and I stayed in a lovely little cabin just north of Duluth. In fact, this whole trip was a wonderful time of sharing with my daughter, and we conversed much together.

When we arrived at the South Farm in the Upsala communities, it was full winter, with a few feet of snow covering everything. The Upsala communities continue to be a big part of our life; you can refer back to Chapter 45 for maps and a description of the life there.

Johanna had returned to her same room with Ray and Paula Brumbach. I stayed in their guest bedroom, an addition onto the trailer. On this trip, I was writing the chapters on setting creation free in *Symmorphy I: Purpose*.

I spent many hours visiting with Ray and Paula through the times I spent in their home. We visited about the Lord and about teaching school (Paula was a teacher in the Upsala School), and about our community and wilderness experiences. There was no sectarian spirit in the Upsala Community. I was received fully as a brother in the Lord who loved Jesus the same as they. I shared my books with several. Ray, especially, devoured my book *The Feast of Tabernacles*. I also visited with John Kiezebrink and shared some of my books with him. John was a warm and welcoming brother and received all that I shared with joy.

The next morning after our arrival, actually January 1, 2016, a number of brothers came to help us move all of Johanna's things from the Budget rental truck up into the upstairs above Paul Beebe's shop. During the day, I went with Johanna to see her new classroom in the school. This was very exciting to me to see her following her mom and dad into the joy of teaching.

That evening, I sat with Johanna at the dinner table in the South Farm Tabernacle. I describe this Tabernacle in *Symmorphy V: Life* as a wonderful example of a well-designed place for the gathering of community. The brothers and sisters gathered around the table this evening were mostly older folks. Yet there in their midst was Johanna, happy and bubbly, and very much a part of their lives. After we were done eating, no one was in a hurry to leave. I did not talk, but just observed how the conversation was filled with so much knowing of one another and so much receiving of Johanna back into their togetherness. This is the knowing of one another that I share of that is central to the life and revelation of God. Of truth, I knew that I was beholding the very face of Jesus Christ.

As I walked back to the Brumbach's home with Ray, I said to him, "You know, Ray, I think that the brethren here need Johanna's bubbly youth as much as she needs your older wisdom." He replied, "Yes, that's exactly right." I went to sleep that night knowing that God had brought Johanna to the right place and that she was utterly safe inside of Him and this precious family.

I drove the Budget Rental truck back to Duluth on Saturday, to drop it off at a Budget place near the Duluth airport. There my brother Glenn picked me up and I went to spend the rest of the weekend in their home. My flight back to Houston would be on Monday.

Glenn was prospering in his construction business, both work he continued to do with Mark Alesch and other connections he made himself. He had done a fair bit of work for a wealthy neighbor and thus he and Kim were able to purchase a very nice house and small property a few miles up the road from Meadowlands, near the small community of Toivola. The house was quite comfortable, although Glenn was doing a fair bit of work to it. He was also building a nice large shop. Their property sloped down to and bordered Sand Creek, a branch of the St. Louis river.

I had a wonderful visit with Glenn. In fact, I felt that for the first time, we were truly knowing one another as brothers. Glenn shared a lot about how he was prospering. The result was that, when I retired to my bed down in the basement amongst all their yet-unpacked stuff, I began to feel quite sorry for myself. The depths of self-pity as I had once known came upon me. I could only contrast my failure and weakness with Glenn's strength and success.

Yet, although I felt like a complete failure in my inability to provide for my family and my dependence on Maureen to work long hours away from home, I did not leave it there. I placed all of that into Jesus and all of Jesus into me, carrying me, and there I rested, though in deep sorrow. Glenn and Kim knew none of that, of course, and after the weekend of wonderful visiting, Kim drove me to the airport on Monday morning and I flew home to Houston.

Not long after, Maureen and I received a letter from Matthew Schneider asking for our permission to begin walking out a year with Johanna. Matthew had loved Johanna from the first times together in class at school (and even sooner), but once they graduated, Johanna had distanced herself from any further relationship, and so Matthew had to wait a few years. Waiting is good. Maureen and I gladly gave our permission and they began their year on January 31, 2016.

A Trip to Nashville

Also in January, I started getting emails from two new readers in Australia, two elderly sisters, Wilhelmina Van der Hoek (Willie) and Cora van Beelen. These two had a long history in both Pentecostal and ultimate reconciliation circles, and their love for Jesus and excitement over the word I was sharing was quite an encouragement to me.

Soon after my return home, I made plans to drive up to Nashville, Tennessee, to spend a few days' fellowship with Ed Carter and his wife, Dora. To help me with that trip, Ed and Dora were the first to respond to my request for financial help with a regular monthly donation.

Not long after, I began to receive a monthly donation from Rachelle Ross as well, a donation which has continued until today. It's not the money that counts, though it helps pay the bills, but rather the gift of herself. Rachelle is very much a part of the ministry of Christ through me. God has always given me just what is needed, and I give Him all thanks.

I now realize that, in having me place my self-pity into Jesus, God took it from me and thus opened the door to my being free to receive His provision.

Then, in mid-March, I drove the now-repaired Suburban to Nashville. In fact, I finally caved in and bought myself a less expensive smart phone for this trip. I don't like phones, but I did need to communicate on the road.

Actually, I drove James to Stephenville first, so that he could go on the medical missions trip to Mexico with Maureen's cousins. Then I spent the next night at a state park in southern Arkansas. I found the Suburban to be very comfortable for staying in. Needless to say, I picked the route that enabled me to collect more counties for my map. Yet I also felt carried inside of a bubble of grace the whole trip.

Ed and Dora Carter had a nice apartment in a larger apartment complex in a small town just to the east of Nashville. I stayed with them for four days, in their spare bedroom. Ed is fun and talkative and he loved the word I share. We visited non-stop for hours and hours. I also noticed several copies of my books all dog-eared and tattered from having been poured over.

I had thought to drive up into Ohio to visit with David Wenger, but he drove down to Nashville and spent a couple of nights in a nearby motel. Thus for about a day-and-a-half, David Wenger was part of our non-stop fellowship. I set before both brothers my need to have someone with the gift I don't have of bringing people together to do that for me and for the word God was giving me. Both were receptive to that need and were willing to consider it. David suggested that I put together radio episodes. He had connections in the Christian radio industry and could help with that. Making such a thing actually happen, however, was a bit beyond what has been practical since then, and so nothing more came of these things.

Nonetheless, I was very excited at the time in my expectation of God that these connections would continue into something real and ongoing. Our fellowship together was rich and very strengthening to all of us. One thing I noted in my conversation with Ed, however, was that when I shared about Christian community, a wall went up in his face. He was not receptive to that part of what I teach and so I did not pursue it.

While I was in Ed and Dora's home, I received a communication from Christopher Küttner in Germany, in which he suggested to me some ideas for an online business that might provide for our needs. I accepted this council as from the Lord and so became very excited about it.

On the way back to Houston, I went into the Ozark region of northern Arkansas. Some readers had suggested I meet with a brother there who had a small community and who ministered deeper truth. I cannot remember the brother's name, except J.C. I did find them and spent a couple of nights there in a bunk house. It was a strange experience, but they finally warmed up to me a bit and I was able to share some good things. I left a copy of *The Feast of Tabernacles* with the brother and continued on back home.

After returning home, I then created a couple of new websites in line with Christopher's ideas and spent a few weeks working on them. As I continued, however, the work became harder and harder for me until I simply could not do one more thing in that direction. And so that "great idea" also came to nothing.

After my visit with him, Ed began calling me on the phone about once a week or so to continue our fellowship. I usually don't do well talking on the phone, but Ed was just the kind of person who made it possible and good for me. These phone calls became a much-needed strength and encouragement to me over the next couple of years.

The Next Parts of Symmorphy

In March, I wrote the final chapter of *Symmorphy I: Purpose* and thus began *Symmorphy II: Essence*, a look at the meaning of key Bible words, especially of "God," "Christ," and "salvation." In April, I started *Symmorphy III: Kingdom* as well, because I had placed a study of John 17, the prayer that birthed the kingdom, into that outline, but I needed that study before I could continue with *Essence*. Once those three chapters were done, I found that attempting to write two books at the same time was not working for me and so I continued with Essence only. Needless to say, that study of John 17 is one of the more important things I have written.

Meanwhile, I continued to fill in the educational parts of *Symmorphy I: Purpose* in order to prepare it for printing. This was a much bigger job on this first text because I was devising everything. With the later *Symmorphy* texts, I simply followed that same pattern of the first. I completed that work and published the print copy through Amazon the first part of May 2016. The chapters of *Symmorphy II: Essence* were my focus, then, until I completed that text in October of 2016.

Writing *Symmorphy I: Purpose* was a critical foundation in my journey to know the Lord. This was the first time that I had done an in-depth, phrase by phrase and word by word study of these verses that I am convinced God intends to be the rule of how we understand everything. I discovered so many things I had never seen before, huge things. I also realized that I did not know anything about Hebrews 10, and it took me some time to work through the wording to even know what it was saying.

Although every one of these verses became much larger in my understanding and in how I related with God, still, it would be the writing of four more *Symmorphy* texts before I could truly say that I understand the basic meaning of these verses and how they fit together.

Strange Distractions

One thing of note through this time was that, after disconnecting with Chris Welch on Facebook, and as part of an effort to draw people to Christ Revealed Bible Institute, I began accepting the many "friend" requests coming my way on Facebook. Requesting to be "friends" with someone else is outside of my ken, however.

And thus over a year or so, I "friended" nearly 5,000 people on Facebook, the limit that was allowed. I learned immediately that each one of those friend requests must be looked at, and so I did scroll through the home page of all of those thousands of people. I did not "friend" any who promoted an attachment to this world or who spoke condemnation against other Christians.

The result of this exercise was small. It did put the word I was sharing before many, but the unhelpful responses quickly became confusing noise to me. I have bailed out of making use of Facebook several times, and I almost never look at the general feed being posted by all those thousands of "friends." The few times I did, I read awful things being spoken by fellow Christians that simply overwhelmed me.

But what I did see was a snapshot view of the Church of Jesus Christ across the English-speaking world. I would guess that about a third were American or European, about a third were African, and about a third were South or East Asian. But of all of these, I would guesstimate that only about ten percent evidenced in their words an actual love towards the Lord Jesus Christ.

On July 31, I received a Facebook message from Dr. Cecil Cockerham, a brother who lived in the Katy area on the far other side of Houston, and who attended the Grace Pointe Community Church on Dairy Ashford, with Pastor Don Keithley. We had visited this church not long before to hear Francis Du Toit of South Africa minister the word.

Dr. Cecil had helped to create an online school called American Seminary and had made a good living from it. He was switching over to developing a similar school with the church and wanted to sell American Seminary to someone who would benefit from it. He had read some of my stuff on Facebook and felt to offer it to me.

I went to meet with Dr. Cecil in a restaurant. He explained the school to me and his reasons for selling it. I was interested as well as desperate for a way to provide for my family and willing to embrace anything that might be the Lord.

A red flag for me came up in our discussion, however, and that is that Dr. Cecil was not willing to share any financial data for the business with me. When I pressed him with the fact the you don't buy a business without a look at its finances, he refused. Later I learned that, not long before, he had inadvertently deleted the entire website and had to pay his technician to recreate everything. All the records of prior students were thus lost.

Nonetheless, I wrote up a proposal for my involvement in the business that included Dr. Cecil's help with marketing. I went again to visit with Dr. Cecil at a dinner in a restaurant, this time with Maureen. Pastor Don Keithley of Grace Pointe Church was also part of our meeting. They expressed that my proposal was great, if I had put a down payment on the business. Dr. Cecil wanted $25,000 down and a total of $125,000 over time. My only option was to work with Dr. Cecil to see if we could generate an income by signing up more students.

On August 17, I sent out a letter titled "My New Job!!!" I was really excited about this direction at first and received it as an open door from the Lord. I was ready to pursue anything that might be God's provision for us and for the word I share.

De. Cecil gave me full access into the website and the courses on offer, which were also delivered through Moodle. I recast a number of the website pages and began to look closely at the courses. This was a two-year program and cost the client $2400. Dr. Cecil had made a lot of money from it in the past.

However, as I looked closely at the courses, I realized that the quality was way too poor for me. I would have to redo everything. More than that, it seemed to me that the total value of everything in the "business" could be no more than $5000, not $125,000, especially since there were no present students. Dr. Cecil assured me that my Facebook friend count of 5000 would be more than enough to get large numbers of students.

I sent copies of Symmorphy I: Purpose to Pastor Keithley and to Dr. Cecil, and part of my visiting with them was about the online Grace school they were starting in the church. This school already included a number of anointed ministries, some of whom were in my Facebook list. I expressed an interest in being part of that larger Bible school, but no response ever came back to me.

In the end, I became uncomfortable with what seemed to me to be a religious manipulation on the one hand and an impractical business idea on the other hand. I could easily create my own school for a few hundred dollars; why did I need a half-broken idea from someone else? I placed the fault upon myself, however, and quietly bowed out.

Nonetheless, this concept of a larger online Bible school was still very exciting to me and so I began to turn Christ Revealed Bible Institute into something more. Of course, business is marketing and I am unable to promote myself. A good salesman signs up all kinds of people to something poor and makes good money. Someone like me, who creates something of great value, but can't sell it, remains poor.

The truth is that I had to look up Grace Pointe Church's online Bible school in order to remember some of the names. I realized that I have felt a contempt in this direction from then until now.

"Lord Jesus, I place this feeling of contempt entirely into You. I know that You think more highly of these brethren than You do of Yourself and that You share that same love with me. Lord Jesus, I bless Dr. Cecil and all these brethren with all my heart."

Where Do I Belong?

As I am writing this little bit in June of 2022, I have a better understanding of the direction God is taking me than I had in 2016. For that reason, I can see more clearly how to place the meaning of this time I am calling "The Season of Symmorphy."

Where I "belong" had not come into view and would not do so until October of 2019, and even then only in its first parts. Through this season of writing these five *Symmorphy* textbooks, God was doing two things inside of me. First the actual writing itself was grounding me in the Bible, in what God actually says and means, in the Word of truth written all through my knowing. This foundation would become a burning fire inside of me to make the gospel clear on the one hand and the false gospel clear just as much on the other hand.

But the other thing God was doing was through my outward circumstances and my eager, but oft misguided desire to be part of something real. He was removing something from me and replacing it with something else. At the time, however, I could not have known the meaning of either one.

Yet I am convinced now that these things, both the clarity of word and what God was preparing inside of me, are essential to the entire Christian Church now and through the Age of Tabernacles.

49. The Season of Symmorphy II

July 2016 - August 2017

"Father, I thank You that You have planted Your Word inside of me so richly and that You have enabled me to hear the meaning of Your Heart. I love Your Words; I love the singing of Jesus in my heart; I love the flow of the anointing onto the page; I love the awakening of Your knowing in the lives of those who read.

"You have given me so much, my Father. You have given me Yourself, and I belong inside of You."

The School Year

In the summer of 2016, James was also taken on as a paid intern at Jesse Jones Park. Through this summer, Maureen and I realized that James's final two years of school needed to be more formal. We communicated with Barbara Beebe at the Upsala Christian School, and the eldership agreed that James could come up to spend his eleventh-grade year in their school. Steve and Cindy Schneider offered James a room in their home for him to stay. James's work through the summer at Jesse Jones park helped pay for his tuition and other costs.

James is the only one of our children who is not a Canadian citizen and so we had to work through the whole process of getting him a student visa, all of which was now online.

Towards the end of August, Maureen flew up to Toronto with James, and then on to Thunder Bay and Upsala. She helped him move into his new room with the Schneider's and saw him situated in his new classrooms, just down the hall from where Johanna taught her classes. James would spend his final two years of high school attending the Upsala school.

Meanwhile, Katrina was now the only one remaining at home. Life was much more quiet for me, which was good and not-so-good, at the same time. This fall Katrina was hired full time as a park ranger with Jesse Jones Park where she would continue for five years. She also began her second year in the theater program at San Jacinto College in Pasadena. We were able to buy a Jeep for Katrina to have for her use.

From Essence to Kingdom

The first half of writing *Symmorphy II: Essence* was a solidifying of my understanding of God's meanings, culminating in a closer look at redemption and salvation. In all that I write, I am reaching for clarity in the knowledge of God and of what He actually says.

But then, towards the end of July, I began a section of *Essence* that I called, at the time, "a looking at darkness." I wanted to see more clearly how the Church turned away from Paul's gospel, never really having known it, and to know what it actually was that Christianity now called "the gospel," something hammered out from the fiction that Jesus is "faraway." This section began with "How Was the Flesh Exalted?"

The important thing for this narrative of my life is this. It is God who has placed inside of me the burning need to KNOW the gospel as He speaks it in the Bible and to understand what this anti-gospel is, where it came from, and how it triumphed inside the Church of Christ throughout the in-part Church Age. The clarity I so desperately needed will come by December of 2020, but it is important to me that you know how it came.

Sometime in the first week of October, I had a dream anointed of God. In my dream, I was standing at the top of a stairway looking down at Jesus in the room below. Jesus was beneath of me. His eyes beckoned to me and I said to Him, "Jesus you are the same as me and I am the same as You. I am a man, just like You, filled with all the fullness of God." When I said that, I knew that Jesus was no longer "beneath of" me, but now part of me, Jesus and I as one together.

I knew, now, that I must share these words with others. The first person I saw next was a girl, around six or seven. Eager anticipation was upon her face as I told her to say, "Jesus, you are the same as me and I am the same as you. I am just like You, a girl filled with all the fullness of God." I knew that in that moment, this little girl was sealed into God and that our bond together was complete, regardless of outward proximity.

In my dream, I continued teaching others to say that same thing, "I am just like You, Jesus, a man/a woman filled with all the fullness of God," and many responded with joy, each now sealed into God, each now part of me and one another. Yet not all would hear.

I noticed a group of "deeper truth" Christians in a room high above me, some of whom I had known. I wanted to speak this word to them, but I could not get up to them, and they showed no interest in coming down to hear.

In my dream, I continued speaking to others, those not "put together," those not successful in either church or world, and they gladly spoke those words of union with Christ. I knew, in my dream, that I had spoken, and was teaching others to speak, the very fulfillment of the First Day of Tabernacles, of being sealed into God and of being made a part of one another.

I completed and sent out the final parts of *Symmorphy II: Essence* through the middle of October and then picked up where I had left off in *Symmorphy III: Kingdom,* with "Christ as Word as Us" and "Christ as a Spirit of Power." I called these chapters as "one of the great milestones of God in my years of seeking to know Him." This was a major step in understanding how Spirit and Word flow together as the environment in which all things exist. Our reality, as it seems normal to me now, was brand new to me this October of 2016.

In the first part of December, I received an email from Lanny Gao, a sister from Athens, Georgia. I asked Lanny recently how she found my website; let me share her response to me.

~~~ Hi Daniel, I went to my mailbox and found out that I wrote you the first email on 12/05/2016. I found your website a couple of months earlier probably (not quite sure) in the month of September, 2016.

Years ago the Lord showed me that the feast of Tabernacles is yet to be fulfilled. I was googling "the feast of Tabernacles" online. After some searching

I found an interesting website "The light house library" (I went back to look for this library after a while and was not able to find it any more). There were quite some good articles that caught my interest. After a little while, I found a series of articles "The Feast of Tabernacles." To my impression, this was the longest one there. I started reading it. Then I searched the name Daniel Yordy, finally I found your website! I delved right in until today.

I couldn't stop reading your materials. I felt I needed to contact you to let you know how blessed I was but I just couldn't stop feasting on your website. It was until December 5, I finally wrote you the first email. You kindly told me that I can ask you if I had questions. To me, I barely had any question to ask, I was just busy taking in everything!

There was tremendous healing taking place in me while I was reading your articles. All these years, I was doubting.... "Does God really love me?" "Am I blessed?" ...because my life was filled with so much hardship and difficulties. When I found out that my heavenly Father truly loves me and all these difficulties and hardship have a great purpose, everything in my life looked different to me ever since. I want to tell you, Daniel, many, many times that I am so blessed by you. You have given me Hope!

I am very thankful for you, dear brother Daniel! – Lanny

☙

Not long after this, Lanny also began sending me a regular monthly donation that has continued until now. The Lord was giving His answer to my heart's cry and to our need.

A Further Turning Point

Through the week of December 19-24, 2016, I wrote Chapter 14 of *Kingdom,* "Not Knowing God." This chapter is right at the mid-point of the five *Symmorphy* texts, and writing it became a major turning point in my life and my knowledge of God.

Lesson 14.2 was titled "Calvinism." In order to write that chapter, I found a copy of John Calvin's *Institutes of the Christian Religion* online and began to read. It wasn't long before I was pacing back and forth through the house calling on the Lord Jesus as I was overwhelmed with the awfulness of what I was reading – a God who "knows evil" and a salvation that leaves wickedness as the only connection between the believer and this "God."

Much more than that, it did not take me long to realize that I was also reading Buddy Cobb, that what Buddy Cobb had preached, the man whom I sat under more than any other in my life, including his "Plan of God," was little more than an expression of John Calvin. I had figured that Buddy Cobb's theology was Calvinist, even when I was at Blueberry, but I never said such a thing, for it would have been hotly denied from every direction.

What was horrifying was to see the dark definition placed against God and the repudiation of the covenant. Calvin said that when we "see God" we will know just how WICKED we are. The Bible says that when we see God, we will know that we are just like Him.

This was all very disturbing to me and I read no more of Calvin beyond what I needed to write that one lesson.

But Lesson 14.3 is titled "A Highway for God." Writing this lesson, then, right after, marked another great turning point in my life, a more complete "turning around." It's not us "going into" God; it's God coming through us into our world.

A Christmas Trip

During Christmas break, in December 2016, Matthew, Johanna, and James flew down from Canada to share several days with us. We rented an Airbnb home, a large and quite comfortable double-wide trailer in an isolated and lovely spot in the hill country of Texas, west of Austin.

Before we went, however, Matthew came to see me early one morning in my little office in the back of the house. He asked me for my permission and blessing to ask Johanna to be his wife. I gave him my blessing with all my heart, but I did place one requirement on him. I requested of Matthew, in return for my blessing, that when it came time for their children to be born, he would study the issue of vaccination carefully, that he would look at the arguments against equally with any arguments for, and then make a decision. I said that if he would become fully conversant in the arguments against, we would accept whatever their decision would be.

I do not know if my son-in-law has kept his agreement with me, nor will I inquire. Rather, Maureen and I continue to do what we have always done towards our children, placing ourselves as intercession before God for their sakes, that God

Himself would arise inside of them.

Claude and Lois came down to be with us over this Christmas. Our dinner this time was an entire English Christmas dinner that I had found in a magazine.

During that day, Johanna came out into the living area with Matthew behind her, a ring on her finger and a beam upon her face. They planned to be married in June, after school was out.

I want to share also an autistic difficulty that happened to me during this short time, for it has bearing on the present. The engine of the Suburban had begun to cut out on me when it was hot. I did not know if this was a fuel problem or an electrical problem. It would still run, but only with low power.

I filled the tank with high-octane gas and it seemed to run better until we hit the steeper climbs of the hill-country. We did make it to the Airbnb, slowly. Kyle and James both insisted that the problem was caused by me foolishly filling it with high-octane fuel. I knew this wasn't correct, but I had no resolving answer.

As we were all in the rental home, conversing together, including with other young men whom I hardly knew, Kyle began to speak what I knew would be a public correction of me regarding my foolish choice to fill the tank with high-octane fuel. In my autistic agony, I could not bear the contempt of young men I did not know, and so I asked Kyle not to continue. He attempted to ask a question concerning what we should do with the Suburban. I stopped him harshly, and he left the trailer.

This was my son, whom I love, and this was the first real breach I had known with him. I could not bear that either, so I followed him and we shared openly together in full respect and again received one another. I realize now that this moment marked the transition from a relationship of parent-child with Kyle to the relationship of friend with friend we enjoy now.

Let me include as well that through this year Kyle had begun to restore his friendship with Shelbie Stephens whom he had known at the local Baptist church through his many visits there growing up. A few weeks after our Christmas trip, in February, Kyle and Shelbie began to date regularly, a relationship that grew from then on.

Driving Uber

In February, just before the super bowl which was held in Houston this year, I signed up to drive with Uber, using Maureen's red Toyota Corolla. Although I would take a break for a few months in the fall, I drove Uber for about a year. The amount one can earn driving ride-share is minimal, still it was better than sitting in my chair in the afternoon and evening doing nothing.

For the most part driving Uber was a good experience. I drove two or three afternoons a week. I learned right away that I would not drive after dark and that driving on the big event days like the super bowl was a mistake. You get caught with short trips in heavy traffic and lose money. With Uber, I would pick up a person near our home first and wherever they wanted to go, that was where I picked up the next person, and so on. I drove to and throughout every part of the Houston area from Conroe to Galveston and from Baytown to Katy. This is the largest most spread out metropolitan area on earth. I carried every kind of person and drove to every kind of drop-off point. Driving someone to the Bush airport was always the most profitable because it was many miles driven on the fastest roads.

I enjoyed getting to know Houston really well, and I enjoyed serving people. Over time, however, the "noise" and press of other people in my car would become too much for me, especially when I made mistakes.

By April, we realized that the red Toyota was insufficient for our needs. We found a newer Toyota Corolla, blue this time, which Maureen bought and which I then used for driving with Uber.

In May, I was driving a customer north on Kirby Drive in heavy traffic. He was late for an appointment and in a hurry. I was in the third lane on the inside with a clear stretch ahead of me. Meanwhile a car was inching through the other two lanes to take a left turn. He pulled into my lane without seeing me. I braked hard, but hit him lightly. Only the outer material of both vehicles was damaged, but the experience shook me greatly. The other driver, a doctor, accepted being at fault and his insurance paid, though when driving Uber, insurance is a tangled mess. We got the blue Toyota repaired and I continued with Uber after the wedding coming up in June.

This accident did show up in my writing as I turned my difficulty into blessing for the sake of my readers.

From Kingdom to Covenant

Through this mid-point of working on *Symmorphy III: Kingdom,* I was also developing the first set of courses for my Christ Revealed Bible Institute program. I had kept a course from Dr. Cecil Cockerham's program on Hermeneutics in which he used R.C. Sproul's book, *Knowing Scripture.* Sproul is also a Calvinist, but without immersion in the Spirit. For my course on studying the Bible, I wanted to use Sproul's book because it was filled with useful things that should be part of understanding the Bible and because it contrasted so clearly with how I read and interpret the Bible.

And so I wrote my own take on interpreting the Bible, titled *Knowing God by Scripture,* as a rebuttal of Sproul's treatment of the Bible as the tree of knowing good and evil. This was my first full "writing to teach" little book, twelve chapters long with three lessons in each chapter. It is a wonderful book, filled with the impartation of life. I wish that all Christians would read it to know what their Bibles are and to know, not the Bible, but God by the Bible.

From January into February of 2017 I wrote the chapters concerning the Church in *Kingdom,* and of the firstfruits of God inside each local gathering. The beauty of the Church as she really is grew in my seeing.

In February, the print copy of *Essence* was finally available, followed by the print copy of *Knowing God by Scripture* in March.

As I wrote the final chapters of *Symmorphy III: Kingdom* through April, I brought back into my teaching and my relationship with God, that full word that I received from God through Sam Fife. As I completed Kingdom I wrote the following.

~~~ "And so it has come full circle. Out from my present knowledge of my full union with the Lord Jesus Christ, the Lord has caused me to know this same word that I received into my heart from age 20 to 21, though I could not know then what it meant. I have faithfully given you that word in this Kingdom text." ~~~

I had a lot going on through this time, including getting ready for our trip back up to Canada for Johanna and Matthew's wedding. I shared about that upcoming trip with my readers on April 23.

Through April, I also found the need to do a complete transcription of the Annie visions, *I Looked and I Saw Visions of God*, which I put into PDF form with my comments in the margin and made it available on my website. This was my fourth and final time reading through this little book. This time was wondrous, for none of these things were beyond my own experience anymore; rather, they were a description of my present knowledge of God.

Then, also this April, as I prepared to write the specifics of my first course for the Christ Revealed Bible Institute program, I encountered a problem when I thought to use Fred Pruitt's book, *Hearts of Flesh*. Fred's approach to writing was similar to mine, that is, to compile a series of letters into a book with only a loose connection between chapters. Scattered through his book were wonderful letters on various aspects of Christ living as us. In between them, however, were letters in which Fred attempted to fit union with Christ together with the Nicene "God." This included giving place for eternal damnation as well as a fulfillment in "heaven-only" of the big verses of the New Testament. In essence, half of his book was what I wanted and the other half would confuse the student with things I would eliminate in the *Symmorphy* courses.

I wrote to Fred, asking him for permission to create a PDF document of just those letters from *Hearts of Flesh* that were useful to the students in the course. He cheerfully gave me his permission, and so I proceeded to do just that. Nonetheless, this experience left me confused inside of a growing need to separate the two gospels completely.

By May I had begun to write *Symmorphy IV: Covenant*. This was an incredibly important task for me. I wrote this in the Review chapter of *Kingdom*.

☙

The burden of writing *Covenant*, however, has come upon me in a manner of which I have not known before. The Hand of God has come upon me, and I no longer write for myself, but for my Father. And in so doing, I find myself, once again, on my face on the floor before all Holiness. Indeed, I fear God.

We are speaking of living inside a Consuming Fire forever. And I see that this Consuming Fire intends to open to us things never before given to humans upon this earth. When I say that, I mean things entirely INSIDE God's Word in the Bible and

by the Holy Spirit, yet things that have been hidden, even from those who wrote those words.~~~

From May through July, however, I sent out the chapters of *Knowing God by Scripture* rather than *Symmorphy IV: Covenant,* even though I was writing the chapters of Covenant at the same time. I just included a link in the *Christ our Life* letter to each next part of *Covenant*. My thinking was that the chapters of *Covenant* were only for those who would seek them out. I returned to sending out *Covenant* in the letter with Chapter 10 "The Ark of the Covenant."

Writing *Symmorphy IV: Covenant* was of great importance to me. My knowledge of God increased enormously through those chapters including things of God that are normal to us now, but that have not been known in Christian thinking.

North to Upsala

Johanna's wedding was coming up in June. Everyone else was planning to fly up, but I preferred to drive, mostly because it would give me opportunity to stop along the way both going up and coming back to visit with readers of my letters.

I especially wanted to stop and visit this person in Kansas who had been sending me a $100 check each month for some time now. He still was not subscribed to my letter, and so I sent a postal letter to the address, not being certain, yet, who this was, asking for his phone number. Thus I called Bill Horton of Atwood, Kansas that May, and told him that I would be driving up to Canada in June and wanted to swing by and spend a couple of days fellowshipping with him.

Bill sounded astonished, but he agreed and welcomed me to visit. This would be the only stop I would make on my way up other than to visit briefly with my brother, Glenn. To most, Atwood, Kansas, is way out of the way; to me, it's just lots more counties to color in on my map.

Johanna's wedding would be on a Saturday, June 24, 2017. I left home in the Suburban on June 13, a week-and-a-half before. I had thought to spend the night on the way to Atwood in the Suburban at a state park in western Oklahoma, but it was much too hot. I got a motel instead. I arrived at Atwood in the middle of the afternoon. Atwood is a small town in northwest Kansas tucked into a small river-valley hollow out of sight of the vastness of the plains.

Bill is about ten years older than I, and he lived in a small three-bedroom home with his elderly mother. Mrs. Horton had mild Alzheimer's and Bill had devoted himself to her care. She was kind and friendly, just forgetful. One of the three bedrooms in the smaller house was filled with books and the second with food stuffs, leaving only the main bedroom that was used by Mrs. Horton. Bill gave me that bedroom for my stay, while the two of them went down to their former home, which was on the market for sale, yet still furnished.

I do not know what Bill was expecting in meeting me, but I was soon quite astonished myself when Bill showed me his copies of my books. He owned all of them up to *Symmorphy II: Essence* at this point, and every one of them was dog-eared, marked up, and filled with tabs. I had no idea that someone else would be so involved with what I have written.

I spent that evening fellowshipping with Bill. I found in him a commitment to the same word I was hearing from God. I spent two nights very comfortably, and did not leave until early afternoon of the third day. We shared, in our fellowship, a desire to know the Lord. On the morning before I left, having determined Bill's level of involvement with the word I shared, I asked him about Christian community, if he was in any way interested in such a thing. He replied definitely that he was.

The Suburban had continued with the occasional lack of fuel flow and thus running at a lower speed in the heat off and on all the way to Atwood. On the afternoon I arrived, Bill went with me to the local shop to see what the problem might be. They looked at it the next day and showed me the part on the fuel line that stuck when it got very hot, thus limiting the inflow of fuel. It would be a simple thing to replace once I could get the part. The mechanic also told me that if it cut out on me, I should stop and fill it up again with fresh gas. That would cool the device back down. Sure enough, that's exactly what happened on the way to Glenn's.

I arrived at Glenn and Kim's on Saturday evening and spent all of Sunday with them. While there, I asked Glenn to order the part needed for the Suburban. I also made the final arrangements with them for James to spend the summer in their home, working with Glenn and Benjamin (James's cousin) in construction. Canada was cooler than the states,

and thus I had no more problem with the Suburban. I spent Monday night in a motel in Thunder Bay near the shore of Lake Superior. While there, I walked around a park area along the harbor and found a wonderful restaurant that I shared later with the rest of my family.

After arriving in Upsala on Tuesday, I wrote the following inside of *Covenant.*, Lesson "8.2 Describing the Holiest," concerning my visit with Bill.

‿

I am sharing all this because I really want to capture for you the practical heart of living inside of God, inside and as His Heart. Thus it was in this mind of Father and I together turning EVERYTHING that might be difficult into goodness and life arising in you that I drove a few hours out of my way going to Canada to spend time with a brother in western Kansas (Bill Horton) who has been reading and practicing what I write for some years now. It was in my heart to be a blessing to him and to lift him up in honor.

Yet when I drove on from there and from that time of fellowship and blessing, I found quite the reverse. In my own consciousness, my blessing of him constituted maybe 10% and his blessing of me the vastly larger 90%. I cannot tell you how deeply I was strengthened and lifted up by seeing the life and reality of this word God has granted me to share as it came back to me through a dear brother alive inside this same speaking of Christ.

Indeed, as this brother spoke Christ back into me, the same word I thought I had taught him, but hearing it myself now on a different level, a level of reality and substance, I find myself walking on a far stronger foundation of confidence than I had known before. This confidence works, now, …as a far clearer seeing of the path forward to the community of Christ that fills my heart.

Johanna's Wedding

Johanna had been living in her own apartment in the upstairs of the Tabernacle at the South Farm of the Upsala community, and that's where Maureen, Katrina, and Shelbie Stephens were staying, along with Johanna's best friend, Jenna, who had flown up with her mother, Carla Zurovec, for the wedding. There was a manufactured home that had been set up on a property used as a business by the community in the past. This property was in-between the

North Farm and the South Farm, just a short walk below the community school where Johanna had been teaching. Johanna and Matthew would be living there after their wedding and it was partly furnished. That is where Kyle and I were staying. James had his own room with the Schneider's at the West Farm. (See the map on page 508.)

This home was not considered part of either community, and thus Johanna and Matthew would be semi-independent for the first part of their married life, something the elders of the Upsala community believed was important. Yet it also meant that I now had little involvement with the brethren, since I was not staying in anyone's present home. I had unhindered time to write each early morning, this time two critical chapters in *Symmorphy IV: Covenant*, "Fire in the Holiest" and "Pro-Knowing."

Maureen and I spent time fellowshipping with Steve Schneider, Matthew's father and an elder in the community, in whose home James was staying. This fellowship was deep and good. Steve shared with us some of the difficulties James had experienced in fitting into a much stricter way of living than he had known at home. I am convinced that Steve was God's best choice for James in that difficulty. Nonetheless, he also spoke of "seeking the will of God," something that also showed up in "8.2 Describing the Holiest." Indeed, it is through this time that "energeia" and "pro-knowing" explode in my knowledge of God.

Lois and Claude came to Johanna's wedding. Sister Delores drove up from Minneapolis, and there were many others whom we knew. Another of Johanna's friends from Family Christian, Serina Borny, also came, but only for the wedding.

Johanna insisted on an outdoor wedding; she is an outdoor girl, with flowers in her hair. Yet there were storm clouds and threatening rain. Her wedding would be in the mown field just below the Upsala community school. A large tent was set up and filled with tables for the reception after the wedding. Next to it were the rows of chairs set up for the wedding.

Here is a picture of me escorting Johanna down the aisle to Matthew waiting in front. I want you to notice four things in this picture. First, I want you to see just how beautiful our daughter is, and second, the deep emotion that is upon me. As I saw Matthew waiting for Johanna, I remembered myself waiting for Maureen. If the picture were clearer, you would see the tears on my face.

Then, I want you to see the dark storm clouds all around, covering the sky, but finally, notice the sunshine upon the wedding itself. This was a most remarkable thing, for the sun was on that wedding through the entire time. Just as the last of the guests entered the reception tent, only then, did the rains fall.

It was a wonderful wedding, of course. Then, during the reception after we ate, different ones got up to share. Both Steve and I shared that we had known years before that God had placed Matthew and Johanna together. Then Kyle got up to share. Kyle was still 25. As he spoke, I was struck by the depth of the anointing that was upon him, and I knew that God had appointed Kyle as a shepherd in His Church. Then the chairs were put up and Jenna Zurovec led the young people of the community in a Texas line dance. That was really fun to watch.

Jenna and her mother were quite impressed with the community and Johanna's life there. I was also very grateful that Shelbie had the opportunity to know firsthand the setting in which Kyle had grown up. She enjoyed every part of it, even though it was all very different for her.

Johanna and Matthew drove east to Quebec City for their honeymoon. On their way back, they stopped at Richter's Herbs near Toronto, the source of herbs we had bought seeds from years before when Johanna was growing things at home. It was exciting to me that they got to stop there. Johanna bought all sorts of herb plants for her new home.

I must add one shadow to this time at Upsala because it is necessary for things to come. Always before, when staying at the Brumbach's and fellowshipping with the brethren at Upsala I had felt fully welcome and found an anointing of the Spirit that I could join together with. This time, I was somewhat isolated in the house Matthew was preparing as their home. Our accommodations were not fully complete, though in all things I give thanks. The problem was that during this whole time I felt the same spirit of condemnation that I had felt from the move in the past. From whence it came, I did not know, but it left me much less interested in having anything more to do with that fellowship.

My Trip Home

As part of my travel plans, I had set up a lengthy trip home with a number of different stops. James rode with me down to Glenn and Kim's north of Duluth where I spent a couple of days getting James settled in for the summer. Glenn had his new shop fully set up by this time. He was able to replace the defective part on the Suburban quickly and easily.

While I was there, I made time to visit with Mark Alesch for a couple of hours. The Meadowlands "community" was now their property and at that point in time Mark and Cindy were the only ones living there, having converted the several buildings into places for people to stay on vacation. I had a wonderful time sharing with Mark concerning the word God was giving to me. I left him with some of my books and placed him on my mailing list.

James spent this summer working with Glenn and Benjamin to earn the money for his next school-year's tuition at Upsala. I drove on from Glenn's to Neenah, Wisconsin to visit again with Richard and Marie Williams and with Rita Robinson. I shared the word with them that evening and through the next day. Marie had arranged for me to stay at a friend of theirs, but when I went there after dark, I found the sleeping arrangement to be utterly unsuitable, to say it kindly. I excused myself and drove back to the William's place and slept in the back of the Suburban. I was set up for that, with a full foam mattress, and was quite comfortable.

Another elderly sister was also with us in the Williams' living room. I believe she was blessed by the word of union with Christ I was able to share with her. She passed on not long after. Marie expressed a desire to receive the Baptism in the Holy Spirit, and so I prayed for her. This is not something I've ever done before or since, but to my complete astonishment, as I was praying, the Spirit of God poured out from her and she was praying in a heavenly language. I also spent a couple of hours riding around and visiting with Richard, as he showed me where he worked.

After a second night in the Suburban, I left early the next morning heading towards Michigan. I had originally hoped to cross Lake Michigan on the ferry, but the timing would not work. Not wanting to go anywhere near Chicago, I drove north through upper Michigan. I took a side route in the center of Michigan to collect a few missing counties before finally arriving at Ed and Dora Carter's place near Flint. This was where they were originally from and had returned there from Nashville prior to this visit.

Ed Carter had continued to call me about once a week through this time. It was easy for me to visit with him and our conversations were warm and fruitful. I was always much blessed in the Lord as a result. For some reason, however, there did not seem to be a connection in the Spirit when I first arrived.

Ed was usually humorous. With a person like that, I am sometimes a chameleon, that is, I take on their mood. We sat in his living room together that evening, and Ed scrolled through the TV, looking for something to watch. When I said that I did not wish to watch a WWII movie, he argued at me as to why that made no sense. To my horror, I fell into the same mood and before long we were arguing AT each other over politics. I can't imagine anything more stupid than arguing over politics.

I went up to their spare bedroom that evening feeling quite depressed. It took great faith to draw the Lord into myself, that Jesus shares all with me.

The next day, as we were sitting around his patio table outside, Ed asked me, a bit harshly, "What are you trying to do, start a cult?" As I shared out from union with Christ in response to such a wild question, Ed finally began to respond back inside the Spirit of Christ and we enjoyed good fellowship together for the rest of the day. I wondered, though I don't know for sure, whether Ed had searched out "Sam Fife" and "the move" online and read all the horrible and mostly untrue stuff one can find.

The next morning I drove on towards Akron, Ohio. I had first wanted to drive back into Canada, into southern Ontario, to visit with Kathy MacDonald, but it was not a good time for her. For that reason, I went on to spend two nights with Dan and Joanne Kurtz near their original hometown of Unionville, Ohio.

I had a wonderful time fellowshipping with Dan and Joanne. They had attended a couple of move conventions again prior to this, just to see how things were going in that fellowship. Dan had embraced Preston Eby's teaching on ultimate reconciliation, so he would never have fit back under Buddy Cobb. Dan shared again many more of his experiences with Sam Fife in the early years of the move communities and of some of the difficult things he and Joanne had faced at Graham River Farm.

The second evening, Lee and Claire Wilkerson, who had been a part of the second Graham River community, came by for supper and fellowship. They lived in that part of Ohio at this time. Dan had a number of my books, but I don't think he had read them much. Instead, he gave them to Lee to read. Lee had also embraced Preston Eby's teaching. Since I started writing my life story, however, Dan has read most of my letters.

My heart was full and rich from my time with the Kurtz's. But I was quite worn out at this point. It took me two long days to make it back home to Houston, arriving home late on Friday, July 7.

Here is what I wrote, then, in *Covenant*, Lesson 9.3 "The Father's Heart."

⌒

I am sharing my conclusions from this time of going from place to place sharing Christ with some VERY different sorts of people. As I went from time spent visiting with one person to time spent visiting with another, whether that time was many hours or ten minutes, I realized that I seemed to be a different sort of person from one interchange to the next. I realized that each one with whom I spoke cast me by their image of me and drew from me only what they wanted. I could not be more nor less than what that one wanted me to be towards them.

You see, as I have traveled, I find that my only desire is to be life as people wish me to be life, to speak Christ as people want to hear from me Christ living as them, and to be silent when people are not interested. Basically, I find myself giving out to them only what people draw out from me. And what each person wants God to be through me to them is very different from one to the next.

A sister wanted to receive from God through me full immersion into the Holy Ghost with speaking in tongues specifically. I have never done such a thing in my life. I just prayed as I write prayers in these letters and to my utter astonishment, the Holy Ghost flooded into her soul and prophetic tongues flowed out of her mouth as rivers. Just like Jesus, I had nothing to do with it. Rather, she, in her own faith and desire, made use of my being there in order to connect with God in her according to that desire.

Another brother also desires to know God through all that I share, yet he is a persnickety sort of fellow who likes to draw people into argument. I have not pointlessly argued politics in 20 years, yet there I was, meeting him at his desire and foolishly arguing over a point that was utterly meaningless to both of us. You see, in times past, I would have gone to bed under total condemnation by such a thing. But I have turned around, and I now see all things as my Father together with me. It was difficult, yes, but I now see that "becoming all things to all men" is not a theatrical exercise, but the very being of God, no matter how excruciating it might be.

Directions for Kyle & for Covenant

This summer of 2017, the Lord opened a most wonderful door for our son, Kyle. During Kyle's time taking electrical courses at San Jacinto College under Mr. Elder, he had organized study groups with the other students and even stood in front of the class at times to help with the teaching. Mr. Elder had recognized Kyle's gift in teaching and told him that after three years experience in the field, he might find a place as a teacher in that program.

Kyle reconnected with Mr. Elder, and with his help applied for a full-time teaching position. Now, Kyle had only three years of field experience and a two-year associates degree from college. He certainly did not "qualify." Kyle was the first of several to be interviewed. During his interview, the college board liked him so much that he was hired to teach full time on the spot and all the other applicants were dismissed.

Kyle is a born teacher, and he has been a full-time instructor in the electrical program at San Jacinto College from the fall of 2017 until the present – five years now.

Then, all of Houston went through quite an ordeal in August, affecting the lives of many, including ours. At the same time, I was finishing the middle part of *Symmorphy IV: Covenant* in August, about to enter into a wondrous new seeing of the Church of Jesus Christ coming up in September.

Map of Upsala Area: Below
The letters are just to the top of the locations.

A. Upsala, a couple of gas stations, etc.

B. The South Farm, where Johanna lived while going to school and where I stayed on my previous visits.

C. Matthew and Johanna's first home.

D. The Upsala School where Johanna taught and where Johanna and James finished their schooling.

E. The North Farm

F. The community hall where the graduations were held.

G. The West Farm where James lived with the Schneiders

H. Lang Lake, in view of the South Farm Tabernacle.

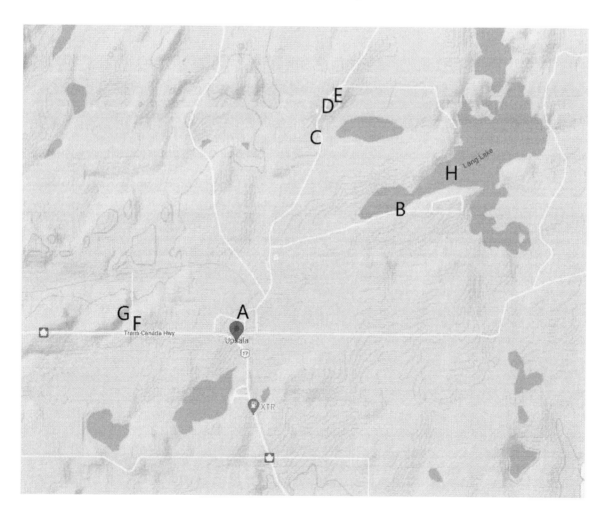

50. In the Crucible of the Word

August 2017 - August 2018

I thought it would be easier to write about recent times because of the joy in which I live every day. It is not easier; it is harder. All the relationships of my past that were painful to me are no longer in continuance. It takes great faith that God is real to place them into the light and to place the Lord Jesus upon me in that moment and upon that brother or sister in my memories.

But now I bring in relationships that are ongoing. And some of those ongoing relationships contain difficulties that are unresolved. Yet my whole life is caught in God's intentions, and He brings forth His completion in me as a direct response to the difficulties.

What I find now is that God is bringing a massive change into my life as of April of 2022. That change includes a transformation of how I now understand my life and the calling of God upon me. To be faithful to future readers, I must include those circumstances that contributed to this transformation.

This August of 2017, I wrote the chapter "Symmorphic" in *Symmorphy IV: Covenant.* I included a discussion of the crossing of the Jordan and the meaning of the priests standing at the bottom of the Jordan with the Ark of the Covenant on their shoulders, standing there until every single Israelite had crossed through the paths of death and entered into the promised land of Christ.

I also learned that my last name, Yordy, is the Hebrew *"Yarden,"* that is, the Jordan River. This has no outward meaning, but it did seal in me that my heart has always been to stand for the sake of all until each little one who believes in Jesus has entered into the life of knowing God.

Harvey & Points North

On August 24, Hurricane Harvey moved over Houston and decided to stay. When the outer rain bands of the hurricane started flowing over Houston, my family was scattered across the city. My wife was in Kingwood caring for the elderly lady she worked for, Melba Turner, through the duration of the floods, having driven there this time in the Suburban. My daughter was on the far southwest side of the city, and my son, Kyle, and I were at home. Soon after the rains started, no one could go anywhere.

Our house was on a slight ridge, so I was not concerned about water inside, that is, not right away. Monday night was the heaviest. Our street was 18" deep in water, but the water was still about 16" below our front door. From Sunday on, we heard helicopters constantly, rescuing people from nearby neighborhoods slightly lower than ours. We also lost power on Sunday and water soon after. We had plenty of provisions, however. On Monday evening, most everyone on our street had stayed. That was the right decision, because the water did not go higher through the night. By Tuesday evening our street was empty of water, even though it was still raining.

Maureen and Mrs. Turner had a different experience. They woke early Tuesday morning with a few inches of water inside the house and rising fast. They were soon rescued by a boat, carrying them to safety. They were able to go to a nice home a couple of miles away, high and dry. Everyone was helping everyone.

On Wednesday, Katrina made it as far as Lakewood church where she helped with processing all the things people were donating for those in need and to help with those who had found shelter there. I drove a long route around in order to take a new change of clothes to my wife. When I arrived in Kingwood, I found that our next task was to drive Mrs. Turner up to Dallas to her daughter's place. Maureen and I drove the long way around back home, packed our stuff for the trip, returned to Kingwood to pick up Mrs. Turner, and went on up to Dallas that evening.

I stayed in Dallas until Friday morning. On my way home I went by the house in Kingwood to check on our Suburban and to get my wife's things. The entire neighborhood had been flooded, three feet inside the homes. The Suburban was ruined; the insurance company totaled it, a second time. I was able to retrieve most of Maureen's things, but the loss inside the home was almost total. Most everything accumulated over many years was now yucky trash, from the up-flow that had come through the toilets.

Maureen remained a number of days in Dallas to help Mrs. Turner settle into a nursing home before returning. That meant that she had no more work, and we had no more income at this point. The park where Katrina worked was entirely inundated including the main building. Her work would now include restoring the park once again. Kyle's new teaching job was postponed for a few days.

James had wanted to come down for a week or so before he returned to his senior year at the Upsala school. He flew down soon after Harvey. Because Maureen had no more work obligation, we drove James back up to Canada, leaving on September 11th.

Johanna and Matthew were now living in the manufactured home on their own space part way between the South Farm and the North Farm. We spent a few days with them. Johanna had filled her flower beds with all sorts of herbs and flowers. Things grow fast and big in the short and wet summers of the North.

We were there over the weekend of the 17th, and so for the Sunday service in the community. While we were there, I wrote the chapter "Believers Together as Incense" in *Symmorphy IV: Covenant*. This was an incredible chapter, and, in fact, a life-changing experience. I was still feeling, however, that sense of "move condemnation" coming against me in the heavens all around through our time there.

We spent an evening with Steve and Cindy Schneider in their home, where James was staying again through his second year at Upsala. After supper, we gathered in their living room and sang praises. Steve is a praise leader. It was a beautiful anointing, but then we sang a song that had once been life to me but now ripped me all to pieces.

I shared this song in the chapter "The Image of God," calling it a song of rebellion. It was the song "Let me enter in." How can one sing for forty years,

"Let me enter in" and for forty years refuse to do such a thing, ever, even with the Way wide and freely open? For actually living inside the Holiest was considered in that fellowship to be deception.

I thought that I might share in the Sunday service, but then I learned that a traveling ministry, one of whom I had never heard, which is strange, would be ministering that Sunday. I really did not want to attend and shared with Matthew and Johanna that we might take a drive Sunday morning. To be honest with you, I was fully fed up with "movism."

Matthew, however, would not hear of it. He sat me down and proceeded to "correct" me in the way I had once known in move culture, that, if I did not go, I would be "missing" God; that is, *perform outwardly to prove you're "in the Spirit."* I meekly submitted and agreed to go. That Sunday morning, however, I wrote the following in the *Christ Our Life* letter, which went out early that morning.

~ I am finding myself in a very difficult place today, not at all outwardly, but entirely inwardly. I am caught in the intense travail of God for His church. I would ask, especially those of you who open this email early on today, that you would place yourself before the Almighty upon the mercy seat of your heart and extend, together with your Father, a bubble of our Holy Spirit for me to walk in as I have never known. And more than that, that the aroma of the gentle blessing of Christ would go forth from me to all in spite of all my personal inhibitions. ~

It turned out that the brother shared a really good word, on entering the Holiest, actually. He was almost there, almost taking the fellowship through the Veil, but not quite, and thus, not at all.

Maureen and I spent a couple of days with Glenn and Kim on our way and then drove across to Atwood, Kansas for another visit with Bill Horton, picking up a whole string of new counties on the way.

We spent two nights, again, in the bedroom that Mrs. Horton usually used, while she and Bill went down to stay in their former home that had not yet sold. We had a wonderful time fellowshipping together. Maureen and Mrs. Horton got on really well. Maureen just naturally brings peace into people's lives.

While I was visiting with Bill, I became very direct with him. "Bill," I said, looking him straight in the face. "When I was here last, I asked you about your commitment to join with me in Christian community whenever the opportunity arises. Is that true? Is that your continued commitment?"

Bill answered me, "Yes, Daniel, it is."

I said, "Good. I don't want to just assume."

For me, and in my life experience in the move, such a word given was certain and true.

On our way back to Houston, Maureen and I learned that Katrina and Kyle had taken in a couple as refugees from the Harvey flooding, Jazz and Clarissa. Clarissa had been a good friend with Katrina during their high school years. They had been living with Clarissa's mom in a single-wide trailer not far from our home. The trailer had been destroyed by the floodwaters, and they were now on their own. Neither of them worked, nor did they really have the ability to hold down a job.

We gave Jazz and Clarissa our spare bedroom and they stayed with us for a year. Kyle helped Jazz get his driver's license, and we slowly prepared him to get and keep a job. At the end of a year, they were able to maintain their own living, and so they moved on. Jazz and Clarissa were always very polite and careful not to intrude. At no point were we troubled by their time with us. Clarissa did attend Lakewood with us and then with Katrina a few times, but Jazz expressed no interest in the Lord. I pray that their time with us will bear fruit in the end.

Give Me a Place to Stand

As I was writing the three chapters in *Covenant* "Believers Together as...," the thought came to me that I could use one of my favorite books, *Patterns of Home: The Ten Essentials of Enduring Design* by Max Jacobson, Murray Silverstein, and Barbara Winslow (2005) as a means of understanding and talking about Christian Community. This was in September, just before we took James back up to Upsala. The joy of this comparison between the patterns of home and Christ Community began to shape how I would write *Symmorphy V: Life,* the most important book to me of my writing career.

Through this fall I completed the chapters of *Symmorphy IV: Covenant* and prepared *Symmorphy III: Kingdom* for printing. *Covenant* was almost finished and *Kingdom* published by the end of November. I was now ready to start *Symmorphy V: Life,* the first chapter of which went out on December 3rd.

On November 12, I sent out a letter titled "Give Me a Place to Stand." I used Archimedes' statement concerning a lever, "Give me a place to stand, and I can move the world." I must explain my purpose at that time in order to set the stage for the great transformation coming to me in the final chapter of this text, "All That I Am."

~~~ I know that the word I share comes from God and the Bible, and that it is the true word of the revelation of Jesus Christ in these final years of this age. Having nearly completed this account, I know the calling of God upon me. Yet I am read by only a handful of people, no more than 40 to 50 at any one time and only a couple of dozen have been engaged with this word I share over several years. How can what I share be of God when only a very few people are receiving it? This contention has been a big deal to me.

My limitation, of course, is Asperger's. Yet my life experience has shown me that when I have walked with another who was anointed in the things I lack, I also could function in the full expression of my abilities. For that reason, I sought for those whom God would join with me to do what I cannot do. This is God's way, that we would need one another. ~~~

I had embraced Solomon's metaphor from the first letter I sent out, **"Cast your bread upon the waters and it will return to you."** And so I wrote in the long-held expectation that the word I share would bring a real community life back to me, a community of people walking together in this wondrous word of Christ our life.

The events of this summer of 2017 had worked together in my thinking into a hope that wasn't from the Lord. I had always liked the Meadowlands area and have looked to the Lord for any indication that we should move there, though none has ever come. I had talked with Mark Alesch about renting a place from them. I imagined that I could live there with James, that Bill and his mother could come and join us, and that we could prepare a place for Maureen to move up as soon as possible.

I really wanted to do this, but I also felt a witness from God against it. By the time I wrote "Give Me a Place to Stand," I had finally given in and accepted that my fantasy was not what God was doing. Yet in this letter, I was searching, somehow, for that context out from which the Word I carry could flow out to many inside the anointing of God.

Here is a bit of what I shared.

⌇

I began this last journey in a sense of knowing the sending of God upon me in a way that I had not known up until now. And finishing this journey through *Covenant* has given me what I did not possess until now. Confidence.

You see, as an Asperger's man, I deplore all fakery and pretending. To consider myself as having been "sent by God" with a word to His Church has never been inside my presentation. I am not given to religious excitement, though I know Spirit deeply. I walked away in tears and loss from everything I had devoted my life to in its entirety because I could not pretend to be something I am not. I require REAL.

...I have inside of me a word given to me by God planted all through the pathways of my heart through many years and inside of deep travail. This word is not for me, but for God's precious people. And as I have completed *Symmorphy IV: Covenant*, God has given me four specific things.

[Those four are (1) a deeper knowing of the Covenant binding God and me together, (2) a new vision of the completed Church as Community (3) readers who are becoming convinced of Church as Community, and (4) ANGER – that we have been robbed of God's meaning of Salvation – Christ Community.]

⌇

I then set out a variety of possibilities for how a Christian Community could begin for us, a place that would include Christ Revealed Bible Institute, a school focusing on the study of Symmorphy. I believed that the provision of such a place would give me the "lever" that would enable the word I share to reach many.

I asked my readers to ask God how they could be part of such a beginning of Christ Community.

As I was finishing this letter, and before I sent it out on November 12, I heard God speak to me. ~ "You provide for them." ~

Well, this was just like God telling me, ~ "Give My people hope." ~ First, I had nothing to give, other than the Word I share. "Provide" meant, to me, the same as **"And they shall nourish her there,"** that is, all provision needed, physical and spiritual, in the time of great need. But this was also the second

time, now, that God has told me to do something, something I have no ability in myself to do.

This was the last time God spoke in this way to me, as of now. Yet I have pondered God's meaning for ~ "You provide for them," ~ and wait upon Him for its fulfillment.

Working on CRBI
In November of 2017, I completed the introductory course for Christ Revealed Bible Institute, "Living in Union with Christ." I chose three texts for the student to study – *The Rest of the Gospel* by Dan Stone, my reduced version of *Hearts of Flesh* by Fred Pruitt, and *The Hyper-Grace Gospel* by Paul Ellis. Dan Stone presented the best introduction to union with Christ in the first half of his book, but when he covered practical living in the second half, he knew nothing of Christ living as us. I used only the first half and then took the student on into Fred Pruitt for the practical living aspects of union with Christ, followed by critical questions and arguments concerning Paul's "excessive" grace with Paul Ellis.

In January and February of 2018, I finalized the Hermeneutics course for CRBI. The three texts for that course were – *Knowing Scripture* by RC Sproul, my own *Knowing God by Scripture* and then my *The Ten Most Important verses of the Bible*. I continued into the third course, Journey to Know the Lord, but did not complete it.

A Trip to New York
Another brother named Pete Douglas, from the New York City area, had also sent me a few emails over the prior couple of years. Pete Douglas and Bill Horton had been long-distance friends for a few years now, though they had never met face to face. I learned from Bill that they conversed regularly on the phone, reading my letters or listening together to the audios. This was quite astonishing to me. They had been introduced to my writing by another brother in the ultimate reconciliation circles who had signed up for my letter through Gary Sigler's "Kingdom Resources" page early on.

I had communicated with Pete about coming to New York to spend a few days fellowshipping in his home. Pete bought my plane tickets, and I flew to New York City on Tuesday, November 28 with a return set for Friday, December 1. I was already writing the first chapters of *Symmorphy V: Life*, and so this trip added things into that text.

Before I left for New York, however, I wrote part of "Gethsemane," my last chapter in *Covenant*. In Lesson 28.3 "I in You," I wrote of signing our fifth signature upon the Covenant, that is, our willingness to be as Jesus towards His Church. I wrote this, ""'Yes, Lord. I will be as You towards our Church, towards all who call upon You in some way. I love our people; I lay down my life for them. I go to Church." When I read this into audio, I knew another level of being sealed into God. I did not know that I was about to enter another nine months of travail in the crucible of the Word.

Sadly, I came down with a bad cold before my flight, but I wanted to go and the tickets were bought, so I went anyhow. I had not been to this part of the country before and so my eyes were glued to the window as we flew past the coast of New Jersey and into John F. Kennedy airport. This was my first sight of New York City from above, and to me it was a vast sprawling mess. You get the impression from movies that Manhattan is its own place, but in reality, it's just one tall "hill" of buildings surrounded by many other similar "hills" of buildings in every direction.

Pete picked me up at the airport, in fact, that was his job, driving people to and from that airport. Pete is a gentle soft-spoken man, around my older brother and sister's age. He shared with me that he had attended Woodstock in his youth, though only briefly. I had been in grade school at the time. Pete's wife was on a trip to Florida at this time, and so we had the house to ourselves.

Pete and his wife live in a nice two-story split-level house on the down slope to Glen Cove on the north shore of Long Island, just beyond New York City proper. From Tuesday evening to Friday morning we shared the deepest fellowship together inside the present Word.

Pete shared with me his and Bill's story. A couple of years earlier, having been introduced to my writing through a mutual friend, Bill had started calling Pete to visit on the phone. Bill is not a reader, but Pete is, and so Bill had wanted Pete to read the chapters of my book, *The Feast of Tabernacles*, over the phone. Pete was suspicious of me and what I wrote, but finally agreed, thinking that it would be good to see how I was wrong. Instead, it went the other direction as they read, and Pete has been a faithful reader and supporter from then until now.

This visit with Pete was so important to me and I value it very much. On Thursday, he drove me around, "collecting counties." We drove up through the Bronx and even into Connecticut just a bit, then back across Westchester county to the Hudson and thus down into Manhattan. We came down the upper west side and then along Central Park. I loved recognizing the Plaza from "Eloise" and the tall building where Stuart Little was carried by the hawk. (I always enjoyed the shows we watched with our children.) We went on down into southern Manhattan and drove a ways down Wall Street. Here the skyscrapers were so close together that we were in what seemed a dark and narrow canyon. We also drove east from Pete's home just a bit, and thus I got all the counties of Long Island. The roads all the way around are winding and convoluted. I must confess that I like Houston and not New York City.

I continued with the bad cold the whole time I was there. Sadly, I learned later that Pete also came down with the same thing after I had left. My trip back home on Friday was the most difficult one I have made. I needed to cough, but dared not, and the pain in my ears through the long descent into Houston was overwhelming. But by the grace of God, I made it home, the difficulty passed, and only the memory of the goodness of God in my time with Pete remains.

The Word Becomes Fire

The nine months from December 2017 through August 2018 are a most critical period of my life. Yet it is only now that what had been "random events" for me have coalesced into my present knowing of God's purpose in my life, His sending of me. My mission from God, found inside my own desperate need, is to separate fully the tree of life from the tree of knowing good and evil all through the Bible and all through Church history and Christian thinking, to set forth the gospel according to the serpent as distinct from the gospel according to Paul and confirmed by John, with no mixture between them.

This was the calling I had embraced when I was 21 years old, to have that pure Word from God for God's people in their hour of greatest need. Yet there is also a second purpose that must come out from this first, and that is to call the Bride into her place as the revelation of Jesus Christ. This second purpose will come in its time.

Every meaningful event inside of these nine months is of importance. For this reason, I want to lay out as carefully as I can this travail again through which God took me, with His WORD burning as fire inside my bones.

In my visit with Pete in New York, I read Preston Eby's recent writing about the harlot of Revelation 17 and 18. Eby was seeing the prostitute church, all those fleshy Christians out there with all their religious nonsense, through the same eyes by which Adam looked upon a wanton and filthy Eve. And then Eby reached for the exact same arrogant Christ as his answer to her that Adam reached for in the garden – contempt and control. I do not mean to speak against Preston Eby, for his overall teaching is of great importance; I speak rather of the inability of all Christian ministries to see Christ in His Church.

Then, likely this December, I received a letter from Joe McCord, a leading ministry in the move and one who had always had an encouraging and positive impact in my life. More than once Jessica, Maureen's sister, had informed me that Brother Joe had quoted from one of my books in the service and had shared his word out from what I had written. I had sent him a few of my books, including *Symmorphy I: Purpose* in response to that initial encouragement.

Brother Joe was very encouraging in his letter to me. Of all the ministries in the move, I think that he had retained the deepest hope in the word Sam Fife had first preached, the Life part of Sam Fife's teaching. His words indicated to me that he was seeing that same hope of LIFE in the things I was writing. He also warned that there would likely be some opposition from other ministries in the move. This letter from Brother Joe was as a quiet seal upon my heart and upon that commitment I had made to God concerning His Church when I was 21 and the same commitment again, as I completed *Symmorphy IV: Covenant*.

Let's Start Again

As I shared, I was writing the first several chapters of *Symmorphy V: Life* through this time, December and January. This text, a manual for Christian Community, is the most important book to me that I have written. I had waited long for the right context to set forth my love for Christian Community and the vision of Church Life God had made me to know. Drawing from all my experience in Chris-

tian Community, all the good and all the not-good, drawing from all my pondering over many years, and weaving it together inside the present word of union with Christ, this was just so important to me. I wanted, with all my heart, to get it right.

More than that, while I was writing *Symmorphy IV: Covenant*, the realization came that I could use one of my favorite books, *Patterns of Home*, as the organizational pattern for this text on Christian Community, and that the ten "patterns of home" presented in that book would correspond directly with the ten ruling verses of the Bible.

You can understand, then, the overwhelming distress growing in me through these months to January 21, 2018, when I sent out Chapter 7 "Protecting the Heart." I was in distress because I was NOT getting it right. The deep cry of my heart for this text to represent my LIFE was not happening. Let me explain why.

Ed Carter continued to call me to visit around once a week. Normally, this fellowship was greatly encouraging to me. Ed was very talkative, and, though he received what I shared, he was also willing to insert his own views into the conversation.

The difficulty began in November when I shared with him what God had spoken to me, ~ "You provide for them. ~ Ed's response was, "That's not union with Christ." That made no sense to me, but I do not respond to such criticism, and so it passed. However, when I began sending out the chapters on Christian Community, the opposition continued and grew. As time went on, I talked less and less and Ed talked more and more. In my frustration, I did what I always do when I cannot express myself in conversation, I wrote my answers inside the flow of the next chapter I was writing. For this reason, Chapters 2-7 of *Symmorphy V: Life* were only half what was from my heart and the other half was argument in response to Ed's opposition to the whole concept of community.

Then, sometime in the third week of January, his conversation became controlling and even accusatory, that I was "losing readers" because of my, apparently, false teaching. I did not respond, but that was it for me. When I give answer to God, shall I say that I did not share what He had put in my heart? I cannot give such an answer, and so I cannot allow such control seeking to turn what I share back into darkness.

The result was that on January 28, I sent out a fiery letter of great strength and vulnerability titled "Why I Write Life Together." Yes, people were unsubscribing, but they belong to Jesus, not me, and He is very good at His job.

Here is some of what I wrote.

⮌

Why do I write? I do not write for you. I do not write for God. I write for me.

I have carried a knowing inside of me, in the depths of my heart, a knowing that I sensed on occasion through my childhood years, a knowing that became a regular part of my life from the age of 21 on. I did not know what that knowing was, nor could I possibly believe it meant something. Yet it was a constant experience that those things that arose in my own mind and heart, out from that knowing, were also the next things preached on by the apostolic ministry in the fellowship of which I was a part. This ongoing experience over many years only increased my agony, because I could not believe in myself and I had no ability to share out from that knowing.

For all those years, until I started writing these *Christ Our Life* letters, that knowing, though insistent, was voiceless.

I write for one reason only. I write to articulate, to somehow "give voice to what's in my heart." And I continue writing because the expression of that once voiceless knowing is not finished. I must know, I am driven to know, the knowing that has travailed in me in unheard cries of agony over so many years, the agony of travail for something that is NOT.

The reason, then, why I send out what I write, making it as available as I can, is the so-far unrequited hope that this great need inside of me, this overwhelming cry, would be fulfilled in my being part of a family of people walking together, loving one another with a pure heart fervently, knowing the same knowing I know and must know, Christ among us in all our interaction together.

As I said, there are three levels of my response to any rejection of my feeble attempts to articulate what I must, to put this knowing that agonizes inside of me out there where I can see it. The outer response is normal, the desire to "prove myself right and them wrong." ... I rarely, if ever, act on those feelings.

I sure wanted to do that recently [referring to the difficult phone conversation with Ed Carter], but then I listened to recent lessons and heard myself teaching myself to lay my life down, to see Christ alone, to bless and not curse. I want the blessing of Jesus through me far more than I want to be right.

But you see, ...the deepest response, the rule of all my going forward. Here is that bottom line, my base response towards any disagreement with my attempts to articulate this burning knowing, a cry for something that does not yet exist, a knowing I must express or die. — I DON'T CARE!

I do NOT write for you. I do NOT write for God. (Such a thing is nothing but religious pretension, manipulating others to exalt self.) I write for me.

Now, I have come to terms with my complete failure to please God or to do what He says, and I rest inside of Jesus inside of such staggering inability. And I have come to terms with my complete failure in the church and in the world, my inability, even to provide for my family, no matter how humiliating such failure continues to be.

But if I were to fail to articulate this agony of knowing inside my heart, then I would be a true failure. I will have failed myself. Such a thought never enters my mind.

And the center of that knowing, its beginning and its end, is that Christ life IS life together. And the birthing of life together has been my only purpose from the first letter I sent out.

[I then give the setting for this word I required of God when I was 22.] I WILL KNOW You, on this earth and in this life – AND – I WIILL KNOW a people who KNOW You. That people is my Jerusalem.

And I will call her into her place, and no one will prevent me. And I will build that wall of protection inside of which the entire Church of Christ across this earth can dwell, and no one will draw me away in order to discuss what is "the truth."

Yet *Symmorphy V: Life* is the most important articulation for me of that knowing I must KNOW. And thus I apologize – to myself – for allowing *"truth, truth, whose got the truth"* to confuse me. Yet all things are Father and me sharing together as one. And thus I see Father, and I see me, and I see that my present approach to *Symmorphy V: Life* does not satisfy us.

When I complete *Symmorphy V: Life*, I must have, before my eyes, a complete and full articulation of that agony of KNOWING that I must express. Such a MUST is greater to me than life or breath. For that reason, I cannot blunder forward, hoping things will come together. Neither can I leave anything remaining that showed up out of distraction.

...In short, I am writing this present series to those who are ready, right now, to join with me in a tangible and intentional Community of Christ on a shared property, ready as the spontaneous arising of Christ as them causes the outward reality to appear. And thus I am writing the specifics of life together to those who are committed to such a way of living.

⌣

I took no more calls from Ed. I am open to any correction of me, but I am closed to any attempt to control that word that flows out from a life lived inside the fear of God. I know my refusal to answer his calls made Ed angry. He did continue to read my letters for a few more months and later asked me a couple of technical questions in an email. I replied with kindness, hoping that he would ask forgiveness for his disrespect. Sadly to me, he eventually unsubscribed, "Please forgive me, I was wrong," seemed to be outside of his present choices.

"Lord Jesus, I bless Ed with all joy. I know that You carry him all the way through the darkness and into life. And I know that Your love towards me is shed abroad in Ed's heart. I am humbled by his love for me."

I still wanted *Symmorphy V: Life* to be everything I must have it to be, and so I started again, rewriting Chapters 2-7. I kept about half, weaving it together with the present flow of the Spirit. Indeed, I think that Chapters 2-5 of that text are among the most anointed and wondrous things I have ever written.

Now, as I wrote this text, using the ten patterns of home to illustrate how the ten ruling verses would shape Christian Community as I envision it must be, I had not really looked closely at the definitions of each pattern to see if that pattern would actually fit with its corresponding ruling verse, I just assumed, by the sense of the Spirit in me, that it would.

You can imagine, then, just how astonished I was, every single time, at how the specific details of each pattern of home opened to us each next ruling verse and placed that verse into life together as

the Church. It was as if I was seeing these verses for real for the first time. In the end, *Symmorphy V: Life* became everything I had hoped it would be, to full measure. I am so grateful to God that He enabled me to express the deepest meanings of my heart and life.

Bill Horton had called me occasionally prior to this difficult experience with Ed. I could also visit easily with Bill over the phone, something that is not typical for me. Without any knowledge of my circumstances, soon after my disconnection from Ed, Bill began to call me to fellowship together even more frequently, up to a couple of times a week. These times of fellowshipping with Bill were important to me and gave me much strength and encouragement.

Jesus and Asperger's

Maureen had obtained work caring for another lady by the name of Carol Hammack soon after we returned after Harvey. She also had similar shorter-term clients for awhile. Because Maureen is compassionate and of utmost trustworthiness, she is in high demand. This next care job was much easier for Maureen than some before. This lady was mildly forgetful, but could take care of her own needs if she was pointed in the right direction. Maureen has worked for Carol from then until now.

During the spring of 2018 I continued to drive with Uber. I had not driven in the fall, but started again around the turn of the year. I mostly enjoyed driving people around and had a number of good experiences. I want to share two experiences that were a bit difficult. I had dropped a lady off in downtown Houston, but had forgotten to sign off on the app, thus adding a mile or so more to her trip. I was flustered from this mistake when I picked up the next person, also in downtown Houston such that when I dropped her off, I almost drove off with her luggage in my trunk. By this time I was so overwhelmed with my mistakes that, as I drove to the Heights to pick up the next rider, I could not bear the thought of more mistakes.

In my overwhelming autistic distress, I placed the Lord Jesus as sharing all with me. That helped, but not really. Then I heard the Lord speaking to me, not as a voice, but in the knowing of my mind, "Daniel, please forgive Me for the mistake I allowed us to endure."

"Oh, yes, Lord," I said, "I forgive You with all joy." Immediately all the agony was gone, and I continued in the joy of the Lord.

The final straw for me, however, was a young Muslim lady whom I drove to the Bush airport. She was late and dared not miss her flight to the Middle East. But then I missed the gate to which she was going and had to drive all the way around, putting her in jeopardy of missing her flight. I went into the right place the second time and quickly came to a stop, dropping her off in heavy traffic. She rushed into the building, and I drove on down, only to discover that her airline was at the far end. I could have driven her there if I had known, but now she would have had to run a long ways down with her luggage. I don't know, but she most likely missed her flight.

Making such a mistake that hurt someone else was just too much for me, and it was my last day driving Uber.

During these months, I wondered if I could obtain a disability income from Social Security due to my inability to maintain a full-time job. I did not research it as much as I should have, for I found out later that if I receive any donations, then, no, I am not eligible, end of story.

Not knowing that, I made an appointment with Dr. Katherine Loveland, professor of Autism Research at the University of Houston. During my time with her, which cost three hundred dollars, she agreed that I was likely Asperger's. I explained that I needed a clinical diagnosis of Asperger's in order to apply to Social Security for disability. She signed me up for a complete evaluation that would cost another $1300 and assured me that she would fill out the forms I needed.

Maureen accompanied me because she also would fill out some questionnaires. I sat with Dr. Loveland and her graduate student assistant as they asked me a series of questions. I was asked what things made me angry. "Being lied to" was my reply. I shared about being scammed and how distressing that was. Then I filled out some long forms. I was alarmed because none of this was scientific or clinical. Over and over, in print and from them, I was asked if I ever thought about committing suicide, to which I replied always in the negative.

When it was finished, I asked the assistant if Dr. Loveland could sign the disability form I had

brought with me. The reply came back that, no, this was not an actual clinical evaluation and Dr. Loveland was not qualified to sign such a form.

The truth is – I was scammed again, and we had another $1600 debt to pay off. Later I received their full report in the mail. It was nothing more than a repeat back to me of everything I had said and of my every response on the forms. Reading all that conveyed a definition of myself as dark and mentally unstable. If I did not walk in the joy of the Lord, I might well have considered "suicide" after I finished reading this "account" of myself.

From then until now I say this. Only those who are Asperger's can write about Asperger's, those who claim knowledge otherwise are just making it up, even contrary to any scientific approach. It's called a scam. And indeed all stories told in this world that do not include the Lord Jesus from beginning to end are also a scam.

But it was a far greater scam, dark and wicked, that made this spring, and April in particular, a time of ANGER.

A Time of Anger

On April 1, Maureen and Katrina planned to go to the Lakewood service. I decided to accompany them. This would be my final time there, and in fact, we sat near where we had sat our first time, up on the south side, looking down.

This Sunday, it was John Gray who would preach. The praise was wonderful, as usual. Then John Gray got up and had us turn to 1 John 4 where he read, **"As He is, so are we in this world."** My initial thought was, "Great, he's going to bring union with Christ into the picture."

What actually happened, however, was that the next twenty-five minutes were the most painful of my life. I tried to hide in disassociation, but I could not. All I could do was bear the intense agony without moving.

John Gray did not preach union with Christ. Rather, he began with the serpent's first words, the assumption that what God says CANNOT be true, unless we make it true by "getting it right." Thousands of good Christian people, all who knew the Lord in the power of the Spirit, were with John Gray in their minds. And well they should have been. He was anointed of God, and I have personally received good words spoken to me by my Father through his preaching. He was "clothed in white," so to speak, yet a serpent was in his mouth that morning.

He began by saying (in so many words), "You SHOULD BE like Jesus – BUT – you, so clearly, are not."

Then, after establishing that God lies, he alternated between three concepts. The first was the image of the super-Christ, a "Jesus" of miracles and outward virtue, far above these fleshy Christians. The second was a condemnation of these thousands of fleshy Christians before him for not measuring up to such an "image of God." And the third was a mighty exhortation that, if they "loved Jesus," they would now pretend with all their might to be like that fake image.

I spent that time in complete horror; I could not escape. I felt as if I was reliving the garden scene all over again. I saw the face of the congregation, thousands of wonderful Christian people, as the face of Eve, imagining that these false words were the very words of God.

Needless to say, God used this experience in my life to penetrate deep into my NEED to set forth a massive distinction, from the Bible, between a gospel of death and a gospel of life.

In order to really KNOW, for myself, what God actually says in His Bible, I had begun my own whack at translating the New Testament, probably in February, which I have called The Jesus Secret Version. My primary resource for this task was www.bible-hub.com, which based its layout on *Strong's Concordance,* which is reasonably reliable.

I did Galatians first and Ephesians for the redo of "Creating Rooms," and sent the rough draft of Ephesians to my readers on March 17. Then, in order to tackle a full understanding of Hebrews 10:19-22, a very difficult verse in its wording, I did the rough draft translation of the second half of Hebrews through the month of April, which I sent to my readers on May 5.

It was in translating the second half of Hebrews that I became very angry, and my anger is right and just, for we have been lied to in the very words of the gospel we thought was trustworthy. The Calvinist translators deliberately altered the wording of this part of Hebrews in order to force God into Calvinist theology, more than any other portion of Scripture, though they have done this same wick-ed practice here and there throughout much of the New Testament, primarily to hide from the reader a Jesus here and now, thus driving Jesus and salvation far away into the delusions of "someday." This is not what the Bible says.

I explain my argument more fully in the introduction to *The Jesus Secret II*, rather than continue here, and will do so even more when I write the introduction to the Jesus Secret version.

The last week of April, I wrote "Parts in Proportion" in *Symmorphy V: Life*. That pattern of home gave me the answer to years of living in community feeling always that something was "out of whack," that something was not quite right. Christ our life is the proportion that was missing.

I did not complete *Symmorphy V: Life* until August of 2018, but this realization concerning Scripture, in it's "white heat," brought a huge change in my need to know God and His gospel.

Katrina and James's Graduations

Katrina graduated from college with a two-year degree in May of 2018. At this point she was working full time at the Jesse Jones Park, continuing to be involved with Texas historical re-enactments.

James was graduating from high school that June, and so we all planned another trip up to Upsala. Everyone else flew, and again I drove, this time having borrowed Kyle's newly-bought small Nissan SUV. I would be bringing James and all his stuff back home.

I drove straight up to Upsala this time. Everyone else was there when I arrived, including Claude and Lois, as well as Matthew, Jessica, and Breanna Sanchez.

James had again gone through a rough patch in his return to the Upsala school, but he had worked through that with Brother Steve, and the Lord had revealed Himself to James in the services. James experienced a change of heart and the remainder of his senior year had gone much better. James is a doer, and not an academic, so he was glad to be out of this time-period of his life.

James graduated on June 9, a Saturday, in the same community hall where Johanna had graduated. It was a good celebration. James gained much from this experience including a lot of practical wilderness skills.

While I was sitting in the graduation service, God gave me a new way of seeing. I saw a precious people who were lost in a theology that teaches them that they are on their own, far away from God, that Jesus does not carry them. They draw as near to the Holiest as they can while never entering in. And I could see in their words and upon their faces that they were frightened deep down inside, just as I had once been.

Yet I also saw Jesus as He is inside of them, value and wealth beyond measure. And in that seeing, I knew the heart of the Shepherd over His people. Jesus carries all regardless, all the way through death and into life.

After the graduation, all of our family went to Sleeping Giant provincial park on a peninsula jutting into Lake Superior just to the east of Thunder Bay. We had rented two sleeping units, travel trailers. We spent two nights there and had a great time together.

Maureen returned to Upsala with Matthew and Johanna for the next couple of weeks and was with Johanna when our first grandson was born, Gabriel Emerson Schneider, on July 1, 2018. She flew back to Houston on July 10.

James and I headed on down the road to Glenn and Kim's place in Minnesota. We spent two days visiting with them before heading out on a third route across to Atwood, Kansas. This practice of visiting Bill Horton was reaping me lots and lots of counties.

We spent two days with Bill. He and James got along really well, and James did some skateboarding on the slopes of Atwood. They had sold their other place at this point, and thus I stayed on a cot in the living room. I don't remember where James and Bill slept. As usual on these trips, I found a special anointing to write early in the morning. I wrote much of Chapter 23 "The Proof of Christ" the first morning at Bill's.

An acquaintance of Bill's in Atwood, Shelia Maune, came over in the afternoon. Bill had signed her up for the Bible Institute program and she was interested in hearing more of what I share. The problem came through lunch. Bill is a natural health person and he was fully aware of my dietary needs. Nonetheless, something I ate that lunch was filled with chemicals; it may have been soybean oil on the asparagus, which he had gotten from some-

one else. It completely wiped me out mentally. As a result, I could not find a focus in the sharing that afternoon and seemed to just ramble on and on. It all felt confusing to me.

James and I drove on from Atwood to Colorado Springs, where we spent a night with Kyle's friend, Will Fonder, who was teaching school there. The next day we drove up to the top of Pikes Peak with Will. They have you park at around ten thousand feet and then bus you the rest of the way – to 14000 feet. I should have stayed at the car park. I was short of oxygen at the top and did not do well until we came back down.

James and I got an Airbnb that night in the midst of the Colorado Rockies, which turned out to be not the best of my Airbnb choices. The next morning we spent a couple of hours at the Royal Gorge of the Arkansas River, over which goes the highest-up bridge in America. This was a great place to see. We drove on to spend the night at the Lubbock Community, in their guest house. The Sanchez's had also taken a family trip, but were back home, now, after James's graduation. We were late getting there because I had to take the long route to get my last two counties in New Mexico, making it the third state to have in the bag. We returned home to Houston the next day.

Clarity and Focus

The discovery of how badly the words that should have been God's words were altered in our Bibles, just as Jesus warned us would happen, set me on a clear and driven path to KNOW how and why and where, and thus to KNOW our glorious Salvation as it really is, as God actually says.

It was a remarkable thing to me how well the ten patterns of home fit the ten ruling verses of the Bible and enabled a much deeper understanding of God's meaning. As I was working my way through those chapters, I pondered the question of the "rules of thinking" that had taken the place of these gospel verses in Christianity.

I now see how important was that brief but horrifying time listening to John Gray speak the entirety of the serpent's lines in Genesis 3:1-5, all garbed in Christian talk and with a captive congregation, as Eve, believing that this preacher was sent by God, followed just after by discovering how the Calvinist translators had altered the wondrous truth of living inside of God with our **hearts sprinkled from an**

evil consciousness to the *"great struggle against sin"* that is, the wickedness of the tree of knowing good and evil, that is, the refusal of Christ Jesus and life.

This powerful set of experiences in April caused me to understand that only one "verse" had taken the place of ten to rule in the minds of all – Genesis 3:1-5. And thus I completed *Symmorphy V: Life* with a chapter, written in July, in which I set out the opposing rules of thinking between knowing God through Jesus as life versus knowing God through the serpent as good and evil.

I had waited to finish my final chapter of *Symmorphy IV: Covenant* until this same time because I needed to know all that God had taught me through writing that course. I had that text completed by the end of July, with the print copy available by the end of August.

I finished writing *Symmorphy V: Life* by August 12. I was fully satisfied that this text had accomplished all the cry of my heart to speak over forty years of life and that *Symmorphy IV: Covenant* had

given me a knowledge of God as my Father as I had never known before.

At this point God had given me two wondrous things. First, He had given me a methodical understanding of Paul's gospel confirmed by John. And second, He had given me a methodical layout of the serpent's perversion of that gospel, turning the entire Bible into the tree of the knowledge of good and evil and away from the tree of life.

Even though I had written the five *Symmorphy* texts in a college textbook format, I was still writing to learn up to their completion. And yes, I freely confess that, until the completion of the *Symmorphy* texts, I did not know the gospel with certainty; I wrote because I wanted to know.

But now, for the first time in my life, I had something to say.

The picture below is Dickens on the Strand, December 2018. Joining us now are Shelibie, in front of Kyle, Matthew, on the right, and Gabriel, in Johanna's arms.

51. Having Something to Say

August 2018 - December 2019

With our children now full adults, there was very little going on in our lives through this time, other than Maureen caring for Carol, and me writing each early morning. Nonetheless, my page limit still seems to fill up quickly.

After my visit with Peter Douglas in New York City, he also began sending me a regular monthly donation that has continued until now. At this point I was receiving around $1000 a month in total. This tremendous provision has made the difference in our financial situation. It has taken some weight off of Maureen and has allowed me to give myself freely to a new urgency of word. This money has always come as freely given, yet more than once, I have said to myself, "Yordy, you'd better get to work in return for all this." It has always been a positive incentive in the Lord.

Yet much more than that, I receive every gift as the impartation of a dear brother or sister into my life, a greater value than I can count. I am a wealthy man.

I must also bring back two individuals in the last chapter, Dr. Katherine Loveland and her graduate assistant. It is easy to brush by individuals such as these and not recognize contempt in one's attitude. This is why we give an account in the presence of God, so that we might place the Lord Jesus on everything.

"Father, I accept that Jesus has cleansed me from all contempt. and I forgive Dr. Loveland and her assistant. I place them into Jesus and bless them, that they might know You."

Sometime through these years I switched over to a Ketogenic diet, most of the time. Eliminating most starches in my diet and including lots of good fats has been the most helpful to me of all natural health attempts through the years. A Ketogenic diet is expensive and takes more work, and so I have not always stuck to it, but I soon feel worse when I don't.

The point is this, the more I hold to a Ketogenic diet the better my mind works and the more I can write. Part of this next time in my life is a massive increase in my writing output, often working on three and even four things at the same time. Yet this increase in writing ability has also been matched with an increase in the anointing and in the urgency in which I write.

For, you see, having completed the season of symmorphy and having passed through the nine months of travail in the crucible of the word, for the first time in my life and writing career, I have something to say.

Knowing Jesus As He Is

And having something to say, the first thing I would write is – *Knowing Jesus As He Is*.

I wrote the twelve chapters of this book from mid-August to mid-November, 2018 with very little interruption. In the final chapters of *Symmorphy V: Life*, I had laid out a series of "rules" from each of the ruling verses of the Bible. I reworked those rules into an orderly list and added a few essential things to round it out. Thus I came up with a list of "36 Rules for Christian Thinking." This list was now the content and organization for *Knowing Jesus as He Is*.

I wrote this little book intending to keep all negative out of it and to set forth only the truth of knowing Jesus in honesty and faith. I also set myself not to add anything "new," that is, no "writing to learn." Instead, I drew from across the span of the five *Symmorphy* texts those things that had become cemented into my certain knowing of – what the Bible says.

It is a big deal to me to say, "This is what God says; this is the gospel." You see, I've never heard anyone say that who was speaking the truth, who regarded what God actually says. And speaking dishonestly about the Bible and our Salvation is not something I dare to do. Such a place is a terrifying and solitary void.

Through this time I was also upgrading my websites to the full layout you now see at www.christrevealed.info. The man who owns the Composr content management system worked on my site personally, for very little cost, to make the full transfer from my old websites to the new. Nonetheless, I put in a lot of work as well, fixing all the bugs in the over two thousand pages in the new format.

Then, my computer of several years, which I had purchased with gifts from readers, finally cratered. I lost the hard drive, and then my backup hard drive got slightly damp and went out as well. I was left with all my work of many years – GONE! I spent a day holding my despair entirely into the Lord. I made an appointment with a technician who had helped me in the past, and it did not take him long to recover all the files from my hard drive. I was so grateful.

What I did, then, was build my own computer (again), using a motherboard my son gave me and buying a number of new parts. Although there was some interruption in sending out letters through this time, I was soon back on track. By the end of October, my website was fairly well finished.

I sent out the final chapter of *Knowing Jesus as He Is*, on November 14.

"Winter" into Spring Writing Season

Along with my list of "The Rules of Christian Thinking," I had also compiled a list of "The Rules of Serpent Thinking" through my completion of the *Symmorphy* texts. Thus I had fully in mind a second book to follow right after *Knowing Jesus As He Is*, which for awhile I titled "Let My People Go." Then I realized that the title was addressing the evil one rather than the firstfruits of Christ, and so I changed it to *Set My People Free*. I wanted this text to be as precise and methodical as Knowing Jesus.

When I attempted to write the first chapters of *Set My People Free*, however, I hit a wall. I was not able to write "what I know." I did not understand the serpent's gospel as clearly as I required.

I already had written letters that were not for these two books, and so I turned to what became a new series/book which I eventually titled *Designed by Word*. My primary purpose for this text became to "write to learn" all the things I needed to know clearly before I could write *Set My People Free* as teaching only.

I wrote *Designed by Word* very quickly, sending out only a few of the chapters in my weekly email, but posting the remainder on the website. I also saw that the several letters I had written just prior to starting *Symmorphy I: Purpose* fitted very well into this book, and so I included them with a bit of re-write.

By the end of December, I sent out the chapter "One Verse to Rule Them All." This was the first time I looked closely at the specific words of the serpent in Genesis 3:1-5 and what they actually meant in relation to the gospel of the revelation of Jesus Christ. Seeing the "gospel of the serpent" so clearly cemented in me a confidence I had not known before this moment. I now had what I needed to counter all the deceit of Nicene and Calvinist theology, and to counter those things out from what God actually says in the gospel.

Knowing Jesus As He Is was available in print copy on Amazon by the first of December. Bill Horton continued to call me on average twice a week for fellowship. He would have called me more often but I found that too many calls became overwhelming to me and so we settled on twice a week. Bill wanted to be involved in making *Knowing Jesus* available to many, and so he sent me the money to have many copies made for us to give away.

On December 2, I sent out a note with my letter asking if any reader would like to receive copies of *Knowing Jesus* in order to pass it around to people who might enjoy reading it. A number of readers responded, and so I sent several copies to each.

Bill also received a larger number of copies which he sent out to others. He sent one to Preston Eby and later received a favorable response from him.

As we worked through this process, however, I was pressed with the need for an introductory letter that would invite someone who loves Jesus to read my little book. And so I wrote the letter that now appears at the front of both *Knowing Jesus As He Is* and *Set My People Free*. It is also found as the only thing on my former website www.ourpath-home.com, which I made simply a landing page to send people to my now single and complete website www.christrevealed.info.

Writing this two-page letter was the most humbling thing I have ever written, for it required me to place myself beneath of any new reader in honor towards the love of God already shed abroad in their hearts towards me. This is the proper position of anyone whom God would send, on their knees in honor and regard towards the least little one who believes in Jesus.

This short letter was ready by the end of December, and thus it went out with the packages of books to be inserted into each. I soon resolved that problem by placing it into the pages of the book itself.

I sent out a number of copies to pastors, both in our area and some I found elsewhere in the United States. I just grabbed a few names at random. I also sent a copy to Johnny Brady, whose church we had attended when we first came to Houston. I never received back any replies and this whole daring enterprise became way too much for me very quickly. Promoting myself is not something I am comfortable doing.

Bill also sent copies to some people he had known in ultimate reconciliation circles including Phyliss Smith. Phyliss was from the Nashville area, but was living in Michigan at this time. Phyliss was deeply moved by the two-page letter that we had included with *Knowing Jesus* and soon began to communicate directly with me. She did not grasp the full meaning of the gospel as I share it right away, but she was drawn by the life and the honesty she found in what I write. I soon sent more of my books to Phyllis.

Another brother who received a copy of *Knowing Jesus* from Bill was Jerry Onyszczak, who lived just to the west of Nashville. Jerry also became excited about what he read and soon began to communicate with me. Eventually I sent him a package of a number of my books including all five Symmorphy texts.. Jerry had written a booklet titled "Total Victory of the Cross of Christ." He sent me a copy, and I found it very useful to me to insert in a yet-to-be-written course inside my Christ Revealed Bible Institute program.

I completed *Designed by Word* by the end of December and then prepared it for print form. I was now ready to begin *Set My People Free*. In fact, for the first time, this first week of January 2019, I had the right outline for that text.

I sent Chapter 1 "Prepare a Highway" of *Set My People Free* out on January 13. I included the following note in the introduction to that letter.

~~~ I am laughing with overflowing joy this morning, for Father and I have walked together through a rough patch for the sake of His people and coming out the other side, I found myself well able to finish the first chapter of *Set My People Free*. I had imagined that I was stuck; I am so glad that I was wrong.

Two new books are now available on Amazon. *Symmorphy V: Life* is simply the most extraordinary book I have ever read. I urge you to obtain a print copy for yourself so that you might have it when the power goes out. Then, *Designed by Word* is a great introduction to this more focused course. Through writing it, I finally understand the power of the evil one in the church of Christ. ~~~

Nonetheless, writing the careful chapters of *Set My People Free* was slow going. I needed another outlet for all the other things arising inside of me. On January 16, I sent out the letter titled "We Do Not Know," which then became the first chapter of a new book, *The River of Life*. My premise was that we do not know what a world of LIFE actually is, for we have never experienced such a thing.

From mid-January, then, until the end of May, I wrote back and forth between *Set My People Free* and *The River of Life*. Many chapters of *The River of Life* I posted only on the website and did not include in the weekly email. Whenever I stalled out in *Set My People Free*, I turned to *The River of Life*, inserting chapters that were the "writing to learn" I needed before I could carefully develop the "writing to teach" required by *Set My People Free*.

On February 17, I included a request in the introduction to my *Christ Our Life* letter for the readers to pray with me. Here is that prayer.

"Father, we ask together that you would release those brothers and sisters who have the gifts that are needed, those whose hearts are to join their gift with ours, so that this word of Christ our life, through Christ Revealed Bible Institute wherever and however it is to be, might be available to Your people across this earth. Father, we ask for this release in Jesus' name, that heaven and earth be loosed, and that Your provision would be poured out for the purpose of gathering many together to learn the Symmorphy Bible Studies program together.

"For that reason, Father, we together believe that we have received all that we ask. We know that these specific brothers and sisters are right now on their way, to join their gifts with mine, that we together might prepare a place for Your people."

⮜

I did not know it, but this was not what God is doing with me in the present season, though it certainly could be God for me in an upcoming time. I place this prayer here, however, as part of my positioning for a great change in focus that will come in 2021.

The middle chapters of *Set My People Free* were hard for me to write, including "One Ring to Rule Them All," and, most of all, "And in the Darkness Bind Them." This was the most terrible piece I have ever written, but at this point, the successful deceit of the evil one in the Church was now fully exposed.

In between these two difficult chapters, I wrote the chapter "I Saw a Scroll" in *The River of Life*. This would be the first of two "game-changers" for me in writing that text. In fact, this chapter, "I Saw a Scroll" was the beginning of the new direction into which God was turning me.

In essence, I now understood that the seals being removed by Jesus were NOT God's judgment against humans, but rather the "Christian" judgment against God and the gospel, and that the removal of the seals is, in effect, a deliverance service for all of God's people caught in the awfulness of Nicene theology. God was now moving towards the present ministry of intercession.

The first of April, after I had completed "And in the Darkness Bind Them," I wrote "How Will They Hear." In that letter, I began a practice in my writing that has grown until now, the inserting of a prayer into the text that we would pray together. Although my readers and I are scattered all across the earth, nonetheless, we are one together in the Spirit and our prayers are effective. Here is that first prayer.

"Father, we thank You that our minds are the servants of Christ, now our only life. We thank you that our minds are the mind of Christ and that as our minds serve the Lord Jesus, so we see and honor our shared life with Him. Father, we ask that You would anoint our minds specifically so that we would be able to see and pierce the darkness that remains in the minds of our beloved brothers and sisters in Christ on the one hand, yet on the other hand be fully free to direct our eyes and our mouth to see and to speak no-consciousness of sins, but

Christ alone concerning our brethren. We ask for this mighty grace, Father, by the authority You have given to us, the name of Jesus, and we believe with You that our precious Holy Spirit is fulfilling right now our shared desire in all power and might."

Then, in the next letter, the prayer began in this way.

"Father, You have placed all authority into our hands, yet You have reserved all power entirely to Yourself and to Your Spirit. For that reason, Father, we are confident that You synergeo with us and we with You in all things. You rely, Father, on our authority to prophesy Christ in full confidence, to call His knowledge forth in all who belong to you, and we rely on the power of Your Holy Spirit to accomplish all that You and we desire."

And it ends with these words.

"Father, we possess together all authority to love one another and to lay down our lives for Your Church. We stand absolutely together inside of that love, and we call forth the weak, the despised, the outcasts, the little ones of this earth, to know and to be the revelation of Your dear Son. And we declare this together in the name of our life and our hearts, the Lord Jesus, knowing that our precious Holy Spirit is accomplishing in power right now all that we speak."

This practice of including a prayer was only intermittent at first, but it definitely is the first step into our present ministry together.

I finished the final chapter of *Set My People Free* the last week of May and sent it out on June 1. I was fully satisfied that I had accomplished my purpose in this "having something to say" little book.

At the same time as I was completing *Set My People Free*, however, I wrote one of the most important chapters in my journey to know the Lord, "Setting Forth Our Souls" in *The River of Life*. Ever since I received a vision of God as the One who carries us in October of 2011, the little verse, 1 John 3:16, had entered into my writing and I could not keep it out, though I did not understand it, nor even like it. Over time, I had realized that an accurate translation would be "set forth our souls" rather than "lay down our lives." But I had no idea what that might mean.

Then, God took me again into Psalm 22, joining with David inside Jesus' soul upon the cross. Inside of the present clarity I possessed concerning the gospel, I understood, for the first time, how it was that Jesus joined us together with the Father inside the agony of His own human soul inside the darkness of the last hour on the cross. And I understood how we are to do the same for our fellow believers. – And we also.

The Summer of 2019

I had the print copy of *Set My People Free* ready by the end of June.

Meanwhile, we had hit a snag regarding the insuring of our house on Fernbank Drive. Things had deteriorated on the house over the years, and I did not have the strength inwardly or outwardly to make the necessary repairs. The insurance company informed us that they would no longer insure our house unless those repairs were made.

James was working on various construction and cabinet-making jobs through this time. He was able to help some, but James was like I was when I was his age, not overly enthusiastic about working for his dad. In my conversations with Bill, he volunteered to come down to help us with the work. Bill came down to Houston twice this summer, once in June, and again in August (I think). Both times he was with us for several days. James took off time from work while Bill was with us and the two worked well together. I also, like James, do better when I am working with another man, and so I was able to assist with the work as well.

We redid much of the outer trim, redid some siding, and painted everything. We had to build out some of the eaves that were just bare rafters. It was great having Bill with us in our home and seeing the needed work progressing well. Bill and I spent much of our non-working time in good fellowship together.

Because we did not finish everything needed the first time, Bill came down again in August, after Kyle and Shelbie's wedding. This second time we were able to finish everything required by the insurance company.

I want to share a couple of instances that happened during Bill's second visit. We were out front. Bill was painting the front door, and I was putting up some window trim. Several people came walking down the street whom we perceived to be Jehovah's Witnesses. Getting entangled in conversa-

tion with people like that is not something inside my autistic framework. I moved to go inside, but Bill, standing in my way and laughing, said that he would call them over. I froze in horror. In that moment, Bill saw in my eyes that my disability is real. He did not call to them, but let me pass.

The second incident was my own foolishness. I can't stand what I call "piddling," that is, wasting time doing unnecessary things in the construction process. Bill, on the other hand, does, in my estimation, a fair bit of "piddling." At one point, he was insisting on doing something that was NOT needed, meaning that he would not be doing something that was needed. In the end, we tussled together over whatever item he was working on as he insisted on doing it and I insisted that he not. This, as I say, was completely foolish on my part.

The next morning early, Bill came out to sit next to me at my computer where I was doing my early-morning writing. I immediately turned to him and apologized for my foolish actions. Yet I took it a step further, into the wondrous truths I was writing. I said to him, "Bill, in all things we place God-Love as our only connection together, regardless of anything that seems to be contrary." I then prayed that very thing in a simple prayer, that our Father as Love is all our connections together, regardless.

As I prayed with Bill, all the constraint I felt inside towards him and towards my own foolishness vanished, and I knew that our Father truly is with us.

"Thank you, Bill, so much, for your friendship, for all you have done for me and for my family, and for your willingness to be taught of the Lord together with me."

Through August I completed the chapters of *The River of Life* and was ready to start whatever came next. But before I bring that in, my son Kyle's wedding to Shelbie Stephens fits in next.

Kyle and Shelbie

Throughout 2017 and 2018, Kyle and Shelbie's relationship had grown until they knew that they wanted to spend the rest of their lives together. There was a problem, though, and that was that Shelbie's father had reservations concerning Kyle and was not willing to give his blessing to their marriage. Because of their respect for him, they waited for a season.

Through these months I visited with Kyle and Shelbie individually concerning the expectation of God through some of the difficulties they faced and we all prayed together that God would turn Mr. Stephen's heart. In July, the Lord spoke to Mr. Stephens while he was worshipping in a Sunday service, that it was indeed of Him for Kyle and Shelbie to marry. Mr. Stephens then freely gave his blessing.

Kyle and Shelbie were married on Friday, August 2, 2019.

A few days before the wedding, Maureen and I went to a restaurant with Kyle and Shelbie and with Shelbie's parents, Herb and Elizabeth Stephens. We had a good time together; there was a mutual kindness.

Maureen's wedding gift to Kyle and Shelbie included the rental of a lovely little park with a gazebo or pavilion on Heights Boulevard in The Heights – Marmion Park. Shelbie loved this area of Houston, as did we all, and especially wanted a wedding in such a pavilion. Although the gazebo was not large, it was just the right size for the wedding and all the guests.

Matthew and Johanna flew down from Canada, with little Gabriel. This was the first time I got to see my first grandson. Claude and Lois came down as well as the Sanchez's. Will Fonder flew in from Colorado Springs.

It was a beautiful wedding, graced by the Lord. Kyle and Shelbie were married by Andrew Johnson, the pastor of the Spirit-filled Baptist Church where Kyle had been attending for some years. We had a reception in the fellowship hall at the church. Kyle and Shelbie then made their first home in an apartment complex just a couple of miles south of our house on Fernbank.

Two Wondrous New Writing Tasks

Around the first of July, I finally began probably the largest and certainly one of the most exciting of all my writing tasks, *The Jesus Secret II*. At this point I had completed the almost-final versions of Paul's letters for the JSV, my own attempt at translating portions of the New Testament.

When I wrote *The Jesus Secret* originally, I was all set to continue with the second volume, that is, Galatians through Revelation. The problem was that the first statement of faith on which to write in Galatians was "I Hold Utterly to Paul's Gospel." What

is Paul's gospel? I did not know just how much I did not know. What I did know was that the anointing to continue vanished from me, and I could not do it.

Through the years since, I had wanted to write that second volume, but how did not come. I toyed with a number of different approaches that went nowhere. Yet Peter Douglas, in particular, expressed how eager he was to have *The Jesus Secret II* in his hands, and so I continued to hold before the Lord how I might start it.

By this summer of 2019, having completed *Knowing Jesus As He Is* and *Set My People Free*, I finally felt that I understood, at least in part, Paul's gospel. To be honest, I did not fully know Paul's gospel until I had completed Romans 8 in *The Jesus Secret II* in October of 2019.

Then, I chose to merge portions of the JSV with the statements of faith; this gave the verses from whence these truths of our being like Jesus actually come. And, because Thessalonians was the second portion of the New Testament written, after James's letter, I began with Thessalonians, placing the order of the books of the New Testament mostly in the order in which they were written. I am convinced that this is an important order for our understanding. The early church did not have Paul's gospel as he wrote it for its first twenty-five years, and it did not have John's gospel in written form for its first sixty-five years. Except for John and the writer of Hebrews, no other New Testament writer actually understood Paul's gospel.

Although *The Jesus Secret II* follows the same concepts as the first *Jesus Secret,* it is much more intense and focused and the truth of Christ as us is far more developed. When I could not write any further in *The Jesus Secret,* I believed at the time that God wanted me to absorb and live in this wondrous relationship of union with Christ before I would return to *The Jesus Secret* at a whole new level. I was completely correct. This is my longest writing task, however. I hope I will have it finished within four years. I have just started on 1 John while writing this chapter of my account, well on my way, albeit slowly, to completion.

Then, the second wondrous (and terrible) writing task I began in August, was this autobiography, **Prepare a Path.** Writing this account is the single most life-changing experience I have known and among the most traumatic.

I had written part of the first chapter, "My Origins," in the spring of 2017 and about my time at Graham River when I was still living in Maple, Texas, but now writing my account would be in earnest.

I had wanted to write this account for years because my life was a tangled mess to me, and I wanted to make some sense of it. When I wrote about my childhood and youth, however, something or Someone else began to take this exercise in a direction I never expected, that I was giving the account of my life required in the presence of a Carrying and a Devoted God. And that my primary task was to place the Lord Jesus upon every moment, circumstance, and person with whom I had interacted.

But my understanding of what God was doing as He wove Christ Jesus all through what I had imagined had been only confusion and loss developed only slowly. The bigger thing for me through the writing of each chapter, was that things that were filled with pain and hidden away were now brought out into the light and HEALED. They were healed because I placed the Lord Jesus into my memories of those difficult things and because I spoke favor and grace into each person with whom I was involved.

I finished with my youth by the end of August and proceeded with pulling in my chapters on Graham River in September. Something else was happening through this August and September, however, that was really exciting to me.

The Zoom Meetings Begin

Through this summer, I had exchanged emails with Jerry Onyszczak, who seemed very eager to learn more, as well as with Phyliss Smith who was moving back to the same area west of Nashville. Jerry suggested that he and I connect on the Zoom app so that we could fellowship face to face. This level of connection long distance with a stranger was a bit much for me, but, as I thought about it, I realized that the Zoom app might actually be a way to bring readers together with me for fellowship. The truth is, this was the Lord, so He enabled me to work through whatever difficulties I might have had.

I communicated with Bill and Pete and we attempted a Zoom meetup on August 25, but ran into a number of difficulties. By September first, I had worked out those connection problems and we had another meeting, this time joined by Christopher Küttner of Germany and Dennis Rhodes of Australia. Jerry Onyszczak may have been with us as well. It was difficult for Dennis, because 8 AM my time was the middle of the night for him.

That same morning then, I included an invitation to all my readers to join with us on Sunday morning, September 7, for our first full Zoom meeting. I do not remember who joined with us when, but from this start, Lanny Gao, Rachelle Ross, and Karen Leigh of South Africa have always been part of our meetings each Sunday. Jerry's wife, Ellie, often joined him in these first Zoom meetings.

Now, I really wanted to impart the word of Christ face to face with Phyliss Smith. I knew that the Lord Jesus wanted her, in particular, to know union with Him. For that reason, I communicated through August with Jerry Onyszczak as well as Bill Horton concerning a trip to Nashville to share this word with several gathered there.

My idea, then, was to use the Zoom meeting to "practice" what I would share in face to face meetings in the Onyszczak's home. I wanted to give an introduction to union with Christ, to symmorphy, and to the wondrous sharing of life with God I was coming to know. I called this short series, "Come into the Feast."

Now, I am limited in the ability to lead conversation and discussion, that is, I can do so only inside of prescribed paths, as a teacher in a classroom. I am also limited in the propensity to prolong conversation in such group settings. For this reason, the Zoom meetings have been primarily a few minutes of greetings and conversation at the start, then I share the Word, then I give opportunity for questions and comments regarding what is shared. My first times of sharing were only 30 to 45 minutes long. They have become longer since.

I want to include something Christopher Küttner shared with me after his first full Zoom meeting with us. – "My feeling during our time together was joy. I could see us as Christ, but the more surprising thing was that I saw my own face as one of you guys, if that makes sense. And as you said, God does what He says He does. And when it happens, it suddenly is clear that it could not be any other way."

Another Trip to Nashville

As I shared, I continued in communication with Jerry and Bill concerning a trip to Nashville. Jerry was very welcoming, that there would be a number of people who would want to gather with us in his home for meetings and fellowship. We set the dates for October 4-6, 2019, Friday through Sunday.

On September 14, I included these comments in my regular letter.

~ I am visiting a small number of brethren near Dickson, Tennessee, the first weekend of October. Bill Horton, from northwestern Kansas, is planning to be there and has helped me enormously in doing that part that is difficult for me to do, and that is arranging all the specifics beforehand. Fellowship is important, and there will be much time for fellowship; nonetheless, it is of great importance to me to impart Christ in power and in specific truth.

For that reason, we have worked out six scheduled "meetings." Friday, October 4 at 10 AM and at 4 PM – Saturday, October 5 at 10 AM and at 4 PM – and Sunday, October 6 at 10 AM and at 4 PM. As far as I know right now, the gatherings will be in someone's home. If you live within a few hours drive of Nashville and wish to join with us, I'm sure you will be welcome.

❧

As I shared, I relied a lot on Bill to interface with Jerry and Ellie to work out all the details of our time with them.

I then created twelve specific "lessons" that would include Power Point presentations. I would teach two lessons per session. In essence, I covered the central ruling verses, beginning with being filled with God in weakness and ending with the ruling verse and our actions of faith.

Now, as a teacher, I wanted to give a dynamic teaching. Yet it had been many years since I had stood up front to share the word, and even a few years since I had been in a classroom. The result was that I over-thought it. I did not know what equipment would be available, and so I purchased a number of items from Amazon that would enable me to present my Power Point slides through a large-screen TV and with a remote control. I charged a few hundred dollars worth of stuff to Maureen's credit card.

I left for Nashville on Wednesday, October 2 in a rented car. At this point in time, we had only the blue Toyota, which Maureen needed. I drove up through Arkansas and stayed in an Airbnb northeast of Little Rock. This was one of the most enjoy-able Airbnb experiences I have had. I went a bit out of my way to Memphis to drive through the two remaining counties in Arkansas that I yet needed. I now had every county in Arkansas.

I arrived at Jerry and Ellie's home near Dickson, just west of Nashville, Tennessee late Thursday afternoon. They greeted me warmly. I would stay in their spare bedroom and the meetings would be held in their living room. Bill had also arrived that day, but was staying with a pastor friend whom he had known in the past.

I was quite tired from the trip, and so I went to bed early. But I hit a snag. I could not sleep. I was in the Onyszczak's home Thursday, Friday, Saturday, and Sunday nights, and I was able to sleep only around four hours each night. I do not do well with such lack of sleep, but I soldiered on.

Now, God was doing something very specific and very important in me through this experience, whatever blessing He wanted to be through me to others. Through the next week after my return home, I wrote the chapter of this text, "Heart with Heart." In that chapter, I refer to this weekend of sharing the word in the Onyszczak's home. I do not want to repeat here everything I shared there, but I would suggest you read through that chapter again to have the full picture.

On Friday morning our first meeting began at 10 AM. I hooked up my new gadgets to Jerry's TV beforehand and got everything working right. In attendance that morning were Jerry and Ellie, Bill Horton, a sister who reads my letters who had driven down from Kentucky but was able to stay only that first morning, Phyllis Smith and another elderly lady who was her friend, and the man and wife of whom I speak in "Heart with Heart."

I will quote this much. ~~~ There was a couple, man and wife, in attendance in the first session on Friday morning. Jerry Onyszczak opened our time together in the Spirit of Christ. Then the sister began to speak in prophetic utterance, directing the service as she wished, in exuberance, in dance, in outflowing abundance. She quoted from the "gospel of Thomas."

I receive all things as from my Father, so this did not bother me at all. Once I started sharing, several times I connected what I was sharing with what she had shared. I did this to honor Christ as her. ~~~

There were fewer people there that afternoon, but I continued the teaching, looking at the One who stumbles under a cross He cannot carry. I had brought a number of my books with me, so they were available for a donation in-between the meetings. We all ate lunch together each day. I also put out a little offering box for donations. I had shared with Jerry my hope that there would be provision for the costs of the trip. That is a normal expectation when one travels to minister, and fully appropriate.

Saturday morning I was even more restrained from lack of sleep, and thus I was stiff during our praise time together. I was able to share the word freely and in the Spirit, however. I share in "Heart with Heart" my experiences that day with the man and wife who had returned just for that second morning service.

Saturday afternoon, after the sharing had begun, several more people came in to hear what I was teaching. One of those was Pastor Bob Taranjo, whom Bill had known from earlier times, along with several from his congregation. I was aware that there was a sense of them "coming to check me out." My topics that afternoon were "The Ark of the Covenant" and "Energeoing and Sustaining All." I believe my sharing was good, and I gave everyone a copy of *Knowing Jesus As He Is* as they left.

Now, the fellowship with everyone, in-between and after the meetings, was mostly very good. Besides the press coming from the man and wife and their wrongful definitions of me, there was a brief, but very discordant note that arose. Jerry was talking excitedly about his vision of the fulness of Christ, what that might mean, yet tinged with "superiority." Inside of that, he mentioned deeper-truth Christians who have passed on and thus who now know what it's all about. Because the heavens are open to us, he intimated that some of these "superior" Christians could visit with us to let us know the truth.

I do not place myself as anything, but this could not continue unchallenged. I said, quietly but firmly, in a moment when all could hear me, "We do NOT visit with the dead." Jerry protested and began explaining himself more fervently. Again I said, in the same quiet and firm tone, "We do NOT visit with the dead."

That ended that present discussion, but later I heard Jerry remonstrate to someone else concerning what right I had to so speak. I don't remember what he said exactly, but his defense of himself was spoken in the same Christian rebellion in which Korah moved.

There is no question in my mind that someone hearing from "superior" Christians, without physical bodies in the heavens, is hearing only demons. First, we must be delivered from our lust for the "super-christ" before we can know a God who places Himself beneath of all.

Neither would I ever, upon hearing such a quiet and firm word spoken to me in the anointing, receive it as anything but God's correction of me. We are in no game.

At the same time, I had pieced together through various things said, that Jerry was glued to Fox News and to the political concerns of this world. He said things that rejected my understanding of how evil actually works.

That evening, Bill and I went for a drive so that we could visit privately together. I was leaning on Bill in a very similar way in which I had leaned upon Don Howat. Bill was my help through all these things. And so we talked through all the difficulties together. In fact, Bill had also been presented with similar difficulties in the place where he was staying. It's not that we came to any conclusion; it's that sharing such things together is what it's all about.

The truth is, however, that I was there for Phyliss, and in all our times of fellowship, I tried to have some quality time with her.

Saturday night was another four-hour-night for me. On Sunday, I really did not have the strength for two more full meetings. Instead, we all gathered around the breakfast table and shared Christ together for a couple of hours. Through this good time, I was able to include the more important things from the lessons I had prepared for the day.

There was only about $75 in the offering, including from the sale of my books. Phyliss also wanted to fill up my car with gas. No other money was provided to offset the hundreds of dollars I had put on Maureen's credit card.

That evening it was just Jerry, Ellie, and myself. We watched a funny movie together, but I could sense that a wall had now come up between them and myself. I retired early, but again, slept even less than four hours. As I pondered why, I guessed that, since my room was in the midst of massive wi-fi connections on three sides, I was basically in a "microwave" box and thus could not sleep long. I cannot know for sure, however.

I woke up just after midnight. I could not bear to lie in bed, so I thought that, since I had prepared that evening to leave early in the morning, I might just as well go now.

I left the Onyszczak home before 1 AM and drove to a nearby grocery store. I got something to drink and then tried to sleep in the car in the parking lot. I was not successful, and so by 2 AM I headed out on my way back to Houston. I got onto the Natchez Trace Parkway and headed towards Alabama. My intention was to get more counties in Alabama and Mississippi and then to turn west on I-10 towards Houston.

Before continuing, I must expand a bit more on my expectations for this trip and what happened to them. I was continuing to wrestle with the huge question – If this word I share is truly of God, then He ought to anoint me to share that word with power.

Here is what I wrote a couple of months later. My topic was the anointing.

~~~ I doubt that any ministry in the Christian church during my life-time was anointed by God with power greater than that anointing which was upon Sam Fife. And the evidence for that assertion was apparent in every direction.

I went to Tennessee in the slim hope that God would prove that the word I share is of Him by anointing me with a slight portion of that in which Sam Fife moved. And please understand this, there is no doubt in my mind that if I had been as Sam Fife preaching in that home, the Spirit of God would have come upon that whole group in mighty demonstrations of power, the pastor attending would likely have become a prominent ministry alongside of me, and all of them would have sold everything and moved into Christian community. They would have been caught in the power and vision of God. That is what happened over and over everywhere Sam Fife went.

I will not complain about the circumstances, but God made sure I knew that He was doing no such thing through me. ~~~

I did almost doze for nearly an hour in a rest stop along the Natchez Trace highway, but I continued on, then, still in the dark. Suddenly, I saw up ahead a flashing light and slowed down. It was a policeman on foot in front of a tree that had fallen across my side of the road. He was waving his flash light down towards the other side of the road, a signal that to me meant proceed cautiously, which I did. But as I drew up alongside of him, he motioned angrily at me, and I rolled down my window. He screamed at me for disobeying him, but finally let me continue on. The normal signal to stop, waving the flashlight as an X, was not what he had done.

I was out of Tennessee and into Alabama not long after the sun came up. I was so glad to be gone from there; I felt like a dog having had his tail caught in the door as he was being booted out. I especially agonized over the fact that no provision had come to cover my costs.

I always enjoy driving through Alabama, and after this trip, I now have only one county left to get in that state. I thought I might get a motel in southern Mississippi for the night. But when I arrived in that area in late afternoon, I could not conceive prolonging the trip. I thought, "I'll just drive a bit further." By the time I was on I-10 heading west, all thought of stopping for the night was gone. Home was in my sight, and I drank all the coffee I needed to get there by 11 PM.

I surprised Maureen, who was not expecting me until the next day. That was one of the longest days of my life, and it was so good to be home.

It was while I was driving down through Alabama that morning that God gave me His Word concerning all my expectations. As I said, I was distressed over the fact that all this trip was now on Maureen's debt on top of not having experienced the anointing in power which I had imagined. But as I checked my email on my phone, I saw that just that morning Lanny Gao had sent me twice her usual monthly donation, enough money to cover the gas, car rental, and Airbnb for the trip itself. I had not actually needed any of those tech gadgets, so that loss would remain on me.

Nonetheless, the moment I saw that money in my account from Lanny, it was God speaking a word to me. Here is how I formulated that word from God in my mind, "Son, I do not give you a ministry 'out there,' but I have given you these precious ones, these few in the Zoom meetings, and I have anointed My word in you for them."

I have not looked for any outward "ministry" since. And God has been faithful in anointing me for His own intentions.

Another "Winter"

From October through December, I felt subdued and a bit discouraged towards God and the flow of Word. I did continue to write and to share in the on-going Zoom meetings each Sunday morning. But I turned most of my time and interests towards another attempt to build an income-producing presence online.

What I attempted to do was to establish two websites, www.thewritingconservatory.com and www.thelearningconservatory.com. I hoped to fill them with valuable content and then earn passive income through many affiliate links, etc. I signed on with another email service as well so that I could increase the flow of traffic to these sites.

I worked hard on these websites for a couple of months, and all that is needed to have affiliate links and internet connections that will draw traffic. The websites are still there and you can see how beautiful they are and how much work went into them. I don't do anything with them now, however.

The problem is that I hit a brick wall. You see, what I knew about making an income on the Internet in 2008 no longer held true. The avenue I tried, Ezine Articles, slammed shut. Then I tried another avenue to gain traffic, but that also had been closed out by how the Internet works today. Then I thought that I would try making a free mini-course to offer on my email signup. I worked hard on that, but I do not do well speaking into a camera for I have no faces to whom to speak. By mid-December, I had completely run out of steam, and so I set aside, once again, this effort to earn money online.

I wrote "Heart with Heart" for my autobiography and sent it out on October 19. As I said, you could read it again, for it also fits here just as much. Then I wrote about my time at the New Mexico community and at Bowens Mill in November and December. I finished "A Song in Great Difficulty" before the end of December.

This was the first time that I had written about my years living at the Ridge. Here is what I wrote in "A Time of Reset."

~~~ Truly, truly, the dark hole inside that has been my memory of Bowens Mill is now filled with love and joy, with memories of good things and with a completely different perspective of the difficult things. This is so wonderful. ~~~

The same was true concerning my New Mexico experience. Writing this account had now become something I had never expected. Not only was there such healing coming to me, healing that has proven to be PERMANENT, but I was beginning to discover a clear and certain purpose of God in the ongoing patterns of my life. This I had not expected.

Nonetheless, I was glancing through pictures of Bowens Mill just a few days ago and marveled at the fact that my only impressions are thoughts of goodness and blessing.

I think that my sharing in the Zoom meetings might have been a bit subdued for the few weeks after my return from Nashville. On November 10, 2019, however, I began an exciting new series called *Tabernacle Teaching*. The Tabernacle of Moses is clearly God's pattern of organization for gospel truth. The writer's of the New Testament all based our salvation on the elements of this pattern and make it clear that this path is God's WAY for the believer. Nonetheless, Christianity hardly knows what that means.

In this series of teachings, I brought in all that I had learned from Sam Fife, entirely filtered into the present word of Christ our life. By the end of December we had progressed into the Holy Place.

Our fellowship together in the Zoom meetings was very precious to everyone. Different people joined with us on occasion or for a short period of time, but from then until now, the gathering has been consistent. Maureen is able to be with us every other Sunday. Then it is Bill Horton, Pete Douglas, and Christopher Küttner, as well as Lanny Gao, Rachelle Ross, and Karen Leigh. Phyliss Smith could never make a direct connection on Zoom work, but she calls me and joins with us by phone about half the time. She is able to hear the others and to share as well.

Even though I do most of the talking, I do not see this as me teaching them, but as God teaching us together. God does not give me His word; He gives US His word.

And as I settled myself with joy into this "limited" place of ministry, so God prepared to open the floodgates of heaven for such wondrous Word about to flow through us together.

I never heard from Jerry again, but I bless him and Ellie with all my heart. I know that Jesus carries them and that He does all things well. I join with the Father in the expectation that some good fruit will come in their lives through my brief encounter with them.

Feeling Like a "Failure"

Chapter 55, "The Meaning of a Life," is one approach to summing up my life story and what I discovered as I wrote this account. As I am doing the final proof, I am reading for the first time my whole account from beginning to end. Often I am in tears; often I am grateful that the clarity I was hoping to convey did come through.

But as I am reading through these chapters now, I suddenly feel very depressed.

You see, I know that if the Word I am sharing is truly of God, then it ought to be flowing through me to many, to God's Church everywhere.

Yet fewer than fifty people read what I share, and how many of them truly connect with God through what they learn from me, I have no idea.

People have bounced away from me all my life. I know it's Asperger's, but I don't understand or know what to do about it.

Nonetheless, I never separate myself from my Father, even when I am feeling like a failure. Rather, I say, "Father, You are sharing even this with me."

And then I understand that, indeed, this is God sharing Himself with me. For has He not spoken, and few hear? Has He not searched for a man who will believe in Him and found none?

People simply do not understand the great sorrow that God bears as billions upon billions of sentient beings, humans and angels, exist inside of Him, inside of His love and by His goodness, and yet they hate Him without a cause.

He comes to His own, and His own receive Him not.

God showed Himself to us as He really is, through a man on his face in the mud under a cross he could not carry, carrying us through a way we could not go, all the way through death and into life.

Yet Christians have turned that one time and place where God shows Himself as He IS into the opposite picture, wherein *the Roman soldiers show us God and the man in the mud shows us our own wickedness.* And they say, "*God is expressing His wrath against us.*"

They will not see themselves inside of that man; they will not accept a God who carries them.

Yes, there is a place inside of God where God Himself feels like a "failure."

Yet the writer of Hebrews is clear in saying that God gave all authority to humans. And Paul is clear in saying that it never enters God's mind to take that authority back.

God carries His own distress inside of His great expectation of faith, inside of the same place He carries us. Yet He also shares with us the same hurt He bears, just a little bit, so that we might know Him, so that we might be His entrance into our world.

By this we have known love, because He set forth His soul for us, and we also are committed to setting forth our souls for our brothers and sisters.

It has been ten years, now, in which God has required me to place myself inside of Him inside of this verse, 1 John 3:16.

I give to my Father every part of my humanity, all weakness and every stumbling step. And I turn, with my God, every circumstance, every moment, every pain, every joy, into goodness for you, dear reader, for your sake.

I want you to KNOW God; I want God to enter your world through you.

52. A New Fire

January 2020 - March 2021

A New Fire Begins

Something opened up inside of me in January of 2020, and rivers of Word began flowing out from the heavens and onto my page. I was simply blown away by the Wind.

I wrote in the letter I sent out on January 11. ~ "Sorry, but there is a fire inside of me that cannot rest until the true Jerusalem is a praise in all the earth, until the knowledge of the Lord flows out to all. And so I must write, for that is what I can do. This next series/book, *A Highway for God,* follows the same desire and purpose as my last book, *The River of Life*. I am approaching the same topic from a slightly different perspective, and out from fresh and present word." ~

I began *A Highway for God* with the same question. ~ What will a world of life be? We know only a world of death, flowing out, every moment, from knowing good and evil, out from self-exaltation and self-cursing. We do not have the slightest bit of experience with the normality found in a world flowing out from the Tree of Life, out from a God who knows no evil through a River of knowing Jesus as the Sustainer of all. ~

A Highway for God is my largest book of the middle size. And it is the most intense and glorious. I'm still too close to it to read it as "something new" and thus to perceive its full impact. But I know that in the writing of it, I was filled with wonder. The premise of *A Highway for God* is that God is entering our world through us. And the most wondrous statement in it is – "My heart is the entrance of God."

Yet at the same time, in this January of 2020, I began to unveil the most difficult time period of my life, which was from 1986 to 1997, my years of involvement with Blueberry Christian Community. And the most astonishing thing happened as I began to write "Blueberry and College." The long-buried memory of how much I loved Blueberry and Covenant Life College resurfaced and took its primary place.

I wrote this on January 18. ~ I have begun working on my first year at Blueberry in a letter titled "Blueberry and College," but it's not finished. I look at it each morning as a boy looks at the cold water of a mountain stream and debates whether to leap in or not. When I am ready to immerse myself in Blueberry, I will do so. Meanwhile, something has happened in my heavens and word is pouring through so fast I cannot keep up. In fact, over and over, my breath is taken quite away by things that seem to be popping out of my fingers onto the page (the first chapters of *A Highway for God*). ~

On January 25, I wrote, ~ Still waiting to take that plunge into Blueberry; I have a distinct sensation, however, of Someone about to push me in." ~ And on January 30, I wrote, ~ I find that writing about my time at the Blueberry Community is one of the costliest things I have done. I share these things for Father's sake. ~

Meanwhile, I had completed Romans in *The Jesus Secret II,* and thus, for the first time, fully understood Paul's gospel. Through the last of January, I also wrote a chapter in *A Highway for God*, titled "My Story," in which I detailed the incredible transformation taking place in me as I saw the Lord Jesus recasting everything that had once been darkness in my memories into life and joy. I wrote the following concerning this writing of my story.

~ I am caught in the grip of my Blueberry story and I am overwhelmed. I want to get as far as I can before taking another prolonged break. My problem is that I cannot separate the difficult times ahead from the good times I am sharing with you at present. The good calls up the memory of the difficult and makes it even more poignant. I am going from being emotionally overwhelmed, to seeing things more truly, to being again emotionally overwhelmed, back and forth. I cannot present to you the years from 1990 to 1998 without honesty, and I cannot present to you those same years in a way that lays any accusation upon anyone. I must see all things as Jesus sees them; I must, with Him, carry all inside my heart through the darkness and into Life.

Writing my life story is becoming an extraordinary experience, beyond extraordinary. I have hardly ever mentioned my time at Bowens Mill. Always before, if I was forced to look across those years, I saw only a dark hole of confusion and pain, yet they were memories that, by the grace of God, held no immediate hold over me. After completing the third chapter on those years, I now look across them and see nothing but goodness and purpose. I never expected this profound transformation. ~

Through February, I wrote about the times of deliverance at Blueberry with Sister Jane Miller and then "Friendship with Maureen." I also completed Colossians & Philemon for *The Jesus Secret II* and began Ephesians.

On March 3, I wrote the following in the introduction to my letter.

~ An incredible miracle has happened in my life over the last several weeks. Beginning my Blueberry account plunged me immediately into all the awfulness of emotion and even fear that I would come to know through the years after our graduation from college and marriage. I continued inside the turmoil of those emotions for nearly a month. Then, it all finally came to peace. Still, I waited a couple of weeks before plunging back in with the writing of this letter. And I find what is to me the most incredible miracle of God I have known, that I can look squarely at every moment and person in my Blueberry experience and sense no shadow at all, but only the goodness of God. There might yet be more emotions to pass through as I go forward, but the purifying fire of God has filled in the most difficult parts with the Lord Jesus.

More than that, I have astonished myself with seeing just how much joy my remembering the entrance of Maureen into my story has become to me now." ~

The World Changes

The events of this world have no actual effect on my daily life except on those occasions when their importance captures my grief and concern.

On March 15, 2020, almost every church in almost every country on earth closed its doors to the congregation and no longer gathered together to worship. And they kept those doors closed for months at the command of petty politicians and strutting would-be local dictators.

This mighty declaration, reverberating throughout the heavens, that the BEAST rules triumphant over the Church of Jesus Christ on this earth, was almost unremarked by most Christians.

I did wear a mask for awhile in order to enter the grocery store to buy our food, but I hated it. I hated it because I was in no way fooled by the claims of a "pandemic" or by the fakery behind the massive psychological warfare being levied against all people on earth to hide their faces from each other, to stay far apart, and to accept the lockdown.

I hate lying; and I hate being surrounded by lying and being required to dance its tune. And no, there was no increase in deaths by respiratory illness anywhere throughout 2020. It was only the spin given to what was not news.

Nonetheless, it is God's people, my brethren in Christ, caught in this nonsense and quietly submitting to the plodding line into death that holds my concern. Because I share heart with God, I care about His people. Because Jesus loves me, I also set forth my soul for their sakes.

But what was I writing through these weeks? I was writing "In the Womb of the Church," positioning my Blueberry experience. And I was writing "Respect" and "Honor" in *A Highway for God*, that is, our high regard for the Church, each one of whom is as Jesus to us.

The point is that the change in the world increased the sense of urgency inside the Spirit inside of me. Yet I was not quite ready for the great change in ministry that would come by the end of August. As I said, very little was happening in my life outwardly through this time. I am sharing my experiences in writing in order to show how God was preparing me for His task for me.

Through March and April, I wrote slowly through the first really difficult times at Blueberry, inside of which Maureen and I were married and Kyle was born. When I write about any part of my life, I feel inside as if it just happened yesterday and all the emotions of that time come up inside of me. This was very traumatic, yet inside the press, I placed Jesus into every difficulty and spoke goodness into all those with whom I interacted at the time.

On May 2, I sent out my letter titled "Thoughts on the Present Crisis." In it I set forth my understanding of the fake "pandemic" as well as what God was doing and about to do through us, His Church.

Through May, I wrote about our time back in Oregon and then our return to Blueberry. On May 28, in the introduction to "Into God's Shattering," I wrote the following. ~ The tangled-up threads of decades of not-understanding are unraveling, and all the path of my life is coming into one simple and straight line, from heart to Hheart. I am astonished and overwhelmed. ~

On May 12, 2020, our second grandson, Konrad Martin Schneider was born. Mother and baby were fine, even though the baby was born before they could make it out the door. Some sisters from the community were there to help and the EMT's arrived just as Konrad came into the world. Maureen had hoped to be there for the birth, but the Covid lockdowns made it impossible.

The Summer of 2020

Throughout June, I was approaching writing about the central point of God's dealings with me, August of 1996. On June 4, I sent out "Becoming an Elder." In that letter, I quoted from David, **"Touch not Mine anointed and do My prophets no harm."** This is indeed God's central test for every human who would know Him.

I received a response from a reader who had lived at Blueberry through this time and who was, in fact, a student in my classroom for one year. This was a person of immense value to me whom I deeply love. She had gone on from Blueberry with her family to another community, one only partly associated with the move fellowship. Her experiences are not my story to give, but her question to me is my story. That question was – what about abuse in the Church?

In response to this critical question, I added another section to my chapter on "Becoming an Elder," which I titled briefly, "Dealing with Abuse." We never speak out from contempt, we forgive all inside of God. BUT – neither do we allow abuse to continue, especially that which uses "God" as a whip to bring shame into the lives of those who love Jesus.

"What Do I Do?" was the significant chapter of my life, detailing my slow and agonizing decision to leave Blueberry. At this time, Maureen had found her calendars through these years in which she had recorded the events of our life. Thus I now had exact dates, especially for our leaving of Blueberry, our long journey through Bowens Mill and immigration, to arrive back again at Blair Valley. Having the dates made these chapters much more specific, something I believe was the Lord.

June 14, 2020 was the last session on the "Tabernacle Teaching" in the Zoom meetings. This was a very fruitful series for us, grounding us in God's organizational pattern for the gospel. Of truth, these series in the Zoom meetings have been among the most important things I have shared, including for myself, that we together might know the Lord.

Then, on June 21, we started a new series on Zoom, a study of individuals in the Old Testament and their relationship with God. I titled this series "After My Own Heart." We started with "God's Riddle" and continued with Cain and Abel, Noah, and then Abraham. This series was the final step in bringing back the Old Testament fully into my knowing and into the present word of Christ our life.

Meanwhile, I had thought to take advantage of the U.S. government's "stimulus" grants for business. A problem came, however, with the SBA not following the legislation, but making up their own rules. And so I was offered a loan at very low interest and generous repayment terms. I received several thousand dollars for my writing business. By law, this should be a grant only, and I have not had to begin re-payment. Whether or not it will be "forgiven," I do not know.

I had redone my computer not long before, but it was not adequate for the type of work I was doing on it. I used the money, then, to build a new computer, the best I have had thus far. This present computer does everything I need and quickly. I purchased the materials to add to my office desk setup, making everything very convenient and at hand.

I also spent some money making my website more "search friendly." I followed the directions given by a number of different "SEO" companies, to little effect, however. The truth is that the most important thing to increase website visibility is links to it from other larger websites. One larger website recommended by some was www.teachable.com.

So I signed on with them with the plan of creating "mini-courses" that might bring in an income while increasing the links going back to www.christrevealed.info.

Through June, then, I developed a series of "mini-courses" to be offered through teachable.com, the first three of which I went on to complete. Each mini-course contained seven lessons, each being a video of Power-Point slides, with exactly twelve slides in each of the seven lessons. The first topic I tackled in this focused way was "Living in Paul's Gospel."

I completed "Living in Paul's Gospel" by the third week of July. This was an important milestone in God's task for me. I did not know fully that for which God sent me into the world; I just knew that I had to put out in front of myself and all Christians a crystal clear, accurate, and brief explanation of a gospel of LIFE as it has never been known in Christianity.

I also completed Paul's letters in *The Jesus Secret II* at this point and turned to Hebrews, beginning with the almost final draft for the JSV. I would work on Hebrews slowly over the next several months.

In May, our daughter, Katrina, had purchased a travel trailer so that she could have her own place to live. To celebrate, we made a trip with the trailer to Waco, Texas, the first weekend of July. We rented a place to park the trailer through Airbnb. It was a lovely setting, and we were the only ones there.

When Katrina first put the trailer onto her pickup, it weighted the pickup down more than is safe. She drove it around for a bit, but when she came back, it seemed that the weight of the trailer was almost beginning to pull the pickup apart. In difficult driving situations, such an imbalance of weight could have resulted in the trailer pushing the pickup in directions Katrina would not want to go. Then our son James borrowed torsion bars and an anti-sway bar from our neighbor across the street and installed them on the trailer/pickup hookup. These bars pulled up the trailer and pickup even with one another tightly.

After a great family time together near Waco, I drove the unit back home and was pleased with how safe it felt. I was driving one unit. When I turned or when I braked, I never felt that the trailer was anything other than part of the pickup. This experience really impressed me. God was about to use it to seal something important inside my heart.

Through July and into August, I completed writing about our time at Blair Valley and then the move to Fort St. John. Finally, during the second week of August, I wrote the chapter, "My Reasons for Leaving" Blair Valley, the move, and Canada.

To understand this present chapter of my life, you could go back and read that chapter again. This is when I wrote it. I do want to include a bit from that chapter here again, because of its importance in what happens next in my walk with God.

~ As I finished writing the chapters on Blair Valley, that image of the trailer weighting down the back of the pickup came to my mind as a clear picture of how my life has been.

Let me explain. The trailer is that large and heavy portion of my life that was my years in the move of God and in Christian community. The pickup is my life since we left that fellowship and we are now in the cab, being driven forward by the power of Christ our only life. My adult life has been two large parts, the first part resting as a heavy weight upon the second part. Most who left the move tried to unhitch and cast off the "trailer" of their move experience from their present life. I am convinced they are doing nothing more than deluding themselves.

The connection between the trailer of my years in the move and the pickup of my present life was our leaving Blair Valley and Canada. That connection has always been weak inside my heart, and sometimes it seems that the years of difficulty might push our present life in the wrong directions because of that weak connection.

The picture of James installing the torsion and anti-sway bars, pulling up the trailer and pickup even with each other, now one tight unit, came to me so strongly as God placed Himself as honoring me through this weak point of my life.

And in that moment, I felt that the two large parts of my life have come fully together as one. I feel whole, complete, and put together. Now, as I am looking forward to writing the second half of my adult life, I am filled with anticipation of the joy of Christ my life entering my experience.

Every particle of my years in the move fellowship is fully complete, fully inside of Jesus, fully filled with blessing and joy. ~

I had not known it, but having this experience in the resolution of my life story meant that God was now ready to hurl me into the next part of His purpose for my life.

A New Ministry

On August 22, the letter I sent out was titled "Pray with Us." I said this in the introduction. ~ It is my intention to begin a time of specific and focused prayer together with those who gather each Sunday in the Zoom meeting. I invite you to join with us, if not inside of Zoom, then in your own time with the Lord. For that reason, I am including a layout here of how our prayers together will develop over the next seven weeks. ~

In my book, *The River of Life*, I had written a short prayer after the description of each removal of a seal from off the Word of Christ written on our hearts. Those prayers were prayers of deliverance for the Church. Nonetheless, they were not prayers actually prayed together out loud at that time.

I extracted those prayers and included them in a shortened list. We then prayed them out loud together in the Zoom meeting, starting on August 23. After seven weeks of praying the removal of the seven seals keeping Christ from being known, we just continued right on with the prayer spoken out loud together at the end of each session from then until now. In all our prayers, we have prayed to know the Lord, and for the deliverance of the Church, all who belong to Jesus all across the earth.

I want to share a bit more about the Zoom meetings and our continuing fellowship together. We had been meeting together almost every Sunday morning for a year now, the same people whom I named, consistently, and with others joining on occasion. We had become comfortable together, and this time of speaking and hearing the word was a key part of our weekly lives.

For the first while, however, the time before and after my speaking what I had prepared seemed disjointed at times. Sometimes the discussion after the meeting went in directions un-related to seeking God together. When that happened, I felt very disjointed, as if something vital to our life was not happening. Our gathering together is an experience of great purpose intended by God. We come together to receive His word planted in our hearts. Casual purposes are fine, just not when the intention is to know God together.

I began starting the session each time by praying an unscripted prayer asking God to plant His Word as Jesus in our hearts. Then, after the sharing time, I spoke a blessing into our lives as a sealing of our time with the Father. I asked the brethren to honor God's purpose for our sharing.

Bill Horton continued to call me around twice a week. Our friendship seemed to be growing and deepening. Bill often wanted to talk about what it meant to be the firstfruits of Christ at the core of Christ Community and the practical reality of loving one another inside of such a life.

On occasion, however, Bill would speak contrary to Christ concerning himself or even speak the "above-you" Christ at me. Each time, I would gently share with him how speaking Christ concerning himself or me would be different. Bill appreciated and embraced these corrections.

Bill's phone calls meant a lot to me and gave me much courage and settled-ness.

September 29, 2020 was our wedding anniversary. Maureen and I had spent thirty years together at this point. Our children had been hoping that we could do something big for this anniversary, maybe even a trip to Quebec City and Prince Edward Island, but the lockdown ended that possibility. Instead, Maureen and I spent the weekend in a nice hotel in The Woodlands. We went down to the zoo in Houston mid-town and then visited a Barnes and Noble book store in The Woodlands Mall.

After thirty years of sharing life together, I can truly say that I would rather be with Maureen than anything else in this life. I also took along a laptop with us, and we were able to join the Zoom meeting on September 27 from our hotel room.

On October 4, we completed the seventh part of the prayer we were praying together to break the seven seals from off the knowing of Christ written upon the hearts of His Church. We were now studying Moses in his heart towards God. Our prayer then turned to the fulfillment of Tabernacles, which season we were then in.

Through October and November, I wrote through the chapters of our time in Lubbock and then Maple, Texas. In the introduction to "A Season of Healing" on November 14, "I wrote:

~ "As I finished posting the last chapter, there arose in me the sense that our time in Three Way was much more important than I had understood, and that I will know more what that means as God takes us into our next step in the present time. This makes me very glad, for we all loved our brief time there." ~

Through November and into December, we were studying David, a man after God's own heart, in the Zoom meetings, and I was writing through my time of teaching in Sheldon ISD and our family life in our home on Fernbank Drive in this autobiography.

From August through December, I also completed two more mini-courses to be posted on teachable.com. The second became "Safe from the Serpent's Gospel," and the third "The Ruling Verses of the Bible."

Thus, by December of 2020, I had completed the first part of God's commission to me, that of presenting a clear, simple, and unmistakable contrast between the two gospels, the gospel of the tree of life versus the gospel of the tree of death. When I went through these 21 short videos again recently, I was struck with the power and distinction of the truth.

Here is a pattern I see only now as I am writing this. It was in November of 1994 that I covenanted with God on a wooded hillside in Oregon, that He would prepare in me a pure word for His people. Soon after that, during the first months of 1995, I began teaching my first rendition of "The Two Gospels" in our service times together.

You will find much similarity between what I taught then and what I teach now, but with one huge difference. I did not know then that it is Jesus who first comes into union with us. That one piece of ignorance meant that I had the two gospels switched!!!

Here it is, twenty-six years later, and God has completed His Covenant with me, that I would have a pure word for His Church. My three mini-courses are the essence of that pure word.

The word I carry was now as clear and simple as I had long hoped it to be, but the ministry of Christ through me was not quite there. From December

of 2020 until the present time, God would take me into the depths of His Mercy Seat, of setting forth my soul for the sake of my brothers and sisters.

Another Trip to Canada

On Thursday, December 17, 2020, Maureen and I got on a plane at the Houston airport and flew to Toronto, and then from Toronto to Thunder Bay. Matthew Schneider picked us up that evening at the airport and we rode with him to their home at the South Farm in Upsala.

This was nearing the height of the Covid hysteria. We were allowed into Canada as Johanna's family, but we were required to wear masks all the way, and enter into a two-week quarantine, not only Maureen and I, but also Johanna, Matthew, and our two grandsons, Gabriel and Konrad. None of us could leave their home for the entire fourteen days, nor could anyone else enter the house.

For a month prior to our trip, Maureen and I had eaten garlic and taken Vitamin C everyday, for we dared not have any sign of sniffles or temperature. Everything about our flight was contrary to me, but we endured it. Then, we were given an app for our phones and we were required to report daily, each of us. The Canadian government made it clear that if we did not obey to the letter, we would go to prison.

It was winter time. Our usual experience in going from southern climes into northern cold had been sickness. Maureen and I continued to eat garlic and Vitamin C, and I wore wool socks on my feet and a stocking hat on my head the whole time. We did succeed in staying well.

Johanna and Matthew were now living in a large single-wide manufactured home a little ways up the slope from Johanna's former home with Ray and Paula Brumbach and straight south of the Tabernacle, on the other side of the large community garden. The manufactured home was sitting on top of a constructed bottom-story the same size and also had a large entry porch added on the south side. Maureen and I were given a bedroom in the bottom floor, just beyond a nice living area. And so we settled into two-plus weeks of immersed time with Matthew and Johanna and with Gabriel and Konrad.

Here is a picture of me reading a book I have always loved, *Green Eggs and Ham*, to my grandson, Gabriel, on the next morning after our arrival. This

is in their upper sitting room, just beyond their dining room. You cannot see, however, that there are library shelves on my right and a wide window filled with light.

Matthew had taken time off from work to be quarantined with us. He made good use of this time by finishing the interior of their entry porch, which had just been rough. This way, they could open it up to be a room of their home. I helped with cutting and installing some of the trim.

I also took on the task of organizing their extensive library scattered upstairs and downstairs. Johanna collects books like me; in fact, many of her books used to be mine. I like doing something like that and soon had all the books neatly lined up in meaningful categories.

Little Konrad was seven months old. He was fairly mobile, though not yet at the walking stage. Konrad is a very definite little boy, sometimes a handful; whereas Gabriel is always wanting to please. Both of them received Maureen and I fully as their "Nina" and "Papa." (Grandma and Grandpa were reserved for Matthew's parents.) Of course, Maureen talked with them most every morning on their smart phones, a practice that continues until now.

Two boys are a handful for anyone, however, and so our being there also gave Johanna a needed break. Johanna then did the mudding and painting

in their front entry job.

We shared a wonderful Christmas together on Friday morning, just the six of us, but with our Houston family also joining in on their smartphones. The little boys got lots of presents; I love giving presents to little boys, and so did everyone else.

I had borrowed Kyle's laptop for this trip, and so I wrote "The Time of the Jesus Secret" through these days, a chapter I want every Christian on earth to understand. I continued conversations with Bill Horton, and he and Peter Douglas joined with me on Zoom for conversation and fellowship.

Then, in my early morning writing/coffee time a most wondrous idea came to me. I realized that I could write another *Symmorphy* text, and not one more, but two. I was far enough away from the more difficult work of completing the educational parts for the first five, and was ready to do it again. In sheer excitement, I wrote out the chapter list for *Symmorphy VI: Mankind* and *Symmorphy VII: Completion*. I shared those with Bill and Pete and they were excited as well.

I had always wanted to write about what we are as humans, and thus to understand, and the discipline of a *Symmorphy* textbook is just the best way to tackle something like that. Then, I still could not write "Our Glorious Salvation," because I needed to write a disciplined textbook on "Completion" first.

Writing more seems only to increase my ambition to write more. Yet writing to learn is only one part of that which carries me forward into the knowledge of God-with-me, the other part is the press of the Mercy Seat, the travail of sharing Hheart with God.

That Friday evening, after Maureen and Jo had gone downstairs to the living room and the boys were in bed, Matthew, my son-in-law, sat down across from me at the dining table.

I will say here only this about our conversation - I did not sleep that night.

We did not converse the next day. Matthew went about his business, and I sat and read a book. This was Saturday. On our first weekend with Matthew and Johanna, I had skipped the regular Zoom meeting. I was looking forward, however, to connecting with the brethren on Zoom for fellowship and sharing the word I had prepared this next Sunday morning.

That afternoon, I asked Matthew where Maureen and I could locate ourselves for that time of fellowship where we would not disturb them. Matthew said, "We'll have to talk about that." The end result was that I sent an email to Bill and Pete stating that I would not be with the Zoom fellowship, but that they should continue without me.

It was another week before the quarantine would be over. We spoke politely about outward essentials, but nothing more was said of any meaning except that I placed kindness and receiving within whatever I said. I also took to heart my inability towards Johanna when she was just a girl, that she had needed a father, and I was not able to be what she needed. In fact, this was the very chapter I was writing at the time, and I was able to place my wrongness towards Johanna into understanding and into Jesus.

We had a couple of days free after the quarantine and we visited with different ones in the community. I was refreshed with good fellowship in the Lord.

Matthew went on to work that next Monday, so it was Johanna who drove us to the airport in Thunder Bay. It's a small airport, and so she parked in the parking lot. It was just a short way across to the terminal. As the three of us gathered to pray together before we went on, I could see in her face that she needed her mom and dad, that she needed to be comforted inside of Jesus. And so I prayed in that direction and blessed her with all my heart. I could see the peace return to her face. How I love my daughter.

Although I do not share here the specific details, the second part of God completing in me His purpose and sending had begun, and it began inside of FIRE..

A "Captain of War"

Our flight home through Toronto again was uneventful. I was very glad to step out of, as it felt to me, the jaws of the beast. Before we left Canada, however, we had been informed by Katrina and James that the toilet in the master bath, right on the other side of a door from my bed, had flooded and ruined the carpet, and that the two of them had moved everything out of our bedroom and removed the carpet. Our house was a mess.

This meant that we could not go home until we had put a new floor into our bedroom. And so we stayed about a week with Kyle and Shelbie at their new place in Splendora, Texas, in their spare bedroom, still living out of our suitcases. This was a good time for me, a peaceful restoration from a difficult experience. We drove down to Fernbank most days and, with the help of our two sons, installed a new floor of vinyl panels in our bedroom. By January 10, we had everything moved back in and could be at home permanently. The good thing was that the old musty carpet was gone.

Having written and sent out "The Time of the Jesus Secret" while in Canada, I completed and sent out "Discovering Christ My Life" on January 16. This was the great turning point in my life story from desire inside of agony to JOY.

At this point, I also wanted very much to convey to my readers and in the Zoom sessions the meaning of God that came through the press of the Mercy Seat. And so I wrote and shared four lessons in the Zoom meetings on "Total War," and placed them as chapters into A Highway for God.

As I was writing and sharing these things, and pondering the prayers we had been praying for the Church, I realized, to my great astonishment, that God had made me a Captain of War. I know how to fight for the Church!

Here is what I wrote for the Zoom meeting on January 17.

~ For seven years, from the summer of 2006 to 2013, I cast down my enemy, and for seven years, from the summer of 2013 to 2020, I filled my 'house' with the knowledge of Christ Jesus causing Father-with-me. Then, in August of 2020, God made me a captain of War. — I had no idea. Filling my house with Christ began in August of 2006, however, and was the cause of that all-out assault of the evil one against me. Christ is always all first, before anything not-Christ could ever vanish away. Christ-All is the cause.

I did not realize it until just recently, but I have slain my thousands, and I have slain my ten thousands. Yet I most certainly had help, an army of mighty angels taking down every powerful, familiar, and desperate demon ordered to insert its words into my sphere. There were no survivors. I do not boast in myself, for there is no 'my' self in which to boast, but only Christ Jesus. Yet the more I see the straight pathway of my life, the more I place my face in worship — "Oh, my Father!"

We are at war! And you are MIGHTY sons with me.

My dad believed in non-violence, deeply and at cost. My brother chose to be a conscientious objector rather than to join the butchery of the evil one. I have not known violence. Well, I hit my sister in the back once because she made me mad. Other than that, it has never been in me to strike against anyone. Nothing would give me greater sorrow than that I should hurt other people, even in self-defense.

Yet from the time I was a little boy, I have been fascinated with war, with military strategy, and with great stories of battle. I have long thought this weird. Don't get me wrong. I am entirely an amateur and armchair 'student' of such things. I like my bigger adventures to be found in a good book or movie.

But suddenly, in this year of our Lord 2020 and now 2021, I find myself thrust into the frontlines of real war and I am astonished that I KNOW exactly what to do. We started in August, and I knew that the thing to do was an Admiral Horatio Nelson — "Attack." – But sir, the French outnumber us and we are not ready. — "I am confident that every man will do his duty. Attack!"

But now, in January of 2021, I hear the voice of Russel Crowe playing General Maximus in my ears. ~

And so we listened together to the clip from the movie, *Gladiator,* in which Russel Crowe calls to those riding into battle with him, "Hold the line. Stay with me. Hold the line." And I shared from that the importance of the fight we are in for the sake of all Christians across the earth, millions upon millions, and that to win together, we give our all – in line together.

Our prayers together became more fierce and direct, and our confidence grew.

In late January, I had a very unexpected experience in a dream. This was not a normal dream, but a real experience. My brother Franz came to me in my dream and said, with great agony and distress of soul, "Daniel, please pray for my children."

Now, how do I place such a thing with my previous assertion that we do not "converse with the dead?" First, I did not speak that without also knowing that there is no veil, no barrier between us and those of us who are in the heavens without physical bodies. At the same time, you will also notice that I did not "visit" with my brother, neither would such a thought ever come to me.

Yet I know this was my brother, and I took his agony of heart upon myself. I have prayed for Franz and Audrey's four children from then until now and have placed them into the keeping and expectation of God. I am not a big "pray-er," but my prayers are inside of faith, and I rest in absolute confidence that God does all that I ask. We also prayed for my brother's children in the Zoom meeting prayers.

I know that when I see my brother again, he will come to me with all of his children KEPT, inside the goodness of Christ. I will have my brother; I will pray for his children.

We did four sessions in the Zoom meetings on our warfare for the sake of our brothers and sisters in Christ all across the earth before returning again to our Old Testament studies. God was raising our confidence and our effectiveness in spiritual warfare for the Church to a deeper level. This level showed itself when we turned Solomon's prayer at the dedication of the temple into our own.

From Hebrews to Symmorphy Again!

I was writing five different things through these months, January through March of 2021. Those five things were the chapters when my life changed in *Prepare a Path*, the Zoom lessons for *After My Own Heart*, the climax chapters for *A Highway for God*, the book of Hebrews in *The Jesus Secret II*, and the first chapters of my return to Symmorphy, *Symmorphy VI: Mankind.*

I am astonished as I look at the weave of all of these together, the topics I was writing all at the same time.

I had Hebrews completed for *The Jesus Secret II* by the third week of March. This meant that from January through March, I was working on Chapters 10-13. This is that portion of Scripture most altered by the Calvinist translators from what was originally written, a deliberate mis-translation that turned the Christian life away from **"no consciousness of sins"** and towards *"the great struggle against sin."*

Of truth, writing *The Jesus Secret II* has been a journey into knowing the Father through knowing Jesus Sent into us. Writing this portion of Hebrews was a key section of that journey.

In *A Highway for God,* right after completing our study on war, I wrote "Calling God In" and "Utmost Purity," and then on into a topic beyond our boldness to enter, "Healing God's Heart" through "Joining Heart with Heart." I think I will find those chapters to be the center of all the change in me that has come since.

When I sent out "Utmost Purity" on February 13, I wrote this.

~ I want to share something incredible with you, something I have only discovered now. In March-April of 1985, I had argued with God in bitterness against John Hinson, and God sided with me, coming to Brother John in a dream, telling him what I told God He ought to say. Twelve years later, in March of 1997, God spoke to me, "Son, you passed the test," because I had refused to place any blame or fault upon Brother John Clarke.

Twelve years later, in March of 2009, God placed four men of great offense before me. And I knew without any question that if I wanted to KNOW Christ in union with me, I would also know Christ in union with them. (This is why I have stalled out again in writing my life story. I haven't found the courage yet to plunge back into God contending with me.) Twelve years later, in January to March/April of 2021, I know what it all means – take your brother with you. ~

Through the middle of February, Texas, including Houston, went through two weeks below freezing, We did experience more than two days without power during the coldest time. We were mostly prepared, however, with lots of candles and a propane heater with propane tanks in storage. The coolest it got inside our house was 65 degrees. Sadly, there were some elsewhere throughout the larger area who did freeze to death. I missed a Zoom meeting as a result of this time without power.

In March, I was able to return to my life story with "Out of the Furnace" and "Shaping a New Path." I was finally into the present season of writing Christ our Life. I also wrote Chapter 1 of my new *Symmorphy* text in March, *Symmorphy VI: Mankind.* It was so much joy to see a whole new level of Word flowing like molten gold into the long-familiar forms of my introductory chapter.

A Familiar Voice

Through these early months of 2021, we were continuing through the relationship with God enjoyed by various Old Testament characters. We spent quite a while with David, and then on to Solomon followed by Elijah and Elisha.

Two more notable things were happening in me through this study. The first was that I was seeing these individuals as friends, as people sharing many similar things with me, people I can know. As James said, "Elijah was a man just like us." Then I realized that David, and all of them, are Christians today, with their focus on the Church of Jesus Christ as the Jerusalem of God.

I now know that all these brothers and sisters from the Old Testament are with us at a personal level and are believing God for us, that Jesus would be proven faithful and true through us into this world.

But an even greater realization dawned on me slowly through this study during these months. I had seen that Abraham had nothing except a Voice speaking to him out of the blue, and that only several times throughout his life.

And suddenly I knew that I know that Voice, for the same Voice who spoke to Abraham also spoke to me across the span of my life with Him. I know the Voice that spoke to Abraham, for it is a Voice that is close and familiar and real in my life experience. I know this now, not in any self-exaltation, but in tears of gladness streaming down my face.

It is from this knowing, then, that I wrote the chapter coming up, "The Meaning of a Life." I place that familiar and honored Voice as the center and structure of my entire life story.

53. A New Altar

January 2021 - December 2021

Understanding Myself

The time period of December 2020 to September 2022 includes some of the most difficult experiences of my life, but it also includes some of my best times, knowing that my Father shares every moment and particle of my life with me. These two, the most difficult and the best, are connected in surprising ways.

I have chosen to place all of the difficult things into this chapter and reserve the continued flow of God's favor in our lives for the next chapter. The reason I must do that is this very altar God has asked me to place myself upon inside of His presence and for the sake of His people.

Now, I say, "God has asked me to place myself upon," because this is how we think, but it's not really the accurate picture, for I do nothing of myself. Rather, God shares all things with me, and it is He, as All-Salvation, who places Himself upon the altar inside of and together with me, as His outward expression in heaven-earth.

One of the most astonishing statements found in the Bible is 1 Corinthians 12:21. **The Head is not able to say to the feet, "I have no need of you."** – God needs His body, for He has no other means by which to enter into His creation to be seen and known. – **We ARE indeed the body of Christ and members of Him as a part.**

And so I finally understand, just now, that I must approach this experience of my life, covering around two-year's time, not from my perspective only, but from God's perspective. For just as He shares all of me with me, so also I share all of Him with Him.

I have just completed and sent out Chapter 55, "The Meaning of a Life." At the same time, I am writing "I Set Forth My Soul" in *Studies in John's Letters*. In fact, as I write, I am going back and forth between "I Set Forth My Soul" and "A New Altar," for they are the same reality.

Only now do I understand my life. Yet I am not alone, for God has always had the same purpose in your life, dear reader.

I am overwhelmed right now as I look across "The Meaning of a Life," and I see the hand of the All-Carrying One upon every moment, with intense determination and driven purpose. And I see this chapter, "A New Altar," fitting into the Passover season of 2021 in the story of my life as the definition of everything. Somehow, I must convey to you the meaning, for I am speaking of 1 John 3:16, God's only entrance into His creation.

Consider these words, written first by Jeremiah, the prophet who wept over Jerusalem and in his tears wrote Lamentation 3, which I have always read as the story of my life.

For this is the covenant that I will make with the house of Israel after those days says the Lord, I will place My laws in their through-minds and upon their hearts I will inscribe them; and I will be God inside of them, and they will be people inside of me. And no one will teach each their neighbor and each their brother saying, 'Know the Lord'; because all will know Me, from the least of them to the greatest of them, because I will propitiate their acts of injustice and their falling short will not be in My thoughts anymore (Hebrews 8:10-12).

There are three threads woven through this expression of the Covenant, and those three threads are all the pattern of my days. I am astonished and overwhelmed, for though I lived this, I knew nothing and planned nothing. **For out from God and passing through God and returning to God are ALL things** (Romans 11). Indeed, if I had known, I would certainly have messed it all up. Yet God did tell me, many times in many ways, but I had no idea what He meant.

The first thread is the Covenant, the primary meaning across the span of my life. The second thread is the Word planted in my heart, the relentless pursuit of my great need over decades. But the third thread is God propitiating my acts of injustice, and that third thread is the most pronounced in the structure of my years.

I have shared with you the pattern of three Passover seasons, with twelve years exactly between them, March/April of 1985 when God spoke my angry words to John Hinson in a dream ~ to March of 1997 when God said, "Son, you passed the test," ~ to March of 2009, when I deliberately placed Brother Buddy into Jesus living as him. – "Do not speak against Mine anointed" and "take your brother with you," that is, three apostolic ministries who were "above me" in the Lord, John Hinson, John Clarke, and Buddy Cobb, all three of whom I had reason to despise, yet God saved me from doing so.

But I like patterns and so I thought – "Well, what about twelve years after and twelve years before." To my complete astonishment, twelve years after is March of 2021, this very month into which I am inserting this chapter, a chapter coming out from the travail of God with me through incredible awfulness and great glory.

Then I looked back at twelve years before, which would be the spring of 1973, the second semester of my junior year at Lebanon Union High School. I thought, "What on earth was I doing and thinking then?" At first it seemed a blank, so I thought through the courses I took that semester. Suddenly, without warning, a six by twelve BEAM came swinging out of nowhere and hit me right between the eyeballs (I'm being poetic).

As I am sitting here writing this morning, I'll be 66 years old in just a few weeks. In all the years of healing from John Eldredge until today, this is the first time God has brought my great wickedness into the light. He has made sure I did not put these things together until right now, neither will I include them in my chapter on "A Time of Darkness." Here is where my acts of injustice belong.

You see, I had thought my sins were fantasy and daydreaming, drugs and rock & roll. And when God said to me just before my season of deliverance, ~ "Even in the darkness, you were still My son," ~ those were certainly among the things He included in my knowing at that time. Indeed, it was in the fall of my junior year when I overdosed on LSD. But those things were peripheral; let me now share the center of my evil self-exaltation.

I think about three men in my early years of the move, Dan Kurtz, Bill Ritchie, and Jim Fant, men of such integrity, honor, and steadfastness whose impact on my life defines me to this day. I think about three other men, Abel Ramirez, Don Howat, and Rick Annett, whose friendships towards me were the friendship of Jesus, friendships that held me steady through the winds of near-insanity.

As I considered the spring of 1973, I saw one man, then two, then three, two of them that spring and the third across my teenage years, three Christian men, three men who were my teachers, three men whom I despised and mocked and cursed.

If I did not KNOW Jesus for me right now, I would be unable to continue.

Let me start with Mr. Philips, my 7th and 8th grade teacher, and P.E. and basketball coach. Yes, Mr. Philips operated inside the "low-grade bully" group towards me, at least as I perceived it. I hated him, and that hatred spanned across my teenage years from 13-19. I would flip a birdy out the window when his car passed us on the road. Later, when I drove by his house in the middle of the night on my way home, drunk and stoned, I blew my horn all the way by, and cursed him and his family with heart and with words.

Mr. Stroup was my U.S. History teacher through my junior year, thus he fits definitely into the spring of 1973. I considered him a very poor teacher, an insipid and shallow man. I passed his course, of course, but I mocked him. On the semester exam, which required all written answers, I filled in absurd and brilliant answers to every question, answers that were just a mockery of him. He gave me a zero, but I exulted in my success. (Later, when Maureen and I lived in Lebanon, Oregon, I saw that Mr. Stroup was the pastor of a nearby Spirit-filled church.)

Then, in the spring of 1973, we had a student teacher in our Chemistry class for the few weeks of his student teaching, taking the place of Mr. Burridge, our favorite teacher. Whatever his teaching skills might have been, and I don't remember his name, he did not know how to connect with teenagers. I think he might have condescended to us, a big mistake on his part. I did not really realize that I was typically the smartest guy in the room. You see, in Mr. Stroup's class, I was by myself without any of my friends in that group. But I had more then once led the other students in rebellion against

Mr. Philips. And, of truth, I was the undercurrent in our total-class, under-the-radar, rebellion against this student teacher. We were successful in that we were not found out and in that he failed his student teaching and could never be a teacher.

Because I will propitiate their acts of injustice and their falling short will not be in My thoughts anymore.

I know now that it is the demon god of "me, myself, and I" who must be appeased - propitiated – by the Love of Jesus until we come down off our high horse and place our foreheads upon the ground in the presence of the One who has always carried us.

"Mr. Philips, I was utterly wrong and wicked towards you and even towards your family; please forgive me." – "Mr. Stroup, I treated you with such disrespect, please forgive me, I was wrong." To the man who was the student teacher, "I was devious and wicked, and I led the whole class to do you great harm. I dare hardly ask your forgiveness, for silence is my best response."

"Lord Jesus, You have already made me clean from all my iniquity and terrible acts of injustice. Indeed, You were with me even through these things, sharing my life with me, though I knew it not. You intended me in every moment, though You did not intend my sins. I ask You, Lord Jesus to release these three men from my darkness and all of its terrible effects, bless them with the knowledge of Your presence and goodness in their lives. Let them know Your joy, even now."

The thing is, however, that redemption makes God's purpose for our lives possible and real, but our redemption itself is not God's purpose, neither is it the meaning of our lives. Something far greater is happening as a result of a life shared with God through Jesus. Salvation is entering through us into our world.

A Tale of Three Stories

The best way for me to convey to you the meaning of this "new altar" now present in my life is to share three stories with you. Two of those are fictional stories, the two most important such books to me that I have ever read, *The Lord of the Rings* by J.R.R. Tolkien and *Hind's Feet on High Places* by Hannah Hurnard. These stories were the call of God ringing inside my soul, calling me to this very moment.

But I want to begin with a third book, one which I read in February of 1996, the beginning of the most important time period of my life. This is a true story titled *The Frontiersmen* by Allan Eckert.

I had begun my time as an elder with the Blueberry eldership, yet I felt so inadequate. I did not understand why I could not move freely "in the anointing" as did all these others, as it seemed to me. I was watching a logging camp by myself in the deep cold, fifty miles from the nearest other human. In my distress, I cried out loud to God, "God, can you not save even me?" I imagined that God did not answer me.

Yet now I know that He did, more profoundly than I can contain. You see, I had nothing to do for several days. Yet I found a large book, *The Frontiersmen*, in someone's bunk and read it. It is the story of Simon Kenton, a man of greater importance than Daniel Boone in the opening of the Kentucky-Ohio wilderness to American settlers. This was an accurate historical account and vast in its scope. Simon Kenton was a man of great stature and the lands of Ohio and Kentucky sloping down to the Ohio River were the most fertile lands on earth.

As a young man, Simon Kenton entered that area in companionship with another young man named Simon Girty. These two young men were drawn to each other as friends so deeply that they were inspired to make a blood covenant together. To them, entering into a blood covenant meant everything; it meant a sharing of all for life. It meant they would be there for each other, regardless.

Yet in the conflict that came to the Ohio Valley, the two Simons found themselves on opposing sides. Simon Girty's heart led him to side with the Shawnee's in their distress, and Simon Kenton's heart led him to side with the American settlers in their distress. The war was over the richest land on earth; elsewhere it was called the War of 1812.

There came a time when Simon Kenton was captured by the Shawnees and forced to run a gauntlet for his life. He ran through the blows most of the way, but just before the end, an old woman caught him hard with her stick and down he went flat on his face in the mud. Death was all he could now expect.

Yet at that moment (this is an accurate story), Simon Girty, the friend of the Shawnees, came into the camp. Girty gave himself as surety for Kenton, and the Shawnees agreed to give Kenton his life and his liberty.

I did not know this was God speaking to me, but God knew, and that's what counts. Let me put into words now, what God spoke, if I had been able to hear.

"My son, when you asked Jesus into your heart, you and I entered into a Blood Covenant together. That means that you and I share all things together. All that I am belongs to you and all that you are belongs to Me. It means that I have your back. Now you are passing through a great gauntlet, carrying the Word I have planted inside of you through great tribulation. You will fail, My son. You will fall flat on your face in the mud, just like Jesus did. Yet I am there, nothing can stand against you, and I will carry you all the way through death and into LIFE."

I know now why *The Lord of the Rings* went deep into me when I first read it at age twelve, the story of a hobbit, stumbling through weakness and failure along a way he did not know, for the sake of his beloved Shire and all free people. To this day, I cannot read Frodo's words, "I will take the ring, though I do not know the way," without tears running down my face.

The depth of truth Tolkien wrote into this "make-believe" story is simply profound. Evil cannot be defeated by strength, but only through weakness. Yet here is the most incredible thing. When Frodo got to his goal, the fires of Mt. Doom, he failed completely. He could not throw the ring into the fire; all he could do was claim it as his own.

How, then, did he win? First, he could never have made it to the crack of doom by himself, for it was the sturdy legs and stout heart of Sam Gamgee that carried him up the last treacherous miles, and with him, the fate of all free folk. Then – this is the most important truth written by Tolkien all through his story – Frodo's victory came from one thing only, step by step along the way, and that was the compassion he showed to Gollum, the least worthy creature on earth.

That's what Gandalf had said, that the pity shown to Gollum may well rule the fate of many.

Finally, the journey of Much Afraid, stumbling each step of the way, in *Hind's Feet on High Places*, spoke to me more than any other Christian book I have read. Much Afraid took a memento of every failure as a testimony of her thanksgiving. But when she finally reached the high places, on the other side of the valley of loss, all she found was a stone altar. There, in her pain and inability, she offered all of herself to the shepherd, that she might belong to him alone.

The truth is, in all three of these stories, it was a life offered in weakness and failure – for the sake of others.

There is a fourth story as well. Of all the things God spoke deeply into me through Sam Fife, the story of Abraham offering Isaac back to God on Mt. Moriah was the most profound to me and went the deepest into my heart.

Now, I want to take you to God's altar for me, my end of the gauntlet, my edge of the fires of Doom, my stone altar of surrender, my offering of Christ back to God. For that purpose, God gave me, not three men this time, but four.

A Tale of Four Men

Over the last two years, God has given me four men, readers of what I write, whose unkind words and unjust actions towards me have ripped me all to pieces inside. Yet these four men love Jesus, are anointed of God, are gifted in differing and good ways, and have blessed and been a blessing to me.

Now, I am accustomed, out from years of living in Christian community, to bear with the stumbling failures and weird ways of other people, with patience and grace. Yet, in the makeup of their present expressions, God chose to give these four, four different traits in their responses towards me that are simply the most difficult human characteristics for me to bear. In short, I partly want to despise them by "exposing" them.

Here is what I just wrote in "I Set Forth My Soul."

‿

My salvation has nothing to do with Jesus "appeasing" God, getting Him to "back off." My salvation has everything to do with a Man receiving me into Himself. It is for this reason that we know that the LOUDEST words in the universe were spoken to God inside of Jesus as He rose to His feet in Gethsemane. – "HERE AM I! I and the children whom You have given Me."

We saw in our study of John's gospel that the most despicable of human responses showed themselves in offence against Jesus the moment after He said those words, in the form of Judas and Peter. It is clear that Jesus had already chosen, personally and in agony, to receive into Himself even those. When He was faced with their deeds, it was already finished inside Himself.

I believe that God transferred all authority from Adam to Jesus that moment when Jesus said, "I will drink Your cup." Jesus, personally and willingly, drank me into Himself, in all my dregs of sin and rebellion. And Jesus, personally and willingly, gave me Himself, His own soul, to call as my own.

I honor Jesus only by receiving with joy all that He has given me – Himself. Then I turn and do the same for my brothers and sisters.

The issue is contempt. Adam ate of death out from contempt, that he might rule over those whom he despised. Contempt versus Honor. There is only one way that I can receive in honor those whose actions towards me are, in my soul, the most contemptuous, those whom I naturally hold in scorn.

He humbled Himself. – Just like Jesus, I must choose humility, the lowest place, taking the blame upon myself, being silent before those who mock. Speaking only the very SWORD of God, "Father, forgive them." This is what Jesus does for me every moment. This is the authority through which God moves in power.

～

When I attempted to write the words and actions of these individuals by name, Maureen reacted with horror. Her reaction forced me to realize my true motivation in writing those things. I really, really wanted to PROVE them wrong. I wanted them to hurt, just a bit, in the way that their words and actions hurt me. I wanted revenge.

At that moment in time, I remain just like Jesus, for He also felt the same things in Gethsemane, that's why it is called AGONY.

And – just like with Jesus, to honor these men is an action of the deepest of humiliation. I must take the blame upon myself. I must be silent. I must speak Christ into and concerning them.

Even now, when I try to write a brief paragraph describing each, I find that I am still giving voice to contempt.

Let me state, then, even more briefly, those four things, which I must do to make sense to you of all of this. – (1) The hard forehead of Calvin's theology, (2) the perverse delight of the flesh to offend, (3) the shallow spin of "amen, amen" that hides a love for the meaningless things of this world, and (4) a low-grade bullying trying to "fix" other people's outward performance. And except for the first, the complete inability to say, "Daniel, I was wrong, please forgive me."

To two I sent a letter attempting to share my own hurt, attempting to do so without placing blame. My attempts were unsuccessful. To the two most offensive communications, I replied with one short line, "Brother, you are as Jesus to me."

Let me place all this into God's purposes through me into this world, now, in the completion of this age. God gave me these four that I might do as Jesus did, that I might place myself beneath of them for their sakes, that I might carry them inside myself with fervent joy, stumbling with me all the way through the darkness and into LIFE.

My decision is 1 John 3:16, God's entrance with power into this world. – **By this we know love, because He set forth His soul for us, for our sakes, and we also are committed to setting forth our souls for the sake of our brothers and sisters.**

But let me continue with the altar of God.

A Dream to Be Shattered

When God first spoke to me concerning Blair Valley in the winter of 1992-93, ~ "Blair Valley is your home" ~, He also began to shape in my heart a new view of Christian Community. This new view was different at the center and core of community from how I had known it up until then in the move fellowship. I have called that new view "the community of my heart," an understanding that grew in me until I was able to put it down on paper in *Symmorphy V: Life*.

In writing this account from then forward, I attempted to give expression to that growing "dream" for a Community of Christ that would be an expression of the true essence of Jesus. I included extra chapters, just to put in front of you my ongoing thoughts concerning this dream.

In late 2012, when I wrote "My Vision" in response to John Gray's wonderful word on "Lazarus, Come Forth," I placed before my readers the thought of an actual return to the Blair Valley property and what it would cost to make it real. I shared that, as we had left that service, God spoke to me, ~ "I will finish the Word I have planted inside of you." ~ This was a promise I perceived to mean the fulfillment of the community of my heart.

Through all these years everything I did and everything I wrote was for one purpose only, our return to community. I am a man of certainty and of commitment. You can see that in this move we were making, from Fernbank to our present home in Shepherd, a place that could become community was the only thing in my mind.

There were two problems, however. The first problem was that much of my thoughts and expressions were, in fact, the imagination of my mind. Yes, it was imagination coming out from what God had planted inside of me, nonetheless, it was, for all practical purposes, useless, and even a blockage to the real.

That is not the entire equation, however. Let me include the other part.

I have stated emphatically from the first that I sent out the *Christ Our Life* letter in November of 2008, that I write for two purposes. My first purpose is to know God, and my second purpose is to call forth a people who know God with whom I can walk daily, that is a Christ Community where my family and I could find our home.

I can say as of this year of our Lord, 2022, my first purpose is fulfilled beyond my wildest expectations. And yet, the first purpose cannot really be complete until the second is also fulfilled. I cannot know God without walking together with other believers of like precious faith inside a shared life together.

Yet I have believed, from the afternoon of August 6, 2006 on, that if I teach people to speak Christ their life, they will be TRANSFORMED, and out from that fruit of Christ, actual Communities of Christ would form.

That was sixteen years ago, sixteen long years in which no such thing has happened.

Yet, as Alexander Pope pointed out, "Hope springs eternal in the human breast."

By the first of June, 2021, we had found the property where Maureen and I presently live. I want to share with you a letter I sent to a brother, though I will not include any names. See this letter only as an expression of my own heart.

⌒

The real question, I think, is what do you want? I know for myself that when all the swirl of thoughts and emotions becomes insufficient, and when I reach deep into the desire of my heart, that is where I find the Lord.

For me, I think, the issue is more centered around what I need. Let me explain.

We have found a property, 1.5 acres on the bottom side of the little town of Shepherd, up 59 from Splendora, where Kyle lives. The land is sloped, which is cool; it has a sandy loam soil, which is great for gardening. It is filled with huge Magnolia trees, which are still shedding their fragrance. The house is cute and comfortable. The shop is just right for James's tools. It doesn't show in the pictures, but there is a single-wide mobile home just below the house. It may not be for sale, we will find out. Nonetheless, the hook ups for it are all in place, and if it were removed, it would be simple to put another unit there.

There is a spot for a third unit on the property, but other than that, it would not suffice for a larger community, but it is what is available, what we can afford, and what would meet our present needs. At the same time, there are many adjoining properties that are vacant and which the owners could be willing to sell. This is entirely outside of the high growth Houston area and the price of empty land here is not being driven up. BUT – I am unable to predict the future.

So – what I want to do is to garden and raise chickens; that is, I like the idea of turning this 1.5 acres into a garden/orchard oasis that would provide much of our food during difficult times. Yet that is where my need comes in. The potential and the newness would inspire me to at least want to try to do the work. On my own, however, I know it could not last long. There is a disconnect in my psyche and I can't bridge it myself.

What I need is someone very like yourself who is enthusiastic about the same vision for the property and who shares the love of the same word and knowledge of God. When there is another man out there working, that disconnect in my psyche is bridged and I can actually go out and put in a few hours a day. And the truth is, I've been like this my whole life.

There are three needs that I have, then. The first is companionship in fellowship, for the same disconnect happens between my desire for regular weekly services and the doing of it. I know from years of knowing myself that someone like you would provide just enough to enable me to initiate such services. My children and wife need this also, especially Kyle.

My second need is physical health. I need physical work, at least a few hours a day, else I don't think my body can stay healthy. And there is no physical work I would like to do better than to garden and raise chickens on a property such as this. It may sound pathetic, but I can't change myself. With a fellow worker like yourself, I am able to enjoy work; otherwise, the disconnect is too great for any enthusiasm to endure.

My third need is to stay alive, with my family, over the next several years. I know that people do not comprehend what things will soon be like. The truth is, staying alive is a lot of work, work I could help with if I'm not by myself, but I think only frustration and rapid decline otherwise.

And so, there is a place here for you, work for you to do, and a fellowship for you to be a part of. The question for you is, what do you want, not what do we need.

It could be that the Lord has appointed you for such a task as this – specifically, to help keep Daniel and his family alive over the next several years. If that were true, I believe it would be a worthy ministry, beyond just saving my own skin. I can't even promise a full Christian Community; that would take at least a third person or family unrelated to either of us. Yet our life together would operate to some degree as community, something we would work out together.

Maureen and I, then, invite you to move to Shepherd, Texas (provided we close on this property) and to be a part of our fellowship together in the word and in the garden.

If the single-wide home does not remain, we would have a small bedroom in our home until we obtained a unit for the space, just below the fixed house. It is important to us that you have your own place so that you feel that you belong. If you chose to come, I would help you move, including renting a truck to bring your stuff down.

Yet the bottom line is what do you want? The truth is, your decision is free entirely from our needs and must answer the desire of the Lord inside of you. If you determine that your place is in (your present location) then we leave you free and blessed in the Lord. Yet if this invitation touches something deep inside of you, then be assured that we here need you and your help even more.

⌒

Let me comment on this letter before continuing. First, nothing in this letter was spoken as a whim. I knew the cost, and I was fully prepared to pay that cost.

Then, Maureen thought this sounded like I need a "savior." Yet I am absolutely convinced that God NEVER intends of us to become "super-heroes" all by ourselves. That since "I can do all things inside of Christ," I ought to produce everything needed out from myself. No – God intends that we NEED one another. I know that I need other brothers and sisters walking together with me daily that I might know the Lord and that I might live.

Finally, I include this letter because I must. This letter sums up forty-five years of desire, of saying, "Yes, Lord," at every point along the way. In it I open myself up, making myself more vulnerable and exposed than anything I have ever written to anyone. This was the first tangible expression of "I will walk with a people who know You," since we left Blair Valley. This is me.

June 9, 2021, then, was the most difficult day since I left move of God community, for there was no response to anything that I wrote. I was caught, through that day and through many days after, in a deep sense of shame, that speaking Christ your life accomplishes nothing, that it transforms no one, that these fifteen years of writing to know the Lord and to call forth a people who know the Lord was one big waste of time. I agonized under the thought to remove all I have written from public availability.

Yet it was also a deep personal humiliation. Let me explain.

I now realize that among the many thousands of people who committed their lives to the word Sam Fife preached was a higher percentage of people of honor and integrity than can be found in any other group. When a reader suggested that there are no people of honor and integrity in the church, I hit back hard. That's the one thing on which I will not be silent, speaking evil falsely against the Church.

Yet through these many days of great failure in June 2021, I thought, "Have I drawn no one of integrity and honor to the word that I share? Does my Asperger's present such an awful outward face that no one true is drawn to me?"

Please understand, the same word God spoke to Elijah applies also to me, "I have 'seven thousand' who have not bowed their knee to pretending." That means that I never actually lost sight of the fact that there are those dear ones who are people of integrity who do read my letters. I am sharing only the depths of what I felt at the time, and nothing of what I did or meant.

After a few days, as the pain and humiliation lessened slightly, I began to do what I always do. "God, what is Your purpose in sharing Yourself with me in this way?"

If I Perish, I Perish

Then, I think it might have been on Tuesday, June 15, as I was considering once again the next session of the Zoom teaching, the second lesson on Esther titled "If I Perish, I Perish," that the Lord first entered my darkness with His Word.

He began by enabling me to see my own fault, that I had been imposing my own mental daydreams on my readers. I began to realize that maybe I was holding others to a higher standard as I had known integrity in the move fellowship, and not that level in which Christ Jesus living as them had carried them through thus far.

In that moment the Lord showed me, out from Esther's story, a level of covenant with Him beyond anything I had known before.

Let me put it into human words. "Son, if you will surrender to me all your practice of imagining your future in any way, including your desire for community, then I will be intercession through you for the sake of our Church." – "God, my Father, I give You this practice of daydreaming about what could be our next step together and about how a Community of Christ might happen, that You might remove it from me. In doing so, You, my God, will be mighty through me for the sake of others."

"If I Perish, I Perish," was possibly the most life-changing thing I have ever written. By the next Sunday morning, June 20, the Lord had restored my heart sufficient to share again in the Zoom meetings and to speak these things out loud to the precious brothers and sisters gathered there. Here are just a few excerpts from that lesson, along with the prayer we prayed together afterwards.

⌇

This was no light matter for Esther. Her enemy had the ear of the king and the law on his side. The chances of failure were so high that to stand for her people was a choice to die. Her final statement, "If I perish; I perish," was no light thing. It was as costly as anything given personally in history. Esther had little hope of success.

We sang it in the move – "If I perish, I perish, but I'm going to see the King." On the one hand, we had no idea what those words meant. On the other hand, I knew hundreds of people in that fellowship who paid every price to be part of what God is doing in the earth. I now understand how rare that quality is.

It became clear a couple of years ago that God has not anointed me to minister the word I share to potentially interested believers. It has now become clear that God has not anointed me to be the beginning of a Community of Christ. This second is probably the greatest sorrow of my life.

To "go in before the King" for the sake of God's people is the costliest thing I have ever faced. Yet this is what Jesus is sharing with me in the present time.

You and I will never know the Father unless we walk together with others of like precious faith. Indeed, I realize how foolish I am to continue writing as if I know anything. Yet God has not anointed me to gather a community together around me, though I have sought for it with tears for 23 years.

Only one thing is left for me. And that is to join with Jesus in the loss of everything, that I might win LIFE for the sake of our brethren. I have no wisdom; I have no strength. But I do have the Lord Jesus, my Savior, arising always inside of me and showing Himself to me through all the course of my life.

We are called for such a time as this, and God has given us a very specific task to do.

If God has not anointed me to minister this word to His Church, and if He has not anointed me to begin a Christ Community, then what has He anointed me to do?

I am beginning to understand the critical importance of the entrance of Word into the human sphere, into the voice of humans alive in the present time hearing and speaking in agreement with that Word. And so God has anointed me to find that Word arising inside my heart and coming to me out from the heavens, and He has anointed us together to believe and to speak that Word inside our world.

I don't know if you wish to join with me in this prayer, for it is a prayer out from the loss of all things dear in this world. If you wish only to listen, that is also the grace of God. The seriousness resting upon us is greater than that resting upon Esther.

"God, our Father, You are mighty and fearsome. We do not stand inside Your presence lightly, for we know the great costliness of Your Salvation. We ask first for ourselves, Father, with strong crying and tears, as Jesus did, that You would save us from death, and especially from the death of holding contempt for others.

"You who carry all, we stand here inside Your presence as Esther stood before the king. Your people, O God, are under overwhelming attack from an enemy they do not comprehend. We know, Father, that You spoke the consequences of sin into our world. We know that Your Son, this Jesus who lives inside of us, crafted, by Himself, all cleansing away of sin. And we know, Father, that You now speak through Jesus inside of us a new Word, a Word of Life for the sake of our brothers and sisters who have been fatally wounded. But we know as well, Father, that Jesus must find faith in the earth.

"It is for one reason only, O God, our Father, that we would be that faith of Jesus in this earth and that is that we might know You, through knowing Jesus Sent as He reveals His mighty Salvation through us.

"Father, we would SHARE, all through our experience and in every practicality, the meaning and power of the cleansing-away wrought by Jesus, that our brethren might live and not die. Lord Jesus, we would know the full meaning of the Ekenosis, of this Redeeming God coming through us, making us part of His poured-out Love.

"We know, Lord Jesus, that the redemption of our brothers and sisters will cost us everything, as it did You. Yet as we suffer the loss of everything we value in this world, Lord Jesus, we are absolutely confident that everything is being turned by us together into the salvation of Your Church.

"Lord Jesus, it is You alone who causes us to share with You the same loss of everything, and the same faith that everything we are and every circumstance coming our way is absolutely and only coming out from our Father. And this narrow and confined place You now share with us, Lord Jesus, we know that it is Father's Heart."

⏝

Yet out from this experience with God would come the most wondrous revelation of God-with-us coming through me into the human experience, coming up in April of 2022, a Word that would change me, along with many others, forever.

Placing Everything upon the Altar

I now know the altar of God and the offering of "a sweet-smelling aroma." I want to share both the beginning of this new fire, now upon the altar of God, and its completion in July through September 2022 as I am finally able to write this chapter, the chapter that is the "climax," the meaning and purpose of my life.

Through July and August of this year, 2022, I watched two mystery shows on TV with an Asperger's character as the lead role in each. The first was *The Extraordinary Attorney Woo* and the second was *Astrid*. The first is South Korean and the second French. In both cases, the actresses genuinely portrayed Asperger's differing characteristics with great skill. The only lack, I think, came from script writers who did not really understand such things from inside of them.

What I love about Attorney Woo was how free she was to express her "weirdness" in public, to do her little dance, especially as she entered a place, and to allow herself to be autistic even in the courtroom. This was beautiful to me, though it is not the normal story of those who are Asperger's. In fact, I loved her "dance" so much that I wept tears, for my severe efforts to hide my Asperger's expressions over years, and especially in community, always drained me of much strength.

Astrid was more realistic towards the pain all who are Asperger's bear all their lives. The story-line included flashbacks to her adolescence in school. She was smarter than all the others, yet they mocked her savagely for her differences, and she had no defense. The story-line also included her joining with a circle of those who were Asperger's who met regularly to help each other through life.

The great grief of all who are Asperger's is the constant attempts of others, low-grade bullies, who think that they ought to "fix" the outward expressions of an Asperger's person so that we might "behave" more appropriately, more "like" them. This practice is relentless, especially in the church, and even more especially in Christian community. It is what makes a place impossible to enter. In fact, it typically comes out that if I want to be like Jesus, then I must be more like them.

Don't get me wrong. There is an expression, spoken in kindness, that gently guides an Asperger's person into knowing how to relate with others. Attorney Woo's father was good at that, instructing Woo that she could not talk about whales, her obsession, while at work. More than that, if I have done something to hurt another, and they or someone else points that out in the kindness of Jesus and in private, then that also is good.

The need to "fix" me, especially in public, is something entirely different.

But the most wonderful thing about Astrid's story was the portrayal of those "normal" people in her life who were to her just like Don Howat and others were to me. The main one of those was an outgoing and very expressive woman, named Raphaëlle, who was the lead detective in the show. She placed herself as Astrid's friend, and inside that friendship, Astrid could venture out into public places that otherwise would be only unbearable pain.

And inside that protective friendship, Astrid could give the brilliant abilities she had to give, a gift she could have given no other way. This was my life; this was Abel Ramirez and Don Howat to me. This was also that safe place for me as "the teacher" in the classroom.

It was Raphaëlle's birthday. Astrid asked an Asperger's friend what she should give her as a present. The friend suggested – give her something that conveys what she means to you.

Astrid braved entering a public pub to offer her gift to "Raph." When Raph opened it, she was astonished to find a thimble. She gulped and said "Thank you," but she had no idea what it might mean.

Later, when it was just the two of them, Raph asked Astrid, "Why the thimble?" Let me paraphrase the answer.

"When someone really wants to sew something, they are faced with a painful task, for a needle is needed and it is sharp and often draws blood. Then they take a thimble and place it on their finger. The needle is no longer able to jab and they can finish sewing things together. You are my thimble, Raph, for your friendship protects me from the pain. That way I can go into a crime scene with you and help weave together the answer without suffering pain."

That thimble became one of Raphaëlle's most precious possessions.

I went out to water my fruit trees right after I watched that episode, on August 17. As I was meditating on the Lord, I thought, "Jesus, You are my Friend; You are my thimble, just like Don Howat was my thimble. It is Your friendship that protects me so that I can give to others all You have given me to give, without placing myself into pain."

When I left the move fellowship, I said, "Jesus, I will know You MORE REAL than Don Howat ever could be." In this moment, twenty-four years later, it was TRUE.

I wept much as I watched these two shows, for the Lord Jesus took me into my own autistic experiences and showed me that it was GOOD, and that He and I together made all my difficulty to be effective goodness for others. It is only out from that moment that I am able to write this chapter.

I know that each person bears much suffering out from different reasons and in different ways. I also know that we cannot know one another's pain unless we truly know our own. The pain of autism is different from pain as known by many. By describing my own pain, I am in no way diminishing anything you also have borne. Rather, I am, with Jesus, sharing myself with you.

I want to go next to that sleepless night when I stumbled into my bed in overwhelming pain over the terrible accusations against God that are Calvin's theology.

In that moment, lying there on my bed, I knew nothing of my present understanding. I was in pain, from the top of my head to the bottom of my gut, but especially through my heart. This is not an emotional or a demonic pain, no demon was in my heavens. This pain carries no bitterness or unforgiveness. Yet it remains. In my twenties, it would have ripped me apart without slacking for a week or more. In my fifties, it would have lasted about forty-eight hours without abatement.

Only one thing ever diminishes that pain, and that is the words of my Bible, the words of the gospel, entering into me, that I might know my Savior. And so it has been since I was nineteen.

As I lay there in the dark, I did what God has taught me to do. With my heart wide open in spite of the pain, with tears on my face, I drew my brother into my heart, upon the Mercy Seat, upon the Blood, and there I joined him together with my Father inside the pain and confusion of my soul, and I set him utterly free of me inside of God.

Except, I took it a step further into God than I had known before. I said, "God my Father, I am willing to stumble through the pain and darkness with You for my brother's sake because I know that You will raise me out from death and into LIFE. – And You will also raise him into LIFE along with me!" I repeated that same declaration often through the night.

The pain continued, however, and to this day I place him inside of God, that through my pain offered in tears, my brother might come to know that Jesus is his only life.

The first part of God's completion in me is the Completion of His Word. Now, this second part of God completing in me His purpose and sending had begun, and it began inside of FIRE. This is the Completion of God's entrance into creation.

If I were to share, blow by blow, the extent and meaning of the pain coming against me over the last two years from these four brothers in Jesus, you would be shocked. For over a year, I wept every single day over the brother's response to my invitation to community. I pleaded with him and with the others, anonymously but regularly, in the lessons I wrote, seemingly to no avail. I searched out every way that I could share how I also had failed (bringing in that time that I lied to Brother Jim Fant, for instance), so that I might give them a door into saying, "Daniel, I was WRONG, please forgive me," and to add NOTHING to it.

Sometime, maybe in January of 2022, I was driving home with my son James. It was after dark. He said something to me that was cruel and awful. I felt inside that I had done enough for him and that now I no longer wanted to maintain a relationship. We drove on in silence for awhile, feeling a savage barrier.

Then, James said to me, "What I said was wrong; I should not have said that."

I want men, especially, to understand what happened inside of me the very moment that those words entered. – ALL sense of a barrier VANISHED from my soul, and I was free to relate with my son inside of love and joy as I normally do. I felt better, even, than if those previous words had never been spoken. I felt the great value of a costly koinonia.

You can be "right" or you can be a friend, but you CANNOT be both. It's called integrity.

Let me return to June of 2021. I have titled this chapter, "A New Altar." It was "new" only in the sense that now I finally accepted its full meaning. This was the same Altar of Incense preached into me by Sam Fife and others in my early years in the move fellowship.

"Lay your Isaac down," became now, "Lay down upon My altar your desire to bring forth a community of Christ in your present life. Surrender it all to Me and think no more of it."

Christ life is life together; it has always been life together. I cannot know God except together with a people who know God walking daily together. To give up the dream of returning to the Community of my heart in the present time is to abandon 45 years of earnest commitment, of desire, and of deep travail in the presence of God.

But all of that now seemed to be nothing more than hot air and straw.

Yet to abandon the thought that our new property at Shepherd could be a community of Christ was to me the loss of everything my life meant.

Yet my grief waited only on the next word from Jesus, and when that Word came, laying it all down upon the altar, as Much Afraid did in *Hind's Feet on High Places*, was my only option. There was no decision to be made, for my decision was made when I was 22.

And so, for the first time in 45 years, I stopped thinking about community, not because I have abandoned anything, but because I have placed it all, with myself, utterly into God, my Father, and He will raise me up. God will give me the Community of my heart, and I will sing for joy.

In the place of my own somewhat imaginary "dream" of starting a new community, my focus and zeal turned fully now upon the entire Church of Jesus Christ all across this planet, now in her hour of greatest need. I had been using the figure of 100 million and more believers in Jesus all across the earth. Our prayers for the entire Church in the Zoom meetings went to a whole new level of confidence and specificity.

All of my life belongs to the Lord Jesus, and He and I together turn everything into blessing and goodness for you, for your sake, dear reader. You also are utterly inside of Jesus; you have never been anywhere else. Place the Lord Jesus Christ upon your entire life, even as I have done, and you will know just as much that your whole life has never been anything other than one seamless story of Christ.

Finally, as I shared, my attempts to write this chapter, through July, August, and September of 2022, threw me into the same confrontations with awfulness inside myself as I had known in the actual interactions. I did not know how to write about these things.

Then, Maureen shared with me the anger of a family member towards me for including them in my life story and making it public. This really frightened me. Out of this fear, I wrote a lesson titled "The Terror of Light," and inserted it into Studies in 1 John. Later, I removed it, because I had written before I received God's final answer.

What I shared on Zoom, this August 21, 2022, and the prayer we prayed together came out from this "terror." I wrote this in response to this dilemma of needing to finish my life story, but being unable to do so. I share it here to convey a small measure of the difficulty of knowing how to write of these things and to show my reaching for, but not quite having, God's ANSWER.

⸺

There is so much in this lesson that could direct our prayers, but this time, I would ask you to pray for me. I have completed my life story except for what now appears to be the most difficult time-period to write about, the twelve months from December 2020 to December 2021. Through this time, God has led me to give my all for the sake of His Church in intercession, yet the mechanism through which that came is a whole series of events filled with autistic pain and inability greater than most in my life.

It is no problem to take the reader into my own pain and failure, the problem lies in the cause of those things from my interactions with others. Yet this is the meaning of my whole life and of God's sending of me.

"Oh Father, how do we give an account of our lives inside of Your presence without giving hurt to those with whom we interact? How do we reveal Your intercession through us without sharing the deep hurt that others have caused?

"Lord Jesus, You are my Friend, close and real, and You protect me from all hurt and dishonesty. Yet these are also my friends, no matter what I feel like in the moment and no matter what foolish mistakes they and I have made. Lord Jesus, how do we walk together inside of the light? How can there be light inside of an unwillingness to be wrong?

"There is no darkness in You, oh Father. Nothing can be hidden. Yet You have sent us to cover one another and your entire Church. Father, Your Love is inside of us. It is so."

⸺

Over the next couple of weeks after this prayer, I went through many severe downs as I attempted to write these things. In the end, I have chosen to unveil my own depths of autistic pain so that you might know the Lord Jesus Christ as He is, but to cover, at the same time, my brothers and sisters.

So, how is it that I am writing this now, in the quiet joy and certainty of this Tabernacles season in late September, 2022, and in the full personification of "I Set Forth My Soul," the completion of the Day of Atonement?

In every instance of about three month's time, in every feeling of awfulness, in every sense of hopelessness, in every wailing cry, in every moment of heart-stopping fear, I knew myself only inside of my Father, I placed God as sharing Himself with me, in all this pain.

And over and over, I said to my God, "Father, take this pain as Your own, and use it to deliver, not only these precious brethren, but also Your entire Church in this hour of her greatest need. God, I give You my pain; give me our Church."

And we also are committed to setting forth our souls for our brothers and sisters. – The altar of God and the offering of a sweet-smelling aroma. The Day of Atonement fulfilled in the Church.

Setting Forth My Soul

I want to pray, now, together with you, dear reader, for I must bring all of this into God my Father, that He might be glorified through all my stumbling failure.

"God, my Father, I drink Your Cup together with You for the sake of my brothers and sisters that I might share Your Heart.

"Father, I know that Jesus has removed from me my acts of injustice towards my teachers in school, placing them into His empty grave. Yet these three men, Mr. Philips, Mr. Stroup, and the chemistry student teacher remain in my heart, even with their offensiveness towards me as I perceived it. I welcome each one of them into this wondrous Fellowship I enjoy with You, Father, even with those actions and words that I perceived as hurt. Let my willingness to share Jesus' suffering be an open door and a short path for each one of them into Your knowledge and joy. If You so chose, I am ready to walk daily with each of them as they are the Lord Jesus to me.

"God, my Father, I open my heart wide towards the brothers whose words and actions towards me over the last couple of years have been difficult, at least as I have perceived it. I humble myself for Your sake, and place myself beneath of them to lift them up, together with You. In every way that I was and am wrong, let me be wrong, with no need for self-defense. Let my open heart inside of You become to each of them a path of Life, a run into Joy, a knowing of Your Fellowship with them. Whether they walk with me in daily life together or not, I receive them with all their human frailties, whatever private pain I might bear. I receive each one as the Lord Jesus to me.

"Father, I pray for each one of my readers, including those who are reading this in the present moment. Use my words, use my life, to open to each one Yourself, Your Heart, Your Joy, Your Life. Embrace each one inside Your Heart, together with me. Cause them to know all of Your fulness filling them full and flowing out from them as Rivers of Life everywhere they go.

"I ask these things inside of Jesus' name and for Your sake, Oh Father, that You might be glorified, and that Your Jerusalem, the Church of Jesus Christ, might be a praise and a joy to all throughout all creation."

Below: Our new home in Shepherd, Texas before we purchased it.

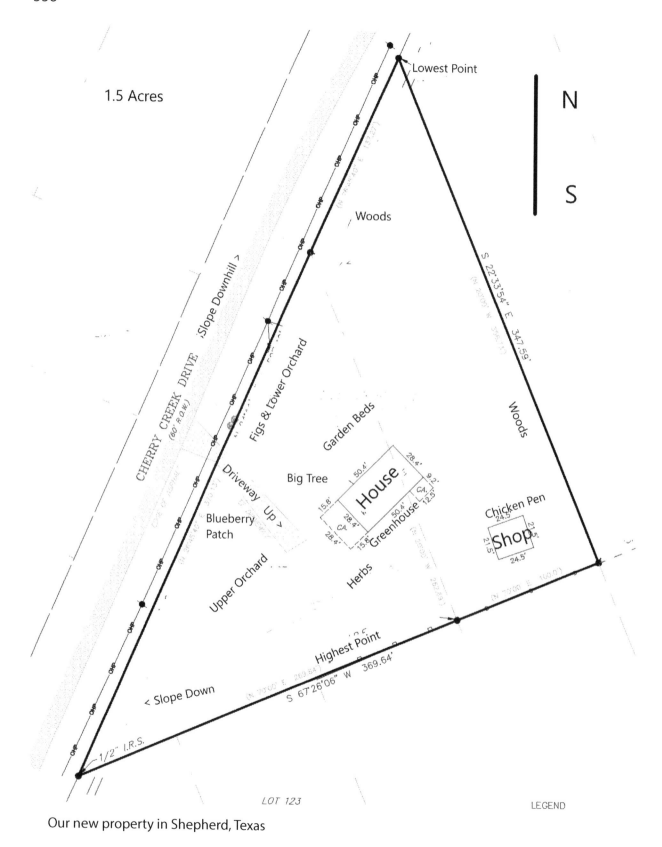

1.5 Acres

N

S

Lowest Point

Woods

CHERRY CREEK DRIVE (60' R.O.W.)

Slope Downhill >

S 22°33'54" E 347.59'

Woods

Figs & Lower Orchard

Garden Beds

Driveway Up >

Big Tree

House

Chicken Pen

Blueberry Patch

Greenhouse

Shop

Upper Orchard

Herbs

< Slope Down

Highest Point

S 67°26'06" W 369.64'

1/2" I.R.S.

LOT 123

LEGEND

Our new property in Shepherd, Texas

54. A New Direction

March 2021 - April 2022

Our Final Months at Fernbank

At this point in time, we had lived in our house on Fernbank Drive for 18 ½ years, the longest time in the same home for both Maureen and me, since we were married and in our entire lives. In fact, if you counted a "home" as at least a month in the same place of "abode," that means we had lived in 17 different homes across the first 12 years of our marriage and family life, prior to moving to Fernbank.

This was where our children had grown up and left home; in fact, it was the only home James remembers. He was just two when we left our prior home in Maple, Texas to come to Houston.

There was much that was good and comfortable and familiar in this house, filled with our things and so many memories. Nonetheless, there was a downside for both Maureen and me, that had become as a great weight sitting upon us.

The primary problem was a leak in the roof, a leak that had begun probably in 2006 or 2007. This leak was at the boundary of the shallow roof over what had once been the outdoor patio and the slope of what had once been the garage, that is, right at the line dividing our dining room from the school room. When we rebuilt the roof after Hurricane Ike in the fall of 2008, I assumed that I was solving the problem. Much to my dismay, the leak continued.

I tried everything I knew over the years, redoing the roof with new coats and new coverings, working on the pipes, chimneys, and air vents, anywhere near the area, redoing the valley. But nothing worked. The leak would move a bit, but it continued.

I know now that the mustiness, and even mold, from the wetting of the interior structure whenever it rained, was a part of my physical weariness. During these months, I had my office in the dining room, and so the leak was several feet in front of me whenever it rained. This was very discouraging.

Then, even though Bill's generous help enabled us to get the outside of the house into a much better condition, still there was much inside that was unfinished.

Another difficulty was Houston and Harris County. We had loved Houston, and had gone to stores and events all across the Houston area through all these years. But suddenly, with the lockdowns and then the new experimental "jabs" being pushed, Houston and Harris county had turned into a beast to us, a nightmare to escape.

I had talked for several years about selling the house, but nothing ever came of that talk because we had no forward direction, no place which would be our next step in God.

Then, during the first part of March, Maureen and I both knew that it was time to move on to a new place. At this point, James was the only one of our children still at home. Katrina was just moving out into her travel trailer. So we called a friend of ours, Jermaine Freeman, who was a realtor, to come talk to us about selling our home. Jermaine had helped Kyle and Shelbie find and then buy their home in Splendora, and so he seemed the right fit for us. Jermaine is a very gentle man and an excellent realtor. We put our trust in him to take us through this humongous journey.

Jermaine spent the evening of March 13 visiting with us about what it would mean to sell our house. After he left, we were firmly persuaded that it was an overwhelming task and wanted nothing to do with it. That, of course, did not solve anything. After several more days, we agreed that we must prepare to list the house for sale.

You can't sell, of course, without having a place to go. Here is what I wrote in the letter sent out on April 10.

❧

We are selling our home. It should be on the market this weekend, and in our area houses are sold within the week. Inflation has pushed up the value of our home nicely, but the money must be parked into an equal value quickly.

This has been our home for over 18 years. Even after a number of efforts to "reduce" in the past, we still have lots of stuff accumulated in a house once filled with children and an over-generous mom and dad. Maureen and I have both gone through the emotional trauma of leaving our "home," but we believe it is time to sell for several strong reasons.

We have been looking for property in the Splendora, Texas area, near where our son and his wife, Kyle and Shelbie, have purchased property. Two properties we thought would work that were within our price range sold before we could put an offer together. So right now we are continuing to pack, putting everything into storage units. We don't really know at this point where we will end up, but are trusting in God for the right place in the countryside to open up.

Because we will soon have buyers trekking through our house peering into everything, we are extra busy this weekend and thus will not be on the Zoom meeting this Sunday... Thank you for your prayers, that the Lord would continue to show His purposes in our life and take us to that perfect place for a community of Christ to begin.

↩

On April 17, I wrote: ~ We have signed a contract with a buyer for our house and hope to close before the end of April. This is an investor and a cash buyer. I hope to send you another letter within a couple of days in which I will share some things God is speaking to us as we are making this move to - we're not sure where yet. ~

Then on April 24, I wrote: ~ The bid for our house was withdrawn and we are back in the market again. Please pray that the right buyer will come and that we will close soon. We have moved most of our belongings to storage units near where our son, Kyle, lives. Every sign is pointing to the fact the we all must be on a country property where we can grow our own food. If anyone wants to join with us, please let me know. We need one another. ~

It was quite a job packing up everything. James helped so much with this task, driving load after load up to our storage units in Splendora.

Kyle and Shelbie had invited us to live with them

in their spare bedroom until we found the right place for us. Kyle shared his hope that we might even build a small home in the back corner of his property.

Then another buyer came along, also an investor, who wanted to remodel our home and then flip it. I walked him through all the problems, but he was earnest, and his offer was very good, the most we could have hoped to expect.

On May 8, I wrote this: ~ We are moving this weekend. We have not yet closed on the sale of our house, but it appears certain, probably sometime this next week. Meanwhile, we are taking the last of our things up to Splendora and will be staying with our son and his wife, Kyle and Shelbie, until we are able to find the right place God has for us. There is no point in looking until we have the down payment for a new property in the bank since you have to move fast in today's market. ~

Before closing out this section, I want to mention briefly the course of my writing through these weeks. Through the end of March and the first of April, I wrote Chapters 2 and 3 of *Symmorphy VI: Mankind*. This was a word of power and glory flowing through me even greater than I knew while writing *A Highway for God*. By the time we moved to Splendora, the first section of that text was completed.

Then, in the Zoom meetings, we were progressing through the prophets, Isaiah, Jeremiah, Ezekiel, and Daniel.

Moving to Splendora

On May 9th, Maureen and I moved ourselves and our primary stuff, bed and computer desk, up to Splendora to our new "home" with Kyle and Shelbie. We still had a few belongings left in the Fernbank home, which we would remove on the day we closed on the sale.

We were right at three months in Kyle and Shelbie's home, a very blessed time. Kyle and Shelbie have a large double-wide manufactured home on a wooded acre just east of the small town of Splendora, Texas. Their guest bedroom was larger than our master bedroom at Fernbank and a large bath was just across the hall. They had not used their large dining room, and so that became my office and sitting area, with my easy chair in the corner. It was a very comfortable arrangement.

James was kind of floating, however. He spent awhile on a foamy in Kyle's office, then he moved into Katrina's small trailer for a while. Finally, after Maureen and I had moved to our new home, Kyle and Shelbie offered James the guest room, where he remained for several months.

The closing on the sale of the Fernbank house went well, on May 19. Suddenly, we had a significant sum in the bank (for a brief time) and the burden of that house was lifted from our shoulders. In myself, I blessed the man who bought our home, that he would prosper in his endeavor. He did. After completely remodeling everything, he sold it a few months later for $90,000 more than the good price he had paid us. I have not wanted to look at the house or any pictures of the changes since. I just leave it all in the peace of the Lord.

We paid off most of our debts, including helping out our children a bit, but we kept carefully a significant sum for a down payment on a new place and for the establishment of a new life there. Because we now had that down payment, we could search for a new home in earnest.

The problem was that this period of time was a seller's market; houses everywhere were purchased within a few days of coming on the market. That meant you could not take time to decide. If you found a suitable place, you had to sign a contract quickly, or it would be sold to someone else.

On May 17, a Monday, Maureen's father, Claude Mack, passed away. On May 21, I sent out this note in my letter.

⟳

Maureen's father, Brother Claude Mack, passed away this last Monday. He was ready to go and his passing was not unexpected. For that reason, we are heading to Lubbock today for the funeral on Saturday and will be there over the weekend. I am so glad that I have given an account of my relationship with Claude over the decades and placed it all into Jesus. Of hearing his passing, my only mental picture of him remains his warm smile to our grandson, Gabriel. That is the only Claude I now know.

We closed on the sale of our house on Wednesday and the money is in the bank. That whole passage is completed, having taken a full two months. We both know that it was entirely of the Lord and that He will lead us forward from here. We are stay-ing at Kyle and Shelbie's house for the interim. The Fernbank address is no longer ours.

⟳

Maureen flew to Lubbock, so that she could spend more time there. I rode with Kyle and Shelbie in their pickup, and James and Katrina drove up together. We arrived Friday in the night. The memorial service was Saturday afternoon. Claude's brothers were there and many other family members as well as many from the move community in Lubbock.

It was a wonderful memorial service, very blessed and fitting, and very family. Afterwards we had a buffet dinner at Lois's church. Many from the move community were there as well, including Brother Joe McCord. Brother Joe was slowly succumbing to old-age difficulties and I could not understand his words to me. Nonetheless, he was quite spry and filled with joy and excitement. I knew he was speaking of my books and was quoting me, and the joy in his expression to me was very encouraging.

We returned to the Houston area Sunday afternoon.

By the end of May, we had located a lovely property for sale in Shepherd, Texas, about twenty miles north of Splendora. Even though it was in the city limits, it was still countryside. The house was smaller, but comfortable, and the property was beautiful. We made an offer and the offer was accepted. Thus we began working through the financing side of things, a task that took two months, but in which we were helped very capably by Jermaine Freeman.

Continuing in Splendora

During the last week of May and then the first week of June, while we were with Kyle and Shelbie, I wrote two chapters of this life story, "Asperger's and Bankruptcy" and "A Vision of God." Contrary to what I had imagined, writing the recent years of my story has been more difficult than the earlier years, and there are longer gaps in-between.

It would be September before I could continue this account.

Through June and July, I wrote voraciously in *Symmorphy VI: Mankind*, from "Being Symmorphic" to "Made from Victory."

Kyle and Shelbie had wanted a patio deck on the back side of their house since they had moved there. Maureen and I turned the money we were now saving by not paying mortgage and electric bills towards the materials needed for this deck. I had gotten some exercise from packing and moving our stuff to the storage units, but I knew that needed to continue.

It was hot summer; so I went out just at sunrise for an hour or so each morning and built the large patio deck for them. Kyle helped some, but he also drove down to San Jacinto College regularly to teach his electrical courses. This bit of regular exercise helped me a lot, with no longer being in a musty environment all the time also contributing to some renewed strength.

It took some time of back and forth with our mortgage agent to finally obtain the financing for the property in Shepherd. Then, it seemed to us that the seller had chosen a poor title company, because there were many more delays. Our move would not happen until August.

Although I was no longer "dreaming" about community, I was very much excited about gardening. I especially wanted to plant a permaculture "food forest," that is, an orchard with many companion plants surrounding each fruit tree. The property in Shepherd seemed well-suited for this. I had to be careful, however, that I not buy things dependent on our closing on that property. Garden seeds we would need regardless, and so I happily ordered a whole bunch of garden seeds.

I also thought that it would be fun and hopefully profitable to attempt a food forest nursery business. I was mulling over these possibilities. I was concerned about world economics, including the supply-chain problems and empty shelves in the stores. I developed a full list of all the things we hoped to do with the new property and what needed to be purchased. The interior of the house was finished nicely, but there was much outside work that would need to be done. The moment we closed on the property, I wanted to turn our money into tangible things before it might be lost.

In the first week of July, Maureen and I went early one morning to Morehead Blueberry farm between New Caney and The Woodlands. This is some twenty acres of blueberry bushes in a beautiful setting in the sandy lowlands of the San Jacinto river, surrounded all the way around by a wall of pine trees. This was u-pick for our own enjoyment of blueberries.

It was an unusual day for a Houston summer, completely overcast and a light drizzle; it felt just like I was back home in Oregon. I am a berry picker, and we went right at it. After about an hour, when we took our full buckets up the front, the owner laughed with us, for we had picked more in that short time than any "newcomers" he had experienced – over $90 worth. In fact, because of the long freeze the winter before, this was his most abundant crop in years.

As we drove away, I felt an energy flowing all through me like I had not known in years. I realized that being outside in the cool morning with my feet on the ground and my hands in the blueberry bushes had given me something important I had been missing. I had already determined that our food forest would focus primarily on different varieties of fig trees and blueberry bushes. As we drove along, suddenly, the name for our new place popped into my mind – The Blueberry Fig.

Soon after, Maureen came up with the catch-phrase – "A Food Forest Family."

On July 25, I added this note to the beginning of my regular letter.

⟿

At this point in our saga in-between, having sold our home of 18 years and waiting to close on a new home, we are still waiting on a survey that must happen before we can sign the papers and the new place becomes ours. At this point, that survey is the only thing lacking. It is supposed to happen on Thursday, but we'll see. The Lord did speak to me that He is taking care of everything, and He has laid on me the necessity of not thinking otherwise.

Meanwhile, Maureen and I are doing all that would be wise before the closing in preparation for our new property. Once we do close, I will become very busy. And this is good, for it seems as if this new place is a fresh start for me. Digging and planting and eating from a new garden can only be healthy for me.

The Zoom Fellowship

Through the summer, I continued writing the flow of the middle parts of *Symmorphy VI: Mankind*. In the Zoom meetings, we finished the Old Testament series, *After My Heart*, on July 18, with Malachi.

At this point, I would normally have started a

new series, but I did not have a topic that resonated with me in the present moment. I did have three uncompleted writing assignments, my life story, *A Highway for God,* and *The Jesus Secret II.* I realized that I could use the need to create something new for the Zoom meeting each week as my incentive to finish *A Highway for God* first. I had been stuck for some time at Chapter 45 "Our Five Superpowers."

This approach worked really well, and so I continued until we had completed *A Highway for God* in October. Sharing my present writing with the Zoom fellowship gave it a spark that I had not had before. I also included occasional lessons from *Mankind* in the Zoom meetings.

Although our connections on Zoom are limited, we had, by this time, come to know one another in Spirit and by face. Our fellowship was maturing – specifically in the sharing together of our prayers for the sake of the Church. I continued to be convinced that God had appointed our little gathering to impact the entire Church in this present season of the unveiling of Jesus Christ and of completion.

I want to share briefly concerning each one who joined together in this fellowship and what they mean to me.

Peter Douglas, of Glen Cove, New York, is a gentle and encouraging man, always lifting others up. Pete often expresses his gratitude for the things Jesus has enabled me to share. He has the grace of shepherding and has led the Zoom fellowship times when I was absent. Karen Leigh, of Cape Town, South Africa, is deeply anointed of the Lord and often has good things to share alongside of whatever I have shared. She often shares of how she also has placed the Lord Jesus upon her life as I have shown. The changes that have come for her are among the most encouraging things that give me strength.

Lanny Gao, from Athens, Georgia, is an eager drinker of every word I share. The intensity of her face draws the word from me in strength. She cares for an autistic child and has known great pain as a mother. She expresses how wonderful it is to her to know that all of her difficulty is God through her. Rachelle Ross, from North Carolina, is a quieter person. I know she has carried great difficulty in her life, as have we all. It is such life to me to see her face, sometimes lined with sorrow, turn to such joy at the end of each session.

Christopher Küttner, of central-west Germany, often shares in the fellowship time. I have been really blessed by his perception of the Spirit. He often mirrors the word that I share back to us. Bill Horton, of Atwood, Kansas, no longer has a working computer for him to be in the face-to-face, but he is usually there on the phone with Pete Douglas to be part of our sharing and prayers. Bill is always a cheerful giver.

Phyliss Smith, from Dickson, Tennessee often joins with us by calling me on the phone. I then place my phone in-between my microphone and speaker so that she can be very much a part of our fellowship. It means a lot to me how Phyliss has embraced the word I share in the knowledge of God. Maureen joins with us whenever she is at home of a Sunday morning when she is not working, about half the time. I do much better with my wife at my side; I expect God for the day soon to come when Maureen can be with me in the services all the time.

Dennis Rhodes, of Western Australia, has joined with us occasionally, but it is typically 11 PM for him and thus late at night. Willie Van der Hoek, of Queensland, Australia, joined with us for a short while, but it is 1 AM for her, and she was not able to continue. She joins often with some of the others for fellowship during her day time. Willie often communicates personally with me. She is one who understands what I teach in applying Christ Jesus to her own life. A few others have joined us for brief visits from time to time.

We are a small group, of no consequence in the church let alone in the world. We share the desire to know the Father through knowing Jesus Sent into us. Each one has embraced for themselves, not only union with Christ, but also the revelation of Jesus Christ through us into our world.

I am confident that our prayers are changing the heavens all around our brethren in this world. I am confident that God is using us for His purposes and desire.

To Cherry Creek Drive in Shepherd

We finally closed on our new home on Monday, August 2. I took a cot up on Tuesday so that I could begin preparing the place for our move. Maureen couldn't stand not being there with me, and so by Friday evening, she joined me in a make-shift set-up. Lois and Jessica drove down that next week to help. The only inside painting to be done was our master bedroom. The three sisters accomplished that together. Finally, we were able to move up our bedroom furniture permanently.

Our time with Kyle and Shelbie was wonderful. We were able to get to know Shelbie a lot more, and she us. I marveled as I watched them, for I saw just how much Kyle loves Shelbie with tender affection and regard. Our departure did seem rather abrupt; we were not really "ready to go." But it is better to move on when things are a blessing; that is not something I have known very often in my life.

Our move to Shepherd is what I am calling "A New Direction." As such, I am bringing to an end the ongoing account of the active part of our life. I want to share with you pictures of our wonderful new place, though, and a brief account of what we are accomplishing here. The picture on page 555 is the house as it was when we bought it. Then, on these pages are pictures as it is in October of 2022. Then, I will continue with the flow of the Word through me until September of 2022.

Maureen and I love our new place all the time. It is such peace to me every time I step outside to do this or that, or even just to walk around. Maureen feels like she is driving home to "vacation" every evening.

Let's begin with our new property layout, on page 556. The property is just under 1.5 acres. We have a very wide ditch area, sometimes deep, which we hope eventually to make a native Texas flower preserve. Note the North-South line. You can see that no line on the property follows the N-S line, neither do the lines of the property correspond to each other. This makes for a very interesting layout. In fact, I have drawn up large sketches of each portion of the property; it contains many unique areas, most of which we have given some sort of name.

The house is about 2/3 of the way up the slope from the road and the yard then slopes on up to the shop, not quite at the highest level. The upper orchard is peach and persimmon trees with a hedge of elderberry bushes along the ditch and property line. The blueberry patch has 17 bushes at present with 7 varieties. There is space for up to 8 more bushes, which will include additional varieties. There are 12 fig trees in the lower orchard, in 7 varieties, along with apple, pear, and plum trees. I am putting in a thick hedge along the property line of edible plants of many kinds, pomegranates and hibiscus, goji and goumi berries, blackberries and muscadine grapes,

The beds are typically 3.5 by 18 feet. I hope to double their number as time goes on. I have found that I must do battle against the moles and the leaf-cutter ants in order to have food crops survive. We are putting in an herb garden just above the front porch of the house.

I find that I can work around ten hours a week, plus or minus. During the hot summer days, I go out just after the sun comes up. In the evenings, we usually let the chickens out to forage for a little while. They're always ready to go back in as the sun goes down.

On the previous page are two pictures, opposite corners of our house outside as it presently is.

We have planted climbing roses that will go up over the trellis. You can see how comfortable and spacious our front patio is. I put the greenhouse on the southeast side of the house in the fall and then enclosed the back porch and opened it to the greenhouse in the early spring. It's a wonderful feeling to step out the laundry room door into the back porch/greenhouse, especially when it's cold out. I built a new potting bench situated on the back porch.

To the left are two pictures on the inside of the house, our living and dining areas.

etc. There are more pomegranates between the big tree(s) and the house. The "big tree" is a huge oak alongside a very large magnolia. The oak dwarfs the magnolia, however. If I were younger, there would be a treehouse high up in the oak.

There are about 18 magnolia trees on the property, some quite large. There are a similar number of oak trees of various sizes, three kinds of oak. There are a "weed" species of laurel trees, which I will replace.

The garden beds are a work in progress. I have 9 in place now, including a lovely asparagus bed.

It is so very comfortable. You can see things that are entirely me and other things that are entirely Maureen, yet they are woven all together beautifully. I've always liked a home that feels lived in. My office where I write is in the back right corner of the living area. My easy chair is at the bottom right of the same picture. There is a large opening between these two rooms; I am standing in nearly the same spot as I take the pictures.

Finally, following are two pictures from the street, looking up across the orchards and gardens.

issues taking place. We did very little on the inside of the house except that Kyle improved our lighting. He also ran power up to the shop, which made it a comfortable place to work.

The insulation was poor. James helped us blow a thick blanket of insulation into the attic. The drainage was non-existent, all the water from above the house and the roof flowed under the house, especially when it rained hard. This had caused the side of the house facing the road to drop by more than four inches. I bought what I needed to pour a deep footer and jack up the house, but that has not happened yet. Meanwhile I have done a lot of work diverting all waters so that nothing ever flows under the house. I have mostly succeeded, but there is still more to do with that project. I also began setting up the gutters into a rain-water collection system for watering our plants. That's about half done, but I am finishing it now.

Cutting down the several trees left a big mess, which we have slowly cleaned up with Katrina's help over the months. We rented a large chipper to turn the branches into mulch for our food forest and sawed much of the logs into firewood, with a lot more to go. The place is mostly cleaned up now, which is nice. We were able to purchase a nice mower and can now keep the grass and weeds trimmed.

On the left top is the lower orchard. There are apple trees and several small fig trees if you look closely. You can also see the beginnings of our hedge. Up the slope are the garden beds. On the right bottom you can see across to the blueberry patch among and just above the pine trees. The big tree is on the left of the picture, the one closer to the house. I just planted a group of hostas that will grow in it's shade.

Through August and September we purchased most of the things we would need to work on our new place. I was concerned we might not be able to acquire things in the future with the supply-chain

But planting my trees and bushes has been the most fun. My nursery ideas have developed slowly, but if commerce continues, I believe that we can make some income starting next year with online sales of food forest plants. I am learning to propagate, though that's not as easy as it sounds.

As I left behind my propensity to dream about community, and especially, to think about what "my next step" might be, I have found ever more the favor of God showing itself in our lives. We can say, with all joy and quiet certainty, "God is good, all the time."

A Fall of Sharing Life with God

On September 11, 2021, I sent out the third lesson of Chapter 14 "The Proving of Christ" in *Symmorphy VI: Mankind*, titled "Sharing Life with God," and on September 18, "Father Among Us." The months of this autumn season of 2021 were truly a joy for me daily as I knew God my Father sharing my life with me every moment. – Joy unspeakable and filled with glory.

In October, I included the book of James for *The Jesus Secret II* in the Zoom meetings, and then continued on to finish *A Highway for God*. I did not have the printed copy of *A Highway for God*, however, until January 20, 2022. It was a long book and took a lot of work. As soon as the print copy was ready, I sent copies out to a number of readers.

It was the first week of November before I finally returned to the next chapter of my life story, "Sealed in the Storm." This was the beginning of some of the more difficult relational experiences in the sharing of this present word. God had to bring me to a place of confidence in Him before I could share some of those things. I also wrote "Time to Turn Around" by the end of November.

On November 14, we began the most wondrous series of teaching thus far in the Zoom meetings, titled *Studies in John*. The outward purpose was that I would share the thinking processes through which I created each next page in *The Jesus Secret II*, along with filling in the boxes for the page. The first lesson was "I Have the Right to Be a Son of God."

This approach increased the immediacy and fire of my writing inside *The Jesus Secret II* pages. At the same time, it involved our fellowship together in the flow of God. This is not from "me"; rather, it is God through us together.

Through December, then, I was continuing with the final third of *Symmorphy VI: Mankind* in my *Christ our Life* letters, and the first chapters of John's gospel in the Zoom meetings.

Early Spring of 2022

On January 1, 2022, I did not have anything from *Symmorphy VI: Mankind* written to send out, and so I shared the lesson titled "I Eat His Flesh" from the Zoom fellowship in my *Christ Our Life* letter. That was a one-off until March when I had brought *Mankind* to near completion and I switched over fully to sending out *Studies in John* each Sunday morning in my letter.

I paused the completion of *Mankind*, then, in March, with only Chapter 28 and the review to go. I wanted to wait to write "A Final Definition" until I had the chance to go through the entire course. Meanwhile, I was determined to finish this account of my life, a process that is only now coming to completion this October of 2022.

I wrote "A Season of Symmorphy I" in January, but was not able to write "A Season of Symmorphy II" until the first part of July, 2022. Then it was another long wait until I wrote these final chapters in August through October, now. This is my last chapter to write.

These chapters, and especially, "A New Altar," were the most difficult of all the chapters of my life for me to share, for inside of them is found the Fire and the Altar of God, the meaning and purpose of my entire life story.

Finally, by the end of March, our *Studies in John's Gospel* had brought us to "Jesus Is Planted inside of Me." This was the season of Passover. Through April, then, we entered into the upper room and John 14. I was now sending out only *Studies in John* in my *Christ Our Life* letter.

On April 17, I shared "I Live inside of Jesus." Through that next week, as I was writing "Jesus Lives inside of Me," the words of God's next step for His Church came flowing onto my page, inside the little box titled "The Way." Even as I considered the meaning of what I wrote, God took me into an experience of Completion inside of Him, a knowing of All Word Fulfilled.

The flow of the wonder of God's completion from Passover to Tabernacles, 2022, is the topic of my final chapter, "All That I Am."

And yet, even though we are enjoying a time together, just the two of us, in a beautiful home on a refreshing property, and inside of God's favor, never do I turn from that moment in time when God will bring us once again into a Community of Christ, into life shared with a people who know God.

On the following page is a picture of Maureen and me at present, October 2022.

55. The Meaning of a Life

July 1964 - November 2022

This experience of giving an account of my life inside the presence of God has changed me forever. It is the most important thing I have ever done in my walk with God. This chapter is a tapestry set forth of God visiting with me from age seven until today, revealing Himself and His word to me. My life is unfettered JOY out from great travail.

Please don't think that I am "boasting of myself" in presenting this layout. I have never known my life in this way; I did not realize the close hand of God upon me. I must set this out just to understand. Yet I am not "special." Your life is the same, if you would place the Lord Jesus upon yourself, one seamless story of Christ.

The Planting of Seed

July 1964 – In response to the picture of my black heart becoming white by the blood of Jesus, I ask Jesus into my heart on the back steps of our home. A "strange warmness" fills me.

July 1965 – I make friends with Henry Miller, our neighbor. Friendship begins to enter my identity of myself.

June 1968 – The agony of travail begins to show itself in my life in tangible ways. I did not know until now that it was always God my Father sharing Himself with me. This agony of travail has never left me. I see now that from the start it was always for the sake of God's people.

July 1968 – A girl in the berry patch asks me what I want to be when I grow up. I give her a true and honest answer, "I want to be married."

Fall 1968 – I read *The Lord of the Rings* for the first time. Frodo's willingness to take the ring to the fire and his victory through weakness sinks deeply into my heart. I did not know yet that it was my Father calling to me.

June 1970 – I make friends with Larry Janssen, a second meaning of friendship. (These first friendships did not endure because the individuals were not true.)

November 1971 – I become friends with Andy Wyatt, a third meaning of friendship.

April 1972 – I spend the weekend with the youth group in a "community" experience at the Albany Mennonite church. Something inside knows that this is right for me.

July 1972 – I read *Prison to Praise*. God plants the seed of "give thanks in and for all things" into my heart. I am filled with the Spirit and with joy. I sit under a teaching for the first time in which the Old Testament patterns are shown to be Christ Jesus towards us. I am deeply intrigued.

October 1972 – I overdose on LSD. I see the gates of the heavenly city closed against me. I wrap myself in the fear-filled imagination that it is permanent.

1975 – Throughout the months of this year, I notice two strange things occurring on a regular basis. On the one hand I sense and sometimes see a "divine presence" protecting me from evil and on the other hand, I feel the winds of the "hound of heaven" pursuing me as I run.

February 1975 – I am again moved by a community experience, something I do not understand.

April 1975 – I begin working with Jimmy Barkley. He is my first true friend and a man with whom I learn the joy of working in harmony together.

August 1975 – My dad lifts me up in his heart to God with tears upon his face, and God speaks to him, ~ "Daniel will return to Me by Christmas." ~

December 1975 – I see a vision of two vault doors slamming shut, similar to what I had seen when I overdosed on LSD, except this time I know that my time of hiding from God is closed to me and I will never return.

A New Level of the Planting of Seed

December 1975 – In my inability to connect with God through faith, I place my finger on the page and read, "For it is impossible... to be restored." I pray, in tears, "Lord Jesus, would you be crucified again for me? Would You put Yourself to open shame again for me?"

– I hear the words, ~ **"My son"** ~ and I see that the gate is open and God will receive me. I am able again to believe. It is two days before Christmas.

I now know that this Voice speaking to me was the same Voice speaking to Abraham, that is, the Lord Jesus, the speaking of God. I have never thought otherwise than that this was God my Father speaking to me. I will include throughout every word spoken by this Voice with this marking: ~ " " ~. Please understand that this Voice speaking to me was not inside my mental thoughts, but rather, coming out from the Spirit of my heart, and that these words were always unbidden by me, usually catching me entirely off-guard, one might say. The meaning of my life is defined by these words.

January 1976 – Andy Wyatt also returns to the Lord and our friendship becomes a fellowship as young men desiring to know the Lord.

March 1976 – I read the Psalms in one sitting. I am filled with a peace I had never known before. I read Watchman Nee's *Release of the Spirit* and follow his example. I ask God to immerse me in His Holy Spirit, and then I believe that I have received.

April 1976 – A sense of God's presence comes upon me as I drive to work. Without any warning I hear ~ **"Will you surrender all that you are to Me right now?"** ~ This is the second time the voice of God speaks to me, and I am overwhelmed. How can I give all that I am to God? I fight and struggle all day. Before I pull into the driveway I give Him answer, "Yes Lord." Before I can make it onto my knees beside my bed I am filled to overflowing with the Spirit of God and am speaking in a heavenly language. This is a powerful planting in me of the seed of "Ask and believe you have received – Be it unto me according to Your word."

May 1976 – I read John's gospel. When I read the words "When the Spirit of truth comes, He will lead you into ALL truth," they leap off the page and into my heart. I seize them as my own, filled with intense longing. Although these were not words spoken directly inside the Spirit of my heart, but rather Bible words becoming me, I have never thought other than that this was the same direct speaking of God as His voice.

July 1976 – I am caught in intense agony inside my gut with the knowing that I am hearing a false "gospel" being preached, but I don't know what that means or what to do about it, especially since my "mental theology" theoretically agreed. I try to read Arthur W. Pink's *The Depravity of Man*, but the book vanishes and I cannot find it.

September 1976 – I want so much to be married, but Paul's comments greatly discourage me. Lying on my bed, I cry out to God to show me His will. I hear the words, ~ **"What does My word say?"** ~ I reply with the only verse in my mind at that moment. "Delight thyself in the Lord and He will give thee the desires of thine heart." ~ **"Is not My word My will?"** ~ This was one of the most important things God ever spoke to me in my life, though I did not know it at the time. (I also did not know that it would be fourteen long and lonely years before my precious wife, Maureen, would walk down the aisle to stand at my side.)

June to December 1976 – I learn from Watchman Nee that I am inside of Christ. This revelation is wondrous to me, though I have no idea what it means. I read T*he Autobiography of Madame Guyon* and *Rees Howells: Intercessor*, and I am deeply moved by the knowledge that a man or a woman can KNOW the living God and that God does all that He speaks. I learn from Watchman Nee that Christ is inside of me. It is a revelation from God to me, but I cannot see what such a thing could possibly mean.

December 1976 – I day-dream of a ministry of Christ Community.

February 1977 – I experience a weekend of Christ Community and I KNOW that it is real and true. I weep in agony, not knowing how I could ever find such a thing. Through these months, I experience some of the greatest agonies of travail that I have known, yet I could not see through them into any resolution or answer.

March 1977 – I ask Jim Buerge if I could come up to British Columbia to spend a season with them. He suggests that I visit Graham River Farm instead. My heart is filled with warmth that this would be the Lord.

A Third Level of the Planting of Seed

April 1977 – I visit Graham River Farm for three weeks. I LOVE Christian Community; it sings together with all the fabric of my heart. I pour over the New Testament and my understanding opens to God's requirement for practical righteousness. Dan Kurtz asks me, "Daniel, where is Christ." I do not reply. He points his bony finger at my heart and says, "Christ is in you." It's true! I KNOW, I KNOW, I KNOW that it is true. I hear Sam Fife on a tape for the first time and am convinced that the man is full of baloney, but I cannot stop listening.

May 1977 – I search my Bible until I see God's pattern of three levels of knowing Him written all the way through everything.

June 1977 – I return to Graham River Farm and to life in Christian community.

July 1977 – I hear Sam Fife preach on a tape the "mystery of a man and a maid." I object strongly, but I search my Bible for weeks until, in a moment, I see God's pattern of the reproduction of life written from Genesis to Revelation with all the truth of God placed upon that primary metaphor.

August 1977 – I hear the words in my spirit, "**That the thoughts of many hearts might be revealed,**" over and over as I go through my daily tasks for weeks. Finally, I search for that line in Scripture and when I find it, it pierces me as the very sword of God. "And a sword shall pierce through your own soul also, that the thoughts of many hearts might be revealed." These were words spoken by God to Mary; they are also words spoken by God to me. I read Watchman Nee's *The Spiritual Man* and to my great embarrassment, I discover that I am a "soulish believer." (Yet I am the same today with all joy.)

September 1977 – I attend my first move convention and hear Sam Fife and the other ministry of that fellowship in person for the first time. I know, now, that this is the move of God, and that God has placed me inside of this fellowship. Sam Fife gives me permission, as it were, to see that my Bible says things that Christianity does not say.

October to November 1977 – In the confusion of my soul, in my loneliness and tears, on my knees beside my cot, I make a covenant with God that, somehow, somewhere, someone will escape all the confusion and enter directly into the knowledge of God – because of my pain and heartache. I am twenty-one years old.

December 1977 – Walking to the barn to escape the job of working on Dan Kurtz's porch, I hear one

word: ~ "**Jonah!**" ~ I turn back in response only to discover not long after to my great joy that I have been working on my own new bedroom. Not only is God planting the seeds of His Word inside my heart, but He is also hammering against my false identity, the made-up stories of self to which I have clung so desperately.

February 1978 – In the February convention, I hear a word as a missionary call concerning the vision of being a provision for God's people all over the earth in their hour of greatest need, a vision of being a Joseph, gathering up word as food for God's Church during a time of great famine. I "raise my hand" inside me to God. I have no idea how I could possibly be part of such a thing, but I want to be, with all my heart, I want to be such a thing for God's entire church during her great travail.

March 1978 – I am riding on the bus down to Prince George, resting in God. I hear His voice, ~ "**You are My son,**" and I am filled with overwhelming peace. After arriving at the Prince George bus terminal, the terror of the Almighty comes upon me. I am shaking visibly. I run into a toilet stall to escape detection and sit down on the closed toilet seat. I see as it were a bony finger pointing straight at me, and I hear the words, ~ "**Will you surrender all that you are to Me right now?**" ~ All I am able to say is, "Yes, Lord." The peace continues, but in deep sobriety.

April 1978 – I read the Annie visions for the first time and my heart is caught by "A Vision of the Holy." I hope that I might be part of such a thing, yet it is entirely beyond me.

June 1978 – I leave home, driving to Bowens Mill in Georgia. I hear "NO" "NO" "NO" for miles down the road. I refuse to turn back. This was the first of only two times that I did not regard this "NO." Yet I know now that my refusal was God my Father showing me my true self. I want one thing. I WANT to KNOW GOD in the midst of His Church at whatever the cost.

September 1978 – I see Sam Fife close-up inside of community for a few weeks. I am deeply moved by the intensity of single-minded devotion towards Christian community and towards Christ revealed in His Church that I see in him.

October 1978 – I hear a word of union with Christ for the first time, preached by Lester Higgins.

I am filled with overwhelming joy, though I have no idea what it means. I look at Sam Fife and see the same joy on his face towards such a word. I hear the most anointed speaking I have ever heard in my life as Sam Fife's words open the heavens to me and I see the woman clothed with the sun, bringing forth the very life of God on this earth out from her great travail.

February 1979 – Sitting in the convention at Headwaters in British Columbia, I hear the voice of God inside my spirit. ~ **"This is My ministry. I have given them My word for you."** ~ I see the same deep sense of travail for the church resting upon Sam Fife.

April 1979 – I hear that Sam Fife has been killed in a plane crash. The thought "we will go on to KNOW the Lord" up-whelms within me. Dan Kurtz shares with me many of his difficulties with the move fellowship. After dropping him off, I drive home. Everything I thought God had taught me is stripped away; nothing remains. In my desperation and great vulnerability, I shout out loud the determination of my covenant with God. "God, I WILL KNOW YOU in this life, and I will walk with a people who know You, right now in this age, right here on this earth." I do not know what such a thing could mean, but I will never be turned aside.

May 1979 – Brother D shares with me of the little community just starting near Albuquerque, New Mexico. A witness leaps in my heart that this is God's next place for me.

A First Furnace of Affliction

July 1979 – I watch Buddy Cobb turn the entire convention away from the Tree of Life to face the false *"struggle against sin."* I have no idea what is happening, but something in me marks this moment, and I know that something is not right.

September 1979 – After my return to the Albuquerque community after a brief visit in Oregon, I feel so very much AT HOME.

November 1979 – Lester Higgins comes through and preaches on union with Christ. I know that it is true, but I cannot see it. Such a thing is far away from me. He leaves in sorrow, and in sorrow, I see him go.

1980 – I hear a true "NO" from God, over and over, concerning a relationship with Roseanna, but I cannot let go. My identity is so tied up in the feel-

ings of my imagination. God has to allow circumstances and the intervention of others to end my wrong direction.

June 1980 – I have the opportunity to drive away from the community and to return home to Oregon. I do not want to stay; I very, very much want to leave. I stay. Why? Very simple. I want to know God in the midst of His Church, no matter the cost.

August 1980 – Richard Hernandez and I spend more time together and become friends. This is another of many chapters of friendship God is writing in my life.

December 1980 – After the community is closed, I see the faces of the Albuquerque elders after the move ministry has spoken to them. I know that God is only kind towards them, but at the same time, I am struck with a deep knowing that you don't mess with God's people, for you are messing with God.

January to May 1981 – Jim Fant teaches me to justify God in all things and find Him right and true. He also teaches me that full deliverance comes only out from my own personal decision to cast down the evil one, regardless.

September 1981 – I experience the most anointed dream I have had. In my dream, Maureen Mack, a girl I had hardly noticed, comes to me in my distress. She says that she wants to know me and I see the kindness in her face. When I am fully awake, I see as in a vision the faces of Maureen's two older sisters, and I know they are not for me. Then I see Maureen's face again, and I hear in my spirit ~ **"Man looks upon the outward appearance, but God looks upon the heart."** ~ I know in that moment that Maureen will be my wife. I do not know that such a joy is still nine years away.

September 1981 to June 1985 – So many times through these years, such joy and anointing arise in me unbidden every time I pass by Maureen. Yet she is closed to me, and I do not know how to talk with her. By the spring of 1985, I can bear the agony no longer, and I harden my heart against such a thought.

June 1981 to September 1982 – I work closely with Abel Ramirez in watchcare over the men in the dorm and in leading parts of the work. In this mature level of friendship Abel demonstrates towards me, I thrive in the anointing. I do not understand, after the Ramirez's move back to Mexico, just how badly I would drop when this relationship is no longer there.

Mid 1981 into 1983 – I listen to a number of Sam Fife's messages until they are written deep in my heart, such words as Abraham offering up Isaac and of Jacob wrestling with God and not letting go. I write out all of "The Hollywood Series" into booklet form. I immerse myself in this word and am astonished without answer when Buddy Cobb tells me that it's not of God. I try again to read Arthur W. Pink's *The Depravity of Man*, but the book vanishes from me and I cannot find it.

1983 – Charley Jones shares with me how God speaks to him to buy this tool and take on that job, how God leads him in joy and provision. I do not share in return that God tells me, "No" even when I just want to buy a screwdriver. As I ponder this contradiction, I understand that God's path for one is not His path for the other, though we walk side by side inside of God.

1983 – I am happily planning to merge the four gospels into one. As I walk from the Tabernacle to the men's dorm, I see a bony finger, as in a vision, pointing straight between my eyeballs. ~ **"What are you doing to My word?"** ~ God's voice this time is harsh and stern. I drop all thought in that moment of ever trying to "figure out the word." From then until now I have done only one thing with my Bible; I have planted all that God speaks as He speaks it deep into my heart with all the intensity of which I am capable.

January 1984 – I step for the first time into the classroom as a teacher. I have found my calling. I love working with teenagers, I love teaching, I love books, I love everything that has to do with school and education. I had never imagined; I had not known myself.

April 1985 – I am very angry with God and totally stressed out over the disaster my life in community has become. I sit in the convention hearing preacher after preacher share the very things I have argued at God in my distress. As I walk back to the Ridge, I raise my hand towards God. "BUT WHAT ABOUT THIS!" I cry. "People are dying in this community and no one cares, no one comes to help." (I do not know that Maureen is thinking the same thing at the same time.) The very next morning John Hinson gets up to preach. He says, "God came to me last night in a dream and He told me that people are dying in my community and no one notices." How can this be? How can my angry words towards God then be spoken by Him to an apostle in the move? My brain registers what just happened, but I have no ability to process it.

April 1985 – I receive a letter from Judy Jones inviting me to come to the Blueberry Christian community in British Columbia.

June to July 1985 – I am determined to take back control of my life from God, and I am distressed to discover that I am completely unsuccessful.

July 1985 to August 1986 – I read widely in world literature, an experience which opens rebellion against God to me. – *If God is all love and all power, why does He let bad things happen to people?* I do not know at the time, but God allows me to taste this rebellion so that I might know His power and goodness when He removes it from me.

November 1985 – I give up. The groaning of word God has planted inside of me is too great for me to bear. I pick up the Annie Schissler book, *I Looked and I Saw Visions of God,* and read it a second time. I do not read far before I am caught in the greatest of horror, that God is doing something wondrous in the earth and that I am not part of it.

February 1986 – I attend the Shiloh convention and am so grateful to be back in a third-feast word. My application to attend college at the Blueberry Community is accepted.

April 1986 – I am determined to IGNORE God's "no" coming hard against my intention to enroll in the local community college. My sister, Frieda, asks me, "Do you think God would take the life of someone who was recklessly going against His direction?" Those words hit me hard, and I know that they are God speaking to me. I know that He would take my life rather than allow me to follow that path away from Him. This is a shocking thought, yes, but I have always been so grateful that God has seized me in His grip and that He will never let me go.

May 1986 – As I attempt to drive back up to Blueberry and to the beginning of my college experience, carrying my huge load of books in my small car, I hear the same words John Janssen had shouted at his son, only now they are the words of my Father to me. ~ **"I will not have those books in My house,"** ~ over and over until I break, turn around and drive home in humiliation.

August 1986 – After the two weddings, I drive back up towards Blueberry, except now, again, I am hearing, "No, no, no" every mile up the highway. This is the second of only two times that I refused to regard the all-too-frequent "NO!" Why did I keep driving? For one reason only. I want to know God in the midst of His Church, no matter the cost.

A Greater Love

September 1986 to May 1988 – I love Blueberry. I love college. These are two of the best years of my life. Plenty of affliction, yes, but I am in the midst of a Spirit-filled church that moves in the grace and love of Christ. I have the astonishing experience, two different times, of a strong elder coming to me to apologize for something hurtful they had said to me. This is in such a contrast to my previous experiences. I learn so much through these years of the normality of the Spirit of God in the midst of the Church.

December 1986 – I am part of a wondrous experience, of sharing with the young people of the community, that is everything my gut tells me Christ Community ought to be.

June 1987 – I have the opportunity to take another path, an opportunity that promises me everything I ever wanted. Yet the thought comes again to me that God would take my life rather than allow me to depart from Him. Needless to say, I do not go.

Summer 1987 – I spend much more time working with Don Howat, now that school is out. His friendship is the largest experience of friendship (other than marriage with Maureen) that I have known in my life. Don always receives me as an equal, and in his encouragement I thrive in the things God anoints me to do. This friendship continues to increase over the next several years.

September 1987 – I sit through Buddy Cobb's course, "The Plan of God." This experience "presses me to the wall," so to speak, regarding knowing what God actually says in the Bible. Buddy Cobb's teaching is confusion to me; I cannot make sense of it, no matter how many Bible verses he uses. I am thirty years old. I make my first determination concerning the set of my face regarding the Word of the gospel. – God's desire comes first, what God wants rules over all. And what God wants is to be seen and known by all through us, His Church. And this God, out from whom all things come, is Love.

Not long after this determination, Romans 8:29 becomes my ruling verse.

November 1987 – I sit through Jane Miller's course titled, "Spiritual Warfare." Of all the ministries in the move, Jane Miller is the closest in anointing and word to that open heavens I had experienced through Sam Fife. I am caught in the overwhelming power of the Spirit. I say to Sister Jane on the first day of deliverance, "Sister Jane, you will pray for me or I will crawl into your pocket until you do." That afternoon, as I sit waiting for my turn to be prayed for, I hear the voice of my Father, ~ **"Even during your time of darkness** (my rebellious teenage years), **you were still My son."** ~ I experience the agony of deliverance, that there is no panacea, that "Yes Lord" is still required. I see the Shekinah glory of God resting upon the precious family at Blueberry. I am convinced of the reality of demonic influence; I see the power of God in open demonstration.

December 1987 – I write these words in a college paper, "I know that my father loved me and sacrificed everything for me." Soon after, I am filled with the knowledge of God's presence with me, for I had forgiven my dad in writing those words. I had "hated him without a cause," for he had always treated me with such respect and kindness. I have known few people in my life more true and more good than my own dad, Emerson Edwin Yordy. And by this grace I know God my Father. I long for that day when he and I and Kyle can walk together as the closest of friends.

February 1988 – I am singing praises in a very anointed service. My experience of overdosing on LSD comes strongly into my mind. With that thought, something like a great angry hornet's nest breaks loose inside of me. I raise my hands up high and cast myself upon the Lord. As I do, bang, a darkness leaves me never to return. I can register in my memory the dark pain that ripped my gut for fifteen years, but I no longer comprehend it. For the first time since adolescence, I no longer need to hide myself in fantasy and daydreams.

April 1988 – I take the Grier speech course and begin my slow journey out from my autistic shell. I write Gene Edward's "A Tale of Three Kings" into a play. God makes real to me the issue of rebellion versus David.

May to August 1988 – I am aghast, for there is Maureen with her parents, and I discover that she is planning to come to school at Blueberry. I spend the summer desperately considering leaving the community, for how can I bear a return to the agony I knew at Bowens Mill.

June 1988 – Upon returning from a trip to Oregon, I have a dream in which I see God's people bound to death and in which I speak to them to live and not die, but they do not hear me.

August 1988 – The Spirit whispers to me, not as the Voice I often hear, but as an understanding, that God does not treat His sons in the way I was fearing, that everything is for a purpose and a season, and that, somehow, Maureen's return into my life will be different.

September 1988 – I do the bravest thing I have done in my life. I ask Maureen Mack what she is taking this year in college. And the most wonderful thing that has happened to me comes next, Maureen talks with me. Before our conversation ends, she says to me, "Daniel, I want to ask your forgiveness for how I treated you at Bowens Mill." Her words are such joy and such pain, both at the same time.

October 1988 – Maureen and I start a covered friendship.

June 1989 – Maureen and I begin walking out a year.

August 1989 – Returning from a trip to Oregon, I look up at the roof construction I had left under Brian Dwyer's direction. He is finishing the last of it. My soul opens to the realization that other people are of great value even when they DIFFER from me. This is one of the greatest changes in my life.

And a Greater Affliction

Spring 1990 – I find myself caught in a great bind between the things I am being taught and what God actually says in the Bible. My school experience and my relationship with Maureen is bringing me out of my autistic shell, yet at the same time, I am without protection and much more vulnerable than I have been before. Before I was oblivious, but now I do not understand the responses of many towards me, for they do not fit with anything true concerning me. I imagine the lie, as it is taught to me, that my will and God's will are violently opposed.

June 1990 – Our words to be married are confirming, but there seems to be an hostility towards our marriage from the elders. I go home to Oregon

by myself. I am pressed with the question of what God requires of me, but I find no answer.

September 1990 – I stand before the family at Blueberry, with my own family also there, and I say, "Now I know that God does what He says He will do." Maureen and I are married, the most important and the best day of my natural life.

August 1991 – Our son Kyle is born inside the close presence of God. I marvel at my wife, how strong she is. For the first time I KNOW that I love her.

September 1992 – Walking together with Don Howat along the air strip at Graham River, sharing strength together as equals regarding the work to begin in the morning, is the greatest and most precious moment of friendship I have known in my life.

November 1992 – I hear the Lord speak, ~ **"Immigrate to Blair Valley."** ~

February 1993 – I hear the Lord speak, ~ **"Blair Valley is your home."** ~ God begins to shape in my heart a new vision for Christian Community.

May 1993 – Our time at Blueberry on student visas comes to an end and we move to Oregon for two years.

A Third Time into the Furnace

October 1993 – God deals with Korah inside of me as I begin my first attempt at writing His word.

January 1994 – Johanna is born at Blueberry in the midst of the Church singing praises to God.

April 1994 to April 1995 – I work with Amos Stoltzfus installing high-end custom cabinets and enjoy a "working together" greater than I have known before or since.

November 1994 – We attend a Thanksgiving retreat. I see how precious all these who belong to Jesus really are to God. On my knees in the prayer hut on a wooded hillside, I place myself into Covenant with God, that He will prepare me that I might have a pure word for the sake of His precious people.

January 1995 – I begin teaching "The Two Gospels." I do not know that I have them switched and that I am missing the central point of the gospel.

March 1995 – I am troubled by the rumors of all the evil things taking place in Oregon. The Lord speaks to me, ~ **"Do not fight giants I have not placed in front of you."** ~

June 1995 – I walk into the worst time of my life. I am hit with the awful realization that in returning to Blueberry, we have come to the wrong place. This sense does not lift from me until we leave in October of 1996.

July 1996 – As I am sitting under the weight of carrying the burden of the second Graham River Tabernacle project all by myself, Brother Milton Vereide speaks words of Christ and of great encouragement into me eye to eye. At the moment of crisis, an experienced builder joins the work and takes on completing the roof. We are now able to finish.

December 1996 – I teach an "improved" version of "The Two Gospels" to the Blueberry family.

January 1996 – I begin my time walking as an elder with the ministry at Blueberry.

February 1996 – I become convinced that there is something terribly wrong with me that prevents me from being "an elder" like the others. While watching a logging camp by myself in the bitter cold, I cry out to God, "God can you not save even me?" I imagine that He does not answer me; I do not know that He already did long ago. I read a book in which I learn the meaning of a blood covenant and gain the picture of running through a gauntlet.

July 1996 – While digging in the soft sand underneath our cabin, I hear God speaking to me, ~ **"Son, you have a sectarian heart."** ~ I respond only with quiet agreement, that He is telling me the truth. I do not "try to do better," yet I know now that from that moment on, a sectarian heart was removed from me.

August 1996 – I face the giant of Korah inside of me, and I find it already defeated and gone. I will not speak against those over me in the Lord nor judge them nor myself. God alone is my Judge, and the Judge of all. I find God right and true in all things.

October 1996 – We drive away from Blueberry.

December 1996 – I lie drunk on our motel bed in California in the despair that I have failed in everything. Yet I rest in God, justifying Him and blaming no one, whether God, myself, or others.

A Long and Slow Healing

January 1997 – Maureen and I are received by Canadian immigration. We are now free to move to Blair Valley.

February 1997 – In my study of the Bible, the words **"Receive one another as Jesus receives you"** first enter my consciousness, even as I place those words into an astonishing list of New Testament verses commanding us to be just like God.

March 1997 – While listening to Brother Ernest Watkins share in the Bowens Mill convention, I hear God speak to me, ~ **"Son, you passed the test."** ~ In that moment, I know that what God is after is something quite different from what most of Christianity thinks, including the move. I know what God truly wants of us, that we would justify God in all things and find Him right and true and that we would place no blame upon any, including ourselves.

April 1997 – Kyle and I arrive at Blair Valley and begin working on our new home.

July 1997 – Katrina is born into our precious and all-too-brief time at Blair Valley.

November 1997 – We "land" as immigrants as we cross from Washington into British Columbia.

December 1997 to August 1998 – A time of peace, a time of quietness and reflection, a time when God can place my dependence entirely into Jesus.

December 1997 to May 1999 – I enjoy a relationship with Rick Annett in which I learn from him the true meaning of friendship.

February 1998 – In the cold and in the loneliness, I despair of ever pleasing God or doing His will. I do not know that the lights are turning on and that I am seeing real for the first time. In my sense of despair I hear the quietest words God ever spoke to me, ~ **"Give My people hope."** ~ I hardly hear those words because I imagine that I have no hope to give. I do not know that the final giant of "any sufficiency in myself" is now gone from me.

February to August 1998 – I know now that I am missing the key point of the gospel, but I have no idea what that is. I become deeply troubled by the contempt for "others" held as an essential element in move-of-God thinking and practice. I become weary of the game of pretending to be "in the Spirit" and all the mask-wearing it entails. I make a firm and final decision that I do not want to be a "son of God" in myself, but that I want to KNOW Jesus, my Savior.

August 1998 – We leave Blair Valley and the move of God and go to Fort St. John.

November 1998 – I discover that there are other people who share the same personality difficulties with me, that maybe there is not something terribly wrong with me. I am numb and frozen inside through all these months, yet I hold to the grace of the Lord Jesus and to nothing else.

February to May 1999 – We enjoy the sweetest of fellowships with the Dickout's and the Annett's even while I see God closing all doors for us in Canada.

July 1999 – I am accepted at Lubbock Christian University, and we accept that God has opened this door for us in Texas.

October 1999 – James is born in our home at the Lubbock community inside the prayers of the Church.

December 1999 – I attempt to fit back under the teaching of the move, and it nearly destroys me. Kyle wonders at the despair and agony he sees on his dad's face.

January 2000 – We separate fully from move community and enjoy full participation with the fellowship of people sitting under Pastor Gary Kirksey. Yet I remain numb and frozen inside.

December 2000 – In an anointed service, I go forward with many for a time of repentance. I say to God, "Oh God, I repent of ever having listened to Buddy Cobb." (Although I needed to do this in that way then, I know now that God had great purpose for placing me under Buddy Cobb's ministry for so many years.) For the first time, I can say to myself, "God loves me." – without any "but" added. Only now can healing actually begin, oh so very slowly.

July to September 2001 – The doors close on moving to Fort Worth and God takes us to a lovely little school in Maple, Texas where I am both the principal and the high school English teacher. This is a place of great peace and goodness for us.

December 2001 – The first knife of God's healing goes all through my soul as I begin to read John Eldredge.

January 2002 – As he shares himself personally with me in his books, John Eldredge teaches me to say "My heart is good; my heart is filled with Jesus." I confess those words with all joy. The agonizing process of placing all my pain into the Lord Jesus and seeing Him there with me in every hurtful moment continues over many months. In actuality the heal-

ing does not become complete until 2021, as I write about this whole time in my autobiography.

August to October 2002 – I get a job teaching school on the east side of Houston, Texas and we move to our family home on Fernbank Drive where our children will grow up.

July 2004 – I stop accusing God of knowing evil.

Fall 2004 to July 2006 – I weep often over the ignorance of God both in myself and in all the church.

A New Word

August 2006 – I hear the most astonishingly wondrous words ever spoken into me by another person when Joel Osteen says, "Speak what God says you are." I rush home to begin writing *The Jesus Secret,* caught in the intense fervor of a door flung wide open to me into the knowledge of God my Father. Years of Bible Word planted deeply in my heart come rushing up into the speaking of Christ my only life.

August 2006 to July 2013 – It takes five years of sitting under Pastor Joel for me to stop all cursing of myself in my own thoughts and two more years for God to seal me into this new mind.

Fall 2007 – I begin to articulate, haltingly and poorly, a many-years-long attempt to show God's people that they have been reading their Bibles using wrong definitions, definitions of death, and that the ruling verses of the gospel ought to be the rule over everything they know about God and His Word.

February 2008 – In a chapel meeting, as I try to hide from a false word being spoken into the children, I wrap myself utterly inside of Jesus. In that moment, "I" seem to disappear and Jesus becomes all that I am in my knowing. I discover Fred Pruitt's writings and begin to learn the joy of my precious union with Christ.

February to November 2008 – I withstand great spiritual assault as every voice I have known hurls its accusations against me that "I" cannot be "Christ as me." I refuse to consider those voices daily until November when they break away and depart from me.

Fall 2008 – God teaches me to place the same union with Christ that I enjoy upon the brothers and sisters with whom I work, in spite of their words that are contrary to Christ and in spite of their false attachment to the world.

November 2008 – I send out my first *Christ Our Life* letter, "Faith Makes Christ in Me Personal." Jesus is my life; I have no other life. Christ is all there is in me.

February 2009 – I am faced with a spirit of hostility from Buddy Cobb towards me and towards my teaching of union with Christ. I am faced again with the potential of "Korah" in my response. I refuse Korah, both towards Brother Buddy and towards Claude Mack. I choose to see that the same Jesus who lives as me lives also as them and carries them through the darkness and into LIFE just as He also carries me.

March 2009 – I read the Annie visions a third time. The things she sees are much closer to me now. From my reading I write, "All of His ways concerning me are perfect. God has never led me wrong. God has never not led me"

Summer 2009 – I write "The Most Important Verses of the Bible" in another attempt to set out God's definitions for how we are to know Him and how we are to understand the Bible.

July 2010 – I learn that I am Asperger's.

October to December 2010 – We go through the deeply humiliating process of bankruptcy. The Lord Jesus writes a deeper meaning of "no sufficiency in myself – all sufficiency in Jesus" upon my heart.

November 2010 – I am humiliated by my autistic difficulties as deeply as I have ever been.

December 2010 – In a visit to a small Pentecostal Church, I see again the beauty of God resting upon His people.

June 2011 – I am again faced with the agony of opposition coming against me, as I perceive it, from Claude Mack and Buddy Cobb. I choose again to place the Lord Jesus Christ upon them inside the same Salvation I would know.

An Ever Increasing Word

September 2011 – I receive a devastating email of the arrogant "Christ" demanding that I "get up out of myself" in order to know this "above-me" deity.

October 2011 – God turns me right-side up and causes me to know Him as He really is, as the One who CARRIES me. I determine to know God ONLY through the image of the Lord Jesus Christ and in no other way, and in particular through that one time and place when we see God as He is – the walk of

the Atonement, a stumbling Jesus carrying us, carried by God all the way through death and into life.

November 2011 - 1 John 3:16 pushes its way into my mind and onto my pages and begins the long process of turning me around.

July 2012 – As we are driving north to Johanna's graduation, I hear God speaking to me, ~ **"Because you have honored My word, I will honor you."** ~ I write "Filled with God," and begin to speak to myself that God fills me with all that He is. For the first time, I know that God shares my life with me, though I hardly know what it means.

September 2012 – I hear John Gray preach "Lazarus Come Forth." I hear God speaking to me, ~ **"I will finish the word I planted in your heart."** ~ I received this concerning my desire for Christ Community, yet it also had a deeper meaning.

December 2012 – God gives me to understand that my heart is His Mercy Seat and that inside my heart, I join all things together with Him. For the first time, I am able to place my Asperger's utterly into God and His goodness and to give all thanks.

May 2013 – I pray a prayer into audio asking God to seal me into Himself as pictured in Revelation 7. My life changes completely. Never again do I accuse God of being separated from me. From here forward, I know Father-with-me in all things, and I call it to be so.

July 2013 – Because of my experience at the end of May, I realize that our season at Lakewood Church under Joel Osteen's ministry has come to an end. It was a season of goodness, and I hold Joel and Victoria in my heart before God with all honor.

April 2014 – I begin to reckon with the reality that since we are saved and since we live only inside of God, the Christian life is to be lived as "turned around" and now going out from God as the revelation of His Salvation in all heaven-earth.

October 2014 – In a dream from the Spirit, I see Charity Titus in the heavens with my mother. After I awake, I hear Sister Charity ask me for my forgiveness, and I know that she has joined with mom to pray for me. The healing towards my time at Blueberry can finally begin.

April 2015 – I write "Sustained" and a whole new understanding of reality enters my consciousness, that all things come out from the good-speaking of Jesus every moment. I begin to write *Symmorphy*

I: Purpose, which is a deeper exploration of the ten ruling verses of the Bible.

June 2015 – I see in a flash God's meaning for Paul's word, *symmorphos,* as sharing all form with the Lord Jesus Christ. Symmorphy enters my understanding.

October 2016 – In a dream, I speak into others to know their union with Christ, that they are the same as Jesus, a man or a woman filled with all the fulness of God. I write "Christ as a Spirit of Power" in which God gives me a far clearer understanding of the power and reality of the bath of living Spirit Word in which we live.

December 2016 – I write "Calvinism" and "A Highway for God" in *Symmorphy III: Kingdom,* and my path turns towards ever greater clarity in hammering out the difference between the two trees in the garden as found throughout the Bible.

Spring 2017 – God restores into my writing the full word He spoke to me through Sam Fife.

April to June 2017 – God's meaning of "energeia" and "pro-knowing" explode into my life in all glorious joy. I read the Annie visions a fourth time, adding comments and turning them into a PDF. I now know everything she sees as part of my present knowing of God.

August 2017 – God plants in me the meaning of standing in the bottom of the Jordan – my last name – until every one has crossed out from death and into life.

September 2017 – Patterns of home enters my understanding of the Church of Jesus Christ and of the ten ruling verses of the Bible.

November 2017 – I write "Give Me a Place to Stand," asking my readers for their part in the establishing of a community of Christ. God speaks to me ~ **"Son, you provide for them."** ~ I do not know what it could mean, for I have nothing outward to give. Then I write the lesson, "And I in You," and speak out loud a commitment to God to be as Jesus for the sake of His Church. I know a further level of sealing in God's purposes for my life.

December 2017 to April 2018 – I am thrown into agony over the Word, what God actually says and what I must write.

April 2018 – I hear a word preached that is as the serpent in the garden and I discover the extent

of the falseness in the Calvinist translations of the Bible. I become very angry. God shows me the essence of what was out of whack in my community experiences.

June 2018 – God shows me His heart inside of mine as a shepherd over His people.

July 2018 – I receive clarity concerning the opposing lists of "rules of thinking." I finally see how Genesis 3:1-5 is the other ruling verse, one verse to "rule" them all.

August to November 2018 – I write *Knowing Jesus as He Is.*

February to April 2019 – I am given a clearer understanding of God's meaning for John's vision as our manual of victory regarding the Church of Christ.

June 2019 – Finally, after eight years of seeking to understand what God means by **"setting forth our souls,"** He shows me its deepest meaning inside of Jesus in Psalms 22.

August 2019 – I begin sending out the first chapters of my life story.

September 2019 – Our wonderful fellowship in the Zoom meetings begins.

October 2019 – God speaks to me that His purpose for me is to give of myself wholly to the little group gathered on Zoom and to no longer look for "ministry" abroad.

November to December 2019 – God brings full healing to my memories of Bowens Mill.

January 2020 – A mighty anointing flows through me as I begin writing *A Highway for God.*

January to April 2020 – It takes me nearly four months to work my way through writing about my first seven years at Blueberry. It is excruciating, but in the end there is only peace remaining and I can think about my time there with joy. I learn what giving an account inside the presence of God is all about.

May to June 2020 – I write of my final time at Blueberry and the test God takes me through. I begin to understand the incredible hand of God that has always been on my life.

July 2020 – I write and complete the mini-course "Living in Paul's Gospel." I finally know what the gospel of life really is and can express it clearly.

August 2020 – God shows me His purpose for my time at Blair Valley and removes from me that wrongful question – what if? We begin to pray for the Church of Christ in our Zoom meetings. We prepare ourselves for war for the Church's sake.

November 2020 – I complete "Safe from the Serpent's Gospel" and now have a full clarity regarding the false gospel as it works in Nicene Christian thinking.

December 2020 – I finish writing about my years teaching in Sheldon ISD and come to peace regarding all of that. I complete the mini-course "The Ruling Verses" and now have God's clarity concerning His thinking for Christians. I am pressed into practicing the Mercy Seat at a level deeper than I have ever known.

January 2021 – Coming out from my experience of the Mercy Seat, I begin to know the reality of sharing life with God beyond what I have ever known. My brother Franz comes to me in a dream and pleads with me to pray for his children. I begin to do just that.

April 2021 – I begin writing *Symmorphy VI: Mankind* as God takes us to a whole new level of understanding who and what we are.

June 2021 – Through a most difficult set of experiences, God removes from me all fantasy regarding my ability to bring forth a community of Christ and turns me, through the teaching on Esther, to a ministry of intercession for His Church. I agree with God to accept nothing as from myself that I be all for the sake of all Christians across the world.

August 2021 – Maureen and I begin a new life at our home in Shepherd, Texas. We begin *Studies in John* in the Zoom meetings and God takes our understanding of His life in us and our prayers of intercession for the Church to whole new levels.

September 2021 to April 2022 – the knowing of Father sharing life with me continues to grow in simplicity, in intimacy, and in JOY.

An Experience of Completion

April 2022 – I begin writing *Symmorphy VII: Completion*. God takes me into a third level of experience with Him, an unfolding experience of completion. I share this with all, both my readers and on Zoom.

June 2022 – Our intercession for all believers in Jesus throughout earth and heaven takes on a level of power and certainty never before known.

July to August 2022 – We complete our most wondrous study of John's gospel as a gospel of LIFE with "Jesus Sends Me," and we begin the study of John's letters with "I Fellowship with God."

August to September 2022 – I pass through the travail of writing "A New Fire," "A New Altar," and "A New Direction." I place myself utterly into God; I will not separate myself from Him. I choose humility with Father in return for the Victory of the entire Church.

September 2022 - I finish writing this account of my life given inside the presence of God. This has been a three-year journey, filled with much travail and much joy. My seeing of my life is utterly transformed, for I have never been alone.

Nonetheless, writing about the great press of difficulty and loss coming through this time places me into the same agonies of heart caused by those specific events as I wrestle through how I am to present these things. As always, God gives me grace and understanding.

Every moment of my life from my conception until now has been "Father with me," sharing everything of me as Himself. My life is joy inexpressible and filled with glory, one seamless story of Christ.

Your life is the same, dear reader, as you call it to be so, as you place the Lord Jesus Christ upon yourself all the way through.

June 2022 – I work on the final parts of this text.

November 2022 - I have the final print copy of my autobiography in hand.

56. All That I Am

April 2022 - September 2022

This is my concluding chapter. I am no longer bringing in the events of my life. Instead, I hope to share with you the tremendous experience of completion that began for me during the Passover season of 2022 and that has continued even to the completion of this account.

All that I am belongs to God. I know that, and have known it in penetrating sweetness ever since I completed writing this account of my life up to that wondrous moment in 2006 of hearing the words, "Speak what God says you are." And I am able to know that all that I am is His because I know that all that is God first belongs to me.

An Experience of Completion

I must articulate this wondrous and ongoing experience of completion that began for me probably on April 22, 2022 but fully opened to me on April 24, which turns out to be the day celebrated as "Easter" by the Eastern Orthodox Church. This is not God endorsing the Eastern Orthodox calendar, but rather God giving certainty to me. Inside of God's patterns, then, the beginning of knowing completion arose from within me through the same days as the Walk of the Atonement, coming to fulness on the day Jesus rose from the dead. (And again, I do not know if that is literal or not; no one does. The point is God's patterns of understanding.)

Now, none of this is to make me "special." All of it is to make Jesus Sent KNOWN to all who will receive Him.

Then, this experience with God came to me inside of writing the second letter on John 14:20, "Jesus lives inside of Me," through the writing of the letter on John 14:23 – "Father Makes His Home with Me." As I filled in the box titled "The Way" on the Jesus Secret page, "Jesus Lives inside of Me," these words flowed out from me.

~ **Living inside of Jesus is my Way to connect with the Father sharing my life with me. Jesus living inside of me is the Father's Way to con-** **nect with me sharing His life with Him, that God might enter creation through me. Life itself is my Way, moment by moment and step by step, not 'to' something, but rather life-unfolding, the living and dynamic expression of God-with-me unveiled new every morning forever. ~**

I knew instantly that I had just written a level of knowing God beyond anything I had ever known before. This word percolated inside of me until I knew it more fully by the time of the Zoom meeting on Sunday morning. At this point, sharing life with God had become the completion of Joy inside of me and the excitement of God arising as every next step.

Then, it would have been somewhere around April 27 or 28, through the next week, as I was writing "Father Makes His Home in Me," that I looked up the meaning of the Greek word *para*, translated, "with." To my astonishment, the phrase "with intimate closeness and participation" was part of the meaning of *para*. I immediately changed the wording of John 14:23 to the following.

We will come to him and will make Our home together in intimate closeness and participation with him.

Here is what I wrote, then, early Sunday morning, May 1, in the box titled "With/Para." ~ I continuously interact with God building our shared home. We work inside each other's presence. We participate intimately together in combining each next step of our shared life into a habitation we live in together. My hands at work are filled with God; God's hands at work are filled with me. God my Father with Jesus comes to me continuously and in every way to make our home together in intimate participation and fellowship. ~

The three experiences in the Christian life could be defined in these short and specific ways. First, being born again is "the peace of knowing Jesus as Savior." Being filled with the Spirit is "the joy of knowing Word as Life," and this third experience, the experience of Completion, is "the certainty of knowing Father with me."

A deep and absolute certainty has come to me several times now, inside this experience as each part of it arises out from my heart. Being sealed means certainty and certainty means completion.

This Is Me

Then, likely on May 12, I was reading a story that could be called a "fairy tale" by Tolkien's definition of "fairy tale." In the story, the main character had an experience of discovering that her gift flowed entirely out from who and what she was and from nowhere else. As I read that experience in the story, I knew the same thing inside of me out from God, that all the flow of Spirit out from my heart fits and sings with, carries and is – ME. This is me.

On May 14 I wrote about this experience in the lesson "the Rule of God." Here is what I said.

∽

The inner working of our human soul is the most important place in the universe to God. Just as God met together with us inside the confusion of Jesus' soul upon the cross, so God meets together with each created thing inside the workings of our own human souls. This is really what I am beginning to understand about Completion. Completion of Word comes out from one action, God and us synergeoing together, making all things GOOD, the very thing God proposed right from the start.

I now know that there is a third experience in God prior to the resurrection of our bodies, a third level of knowing God that is the emanation of Life.

Receiving from God this third experience is equal to, yet far greater than, being born again and being immersed into the Devoted Spirit. The result of this experience over the last few weeks is that I KNOW that a shared life with God is part of myself and true to who and what I am. This experience has come to me as an unfolding to permanence, one might say. It is a knowing out from Joy.

The experience of being conceived of God comes to us. The experience of being immersed into the Spirit comes upon us. But this experience of Completion flows out from our own person, out from our own heart and soul, Father with us.

The rule of God contains no shadow of "rule over" or of "command and control," or any outward

or imposed darkness. Joy is the center of my person, and the rule of God flows out from that JOY in complete harmony, not just with, but as all that I am. In my knowing, God remains God and I remain me, and there is no confusion of person. Nonetheless, our sharing of life together is so complete such that we are the same note, tune, and rhythm.

"The same note, tune, and rhythm" is the meaning of synergeia. The rule of God forever is synergeia, the full entwining of God's life force and my life force as one together, such that the flow of "this Treasure through my earthen vessel," is simply normal and natural to me.

I remain fully human, yet I am also Joy. I am Joy inside my person, and I am Excitement towards every forward step. The flow of Life through me is normal and natural to myself, and it is normal and natural to God my Father. My mind thinks only in terms of all completion of Word fulfilled as the outflow of my own person, Christ Jesus my life.

I am not boasting "of myself." What I am trying to do is to make this present experience as clear as I can express it. You also will have this same experience with God, yet your knowing of this act of Completion will be true to your own heart and person and to how God has always synergeoed with you.

You will not have this experience as a result of any "Pentecostal travail," which is little more than unbelief on the one hand and a longing for superiority on the other. There is one path to this experience, and I have shown you that path. In fact, the four actions of Love, described in 26.2 "Revealing God-Heart" in *Symmorphy VI: Mankind*, becoming how you think and live, is that path. Giving thanks and expecting God – for the sake of others.

Synergeoing with God is now the only knowledge I have of myself. And I know synergeoing as the fulfillment in me of every gospel Word spoken by God and written in the Bible. This synergeoing with God, this fulfillment of every gospel Word, is normal and natural to me, it flows out from what I have always been and how I know myself. And it is permanent, regardless of the winds or the waves.

Yet this flow of synergeoing is the Rule of God, a Rule that contains no carnal effort on my part. What removed carnal effort from me? – The revelation that my every next moment is Father sharing with me the building of our Home together, a dwelling place for us and for all.

Yet this experience of completion continued to happen in my life. In the early morning of May 22, in preparation for the Zoom meeting in which I shared this Experience of Completion, I finished the lesson 2.1 "The Principles of Completion."

The Principles of Completion

Salvation has two parts, redemption first and then completion. Redemption in our experience is instantaneous and total. God places us into completion, that is, into Christ, the moment we receive Jesus as our Savior. Yet our knowing of completion comes slowly over time.

Here are the seven principles of completion.

1. Every Word Fulfilled. **Jesus said to them, "... Everything must be fulfilled that is written about Me in the Law of Moses, the Prophets, and the Psalms"** (Luke 24:44). When? – In this present age. Where? – On this present earth.

MUST BE! Let's bring Jesus' words into our present day. "Everything that is written in Paul's gospel and confirmed by John concerning Me inside My Church MUST BE FULFILLED."

Consider this Word of Jesus that must be fulfilled. – **"Love one another in exactly the same way that I have loved you."** If this Word is not fulfilled in totality, exactness, and permanence inside the present church, then there is no God and Jesus was blowing smoke.

This first principle of completion requires every believer in Jesus to contend face-to-Face with God concerning His Word. Pause a moment and think about the absolute certainty of every Word fulfilled.

2. Synergeoing Together. **For this is age-unfolding life, that they may know You, the One true God, and Jesus Christ whom You have sent** (John 17:3). To KNOW God is Life; not to know God is death. Neither the meaning of "to know" nor the God we are to know has any end. Nonetheless, there is a sealing into completion that marks a knowledge of God that is Life.

This experience in a believer's life of being sealed into completion results in the full knowledge of sharing life with God and synergeoing with Him to make all things good, especially every next step taken. Sharing Life with God, that is, symmorphy, is the end purpose of Covenant; synergeoing with God is the outflow of Kingdom.

Completion means that God and the believer take every next step together, entirely by an equality of faith in one another, that is, Christ Jesus. Completion means true and continuous friendship with God.

We have defined friendship elsewhere as being a commitment to walk together in full equality of heart and with fully shared and open words and actions of harmony and honesty. It means enjoying one another inside of the deepest respect. Nothing is greater or more valuable than to synergeo with God as equals inside a fully shared Word, making all things good, calling all things into life. My bond of friendship with God is the only thing worth knowing.

3. Full Assurance of Faith. **Let us approach [everything inside the Holiest] with a true heart, in full assurance of faith** (Hebrews 10:22). – **For we have become partakers of Christ IF INDEED the source of our substance and assurance we should hold firm until all completion** (Hebrews 3:14).

Look at me, God; I belong to You. Let it be to me according to Your Word (Luke 1:38).

Full Salvation is friendship with God. Friendship is full assurance of faith in one another. God always initiates; my response to Him is always giving back what He first gives to me. My certainty that God is speaking me in truth comes out from God's certainty in me first, that I speak in truth.

God knows me, for I come out from His thoughts through the good-speaking of Jesus; God entrusts Himself to me, that I speak the truth. This trust enables me in return to embrace all that God speaks as the truth and to know that all that God is belongs to me.

4. The Ability of Christ. **...the finest details of the Energeia, the mighty continuous and swirling action of His ability to cause ALL to be subject to Himself** (Philippians 3:21). – **Christ, Who is energeoing all down to the finest details of the counsel and deliberate wisdom arising out of God's desire** (Ephesians 1:11).

Jesus is capable of doing symmorphy. Jesus is capable of connecting God and me together in a shared life, in all things. Jesus is capable of living as me. Jesus is capable of taking my human qualities and making them part of God.

Jesus is the most able Being in the entire universe, for He is able to do what neither God nor we can do. God cannot connect with us apart from Jesus. We cannot connect with God apart from Jesus.

More than that, the life I now live inside this sphere of flesh, I live entirely inside the sphere of the faith of the Son of God, this one having loved me and having given Himself entirely for me. – I have all the faith in the universe.

5. The Place of Church. The Church is His body, the fullness of Christ, that is, the full meaning that is Christ filling full all inside of all, that is, Jesus filling with Himself everything in everyone (Ephesians 1:23). – This is My full completion, that you love one another in full reciprocity just exactly as I have loved you (John 15:12). – Beloved, if God so loved us, we also are committed to loving one another (1 John 4:11). Friendship with God means friendship with one another, otherwise no friendship with God actually exists.

The gathering together of the Church is the place of Salvation; it is where true friendship with God takes place. Behold, how good and how pleasant it is for brethren to dwell together in unity! – For there the Lord commanded the blessing—Life forevermore (Psalm 133).

The place of Church, then, is as true for God's Completion as it is for ours. God cannot be complete except in Church. We cannot be complete except in Church. No one wants to go to heaven, for death cannot save anyone. Everyone wants to go to Church, even if they imagine otherwise. Salvation is NOT heaven; salvation is Church.

6. The Fulness of Time. The principle of the fulness of time is based upon God's law of the relationship between substance and appearance. For that reason, this principle has two parts. The first part of this principle asserts that everything is already complete, though we may not see it outwardly. Then, the second part is a short time-period set by God in which everything will be seen as it truly is. That which has always been true remains, while the lie is KNOWN as a lie and then vanishes away.

God's completion requires that everything be seen to be fully what it is by all. This apocalypse is certain.

7. Calling Completion. This One who is continuously giving life to the dead and calling into existence things not existing (Romans 4:17).

– Look at me, God; I belong to You. Let it be to me according to Your Word (Luke 1:38).

The reality of God requires that we call Completion into our lives. We do this through full assurance of faith.

Calling completion is our active role. The Devoted Spirit, entirely on our side of things, anoints us to call, but calling completion upon ourselves is something we alone must do. Yet calling forth completion is always for the sake of others, and thus our call is always synergeoing with God, making all things good and true, that is, Complete.

I am just overwhelmed, even by this first time through this list, for these things are so clear and so simple and so overwhelmingly powerful and wondrous. We live in all Salvation now. Our Salvation is Glorious and Complete.

The Flow of the Anointing

On May 22, then, we prayed together this prayer of completion.

⤶

"God, my Father, I ask You to give me a third experience in knowing You. In my first experience of knowing You, You sent Jesus into my heart that I might be conceived of Your incorruptible Word. In my second experience of knowing You, You immersed me into Your Devoted Spirit, sending Your Spirit into every part of my human soul, that I might know that Your Word is true.

"In this third experience in knowing You, Oh God, I ask that You seal me forever into LIFE and into the Completion of all Salvation and of all that You speak. Father, cause me to KNOW that You share every part of my daily life with me. Cause me to KNOW that I synergeo with You turning every single next step and moment and circumstance into all goodness as our dwelling place.

"God our Father, save me forever from any thought that You might be separate from me, that You might not be sharing my life with me. Save me forever from any thought that You and I together do not turn all things towards goodness for the sake of others.

"Seal me into my commitment to You, Oh God, into the full equality of friendship with You, face to Face and heart to Heart, even as You are first committed to me. Let the completion of Your Word flow out of me as my entire human person joined with You in all familiar companionship. Let the ability of Your Son cause You and me to know one another in intimate participation together.

"God, seal me right now into Your Glorious Salvation, into all completion of every Word You speak, into the full knowledge of Your intimate friendship with me, into all honesty and into no need of any sufficiency in myself. Seal me into the River of our precious Devoted Spirit flowing out from our persons together, setting creation free.

"I ask for this experience from You, Oh God, my Father, inside of the name of the Lord Jesus Christ, that He might be proven faithful and true in all that You speak. And in asking I believe with full assurance of faith that I have received all that I have asked. And in believing that I have already received, I wait upon You in confident expectation that this experience of being sealed into Your Completion, into all the fullness of LIFE, will arise from inside of me, inside of my knowing of myself and of You with me, that I am forever just like the Lord Jesus Christ.

"I give You all thanks, my Father, and I wait in confident expectation upon Your arising in me every moment."

Now, part of what I shared, though only briefly, of what I mean by "This is me" arising out from my own being, out from Father and me sharing life together in every next step, was the meaning pictured for us in Zechariah 4, of the anointing oil flowing out from the olive tree in the presence of God.

God has anointed me to know His Word by the Spirit and made personal. God has anointed me to be a channel through which a pure Word flows out from the throne and into the understanding of the Church in all heaven-earth. This is the Joy of my life, what makes me sing. This is what makes every moment of 65 years of what I thought was heartache and loss to be more valuable than I could imagine.

The Removal of Korah

Through the next week, May 23-28, I got all excited about writing the Chapter "The Meaning of a Life" for my autobiography. As I filled in the story of each significant moment of God speaking to me from the age of seven on, I was overwhelmed as I saw direct connections between experiences that

I had before thought were random and haphazard. I could no longer deny that God had His hand of great purpose upon my life every step of the way.

Inside of that experience was seeing the incredible thirty-year pattern of God dealing with contempt inside of me through which He not only removed it from me out from Covenant, but through which He proved Christ as me, that I had "passed the test," not just in a moment, but perpetually.

My decision to see Buddy Cobb and Claude Mack as Christ living as them, as Jesus to me, was not any back and forth, but rather the only possibility for me. My decision was made thirty years earlier, when, in my great desperation, I covenanted with God that I would KNOW Him and that I would walk with a people who KNOW Him.

When I saw, in a moment's flash, as this ongoing Experience of Completion, that removing "Korah" from me, full and complete, was God's purpose through thirty years of agony. I saw that "Korah" gone from me was God's permission to me to stand certain inside His calling. You see, "**He humbled Himself**" is the only entrance of God into the visible seeing of His creation.

I also saw, as I wrote "The Meaning of a Life," that the full intensity of travailing with God for the sake of His people actually began when I was twelve years old. In fact, God speaks through anything and in such a way that we can understand it. For that reason, God used a "fairy tale" to convey His meaning to a twelve-year-old boy, for my heart was taken by the story of a hobbit named Frodo Baggins who was willing to take on a task he could not do and who accomplished that task through weakness and because he failed at every crucial moment.

Frodo's words in "The Council of Elrond," – "I will take the ring (to the fire), though I do not know the way" – became the story of my life, and I could not read those words from then until now without weeping.

To "take the ring to the fire" is to be rid of the contempt of Adam for others, the wicked hatred of humans against God. It is the certain downfall of the evil one. As figurative speaking, it is the same as being rid of "Korah."

Through the week of May 30 through June 5, I continued to work on "The Meaning of a Life." As I did so, the meaning and significance of different things God spoke to me over the years took on a FAR larger scope than I had ever considered before.

~ **"Is not My Word my Will?"** ~ had already established the certainty of completion in me and was the first part of my writing "The Principles of Completion," that every word must be fulfilled.

Then, ~ **"Because you have honored My word, I will honor you,"** ~ became the quiet certainty of authority in the Word given to me by God, the knowing of the Word as it really is now flowing through me.

Through this same week of May 30 through June 5, I was also writing the lesson for the Jesus Secret Page, "The World Hates Me." As I completed that early in the morning on June 5, I understood why Jesus could save us ONLY inside the confusion of His own soul upon the cross, by choosing never to drive Father away from Himself and by choosing to include us inside Himself joined together with the Father.

Our Salvation happened only inside Jesus' own soul, inside His own confusion and almost-lostness shared fully with us. **And we also – for the sake of our brothers and sisters.**

Drinking of One Spirit

Then, as I was writing "The Spirit Leads Me," the next massive part of this ongoing Experience of Completion happened to me, let's say on June 7 or 8. I saw that because we drink of one Spirit with all who belong to Jesus, we can stand inside of God as the entire Church making our words to and out from God to be her words as well, that we can do in God what our millions of brothers and sisters cannot do, as them and for their sakes.

Out from this knowing, I wrote the first prayer of standing inside of God as the Church and for her sake in the early morning of June 12, as I was preparing for the Zoom meeting. I did not know on June 12 that, according to the Eastern Orthodox calendar, this was the Day of Pentecost. Here is what we prayed on that day.

❧

"God, our Father, we belong to You because You first belong to us. We are devoted to You because You first are devoted to us. Inside of our shared Spirit, Oh God, we join with You in travail for the sake of Your entire Church.

"God, we know and drink of the same Spirit that fills all who belong to Jesus, and we are members with them of Your same body. We are, right now, the voice of that body and we speak as her with authority and in the power of the Devoted Spirit. God, cause the Fire of Your Spirit to burn, cause all eyes to open, cause all pretending and arrogance to be cast off, cause Your knowing to arise inside of all.

"God, our Father, we are in travail with You, inside our shared Spirit, with groanings too deep to express, that LIFE, that the KNOWLEDGE OF GOD, would be birthed inside of creation, here upon this earth. God, we tolerate no more the infidelity and the game-playing that has been Your people inside this world. Not one remains inside the prostitute. We speak even for those who are so foolish as not to be filled with Your Spirit, that they also would be snatched out of their darkness.

"God, we will not let You rest until You have made the Church of Jesus Christ, our Jerusalem, to be a praise and a joy among all humans in this world, the revelation of Jesus. Let our 'Yes, Lord,' be the 'Yes, Lord,' of all, in Jesus name."

❧

Upon praying this prayer together in the Zoom meeting, I understood that I (and we) had taken the first significant step out from the Holy of Holies as the Ark of the Covenant going forth into and as the Church. I understood that Church, Christ Community as I will know it, must come first out from those who speak as and for the Church inside the presence of God. And right now, on June 23, as I am writing this, I am utterly overwhelmed that June 12 was the Day of Pentecost, the birthing of the Church.

At the Bottom of the Jordan

As early as June 8, I had started to write the lesson for the Jesus Secret page "The Meaning of Life." I had it mostly finished by June 14, though without the last two boxes filled in. Here is part of what I wrote in that lesson. The numbered sections are part of the definition of "to know."

❧

The fifth level of knowing God, then, remains in the Holiest until that full experience of completion as God has now brought to us. (Third or fifth depends on perspective, that is, we can speak of "three" levels of knowing God and we are complete, or, we can speak of seven levels of knowing God, of which three take place inside the Holiest.)

5. To share Hheart with God; to be penetrated with the meaning of "**And we also**"; to embrace a view of the Church as the passion of Jesus inside; to know the Spirit of intercession for the sake of others; to be the Mercy Seat of God, the throne of heaven; to know sharing life with the Father every moment; to be sealed into all completion.

The sixth level of knowing God, then, is knowing God inside His Church, that is, knowing one another. And the seventh level of knowing God is the experience together as the Church of God-known through us. We could even add an eighth level, and that would be the resurrection of our bodies which will seal us forever into a life shared with God and with one another in all outward appearance, that is, all expression of God-known.

6. To commit one's self to speak as and for the entire Church; to commit one's self to walk together with other believers in Jesus; to know one another inside God-among-us, that is inside of Love; to love one another with pure hearts fervently.

7. To be God-made-known, both individually and together; to be Love revealed; to be the Salvation of God made visible; to know the full expression of God in outward appearance; to thrill with the joy of Father released to be Himself as He pleases.

↩

On June 10 or 11, I happened to watch a YouTube video regarding Tolkien's world titled "Who is Cirdan? Legends of Middle Earth." I had not known this character's life, yet as I listened, such joy arose in me, for it spoke of the same longing I have known, what I always wanted to be.

I did not know it was the Day of Pentecost that Sunday morning, but as I was sharing the lesson, "The Spirit Leads Me," in the Zoom meeting on June 12, I wasn't certain if I should mention what I had learned from this YouTube video or not. Then, I realized that the story of the Ark of the Covenant at the bottom of the Jordan was the same metaphor and I was able to share both.

The four priests who carried the Ark on their shoulders were the first into the waters of the Jordan. As the water swirled around their feet, suddenly the flood waters all the way across the river backed up and formed a wall to their right with a dry path

all the way into LIFE. Those four men then stopped in the middle of the river bed at the lowest place on earth. I like to picture them having turned to face south, with the wall of death held back behind them and facing the children of Israel crossing before them, beginning with Salmon, the prince of Judah, the forefather of David. I picture every single Israelite from the least to the greatest turning to gaze upon that Ark, the presence of God, held there in the lowest place on earth, held there that they might have a Way into life, that all might enter into Christ.

Those men stood there, unmoving, until every single little one of all the children of Israel had crossed over into the Promised land. Only then did they also turn, in defiance of death, and walk up into life.

This is also what Cirdan had done. He had devoted his life for 10,000 years to make sure that every single elf in Middle Earth who wanted to cross the sea to the undying lands was able to do so. Cirdan was the last to cross, even though his heart had wanted to be the first. He was the last to cross, because he had accepted the mission of making sure every single one who belonged to LIFE had passed through the Way that led to life.

I do not know what it means, but this is the calling that sings to me. My last name is Yordy, which is an anglicized form of the German form of the original Hebrew word, Yarden, also translated into the English as "Jordan." My last name is the Hebrew *Yarden*. To me it means one who stands with Father beneath of all and for the sake of all, that each little one who believes in Jesus might enter into the full meaning of the knowledge of God, that is, into LIFE.

God Is My Judge

On June 14, my son, Kyle, took me as a Father's-day gift to a special meal being offered at the restaurant where my daughter, Katrina, works. She was the one serving the tables of all those who had signed up for this special meal. It was an excellent meal, but the point of the story is that the meal included many samplings of Samuel Adams drinks, and by the end I had drunk just a bit more than might be called proper.

On Wednesday morning, June 15, as I was sitting at my computer with my coffee, feeling a bit foolish in my hangover, I did as I always do, I said, "Father, You are sharing even this silly foolishness with me." Immediately I knew the presence of my Father, swallowing up into Himself all my humanity. Then, I listened again to the voice on Microsoft Word reading to me what I had written in "The Meaning of a Life" for my autobiography.

As I was listening to the incredible flow of God with me over many years, and as I was thinking of the travail I shared with God for the sake of His people, the next great part of the Experience of Completion arose from inside of me.

This is what happened. I thought about all the people in my life, and I saw them all without any pain at all. My heart enlarged inside of compassion and I thought to myself, "It is so easy to forgive every single person and to receive each with all joy." Then I thought of Lloyd Green, and I saw him, as in a vision, as a frightened and lonely little boy, and I thought, "It is so easy to forgive Lloyd Green and to draw him out from the un-known-ness and into my heart."

All pain is gone. ALL PAIN IS GONE! Indeed, it is easy for me now to see that all my pain was entirely self-inflicted. What Lloyd Green did to me was wrong, even wicked. But I was the one who had taken that experience and used it to beat myself inside of darkness. – Simply because I had not given thanks and had not called that experience as God sharing all things with me.

I turned, then, and added more to the lesson, "The Meaning of Life" in *Studies in John*, including the first part of the prayer. Here is what I wrote.

❧

We will continue to go back and forth between metamorphy and synergeia in our prayers; however, we will also continue to speak as the Church for her sake.

Last time, I did not arrive at the wording I wanted until the last line, "Let our 'Yes Lord,' be the 'Yes Lord' of all." God's people are sheep. They do not know the way and are afraid of getting it wrong and losing Salvation. Just as we needed Jesus to speak for us before God, so our brothers and sisters need us to speak for them. And we also.

Standing for the Church for her sake is our first step into the sixth level of knowing God as the Ark of the Covenant.

What Is the Church? I want us to fix in our un-derstanding, our "mind's eye," for whom it is we are praying. Cast your mind across all Christians you have known of every stripe, color, and flavor. Cast your mind across every country and people-group on earth. Reach out to include every sect, and denomination. Include all in the heavens out from all human history. Include those who do not yet know the Lord Jesus, but who will. Consider Christians you don't like. Draw into your mind the faces of those you once despised.

In this third part of experiencing completion; God will enlarge you to be compassion for ALL.

❧

At the same time, as I was listening to "The Meaning of a Life" being read to me, I understood that my first name, Daniel, meaning "God is my judge," is simply the best sentence one could come up with to define the meaning of my life up until now. – God is my judge. And David, my middle name, is the Beloved, the one who shares heart with God, the one who will not let go of God until Jerusalem is a praise in all the earth.

I began to understand, now for the first time, God's second commandment to me, in instructing me to give to His people. The first time God told me to do something it was, ~ **"Give My people hope."** ~

The second time God told me to do something was while I was writing the letter "Give Me a Place to Stand." These words came to me from the same Voice inside of me, ~ **"You provide for them."** ~ Meaning, don't just ask God's people to provide for you, rather, you also provide for them." Just as I had no hope when God instructed me to give His people hope, so I had nothing to give when God told me to provide for His Church.

Understand that I heard the words ~ **"You provide for them"** ~ in the context of the Church entering into her time of greatest need and in the context of **"and they shall nourish her there."** And so, on this same eventful morning, June 15, I understood that the greatest provision that could ever be given to God's people on this earth right now is to speak in the presence of God as her and for her sake.

Now, that is where it stands thus far, as I am writing this morning, on June 16, 2022. And I am busy with this account right now because a further part of this Experience of Completion has begun in me even this morning.

You see, none of this is me exalting myself. That's the whole point. I am a total failure in everything. It is God my Father, sharing my life with me, who is exalted. And God is exalted as you, dear reader, come to know Him inside this Experience of Completion as I also know Him now.

Every moment of your life has been as filled with purpose and with Father sharing everything with you as mine has been. CALL IT TO BE SO, and you will see. This is knowing God; this is the path of Life.

For the Sake of the Church

This morning, even though I haven't yet shared "The Meaning of Life" with the Zoom meeting, I opened the next lesson for the Jesus Secret page titled "I Know Jesus Sent." I wrote the first sentence and then sat here considering how to shape this wondrous reality. I looked at the word "Sent" and saw just how critically important it is and what it means.

To be SENT means that Jesus came into us out from Another, that is from God, with great purpose. Jesus cannot "rest" until He has fulfilled inside of us everything for which the Father Sent Him. To be sent means that you must accomplish the purposes of the one who sent you. You are where you are for the sake of One greater than you. And from an early age, you have been "about Your Father's business."

Because, you see, even though this is Jesus Sent into us, the last page of *The Jesus Secret II* for John's gospel is "Jesus Sends Me." – "**Just as the Father sent Me forth, so I also send you.**"

Every one of these parts of this great Experience of Completion that is arising as rivers out from Father and us sharing life together, is centered in the entire concept of CERTAINTY.

God is – and now I KNOW that He is. – To KNOW that I am sent into this world in exactly the same way and for the same purposes that God sent Jesus, is to know utter and quiet CERTAINTY in the unfolding of every present moment.

I wrote this narrative up until this point on June 16. Now, in the early morning hours of June 23, 2022, I am writing the next bit. I will begin this part, then, with what we, in our small gathering on Zoom, prayed together for the sake of the Church of Jesus Christ throughout heaven-earth on Sunday morning, June 19.

"God, our Father, we stand here inside Your presence, in intimate participation with You and with one another, as, and for the sake of Your entire Church in heaven-earth. Enable us to speak for their sake what others are not able to speak, not until their eyes are opened to the Path of Life.

"As and for the sake of the entire Church, we repent, Oh God, of not desiring to know You above all things. Cause us, with all who belong to Jesus, to KNOW You.

"As and for the sake of the entire Church, we repent of 2000 years of turning Your gospel away from the tree of life and into the tree of knowing good and evil. Cause us, with all who belong to Jesus, to see John 14:20 as our only LIFE.

"As and for the sake of the entire Church, we repent of having not obeyed the one command of the gospel that counts. Cause us, with all who belong to Jesus, to put the Lord Jesus Christ upon all that we are, with no thought regarding our human weakness.

"As and for the sake of the entire Church, Oh God, we close our mouths about ourselves. It is so good to be utterly and completely WRONG; apart from Jesus we can do nothing.

"As and for the sake of the entire Church, we stand upon firm and we SEE the Salvation of God, the Lord Jesus Christ fulfilling all. We SEE all sin purged away; we SEE no more disconnection from God. We SEE a life shared with our Father forever. – For ALL who belong to Jesus."

"As and for the sake of the entire Church, we stand inside of You, Oh God, and inside the Completion of every word You speak. Let our confidence in You be their confidence in You. Let our rejoicing in a shared life with You be their overflowing Joy.

"Father, let our travail stand in for theirs; let our groaning for the resurrection, for our bodies swallowed up by life, be their faith in You.

"Father, cause Your people all across the earth and throughout the heavens to KNOW YOU, that we might also KNOW YOU, together with them. For God, we will not let You go, we will give You no rest, until every least little one who loves Jesus has passed out from death and into LIFE.

"Let it be so; it is so, inside of the name of Jesus."

I knew, the moment we finished praying this, that we together had just uttered the most powerful prayer I have ever known, and likely more impactive than any prayer during the in-part Church age. It was no surprise to me that, over the next few days, I sensed a massive counter-attack in the heavenly realms against us. I gave it no mind, for these evil angels are ON THEIR WAY OUT! This next paragraph, however, is what I wrote first this morning.

~ So, yea. I haven't even finished setting forth what is up to this moment on June 23, 2022 when the next experience of completion comes out from Father and me together. How can I explain it. Yet it must be explained and its path must be shown. ~

Praying for the Church

The next portion of this Experience of Completion that came to me this morning is the full realization that being a ministry of Christ to His Church MEANS that I, standing inside the presence of God, sharing life with the Father, DO for my brothers and sisters what they cannot do for themselves, that is, I say every "Yes, Lord," for their sake.

I now have the full answer to why it is our brethren cannot hear or see the Salvation of God. It's because they can't. You see, neither could we. We needed Someone to stand for us in the presence of God and to speak for us what we ourselves could not speak. Since this is what Jesus does for us, – and we also – means that we turn and do the same for all believers in Jesus who also cannot, just as we could not.

Again, this is not "replacing" Jesus' completed atonement. Rather, it is two things. First, it is Jesus sharing with us a small measure of what He Himself is and does. But second, God has set out from His own nature that He cannot penetrate into human affairs except He comes through humans who are alive now upon this earth. Jesus must find faith IN the earth.

And thus I see why it is God has had me pencil out the pathway of my life, for it is evident that I am NOT different, that I am NOT special, but that I am a bumbling human in this world like everyone else. That means that whatever is true of Father with me is also true of Father with you your whole life, just as much. Call it to be so.

It is an easy thing to say, "Yes, Lord." And it is an

easy thing to say, "Yes, Lord," for the entire Church of Christ. I think back now to my decades of screaming and hollering against God. Jesus spoke the truth, I hated Him WITHOUT a cause. Then I saw that the time period through which I fought and struggled against God dragging me into the Joy in which I now live was right at forty-nine years, from the summer of 1964 when I asked Jesus into my heart at age seven until May of 2013, at age fifty-six, when God sealed me into Himself, into His Jubilee, never to imagine myself separate from Him ever again.

Why did I fight against God so hard for so long? – Because I was stupid! – It is so good to be WRONG.

You can't! But I can, inside of Jesus, for your sake. And so I do, together with Father.

And how is it that I have the authority to do so? – Simple. – GOD IS MY JUDGE, utterly and completely. I have no other judge.

Never, in all the history of the Church, did God ever intend for Christian ministry to condemn those who cannot please God, but rather, to stand for the sake of others just as Jesus stood for them.

Let me insert this list, now, of the lesson titles from *Studies in John* and the Sunday in which I shared them on Zoom and in which we prayed the prayer together. This is momentous. – Also realize that I typically began to write each next lesson the next morning, Monday, after the Zoom meeting.

April 10 – The Place of Life (Intro to John 14:20)
April 17 – I Live inside of Jesus
April 24 – Jesus Lives inside of Me (Passover)
May 1 – Father Makes His Home with Me
May 8 – I Bear Much Fruit
May 15 – I Love My Brethren
May 22 – An Experience of Completion
May 29 – My Brethren Love Me
June 5 – The World Hates Me
June 12 – The Spirit Leads Me (Pentecost)
June 19 – The Meaning of Life
June 26 – I Know Jesus Sent
July 3 – I Know the Father
July 10 – I Am with Jesus in God
July 17 – The Path of the Atonement
July 23 – The Way of Life
July 30 – Jesus Sends Me

Every Single One

It is now June 25. Yesterday and this morning I filled in the list of each letter I sent out from *Sym-*

morphy I: Purpose to Symmorphy V: Life, including the introduction I wrote for each letter. I realized that I needed to fit a number of things more into those chapters of my life story.

Yet in doing that, my understanding of God's purpose for my life became simple and plain. When I shared my present understanding with Maureen, she said, "That's good, Daniel." From a Mack, that is a full commendation.

I have allotted two pages only for the introduction to my autobiography. Proclaiming myself as "somebody" in the face of others is more abhorrent to me than I can express. Yet, in those two pages, I must set before you in quiet simplicity the hand of God upon me and the purpose of my life for your sake, that you also might enter into all the knowledge of God, that you also might know that God has shared your life with you just as much.

I must set before all readers why they must read this account.

God removed from me the fulfillment of immediate Church and then turned my focus to His entire Church throughout all heaven-earth. Jesus has found Himself as faith in the earth; God has found Himself as a man after His own heart. I am privileged to share with Them all that I am.

I will stand here at the bottom of the Yarden, in the lowest place on earth, as the very Ark of God, and with death at my back. I will stand here, as God is my judge, until every single one who belongs to Jesus, from the least to the greatest, has left the wilderness of their own ignorance of God and has crossed into the full meaning of all the fulness of Christ.

Only when that last little one has passed out from death will it be acceptable to me to turn, and, with those who have chosen to stand with me, then enter into all outward expression of God among us.

This is me; this is what makes me sing.

Yet what does it mean that every single Israelite, crossing through death and into life, has turned to look upon the Ark of the Covenant here at the bottom of the Jordan?

It is the anointing of KNOWING the pure Word out from God, KNOWING that Word as Christ living as them, that each one receives. This also is me; this also is what makes me sing.

All Word Fulfilled

It is now October of 2022, as I am finishing this final chapter. The travail of these last few months is found in the earlier chapter, "A New Altar." I want to share with you now what I wrote on October 3.

❦

I am ever more overwhelmed as I now see ever more the perfection of God in the events of my life. And what I am after is to unveil to you what really happened inside of me on August 6, 2006, when I heard the words, "Speak what God says you are." What I heard in that moment, shouting into me as all the Voice of God, was the COMMAND – Believe you have received ALL WORD FULFILLED!!!

We begin with a challenge to all ministers and teachers inside of Christianity. – Why do you not ask God to fulfill His Word as He means it inside of you and then believe that you have received what you ask?

You see, the issue is always the Spirit of Truth VERSUS the spirit of anti-Christ. And the spirit of anti-Christ seems to prevail.

There is NO knowing of Word or Truth or God apart from being immersed into the Spirit, apart from being filled to overflowing with the knowing of the Spirit. And so I want to trace out this Great Contention across the whole course of my life.

I have spoken of "running the gauntlet." That gauntlet was right at ten years in length from February of 1988 to February of 1998. At every step of that run, I was being beaten by two gospels, one on either side of me. God's intention was for me to FAIL and, in total failure, to despair. God was after "no sufficiency in myself" as driven by the complete opposition of these two gospels.

Those two gospels are Christ versus anti-Christ, knowing God through Christ inside my heart VERSUS the savage separation between Christ and me.

God positioned these two opposing words on either side of me in the fall of 1987, around my 31st birthday. The gospel of separation was Calvinism filtered through Buddy Cobb, all Bible verses, all in the wrong places. And the gospel of knowing God, that is, Life, came through Jane Miller in the demonstration and power of the Spirit. My nous, my intellectual mind, went with the first, and my phroneo, my heart-gut mind went with the second. But I was not released to RUN until February of 1988, when

God removed from my gut the demons of fear from LSD.

These were the most intense years of searching my Bible so that I might KNOW what God actually says, especially at the beginning of that run, ages 31 to 33. Here was my conclusion after that run was over, an absolute Covenant with God inside of me. – JESUS WILL BE more real inside of me than Don Howat and Abel Ramirez ever could be outside of me. In other words – the Person of JESUS will fill my flesh. Yet that Person is also every Word God speaks.

Here are the Words God planted in me prior to this RUN and then the Words He planted in me through the beginning of the gauntlet.

Although I asked Jesus into my heart when I was seven, God began His relationship with me at age nineteen with two words, audible in my spirit, His Voice saying, ~ **"My son."** ~ Those two words made everything utterly Personal to God and utterly personal to me. I have never thought differently.

Prior to God making everything personal between Him and me, God planted two mighty things inside of me. The first came when I was twelve. God planted in my heart-gut mind a love of the fantastic (Spirit) and a hatred of dishonesty. And inside that planting was a call to intercession out from knowing God.

The second word came when I was fifteen. – **Give thanks in and for all things.** You see what that Seed did? It began the turn away from controlling my outward and towards the fulfillment of every Word God speaks inside of me.

Then, after God made it personal between Him and me, He planted four critical words into me prior to the great RUN yet ahead. The first of those four words was through Watchman Nee – Ask God to fulfill His Word inside of you and then believe you have received all you have asked.

The second was a word of the Spirit, the words coming alive and personal inside of me. – **"The Spirit of Truth WILL lead you into all truth."** The third was the voice of God inside my heart. ~ **"Is not My Word My will?"** ~

And the fourth came through Sam Fife, the single most important word he preached into me. – **"It is the Spirit that giveth life; the flesh profiteth nothing. The words that I speak to you are Spirit and they are life."**

Let's list these seven words.

1. Love the fantastic and dream of what could be; hate dishonesty and all lying about what is.
2. Give thanks inside of and for the sake of all things.
3. It's utterly personal between Me and you, My son.
4. Ask Me to fulfill My word in you and then believe You have received – and I will fill you with My Spirit.
5. My Spirit will lead you into all truth.
6. My will and desire is My Word fulfilled in you.
7. The Words of Jesus are Spirit inside of you and your life.

I may not have been able to tell you at the time, but these words were ABSOLUTE inside of me before I was thirty.

One final note before the Word that came into me at the beginning of the gauntlet. When I was 26, God confronted me with dire instruction. – "Do NOT put My Words into your intellect, but plant them as I speak them inside your phroneo, your heart-gut mind."

⤿

Then, read the chapters "The Season of Deliverance I and II" to get the power of the gauntlet God sent me down and the deep issues inside of it. It is so important to me that you KNOW the seven words God planted in me and then told me to RUN!

I was running for my LIFE. And in that run, I searched my Bible to KNOW what God was really all about.

The first two that came to me from that search was the BATTLE. – *"Yeah hath God said,"* VERSUS **"Let it be to me according to Thy Word."** The second two were the goal, the end of my run. – **"Conformed to the image of His Son,"** the ruling verse of the Bible, and – **Enter BOLDLY into all that is God,** Hebrews 10. The third two were the how – **"Cast down the accuser,"** and – **"Rivers of Spirit flow out from your belly."**

Yet there was a seventh word, one I could not have said.

That seventh verse was at the heart of my great test, God's removal of Korah from me in the proving of Christ, and His voice to me, ~ **"Son, you passed the test."** ~ That verse I can place only now – By this we have known Love because He set forth His soul for us AND WE ALSO are committed to – Love one another.

Listen to the voices screaming at me for ten years, beating me with whips, the "God" of Calvinism. – God hates you. God is against you. You are in trouble with God. Hear and obey, loser. Know your place, loser. Your will is always at war against God. What you think is your calling is NOT of God. What you think is God speaking to you is NOT God speaking. You don't know yourself, but I do, and you are the proudest man I have ever known.

All these and so much more, welded intrinsically into so much speaking of 'word' at me. This is the spirit of anti-Christ speaking against Christ now come in Daniel Yordy's flesh. And all with Calvin's crowning words, "When you see God, you will KNOW just how EVIL you really are."

Yet in all of this, I have left out the one Word that defined my own heart every stumbling step of that way. That one Word that came out from God's first words spoken to me, "It's all personal between you and Me, My son." Here is that word that I HAD TO KNOW. – If a man love me, he will keep my words: and my Father will love him, and we will come unto him, and make our abode with him.

This was LIFE or DEATH for me, and I did not want to die. I MUST have Father make His home with me; therefore I MUST keep His Word.

And this was my ABSOLUTE despair at the end of that gauntlet in February of 1998. – "I cannot keep His Word." And the Absolute Covenant with a God who makes everything personal between Him and me, coming out from that despair, "I must have a Savior. I will know Jesus for real, and I will know nothing else."

Yet what was it inside my own character that kept that path in a straight line? – It was my love of the fantastic, that is, "Christ, not I, yet I live," that is, Jesus in my flesh, and my hatred of dishonesty, that is, "I, not Christ."

I count at least 25 powerful things planted by God as His Word inside of me. Every single one of those Words reverberated all through my being. And I have left out, though it was also very much there – that you might be filled with all the ful-

ness of God. And on August 6, 2006, when Joel Osteen said, "Speak what God says you are," every single one of those Words EXPLODED in all THIRST and all GLORY inside of me.

But then also, through the nine months of February to November, 2008, every single one of those anti-Christ voices screamed and wailed against me without let-up, AND I REFUSED THEM. I cast them down.

Let's paraphrase 1 John 4:4-5. – You are out from God, little children, personal between you and the Father, and have defeated the anti-Christ spirit and cast it down, because the Jesus who is inside of you, come now in your flesh, the Completion of all that God speaks, is greater than the one who speaks his anti-Christ nonsense in the present world.

⤚

I Have a Dream

I have a dream.

I dream of the Church of Jesus Christ now upon this earth. I see her clothed with the Lord Jesus Christ; I see her bringing forth the knowledge of God into creation.

I see the Church, that she comes out from Jesus' side upon the cross. I see the Blood and the Water flowing out together, mixing into the dirt of the earth, the very Bride of Christ. I see the Lord Jesus coming into His Church by the Spirit of Truth on the day of Pentecost. I see that Jesus is all inside of all who belong to Him.

I see the Church, a hundred million and more believers in Jesus all across this planet, walking together as the revelation of Jesus Christ in all of His glory revealed, right here on this earth, right now in this age.

You see, I care about God, that He would gain the desire of His Heart, to be seen and known by all creation through His only body, Christians loving one another with pure hearts fervently.

I dream of a firstfruits of Christ, giving their all for the sake of the Church, ready to sacrifice everything that they might be a point of gathering together. I see Christians everywhere gathering together around God's firstfruits into

Christ Communities, more than a million Christian Communities across every land and among every people on earth.

I see the New Jerusalem coming out from God upon the earth inside of heaven.

I see Christians loving one another, with every thought that Father might be glorified through their gathering together, placing God Himself as all their connections together, a people filled with all the fulness of God.

I see Christians who place the Sacrifice of Jesus, **one unlimited sacrifice for sins**, as their only core, their only foundation, their absolute protection, their all.

I see Christians loving one another out from God, out from their personal union with the Lord Jesus Christ connecting them always with God and with one another.

I see great movements of the Devoted Spirit flowing inside of each community of Christ, among the Churches together, and out from them into all human society. I see the Word of the gospel being spoken everywhere.

I hear the ruling verses of the Bible on the lips of a hundred million or more Christians, spoken as their own self story, spoken together as the testimony and witness of Christ.

I hear the people of this world in awe, saying, "Now we know that God is true, for we can see Him. We can see Christians loving one another with all commitment and in all liberty. We know we are seeing God. We know that God sent Jesus into our lives."

I see Christians loving one another, committing their lives to each other and to the gathering together. I see sacrifice, I see steadfastness, I see faithfulness, I see giving, all in full reciprocity, back and forth, as the very revelation of God. I see Christians treating each other with utter respect and in the highest regard.

I see every Word spoken by Jesus and His apostles fulfilled in all completion right here on this earth, right now in this age, inside a hundred million or more believers in Jesus - the absolute proof that God is telling us the truth.

This is my story; this is my dream. This is the commitment of my heart and life. I know the cost; I know the tears. I know the joy unspeakable and filled with glory.

For Father's sake - a people for Father's sake. That God might be known by all.

I will know God in full, in all that God intends, and I will walk with a people who know God in the same way, right here on this earth, right now in this age.

I will walk in committed Christian Community with all who love Jesus made visible.